THE REAL ESTATE HANDBOOK

The Real Estate Handbook

edited by

MAURY SELDIN

Professor of Real Estate and Urban Development
School of Business Administration
The American University

DOW JONES-IRWIN   Homewood, Illinois   60430

This publication is designed to provide accurate and
authoritative information in regard to the subject matter
covered. It is sold with the understanding that the
publisher is not engaged in rendering legal, accounting, or
other professional service. If legal advice or other expert
assistance is required, the services of a competent
professional person should be sought.

*From a Declaration of Principles jointly adopted by a Committee
of the American Bar Association and a Committee of Publishers.*

ISBN 0-87094-184-4

Library of Congress Catalog Card No. 79–51783

Printed in the United States of America

1 2 3 4 5 6 7 8 9 0 K 6 5 4 3 2 1 0

DEDICATION

The first chapter in this work is written by a man whose enthusiasm for and commitment to the practice of real estate have set the highest standards of conduct for over 60 years. The editor, the advisory board, and the publisher of this book dedicate it to him with much affection and gratitude.

PREFACE

The Real Estate Handbook answers questions you have been asking about real estate or should have been asking if you are in the business or any of the related fields.

It is rapidly becoming the standard reference work because it provides authoritative information on a broad range of real estate subjects organized so that you can learn what you need to know by reading a chapter among a cluster of chapters. In some cases, additional references are provided for those who desire more detail. Frequently, the chapter author has written a book on the subject or, at least, monographs or articles. Much is also based upon the author's front line experience.

The *Handbook* is organized to provide five major parts containing the 67 chapters plus an appendix on professional designations. The opening part, on Real Estate Transactions, focuses on the decisions you need to make when buying/selling or borrowing/lending from the standpoint of what you agree to do. You need to understand the business and legal consequences of what you agree to do.

The second part deals with the variety of analyses including appraisals, feasibility, and other studies. The third part is on marketing which in addition to the regular business aspects covers the ever increasing regulatory morass.

The fourth part, on financing, discusses the traditional financing sources plus new sources for money and an orientation about the mortgage market for both borrowers and mortgage investors.

The fifth part tells about ten different types of real estate investments in terms of type of use plus a chapter on condominiums and joint ventures/syndicates. The capstone chapter guides you in the process of selecting a real estate investment.

This book is a reference work which will be used time and time again. Yet, it is so structured that it is five books in one. Each section can be read as a separate book, each chapter as a separate chapter, and there is a complete index for those who want information which transcends the various chapters.

The Real Estate Handbook is the most authoritative work in the field. The authors or coauthors of 67 chapters include current or past presidents or chief operating officers of the following organizations:

American Bankers Association

U.S. League of Savings Associations

Mortgage Bankers Association of America

Securities Industries Association

National Association of Home Builders

ULI—The Urban Land Institute

The American Real Estate and Urban Land Economics Assn.

Lambda Alpha, the International Land Economics Fraternity

Rho Epsilon, the National Professional Real Estate Fraternity

American Institute of Real Estate Appraisers

Institute of Real Estate Management

National Marketing Institute of the National Association of Realtors

In addition, the author list includes chief economists or other high staff persons and/or key officers or chairpersons of committees or divisions of numerous other organizations. While no organizational endorsement is expressed or implied, these are the people who are on the front line in organizational work.

Additionally, the author list includes persons who hold the following professional designations: MAI, Member, Appraisal Institute (14); SRPA, Society of Real Property Appraisers (8); CRE, Counselor in Real Estate (7); SIR, Society of Industrial Realtors (4); SREA, Society of Real Estate Appraisers (3); CPM, Certified Property Manager (3).

The academic community is represented by about 20 fulltime faculty members from across the country and by another 20 part-time faculty members most of whom are practitioners in the business or related professions.

The chapter authors have previously written or been coauthors of over 50 hardcover books on real estate or related subjects. Their articles and book chapters number well into the hundreds.

The Editor-in-Chief wishes to acknowledge the assistance and cooperation of a great many people who worked on this project. First, there is the Editorial Board who provided review and consultation. These people are W. Donald Calomiris, Wm. Calomiris Investment Company, Washington, D.C.; John P. Dolman, Jackson Cross, Philadelphia; Joseph B. Doherty, Doherty Realty Agency, Andover, Massachusetts; Dr. Michael Sumichrast, National Association of Home Builders, Washington, D.C.; Percy E. Wagner, Chicago; and Dr. Arthur M. Weimer, Indiana University and United States League of Savings Associations, Washington, D.C.

Additionally, the individual chapters of the handbook were reviewed by numerous experts to assure technical competence. These people are Dr. Nathan A. Baily, Mortgage Bankers Association of America, Washington, D.C.; Dean Boyes, Senior Vice President, First National Bank of Portland, Oregon; James C. Brincefield, Jr., Esq., Brincefield, Middleton, Reiner and Tremaine, Attorneys at Law, Alexandria, Virginia; Gavin

A. Brown, Mortgage Bankers Association of America, Washington, D.C.; Professor D. Barlow Burke, The American University, Washington, D.C.; Dr. Fred E. Case, University of California, Los Angeles; Elliot H. Cole, Esq., Patton, Boggs & Blow, Washington, D.C.; E. Lee Curtis, CPA, Gronsbell, Halt, & Curtis, Ltd., Alexandria, Virginia; Dr. Harold A. Davidson, President, Harold Davidson and Associates, Inc., Los Angeles; John J. Dennis, II, Century 21, Rockville, Maryland; Max J. Derbes, Jr., Max J. Derbes, Inc., Realtors, New Orleans; Roy P. Drachman, Roy Drachman Realty Company, Tuscon; Anthony M. Frank, Chairman and President, Citizens Savings and Loan Association, San Francisco; Dr. James P. Gaines, University of South Carolina, Columbia; David R. Ganis, Vice President, Paine, Webber, Jackson and Curtis, Inc., Chicago; Bill Gattis, Bruce Mulhearn Inc., Realtor, Bellflower, California; Bernard P. Giroux, District Real Estate Manager, The Great Atlantic and Pacific Tea Company, Inc., Paterson, New Jersey; Martin A. Goodman, Leo Eisenberg and Company, Realtors, Kansas City; Stewart Grill, Evanston, Illinois; Charles M. Gronsbell, CPA, Gronsbell, Halt & Curtis, Ltd., Alexandria, Virginia; Victor E. Hanan, License Specialist, Herndon, Virginia; Lloyd Hanford, Jr., Lloyd Hanford, Jr. and Company, Real Estate, San Francisco; Thomas L. Howard, Esq., Colton & Boykin, Washington, D.C.; Ephraim Kranitz, Esq., Los Angeles; Norman E. Lauer, Arlington, Virginia; Thomas J. Meyer, Muriello/Meyer and Associates, Elk Grove Village, Illinois; Professor Alton Penz, Carnegie Mellon University, Pittsburgh; Kenneth M. Plant, President, Captial City Federal Savings and Loan Association, Washington, D.C.; Professor David Reitzel, Chairman, Department of Business Law, The American College, Bryn Mawr, Pennsylvania; Anthony Reynolds; Reynolds and Reynolds, Inc., Washington, D.C.; R. Bruce Ricks, Becker and Ricks, Partners, San Francisco; Joseph R. Schuble, Dreyfuss Brothers, Inc., Bethesda, Maryland; Malcolm Sherman, President, Phipps Land Company, Inc., Atlanta; Donald J. Snider, Vice President, Snider Brothers, Inc., Realtors, Wheaton, Maryland; Marcia Grier Spencer, Marketing Officer, North Carolina National Bank, Charlotte; Professor Howard Stevenson, Harvard University, Cambridge; Jay J. Strauss, President, B. B. Cohen and Company, Chicago; Professor Leonard P. Vidger, San Francisco State University, San Francisco; Donald R. Waugh, Jr., Senior Vice President, The Equitable Life Assurance Society of the United States, Erick West, Erick Incorporated, Silver Spring, Maryland; Alvin J. Wolff, Alvin J. Wolff, Inc., Realtors, Spokane, Washington; Michael S. Young, Shlaes and Company, Real Estate Consultants, Chicago.

In addition, there was outstanding staff support headed by Irmgard Svenson who served as secretary for the project and from time to time was assisted by Susie Seldin, Judy Seldin, Robin Janick, and Rachel R. Seldin. A special note of thanks goes to the copy editor, Gene Zucker.

December 1979   MAURY SELDIN

Contributing Authors

Alexander, Willis W. (Chapter 42)
Executive Vice President, American Bankers Association

Banks, Lawrence S. (Chapter 22)
Appraiser-Real Estate Analyst

Beaton, William R. (Chapter 39)
Professor of Real Estate, School of Business & Organization Sciences, Florida International University

Bechhoefer, Ina S. (Chapter 56)
Research Associate, Homer Hoyt Institute and Metro Metrics, Inc.;

Blackwell, Marion Jr. (Chapter 60)
President, Sharp-Boylston Company

Bloom, George F. (Chapter 13)
Professor of Real Estate Administration, School of Business, Indiana University

Boyce, Byrl N. (Chapter 19)
Professor of Finance and Real Estate, School of Business Administration, University of Connecticut

Boykin, James H. (Chapter 12)
Alfred L. Blake Professor of Real Estate, School of Business, Virginia Commonwealth University

Brenner, Donald (Chapter 2)
Attorney at Law; Associate Professor of Real Estate and Business Law, School of Business Administration, The American University

Brown, Gary Alan (Chapter 44)
Associate Counsel, National Association of Real Estate Investment Trusts, Inc.

Brueggeman, William B. (Chapter 38)
Corrigan Professor in Real Estate, School of Business Administration, Southern Methodist University

Callery, T. Grant   (Chapter 6)
Attorney at Law, Winkelman and Delaney

Calomiris, W. Donald   (Chapter 33)
*Executive Property Manager and Treasurer, William Calomiris
Investment Company*

Chertkof, Howard L.   (Chapter 27)
Real Estate Broker and Developer, Howard L. Chertkof & Company

Clancy, Joseph P.   (Chapter 45)
Manager, Real Estate Division, Ravenhorst Corporation

Donnell, John D.   (Chapter 8)
*Professor of Business Administration, Chairperson of Business Law,
Graduate School of Business, Indiana University*

Field, Charles G.   (Chapter 25)
Associate, Troy, Malin & Pottinger, Washington, D.C.

French, William B.   (Chapter 5)
*President, William B. French & Associates, Inc., Real Estate Consultants
and Brokers*

Freshman, Samuel K.   (Chapter 46)
Freshman, Marantz, Comsky & Deutsch Law Corporation

Garrigan, Richard T.   (Chapter 18)
*Associate Professor of Real Estate and Finance, Graduate School
of Business, DePaul University*

Gettel, Ronald E.   (Chapter 23)
Real Estate Appraiser and Consultant

Good, Sheldon F.   (Chapter 35)
President, Sheldon F. Good & Company

Gottlieb, Roy D.   (Chapter 65)
Chairman, President and Chief Operating Officer, Kenroy Inc.

Greenblatt, Stanley D.   (Chapter 31)
*BS, SIR, Partner in firm of Stanley D. & Alan L. Greenblatt, Industrial
and Commercial Real Estate Sales, Rentals, Appraisal, and Management*

Grewell, Bruce   (Chapter 26)
Attorney and Real Estate Broker, Gulledge Corp., Alexandria, Virginia

Halpin, Michael C.   (Chapter 16)
President, Michael C. Halpin Consultants

Hanan, Catherine B.   (Chapter 3)
*Former Associate of Levinson & Lieberman, Attorneys; currently
practicing in Century City, California*

Haney, Richard L. Jr.   (Chapter 51)
Associate Professor of Real Estate and Finance, Texas A&M University

Harps, William S.   (Chapter 15)
First Vice President, John R. Pinkett, Inc.

Hart, John C.   (Chapter 59)
Developer of land, residential, commercial and industrial sites

Hartman, Donald J.   (Chapter 63)
Executive Vice President, Carl Rosman & Company

Harvey, Robert O.   (Chapter 21)
Professor and Chairman, Real Estate and Regional Science, School of Business Administration, Southern Methodist University

Hewitt, Charles M.   (Chapter 24)
Professor of Business Law, Graduate School of Business, Indiana University

Hoyt, Homer   (Chapter 61)
President, Homer Hoyt Associates

Hysom, John L.   (Chapter 17)
Professor in charge of the Real Estate and Urban Development Program, at George Mason University; President of J. L. Hysom & Associates

Inbinder, Alan J.   (Chapter 65)
Partner, Kenroy Associates

Jacobe, Dennis J.   (Chapter 52)
Economist, United States League of Savings Associations

Jacobson, Norman L.   (Chapter 30)
Secretary and Treasurer, Wagner-Jacobson Company, Inc., Realtors®

Jones, Oliver E.   (Chapter 47)
Oliver Jones & Associates, Consulting Economist

Jundt, Dwight W.   (Chapter 64)
President, Jundt Associates, Inc.

Kaufman, David M.   (Chapter 62)
President, David M. Kaufman Associates, Inc., Realtors® and Auctioneers

Kellogg, John S.   (Chapter 4)
Attorney at Law

Kendall, James N.   (Chapter 40)
Director, Public Information, United States League of Savings Associations

Kendall, Leon T.   (Chapter 18)
President, Mortgage Guaranty Insurance Corporation

Kettler, Milton E.   (Chapter 29)
Director and Chairman of the Board, Kettler Brothers, Inc.

Kidd, Phillip E.   (Chapter 47)
Director of Economic Research, McGraw-Hill Information Systems Company

Kinkade, Maurice E.   (Chapter 41)
Senior Vice President, The Poughkeepsie Savings Bank

Kokus, John Jr.   (Chapter 55)
Associate Professor of Real Estate and Urban Development, School of Business Administration, The American University

Lancaster, Joe J. Jr.   (Chapter 32)
President, Henry S. Miller Management Corporation

Levinson, Burton S.   (Chapter 3)
Levinson & Lieberman, Lawyers

Lewis, John R. (Chapter 57)
Professor, Risk Management and Real Estate, College of Business, The Florida State University

Lipsey, Robert H. (Chapter 9)
Kenneth Leventhal & Company, Certified Public Accountants

Lyon, Victor L. (Chapter 34)
President, Victor L. Lyon, Inc.

McCandless, Donald C. (Chapter 14)
D. C. McCandless & Associates, Inc., Real Estate Consultants

Marcis, Richard G. (Chapter 53)
Deputy Director, Office of Economic Research, Federal Home Loan Bank Board

Mehler, I. Barry (Chapter 10)
Partner, Ernst & Whinney

Messner, Stephen D. (Chapter 19)
Head of the Finance Department, School of Business Administration, University of Connecticut

Monte, Nicholas R. Jr. (Chapter 49)
President, L & M Realty of New Jersey

Mulhearn, Bruce T. (Chapter 28)
Bruce Mulhearn, Inc., Realtor

Muriello, Frank J. (Chapter 58)
Muriello/Meyer & Associates, Real Estate Appraisers and Consultants

Murray, Thomas F. (Chapter 43)
Financial and Real Estate Consultant

Ramseyer, William L. (Chapter 66)
Executive Vice President, Questor Associates

Rapkin, Chester (Chapter 48)
Professor of Urban Planning, School of Architecture and Urban Planning, Princeton University

Reid, Robert J. (Chapter 26)
President, Home Owners Warranty Corporation, National Housing Center

Sachs, David (Chapter 26)
Partner, George S. King Company, Real Estate

Seiders, David F. (Chapter 39)
Senior Economist, Division of Research and Statistics, Board of Governors of the Federal Reserve System

Seldin, Maury (Chapter 67)
Professor of Finance and Real Estate, School of Business Administration, The American University

Shenkel, William M. (Chapter 7)
Professor, Department of Real Estate and Urban Development, College of Business Administration, The University of Georgia

Smith, Halbert C. (Chapter 11)
Professor of Real Estate and Urban Analysis and Director of the Real Estate Research Center, University of Florida

Strunk, Norman   (Chapter 40)
Executive Vice President, United States League of Savings Associations

Sumichrast, Michael   (Chapter 20)
Vice President and Chief Economist, National Association of Home Builders

Thygerson, Kenneth J.   (Chapter 54)
Chief Economist and Director, Economics Department, United States League of Savings Associations

Treadwell, Donald J.   (Chapter 26)
President, Treadwell Real Estate Company

Wagner, Percy E.   (Chapter 1)
Real Estate Appraiser and Counselor

Warner, Arthur E.   (Chapter 50)
Chairprofessor of Real Estate, Property Finance and Urban Development, College of Business Administration, University of South Carolina

Weimer, Arthur M.   (Chapter 67)
Economic Consultant, United States League of Savings Associations

Weitzman, Herbert D.   (Chapter 32)
President, Commercial Retail Division, Henry S. Miller Company, Realtors®

Wiedemer, John P.   (Chapters 36 and 37)
Lecturer, Real Estate Finance, College of Continuing Education, University of Houston

Winkelman, Steven A.   (Chapter 6)
Attorney at Law, Winkelman & Delaney

Woodward, Lynn N.   (Appendix)
Assistant Professor of Administration and Professorship of Real Estate and Land Use Economics, Wichita State University

CONTENTS

The Duty of Fidelity. The Contractual Liability of the Agent to a Third Party. Exceeding the Agent's Authority. The Agent as Conduit. The Agent's Liability for Torts.

Mortgage Equity Method. The Use of Capitalization. Limits and Application of the Income Approach.

How Property Taxes Work: *The Ad Valorem Concept. Classified Property Taxes and Other Modifications of the Ad Valorem Concept. Inconsistent Appraisals. Legal Assessment Standards. De Facto Levels of Assessment.* Property Tax Administration. Appeal Processes. *The Success of Appeals.* Checking an Assessment for Fairness: *The Availability of Records. Grounds for Reduction.* Preparing to Challenge an Unfair Assessment: *Assessment Comparables. Cost versus Value. Market Data Comparisons. The Income Approach.* Nonappeal Methods of Getting Taxes Reduced. Forecasting Future Assessments. Monitoring the Tax Burden.

PART III   Real Estate Marketing

The Passage of the Sherman Act. Penalty and Enforcement Provisions of the Sherman Act: *Criminal and Civil Proceedings. Consent Decrees.* Main Regulatory Provisions of the Sherman Act: *Section 1. Section 2. Monopolizing.* Elements Necessary to Prove a Violation of the Sherman Act: *Jurisdiction and Violation. Application to "Local" Activities. Activities in Restraint of Trade.* Other Important Areas of Law Related to Competition: *Tort Law. Trademarks. Interference with Contracts. Interference with Economic Expectations. Ancillary Restraint Contracts.*

THE REGULATION OF INFORMATIVE CONTENT: The Truth-in-Lending Act: *Purpose. Scope. Enforcement. Information.* The Interstate Land Sales Full Disclosure Act: *Purpose. Scope. Enforcement. Information.* The Real Estate Settlement Procedures Act: *Purpose. Scope. Enforcement. Information.* REGULATION OF THE PRODUCT: Mobile Homes Construction and Safety Standards: *Purpose. Scope. Enforcement. Information.* Energy Performance Standards for New Buildings: *Purpose. Scope. Enforcement. Information.* CONDOMINIUMS: A NEW AREA OF CONCERN. CONCLUDING OBSERVATIONS.

REAL ESTATE LICENSURE: Types of Licenses. Application for Licenses. The Real Estate Commission. Administration. Examination. Regulation. Changes. Narello. SELF-REGULATION OF THE REAL ESTATE INDUSTRY: Evolution of the Code of Ethics. The Code of Ethics and Licensing Laws. The Code of 1924. The Success of the Realtor®. The Code Revision of 1974. Implementation of the Code of Ethics. Parallel Developments. WARRANTIES ON RESALE HOUSING: Background. Available Coverage. Legal Restrictions on Home Warranties. HOME BUILDER WARRANTIES: The Ten-Year Warranty/Insurance Program. Dispute Settlement by Conciliation-Arbitration. HOW National Construction Standards. The Relationship between HOW and the Federal Government.

ments. Residential Income Properties: *Apartment Properties. Single-Family Rental Properties.* Commercial Features of Loans: *The Application. The Financial Statement. The Appraisal. The Property Survey. Title Information. Additional Requirements.* The Costs of Commercial Loans: *Interest and Discount. Service Charges.* Obligations on a Commercial Mortgage Loan: *Repayment Terms. Restrictive Covenants.* Federal Income Tax Considerations: *Appreciation. Depreciation. Passing by Will or Descent. Refinancing.* Methods of Financing Other than Mortgage Loans: *Seller Financing. Supplier Financing. Balloon Notes. Endorsement. Reappraisal. Purchase and Leaseback. Syndication.*

PART V   Real Estate Investment

ings. The Evaluation of Industrial Investments: *The Income Stream. Reversion. Investment Considerations.* Leases and Leasing: *The Gross Lease. The Net Lease. Lease Terms and Options.* The Financing of Industrial Real Estate: *Cash. The Mortgage. Mortgage Lenders. The Purchase-Money Mortgage. Contract for Deed. The Sale-Leaseback. Syndication. Revenue Bonds. Leverage.*

Avoiding Personal Liability. Protections. Negotiating Strategies: *The Offer. Legal Matters. Basic Provisions. The Seller's Response. Acceptance.*

PART I
Real Estate Transactions

THE CONCEPT
OF PRIVATE PROPERTY

Percy E. Wagner

*P*ERCY E. WAGNER, PhB, CRE, MAI, CPM, SRPA, Real Estate Appraiser and Counselor, Chicago, Illinois.

Advisory Board member, The Real Estate Handbook *(Dow Jones-Irwin). Since 1940 dean, Real Estate Institute, Central YMCA College, Chicago. Past president, American Institute of Real Estate Appraisers; Illinois chapter, American Institute of Real Estate Appraisers; Chicago Real Estate Board. Past chairman, Real Estate Examining Committee, State of Illinois. Formerly chief valuator, Federal Housing Administration, State of Illinois; zone manager, Midwest states, Federal Housing Administration; vice president, National Association of Real Estate Boards. Coauthor,* Modern Real Estate Practice *(Homewood, Ill.: Dow Jones-Irwin, 1974). Contributor,* Encyclopedia of Real Estate *(Englewood Cliffs, N.J.: Prentice-Hall, 1973).*

The possession of land is the key to understanding the origin and continuity of private property. It is a manifestation of the human instinct for self-preservation and the most important ownership right of both the prehistoric people who fought for their caves and present-day owners and renters.

Club, spear, or sword were used by the cave dwellers of 8,000 years ago—and are used by the Bushmen of today—to protect their squatter rights. The right of possession in our developed societies is conveyed by a legal process and protected by a state or central power. The right of possession has thus shifted from defense by physical strength to defense by a legal system of justice.

The Bundle of Rights

Primitive man was alone in his battle for shelter and food. His physical prowess gave him the right to his dwelling. He protected the plot of land which he cultivated and repulsed intruders by his strength and skill. He had possession of the complete bundle of rights which we call ownership.

As the population of an area increases, individual defense becomes more difficult. The cave dweller found that joining with others gave him greater security against potential intruders. Thus the benefits of a common defense were a factor in the origins of tribal life.

In clustering for the common good, the individual voluntarily surrendered some of the rights he had. It was as though some sticks in the bundle of rights were transferred to the communal government. In this process rules of conduct were established and the "common law" of tribal life was enacted. The establishment of these "rules" for living together diminished the rights possessed by the individual.

As tribal life expanded and population grew, the protection of the group from foreign enemies required the consolidation of various tribes and resulted in the formation of a strong central authority. However, this loss of tribal control to a central authority did not invalidate the individual's right of possession. The individual retained possession of his land and paid for his protection with tithes, rent, tribute, or servitude. Step by step, historic man released sticks of the bundle of rights in exchange for protection, but he retained possession of a portion of the fruits of his labor and of the right to pass on his retained rights to his progeny.

The bundle of rights includes not only the right to possess land and the right to transfer the ownership of land to others but the right to leave land to others, the right to let others make limited use of land without owning it and the right to use land as collateral for loans. These and other rights are discussed in succeeding chapters, especially Chapter 2.

The Legal Concept

The legal concept of property was well stated by George W. Thompson in *Law of Real Properties* as follows:

> Private and Real Property by its very nature has always been a monopoly. The very essence thereof is that the owner could do with it as he saw fit providing always that he does not interfere with the rights of others. . . .
>
> Man as an animal had and has a sense of possession. Personal property preceded realty ownership as man was free to rove and there was no need for the use of a particular parcel. As group or family living emerged the individual possession of things became necessary. The raising of food remained the effort of the individual or the family although hunting was done by groups or clans. The natural development was for man to have a sense of proprietorship and areas become defined to which the individual claimed possession. Primitive man has no method of defining his property but rule by possession defined to him and his neighbor his property. Man's

nature develops laws for his dependence and controls his action and well being.

Through the centuries, laws governing property developed from customary practices. Such laws are in contrast to legislated usage.

Under early legal systems, title to the land was vested in the supreme sovereign power or the Creator. The individual tiller could get some lesser interest of possession and use, but with restrictions on the transfer of his interest.

Early evidence of the granting of the use of land is contained in the Bible. In Genesis 12:7 we find a promise by God to grant the use of land to Abram, the patriarchal head of the Hebrew people. When Abram returned from Egypt with his nephew Lot, the promise was fulfilled. Genesis 13:17 states that Lot was asked to inspect his land by walking through it. The Book of Numbers, 34:3–13, contains description by metes and bounds. Evidence of the right of inheritance is found in Genesis 13:15 and in Numbers 34:13, which says: "For all the land which thou seest, to thee I give it and to thy seed forever." The method for redeeming property that had been sold or lent which carried with it the right of repossession is described in Leviticus 23–34.

Early Systems of Property

In ancient times land was owned by emperors, kings, and other large owners and was parceled out to families that dwelt on their small tracts. The small landowner could mortgage his property and would pay his debt from the proceeds of his crops. If default occurred, his possession was never questioned. Even though he had given the land as security, the debt was regarded as a personal obligation and could not be met by the surrender of the property. The title to land was always vested in the sovereign state, whether that title was created as a gift of God, a God-created dynasty, or a conqueror.

Japan. Japanese history is dated from the advent of Emperor Jimmu, in 660 B.C. As the descendant of God, the emperor was the sole proprietor of the land within his realm and had full power to dispose of it. Feudal families bound to the emperor received rights of possession and distributed land to their subjects. Peasants tilled the soil and retained possession by the payment of tribute or services.

China. According to John Gunther *(Inside Asia),* known Chinese history began in 2800 B.C. when communities in the Yangtze and Yellow River valleys joined in a loose empire. Dynasties were established in about 1750 B.C. Feudalism spread, with central authority resting in the emperor. The economic life of China has been primarily agricultural. Through the centuries the peasant tilled the soil and paid tribute for possession of the land. Crop sharing was the prevalent manner of rent payment. The peasant had an inherited right of possession and was attached to his land from the cradle to the grave. The inheritance of possession caused families to divide their plots into small, intensively cultivated parcels.

India. Little is known of the history of India prior to 1500 B.C., when nomads from the north invaded India through the Afghan passes. During the 14th century B.C. the Moguls controlled landownership but the peasant remained in possession. Under British rule and maharaja domination, large landholdings were under the control of maharajas. The landowner paid taxes to the state, and the tenant peasant paid rent to the landowner. The peasant remained in possession of the land, and upon his death his plot was divided up among his descendants. The right of inheritance was never disturbed, and thus many families came to hold less than one acre.

The Mideast. The oldest record of landownership dates from the empires of Egypt, Babylonia, and Assyria. Under these empires, the land was owned by the king and the peasant and shopkeeper paid rent to the king or his emissary. Rent was paid in either produce or coins. Large landholdings were accumulated by some peasants and merchants.

The Egyptian feudal age began in about 2000 B.C. It is viewed by some as the forerunner of the European Middle Ages. During the Egyptian feudal age the peasant paid rent by sharing his produce or his labor with the landholder.

The Roman Empire. The Roman Empire created a wider ownership of land. All of the lands conquered by the empire became its property. However, the empire tolerated the private ownership of land by families. The peasant tilled the soil and paid rent to the landlord, and the landlord paid taxes to the state. When the payment of rent in produce became burdensome to the landlord, it was replaced by payment in coin. In the later years of the Roman Empire, inheritance taxes became confiscatory, causing the breakup of large family holdings.

Feudal Europe. With the fall of the Roman Empire the feudal system of land control spread throughout Europe. Strong leaders established small kingdoms and then in concert with the Church of Rome parceled out their landholdings to relatives and associates. The tillers of the soil became slaves, serfs, or tenants. The slave was the property of his master with no reward beyond subsistence. The serf held a small plot and provided his own food and clothing. After paying tribute to his lord, he could create a surplus for his own use. When his status allowed him to move from plot to plot, he became a peasant. The peasant paid rent or tribute to the lord for the use of his land.

Throughout the Middle Ages and centuries of domination by the Church and subservient knights, princes, and emperors, the peasants and serfs retained possession of their land. Wars among France, Germany, Austria, Hungary, and Italy caused little change in their condition. The kings and the nobility fought for control of the land and exacted tribute for its use, but allowed possession to remain with the tiller of the soil.

The English System

Common Law. The laws on land tenure and personal property in the United States and most European countries have evolved from the common law of England. Feudalism existed in England prior to its invasion by William the Conqueror in 1066. The kings of England were absolute owners until the nobles forced King John to sign the Magna Charta in 1215. This gave the nobles greater control over their lands, and the common law of land use and control developed. The right to tax and to demand military service remained with the king and the nobility, and the state protected the tenant and peasant.

The Enclosure Laws. The possession of designated land was fostered by the enclosure laws of England, which were upheld as common law by decisions of chief justices in 1468 and 1484. These decisions held that a "tenant by custom is as well inheritor to have his land according to custom as he hath a freehold at the common law" and that

> a tenant by custom who continued to pay his service could not be ejected by the Lord of the Manor. Tenant possession was protected by these rulings and the manor court rolls recorded decisions of the local court which served as proof of title. The enforcement of the enclosure laws came about by the changing economy of England. Pasture land and grain growing areas did not require the fencing of property. As sheep raising developed and wool became an important agricultural product the land owner (tenant) was forced to enclose his land.

The Small Holdings Act. There was little change in landholding for several centuries until a movement for the breakup of large estates occurred during the 19th century. Laws were enacted which enabled the tenant farmer to buy his land either directly or through the intercession of the government. The Small Holdings Act of 1892, passed by the British Parliament, gave the city councils a mandate to acquire land suitable for agricultural purposes and to rent or sell it to persons who would cultivate it. The price would be fixed by appraisal. The down payment would be at least 20 percent, and the balance of the debt would be payable in 50 years or less. Tenant farmers were thus given the opportunity to buy their holdings from their landlords.

An opportunity for home ownership was also provided by the Small Dwellings Acquisition Act of 1899, which empowered the local authorities to make 80 percent loans to purchasers of small houses.

The Social Contract

These acts of Parliament came late to the English people. For centuries before, continental European countries were gradually reforming their concepts of private landownership and of the rights of the citizen to own land and to be free of the shackles of the state. A major proponent of the view that the citizen should be a free person who cannot be shackled by a central power was Jean Jacques Rousseau, who proclaimed that the individual is the ultimate sovereign power. Rousseau declared that the acts of government should reflect the will of the electorate. The philosophers of the 15th, 16th, 17th, and 18th centuries debated at length the human rights of the people. The French Revolution of 1789–99 was the culmination of the effort to make the citizen the basis of governmental power.

Although, in Rousseau's view, the governmental power stems from the electorate, Rousseau also believes that the elected government is the controlling influence in the affairs of the people. Such a government is not a pure democracy but a delegated form of social control. In *The Social Contract,* Rousseau expounds the theory and practice of democratic government, in which the people are the power in government and government embodies the will of the people. This system of government was realized in life by the American Revolution.

Property in the American Colonies. The American colonies were created by grants of land from the kings of England. Through the influence of English kings, Lords Baltimore, Hopton, and Alexander formed trading companies. The Plymouth Company, the London Company, and the Massachusetts Bay Company were intended to be a source of taxes and of profit to the shareholders. British customs and laws were accepted in the American colonies.

In the 15th and 16th centuries Spain and France obtained land in the Americas by conquest. Their landownership customs and laws governed their acquisitions. However, except where they established military installations, the native Indian remained in possession.

Effects of the American Revolution. The American Revolution resulted in the passage of title from the British king to the individual colonies. The colonies then conveyed their rights to the government of the United States.

Each of the various states has retained some of the customs and laws of the country from which the United States received its title. Thus the Spanish and French laws on ownership by husband and wife and on inheritance have remained effective in the former Spanish and French territories.

Although some of the original laws governing property have been changed by state legislative action, the right to tax, eminent domain, escheat, and the police Power have been retained by the states and granted to local governments. The federal government has some power over those lands which border bodies of water which serve interstate commerce.

Federal Land Grants. As original landowner, the U.S. government distributed land to its citizens by grants for service to the government or by sale. Veterans of the Revolutionary War, the War of 1812, the Civil War, and other conflicts were granted homestead rights which required living on and tilling the land for a specified period of years. Homesteading was not abolished until 1976. Other grants were given to holding companies and railroads as compensation for opening the Great Plains and connecting the Atlantic and Pacific oceans. Valuable mineral and oil lands are owned by the government, and leases are entered into for exploration.

At present, the federal government has title to over one third of the land area in the United States. Its two largest acquisitions by purchase were the Louisiana Purchase from France and the purchase of Alaska from Russia.

The Rights of Government and Limitations on Government. The ownership of land is affected by the rights retained by government. The three
rights withheld by government are the right to tax, the right to purchase
(eminent domain), and the right to regulate (the police power). Escheat
is a right which returns to government land forfeited because proof of
inheritance is lacking. The right to tax and the right to regulate land
use for the benefit of the public have seriously affected the desirability
of landownership and land development. Property taxes have risen
greatly. Restrictions on land use and development through zoning ordinances, environmental regulations, and other constraints have become
increasingly burdensome since the Supreme Court upheld the right to
zone property for the public welfare in 1926 *(Village of Euclid v. Ambler
Realty Co., 272 U.S. 365).*

The right of government to regulate the use of land is restrained by
the 5th and 14th amendments to the U.S. Constitution. The 5th Amendment bars the government from taking property for public use without
just compensation to the owner. The 14th Amendement makes the 5th
Amendment applicable to state laws and grants the rights to equal protection of the law, due process of law, and travel. The right to travel
includes the right to migrate and settle within the United States.

The 5th Amendment grants the government the power of "taking,"
provided that certain criteria are met, namely, that the land is taken
for a public purpose, that just compensation is paid to the owner, and
that the taking promotes the public health, safety, morals, or welfare.
The concept of public use has been interpreted broadly, and reasons
for governmental expropriation of private property for public use are
not difficult to find. The public welfare clause is loosely interpreted by
a definition of the Surpreme Court in *Berman* v. *Parker,* 348 U.S. 26
(1954): "The concept of the public welfare is broad and inclusive—the
values it represents are spiritual as well as physical, aesthetic as well
as monetary. It is within the power of the legislature to determine that
the community shall be beautiful as well as healthy, spacious as well
as clean, well balanced as well as patrolled." Thus, if the courts rule
that "public use" or the police power of the state warrants the taking
of private property and that just compensation has been paid, then ownership, including the possession of private property, can be taken from
the private citizen, the corporate owner, or any other legal titleholder.

Value in Taking. The "takings" clause involves establishing the value
of the condemned property, and several theories of value are presented
in testimony. The fundamental question is whether "value" is taken.

One theory is that the use of private property should not injure one's
neighbor, and that no compensation should be paid if property is taken
to prevent it from harming the public. One of the oldest precepts of
the common law is that "no man may use his property so as to injure
his neighbor." In *Mugler* v. *Kansas* the Supreme Court in 1887 upheld
a law which prohibited the manufacture and sale of liquor in Kansas
and thereby made Mugler's brewery worthless. No compensation was
paid because the removal of a nuisance was not considered cause for

compensation even though removing the nuisance destroyed a business use of the property.

A second theory holds that compensation must be paid where a taking incurs private harm in order to achieve a public benefit. The balance of benefit and harm presents difficult decisions for courts.

A third theory, somewhat debatable, is based purely on financial loss. This theory holds that where a confiscation of property leaves the owner with no reasonabe use of his or her land, a taking has occurred and compensation must be paid.

A fourth theory, also debatable, involves a question "which bears the greatest weight in achieving the government policy of the taking or the intrusion into privately held property." In 1894, the *Lawtin* v. *Steele,* 152 U.S. 133, 137, the Supreme Court held: "To justify the State . . . in interposing its authority in behalf of the public it must appear first that the interests of the public . . . require such interference, and second that the means are reasonably necessary for the accomplishment of the purpose, and not unduly oppressive upon individuals."

The various theories on the right of taking cause the courts to interpret statutes courts according to circumstances. Thus the Supreme Court's precept is indisputable: "There is no set formula to determine where regulation ends and taking begins" *(Goldblatt* v. *Town of Hempstead,* 369 U.S. 590, 594 [1962]).

Court Decisions. In applying the 14th Amendment, the Federal courts uphold laws enacted at various levels of government if these laws are reasonable and not arbitrary and if they bear a reasonable relationship to a permissible governmental objective.

One landmark Supreme Court decision involved the "Belle Terre ordinance," which restricted the use of one-family dwellings to *(a)* one or more persons related by blood, adoption, or marriage, living and cooking as a single housekeeping unit, or *(b)* not more than two persons unrelated by blood, adoption, or marriage, living and cooking together as a single housekeeping unit. The ordinance was upheld as reasonable and not arbitrary and as bearing a reasonable relationship to permissible governmental objectives, and the Court stated that "the police power is not confined to the elimination of filth, stench and unhealthy places."

Exclusionary zoning has been under attack, and in the *Southern Burlington County N.A.A.C.P.* v. *Township of Mount Laurel* case the Supreme Court held: "As a developing municipality, Mount Laurel must, by its land use regulations, make realistically possible the opportunity for an appropriate variety and choice of housing for all categories of people who may desire to live there, of course including those of low and moderate income." This decision emphasized the objective of making low-income housing feasible and obtainable.

Exclusionary regulation was upheld by the Supreme Court of New York in its decision on an ordinance passed by the town of Ramapo. The growth plans embodied in the ordinance were intended "to provide a balanced cohesive community dedicated to the efficient utilization of land." The ordinance also made provision for low- and moderate-income housing on a large scale.

The federal district court of California struck down a growth control ordinance on those grounds: "A zoning regulation which has as its purpose the exclusion of additional residents to any degree is not a compelling governmental interest nor is it one within the public welfare." The U.S. court of appeals reversed this decision on the ground that the plaintiff was asserting claims "on behalf of a group of unknown third parties allegedly excluded from living in Petaluma." The court then ruled that "the concept of the public welfare is sufficiently broad to uphold Petaluma's desire to preserve its small town character, its open spaces and low density population and to grow at an orderly and deliberate pace." As the U.S. Supreme Court refused to hear the *Construction Industry Association of Sonoma County* v. *City of Petaluma,* 375 F Supp. 574 6 ERC 1453 N.D. Calif. (1974), it is assumed that the Petaluma ordinance will be adopted by many other communities.

Varied court rulings with respect to takings emphasize the complexities and difficulties inherent in land use regulation. Further clarification will come from future court decisions.

Environmental Regulation.   The basic law on federal environmental legislation is the National Environmental Policy Act, which became effective January 1, 1970. This act established the following purposes for federal environmental policy:

1. To fulfill the responsibilities of each generation as trustee of the environment for succeeding generations.
2. To assure for all Americans safe, healthful, productive, and aesthetically and culturally pleasing surroundings.
3. To attain the widest range of beneficial uses of the environment without degradation, risk to health and safety, or other undesirable and unintended consequences.
4. To preserve important historical, cultural, and natural aspects of the national heritage and to maintain, wherever possible, an environment which supports a diversity and variety of individual choice.
5. To achieve a balance between population and resources which will permit high standards of living and a wide sharing of life's amenities.
6. To enhance the quality of renewable resources and approach the maximum attainable recycling of depletable resources.

To achieve these objectives, federal agencies must prepare an environmental impact statement before undertaking an action that will have environmental consequences. This statement must include information on:

1. The environmental impact of the proposed action.
2. Any adverse environmental effects which cannot be avoided should the proposed action be implemented.
3. Alternatives to the proposed action.
4. The relationship between local short-term uses of the environment and the maintenance and enhancement of long-term productivity.
5. Any irreversible and irretrievable commitments of resources which would be involved in the implementation of the proposed action.

National parks and federally owned lands are administered by the following agencies:

1. The Forest Service of the Department of Agriculture.
2. The Bureau of Land Management of the Department of the Interior.
3. The Fish and Wildlife Service of the Department of the Interior.
4. The National Park Service of the Department of the Interior. (For additional information on environmental legislation, see Chapter 22.)

These agencies must comply with NEPA regulations.

State and Local Land Use Controls. Controls by states, counties, and municipalities are proliferating. Zoning and building restrictions for the purpose of population control and the efficient use of natural endowments are having an increasing impact on landownership.

The following programs are implemented by state agencies:

1. Land use value–tax assessment laws.
2. Surface mining regulation.
3. Floodplain regulation.
4. Power plant siting.
5. Wetlands management.
6. The management of critical areas.
7. Coastal zone management.
8. State land use management.

In most states, one or more of these programs are in effect.

State enabling acts grant cities, counties, and villages the power to affect the use of land by their citizens. The states have the power to enact legislation that will protect the health, safety, morals, and general welfare of their people, and in turn they have granted this power to a degree to local governments. Because of the continuing activity of state and local governments in land use legislation, land developers should check with the local authorities for current legislation and regulations affecting their proposed projects.

As general guidelines for those concerned with land use problems, the following questions must be answered:

1. What laws bearing on land use decisions have been enacted by the state?
2. Which agencies, boards, commissions, offices, departments, divisions, or other bodies have been given the responsibility of implementing and enforcing these laws?
3. What procedures must these bodies follow?
4. Are permits, licenses, or approvals required by law?
5. If so, to what types and dimensions of development projects do they apply?
6. What provisions have been for citizen participation in the implementation and enforcement of the law? For public hearings or meetings? For public notice of the filing of permit applications?

These questions must be answered in relation to the laws of the state. However, the citizen must also become acquainted with the laws that have been enacted by local government bodies under state-delegated powers.

The principal concerns of states land use legislation have been:

1. The protection of Wetlands and Shorelines.
2. Coastal zone management.

3. Floodplain controls.
4. The preservation of wild, and scenic rivers.
5. Critical area programs.
6. Agricultural use tax assessment.
7. The management of state lands.
8. Boards of land commissioners.
9. Fish and wildlife protection.
10. The protection of water resources.
11. Soil conservation commissions or boards.
12. Air pollution.
13. Solid waste management.
14. Noise pollution.
15. Comprehensive state planning.
16. The state A-95 clearinghouse.
17. Transportation programs.
18. State National Environmental Policy Act review.
19. Land subdivision registration.
20. Power plant sitting.
21. Strip mining.
22. Oil and gas commissions.
23. Statewide land use programs.
24. Land use control—National Resources Defense Council, Inc.

Although states have passed enabling legislation to form regional planning commissions the preponderance of land use control still lies with local governments through their use of:

1. Zoning.
2. Municipal planning.
3. Subdivision control.
4. Official maps.
5. Building codes.
6. Capital improvement programs.
7. Local conservation commissions.
8. Local real property taxes.

Each of the above has a great influence on land use programs and should be studied in order to ascertain local land use conditions.

Land use control has been granted to local governmental bodies by the provisions of state constititutions, by home rule acts of the state legislatures, and by specific state legislation that deals with particular areas. The great number of local governments and the proliferation of authority render even a sketchy account of local controls impossible. Each village, county, region, and state has its particular authority and must be studied for its impact on real estate ownership.

Court Attitudes. Although there have been a vast number of court decisions on land use control, relatively few have reached the U.S. Supreme Court. In recent treatise, *American Land Planning Law,* Professor Norman Williams found that 75 percent of the cases were heard in 13 states that the decisions fell into four distinct categories: (1) those that favored the municipality; (2) those that favored the developer; (3) highly erratic decisions; and (4) the good gray middle. These categories include recent litigation, and there is no evidence that the trends will change in the near future.

Since 1926 the U.S. Supreme Court has heard 12 land use cases and 2 related cases. The land use cases are:[1]

Village of Euclid, Ohio et al. v. Ambler Realty Company, 272 U.S. 365 (1926).

Zahn et al. v. Board of Public Works of City of Los Angeles et al., 274 U.S. 325 (1927).

Gorieb v. Fox et al. 74 U.S. 603 (1928).

Nectow v. City of Cambridge et al., 277 U.S. 183 (1928).

State of Washington ex rel Seattle Title Trust Company v. Roberge, Superintendent of Building of City of Seattle, 278 U.S. 116 (1928).

Village of Belle Terre v. Boraas, 416 U.S. 1 (1974).

Warth v. Seldin, 422 U.S. 490 (1975).

Hills v. Gautreaux, 425 U.S. 284 (1976).

City of East Lake v. Forest City Enterprises, Inc., 426 U.S. 668 (1976).

Young v. American Min-theater, 427 U.S. 50 (1976).

Metropolitan Housing Redevelopment Corp. v. Village of Arlington Heights, 429 U.S. 252 (1977).

Moore v. City of East Cleveland, U.S. 97 S. Ct., 1932 (1977).

The two related cases were:

Berman v. Parker, 348 U.S. 26 (1954).

Town of Hempstead v. Goldblatt, 369 U.S. 590 (1961).

A briefing of each case may be found in the August 1977 issue of the Urban Land Institute's *Environmental Comment.*

Consumer Protection Legislation. The Interstate Land Sales Full Disclosure Act of 1969 is of considerable importance to the real estate industry. It requires that:

1. A "statement of record" be filed with the Office of Interstate Land Sales (OILSR) of the U.S. Department of Housing and Urban Development.
2. A person be furnished with a printed "property report" which meets all OILSR requirements before he or she signs any contract or agreement for a lease or purchase.

The act also makes it unlawful for an agent offering to sell or lease subdivision lots:

1. To employ any device, scheme, or artifice to defraud.
2. To obtain money or property by means of a material misrepresentation with respect to information included in the statement of record or the property report or with respect to any other information pertinent to the lot or the subdivision.
3. To engage in any transaction, practice, or course of business which operates or would operate as a fraud or deceit upon a purchaser.

---

[1] Reprinted from the August 1977 issue of *Environmental Comment* with permission of ULI–the Urban Land Institute, 1200 18th Street, N.W., Washington, D.C. 20036.

Provisions of the act exempt such operations as the following:

1. Subdivisions of less than 50 lots.
2. The sale of lots in subdivisions offering plots of five acres or more.
3. The sale of cemetery lots.

Exemptions are also provided for:

1. Property which is free and clear of all liens, encumbrances, and adverse claims.
2. Property which has been inspected by the purchaser and the purchaser's spouse before they sign the contract.
3. Instances in which the developer has obtained OILSR approval of a statement detailing all reservations, restrictions, taxes, and assessments applicable to the land and furnished the statement to the purchaser prior to the signing of the contract, and the purchaser acknowledges receipt of the statement.

From time to time other exemptions have been allowed, and a developer would be wise to find out what are effective at the time of development.

Fraudulent land sale operations have been greatly reduced by the act, which has been particularly effective in resort areas and in areas that appeal to retired persons.

Increasing Limitations a Property Right. The right to use private property becomes more restricted as court decisions favor limitations by governmental bodies. Part of this limitation occurs through the use of building codes, zoning, and planning regulations. Part occurs under the guise of property service and the creation of new public services which result in higher taxes.

The development of restrictive land uses is not without its merits. The public interest must be served when problems of urban growth, environmental damage, and population shifts are faced by government. Change is an axiom of life, and change in land use is no exception.

The demand of tenants for a "bill of rights" has caused the enactment of laws governing the relation between landlord and tenant. Leases spelling out the respective responsibilities of landlord and tenant have been standardized. State legislatures are enacting laws which give right of occupancy or purchase to tenants of buildings whose conversion to condominium ownership has been proposed. The rights of ownership and tenancy are often abridged in practice where laws do not govern.

Possession: The Key Right. The many sticks in the "bundle of rights" in real property have dwindled, leaving mainly the rights of possession, restricted sale and leasing, and inheritance. To the owner of residential property, "possession" is subject to whatever limitations the local government imposes. To the tenant, possession is subject to the terms of the lease and the landlord-tenant law in effect. To the owner of commercial property, use is regulated by local zoning, health restrictions, inspections of compliance, and numerous other legal devices to protect the health and welfare of the public.

In a nation dedicated to the ownership of private property and the right of free speech, we may rely on the conclusion of Attorney Richard Babcock:

The blunt fact of history these last 50 years is that the state courts having to deal with zoning on a burgeoning scale understand what the game is all about. The federal courts, having all but abandoned zoning since the mid-20s, have not the vaguest comprehension of what is going on since the United States Supreme Court in *Ambler Realty Co.* v. *Euclid,* 272 U.S. 365 (1926) decided that zoning was the epitome of municipality civility, a view which 50 years of suburban wall building has not challenged.

This conclusion by an eminent attorney on municipal law gives substance to the fact that land use is a matter of public interest and that its use is controlled by those interested in its possession.

Although the bundle of rights is dwindling in number, the right of possession has survived through the centuries and in a free country it is likely to remain in the bundle for centuries to come.

This chapter has not discussed the rights of ownership that are related to freehold estates and less than freehold estates. These rights are explained in Chapter 2.[2]

---

[2] The author wishes to acknowledge the assistance he received from the following in the preparation and writing of this chapter and to express his appreciation for the permission he has been given to quote from the articles and books mentioned.

Einsweiler, *Land Use,* publication of the American Right of Way Association, January 1977.

"Rights to Own Land Dates from Antiquity," *Lawyers Title News,* March 1966.

Gwyneth McGregor, "Taxation in the Ancient World," parts 1 and 2, *Canadian Tax Journal,* July–August 1956.

Beverly Dordik, Librarian, National Association of Realtors® Library.

"Supreme Court Land Use Cases, 1926–1977," Urban Land Institute, *Land Use Digest,* August 1977.

Elaine Moss, ed., *Land Use Controls in the United States,* Natural Resources Defense Council, Inc., New York.

Richard F. Babcock, attorney, Chicago, Ill., *The Zoning Game.*

John Gunter, *Inside Asia* (Westport, Conn.: The Greenwood Press), 1974.

FORMS OF OWNERSHIP

Donald R. Brenner

*D*ONALD R. BRENNER, JD, Attorney at Law, Associate Professor
of Real Estate and Business Law, School of Business Administration, The American University, Washington, D.C.

Member, Bar of Ohio, Maryland, District of Columbia, U.S.
Supreme Court. Private law practice and legal consultant,
Washington, D.C. Formerly congressional administrative assistant. Member, International Fraternity of Lambda Alpha, honorary professional land economics fraternity. Lecturer and author in various legal areas, especially real estate law. Author
of "Legal Lines" in Realtor and National Capital Area Realtor.

The principal purpose of this chapter is to explain the various kinds
of ownership and their legal meaning and effect, and to assist the purchaser in selecting the proper and most advantageous form of ownership
when acquiring title to real property. "Forms" of ownership refer (1)
to the nature of the ownership and the rights acquired and (2) to the
relationship between and among owners who are acquiring the same
or similar ownership interests. It must be noted that although generalizations may be made, the most advantageous kind of ownership and
title depends on many factors, such as the circumstances of the purchaser and, in some instances, of the seller, on the relationship of the
parties, and on the purpose for which the transfer is being made. In
addition, it depends on laws which vary from state to state.

A second purpose of this chapter is to point out and explain the advantages and disadvantages of the various kinds of ownership. Again, there
are differences in state laws so that the guidelines are generalized statements.

Methods of Acquiring Real Property

Before form of ownership itself is discussed, it is important to explore
some of the more common methods of acquiring real property.

Original Title. When this country gained its independence, much of the land within the borders of the original 13 states had already been granted to individuals by the country which had previously acquired sovereignty over the land by discovery, settlement, forcible taking, or treaty. After independence, each state declared its sovereignty over lands within its borders that were either vacant or unappropriated. Some land, such as the Northwest Territory, came under federal jurisdiction by grant from the several states having claim to it. Land acquired from France, Spain, and Mexico forms most of the United States proper, other than the original 13 states and the Northwest Territory. The U.S. government still owns land, some of which private individuals may acquire by government grants or patents.

Contract or Agreement. In this country, most property is acquired through agreement of the parties—buyer and seller, or grantee and grantor (see below and Chapter 3).

Judicial Sale. A considerable number of transfers of property result from foreclosure sales or from sales for delinquent property taxes (see Chapter 7).

Adverse Possession. The principle of adverse possession is based on a theory of a lost grant and requires the following: (1) actual possession, (2) possession that is open and notorious, (3) exclusive possession, (4) continuous and uninterrupted possession, (5) possession under a claim of right, and (6) possession for the required statutory period. A person who has satisfied all of the above requirements bars any remedy for recovery of possession by the record holder of title, and acquires a title that the courts generally will not set aside.

Descent or Devise. Real property may be acquired by will or in the absence of a will through the laws of descent and distribution of the state in which the property is situated.

Accretion. Accretion is an accumulation of soil or land to an already existing property through the forces of water. For example, land added to property by the action of water in bringing soil to the shore is called "alluvion"; land added by receding water, is called "reliction."

Classifications of Ownership Rights in Real Property

Ownership rights in real property may be classified into several categories that are commonly called "estates." These may be further classified and identified according to size, legal nature, and the extent of the right created. Estates may also be considered in relation to the length of time of enjoyment of the estate, and to the number and relationship of persons holding rights in and to the property. The major classifications are: (1) freehold estates, (2) nonfreehold estates, and (3) concurrent estates (or coownership). In addition to the above, there are what is called incorporeal interests in real property, or interests relating to rights involving the use of land but not its possession, such as easements, licenses, covenants, and profits. There are also future interests in property, such as those created by will, by life estates with reversions or remainders, and by law in the absence of a will.

Freehold estates are:

1. Fee simple.
2. Fee tail.
3. Fee simple determinable.
4. Life estate.

Nonfreehold estates are:

1. Tenancy for years.
2. Tenancy from period to period.
3. Tenancy at will.
4. Tenancy at sufferance.

Concurrent estates, often referred to as cotenancy, are:

1. Joint tenancy.
2. Tenancy in common.
3. Tenancy by the entirety.
4. Community property.

(See Exhibit 1)

Freehold Estates

Fee Simple. The fee simple estate, also called fee simple absolute, is the broadest form of real property ownership and the "highest" in quality. For all practical purposes it may last forever, and its owner has total rights which are superior to all other rights. Those rights are subject, however, to certain claims, such as leases, liens, mortgage obligations, and eminent domain. The owner may use his fee simple rights during his lifetime, so long as he does not maintain a nuisance on his property. He may sell, encumber, lease, or dispose of all or part of his rights, and he may dispose of his rights by will.

In summary, the owner of a fee simple estate may: (1) use the property as he sees fit; (2) abuse the property so long as a nuisance does not result; (3) have exclusive use and enjoyment of the property; (4) enjoy the benefits or profits from the property; (5) dispose of the property during his lifetime by deed or by a will which is operative at death.

The owner "in fee" is vested with and has control over what is called the "bundle of rights" in the property. This means that he has rights superior to all other rights, rights from which all lesser estates in property flow. He may grant or convey all or part of his rights and may use his property for any lawful purpose so long as that use does not jeopardize the health, safety, or welfare of others and does not damage the property of others. There are certain restrictions on the use of property, whether owned in fee or otherwise, such as regulation pursuant to the police powers of the federal, state, or local government, and the power of eminent domain, which is the right of any duly constituted government to condemn privately owned property for public use upon the payment of a just compensation.

EXHIBIT 1
Comparisons between Basic Freehold and Nonfreehold Estates

Freehold	Illustration	Similarities	Dissimilarities
Fee simple	Grantor to grantee and to heirs of grantee	Possession and legal estate for indefinite period of time	Interest in real property which is inheritable
Fee tail	Grantor to grantee and to heirs of grantee	Possession and legal estate for indefinite period of time	Interest in real property which is inheritable
Life estate	Grantor to grantee for life of grantee	Possession and legal estate for indefinite period of time	Interest in real property which is not inheritable
Nonfreehold			
Estate for years	(1) Grantor to (2) grantee for specific number of years	Possession and legal estate	Interest in personal property which is not inheritable
Tenancy from period to period	Grantor to grantee from year to year, month to month, etc.	Possession and legal estate	Interest in personal property which is not inheritable
Tenancy at will	Grantor to grantee at will of grantor or by mutual agreement	Possession but no legal estate	Interest in personal property which is not inheritable
Tenancy at sufferance	Grantee remains after expiration of tenancy without permission of grantor	Possession but no legal estate	No property interest

(1) Lessor.
(2) Lessee.

Fee Tail. A fee tail, or estate "tail," is granted to a person and to "the heirs of his body." At common law the purpose of the fee tail was to provide a mechanism for keeping a property in the same family so long as there was a family or issue of a family member. The fee tail provided that a conveyance could not be made to defeat the right of the owner's heirs or of the reversionary interest of the grantor in the event that the line of heirs terminated. However, if the bloodline came to an end, title to the property reverted to the original grantor. The fee tail never quite caught on in the United States—only 4 states permitted such an estate without limitation; other states modified the fee tail; and 33 states prohibited its use.

Fee Simple Determinable. A fee simple determinable, sometimes called a "base" or "qualified" fee, is a conveyance whose grantee has all the rights of a fee simple holder except that upon the happening of a certain or designated event, the time of which must be uncertain at conveyance, the estate immediately terminates and the fee reverts to the grantor. The event wich terminates such an estate may be one which is certain to take place time of it is not known, or it may be one which will actually never happen. If and when the reversion takes place, the original grantor becomes the real owner in fee simple and may claim immediate possession of the property.

Life Estate. A life estate is one whose duration is limited to the life of the owner or to the life or lives of another person or other persons. A life estate is a useful mechanism for providing someone with the use of property during his or her lifetime. Such an estate may be terminated on the happening of a certain event, such as the death of the life tenant, or of an uncertain event, such as the remarriage of one's wife. At the termination of the life estate, the rights of the tenant for life merge into the fee. If the grantor has retained the fee, the fee will "revert" to him; if, however, the grantor has given a life estate to one person and the fee after termination of the life estate to another person, the fee will go to the "remainder" person.

Life estates are generally classified as follows: (1) conventional, or those created by agreement or act of the parties; and (2) legal, or those created by statute, such as dower and curtesy, and homestead rights.

Dower is the widow's right to take part of her husband's real estate for life, its historical purpose being to protect a widow and her children and to provide them with a place to live and, perhaps, with means of support. At common law, the widow's dower right was a life estate in one third of the real property owned by her husband during his lifetime. This right has been changed by statute, and one must look to a particular state for the applicable prevailing law.

Curtesy was, at common law, the counterpart of dower, that is, the husband's life estate in property owned during the lifetime of his wife. Modern statutes have altered or abolished curtesy, and it is necessary, again, to examine the laws of a particular state for the applicable prevailing law.

The word *homestead* means "dwelling house," and the purpose of state homestead laws is to secure the family dwelling from the reach of creditors. In other words, even after creditors have obtained a judgment against the head of the household, the homestead law prevents them from evicting his or her family from their home. The homestead laws of the various states which have them are not uniform.

Because a life estate is the conveyance of an interest in real property, it must be accomplished by a written instrument in order to satisfy what is called the statute of frauds, which was called "an act to prevent frauds and perjuries" when it was originally enacted in England in 1677. The purpose of this statute was to lessen the incidence of fraud by requiring that certain contracts be in writing and signed by the person from whom performance was sought. All of our states currently have similar statutes.

It is of interest to note that this country has regarded the acquisition and ownership of real property as sacrosanct. Therefore, contracts involving the acquisition or the divestiture of real property have been considered important in the eyes of the law. For this reason, the statute of frauds applies to all contracts which create or transfer an interest in land and to contracts involving life interests, mortgages, easements, and leases for more than one year.

Nonfreehold Estates

If one merely wishes to have possession of real property, either for a long or a short time, but not to acquire title to it, a nonfreehold, or "lease," interest will accomplish the purpose. Through this mechanism the lessee, or tenant, will acquire certain rights, such as possession, quiet enjoyment, the right to use the property for a particular purpose, and the right to remain in possession under certain stated conditions. Unless the lessee subsequently acquires the property, by purchase or otherwise, the property rights revert to the owner (lessor).

Tenancy for Years.   A tenancy for years, sometimes called an estate for years, includes leasehold interests which by agreement are to continue for a stated time—the time may be a year, less than a year, or 99 years. In the tenancy for years, the lessee has the right to use and possess the property under lease to the exclusion of all other persons so long as he or she abides by the provision of the agreement and any conditions and covenants contained therein. Upon termination of the lease, the lessee must give up the property to the lessor in the same condition as it was at the beginning of the tenancy, ordinary wear and tear excepted.

Tenancy from Period to Period.   A tenancy from period to period, sometimes called a tenancy from year to year, may be created by agreement of the parties, in which case the tenancy continues for successive like periods until one of the parties gives proper notice of termination. It may also be created by what is called "operation of law." This occurs when such a tenant remains in possession of the premises with the knowledge and consent of the landlord. As a general rule, the subsequent tenancy will then be for the same period as the original one, provided that the original tenancy was for less than one year, if the original tenancy was for more than one year, the subsequent tenancy will be for no more than one year. The parties may agree on a daily, weekly, monthly, or yearly period. In most states the period of notice required for termination must equal the period of the tenancy. However, a tenancy from year to year usually requires six months' notice.

Tenancy at Will. A tenancy at will may be created either by agreement or by circumstances surrounding the relationship and conduct of the parties. Its duration is indefinite, and either party may terminate by giving proper notice as required by statute or by the practice of the given locality or community.

Tenancy at Sufferance. A tenancy at sufferance is created when a tenant originally in lawful possession of the premises refuses to quit the premises after the lawful tenancy has expired. A tenancy at sufferance is also deemed to exist after foreclosure or when the mortgagor refuses to give up possession to the purchaser after rights of redemption have expired. Because such a tenant is considered to be in possession without a right of possession, no notice is required to be given him. If the owner agrees, however, a "holdover" tenant may remain in possession and a tenancy at sufferance may be converted into a tenancy at will or a tenancy from period to period.

Concurrent Estates (Coownership)

When title to real property is taken in the name of a single person (or organization), the property is owned in "severalty"; however, if title is taken in the names of two or more persons (or organizations), ownership of the property is vested in coowners and a concurrent estate results. The usual types of coownership are joint tenancy, tenancy in common, and tenancy by the entirety. In eight states partnership tenancies and community property are also regarded as types of cotenancies. Other forms of coownership are the condominium and the cooperative.

Joint Tenancy. A joint tenancy is the coownership of a single estate in real property by two or more owners or grantees; the result is one title. A joint tenancy may be created by grant, purchase, or will; it cannot be created by operation of law.

A joint tenancy requires four distinct "unities" at its creation: (1) *unity of time,* meaning that all of the cotenants take their interest in the property at the same time; (2) *unity of title,* meaning that all of the cotenants derive their interest from the same deed or will; (3) *unity of interest,* meaning that all of the cotenants have exactly the same legal interest in the property; and (4) *unity of possession,* meaning that all of the cotenants have the same right of possession of the property.

The death of one joint tenant does not terminate the tenancy. It merely reduces the number of cotenants, and the cotenants who remain succeed to the rights of the deceased cotenant by operation of law. In other words, there is no need to redeed the property or go through another transfer. The last surviving cotenant becomes the sole owner, and upon his death the entire estate passes either by will or, in the absence of a will, by the laws of descent and distribution.

EXHIBIT 2

	Characteristics	Creation	Coownership Rights	Termination
Joint tenancy	Single estate; one title; death does not destroy remaining tenants' take	Grant, purchase, devise. Title, time, interest, or possession	Rights of possession for each tenant	When any one of the four essentials is destroyed—if one conveys—grantees hold as tenants in common
Tenancy in common	Two or more hold separate title; on death title to heirs	Government, purchase, devise, or operation of law	Only unity needed is possession—need not be acquired at some time	By partition, merger of interests—one tenant may sell or devise his or her interest
Tenancy by the entirety	Joint tenancy between husband and wife; right of survivorship; four unities of joint tenancy with one indivisible legal unit	Government, purchase, or devise (but not by operation of law)	Possession and survivorship	Must be by act of both husband and wife—mortgage by one will not impart right of the other; upon divorce, parties will be tenants in common
Community property	Property owned in common by husband and wife, generally after marriage; property acquired by either husband or wife during marriage by gift, will, or inheritance is separate property	Property acquired during marriage, generally by purchase	Separate property free from interest or claim by spouse—generally no dower or curtesy	Parties may divide the property;—on divorce, each takes one half; in many states each may will one half; but if no will, survivor may take all
Partnership	Title in firm name; each partner holds as tenant in partnership	By deed or purchase	Common rights with other partners	On death of one partner, title in other partners or dissolution

This right of survivorship is the most distinctive aspect of a joint tenancy, because of the fact that the interest of a deceased cotenant does not pass to his heirs but to the surviving coowners. In a strict legal sense, when one joint tenant becomes deceased, the surviving joint tenants actually take nothing from him. What they take is taken from the originally conceived conveyance, the whole of which the joint tenants have owned undividedly since its inception.

A joint tenancy may be terminated by destroying any of the four unities. A tenant may accomplish this by grant or sale during his lifetime, but not by will, because the right of survivorship takes precedence over the purported devise. Termination may also be effected by partition or any other act which destroys any of the four unities. In the event of a sale or a transfer of interest by any of the joint tenants, the grantee does not acquire the grantor's status or rights as a joint tenant. Instead, he becomes a tenant in common with the remaining joint tenants.

Tenancy in Common. A tenancy in common is the coownership of a single piece of real property in which two or more owners hold separate title to the same property, each separate estate being of inheritance. In other words, the element of survivorship, so prominent in the joint tenancy, is not present. Upon the death of a tenant, his interest passes to his heirs and not to the surviving tenant or tenants. A tenancy in common requires but one "unity" at its inception, that of possession, and it may be created by grant, purchase, will, or by operation of law. In other words, unlike the interests in a joint tenancy, the interests in a tenancy in common need not be acquired at the same time or by the same deed or conveyance, and need not be equal in size. The result is that each tenant in common holds an undivided part of the whole and that no tenant in common holds the whole as in the joint tenancy.

Each tenant in common may dispose of his interest by deed or will, and upon the death of a tenant in common his interest passes by operation of law to his heirs. A tenancy in common can be terminated by partition of the property, by the merger of the entire interest in one person, or by the death of a cotenant.

Tenancy by the Entirety. Tenancy by the entirety is a unique form of coownership in that its concept is based upon the common-law principle of the "unity" between husband and wife. Therefore, this type of coownership is limited to the husband and wife relationship. It is a peculiar kind of cotenancy in which each party owns the entire estate and the survivor takes the whole of the estate and the heirs no part. Five "unities" are essential to the creation of a tenancy by the entirety— the first four as in a joint tenancy, the fifth that of a husband and wife. According to common-law principles, husband and wife are considered as one indivisible legal entity, so if they take property as tenants by the entirety, they take it as one.

A tenancy by the entirety may be created by grant, purchase, or will, but not by operation of law. As a general rule, neither the husband nor the wife can convey or otherwise dispose of any interest in this jointly held estate without the consent of the other, nor can either the husband or the wife alone sever or destroy the tenancy. Creditors of one spouse are unable to levy against the entire estate, though creditors of both spouses may execute against the interests of both. If the parties to a tenancy by the entirety become divorced and continue joint ownership of the property, they become tenants in common and the tenancy by the entirety is destroyed. In a broad legal sense, the real purpose of tenancy by the entirety is to protect the family unit by making it impossible for one spouse to transfer any interest in the ownership of real property without the consent and participation of the other.

Community Property.   The idea of community property, which originated in Spain and later became popular in Mexico, has been adopted by some of our Western and Southwestern states. Under community property laws, a husband and wife each have an equal ownership in real and personal property acquired during their marriage, irrespective of the origin of the funds used to purchase that property. Some state community property laws make provision for separately owned property, especially that acquired before marriage. There is no uniformity among those states in which community property exists as to the disposition of the property in the event of divorce or the death of one party.

Cooperatives and Condominiums

Cooperatives and condominiums are "special" types of coownership that give the owner of a unit in a multi-unit building the rights and indicia of ownership possessed by the owner of a single-unit building. Cooperatives and condominiums have become popular because of population growth, rising land costs, and tax advantages.

Most persons think of cooperatives and condominiums as high-rise structures, or what are commonly called "vertical" subdivision developments. Most people also think of cooperatives and condominiums in terms of residential use. However, there is no reason why cooperatives and condominiums cannot be "horizontal" subdivision developments or why they cannot be employed for commercial use.

The cooperative concept has been used in this country for many years. Originally it was used almost exclusively for apartments. The condominium concept was rarely used until about 20 years ago.

The National Housing Act, passed in 1961, gave impetus to both the condominium and the cooperative by authorizing FHA mortgage insurance for single units within multi-unit structures. Many states have since enacted "horizontal property" acts, which are designed to spell out condominium project procedures.

The cooperative or the condominium offer the prospective purchaser several broad advantages:

1. Although the unit may be "apartment-like," the interest acquired is one of private ownership.
2. The cost of the building is shared by all the owners, not one of whom, in all probability, could alone afford the initial purchase cost of the property.
3. There may be income tax advantages comparable to those of the sin-

gle-home owner, such as deductions for interest on monies loaned for purchase and deductions for taxes.

4. The location of a condominium or cooperative building is likely to be in choice parts of the community which are economically suitable for single-unit dwelling.
5. The purchaser acquires the rights, privileges, and pleasures of home ownership but is free from such responsibilities as yard and roof maintenance.
6. A large and well-maintained and -monitoried building with close neighbors and mechanically controlled security devices gives some people a sense of security.

The disadvantages of cooperative or condominium ownership include the following:

1. There is a lack of privacy and the feeling that one is living in a "communal" atmosphere.
2. All of a building's owners must follow certain rules and regulations, some of which may be annoying or even incompatible with the use or enjoyment of the premises.
3. At certain times it may be more difficult to sell a cooperative or condominium unit than a single-family detached dwelling because of the rules and regulations governing the cooperative or condominium or because of the nature of the property being sold.
4. Each owner may have little control over the long-term character of the building, including who his neighbors are.
5. It is difficult, if not impossible, to obtain private financing for the purchase of a cooperative.

The Cooperative.   The usual form of a cooperative is that of the corporate structure. That is, title to the entire property, both land and building, is vested in a corporation. A person who desires to occupy a unit must purchase shares of stock in the corporation. This entitles him to what is called a "proprietary" lease, which in turn entitles him to the occupancy of a unit or units. The number of shares purchased depends upon the cost of a particular unit. In other words, each purchaser is issued that number of shares in the corporation which corresponds to the value of his unit. The costs of upkeep, maintenance, and operation are apportioned among the various shareholders in proportion to the number of shares owned by each.

Each owner has a dual role within the cooperative structure: he is a tenant of the corporation by virtue of his lease, and he is a part owner of the corporation by virtue of his ownership of shares of corporate stock. Each owner has the right to the enjoyment of both his own unit and the common areas of the building.

A cooperative is usually financed by having the corporation execute a single mortgage covering the whole project, it being difficult and uncommon for individual members to arrange separate financing. The control of the cooperative rests with those who have purchased shares in the corporation. Each shareholder generally has one vote, no matter

EXHIBIT 3
Comparison between the Condominium and the Cooperative

	Organization	Advantages	Disadvantages
Condominium	By statute which includes: 1. Condominium declaration 2. Bylaws 3. Separate deed for each unit	Fee simple ownership for each unit Common areas held by owners as tenants in common Ease in selling Ease in financing Ownership without certain property obligations Tax considerations	Limited space and no "yard" Proximity of neighbors Usually a high-rise building Subject to condominium rules and regulations Market conditions may affect ability to finance or sell

Cooperative	1. Business trust
	2. Corporation which includes:
	  a. Corporate charter or articles of incorporation
	  b. Bylaws
	  c. Proprietary lease in each unit
		Ownership of corporate stock or membership certificate plus proprietary lease of individual unit and common areas
		Individual stock owners control the corporation that owns and manages the property
		Each owner has one vote; the majority rules
		Individual unit owner has voice in voting on acquisition or transfer of stock
		Tax considerations
			Limited space and no "yard"
			Proximity of neighbors
			Usually a high-rise building
			Subject to bylaws and cooperative rules and regulations
			Market conditions may affect ability to finance or sell
			Inability to finance each individual unit
			Subject to rule of majority

how many shares he owns. The majority rules as to management policies and budgetary matters. Many cooperatives attempt to restrict the sale or transfer of ownership by making leases or the sale of shares subject to approval by the majority in ownership or their elected representatives.

The Condominium. The condominium has many of the same elements of ownership as the cooperative. However, there is one major difference: each unit of a condominium is owned in fee by the purchaser, and all common areas, such as hallways, elevators, sidewalks, roof, and mechanical systems, are owned by the owners as tenants in common. What the purchaser acquires is the individual ownership of a unit in a multiunit building along with an individed interest, as a cotenant in common, in those areas used by all owners. The costs of upkeep, maintenance, and operation are apportioned among the various owners, generally on the basis of the square footage of their units.

The condominium owner may finance his unit by mortgage, may insure his unit, and may sell or transfer his unit as if it were a single dwelling. The right to use common areas is included in the sale or transfer of each unit. Many states have adopted statutes, commonly called condominium acts or horizontal property acts, which are designed to codify the organizational requirements and the general management guidelines of condominiums.

In summary, the condominium, unlike the cooperative, gives the individual ownership rights in each separate unit, permitting greater latitude in original financing and subsequent borrowing. An encumbrance placed against a condominium is on the individual unit; one placed against a cooperative is on the entire building. In choosing between the condominium and the cooperative, one must consider such matters as basic personal objectives; personal preference; the laws of the given state, county, or city; tax benefits; and market conditions.

Real Property Partnerships and Corporations

Partnerships. A partnership is generally defined in the law as the association of two or more persons for the purpose of carrying on a business or a venture for profit. The sharing of profits gives rise to a like sharing of obligations and debts. Pursuant to the principles of partnership law, each partner is a principal and an agent—he has authority to act for the firm in the course of conducting the ordinary and usual business of the firm, including executing assurances and documents necessary to carry out firm business. A partnership structure is an odd one, in that a partnership is not regarded as a "legal" entity. In other words, the partners maintain their individual identity in a legal sense, although they are associated for the purpose of their business or profession. As a result of this structural oddity, each partner becomes jointly and severally liable for firm debts, which means that each is individually liable for firm debts in addition to being liable as a partner. At common law, prior to the adoption of the Uniform Partnership Act, real property could not be held in the name of a partnership because the partnership was not a legal entity, and title had to be conveyed in the names of the partners. Consequently, if a deed named a partnership as a grantee without naming all or one of the individual partners, title would not pass. Under the Uniform Partnership Act, however, real property may be acquired by a partnership. It may be deeded to and held in the firm name, and it may be conveyed in that name.

If real property is acquired and held by a partnership, no individual acquires title to the property or any part of it. Each partner, acting as the principal of his partner or partners and as the agent for his partner or partners, holds the property as a partnership "tenant" for and with his other partner or partners. A major disadvantage of this type of ownership is that each partner assumes unlimited responsibility for the debts and liabilities of the firm, and in addition he may be responsible for the negligent or wrongful acts of the other partners, based on the theory that each partner is the principal of the other partners. In the partnership, as in any other agency relationship, the principal is liable for the act of his agent so long as the agent acts within the scope of his authority and pursuant to his agency relationship (See also Chapter 10.)

General partnership practice, following principal-agent practice, permits each partner to execute a deed conveying partnership property if this is done in the normal course of conducting partnership business, or if the regular business of the partnership is buying and selling real property.

The General Partnership. A general partnership is one in which each partner has the right and the authority to share in the control and operation of partnership affairs. At the same time, each general partner assumes joint and several liability for firm debts and obligations.

The Limited Partnership. The limited partnership is a structural device that is generally used primarily for ease in investment acquisition and financing rather than for the purpose of coownership. It has two classes of partners, general and limited. The general partners assume general liability, and the limited partners assume liability only for the amount of their investment. The general partners, however, have control of the management and operation of the venture, whereas the limited partners do not.

In recent years the limited partnership has been a popular way to structure real estate building ventures because of the apparent ease with which it has attracted large numbers of investors who wish to invest in a building venture with limitation of personal liability, who have no desire or time to become involved in the management or operation of the venture, and who seek other benefits, such as depreciation write-offs for tax purposes.

One of the attractions of both general and limited partnerships is that income earned by the partnership is taxed to the partners as individuals; the partnership itself does not have a tax liability.

Real Estate Corporations and Subchapter S Corporations. Real estate corporations and the so-called Subchapter S corporations have a special attraction in that they afford the investor immunity from personal liability not available in a partnership. These are similar to any other type

EXHIBIT 4

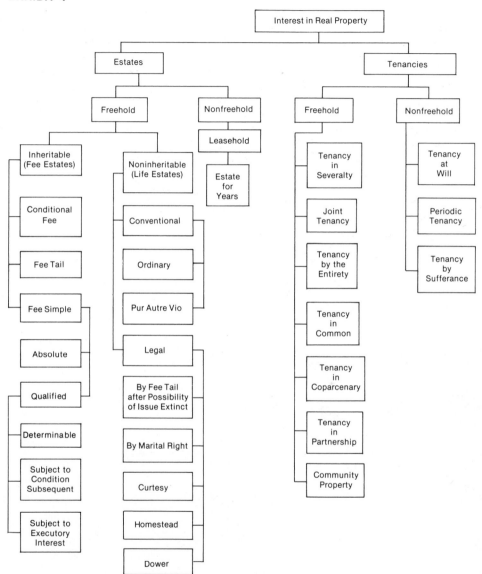

of corporations in that their debts and liabilities are generally those of the corporation and not of the shareholders, directors, or officers.

The corporation does have certain disadvantages, however, one of which is what many regard as double taxation—the corporation is taxed on its income, and the shareholders are then taxed on the dividends paid to them. In addition, employees of the corporation are taxed on their salaries. Another disadvantage is that individual shareholders may have little or no voice in the management and operation of the corporation, since the majority in stock ownership controls the corporation's affairs. In other words, the owner of 51 percent of a corporation's outstanding shares can elect the board of directors, who in turn elect the officers each year.

The Subchapter S corporation, a device created by federal tax regulations, is regarded as a legal corporation but has the option of being taxed as a partnership. The number of shareholders is limited to ten, and all income is taxed directly against the shareholders. There are limitations on the use of Subchapter S corporation for firms whose main source of income is passive, such as from real estate investments. Competent legal and accounting advice should be sought before this type of corporate structure is chosen.

Some additional discussion of the forms of ownership is included in the next chapter, which focuses on the transfer of ownership interests.

OWNERSHIP TRANSFER

Burton S. Levinson

Catherine B. Hanan

*B*URTON S. LEVINSON, LLB, Levinson Lieberman, Lawyers, Beverly Hills, California.
 Lawyer and consultant to title insurance firms, escrow organizations, and Realtors®. Formerly professor of law, University of San Fernando College of Law. Author of numerous legal publications dealing with title insurance and general real estate matters.

CATHERINE B. HANAN, JD, Former associate of Levinson & Lieberman, Attorneys, Beverly Hills, currently practicing in Century City, California.
 Lawyer and consultant with emphasis on real property and title insurance defense litigation. Member' Real Estate Committee, Beverly Hills Bar Association. Formerly director, UCLA Community Resource Center. Coauthor of various publications.

The Acquisition of Title to Real Property

There are striking differences between the transfer of title to real property and the transfer of title to personal property.

The acquisition of title to real property is ordinarily accompanied by an instrument in writing, whereas simple delivery of the property may suffice for the passage of title to personal property. Furthermore, documents affecting title to real property are stored in public depositories so that the public may ascertain the owners of the property from those records. Generally speaking, however, the ownership of personal property cannot be determined by an examination of public records— the notable exception being security agreements which affect personal property.

The transfer of real property did not always require the delivery of a written instrument. In early common law, a freehold estate in land was conveyed by a method known as "feoffment." Feoffment required no written instrument but rather a delivery of possession of the real property involved. Evidence of the delivery of possession was provided in a ceremony known as "livery of seisin" whereby some object symbolic of the land, such as a twig or a clod of dirt, was delivered in the presence of witnesses. No deed, writing, or document of any kind was necessary to validate the transfer, although such a document might be offered as an optional accompaniment to the transfer.

The statutes of frauds, which was enacted in 1676, required a written document to accompany any transfer of any interest in real property. By virtue of the statutes of frauds, what had been an optional additional document became an essential part of every transfer.

The American system of recording evidence of one's ownership of land in the public registry was first adopted by Plymouth Colony in 1636. The present American recording system is an outgrowth of that original colonial practice of perpetuating evidence of land ownership.

Both the legacy of the recording system and the requirements of the statutes of frauds have made transfers of real property more complex than transfers of personal property. Where the statute of frauds requires that certain transactions which affect land must be evidenced by written documentation, the recording system provides an even stricter standard that may make even a written document insufficient to protect certain rights unless the document is deposited in the public registry.

Although the recording system may contain all the documents which affect title, it cannot be said to be a statement of title itself. It is simply a place in which is deposited evidence of title from which one may form his or her own conclusions as to the state of title. Therefore, each recorded instrument of transfer is both an instrument of conveyance as well as a component of "title."

The sale of real estate is a two-step process. The first step is the land sale contract itself. The second step is the closing transaction in which after a specified time, usually between 30 and 90 days, money and deeds are exchanged and the deed placed of record. The time lapse allows investigation into the title of the property. Because of the present conveying system, with documents and recording depository, title is transferred only after a search verifying the seller's ownership in title.

Title may be acquired in a variety of ways:

1. By public grant.
2. By private grant.
3. By involuntary alienation.
4. By descent.
5. By devise.
6. By escheat.
7. By dedication.
8. By accretion.
9. By eminent domain.

10. By abandonment or forfeiture.
11. By adverse possession.
12. By estoppel.

Title by Public Grant. The term *public land* means all land belonging to the federal government, but technically it refers only to unoccupied government lands which are subject to sale or general disposal under general land laws. The U.S. title to public lands is a perfect title held in fee simple with the exclusive right of possession. Congress has exclusive control of public lands and virtually unlimited authority to dispose of them.

Title by public grant may be made by Congress in a number of ways. Congress may make a direct grant by a self-operative act which requires a patent or other instrument, such as with school grants to the state or railroad grants. Or Congress may provide for the disposal of land under public land laws administered by the Bureau of Land Management (formerly known as the General Land Office). Various land laws have prescribed the conditions and modes of disposal of public land. However, Congress can withdraw lands from disposition under public land laws. Ordinarily, government lands are not subject to disposition under public land laws until they have been surveyed.

Title by public grant may be quite complicated, especially in areas in which various sovereignties have made such grants. In California, for instance, land can be divided into three categories according to the origin of title.

1. Mexican grants, mostly rancho and pueblo lands, title to which was derived from Mexican and Spanish authority before California became a part of the United States.
2. Public lands of the United States, including all lands passed to the United States on Mexico's secession from California, but excluding state lands and Mexican grants.
3. State lands embracing lands granted by the U.S. Congress to California out of the public domain to furnish it with funds for education, reclamation and other purposes.

A patent is a government conveyance passing title from the United States to a grantee or patentee. The patent is issued when an entryman makes and perfects a claim for a homestead or a preemption right in compliance with certain public land laws. Originally, patents were signed by the president or by a clerk in the General Land Office who was designated to sign for him, and were countersigned by the recorder of the General Land Office. However, effective in 1948, all patents are now issued and signed by the Secretary of the Interior or by an employee or officer in the Department of the Interior to whom this authority has been delegated.

A patent is similar in form to other conveyances. It contains recitals showing compliance with the law, with the congressional act under which it is issued, and with prescribed exceptions or conditions. A patent is a kind of quitclaim deed, so that it does not pass after-acquired title and it conveys no title at all if the United States never owned or previously conveyed the land.

The issuance of a patent is evidence that a determination has been made by the Bureau of Land Management of the existence of facts that authorize the patent. This evidence is judicial in character, and it may be conclusive. However, a patent is not conclusive if the bureau had no jurisdiction to dispose of the land, for instance, when Congress had made no provision for its sale or had made its sale subject to the rights of good faith purchasers and to the effect of the statute of limitations. A patent is also not conclusive if the bureau had no jurisdiction to dispose of the land because the land had been disposed of previously, or because substantial rights had been acquired in the land, by settlers or others.

A title based on public grants by patent is further fortified by the application of the statute of limitations, which bars suits by the United States to vacate and annul any patent more than six years after its date of issuance, and the rule that bona fide purchasers for value who succeed to a patentee's interest are protected against an action to annul a patent even if it was obtained fraudulently.

Local land office records should be examined in every case in order to show that any claim adverse to the patentee has been disposed of. Furthermore, the records of the Bureau of Land Management should be examined if the local records are incomplete or if other special problems make this necessary. In addition, instruments and other matters in the chain of title cannot be disregarded simply because they precede the issuance of a patent.

Title by Private Grant. Title by private grant refers to the voluntary transfer of real property, such as by written instrument conveying title to real property. By private grant, one usually refers to a deed executed voluntarily by the owner of real property or by a person with an interest in such property.

Title by Involuntary Alienation. A transfer by operation of law is sometimes referred to as an involuntary alienation. This method of acquiring title includes title acquired pursuant to execution sales, judicial decree, or statute (such as bankruptcy). The acquisition of title by involuntary alienation is governed by compliance with the specified statutory provisions and requires no voluntary act on the owner's part, such as in the conveyance by private grant where transfer is made by deed. In bankruptcy, the transfer is not automatic but requires the eventual execution of a deed, such as a trustee's deed, a tax deed, a commissioner's deed, or a sheriff's deed. When examining title to real property, one frequently finds that title to property has been acquired by the operation of law, for example, in bankruptcy proceedings, foreclosures of mortgages and trust deeds, foreclosures of mechanics' liens, and tax sale proceedings.

Title by Descent and Devise. Title to real property is acquired by descent by succession if an owner dies without disposing of the property by will.

Title acquired by devise is, of course, the receipt of the property of an owner who died with a will.

Title by Escheat. If a person owning real property dies without a will and without heirs, title to the property reverts to the state as the original owner. Furthermore, the law formerly provided that real property acquired by an alien ineligible for citizenship escheated to the state upon the death of the alien.

Title by Dedication. Title by dedication refers to title acquired by the public when a landowner evidences his intent to have his real property devoted to a public use.

Title by Accretion. Title by accretion is the means by which an upland owner acquires title to land which forms gradually because of the movement of water along a riverbank or other body of water.

Title by Eminent Domain. Title by eminent domain is the method by which property is taken for public use by the United States, by an individual state, or by agencies designated to do so through condemnation proceedings.

Title by Abandonment or Forfeiture. The abandonment or forfeiture of title—for example, the abandonment by a lessee of his leasehold interest or the forfeiture of a contract purchaser's interest for breach of a contractual condition—is, strictly speaking, not a method of transferring title from one person to another, but rather results in the extinguishment of a right or interest in favor of another.

Title by Adverse Possession. Title by adverse possession may be acquired if an occupant of real property maintains adverse possession of land for a period prescribed by law as sufficient to bar an action by the legal owner for the recovery of the land. Such occupancy confers title which may prevail against all except the state or another public entity.

Title by Estoppel. Title to real property may be acquired by equitable estoppel when justice and equity require that this be done. For example, the doctrine of after-acquired title is based on the acquisition of title by equitable estoppel. Where a person purports by a proper instrument to grant real property in fee simple and subsequently acquires any title or claim of title to that property, this passes by operation of law to the grantee. Therefore, when A who does not have title to Greenacre purports to transfer Greenacre in fee simple to B, a subsequent acquisition of Greenacre by A will operate to pass the title to B. This doctrine of after-acquired title is based on the acquisition of title by estoppel.

However, it is important to note that a quitclaim deed ordinarily has no effect on title acquired by the grantor after the date of the deed. Furthermore, the doctrine of after-acquired title or title by estoppel does not apply to patents from the United States or an individual state, which purport to convey only the present interest of the grantor, or to a sheriff's deed on execution sale. Title by estoppel does not apply to a deed by an administrator, executor, or guardian or to a quitclaim deed of a sheriff on default and sale under a deed of trust.

Deeds

A writing voluntarily transferring title to real property is commonly referred to as a deed.

Any interest in real property may be transferred, including a fee simple, an easement, an undivided interest, a life estate, timber and mineral interests, a vendee's interest, or a lessee's interest. However, a mere possibility, unless coupled with an interest in real property, may not be transferred.

The transfer of an interest in real property transfers all interests incident to it, unless express exceptions have been made by the instrument.

A deed transferring "all property owned and subsequently acquired" without specific description, is valid for all property actually owned as of the date of the deed. But the subsequently owned property is not conveyed since the interest transferred must have either an actual or a potential existence. It cannot be just a possibility.

At a minimum a valid deed requires:

1. A written instrument.
2. A grantor who possess the legal capacity to convey.
3. A grantee.
4. Words of conveyance.
5. A sufficient description of the property.
6. The signature of the grantor.
7. Delivery to the grantee.

Other requirements vary with each state. Some states require that the consideration for the transfer be specified; other states require that the grantee be competent; and still other states require that the deed be acknowledged or attested.

Requirements. *1. A Written instrument.* With the exception of an estate at will or a grant of an interest for a term not in excess of one year, all interests in real property can be transferred only by operation of law or by written instrument.

This requirement stems from the English statute of frauds, which was probably enacted because transfers of real property were considered so important that they needed the higher evidentiary value a writing provided.

2. A Grantor. The grantor must be a party with the legal capacity to act. His name must appear in the caption of the deed, or he must be otherwise described sufficiently to identify him.

Many problems with title arise because the grantor lacks the capacity to enter into a conveyance. State law determines capacity.

3. A Grantee. The grantee must be a legal entity capable of acquiring title to real property. The grantee must be designated in such a manner as to be identifiable. Mistakes as to the name of the grantee cannot be cured by a correction deed, except in the case of a mere recital, such as a tax or trustee's deed.

4. Words of Conveyance. Appropriate words manifesting the grantor's intention to divest himself of the title must appear in the deed. Such words of conveyance include the following: "grant," "release, remise, and quitclaim," "release and quitclaim," "release," "convey," "assign," "bargain," "give," "remise," "sell," and "transfer." Many states designate specific words as words of conveyance.

5. A Description. A deed must sufficiently describe the property being conveyed to properly identify it.

6. *The Signature of the Grantor.* A deed must be signed by the grantor or by his agent duly authorized in writing. Signature or subscription includes a mark when the person cannot write his name, provided that the state's legal requisites for witnesses, attestation, and acknowledgment are met.

7. *Delivery to the Grantee.* Delivery may be actual or constructive. Actual delivery occurs when the grantor hands the deed to the grantee with the expressed intent of divesting himself of the title. Constructive delivery occurs when the grantor expresses the intention of divesting himself of the title to the grantee but does not hand over the deed.

Deeds that are given in contemplation of the grantor's death, deeds that take effect upon the grantor's death, and deeds that are not to be recorded until after the grantor's death raise questions as to the sufficiency of delivery for the purposes of inheritance laws. Under federal law, any transfer made without adequate consideration within three years prior to the grantor's death is considered to have been made in contemplation of death and may be subject to federal estate tax. Such a deed may also be subject to state inheritance taxes.

A deed may be clear in its intent to convey an interest in real property, or ambiguities in its language may create doubt as to the interest being transferred. A deed is ordinarily construed in favor of the grantee. In some states a reservation in any grant or grants by a public officer or body as such to a private party are interpreted in favor of the grantor. Where a person purports by proper instrument to grant real property in fee simple and subsequently acquires any title or claim of title thereto, it passes by operation of law to the grantee. In effect, when A who does not have title to the lot purports to transfer the fee title to B, a subsequent acquisition of the title by A will operate to pass such title to B.

A quitclaim deed, however, ordinarily has no effect on title acquired by the grantor after the date of the deed. A deed by which a grantor "bargains, sells, and conveys" does not limit the estate conveyed to his present interest.

The doctrine of after-acquired title does not apply to patents from the United States or a state to a deed which purports to convey only the present interest of the grantor, or to a sheriff's deed on execution sale. Nor does it apply to a deed by an administrator, executor, or guardian; a quitclaim deed or a sheriff's deed on default; and sale under a deed of trust.

Warranty Deeds. If a deed is given on a property with no warranty in it, there is no implied warranty of marketability. Once a deed is given, the title is conveyed and the implied warranty on the contract to convey real property no longer applies.

If the buyer accepts the deed as given, this implies that the contractual relations have been complied with and there is no redress, except if the deed contains a warranty as well.

In general, a warranty deed warrants against all defects, and a special warranty deed warrants against all defects arising before and during the time that the grantor was connected with the property.

A general warranty deed contains three warranties: (1) A *covenant of seisin,* which warrants that the grantor has title to convey to the grantee. This covenant is either broken at the time it is made, or it is never broken at all, for it covenants a present fact. (2) A *covenant of encumbrances,* which warrants that there are no encumbrances on the property. This covenant is also either broken at the time the deed is made, or it is never broken at all. (3) A *covenant for quiet enjoyment.* This covenant is not broken until the quiet enjoyment of the grantor is disturbed at some future date. By the terms of the covenant the grantor warrants that he will defend the title against any problem with the future enjoyment of the property.

Maryland is the only state which requires the recordation of a deed in order to pass title. In all the other states, title passes with the delivery of the deed.

The seller is usually responsible for preparing the deed, though in some localities this responsibility is borne by the buyer.

If the purchase agreement does not specify the types of warranties in the deed to be used, it will be presumed that a special warranty deed was intended. A special warranty deed does not obligate the grantor for any liability for a loss arising from some title paramount to his own, but holds him liable for any encumbrances created or suffered by him. A special warranty deed also warrants that the grantor will defend the property unto the grantee and the grantee's heirs, representatives, and assigns against the lawful claims and demands of the grantor and all persons who make claims by, through, or under the grantor.

A general warranty, on the other hand, warrants that the property is free and clear of all encumbrances and that the grantor covenants to defend the grantee's title against the whole world. Under the terms of a general warranty deed, a grantor must forever warrant and defend the property and every part thereof unto the grantee and the grantee's heirs and assigns against the lawful claims and demands of any person whatsoever.

Quitclaim Deeds. A quitclaim deed merely conveys the title or interest that the grantor may have in the property described, rather than the property itself. No covenant or representation that the seller has any interest whatsoever in the property is made with respect to such a deed. The seller simply releases whatever interest he may have at that time.

The quitclaim deed has no binding effect against anyone except the seller and claimants through or under the seller. Under the system of transference of real property title, it is merely the transfer by the grantor of whatever ownership he may have. The seller's warranty does not assure the buyer of title. The acceptance and recording of the quitclaim deed is not an adjudication as against the world. In order to have some reasonable reliance upon the conveyance of the grantor, his title must be traced in order to be sure that he has a better claim to the property than anyone else. Only by examining the relevant documents can one determine whether a marketable title is being conveyed.

Grant Deeds—Implied Covenants. When used in any conveyance of an estate of inheritance of fee simple, the word *grant,* unless restricted by express terms, implies on the part of the grantor for himself and his heirs that the grantor has not already conveyed the estate to any other person, and that the estate conveyed is free from encumbrances—including taxes, assessments, and liens—made or suffered by the grantor or by any person claiming under him.

A quitclaim deed may be in the same form as a grant deed, with the word *grant* changed to *quitclaim*. A quitclaim deed conveys all of the right, title, and interest owned by the grantor at the date of such deed.

A quitclaim deed, however, ordinarily has no effect on title acquired by the grantor after the date of the deed. A deed by which a grantor "bargains, sells, and conveys" does not limit the estate conveyed to his present interest.

Void and Voidable Deeds. Deeds which are void and pass no title, even in favor of innocent purchasers for value, include:

1. A deed from a person whose incapacity has been judicially determined, that is, a person for whom a guardian has been appointed.
2. Forged deeds.
3. A deed from a minor under 18 years of age.
4. A deed executed in blank on which the name of the grantee has been inserted without the authorization or consent of the grantor.
5. A purely testamentary deed, that is, a deed which the grantor does not intend to become operative until his death.

Deeds which pass title subject to being set aside in appropriate judicial proceedings include:

1. A deed from a person of unsound mind whose incapacity has not been determined.
2. A deed from a person over 18 years of age and under 21 years of age, except for a lawfully married person. (This is the law in California, but the requirements vary in other states.)

The Torrens System

In the early years, purchasers of property could examine the records contained in the public depository and easily determine the state of title to real property. But as time passed and the volume of land transfers grew, the documentation necessarily increased, various recording problems developed, and the need to establish sophisticated recording indexes and other devices arose.

At one time, it was thought that the adoption of a land registration system would solve the problems inherent in a system which relies upon repeated reference to a public depository. This land registration system was referred to as the Torrens system.

Basically, the Torrens system involves the registration of title to land as opposed to the recordation of the evidence of title contained in deeds and other instruments. The Torrens system sought to make a certificate of registration conclusive evidence of title to real estate. Twenty states adopted the Torrens system between the turn of the century and 1917. Its use was made optional, however, and extensive use of the system was limited to relatively small geographic areas within such states as Illinois, Massachusetts, Minnesota, New York, and Ohio.

Although the Torrens system was not widely used in this country, ideally it would have eliminated the need to conduct exhaustive searches and to rely on ancient documents which might be destroyed or lost through natural or unnatural catastrophes. In fact, nearly half of the states which originally adopted the system have abolished it. In California, for example, the Land Title Law (Torrens Act) was enacted in 1879 and repealed in 1955. Title companies now operating in California have the additional burden of incorporating within the regular chain of title various documents registered in accordance with the Land Title Law.

Although the practical outcomes of the Torrens acts have varied from jurisdiction to jurisdiction, the apparent failure of the system to supplant recording systems centers on four problem areas.

First, there is the fear that when title is put into a piece of paper that is viewed as conclusive, parties may be more easily defrauded by a manipulation of that paper.

Second, the initial registration costs deterred many owners from registering.

Third, a number of exclusions and exceptions, such as tax liens and other interests, could not be included in the registration process and therefore had to be listed on the registration certificate. Thus, it became necessary to consult the standard public records for information on these interests.

Fourth, and most important, the absolute conclusiveness of the certificates of registration, which was the basic inducement for registering was not established. In most jurisdictions, court decisions held that the registrations were not to be considered conclusive. These judicial determinations obviously undermined the effectiveness of the Torrens acts.

Title Insurance

The public recording depository contains documents which have a bearing upon title to real estate and preserve all evidence of real estate ownership. Such a depository also gives people notice of the state of title and of specific priorities between different parties in interest. With the increased number of land transfers, recording systems became cumbersome, and various indexing systems, as well as title insurance, came to the forefront. Due to the varying types of recording procedures, title searches vary throughout the United States.

In the West and the Midwest, it is often customary to trace all titles back to a patent from the government. In the East, such a title search may be impossible and it has often become traditional to trace title back a predetermined number of years or until a warranty deed is encountered. In Massachusetts and Connecticut, it is common to search back some 60 years. In other states, terms of 45 to 50 years suffice.

In the New England states and in some Middle Atlantic, Southern, and Midwestern states, an attorney conducts title searches and renders an opinion. That is, an attorney makes a search of title among all public land records and prepares an abstract of title from his notes. The attorney then formulates his opinion on the basis of his abstract and gives that opinion to the potential buyer.

Other areas of the East, the Midwest, and the West simply rely upon an abstractor. An abstractor searches title on a given property and complies an abstract which reflects all the located instruments on record affecting that property. The abstractor certifies that the abstract is a complete and accurate copy of his notes. With each ensuing transfer, he updates the abstract and passes it on to the new owner. A potential buyer's attorney may give an opinion of title from an examination of the abstract, or the abstractor himself may issue a title certificate based on the abstract.

Another method of title search and appraisal is obtainable through the title insurance process. Title insurance is issued only after a careful review of the documents which form the public record. Most title companies maintain a title plant and transfer the public record into a highly organized and efficient index system of their own. Certain title companies have utilized computers in order to avoid duplication of services and to better utilize resources, particularly in highly developed metropolitan areas where the documentation of transfers is voluminous. After the title search, an opinion of the title is made by attorneys or laypersons employed by the title company. The title insurance process usually eliminates the need for any activity by the attorney of a prospective purchaser of real property. Consequently, more and more U.S. real estate transactions are being handled by title insurance companies.

The Rationale for Title Insurance. Those who take property always run the risk of not taking the best title to the property. The grantor may have held his title subject to a defect, or he may have granted to another the same property he purported to convey to the grantee. To minimize such risks, buyers made their purchases conditional upon a title searcher's examining the record and declaring that the title was "marketable."

Traditionally, lawyers have searched the title records on behalf of the buyer or the holder of an encumbrance. In the past century, however, spurred by the need to reduce the costs and the delay occasioned by an attorney's title search and report, this function has been taken over by title insurance companies.

A good explanation of the purpose of title insurance can be found in this California Insurance Code definition:

> "Title insurance" means insuring, guaranteeing or indemnifying owners of real or personal property or the holders of liens or encumbrances thereon or others interested therein against loss or damage suffered by reason of:
>
> *(a)* liens or encumbrances on, or defects in the title to said property;
> *(b)* invalidity or unenforceability of any liens or encumbrances thereon;
> *(c)* incorrectness of searches relating to the title to real or personal property. (California Insurance Code, §12340.1)

How Title Insurance Works. The title insurer either conducts a search in its "plant" or relies on a search by an abstract or title company.

In its "plant" the title insurer maintains all instruments and up-to-date records affecting each parcel of property within the geographic area in which it does business. These instruments and records include tax records, liens, partition suits, marital dissolution suits, bankruptcy proceedings, conveyances of the property, and mortgages or deeds of trust encumbering the property.

After the title insurer completes its search, it analyzes the information, assesses the risks of the defects in the title, and issues a title insurance policy for a premium reflecting that risk.

Title insurance companies guarantee that the title is marketable (free from all but trivial defects). If the insurer comes across a glaring defect, it will either amend the policy so that the insurer is not guaranteeing the title against any loss caused by that defect or it will insist that the defect be cured before the policy is issued.

When title insurers become liable, this usually happens because an error has been made in compiling the search report (for example, the person who conducted the search may have missed a mortgage on the property) or because a legal instrument was incorrectly evaluated (for example, only one of the parties holding title signed the deed to the grantee, and the title insurer failed to realize that all of the parties should have signed it) or because of some defect in title was disclosed by the record.

Off-the-Record Risks.   Many transactions involving land are void, though they may appear to be perfectly good in the record. A married person may appear to pass title to a grantee, but if the spouse does not join in the conveyance, he or she may later assert his or her community property, dower, or curtesy interest. Guardianship or conservatorship proceedings for the grantor that are pending in another jurisdiction may not be revealed in the public records of the county in which the conveyance was recorded. Delivery of the instrument affecting title to real property with the intent to pass title is a requisite to the instrument's validity. The intent is often not revealed in the public record. These are a few of the risks that title insurers protect against. In addition to guaranteeing the title, the title insurer also promises to defend it in litigation.

Types of Coverage.   Owners and lenders are the two main classes of policyholders who obtain title insurance. The owner's policy provides protection of an ownership interest in real property. The lender's policy insures the priority and validity of a trust deed or mortgage on real property.

However, in addition to owners and lenders, there are a small number of persons not possessing a recorded interest who seek title insurance. Among them are persons who possess an unrecorded interest in real property, attorneys who want to issue an opinion on title, or optionees under an option to purchase.

Both the owners' and lenders' title insurance policies have become indispensable in real estate transactions. Unless title insurance can be obtained, prospective purchasers or lenders will refrain from consummating such transactions.

Time Limit. A title insurance policy is issued on a one-time premium payment. The insurer is protecting against defects in the title that exist as of the day the policy is issued. The policy protects the owner as long as the title remains in his hands. It also protects those who take the property by operation of the law from defects at the time the policy is issued.

Owners' and Lenders' Policies. Title searches and title insurance arose from the need of the purchaser of real property or the holder of an encumbrance upon real property to protect the investment.

The purchaser of real property wants assurance that he possesses marketable title to it. Marketable title may be defined as title sufficiently free from defects that a prudent purchaser would be willing to take title. Marketable title generally includes title to both the legal and the equitable estate, is free from unknown encumbrances, and is both defensible and salable.

A typical owner's policy provides protection against any off-the-record defects, any on-the-record defects that the title insurer failed to except from the policy, and any interpretation of an instrument in the record which differs from the interpretation stated in the policy. Usually, the owner's policy does provide protection against defects of which the owner could learn by inspecting the property.

The upward limit of an owner's policy is generally the value of the property at the time the policy is issued. Only rarely does a defect result in the loss of the entire property; the risk from most defects is usually significantly less than the face value of the policy.

The lender's policy serves a different purpose. It guarantees to the amount of the loan that there are no prior encumbrances or defects which would render the loan worth less than its face amount. Occasionally the lender also takes insurance to guarantee the enforceability of the loan.

Unlike an owner's policy, a lender's policy is freely transferable and automatically inures to the benefit of any transferee of the mortgage or deed of trust which is insured.

The value of the lender's policy diminishes as the loan is paid off.

Special Title Problems

Ownership by Foreign Investors. Generally, citizens of other nations have the same land ownership rights as the local citizens. However, the exceptions to this rule demand a thorough examination of the applicable state law in transactions involving aliens.

Missouri, for instance, forbids aliens from acquiring land, except by descent or devise, unless they have announced an intention to acquire citizenship. Some states, such as Nebraska, stringently limit the powers of alien landowners.

If a citizen holds an encumbrance on or buys property owned by a foreigner, he must check the applicable state's law to be certain that the alien is not prohibited from owning the property and that the state does not limit the alien's right to transfer or encumber the property.

Pursuant to the provisions of the Trading with the Enemy Act, during times of war between the United States and the foreign citizen's nation the federal government administers the property. This may also affect the condition of the title.

Minors and Incompetents.   As was indicated in the section on deeds, it is generally assumed that a person making a conveyance is of legal age and mentally competent. Title problems may arise, therefore, if an instrument has been executed by a minor or by a mentally incapacitated person. Obviously, an examination of the record would not reveal such a title problem.

Public policy generally affords protection to minors. Consequently, a conveyance by a minor is usually voidable. Most states hold that until a minor reaches majority any conveyance of an interest in real property by that minor is subject to his or her repudiation. After a minor attains majority, however, statutory limitations may prevent the repudiation of a transfer made when the transferee was a minor unless that repudiation occurs within a reasonable time after majority has been attained.

Certain jurisdictions, such as Nevada, have statutes which deprive a minor of the option of disaffirming specific types of real property conveyances made during his or her minority. In Nevada, a minor may not disaffirm the conveyance of a mining claim made during his or her minority. Furthermore, some statutes empower minors in certain circumstances to execute a conveyance without the ability to disaffirm it. Veterans who are minors and have executed conveyances of interest in real property, may find that such conveyances are binding upon them. Moreover, minors who are nearing the age of majority or who have entered the armed forces or married, may have "attained majority" for the purpose of conveying real property. The current trend seems to be that arbitrarily fixed age requirements for majority do not apply to minors who have engaged in "adult activities" such as matrimony.

Conveyances by mentally incapacitated persons, like conveyances by minors, are usually voidable. Under certain circumstances, however, such conveyances may not be repudiated. For instance, if the buyer or grantee is a bona fide purchaser without notice of the incapacity of the seller, a subsequent repudiation by the conservator or guardian of the seller will not void the conveyance. In addition, various statutes of limitation bar repudiation by the incompetent or his or her representative.

Trusts.   In a land trust arrangement, an owner of property by will, deed, or declaration of trust designates the trustee to administer the property on behalf of the beneficiary. The trustee holds title to the property in his own name, for the beneficiary.

Because the trustee holds title, a deed in which he is the grantor will appear valid on its face. However, the trustee maintains a fiduciary relationship with the beneficiary, that is, he owes the beneficiary the highest possible duty of care in his administration of the trust. In many states, if the grantee knows that the grantor is a trustee, he may be held to have been put on notice to learn whether the trustee is authorized to enter into the transaction.

Problems with trusts arise because grantees mistakenly believe that the grantor as trustee has the capacity to convey the property. Usually the instrument creating a trust spells out the trustee's powers. In some states a trustee's power to sell or encumber property is inferred from the grant of trusteeship to care for the property in the best interest of the beneficiary. In other states, however, all transfers not expressly authorized are void. The best way to avoid title problems when dealing with trustees is to examine the terms of the trust and the applicable state's interpretation of the trustee's powers.

Taxes. Real property is subject to liens for unpaid taxes, and anyone who takes title to property runs the risk that his grantor failed to pay some or all taxes during his ownership.

Tax liens may be imposed by any number of federal, state, and local units. These agencies have the power to put a lien on the property to secure the unpaid balance of taxes. If the taxes remain unpaid, they can have the property sold at a tax sale to pay off the lien. Often the title search will reveal that a previous owner acquired his interest through a purchase at a tax sale. If the tax sale was defective (as determined by the particular state law), subsequent grantees risk the loss of their interests until either the person whose land was sold loses his right of redemption or the grantees hold the property long enough to obtain title through adverse possession.

Most unpaid federal taxes, such as the income tax, the excise tax, and the gift tax, and unpaid state and local taxes must be recorded in the public record to be effective. A bona fide purchaser who take a property for value and without notice of the lien, takes the property free of unrecorded tax liens.

One major tax lien, that of the federal estate tax, attaches at the moment of death. This lien is effective without recordation, and all purchasers take title subject to it. Many states have similar inheritance tax laws, under which liens arise without requiring recordation.

Certain special proceedings may have a drastic impact on title. Mechanics' liens to secure payment for improvement upon real property are statutorily granted in most states. Such liens are often effective even if they have been recorded incorrectly.

Property transfers that a bankrupt has made within a statutorily designated period before the initiation of bankruptcy proceedings are voidable by the trustee or receiver.

REAL ESTATE CONTRACTS

John S. Kellogg

*J*OHN S. KELLOGG, LLB, Attorney at Law, Denver, Colorado. Formerly chief executive officer, Attorney's Title Guaranty Fund, Inc. Qualified and testified as expert witness on real estate law in U.S. district court in Denver. Member, Title Standards Committee, Section of Real Estate Law and Titles, Colorado Bar Association. Former director, Real Property Division, Section of Real Property, Probate, and Trust Law, American Bar Association. Former chairman, standing committee on Lawyers' Title Guaranty Funds, American Bar Association. Former conferee representing American Bar Association at National Conference of Lawyers, Title Insurance Companies, and Abstractors. Editor, Probate and Property, periodical publication of American Bar Association Section of Real Property, Probate, and Trust Law. Author, "Property Rights and Other Aspects of Land Transactions," in The Fannie Mae Guide to Buying, Financing, and Selling Your Home (Garden City, N.Y.: Doubleday, and pocket part supplement and original text relating to real estate titles in King's Colorado Practice, St. Paul, Minn.: West).

Although it is possible for a buyer and a seller to agree on all the terms of a real estate sale orally and then to proceed immediately to transfer the ownership by deed, real estate transactions rarely occur in this way. There are too many complications, caused mainly by the fact that the subject of such transactions is the transfer of rights in real estate that are not visible or tangible, making it impossible for the prospective buyer to look at the real estate and thus determine all he needs to know. Accordingly, the actual transfer of real estate rights is usually preceded by the formation of a purchase contract between the seller and the buyer in which the buyer indicates exactly what rights he must get, what and how he will pay for them, when and where the transfer will take place, and what will be done if changes in the property occur between the time that the contract is made and the time that the transfer of title from the seller to the buyer takes place. The purchase contract will also indicate whether the buyer's obligation to buy is absolute or whether it is conditional upon certain contingencies, such as his ability to obtain suitable financing.

In general, the purchase contract is a simpler matter for the seller than for the buyer, because the seller usually wants to sell all the interests he has in the subject property. Since he is getting out, he is less interested in what those interests are than is the buyer, who has definite ideas about what he wants to do with the property.

This does not mean, however, that the seller can afford to be casual and haphazard at this point, for he could very easily find himself overcommitted by the contract, that is, be obligated to sell more than he owns and thus be faced with two uncomfortable choices: either to acquire what he promised to sell which would probably be costly and might be impossible, or to pay the buyer damages.

Because of the overriding importance of the initial contract, you should use legal counsel *before* you sign anything.

Major Contract Elements

The Legal Requirements of Real Estate Contracts. Contracts for the sale and purchase of real estate must meet the legal requirements applicable to all contracts, and in addition, must be in writing. The essential elements of real estate contracts are:

1. Competent Parties. Buyer and seller must be legally competent to enter into contracts. The parties to a contract may be individuals, partnerships, governmental bodies, corporations, trustees, and depending on local law, trusts, joint ventures, unincorporated associations, and religious organizations may be legally competent for this purpose. Whenever you deal with a person who claims to be acting other than in his own individual capacity, it is wise to verify the legal competence of the entity that the person represents, and the authority of the person to represent it, in connection with your particular transaction.

2. Mutuality of Obligation. Both parties must undertake some kind of obligation.

3. Offer and Acceptance. In the real estate field, the most common format is for the buyer to submit an offer to the seller which becomes a contract upon acceptance by the seller.

4. Definiteness and Certainty. The words of the contract together with applicable law must include everything necessary to define the rights of the parties.

5. Consideration. Something must be given in exchange for the undertakings. The respective promises of the parties generally satisfy this requirement.

6. Statute of Frauds. The contract must be in writing and signed by the parties charged with obligations thereunder.

7. Mistake, Duress, Fraud, Undue Influence. These defeat what would otherwise be valid contracts. The basic concept is that the contract document does not express a true "meeting of the minds" of the parties. Do not think, though, that you can fail to check your transaction thoroughly at the outset and then, if you don't like the result, get out of it by claiming "mistake" on your part. It's not that easy.

Special Considerations for Sellers. Your first problem as a prospective seller of real estate is to determine specifically what you want to sell.

1. All or Part? You must be prepared to describe exactly what you wish to sell. If you own a large tract of land you may wish to sell only part of it. If so, you must consider the effect of such a sale upon the retained portion. For instance, will you need an easement for ingress and egress over the part to be sold in order to use the part to be retained? If so, this must be provided for at the beginning. Or perhaps the buyer of part of your tract will need an easement over the portion that you will retain. Will it make any difference to the portion you retain if the buyer changes the existing type of use or erects buildings? If so, you may wish to impose restrictive covenants to limit such acts. The real point is that if you are not selling out completely, you should think through the transaction at the beginning so that you can provide the necessary protections for your remaining property. If these are not included in your contract, it will probably be impossible to get them later.

2. Is Personal Property Included? Especially in the sale of residential real estate it is necessary to be specific about which personal property goes with the house and which does not. If nothing is specified, the law is that the real estate includes the land, structures permanently attached to the land, and items of a permanent nature attached to the structures. For example, the heating system is part of the house, but what about the "built-in" dishwasher? This is an area of great uncertainty in the law, so the answer is to be specific in your contract. As a seller, you should make a specific exception in your contract for every item you intend to keep.

The personal property and "fixture" problems exist with the sale of any improved real estate, but in the case of business properties it is more likely that everything associated with the business will be included in the sale.

3. Pricing and Timing. Naturally you want to receive as much as possible for your property. With some kinds of property, prices tend to remain relatively stable, or at least to change at a rather uniform rate, while with other types there may be significant seasonal variations. If you are inexperienced you would probably be well advised to get professional assistance in this area.

4. Taxes. There are severe and constantly changing tax effects of real estate sales. The taxes depend upon a variety of factors. If there is a taxable gain on such a sale, it may be to your advantage to spread it over a period of time through the installment sale technique. If the gain comes from the sale of your personal residence, the tax on it will be deferred if, within the statutory time periods allowed, *(a)* you invest the proceeds in another residence either by buying an existing home or by building a new one and *(b)* you occupy the new home as your residence. In any event, if how you structure your sale will affect the tax consequences, the only time you can obtain the most advantageous provisions in your contract is before you sign it, so check out this aspect as soon as possible. If you need expert advice you can get it from a variety of sources—real estate brokers, lawyers, accountants, bankers, and even the Internal Revenue Service itself. In addition, many specialized publications keep current in this field. Your public library will probably have some of them.

5. *Special Problems.* The ownership of real estate is the ownership of legal rights in land. No person ever owns all of the existing or potential rights in any piece of land, so when you are preparing to sell the rights you do own, be sure not to allow the legal description to exceed the rights you own and have authority to convey. If you received an owner's title insurance policy or an abstract of title and an attorney's opinion when you acquired the property, the document will give you a good idea of what your rights were at that time. Such rights may, however, have been changed since you acquired the property, either by actions you have taken (leasing some or all of the property, borrowing money and securing the loan by a mortgage or deed of trust on the property, getting married, etc.) or by actions which you could not control and maybe even did not know about (zoning changes, lawsuits, etc.). Therefore, you should check your current status as to rights in the property. It may be that unless your wife joins in the contract she will not be obligated to sign the deed to the new buyer, and that the new buyer will not receive good title unless she does. If you have become legally obligated to convey, you'd better be sure you're in a position to do so.

If you have mortgaged your property, be sure that the mortgage does not prohibit you from selling without first paying off the balance of the loan. If it does, you must take this into account. It may be that if the lender approves the credit of your buyer, the lender will waive the "acceleration" provision. Any understanding between you and your lender on this should be in writing. The subject of acceleration clauses, sometimes referred to as "due on sale" clauses, is currently a lively one in the courts and in state legislatures, so the legal implications of such a clause will depend on where you are, when the mortgage was made, and the precise language of the clause.

6. *Finding a Buyer.* Selling real estate is like selling anything else— the better it looks, the more likely the sale. So consider what can be done at relatively low cost to improve the appearance of the property. Don't however, carry the improvement idea to excess. For example, if you are selling a house with a built-in dishwasher in good working order, replacing the dishwasher with a newer model would probably not help you sell the house.

Potential buyers can be located in various ways. Newspaper advertisements, signs on the premises, word of mouth among friends, and shopping center or company bulletin boards are possibilities. Unless you have an exceptionally "hot" property to sell, however, you will probably sell it faster and at a more realistic price if you give the job of finding a buyer to a professional real estate broker. Matching buyers with sellers is the broker's principal service, and the broker has many advantages that you don't have to help accomplish the mission. The broker knows property values, how to advertise, how to show the property, what fix-up would be beneficial, and how to get the prospective buyer to make up his mind.

But using a broker has its hazards, too. For one thing, the broker expects a listing agreement (see Chapter 8). Although the listing agreement contains all the essential terms upon which you are willing to sell, it may give the broker an exclusive right to sell for a fairly long period of time. This means that if the broker finds a buyer who is ready, willing, and able to buy on the terms that you prescribed in the listing agreement, you will owe the broker his commission even if, for some reason, you don't want to sell to that buyer or on those terms. There have even been cases in which property owners have listed with more than one broker and have had to pay more than one commission on a sale. Furthermore, if during the period of the listing agreement you find your own buyer without the help of the broker, you will still owe the broker a commission even if the deal you make is less favorable to you than the terms in the listing agreement.

If finding a buyer is not a major problem for you, then you can undoubtedly handle the transaction without using a real estate broker and you can get the technical help you need from other sources, mainly your lawyer. In some communities title companies will assist you in completing the transaction once you have entered into a contract with your buyer, but they cannot help you or represent you in negotiations with the buyer.

Special Considerations for Buyers.   The buyer's point of view in a prospective real estate transaction is naturally different from that of the seller. As a buyer, your first problem is to determine what you expect to accomplish through the purchase of real estate and then to see how close the available parcels of real estate will come to fulfilling your objectives. Here are some matters to consider.

1. The Location.   Land won't move, so if you don't like a parcel of real estate where it is, including its surroundings, forget it. In evaluating a particular parcel, you should consider whether the use you wish to make is permitted under zoning laws and whether the water, sewer, school, fire, and other public services are adequate. You should also consider the future. What changes have been planned or are being considered by public authorities? Suppose, for example, that you wish to purchase a building from which to conduct a business. You find one that is suitable in all respects, but learn that the area has been rezoned so that the business use can be continued under a "grandfather" clause, but that if the building should be damaged or destroyed, it could not be rebuilt and used for business. You might choose to look for another property to buy. Similarly, suppose that you find a house that you consider suitable. Consider not only the present but also the probable future conditions regarding schools, traffic patterns, neighborhood patterns, and all the other attributes of the property that make it suitable or unsuitable for your needs.

2. Financing. Be sure not to commit yourself to a purchase you cannot handle financially. More will be said about this when we discuss contingencies in the purchase and sale contract.

3. The Seller's Representations and Obligations. In general, every representation made by a seller and every obligation undertaken by a seller and expressed in the purchase and sale contract will be deemed to have been fully performed upon the delivery of the deed to the buyer. Therefore, if there are obligations that you expect the seller to perform after the closing, be sure to provide in the contract that such obligations will survive the delivery of the deed. For example, the seller may have agreed to repair the garage door opener, but at the closing you may find that the repairs haven't been made (or worse, you may not find out), but you go ahead and close and accept the deed. Under the doctrine of merger, the seller's duty is discharged unless you have provided in the purchase and sale contract that such obligations shall survive delivery or unless you make a separate agreement upon something that you find out at the closing has not been done.

4. Insurance. Often a real estate sale contract will call for the seller to assign to the buyer insurance policies covering physical hazards such as fire and windstorm, with the buyer reimbursing the seller for the prepaid but unearned premium covering the time from the closing of the sale transaction to the expiration of the policy or period for which premium was paid in advance.

There are several hazards in this approach. One hazard is that the assignment may not be effective until the insurance company approves it. If a loss occurs in the interim, the company may deny coverage. Another hazard is that the "homeowner's" insurance frequently issued in connection with single-family dwellings may not be assignable to a new owner who does not occupy the house or to a new owner that is a corporation or partnership rather than an individual.

All of the problems of notice to the insurer, approval by the insurer, and ineligibility of the buyer to take the seller's insurance will be avoided if the buyer does not contract to purchase the unused coverage and instead buys his own coverage from the agent of his choice. The buyer should make the arrangement for insurance coverage with his agent before the closing and should obtain a written binder so that the coverage will be effective the instant title passes to the buyer.

Contract Provisions

Types of Contracts. The most important thing to know is that there are no standard real estate contracts. Printed forms, yes. Forms that certain sellers (such as subdividers) insist upon, yes. But legally the parties are free to make whatever agreements they choose and to express those agreements in the purchase and sale contracts.

Most purchase and sale contracts fall into one of two types: either the option type, in which the purchaser has an option to buy the property and loses his down payment (option money) if he decides not to buy (assuming that the seller is not in default), or the specific performance type, in which the seller can require the purchaser to buy, or respond in damages. It should be noted that in both cases the seller can be required to sell. Thus, the difference between the two forms of contract relates to the remedies available to the seller in case of default by the buyer.

Two other forms of contracts should be mentioned. One is called a land contract or a contract for deed. In reality, this is a financing arrangement which allows the purchaser to buy the land on the installment plan, with payments extending over a period of years. Such provisions can be included in either the option or specific performance type of basic contract. The other form is for exchange of lands. In this form, some or all of the purchase price is covered by the buyer giving land to the seller instead of money. Again, this is really a variety of either the option contract or the specific performance contract.

Although there are no standard contracts, there are standard forms with blanks to be filled in. In Colorado, the state Real Estate Commission has prescribed a series of these. Real estate brokers are required to use them without changing them except to fill in the blanks. For residential sales, there are two types, as explained above, the Receipt and Option Contract (Figure 1) and the Specific Performance Contract (Figure 2). The only difference between the two is in paragraph 9, relating to the seller's remedies in case of default by the buyer.

You will see how these forms work when we discuss various contingencies that should be provided for in real estate contracts. Some of these contingencies are covered by the printed part of the forms and some must be handled in the blank spaces.

Contingencies. From a practical standpoint, it is in the recognition of contingencies that should be provided for and in the specific manner of providing for them that the importance of the real estate contract is greatest. The reason for including specific provisions in the contract covering various contingencies is to deal in advance with two classes of unknowns, and thus avoid later misunderstandings. First, there are existing facts which are unknown to the buyer and cannot be ascertained until after the contract has been made. For example, the tract to be sold may contain 42.35 acres and the seller may have represented this to be the case. Suppose, however, that the seller has forgotten that when the highway was widened a few years ago three acres were taken from this property. If the real estate contract provides for a survey to determine boundaries and acreage and for a price adjustment in case the acreage is greater or less than has been represented by the seller, both parties are protected. If no such provision is made and the tract turns out to be three acres short, what happens? Does the buyer have to buy and pay the agreed total price? Does the buyer have the right to reject the entire deal? Does the buyer have the right to purchase the property, but at a lower price? If so, how much lower? All such questions can be avoided through contingency planning in the contract.

The second class of unknowns are those relating to events which may occur between the time that the contract is signed and the time that the settlement or closing takes place and the title passes from the seller to the buyer. Suppose that the subject is a house and that it burns to the ground during this interim period. The same kinds of questions arise as in the acreage example. In addition, what if the seller had insurance against fire? Who gets the insurance proceeds?

In drafting provisions to deal with contingencies, the following matters should be covered:

1. The contingency should be accurately described.
2. If procuring the event which is the subject of the particular contingency (such as the buyer being able to obtain a certain loan) requires affirmative action by either the seller or the buyer, or both, or the cooperation of either or both, the duties to act or cooperate should be spelled out.
3. If the contingency is an act to be done or a fact to be ascertained, there should be a time limit and an express provision of what will happen if the time limit is reached and the act has not been done or the fact ascertained.
4. A standard of evidence as to the existence or nonexistence of the fact or as to whether the act has been done in time should be agreed upon and expressed in the contract.
5. The given provision should include what kind of notice is to be given in relation to the contingency and when it is to be given and the result if no notice is given.

These elements will be more clearly seen when we consider some of the relatively common contingencies which are encountered in real estate contracts.

Specific Contingencies. *1. Damage to or Destruction of Improvements.* This risk always exists with respect to improved real estate. For this reason, most printed contract forms include provisions on the subject. Just because the provisions are printed, it does not follow that they must be used. Examine the printed language, and if it does not fit your situation, strike it out and substitute something that does. If your contract does not deal with this matter, the law will step in and determine the results for you if damage or destruction should occur between the signing of the contract and the settlement. However, what the result will be is anything but certain. For one thing, there will probably be a difference in result depending upon the degree of damage. Furthermore, in a majority of the states the law puts the risk of loss on the buyer, but a substantial minority take the opposite view.

Consider the provisions in paragraph 8 of the sample Colorado forms (Figures 1 and 2). The paragraph divides damage into two classes, damage in the amount of not more than ten percent of the total purchase price, and damage in excess of that. First, note that the key to minor damage is ten percent of the total purchase price. Assuming that the "price" or "amount" of the damage can be readily determined (difference in value before and after? cost of repair?), the base is the total purchase price of everything being sold under the contract, not just the value of the improvements. Thus, if in a given case the land value is relatively high as compared with the value of improvements, or if a considerable

FIGURE 1

RECEIPT AND OPTION CONTRACT
(RESIDENTIAL)

_____, 19____

RECEIVED FROM _____,
Purchaser (as joint tenants), the sum of $_____, in the form of _____
to be held by _____, broker, in his escrow or trustee account,
as earnest money and part payment for the following described real estate situate in the_____
County of_____, Colorado, to wit:

with all improvements thereon and all fixtures of a permanent nature currently on the premises except as hereinafter
provided, in their present condition, ordinary wear and tear excepted, known as No._____
_____
which property purchaser agrees to buy upon the following terms and conditions, for the purchase price of
$_____, payable as follows: $_____hereby receipted for, $_____

1. If a note and trust deed or mortgage is to be assumed, the purchaser agrees to pay a loan transfer fee not to
exceed $_____ and it is a condition of this contract that the purchaser may assume such encum-
brance without change in its terms or conditions except_____
_____

2. Price to include any of the following items currently on the premises: Lighting, heating and plumbing fixtures;
all outdoor plants, window and porch shades, venetian blinds, storm windows, storm doors, screens, curtain rods, drapery rods, central air conditioning, ventilating fixtures, attached TV antennas, attached mirrors, linoleum, awnings,
water softener (if owned by seller), fireplace screen and grate, built-in kitchen appliances, wall to wall carpeting
_____;
all in their present condition, free and clear of all taxes, liens and encumbrances except as provided in paragraph 4;
provided, however, that the following fixtures of a permanent nature are excluded from this sale: _____
_____

3. An abstract of title to said property, certified to date, or a current commitment for title insurance policy in an
amount equal to the purchase price, at seller's option and expense, shall be furnished the purchaser on or before
_____, 19_____. If seller elects to furnish said title insurance commitment, seller will
deliver the title insurance policy to purchaser after closing and pay the premium thereon.

4. Title shall be merchantable in the seller. Subject to payment or tender as above provided and compliance with
the other terms and conditions hereunder by purchaser, the seller shall execute and deliver a good and sufficient
_____warranty deed to said purchaser on_____, 19_____,
or, by mutual agreement, at an earlier date, conveying said property free and clear of all taxes, except the general
taxes for 19_____, payable January 1, 19_____, and except_____
_____;
free and clear of all liens for special improvements now installed, whether assessed or not; free and clear of all liens
and encumbrances except easements for telephone, electricity, water and sanitary sewer, and except _____
_____;
and subject to building and zoning regulations, and restrictive covenants of record. Any encumbrance required to be
paid may be paid from the proceeds of this transaction.

5. General taxes for 19_____ shall be apportioned to date of delivery of deed based on the most recent levy and the
most recent assessment. Prepaid rents, water rents, sewer rents, FHA mortgage insurance premiums and interest on
encumbrances, if any, and_____
_____
shall be apportioned to date of delivery of deed.

FIGURE 1 *(continued)*

6. The hour and place of closing shall be as designated by _____

7. Possession of premises shall be delivered to purchaser on _____

subject to the following leases or tenancies:

If the seller fails to deliver possession on the date herein specified, the seller shall be subject to eviction and shall be liable for a daily rental of $_____ until possession is delivered.

8. In the event the premises shall be damaged by fire or other casualty prior to time of closing, in an amount of not more than ten per cent of the total purchase price, the seller shall be obligated to repair the same before the date herein provided for delivery of deed. In the event such damage cannot be repaired within said time or if such damage shall exceed such sum, this contract may be cancelled at option of purchaser. Should the purchaser elect to carry out this agreement despite such damage, such purchaser shall be entitled to all the credit for the insurance proceeds resulting from such damage, not exceeding, however, the total purchase price. Should any fixtures or services fail between the date of this agreement and the date of possession or the date of delivery of deed, whichever shall be earlier, then the seller shall be responsible for the repair or replacement of such fixtures or services with a unit of similar size, age and quality or an equivalent credit.

9. Time is of the essence hereof, and if any payment or any other condition hereof is not made, tendered or performed as herein provided, there shall be the following remedies. In the event a payment or any other condition hereof is not made, tendered or performed by the purchaser, then this contract shall be null and void and of no effect, and both parties hereto released from all obligations hereunder, and all payments made hereon shall be retained on behalf of the seller as liquidated damages. In the event that the seller fails to perform any condition hereof as provided herein, then the purchaser may, at his election, treat the contract as terminated, and all payments made hereunder shall be returned to the purchaser: provided, however, that the purchaser may, at his election, treat this contract as being in full force and effect with the right to an action for specific performance and damages.

10. In the event the seller fails to approve this instrument in writing on or before_____
19_____, or if title is not merchantable and written notice of defects is given to the seller or agent within the time herein provided for delivery of deed and shall not be rendered merchantable within 30 days after such written notice, then this contract, at purchaser's option, shall be void and of no effect and each party hereto shall be released from all obligations hereunder and the payments made hereunder shall be returned forthwith to purchaser upon return of the abstract, if any, to seller; provided, however, that in lieu of correcting such defects, seller may, within said 30 days, obtain a commitment for Owner's Title Insurance Policy in the amount of the purchase price showing the title to be free from such defects and seller shall pay full premium for such Title Insurance Policy.

11. Additonal Provisions:

12. Upon approval hereof by the seller, this agreement shall become a contract between seller and purchaser and shall inure to the benefit of the heirs, successors and assigns of said parties.

_____   Agent _____
Purchaser   Date

_____   By: _____
Purchaser   Date

Seller approves the above contract this_____ day of _____, 19_____ and agrees to pay a commission of _____% of the gross sales price for services in this transaction, and agrees that, in the event of forfeiture of payments made by purchaser, such payments shall be divided between the seller's broker and the seller, one-half thereof to said broker, but not to exceed the commission, and the balance to the seller.

_____   _____
Seller   Seller

Purchaser's Address _____

Seller's Address _____

FIGURE 2

The printed portions of this form approved by the
Colorado Real Estate Commission (SC 21-10-75)

SPECIFIC PERFORMANCE CONTRACT
(RESIDENTIAL)

_____, 19_____

RECEIVED FROM _____,

Purchaser (as joint tenants), the sum of $_____, in the form of _____

to be held by _____, broker, in his escrow or trustee account,

as earnest money and part payment for the following described real estate situate in the _____

County of _____, Colorado, to-wit:

with all improvements thereon and all fixtures of a permanent nature currently on the premises except as hereinafter provided,

in their present condition, ordinary wear and tear excepted, known as No. _____

_____which property

purchaser agrees to buy upon the following terms and conditions, for the purchase price of $_____,

payable as follows: $_____ hereby receipted for, $_____.

1. If a note and trust deed or mortgage is to be assumed, the purchaser agrees to pay a loan transfer fee not to exceed
$_____ and it is a condition of this contract that the purchaser may assume such encumbrance without change in its
term or conditions except _____

2. Price to include any of the following items currently on the premises: Lighting, heating and plumbing fixtures; all
outdoor plants, window and porch shades, venetian blinds, storm windows, storm doors, screens, curtain rods, drapery rods,
central air conditioning, ventilating fixtures, attached TV antennas, attached mirrors, linoleum, awnings, water softener (if
owned by seller), fireplace screen and grate, built-in kitchen appliances, wall to wall carpeting

all in their present condition, free and clear of all taxes, liens and encumbrances; except as provided in paragraph 4; provided,
however, that the following fixtures of a permanent nature are excluded from this sale: _____

3. An abstract of title to said property, certified to date, or a current commitment for title insurance policy in an amount
equal to the purchase price, at seller's option and expense, shall be furnished the purchaser on or before
_____, 19_____. If seller elects to furnish said title insurance commitment, seller will
deliver the title insurance policy to purchaser after closing and pay the premium thereon.

4. Title shall be merchantable in the seller. Subject to payment or tender as above provided and compliance with the other
terms and conditions hereunder by purchaser, the seller shall execute and deliver a good and sufficient
_____warranty deed to said purchaser on _____, 19_____, or, by mutual
agreement, at an earlier date, conveying said property free and clear of all taxes, except the general taxes for 19_____, payable
January 1, 19_____, and except _____

free and clear of all liens for special improvements now installed, whether assessed or not; free and clear of all liens and
encumbrances except easements for telephone, electricity, water and sanitary sewer, and except _____
_____;

and subject to building and zoning regulations, and restrictive covenants of record. Any encumbrance required to be paid may
be paid from the proceeds of this transaction.

No. SC 21-10-75. Specific Performance Contract (Residential)—Bradford Publishing Co., 1824-46 Stout Street, Denver, Colorado—10-75

FIGURE 2 *(continued)*

5. General taxes for 19_____ shall be apportioned to date of delivery of deed based on the most recent levy and the most recent assessment. Prepaid rents, water rents, sewer rents, FHA mortgage insurance premiums and interest on encumbrances, if any, and _____

_____

shall be apportioned to date of delivery of deed.

6. The hour and place of closing shall be as designated by _____

7. Possession of premises shall be delivered to purchaser on _____

_____

subject to the following leases or tenancies:

If the seller fails to deliver possession on the date herein specified, the seller shall be subject to eviction and shall be liable for a daily rental of $_____ until possession is delivered.

8. In the event the premises shall be damaged by fire or other casualty prior to time of closing, in an amount of not more than ten per cent of the total purchase price, the seller shall be obligated to repair the same before the date herein provided for delivery of deed. In the event such damage cannot be repaired within said time or if such damage shall exceed such sum, this contract may be cancelled at option of purchaser. Should the purchaser elect to carry out this agreement despite such damage, such purchaser shall be entitled to all the credit for the insurance proceeds resulting from such damage, not exceeding, however, the total purchase price. Should any fixtures or services fail between the date of this agreement and the date of possession or the date of delivery of deed, whichever shall be earlier, then the seller shall be responsible for the repair or replacement of such fixtures or services with a unit of similar size, age and quality, or an equivalent credit.

9. Time is of the essence hereof, and if any payment or any other condition hereof is not made, tendered or performed by either the seller or purchaser as herein provided, then this contract, at the option of the party who is not in default, may be terminated by such party, in which case the non-defaulting party may recover such damages as may be proper. In the event of such default by the seller, and the purchaser elects to treat the contract as terminated, then all payments made hereon shall be returned to the purchaser. In the event of such default by the purchaser, and the seller elects to treat the contract as terminated, then all payments made hereunder shall be forfeited and retained on behalf of the seller. In the event, however, the non-defaulting party elects to treat this contract as being in full force and effect, the non-defaulting party shall have the right to an action for specific performance and damages.

10. In the event the seller fails to approve this instrument in writing on or before _____
19_____, or if title is not merchantable and written notice of defects is given to the seller or agent within the time herein provided for delivery of deed and shall not be rendered merchantable within 30 days after such written notice, then this contract, at purchaser's option, shall be void and of no effect and each party hereto shall be released from all obligations hereunder and the payments made hereunder shall be returned forthwith to purchaser upon return of the abstract, if any, to seller; provided, however, that in lieu of correcting such defects, seller may, within said 30 days, obtain a commitment for Owner's Title Insurance Policy in the amount of the purchase price showing the title to be free from such defects and seller shall pay full premium for such Title Insurance Policy.

11. Additional Provisions:

12. Upon approval hereof by the seller, this agreement shall become a contract between seller and purchaser and shall insure to the benefit of the heirs, successors and assigns of said parties.

_____ _____   Agent _____
Purchaser   Date

_____ _____   By: _____
Purchaser   Date
   Seller approves the above contract this _____ day of _____, 19_____ and agrees
to pay a commission of _____% of the gross sales price for services in this transaction, and agrees that, in the event of forfeiture of payments made by purchaser, such payments shall be divided between the seller's broker and the seller, one half thereof to said broker, but not to exceed the commission, and the balance to the seller.

_____   _____
          Seller   Seller
Purchaser's Address _____

Seller's Address _____

amount of fixtures and personal property, such as household furniture, is included, the damage to the improvements would have to be relatively greater before it would trigger the purchaser's option to cancel the contract. The point to remember about printed provisions, suggested provisions in books such as this, provisions drafted by an attorney (yours or the other party's), and especially provisions that you produce yourself is that you should think through the meaning and effect of the provisions under the facts and circumstances of the case at hand.

Suppose that we were to substitute the following for the first two sentences of paragraph 8 of the sample form: "If the premises should be damaged before the closing date, the seller shall be obligated to repair the same, but if the repairs are not completed by the closing date, the buyer shall have the option of canceling the contract and receiving back any payments theretofore made or of closing despite the damage, in which case the purchase price shall be reduced in the amount needed to complete repairs." This would avoid having to measure the amount of damage against the total purchase price and would also make it unnecessary for the buyer to be concerned about the seller's casualty insurance. If the buyer and seller could not agree about how much to reduce the purchase price to complete repairs, an alternative might be to place an appropriate portion of the purchase price in escrow to pay the repair bills and when all had been paid, to remit the balance to the seller. If no agreement could be reached, the buyer could cancel the contract.

2. *Buyer's Need to Obtain Loan.* Although many real estate contracts contain provisions making the buyer's obligation contingent upon his being able to obtain a loan secured by a mortgage (or trust deed) on the premises, more often than not the language of such provisions seems to be inadequate to meet the criteria previously suggested for contingencies. The following clause, admittedly somewhat wordy, is based upon a suggested form contained in *Contracts and Conveyances of Real Property* by Milton R. Friedman, published by the Practising Law Institute.

This contract is subject to purchaser's obtaining a commitment by (date) from a lending institution for a purchase money mortgage of at least $___ ___ with interest rate not over ___ percent per annum and a loan fee not over ___ percent of the loan, payable in equal monthly installments over a period of not less than ___ years. Purchaser will endeavor in good faith to obtain such a mortgage, and both seller and purchaser will cooperate to supply any prospective mortgagee with such information as may be requested, and purchaser will pay the customary charges of the mortgagee and will execute and deliver the mortgage instruments and other papers customarily used by the lending institution. If purchaser shall be unable to obtain a commitment within the time allowed, purchaser shall so notify seller by such date, and seller shall return to purchaser any sums theretofore paid on account of the purchase price hereunder, and upon such return this contract shall have no force or effect and neither party hereto shall have any rights against the other hereunder. Rejection of purchaser's bona fide application by two lending institutions shall be conclusive proof of purchaser's inability to obtain such mortgage. Notwithstanding the foregoing provisions of this paragraph, seller shall have five days after receipt of notice from purchaser of his inability to obtain such mortgage to elect to become purchaser's lender on terms no less favorable to purchaser than above set forth, in which event the promissory note and mortgage to be executed by purchaser shall conform to [identify standard note and mortgage forms] or [the blank instruments attached hereto marked Exhibit A and Exhibit B].

The above paragraph not only satisfies the buyer's need not to be committed to buy unless he can finance the purchase, but also gives the seller a second chance to sell even if outside financing is not available.

3. Buyer's Need to Sell Other Property. Often the buyer will want to be able to avoid his purchase unless he can sell some property he already owns. Most frequently this requirement is associated with residential purchases. One initial question is whether the contingency is the actual sale of the buyer's property or merely the obtaining by the buyer of a valid contract of sale. If the latter is the test by which the buyer's obligation to buy will be measured, the buyer runs the risk that even though he has a valid contract to sell his present property, he cannot enforce it. For example, suppose that the party who executes the contract to buy the present property takes bankruptcy before closing. The buyer might be better protected if he were not obligated to buy unless he first actually sells his present property, but in that case a problem over timing could easily develop. Obviously at the time that the buyer signs the contract with the contingency in it he hasn't yet found a buyer for his present property. Thus, the closing date for the buyer's purchase is likely to be ahead of the closing date for his sale. The following clause is offered for consideration in this situation:

This contract is subject to buyer's obtaining a valid contract for the sale of buyer's real property described as [legal description] at a price of not less than $_____, subject to such contingencies as buyer [under this contract] shall agree to, on or before [date]. Buyer agrees to list said property with a reputable real estate broker. Unless buyer notifies seller of his inability to sell such property on the day before this contract is scheduled for closing or on the day before the date to which the closing on this contract has been extended, buyer shall be deemed to have waived this contingency.

4. Buyer's Need for Rezoning. The need for rezoning contingency provisions can arise in connection with any kind of property which is subject to zoning, but it will arise most often in situations where the buyer is buying large amounts of land for development. For example, the land may be a farm and zoned for agriculture. The buyer may plan to build houses on part of it and a shopping center on the rest. To accomplish this, the land will have to be rezoned. Getting it rezoned will probably require the cooperation of the seller. The buyer will want to have a firm contract so that if the rezoning is granted, he can obtain the property at the agreed price. At the same time, the buyer will not want to be committed to buy the land if rezoning is not available. Points to keep in mind in drafting the contingency clause are; *(a)* provide for adequate time to get the rezoning (it will probably take longer than either the seller or the buyer expect); and *(b)* have the seller agree to cooperate in the effort to rezone. Although it would normally be in the seller's interest to cooperate, as the land will sell for a much higher price if it is rezoned, there are dangers that antirezoning pressures will be put upon him and he will be in a better position if he is obligated by contract to cooperate.

Sometimes a buyer will wish to have the right to purchase land at a fixed price and, to keep the price down, will not wish to tell the seller of his plans in advance of making the contract. In such circumstances a straight option to purchase will work. In this type of contract the buyer pays for the right to purchase the property at a later time for a stipulated price. If the buyer ultimately decides not to purchase, the seller will have been compensated for keeping the property off the market. In some cases the amount paid for the option can be applied to the purchase price if the buyer ultimately buys. This is a matter for negotiation by the parties. In using options, care should be taken to check state law as to limitations upon how long an option can legally run, or how long a recorded option agreement continues to provide constructive notice of the buyer's rights.

5. Buyer's Need to Assume Existing Loan.   Under the terms of some mortgages a new owner can take the place of the former owner without needing the agreement of the mortgage holder. In recent times, however, it has become common for lenders to include acceleration clauses in their mortgages. Under these clauses the lender has the right to call the entire outstanding balance of the loan immediately due and payable if there is a transfer of ownership rights in the property without the prior consent of the lender. As a practical matter, lenders use this device to give them the opportunity to check the creditworthiness of the new buyer and also to increase the interest rate on the loan if the new loans then being made command higher interest rates than were called for by the old loan. The language of acceleration clauses varies widely, so the mortgage at hand must be examined to determine precisely what will trigger the clause and what rights the lender will have. In addition, acceleration clauses have been the subject of recent state legislation and judicial decisions, so these areas must be checked before you will know exactly where you stand.

As a buyer, if you intend to assume an existing loan, be sure to examine the mortgage for an acceleration clause, and if you find one, provide a contingency in the purchase contract so that if the lender doesn't approve you, or will approve you only if the interest rate is increased to a level higher than you are willing to pay, you will be released from the contract.

You should also understand the difference between taking property "subject to" an existing loan and "assuming" the loan. If you take a property subject to a loan, you have no personal liability on the underlying debt. Thus, in the event of default, the lender could enforce the mortgage against the property but could not have a judgment against you personally for any deficiency in the amount realized through foreclosure as against the unpaid balance of the loan. On the other hand, if you assume a loan, you undertake a personal liability to pay. This does not automatically release your predecessor from liability. The lender just adds you to the others to whom he can look for payment.

As a buyer, you should also be aware that you need not sign a document in order to assume liability on an existing loan. It would be easy for you to become personally liable without actually knowing you had done so. The typical way for a buyer to assume a loan is through words in the deed conveying the property from the seller to the buyer. For example, the deed may have a clause reading, "Subject to first mortgage dated September 1, 1972, and recorded September 4, 1972, in Book 2345 at page 67 of the county records given by John Smith and Mary Smith to Local Mortgage Company to secure payment of $95,500.00 which mortgage grantees assume and agree to pay." If you accept the deed, you've assumed.

6. Contingency Checklist.   There is no limit to the subjects which should be handled as contingencies. The following matters should be checked when you are preparing to enter into a purchase and sale contract, and if they are pertinent, you should include contingency clauses to deal with them:

Acquisition of other property (buyer trying to assemble larger tract).

Acreage (price dependent upon amount of land).

Annexation.

Approval:
   By buyer's attorney.
   By court (sale from estate).
   By directors, shareholders
      (seller's or buyer's).

Assumption of loan.

Completion of improvements.

Inspection of premises:
   By buyer.
   By architect or engineer.
   By pest or termite control company.

License or permit.

New loan.

Sale of other property.

Soil conditions.

Survey:
   Of boundaries.
   Of encroachments.
   Of amount of land.

Termination of leases.

Title:
   Curing of defects.

Utilities.

Zoning.

Other Aspects

Assignment of Real Estate Contracts.　As with contracts generally, a contract for the sale and purchase of real estate can be assigned by either party. It is unusual for the seller to assign, but fairly common for the buyer to do so.

The statute of frauds requires that the assignment be in writing.

Covenants and agreements in the contract which are personal in nature continue to obligate the original party even after assignment. For example, if the contract calls for the seller to take back a purchase money mortgage from the buyer, the seller is entitled, where applicable, to have the personal liability of the original buyer on the promissory note. The seller can, of course, waive this right and accept the buyer's assignee as the maker of the note.

Assignment enables a buyer who does not wish to be identified to obtain a contract to purchase in the name of a nominee who will later assign the contract to him. This technique is frequently employed by buyers who seek to assemble property by making purchases from various owners. Using a different nominee in each case reduces the likelihood that the sellers will realize what is happening and raise their prices.

Care should be taken in selecting the nominee. In some jurisdictions, court judgments are automatically liens upon any interest in real estate owned or acquired by the judgment debtor. If your nominee has a judgment against him, it will attach to his interest in the contract as if he were the real party in interest.

A provision in a contract that it will become null and void if assigned without the consent of the other party will probably be enforced by a court.

In assigning a contract, the original buyer (assignor) does not warrant or guarantee the seller's title to the property or the value of the property. He does, however, warrant that the contract is genuine and that the signatures are authentic. (See also Chapter 6.)

Closing.　The closing, sometimes called the settlement, passing papers, or the law day, is the process by which the purchase and sale contract is performed by the parties. Here the various legal instruments are executed and delivered, and financial adjustments made. This process can be smooth and pleasant if the transaction is based on a good contract and if the various functionaries who prepare the documents and supervise their execution are experienced and their efforts well coordinated. On the other hand, a closing can be a disaster if adequate preparation is not made.

The most important step to ensure a good closing is for the parties (seller, buyer, lender, real estate brokers, title insurance company) to agree on who will have overall responsibility. Next in importance is to insist that all documents be prepared and submitted to the parties in advance. This allows time to find errors, make corrections, raise and resolve objections, and become familiar with the documents so that the actual closing will be an efficient and orderly procedure. Here your lawyer can help you make sure that the instruments you sign and the instruments you get are correctly drawn and properly executed.

Closing costs have received considerable publicity in recent times. In the minds of most people, every item for which payment must be made or arranged at the closing is lumped together, even though some of these items are not really closing costs. For instance, if the buyer takes over the unused portion of prepaid sewer charges and reimburses the seller therefor, the item is not a closing cost but the purchase of sewer service. If the buyer is assuming the seller's loan and the buyer pays for the seller the balance in an escrow fund that the lending institution has required to cover taxes and insurance, the amount paid isn't a cost at all—it's an even trade of dollars.

Here are some common items that may be encountered as "closing costs":

"Points" charged to the seller when the buyer obtains a new FHA or VA loan. This is a form of discount to increase the yield of the mortgage to the investor so as to make it competitive with other loans having a higher interest rate than the law allows for FHA and VA loans. The law will not allow the borrower (buyer) to pay these points.

Title examination fee or title insurance premium.

Survey fee.

Attorney's fee.

Credit report.

Loan origination fee.

Mortgage assumption fee.

Closing service fee.

Termite or other inspection fee.

Recording fees.

Documentary tax or fee.

Transfer tax or fee.

Real estate sale commission.

Prepaid expenses:

Tax and insurance escrow.

Special assessments, such as assessments for roads, sidewalks, sewers, etc., provided by municipality.

Credit life insurance premium.

In some parts of the country, notably the Southwest and the West Coast, the closing function is frequently handled by an escrow company. Under this system the various documents and funds are delivered to the escrow company, which holds them until every document needed to complete the transaction has been properly prepared and delivered. When the last paper arrives, the escrow company records the deed and the other papers that should be recorded, makes sure that nothing adverse has been recorded since the previous check of the records, and then disburses the funds.

After closing, be sure to set up a file for the financial records pertaining to the transaction. You will need them for tax purposes.

Title Matters. 1. *Marketable Title.* Marketable title, sometimes called merchantable title, is a term of great significance in real estate contracts, as it is the measure of the quality of title that the buyer is entitled to receive unless the contract specifies some other standard. The term, however, does not have a universal meaning. For example, a large number of U.S. land patents were issued subject to the right of the proprietor of a vein or lode to extract or remove his ore therefrom, should the vein or lode be found to penetrate or intersect the premises granted by the patents. In some localities this reservation has been treated as insignificant for many years, so that its existence would not render a title unmarketable. In these localities a buyer could not refuse to buy simply because of that patent restriction, even though no mention of it was made in the contract to purchase. In other localities the opposite is true. Accordingly, while marketable title signifies legal sufficiency of the rights to be conveyed, in many cases it also has a practical meaning that is based on custom.

Many courts and writers have wrestled with the problem of defining marketable title and have had only slightly more success than the courts and writers that have wrestled with the definition of pornography. The definition most frequently used in Colorado is taken from the decision in *Federal Farm Mortgage Corporation* v. *Schmidt,* 109 Colo. 467, 126 P. 2d 1036 (1942). The court adopted a definition found in Thompson or Real Property, and stated it as follows:

> A purchaser of land, before he is required to pay the purchase price, is entitled, unless stipulated to the contrary, to receive a marketable title, a title that is fairly deducible of record and not depending on matters resting in parol. The term "marketable title," when applied to real estate, means a title free from reasonable doubt. It means a title that is reasonably free from such doubts as will affect the market value of the estate; one which a reasonably prudent person with knowledge of all the facts and their legal bearing would be willing to accept.

Hardly a scientific, objective definition! The readers of this chapter, then, whether prospective buyers or sellers, would be well advised to find out what a marketable title means in the jurisdiction where the land lies before undertaking to deliver or agree to receive such a title.

2. *Evidence of Title.* How do you know whether title to a given parcel is or is not marketable, assuming that you understand the applicable definition of marketability? This leads to a consideration of the sources and types of evidence relating to real property rights, what they are and who has them.

In almost all of the states, title evidence stems from a system of public records that is usually kept at the county level, although there are exceptions, such as Connecticut, where the town is the record keeper. In a geographically small, but nevertheless significant, part of the country, various systems of title registration are in operation. These are adaptations of the Torrens system, which originated in Australia and is widely used there and in many other parts of the world. The definition of marketability given above relates to the recording system and not to the Torrens, or registration, system.

a. The recording system. The central concept of this system is that transfers of rights in land will not be effective as against parties who do not have actual knowledge of transfers until the instruments by which the transfers are made have been recorded with a designated public official. Upon being recorded, such instruments are available for examination by the public, and the public is then charged with knowledge of them (constructive notice) whether or not a member of the public has, in fact, looked at them or knows of their existence.

The official who keeps the records (recorder, register of deeds, clerk, and even probate judge are names given in various localities to this officer) is also required to keep an index of them to enable members of the public to locate documents more readily. Most recording offices keep only a grantor-grantee index in which the names of the various grantors and grantees of recorded instruments are listed alphabetically. In the simplest systems (from the point of view of the recorder) the alphabetization is merely a list in which each name beginning with *A,* for example, is added in chronological order of recording to the other *A* names. The advent of the computer has permitted many more progressive recorders to put grantors and grantees in strict alphabetical order and to merge listings to cover a year or more in a single list. This obviously saves much time for those who use the indexes.

Jurisdictions differ as to whether the index is or is not a part of the official record. In some jurisdictions, constructive notice attaches immediately upon recording the instrument, whether or not it is correctly indexed. In a lesser number of jurisdictions, there is no constructive notice unless the instrument is properly indexed.

b. Abstract of title. The obvious difficulties that the recording system presented for users led to the founding of businesses for the purpose of maintaining private indexes and summarizing the instruments and selling the product (abstracts) to the public.

Since the party wishing to know about land titles usually has a certain parcel of land in mind, not the names of parties who have held interests in that parcel of land in the past, an index of records based upon parcels of land rather than the names of people is more useful. However, most public recording offices do not maintain land-related indexes (tract indexes). The abstract companies, however, do.

In recent years the summarizing aspect of abstracting has been largely replaced by the technique of using photocopies of recorded instruments as pages in the abstract.

Suppose that you learn what recorded instruments relate to the parcel of land in which you are interested and that you either examine them in the recorder's office or look at an abstract. How do you know the state of the title?

Unless you are able to judge the legal effect of each instrument and know whether or not it is properly executed and acknowledged, and so on, you don't really know much more than you would if you hadn't bothered to look. Lawyers (at least some of them) can interpret these instruments and, after examining them, will give you a written opinion setting forth their conclusions.

There are still some risks. For example, suppose that one of the deeds on which the buyer must rely for a good title is a forgery. This would not normally be detectable by looking at the recorded instrument (unless you're a supersleuth or it's a really bum forgery) or at a picture of it, and certainly not by looking at a summary of it. This problem, and others like it, led to the establishment of still another business, title insurance.

3. Title Insurance. Essentially, a title insurance policy is a contract under which title insurance company agrees to indemnify the insured (owner or lender) against loss sustained by the insured because the title is not as described in the policy. The policy will contain an upper limit of liability and a rather lengthy list of matters against which the title company does not insure. Some of the noninsured matters are printed in the policies as exclusions from coverage or as standard printed exceptions. More specific exceptions are typewritten in the policy.

Nearly all title insurers use the American Land Title Association (ALTA) policy forms. There are two main styles of owners' forms. Form A does *not* insure marketability of the title; Form B does. There have been a series of loan policy forms which have been changed to keep up with changing financing techniques and practices.

You may not really know the limits of your protection when you look at a title insurance policy (or the commitment for a title insurance policy, which is the preliminary document issued by the title insurer before the closing of the current transaction, setting forth the state of the title at that time and indicating what must be done in order to obtain the policy after the closing and what specific exceptions will appear in the final policy). If you have any doubts about whether you are receiving the protection you need, the services of an experienced real estate lawyer will be most worthwhile.

You should also be aware that the protection offered in the commitment of the title insurance company is not necessarily a take-it-or-leave-it matter. Coverages are negotiable, and if you need protection that seems to be lacking, discuss this with the title company. Here again, a real estate lawyer can be very helpful. Such a lawyer will be able to evaluate your needs and will know how to deal with the title company.

Title insurance is a contract of financial indemnity for losses, not a guarantee that the owner can keep the property, for example, even if his title is defective. Often a title insurance company will regard the chance of loss as so remote that it will insure against a known peril. The policyholder should understand this.

An example of this principle occurred when Colorado adopted the Uniform Probate Code. It contained some provisions (since repealed) that endangered titles. A large title insurance company which refused to insure against this particular risk found that other title companies were issuing policies that did not mention or exclude it. The company published a bulletin on the subject which said: "A title company insulating a buyer from monetary loss is not the whole story. In a dispute, an insured buyer is required to cooperate with the insurer, produce proof to the insurer, testify for the insurer, and make claim free of the insurer's defenses. In other words, the insured buyer or lender has substantial trouble. This means that a title company's willingness to insure (provided their underwriter approves) does not shelter your customer from substantial inconvenience." This forthright statement is accurate and applies to all coverages. It does not mean that title insurance is worthless, but it does give an idea of the limits of this form of protection. (For additional information on title insurance, see Chapter 3.)

4. Registered (Torrens) Title.   The essence of this system of title evidence is that the state government establishes a means whereby all rights to land (except for certain enumerated types of rights) are determined by a court decree that is then registered in a public office. Thereafter the registrar issues official certificates of title to the holders of various interests in the land. Transfers can then be made only by surrender of the outstanding certificates (or accounting for their loss) and the issuance of new certificates. This part of the system is not unlike the way in which titles to automobiles are usually handled. Nothing counts unless it is shown on the certificate of title.

Problems in using this system have prevented its widespread adoption in the United States. First, it is expensive to get a parcel registered initially, as this requires (in order to meet due process mandates of federal and state constitutions) a separate lawsuit in which all interest owners are joined. Next, in many of these systems there is little financial backing to cover in case of error. (Title insurance can supply this and is often used in conjunction with registered titles.) Third, there are property rights that are not included in the system. This materially reduces the system's efficiency, as the traditional title search and examination must still be made with respect to the excluded interests. Examples of excluded interests are railroad and public utility rights-of-way and claims arising under the constitution or laws of the state or the United States, which need not be recorded to be effective. (For additional information on the Torrens system, see Chapter 3.)

5. Warranties.   Among the most widely used forms of conveyancing instruments are the quitclaim deed and the warranty deed. The quitclaim deed merely conveys whatever interest in the land the grantor of the deed may have, and it does not represent that he has any at all (see Chapter 3). I could safely give you my quitclaim deed to the Empire State Building (or the Brooklyn Bridge) and you wouldn't get anything nor would you have any enforceable claim against me.

When the warranty deed is used, the grantor warrants (guarantees) that he has good title as described in the deed, has power to convey, that the title is free of defects or encumbrances not specified in the deed, that the grantee will enjoy quiet and peaceable possession of the property, and that if such possession is attacked, the grantor will defend. Warranties vary somewhat from one jurisdiction to another, but the practical effects of warranties are about the same everywhere.

Although warranties are helpful, they do not insure good title or anything else. The enforcement of warranties is subject to statutes of limitation. Even if there is a breach of warranty and enforcement is not barred, you may have difficulty locating the warrantor, and if you do locate him, you may find him financially unable to respond. (See also Chapter 3.)

Governmental Regulations. Governmental regulations relating directly to what uses may or may not be made of a given parcel of land, or what types of improvements may be made, where such improvements may be located, what their physical characteristics may be, and so on, had their beginnings as purely local matters aimed at the promotion of the health, safety, and welfare of the public at large. Thus it was felt proper to segregate factories and homes in separate parts of a city.

In more recent times the protection of "consumers" has become a stated objective of governmental regulation not only of land uses, structural soundness, and so forth, but also of the financial aspects of land transactions. Furthermore, direct federal regulation has been added to local and state regulation. (For discussion of federal laws directed toward consumer protection, see Chapter 25.)

In making real estate contracts, it is important to know what regulations currently apply to the land you are dealing with, to the uses you intended to make of it, and to the financial arrangements. Otherwise a contract that seems to be totally satisfactory to the buyer and the seller may later prove to be unsuitable for its purpose because of the impact of governmental regulations.

It is impossible to give a complete listing of the specific governmental regulations that may be involved in a given real estate contract or to say how to deal with them in a particular case. What can be done is to list the types of governmental regulations currently in vogue, to explain something of their objectives and how they are administered, and then leave it to you to investigate the specifics when you are preparing to enter into a real estate contract.

1. Local Regulations. The most common local regulations are zoning and building codes. These codes are generally administered by cities or counties. Zoning relates mainly to kinds of uses (residential, commercial, industrial, agricultural, etc.) and to density of occupancy (single-family dwellings, apartments, duplexes, etc., and the amounts of land which must be left open around the improvements).

As with all governmental regulations, you need to know three things about zoning and building codes: (1) what regulations apply now, (2) what regulations will be necessary for or compatible with the intended use, and (3) what changes are in prospect.

Building codes address themselves to the safety of both building occupants and the neighborhood.

The trend in zoning has been toward much more specific regulation. That is, you may be required to submit a plan for a certain improvement, and if the plan is approved, you can build the improvement but you can't change the specifications. Earlier zoning was in more general terms. If land was zoned "residential," you could build any kind of residential structure without any further zoning approval. A little later it became common to subdivide "residential" into such categories as single-family dwellings with no conduct of business allowed in the home, single-family dwellings with conduct of business allowed in the home, and to require various minimum lot sizes.

Another recent trend in zoning has been to allow buildings to be clustered and the open areas combined so that there is more flexibility in the location of buildings than with the earlier forms of zoning, where each building had to be surrounded by its own open space. This newer approach is often called planned unit development (PUD).

The latest trend in local governmental controls affecting land is the attempt to control the rate and the location of municipal growth regulating the supply of public utilities, such as gas, water, electricity, sewer, and roads, or by limiting the number of building permits. Illustrations of these techniques are found in the cases of *Golden* v. *Planning Board of Ramapo,* 30 N.Y. 2d 359, 285 N.E. 2d 291 (1972), and *Construction Industry Assn. of Sonoma County* v. *City of Petaluma,* 375 F. Supp. 574, N.D. Calif. (1974).

It is safe to predict that this type of land use regulation will continue to be attempted and litigated. For a comprehensive treatment of the subject, see the Urban Land Institute's three-volume work, *Management and Control of Growth: Issues—Techniques—Problems—Trends.*

2. State Regulations. The states have come to feel that how an individual landowner uses his land may affect the state in general. This has led to land use regulations at the state level. In some states the counties and cities are required to enforce the regulations, and in other states the regulations are enforced at the state level. Many of the state regulations concern requirements for land subdivisions. For example, Colorado has state laws governing all subdivisions into tracts of 35 acres or less within unincorporated areas. Environmental protection and historic preservation are also coming under state regulation.

3. Uniform State Laws. Traditionally, land laws have been thought to be peculiarly local. With the increase in the interstate mobility of population and the interstate financing of real estate transactions, many have felt it desirable to strive for more uniformity in state laws. The National Conference of Commissioners on Uniform State Laws drafts and proposes "uniform" state laws on a wide variety of subjects. Currently there three such laws in the field of real estate have been drafted for submission to the legislatures of the states. These are: (1) the Uniform Land Transactions Act which, deals with general property rights, mortgages on land, and liens on land given to those who supply labor or materials for the construction of improvements on land; (2) the Uniform Simplification of Land Transfers Act, which deals with land records and the process of conveyancing; and (3) the Uniform Condominium Act.

LAND CONTRACTS

William B. French

*W*ILLIAM B. FRENCH, LLB, Realtor®, President, William B.
French & Associates, Inc., Real Estate Consultants and Brokers,
South Bend, Indiana.
Adjunct instructor of real estate, Indiana University. Law
instructor at Indiana Realtors Institute and Certified Auction-
eers Institute. President, Great Lakes Real Estate Exchange Club.
Past chairman, Probate, Trust, and Real Property Section, Indi-
ana State Bar Association. Member, editorial board, Real Estate
Review. Author, Indiana Real Estate Law and Practice Manual,
for Indiana Real Estate Commission, 1971; and Understanding
Your Trust Department (Indianapolis, Ind.: R. & R. Newkirk,
1976). Coauthor, Law of the Real Estate Business (Homewood,
Ill.: Richard D. Irwin, 1979); and Guide to Real Estate Licensing
Examinations (Boston: Warren, Gorham & Lamont, 1978).

The land contract or contract for a deed is quite similar to the typical
contract of sale, with two important differences:

1. The final performance of the duties of both parties (payment for
and conveyance of the property) is not immediate but is postponed for
a lengthy period of time.

2. The burdens and risks of ownership normally retained by the seller
until closing are shifted to the buyer long before he or she obtains full
legal title to the property.

The combination of these two exceptions has converted the land contract
into a security device, with the seller retaining the strongest security
recognized: absolute legal title. During the term of the contract the buyer
holds the rather tenuous "equitable title," the mere right to compel the
seller to convey the legal title after the buyer has completely performed
his side of the contract.

It should be clear from the above working definition that there can
be considerable latitude in the agreement between the buyer and the
seller under the well-recognized doctrine of "freedom of contract," so
that the land contract is a very flexible device that can be adapted to

fit a wide variety of transactions. In fact, however, the doctrine of freedom of contract is itself subject to a severe practical limitation: the
relative bargaining positions of the parties. As a direct result of the
fact that the product involved is usually housing or shelter, the buyer
under the land contract has historically been in the poorer position and
the seller has literally dictated the terms of the contract.

Until recently our courts have not looked beyond the literal terms
of such contracts and the doctrine of freedom of contract has protected
many abuses. In recent years, however, the consumerist movement has
forced our legal system to look beyond the form of the contract, to look
at its real substance, and to demand essential fairness no matter what
the contract provides. Our courts now recognize the land contract as a
security device and have found new meanings for and reached different
conclusions on basic contract law. Many courts now interpret a land
contract as a mortgage and insist that formal foreclosure proceedings
be followed as opposed to a straight cancellation and forfeiture. It is
appropriate, therefore, that we reexamine the use of the land contract
in the real estate business today.

Even though the use of the land contract for purposes of residential
sales may have achieved notoriety in the residential area, the land contract has long been recognized as a vehicle for obtaining favorable income tax consequences for the seller of appreciated real estate. The
land contract provides an excellent way in which to qualify a sale for
installment treatment of long-term capital gains. Greatly oversimplified,
the land contract can be used to spread the recognition of the capital
gain over a period of many tax years for the seller. Here too, however,
the use of the land contract as a tax-saving device has achieved a degree
of "notoriety" in the sense that it is popularly seen as a safe, sure, simple
way in which to minimize the tax upon capital gain. Would that this
were true. The fact is that the structuring of such a sale, against the
backdrop of business reality, is anything but simple. Two major tax
law revisions, in 1969 and 1976, have forced a revaluation of the land
contract (or any other device) as a means to obtain installment treatment
of the capital gain, *and* whether the gain is long term or not is now
in serious doubt. This is particularly true with property which has appreciated in market value while it has been *de*preciated for income tax
purposes.

All of the above matters will be explored in detail in this chapter.

Status of the Title to Real Estate during the Term of a Land Contract

Legal title to the property remains in the seller. As a result, he has
significant powers to deal with it, subject only to the rights of the buyer
(borrower). The seller may:

1. Mortgage the property (or deed it in trust) to secure a borrowing.
Theoretically, in the absence of a contract provision to the contrary,
the only limitation upon this power is the mortgage loan value of the
property without deduction of the value of the interest acquired by the

land contract buyer. Technically, if the loan exceeds the contract balance, there has been an anticipatory breach of contract by the seller.

2. Sell the property to a third person. Such a sale must be subject to the rights of the land contract buyer, of course, since one can sell no more than he owns. Although technically not essential to the completion of the transfer of title, such a sale as a matter of course is coupled with an assignment of the seller's rights (and obligations) under the land contract.

Equitable title to the real estate passes to the buyer under the land contract at the time that the contract is executed. Typically, the buyer assumes all of the burdens of ownership, such as payments for taxes, insurance, and maintenance (though, at least ministerially, some of these burdens may be retained by the seller). The buyer also has some of the rights of ownership:

1. The buyer may sell (by assignment) his rights under the land contract, but he may not thereby relieve himself of his obligations unless the contract so provides.

2. The buyer may also pledge his interest to secure a debt even though he has no legal title to support a valid mortgage or deed of trust. Typically, such an interest would be of little attraction to normal sources of mortgage funds unless it was well seasoned and the buyer's equity was substantial.

3. The buyer may use the property for any lawful purpose. For example, if it is, residential property, he may rent it out to others during the term of the contract.

When to establish the quality of the title is a question which logically raises itself at this point. It is well established that in the absence of contractual agreement the buyer of real estate is not entitled to evidence of the seller's title or to any assurances other than those included in the ultimate deed. It has become customary, however, in all sale contracts of real estate to require an abstract continuation or title insurance prior to the transfer of title. In a sale by land contract there are two possible points at which the contract may require this:

1. The title work may be delayed until the time at which the final payment is due and when title is to be conveyed. In small dollar volume sales of residences, where there is a high risk that the contract will never be completed, the seller will not want to incur the expense involved in "proving" his title at the outset of the contract.

2. The situation is somewhat different, however, in the case of the purchase of vacant land upon which the buyer intends to erect improvements during the term of the contract. In such a case the buyer will clearly desire and should demand assurance of the quality of title at the very outset.

In either event the negotiation of this matter into the contract should receive consideration at the time the land contract is drafted.

Remedies of the Parties in the Event of Breach of Contract

Breach of Contract by the Seller.   If the seller breaches the land contract, the buyer has several possible remedies, and depending upon the nature of the breach, he may have the option of choosing among them.

If the buyer has fully performed the contract and makes demand for conveyance, and the seller *refuses* to convey, the purchaser may:

1. Bring suit for the damages suffered as the result of the seller's refusal to perform. This is a civil suit, and the measure of damages will be the difference between the price that the buyer has paid and the price that the buyer must pay in order to obtain comparable property.

2. Bring suit to rescind the contract and sue for the return of all payments made during the term of the contract plus the cost of improvements made. This amount, if the buyer prevails, will be reduced by the fair *rental* value of the property during the time he occupied it. It would be unfair to permit the buyer to have had essentially free occupancy for a period of years, even though the seller is a wrongdoer.

3. Bring suit for specific performance of the contract and ask that the court *order* the seller to convey the property. This last remedy is considered an extraordinary one, but it is available when real estate is the subject matter of the contract. The penalty for the failure of the seller to comply with such a court order is a finding of contempt of court and possible imprisonment until the order is complied with.

At the outset of this section it was noted that the above elections of remedies are available when the seller *refuses* to perform. If the seller is *unable* to perform (because he never had title or because he parted with it during the term of the contract), the extraordinary remedy of specific performance may not be available against the seller since the court can hardly compel him to do that which he is powerless to do.

Breach of Contract by the Buyer. If the buyer breaches the contract, the seller has a variety of remedies, some of which have become of doubtful value in light of the consumerist movement:

If the buyer has defaulted by failing to make payments when due (or for other violations included in the contract), the seller may sue to cancel the contract and to have the possession of the property returned to him. His additional remedies are very similar to those of the buyer. That is, he may:

1. Sue for money damages caused by the buyer's breach, and the measure of these damages will be the difference between the agreed-upon price and the price at which he is now able to sell the property. He must "mitigate" damages by selling the property, and he must also grant credit to the buyer for payments against principal that have actually been made.

2. Bring suit to rescind the contract and keep all payments made by the buyer. Because this remedy is a kind of forfeiture, it has been hotly contested in recent years. Courts considering such cases have been prone to find this form of relief unconscionable when the buyer has built up a substantial equity, and they have begun to require mortgage foreclosure proceedings as the proper remedy in order to permit the buyer some measure of protection. This attitude reflects the fact that modern courts will now look seriously at the bargaining positions of the parties at the time the contract was negotiated.

3. Bring suit for specific performance by the buyer. This remedy of the seller is highly questionable, since money is not unique, whereas

real estate has always been considered unique under our law. The unavailability of this remedy to the seller leaves him in the law courts and not the equity courts, so that the severe pressure represented by contempt of court is unavailable. *No law court ever ordered a defendant to do anything.* All that the law court does is establish the fact that damages are due the successful plaintiff. It is then up to the plaintiff-seller to seek "execution" of the judgment, a sometimes lengthy and fruitless effort if the buyer is in a poor financial position.

Recordation of the Land Contract

The recording of land contracts is a matter that is frequently determined without a great deal of thought by the parties. It is a point upon which the relative strength of their bargaining positions is frequently determinative of the issue. However, there are instances in which the stronger party may exercise his power to save a small amount of money at a potentially far greater later expense. The matter is considered below from both the seller's and the buyer's standpoints.

From the seller's standpoint it is generally felt that recording the land contract is both unnecessary and undesirable because it "clutters" up the record title and because in the event of default either a legal action or a recordable quitclaim deed is needed from the defaulting buyer to set the contract aside and clear the legal title. Both may be costly. As a result, countless unrecorded land contracts are in existence today, most of them covering properties that were of modest value at the time the contracts were executed. There are two potential problems with the use of this approach:

1. The defaulting buyer and the seller do not always part friends, and obtaining a deed from the buyer may prove to be impossible should the need for it ever arise. In theory, the need should never arise. However, over time a variety of things may happen that will find their way into the record and later be picked up by an alert and careful title examiner. One common example is the filing of a mechanic's lien against the property and the contract buyer. Even though such a lien may be invalid, the mere fact that it is a matter of record will put the title examiner on inquiry. Such an examination will usually take place when the property is being sold outright, and the expense of clearing the title may be far greater than it would have been at the time of default.

2. Dramatic changes in the value of the property may occur. This is particularly true of vacant land surrounding a metropolitan area which experiences a period of sustained growth. Even though nothing in the record betrays the existence of the old land contract, the buyer who has been defaulted on an informal basis may return to the scene (usually about one week before the closing of the sale to a developer) and suggest that he still has an interest in or claim to the property by virtue of the old land contract. Valid or not, and even if it constitutes sheer blackmail, the claim must be dealt with. This is usually a rather

expensive matter from the seller's standpoint, and it comes at a time when he is under great pressure—hardly a strong bargaining position.

In view of the above possibilities (not to mention the "sharing" of condemnation awards and the like) it is suggested that even where the seller has the upper hand in negotiating this clause, some thought should be given to the question of whether recording the land contract is the expensive nuisance that it appears to be.

From the buyer's standpoint the recording of the land contract may or may not be of great consequence. It is clearly advantageous to have some claim of record in all such purchases to strengthen the buyer's claim to the equitable title so as to give record notice to all third parties. However, the land contract is much more important in some situations than in others. Two such situations are discussed.

In the first situation, where the subject matter of the land contract is a single-family dwelling *and* the buyer is in physical possession of it, third parties dealing with the legal titleholder are obligated to know that the resident buyer is asserting some claim to the right of possession. They have a duty to inspect the property and take title subject to the claims of the resident buyer, and this is true even if the land contract is not recorded. If, however, the property being purchased is a vacant lot or a parcel of land and the contract buyer is *not* in possession, then there will be no notice of his claim that will be evident from an inspection. If the contract is unrecorded, there will also be no record notice to the third party. In the absence of any *actual* knowledge of the existence of the contract the third party can qualify as a "bona fide purchaser" and his purchase from the record titleholder will cut off the buyer's equitable title, leaving the buyer with a suit for damages against the seller. Clearly, therefore, in land contract purchases of vacant property the buyer should insist upon a land contract in recordable form.

The second situation is related to the time at which title should be examined and cleared. There are frequently land contract sales of property upon which the buyer will place substantial improvements. Sometimes the purpose of the land contract is to obtain for the seller installment treatment of long-term capital gain for income tax purposes. In such a situation it is not uncommon for the buyer to have the upper hand in negotiating this point. Clearly, he should demand a recordable land contract. (The use of the land contract for such sales is discussed in detail later. However, it should be suggested here that in situations involving high-cost development and the use of borrowed funds, the buyer may require a great deal more than just a recorded land contract: he may have to have legal title, at least on a piecemeal basis, in order to secure his borrowings. Such arrangements can become extremely complex.)

From the above discussion it should be evident that since the seller will have legal title to the property during the term of the land contract, the buyer who does not insist upon and obtain a contract in recordable form must have faith in the seller's integrity and financial responsibility. A good rule in such situations is: Know your seller.

Typical Land Contract Provisions

In order to illustrate the more important terms and conditions used in land contract sales, a simple form of land contract appears in Figure 1. It will be apparent to the reader that this sample contract is of the

FIGURE 1

Land Contract

This agreement is made and entered into this _____ day of

_____, 19__, by and between _____

_____, of _____ County, State of

_____ (hereinafter referred to as "Seller"),

and _____, of

_____ County, State of _____

_____ (hereinafter referred to as "Purchaser"), and witnesses that:

For and in consideration of the performance of the acts and the payments required by this agreement by Purchaser, Seller agrees to sell and convey

the real estate located in _____ County,

State of _____, commonly known as _____

_____, the legal description of which

is as follows:

_____

_____

_____ (hereinafter referred to as "the prop-

erty").

The total sale price shall be _____

_____ (\$_____) dollars, of which Seller here-

by acknowledges receipt of _____

_____ (\$_____) dollars, as the initial payment from

Purchaser.

If Purchaser shall pay to Seller at _____

_____ (or at such other place as Seller

shall from time to time direct in writing) not less than _____

_____ (\$_____)

dollars on the _____ day _____, 19__, and on the

_____ day of each succeeding month until the sale price, plus interest

FIGURE 1 *(continued)*

thereon at the rate of _____ percent per annum, computed

_____ on the then unpaid balance, is fully paid;
and if until full and complete payment is made in accordance with this
contract, Purchaser shall:
(1) pay when due and payable the real estate taxes starting with the

payment due on the _____ day of _____, 19__, and all
taxes coming due and payable thereafter; the existing special assessments

on said land described below: _____

_____

_____

and all special assessments levied thereon after the date of this contract;
any and all other charges of any kind hereafter levied or assessed against
the property and which are not created or caused by Seller; and shall
provide to Seller evidence of payment of all such taxes, levies, or assessments on or before the next installment payment date after such payments
become due and payable;
(2) insure the buildings and improvements presently on the property,
if any, and deposit with Seller a paid-up policy or policies of insurance
issued by companies satisfactory to Seller to cover the improvements
against loss or damage through fire or hazards covered by the commonly
used Extended Coverage Endorsement in the amounts determined by
Seller; or, in the event that Purchaser fails to pay premiums upon such
insurance when due, Seller may pay them and add the amount of the
premiums to the unpaid balance then due under this land contract; such
policies shall provide by endorsement that any loss shall be payable to
Seller or Purchaser as their respective interests may appear;
(3) maintain the property, both land and buildings, in good condition
and shall permit Seller to have access to the property during reasonable
hours for the purpose of inspecting the property;
(4) refrain from using or permitting the property to be used for any unlawful purpose or purposes which will depreciate the value of the property;
(5) neither remove nor alter any existing buildings nor build new structures of any kind without first obtaining the written consent of Seller;
(6) not violate any restrictions, conditions, or covenants to be included
in Seller's deed, said restrictions, conditions, and covenants being hereby
made effective as of the date of this contract and are as follows:

_____

_____

_____

(7) neither assign this contract nor lease the property or any part thereof
without first obtaining the written consent of Seller; should Seller consent
to any assignment of this land contract, Purchaser shall be obligated to

FIGURE 1 *(continued)*

pay Seller only for the costs of obtaining necessary credit information on the assignee; *then and in that event and at the time of final payment,* Seller shall execute and deliver to Purchaser a good and sufficient general warranty deed conveying the property to Purchaser in fee simple, subject to:

(a) all taxes, assessments, and charges described in clause (1), above, and those coming due and payable thereafter;

(b) all liens, encumbrances, or other defects of title to the property created or caused by Purchaser;

(c) applicable zoning regulations in effect on the date of this contract or imposed during the life of this contract;

(d) existing restrictions, conditions, and covenants now of record which affect the use of the property;

(e) all restrictions, conditions, and covenants specified in clause (6), above.

Seller further agrees to provide Purchaser (or his assignee) at the time of the delivery of the deed, at Seller's option, either: an abstract of title certified to the date of delivery of the deed, showing merchantable title in Seller subject only to such limitations upon Seller's deed as are specified in this contract; or, an Owner's Policy of Title Insurance in the full amount of the purchase price specified above, said policy to be subject only to such limitations, liens, or encumbrances as are assumed by Purchaser pursuant to this contract.

Interest shall, at the end of each _____ period, be computed upon the principal balance due and owing at the commencement of such period and added to the unpaid principal balance due and owing at the commencement of such period. From the balance thus obtained shall be deducted all payments made by Purchaser during said period, applying those payments first to the interest and the excess to reduction of the principal balance. The amount remaining after so applying Purchaser's payments shall stand as the unpaid principal balance for the next

succeeding _____ period.

Seller may place or maintain a mortgage or deed of trust on the property for an amount not in excess of the then unpaid balance of the purchase price under this contract. Purchaser agrees that any lien created by such action of Seller shall be senior and prior to any claim of Purchaser under this contract, *provided,* however, that in the event that Seller shall hereafter create such a lien upon the property, Purchaser is entitled to written notice of such proposed action, which notice shall disclose the name of the lender, the principal amount of the debt, the rate of interest, and the terms of payment, including the final payment date. In the event that the Seller's lender requires documentation to the effect that its lien shall be superior to any claim of Purchaser pursuant to this contract, Purchaser agrees to execute any documents reasonably required to accomplish that end. However, Purchaser shall not be required to execute any document which would make Purchaser personally liable for the repayment of such debt incurred by Seller. After the execution and recording of any such mortgage or deed of trust Purchaser shall have the continuing right to pay down the balance due of the purchase price under this contract to an amount equal to the

FIGURE 1 *(concluded)*

then unpaid balance of Seller's debt and to demand the general warranty deed provided for herein. In such event Seller shall promptly deliver such deed to Purchaser, which deed shall, however, specifically provide that it is subject to the indebtedness and that Purchaser personally assumes and agrees to pay that indebtedness. This assumption of Seller's obligation by Purchaser shall be exercised in accordance with the terms and conditions of the mortgage or deed of trust, but when so exercised shall constitute full and final payment of Purchaser's obligations under this contract.

Time is of the essence of this contract. Should Purchaser fail to perform any act or acts or to make any payment required by this contract timely in accordance with the terms of this contract, then all payments made prior to such default shall be retained by Seller as liquidated damages and compensation for the use of the property prior to the time of default and Seller shall thereafter have no liability or obligation to Purchaser under this contract. Immediately upon default, and without further demand or notice by Seller, Purchaser agrees to surrender to Seller peaceably immediate possession of the property together with all buildings and improvements thereon. Should Purchaser, upon default, fail to surrender possession as provided above, then Seller may proceed in any action at law or in equity for possession of the property and for damages suffered as the result of Purchaser's default.

Purchaser may make payments in excess or in advance of the amounts or times due under this contract and may pay the entire amount of the unpaid balance of the purchase price at any time without penalty for prepayment and with interest computed to the date of such payment.

Possession of the property shall be given by Seller to Purchaser on the _____ day of _____, 19 __ .

Further conditions to this contract are as follows _____

_____

_____

_____

_____

Both Purchaser and Seller expressly agree that this contract shall be binding upon, apply to, and inure to the benefit of their respective heirs, successors, and assignees in the same manner and to the same extent as it binds or benefits the parties themselves.

In Witness Whereof, the parties have signed, sealed, and delivered this contract in duplicate, each of which shall be an original, the day and year first written above.

Seller_____   Purchaser _____

Seller_____   Purchaser _____

Assignment by the purchaser, acceptance by the assignee, and acceptance of the assignment by the seller could be included in the land contract form at the outset. The same is true of the formal acknowledgment which is required if the contract is to be recorded. These are omitted here for the sake of brevity.

"garden variety." It is presented here solely to illustrate the points which are discussed in the succeeding pages. Only the significant elements are discussed. It is our purpose here to highlight and explain the significance of the boiler plate clauses which we use on a day-to-day basis, as well as to suggest modifications that may be made to adapt the simple land contract to more sophisticated transactions. Nevertheless, the reader should keep in mind that even the ordinary straightforward conditional sale of real estate for which the land contract is commonly used is not a simple sale because of the extended period of time involved for the performance of its terms by both parties.

The Real Estate Tax and Assessment Clause. The shifting of the burden of payment of real estate taxes to the purchaser has become standard in sales by land contract. This transfer has some basis in pure logic: it is, after all, the purchaser who is occupying and using the property, so that it is hardly unconscionable to expect him to pay the taxes levied against the property. As with the burden of casualty insurance, it is not uncommon for the seller to reserve the ministerial function of paying these taxes (in order to protect his security, the legal title) and to add this cost to the remaining balance due under the contract. The imposition of the ultimate liability for real estate taxes on the contract buyer has become so commonplace that it is seldom a matter of discussion, let alone negotiation in the true sense of that term. Not only is the burden of tax payment shifted to the buyer, but also the risks of increased tax rates and increased valuations for tax purposes.

Nevertheless, the inclusion of a well-drafted real estate tax clause is important to both the seller and the buyer because of its impact upon the true total cost of the property. There is, however, another important reason for clearly defining the real estate tax liabilities of the parties, namely, the federal income tax consequences to each of them. Local real estate taxes are generally deductible against the ordinary income of the party who pays them. In order to be deductible, however, they must be the legal obligation of the party claiming the deduction. Another familiar general rule in the federal income tax area is that when the legal obligation of the taxpayer is paid by another party, the taxpayer has received reportable income. In short, what are the income tax consequences to the seller and the buyer when the burden of paying local real estate taxes is shifted to the buyer while the seller retains the legal title?

In the typical, short-term contract of sale of real estate the Internal Revenue Code appears to clearly dictate that the proration or apportionment of real estate taxes which are already the legal obligation of the seller results in the deductibility of these taxes by the seller no matter who pays them. The only real question is whether the taxes are deductible in the year of sale or at the time they are actually paid. In the case of the long-term land contract sale, however, the income tax consequences are not quite so clearly defined and they are generally ignored during the negotiations. In general, the obligation to pay real estate taxes is that of the holder of the legal title to the real estate. Where such taxes are deductible for federal income tax purposes, then the owner is clearly entitled to the deduction. The real issue is: Can this obligation be shifted by private contract in such a way that the buyer is not only obligated to pay these taxes but also becomes entitled to the deduction? It now appears clear that such is the case. The IRS has ruled that if a sale by land contract imposes the tax burden on the buyer, then the buyer is entitled to an income tax deduction for the payment of the real estate taxes even if under state law this burden is the obligation of the legal titleholder, the seller. The transfer of title is not the test for federal income tax purposes; the test is whether or not there has been a taxable transfer *and* the buyer has taken possession. Both of these elements are typically present in a sale by land contract.

It also seems both appropriate and fair to shift the burden of assessment payments for municipal improvements (such as streets, sewers, and water) to the contract buyer. Again the rationale would be that these improvements increase the value of the property being purchased and should be paid for by the ultimate owner. It is important that the transfer of this burden to the contract buyer be clearly spelled out in the contract since the general rule would otherwise impose the burden upon the holder of record title, the seller.

2. The Insurance Clause. During the term of the land contract it is apparent that both the seller and the buyer have an interest in the property and its improvements and that each may insure that interest. That is, each has an "insurable interest" to be protected. What is not clear, however, is the question of who has the *duty* to insure. Actually, neither party has a duty to insure his own interest, let alone the other party's interest. This is a matter which must be covered by the contract, and the typical resolution is a clause requiring the buyer to obtain and keep in force adequate insurance for the benefit of both parties. This is yet another burden of ownership that is transferred to the buyer during the term of the land contract. Many such clauses are drafted with something less than precision, some simply providing that the seller have the right to approve the insurer and others providing further that the amount of the insurance be acceptable to the seller. In today's world of rapidly escalating replacement and repair costs (let alone the increasing premium rates for insurance) the insurance clause should be given careful consideration so that both parties are adequately covered. The flexibility provided should be such that the insurance proceeds will truly reflect the losses suffered by the parties. One possible solution to the problem is to permit the carrier selected by the parties to arbitrate this matter on the basis of the most recent experience in the industry plus a national index of increasing replacement costs.

In many insurance clauses the seller reserves the right to procure insurance on the property in the event that the purchaser fails to do so. The amount thus expended is added to the contract balance and is ultimately paid for by the buyer, along with interest on the expenditure made by the seller. Where the financial strength of the buyer is doubtful, this may be provided for in the contract at the outset, so that the seller can be sure that there is adequate coverage at all times without relying upon the buyer to obtain it.

3. The Maintenance and Inspection Clause. It is quite common under the sale by land contract to impose upon the buyer the obligation to properly maintain the property and the improvements on it. This is but one of the burdens of ownership generally cast upon the buyer during the term of the contract. It is, of course, in the best interests of the buyer to properly maintain the property because he will ultimately own it. However, this is not the true motivation for the maintenance clause. The real purpose of the maintenance clause is to require the buyer to protect and preserve the seller's security. Making this a positive requirement means that a failure of the buyer to comply will constitute a breach of the contract so that it can be terminated by the seller and the property retaken. At the same time, such a clause is difficult to monitor unless the contract reserves the right of the seller to enter and inspect periodically to verify that necessary maintenance is in fact being performed. In view of the nature of the buyer's interest in the property under a sale by land contract it is doubtful that the right of inspection would exist without such a clause.

4. The Improvements Clauses. In connection with a sale by land contract the matter of existing and contemplated improvements should be considered by both parties. The seller will want to restrict the right of the buyer to physically remove existing improvements from the property, assuming that the use of those improvements is the primary motivation for the contract in the first place. This is typically the case for residential property. In other instances, however, the improvements may be of no value and a hindrance to the proposed use of the property by the buyer. This can easily occur when dilapidated outbuildings are occupying tillable acreage, and the parties may contemplate their demolition and removal. Whatever the case, their contract should clearly spell out their intentions in order to avoid later disputes.

Where improvements are to be *added* to the property by the buyer during the term of the contract, a far different question is presented. Historically, the seller has been content with a contract which is silent on this point on the theory that the buyer's improvement of the property enhances the seller's security and that in the event of a subsequent breach by the buyer, improvements have become part of the land under the law of fixtures and will become the seller's property under the typical forfeiture clause. From the buyer's standpoint, of course, some protection against this result is highly desirable. Given the already noted trends in the law which applies to land contract sales, it is very likely that under this theory such a forfeiture would "unjustly enrich" the seller. The buyer, already has a great deal of protection even if the contract is silent. Nevertheless, a clearly drafted clause outlining the rights of the parties is desirable in order to avoid costly litigation to resolve the matter.

The seller may wish to include a provision in the land contract which restricts the right of the buyer to add improvements since it is not true that every "improvement" will enhance the value of the property. This notion is not applicable merely to situations in which shacks or other undesirable structures are placed upon a property. It may be very important to the seller who is subdividing a development. Permitting the buyer to add improvements which are inconsistent with the value of the parcel of land he is buying might have a serious downside impact on the value of the as yet unsold lots.

5. *The Use Clause.* Whether and to what extent the buyer's use of the property will be restricted (other than by local ordinances, including zoning) must be established in the contract itself. The seller will frequently require more protection than just a prohibition against illegal use. Indeed, he must require that the buyer refrain from breaching any existing private or restrictive convenant since such violation might jeopardize his legal title. At the same time, any additional restrictions upon the use of the property which the seller intends to include in the ultimate deed must be established in the contract so that the buyer will be legally obligated to accept them. Such protection is also necessary in order to protect the value of any property retained by the seller, whether he intends to keep it or to sell it to others. For example, if the property being sold is a parcel that will be included in a planned subdivision which will be subject to protective covenants in all deeds, it is essential that these same covenants be spelled out in the land contract. Otherwise the additional lots to be sold may have far less value.

6. *The Assignment and Lease Clause.* Many land contracts contain an absolute prohibition against assignment. In the absence of any provision at all the land contract would be freely assignable by the buyer just as almost all other contracts may be assigned. This particular form of contract contemplates the possibility of assignment but permits the seller to retain a strong element of control by requiring his approval prior to assignment. Under general contract rules the fact that the purchaser assigns his rights under the contract in no way relieves him of primary liability for the performance of his duties under the contract. As a practical matter, however, the seller may be quite content to have an assignee substituted for a buyer who turns out to be financially irresponsible.

It is also quite common to include in the land contract a prohibition against the buyer's leasing of the property to a third party during the term of the contract. Typically, the reasoning behind such a prohibition is the concern that the tenant may be less responsible than the contract buyer in caring for the property.

7. *The Mortgage Clause.* If there is already a mortgage or a deed of trust against the property at the time the land contract is executed, whether or not this fact is made known to the buyer, the lien thereby created will not be affected by the sale and the contract buyer's rights will be subservient to those of the lienholder.

Even where there is no such preexisting secured debt upon the property, however, the seller may find it necessary or desirable to create such a debt after entering into the land contract. Because this action has a negative impact upon the seller's ability to perform his side of the bargain, it seems that the contract buyer is entitled to be notified of such intended action by the seller. The lender, *if aware of the land contract,* will insist upon the contract buyer's acquiescence in and recognition of the superiority of the lien of the mortgage or deed of trust.

It would be a little too much to expect the contract buyer to assume any personal liability for his seller's debt. However, the use of a clause of the type illustrated here can be quite helpful in assisting a marginal buyer in establishing an equity in the property in substitution for a significant cash payment which would qualify him for mortgage financing because this clause permits the buyer to obtain legal title by assuming and agreeing to pay the secured debt when it is equal to the balance due under the land contract. Care should of course be taken to see that the mortgage is assumable and under what terms an assumption will be permitted by the lender. (The lingering liability of the seller for the repayment of the debt is not considered here, but it is certainly a factor in determining the willingness of the seller to permit an assumption by the contract buyer.)

The prevalence of the "due on sale" clause in modern mortgages must be kept in mind if the reason for using the land contract is to avoid triggering the due on sale clause in an existing mortgage on the property. There are two possible problems to consider. The first is whether under local law or *the mortgage instrument itself* the sale by land contract is a present sale which will trigger the due on sale clause, thereby accelerating the payment of the debt secured by the mortgage and defeating the purpose of the parties to the land contract. Many newer mortgage forms will specify that a sale by land contract is a present sale for purposes of accelerating payment of the mortgage debt. Once this matter is resolved, and assuming that the due on sale clause has been triggered, the second problem that must be considered is whether or not due on sale clauses are enforceable at all under applicable state law. Until the present time most states have upheld such clauses under the doctrine of freedom of contract. However, in a recent case the Supreme Court of California held that such clauses are not automatically enforceable even if there is an outright sale of the property. The court did not outlaw the use of such clauses but decided that in order to enforce them lenders must show foreseeable harm or impairment of their security. Otherwise, such a clause represents an unreasonable restraint on the alienation of real estate. It appears that neither of these questions has been finally settled in the courts so that caution and knowledge of local law are needed before mortgaged real estate is sold by land contract.

8. The Liquidated Damages Clause. Under the basic doctrine of freedom of contract, courts have traditionally upheld a good faith effort by the parties to determine in advance what damages will result from a breach of their contract. This is particularly true in cases where it would be difficult or impossible to accurately determine the *actual* damages at the time the contract is breached. The inclusion of such a clause eliminates the need for time-consuming and expensive litigation. It is therefore quite appropriate for the parties themselves to establish this amount in their agreement, and such clauses are enforceable. There is, however, the possibility that one party or the other may be in a commanding bargaining position and may force upon the other a "liquidated damages clause" which is so onerous that a court will interpret it to be a "penalty clause," an economic club which the court will find unenforceable.

In connection with low-priced residential properties, where the down payment is very low, the buyer's financial strength questionable, and the risk great that the contract will never be paid in full, liquidated damages clauses frequently appear to be penalty clauses. On the surface such a clause might appear to be an obvious penalty as opposed to a true attempt to arrive at what the seller's damages might actually be in the event of a default. Clearly, under such a clause the buyer would lose any equity that he might have accumulated. In point of fact, however, the clause may be eminently fair to the defaulting buyer since it is quite possible that his payments did little more than cover the fair rental of the property, taxes, and insurance, while the property was in fact depreciating in value.

The point is that the wording of the clause itself is not the determining factor in characterizing it as a liquidated damages clause or a penalty clause. One must apply the clause to the actual situation in order to see its economic impact upon the parties. The recent trend in the courts has been to follow this procedure and to characterize such provisions as penalties only where the buyer has built up a "substantial" equity. Where the equity is insignificant, such clauses are still being upheld. The important change which has occurred is that our courts will now *entertain* such suits in the first place. It is clear that in negotiating and drafting the liquidated damages clause, more care is now necessary to ensure that the clause will meet the test of essential fairness.

9. The Prepayment Clause. By the very nature of general contract law, where terms of payment and delivery are specified with reasonable certainty, there is generally no right on the part of one party to tender performance ahead of schedule and to demand immediate performance by the other party. It is therefore essential that a prepayment clause be included in a land contract. Such a clause has become "boiler plate," and it is seldom given much thought by the parties in "negotiating" or reviewing a typical form land contract. However, in certain instances the inclusion of such a clause may be very dangerous to the seller from an income tax standpoint. The use of the land contract in order to obtain installment treatment of the payments for income tax purposes is discussed in detail later in this chapter. At this point it is important only to note that the seemingly unnecessary and innocuous prepayment clause may have important implications for both parties. From the buyer's standpoint, it may be crucially important to obtain title earlier than scheduled so as to be able to obtain mortgage financing for improvements or for any other purpose which requires the security of a mortgage upon the real estate. The basic problem is, of course, that the buyer does not have the legal title which is necessary to create a valid mortgage or deed of trust lien, and the typical commercial lender will seldom be willing to accept anything less as security for a loan secured by the real estate. Wraparound mortgages may represent a solution to this problem.

Federal Taxation on Installment Sales

As was noted at the beginning of this chapter, the use of the land contract as a vehicle to obtain installment treatment of sales which generate capital gains has received a great deal of attention in recent years. For this reason the discussion below is somewhat detailed, the basic premise being that obtaining installment treatment by use of the land contract is not as simple as it seems to be. Due to tax reform legislation in 1969 and 1976, there are many pitfalls to be avoided. The structuring of the successful "tax-mitigating" sale must be done carefully. Nevertheless, the land contract remains a very important and useful device for the achievement of installment treatment.

Qualifying the Sale under Section 453. Under the present Internal Revenue Code, when the seller of appreciated real estate realizes a long-term capital gain, it is possible to "spread" that gain over two or more years with significant tax savings, provided that certain conditions are met which qualify the transaction as an installment sale under Section 453 of the Internal Revenue Code. The basic conditions which must be met to so qualify the sale are:

1. The seller-taxpayer must qualify for and affirmatively elect installment sale treatment.
2. The initial payments received by the seller in the year of sale cannot exceed 30 percent of the selling price.
3. The interest rate must be high enough to avoid the imputation of interest at the rate considered to be reasonable by the Internal Revenue Service (currently 6 percent simple interest).
4. Sales of appreciated property to related parties or their trusts cannot qualify for installment treatment except under unusual circumstances.

The structuring of a sale of low-basis, appreciated real estate assets is a delicate task that should be handled carefully because of the technical nature of the tax rules and the manner in which they are interpreted and applied. Therefore, each of the above conditions is discussed separately.

Affirmative Election by the Seller. The seller-taxpayer must affirmatively elect to treat the sale of appreciated property on the installment basis. This election to treat the sale as an installment sale and to benefit from spreading the gain over several tax years does not affect or change the character of the profit realized from the sale. That is, the seller must clearly qualify for long-term capital gain treatment in the first place. If he does not so qualify, then, even though he receives payments in a deferred payment plan, these payments will be classified as ordinary income. (Even this may be beneficial to a person who is classified as a "dealer" as opposed to an "investor.") Under the present state of the tax laws it is obviously advantageous to qualify for long-term capital gain treatment in the first place.

The 1976 Tax Reform Act introduced a significant change in the length of time that a capital asset must be "held" or owned before it can be sold at a profit and still qualify for long-term capital gain treatment. Under that act the "holding period" was increased from six months to one full year for sales which occur in 1978 and subsequent years. (An interim rule of nine months applied for sales in 1977.) For many real estate investments this increase in the holding period may be of little consequence. However, the impact of the increase upon the option market may prove to be very dramatic, since the negotiation of the purchase of an option to purchase real estate for such a lengthy period will be more difficult and costly.

The Initial Payment Test. The basic rule, that the initial payments received by the seller in the year of sale may not exceed 30 percent of the selling price, is deceptively simple to state. It is in the application of the rule that several perils are encountered. Before applying the percentage rule, one must first establish the selling price to which the rule applies. Normally, this is relatively simple to determine, but there may be serious problems if the sale involves the assumption of an existing mortgage or obligations under a deed of trust. (This may even be true when the sale is "subject to" existing security devices even though there is no *assumption* of the obligation, since the IRS perceives no difference between the two.) When the buyer's assumption of the seller's obligation is involved, fortunately, that assumption is not considered a part of the initial payment, *unless* the amount of the assumed mortgage exceeds the seller's adjusted basis. Any mortgage balance amount which exceeds the adjusted basis must be counted as part of the initial payment. Assume, for example, that the seller's adjusted basis for tax purposes is $50,000, that the sales price for the property is $75,000, and that an existing mortgage of $60,000 will be assumed by the buyer. Then the excess of $10,000 (mortgage balance of $60,000 less the adjusted basis of $50,000) is considered part of the initial payment, thereby reducing the amount of cash which the seller may receive without exceeding the 30 percent limitation.

In addition to being wary of the problems posed by the assumption of a mortgage debt by the buyer, the seller must be wary of the assumption by the buyer of any other personal obligations of the seller in connection with the property. An assumption of real estate tax payments which are the seller's personal obligation, for example, will be counted as part of the initial payment. Obligations such as assessments for municipal improvements and other liens against the property must also be considered in determining the full amount of the initial payment.

Another important point to consider in the sale of property which has appreciated in value (and even property which has *not* appreciated) and has been *de*preciated for income tax purposes is the matter of "recapture" of accelerated depreciation (as *ordinary income*) claimed in years prior to the sale. Both the 1969 and the 1976 Tax Reform acts are relevant.

The 1969 act introduced the concept of recapture of all depreciation taken in excess of straight-line depreciation unless the property (depending upon its character as residential, commercial, industrial) were held for an extended, specified period of time. A sale prior to the expiration of that time resulted in a recapture in the year of sale of the excess depreciation taken as ordinary income. In an installment sale the first monies received by the seller are presumed to be the recaptured excess depreciation and are, therefore, treated as ordinary income instead of capital gain. As a result, much or all of the initial payment may be ordinary income to the seller in the year of sale. This can be a serious problem to the seller, and it may require that the sale be very carefully timed so that it takes place near the end of the seller's tax year, with the second payment scheduled just after the beginning of his next taxable year. This will provide the funds that are needed to meet the income tax liability generated by the sale.

The second shoe dropped when the 1976 act became law was that all excess depreciation taken after 1975 became subject to recapture as ordinary income in the year of sale *no matter when the property was sold*. That is, the holding period specified by the 1969 act will not shelter or diminish the excess depreciation taken after 1975. Clearly, if the timing of the sale under the 1969 act was worthy of consideration, it is even more critical under the 1976 act. (In passing, it should be noted that the recapture rules under both acts apply even when the sale is involuntary.)

The Imputed Interest Problem. It is a temptation to the seller to attempt to have the entire amount of the payment received treated as long-term capital gain. Theoretically, the land contract could be so structured that all payments made during the term of the contract are principal only and no interest is charged by the seller. In fact, many land contracts have been so structured. As far back as 1963, however, the tax laws were revised to reflect business reality and the true nature of the land contract: no one extends credit over an extended period of time without charging interest. Therefore, even if the contract clearly states that no interest is being charged, the IRS will "impute" a realistic interest rate. At present, if the contract does not provide for an interest rate of at least 6 percent, the IRS will "impute" or "read into" the contract an interest rate of 7 percent, compounded semiannually. This is a two-edged sword from the seller's standpoint:

1. A portion of each payment received during the life of the contract will be interest income, taxable at ordinary income tax rates instead of capital gain rates.

2. More important, the rule has an impact in the year of sale in determining whether or not the 30 percent limitation has been exceeded. For example, if the contract provides for a sale at $200,000 with no interest to be charged, the imputation of 7 percent interest, compounded semiannually, will be deducted from the $200,000 in determining the purchase price to which the 30 percent limitation applies. If the initial payment was 30 percent of $200,000 ($60,000), then 30 percent of the

discounted purchase price must be less than $60,000 and the limitation has been exceeded because the initial payment is too high. This destroys the whole scheme and disqualifies the sale from installment treatment, making *all* of the taxes due in the year of sale.

Clearly, the inclusion of a realistic rate of interest in the land contract is an important matter for both the seller and the buyer. From the buyer's standpoint, the amount of interest paid is deductible against ordinary . income, and a statment in the contract itself of the interest being paid is clear evidence of his entitlement to the deduction. At the same time, at least a portion of the payment for the property is being made with before-tax dollars. From the seller's standpoint, since part of each payment will be characterized as ordinary interest income, he is receiving payment in aftertax dollars. In a transaction of major proportions this "swing" can have an important impact upon the purchase price. Consequently, knowledge of the imputed interest rule (which is subject to change from time to time) is an essential tool in the negotiating process.

The Related Parties Problem.   Whenever there is a transfer of property between related parties, which results in a savings of income taxes or the unified gift-estate tax adopted by the 1976 Tax Reform Act, whether the transfer is direct or indirect by virtue of the use of a trust, close scrutiny of the transaction by the IRS can be anticipated. More than this, the tax advantages contemplated will almost certainly be lost unless there is the intervention of a truly independent third-party trustee. In extreme cases where an extraordinary capital gain, a windfall, has been earned by the astute investor, the concept may be worth considering. In order to have any chance of success it is usually necessary to utilize a complex arrangement made up of a corporation, an irrevocable trust, and a carefully executed corporate liquidation.

Comparison of Installment Sale and Cash Sale.   In the calculations set out below it is assumed that the seller is an investor (as opposed to a dealer) and that the sale will qualify for long-term capital gain treatment. Assuming an adjusted basis of $50,000 and a gross sale price of $100,000, the first year's transaction would look like this:

Contract sale price	$100,00	
Expense of sale	6,000	
Amount realized		$94,000
Adjusted basis		50,000
Gross profit (total gain realized)		$44,000
Percentage of gain to contract price .		44%
Payment received in year of sale . . .		33,000
Gain taxable in year of sale (44%) . .		13,200

In each subsequent year of the contract, 44 percent of each payment received would be taxable at capital gains rates.

If the above transaction had not been an installment sale, then the full $44,000 would be taxable in one year even though the seller received only $30,000. (This may be advantageous if the seller has capital losses in that same year to offset against the gain.) Most important, however, if the payment in the year of sale (whether in cash or indirectly) exceeds $30,000, say $31,000, the sale is disqualified for installment treatment and the full $44,000 is taxable in the year of sale. Because of the danger of the unnoticed constructive receipt during the year of sale, most contracts of this nature provide for something less than 30 percent just as a precautionary measure. Finally, the contract must, for the seller's protection, provide in no uncertain terms that the buyer may not prepay any installment during the first year, so that the risk of losing the installment treatment of the gain is eliminated. This is a very sensitive point where there is an assumption of the seller's obligation under a mortgage or a deed of trust.

The Revenue Act of 1978.   The change initiated by the 1978 act to tax 40 percent of the capital gain, as opposed to 50 percent prior to November 1978, raises the question of how valuable installment treatment of capital gain will be in the future. The reasons for this assertion are as follows: *(a)* the capital gains tax will be lower, and *(b)* the payment of the purchase price over a period of years is likely to be made with cheaper dollars. The point is that the immediate savings in income taxes resulting from the installment sale may be more than offset by the erosion in the value of the dollars received during the life of the contract. One apparent solution is to simply increase the price of the property to compensate for anticipated devaluation. However, the prevailing market will determine the effectiveness of this approach.

MORTGAGES AND TRUST DEEDS

Steven A. Winkelman

T. Grant Callery

*S*TEVEN A. WINKELMAN, JD, LLM, Attorney at Law, Winkelman
and Delaney, Washington, D.C.*

*Senior partner, law firm of Winkelman and Delaney. Adjunct
professor in the fields of wills and trusts and the Estate Planning
Seminar, Georgetown University Law Center. Member of the
Washington, D.C., Bar Association and the American Bar Association. Author, "A New Look at Sprinkling Trusts," in* The Best
of Trusts and Estates *(New York: Matthew Bender, 1966); "The
Trust and the Trustee,"* Taxes, *August 1960; and "Practical Appraisal of Sprinkling Trusts,"* Trusts and Estates, *June 1960.
Coauthor, "Participation, Coverage, and Vesting under the Pension Reform Act,"* Trusts and Estates, *January 1975.*

*T. GRANT CALLERY, JD, Attorney at Law, Winkelman and De-
laney, Washington, D.C.*

*Member, American Bar Association and District of Columbia
Bar. National director and chairman, Council on Younger Lawyers, Federal Bar Association. Author of various articles. Coauthor, "Participation, Coverage, and Vesting under the Pension
Reform Act,"* Trusts and Estates, *January 1975.*

The Mortgage Concept

Historical Overview. A mortgage may be said to be the conveyance
of property for the purpose of securing a debt. The use of an interest
in real estate for collateralizing loans has preconquest Anglo-Saxon
roots. In the 12th century the concept of the gage of property developed.
Under this device the borrower (the gagor) would transfer all of the
incidents of ownership of either real property or chattels to the lender

(the gagee) in return for the loan of funds. When the loan was repaid, the property would be reconveyed to the borrower. There were numerous variations on the device, but the distinction most important to the development of modern law was the one relating to the right to the rents and profits from the property. If the gagor was entitled to such proceeds or entitled to have them applied to reduction of the indebtedness, the arrangement was denominated a *vivum vadium* (a live pledge). If, on the other hand, the mortgagee was entitled to receive the rents and profits without applying them to the reduction of the debt, the benefit of ownership was thought to be dead to the borrower and the device was referred to as a *mortuum vadium* (dead pledge) or a *mort gage.* The ecclesiastical courts of the period frowned upon this device because the charging of any interest at all was, at that time, a violation of the usury law and the retention of the proceeds of the property by the gagee was considered to be the payment of interest.

In the 14th century, therefore, there developed the classical common-law mortgage, which is the direct forerunner of the modern mortgage. This instrument was in the form of a deed of the land from the mortgagor to the mortgagee. The deed passed all of the incidents of ownership, including the right to possession of the property. The only qualification in the deed took the form of what was known as a defeasance clause, which stipulated that upon repayment of the indebtedness at an appointed time (the "law day") the conveyance would become void. During the early years of the common-law mortgage, the device could work very harshly against the mortgagor. If the payment was not tendered or made upon the law day, the right to reconveyance was irrevocably extinguished.

As time passed, however, the finality imposed by nonpayment on the law day became less and less acceptable to the people and the government. The courts of chancery or equity came to accept petitions whereby the mortgagor was allowed to redeem his property from the mortgagee at a date after the law day by tendering full payment with accrued interest. This right was called the equitable right to redeem or the equity of redemption.

As the equity of redemption became routinely available to the mortgagor, the mortgagee's title was forever clouded by the existence of the delinquent borrower's equity of redemption. To remedy this situation the mortgagee turned to the equity courts. The solution arrived at was the process known as strict foreclosure, under which the court, in response to the mortgagee's showing of a default, would order the mortgagor to pay his debt along with costs and interest within a stipulated period or be forever barred, or foreclosed, from exercising the equity of redemption.

Mortgage Theory. Predicated upon the evolution of the common-law mortgage, two major mortgage theories and a third, hybrid theory have developed in the United States. These are generally referred to as the title, lien, and intermediate theories. The distinctions are now rather blurred, since each state, whether denominated as title or lien theory, has elements of both.

The title theory in its pure form is more closely akin to the early concept of a mortgage than the lien theory, and as its name implies, it gives the mortgagee actual title to the property securing the indebtedness. The title theory was transplanted from England to the United States in the early days of our history, but it has been largely replaced by the lien theory, which represents recognition of the fact that a mortgage is really only security for a debt and that the ownership of the mortgagor should be impaired only to the degree necessary to provide the necessary security. Under the lien theory, therefore, the mortgagor is considered to be the true owner of the property, with the mortgagee having no right in the property other than as security for the debt. The mortgagee's right to possession arises only upon foreclosure of the mortgage. The lien theory prevails today in a majority of states.

The third mortgage theory, a hybrid between the strict title and lien theories, is generally called the intermediate theory. Under this theory the mortgagee holds no practical incidents of title as long as the mortgagor is not in default, the mortgagee's rights being accelerated, not upon foreclosure, but upon default by the mortgagor. This theory is in effect in only a few states. As has been mentioned, although states adhering to the title theory vest the incidents of ownership in the mortgagee, the practical drawbacks of actual possession, such as the need to manage the property and to account to the mortgagor, make possession by the mortgagor while the loan is current the universal practice.

Mortgage Theory and Leases. In addition to possession, a second major area in which mortgage theory governs the rights and obligations of the parties' duties relates to leases of the mortgaged property. The result obtained in any particular situation is governed by the interplay of two elements: the time at which the leasehold began and the applicable theory in the jurisdiction. What combinations are found?

We will first look at the situation in which the lease predates the mortgage. In title theory states, a mortgage is given subject to a preexisting lease unless the lease contains a provision that the lessee will agree to subordinate his lease to a subsequent mortgage. If no provision to that effect is included, the mortgagee must honor the lease. In title theory states, since the mortgagee has the right of possession, he also has the right to collect the rents for the period of the lease term subsequent to the giving of the mortgage. In lien theory states, as would be expected, there is no such entitlement, and as a matter of practice, even in title states the lessee may generally continue to pay rents to the lessor until such time as the mortgagee demands that future payments be made to him. It is normal for the mortgagee to leave the mortgagor in possession of both the property and the rents since a lender seldom wants to involve himself with rents unless problems in the mortgagor's repayment of the debt arise or can be foreseen.

Where the mortgage predates the lease, the mortgagor in lien states may receive the economic benefit of the lease made until foreclosure occurs. However, in such states the mortgagee may impose restrictions on the right to lease the premises as a condition for making the mortgage loan.

In title theory states, the shift of the incidents of ownership to the mortgagee creates an interesting and unusual situation with regard to leases and rents. Since the mortgagee has title, all that the mortgagor retains, from a legal standpoint, is a reversionary interest in the property upon repayment of the debt. That being the case, a mortgagor in possession technically lacks the power to enter into a lease of the property. This lack of authority creates a situation in which the mortgagee lacks privity with the lessee and cannot, therefore, compel direct payment of the rent. On the other hand, since the mortgagor had no authority to let the property, the mortgagee may, at will, enter into possession and evict the tenant. Again, the actual results are usually less harsh. The mortgagee, upon taking possession, will normally desire to retain the tenant and will enter into a separate lease with him, often a continuation of the mortgagor's lease. Such action is referred to as an attornment agreement.

Regular or Legal Mortgages. The form taken by the mortgage today in most real estate transactions is that known as a legal mortgage. The requisites for such a mortgage vary from state to state, but an overview of the common elements will give the reader a checklist against which to compare the documents encountered in a given situation. Again, the prevailing mortgage theory will influence the degree of importance attached to the formalities of the mortgage. As would be expected, in title theory states, strict adherence is the rule, whereas lien theory states place less emphasis on formalities. This is to be expected since the mortgage in a title state must actually convey title.

The most universal requirement for a mortgage is that it be in writing. This has been a requirement for all contracts dealing with real estate since the inception of the statute of frauds.

The grant of the property to the mortgagee is generally worded to comply with the rules governing conveyances in the given jurisdiction. This is most important in the title states, since in such states mortgages must so comply, and it may even be required that the grant contain words of inheritance, that is to say, that the property is conveyed to the mortgagee "and his heirs," if it is to be valid. In lien states the mortgage may be worded as a conveyance of the fee or it may more truly reflect the limited interest conveyed.

In addition, the mortgage will include a description of the property. Although the usual practice is to use the legal description of the property as found in the land records of the jurisdiction, this is not necessary, and any description by which the property may be identified is sufficient.

Perhaps the most important element of a legal mortgage from the mortgagor's standpoint and the element distinguishing the legal mortgage from a straight deed is the defeasance clause. Although the absence of such a clause will not invalidate a mortgage, the importance of the clause lies in the fact that it sets forth the conditions upon which the mortgagee's interest will cease. The defeasance clause will state what must be done for full title to again vest in the mortgagor. Although the defeasance is normally a part of the mortgage itself, it may take the form of a separate agreement entered into by the parties.

Finally, a legal mortgage will incorporate a statement of the debt which it secures. As security is the entire purpose of the mortgage conveyance, there must be an underlying debt for a mortgage to exist. An adequate statement of the debt is important to the mortgagor as this debt is intertwined with the defeasance in determining when the mortgage relationship is to cease. In addition, a statement of the debt enables third parties who may purchase or take some other interest in the property to become fully aware of the extent to which the property is encumbered. The normal form for description of the debt is by accurate reference to the written debt obligation.

Equitable Mortgages.   Another class of mortgages deserves mention, though it is not an alternative form in the sense that it would be chosen in lieu of a regular mortgage or a deed of trust. This is the equitable mortgage, which may arise if a court sitting as a court of equity views the circumstances as having created a mortgage.

One of the most common ways in which an equitable mortgage may arise is the giving of a defective legal mortgage. If a loan is made and the mortgagor executes a document that purports to be a mortgage but fails in some way to meet the technical requirements of a legal mortgage, the equity court will look to the intention of the parties and will treat the document as a mortgage. The need to look to the equity court under these circumstances is, of course, greater in title theory states, since the formalities take on greater meaning in those jurisdictions.

The equitable mortgage also becomes important in a situation in which the document given by the mortgagor to secure the indebtedness is, on its face, an absolute deed lacking the defeasance clause that would make it recognizable as a legal mortgage. Again, should the debt be staisfied and the mortgagee refuse to reconvey, the equity court will view the deed in light of the purpose for which it was given and will treat it as an equitable mortgage. There is, in fact, a presumption upon a showing that the conveyance was to secure a debt that the deed is an equitable mortgage. Furthermore, courts of equity will allow the use of parol or oral evidence as to the circumstances surrounding the conveyance for the purpose of establishing the true nature of the conveyance.

The courts will also find the existence of equitable mortgages in situations in which an individual advances monies to enable the purchase of land by another, but title is given in the name of the lender and the borrower conveys nothing but an equitable interest in the security in consideration of the loan. An example would be the beneficiary of a trust securing a loan by conveyance of his beneficial interest in the trust assets. At common law, in which the title theory prevailed, any mortgage junior to the first mortgage was necessarily equitable since the mortgagor retained only the equitable right to the reversion. In the United States, however, the courts have generally held that properly drawn second mortgages are to be considered legal mortgages.

Deeds of Trust

Next to the legal mortgage, the deed of trust is the second most important form of security in use in the United States today. This form accomplishes an end similar to that of the mortgage, but it is somewhat different from the mortgage in its operation. The interest in the property is conveyed, not to the mortgagee, but to a third party or third parties, usually independent of the transaction (though in practice chosen by the mortgagee), and the conveyance is in trust. The trustees hold nothing but naked legal title (in title states), and they hold it for the purposes of the trust. Both the mortgagor and the mortgagee are beneficiaries of the trust *(cestuis que trust),* since the ultimate conveyance or reconveyance will be made to one of them, depending upon the type of termination that occurs. The primary differences between using a deed of trust and using a normal mortgage lie in the procedures upon default. As long as the obligation giving rise to the deed of trust is current, the operation under a deed of trust is very similar to that under a mortgage.

There is great variation in the statutory provisions governing deeds of trust, and careful attention must be paid to the nuances of practice in the given jurisdiction. The most important element of a deed of trust is the power of sale. This provision, the mechanics of which will be discussed later in the chapter requires the trustee to sell the security upon default by the borrower. Under a power of sale, no judicial intervention is needed in the foreclosure process. The trustee merely follows the notice and sale procedures set forth in the deed of trust and allowable under statute and may convey the property free of any equitable right to redeem (though it is subject in some states to a statutory right).

Various qualifications of trustees which are set forth in the statutes. The trustees must, of course, be competent, of age, and "sui juris," or without legal disabilities. In addition, a number of states require that they be residents of the state in which the property is located and forbid foreign corporate trustees from serving. The statutes may also require that trustees unrelated in a business or personal sense to the lender exercise the power of sale.

The trustee's duties upon default are set forth in the document and must be exercised in good faith and without prejudice since the trustee occupies a fiduciary (trust) relationship with both parties. Upon the payment in full of the obligation, it is, of course, the trustee's duty to reconvey all title to the mortgagor or, if the property has been conveyed, to the mortgagor's successor in interest.

Both the advantages and the disadvantages of the deed of trust arise from the utilization of an independent trustee. The primary advantage is that the power of sale speeds up and eases the foreclosure procedure considerably by making recourse to judicial process unnecessary. The use of an independent party also facilitates the transfer of the debt by the mortgagee, since there need be no coincident transfer of the security interest. The same element which gives rise to the advantages of a trust deed also creates certain disadvantages. For example, the release procedure may be complicated because a trustee who is not a principal in the loan will not have firsthand knowledge that the obligation has, in fact, been satisfied and will require documentation in the form of canceled notes or surety bonds if the note has been lost or destroyed. However, the advantages seem to outweigh the disadvantages, as is evidenced by a trend toward the increased use of this form of security.

The Mortgage Debt

The very essence of a mortgage is that a debt must exist. The form and nature of the obligation, however, can vary considerably. The most common form is that of a promissory note running from the mortgagor to the mortgagee and executed as a part of the overall financing transaction at the time of settlement on the property. This note will normally refer to the existence of the mortgage or trust deed and state that it is secured thereby. The mortgage will also identify in some detail the note which it secures. In order to create a relationship that will fit into the flow of commerce, the note should be negotiable and must, therefore, conform to the requirements of the Uniform Commercial Code (Article 3). This is the standard format, but by no means the only one. Any obligation which can be reduced to a sum certain can be secured by a mortgage. In addition, the obligation need not be that of the mortgagor. Property may be given as security for the payment of a debt of a third person upon which the mortgagor has no liability.

Personal Liability.   Another aspect of the debt that creates problems is the extent of the mortgagor's personal liability. This must be the subject of negotiations between the parties. In general, the mortgagor will be personally liable on a mortgage if the note contains an admission of indebtedness or a promise to pay the amount due on the note. It is, therefore, important from the mortgagor's standpoint to include in the mortgage document constituting the agreement between the parties, a provision that the mortgagee will look solely to the property for payment of the debt. Such a mortgage is known as a nonrecourse mortgage. Without such language, it is likely that the mortgagee will be entitled to obtain a deficiency judgment should foreclosure be required. Some aspects of deficiency judgments will be discussed in the portion of this chapter relating to foreclosure.

Assignment of the Mortgagee's Interest.   Under modern legal theory, a mortgage is an assignable right (a chose in action) which may generally be assigned at the will of the mortgagee. The method of assignment varies according to statute, but title theory states are likely to require that an assignment take the form of a valid conveyance of realty, whereas lien jurisdictions tend to be less precise about the format of the assignment. Without an agreement to the contrary, it is usually unnecessary to obtain the mortgagor's consent to assignment of the mortgage, though notice must be given after assignment has occurred. Since the debt and the security are inextricably interrelated, it is generally the rule that an assignment, whether of the mortgage or, on its face, of the debt alone, acts as a transfer of both the debt and the security. In lien theory states the debt and the security are inseparable, but even in title theory states, where the mortgagee may technically transfer the security and the debt separately, there is a presumption, without a clear indication to the contrary, that the transfer of either the debt or the security is in fact a transfer of the mortgage.

The assignment of a mortgage transfers all interests of the mortgagee to the assignee and gives the assignee all the rights and obligations of the original mortgage. The exact status of the assignee depends to some degree upon the character of the evidence of indebtedness. If the debt takes a nonnegotiable form, then the assignee receives the mortgage subject to all the claims and defenses that might have been available to the mortgagor against the original mortgagee. If, however, the debt is in negotiable form (as that term is defined by the Uniform Commercial Code), the assignee, if a purchaser of the note or mortgage for value (called a holder in due course), takes the mortgage free from any defenses which the mortgagor may have had against the assignor and of which the assignee is not on notice. In this way, an assignee may find himself in a better position than that of the assignor. In practice, an assignee of a nonnegotiable debt may receive benefit similar to that of a holder in due course by obtaining from the mortgagor prior to the assignment a statement which says that no defenses to collection exist and which sets forth the amount due on the mortgage. This is called an estoppel certificate, and it precludes the mortgagor from asserting any defense at some future time.

Assignment the Mortgagor's Interest.   The mortgagor also has an interest in the security which is capable of transfer to a third party. After giving a mortgage, the borrower retains a diminished interest in the security, that being the right to the reversion of full ownership upon payment of the debt. Since the mortgagor is in possession, however, he is capable of assigning his possessory interest. Although this ability is theoretically unhampered, in practice the mortgagee will often make such transfer subject to his approval and will state in the mortgage that transfer without approval will render the debt payable in full. When a conveyance of the mortgaged property occurs, this does not affect the validity or enforceability of the obligation. There are basically two ways in which the transferee will take the property—either subject to the mortgage or by assuming the mortgage—and the manner chosen will govern the rights and liabilities of the parties.

When one purchases property upon which there is a mortgage and takes title subject to that mortgage, the understanding is that the real estate itself will be the only security source for repayment of the loan. In effect, the original borrower now becomes only a guarantor of the mortgage, with payments normally made by the transferee. There is, however, no liability on the debt placed upon the transferee. The transferee's incentive for making the payments is that upon paying off the loan the transferee will take title free and clear of any encumbrance. Should payment not be made, the mortgagor is still liable on the debt and may proceed against the real estate for reimbursement or satisfaction of its liability.

The second manner in which mortgaged land is transferred is by assumption of the mortgage by the transferee. Assumption is distinguished from taking subject to a mortgage in that the transferee agrees to be bound by the debt and thus becomes liable for its payment. The assumption may be expressly provided for in the deed going to the transferee, or it may be provided for by a collateral agreement or even an informal oral agreement. In an assumption, however, the mortgagor is not relieved of liability for the laon. As the mortgagor's position relates to the assignee, the latter becomes primarily liable, but from the standpoint of the mortgagee, recourse may be had against either the mortgagor or the assignee unless the mortgagor is specifically released from liability.

Prepayment. The concept of the law day, or the preset date upon which a loan becomes payable, is the most important condition triggering defeasance of the security. Although the payment of modern mortgages is often amortized over the life of the loan rather than made at one time, the obligation must still be satisfied according to the amortization schedule.

Questions often arise regarding the timing and the effect of satisfaction of the debt. Historically, the debt was due on the law day and no earlier or later payment was contemplated. Payment of the debt at the appointed time is all that is required to terminate the interest of the mortgagee in the property. Practically, of course, because mortgages are recorded, the termination must be made "of record."

At common law, no right to prepay a mortgage debt exists. The lender is entitled to know the exact period of time for which the loan will be out and his money earning interest. Recently, however, practice and some statutes have come to recognize a privilege of prepaying a mortgage, particularly if the interest rate exceeds certain levels. The rationale for allowing such prepayment is that a borrower who requires funds when the interest rates are abnormally high should not be precluded from refinancing if the rates dip.

In return for giving the borrower the right to prepay the loan, the lender will often impose a penalty fee for the exercise of that privilege. Such penalties may be controlled by the market or by statute, and they are generally imposed most stringently during the early part of the loan term as a deterrent to rapid refinancing predicated upon small fluctuations in interest rates. A prospective mortgagor will normally negotiate for the inclusion of a right to prepay without penalty, and after ascertaining the maximum allowable penalty, he should ask possible lenders about their current policy regarding penalties. The loan commitment should specify the terms of prepayment being offered.

Termination of the Mortgagee's Interest. Although payment of the debt may technically terminate the mortgage relationship, certain other acts may be necessary in order to place the parties in the proper relationship to each other. In titles states, a reconveyance of the title to the mortgagor is necessary. This act is unnecessary in lien states, since there was never an actual transfer of title.

From a practical standpoint, however, written releases of mortgages and deeds of trust are used in all states because the loan and the security are normally recorded in the land records of the jurisdiction in which the property is located. Upon satisfaction of a mortgage debt the mortgagee will normally cancel the note and execute a release in recordable form so that the records will indicate the lifting of the encumbrance on the property, making it once again fully marketable. In trust deed jurisdictions a similar release must be obtained, but the mechanics differ slightly. The release must be obtained from the trustee holding the security. Upon satisfaction of the debt, the mortgagee will normally cancel the note, which may then be presented to the trustee, who will then execute a release that the mortgagor may have recorded, though other methods of proof are sometimes used.

Each jurisdiction has requirements for documents which are "recordable" in form. This generally means that a specified form of notarial attestation of the signatures must be a part of the document. As it is quite important that the release of the mortgage be recorded to evidence the mortgagor's unencumbered title, care must be taken to obtain a release and to ensure its compliance with the recording rules of the given jurisdiction. Just as the mortgagee may generally insist upon timely payment of the debt, the mortgagor may rely upon release of the mortgage if such payment is properly tendered. For tender to be made properly, it must generally be of the full amount due (including any accrued interest and costs) and must be made unconditionally to the mortgagee or his agent. Specific variations on these requirements are governed by the law of contracts as developed among the states.

Should the mortgagee refuse a proper tender of payment, the effect will be to release the mortgage lien and to free the mortgagor from the payment of any further interest on the loan. Tender does not, however, relieve the mortgagor from his liability to repay the loan amount due at the law day. The rules governing tender after the due date of the loan vary considerably, but it should be sufficient to note here the general rules that in title states late tender without acceptance does not discharge the mortgage, whereas in lien jurisdictions it does, so that a mortgagee in lien jurisdictions is much less likely to reject a tendered payment.

Priority of Claims

If multiple mortgages attach to the same property, the rights of the various mortgagees become quite important. There are two basic methods of determining priorities in mortgages, the first being the common-law rules and the second being the rules set by the recording statutes of the various states. In the United States the second method has largely superseded the first.

It may be stated as a general rule of successive legal mortgages that the first in time has precedence over the others. A legal mortgage will also prevail over any subsequent equitable mortgage. The rationale for this result is obvious in title theory states where the superior position of title holding certainly deserves priority to a lesser estate conveyed subsequently. However, where prior equitable mortgages and subsequent equitable or legal conveyances exist, the result may differ, depending upon the equities of the parties.

The actual result in a given case may turn on what is known in the law as the concept of the "bona fide purchaser." As used here, this term refers to an individual purchasing and interest for value in an arm's-length transaction and without any knowledge of prior liens on the property. In the absence of a recording act provision to the contrary, a bona fide purchaser of legal title to property will take free of the liens of prior equitable mortgagees. In the case of multiple equitable mortgagees, however, the first in time will prevail unless the person obtaining a subsequent equitable interest is able to show that a prior holder lacked bona fides in acquiring the prior interest. Among equal equities it is axiomatic that the prior equity will prevail.

Recording Acts. As a practical matter, priorities in the United States are largely governed by the recording acts currently in effect in all 50 states. Although these acts may vary in their operation from state to state, certain basic elements are common to all. First developed in England, recording acts require the placing of all deeds, mortgages, and other documents conveying interests in land into a master index maintained by the jurisdiction in which the property is located. It should be noted that recordation of a deed is not necessary to convey title or a lien between a purchaser and a seller or between a mortgagor and a mortgagee. The deed is effective among the parties to it without recordation.

Recordation is, however, necessary in order to make the transaction binding upon third parties in their dealings with the property. The underlying purpose of a recording statute is really to create public notice of all transactions encumbering or conveying title to real estate. Recordation is held (within some operational limits) to place all subsequent takers of an interest in property on constructive notice of the recorded transaction. It can be seen that this is of great importance in determining priorities where the concept of a bona fide purchaser could cut off the equities of an earlier interst in the property, since a lack of notice is required for one to qualify as a bona fide purchaser

Chain of Title.   As a practical matter, some limits had to be placed on the search of the land records necessary for a prospective purchaser or mortgagee to satisfy himself that no senior encumbrances existed. To this end, the concept of "chain of title" was developed. Most jurisdictions maintain a grantor-grantee index of real estate transactions. In this indexing system, one who is comtemplating a transaction involving a parcel of land may trace the title by going to the index and looking under the name of the individual who proposes to make the conveyance in question. Any prior conveyances by that grantor will be shown in the index. The search process may then be continued back to the original conveyance of the property by tracing each grantor back to his predecessor in interest. This search develops the chain of title on the property, and the person acquiring the property interest is considered to be on notice only of what appears in the chain.

In a smaller number of jurisdictions, a plat index which follows not the parties but the parcel of property is kept either in addition to or instead of the grantor-grantee index. If that is the case, a diligent or reasonable investigation must be made of this index, too, before one will be released from the imputation of constructive notice.

Notes. There are some variations in the application of the recording acts among the states. The greatest number of states hold that in order to defend title based upon lack of notice, it must be shown not only that there was no notice of record but also that there was no notice of the prior encumbrances. A lesser number of states base their priorities solely on recording, thereby ignoring the effect of actual notice. This simplifies the application of the statute, but at the cost of utilizing a legal fiction and also perhaps of causing certain "races to the courthouse" to set priorities at times differing from those of the actual conveyances. A third group of states require a lack of actual notice but also require that the subsequent purchaser record his interest before the time at which the previously unrecorded prior interest may be placed in record.

The recording systems and statutes used in the United States are of great significance to persons entering into mortgage transactions, and great care must be taken both in searching the title and in insuring prompt and proper recordation in accordance with the particular statute in force.

Acceleration and Foreclosure

The remedy of foreclosure on a mortgage becomes available to the mortgagee upon default by the mortgagor. In earlier times, the determination of a default that gave rise to this right was relatively simple. The debt was payable in full on the law day, and if it was not paid, the loan was in default. In modern practice, however, the amortized mortgage gives rise to questions as to the extent of the right of foreclosure upon the mortgagor's default in a single payment.

For all practical purposes this problem has been solved by the development of the acceleration clause, which is now found in almost all mortgages and mortgage notes. This device allows the mortgagee to declare the entire mortgage balance due and payable upon the happening of any one of a number of specified events. The clause nicely skirts the problem of partial default because invoking the clause enables the mortgagee to escalate such a default into a total default.

Almost every mortgage or deed of trust now written contains a clause allowing acceleration, at the option of the mortgagee, upon a default in any payment of principal or interest. This standard acceleration clause must be distinguished from an automatic acceleration (called ipso facto acceleration) which causes acceleration immediately upon occurrence of the act of default, thus starting the foreclosure machinery even if the mortgagee does not wish to foreclose. Automatic acceleration clauses should be avoided in any mortgage transaction since they serve the purposes of neither the mortgagee nor the mortgagor.

In addition to default on a payment, frequent causes for acceleration include failure to maintain the required insurance on the property and failure to keep current with taxes or to make such escrow deposits as the mortgagee may demand. Furthermore, it will often be found, as mentioned earlier, that transfer of the property by the mortgagor without the consent of the mortgagee will be a ground for acceleration. Acceleration may be had upon any other occurrence, but only if this is set forth in the mortgage or the note.

A properly drafted acceleration provision will allow the mortgagee to accelerate in a given situation. Often, if there is a merely technical violation or a single nonpayment by an otherwise diligent mortgagor, the mortgagee will not exercise the right, but will accept delayed payment (perhaps with a penalty if the mortgage provides for one). A mortgagee generally need not give any notice of acceleration other than beginning foreclosure procedures. Payment or tender of the amount due prior to the election to foreclose will cancel the right to foreclose, but payment after the election to foreclose will not preclude the mortgagee from proceeding with foreclosure. The fact that a mortgagee does not elect to accelerate upon the occurrence of one act allowing foreclosure does not preclude the election to foreclose if that act is repeated in the future. During the drafting stage of any mortgage transaction, care should be taken to ensure the inclusion of parallel acceleration clauses in both the note and the mortgage so that a single foreclosure action will be possible on both the debt and the security upon acceleration.

Strict Foreclosure. Upon exercise of the acceleration option, the mortgagee is able to foreclose the mortgage. Foreclosures are generally classified as either judicial foreclosure, foreclosure under a power of sale, or strict foreclosure. Perhaps the least common current foreclosure method is the oldest—strict foreclosure. In essence, the mortgagee goes to the equity court, presents proof of default, and asks that all incidents of title be vested in him. If the mortgagor presents no defense, the court sets a period (sometimes no more than 30 days) after which the mortgagor has no further right to redeem ownership. The mortgagee can then do as he wishes with the property.

The inequities which can arise under strict foreclosure are obvious. Theoretically the mortgagee can obtain full title to a valuable parcel of property where the outstanding indebtedness is very small in relation to the value of the property, and still have recourse on the debt. For this reason, many states do not allow strict foreclosure and in those states where strict foreclosure remains available its potential for the unjust enrichment of the mortgagee has been eliminated either by statute or by the courts.

Foreclosure by Judicial Sale. The most common method of foreclosure found in the United States today is known as foreclosure by judicial sale. This method of foreclosure is conducted under the supervision of the equity court having jurisdiction over a property. The method was developed in order to eliminate some of the inequities of strict foreclosure. The theory of the judicial sale is that the court will order and supervise the sale of the property, from which funds will be made available to satisfy the debt.

The mortgagee files a petition setting forth the default and the extent of the debt, and seeking to have the court enter a decree ordering the sale of the property. In some states the mortgagee may also seek entry of a deficiency judgment for any amount not paid by the sale proceeds.

The court will generally enter a decree giving the mortgagor a stated period during which to redeem and ordering the sheriff or other officer of the court to conduct a public sale after such notice and in compliance with such procedural safeguards as the statute may require.

After the judicial sale has been made, the court must confirm the result. The proceeds of the sale then pass with judicial oversight and are used for the payment of taxes and costs and for the satisfaction of the indebtedness and any other liens outstanding. The surplus, if any, is turned over to the mortgagor.

It is important from the mortgagee's standpoint to ensure that proper parties defendant are named in the action. The petitioner is normally the mortgagee or his assignee. A single defendant or multiple defendants may be named. It is necessary to name all persons having any interest in the mortgaged property, since all interests in the order of their priority will have to be satisfied from the proceeds of the sale. Obviously, the principal defendant will be the mortgagor (or his or her heirs or estate). If the mortgagor is married, his or her spouse will have to be named to clear any possible marital interest in the property, as will all holders of mortgages junior to the mortgagee, and any judgment or other creditors of record whose interests may encumber disposition of the property. The failure to join a defendant will not void the sale, but it will impair its effectiveness, since the proceeding will not foreclose an omitted defendant's right against the property.

Power of Sale.   The third of the major foreclosure methods in use in the United States today is disposition of the property under what is known as a power of sale. The primary advantage of a judicial sale of property is that judicial supervision tends to provide safeguards that the property will be sold at a fair price. The primary disadvantage is that the process can be slow and involved. The power of sale considerably streamlines the foreclosure process.

The power of sale is a contractual agreement in a mortgage or a deed of trust (it is almost universally included in deeds of trust) which provides that upon default or acceleration the mortgagee or the trustee has the authority to sell the property at public sale. The agreement will set forth the specific acts of default that will bring the clause into operation as well as the notice requirements, the conditions, and the procedures of the sale. The provisions on the sale must comply with the statutory scheme for powers of sale in the given jurisdiction and must be scrupulously adhered to, since the courts, if asked to review such a sale, will expect total compliance. This is understandable, since the lack of judicial supervision creates great possibilities for misuse.

The power of sale clause will generally require publication of notice of the sale, including a description of the property and the time and place of the sale. The sale itself must be a fair and impartial public auction, and the holder of the power of sale must use the sale proceeds just as the court would under a judicial sale—the costs of the sale are paid; the debt is settled; other liens are paid in order of priority; and the remainder, if any, is distributed to the mortgagor. The seller normally seeks a court accounting regarding the disposition of the proceeds so that the court may determine the priorities of the various parties.

It is the general rule that the mortgagee cannot purchase the property in a foreclosure sale under a power of sale without the consent of the mortgagor. This is obviously necessary in light of the fact that the individual conducting the sale must impartially administer the proceedings. When a trustee conducts the sale, however, the mortgagee may "bid in" the property for the amount of the debt, since the sale is being conducted by an independent entity.

In sum, the foreclosure of mortgages under a power of sale is the most expeditious manner of foreclosure. If the procedures are followed closely, the sale will be effective and smooth in most cases. Should problems arise, however, recourse to judicial supervision or to a judicial sale is available in all states.

Defenses to Foreclosure. Few defenses that will preclude foreclosure are available to the mortgagor. In order to raise a valid defense, the mortgagor must set forth a reason that goes to the heart of the mortgage relationship. Agreements surrounding the mortgage or ancillary agreements between the mortgagor and the mortgagee will generally not support an action to stop foreclosure.

Satisfaction is perhaps the most important defense to a foreclosure action or sale. As has been indicated, the mortgagor may generally tender payment up to the time of sale. Such tender of payment and its acceptance, even during the notice period, can generally be set forth as a valid defense.

As with most contractual agreements, certain defenses to the validity of the mortgage itself may be raised by the mortgagor. These may include such defenses as the following: that the mortgage was entered into on the basis of fraudulent representations, that duress was used to force the mortgagor to enter into the mortgage, or that there was insufficient consideration for the mortgage. The nature and the quantum of proof needed to sustain such defenses will be governed by the general principles of contract law of the particular jurisdiction.

In addition, various general legal defenses, such as statutes of limitation, waiver of the right to foreclose, and laches (delays in enforcing a right to the detriment of others), may under certain circumstances preclude the ability of the mortgagee to consummate a foreclosure proceeding.

Deficiency Judgments. Assuming the validity of the mortgage and of the foreclosure proceeding, a matter of concern to both the mortgagor and the mortgagee is the resolution of a situation in which the sale of the property fails to yield enough funds to satisfy the indebtedness. To what extent is the mortgagor personally liable? As a general principle, if the mortgagor has executed a promissory note or some other evidence of indebtedness in favor of the mortgagee, there is personal liability for full repayment of the debt and the mortgagee is entitled to obtain a deficiency judgment to achieve that end.

The method by which the deficiency judgment is obtained varies among the states. In certain jurisdictions the mortgagee may ask for such a judgment as part of his foreclosure petition, and in others the judgment is sought after the sale of the property, especially where a power of sale avoids prior judicial involvement. Furthermore, some jurisdictions subscribe to the so-called one-action rule, which forces the mortgagee to consolidate his recourse into a single foreclosure action whereby sale is made and a deficiency is issued only for the amount not satisfied by the sale proceeds. This precludes multiple lawsuits to cure a single default. Although a question may arise as to the adequacy of the sale price and, therefore, the propriety of the deficiency, the courts will normally uphold the price received at a procedurally proper sale and award a personal judgment against the mortgagor for the balance.

There are some limitations on the availability of a deficiency decree. First of all, a provision in the mortgage may state that the mortgagee will look only to the security for satisfaction of the obligation. Although such a clause is not usually acceptable to a lender, the mortgagor may secure it in negotiating his loan. Second, some states set statutory restrictions on the availability of deficiency judgments. These so-called antideficiency statutes limit or eliminate the availability of deficiency judgments under varying circumstances. For example, in a few states deficiency judgments are not available as a remedy for default on a purchase money mortgage by virtue of statutory provisions.

The Right of Redemption.   One final topic must be touched upon in this discussion of mortgage foreclosure, and that is the incidents of the mortgagor's right of redemption which survive in our legal system.

The equitable right of redemption, discussed at the beginning of this chapter, remains intact to some degree, but it is of less utility today than it was in earlier times. After the mortgagee has begun his foreclosure proceedings (or taken possession) and throughout the period set by the court prior to the sale, the mortgagor may bring his own bill in the equity court to redeem his title by paying off the debt. The sale extinguishes this right for any party defendant in the foreclosure suit. An omitted party, however, is not foreclosed by the sale and may exercise his equity of redemption until he is barred from doing so by a statute of limitations. In the absence of a foreclosure action, the mortgagor's equity of redemption will also continue until the expiration of the statute of limitations. In most states the statute of limitations allows considerable time (sometimes more than 20 years) to recover the possession of realty. Although the equity of redemption is occasionally exercised today, its importance for lenders, such as banks, which would prefer to avoid possession and foreclosure, has diminished.

Another form of redemption, operating after foreclosure, is of more recent origin and is mandated by statute in about half of the states. The right to statutory redemption is given to the mortgagor and usually to junior mortgages. The statute will set a period of time following the foreclosure sale during which the specified parties may regain title to the property by tendering full payment of the foreclosure sale price plus interest and perhaps costs. Most of the statutes allow redemption from six months to two years from the date of sale. The mortgagor generally retains possession during the redemption period, with the purchaser getting an interim certificate of sale. Upon the expiration of the redemption period, the purchaser will obtain a deed from the court and no further right in the property will exist in the mortgagor. Should the redemption be exercised, however, the purchaser will receive the return of his funds and title will revest in the mortgagor. Since this type of redemption is governed solely by statute, its mechanics must be thoroughly researched for each jurisdiction.

LEASE ARRANGEMENTS

William M. Shenkel

*W*ILLIAM M. SHENKEL, PhD, CPM, *Professor, Department of Real Estate and Urban Development, College of Business Administration, University of Georgia, Athens, Georgia.*

Organized and served as past chairman of the Department of Real Estate and Urban Development, College of Business Administration, University of Georgia. Senior member, in the American Right of Way Association. Former president, Georgia chapter, Institute of Real Estate Management. Author, Marketing Real Estate *(Englewood Cliffs, N.J.: Prentice-Hall, 1980);* Modern Real Estate Management *(New York: McGraw-Hill, 1980);* Modern Real Estate Appraisal *(New York: McGraw-Hill, 1978);* Modern Real Estate Principles 2d ed., *(Dallas, Tex.: Business Publications, Inc., 1980);* Real Estate Finance *(Washington, D.C.: American Bankers Association, 1976):* The Real Estate Professional *(Homewood, Ill.: Dow Jones-Irwin, 1978). Coauthor,* The Professional Real Estate Broker *(Homewood, Ill: Dow Jones-Irwin, 1978).*

Leases vary from two-page, printed contracts to extremely lengthy legal documents tailored to the specific situation. They are widely used for virtually all types of improved and unimproved property.

Lease Advantages

Leases may be viewed as a means of financing real estate. As an alternative to the sale of his or her property, the owner lends the property to the tenant, much as a banker lends money to a borrower. The tenant pays for the use of the borrowed property as he or she uses it. The tenant may find it preferable to lease land and buildings rather than purchase them outright. He or she does not have to tie up capital in owning, and may deduct all the lease payments if they are a business expense. In addition, leasing may give more flexibility in changing location—depending on the terms of the lease and the real estate itself.

Advantages to Owners. Although some owners are legally barred from selling through restrictions on the transfer of interest, most owners who lease their property do so because of the economic advantages that this offers.

Owners Defer Capital Gain Taxes. When real estate is sold, the owner may be liable to federal capital gain taxes, especially if the property has been held over a long term and has substantially appreciated in value. The payment of taxes would reduce the amount of capital available for investment. Thus, it may be advantageous for real estate owners to postpone capital gain taxes by continuing to lease property which might otherwise be sold.

Owners Create Income Comparable to That Provided by an Annuity. The owners of some real estate have the option of selecting tenants who will provide management-free income. An owner who leases to a reputable, nationally known, and financially strong company on a triple net lease gets an income with a high degree of security and no management problem. In this way, owners benefit from income earned from tenants with proven financial resources. Less qualified tenants may produce more net income, but entail greater risks and require more of the owner's time.

Tenants Improve Leased Land. Owners may negotiate with tenants to improve undeveloped property. In such instances, owners may look toward the enhancement of property value as part of their compensation. When a lease expires, the owner may lease the developed property for higher rent. This arrangement may be useful for land that needs development in order to earn maximum income.

Other Financial Advantages. Good tenants add to the value of property. Depending on the terms of the lease, which it is assumed are not onerous to the owner, property leased on a long-term basis—over 15 years—may become marketable if it is leased to nationally known companies. The good credit of a national tenant increases the value of a property. Without the lease, the income of the property may be lower, more remote, and less certain. In short, a favorable lease may convert vacant, unproductive land into an income-producing asset.

In addition, owners may benefit from the superior financing capability and the proven business ability of tenants. If vacant land has potential as a shopping center, arranging a net ground lease with an experienced shopping center developer would probably create more income for the owner than would proceeding independently in shopping center development. Indeed, owners earn the highest possible land rent by deliberately soliciting experienced tenants who have specialized knowledge and capital resources to improve property.

Leases permit owners to accept less rental income in return for tenant improvements. The owner sacrifices current income for expected capital appreciation. Some leases convert run-down or undeveloped property into well-maintained, developed property which is improved as required by lease terms. In other words, tenant maintenance and improvement may be recoverable by the owner in the form of capital gains.

Advantages to Tenants. For the tenant a lease may represent a form of credit that enables him or her to acquire long-term use of a property without a large initial capital investment. A lease may give the tenant economic advantages that are not found in fee ownership.

Give Tenants Maximum Financing. Suppose that the tenant leases for 50 years land that has a present value of $1 million and agrees to pay an annual rent of $80,000. To the tenant, the $80,000 is equivalent to interest on a $1 million loan, and the tenant does not make annual payments to amortize principal. At the same time, the lease is usually long enough to allow the tenant to recover his investment from business operations. More important, the tenant secures financing equal to 100 percent of the land value. A 100 percent mortgage secured only by vacant land would be difficult to obtain.

Rent Is Income-Tax Deductible. Though owners may deduct depreciation allowances for buildings used in business, the same privilege does not hold true for vacant land because for income tax purposes, land is not depreciable. For highly valuable land, for example, downtown parking lots, it is often advantageous to lease the site and deduct the rent for income tax purposes. If the land were purchased, the parking lot owner would not have lease payments to deduct as an income tax expense. In sum, net ground leases are often financially advantageous if the land is highly valuable in relation to the depreciable building value.

Minimize Capital Requirements. Provided that certain legal and financial requirements are met, leasing may enable tenants to increase the rate of return on equity. Tenants with proven ability and financial means might be able to obtain 100 percent financing of both land and buildings by combining a ground lease with a first mortgage. For example, a tenant might finance a $400,000 new building under a first mortgage and lease a $100,000 site from the landowner.

Certain other financial advantages may accrue to tenants. First, leasing may enable a tenant to secure a better location than would be attainable without leasing. Even if the tenant prefers to own, he or she may elect to lease because the property available for purchase represents a less profitable business location. Second, under a long-term lease, tenants by good management and capital investment can create estates that are marketable as other real estate interests. It will be shown later how tenants benefit from the rising values of their estates.

Elements of a Valid Lease

Like other real estate instruments, leases must conform to the requirements of an enforceable contrac In most states, leases that are enforceable for more than one year must be in writing. At a minimum, a valid lease would require:

1. A beginning and an ending date.
2. Identification of the owner and the tenant.

3. A legal description of the property leased.
4. The rental terms, including the time and place of payment.
5. The signatures of the parties to the lease.

Further, an enforceable lease must be for a legal purpose; it must be executed by competent parties; it must be signed, witnessed, and acknowledged according to state law. By convention, leases also include certain legal elements, although, unlike other real estate documents, leases are not governed by a fixed format or a common set of terms. However, certain elements are common to most commercial leases.

To illustrate, it is convenient to group these elements into six categories: (1) introductory terms, (2) financial rights, (3) building improvements, (4) miscellaneous rights, (5) insurance requirements, and (6) other legal requirements. The main purpose in explaining these elements is to show the importance of each, so that proper legal counsel may be consulted in dealing with real estate leases.

Introductory Terms. Leases generally begin with definitions of technical terms. In this introductory section, the parties to the lease are identified and the property under lease is legally described.

For example, consider leases that base rents in part on annual gross sales. In such instances, questions arise on whether bad debts, merchandise returns, sales taxes, or excise taxes should be included in gross sales. In defining gross receipts, such leases usually state:

> Gross receipts means all income, including money and any other thing of value, received by or paid to lessee or its affiliates. . . . (1) "Gross receipts" shall not include amounts collected and paid out for sales or excise taxes imposed by a duly constituted governmental authority where such tax is billed to the purchaser as a separate item. (2) It shall not include credits for the exchange of goods or merchandise between the stores, if any, of lessee or its affiliates where such exchange is made solely for the convenient operation of business and not for the purpose of consummating a sale previously made directly or indirectly from or on the leased premises. (3) It shall not include the amount of any refund where the merchandise sold, or some part thereof, is returned by the purchaser and accepted by lessee or its affiliates. (4) It shall not include income from the sale of fixtures.

Ordinarily this part of the lease will conclude by giving the lease beginning and ending dates.

Financial Rights. The purpose of the lease determines the financial terms. Leases must detail the circumstances of the rent payment:

The place of the rent payment.

The time of the rent payment.

The amount of the rent and its calculation.

Accounting procedures associated with the calculation of the rent.

If the lease covers the tenant's construction of a building on leased land, the financial terms must ensure the tenant's completion of the building as promised. Usually, tenants must provide security guaranteeing the completion of the building and the payment of all claims for work and construction materials. A corporate surety bond in an amount equal to the cost of the building satisfies this provision. The bond remains in force until the building is completed according to the terms of the lease.

Alternatively, the tenant is often allowed to deposit in escrow bonds, cash, or other securities sufficient to pay the cost of building construction. The escrow agreement typically provides that at least 15 percent of the funds will be withheld until the time for filing mechanics' or material liens expires.

Building Improvements. This portion of the lease ensures that property will be developed according to its highest and best use. The owner controls the type of building and its construction, maintenance, and repair. Tenants proposing to lease land on which new buildings will be constructed must ordinarily submit architectural plans for the owner's approval. This restriction ensures that property will be developed to its maximum potential. Typical language reads:

> The lessee shall submit the general plan and architect's design for the complete development for the entire leased premises. The lessor shall either prove or state reasons for disapproval of plans and specifications within thirty (30) days after their submission.

Further, it is in the owner's interest to provide for proper property maintenance:

> All improvements placed on the leased premises shall be constructed in a good and workmanlike manner and in compliance with applicable laws and building codes. All parts of the buildings exposed to perimeter properties shall present a pleasant appearance, and all service areas shall be screened from public view. The lessee shall, at all times during the terms of this lease and at the lessee's sole cost and expense, maintain the premises and all appurtenances thereon in good order and repair and in a neat, sanitary, and attractive condition.

Such a lease usually specifies a minimum building cost and provides for a final date of completion. Failure to observe these restrictions places the tenant in default, giving the owner the right to cancel the lease.

Miscellaneous Rights. In considerable detail, leases define the right of tenants to sublease, to assign the lease, and to grant utility easements or rights-of-way. The liability for the payment of property taxes should be clearly explained.

Most owners reserve the right to approve subleases, especially if the lease is based in part on a percentage of gross receipts. Here the owner has a vested interest in the competence, financial ability, and credit status of the subtenants responsible for rental payments. The right to approve subleases helps ensure that only responsible subtenants who are likely to observe the provisions of the lease will be selected.

A lease assignment refers to the transfer of tenant rights to a third party. Again, if an owner withholds the right to approve assignments, he or she has a final voice in selecting new tenants who will responsibly observe terms of the lease.

Complex legal questions are avoided if the original lease makes provision for the right to supply utility easements and streets over the life of the lease. The clause on property taxes may give the owner the right to terminate the lease if the tenant does not pay property taxes.

Insurance Requirements. In building leases, insurance provisions play an important role in preserving the owner's interest. Such provisions insure against loss or damage by fire in an amount equal to the insurable value of buildings. Building leases usually require that insurance funds for the repair, restoration, or replacement of damaged structures be deposited in escrow. In addition, tenants are required to carry personal liability insurance for property damage and personal injury.

Other Legal Requirements. Leases usually include certain clauses that cover:

Eminent domain	Obligations of the tenant
Tenant default	Status of subleases
Attorneys' fees	Payments and notices
Partnership between owner and tenant	

These lease clauses define the rights of the parties over the life of the lease. They explain under what circumstances the lease will be terminated and detail the rights of both parties in the event of a partial taking by government under eminent domain. They define the circumstances in which the tenant may be held in default. The responsibility of both parties for the payment of attorneys' fees in the event of litigation is carefully stated. It is stipulated that the lease agreement creates no partnership relationship between the owner and tenant. Added obligations of the tenant and the status of sublease interests in the event of tenant default are specified. Some leases require certain tenant payments, legal notices, and other duties prescribed by state law. In sum, these necessary lease provisions—and others—show that leases are complex instruments requiring a careful economic and legal review so that the parties to the lease may gain maximum benefit.

Estates Created by a Lease

It is important to recognize the legal estates created by a lease. Close attention should also be focused on the legal interests held by the owner and the tenant.

Less than Fee Simple Estates. Though leases grant tenants the right to the exclusive use of real estate, the right is called less than a fee simple estate since it is limited in time. The estate acquired by a tenant, who is the *lessee,* is termed the *leasehold* estate or interest. The owner of the title, who grants a lease, becomes the *lessor* and acquires the *leased fee* estate. Simply stated, the tenant agrees to pay rent and observe other terms of the lease in return for the right of exclusive use and possession as defined by the written lease. At the termination or cancellation of the lease, the leasehold interest ends and property ownership and the rights of use and possession revert to the fee owner. These relationships are shown in Figure 1.

There are two other relevant points. (1) If the lessee *subleases* to a third party, the lessee is still responsible to the lessor as agreed in the

FIGURE 1
Estates Created by a Lease

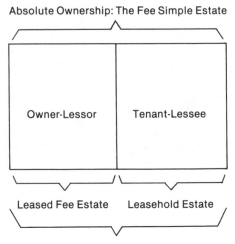

Absolute Ownership: The Fee Simple Estate

Owner-Lessor   Tenant-Lessee

Leased Fee Estate   Leasehold Estate

Less than Fee Simple Estate Interests

lease. The sublessee becomes responsible to the lessee. The sublease, in effect, creates a new estate. (2) However, if the lease is *assigned,* the new lessee steps into the shoes of the original lessee, becoming directly liable to the lessor. The original lessee is excused from the lease and is no longer a party to the agreement. No new estate is created by a lease assignment.

In these lease agreements, it is possible to create one of four types of tenancies: *estates for years, periodic tenancies, tenancy at will,* and *tenancy at sufferance.*

Lease Tenancies. The simpler leases, for one year or less, may be fully enforceable even though they are evidenced only by an oral agreement. The rights of the owner and the tenant are controlled by written or oral agreements and state law.

Estates for Years. A leasehold estate that continues for a definite time is known as an estate for years. The time may be virtually any period: six months, one year, five years, or even 99 years. (By custom, leases do not extend beyond 99 years.) During this time, subject to the lease agreement, the lessee has the exclusive right of possession. From the standpoint of both parties, this is the preferred estate.

Periodic Tenancies. Also referred to as leases from year to year, periodic tenancies continue indefinitely until one of the parties gives notice of termination. Suppose that you rent an apartment for 30 days and that each month thereafter you agree with the owner to lease for another month by paying a month's rent in advance. This arrangement may continue indefinitely until either party gives notice of termination. State law usually governs the period of notice required to terminate a periodic tenancy. A 30- or 60-day written notice is not an unusual legal requirement.

Tenancy at Will. This type of tenancy meets the convenience of owner and tenant when a written lease terminates. If the tenant continues in possession *with the express approval* of the owner, after a lease expires, the tenant holds a tenancy at will. Again, state statutes govern the requirements of statutory notice—the time, the form of notice, and the method of terminating a tenancy at will.

Tenancy at Sufferance. The least desirable type of tenancy, tenancy at sufferance refers to continued unlawful possession by a tenant. It occurs when a tenant who has entered the premises lawfully under a lease continues in possession *without the owner's permission* after the lease has expired. In effect, the tenant has no rights since his or her occupancy lacks the express consent of the owner. Tenancy at sufferance remains in effect until the owner consents to the occupancy, changing the tenancy to a tenancy at will, or until the owner takes action to repossess the premises. Most states require no notice to terminate a tenancy at sufferance. For this reason, the tenant at sufferance has no economic interest to mortgage, assign, or sublease.

Rental Terms

The rental terms are critical to the lease. These may be adjusted to the specific requirements of the owner and the tenant, based on their concept of how property values will change in future years. In some cases, rental adjustment clauses fit the financial demands of the tenant while maximizing owner receipts. The parties to a lease are pretty much confined to five types of rental agreements, which in special circumstances may be offered in combination: (1) fixed rents, (2) graduated rents, (3) percentage rents, (4) reappraisal leases, and (5) index leases.

Fixed Rents. Some owners are reluctant to base rents on fixed dollar amounts because they anticipate continued inflation. Yet, in some cases, owners prefer fixed rents. For instance, suppose that land acquired ten years ago for $50,000 is now worth $500,000. Suppose further that a tenant proposing to construct a new building on the land must negotiate a fixed rent schedule because mortgage lenders will not approve rising and uncertain rent schedules. If the owner negotiates a lease for 25 years at a fixed annual rent of $50,000, each year of the lease the owner will recover the original value of his investment. Though the rent may decline in purchasing power over the life of the lease, the owner who relates the rent payment to the original investment cost may favor a fixed rent.

Fixed rents are advised for relatively short leases. One-, two-, or three-year apartment leases provide for fixed monthly rents. The owner is protected from rising costs by the ability to negotiate rents at the market level when such leases are renewed.

In some circumstances, however, a fixed rent schedule is poorly adapted to owner-tenant needs and a graduated rent schedule may prove more suitable.

Graduated Rents. Some properties are developed in anticipation of future growth. Given a rapidly rising population, a shopping center may have good future prospects but low immediate earnings. Graduated rents are suited to this situation.

A 65-year net ground lease, providing for the construction of a $450,000 nursing home on a five-acre site, specified a graduated rent schedule over the first five years:

Year	Annual Ground Rent
1	$ 3,200
2	6,400
3	9,600
4	13,000
5	16,000

In this example the landowner approved lower rent in the initial years while the nursing home improved its occupancy rates. After the first ten years the rent was to be revised in accordance with a reappraisal of the land.

Under the graduated rent schedule, the owner subsidizes the tenant by reducing the rent to uneconomic levels until the tenant has developed the property or is benefiting from increased population and promotion. For example, it would be prudent for the tenant to lease land for $10,000 a year for three years and to agree to pay rent of $50,000 a year afterward, when the property (for example, a new shopping center) is expected to be more profitable.

Generally it is risky to graduate rent upward over relatively long periods—10, 20, 30, or more years. In practice, rent schedules are graduated only during the early years of a lease and represent temporary rental adjustments while the tenant is developing a property.

However, certain long-term building leases, say over 25 years, call for reduced rent if the tenant exercises renewal options, since it is reasoned that the owner will have recovered the value of the building over the initial 25 years and will be entitled to only a return on the land afterward. Such leases are exceptional.

Percentage Leases.   Percentage leases frequently combine minimum fixed rents with rents based on a share of gross sales. They are popular in leasing retail space. The minimum rent (1) provides the necessary guarantee for financing building improvements and (2) eliminates the marginal tenant who lacks the merchandising ability, financing, or know-how needed to maximize land use. The percentage rewards the owner according to the productivity of the site—the higher the retail sales, the higher the rent. The tenant, in turn, pays higher rents only if he or she benefits from a higher sales volume.

The credit of the tenant and custom largely determine the amount of the percentage. In shopping centers, the major tenants who attract shoppers are able to negotiate below-market rents and low-percentage rents—largely because of their bargaining power. Percentage rents for shopping center tenants reported in the last survey of the Urban Land Institute show a median percentage rent of 2.5 percent of gross sales for junior department stores leasing space in neighborhood shopping centers. Higher percentage rents are usually found for high-markup, lower-volume retailers, for example, optometrists, who pay a median percentage rent of 7.5 percent of gross sales.

The typical rental clause would require, say, "4.0 percent of gross income in excess of $600,000." The minimum sales figure, which varies by tenant and location, is found by dividing the minimum annual rent by the customary percentage figure. For example, if the minimum annual rent is $24,000 and the customary percentage rent is 4 percent, normally the percentage rent would not apply until gross sales exceeded $600,000 ($24,000/0.04).

It should be pointed out that percentage rents are inappropriate for some businesses. They are not applied to businesses based on personal services, for example, the businesses of dentists, doctors, or accountants, and they are unusable for certain industrial operations—warehousing, industrial plants, and other nonretail operations. Moreover, they are difficult to enforce for relatively small tenants with poor accounting and record systems.

Reappraisal Leases. Leases extending over relatively long terms, for example, more than 25 years, may call for reappraisals to establish fair market rent at periodic intervals. Such a clause is common in leases that give tenants the option to renew at the end of 20 years, 25 years, and the like. This approach is used in FHA mortgages on dwellings constructed on leased land, which are very common in the state of Hawaii. Usually the tenant and the owner each select an appraiser, and the two appraisers select a third appraiser to make up an appraisal board that submits its estimate of fair market rent. The reappraisal clause further requires that the lessor and the lessee share equally in the cost of the rental reappraisal.

To illustrate, a 75-year lease which called for reappraisal of the rent every 10 years provided that

> such rent shall be a fair return on the then market value . . . determined by three impartial real estate appraisers, one to be appointed by each of the parties hereto and the two appraisers thus appointed shall appoint a third appraiser. . . . The three appraisers so appointed shall thereupon proceed to determine the matters in question, and the decision of said appraisers or a majority of them shall be final, conclusive, and binding upon both parties hereto.

Although on its face the reappraisal lease seems fair, the owner and the tenant have the right to appeal in court. Some observers claim that reappraisal leases invite expensive court litigation to settle conflicts on the fair market rent.

Index Leases. Index leases adjust rent according to the value of the dollar. Under such leases, rent rises or falls proportionately with changes in some price index—for example, the consumer price index or the wholesale price index.

Suppose that the rent is adjusted upward every two years according to changes in a selected price index. Suppose further that in the first month of the lease the base index was 186.9 and that two years later it is 214.3. The rent would then be adjusted upward as follows:

Price index in the first month (base index) = 186.9
Price index at time of adjustment (current index) = 214.3

$$\text{Rental adjustment factor} = \frac{\text{Current index}}{\text{Base index}}$$

$$\frac{214.3}{186.9} = 1.14$$

In this example, the price index has moved upward by some 14 percent. If the monthly rent was initially $3,000 per month, changes in the price index would require a monthly rent of $3,420 (1.14 × $3,000).

In sum, to apply percentage adjustment clauses:

1. Determine the base index—usually the price index for the first month of the lease.
2. Determine the current index for the month when rental adjustments are required.
3. Divide the current index by the base index to give the rental adjustment factor.
4. Multiply the initial monthly rent by the rental adjustment factor.

Note that index leases adjust rent so that the tenant and the owner neither gain nor lose from price inflation. In this sense, the index lease corrects for the effects of inflation.

The method is appropriate for long-term leases where there is continuing and erratic inflation. However, it will be appreciated that real estate values, retail sales, and the market rent for a specific property may not change proportionately with national price series. The local real estate market for commercial real estate may vary widely from general price trends.

Net Ground Leases

A net ground lease has significant financial advantages to the owner of vacant land and to the tenant who develops that land. Under this arrangement, the owner conveys land use rights for a relatively long term, 25 years to 99 years. The tenant pays rent based on a reasonable return on the market value of the land, and constructs a building suited to his or her purposes. At the end of the lease (or in the event of tenant default), the building and land revert to the owner. These are called "net" leases since the rent is net to the owner; the tenant pays property taxes and insurance.

Under the net ground lease, the owner converts vacant land to productive real estate. He or she benefits from tenant improvements, and with above-average tenants the income from a net ground lease may justify a higher market value than would prevail for the vacant land without tenant improvements.

Financing Net Ground Leases. The tenant gains from minimizing the equity, and if lease terms are favorable, the tenant may increase the rate of investment return by combining a mortgage with a ground lease.

To show this effect, assume that the land under lease has a market value of $75,000 and that the tenant proposes a land improvement of $225,000 and agrees to an annual rent of $8,000. Assume further that mortgage financing for 20 years at 9 percent is available to finance improvements under a loan-to-value ratio of 66⅔ percent.

Under these assumptions, leasehold financing will show a higher return on equity than will mortgage financing of the fee. Leasehold financing is compared to mortgage financing of the fee in the example in Table 1. With a proposed property value of $300,000 (land, $75,000; land improvements, $225,000), the maximum loan under the assumed conditions would be $200,000. To show the return on equity after mortgage service and ground rent, assume also a net rental of $35,000 on land and building. Under these circumstances, a first mortgage of $200,000 would require an annual debt service of $21,600, resulting in a net income after mortgage payments of $13,400—a return on the $100,000 equity of 13.4 percent.

If, on the other hand, the site is leased without subordination, a loan of $150,000 would be necessary (two thirds of $225,000). After the deduction of rent ($8,000) and mortgage service requirements ($16,200), the tenant would receive a net cash return of $10,800, or a return on equity of 14.4 percent ($10,800/$75,000).

With subordination of the leased fee, the lender would regard land and building as security, which would permit a maximum loan of $200,000. After the deduction of ground rent and debt service of $29,600, a net income of $5,400 remains, which represents a return of 21.6 percent on a $25,000 equity.

Net Ground Lease Illustrated. The owner of two acres of commercially zoned land in Palm Springs negotiated a 60-year net ground lease that

TABLE 1
Leasehold Financing Compared to Conventional Financing

Item	Mortgage Financing	Leasing without Subordination	Leasing with Subordination
Minimum loan	$200,000	$150,000	$200,000
Equity	100,000	75,000	25,000
Net rental from tenant	35,000	35,000	35,000
Ground rent	—	8,000	8,000
Annual payments (20 years, 9 percent rounded)	21,600	16,200	21,600
Total charges	21,600	24,200	29,600
Net after ground rent and mortgage payments	13,400	10,800	5,400
Ratio of equity to down payment	13.4% ($13,400/ $100,000)	14.4% ($10,800/ $75,000)	21.6% ($5,400/ $25,000)

provided for a minimum annual rent of $16,000, representing a 7 percent return on $218,000, the market value of the land. The lease required the owner to construct a two-story retail office building within two years for an amount of not less than $300,000. The owner financed the construction of the building with a $250,000 mortgage. Since the building was a multiple-tenant structure with retail stores on the ground floor, the lease further provided a rent equal to 25 percent of sublease rents or $16,000, whichever was greater.

At the end of five years, the percentage rent totaled approximately $28,000. If this income were capitalized at a 7 percent return, its value would be $393,120. (The income capitalized by the factor for the present worth of one per annum at 7 percent equals 14.04 × $28,000.) If this income were capitalized at 9 percent, the value of the rental income would be $309,400 (11.05 × $28,000).[1]

This example shows the economic advantage in negotiating a lease that provides for rent which, when capitalized, produces a value greater than the market value of the unimproved land. Assuming that the building cost $300,000 and that the land was initially worth $218,000, the tenant developed an investment worth $518,000 with a capital investment of $50,000. Before negotiating the lease, the tenant undertook a rental market study showing the potential demand for office and retail space at that location.

Sale Leasebacks

Sales leasebacks, which are attractive investments to institutions, appeal to large firms as a means for financing expensive buildings. In operation, real estate is leased back by the seller, usually over the remaining economic life of the building. Figure 2 illustrates the arrangement in which the seller becomes the lessee and the purchaser simultaneously becomes the lessor.

It is difficult to understand the appeal of a sale leaseback without recognizing that:

1.   Different individuals and institutions have widely different income tax rates.
2.   Capitalization rates affecting investors and owners vary under different investment objectives and conditions.

Further, a company which earns a 20 percent return in operations may prefer to lease its premises at a rent equal to, say, a 9 percent cost of capital.

Advantages of Sale Leasebacks. Financial institutions supplying mortgageable funds are usually restricted in the maximum loan that they may make on a single property—for insurance companies the maximum loan is generally 66⅔ or 75 percent of the appraised value. However, under a sale leaseback an insurance company may invest in the

---

[1] Consult present worth of one per period tables to calculate the present worth of a constant annual income, capitalized at 7 and 9 percent for 60 years.

FIGURE 2
Sale-Leaseback Financing

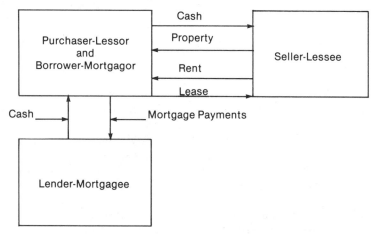

full value of the property (the purchase price) and earn rent representing a favorable return on the investment, including amortization of the purchase price. In short, the sale leaseback appeals to institutional investors because they may invest larger sums on individual properties at returns which are higher than mortgage interest rates. Moreover, if the sale leaseback includes depreciable buildings, the purchaser-lessor may deduct depreciation from other taxable income under the present law.

The decision to enter a sale leaseback transaction as a lessee rests on purely financial grounds. Though the lessee loses the advantage of depreciation deductions, this is offset by the full deduction of rent as an operating expense against taxable income. In addition, the lessee exchanges a fixed asset for current funds (the purchase price) while continuing to use the property under the terms of the lease.

For some institutions, the return on capital in operations is greater than the aftertax cost of lease payments. The aftertax cost to the lessee is found by subtracting from the rent the product of the rent multiplied by the tax rate of the lessee. For example, a corporation that is subject to a marginal tax rate of 46 percent and leases back vacant land at an annual rent of $10,000 would have an effective rental expense of $5,400 per year:

Annual rent	$10,000
Less 0.46 × $10,000	− 4,600
Aftertax rental expense	$ 5,400

If the lease includes a building, and if the annual rent exceeds annual depreciation, the lease results in a larger annual tax deduction.

Sale Leasebacks on Land Only. A sale leaseback on vacant land provides capital to developers. For relatively valuable land, such as a regional shopping center site, the landowner-developer may elect to sell the land, leasing back the land for a term longer than the economic life of the proposed construction. Under this arrangement, the developer sells the land to an investor and uses the proceeds of the land sale to construct a building. The investment return to the buyer is related to the sale price of the land. More commonly, the investor-lessor will be a long-term lender who also grants a permanent mortgage loan for the proposed building.

Some lenders will purchase land only after the developer completes the building construction. In effect, this arrangement provides for a *take-out commitment* in addition to the prior commitment for a permanent mortgage loan, allowing the developer to gain temporary financing to cover the cost of construction. When construction is completed, the developer sells the land to the investor and leases it back. The developer, who is now a tenant, gains from the tax deductions on rent and gains further from the deductibility of depreciation on the building. If the tenant defaults, the building reverts to the owner-investor; the building, therefore, serves as security for rental payments called for by the ground lease.

Sale Leasebacks on Land and Building. Since the seller-lessee benefits from 100 percent financing in the sale leaseback of a building, this arrangement is attractive to firms that prefer to invest available capital in company operations rather than real estate. Such firms reason that their aftertax return is higher on investments in company operations than on the money they might save on rental payments by investing in real estate.

The attractiveness of a sale leaseback is further increased if a company has occupied the building for a considerable time, so that the remaining depreciation allowance for taxes is relatively small. Or consider a company that has a building on a highly expensive site: a downtown office building constructed on expensive land that is not depreciable. By engaging in a sale leaseback, the company benefits from the tax deductibility on that portion of the rent paid for the use of land.

Finally, it should be noted that the investor usually looks to the credit of the seller as security for the rent. Leases to major firms—such as J. C. Penney or Sears—are judged primarily on the financial standing of the company. Rent is customarily based on a return on the sale price which earns a slight premium above the prevailing bond rate. If the sale leaseback covers more specialized property (for example, hotels, office buildings, and shopping centers) and less creditworthy tenants, the purchaser-lessor typically charges a higher rate of return and negotiates for shorter term leases. Here, the lease is based on the potential income-earning ability of the property.

Build-Lease Arrangements

The simplest build-lease arrangement is that of the investor who purchases the land, negotiates a long-term lease with a nationally known tenant, and on the basis of the lease secures a mortgage to construct a building for the tenant. Mortgage payments are made from rental receipts, and, because the typical tenant is financially strong, the investor then sells the leased fee to others who purchase rights to the rental income. The capitalized value of the rental income is greater than cost, providing a profit for the investor.

A variation of this technique is illustrated by the financing of some hundred Safeway stores.[2] In this case, the investor agreed to purchase the stores at a price equal to the land and building cost. Simultaneously with each store sale, Safeway leased the building back for 30 years at a rental based on the purchase price. Subsequent to the initial term of 30 years, the agreement provided for four five-year renewal options at rents graduated downward. Safeway was given the right to cancel the lease during the first year at a purchase price based on a stated amortization rate.

The second part of this leaseback turned on the resale of individual stores to investors at a lower capitalization rate than the rate used to calculate the leaseback rental. This, in effect, produced a price higher than the acquisition cost. The contract and sale required a 20 percent cash down payment, with a purchase money mortgage given to the original investor for the 80 percent balance. The purchaser gained by collecting higher rents from Safeway than the mortgage charges, giving a high-leverage return on his 20 percent cash equity. At the same time, the purchaser benefited from building depreciation deductions—an attractive feature for investors in the 70 percent marginal income tax bracket.

To sum up, build-lease arrangements are adapted to the needs of companies with superior credit. By agreeing to lease, such a company acquires the use of land and of a new building designed for its specific purposes and constructed, in effect, under 100 percent financing terms. Because of the excellent credit standing of the tenant, mortgages are obtainable on the leased fee interest on highly favorable terms. The lease provides for rental payments greater than the mortgage payments. The leased fee is then sold to investors with relatively high marginal income tax rates.

Investors gain from the income tax deductibility of building depreciation and mortgage interest. Tenants, in turn, acquire the use of buildings adapted to their needs with no capital outlay. In addition, they benefit from the income tax deductibility of rent. Even the mortgage lender gains: mortgage payments are secured (1) by the superior credit of the tenant, who makes rental payments in excess of the mortgage payments, and (2) by the value of the new building and the land that are pledged as security for the mortgage.

---

[2] For additional detail, consult H. Jackson Sillcocks, "Financial Sense in Sales and Real Estate Leasebacks," *Real Estate Review,* Spring 1975, vol. 5, no. 1, pp. 93–95.

AGENCY LAW IN REAL ESTATE TRANSACTIONS

John D. Donnell

*J*OHN D. DONNELL, JD, DBA, Professor of Business Administration, Chairperson of Business Law, Graduate School of Business, Indiana University, Bloomington, Indiana.

Member, American Bar Association, American Business Law Association, and Law and Society Association. Former editor in chief, American Business Law Journal, and coeditor, American Business Law Journal. Author of numerous articles on legal and management topics in Business Horizons, Journal of Small Business Management, American Business Law Journal, and Business Lawyer. Author, The Corporate Counsel: A Role Study. Coauthor, Business Law: Principles and Cases; and Readings and Cases in Business Law.

The principal body of law governing real estate brokers and real estate salespeople in their relationships with clients is agency law. This is an ancient body of law that developed primarily from the transnational law merchant of the Mideastern and European traders. The law merchant was eventually incorporated into the English judge-made or common law, and that law was transplanted to America by the English colonists. It continues to develop and change, mostly through the decisions of the judges of the various states. However, most states impose certain statutory requirements on the conduct of a real estate business, and such requirements occasionally modify some of the common-law rules.

Agency law deals with the reciprocal rights, duties, and liabilities of the three parties to the triangular relationship between the principal, the agent, and the third party with whom the agent deals for and in behalf of the principal. The principal is the party—either a buyer or seller of real estate—who employs the broker. Agency law also covers the reciprocal duties of the broker and the broker's employees—including salespersons.

The general body of agency law, rather than special rules, is applicable to real estate brokers and salespersons, although the large number of reported cases involving real estate brokers provide more specific guidance in handling many common problems in the real estate area than do cases involving other sorts of agents. The pertinent statutes, on the other hand, tend to be directed specifically to real estate brokers and salespersons.

The basic rules of agency law are relatively few and simple. They may be summarized in nine statements. These statements are presented below, followed by a discussion of their applicability to real estate brokers in their relations with clients and employees. Because they are so closely related, the first and second statements and the fifth and sixth statements are discussed together. Both the rules developed by the judges in deciding specific controversies before them and the statutes passed by legislatures that apply to real estate brokers differ somewhat in the 50 states. However, it is believed that there is sufficient consistency to make this summary useful.

The Broker-Agency Relationship

1. *The agent has a duty to act for the principal with complete fidelity to the principal's interests, to follow the principal's instructions, to exericse due care in conducting the principal's business, and to account to the principal for whatever property belongs to the principal.*

2. *The principal has a duty to reimburse the agent for his proper expenditures on behalf of the principal and to compensate the agent according to the contract between them, express or implied.*

A Written Contract of Employment. The duties of the broker to his client are, for the most part, determined by the agreement (contract) between them. Except where required by statute, this agreement need not be in writing. However, a written contract is highly desirable. This is because the existence of a writing tends, if it is carefully read and understood by both parties, to minimize misunderstanding and dispute. A written contract also provides evidence of the agreement should the parties later disagree as to its terms or even its existence. It should clearly state the respective duties of the broker and the client, the compensation to be paid, and when that compensation had been earned by the broker. An attempt should be made to foresee events that might lead to misunderstanding and dispute, and the terms of the contract should provide solutions to problems that might arise should these events occur.

The principal and the broker can, but need not, use a standard form contract prepared by a lawyer for an association of real estate brokers or one that the broker may have had prepared for use in his business. The principal and broker can draft their own individual contract, but to avoid dispute and possible litigation the broker would be wise to use either a standard form contract with which he is entirely familiar or to engage a lawyer to draft one for the specific, out-of-the-ordinary case.

By statute a number of states require that the employment of a real estate broker be evidenced by at least a memorandum of agreement. The statutes were enacted because of the large number of disputes taken to the courts by brokers seeking a commission and alleging that they had been employed by the defendants. These statutes usually define such employment as acting for another for compensation in attempting to buy, sell, exchange, or rent real property or in negotiating a loan secured by real estate. They usually specify that only a licensed real estate broker or a licensed salesperson employed by a broker can serve as an agent for those purposes. This protects the principal from a volunteer who may later claim that the employment agreement was oral.

Under the common law a volunteer could not recover a commission even if the client were aware that the volunteer was a real estate broker, since the broker might well be employed by the other party to the transaction. For example, a broker who merely asks an owner if he will sell his property is not entitled to a commission from the owner if the latter agrees to sell at a given price and the broker then finds a buyer at that price. No explicit promise to compensate is required; however, an agreement to pay the customary commission or a reasonable commission is frequently found by the courts to have been implied.

In the absence of restrictive legislation, the principal and the agent are free to agree upon such terms as they wish, except that, for public policy reasons, the courts will not permit an agent to contract away completely his fiduciary duty to the principal—that is, the duty to act in the best interests of and in complete loyalty to the principal. This duty will be discussed below in detail.

Types of Listings.   One of the most important terms to be specified if the principal wishes to sell real estate is the type of listing. The principal can empower the broker to complete the sale of the property, either through his own efforts or the efforts of other brokers, but normally the broker's function is merely to find a buyer with whom the principal will contract to sell. If that is so, there are four types of listings: open (or general), exclusive right to sell, exclusive listing, and multiple listing.

An *open* or *general listing* merely constitutes the contracting broker as an agent of the owner for the purpose of finding a buyer for the property. Under this type of arrangement the owner may contract with more than one broker, and the first of these brokers who finds a buyer ready, willing, and able to make the purchase is entitled to the agreed-upon commission, unless the owner first terminates the agency or makes the sale himself.

An *exclusive right to sell,* at the opposite extreme, entitles the listing broker to the agreed-upon commission if the property is sold, without regard to who finds the buyer. Even if the owner sells it without any participation by the agent, the agent is entitled to the commission.

An *"exclusive agency,"* or *"exclusive listing,"* however, does not prevent the owner from completing a sale on his own and avoiding the payment of the commission. Careful drafting of the agreement is necessary to make the arrangement an exclusive right to sell.

A *multiple listing* occurs when the listing broker is a member of a group of brokers who have an arrangement to exchange listings. Normally the listing broker obtains an exclusive right to sell but permits other brokers in the group to show the property to prospective buyers, with the understanding that if a sale is made through the efforts of a broker other than the one who obtained the listing, the commission is split between the two brokers on a prearranged basis.

A prospective purchaser may also enter into an exclusive agency contract with a broker, whether or not it is understood that the broker is to receive his commission from the seller or from the buyer. If the buyer consummates a purchase other than through the broker, the agent is entitled to damages from the principal equal to the commission that would have been paid by the seller or to the commission promised by the prospective buyer, depending on the nature of the agreement.

Other terms of the agency contract also need to be carefully drafted. The duration should be specified; otherwise it terminates after a "reasonable time," reasonable depending on the nature of the property—longer for a special-purpose business building than for a developer's single-family dwelling. If no time is specified, the principal can terminate the agency at any time without liability for the commission, so long as he acts in good faith, unless perhaps negotiations have been substantially completed. If a time is specified, the principal still has the power to terminate but would be liable for damages if the broker has expended money or effort in pursuing the objective of the agency. A sale of the property terminates the agency. However, whether damages for premature termination are due the other party depends upon the agency agreement. Obviously there would be none where the broker has an open or general listing contract and the owner or another broker has completed the sale. Even though most courts find no duty of the owner to notify other brokers, some will award damages for his efforts to a broker who had found a ready, willing, and able buyer after a previous sale by an owner who failed to notify the broker.

When the Commission Is Earned.   Normally, a seller's agent who has found a buyer "ready, willing, and able to buy" has earned the commission. There are no precise legal definitions of these words, but if the buyer is financially able to meet the terms, the completion of a contract of purchase and sale entitles the agent to the commission. Unless the broker for a seller is aware of a defect in the title, he has earned the commission even if the deal falls through because of such a defect. Likewise, a refusal of the seller to convey title does not defeat the broker's right to the commission.

If a prospective buyer offers less than the listing price or varies some other material term of the listing, the seller need not accept the offer. If the seller does, however, the broker is entitled to the commission on the sale price. Where some other arrangement is intended, it is important to specify the arrangement clearly if controversy and perhaps a lawsuit are to be avoided. For example, the listing agreement may specify *no deal, no commission.* Then the commission is contingent upon the completion of the transaction. Or the agreement may provide for the receipt of a net sum by the owner. In that case the broker is entitled to his full commission only if the buyer receives the stipulated amount after all expenses, including the commission, have been paid. At least one case has held that the broker is entitled to no more than the agreed-upon commission or, if none is specified, a reasonable commission even though the sale price nets the owner more than the specified amount. However, clearly stated agreements that the broker is to receive anything paid in excess of the stated net price have been enforced.

Under both the open listing and the exclusive agency arrangements, controversies sometimes arise as to whether a particular broker who has been involved but may not have handled the entire transaction is entitled to the commission. Courts grant the commission to the broker if he was the procuring cause of sale. Where two or more brokers have each dealt with the buyer who contracts to make the purchase or who is "ready, willing, and able," the broker who brings about substantial agreement between that buyer and the seller is the one entitled to the commission even if there is a brief hiatus and another broker later completes the transaction. A broker would, of course, also be entitled to the commission if the owner completes the sale after negotiations have been substantially completed with the aid of the broker.

The custom in contracts with real estate brokers is for the broker to assume the cost of advertising and showing the property. The same is true where the broker is to find property for a buyer. If this arrangement is not to be implied, the agreement should specify any expenses for which the broker is to be reimbursed. Spelling out the arrangement on reimbursement, if any, for legitimate expenditures is desirable because of the general agency rule that entitles agents to reimbursement.

The Duty of Due Care. A broker is liable for damages to the principal caused by the broker's negligence. For example, if as a result of having been misplaced and forgotten an offer to purchase is not delivered to the owner until after it has expired, the broker is liable for any loss by the owner suffered because of the broker's lack of due care. A failure to get the signature of a co-owner on a contract to sell property would impose liability on a broker acting for a purchaser who lost the purchase due to the broker's negligence. This would also be true if a broker gave misinformation as to the sale price of nearby property, the state of the local real estate market, or other matters concerning which the broker should be informed if the misinformation adversely affects the price at which the owner lists and sells the property. There would, however, be no liability for an honest opinion as to value or as to other matters of judgment.

The Duty of Fidelity. The vulnerability of brokers for a breach of this duty is likely to increase in our post-Watergate era. Expectations, and probably standards, for avoiding conflicts of interest are rising in American society as a whole. Real estate brokers and their salespeople are frequently in situations where there is or may appear to be a conflict between their duty to the party who has employed them and who is liable for the commission and their duty to or their interest in the opposite party to the transaction.

The law has long imposed a duty upon agents to act in complete loyalty to their principals. It has not permitted agents to benefit themselves at the expense of their principals, and if an agent has put himself in a position in which his interests might conflict with those of the principal, courts have not hesitated to protect the principal. Sometimes, in order to keep the agent from benefiting from a violation of his duty of loyalty, courts have permitted the principal to gain a windfall. For example, if a broker who is given authority to sell land for the owner sells to himself without the knowledge of the owner, a court may permit the owner to recover the land when he learns of the agent's duplicity, even though the agent assumed considerable economic risk and expended his own funds in improving the land and the land is now worth much more than it was when the agent purchased it.

Certain prohibitions are clearly established in the law. A broker may not, without first disclosing the fact, buy from or sell to the client, nor may a close relative or a corporation in which he holds the major interest. Obviously, the broker is in a conflict of interest situation when his or her spouse is the buyer procured by the broker for the owner. Even though the spouse pays the full asking price, the broker has breached his or her fiduciary duty to get the highest possible price for the property. It is assumed by courts that the broker is also interested in a "good deal" for the spouse and that this interest may be enough to affect the broker's judgment.

An agent is not permitted to serve both parties to a transaction unless the dual agency is known to both parties. For example, if a broker has a listing of some property that might be appropriate to another client who has agreed to pay him a commission for finding suitable property to purchase, he should disclose this fact to both parties. Where a court views this as a dual agency, then the agent is not entitled to a commission from either party and either party can rescind the contract.

The difficulty sometimes is determining who, if anyone, is the broker's principal. A broker may be employed by either a seller or a buyer merely to locate a prospect (buyer or seller) with whom the party first contacting the broker can negotiate a contract. Courts have permitted brokers in such instances to collect commissions from both the seller and the buyer, finding no wrongdoing—no dual agency—because the broker is acting only as a middleman or finder. If sued for breach of duty where he has collected two commissions or acted for both parties, a broker usually claims that he was merely a middleman, that he had no discretion in negotiating terms, and that the client did not expect to rely upon his judgment. Such is clearly not the case, however, where the broker is given power to complete a transaction, and it is doubtful in the typical situations in which an owner lists property with a real estate broker.

Most clients employing a real estate broker to find a buyer for their property expect to and do rely upon the broker's advice as to price and terms. Since the client will pay the commission, he expects, reasonably, that the broker will be faithful to his interests. Court decisions are generally consistent with that expectation. Furthermore, the increased sensitivity of our society to conflicts of interest is likely to result is more lawsuits and perhaps decisions against brokers in what have heretofore been only "gray areas."

Two examples must suffice. First, it is often in the broker's interest to sell the property as quickly as possible with the least possible effort and advertising expense. This will usually be in conflict with the owner's interest in getting the highest possible price. It is even likelier that an inherent conflict of interest will exist between a broker who is a developer and a client who has listed for sale property similar to that of the broker. The growth of condominiums has greatly increased this problem. Here the broker's interest may be to steer prospective buyers toward the purchase of one of his own properties rather than that of the client. On the other hand, the developer may be the broker who can best find a buyer because of his familiarity with and known connection with the development.

Prospective buyers to whom the broker shows property are also likely to view themselves as clients of the broker, and brokers are tempted to encourage this view, both because it may increase the chances of a sale and because often the owner is leaving the neighborhood while the prospective buyer may influence others to become clients as well as be a potential client himself. In the past the courts have generally refused to recognize any fiduciary duty of the broker to the prospective buyer when the broker has been employed by the owner. In a few recent cases, however, courts have given the prospective buyer recovery against the broker where the broker misrepresented to him the minimum price that the seller would accept or failed to transmit an offer to buy to the seller. Efforts of real estate brokers to gain recognition as professionals tend to make it likelier that courts will find liability for any lapse in a broker's conduct that harms either the original client or the person with whom the broker deals on behalf of that client.

The Contractual Liability of the Agent to a Third Party

3. *When the agency is disclosed, any contract made for the principal within the authority of the agent is the principal's, and only the third party and the principal, not the agent, are bound on it.*

In the usual situation the duty of a real estate broker serving either a seller or a buyer of property is merely to find someone who will buy (or sell) on terms favorable to the client. In this case, and frequently even when the broker is authorized to complete a contract for the client, the broker will be acting as agent for a disclosed principal. That is, he will make the real party in interest, the client, known to any third parties with whom he deals with respect to the property. If the client (principal) is disclosed even though the broker completes the contract, the broker will not be a party to it and will not be liable to the third party for the obligations assumed in the contract. To make it clear that the broker is not a party, the broker should sign the contract in the form "T. Principal, by J. Broker, her agent."

4. *When the identity of the principal is not known to the third party, the agent is liable on the contract to the third party if the third party*

chooses to hold the agent liable. However, both the principal and the third party can enforce the contract against each other.

Occasionally a client who has or is reputed to have great financial resources or who wishes to buy several contiguous parcels of property employs one or more real estate brokers to purchase the real estate while keeping secret his existence and identity. This may avoid the inflated price demands that would otherwise be made by the seller in such circumstances. However, whether the third party assumes that he is dealing with the broker as principal or knows that he is dealing with an agent, so long as the principal is not disclosed, the broker becomes a party to the contract and is liable on it. Therefore, if for any reason the client refuses to complete the purchase or sale, the third party can recover any damages from the broker. Of course, the broker is entitled to reimbursement from the client under statement 2, assuming that the broker has acted within his authority.

The agent can avoid personal liability to the third party if the third party so agrees. However, under contract law such an agreement of sale or purchase is unenforceable since the requisite two parties are not present.

Exceeding the Agent's Authority

5. *The third party may be able to hold the principal liable on a contract made by a purported agent or by an agent who has exceeded his actual authority (express or implied) on the basis that the principal gave the agent or purported agent apparent authority or had ratified the unauthorized act of the agent or purported agent.*

6. *The agent is liable to the third party if the agent has acted beyond his authority unless the principal ratifies the act.*

Although these statements generally apply to unauthorized acts of agents, real estate brokers are more likely to become involved in their application as employers than as agents. A real estate salesperson as well as any other employee of a real estate broker is explicitly authorized to perform certain acts on behalf of the broker as employer. Since few agreements of employment and later directions and authorizations by an employer are likely to cover every conceivable situation, there are times when it may be beneficial for the employer if the employee performs an act not specifically authorized by the employer. Indeed, implied in every duty assigned is the authority to do what is usual and necessary to perform that duty. For example, the broker in a small office may leave a salesperson in charge of the office for several days while the broker takes a vacation. If an unforeseen situation arises that requires some action before the broker can be reached, the salesperson may have implied authority to act. If a tornado damages the building in which the business is conducted, and which the broker owns, the salesperson left in charge would clearly have implied authority to make emergency repairs or to take steps necessary to protect the building and the business, such as boarding up a broken window.

The test of whether or not an act performed by an employee is within the implied authority of the employee is whether a reasonable employee would believe, under all of the circumstances, that he had such authority. If so, then the employer is liable to a third party with whom the employee contracted on behalf of the employer, such as a repair service that boarded up a broken window or placed canvas over a damaged roof, even though the employer might have handled the matter differently and denies liability.

The agent's actual authority includes both implied and express authority. The principal, however, may also be held liable for acts of an agent within the agent's apparent authority. Although sometimes overlapping implied authority, the test for apparent authority is what a person dealing with the agent would reasonably believe was within the agent's authority in acting for the principal. This reasonable belief must be based upon what the principal has said or done or what the principal has failed to say or do, not on representations made by the agent. Or a purported principal may be held liable on a contract made on his behalf by a person who has never been employed by the principal as an agent if it would appear to a reasonable person in the third party's position, on the basis of the actions of the purported principal, that the person making the contract was an agent of the purported principal. For example, a broker might have an arrangement by which another broker carries on his own real estate brokerage business out of the office of the first broker. The first broker would be liable on contracts made by the other broker of the kind usually made by salespeople of the first broker's office or of other real estate brokers in the community if the other broker purports to be and reasonably appears to be a salesperson of the first broker.

Even when there are no acts of the principal or purported principal that could be interpreted by a reasonable third party as indicating authority in the agent or purported agent, the principal may become liable on a contract entered into on his behalf through ratification. Several requirements must be met if a court is to hold that a ratification has occurred, but it is important for a broker to avoid accepting any benefit from an unauthorized contract after learning of it, since he may be held to have ratified the contract if he accepts benefits with knowledge of all the facts. It is desirable to repudiate any unauthorized contract as soon as one is aware of it, although this is not required.

The Agent as Conduit

7. *The principal is considered to have received any notice given to the agent and to have any material knowledge that the agent has concerning the transaction, and the agent has a duty to so inform the principal.*

This rule imposes a duty upon the broker to inform the client promptly of any fact that has any bearing on the transaction being handled for the client that may come to the attention of the broker. For a broker acting for a seller this would include full disclosure to the client of all information relevant to the sale of the listed property. It would include prices of comparable property recently sold in the neighborhood (both before and after the listing), changes in market conditions that might affect the value of the property, and disclosure of any potential conflict of interest that the broker may have—such as an interest in similar properties as a developer. The broker has a duty to give the client information known to him concerning the lack of creditworthiness or reliability of an offeror. Here the broker must avoid passing on mere rumors, or a suit for defamation could result.

8. *The principal is bound by contracts made by subagents if the agent has been given authority to employ subagents.*

The broker's client is bound by contracts made by the broker's employees to the same extent as he would be if the contracts were made by the broker. It is customary for brokers to employ salespersons to seek buyers for the owner. Where a broker is given authority actually to enter into a sale contract, such a contract entered into on behalf of the owner by a salesperson of the broker is probably not binding on the owner unless he has at least impliedly given the broker authority to appoint a subagent. The negotiation of such a contract requires skill and special knowledge. A court would probably find that the owner intended to rely upon the broker's personal judgment.

Under a multiple listing arrangement the broker is clearly authorized to use the other brokers in the group as subagents in finding a buyer. The original broker is entitled to the commission and is then bound to divide it with the broker arranging the sale on the basis agreed upon by the group.

The Agent's Liability for Torts

9. *An agent is always liable to any third party for the agent's own wrongdoing (tort). The principal is usually liable for the agent's misrepresentations and other wrongdoing in connection with a transaction being conducted for the principal. However, the principal is not liable for the physical torts of a professional (nonemployee) agent.*

Every individual is legally responsible for any tort he commits except wrongs committed completely innocently (and there is even liability for some innocently committed torts). For example, if the owner of a house tells a real estate broker that the listed house has six inches of rock wool insulation under the floor of the attic and the broker or one of his salespersons so informs a purchaser, neither the salesperson nor the broker is liable for the misrepresentation if he had no reason to doubt the owner's statement and no ready means of checking it. The owner alone would be liable. However, if the broker and his employee were aware of the fraud, any of the three—owner, broker, and employee—would be liable for damages to the purchaser. The purchaser could gain only one recovery, but he could choose to sue the owner who originated the deception, the employee who made the false representation, or the broker. The broker is liable under the doctrine of *respondeat superior* (the master must answer for the wrongs of his servant) for any tort committed by an employee in the course of his employment.

The same options would be open to the purchaser if the broker's employee said that there was insulation although he was aware that there was none. The rationale would be the same except for the case of the innocent owner. The owner, however, could be held liable for the fraud because it was committed by his subagent to induce the sale and was the sort of representation that real estate salespersons are expected to make.

The owner would not be liable for damages to a prospective buyer who is injured in an auto accident caused by the negligence of the broker's saleperson. Since the broker is what is known as a professional agent—that is, he or she is employed to accomplish a specified result without any control by the owner over the broker's or his employees' activities in finding a buyer—the principal (owner) is not liable for the physical tort resulting in injury to the third person. As the employer of the salesperson, however, the broker can be held liable for the tort, again under the doctrine of *respondeat superior*. The situation with respect to liability would be the same if the salesperson got into an altercation with a prospective buyer, injuring the prospect with a punch in the face. Either the salesperson or the broker, but not the owner, would be liable.

The trend in tort cases, especially where fraud is alleged, has been running strongly in favor of consumers and other victims whom the courts may see as vulnerable because they lack knowledge or experience or where the risk is common, if not necessary, in the defendant's business. Even where a broker or his salesperson makes a representation in the belief that it is true, if it turns out to be false and the court thinks that the broker should have first ascertained the facts, the broker is likely to be held liable for fraud. For example, a broker was so held where he had represented a relatively new furnace to be in good condition when, unknown to the broker, it had a cracked boiler whose condition had been concealed by the owner. Since many errors and omissions insurance policies exclude coverage for fraud, such cases can be devastating to the defendant broker.

The above exposition of agency law as applied to real estate brokers is necessarily brief and general. The principles stated, however, can frequently be extrapolated to different but similar situations. This can, of course, be misleading, because often two or more legal principles conflict. For specific application, competent counsel should be consulted.

FEDERAL INCOME TAXATION

Robert H. Lipsey

*R*OBERT H. LIPSEY, CPA, Kenneth Leventhal & Co., Certified Public Accountants, Washington, D.C.

Partner in charge of tax services for the East Coast offices of Kenneth Leventhal & Company. Member, American Institute of Certified Public Accountants, Tax Division, Subcommittee on Special Entities and Industries. Instructor in real estate taxation for Maryland Association of CPAs.

Taxable Income and Capital Gains Taxing Income and Profit

Investors realize economic benefits from real estate in a number of ways. Rental properties may produce rental income greater than the total operating outlays, resulting in positive "cash flow." Prudent purchases of any real estate at the right price may result in a resale profit. Some sophisticated investors expect very little economic benefit from their investments in real estate—the available income tax benefits are their primary goal. Resale profits are often taxed at very favorable rates as "long-term capital gain," provided that the investor does not engage in so many transactions that the IRS could subsequently treat him as a "dealer" who buys properties primarily for resale to customers in the ordinary course of his trade or business.

Taxable Income and Cash Flow. An investor must know a property's expected positive or negative cash flow in order to determine his ability to purchase and hold the investment.

It is also important that he knows its taxable income because he may have an addition or reduction in tax as a consequence of the investment.

1. *Cash flow:* A property produces "positive cash flow" when its operating income exceeds all of the cash outlays necessary for its operation (generally over a year). If the outlays exceed the income, the property has "negative cash flow." Outlays simply mean all cash payments out, and income generally means all rental income.

Example: A potential investor is provided with the following facts regarding a small duplex home which is for sale by its owner:

Present owner (annual totals)		
Gross rental income		$7,200
Outlays		
Operating expense: utilities, maintenance, repairs, miscellaneous expense	3,100	
Real property taxes (assessed at $40,000)	1,000	
Mortgage on $20,000 balance (assume $160 per month)	1,920	
Total outlays		$6,020
Positive cash flow		$1,180

The owner asks $50,000 for the property, with 20 percent down, and offers a $40,000 mortgage to the investor, with payments of $320 per month.

Investor's figures (annual totals)		
Gross rental income		$7,200
Less outlays		
Operating expenses	3,100	
Real property taxes	1,000	
Mortgage	3,840	
Total outlays		$7,940
Negative cash flow		($ 740)

If every other factor about the property is positive, the investor must still understand the need to provide $740 per year simply to cover his cash deficit (negative cash flow) and he must anticipate a rise in the property taxes because of the increased price ($50,000) as compared to the value on which the previous assessment was based ($40,000).

2. *Taxable income:* In order to determine the taxable income from a particular investment, the cash flow (either negative or positive) is adjusted as follows:

$$\text{Cash flow} + \text{Mortgage principal (amortization)} - \text{Depreciation}$$
$$= \text{Taxable income}$$

The amortization of mortgage principal must be added to cash flow because it is not deductible for tax purposes. This is entirely logical, considering that the loan funds are not taxed as income when the borrower receives them.

Depreciation is a tax-deductible expense that is not represented by cash outlays. The theory of depreciation is that all buildings (including such components as the roof, heating and air conditioning systems, and plumbing) will eventually wear out or become functionally obsolete and that in either case a portion of this loss must be estimated annually over the "useful life" of the investment and treated as an expense. Investors must determine a "reasonable" estimated useful life for a building based on all the pertinent facts and circumstances. The age and condition, location, type of use, length of mortgage, and so on, are often used to help make this "guesstimate," and there may be a certain amount of bargaining if the taxing authorities disagree with the owners.

We can utilize the example from the cash flow discussion above to illustrate.

```
Present owner
  Positive cash flow ......................................    $1,180
  Add: Assumed amortization of principal ...................       960
  Subtract: Depreciation (33⅓-year useful life;
    straight-line method; $28,000 building cost)
    (land was $12,000) ....................................      −840
  Taxable income ..........................................    $1,300
Investor
  Negative cash flow ......................................    $(740)
  Add: Assumed amortization of principal ...................      +400
  Subtract: Depreciation (25-year useful life;
    straight-line method; $32,000 building cost)
    (land was $18,000) ....................................    −1,280
  Taxable gain (loss) .....................................   ($1,620)
```

Assuming that the investor is in the 45 percent tax bracket, his annual taxes would be decreased by 45 percent of $1,620 or $729. His negative cash flow of $740 is offset by the tax savings. Thus, the tax advantage is clearly critical in this case.

Keep in mind that the cost of land must not be depreciated since land does not wear out. Also bear in mind that the straight-line method used in the example is only one of the available depreciation methods and that the use of an overall "composite" life for depreciation may be less favorable from a tax standpoint than would the breakdown of building costs into separate "components." These matters will be discussed further in the chapter.

Taxation of the Proceeds of Real Property Sales. The tax impact on a sale of real property is not always apparent without a careful analysis of various data.

1. Basis. If a property has been "purchased," its tax basis is determined by its cost, including the mortgages to which the property is subject. Even if a property is subject to a "nonrecourse" mortgage (that is, the creditor can look only to the property for payment), the mortgage is considered to be part of the cost.

2. Adjusted Basis. The most common adjustment to basis is depreciation expense. Since this is an annual estimate of the exhaustion of the building, it reduces the tax basis continually.

3. Taxable Gain or Loss. The proceeds of sale may be all cash, part cash and part transfer subject to existing mortgages, or the actual assumption of existing mortgages. The taxable gain or loss is determined by subtracting the property's adjusted basis from the proceeds of sale, including the relief of mortgages as though the seller had received the money. If the proceeds exceed the adjusted basis, a taxable gain has been realized; if the proceeds are less than the adjusted basis, there has been a taxable loss.

4. The Tax Rate on Gain or Loss. Property purchased primarily for resale at a profit by "dealers" in real estate would be treated as though it were "inventory" subject to ordinary tax rates on gains from sales. The gain or loss would be considered additional income and would be combined with any other ordinary income in the seller's tax returns.

Investors who are not considered dealers with respect to real estate investments are usually able to treat the sale of property at a profit as a long-term capital gain, subject to a substantially reduced rate of tax as compared with ordinary income. The property must have been owned more than one year, and generally the investor can be assured of favorable capital gains rates if the property was rented for more than one year. Whether profits on real estate sales are subject to tax as ordinary income or at long-term capital gains rates is a subject that has been litigated frequently, and taxpayers have generally, fared well in the courts. The occasional investor in real estate should encounter no challenge to treatment of his gains as capital gains. In general, such gains are taxed as ordinary income to the extent that the investor claimed accelerated methods of depreciation in excess of straight line. This subject is discussed below.

Sale of investment property at a loss will result in a long-term capital loss if the property has been held over one year and if it has not been rented or used in the taxpayer's trade or business for at least one year. Long-term capital losses are of limited tax benefit because each two dollars of loss offsets only one dollar of ordinary income and because the total annual deduction is limited to $3,000. In this situation, investors sometimes argue that they are really "dealers." This tactic must be weighed very carefully because of its potential adverse impact on profitable future sales.

5. Pretax Proceeds. Sale at a taxable profit sometimes occurs even where there are minimal cash proceeds because of mortgages on the property.

> *Example:* Investor A bought an office building held for rent in 1972. His total cost for the land and building was $375,000, and his depreciation deductions for 1972 through 1978 were $9,000 each year. He originally made a down payment of $45,000 and obtained a first mortgage of $330,000. In 1975 he placed a second mortgage of $60,000 on the property, using the proceeds for repairs and maintenance and to help cover negative cash flow. On January 1, 1979, he sold the building for $400,000. The mortgage balances at the time of sale were:

First mortgage	$315,000
Second mortgage	57,000
Total	$372,000

The taxable gain and the cash proceeds were as follows:

Basis	$375,000
Adjustments (depreciation 1972–78 @ $9,000 per year)	63,000
Adjusted basis	$312,000
Sale proceeds	$400,000
Adjusted basis	312,000
Gain on sale	$ 88,000
Total sale proceeds	$400,000
Mortgage balance	372,000
Cash proceeds	$ 28,000

The gain was more than twice the cash proceeds.

6. Aftertax Proceeds. After mortgages are satisfied, the cash proceeds are subject to further diminution for federal and state income taxes on the taxable gain. The office building should qualify as an asset used in a trade or business more than 12 months and therefore the $88,000 gain should be subject to tax as a long-term capital gain. At this writing the direct tax would be as follows:

Gain on sale	$88,000
Capital gain deduction (60%)	52,800
Taxable portion	$35,200
Income tax (assume 50% marginal rate)	$17,600
State tax (assume 6% of $35,200)	2,112
Total taxes—direct	19,712

In addition to the tax burden shown here, the long-term capital gain may cause the taxpayer to be subject to the alternative minimum tax, enacted in the Revenue Act of 1978.

The above discussion is intended to create an awareness of the difference between the terms *gain* and *cash*. A more typical case might be shown by assuming exactly the same facts, except that no second-mortgage loan was needed and that only the $315,000 balance of the first mortgage existed at the time of sale. The figures are then revised as follows:

Sale proceeds	$400,000
Mortgage balance	315,000
Cash available	$ 85,000
Tax liability—direct	19,712
Net cash to investor	$ 65,288

Accounting Methods—Choices

Depreciable Base. The investor is usually confronted with tax accounting alternatives relating to the amount of depreciable base and

the "composite" versus "component" method accounting for depreciation.

1. Land allocation. An attempt must be made to determine the portion of the purchase price attributable to land. This is necessary because
the cost of land is not depreciable for tax purposes. Various methods
are used to make this allocation—appraisals, assessment by the real
estate tax authorities, reference to similar sales of land, and so on. Although none of these is necessarily the "best" method, the most frequent
approach of the IRS tax examiner is to apply the land-building proportions of the real estate tax assessment to the overall purchase price.

> *Example:* A building sold for $100,000. The local real estate tax assess-
> ment had been fixed at $20,000 on the land, $30,000 on the building, for a
> total of $50,000. Unless a better means of determining fair market value
> is found, the IRS would probably utilize the following method to determine
> the cost of the land:
>
> $$\text{Assessed value} - \frac{\text{Land \$20,000}}{\text{Total \$50,000}} \times \$100,000 = \$40,000$$
>
> The investor would be able to compute depreciation on only $60,000, the
> cost allocable to the building. If a reliable appraisal were obtained, or if
> another basis for making the allocation exists, the portion of the cost avail-
> able for depreciation might be substantially increased.

2. The Composite Method versus the Component Method. Depreciation may be computed over a "composite" useful life—an estimate
applied to the cost of the building as a whole—or over the estimated
useful life of each separate building component, provided that the costs
of those components are ascertainable. In order to utilize component
depreciation for an older building, definitive allocations of cost to specific components should be made by construction or engineering experts.

> *Example:* A building was constructed in 1978 at a total cost of $300,000.
> The composite life currently in use for similar buildings was 33⅓ years.
> The component lives, and costs, and straight-line depreciation were deter-
> mined to be as follows:

Component	Cost	Estimated Life	Annual Depreciation
Shell (masonry, etc.)	$175,000	45 years	$ 3,889
Plumbing and electricity	50,000	25 years	2,000
Heating, ventilation, and air conditioning	45,000	20 years	2,250
Carpets, appliances, etc.	30,000	5 years	6,000
	$300,000		14,139

> The component depreciation is thus $14,139. The composite depreciation
> would amount to $9,000 annually (3 percent times $300,000). So, for the first
> five years the component method produces $5,139 more depreciation per
> year.

The more rapid depreciation obtained by using the component method
is a significant tax benefit in most cases. The cost of an engineer's study

or some other expert opinion regarding an older property's component costs should be more than offset by the tax benefit of the increased depreciation.

Useful Life. Buildings and their component parts must be depreciated over their estimated useful lives, which are determined by considering all the facts and circumstances in the situation. The more important facts and circumstances include the age, condition, type of use, location, and zoning of a particular building. For example, an older frame structure that is used as a summer beach house in New Jersey would suffer greater physical depreciation than would a new frame residence in the suburbs of Washington, D.C. A building should depreciate faster if it is used for heavy industrial production facilities than if it is used for light industrial activities. Components must be individually evaluated to determine their useful lives for depreciation purposes. The investor should also be aware that the depreciation of a building can sometimes involve extensive argument with the tax authorities over important nuances. For example, the IRS sometimes takes the position that the initial painting cost of a new building must be considered part of the "shell," whereas many investors depreciate this cost over its separate estimated useful life. Although the issue may seem trivial, the tax effect can be significant and the discussions go on and on.

Accelerated versus Straight-Line Depreciations. Certain types of properties may be depreciated for federal tax purposes at rates faster than straight line. Table 1 describes the availability of various depreciation methods for different types of real property.

Special depreciation rules also allow straight-line depreciation over 60 months for qualified rehabilitation expenditures on low-income housing and certified historic structures.

Comparison of Methods—Computations. Straight-line depreciation is calculated evenly over the expected useful life of the property.

The *sum-of-the-years'-digits* method allows greater amounts of depreciation for the early years and lesser amounts in later years. The formula is determined by applying a fraction whose numerator represents the number of years remaining to be depreciated and whose denominator is the sum of the years' digits in the entire estimated useful life.

Example: Assume that a component is depreciated over a seven-year estimated life using the sum-of-the-years'-digits method. The first year's depreciation is determined as follows:

$$\frac{7}{28} \times \text{Cost} - \text{Depreciation}$$

The numerator is the years remaining. The denominator is $1 + 2 + 3 + 4 + 5 + 6 + 7$.

This is a *shortcut method* for determining the denominator:

$$\frac{(\text{Number of years}) \times (\text{Number of years} + 1)}{2}$$

or

$$\frac{7 \times 8}{2} = 28$$

TABLE 1

	Straight Line	Sum-of-the-Years' Digits	200 Percent Declining Balance	150 Percent Declining Balance	125 Percent Declining Balance
New residential	X	X	X		
Used residential—20 years' life or more	X				
Used residential—under 20 years' life	X				
New commercial	X			X	
Used commercial	X				X

If the cost of a component was $50,000, the first year's depreciation would be $12,500, or

$$\frac{7}{28} \times \$50,000 = \$12,500$$

The next year's depreciation would be $\frac{6}{28} \times \$50,000$, or $10,714, and so on.

Declining balance depreciation applies the permitted rate consistently to the remaining undepreciated cost of an asset. The 200 percent, 150 percent, and 125 percent are based on the estimated straight-line depreciation rate of an asset. An asset with a 40-year estimated life has a straight-line rate of 2½%; i.e. $40\overline{)1.000}^{\,0.025}$

If a 200 percent declining balance rate is used, 5 percent of the remaining undepreciated cost may be deducted each year for depreciation; if 150 percent rate is used, 3.75 percent may be deducted.

Example: An asset costing $50,000 with a useful life of 20 years is depreciated at 200 percent declining balance. The computations are as follows:

Year	Adjusted Basis	Life Years	200 Percent Rate	Annual Depreciation
1	50,000	20	10%	5,000
2	45,000	20	10%	4,500
3	40,500	20	10%	4,050
4	36,450	20	10%	3,645
.	.	.	.	.
.	.	.	.	.
.	.	.	.	.

Comparison of Methods—Important Side Effects. The excess of accelerated depreciation over the straight-line annual deduction is treated as a "tax preference" item. Although that description may sound quite innocent, it is not! In general, the tax preference amount can be taxed at 15 percent by the minimum tax (if the total "preferences" exceed $10,000) and the taxpayer's earned income may lose the benefits of the 50 percent minimum tax rate to the extent of the preference amount. Due to these provisions a decrease in the regular tax that is obtained by utilizing accelerated depreciation may result in a larger increase in the overall tax.

Upon sale at a gain the excess of accelerated depreciation over straight-line depreciation is (with certain exceptions) taxed as ordinary income. Even where a property has been held for rent for a number of years, the full amount of this "excess" will be taxed as ordinary income, to the extent of any gain on sale.

The rules in this area have been changed frequently. However, for depreciation claimed after 1975, the full excess is recapturable with a limited exception for certain specifically defined "low-income" rental housing. The recapturable excess depreciation for the period after 1975 is decreased by 1 percent for each month that the property has been held over 100 months. For property owned before 1976 (whether or not it was low-income housing), accelerated depreciation must be recaptured in differing proportions upon profitable sale.

The combined considerations of minimum and maximum tax and ordinary income upon sale at a gain must be carefully weighed when an investor determines his or her depreciation methods.

Cash versus Accrual. Individuals considering a real estate investment are ordinarily cash-basis taxpayers who report income only as it is received and deduct expenses when these are paid. The accrual method of accounting records income when it is earned and expenses when they are incurred, regardless of the dates of cash payment. Where a taxpayer operates a trade or a business and keeps its books on the accrual method, that method may be used for tax purposes even though the same taxpayer uses the cash method to report other income, deductions, and so on. An operating rental property is generally considered a separate trade or business for this purpose. The primary tax advantage of using the accrual method is that it confers the ability to deduct expenses before they have been paid. This may be only a temporary first-year benefit, since the accounting method may not be changed without specific IRS permission after the initial year. In certain situations, however, very significant one-time fees and expenses may be involved, and the tax benefit may be of major importance.

Construction Period Expenses. It is mandatory for individuals, partnerships, subchapter S corporations, and certain closely held corporations to capitalize interest and taxes incurred during the construction period for most real estate. (The law excepts low-income rental housing construction, on which interest and taxes may be deducted as they are paid or incurred.) The capitalized amounts are permitted to be amortized and deducted over a period of years that depends on when the expenses are incurred and whether the construction is residential or not. If the constructed property is sold, any construction period interest and taxes that have been capitalized would be treated as additional costs of the property, to the extent that they have not been amortized.

All taxpayers, including corporations, are allowed to elect to capitalize interest and/or taxes incurred on real property while it is unimproved and unproductive, and to switch their practice of either deducting or capitalizing each year. Once construction has begun on a project, an election to capitalize an item of interest and/or taxes would be binding until the completion of the project. The ability to use this election is a very important tax-planning mechanism for many land developers. Where items of interest or taxes are electively capitalized, the mandatory capitalization and amortization rules are not in force. If a taxpayer does not electively capitalize interest and taxes, the mandatory capitalization and amortization rules (referred to in the previous paragraph) are applied.

The Uses of Financing

The Impact of Financing. The impact of financing on most real estate acquisitions cannot be overemphasized. Most investors will take a hard look at a less-than-perfect investment opportunity if the financing is right. Sellers often take back a first or second mortgage to ease the purchaser's financial burden and increase the selling price to themselves. The costs of financing—including interest rates, "points," servicing fees, and commitment fees—vary with different lenders, and motivation of some sellers in offering self-financing to a purchaser is to reduce such costs to themselves.

1. Cash Requirements. If the customary practice in the area is to have a 20 percent down payment and an 80 percent mortgage, the cash required for the 20 percent down may eliminate a large number of potential purchasers for a particular property. A high-income investor may not wish to tie up 20 percent in cash to purchase a $1 million apartment project, even though he would be an excellent property owner in every other respect. The cash necessary to make the purchase may be reduced by the seller granting a first or second mortgage, or by third parties lending more than the usual 80 percent. Sometimes investors join together in partnerships to acquire interests in a project, and this is often accomplished with a limited partnership.

2. Leveraging and Taxable Income. Investors must be careful not to create too much debt load for the property to carry. A strong rental location with a good history of rent increases may permit highly leveraged financing with favorable impact on taxable income.

> *Example:* An investor is considering the purchase of a ten-year-old office building at a total cost of $400,000. The seller will take back a $300,000 first mortgage with a 30-year term at an 8½ percent interest rate. The building is in relatively good condition, fully rented, and well located. A current appraisal of the property valued it at a total of $420,000—$105,000 for the land and $315,000 for the building. It is believed that a 25-year composite useful life could be justified for depreciation purposes. The investor's top tax bracket is 50 percent, and he has found a mortgage company willing to lend an additional $50,000 at 11 percent on a 20-year second mortgage.

The income and expense, mortgage amortization, and depreciation are as follows:

Rental income	$ 65,000
Operating expenses	22,000
Real estate taxes	5,000
Depreciation	
Basis—land and building	400,000
Depreciable base—building (utilizing appraisal proportion of 75% for building)	300,000
Rate of depreciation (25-year straight line)	4%
Amount	$ 12,000

Mortgage payments (principal and interest—annual amounts)

First mortgage (8½%, 30-year term, $300,000)	$ 27,672
Second mortgage (11%, 20-year term, $50,000)	6,192

	First Mortgage	First and Second Mortgage
Rental income	$ 65,000	$ 65,000
Operating expenses	(22,000)	(22,000)
Real estate taxes	(5,000)	(5,000)
Mortgage payments		
First mortgage	(27,672)	(27,672)
Second mortgage	—	(6,192)
Positive cash flow	$ 10,328	$ 4,136
Amortization		
First mortgage	2,268	2,268
Second mortgage	—	730
Depreciation	(12,000)	(12,000)
Taxable income	$ 596	$ (4,866)
Tax (cost) benefit — 50%	$ (298)	$ 2,433
Cash flow	10,328	4,136
First-year benefit	$ 10,030	$ 6,569
Initial investment	$100,000	$50,000

The higher proportion of the purchase price obtained by financing often increases the direct percentage of return on the actual dollars invested. The above example shows first-year combined benefits of more than 13 percent on a $50,000 investment, compared with around 10 percent on a $100,000 investment. Each deal must be carefully evaluated, and the investor must also compute the expected cash flow and tax benefits for several years in order to make meaningful judgments.

In the above example, this can be accomplished by making certain assumptions:

1. That the rental income and expenses will not increase or decrease. This assumes that increased expenses will be offset by increased income, so that the projected cash flow and taxable income will remain unchanged.
2. That the depreciation will remain at $12,000 annually (though recognizing that the IRS *may* claim that the 25-year estimated life is too short).
3. That the first and second mortgages will have increasing amounts of principal amortization. From mortgage amortization schedules, these amounts are determined to be as follows:

	$300,000 First Mortgage (30 years, 8½%)	$50,000 Second Mortgage (20 years, 11%)
1st year	$2,268	730
2d year	2,468	813
3d year	2,686	907
4th year	2,923	1,012
5th year	3,182	1,129

Reference to the previous example shows that the figures do not change drastically after five years.

	First Mortgage	First and Second Mortgages
Cash flow	$10,328	$ 4,136
Depreciation	(12,000)	(12,000)
Fifth year amortization	3,182	3,182 1st
		1,129 2nd
Taxable income (loss)	$ 1,510	($ 3,553)
Tax saving (cost)		
(assumes 50% rate)	(755)	1,776
Fifth-year benefit	9,573	5,912

The annual benefit in the fifth year is nearly 12 percent of the original $50,000 investment compared to around 9½ percent with the one mortgage at $300,000. Leveraging clearly results in higher returns for the investor in this example.

3. Mortgage Default and Foreclosures. The mortgage instrument provides a mechanism for a sale of the property by the mortgagee upon default by the mortgagor. During a period of mortgage default, the tax accounting methods used by the lender and the borrower can become quite important. Taxpayers using the cash method generally reflect interest deductions and income only when these are paid or received. Taxpayers using the accrual method reflect expenses when they are incurred and income when it is earned, without regard to actual cash payments.

Foreclosure is a legal proceeding which results in a sale of the property for payment of the defaulted underlying loan. Various other types of voluntary reconveyances are often negotiated by the parties, and the tax consequences to the property owner are generally the same. The reconveyance is usually treated as a sale to the lender for the unpaid mortgage balance unless the borrower is insolvent after the reconveyance. The gain or loss for tax purposes is obtained by comparing the owner's adjusted basis with this unpaid balance. If accelerated depreciation has been claimed on the property, any gain from the reconveyance or foreclosure would be at least partially subject to ordinary income taxation, as if the property had been sold for cash. In general, gain or loss would be similarly subject to the rules for the taxation of sales.

Two special situations should be mentioned for completeness: (1) cancellation of debt and (2) the mortgagor's insolvency.

Cancellation of Debt. If a mortgage is foreclosed and the borrower can establish that the property's value is less than the unpaid mortgage, under certain circumstances the borrower can elect to reduce his adjusted basis of other assets by the excess of the mortgage balance over the property's fair market value. Gain or loss on reconveyance is then measured by comparison of the adjusted basis of the reconveyed property with its demonstrated fair market value.

The Mortgagor's Insolvency. No gain is taxable upon debt cancellation where a debtor's liabilities exceed the fair market value of his assets immediately before and after a debt cancellation. This rule has been extended by the courts to cover a conveyance of property by an insolvent taxpayer. The test for insolvency is unrelated to bankruptcy and is essentially the comparison of the mortgagor's assets and liabilities at their fair market values. (See also Chapter 6.)

Tax Shelters. A "shelter" defers current tax payments into the future. The longer this deferral can be maintained, the more the investor is able to use the government's dollars in order to realize additional income. Many tax shelter deals also anticipate tax write-offs against current years' ordinary income (up to 70 percent benefit) with future payments as long-term capital gains at reduced tax rates. Most tax shelters are sold to groups of investors who purchase limited partnership interests. A limited partner or investor in real estate is permitted to deduct taxable losses greater than his invested capital to the extent of his share of "nonrecourse loans."

Extreme Leverage. Many tax shelter deals are highly leveraged to minimize the cash required and maximize the return on investment. This is often a desirable factor in a particular investment opportunity. Certain tax shelter deals are designed to yield extreme write-offs by arbitrarily setting a very high purchase price that will never be paid to the seller. The price is secured by a nonrecourse mortgage (the property is the sole security) that artificially inflates the adjusted basis, allowing very high depreciation deductions. Since the underlying property produces little income, the amortization of mortgage principal is almost nonexistent. Occasionally, extreme leverage will be supportable under the specific circumstances. However, a potential investor should make all possible inquiries into the economic viability of the deal.

Section 8 and Other Subsidy Programs. Various government subsidy programs are in place to provide rental housing for low-income persons and families. Section 8 is a rental subsidy of the federal government, and other such programs are provided by some states and localities. The rents charged and the operative rules of subsidized housing programs usually provide little or no positive cash flow to investors. The typical investor in such programs is primarily interested in using them as tax shelters to offset his other taxable income. Special rules in the Internal Revenue Code favor investments in low-income housing over other real estate investments. These include the following:

1. All interest and taxes during the construction period may be deducted.

2. Accelerated depreciation in excess of straight-line is not subject to recapture at ordinary income rates if the property has been held for 16 years and 8 months. If such a property has been held for at least eight years and four months, the accelerated depreciation subject to recapture decreases at the rate of 1 percent for each additional month that the property is held.

Negative Capital. Nearly all subsidized housing projects utilize nonrecourse mortgages, and with tax shelter as a primary objective, the investors in a partnership will frequently have deducted more tax losses than their cash investment at an early point in the partnership's activities. The excess deductions are known as a limited partner's "negative capital." This amount will become taxable income in the year the property is sold, the partner withdraws from the partnership, or the mortgage is foreclosed. Accelerated depreciation claimed by the partnership is subject to partial recapture upon the sale of a partner's interest, so that he may be required to report part of the "gain" as ordinary income. The law is unclear as to the income tax consequences of the death of a partner with "negative capital" in one or more limited partnerships. It appears that these amounts may become taxable income to the estate of the deceased partner. However, the law was changed in 1976 and again in 1978, and tax practitioners are not in agreement on this matter.

Getting Out of a Real Estate Investment. Differing tax consequences result from the liquidation of real estate investments, a number of which have been discussed earlier in this chapter.

1. The sale of a property results in a taxable gain or loss, which is taxed as either ordinary income or long-term capital gain, as has been discussed above.

2. Withdrawal from an investment as a limited partner in real estate results in gain or loss as though the interest had been sold. *Negative capital* situations have been discussed in the preceding section. A withdrawal by a partner with a positive capital would result in a capital loss to that partner equal to the amount of his capital account.

3. Foreclosure is generally, treated as if the property has been sold for the amount of the outstanding mortgage.

4. Where a property is sold and not more than 30 percent of the selling price is received in cash in the year of sale, the seller can elect to report the gain over the period that he collects the sale price instead of reporting the entire gain in the year of sale. The terms of such an installment sale are often dictated by the seller, who specifies what amount he will accept as a down payment, the period of the remaining payments, and so on. The installment method has several advantages.

a. If the installment method is not used, the tax payable on the total gain would sometimes be greater than the total cash received in the year of sale.

b. Reporting only portions of the gain each year instead of "lumping" the entire amount in one year may place the taxpayer in a lower marginal tax bracket.

c. If the original sale qualified for favorable long-term capital gain rates, the installment payments received in later years will (to the extent that they are taxable) so qualify.

> *Example:* Investor B has parcel of land that he has held for three years and now wishes to sell. His adjusted basis is $40,000, and he has received an offer of $80,000, with $20,000 down in 1979. He would hold for $60,000, an 8½ percent first mortgage payable over six years, $10,000 each on December 1, 1980, through December 1, 1985, plus interest. If he wishes to do so, he could report this as an installment sale.

Selling price	$80,000	100%
Adjusted basis	40,000	50%
Taxable gain (gross profit)	$40,000	50%

Thus, 50 percent of the selling price is taxed as gain. Each year's collections, taxable gain, and income taxes on the gain are as follows:

Year	(1) Collec- tions	(2) Taxable Gain	(3) Long Term Capital Gain Deduction	(4) Amount Added to Other Income (2 − 3)	(5) Income Tax as Gain (assume 55 percent marginal tax rate)
1979	$20,000	$10,000	$ 6,000	$ 4,000	$2,200
1980	10,000	5,000	3,000	3,000	1,100
1981	10,000	5,000	3,000	2,000	1,100
1982	10,000	5,000	3,000	2,000	1,100
1983	10,000	5,000	3,000	2,000	1,100
1984	10,000	5,000	3,000	2,000	1,100
1985	10,000	5,000	3,000	2,000	1,100
	$80,000	$40,000	$24,000	$17,000	$8,800

In addition to reporting the gain on the installment sale, would report interest as it is earned or collected. (See also Chapter 10).

5. "Deferred payment" sales of real property do not qualify for installment sale treatment when the seller receives more than 30 percent of the price during the year of sale. Contingent sale prices will also disqualify a transaction from installment reporting for tax purposes. In either case, the seller is required to treat the sale as a deferred payment sale for tax purposes. The property is treated as though it had been sold immediately even though payments may be required over a period of time. However, the purchaser's contract or promissory note can be sold, usually at a discount, depending on the credit rating of the maker, the interest rate, and so on.

Example: Mr. A sells a farm for $200,000, of which $75,000 is received as a down payment. The purchaser agrees to issue a promissory note of $125,000, payable at $12,500 per year, plus simple interest at 6 percent. Mr. A's adjusted basis for the property is $60,000. Mr. A realizes, too late, that he cannot utilize the installment method when payments in the year of sale are more than 30 percent. He considers selling the note to various institutions and learns that they would pay only 60 percent of the face amount because of the low interest rate on the note. If he uses the deferred payment method for tax purposes, the sale would be reported as follows:

Sale proceeds—cash	$ 75,000
Notes—$125,000 @ 60%	75,000
Total	$150,000
Basis	60,000
Gain in year of sale	$ 90,000

In addition to reporting the taxable gain (which might qualify as a long-term capital gain), Mr. A would be required to report 40 percent of each dollar of note collections as additional income since his adjusted basis of the note is only 60 percent of its face.

Note amount	$125,000
Reported in year of sale	
(60 percent times $125,000)	75,000
Collections with no tax basis	$ 50,000

These subsequent collections would be taxed as ordinary income if the note was originally issued by an individual, even where the original sale qualified for capital gain treatment. Gain realized on the collection of a note issued by a corporation may be taxed as long-term capital gain.

In rare cases, a purchaser's contract to pay in the future is considered to have no value and no gain is reported until the collections actually received exceed the seller's basis. These cases involve *sales on contract,* a method that the IRS is very reluctant to allow upon audit of returns.

Tax-Free Trades. Real property held for investment or the production of income may be traded tax free for other real property held for those purposes. ("Inventory" property held primarily for sale to customers may not be traded tax free.) Where such trades are arranged, any cash or other property used to equalize the values is taxed up to the amount of the gain. Mortgages to which the traded property is subject are not treated as other property to the extent that the mortgages on the property received equal or exceed the mortgages on the property given up. Tax-free exchanges can involve three-way transactions in which a prospective purchaser is required to purchase a property suitable to the present owner of an investment property that is to be traded. The courts have accepted numerous forms of tax-free trades, and the investor facing a large tax on the sale of his property can often utilize this flexibility. (See also Chapter 10).

Impact at Death. The 1976 Tax Reform Act introduced "carry-over basis," "fresh start," and numerous other terms to the income tax laws. The changes it introduced were so extensive and required so much additional clarification that the rules were deferred by Congress for three years in the Revenue Act of 1978. Prior law allowed property acquired from a decedent to take a stepped-up basis for income tax purposes, equal to the property's value at the date of death, or six months later in certain cases. The carry-over basis rules arbitrarily assume that appreciation occurred evenly over the period that the property had been held. Under this formula, appreciated property held at the decedent's death takes the decedent's basis without adjustment if the property was acquired after 1979. Property acquired before January 1, 1977, is subject to an adjustment to allocate appreciation over the time that the property was owned. The tax basis of such property is deemed to be stepped up to include the pre-1977 appreciation.

> *Example:* Assume that the decedent acquired land five years prior to December 31, 1976, and that his date of death is ten years after December 31, 1976.

Fair market value at date of death	$7,000,000
Adjusted basis	1,000,000
Increase in value	$6,000,000

Formula for addition to basis is:

$$\frac{\text{Number of days property held prior to January 1, 1977}}{\text{Total number of days property held}} \times \text{Amount of appreciation}$$

$$\frac{5 \text{ years} \times 365 = 1,825 \text{ days}}{15 \text{ years} \times 365 = 5,475} \times \$6,000,000$$

One third × $6,000,000 .... $2,000,000
Decedent's basis 1,000,000
Beneficiary's basis $3,000,000

If the estate or the beneficiaries sell the property at its $7 million value, a $4 million income tax gain would be realized. This example is somewhat oversimplified for ease of illustration. However, the entire income tax gain results from the carry-over basis rules enacted in 1976.

TAX CONSIDERATIONS IN THE FORMS OF OWNERSHIP AND TRANSFER

I. Barry Mehler

I. *BARRY MEHLER, MBA, CPA, Partner, Ernst & Whinney, Washington, D.C.*

Partner in charge of tax services in the Washington, D. C., offices of Ernst & Whinney. Lecturer on Income Tax, The American University. Member AICPA. Author of articles for various professional journals, including Taxation for Accountants *and* The Certificate.

An introduction to the complexities of the Internal Revenue Code (IRC) and U.S. Treasury Regulations is necessary for an investor in that the methods used in his transactions can have a major impact on the taxable outcome of his investments. This chapter alerts the investor to some of his choices in structuring the form of his investments and to the types of tax advantages, disadvantages, and problems that accompany those choices. The information presented here will not make the reader a tax expert, and it is strongly recommended that he seek *competent* tax advice before making any real estate investments.

The Tax Consequences of Various Forms of Business Organization

The selection of the form of business organization has important tax ramifications. The most widely selected forms adaptable to real estate operations are corporations, both regular and subchapter S (Sub-S), and partnerships, both general and limited. The individual proprietorship will not be discussed in this chapter.

The Corporate Form—Regular. A corporation is a separate legal entity which generally has a perpetual existence, centralized management, limited liability, and free transferability of ownership. Investors in real estate should be aware that when a corporation is created to hold real estate, the investment, which is now stock, becomes personal rather than real property and is subject to personal property rules.

One advantage of a corporation is its treatment as a separate legal entity and therefore as a separate taxable entity. The corporate tax rate at this writing is as follows:

Taxable Income	Tax Rate
$0–$25,000	17%
$25,000–$50,000	20
$50,000–$75,000	30
$75,000–$100,000	40
Over $100,000	46

For many taxpayers in higher brackets, the retention of funds at the corporate level permits greater capital accumulation, since in this way less is lost to taxes.

A corporation offers the advantage of unlimited deductibility of investment interest expense. An individual, on the other hand, is subject to a $10,000 limit (in most cases) on investment interest expense in excess of net investment income.

As to disadvantages, if a corporation has a net operating loss, it may be carried forward for seven years. This could prove to be a disadvantage if the loss situation is not turned around in time to utilize the loss carryforward, which expires after the seven years. An individual, on the other hand, may carry forward a disallowed excess interest deduction indefinitely.

The expiration of net operating losses carried forward after seven years can be a considerable problem for a real estate investment corporation for other reasons as well. Due to high deductions from depreciation on real property in the early years, a real estate investment corporation could easily sustain continued losses. The depreciation taken will lower the basis of the property held, whether or not any tax benefit is derived by the corporation, and when the property is sold at a later date, this lower basis will be used to determine the gain on the sale.

Another disadvantage of a corporation is the existence of double taxation, that is, the taxation of earnings on a corporate level and the taxation of dividends on an individual level.

Several potential problems are associated with the corporate form. These relate to collapsible corporations, the accumulation of earnings, and personal holding companies.

A collapsible corporation is one in which a project is started but little or no income has been realized, and then it is liquidated with assets distributed at fair market value to the shareholders. The purpose of this device is to have the profit to be realized taxed at capital gain rates on liquidation rather than at the ordinary rates on income received by the corporation. This generally applies to a situation similar to the following: A corporation begins construction of a town houses or apartment project. While the project is under construction, an offer to buy it is received. The owner of the project would like to liquidate the corporation, realizing gain to the extent that the fair market value of the project exceeds his basis and paying capital gain rates at the individual level. The project would then be sold to the buyer at the same fair market value, and there would be no gain or loss on the transaction.

The problem is that the rules for a collapsible corporation state that unless a project is completed to a point at which one third or more of the *profit* is recognized by the corporation, the transaction described above will result in ordinary gain, not capital gain. This rule became effective in 1950 after many people had used collapsible corporations to bypass taxation at ordinary rates. The author cautions the reader, however, that this explanation is a vast simplification of a subject complicated enough to take the full length of this chapter.

The second problem relates to the accumulation of earnings within the corporation which are not necessary to the reasonable needs of the business. The Internal Revenue Service possibly could take the position that the accumulation is to avoid paying dividends which would be taxed to its shareholders. The burden of proof to disprove this contention by the IRS rests on the corporation. The Internal Revenue Code states that only amounts in excess of $150,000 will be considered excess (i.e. the first $150,000 of accumulated earnings will not be challenged). If no business purpose for the accumulation can be proven, a penalty tax is applied at the rate of 27½ percent of the first $100,000 above the $150,000 and 38½ percent of all amounts in excess of $250,000.

Personal holding company rules were created by Congress so as to prevent investors placing their personal investments in a corporation in order to have the income taxed at a lower rate. If a corporation is deemed to be a personal holding company, the tax on undistributed personal holding company income (ordinary income less regular corporation tax less dividends paid) is 70 percent. Corporations in the real estate field need to be aware of this potential problem because the personal holding company rules apply to passive income.

Two tests determine personal holding company status:

1. *Stock ownership.* More than 50 percent of the outstanding stock of the corporation must be owned directly or indirectly by five or fewer individuals during the last half of the taxable year.

2. *Personal holding company income.* At least 60 percent of the ordinary gross income of the corporation must consist of certain types of passive income, including rents, royalties, dividends, and interest. For this test, *gross* rental income before expenses is used. An exception to protect companies engaged in the business of producing income from rent, mineral, oil and gas royalties, copyright royalties, and produced film rents is the 50 percent test. If the income from one of these sources exceeds 50 percent of the company's ordinary gross income as adjusted, such companies can be exempt from personal holding company status. Once again caution is urged. The rules are complex and one must have competent advice.

The Corporate Form—Sub-S. The Subchapter-S corporation is similar to a regular corporation in its legal attributes and form. However, the shareholders of a Sub-S corporation elect to be taxed at the individual level rather than the corporate level, except as detailed below.

Sub-S income or loss is ordinarily computed at the corporate level in a manner similar to that of regular corporations. Shareholders then report this income or loss on their individual tax returns, whether or not the income is distributed. Unlike regular corporations, Sub-S corporations have no allowable net operating loss carry-back or carry-forward, as losses flow through to shareholders in the year of loss; however, these losses may be deducted by shareholders only to the extent of the shareholders' basis in stock and loans. A shareholder's basis is limited to the adjusted basis of the shareholder's stock plus the adjusted basis of any loans that the shareholder has made to the corporation. Any losses over this limit are lost forever, unlike the partnership where losses are carried over and used in future years. The amount of loss allocated to a shareholder is prorated on the basis of the percentage of his stock and the number of days in the year that he held the stock.

' An exception to being taxed solely at the shareholder level is that capital gains tax may be imposed at the corporate level under certain circumstances when appreciated property is transferred to the corporation in the first three years following the Sub-S election. There are special rules relating to this area that must be considered.

To be eligible for a Sub-S, the following requirements must be met:

1. Ten or fewer shareholders (up to 15 after 5 years). This has been raised to 15 for 1979 by the 1978 Tax Reform Act. Husband and wife will be counted as one shareholder regardless of how their stock is held.
2. Only one class of stock.
3. All shareholders must be individuals, grantor trusts, or voting trusts (not other types of trusts, partnerships, or corporations).
4. A nonresident alien may not be a shareholder.
5. The corporation must be a domestic corporation and must not be a member of an affiliated group eligible to file a consolidated return.

Certain restrictions are placed on a Sub-S corporation that may affect its application in real estate operations. No more than 20 percent of the corporation's *gross* receipts may be from rents, interest, gains from sales, or exchanges of stocks and securities or other passive investment income. An exception is made in the first two years if the investment income is less than $3,000.

The advantages of using a Sub-S corporation are the elimination of double taxation, the ability to pass through any losses of the corporation to the shareholder (restricted as noted above) and the corporation's option of choosing a fiscal rather than calendar year end. This latter advantage has great appeal when trying to spread income over a two year period. For instance, a construction project is set up in a subchapter-S corporation and when half of the income is realized, the corporations chooses to end its year. It thereby throws the balance of the income into the second year of the individual shareholders.

Disadvantages, as noted before, are the passive income limitation, and the limit on net operating loss deductions allowed to each shareholder. Tax preference items are also passed through to the shareholder to be accumulated with other tax preference items of the individual. A further disadvantage can occur if the corporation loses its Sub-S status and there is undistributed taxable income, that is income that was taxed during a previous year but was not distributed before 2½ months after the close of the year. Any future distributions will come from the now regular corporation's earnings and profits and will be taxable dividends until all current earnings and profits are exhausted. Only then can the previously taxed, undistributed taxable income be distributed tax free.

Special Situations. Before a corporation's stock is issued, an advantage available to all corporate shareholders is an election under Section 1244 to have the corporate stock treated as "small business stock." This election is independent of the Sub-S election, but it is often used by Sub-S corporations. The election operates as an incentive to the creation of small businesses by allowing an ordinary deduction rather than a capital loss deduction should the businesses fail. *Very specific requirements must be adhered to* if this election is to succeed. The limit for treatment as ordinary loss to a taxpayer is $100,000 on a joint return. Above that limit, the loss becomes capital.

Corporations for use in real estate investments may be established in three ways:

1. *Purchase assets from an outsider.* This involves the purchase of an ongoing corporation.

If an individual purchases and holds the stock of a corporation with real estate, the basis of the corporation's assets will remain at their historic value. For example, if an individual purchaser, B, buys Corporation X for $500,000 and Corporation X has a building whose basis net of depreciation is $100,000, this basis remains $100,000 after the purchase of Corporation X by B.

A solution to this problem is for B to set up his own corporation, purchasing its stock with his $500,000. This corporation then purchases the stock of Corporation X for $500,000 and liquidates Corporation X. Such a liquidation can only be accomplished within two years of the purchase of Corporation X's stock, whose sellers are taxed at capital gains on the sale of stock. Under these circumstances, the basis of Corporation X's asssets (the building) is determined by IRC Code 334(b)(2) based on the purchase price of Corporation X. Here there is a step-up in the basis of the building of $500,000 (to be used for depreciation and figuring gain or loss on the sale of this asset) with no immediate tax consequences. This liquidation can only be accomplished within two years of the purchase of stock. Sellers are not affected by this transaction and are therefore taxed at capital gains on the sale of stock. Competent advice is necessary in structuring this type of transaction.

A purchaser may want to buy only the assets of a corporation. To avoid double taxation on the seller (a corporate tax on the sale, a shareholder tax on the liquidation), the corporation should adopt an IRC Code 337 plan of liquidation. This plan *must* be adopted *prior to* the sale. Its use results in only one tax at the individual level rather than double taxation. The requirements for this treatment are strict, so competent tax advice again is urged.

2. *Transfer assets owned by individuals, groups, or partnerships into a newly formed corporation or an existing corporation in exchange for the stock and securities of the corporation.* Under IRC Section 351 this transfer is tax free as long as these conditions are met:

a. The basis of the transferred assets exceeds the basis of the transferred liabilities.

b. The transferors are in control of the corporation immediately after the exchange. IRC Section 368(c) defines control as ownership of at least 80 percent of the total combined voting power of all classes of voting stock *and* at least 80 percent of all other classes of stock.

3. *Sell assets that the taxpayer owns to a corporation controlled by the taxpayer.* The advantage of selling an asset rather than exchanging an asset for stock or securities lies in the treatment of the basis of the asset after the transaction. In the tax-free exchange, the basis of the asset is the same for the corporation as it was for the transferor. In the sale of an asset, the purchase price becomes the new basis. When property is sold on the installment basis (to be discussed later), there is the double advantage of the step-up in basis and delayed recognition of the gain on the sale. If selling the asset to the corporation is the method chosen, the sale must be carefully constructed so as to avoid the purview of Section 351, as this section is mandatory, not elective.

Partnership.   The partnership is a heavily utilized vehicle in real estate investments. It is defined as a relationship of two or more people who join together to operate a trade or business, with all of them contributing money, property, or services and all of them expecting to share in the profits and losses. Each general partner bears full liability for the acts of the other partners in relation to the partnership. A partnership is not taxable entity. The individual partners report their share of partnership income or loss, bonus depreciation, tax preference items, and investment credit on their own personal returns.

The primary advantage of using the partnership form of organization is that this eliminates the problem of double taxation, since the partners and not the partnership are taxed. In real estate ventures, large losses from depreciation are often passed through in early years. A partner may offset these losses against his other income and carry over or carry back any residual amount.

If certain rules are followed, the Commissioner of the Internal Revenue Service will grant permission to have a partnership year end up to 90 days prior to the year-end of the principal partners (for example, if the partners are on a calendar year, the partnership year can end on September 30). This offers the individual partners an opportunity for personal tax planning.

The primary disadvantage of the partnership form is the unlimited liability of general partners. Another disadvantage is that partnership income is taxable to the partners whether or not distributed. Also there is the limit on use of property available for investment credit applied to a partnership as an entity. Thus, the limit of $100,000 on the availability of used property for investment credit is the same for a partnership as for an individual, and the partnership must apportion this amount among its partners. Bonus depreciation is limited for partnerships in a similar way. The $2,000 limit (20 percent × $10,000) is applied on the partnership level and divided among the partners for use individually.

A potential problem of partnerships can arise in connection with the condemnation of property. The proceeds from the condemnation are considered as belonging to the partneship only, and in order to avoid gain the *partnership* and not the individual partners must be the entity that reinvests the proceeds.

The Tax Reform Act of 1976 barred the retroactive allocation of partnership gain or loss for the years beginning after 1975. Instead, partnership income is allocated to incoming and outgoing partners only for the portion of the year during which they were partners. Further, special allocations (such as for depreciation) are not allowed unless they have substantial economic effect. Questions under this paragraph should be referred to your tax adviser.

When a partnership is established, the partners contribute capital (money, property, or services) and articles of partnership are drawn up which set out the various partners' shares in profit and loss and any other special conditions that the partners agree upon. If the partnership agreement contains percentages for the allocation of profit and loss, distribution in proportion to the partners' shares in the capital account is assumed. As in the exchange of property for the stock of a corporation, when a partner contributes real property to a partnership, the partner receives personal property in return (a partnership interest). No taxable gain or loss occurs when property, including money, is transferred. If services are rendered for an interest in the capital of the partnership, the value of the partnership interest is immediate ordinary income (compensation) to the partner. If a partner is entitled to receive only a share of future gains and losses, no taxable event takes place until the gains and losses are realized. A problem arises in the transfer of depreciable assets, whether the transfer is to a partnership or a corporation, as the property becomes used property (first-user rights are lost) and may be subject to a slower rate of depreciation. Table 1 shows the differences between the rates for new property and the rates for used property.

TABLE 1

Types of Assets	Maximum Rates Allowed	
	New	Used
Commercial	150%	S/L
Rental residential*	200	125%

* Eighty percent of the gross rental comes from the dwelling units; otherwise the commercial rates apply.

A special situation arises when an interest in a ongoing partnership is purchased at a price higher than the basis of the selling partner in the partnership. A special election may be made by the partnership giving the new partner a special basis in the partnership properties on which he will compute his depreciation, gain or loss. Here is an example:

The assets of the old partnership are:

Cash	$12,000
Property	30,000
Total value	$42,000
Fair market value	$54,000

The value of each partner's assets is:

	X	Y	Z	Total
Cash	$ 4,000	$ 4,000	$ 4,000	$12,000
Property	10,000	10,000	10,000	30,000
	$14,000	$14,000	$14,000	$42,000

Partner X sells his interest to P for $18,000. If the partnership elects the special rules for increasing basis, the new allocation will be:

	P	Y	Z
Cash	$ 4,000	$ 4,000	$ 4,000
Property	14,000	10,000	10,000
	$18,000	$14,000	$14,000

Depreciation may then be computed on these values, with P having a higher deduction than Y and Z.

A Special Hybrid—The Limited Partnership. The limited partnership in organizational form is a hybrid between a corporation and a general partnership. Limited partners are liable only for the amount they invest in a partnership, and only the general partner in a limited partnership retains unlimited liability.

Much has been written about the "at risk" provision of the Tax Reform Act of 1976. Real estate investment was included in the first draft of the bill but was eventually exempted. This exemption was continued in the 1978 Tax Reform Act. Consequently, the limited partnership is still a much-used tax shelter because it allows losses to pass through to limited as well as general partners in excess of their capital invest- ments where there is debt on the property for which no partner is liable (the lender looks only to the property). Then each partner, limited and general, is considered to have assumed part of this liability, thus increas- ing basis and the ability to take losses.

As in other transactions, one must remember that careful structuring of the limited partnership is necessary for successful tax benefits.

Tax Consequences of Real Estate Financing

Mortgages in the Ordinary Course of Business. 1. *Financing transactions.* Mortgage financing is the standard method for the tax-free financing of real estate. The creation of a liability is not a taxable event, and the leveraging obtainable by mortgage financing allows the investor to retain funds for other uses. Tax benefits may be realized by virtue of interest deductions, especially in the early years, when the payments consist mostly of interest. The investor must always be aware that the payments will later consist mostly of principal. If he is using accelerated depreciation, the time when his taxable income exceeds his cash flow from the project will be hastened. Refinancing may alleviate this problem.

Another technique for generating tax-free fund flows from real estate is to set up a land lease with a high-quality tenant. The lease could then be used as collateral for a bank loan. The loan proceeds are tax free, the interest is deductible, and the rent, although taxable, will provide some or all of the funds for amortizing the mortgage. In this way the investor can keep the property for sale later and have funds available for use now. In the meantime the property may continue to appreciate.

One word of caution is mandated here and applies throughout. Many of the planning examples are based upon court cases. They contain various degrees of risk and should be discussed with experienced tax professionals before any actions are undertaken. Sometimes the improper wording of documents or an improper sequence of transactions is sufficient to destroy the beneficial tax aspects of a plan.

2. *Construction Period Interest.* The 1976 Tax Reform Act requires construction period interest to be capitalized in the year it is paid or accrued, and amortized according to special rules that phase such interest into what will eventually be a ten-year amortization period. This period begins in the year that the interest is paid or accrued. The remaining balance must be amortized beginning in the *latter* of (1) the taxable year in which the property is ready to be held for sale or to be placed in service or (2) the first taxable year following the taxable year in which the interest is paid or accrued. The length of the amortization period is phased in according to special rules, depending on whether the property is nonresidential real property, residential real property, or low-income housing (see Table 2). Real estate taxes are affected in a like manner and must also be capitalized and amortized according to the same rules.

Tax-Free Transfers. Normally the transfer of assets to a corporation or a partnership, which is controlled by the donors of the property, is tax free, and the basis of the assets transferred less the liabilities becomes the basis for the stock or partnership interest. Problems may arise when the basis of the assets transferred is exceeded by the liabili-

TABLE 2

Tax Year Amortization Is Paid or Accrued

Nonresidential Real Property	Residential Real Property	Low-Income Housing	Percentage Allowed for First-Year Deduction	Remaining Percentage	Remaining Years to Be Amortized*
82	78	76	25%	75%	3
83	79	77	20	80	4
84	80	78	$16\frac{2}{3}$	$83\frac{1}{3}$	5
85	81	79	$14\frac{2}{7}$	$85\frac{5}{7}$	6
86	82	80	$12\frac{1}{2}$	$87\frac{1}{2}$	7
87	83	81	$11\frac{1}{9}$	$88\frac{8}{9}$	8
88 and after	84 and after	82 and after	10	90	9

* This amortization begins the latter of (1) the taxable year in which the property is ready to be held for sale or to be placed in service or (2) the first taxable year following the taxable year in which interest is paid or accrued.

ties. Note that the test is the aggregate basis of all the items transferred in a particular transaction. Therefore, lumping several assets together may remove the stigma of an overmortgaged asset. When the aggregate liabilities exceed the aggregate assets, the difference is considered "boot" and is taxable to the transferor.

In order to maintain a tax-free transfer of property to a controlled corporation or partnership, a bona fide business purpose must be established. In one case, an individual transferred appreciated property (stock) to a corporation that he owned, receiving additional stock of the corporation in return. The corporation had a loss situation and considerable debt. The property was then sold, the debt paid, and no tax was paid by the corporation. The IRS challenged the transaction, but the trial court upheld the treatment. The finding of a valid business purpose was central to the success of attributing the sale to the corporation rather than the individual. In this case, the corporation was controlled by a major stockholder. Prior to the transfer of the appreciated securities, the stockholder had entered negotiations for the sale of the corporation and had been advised by both the purchaser and his own bank to reduce the corporation liabilities. The path chosen was the one selected by the shareholder, and it was accepted by the court as a valid business reason for the transaction, and, therefore, the successful tax result was allowed to stand.

Options and Installment Sales

Options. The option to buy real estate is a tool for deferring income on a sale. The benefit of the option to the seller is that the money he receives for it is not taxable. The advantage of the option to the buyer is that it enables him to commit less funds for a specified period of time during which he can secure financing, find another purchaser at a higher price, or change his mind.

The seller of an option ordinarily provides that the option payment will be applied against the sale price. Once the option is exercised or expires, the tax consequences will be based on the character of the property underlying the option and on the holding period. If, for example, Mr. Jones acquired a two-year option for $10,000 to purchase 20 acres of land in June 1977 and he sold the option for $20,000 in September 1978, he would have capital gains of $10,000.

Installment Sales. Any sale of real property may be reported by the use of the installment method. The common definition of an installment sale is that it is a transaction in which the purchaser receives one or more deferred payments over time for the transfer of title to property. The tax definition is more rigid—for a transaction to qualify as an installment sale, there must be *two or more payments* payable in *two or more taxable years.* The aggregate of payments in the first taxable year (previous option payments and the down payment, plus payments on notes) cannot exceed 30 percent of the sale price. The sale price is the entire cost of the property—cash, the fair market value of property given to the seller, and any debt assumed by the purchaser. The 30 percent payment in the first year does not include any interest paid, but it does include all cash and property received in the year of sale and the excess of any assumed mortgage over the seller's basis in the property transferred. An election to report on the installment basis must be made on the tax return. Installment sale reporting is available only when property is sold at a gain—all losses must be recognized in the year that the transaction takes place.

An obvious advantage of using the installment method for tax-reporting purposes is that the method relieves the taxpayer of the burden of paying taxes on income that he has not yet received. The installment method also spreads capital gains, and it may enable the taxpayer to take advantage of lower tax rates.

The disadvantages are twofold. The first one is the economic risk in the deferral of receipt of all the money from the sale. The second disadvantage is the danger of uncertainty in the changes of the tax law. Although the holding period and the amount of gain are fixed, the nature of the gains and the tax rates relating thereto are generally determined by the law and facts in effect in the year of receipt of the proceeds. With the potential changes on tax reform, a party planning to enter into a long term installment sale today should certainly weigh this problem carefully.

The main problem to watch for in installment sales is the 30 percent rule. When selling mortgaged property, the taxpayer must be careful not to go over the 30 percent limit. As has been noted, if a mortgage on property is in excess of the seller's basis, the excess must be included in the calculations of the payments for the first year.

Another potential problem arises if the seller has to take the property back voluntarily in foreclosure. In some cases the IRS may assert that this transaction is a taxable event, and the amount by which the fair market value of the property exceeds the remaining tax basis at the time that the property returns to the original seller is gain that must then be recognized immediately in the tax return. Proper tax planning can chart a course to the least costly tax alternatives. (For additional information on installment sales, see Chapter 9.)

Trading as Tax Deferral

A general rule of taxation is that the entire amount of gain realized upon the sale or exchange of property (including real estate) is taxable. In certain instances, however, Congress has deemed it inappropriate to tax the realization of gain if the taxpayer's investment after an exchange continues to be in substantially the same type of asset. Here the gain becomes subject to tax when the taxpayer discontinues his investment. This section will discuss one such opportunity for the deferral of taxes, tax-free exchanges under Section 1031 of the Internal Revenue Code. Section 1031 provides a technique whereby no gain is "recognized" if qualifying property is exchanged solely for property of a like kind. For the purposes of this section, "realization" of gain takes place at the time of the sale or exchange and "recognition" of gain is the reporting for federal income tax purposes. Qualifying property can be property that is used in a trade or a business or property that is held for investment, but it cannot be property that is held primarily for sale or personal use. Thus real estate that is either used in a trade or business or is held for investment will qualify under Section 1031, whereas real estate that is held by a "dealer" as inventory or by an individual for use as a personal residence will not.

In order to defer the recognition of gain, qualifying property must be exchanged for property of a "like kind." In the case of real estate, the phrase "like kind" has been defined broadly. Although the exchange must be an exchange of real estate for real estate, within this basic parameter the latitude is great. City real property may be exchanged for a farm; unimproved real estate may be exchanged for improved real estate; a single property may be exchanged for two or more properties.

If property other than property of a like kind is received, then the gain, if any, will be recognized to the extent that such property is received. Such nonqualifying property, commonly called "boot," may be the amount of money received, the liabilities of the taxpayer that are assumed by another, or the fair market value of other nonqualifying property received. If the taxpayer has a loss, that loss is not recognized in the exchange despite the presence of boot. The following examples illustrate the effect of boot in like-kind exchanges.

> **Example 1:** A taxpayer exchanges a building with a basis of $50,000 for a building with a fair market value of $190,000 plus $10,000 in cash. The taxpayer has a realized gain of $150,000, of which $10,000 will be taxed.
>
> **Example 2:** Suppose that in Example 1 the building exchanged by the taxpayer was subject to a mortgage of $50,000 which was assumed by the other party to the exchange. Further assume that the building received by the taxpayer was unencumbered by debt. The taxpayer would report income of $60,000, which is the sum of the cash he received plus the liabilities that were assumed by the other party.

In real estate transactions it is important to understand the tax treatment of liabilities. It is uncommon for a piece of property to be unencumbered. For purposes of a tax-free exchange under Section 1031, the assumption of a liability by the other party to the exchange will be boot only if it exceeds the liabilities assumed by the taxpayer plus any cash paid by the taxpayer. In other words, mortgages are "netted" for the purpose of determining whether there is boot.

> **Example 3:** A trades a building to B which has an adjusted basis of $100,000 and a fair market value of $220,000, and is subject to a mortgage of $80,000. B's building (now A's) has a fair market value of $250,000, is subject to a mortgage of $150,000, and has an adjusted basis to B of $175,000. A received B's building plus $40,000 in cash.
>
> Although A has a potential gain of $120,000 ($100,000 basis − $80,000 mortgage for $250,000 fair market value − $150,000 mortgage + $40,000 cash), he will recognize only $40,000, the amount of cash received. This is because the $80,000 mortgage that A is relieved of is exceeded by the

$150,000 mortgage that A assumes. If B's mortgage had been only $60,000, A's recognized gain would have been $60,000 ($40,000 cash plus the $20,000 difference in the liabilities exchanged).

The deferral of gain in the context of a tax-free exchange is just that—deferral, and not elimination. The price paid for the deferral is a lower basis both for depreciation and for determining gain or loss in the future. Generally the basis to the taxpayer for property received in a tax-free exchange is the basis of the taxpayer in the property transferred, with certain important adjustments. These adjustments are that the basis is reduced by the amount of any money received (including liabilities), increased by the amount of gain recognized, reduced by the amount of loss recognized, and increased by the amount of any liabilities assumed. Thus in Example 3 A would have an adjusted basis in the property he receives of $170,000 computed as A's original basis of $100,000 in the property transferred, plus the $150,000 liability he assumes, less the $40,000 cash he receives and the $80,000 liability of which he is relieved, and finally increased by the $40,000 gain he recognizes.

The Internal Revenue Service recently stated in Revenue Ruling 78–135 that exchanges of general partnership interests would not qualify as tax free under Section 1031.

Tax-free exchanges provide remarkable flexibility for the deferral of gain in real estate transactions. That flexibility is most evident in triangular, or three-party, exchanges, a technique by which the taxpayer seeks to avoid gain on the disposition of appreciated property. The three parties typically involved are: A, who wants to dispose of his appreciated property (to B); B, who wants to acquire A's property for cash; and C, who has like-kind property that A would like to acquire tax free to replace the property that is being acquired by B rather than receive cash from B and report the gain. With proper structuring, all the parties to such an exchange can realize their objectives. Typically the transaction in question might be structured so that B purchases C's property for cash and then exchanges it for A's property. A will recognize no gain or loss, provided that he does not actually (or constructively) receive cash. C, on the other hand, will recognize gain or loss. The transaction as to B is not taxable. Triangular exchanges are subject to a great deal of scrutiny and should be entered into only with the advice of a competent tax adviser. (See also Chapter 34.)

The Sale or Exchange of a Personal Residence

Section 1034 of the Internal Revenue Code provides a tax deferral for taxpayers who sell a personal residence and then replace that residence within a specific amount of time. This provision was enacted out of a recognition by Congress that a taxpayer's change of personal residence was often a response to a change in the size of his family, his place of employment, or other factors beyond his control. Taxation is deferred until the taxpayer disposes of a principal residence and does not replace it or replaces it at a lesser price (trades down). It should be noted that the nonrecognition provisions of Section 1034 are mandatory; where Section 1034 applies, gain is automatically deferred.

Section 1034 has several basic requirements. One requirement is that the property sold and the property acquired must both be "principal residences" of the taxpayer. A taxpayer can have only one principal residence. Thus in most cases a second home in the mountains or at the beach will not be a principal residence. A principal residence may include, however, a houseboat, a house trailer, a condominium, or an apartment in a cooperative. If the property used by the taxpayer as a principal residence has more than one use, an allocation among those uses must be made. For example, if the taxpayer uses part of his property in his trade or business, only the portion attributable to use as a personal residence will qualify for Section 1034 deferral.

The new residence acquired by the taxpayer can be bought, constructed, or acquired by exchange. The time for replacement, however, depends upon how the new residence is acquired. If the new residence is purchased (already constructed), then its purchase and its occupancy as a principal residence must occur within a three-year period beginning 18 months before the sale of the old residence and ending 18 months after such sale. If the taxpayer constructs his own residence (defined to include either building it himself or contracting to have it built), then he must have commenced construction not later than 18 months after the sale of his old residence and must occupy the new property as his principal residence within two years of the sale of the old residence. Special time limits exist for members of the armed forces and persons working overseas. The applicable 18-month or 2-year period is suspended during the time that a member of the armed forces is on extended active duty and that a person is working overseas, provided that a qualified replacement with a new residence occurs within four years.

Under Section 1034, *gain will be recognized* under certain circumstances despite an otherwise qualified replacement with a new residence if the adjusted sale price of the old residence exceeds the cost of purchasing the new residence. The adjusted sale price of the old residence is the amount received for it less certain expenses incurred to "fix up" the residence for resale. To be eligible to reduce the sale proceeds for Section 1034 purposes, such fix-up expenses must have been incurred within 90 days of the date of the sale contract, must be paid for within 30 days after the sale, and must not be otherwise deductible. Such expenditures might include painting, wallpapering, and the like. Although these expenses may not be added to basis to reduce gain, they are permitted to be deducted from the sale price of the old residence to determine initially whether any gain at all must be recognized. Thus the timing of fix-up efforts could have a significant tax benefit.

> **Example:** A taxpayer sells his old residence for $19,000 (after reduction for commissions and other selling expenses). His basis is $17,500, so he has a realized gain of $1,500. The cost of his new residence was $18,000, so if he has no fix-up expenses he will recognize $1,000 of the $1,500 gain

he realized. If, however, the taxpayer has $300 of fix-up expenses, then he would recognize only $700 of gain (computed by subtracting the $300 in fix-up costs from the sale price of $19,000 to arrive at an adjusted sale price of $18,700). Do note that to the extent that the purchase price is less than the adjusted sale price, gain is recognized in full, not prorated.

Section 1034 has built into it some flexibility regarding changes that may occur in the marital situation of the taxpayer. It will apply if a single joint residence used by a husband and wife who separate is replaced by two residences, one of which is used by each. No gain will be recognized as long as each of the residences acquired exceeds in cost the proportionate share of cost attributable to the purchaser from the old residence. Similarly, a separate residence may be replaced by a joint residence. If two taxpayers marry, sell their respective individual residences, and purchase a joint residence, Section 1034 will apply to prevent recognition of gain if the other requirements are met.

The 1978 Tax Reform Act eliminated problems that arose in the old law if a new residence was both acquired and sold by a taxpayer during the 18-month period before the sale of the old residence. Section 1034 now applies to such a new residence.

A special tax relief provision exists for persons over the age of 55 who sell their home and do not reinvest the proceeds in a new residence. This provision permits an election of a direct reduction of the amount of taxable gain as the first $100,000 of gain can be excluded on sales made after July 26, 1978. This break is available only once in a lifetime. In order to qualify for the over-55 exclusion, the taxpayer must have owned the property three years out of the five years preceding the sale.

PART II
Real Estate Analyses

VALUE CONCEPTS

Halbert C. Smith

*H*ALBERT C. SMITH, DBA, SRPA, Professor of Real Estate and
Urban Analysis, Director, Real Estate Research Center, College
of Business Administration, University of Florida, Gainesville,
Florida.
    Past president, American Real Estate and Urban Economics
Association. Formerly chief economist, Federal Home Loan Bank
Board. Director, First Federal Savings and Loan Association of
Mid-Florida. Educational consultant to Florida Real Estate Com-
mission. Author, Real Estate Appraisal, (Columbus, Ohio: Grid,
1976); and Real Estate Appraisal, Finance, Investment, and Business Management (Florida Real Estate Commission, 1978). Coau-
thor, Real Estate and Urban Development rev. ed., (Homewood,
Ill.: Richard D. Irwin, 1977).

Value is the central criterion for most real estate decisions. Whether
to buy, sell, lease, or rehabilitate and at what price and time are typical
real estate decisions that hinge upon value. Buyers do not want to pay
more and sellers do not want to receive less than the value of a property.

Thus, the estimation of value is a crucial step in most real estate
decision making, especially when it comes to a decision to build, rehabilitate, or rent.

The estimation of value might be rather simple and straight-forward
if appraisers and other real estate decision makers agreed upon the
nature and components of value. If the concept of value contained only
a single element, and if one definition fitted every case (and was agreed
to by decision makers), valuation would be reduced to a mechanical
process. Appraisal procedures would be tailored to the value concept,
and the same items of information dealing with agreed-upon elements
of value would be gathered for every real estate decision. For example,
population data, income data, zoning information, community growth,
property expenses, and a standard rate of return could be fed into a

computer which would render a value conclusion accepted by both the buyer and the seller. A real estate decision would often be implied by the computerized value conclusion.

Value, however, is such a complex concept that neither its nature nor its elements can be standardized and mechanized. The concept is multifaceted, emphasizing supply considerations for some purposes and demand considerations for other purposes. Value-determining elements change in importance for each decision. Population growth may be an important element of value for one type of property (say undeveloped land), but less important for a basic industry that ships its products out of the community.

Although the importance of value-determining elements changes for each decision, greater consistency among value conclusions can be expected if value estimators and other real estate decision makers attain an understanding of value concepts. Although nonprofessionals may assume that such an understanding exists, this is probably because they are unaware of the many definitions of value that have been proposed, the long history of value conceptualization, and the relatively new concepts, such as probability, that are beginning to be incorporated into theoretical treatments of value but are not widely understood and accepted by real estate professionals.

It seems evident, then, that the greater the degree of understanding and agreement about the concepts of value by real estate decision makers, the narrower the areas for judgment will be. Differences of opinion will always exist regarding the elements of value and their weights. However, needless confusion deriving from lack of understanding and agreement about the relevant concepts can be avoided by a thorough consideration of the current developments regarding value.

In addition to narrowing the range for judgment, an understanding of value concepts should help determine the appropriate valuation methodology. For example, if the classical view of land value as a price-determined commodity were accepted, land would be regarded as a residual claimant after labor, capital, and entrepreneurship had received their fair returns. If, on the other hand, the claim of land values is regarded as equal to that of the other factors of production, a market return competitive with that of other investments can be assigned to land.

The History of Value Theory

Supply-Oriented (Classical) Value Theory. The classical economists—Adam Smith, Thomas Matthews, David Ricardo, John Stuart Mill, and Johann von Thünen—regarded value as primarily the resultant of supply forces. Implicitity, they believed scarcity to be the primary value-creating fact of life. Without scarcity, value would not exist. Thus, the essential problem in identifying the sources and amounts of value was to measure the inputs of value into a commodity or product. The factor of labor was regarded as the essential input to value by the earlier classical economists—Smith, Malthus, and Ricardo. Thus, the cost of labor measured the value of the items produced.[1]

The classical economists made an important distinction between land and the other factors of production. Since land was not created by human labor, land value could not be regarded as a function of labor input. Therefore, Smith and Malthus contended that the return to land was determined in the labor and capital markets. They considered labor and capital to be mobile and to have a higher priority than land for obtaining a return. They did not consider productivity and utility to be determinants of value, except to the extent that labor was productive. The return to land—and thus its value—was determined as a residual only after labor and capital were paid their just returns.

Adam Smith (1723–90) distinguished value in use from value in exchange, and price from value. Value in use was the inherent usefulness of a commodity or product, whereas value in exchange was a function of the marketplace. The air we breathe, for example, has high value in use but low value in exchange. Ornamental diamonds, on the other hand, may have little functional utility but high value in exchange.

Smith considered value to be the price that would occur naturally, while regarding price as a fact determined by the vagaries of the market. Price was the sum of money that was actually paid for a product or commodity. Value was the price that would prevail in a large, active market of well-informed buyers and sellers bidding against one another. The values of labor and capital were established in their own markets, whereas the value of land was derived from other markets.

In his extension of Malthus' land value theory, David Ricardo (1772–1823) viewed land as being composed of various grades of quality. Land of the highest quality would be used first, land of the next highest quality second, and so on, until the last (marginal) grade was brought into cultivation. Since the lower fertility of the lowest grade of soil meant that higher costs must be incurred to produce the same quantity of grain as that obtained from higher grades of land, the owners of the higher grades of land had an advantage over the owners of the lower grades. The costs of labor and capital applied to the lowest grade (highest cost) land determined the product's value. The owners of higher grades of land incurred lower costs, and the differential gave higher quality land an advantage that determined its value. Since this differential was not caused by the application of labor or capital, the surplus was regarded as unearned. That unearned surplus was technically known as rent.

A German economist, Johann Heinrich von Thünen (1783–1850), added the element of location to land value theory. He theorized that unused or undeveloped land would not be brought into production unless the added income was expected to provide a return on the labor and capital invested equal to the current rate of interest. He recognized that the added income was a function of the land's location in relation to "the isolated city," as well as to its fertility relative to other parcels.

---

[1] See especially Adam Smith, *The Wealth of Nations,* book 1.

Thünen applied the same type of analysis to land already in production. Increments of capital and labor would be applied to land already in use until the value of the marginal units of labor and capital equaled the value of the additional (marginal) revenue to be obtained. The transportation costs of shipping commodities to the city would determine whether it was more profitable to apply more labor and capital to land already in production or to develop new land. Later economists termed these concepts the intensive and extensive margins. The intensive margin is represented by the last profitable increment of labor and capital, and the extensive margin is represented by the last parcel of undeveloped land which can be developed profitably. "The cost of overcoming the friction of distance serves as the balancing force between the intensive and extensive margins."[2]

Supply-oriented theories of value continue to play an important role in the prevailing value concepts and valuation methodologies. The cost approach now used by appraisers is based upon classical theory and its assumption that the cost of production equals value. In modern appraisal practice, adjustments are applied to cost for the incurrence of depreciation (physical, functional, and locational); however, the relevance and accuracy of these adjustments are subject to question. (See Chapter 15.)

Another carry-over from classical theory is the assumption that land income is residual. The land residual technique of income capitalization and the concept of highest and best use both employ the residual theory of land value. Land is assumed to obtain a return only after the other factors of production are adequately compensated.

Demand-Oriented (Marginal Utility) Value Theory. Demand-oriented theories of value pay scant attention to the cost of production. These theories emphasize utility, and they measure the value of a commodity or product by the price paid for the last (marginal) unit produced and sold. Thus, if a builder constructs one or two houses that he sells for $60,000, but then constructs ten more identical houses and, because of efficiencies of scale, is able to sell the last two houses for $50,000, the value of all the houses is established at the latter price.

The marginal utility theory was developed primarily by the Austrian economists Menger, von Wieser, and Böhm-Bawerk in the late 19th and early 20th centuries. These economists measured utility by the income to be obtained from a commodity or product. They also advanced the idea that income to be obtained in the future had to be discounted at the rate necessary to forgo the present use of capital. Böhm-Bawerk in particular advanced the discounting process by stating, "It [interest] therefore constitutes the most direct consequence conceivable of the difference in value between present and future goods."[3] The value of a commodity or product was thus regarded as the sum of discounted

---

[2] Halbert C. Smith, Carl J. Tschappat, and Ronald L. Racster, *Real Estate and Urban Development* (Homewood, Ill.: Richard D. Irwin, 1973), p. 46. © 1973 by Richard D. Irwin, Inc.

[3] Eugen von Böhm-Bawerk, *Positive Theory of Capital,* trans. George D. Muncke (South Holland, Ill.: Libertarian Press, 1959), p. 291.

future payments, the size of the payments being determined by the utility of the marginal unit.

The income capitalization approach in current-day appraisal methodology is a direct descendant of marginal utility theory. The conversion of a forecast, future income stream into a lump-sum, present value by means of a capitalization process is an explicit application of the theory. The capitalization rate embodies Böhm-Bawerk's concept of the rate of interest necessary to forgo the present use of capital on similar, competing projects. The forecast earnings are the measure of a property's marginal utility. (See Chapter 13.)

Market Equilibrium–Oriented (Neoclassical) Value Theory. To the brilliant English economist Alfred Marshall (1842–1924) must be given the credit for realizing the significance of supply-oriented and demand-oriented theories of value. In his *Principles of Economics,* Marshall synthesized supply and demand concepts into an integrated theory of value.[4] His well-known scissors analogy explained value as the price resulting from the interacting forces of supply and demand. Just as both blades are necessary to the operation of a pair of scissors, so both the forces of supply and the forces of demand are necessary to the operation of a market. For Marshall, price (value) was determined by the point of equilibrium between the schedules of supply and demand.

Later in the 20th century, John Maynard Keynes (1883–1946) revolutionized the concept of market equilibrium by his view of the general (macro) economic effects of saving, investment, and consumption. In *The General Theory of Employment, Interest, and Money,* Keynes developed the thesis that full employment is not achieved at the point of equilibrium between saving and investment.[5] The nature of the consumption function (a relationship of increasing consumption in relation to income, but at a decreasing rate) tends to produce less saving and investment than are required to maintain full employment over the full course of a business cycle. Government stimulus is thus required during some stages of the business cycle to maintain employment at a satisfactory level and to nudge the economy away from a recessionary tendency and into a growth pattern.

Although it pertains to a nation's level of economic activity, Keynes's theory is pertinent to value theory in that it deals with equilibrium tendencies and with policy actions to maintain economic activity, and thus values. The market equilibrium theory explains the market forces that determine the values of individual parcels of real estate. The theory is reflected in the sales comparison approach used by current-day appraisers. In this approach, appraisers attempt to look at various elements of supply and demand in a market and to measure them directly from the transaction prices that actually occur. (See Chapter 14.)

Institution-Oriented-(Eclectic) Value Theory. Institutional economists have not advanced a systematic or integrated theory. Rather, they have

---

[4] Alfred Marshall, *Principles of Economics,* 8th ed. (London: Macmillan, 1920).

[5] John Maynard Keynes, *The General Theory of Employment, Interest, and Money* (New York: Harcourt, Brace, 1935).

made a wide variety of contributions to our thinking about economic problems in general and value theory in particular. Many of these writers have provided necessary social reflection and criticism which have influenced public attitudes and social action.

One of the best-known critics of contemporary society and economic assumptions was Thorstein Veblen. He contended that the institutions of private property and technology lead to a "pecuniary culture," in which members of the leisure class consume unproductively merely to impress others—a phenomenon he termed "conspicuous consumption." Industries become businesses, whose function is to make a profit rather than to make needed products. Absentee owners and hired managers tend to accentuate profits rather than needs. Although Veblen was unwilling to predict the downfall of the capitalist system (or any other system), he did believe that capitalism would lead to ever greater concentrations of power and group conflict. In his view, society is in a continuous state of change which cannot be predicted but can only be observed.

Henry George (1839–97) was another institutionalist whose ideas gained a wide public following. He was not a professional economist, and his writings were emotional rather than analytic and systematic. He contended that private ownership of land led to the conditions of poverty that he observed in large cities. He believed that the land should belong in common to all people and that it should not be a vehicle for the concentration of wealth and power by some to the exclusion of others. He sought to discourage landownership through the levying of a heavy tax on land. George became known as the advocate for a single tax on land through his book *Progress and Poverty,* and this idea continues to attract many adherents.[6]

Modern Value Theory.   Current-day value theory rejects most of the elements of classical value theory. It views land as equal to the other factors of production in priority of claim. It does not regard land income and value as residual; rather, it sees land as economically mobile, in the sense that several parcels may compete with each other for a given use. Furthermore, it does not regard rent as an unearned increment or surplus, but as payment for the benefits to be obtained from the use of land. As Richard U. Ratcliff, the foremost proponent of modern value theory, has stated:

> We view land as a factor of production with an economic behavior little different from that of the other basic factors. We incline to the view that rent is a return to land for the contribution that it makes in creating want—satisfying goods and services; rent is compensation for the productivity of land in the same sense that wages are the payment for the productivity of labor. Land is valuable because it is scarce in supply in relation to the demand for its services. Rent is no more unearned than wages or interest, save in an abstract sense; in the same sense, wages might be considered in part a return on innate human intelligence. Rent is not exploitative, for it takes nothing from the worker, from the owner of capital goods, or from the consumer; rent is a measure of contribution not of extraction or reduction.[7]

---

[6] Henry George, *Progress and Poverty* (New York: Robert Schalkenbach Foundation, 1948).

[7] Richard U. Ratcliff, *Urban Land Economics* (New York: McGraw-Hill, 1949), p. 365.

The modern view of land value attaches no relevance to the distinction between price-determined and price-determining goods. Instead, it applies the neoclassical equilibrium explanation of prices to land. It attaches no special significance to the marginal units or their cost of production, although it would not abrogate the concepts of the intensive and extensive margins.

Modern value theory has undoubtedly developed to explain land prices in urbanized, Western societies. Older explanations of agricultural land values failed to take account of the contributions of human beings in the production of urban locations. The "original and indestructible powers of the soil" visualized in Ricardian rent theory are not the value-creating forces of city sites. Modern land values can in most cases be regarded as the direct result of the application of labor, capital, and entrepreneurship. Land in this sense is made by human beings and not a gift of God, and it provides differential advantages to some owners over others. These advantages and the returns they yield are obtained by bearing risks and incurring costs.

Market Value versus Other Types of Value

Many definitions of market value have been proposed or espoused over the years. These definitions spell out requirements or assumptions of value. For example, some definitions emphasize that value is the "highest price" that could be expected in an arm's-length transaction. Others cite the requirements of "fairness," "arm's-length bargaining," lack of "duress," and a "prudent" buyer or stress the future aspects of value by defining it as "the present worth of future benefits." Still others have noted that value is the price that *should* prevail in a viable, active market of well-informed sellers and purchasers.

Market Value under Perfect Competition. Most definitions of market value contain one or more elements of market value under conditions of perfect competition. Just as physicists consider the theoretical implications of an unattainable perfect vacuum, so economists and appraisers may find it useful to begin their analysis of value by considering the nature of value in an unattainable perfect market.

In a perfect market, the following criteria must be met:

1. Homogeneity of products.
2. A large number of buyers and sellers.
3. Buyers and sellers small in size, such that none can influence the market price.
4. No external influence.
5. Agreement as to expectations of the future.
6. Complete knowledge by all buyers and sellers as to possible uses.

If these criteria were met, the market price would, by definition, equal value, as shown in Exhibit 1.

In the model of pure competition, sellers can sell all of the product they desire at the market price, average revenue *(AR)*. They receive for each additional (marginal) unit the same amount of additional (marginal) revenue that they receive for all other units. In order to maximize

EXHIBIT 1

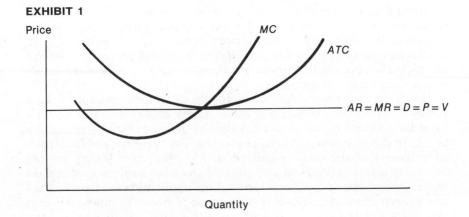

profit, they tend to operate at the level of output at which marginal cost *(MC)* equals marginal revenue. In long-run, pure competition, no profit is shown. However, a fair, reasonable profit is included as a cost. This cost is the amount that must be received by producers to induce them to stay in business. Also, in long-run, pure competitive average total costs will reach a minimum at the point of tangency with the average revenue curve. Under these conditions, $AR = MR = D = P = V$. By definition, value equals the price that would occur in a perfect market.

Needless to say, the requirements for a perfect market cannot be attained. Moreover, the real estate market is usually considered to be one of the least perfect markets: no two properties are exactly alike; there are few buyers and sellers at any given time; a buyer or a seller may be able to influence the market; there is much external influence (by government), and there is usually disagreement as to (1) a property's most profitable use and (2) expectations of the future. In contrast, the wheat market is regarded as relatively perfect. Wheat is homogeneous within grades; there are a large number of buyers and sellers; a single buyer or seller cannot usually affect the market price; and a futures market helps dilute the impact of differing expectations for the current market price.

Since the real estate market is relatively imperfect, one might (as did the classical economists) tend to view real estate primarily from the monopoly side.[8] But even if it is granted that each parcel contains

---

[8] See Edward Chamberlin, *Monopolistic Competition* (Cambridge, Mass: Harvard University Press, 1939), appendix D, "Urban Rent as a Monopoly Income," pp. 214–17, for the viewpoint that income to real estate represents a monopoly return. This viewpoint derives from the contention that each parcel of land is unique in its locational characteristics and, therefore, cannot be considered as in direct competition with other parcels of real estate in supplying specific locational needs. According to Chamberlin, the locational characteristic of urban land is different from that of agricultural land. Urban land carries its market with it, and the rent paid represents the value of the monopoly privilege of providing retail services *at that particular place.*

some unique (and thus monopolistic) elements, it is also true that each parcel must compete with close substitutes. This aspect of "economic mobility" lies at the heart of the modern theory of land value. In this view, real estate, like most economic goods, is regarded as falling into the category of monopolistic competition. Goods that fall into this category contain unique, monopolistic elements, yet are in competition with close substitutes.

In a book on appraisal terminology jointly sponsored by the American Institute of Real Estate Appraisers and the Society of Real Estate Appraisers, the following definition of market value is offered.[9]

> The highest price in terms of money which a property will bring in a competitive and open market under all conditions requisite to a fair sale, the buyer and seller, each acting prudently, knowledgeably and assuming the price is not affected by undue stimulus.
>
> Implicit in this definition is the consummation of a sale as of a specified date and the passing of title from seller to buyer under conditions whereby:
>
> 1. Buyer and seller are typically motivated.
> 2. Both parties are well informed or well advised, and each acts in what he or she considers his or her own best interest.
> 3. A reasonable time is allowed for exposure in the open market.
> 4. Payment is made in cash or its equivalent.
> 5. Financing, if any, is on terms generally available in the community at the specified date and typical for the property type in its locale.
> 6. The price represents a normal consideration for the property sold unaffected by special financing amounts and/or terms, services, fees, costs, or credits incurred in the transaction.

Note that the requirements of this definition are somewhat similar to those of perfect competition: there is a competitive, open market; the buyer and seller must act prudently; no undue stimulus is allowed; and the buyer and seller are well informed and typically motivated. Yet the requirements are not as stringent as the requirements of perfect competition. It is a definition that has been characterized as a "semiperfect market" definition of value.[10]

Market Value versus Investment Value. Investment value is the worth of a property to an individual or an organization (e.g., a business firm or a government agency). The individual or organization may be an owner, a seller, or a potential buyer whose investment values may or may not equal market value. The owners' or sellers' investment value is the minimum price that they would be willing to accept, whereas the buyers' investment value is the maximum price that they would be willing to pay.

Both buyers and sellers establish their investment values by assessing the risk and future productivity of a property in relation to their needs and preferences. Although a buyer and a seller might concur in their

---

[9] Byrl N. Boyce, ed., *Real Estate Appraisal Terminology* (Cambridge, Mass.: Ballinger, 1975), p. 137.

[10] Halbert C. Smith, "Value Concepts as a Source of Disparity among Appraisals," *Appraisal Journal*, vol. 45, no. 2 (April 1977), pp. 203–9.

analyses of a property's risk and productivity characteristics, their individual needs would seldom be the same. For example, a seller may need funds for other purposes, while a buyer may be seeking an investment medium. Or a seller may have used all of the tax shelter benefits that a property can offer him, while a buyer may be able to attain additional tax shelter from the same property.

Buyers and sellers often disagree in their assessments of a property's risk and productivity. Forecasts of income sources and amounts may vary between buyer and seller. Similarly, expenses may be more controllable by the buyer than by the seller.

Competition among buyers for similar properties and competition among sellers offering properties results in transactions. The transaction prices for similar properties form a distribution that can be used in estimating market value. The greater the similarity among properties, the more active the market, and the more knowledgeable the buyers and sellers, the tighter the distribution of prices around the mean value will be. Since the mean value of the distribution of investment values would be the best estimate of market value, the concepts of investment value and market value are linked through the competitive market process.

It should be pointed out that each transaction price will be equal to or above the seller's investment value and equal to or below the buyer's investment value. In a viable, competitive market, competition among sellers of similar properties precludes an individual seller from extracting the maximum investment value from a potential buyer. Similarly, competition among buyers precludes an individual buyer from requiring a particular seller to accept a minimum reservation price for a property. Thus, a ceiling for transaction prices is established by competition among sellers and a floor for transaction prices is established by competition among buyers. Individual transaction prices are negotiated between this ceiling and floor, with market value conceptually being the most probable selling price.

Other Types of Value. Types of value other than market value and investment value are sometimes discussed in relation to real estate issues or transactions. None of them is conceptually so important as market value or investment value. However, the concept of market value may be clarified by defining some of these other types of value.

> *Assessed value:* A dollar amount assigned to taxable property by an assessor for the purpose of taxation; frequently a statutorily determined percentage of market value.
>
> *Condemnation value:* Value sought in condemnation proceedings is market value. In the instance of a partial taking, adjustments to the value of the part taken may be made for damages or special benefits to the remainder property.
>
> *Excess value:* Value over and above market value which is ascribable to a lease that guarantees contract rental income in excess of market rental at the time of appraisal.
>
> *Forced "value"; liquidation "value":* The price paid in forced sale or purchase when time is not sufficient to permit negotiations resulting in

the payment of market value; should be called "forced price" or "liquidation price."

Going concern value: The value of the business enterprise and the real estate it occupies; includes goodwill.

Insurable value: The value of the destructible portions of a property.

Intangible value: Value not imputable to any part of the physical property, such as the excess value attributable to a favorable lease, or the value attributable to goodwill.

Leasehold value: The value of a leasehold interest; the right to use, enjoyment, and profit existing by virtue of the rights granted under a lease instrument.

Mortgage value: Value for mortgage lending purposes.

Stablized value: A long-term value estimate which excludes from consideration an abnormal relation of supply and demand; or a value estimate which excludes from consideration any transitory condition that may cause excessive cost of construction and an excessive sale price.

Several of these types of value are essentially derived from market value. They simply reflect specific purposes or uses to which market value is put. For example, assessed value, condemnation value, insurable value, leasehold value, mortgage value, and stabilized value each reflects a specific purpose or use for market value.

Value Theories and Appraisal Techniques

The various theories of land value have been adapted to the appraisal process. The classical theory—relying upon the ideas of the labor cost of production, land value as a residual, and the distinction between price and value—is manifested in the cost approach of the traditional appraisal process. This process sees an improvement's value as deriving primarily from its cost new. To the extent that value losses have occurred from this cost new, depreciation is subtracted. Many elements of depreciation are also measured by their "costs to cure." In the traditional appraisal process site value is treated as a separate problem (and thus, in a sense, residual). (See Chapter 15.)

The marginal utility theory is directly applied in the income capitalization approach. Expected future earnings are discounted at the rate of interest necessary to compensate employment of the capital in another use. The level of future earnings is established by the price obtainable from the last (marginal) unit.

The classical theory enters the income capitalization approach in the land (site) residual technique. In this technique, income allocable to labor, capital, and entrepreneurship (as manifested in the improvements) is subtracted from a property's total net operating income. The remaining (residual) income is assigned to the land and is capitalized at the appropriate interest (discount) rate.

Highest and best (most profitable) use is an application of the land residual technique and thus relies upon both classical and marginal utility theories. As shown in Exhibit 2, the estimation of highest and best use involves the estimation of the income residual to land under alternative uses.[11] The use producing the highest present value of the land is its highest and best use. If all of the alternative uses can be expected to produce income for the same time period and can be discounted at the same rate, the use providing the highest income will yield the highest present value—and thus will be the highest and best use. (See Chapter 13.)

Note that in Exhibit 2 the least costly improvement (the store building) is the site's highest and best use. It should be evident that it is not cost, size, or total income but the relationship among these elements that establishes highest and best use.

EXHIBIT 2

	Use		
	Office Building	Apartment Building	Store
Cost	$200,000	$250,000	$180,000
Net operating income	35,000	40,000	35,000
Return to improvements (12%)	24,000	30,000	21,600
Return to land	11,000	10,000	13,400
Value of land (at 10%)	110,000	100,000	134,000

The neoclassical theory of market equilibrium serves as the basis for the comparable sales approach in appraisal.[12] In this approach, the market prices of properties similar, or comparable, to a property being appraised are assumed to reflect its value. Adjustments to the price of each comparable are allowed for: (1) transactional differences (financing and conditions of sale) between the comparable and the subject property; (2) market conditions that varied between the time of sale of the comparable and the time of appraisal of the subject property; (3) locational differences; and (4) physical differences. Nevertheless, the essential assumption of the approach is that the transaction prices represent the equilibrium forces of supply and demand in the market. (See Chapter 14.)

Current Issues Involving Value Concepts

The juxtaposition of modern value theory with the older theories, especially classical theory, has led a few appraisal scholars to question the relevance and applicability of the widely accepted definitions and procedures of current appraisal practice. Modern value theory rejects the "semiperfect market" definition of market value as unrealistic. Transactions for comparables and a subject property frequently do not

---

[11] The example is taken from Halbert C. Smith, *Real Estate Appraisal* (Columbus, Ohio: Grid, 1976), p. 7.

involve well-informed buyers and sellers; "undue" stimulus often exists; transactions sometimes occur at less than arm's length; the highest expected price is perhaps seldom attained; financing may not be obtained at generally available terms; payment may not be in cash or its equivalent; and a reasonable time may not be allowed for exposure to the market.

In recognition of these types of difficulties with traditional definitions of market value, Ratcliff has suggested that market value be defined as the most probable selling price. In this definition, the highest price and the other requirements of a "semiperfect market" are no longer necessary. Rather, the market is accepted as it is—with all of its imper-

EXHIBIT 3

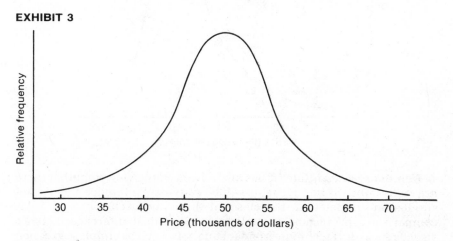

Price (thousands of dollars)

fections and irrationalities. The appraiser's job becomes one of predicting a property's market price by giving full consideration to all of the imperfections—not by assuming them away. As Ratcliff states the case, "In the absence of instructions to the contrary, the appraiser must assume that the client seeks a prediction of market value under conditions as they actually exist; for it is under these conditions that his decision must be made or his problem must be solved."[13]

Probability Distributions for Value. If valuation is a matter of prediction, and if value is the most probable transaction price, it follows that there are less probable—even least probable—prices. In other words, value is composed of a range of values, and a probability distribution is associated with that range. For example, a property might have a most probable transaction price of $50,000 with a probability distribution as shown in Exhibit 3. Note that this distribution is a symmetrical normal distribution, indicating that prices the same distance on either side of $50,000 enjoy the same probability of occurring.

---

[12] The comparable sales approach is also referred to as the sales comparison or market data approach.

[13] Richard U. Ratcliff, *Valuation for Real Estate Decisions* (Santa Cruz, Calif.: Democrat Press, 1972), p. 12.

A more realistic distribution may be one that is skewed toward the lower prices, such as that shown in Exhibit 4. In this distribution, it is less probable that the transaction price would go above $55,000 than that it would go below $45,000. Indeed, it is about as probable that the price would go below $35,000 as that it would go above $55,000.

EXHIBIT 4

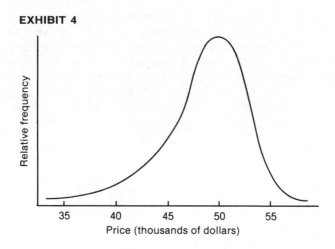

Price (thousands of dollars)

New Approaches. Ratcliff has also advanced the viewpoint that there are really only two approaches to value—statistical inference and market simulation—rather than the classical three approaches of cost, sales comparison, and income capitalization. Statistical inference includes various statistical techniques of data analysis, such as simple regression analysis, multiple regression analysis, factor analysis, and parametric and nonparametric probability analysis.

In place of the traditional comparable sales approach, Ratcliff proposes a manual regression procedure, in which comparables and the subject property are rated according to various features (such as location, neighborhood, and physical condition). Each rating is multiplied by the feature's weight to obtain a weighted rating. The weighted ratings and selling prices are then plotted on a graph, and a straight line is fitted visually to the plotted points. The selling price of the subject property can then be inferred from the graph. For example, consider the appraisal of a single-family residence shown in Exhibits 5 and 6.[14]

Note that only the characteristics causing value differences among the properties were included. All of the properties were located in the same neighborhood; thus, location and neighborhood were not included as productivity features producing value differences. A sale price of about $26,000 can be inferred from the visually constructed regression line.

Market simulation involves determining the way in which market

---

[14] The example is taken from Smith, *Real Estate Appraisal,* pp. 134–36.

EXHIBIT 5
Statistical Inference: Single-Family Residence

Productivity Feature	Weight	Rating/Weighted Rating						Subject
		A	B	C	D	E	F	
Space utilization	25	3/75	3/75	3/75	1/25	1/25	3/75	2/50
Visual appeal.....	20	3/60	1/20	4/80	3/60	2/40	2/40	3/60
Heating and cooling	10	4/40	4/40	4/40	4/40	4/40	1/10	4/40
Physical condition	20	2/40	1/20	3/60	2/40	2/40	2/40	2/40
Maintenance cost..........	15	2/30	1/15	3/45	2/30	2/30	2/30	2/30
Site	10	3/30	2/20	4/40	1/10	2/20	3/30	1/10
	100	275	190	340	205	195	225	230
Selling price ($000)		24.0	26.5	22.5	27.0	27.5	25.0	?

participants arrive at prices and then replicating that process. For example, if buyers typically set prices for a particular type of property by means of a gross multiplier (monthly or annual), the appraiser would apply such a multiplier to the income of the property in order to predict the most probable selling price. Or if buyers establish a price by estimating the cost of a new, substitute property, this procedure would be employed by the appraiser. Other procedures used by the market might include the capitalization of stabilized net operating income and the capitalization of cash flows. Any such process used by market participants would be employed by the appraiser in the market simulation approach.

EXHIBIT 6
Scatter Diagram: Weighted Ratings and Prices

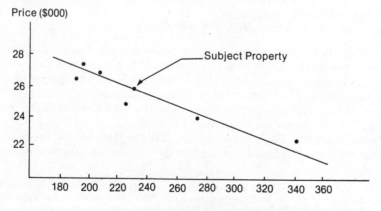

A Conceptual Framework for Technological Advances

The Ratcliffian framework provides a convenient structure for technological advances in data analysis.[15] Statistical inference accommodates such applications as multiple regression analysis, factor analysis, and probability tests for significant differences. Market simulation includes such applications as computerized cash flow analysis and capitalization, sensitivity analysis, and net present value analysis.

Multiple Regression Analysis. Multiple regression analysis is one of the most powerful and useful statistical techniques applicable to appraisal. It requires a relatively large number of observations (properties) and is performed by computers, using standardized programs. Least squares regression is used to estimate the relationships among the independent variables (value-determining characteristics) and the dependent variable (transaction prices). These relationships are expressed in the following form:

$$Y = a + b_1 X_1 + b_2 X_2 + b_3 X_3 + \cdots b_n X_n + e$$

where

Y = Dependent variable (price)
a = Constant (Y-intercept)
b = Coefficients
X = Independent variables (value-determining characteristics)
e = Unexplained variance

For example, one recent regression analysis of 43 single-family residential properties produced the following relationships:

$$Y = 4.58 + 0.332 X_1 - 0.84 X_2 + 2.19 X_3 + 1.84 X_4 + 1.42 X_5$$

where

Y = Price ÷ 1,000
X_1 = Square feet of livable area ÷ 100
X_2 = Effective age
X_3 = Ranking of location
X_4 = Ranking of construction
X_5 = Lot size in square feet ÷ 1,000

A property considered to be in the same market would be appraised by substituting its values of the independent variables into the equation and carrying out the arithmetic procedures. Standard errors of the b coefficients would indicate whether they are significantly different from zero, and the standard error of the estimate would indicate the degree of dispersion around the estimated value of Y.

Factor Analysis. Factor analysis is a statistical technique for reducing a large number of variables into a few factors. Usually there is consider-

---

[15] The Ratcliffian framework omits the traditional cost approach, which is regarded as conceptually irrelevant and practically unreliable for estimating market value. Replacement cost is an acceptable technique under market simulation when a new property is a viable alternative to the purchase of a subject property.

able correlation among several of the variables, and they can be combined and represented by one factor. For example, the square feet of livable area, the square feet of the site, and the number of stories may all be represented by one factor called size. The statistical procedures are beyond the scope of this chapter; they involve the rotation of axes among the observed values of the variables to determine which ones are most closely related.

Although one recent study showed that factor analysis in combination with multiple regression analysis provided no greater predicting power than did multiple regression analysis by itself, factor analysis should not be dismissed.[16] It may be useful for complicated properties involving large numbers of variables whose impact upon value is not understood.

Probability Analysis. Various probability applications can be used to test whether particular values are contained within a population or are significantly different from other values. Parametric applications include tests of differences between means and proportions. They require a determination of the probability that a value falls within a specified distance (measured in standard errors) from the mean of a standard distribution. For example, the probability that a site (which varies in size from the mean size site) is inside or outside of the population (market) of relevant sites can be determined.

Nonparametric statistics include such tests as chi-square, the sign test, the median test, the Mann-Whitney U test, the Wald-Wolfowitz runs test, and the Kruskal-Wallis H test. These tests require no assumptions about the shape of the parameter distribution, yet allow the analyst to test for significant differences between various aspects of data sets. For example, chi-square is used as a test of significance when data are expressed in frequencies, and the H test is used to test whether or not a group of independent samples is from the same or different populations.

Cash Flow Analysis. Investment values can be calculated for after-financing, aftertax cash flow. The present values of forecast cash flows for a given number of years (say ten) can be calculated and summed to obtain the investment value for a given investor. The discount rate used must meet the investor's requirements.

Internal Rate of Return and Sensitivity Analysis. If a given price is assumed, an investor's internal rate of return can be calculated. The effects of changes in income or expenses on the return can be calculated to show its sensitivity to such changes. (See Chapter 18.)

Net Present Value. The net present value of a property is its value after capital outlays have been deducted from its discounted net income or cash flow. The property's net present value can be estimated and compared with the net present values of other investment properties having comparable risk characteristics.

All of these techniques may be used by investors in determining the prices they will pay for income-producing properties. Thus, they can be used by an appraiser under the market simulation approach. The

---

[16] Frank W. Schieber, Jr., "Factor Analysis in Income Estimation for Real Estate Valuation," University of Florida, unpublished M.A. thesis, 1976.

relevant value concept recognizes that market value is the expected value of transaction prices of competitive properties.

Summary

Concepts of value have their origin in economic theory. The chapter traces such concepts from the classical economists through the marginal utility and neoclassical economists. Each economic school of thought has contributed particular insights into the nature of value—the supply side has been emphasized by the classical economists; the demand side by the marginal utility economists; a synthesis of supply and demand by the neoclassical economists; and specific points of criticism and analysis by the institutionalists.

Modern value theory and its applications to property valuation are discussed at some length. This view holds that urban land values are created by human beings and are no more the result of exploitative or monopolistic aspects of the market system than are labor or capital. Rent is a return to land for its productivity and for the risk that must be borne to hold land.

The concept of market value is related to investment value and some other types of value. Market value as defined under perfect competition and "semiperfect" competition is contrasted with market value defined as the most probable selling price. The most probable selling price is best predicted by the use of a two-approach system—statistical inference and market simulation. Such a system has the added advantage of providing a logical framework for technological advances in professional appraisal.

PROPERTY INCOME

James H. Boykin

*J*AMES H. BOYKIN, PhD, MAI, SRPA, *Alfred L. Blake Professor of Real Estate, School of Business, Virginia Commonwealth University, Richmond Virginia.*

Associate professor and director, Real Estate and Urban Land Development Program. Member, Education Coordinating Committee, Virginia Real Estate Commission. Consultant to numerous developers, financial institutions, and agencies. Member, Editorial Board, Appraisal Journal. *Author of numerous articles in* Appraisal Journal, Mortgage Banker, Realtor, Real Estate Today, Skyscraper Management, Real Estate Review, Journal of Small Business Management, Real Estate Appraiser, and The Valuer *(Australian Institute of Valuers). Author,* Financing Real Estate *(Lexington, Mass.: Lexington Books, 1978);* Mortgage Loan Underwriting *(1975); and* Industrial Potential of the Central City, Research Report no. 21 *(Washington, D.C.: Urban Land Institute, 1973). Editorial consultant, The Appraisal of Real Estate, 6th ed. (Chicago: American Institute of Real Estate Appraisers, 1973); and* Industrial Real Estate: An Annotated Bibliography *(Washington, D.C.: Society of Industrial Realtors, 1969).*

The purpose of this chapter is to explain how property values are related to property income as well as how a variety of conditions cause changes in the level of property income. The two basic categories of property income are gross income and net income. Our concern here is with maximizing the stream of net income relative to the capital invested in land and building.

Income and Market Operation

The income stream sets the upper limit of affordable construction costs. (The construction costs, in turn, set another upper limit—the amount that an investor is justified in paying for a property.)

Rents and Return. A prospective investor—either an equity investor or a mortgage lender—should consider an income-producing property primarily from the standpoint of its ability to generate income that will cover the expected expenses and still provide a desired return. The seller of a property or his agent may give any number of reasons why the rents have not been raised for several years, but may hasten to add that there is a potential for increasing these rents substantially once the property has been purchased and placed under new management. The present rents may indeed be low, but has the correct reason been given? The present owner obviously has nothing against earning a higher return on his investment. Therefore, given a situation in which the rents and the return are low, the prospective investor must analyze the condition of the property, its relative attractiveness and level of maintenance, and the rental market for properties of the type under consideration.

Gross Rents. Among the first items that a prospective investor should obtain are copies of all leases. These should be examined in order to ascertain lease lengths, lease expiration dates, rentals, and any concessions that have been made by the owner. An office building nearly all of whose leases were expiring within the next few months would obviously not be as desirable as one whose lease expiration dates were evenly distributed over the next year.

The absence of signed leases—this is sometimes the case for lower income tenant property—should alert the investor to be cautious about purchasing a property. Whether there are one-year leases or multiyear leases or verbal short-term leases, the prospective investor must determine the vacancy and collection losses. If the owner has difficulty in recalling this ratio and can only make such general comments as "we seldom have any vacancies" or "the occupancy is quite high," it is necessary to check out the vacancy rate. One way to do this is to ascertain the property management commission rate and then to divide that into the commissions earned over the past year. For example, if on the average the leases called for a $200 monthly rental over the past year, the potential gross income for a 20-unit apartment building would have been $48,000. If the property management commission on the basis of a 6 percent rate was $2,592, then the vacancy and collection losses would have been $4,800. Another way to determine these losses is to compare the collected rent with the potential gross income of the building.

As the leases are studied, the reviewer should determine their "netness." If the lease requires that the tenant pay all expenses, then all of the rental would be available to the owner. This is termed an absolute net lease, or sometimes a triple net lease. Thus, if two 20-unit apartment properties are being considered for purchase, and both have a $200 a month rental income per unit, the one which requires the tenant to pay more of the operating expenses would be the more valuable property.

The sharply rising cost of utilities and property taxes has become a major concern for investors. Sometimes it is possible to use "expense stops" that will either partially or completely shift such costs to the tenant. This strategy becomes especially important for poorly insulated older properties with central heating or air conditioning systems. For such properties, metering the fuel to each individual unit usually requires very expensive conversion costs. In the long run, it may become advantageous for the owner to bear the expense of properly insulating a property to reduce fuel costs. Otherwise, the tenants will eventually choose less expensive quarters.

The inflation of real propery values has been quite attractive to investors upon selling or refinancing real property. However, increasing property values cause higher real estate taxes, which take a greater share of the income available to the investor. Higher real estate taxes can reduce the value of a property if its income is not increased proportionately.

Although the existing rentals may initially appear to be high enough to justify the purchase price for a property, the investor must consider the possibility that concessions have been made. Concessions that would overstate the actual rental received include unusually low security deposits, the provision by the owner of draperies in apartments or of unusually expensive interior partitioning and mechanical equipment in stores or offices, and rent-free occupancy for several months.

Expenses. As has been stated, the investor should determine the netness of the leases and whether the expense-sharing arrangement between the owner and the tenants is typical and will maintain a desired level of income for the owner over the term of the leases. It may be necessary to reconstruct the owner's income statement inasmuch as there is often deferred maintenance during the last year of the holding period. Deferring maintenace enables the owner to increase the net operating income of the property over a short period, which in turn gives the property the appearance of having a higher value. To determine the normal expense burden and thus avoid overvaluing a property, income and expense statements should be obtained for a three-year period.

If the owner can disguise operating (or periodic) expenses as capital expenditures, then the reported net operating income would be unjustifiably high. Sometimes it is helpful to use a standarized operating expense guideline for a particular type of property. Standardized operating expense ratios may be a useful screening device. They can enable the prospective investor to gauge the reasonableness of the reported expenses. If a particular expense departs considerably from the standard ratios, closer attention should be given to it.

It is usually necessary to reconstruct the income statement supplied by the owner in order to analyze insurance premiums and recurring decorating expenses, eliminate franchise taxes, add income taxes, and properly report management fees. The management fee should be based on "collectible income" or "effective gross income," that is, on the income that remains after vacancy and collection losses have been allowed for. It should be paid only on the rents actually collected, not on the rents specified in the leases. This arrangement gives the property manager an incentive to pursue slow-paying tenants and maintain high occupancy. The expense statement should include an allowance for short-life items which would need to be replaced over the productive life of the building, the investor's anticipated holding period, or the mortgage term. Otherwise, the net operating income will be overstated and the property value inflated.

Borrowed Money. A potential investor in a real property investment is concerned about whether the property can adequately secure his equity investment and be able to obtain a mortgage sufficient to complement his down payment. Thus, he turns his attention to the amount of borrowed money available for this class and age of property while simultaneously comparing the probable debt service and operating expenses with the probable income that the property will generate. If the property appears to be a sound investment that will have high occupancy and minimal income fluctuation, and will require modest repairs, then the strategy would be to increase the ratio of borrowed capital funds to equity funds. An important consideration at this stage is whether the property can carry itself; that is, the rental income should more than offset the mortgage payments and operating expenses. If this is unlikely, then a smaller loan should be obtained—if such a revised mortgage arrangement is acceptable to the investor.

Another mortgage-financing concern of the investor is the cost of borrowed money (i.e., the interest rate and term, the ability to obtain secondary mortgage financing, and the ability to refinance at a later date without onerous prepayment terms). In some cases, lenders require a participation in the profits or the income stream of a property. Depending on how this participation is structured, the investment can vary from attractive to unprofitable. In the tight money markets of the late 1960s and mid-1970s, such participation financing, which then favored lenders, was disparagingly labeled "arm and leg financing" by some developers and investors. At that time many potential investors shunned this type of financing or simply awaited the return of more favorable terms.

Depreciation. There are two major concerns when considering depreciation for an investment property. The first is the present condition of the property and the degree of depreciation (value loss) actually suffered by the property, as well as the probable extent of the repairs needed during the investment period or over the anticipated remaining useful life of the property. This period should comfortably exceed the mortgage term. The second is the depreciation schedules for various classes of property permitted by the Internal Revenue Service. For example, two residential rental properties of the same age may operate under two different depreciation schedules if one is owned by an original owner using an accelerated depreciation while the other is owned by a second owner who acquired the property as a used property (see Chapter 9).

Return. There is no dispute among real estate investors that a real estate investment should produce an adequate return. However, each investor uses different criteria for judging the soundness and profitability of such investments. These diverse criteria arise from the different motivations that prompt investment in real estate. Some investors prefer a reliable, though conservative, income stream. Other investors use real estate to shelter income from other earnings. Still other investors seek sizable profits from the resale of real estate.

There are two principal classes of investors in real estate—equity investors and complementary investors. Equity investors are organized through a variety of legal forms of individual ownership, coownership, or group ownership, such as sole proprietorship, joint tenancy, tenancy in common, and tenancy by the entirety. They may be organized in limited and general partnerships, corporations, and real estate investment trusts. Complementary investors are institutional investors which provide debt capital. This group includes financial intermediaries such as savings banks, commercial banks, savings and loan associations, mutual savings banks, finance companies, credit unions, life insurance companies, and even pension funds.

Whatever the investor's nature or motivation, there are three basic techniques by which the profitability of an investment may be evaluated. These are (1) return on the value of the property, (2) return on the investor's equity prior to income taxes, and (3) return on the investor's equity after taxes. In addition, an investment should be analyzed over its projected optimum holding period to reveal the probable return on investment (ROI) from its income stream and the proceeds from the sale of the property.

Each of the three tests of profitability has its particular purpose. All of the tests can enlighten the investor. Using the first test, a property's net operating income (NOI) is divided by its purchase price. This test considers the property as if it were unencumbered by mortgages. This rate is quite informative when it is compared to the rate for other similar properties or to the investor's desired return. The rate can enable an investor to ascertain whether the property produces a sufficient return to warrant an investment in it.

The second measure of profitability (sometimes known as "cash on cash") is a comparison of the cash flow generated by a property with the owner's equity investment. This analysis includes a consideration of the influence of financing on the return from the property. A key consideration, from the point of view of both the equity investor and the mortgage investor, is whether the property generates sufficient income to cover the operating expenses and mortgage payments (debt service) while still maintaining an ample margin of safety.

The third test considers the tax impact of the investment. Ideally, a property will have positive cash flow that more than covers the operating expenses and debt service. However, many investors in the upper tax brackets will accept a large negative cash flow. Such investors may apply the associated "tax loss" to offset other income, thus reducing the taxes on that income.

Returns and Construction. Before constructing a building or a project, both the developer and the lender ought to be assured (1) that there is a strong market for the space it provides, (2) that the income it produces will at least offset the operating expenses and the mortgage debt service, and (3) that the value created will at least equal the cost of producing the property. This last consideration is illustrated by two terms used by mortgage lenders—"economic value" and "physical value." A developer may try to justify a mortgage loan on the basis of the expected cost of creating a project. However, this rationale is certain to be rejected by mortgage lenders. What the developer should emphasize is the present worth of the property as revealed by the sale of similar properties or by capitalizing a stabilized income stream generated by the property.

If a property's economic value is to be maximized, then it is imperative that the developer use great care in:

1. Selecting an area with a strong market potential for the proposed project. It is far safer to begin by identifying a potential market for a project than to begin by obtaining a site or devising a concept and subsequently trying to "fit" the market to the site or the concept.
2. Choosing a highly accessible site of the proper size—neither so large that it jeopardizes the developer's ability to hold the property nor so small that it prevents a properly designed development or necessitates acquiring additional property later at much higher prices.
3. Obtaining a skillfully conducted market analysis to:
   (a) Determine whether there is a sufficient demand for the proposed project.
   (b) Account for existing and probable future competition.
   (c) Provide information that will enable the architects to design an appealing and profitable development.
4. Constructing the project according to the information provided by the market analyst and the architect.
5. Skillfully managing the project so as to maximize the appeal, marketability, physical soundness, ease of maintenance, and net operating income of the project.

In considering a potential project, it is most important that the developer avoid "wishing his way to success." A tough-minded examination of all relevant information should be made by the developer before he commits himself or the funds of investors to the project. Sometimes options can be used to control a property prior to its purchase in order to raise the money needed, to study various pertinent matters, or to await certain desired municipal actions. However, since the use of an option generally forces the prospective purchaser to make some concessions in price or terms, it can be argued that most of the necessary research should have been done before approaching the property owner with an offer to purchase.

One of the greatest potential errors that a developer can make is to underestimate the time required to launch and market a project. Invariably there are delays at every stage. These delays may be caused by government inspections, permits, and approvals, especially those involving environmental concerns. The anticipated opening date for a local street or an interstate highway interchange may be delayed for years or even canceled. There may be delays due to work stoppages or slow delivery of materials. There may be unanticipated legal difficulties and engineering redesign requirements. The competition may be keener than expected. All of these increase the time, and cost of holding a property.

Some developers are inclined to "buy anything as long as it is cheap." This unsound strategy has caused some developers to fail—especially during the era of gasoline shortages that began in the fall of 1974. Remote tracts of land, although relatively cheap, may fail to generate sufficient demand for an intended use. In addition, a completed project may not be competitive with other projects until public utilities have been extended to it. Decisions based upon estimates of the availability of such utilities may be quite risky.

Cyclic Operation. The owner of an income property is not only concerned with the initial return on his investment but also desires to maintain a desired rate of return on the investment over the term of the leases. In recent years, expected returns have been undermined by rapidly escalating maintenance, fuel, and utility costs as well as rapidly rising property taxes. These mounting expenses have eroded net operating income—even on one-year apartment leases. Multiyear leases can create even greater revenue problems. To prevent this, astute owners have begun using various "expense stops" or escalator clauses. Escalator clauses shift part of the rising operating expenses to the tenant in order to maintain an acceptable level of income for the property owner.

Such cities as New York and Washington, D.C., have enacted rent controls for apartment properties. In these cities, investors left with unprofitable investments have deferred maintenance in order to retain a positive cash flow. In some dire situations they have even abandoned their properties—leaving the cities with rapidly deteriorating properties and a greater shortage of sound housing than would exist otherwise. Given such experiences, it is important to consider the municipal attitude toward rental and other property controls before investing.

Inflation has continued to push interest rates up in recent years. FHA and VA interest rates were 4 percent in 1945 and rose only 1½ percent over the next 22 years. During the 1970s these interest rates became quite volatile, changing some 20 times. In 1974 and 1975 alone they changed ten times, a high of 9½ percent being reached during the summer of 1974.

The level of interest rates influences the volume of both real estate sales and real estate construction. For instance, rising interest rates in 1955–57 caused housing starts to decline. In 1958, interest rates declined and housing starts rose. In a more recent period, 1972–75, interest rates rose from 4 percent to 11 percent[1] while housing starts declined from 2½ million units a year to less than 1 million units a year. Part of the upward pressure on interest rates has been caused by gigantic federal deficit spending. During the ten-year period from 1961 through 1970, federal deficits totaled $66.1 billion; in only one of those years was there a surplus—$3.2 billion in 1969. The forecasted deficit for 1978 was $61.3 billion, which is about equal to the entire accrued debt for the years

---

[1] Average of monthly average yields on prime commercial paper, four–six months; prime bankers' acceptances, 90 days; federal funds rate; and three-month government bills.

1961–70. Thus, the federal government's drain of funds from the private sector and pressure on interest rates will remain a key factor in the cyclic nature of real estate construction and sales.

The relative levels of demand, supply, and construction activity within a market should be closely monitored at all times. It is imperative to accurately identify the specific submarket for which a project is being developed as well as all competitively located space and service alternatives. Simply observing the relative scarcity or backlog of housing within a metropolitan area misses the essential points—being aware of the direction of urban development, the size and the amenities of existing and proposed housing, employment trends, proposed sewer line and street extension programs, the housing units scheduled for construction in the near future, and the relative demand for different types of units in different price ranges. Such concerns are pertinent to the analysis of all types of real estate development and investment. If a market is underbuilt, discover why. It may be that tenant militancy or inept municipal government housing policies have caused investors to shun this market.

Forces Affecting Rents

Inflation—Prices and Values.   Historically, an appealing attribute of real estate as an investment has been that inflation enhanced real estate values rather than eroding them, as happened with some alternative investments. Table 1 illustrates this point by showing that from 1967 through 1977 an investment in a single-family home grew by 23 percent, whereas money invested in savings accounts and common stock declined in value. In fact, common stock investment over this period, ignoring dividends, was little better than holding cash.

Changes in the Quality of Locations.   Location is perhaps more important than any other attribute of a real estate investment. This concept, however, has been overly simplified to the point of encouraging faulty decisions. A business location, for example, must be viewed in the context of an existing or a proposed enterprise, compatibility with the intended use, level of traffic flow, the accessibility of traffic, and proximity

TABLE 1
Value of One Dollar Invested in 1967

	Purchasing Power of the Dollar		
Investment	*1967*	*1972*	*1977*
Single-family home	$1.00	$1.14	$1.23
Corporate bond	1.00	1.13	1.18
Savings account	1.00	1.04	0.93
Common stock	1.00	0.95	0.58
Cash	1.00	0.80	0.55

Source: *Real Estate Status Report* (Washington, D.C.: National Association of Realtors®, October 1977), p. 4.

to the sites of other important activities such as employees' residences. In addition, a balance must be struck between the sale price or rent and the nature of the business. Not every business needs exposure to vehicular traffic or a downtown retail location. Moreover, not only the present market but future growth patterns must be considered. Business at a given site may be greatly reduced in the future by the development of interceptor sites between that site and population nodes. What is a good, easily accessible site today may be bypassed tomorrow.

It is difficult to generalize as to the proper location for a given class of tenants or business establishments. For example, one may say that the inbound side of a traffic artery (that is, the side immediately adjacent to traffic coming into a city) is a proper location for a motel. This may generally be true, but sometimes motels are more advantageously located adjacent to major industrial complexes, since sales representatives may prefer to stay close to such complexes. Clothes cleaners generally prefer to locate on the inbound side of a traffic artery so that customers may drop clothes off on the way to work in the morning. Sites on the far right corner of an outbound traffic artery are generally chosen for gasoline stations so that customers may be serviced after they have passed through a traffic signal on the way home from work. It is then relatively easy for them to reenter the artery as the outbound traffic is halted by the traffic signal.

From the above discussion on site selection it should be clear that a well-conceived business idea will not succeed unless the site is properly selected. A site that is for one activity may cost too much or may lack the necessary traffic for another use. In order to select the proper site it is necessary to understand the marketing policies of the given industry, the consumer behavior of potential customers, and population, traffic, and development trends within the given market area.

Residential site selection emphasizes convenience and privacy. A neighborhood of single-family residences should be convenient to churches, parks, stores, and schools. However, convenience to schools no longer exists where there is court-ordered busing of schoolchildren beyond their neighborhoods. Another desirable feature is access to employment centers, but without having major traffic arteries penetrate the neighborhood. The neighborhood should also be zoned for compatible uses, have adequate public services, and a reputation for safety from human assault as well as from natural hazards, such as unstable soil.

Forces Affecting Expenses

Taxes. Several different types of local taxes may influence the site selection of a business establishment. If the aggregate of local, business, inventory, personal, and real property taxes is decidedly higher in one jurisdiction than in another which provides similar amenities, then the latter community will generally be preferred. A decision to relocate to a lower tax jurisdiction may be postponed because of strong community ties; a favorable long-term lease; established linkages with adjacent establishments, suppliers, or transportation facilities; or the considerable expense of removing equipment or of recruiting and retraining new employees at another location.

Essential considerations in the analysis of local real estate taxes are: (1) the balance and diversity of revenue sources, (2) the age and quality of taxable real properties, (3) the level of public service expenditures such as welfare and fire and police protection, and (4) the share of the local revenue burden that is carried by real property—especially income property. Consideration of each of these features will enable the analyst to make a reasonably reliable judgment about the probable level of the real estate tax burden and about the impact of that burden upon the expenses for a particular property.

Persistent high levels of inflation exert an upward push on property taxes. In response to this ballooning expense, competent investors insist that escalation clauses be used to safeguard their expected level of return.

The burden of real estate taxes is often not fully expressed when it is related to the value of a property. Although annual real estate taxes may be only 3 percent to 5 percent of the value of a property, the burden of such taxes becomes much more severe when the taxes are related to the net operating income of a property. If, for instance, a property produces a 10 percent return on value before taxes, then a 5 percent property tax would be equivalent to 50 percent of the net operating income. This situation is illustrated by the following example:

Property value	$100,000
Property tax (5% × property value)	5,000
Return on value (10%)	10,000
Tax as a percentage of net operating income*	5,000/10,000 = 50%

* This could be any defined income, such as cash flow before or after income taxes.

Utilities. Utility expenses should be viewed from several perspectives. If public utilities are unavailable, then private facilities must be provided. Private water and sewer systems are often inefficient or incapable of providing a sustained level of required services. If private or public systems are inadequate, operating costs may increase due to the levying of special assessments to fund additional facilities. Otherwise, makeshift arrangements may have to be devised by the owner or even by the tenants. The problem cannot be solved simply by shifting the burden to the tenant since less expensive and more reliable service will invariably be available elsewhere.

Other Expenses. Property income is reduced by other expenses besides taxes and utility expenses. Whatever those expenses, it is important to remember that although the gross income for different properties may be similar, because of different expense-sharing arrangements, like properties will have different net operating incomes and therefore different values. As has been noted above, owners often conveniently overlook certain operating expenses and repairs when selling a property.

They also tend to reduce or even ignore maintenance. However, you may be confident that all such expenses will have been reported for federal taxes; thus, tax statements are a helpful source of information. Also, examining income-expense records for several years makes it possible to detect a normal level of expenses. In addition, reference can be made to various operating expense surveys for different classes of real property to see whether the reported expenses are in line.[2]

The Changing Cost of Money

Most of the preceding discussion focused on cyclic and other forces affecting rental income, building operating expenses, and the return on invested capital. Also considered was the importance of maintaining a proper balance between the construction cost of a project and the income which it can be expected to produce. Still another cost that requires the careful scrutiny of the investor is the cost of borrowed capital. The cash flow concept is well suited to account for the recurring expense of mortgage payments—which are normally expected to endure beyond the typical holding period for an income-producing real estate investment.

Cash flow accounts for rental income received less operating expenses and debt service. This may be expressed as:

	Gross rental income
minus	Vacancy and collection losses
equals	Collectible rental income (Effective gross income)
minus	Operating expenses
equals	Net operating income (NOI)
minus	Debt service (DS)
equals	Cash flow (CF)

From the above $NOI - DS = CF$ relationship it can be seen that if net operating income remains unchanged while debt service is reduced, cash flow increases. Thus, it is advantageous for a mortgagor (borrower) to reduce the amount of debt service, or the annual mortgage payments. For a given loan amount, this can be accomplished by reducing the interest rate, extending the repayment period, or deferring the principal payment via a "balloon" payment. This balloon payment may be for part or all of the original loan principal.

For a level-payment mortgage, which is typically used, each payment and in turn the total annual payment is constant. From this fixed relationship has evolved a widely used term, the "annual mortgage constant." An annual mortgage constant is an annual mortgage payment which consists of principal and interest payments. It may be expressed

---

[2] For instance, see: *Dollars & Cents of Shopping Centers, 1975* (Washington, D.C.: Urban Land Institute); *1977 Downtown and Suburban Office Building Experience Exchange Report* (Washington, D.C.: Building Owners and Managers Association International); *Trends in the Hotel/Motel Business,* 1975 ed. (Chicago: Harris, Kerr, Forster & Company); and *Income/ Expenses Analysis: Apartments, Condominiums, and Cooperatives,* 1976 ed. (Chicago: Institute of Real Estate Management).

as a dollar amount or as a percentage of the original amount of the mortgage. Suppose that a 75 percent loan-to-value, 30-year, 10 percent, monthly payment mortgage could be secured for a property valued at $100,000. The loan would be repaid by monthly installments of $658.19, or $7,898.28 annually. Relating this annual amount to the original amount of the mortgage ($7,898/$75,000) produces an annual mortgage constant of 10.53 percent.

Suppose that the same property produced an NOI of $12,000. This would leave a cash flow of $4,101.72 and a return on the $25,000 original equity (ROE), also known as cash on the down payment (COD), of 16.4 percent.

In order to increase the CF and ROE (or COD), the investor may try to extend the mortgage term. Assume now that a 35-year, 10 percent, 75 percent loan-to-value mortgage is available. If it were, the annual mortgage constant would be 10.32 percent ($7,737.12/$25,000); the cash flow, $4,263; and the ROE, 17.1 percent.

Another way to increase the ROE, though lowering the cash flow, is to increase the loan amount. By obtaining a 10 percent, 35-year, 80 percent loan-to-value mortgage, the borrower would reduce the initial equity to $20,000. The annual debt service based on the same annual mortgage constant would be $8,256 (10.32 percent × $80,000); the cash flow is reduced to $3,744; but the ROE is increased to 18.7 percent.

Leverage, nevertheless, may be carried to an undesirable extreme. A high degree of prudence must undergird the use of leverage and financing in general if the income and value of real property are to be maximized. If a higher loan-to-value ratio can be negotiated by the borrower, a shorter term or higher interest rates, or both, may have to be conceded in exchange. If so, then at some point increased leverage will reduce the ROE and magnify cash losses rather than gains. Suppose, for example, that a 90 percent loan were available for the above property, but that in order to obtain the loan the mortgage term were reduced to 20 years and the interest rate increased to 10½ percent, producing an annual mortgage constant of 11.98 percent. Thus, the annual debt service becomes $10,782; the cash flow is reduced to $1,218; and the ROE drops from 18.7 percent to 12.2 percent.

Leverage magnifies the gains or losses that may result from the use of borrowed money. The next chapter explains analytic techniques for valuing property based upon income with and without the use of leverage.

VALUE ANALYSES: THE INCOME APPROACH

George F. Bloom

GEORGE F. BLOOM, DBA, MAI, SRPA, Professor of Real Estate Administration, School of Business, Indiana University, Bloomington, Indiana.

Founding president, American Real Estate and Urban Economics Association. Past Education Committee chairman, American Institute of Real Estate Appraisers. Member, Lambda Alpha, Rho Epsilon, NACORE. Director, Indiana Realtors Institute. Coauthor, Real Estate, *7th ed. (Santa Barbara, Calif.: Wiley/Hamilton, 1978); and* Appraising the Single-Family Residence *(Chicago, American Institute of Real Estate Appraisers, 1978).*

Concepts of the Income Approach

The key to the income approach is net income, by whatever name it may be called—net operating income, net income before recapture, effective net income, or a variety of other names that are used by appraisers and other analysts. Whatever the name, the calculation of "nets" must follow the same guidelines so that all net incomes which are converted into a market value estimate are the same for all users and all purposes.

Because the subject was handled thoroughly in the previous chapter, no further mention is made of other kinds of income than "net used for capitalization purposes," which is what was referred to as "net operating income." For present purposes, we are talking only about the net operating income used by appraisers and analysts.

In applying the income method of valuation, the analyst must thoroughly understand the three variables of net income—how much, how long, and at what risk. These variables are often referred to as quantity, duration, and quality. In analyzing these characteristics of net income, one must understand and consider the past status and the current status of net income, and then make a projection into the future. Many of us can do the first and second of these analyses very well, but projecting reliably and confidently into the future is another matter, of course.

Historical information and its consideration are essential in the capitalization process. Historical information must be used in its proper perspective, however, because past experience is not necessarily the key indicator of the future. Nevertheless, the thorough analyst must have a complete understanding of historical experience as it applies to the particular properties being analyzed, to all other real estate of a like kind, and, in fact, to the entire real estate investment market. Such experience must cover income and expenses, capital replacements, and management problems. The impact of past financing on the properties being appraised is, of course, likewise critical.

The current status of the properties being appraised must also be studied thoroughly. Most of us feel that we know where we are and that we can identify the relative position of an activity without too much difficulty. The simplicity of this type of analysis, however, is greatly exaggerated. In fact, if we were able to reliably determine the present position in its life span of a property being appraised, then we would have the property pinpointed as to its past and as to its remaining economic life. Such a determination requires a complete analysis of the market of which the property is a part. Typically, this step has been underemphasized by many analysts, and unwary equity investors and mortgage leaders have paid the price. Even analysts with little real estate investment experience recognize that when considering the market value of an investment property such as an apartment house, an investor or a mortgage-lending officer needs to know as much about the current status of the market of which the subject property is a part as about any other element of analysis. Certainly the trend of rental rates, expenses, and vacancies, the impact of zoning, and a multitude of other points regarding the apartment market must be understood before the analyst can proceed.

Another obstacle to a thorough analysis of the current status of a property is the collection of factual data. It is perhaps as difficult to assemble factual data on a real property as on any other income-producing facility or operation. Much of the necessary data is considered confidential and private. Some of the record keeping is inadequate. If such is the experience with one property, the cumulative industry activity magnifies the difficulties of acquiring data on which to base a sound decision.

The third requirement of the analyst, from which there is no escaping, is that of projecting into the future. The entire concept of capitalization is based upon the projection of net income into the future. The economic life of real estate is relatively long compared to that of other kinds of economic goods. Projections of 10, 20, and 30 years, or longer, are not at all unusual. Not only is the analyst charged with projecting the *level* of the net income stream and *how long* it will be earned, but he or she must also project the *risk characteristics* of that income throughout the life of the income-producing property. It is frequently stated that there is no way to accurately predict the future. A person who could do so would be rich overnight. What the analyst does, however, is to project the competitive character of the real estate being appraised to the best of his or her ability, based on the information available, good judgment, education, experience, and the application of methods and techniques.

Capitalization appears to many to be a strictly mechanical, mathematical procedure. It is true, of course, that it is a mathematical process, sometimes involving tables as well as calculators and computers. Capitalization is much more fundamental, however, than a merely arithmetic procedure. It involves a basic understanding of the complex appraisal process, which is discussed in detail later in this chapter.

Capitalization is a discounting process. It is a procedure by which future income is discounted, or reduced to present-day values. It is generally recognized, but too often forgotten, that a dollar which we cannot use until tomorrow is worth less than a dollar available for use today. To paraphrase an old adage, "A dollar in hand is worth two in the bush." Inasmuch as the income stream for dollar-producing real estate may be projected many years into the future, capitalization involves reducing to their present capital value the net dollars to be earned over a period of years.

After a net income figure has been reached, the capitalization process is one of selecting appropriate methods and techniques. These methods and techniques vary from rather simple ones to very complicated mathematical programs. Even the simplest, however, involve the same thorough understanding of the process and the same types of data and information as are required for the more complicated ones. Four methods and techniques of capitalization are described in detail in the procedural section of this chapter.

One word of warning regarding the capitalization of income from real estate. Most investment real estate is made up of two components, land and improvements. These are dissimilar economic goods, inasmuch as land is perpetual and buildings depreciate, wear out, and are ultimately removed. There is need, therefore, to consider the different characteristics of these two primary components and the special analytic techniques involved in converting to present worth the income they throw off.

Figure 1 illustrates the different characteristics of land and improvements. Let us assume that land and improvements each earn a net of $10,000. The two are not necessarily together—that is, the land may be in a separate use and the building may be pictured as a leasehold interest on a separate site. Let us also assume that the applicable risk rate to both is 10 percent. Based on acceptable theory, land earns income in perpetuity and does not wear out. In other words, there is no termination of return to land and that condition justifies capitalization of land by the risk rate in perpetuity. The required return to the land, then, is $1,000 per year. If the risk rate is 10 percent and the indicated value based on capitalization in perpetuity is $10,000, this formula is used: $I/R = V$. Anytime that two of the three components are known, the third can be found. If the rate is unknown, this formula is used: $I/V = R$. If the value and the rate are known, the formula is $V \times R = I$.

To illustrate the difference between land and improvements in Figure 1, the right-hand column shows income to improvements. Starting again with the value of $10,000, the capitalization rate or total rate of return must include not only return *on* the investment of $10,000 but also a recapture *of* the depreciating asset (improvement) over its estimated remaining economic life. If the estimated remaining economic life is 20 years on a straight-line basis, 5 percent per year must be recaptured,

FIGURE 1

Land		Improvements	
Value	$10,000	Value	$10,000
Risk rate	10%	Return on	10%
Return in dollars	$ 1,000	Return of	5%
		Capitalization rate	15%
		Dollar return	$ 1,500
Return in dollars	$ 1,000	Return in dollars	$ 1,500
Capitalization rate	10%	Capitalization rate	15%
Indicated value	$10,000	Indicated value	$10,000

thus increasing to 15 percent the total that the depreciating asset must earn. A 15 percent return, or $1,500, represents a $1,000 return *on* the improvements, and the balance of $500 represents a return *of* a portion of the original capital investment, so that the total investment may be recaptured over the remaining economic life of the improvements. Continuing in the right-hand column under improvements, if $1,500 net income per year is allocated to the improvements and the capitalization rate is 15%, then $I/R = V$ produces $1,500/0.15 = $10,000. This example indicates that the two contributors of income must be processed differently.

Procedures of the Income Approach

In capitalizing net income, the analyst has a choice of methods and techniques and combinations thereof. As stated above, the starting point of capitalization is the development of net income, described as net operating income (NOI) or net income before recapture (NIBR). The same net income is used, regardless of the type of method and technique selected. Furthermore, it is a special kind of net income, different from "nets" used by many others in related fields. All kinds of net figures, such as cash flows and bottom line figures, are used in real estate analysis. The net income used by appraisers in the development of a capital value, however, has been described by some as being "what it should" net. Furthermore, it is a "net" figure that is averaged or adjusted for the beginning year and is typically applicable for the remaining economic life of the investment. The "should" concept reflects good professional management of the property, excluding both the marginal management at the bottom level and the superior management at the top level. Neither extreme should be used in the development of the appraiser's net income.

The development of net income for capitalization purposes also differs from other "nets" with respect to calculations of expenses. Most nets are developed by subtracting from acutal gross income earned such fixed expenses as real estate taxes and property insurance. General operating expenses include such things as utilities, routine repairs, maintenance, and management. One additional expense category is included in the appraiser's expenses. It is called "replacement," and it is not typically considered by most investors. Parts of buildings do wear out and must be replaced from time to time. Inasmuch as buildings last for several decades, it is usually necessary to replace the roof every 15–20 years, to replace the entire heating and cooling system every 10–12 years, and to make similar major replacements of other items that wear out and have a much shorter life than the building as a whole. Carpeting, water heaters, ranges and refrigerators in furnished or semifurnished apartments, and with many other items of this type are major in character and do not last as long as the economic life of the building. Thus, a special dimension is added to net income for the appraiser.

The impact of replacement costs on the capitalized value is one of reducing it in comparison with other kinds of values. It is necessary to recognize this difference before one can embark upon any kind of comparison between the capitalized values of the income approach and other kinds of capital value.

The Selection of Methods and Techniques of Capitalization

Figure 2 indicates some of the most popular methods of capitalization. Less frequently used methods are not shown on this chart. Students of appraising should become familiar with these methods by reading other sources, such as *The Appraisal of Real Estate,* (7th ed., 1978) published by the American Institute of Real Estate Appraisers.

FIGURE 2
Methods and Techniques of Capitalization

Methods	Techniques	Capitalization Rates
Direct	*	Overall rate (OAR)
Straight-line	Residual (land and building)	Risk rate for land; risk and recapture for building
Inwood annuity	Residual (land and building)	Factors developed from risk rate and annuity tables
Ellwood mortgage equity	*	Special rate

*None applicable.

It is difficult to show in chart form the combinations of the most popular methods and techniques and capitalization rates that these methods use. Charting the alternatives may be dangerously oversimplifying a more complicated procedure. This chapter seeks to present an introduction to capitalization, to assist in its proper application, and to furnish guidelines for those who review the appraisals of others. The reader should recognize the obvious limitation of coverage and refer to additional sources.

The first method is appropriately designated the direct method. It is by far the most direct method of capitalization—a rather simple arithmetic process of dividing net income by a capitalization rate to develop a capitalized value. In formula form, it reads $I/R = V.$ If capitalization were truly that simple, sixth-grade arithmetic students could easily calculate valuation figures. Complications arise in the development of the rate to be used. I represents the net income that has been discussed in this chapter. R represents the capitalization rate that is to be used for this particular method. It is called the "overall rate" (often expressed as OAR). The method relies heavily upon the proper development of the overall rate. In its weighting and allocation, this rate must express the amount of risk involved in the total venture, including the annual amount of recapture that is needed to accumulate the original investment in the building and the appropriate risk rate. The overall rate is extracted from the market. There is no way in which an overall rate can be developed other than from the direct market (which is probably another reason for the name used for this method). An overall rate may be developed from the market by the proper analysis of investment properties of like nature which have sold recently and for which reliable selling prices and net income figure can be developed. The formula is $I/V = R$. An illustration of overall rate development from one selected comparison (but please bear in mind that you must have enough sampling from the market to justify the development of a representative overall rate) is: assume that an investment property recently sold in the open market for $100,000. The appraiser develops a net operating income of $10,000 based on the steps outlined previously. The above-stated formula is used with the verified figures: $10,000/$100,000 = 10 percent, the overall rate.

The key to the application of the direct method of capitalization is the proper selection of the overall rate. About 90 percent of the appraiser's time on this method is spent in developing the rate. The appraiser begins the capitalization with the net income already developed, so most of his time is directed to extracting from the market an overall rate with which to capitalize.

The second method of capitalization shown in Figure 2 is the straight-line method. This is one of the most basic appraisal methods and the earliest one developed in traditional appraisal theory and practice. For the beginning student of appraisal, in particular, the straight-line method is of utmost importance because it requires an understanding of basic appraisal theory, the proper allocation of "net income" between land and improvements, the selection of applicable "cap rates" for each, and the application of the residual technique. The land residual technique is a respected and reliable technique for developing values. The building residual technique follows the steps of first allocating "net" to the land and the residue (that which is left) to the building. The straight-line method of capitalization is used *only* when the property being appraised produces a declining income stream over its remaining economic life. It is used on apartments and other residential types, and on properties having short-term leases, such as some office buildings. If the income stream is not declining, then the Inwood annuity method (to be discussed later) is the appropriate method to use.

The land residual technique combined with the straight-line method is also used as a test of the highest and best use of a site. This requires

FIGURE 3
Land Residual Technique—Straight-Line Method

Net operating income (NOI) to the property		$34,000
Market value of improvements	$200,000	
Capitalization rate applicable to improvements	14%*	
Return to improvements		28,000
Residual net income to land		$ 6,000

$$\text{Land income capitalization} = \frac{\$6,000}{10\%\dagger}$$

$$= \$60,000 \text{ indicated market value of the land}$$

* 10 percent risk rate + 4 percent recapture rate.
† 10 percent risk rate.

the proper allocation of net income to the building, with the residual remaining to the site. The number of dollars allocated to the site is then capitalized to develop the market value of the land being appraised. If that value does not basically match the indicated market value for the site that has been extracted from the market (market data approach), this is evidence that the building is not the appropriate development for the site. If, however, the capitalization of the residual to land produces an indicated market value that basically conforms with that which has been extracted from the market, this testifies that the improvement is the proper one and, in fact, develops the site to its highest and best use. An example of this technique is shown in Figure 3.

Of concern in Figure 3 may be the development of the rates. Briefly (but certainly not adequately), the rate development can be described in this manner. Both contributors to income (land and improvements) are entered into with the same degree of risk. In the example shown in Figure 3, 10 percent was used as the appropriate risk rate for this kind of investment. The development of the capitalization rate for the building, however, involves a different technique because in addition to the risk involved in the ownership of the building, there is also the requirement that the building be replaced over a 25-year period, or at least that the original investment in the building be recaptured over that period of time. A 25-year recapture period requires that 4 percent be recaptured on a straight-line basis each year, developed in this manner:

$$\text{Recapture rate} = \frac{100\%}{25 \text{ years}} = 0.04, \text{ or } 4\% \text{ per year}$$

By adding the 10 percent risk rate to the 4 percent recapture rate, a 14 percent capitalization rate is developed for the building. This capitalization rate represents the amount that must be returned each year, based on the original investment, in this case $200,000. In order to justify the

FIGURE 4
Building Residual Technique—Straight-Line Method

Net operating income to the property		$34,000
Market value of the land	$200,000	
Risk (return) rate applicable to land	10%	
Dollar return to the land		20,000
Residual to the improvements		$14,000

$$\text{Capitalization of improvement} = \frac{14,000}{14\%^{*}} = 100,000$$

* See above discussion of the land residual technique for an explanation of the capitalization rate for improvements.

investment, it is necessary that $28,000 of the $34,000 net income be allocated to the improvements, leaving $6,000 as a residual to the land. Having developed the amount of net income attributable to the land as a residual, the next step is to convert the annual income into a capital value. This is done by dividing the annual net income by the 10 percent risk rate, producing a $60,000 indicated market value of the site.

If this technique is being used as a test of the highest and best use of the site, the result is compared with the indicated market value developed by the direct market application (as is explained in detail in Chapter 14). If the direct market reflects that sites of this kind have been selling in the range of $60,000, then the building is the appropriate use and the site is in its highest and best use.

If the market value developed by the direct market approach is in the range of $200,000, then it would be necessary to resort to the straight-line method of capitalization using the building residual technique to properly allocate a fair share to the land. This is illustrated in Figure 4.

The building residual technique develops a market value of $100,000 for the improvements. The building residual technique is most frequently used for property that produces a declining income stream or for property that is not protected with long-term leases or the equivalent.

The Inwood Annuity Method of Capitalization with Residual Techniques

Some properties earn income which has the characteristics of an annuity, such as a 20-year lease with a triple A corporate entity. An annuity or an amount assured for the next 20 years would be a relatively low risk as contrasted with some kinds of speculative investments. When such conditions prevail, the property has a different income potential

FIGURE 5
Land Residual Technique—Inwood Annuity Method of Capitalization

Net operating income to the property		$41,000
Market value of improvements	$200,000	
Capitalization rate applicable to improvements based on a 10% risk rate for 20 years	8.514*	$23,500
Net income attributable to land		$17,500

Capitalization of land income into market value of land $= \dfrac{\$17,500}{10\%} = \$175,000$

* This is a factor (a whole number) extracted from "present value of $1 per annum" tables. An illustration of the 10 percent table:

End of Years	What $1 Payable Yearly Is Worth Today
1	0.909091
5	3.790787
10	6.144567
15	7.606080
20	8.513564
25	9.077040

than does a property with a declining income stream. As such, the capitalization method must vary to fit the different circumstances. Both land and building residual may be used with the Inwood annuity method of capitalization. A major difference is in the type of capitalization rate that is used. Because the income is not declining, there is no need for straight-line recapture of the original investment in the building. Rates are therefore developed by using "present value of one per annum" tables. Such tables are available from many sources. The tables are organized on the basis of the rate and the number of years involved. The product of time and rate reflects the discounted value of a series of dollars which the recipient must wait to receive.

The building residual technique is also used in conjunction with the Inwood method of capitalization. If this is done, the market value of the land is a known factor, either through the direct market comparison approach or through the land residual technique. Special attention should be given to the proper application of this value as it applies to the building. Contrasting with the land residual technique, in which the factor was used as a divisor, the factor becomes a multiplier when it is used as a capitalization rate.

The Ellwood Mortgage Equity Method

The fourth method shown in Figure 2 is the Ellwood mortgage equity method. It is a relatively recent innovation in appraisal theory and practice. Pete Ellwood, a longtime insurance company mortgage officer, used empirical evidence over many years to develop this method. He recognized that the value of an investment to the investor lay not only in the net income it produced but also in two other components (from which the name was derived)—the mortgage and the equity. The terms of the mortgage (interest rate, loan-to-value ratio, length of the note, and many others) affect investor decisions. Investors in many markets are willing to pay more for an investment if the financing is favorable to them; thus this factor is reflected in the Ellwood method's development of the capitalization rate. Ellwood also discovered that the growth or decline of equity was a factor in investment decisions. Equity is the amount of money required at the time of purchase in addition to the amount that can be borrowed. Throughout the life of the investment however, the equity obviously changes, in one or two ways. As mortgage payments are made, the amount of the obligation is paid off, thereby increasing the amount of the equity. Also, in recent years, properties have benefited from appreciation, that is, after 15, 20, or 25 years, they have sold for more than the investor paid for them. Investors realize that both property appreciation and property depreciation affect the overall yield during the holding period. The Ellwood method considers such factors.

In applying the Ellwood method, the residual techniques can be used and a special rate is developed. A special algebraic formula is used to develop a mortgage equity rate which considers the items indicated above as well as the traditional items included in the capitalization rate, namely risk and recapture. Most commonly, the mortgage equity method of capitalization uses property residual, that is, it allocates the income neither to land or building but permits it to remain unallocated to the property as a whole. Then the rate used is similar to the overall rate described in the direct method. There are other situations in which either building residual or land residual can be used in the mortgage equity method.

The Ellwood method has been recognized as a major contribution to appraisal theory and practice, and is gaining in popularity. It is by far the most complicated method for the development of a capitalization rate. Because it is relatively complicated compared to the other methods, certain formulas have been developed to assist in the calculation of the rate. Since the Ellwood method permits building in a great amount of speculation on the part of the analyst, it must be used with exceptional care. And, of course, any income approach technique must be used with great care.

The Use of Capitalization

Inasmuch as many appraisal problems are concerned with income-producing property, the use of the capitalization technique is common.

Sometimes it is used as an additional source of guidance along with either the market approach or the cost approach. It is also subject to either intentional misuse by the clever or to misuse without plan or devise by the misinformed. A major cause for differences of answers in the appraisal process is not the data used or the application of the methods and techniques, but a lack of common understanding and acceptance of the type of value that is to be estimated. Chapter 11 discussed a wide range of value concepts. If each person making an estimate of value were permitted to use his own definition and understanding, then there might be as many dollar estimates as there were definitions. On the other hand, if each valuation were based on a commonly accepted and understood definition of market value, with agreement and understanding of each component, then the only explanation for variances in answers could be the data used or the application of methods and techniques. For his own protection, the novice in this field should, at a minimum, maintain a firm position regarding the definition of market value. Unfortunately, because this step appears to be so unimportant and simple, it is quite often left dangling. The next few paragraphs discuss various interpretations of the term *market value*. It is not the intent of these paragraphs to resolve the differences in the interpretations and applications of such definitions, but to properly identify each and explain its development.

The professional appraiser is subject to a well-established definition of market value. The courts, over a period of time, have made an attempt to clarify the meaning of market value. Educational programs of the professional appraisal organizations devote time to the subject of market value. Market value is now generally recognized as an objective expression which attempts in the best manner possible to reflect the results of an effective marketing system. The subjectives (likes, dislikes, biases, prejudices) have been removed, as have special types of value couched under the term *market value*. By definition, there can be no market value for just one buyer or seller—a market value must apply broadly to all of the persons involved in a particular market.

On the other hand, investors' value figures may be very subjective; therefore, investors have certain limits within which they are willing to become involved. One of the most common factors affecting value for investors is the particular investor's tax situation. Real estate investment has long been affected by changing income tax regulations. It is quite common, therefore, for investment decisions to be made for special reasons that are not applicable to all of the investors in a market. There are endless numbers of situations in which investments are made for personal reasons. A property may be worth more to a particular investor because its close proximity to other property that he owns and operates would add "plottage" value to his entire holding. That investor, therefore, is justified in paying more for the property than any other investor.

Financial institutions acting as lenders in the mortgage loan process also have a special type of value, sometimes referred to as mortgage loan value. Such institutions have a fiduciary responsibility to make "safe" loans. Therefore, they tend to take a conservative position toward the real estate on which loans are being considered. Some such institutions ask for market value estimates on the basis of which decisions regarding the terms of loans are then made. Other institutions alter the standard acceptable definition of market value by adding further considerations to their definitions of market value. Real estate brokers quite often use a much broader explanation of market value than the standard definition, in line with their obligation to match the property being sold with the best buyer. They must look for potential buyers with special interests. Their definition, then, may be very subjective.

Our final word of caution, then, is to recognize that there are a variety of values, and that there is a wide range of understandings regarding market value. In order to reduce the range of value estimates and to improve the understanding and communication of such estimates, the primary requirement is a universal understanding and acceptance of market value. If this is unrealistic, then the essential step is to understand and consider the wide range of definitions regarding market value and to adjust accordingly. (See also Chapter 11.)

Limits and Application of the Income Approach

Some users of capitalization do so by rote, without fully understanding the complexities of the methods. It has been stated that some well-informed individuals can apply the income approach to reach any previously defined valuation figure merely by juggling the components of the approach. This is true, and it is one of the major dangers of the system. The capitalization methods and techniques were developed by highly qualified professionals who were committed not to a predetermined answer but to an approach that would lead to an entirely defensible and justified answer. It is not the arithmetic process that is complicated in this approach (sometimes only simple math is involved) but the data which go into making up the figures used. The Ellwood mortgage equity method lends itself to greater misuse than any of the other capitalization methods. It is more complicated and it has a great number of steps, and thus it permits inputs of data which may not properly reflect the attitude of the open and effective market.

Great care must be applied in using any of the capitalization methods and techniques. The results are only as good as the data used. Like the output of a computer, the result of an appraisal is only as good as the information fed into it. The methods and techniques of capitalization are indeed a prime source of real estate market value indications, but only if and when they are properly applied by professionals who use the support data in the proper fashion.

VALUE ANALYSES: THE MARKET COMPARISON APPROACH

Donald C. McCandless

*D*ONALD C. McCANDLESS, MAI, CRE, SRA, D. C. McCandless &
Associates, Inc., Real Estate Consultant, Bethesda, Maryland.
Formerly senior vice president, Real Estate Research Corporation. Past president, Washington metropolitan area chapter, Society of Real Estate Appraisers. Vice chairman, Education Committee, American Society of Real Estate Counselors. Seminar
instructor and lecturer on marketability analysis and valuation. Author of articles for Appraisal Journal and The Appraiser.*

The Concept and Logic of the Market Comparison Approach

Value estimation by market comparison is the most widely used
method of real estate valuation.

The basic concept of this approach is the same as that of every mercantile transaction, namely, that *market price is determined by comparison among similar products offered in the same market.*

Everyone who buys or sells anything understands the concept and
practices it, from the earliest choices at the candy counter to the selection
of an automobile.

The concept upon which the market comparison approach is based
has certain underlying assumptions about:

1. General economics.
2. The conditions and trends expected, or the observed reactions of
   the real estate market to those general economic conditions.

The most important element of the logic underlying the market comparison approach is the principle of substitution. This economic principle states that *when one commodity can be substituted for another,
the price of the commodity tends to be no higher than that of its substitute.* When applied to the pricing and sale of real properties in the
market, this principle is amended to equate "commodity" with "proper-

ties having equal utility" and to add an element of *time,* that is *that a property and its substitutes are available to a purchaser without undue delay.*

An additional assumption of the market comparison approach is that it is applied within a time frame when the supply and demand elements of the particular submarket under consideration are approximately in the same degree of balance or imbalance.

The assumption that the buyer and the seller are "reasonable" persons, intimately acquainted with the character of the market they are dealing in, is a caveat of the traditional concept of this and all other approaches to value estimation.

Corollaries to the principle of substitution apply to varying market conditions of supply and demand.

1. *Seller's market:* When the market price exceeds the cost of reproduction, new units will be produced to meet demand.
2. *Buyer's market:* When the number of units available for purchase (or rent) increases more rapidly than demand, prices tend to decrease.

Even the casual observer of market trends is aware of the forces which have historically tended to create imbalances between supply and demand. Since real property can neither be created nor consumed with the rapidity of most commodities, it has been subject historically to periods of oversupply and shortages. The assumption, therefore, that the "normal" market reflects a condition of balance between supply and demand may or may not be applicable at a given point in time. It is further assumed that if market forces are permitted to respond freely, they tend toward balance.

From this precept—that the market forces in a free market are constantly seeking to establish a reasonable balance between supply and demand—the logic of the market comparison approach is that the aggregation of sales of comparable properties is a reliable indication of value.

Subjectivity, Utility, and Forecasting. Other important ideas underlying the market comparison approach are so closely linked that it is best to consider them together.

Any system or procedure which is designed to produce an objective conclusion must identify the basic elements, explain their mutual reaction, and isolate the significant variables. Because of the uniqueness of each parcel of real property and the inherent complexities of each real estate transaction, it is difficult to deal objectively with a major real estate submarket or even individual real estate transactions in the manner that physical phenomena may be studied in a laboratory.

Although a generalized idea of potential utilization may be assumed for most properties, each prospective purchaser views the same property differently as to the way it meets or may be adapted to his needs and objectives. Each of the assets and liabilities of the property is measured qualitatively and quantitatively against the purchaser's individual standards. Such detailed judgments are made in the context of the prospective purchaser's experiences and knowledge.

In addition to the variety of judgments which may be made about reasonably discernible factors, each purchaser approaches the question of price with his individual anticipations about future economic events, both in general and as they relate to the specific property.

The discussion above has been confined to the standpoint of the purchaser. However, the same processes hold equally true for the seller.

Thus, every real estate transaction possesses a greater or lesser degree of subjectivity inherent in individual views of potential uses and individual forecasts of economic events. The market comparison technique is therefore a means of arriving at a relatively objective consensus of value by analysis of aggregated market decisions.

Sale/purchase prices between private sellers and buyers are assumed to represent the conclusions of negotiations in which each principal has achieved a reasonable and rational solution to his desired investment or use objective. An old brokerage truism may serve to illustrate this point: *A seller who turns down an offer has in effect purchased the property at the offered price.*

The Processes and Techniques of the Market Approach

Of the three neoclassic approaches to estimating real property values—cost, income, and market—the market approach is the only one which may be used without the need for one of the other two.

As has been pointed out in other chapters, the cost of replacement is, by itself, not necessarily an indication of the price that a property may bring in the market. In the case of a new house, the actual construction cost may be significantly greater or less than the probable sale price in the market. In the case of a used property, measurement of all the items of depreciation, except curable physical deterioration, is related to the use of market comparison elements. In any event, a conclusion of value based solely on the cost approach is suspect.

The income approach conclusion may be prepared with great care and executed with apparent precision. However, it also cannot be considered alone as a completely reliable indicator of value without the support of a market approach estimate.

A user's examination of the market approach in a formal appraisal should include at least two major questions.

1. *What is the appraiser's definition of the value to be estimated?*
2. *What is the purpose of the appraisal?*

In most cases the classic definition of fair market value is said to be the objective of the appraiser's work. However, this definition has acquired a precise meaning only in valuations for litigation purposes. The unlimited variety of other reasons and circumstances which create a need for appraisal services must of necessity be classified and defined in terms which are specifically related to the character of the property and the needs of the user.

Richard U. Ratcliff states in the foreword to *Valuation for Real Estate Decisions:*

"1. The end-product of valuation must relate to the problem or the impending decision of the client which gave rise to the appraisal assignment.

"2. In most appraisal assignments, the client requires a prediction of the probable selling price of the subject property if exposed to the market."

It is Ratcliff's thesis that although many special value terms may express the special needs of clients, market value is *the most probable predicted selling price in the market.* It is typically the answer to users' needs. The statement of a standard, formal definition of the value estimate by the appraiser may thus not only be inappropriate to the particular valuation problem but may also be meaningless to the user.

For most appraisal assignments other than single-family homes and cases at law, it would probably be preferable for the value estimate objective to be stated in informal terms setting forth its basic elements. In the absence of a pertinent value definition, the user must look to the manner in which the data of the market approach have been interpreted and processed to ascertain what value the appraiser had in mind.

Comparability

Similarity of Use and Motivation.   There should be a recognizable pattern of similarity of actual or potential uses between the comparable properties and the subject property. The analysis of highest and best use should be a clear presentation of the appraiser's opinion of the subject's most profitable and permitted use and of his reasons for his conclusions.

The selection of comparables whose actual or potential uses coincide with those of the subject property provides some assurance that the perceived or reasonably implied motivations of the purchasers of the comparables would be similar to those of a purchaser of the subject.

In certain instances the market data will include purchases for both investment and user-owner occupancy. In larger submarkets an appreciable difference in prices may result from these differences in motivation.

Common examples illustrating such differences can be observed in older, deteriorated residential neighborhoods which again become desirable due to social or economic shifts in the market. Single-family houses and small multifamily buildings in such neighborhoods will usually reflect significant differences in selling prices for similar properties in the earlier stages of private redevelopment. Lower sale prices are usually paid by knowledgeable speculators or redevelopers to sellers who are not aware of the probable turnaround in the fortunes of their neighborhood. The highest prices are generally paid by user-purchasers who intend to perform their own rehabilitation.

In almost all cases, sale prices of small warehouse properties to users will be significantly higher than prices of similar warehouses sold to investors. Without examining the reasons for this particular phenomenon, the point is that if such a situation is observed in the aggregated data, the sales having the different implied motivations should be grouped and analyzed separately.

These kinds of circumstances clearly illustrate the limited applicability of a market value definition whose objective is "highest price" as contrasted with "most probable sale price."

Another example reflecting motivational differences is frequently found in sales of tracts of raw land. A purchaser for immediate development can be expected to have an entirely different economic context and therefore a willingness to pay a higher unit price than the price that a purchaser-investor who buys for long-term appreciation would be willing to pay.

In instances where the market data analysis reflects significant differences resulting from the existence of different classes of purchasers having motivational differences, it is incumbent on the appraiser to give value estimates applicable to each of the potential classes.

Probable Use. To ascertain the quality of the market approach in a formal appraisal it is frequently necessary to test the appraiser's approach to the "most probable use" thesis of his analysis of highest and best use. The ultimate support for his conclusions must be found in the overall market analysis portion of the report. The conclusions of this analysis must be reflected by the comparables which are selected and the processing of these data. If the continuing or ultimate use of the subject is not the same as that of the comparables used in the market appraisal, the appraiser has confronted his client with an ambiguous report whose conclusion is highly questionable.

The determination of highest and best use (most probable use) is the key to all of the processing which follows. A faulty determination will ultimately lead to an erroneous value conclusion.

If a house of the same age as all of the houses in a newer subdivision is the subject of appraisal, there is little doubt that its current and future permitted and profitable use will be as a residence. However, a careful study of alternative available or potentially available uses is required under the following circumstances:

1. When an improved property is unsuited for its designed use.

    Example: An old single-family house in a very poor condition in a good residential neighborhood.
    The questions to be answered are whether it would be more profitable to thoroughly modernize, cosmetically refurbish, or demolish the improvement. The basic question is what the prospective contribution of the house, as is, would be to its value after an owner or a purchaser has adopted one of these programs.
    The first steps are to determine as precisely as possible what the deficiencies of the improvement are and what the costs of curing them would be. With these figures in hand, comparisons can be made with market sales data. What would the lot be worth vacant? How much money would be realized from probable sale prices forecast by reference to market sales under thorough or cosmetic renovation, less the cost of such renovation? Computation of the costs should include a return on the investment for renovation, taxes, management, rental loss, and sales commission.
    A final conclusion of most probable use must also measure the prospective marketing risks of alternative programs.
    The same process would be required for analysis of most probable use

for underimproved or overimproved commercial and industrial properties which are particularly suited for owner occupancy.

2. When an improved or an unimproved property might achieve a higher value by a change in zoning.

Example: A large farm is within an area designated on the current preliminary master plan for rezoning to medium-density apartments.

The question is whether to appraise the property as farmland or as developable apartment land.

The first step is to determine whether the property has the locational and physical qualities to be attractive for such development. Assuming, for the moment at least, that it could be rezoned, does it possess the requisite attributes of a successful apartment development? If highway access or adequate sewer and water facilities are not available in the foreseeable future, there is no need to proceed further. Or, if suitable tracts with such facilities are already available in more desirable areas, there is no need to find out whether final zoning approval might be granted.

If the property possesses or can acquire the requisite facilities and is acceptable locationally for apartment development, then the appraiser must address himself to the possibilities of actually obtaining the zoning proposed in the preliminary plan. At this point he must become involved in a study of the political climate regarding growth and the capital budget programs for highways, sewer treatment, siltation and storm water control, and a dozen other items within the jurisdiction in which the property is located. The temper of the local populace toward such a development must be judged, since approval for a new project is probably subject to public hearings. All of these questions require definition and research in order to produce judgments about the probabilities and risks surrounding the basic feasibility of such a project. This accumulation of judgments, based on the best facts available, must precede any test of financial feasibility based on a development approach to the current market value.

The determination of the highest and best use of a transitional property is not easy. All reasonable alternatives should be investigated—at least to the point where they can be dismissed. The relative financial results of the most reasonable alternatives can be estimated by a combination of development models utilizing discounted cash flow techniques. The market comparison approach is useful in putting the whole process in perspective.

To reiterate, a proper determination of highest and best use is essential to the ability to properly utilize the market comparison approach—or any other approach—to real estate valuation.

A basic criterion which must be applied to the selection and adjustment of comparable sales is that *the appraiser should have a keen perception of the underlying economic conditions and the specific real estate market conditions at the time that the comparable property was purchased and should be prepared to relate those conditions to the conditions which are effective as of the date of valuation.*

The factual bases for selecting and using market transactions as useful comparables are not usually revealed by cursory examination or the use of blanket assumptions.

Having come to a clear understanding of the purpose of the valuation and the characteristics of the property under valuation, the user should address his examination of the market approach to the character of the transactions which are cited as prospective comparables for use in estimating the value of the subject property.

If the comparables are similar to the subject in location, size, use, and age, and if sales or rentals have occurred shortly before the date of valuation, there should be no problem in following the rationale. Seldom is such an ideal data background available. Most commonly, directly comparable property transactions are limited in number and differ significantly from the subject property in location, size, or quality.

In a misguided effort to cite what they feel is an adequate number of transactions as basis for their estimate, some appraisers will refer to many inappropriate transactions. Inappropriate comparable transactions include:

1. Properties having economic uses which are obviously different from those of the subject.
2. Conveyance dates so many years or months prior to the valuation date that they cannot be related.
3. Gross differences in size and quality between the subject and the comparable.
4. Acquisitions by public authorities having powers of condemnation.
5. Conveyances between individuals or entities that have close personal or business relationships.

A market data array which includes many inappropriate sales may be inserted as a smoke screen to conceal the fact that the appraiser has made a subjective (and possibly predetermined) value conclusion.

The concept of the market comparison approach is applied in detail in the adjustment process. To be used effectively, this process must begin with a thorough preliminary analysis of the "fit" between the property and the characteristics and requirements of the various sale markets for which it is potentially useful.

The great depth of certain submarkets, such as those for moderately priced single-family homes and rental apartments, will usually produce a large enough number of similar units and transactions to permit reasonably generalized conclusions to be drawn about the characteristics of demand as reflected by unit sale or rental prices.

Investment properties other than apartments represent considerably smaller submarkets and require a more precise knowledge of the various components and their relative importance in the production of income and, therefore, value. Since relatively few recent transactions of comparable investment properties are available at a given point in time, the accuracy of adjustments is heavily dependent upon the amount and the reliability of the data regarding the comparable properties and the circumstances surrounding the sales.

Complete knowledge as to the physical condition of improved comparables as of the date of the sales or as to the circumstances of the sales is frequently unavailable to the appraiser, and therefore he must make certain judgments in applying adjustments. These judgments are related to his knowledge and interpretation of broad market principles and the implied reactions of the investors in the particular submarket to existing market conditions.

For instance, if the appraiser's definition or concept of the value of property in the submarket includes as one of its criteria a transaction which is all cash to the seller, then a comparable sale in which the seller takes back a large deferred purchase mortgage subject to a new mortgage should result in a downward adjustment of the comparable to reflect the present discounted value of the deferred purchase money mortgage.

A further example of an appraiser's use of judgment is provided by the time adjustment. If the appraiser's value concept includes the idea that real property prices increase directly in proportion to indices of general inflation, he may adjust a past sale by calculating the difference in the consumer price index between the date of the sale and the date of the appraisal. This procedure may be viewed as a somewhat more accurate measure than a time adjustment of 10 percent per year compounded annually that the appraiser pulls from the air. However, in some investment submarkets net income trends are inversely related to general economic inflation. In such instances a small or even a negative adjustment is a more accurate reflection of the effect of differences in time than is an increase that reflects the increase in the consumer price index.

Gross aberrations of typical transactions accepted for comparison purposes occur when a sale price is either substantially higher or lower than the observed range of sale prices reflected by actual sales. Such differences can usually be related to special circumstances which have to do with a lack of knowledgeability on the part of the buyer or the seller, with a special need for quick liquidation, or with a special need for acquisition.

Purchases of properties reflecting large actual net losses in operating income to shelter taxable income from other sources, or sales made to avoid foreclosure are also market aberrations. Although such transactions may illustrate highest or lowest prices, they usually cannot be used directly to indicate the market. They are not to be considered as reliable data for estimating market value unless no other transactions are available. Such a situation might arise where the market for a particular type of property is severely depressed and although there are many offerings, no conventional sales occur. Special attention must be paid to the identity and interest of the purchaser in foreclosures, auctions, or trustee's sales in an exceptionally depressed situation. If the purchaser represents a defaulted mortgagee, the "sale price" is usually only the amount of the unpaid indebtedness.

Units of Comparison.   Appraisers, users of appraisals, investors, and mortgage bankers are always in search of readily and easily ascertained units of measure—"rules of thumb." Such rules of thumb may be useful when quick, preliminary "ball park" estimates of property value are needed. However, they are not to be used or taken seriously in an appraisal. One of the skilled appraiser's strong suits is his ability to manipulate pertinent data in such a manner as to produce useful units of measurement, namely, dollars/square foot of land area, dollars/cubic foot of building area, net or gross income multipliers, dollars/square foot of net rentable or sales floor area, dollars/square foot of gross permitted floor area, and so on. These units of measurement must represent analyses of properties which possess a high number of significant common characteristics to be meaningful and useful.

For instance, an attempt to use a unit price of dollars/square foot of gross floor area of an older 34-unit garden apartment by averaging the dollars/square foot of gross floor area of four modern high-rise apartments and two garden developments, each comprising 300 units, as a useful market indication of value is obviously an exercise in futility.

The chief problem with attempting to apply rules of thumb to real estate decisions is lack of definition of the sources and specific characteristics of the data which produced them. An attendant problem is that rules of thumb tend to perpetuate themselves, regardless of changes which occur in the market. In settled communities in an earlier time, most real estate decisions about value were made by rules of thumb. Since the 1920s, in the United States the constant and violent changes in the real estate market have made an anachronism of rules of thumb (except perhaps in the smallest rural areas). Comparison of apples with apples is impossible to find in real estate, except in brand-new, cookie-cutter-type subdivisions.

Comparables must be made to be comparable. The first step of the appraiser is to find a number of reliable sale transactions where a reasonable number of critical elements are similar to those of the subject property. His next step is to measure the number and size of the dissimilarities between the individual properties selected and the property under appraisal. This may lead to selecting out some of the properties he considered initially as potential comparables.

The third step is to individually study the remaining properties from all aspects in order to measure the dissimilarities between them and the property under appraisal. Not only are significant physical differences measured, but also differences as to character of the transaction which he is using in his value concept.

Applications of Statistical Analyses. Statistical analyses can produce more objective and precise measurements of differences among data. Statistical techniques possess a large existing and growing potential for assisting real estate value-estimating theory and practice.

For instance, the question of measuring differences in prices as affected by size differences frequently arises in estimating the value of vacant, unsubdivided land. What adjustment is the appraiser to use for size differential when his subject tract is 120 acres and the comparables range from 80 acres to 200 acres? This is a far more complicated problem than the superficial treatment of using a hand-applied percentage adjustment for size of 10 percent to 30 percent might suggest.

No precise measurement of the price effect solely attributable to size can be made unless and until adjustments are made for all other significant variables among the comparables. The use of regression formulas can produce a reliable selection of significant variables and a prediction of their relative impact on price or value based on qualified samples.

Although the potential uses and benefits of such statistical tools are great, the tools must be used in those situations to which they can be reasonably adapted. Their application to analyses of real estate sales pointed to value estimate conclusions should be regarded with suspicion unless the internal functioning of the real estate market is explicit in the manner in which the conclusions are applied. The lay nonstatistician is inclined to damn this form of data manipulation out of hand, to accept it blindly, or simply to view it with suspicion. A negative reaction is warranted unless the statistical process is accompanied by a believable explanation.

The user of a report containing computations based on mathematical formulas should be aware of two basic facts.

1. The validity and reliability of statistical analyses are related to the number and quality of the inputs. Colloquially, the computerized processing of inappropriate data is referred to as "garbage in, garbage out." The reliability of the identification of significant variables and the measurement of their relative effects upon price/value by statistical inference require the input of an adequate sample of sales or events. The reliability coefficient or confidence level is immeasurably better if more than 30 single-family comparable sales are used than if a regression analysis is used with a sample of 10 sales.

2. The conclusions of a regression analysis of ten shopping centers are far superior to the conclusions of a regression analysis applied to ten industrial manufacturing plants. Shopping centers have many elements in common, whereas there are seldom many elements in common among manufacturing plants.

Statistical analysis is useful in refining the measurement of significant elements and their qualitative and quantitative effects on price/value, but only if these elements have a reasonable number of explicit similarities.

Statistical analyses have great advantages when they are applied to mass appraisal problems, such as reassessments in large cities, or to mass acquisitions. However, like the more pedestrian techniques, their use and dependability must be based on the completeness and appropriateness of the data input.

In the final analysis, the credibility of the market approach is dependent not only upon the selection of appropriate comparables but upon the appraiser's detailed physical description of those comparables. The appraiser should also provide at least a brief comment on motivation and some comments as to his interpretation of the facts as they relate to the subject property.

Time and Financing Adjustments

Time Adjustments. All valuation estimates are applicable as of a specific date. Appraisal value estimates are made as of the date when the appraiser inspects the property unless there is a special reason for choosing another date. Valuation estimates as of a date in the past (retrospective) are generally made in connection with meeting a legal requirement, that is, for inheritance tax purposes, condemnation, establishing a base for depreciation, and so on. Appraisals for acquisition and development loans are projections of the market value of the property upon completion as of a time in the future.

For many years, security market analysts have assembled masses of historical statistical data for the purposes of explaining past price fluctuations and forecasting future movements of a class of stock. Numerous systems have been developed for projecting trends in the security markets.

On the whole, the real estate valuation market approach is organized in the same fashion. However, because of the inherent differences between securities and real estate, the methods vary in determining what is a reasonable price at which to buy or sell at a specific point in time.

Leaving aside consideration of the many differences between securities and real estate, the immediate purpose of our analogy is to point up the fact that all investment or divestiture decisions—for even short-term speculations—are made within a context of *historical* price movements *plus* a forecast of *future* price movements. The "reasonable" purchaser in the market comparison approach expects that the value of the property which he purchases today will not decline significantly in the foreseeable future. The "reasonable" seller is presumed to believe that his property will not bring a much higher price in the short-term future.

Adjustments for Financing. Adjustments of comparable sales to subject based on the financing of the comparable transactions are generally made within two major contexts: (1) the requirements of the purchaser or seller or (2) typical terms as found in the market.

Appraisals for use in condemnation must invariably be based on the fact that the condemnee will receive all cash. In circumstances where it is known or assumed that the purchaser or seller of the subject property intends to make or require an all-cash transaction, each of the comparables must be adjusted accordingly. An all-cash transaction is usually accomplished by the assumption of existing indebtedness or the placement of a new senior mortgage. The purchaser pays cash (equity) above the mortgage financing which he obtains (or assumes). No deferred money trust or mortgage is taken back by the seller.

The classic assumption underlying adjustments for financing is that a transaction which is all cash to the seller is unaffected by the amount or terms of any secondary financing.

If the value of the subject property is estimated on the assumption of an all-cash-to-seller transaction and some of the selected comparable transactions include secondary financing *held by the seller,* a downward adjustment of the comparables' indicated sale price should be made. Technically this adjustment can be computed by discounting the anticipated income from the deferred purchase mortgages treated as an annuity to estimate the present worth. The amount of discount can be ascertained within a reasonable range in larger metropolitan areas where a market for such notes is present.

Less complicated methods of calculation are ordinarily used. To illustrate, if the private market for notes with typical terms on small investment properties is computed as 3 percent/year for a five-year amortizing term, the present worth of such a note is 85 percent of its face value.

The adjustments for deferred purchase financing which are exceptionally favorable to the purchaser—such as interest only during the term of the first mortgage or when the purchaser puts up no equity—indicate that the price is probably considerably higher than it would have been with more typical financing or that the seller was under unusual compulsion to sell. The amount of the downward adjustment is based on the appraiser's judgment of the market value of such notes.

Most sales of single-family houses are based on typical terms. "Typical" is defined for this purpose as the loan-to-value (sale price) ratio, term, and interest rate which predominate in the current submarket of which the subject property is a unit.

Let us assume that the ratio of the typical first mortgage for 20–30-year-old houses in the $40,000–$50,000 range is between 66 percent and 70 percent of the sale price. Equity payments reflected by market transactions are equivalent to 20–30% of purchase prices, with small deferred purchase money trusts, if any, taken back by sellers.

In another part of the same metropolitan area it is observed that new houses are selling in the same $40,000–$50,000 price range with 90 percent first mortgages requiring a 10 percent down payment.

The question: Which set of terms is a more reliable measure of value? The answer: *As long as the comparables are typical of the type and location of the subject property, the financing terms which are typical of the submarket are the basis for adjustment.* In fact, in most areas single-family residential sales for *typical terms* are a more reliable indication of market value than a cash sale because they reflect the terms under which the bulk of all transactions are made within the given submarket.

Some classes of property are frequently sold on terms which are designed to give the seller the advantage of federal tax laws regarding capital gains. This occurs most frequently with single-family residences, farms, vacant land, and small investment properties which have been held for more than five years and whose seller owns the property free and clear or has only a small unpaid mortgage balance. By taking a maximum of 29 percent of the purchase price in cash and giving back the balance in a deferred purchase money trust the seller is able to achieve advantageous tax treatment of the capital gain between the acquisition price and the sale price.

Again, if the submarket transactions show terms occurring frequently in the market, or if it is known that these are probably or logically the terms which the owner of the subject property would accept, then this is the criterion for any adjustment of comparables.

Application of the Market Approach

The purpose of this section is to highlight the most important elements in the application of the market approach to appraisal of the principal types of property.

Single-Family Dwellings. The market approach process for single-family dwellings is focused on adjustments of quantitative and qualitative differences between the subject property and comparable properties.

The significance and amounts of adjustments must be related to market observations rather than measured solely by the cost of substituting the missing or additional element.

Quantitative Adjustments. The key criterion for the comparison of single-family residences is the number of bedrooms. Regardless of the volume of space in a house, the number of bedrooms is the first element of similarity that should be used. In a market area, there is usually a rather precise relationship between the number of baths or lavatories and the number of bedrooms.

The most useful unit of comparison for quantitative adjustment among similar houses is square feet of livable area. Livable area is usually defined as all of the finished space above grade or accessible at grade which can be used in all seasons. Excluded from livable space are finished basements that are entirely below grade, open or unheated enclosed porches, and other areas.

Variations in the number of stories or levels is a key element in the reliability of comparables. One-story bungalows or ramblers represent a somewhat different market from 2-story or 1½-story houses.

Qualitative Adjustments. Locational adjustments for single-family homes are related to differences in site value. If some pertinent comparable sales properties are in a different neighborhood than the subject property, an adjustment may be needed. The basis of such an adjustment is related to any differences in typical vacant site prices between the neighborhood of the subject property and the neighborhoods of the comparable properties.

In addition to significant locational differences, variations from typical size and topography within the subject's neighborhood should be evaluated. Size adjustments based on direct mathematical relationships such as frontage/depth ratios and differences in area may exaggerate the actual degree of differences in market prices. Adjustments for topography should only be made if the site of the subject property or the sites of the comparable properties are untypical of the neighborhood in which they are located.

Significant differences in site value attributed to amenities cover a broad range of elements, such as the landscaping, the view, the distance from the street, the distance from shopping or schools, the condition of adjacent houses, and the lot shape. Most such elements are subjective to some degree. It is difficult to determine the precise significance of such differences and even more difficult to measure them in dollars. In most appraisals, adjustments for differences in amenities between the subject property and comparable properties will offset each other so that no net adjustment needs to be made. Adjustments for significant differences in amenities are probably best expressed by expanding the range of the probable selling price.

Adjustments Measured by Differences in Cost. Adjustments for significant differences between the comparable properties and the subject are typically related to cost. However, the estimated cost new of an element which is possessed by one property and not by the other may or may not be the proper measure of difference in value.

The actual relationship of the adjustment to the cost new of a substitute is related to how essential the element is typically regarded in the market. This is again an area where the appraiser's experience and knowledge of the market is critical to making a reasonable adjustment.

> *Example:* The subject property is located in a mature neighborhood where most, but not all, of the comparable sale houses have detached garages. The subject does not have a garage. The cost to construct a new garage on the subject is approximately $3,000.
>
> Is it proper to adjust the subject downward by $3,000 as related to those comparables which have garages?
>
> Assuming that the garages of the comparables are all of the same age, size, and quality of construction, the question of the amount of adjustment must be related to the appraiser's observations as to the probable value which a typical purchaser would place on the absence of the garage.
>
> The first step is to acknowledge that the garages of the comparable properties are not new. Some depreciation must be taken. For purposes of illustration, let us say that the appraiser estimates that one third of the economic lives of the comparable properties with garages is exhausted. Thus, the base for adjustment is actually $2,000—not the cost new of $3,000.
>
> The broker has observed that although garages predominate in the neighborhood of the subject property, they are a rarity in similar neighborhoods. He may decide, therefore, that a deduction of $2,000 exaggerates the effect that the absence of a garage would have on the probable sale price of the subject property.

Climatic conditions play a role in cost adjustments. Basements are found in most single-family homes in the Northern and Midwestern states but are rarely built in the Southern and Southwestern regions of the United States. The amount of adjustment for a basement in a California house may be nominal as related to its cost. An untypical basementless house in Minnesota may require a downward adjustment which is close to the cost of a new basement—particularly in view of the prospective differences in heating costs since the energy crisis.

Land. Estimating the probable selling price (value) of unimproved land is generally regarded as more difficult than estimating the probable selling price of many typical types of improved property. Some of the principal problems which may be associated with such an appraisal have been discussed generally in earlier portions of this chapter. More detailed presentations of various aspects of land use, contribution, and value are contained in Chapters 16, 21, and 65.

The conclusion of the highest and best use analysis determines whether the subject is an economic entity which can or cannot be used as is.

The adjustment process of the market approach for land value estimates requires a clear understanding of the characteristics of the basic economic unit for which the property is best suited. "Economic unit," as used in this instance, relates to the appropriateness of the property's physical and locational characteristics as well as to the market demand for the property.

Physical Characteristics. The basic determinant of the appropriateness of urban property comparables is whether the subject property is large enough to support the improvements of the comparables. If the best use of the 10,000-square-foot site appears to be a service station, but the minimum site size required by the oil companies is 20,000 square feet, then we had better restudy our conclusion. Assembly with an abutting property for the same use may be a possibility. If not, the best use could be for a fast-food shop. The oil companies' minimum-size criterion is derived from their economic experiences. Service stations with sites under 20,000 square feet are losers.

Similar market tests for economic size are applicable to all types of uses. A site proposed for a regional shopping center which cannot support a minimum of 1 million square feet of gross leasable area is not acceptable. In a downtown area where the median of the range of new office building sites is 30,000–40,000 square feet, it is highly improbable that a developer would find a 10,000-square-foot site attractive.

Estimates of the Actual Yield of Residential Subdivisions. Applying the market approach to a parcel of vacant land suitable for single-family detached homes should be done with particular attention to the net number of building sites which it will yield. This is the key unit price in developing the value estimate.

The maximum potential yield is usually established by the zoning classification. However, maximum yields stated in ordinances are frequently purely theoretical or are keyed to situations in which there are no physical constraints.

If an appraisal has been made without the benefit of a competent engineering study to determine the site yield, it is the responsibility of the appraiser to make an estimate for the purpose of adjusting comparable sales of undeveloped parcels.

> *Example:* The subject property comprises 50 acres of undeveloped land accessed by a 90-foot right-of-way which ends at the property line. It has no other road frontage. Zoning permits a maximum of 3.0 homesites per gross acre at a minimum of 12,500 square feet each, or a potential of 125 sites.
>
> Three sales of similarly zoned parcels, from 40 acres to 70 acres in size, sold for $15,000/acre to $20,000/acre. The net lot yields of the comparables were from 2.5 lots/acre to 2.75 lots/acre, reflecting a tight price range of from $7,500 to $7,300/site, in the raw.
>
> Each of the comparables has substantial frontage on at least one existing road.
>
> Assuming that there are no significant differences between the subject property and the comparable properties as regards elements of location, topography, shape, time, the availability of utilities, and subsoil conditions, the subject property's lack of road frontage will result in a lower lot yield due to the fact that all of the roads serving the subdivision must be internal.
>
> Superimposing a sketch of a simple road pattern to scale on the plat of the survey of the subject property reveals that the maximum yield may be about 1.5 lots per acre, or a total of 75 lots rather than the 125 potential. The indicated value of the subject tract by comparison is therefore estimated as follows: 75 sites at $7,300 = $547,500 or 75 sites at $7,500 = $562,500, giving a range per acre as follows: $547,500 ÷ 50 acres = $10,950 per acre,

$562,500 ÷ 50 acres = $11,250 per acre. Some adjustment may be warranted for the larger size lots.

Differences in any of the significant physical elements can increase or decrease the potential yield of the subject property as compared with the yield of the comparables. Such differences will usually produce variations in prospective development costs which should also be considered a part of the adjustment process.

The volatility which yield and development costs impose on the value estimate arrived at by comparing raw tracts for subdivision purposes makes it highly advisable to have a preliminary lot and street layout prepared by a competent engineer/land planner. Appraisers are expected to have a thorough working knowledge of subdivision regulations, but they are seldom competent to make reliable engineering interpretations on a specific tract.

The value of large undeveloped tracts whose highest and best use is for subdivision and phased developments for residential, commercial, or industrial use should be estimated by an approach which discounts the estimated net proceeds from sales of individual finished sites or groups of finished sites over a projected marketing period as well as by direct market comparison. This is effectively an income process, but it is frequently cited as an alternative market approach.

The projected flow of net income for each time period is based on the sum of forecast retail or wholesale unit sale prices multiplied by the number of units sold, less all expenses incurred for the time period. This approach can produce a more precise estimate, dependent on the accuracy of the inputs, as a detailed model of the projected financial experience.

Typically, such phased developments incur the heaviest expenses at the beginning of development and before there are any receipts from sales. The earliest time periods will reflect negative cash flows attributable to interest on acquisition and development loans plus out-of-pocket expenditures for planning, engineering, utility installation, and operating overhead.

Sales usually start at a relatively low level and then increase in volume. The annual expected expenses for ongoing site development work, taxes, and sale costs are deducted from estimates of the gross sale proceeds to produce a series of anticipated net cash amounts over the sellout period. The flow for each period is discounted to present worth (the current date) using a market accepted rate of return for the development and sell-off of the lots as a speculative *investment.*

An entrepreneurial profit must be deducted from the sum of the discounted flows to arrive at the estimate of the value of the raw tract as is. The following method could be used as a check on the direct comparison approach, or in the absence of suitable comparable sales it could be used alone.

Purpose: Estimate the value of a vacant tract, as is, by the development method.

1. Enumeration of all pertinent market facts, conclusions, and estimates.
2. Estimates of development time costs and sales.

3. Computation of all anticipated costs and income based on most probable terms of purchase of raw tract, financing, development, and sales through a series of time periods from purchase through sell-out.
4. Discounting net income for each period to present worth.
5. Deduction of allowance for entrepreneurial profit. The remainder is an estimate of the vacant, as-is value of the subject tract of land.

Income Property. The market approach process for the valuation of improved income-producing properties requires concentration on the comparability of both physical and income-producing qualities.

Gross Income Multipliers. The most common unit of comparison for income properties is the gross income multiplier (GIM). This unit is the dividend obtained when the sale price of a property is divided by the gross annual income for the year in which it was sold.

TABLE 1
Comparable Apartment Buildings

Sale No.	No. of Units	Gross Income Year of Sale	Sale Price	GIM
1	300	$835,000	$5,000,000	5.99
2	320	850,000	5,500,000	6.47
3	148	460,000	2,780,000	6.04
4	340	800,000	4,250,000	5.31

If the comparable sale properties in Table 1 represented straightforward transactions and the properties were in reasonably good physical condition and without unusual financing, the comparables would indicate that the market price range for such projects is between 5.5 and 6.5 times annual gross income.

Sale 3 might be initially suspect because this comparable has substantially fewer units than do the other three comparables. However, this does not necessarily make for unreliability in large apartment developments if the quality of the structure, the neighborhood, and the rental rates are similar.

Gross differences in the quantities of space in commercial properties may very well affect GIM because of the character of this market and the amount of competition in it. For example, in several U.S. urban markets four-flat buildings consistently bring a substantially higher price per unit and a lower GIM than do large garden developments in similar locations and of similar size and quality. The explanation is that many small investors and owner-occupants are competing for the four-flats and that relatively few investors are competing for the large developments. Again, motivation and economic outlook must be considered.

One of the weaknesses of the GIM is the sensitivity of the multiplier. Small changes in the multiplier make for big changes in value. The general rule is that the greatest reliability for the use of GIM is achieved for smaller properties where there are many units of the same quality and size in the same or similar markets.

Net Income Multipliers. The main advantage of using net income multipliers over GIM, is that differences in expenses may be considered. The ratio of expenses to income may be used as a key criterion for the selection of comparables and adjustments between comparables and the subject property. Unfortunately, the appraiser may not have access to the detailed operating data of many (or possibly any) of his comparable sales.

Other Units of Comparison. There are many possible units of comparison which, used appropriately, can give highly reliable indications of value.

As discussed earlier in this chapter, the most common unit is dollars per square foot of floor area. The gross, net, and rentable areas of most buildings are readily available from assessors' offices, building departments, and mortgagees. These figures are also much more easily obtained from sellers or purchasers than is information about net income.

The most useful building area measurements for different types of income properties are:

$$\$/\text{sq ft of building (including land)} - \frac{\text{Sale price}}{\text{Building area}}$$

Apartment Buildings—Net Rentable Area. The net rentable area of apartment buildings is all the area available for rental occupancy. This is the sum of the net areas of all rental units, or alternatively, it is the gross interior area of the structure *less* the common areas, that is, lobbies, hallways, elevator shafts, and fire towers. The comparable properties and the subject property should have approximately the same distribution of unit types. This unit is more accurate for comparison than $/D.U.

Office Buildings—Net Rentable Area. This can be the gross interior floor area exclusive of below-grade storage and mechanical areas, *less* the entrance lobby, elevator shafts, utility stacks, and in the case of multi-tenant buildings, elevator lobbies, toilets, and janitor closets. The method of measurement may vary with the geographic area. The Building Owners and Managers Association standard method of measurement is applicable in most areas, but with notable exceptions in New York City, Washington, D.C., and San Francisco. Adjustments must be made for differences in storage and interior parking.

Stores and Shopping Centers—Gross Leasable Area. Gross leasable area is usually defined as all the space within demising walls, less common areas and mechanical rooms. In covered malls, gross leasable area may well include the mall area.

Industrial Buildings—Gross Building Area. The universal method of measurement for industrial buildings is gross building area measured on the *exterior* of exterior walls. The most common adjustments to the unit price are made for (1) differences in clear height in storage areas and (2) significant deviations from the typical ratio between finished and unfinished space.

If, for instance, the subject warehouse has in common with practically all other warehouses in your area 6 percent of interior space finished for offices, and one of the comparables has 12 percent of the gross building area finished in offices, the unit or sale price of the comparable should be adjusted upward or downward, depending on the circumstances of the sale of the comparable. Did the purchaser of the comparable need the additional office space, or did he discount it as being superfluous to his needs?

Adjustments for the Site Area of Income Properties. A relatively common major adjustment in the market approach process is that made for the site area of income properties.

Assume that the areas of the subject property and the comparable properties are improved and conform with the minimum requirements. In order to ensure that adjustments are made consistently, the appraiser should analyze the size or capacity of the site as a ratio of building size. For instance, the relationships among an array of comparable sales of shopping centers are shown in Table 2.

TABLE 2
Comparable Shopping Centers

Sale No.	Gross Leasable Area (GLA)	No. of Parking Spaces per 1,000 sq. ft. GLA	Unit Sale Price ($/sq. ft. of GLA, including land)
1	200,000	6.0	$28.50
2	250,000	5.7	31.00
3	350,000	5.5	32.00
4	300,000	10.0	35.65
5	450,000	5.5	30.00

This comparison shows that Sale 4 has almost double the median of the ratio of parking spaces to gross leasable area (GLA) of the other four sales. If 5.5 spaces per 1,000 square feet of GLA, averaging 300 square feet per space after allowing for aisles, walks, and so on, is the median for successful shopping centers, then Sale 4 includes a quantity of excess land. The amount of excess land could be computed as follows:

Land in parking .... 900,000 sq. ft.
Land actually required for parking
   300,000 square feet of building requiring 5.5 spaces per
     1,000 square feet of building calls for 1,650 spaces
     (300 thousands of square feet times 5.5)
   Then, at 300 square feet per space for 1,650 spaces
     (300 × 1,650) the required area is .... 495,000 sq. ft.
Thus, the excess area is .... 405,000 sq. ft.

If the appraiser estimates the land value of the comparable at an average of $2.00/square foot, the value of the excess land is approximately $810,000. The price of Sale 4 was $10,695,000, or a unit price of $35.65/square foot of GLA. However, this price included 405,000 square feet of additional land which was not required by the present center but was available for expansion or resale. The unit price for comparison purposes should be adjusted by reducing the size of the site and extracting the imputed value of the excess land.

Sale price	$10,695,000
Value of excess land	810,000
Adjusted sale price	$ 9,885,000
Indicated unit value of 4 after	
extracting excess land	
($9,885,000 ÷ 300,000 sq. ft.)	$32.95

The unit price after deducting for excess land is a much more reasonable and accurate basis for more refined analysis and adjustments.

Adjustments to unit prices which include the value of the land must be made for significant deviations from the normal site in frontage and in gross or usable land areas. The subject property must, of course, be adjusted if the ratio of its site area to its building area is considerably higher or lower than the range reflected by comparable sales.

Sales Subject to Lease.   The research on sales of income properties includes ascertaining the status of leases which were in effect as of the date of the sales. The quality of tenants and the terms of existing leases are important elements in evaluating both the sale prices of comparable properties and their adjustment to the subject property. In the market approach the unit prices of comparables generally fall into a range that results from the quality and the terms of leases.

1. *High:* Recently executed leases with high-quality, established tenants at current market rents, with standard provisions for escalations and the pass-through of operating expenses and taxes over the base year.
2. *Average:* Leases executed a few years ago, with good to fair tenants and standard provisions for escalation and expense pass-through.
3. *Low:* Long-term leases executed some years ago, with less-than-standard provisions for escalation and the pass-through of increases in operating expenses and taxes. Usually these properties will also have a history of higher than normal vacancy and substantial accrued maintenance.

Comparable sale data are based on the conveyance of fee interests. When sold subject to a lease the sale reflects only the price paid for the leased fee. The amount of the difference between current economic rents and contract rents, as well as terms for adjustments as covered by lease terms, determines the degree to which the price paid for the leased fee is indicative of the price for the full fee interest in the property.

Nonresidential Properties—User and Special Purpose.   Certain nonresidential properties are classified as special purpose because of an observed propensity of owner-occupants to purchase them. This situation is most common for smaller industrial-type warehouse or fabricating buildings and small commercial-residential properties. Such properties are generally too small to attract much investor interest and, more important, usually provide only marginal returns. In active markets, the sale prices of these properties may be higher than can be justified by income capitalization. The reason is that owner-occupant purchasers are usually more influenced by personal locational preference than are investors. Further, in their estimate of value they generally give greater weight to the cost new of a substitute building than does the investor, who gives greatest weight to income potential. Owner-users are also seeking the tax benefits of ownership. In short, the motivations of owner-occupant purchasers of nonresidential properties are much the same as those of home purchasers.

Nonresidential properties which can be termed truly special purpose usually contain buildings that have been designed or adapted for a specific function or process for which there is an extremely small market. Churches, schools, recreational facilities, and certain industrial plants are generally considered special-purpose properties.

The appraisal of such properties is difficult because of the limited amount of market data. Furthermore, the available market data is usually difficult to correlate because the sales of such properties usually involve special circumstances. When a substantial improvement is involved, it is advisable to extend the search for comparable market data beyond the geographic limits of the immediate market area.

The general procedure for estimating the value of special-purpose properties should begin with an estimate of the value of the site, as vacant, for its most probable and profitable economic use. The valuation of the property as an entity (building and site) for its designed use should follow the same procedures of comparison and adjustment that are applicable to conventional properties.

If the appraiser has concluded, in the highest and best use analysis, that the most profitable use of the subject property would be achieved by rehabilitating the property and adapting its improvements to a use other than the designed use, then the market data research should include sales of similar properties which were converted to other uses. In these cases, adjustments between comparable properties and the subject property are based on the quality and condition of the building shell and the adaptability of the building and its mechanical systems to a marketable use.

Some appraisers tend to define special-purpose properties too broadly and to value such properties by the reproduction cost new less depreciation process. The true tests of a property's special-purpose character are a thoroughgoing analysis of highest and best use and analyses of market data, except in certain limited circumstances in which the property is to be acquired under eminent domain.

VALUE ANALYSES: THE COST APPROACH

William S. Harps

*W*ILLIAM S. HARPS, MAI, SREA, First Vice President, John R. Pinkett, Inc., Washington, D.C.*

Has specialized in appraising all types of urban real estate since 1950. In 1955, became one of first seven appraisers appointed to perform Urban Renewal Re-Use appraising in the United States. Has taught all required courses for the American Institute of Real Estate Appraisers MAI designation at major U.S. universities. Has taught for the Society of Real Estate Appraisers. Lecturer in real estate, The American University, Washington, D.C. Past president, Chapter 18, American Institute of Real Estate Appraisers; Washington Board of Realtors®. Formerly member, Board of Directors, National Association of Realtors®. Member, Board of Directors and executive committees, Perpetual Federal Savings and Loan Association, Washington, D.C.; and the National Bank of Washington, Washington, D.C.

There are three approaches to the value of real estate. These are the market comparison approach, the income approach, and the cost approach. All three approaches are pertinent to the appraisal of some types of properties. Any one of the approaches may be most pertinent to the appraisal of a specific type of property. Each approach relies for its validity on the principle of substitution. As applied to the cost approach, the principle affirms that the value of a property cannot exceed the cost of acquiring an equally desirable substitute of equivalent utility, provided that the substitution can be made without costly delay and expense. Value may exceed cost if the substitution requires costly delays in land acquisition, planning, zoning, building, and the like. Value may be less than cost if depreciation affects the property.

Traditionally, the basic steps in the cost approach have been as follows:

1. Estimate the land value from comparable market data, or by abstraction or by the use of a land residual technique.
2. Estimate the reproduction cost new or the replacement cost new of the improvements, except for site improvements.
3. Estimate the accrued depreciation from all causes as of the date of the appraisal.
4. Deduct the accrued depreciation from the estimated cost new to obtain the depreciated cost of the improvements.
5. Add the land value and the value of site improvements at their depreciated cost to the depreciated cost of the improvements to obtain the indicated value of the property.

Modern appraisal thinking has questioned the inclusion of the land value estimate in the cost approach. Land value estimates are used in the building residual technique of the income approach and in one method of comparing properties in the market comparison approach, and they are themselves most often obtained by use of the market comparison approach.

Use of the Cost Approach

The determinants of the use of the cost approach are (1) the purpose of the appraisal, (2) the type of property, and (3) the use of the property at the time of the appraisal.

As Julius L. Sackman has stated:

> It is important to note that the purpose of the valuation has a crucial bearing upon the validity of the method of valuation. The underlying differences in purpose create the need for differences in approach. Thus in fire insurance cases, the land having survived the holocaust, the destroyed structure is valued separate and apart from the land. In eminent domain, the improved property (land and building) must be valued as a single entity; buildings are not generally bought and sold separately from the land. (*Appraisal Journal,* January 1968)

Certain property types are classified as special-purpose properties. Such properties are characterized by a special physical design that fits them for a particular use, lack of a market except for user-owner, and the absence of a feasible alternative use as of the date of appraisal. The clause "as of the date of appraisal" is considered extremely important. For example, a church which is being appraised for condemnation purposes because it lies in the path of a proposed highway is unquestionably a special-purpose property if as of the date of appraisal it is an operating church occupied by a congregation. If the same church has been vacant for three or four years and is located on the edge of a residential neighborhood that is changing to industrial use, treating it as a special-purpose property might lead to an unreasonably high estimate of value.

Pertinent definitions at this point are as follows:

Value in use: The value of a property to an owner who may have no intention of exposing the property on the open market. Value in use computation is generally appropriate when: (1) the property is fulfilling an economic demand for the service it provides; (2) the property improvements have a remaining economic life expectancy; (3) there is responsible ownership and competent management; (4) diversion of the property to an alternative use would not be economically feasible; (5) continuation of the existing use by the present occupants or similar occupants is assumed; (6) due consideration has been given to the property's functional utility in serving the purpose for which it was constructed. (*The Appraisal of Real Estate,* 6th ed., p. 23)

Special-purpose property: A property devoted to or available for a purpose, such as a clubhouse, a church, a public museum, and a public school. Such property also includes buildings having value which cannot be converted to other uses without large capital investment, such as hospitals, theaters, and breweries. (Bryl Boyce, *Appraisal Terminology and Handbook*)

Replacement cost: The cost of creating a building or improvements having the same or equivalent utility, on the basis of current prices and using current standards of material and design.

Reproduction cost: The cost of creating a replica building or improvement, on the basis of current prices and using the same or closely similar materials. (*The Appraisal of Real Estate,* 6th ed., p. 215)

Reproduction Costs versus Replacement Costs

Except in cases where no prudent person would consider reproducing a property exactly as it was or where construction methods and materials have changed to such an extent that the estimate of reproduction costs is not possible, reproduction cost new is to be preferred to replacement cost. This is especially true in condemnation cases. When confronted with cost-new estimates based on replacement costs, judges have ruled "that the building whose cost you have estimated is not the building you have appraised." Further, there is always a chance of applying double depreciation when replacement cost is used rather than reproduction cost. The most logical reason for using replacement cost is that certain functional inadequacies or superadequacies are eliminated in the cost-new estimate, regardless of the skill or judgment of the appraiser. An estimate of physical depreciation or additional functional obsolescence may be less convincing to a reader or a court when a replacement facility rather than a replica of the building being appraised is utilized as the new building.

A partial list of properties which might be considered special purpose, depending on the objective of the appraisal, are as follows:

1	airport	4	banking structures
2	amusement centers	5	blast furnaces
3	aqueduct rights-of-way	6	brick kilns

7	bridges	26	oil storage tanks
8	cemeteries	27	oil tank farms
9	chemical plants	28	parks, (city, state, or private)
10	churches	29	patriotic halls
11	city halls	30	pier warehouses and docks
12	clubhouses	31	post offices
13	courthouses	32	public beaches
14	customhouses	33	public transportation
15	exposition buildings		(real estate)
16	forest preserves	34	racetrack grandstands
17	grain elevators	35	radio broadcasting stations
18	gravel pits	36	railroad rights-of-way
19	hospitals	37	railroad roundhouses
20	mines and mineral deposits	38	reservoirs
21	monumental office buildings	39	schools and colleges
22	monuments	40	skating rinks
23	museums	41	state capitols
24	music centers	42	streets
25	oil fields	43	theaters

In addition, many buildings used for industrial and manufacturing purposes and most buildings used by utility companies under the control of a public utility commission are special-purpose properties.

It can be seen from the above list that an estimate of value based on the cost approach may be extremely complex. Unless the appraiser is also an experienced cost estimator, he will need to retain other experts to determine the replacement cost new, reproduction cost new, physical depreciation, and functional obsolescence of the equipment. In many appraisals for condemnation purposes, equipment may be considered a part of the real estate under certain circumstances. These circumstances may differ in state law or in federal law. Generally, the equipment may be included as part of the real estate if the equipment cannot be moved without seriously damaging it or if it cannot be moved without seriously damaging the real estate.

In his article "Limitations of the Cost Approach," Julius Sackman states:

> Clarity of presentation requires that the cost factor in the determination of value be considered:
> 1. as a criterion of value, 2. as evidence of value, 3. as a check on other approaches, 4. as support for expert opinion.
>   The rule to be followed is that cost as evidence of market value, should be restricted to those cases where:
> 1. the property involved is unique, 2. or, is a specialty, 3. or, there is competent proof of an absence of market data.
>   When it is utilized, it can be properly valuated only if we remember that:
> 1. except in unusual situations, it fixes the ceiling for value (if new). 2. it should be given weight only when the other approaches are unavailable. 3. care must be taken to make full allowance for physical and functional depreciation. (*Appraisal Journal,* January 1968)

These remarks are intended to apply mainly to appraisals made for condemnation purposes.

The cost approach is also utilized in many appraisals of proposed investment properties for loan purposes. Lenders want to know that they are not lending an amount in excess of the cost of construction plus the land value, or in an amount exceeding their desired percentage of loan to value.

Steps in the Cost Approach

I. Land value estimate
  A. From comparable sales.
  B. From abstraction.
  C. From a land residual estimate.
II. Cost-new estimate
  A. Reproduction cost.
  B. Replacement cost.
  C. Indirect costs.
  D. Methods of estimating.
    1. Quantity survey method.
    2. Unit-in-place method.
    3. Comparative method.
      a. With known building.
      b. From cost service of material in place.
III. Accrued depreciation
  A. Physical depreciation.
    1. Curable—measure is cost to cure.
    2. Curable postponed—measure is percentage cost to cure.
    3. Incurable—measure is age life or straight line on physical bases.
  B. Functional obsolescence.
    1. Curable.
      a. Due to a deficiency, not a new addition. Measure is cost to cure.
      b. Deficiency involving a new addition. Measure is excess cost to cure.
      c. Due to an excess. Measure is reproduction cost minus physical depreciation already charged, plus cost to cure.
    2. Incurable
      a. Due to a deficiency. Measure is capitalized net rent loss, or gross rent loss times gross rent multiplier.
      b. Due to an excess. Measure is reproduction cost minus physical depreciation already charged, plus cost to carry.
  C. Economic obsolescence. Measure is capitalized net rent loss or gross rent loss times gross rent multiplier.

Accrued Depreciation

As it applies to improved real estate, depreciation, is loss in value from any cause. Accrued depreciation is loss in value which has taken place prior to the date of appraisal. According to the text *The Appraisal of Real Estate* (6th ed.), "Accrued depreciation is the actual depreciation existing in the improvements at a given date; or the difference between the cost of reproduction new of the improvements, as of the date of appraisal, and the present value."

Depreciation may be estimated by direct or indirect methods. The direct methods of estimating depreciation involve careful inspection of the improvements, noting their physical condition and their functional deviations from the norm or from a new standard being applied as of the date of appraisal, and analysis of the location to determine whether forces external to the property adversely affect its life, utility, and profitability.

The indirect methods of estimating depreciation utilize as a measure of accrued depreciation the difference between the cost new and the current value of the subject property, as indicated by the market comparison approach or the income approach, or by the analysis of closely comparable properties to determine the rate of depreciation that is reflected in their sale prices.

The direct methods of estimating accrued depreciation are the straight-line method utilizing physical life, the straight-line method utilizing economic life, and the breakdown method. In any case, if the only approach to value available to the appraiser is the cost approach, the breakdown method, when correctly applied, is the most reliable.

An Indirect Method for Estimating Accrued Depreciation. The indirect method that utilizes *comparable sales* in the appraisal of a dwelling is as follows:

1. Estimate the cost new of improvements as of the date of sale (less site improvements).
2. Estimate the land value based on comparable land sales as of the date of sale.
3. Deduct the site improvements, other improvements, and the land value from the sale price.[1]
4. Deduct the penalty for financing due to VA, FHA, or other insured financing and premiums for secondary financing if the market conditions indicate that the deduction is warranted.
5. Subtract the remaining cost from the cost new to arrive at the depreciation.
6. Divide the depreciation by the cost new to obtain the percentage of depreciation for the comparable.
7. Divide the percentage of depreciation by the age of the property to obtain the annual depreciation ratio.

The following is an application of the technique outlined above to a single-family dwelling containing 1,168 square feet. This dwelling is approximately the same in size and age as the subject property, and it is located in the same neighborhood. The improvement is the highest and best use of the land.

---

[1] Other improvements could be a recreation room, front porch, extra bath, storm windows.

1. Land, based on land sales .... $ 3,800
2. Cost new @ $28.50 per sq. ft.   33,288
3. Price with VA financing (loan $22,500) $23,500
    Deduct loan   3,800
    Deduct storm windows   250
    Deduct site improvements   750
    Deduct points for VA financing
      (0.04 × $22,500)   900
    Remainder   17,800
4. Cost new................................. $33,288
    Less remainder   17,800
    Equals depreciation...................... $15,488
5. Calculation of depreciation rate
    $15,488 ÷ $33,288 = 47% depreciation
    0.47 ÷ 33 = 1.4% per year

Based on this single comparable sale, the ratio of depreciation applicable to the subject property, exclusive of extras, would be 1.4 percent a year. If several such comparable properties were available, and if the range of annual depreciation ratio were from 1.2 percent to 1.45 percent, it would be reasonable to assume that the ratio applicable to the subject property would fall within that range, say 1.3 percent a year. Thus, if the subject property were 30 years old, the amount of depreciation would be 1.3 percent a year, or 39 percent. Of course, adjustments would have to be made for such extras as storm windows, fences, garages, and recreation rooms if these were not included in the subject's cost-new or site improvements. This method, is actually a variation on the market comparison approach rather than the cost approach. On the other hand, a value arrived at by using this method would be as valid for a single-family dwelling as any other method available to the appraiser. The method could be applied to properties other than single-family dwellings, provided that a high degree of similarity existed among the comparable properties.

The Direct Method for Estimating Accrued Depreciation. The simplest application of the direct method of estimating accrued depreciation is to divide the observed effective life of the improvements as of the date of appraisal by the sum of their observed effective age and their future economic life. This method encompasses all types of depreciation, with the possible exception of some types of physical curable (repairs). The future economic life of a property is generally determined by considering the property's physical condition and the extent of its functional and economic obsolescence. An example of this method is as follows:

Actual age of property ....   20 years
Property has been well cared for, with considerable
    preventive maintenance. Effective age of property ....   10 years
Future economic life of property ....   40 years
Sum of effective age and future economic life
    is 10 years + 40 years ....   50 years
Depreciation is therefore 10 years ÷ 50 years, or 20%

If the effective age of the property were equal to its actual age, the numerator would be 20 years instead of 10 years. If the future economic life of the property were estimated at 35 years, then the sum of the future economic life and the effective age would be 20 years plus 35 years, equals 55 years, and the depreciation would be 20 years divided by 55 years, or 36 percent.

It should be that the future economic life used in this method should be the same future economic life as that used in the income approach to value if the capitalization technique requires the use of a future economic life.

If instead of future economic life the future useful life of improvements is utilized, the depreciation estimated would be incurable physical depreciation. For the same property used in the preceding example, the appraiser might estimate that the future useful life of the improvements is 60 years and that the effective age is again 10 years. In that case, the incurable physical depreciation would be the effective age divided by the sum of the effective age and the future useful life, or 10 years divided by 70 years (10 years plus 60 years) equals 14.3 percent.

The appraiser would then have to give consideration to curable physical depreciation, functional obsolescence, and economic obsolescence, and either a full or a modified estimate by the breakdown method would be indicated. Theoretically, whichever method is utilized, the answers would be similar if not identical, depending upon the skill, experience, and judgment of the appraiser.

A modified example of the breakdown method of estimating accrued depreciation is set forth below. This modification utilizes general building components—for example, structure and finish; heating, ventilating, and air conditioning; plumbing; and electrical systems—rather than a complete engineering breakdown of all components, including excavating, masonry, roof deck, roof finishing, framing, flooring, finish flooring, and so on. This modified breakdown method is considered to be more practical because it is more likely that the appraiser will be able to obtain the contractors' and subcontractors' bids by trades than that he will be able to obtain the complete work sheets of the contractors and subcontractors. Further, if the appraiser is estimating cost new on a unit-in-place method, it is more likely that he will be capable, with the use of cost services, of estimating the cost of general building components than that he will be capable of estimating the cost of all components.

Classification of Depreciation and Obsolescence

Physical—Curable
Worn roof covering.
Rusted downspouts and gutters.
Broken or worn walks and drives.
Poor maintenance of exterior walls.
Worn trim.
Worn floors.

Worn wall finish.
Worn trim finish.
Worn bath fixtures.
Worn kitchen fixtures.
Worn plumbing and water supplies.
Worn and overaged heating and ventilating equipment.
Worn electrical switches and fixtures.
Cracked basement floor.
Badly maintained garage.
General wear and tear that is economically curable.

Physical—Incurable
Loss in value resulting from the wearing out of irreplaceable items.
Damage to concealed foundations, exterior walls, load-bearing members of roof.
Structural defects.

Functional Obsolescence—Curable
Crack or failure in foundations having other causes than structural defects or poor workmanship.
Undersized and weak roof members.
Insufficient downspouts and gutters.
Walks and drives not in place or insufficient.
Inadequacy or absence of baths.
Obsolete bath fixtures.
Fixtures or finish below neighborhood standards.
Poor kitchen layout.
Inadequate kitchen cabinets.
Obsolete kitchen fixtures.
Obsolete plumbing and water supply system.
Inadequate plumbing and water supply system.
Inadequate or insufficient heating and ventilating system.
Obsolete heating and ventilating system.
Inadequate electrical wiring.
Outdated electrical fixtures.
Insufficient electrical service.

Functional Obsolescence—Incurable
Oversized foundations.
Cracked foundations.
Oversized roof members.
Roof covering substantially better than those of neighborhood.
Roof covering substantially worse than those of neighborhood.
Eccentric trim.
Poor workmanship in structural framing, oversized or undersized structural framing.
Poor workmanship in floor and roof slabs, oversized or undersized floor and roof slabs.
Overimprovement or poor quality of workmanship in finished floor.
Poor quality and workmanship in walls.
Poor quality and workmanship in trim.
Bath fixtures above neighborhood standard.
Kitchen equipment above neighborhood standard.
Plumbing and water supply system above neighborhood standard.
Superadequacy in heating and ventilating.
Superadequacy in electrical wiring.
Garage too small or superadequate.

Architecture poor or unusual—bad floor plan, excessive ceiling height, poor plot plan.

Overadequacy or underadequacy of capacity of plant.

Excessive wall thickness.

Any functional characteristic of a building which has become nonfunctional by reason of new materials, new techniques, or decreased costs, such as ventilation furnished by monitor roofs prior to the economic feasibility of mechanical ventilation systems.

Economic Obsolescence

Architectural overimprovement or underimprovement for neighborhood.

Nuisances such as smoke, dirt, noise, odor, traffic, zoning, change in use, rent control, excessive taxes, and inadequate transportation, shopping, schools, and parks.

Local, regional, and national legislation[2]

EXAMPLE OF THE COST APPROACH (COST-NEW ESTIMATE AS OF JULY 1, 1978)

Summary of the Construction Details (full description would be elsewhere in the report under the description of improvements)

Type	Public bus garage
Built	1935
Area	43,000 sq ft ground floor
Stories	One plus mezzanine and furnace room; mezzanine for offices, drivers' washrooms, locker rooms, check-in and checkout rooms, etc.
Construction	Brick-steel
Walls	Solid brick
Ceiling	24 ft to eave; 39 ft to top of monitor roof
Cubic content	1,500,000 cu ft
Column space	80 ft under monitor roof E-W; 30 ft perimeter N-S
Heat	Low-pressure steam-oil for offices, washrooms, etc.; blowers in garage and storage area
Office and other finished area	3,800 sq ft in mezzanine
Sprinkler	Wet system
Toilets	Adequate for male drivers, superintendent's office, employees; none for female drivers
Area of site	152,000 sq ft valued at $3 per sq ft
Available for parking buses	88,000 sq ft for 160 buses (40 buses park indoors)
Available for parking cars	18,000 sq ft for 52 cars (total parking needed: 120 spaces)

---

[2] Many of the items on this list are from a paper presented by Robert V. McCurdy, MAI, CRE, Baltimore, Maryland, at a meeting of the Central Atlantic Region of the American Institute of Real Estate Appraisers in Atlantic City, New Jersey, 1958.

Other Functional or Nonfunctional Features

Brick-enclosed area in one corner of building, 32 feet by 16 feet, formerly used for drivers to turn in cashboxes from buses, change counting, and overnight storage of cash. Use was abandoned ten years ago when modern facility was erected adjacent to entrance where all buses had to pass. This excess structure was 12 feet high, had two walls and a concrete roof, and contained plumbing facilities and a small, separate gas warm-air furnace.

Physical Condition

Sound, normal wear and tear based on comparison with other old garages; 150 wire-glass panes, 15 inches by 20 inches each, need replacing; decorate office area; need some repair of plumbing fixtures and replacement of steam valves; replace 120 linear feet of five-foot downspouts (copper); replace 1,000 square feet of asphalt tile.

Reproduction Cost

By unit-in-place method. (Cost new actually included indirect costs. They are separated out to illustrate the method.)

	Cost
43,000 sq ft	$ 950,000 (rounded)
Sprinkler system	40,000
Coin room (16 ft × 32 ft × $15 per sq ft)	7,680
Cost before indirect costs	$ 997,680
Indirect costs (18.5%)*	$ 184,571
Title expenses, surveys, soil tests, legal expenses, casualty insurance and taxes during construction, commissions and points paid for financing, construction loan interest, architect's fees, engineering and administrative expenses during construction, etc.	
Total cost new	$1,182,251

* 184,571/997,680 equals 18.5%.

Component Breakdown for Depreciation Purposes

Can be estimated using historical percentages obtained from contractors or from analysis of the unit-in-place estimate.

Structure and Finish........	70.8%	$706,358 × 1.185 = $	837,034
Sprinkler	4.0	$ 39,907 × 1.185 = $	47,290
Heating and ventilation	8.0	$ 79,814 × 1.185 = $	94,580
Plumbing	10.2	$101,763 × 1.185 = $	120,589
Electrical	7.0	$ 69,838 × 1.185 = $	82,758
	100 %		$1,182,251

$$\text{The cost per square foot of structure} = \frac{\$837,034}{43,000} = \$19.466/\text{sq ft}$$

$$\text{The cost per cubic foot of structure} = \frac{\$837,034}{1,500,000} = \$0.56/\text{cu ft}$$

Accrued Depreciation Estimate

Curable Physical Depreciation

Replace 150 panes	$2,200
Paint office area	$1,900
Point up plaster in corners where needed (included above)	
Miscellaneous plumbing repairs	$1,000
Replace 16 steam valves	$ 160
Replace 120 linear feet of five inch (diameter)	
copper downspouts	$1,200
Replace 1,000 sq ft of asphalt tile	$1,200
Total physical curable	$7,660

The cost of repairs may be estimated by the appraiser if his experience warrants, or it may be estimated by a contractor or by the management department of the appraiser's office.

The total curable physical depreciation is only 0.65 percent. This *small* amount may be deducted from the component of which it is a part or from the structure as a whole. If it is deducted from the structure, the remainder would be calculated as follows:

Cost new	$1,182,251
Less physical curable	7,660
Remainder	$1,174,591

or

Structure	$ 837,034	
Less panes, decoration, and tile	5,300	
Remaining structure cost		$ 831,734
Plumbing	$ 120,589	
Less	2,360	
Sprinkler		118,229
Heating, etc.		47,290
Electrical		94,580
		82,758
Remainder		$1,174,591

The remainder is the same, *but* the components subject to further depreciation differ. For consistency, this example will deduct the curable physical depreciation from the affected component.

Based on conferences with the chief engineer and on the appraiser's experience, the components with lives shorter than that of the whole property are estimated to have effective lives and useful lives as follows:

	Cost New	Life New	Effective Age	Remaining Life	Depreciation Percentage	Depreciation	Depreciated Cost
Sprinkler	$ 47,290	40 yr	20 yr	20 yr	50 %	$ 23,645	$ 23,645
Heating and ventilation . . .	94,580	40 yr	25 yr	15 yr	62.5	59,113	35,467
Plumbing	118,229	40 yr	25 yr	15 yr	62.5	73,893	44,336
Electrical	82,758	40 yr	20 yr	20 yr	50	41,379	41,379
					Depreciation	$198,030	
					Depreciated cost		$144,827

Incurable Physical Depreciation

Age of the building is 43 years. It was heavily built, and it has had good maintenance. The structure is estimated to have a useful life of 90 to 100 years (based on a comparison with two streetcar barns built in 1895 which were converted to bus garages in 1940, and are still in use). On an age-life basis, the structure is estimated to have a future useful life of about 50 years. Therefore,

$$\frac{43 \text{ years}}{43 \text{ years} + 50 \text{ years}} = \frac{43}{93} = 46\%$$

And

$$0.46 \times \$831{,}734 = \$382{,}598$$

Summary of Physical Depreciation

Physical curable .... $ 7,660
Physical deferred on short-lived components 198,030
Physical incurable 382,598
    Total physical depreciation $588,288

Percent physical depreciation

$$\text{charged at this point} = \frac{\$\ 588{,}288}{\$1{,}182{,}251} = 50\%$$

Curable Functional Obsolescence due to a Deficiency

The deficiency is the lack of restrooms and lounge facilities for women. This is a source of friction with the union. Space is available in several places. The cure requires a new addition. It is an excess cost to cure. The contractors' cost is $40,000 to enclose 1,000 square feet, creating three rooms, a locker, a lounge, and rest rooms with 6 water closets in metal stalls, 4 lavatories, 4 mirrors, 4 sanitary dispensers, 3 stall showers, 30 lockers, tile floor and wainscoting in the toilet rooms, heat, light, and so on.

The estimated cost of including these rooms and this equipment in the reproduction cost-new estimate would have been $30,000. The excess cost to cure is therefore $40,000 less $30,000, or $10,000.

Curable Functional Obsolescence due to Excess

The excess structure—512 square feet in size—is in the corner of the building and was formerly used as a coin and counting room. The measure is the reproduction cost, minus physical depreciation already charged, plus the cost to cure.

$$\text{Reproduction cost: } \$7{,}680 \times 1.185 = \$9{,}100$$

The small section contained plumbing, heating, electricity and sprinkler. The overall percentage of physical depreciation is 50%. Since this has already been charged against the whole property, it must be deducted from the reproduction cost new here.

And $9,100 × 0.50 .... $4,550
Cost to cure (to repair floor, walls, cap
  off utility lines, clean up, and haul) $1,500
    Total functional curable due to excess $6,050

Incurable Functional Obsolescence due to a Deficiency

Measure is capitalized net rent loss.

Total off-street parking needed .... 120 spaces
Total available .... 52 spaces
Deficiency................................. 68 spaces
Area per car needed .... 350 sq ft
And 350 sq ft × 68 .... 23,800 sq ft

Market research, indicates that industrial users in the general area pay from 40 cents to 60 cents more rent per square foot of gross floor area for a building with adequate parking than they do for a building with little or no parking. The subject building has some parking for employees' cars, and during the day some of the space occupied by the buses can be used for this purpose. The appraiser's judgment is that additional space for 34 cars would equate the subject property to the buildings with adequate parking.

The reasonable penalty is therefore 50 percent of an average of 50 cent a square foot, or 25 cents. And 43,000 square feet[3] × 0.25 cents/square foot equals $10,750.

The market indicates that the only charges against this gross rent figure would be taxes (for the additional land), agent's commission (a charge against income on a constant percentage basis), and a vacancy loss (a percentage charge against gross income). These charges are estimated at 20 percent.

$$\text{Net income} = 0.80 \times \$10,750 = \$8,600.$$

The appraised property is a public utility. The income approach is not warranted. However, market research clearly indicates an interest rate of 10.5 percent.

And $8,600 capitalized at 0.105 is $8,600/0.105, or $81,905.

Incurable Functional Obsolescence due to Excess Height

The excess height is mainly under the monitor roof. The monitor roof has an average excess height of 15 feet. The roof is over 21,700 square feet of the 43,000 square feet of the building. The cubage of the excess height is therefore 15 feet × 21,700 square feet, or 325,500 cubic feet.

The measure is reproduction cost minus physical depreciation already charged plus the cost to carry. The reproduction cost is 325,500 cubic feet × 56 cents, or $182,280.

The physical depreciation already charged is 50 percent.
And 0.50 × $182,280 is $91,140.

Cost to Carry

Maintenance on monitor roof
  Windows (estimated) $1,200/year
  Cost to heat space 1,500/year
Additional fire insurance required because of
  replacement cost clause .... $ 315
    Total $3,015

Rate considered warranted is 10.5%, and $3,015/0.105 = $28,714

---

[3] The area of the building.

TABLE 1
Summary of Functional Obsolescence

Functional curable	
Due to deficiency	$ 10,000
Due to excess	6,050
Total	16,050
Functional incurable	
Due to deficiency	$ 81,905
Due to excess height	91,140
Cost to carry	28,714
Total	$201,759

Economic Obsolescence

None was present. However, if we assume that location is two blocks from city's main sewerage treatment plant, that odor adversely affects employment, and that turnover is exceptionally high, rental rates from high grade tenants occupying warehouses and small manufacturing plants are an average of $0.30 a square foot less in this neighborhood than in competing neighborhoods. The penalty for the locational or economic obsolescence is $0.30 and $0.30 a square foot × 43,000 square foot = $12,900 (rent loss). The net portion of the $12,900 is estimated at 80%.

And 0.80 × $12,900 = $10,320.00.

The market proved discount rate of 10.5% results in value loss as follows: $10,320/.105 = $98,286.

Summation of the Cost Approach

Reproduction cost new			$1,182,251
Less accrued depreciation			
Physical curable	$ 7,660		
Depreciation on short-lived components ..	198,030		
Physical incurable	382,598		
Functional obsolescence—curable	16,050		
Functional obsolescence—incurable	201,759		
Economic obsolescence	None		
Total accrued depreciation			$ 806,097
Depreciated reproduction cost			$ 376,154
		Say	$ 376,000
Add other improvements at depreciated cost			
Paving in parking area			
(106,000 sq ft @ $0.50)	$ 53,000		
Driving aprons	$ 5,000		
1600 LF chain link fence around parking area	$ 6,400		
Landscaping	$ 5,000		
Total other improvements			$ 69,400
All improvements			$ 445,400
Land value estimate			$ 456,000
Total value from cost approach .			$ 901,400
Rounded $ 900,000			

Alternative Method Utilizing Economic Life

The appraiser is familiar with older bus garages. Judgement suggests that the effective age equals actual age and that the future economic life is 20 years. The point of view is that repairs must be made to preserve the property. They must be deducted in addition to percentage depreciation.

Cost new	$1,182,251
Needed repairs	7,660
	$1,174,591

Age of improvements .... 43 years
Future Economic life .... 20 years

$$\text{Accrued depreciation} = \frac{43 \text{ years}}{20 \text{ years} + 43 \text{ years}} = \frac{43}{63} = 68.25\%$$

And 0.6825 × $1,174,591 =	$ 801,658
Repairs	7,660
Total accrued depreciation	$ 809,318
Reproduction cost new	$1,182,251
Less accrued depreciation	809,318
Depreciated cost	$ 372,933
Say	$ 373,000

This compares with $376,000 by the more detailed method, based on the appraiser's judgment as to effective life and future economic life.

SUMMARY

The cost approach is the single approach that is available to the appraiser in all appraisals of improved properties. This is its strength. When an improvement is new and a proper use for the site, and adequate comparable land sales are available, the value estimate based on the cost approach is as valid as any other. The major weakness of the cost approach is the difficulty of estimating accrued depreciation. That difficulty increases with the age of the improvements. Obviously, the validity of the results obtained by the cost approach decreases with the age of the improvements.

However, in all cases in which the cost approach is pertinent, accrued depreciation must be estimated. Skill in the estimate requires judgment and experience. The starting point is a thorough inspection of the neighborhood and a detailed inspection of the property. Economic obsolescence flows from the neighborhood, and physical depreciation and functional obsolescence flow from the property. The mid point is the accumulation and analysis of a mass of data in the appraisal files. The data should include the ages of properties sold, their condition, the most probable land value, sale prices, and highest and best use. The end point is the acquisition of the skill needed to process a cost approach to value that is convincing to the appraiser and the appraiser's clients.

FEASIBILITY ANALYSES AS A PROCESS

Michael C. Halpin

*M*ICHAEL C. HALPIN, *President, Michael C. Halpin Consultants, Santa Clara, California.*
Formerly vice president of corporate development of a multi-state housing development corporation and president of one of its subsidiary companies. Formerly corporate architect for Litton Industries. Author, Profit Planning for Real Estate Development *and more than 30 articles in publications serving the real estate development, investment, and financial communities. Contributor to a book on real estate venture analysis. Frequent conference and convention speaker, a guest lecturer, at leading universities, and a columnist.*

The Problems

Feasibility Analysis a Problem-Solving Process. Feasibility analysis is a problem-solving activity. Too often the results of feasibility analysis are irrelevant because the analyst did not know what the real problems were to begin with, or did not attempt to define the real problems before providing the "solutions" or findings, or did not solve the problems.

The decision maker (e.g., the investor or the developer) determines the purpose of the analysis (e.g., what should be developed on a property or whether a proposed development makes sense), and the analyst defines the objectives of the analysis. The feasibility analyst's function is to identify the problems and then to formulate an objective in light of the problems recognized. In identifying the purpose which prompted the feasibility analysis, the investor or developer may not have taken into account related problems.

Problems are rarely what they appear to be from a superficial analysis. Superficial analysis generally uncovers symptoms rather than underlying causes. A problem is a cause which interferes with the accomplishment of an objective—a cause, not an effect. The feasibility analyst must dig down to the cause and not be deceived and sidetracked by the effect disclosed in that process. A beginning point in problem analysis is to state what the problems appear to be. From that point the circumstances surrounding the apparent problems are examined. This examination should focus on the most critical information, as too much information will confuse rather than clarify.

Among the most critical information that should be uncovered is why an apparent problem exists. How did it develop? What other symptoms can be identified and associated with it? Why does it occur in one situation and not in another? This type of fact-finding will lead to the identification of the real problem.

Defining an organization's or an individual investor's objectives, constraints, and real problems is a most important aspect of a feasibility analysis. The objectives should be stated in terms of measurable results whose accomplishment will eliminate the cause of the problems. How to eliminate the cause is not considered at this point.

When the objectives have been established, standards must also be established to confirm when and how well the objectives have been achieved. Objectives change and problems take on different dimensions with the passage of time. Consequently, both long- and short-term objectives and solutions must be developed.

Much can be said for spontaneity, intuitive hunch and entrepreneurial audacity in decision making. However, rational, deliberate, planned decision making is necessary to balance the kinds of spontaneous, intuitive, entrepreneurial drives that management often exhibits. Spontaneous decisions are often based on previous conditioning or previously successful modes of operations. They may be rooted in inappropriate comparisons or experience, or the decision maker may not really understand what the problem is, in which case almost any decision will be inappropriate. Adherence to a rational, planned decision-making process (or feasibility analysis) will provide a better safeguard against the ravages of change than will shoot-from-the-hip decision making.

Spontaneous decisions tend to be applications of old solutions to new problems. The analyst, however, should seek to improve what has been done well in the past and not merely repeat old solutions. Each decision should represent an advance over past technology and accomplishments.

Feasibility analysis is concerned with properly identifying the investment or development problem, with structuring or evaluating the objectives, and with formulating or evaluating an action plan to accomplish those objectives. It is the process of maximizing the opportunities and neutralizing or minimizing the obstacles in order to achieve the optimum solution to the investment or development problem.

The components of feasibility are not generally analyzed in a single report produced by a single individual. The total feasibility analysis represents a consolidation of the efforts of numerous specialists. The feasibility report may utilize work and reports by others as backup to the final consolidated report.

Feasibility Analysis Contrasted with Appraisals. The purpose of a feasibility analysis is to evaluate the risk and the reward to a specific investor/

developer for a specific project or development concept or for a specific site that is to be acquired or developed. Feasibility differs from appraisal in that appraisal concerns itself with value to the market in general, whereas feasibility is concerned with usefulness to a specific sponsor. Feasibility also differs from appraisal in that appraisal theory assumes rational behavior in the marketplace, whereas feasibility analysis attempts to maximize return by encouraging irrational or emotional behavior in the marketplace through skillful marketing. The appraisal concept of fair market value is objective and dependent on average conditions. Feasibility analysis, however, arrives at investment value as related to a specific opportunity by including subjective considerations which add to or subtract from fair market value.

A feasibility study is concerned with the specific opportunities and constraints associated with a specific site and a specific sponsor, whereas an appraisal assumes a fictitious buyer classified as "economic man" and uses aggregate data which represent the market as a whole in order to develop a value which is an average of market conditions. Since events are influenced, not by average conditions, but by specific conditions bearing on specific situations, any such attempt to create an average situation out of a diverse cross section of specific situations is fictional and potentially misleading.

The analysis and findings of a feasibility report can be utilized by the reader not only to make a go or no-go decision but also to develop comprehensive planning, organizational, marketing and merchandising strategies for implementing the conclusions of the report. For example, the buyers or renters identified in the report may become the target of a merchandising campaign.

In an appraisal, on the other hand, the methodology merely supports and defends the conclusion, and the appraiser merely needs to inform the reader of the methodology being employed in sufficient detail for the reader to able to follow the manner in which the final conclusion of value was reached. Thus the reader's interest in the methodology and findings of a feasibility report goes far beyond his or her interest in the methodology and findings of an appraisal.

An appraisal may be adequate for a lender who can average his risks over a large number of investments and desires no entrepreneurial involvement. But the developer or investor who is risking everything he has on a single development seeks to maximize value added through entrepreneurial involvement and needs a more specific measure of safety and risk than is provided by an appraisal. Such an investor needs a feasibility study to show him the specific constraints of the market and specific opportunities to outperform the market, through skillful marketing and entrepreneurial audacity.

An appraisal and a feasibility study are also distinguished from each other by the viewpoint of the analyst. The appraiser observes what has been successful in the past and stresses historic patterns and average market conditions. The feasibility analyst is concerned with what might be, with creating or identifying opportunities. Thus the appraiser is more likely to recommend the development of a product in an area where it abounds, whereas the feasibility analyst is more likely to recommend the development of a product in an area where it is scarce.

Traditional appraisal methods have been criticized as not being clear or convincing enough due to the manner in which they reach value conclusions. Appraisal leaves much room for manipulation and vague assumptions. This is not to say that there is a lack of appraisal theory as regards valuation problems but that appraisal theory may be unsuited to the solution of specific problems.

Many factors determine value, including consumer emotions and attitudes. However, when the "economic man" that is assumed in appraisal theory—the buyer and seller who have equally desirable alternative courses of action and an equality of knowledge—does little to encourage the study of buyer profiles, submarkets, unmet buyer needs, and the impact of skillful marketing and merchandising or value. The "economic man" of appraisal theory assumes that comparables are equally desirable, whereas the skillful entrepreneur seeks to create monopoly situations in which the buyer believes that there is no equally desirable comparable on the market. Thus, appraisal theory, unlike feasibility theory, is not well suited to measure the value and risk associated with marketing monopolies.

Types of Analyses

Acquisition Feasibility versus Developmental Feasibility. The acquisition of an existing property does not pose as complex an investment/feasibility decision as the development of a new property. Once a building has been constructed, there are fewer uncertainties. An operating building has already been tested in the market and has produced a historic cash flow and a return on investment measure of performance. Although the acquisition of an operating property is less complex than the development of a new property, superior performance in either acquisition or development requires superior feasibility analysis. Serious mistakes in either acquisition or developmental feasibility generally cannot be compensated for by any amount of subsequent superior performance in other areas.

Both acquisition and developmental feasibility require as a first step a complete identification of investor objectives and constraints. In light of those objectives and constraints an acquisition policy is developed to guide subsequent activities, identify and qualify compatible investment categories, identify and rank competing investment opportunities, manage acquired properties, and guide resale and refinance decisions.

Developmental feasibility is more complex and more expensive to implement than acquisition feasibility. A developer cannot afford too many dry runs and must possess a good intuitive feel for the feasibility of a development before launching a thoroughly planned and researched feasibility analysis. By contrast, an investor who acquires developed properties will typically evaluate numerous properties before making an acquisition.

Developmental feasibility requires the completion of more phases in the analysis before a potential opportunity can be accepted or rejected. Indeed, the demands of environmental and legislative bodies and radical fluctuations in construction costs and money market rates often compel the developer to complete a significant amount of the preconstruction development process before feasibility can be reliably indicated.

Other Types. The components of feasibility analysis may be economic feasibility, legal and political feasibility, performance feasibility.

Economic feasibility evaluates the suitability of an investment as related to the following questions:

1. Does the indicated return meet or exceed the minimum investment standards of the sponsor?
2. Are the equity requirements within the means specified by the sponsor according to his sources or other available sources?
3. Will the market absorb the product fast enough to make it a profitable investment?
4. Are the absorption income and expense projects reliable and consistent with industry standards? Do they allow a margin for error or unforeseen circumstances?
5. Is the proposed investment package as attractive to lenders as competing investment packages, or more attractive?

Legal and political feasibility considers the practicalities of the investment as related to the following questions:

1. Is the property correctly zoned for the proposed use? If not, will the rezoning be legally and politically feasible within a reasonable time?
2. Are there legal environmental, political, or social considerations that would jeopardize the use of the property as zoned or proposed?
3. Are there legislative or environmental and social trends that would jeopardize or hinder the ongoing operation of the proposed investment?
4. Does the proposed investment conform to existing codes, ordinances, deed restrictions, and state and federal laws?
5. Is title to the property clear of restrictions that would impede the development as proposed?
6. Is the development entity properly structured from a legal and tax standpoint?
7. Have all tax considerations been properly analyzed and structured?

Performance feasibility and especially compatibility with sponsor objectives consider the stability of the investment as related to the following questions:

1. Is the proposed investment a sound strategy for implementing sponsor objectives?
2. Is the proposed investment feasible within the limitations imposed by sponsor constraints? Does the sponsor possess the management team and the consultants that are required to implement the investment program?
3. Are the required separate contractors, subcontractors, workers, and materials suppliers available and capable of performing according to the performance schedules?
4. Are the performance schedules complementary, and are they in a sequential order that will avoid conflicts or bottlenecks in implementation?

5. What resources are required, and are they available?
6. Are there conflicting or prior commitments of those resources?
7. What is the desirability and value of the plan in achieving objectives, as compared to available competing plans?
8. In relation to other plans and objectives, does the plan represent duplication, conflict, or working at cross-purposes?
9. Can the plan be effectively administered through control devices, within the capabilities available to the organization?
10. Have the capabilities of the organization as related to the proposed plan been objectively evaluated?
11. Are the objectives realistic as related to the opportunities, and are they expressed in a comprehensive manner?
12. Has the market research been responsive, and are the premises based on facts arrived at from objective analysis rather than preconceived ideas?
13. Does the plan take into account the dynamic, cyclic nature of the market and provide for alternative courses of action if the actual conditions do not confirm to the projections?
14. Are the financial data realistic and consistent? Are they based on reliable information or on horseback figures?
15. Have the opportunities expressing the highest and best use consistent with the organization's resources and the economic environment been identified?
16. Have the problems and pitfalls been properly evaluated?

The Process

Establishing Objectives and Constraints. No day's work should be entered into by an organization which is not part of a monthly, quarterly, annual, and long-range plan. Appropriate economic action requires an integration of long-term and short-term plans and objectives. Long-term plans look far ahead to ultimate objectives; short-term plans prescribe what must be done in the immediate future.

Before entering into any development or investment program, a clear identification of the objectives is critical. Public companies generally have a different set of objectives than do privately owned companies, and within each type of company there may be varying sets of objectives, depending on the opportunities available and the company's present internal needs. Also, a company may be locked into an undesirable situation from which it cannot be readily extricated, and it may be looking for a solution that is no more than the better of two evils.

Stating long-term and short-term goals determines the ways in which capabilities and resources are to be utilized. Thus such goals provide a framework which establishes a perspective for subsequent decisions. The more specific and better understood an objective is, the more specific and appropriate the action to achieve it will be. The more specific and appropriate the action to achieve an objective is, the greater is the probability that the objective will be achieved.

Both organizations and individuals often tend to expend resources on "correcting" symptoms rather than on discovering and correcting the causes which produce those symptoms. The manner in which resources are consumed in the present largely determines the range of alternatives in the future. An overemphasis on solving immediate problems as they occur, as opposed to planning the execution of objectives, will greatly diminish the scope of future alternatives.

Custom-Fitting Opportunities to Objectives and Constraints. The challenge in establishing the feasibility of a real estate development or investment is to match the correct development concept or product to the needs identified in the market and also to complement or work within the objectives and constraints of the developer or investor. The better the match of the product with market need, and with organizational objectives and constraints, the better the chances of success.

Objectives must be properly structured from the outset because a better order is equivalent to vast amounts of effort or capital. Profit is the fruit of a better order and of timeliness in meeting the right opportunity with the right concept, resources, and capabilities.

Market needs are broad and varied. They provide numerous opportunities for profit. Some of these opportunities will be more suited than others to the unique capabilities and resources of a particular company or investor. Success in turning opportunity into profit depends on the extent and depth of the opportunity and on the capabilities and resources that the organization can devote to the opportunity.

An organization or an investor is limited in the number and types of opportunities that can be pursued within the constraints of capabilities and resources. The success rate will be higher where there is a good match among opportunity, capability, and resources. Opportunity must also be evaluated as it relates to the long-range objectives of the organization or the investor. An opportunity within easy reach may not be as attractive as one on the fringes of one's capability if the latter blends more harmoniously into one's long-range objectives and the former offers short-term benefits at the expense of long-range objectives.

If the interrelationship of the available opportunities with capabilities and resources is not correctly evaluated, objectives may be unrealistic. Working toward unrealistic objectives will cause even the best-laid action plans to be ineffective and wasteful of resources.

The evaluation of an opportunity and decisions as to objectives must include an analysis of the organization's or the individual's strengths and weaknesses, capacity and resources, as related to the opportunity, the competition, and the socioeconomic environment. Objectivity is important in the evaluation process. The facts must be placed on the table early, to ensure that all known strengths and weaknesses can be considered early enough to build a firm foundation for subsequent strategies. Objectives should be formulated to capitalize on the most promising opportunities.

Classifying and Ranking Data according to Priority. The data utilized for feasibility analysis can be grouped into two basic information classes: Class 1, information which influences project feasibility but is beyond the control of the developer or the investor; and Class 2, information which can be influenced by the decisions and actions of the developer/ investor.

Class 1 information comprises aggregate market data which present a panorama of the overall situation confronting the developer/investor. Aggregate data help the developer/investor to the economic setting and the major trends of the market. Aggregate data provide clues to market opportunities, but seldom can a developer or investor identify a specific marketing opportunity from aggregate data alone. Aggregate data generally represent a situation that is too large in scale to be influenced by individual developers or investors unless they are very large. Aggregate data by definition deal with large amounts of information and with statistical averages or means. Successful projects are not designed around aggregate conditions but around very specific conditions, that is, around a very specific type of product for a very specific market in a very specific location with a very specific need to be served.

Class 2 information provides close-up shots to identify specific opportunities within the panorama presented by aggregate data. It identifies submarkets, competitor weaknesses, and specific merchandising and product opportunities, and it relates to the opportunities and constraints of a specific property. Neither the investor nor the developer wants to compete as an equal with others in a market situation. Successful developers/investors seek to insulate an opportunity from general supply and demand factors by creating a competitive edge within a portion of the market which they can control to some degree, while reducing the influence of the uncontrollable. Class 2 data emphasize individual consumer and investor needs and motivations rather than making broad statements of consumer action and supply and demand. Both Class 1 data and Class 2 data have their place in feasibility analysis. The Class 2 data coming within the scope of influence and the span of control of a developer or an investor will generally have a greater influence on the outcome of a development than will Class 1 data. Class 2 data should be emphasized accordingly in the feasibility analysis.

The more specific the data relating to market need by submarkets, price range, product features, locational preferences, and competitive position, the greater is the ability of the developer/investor to control the safety and risk. Very specific data coming within the scope of influence and the span of control of the developer/investor can be influenced by the developer/investor in such a way as to produce monopoly situations to one degree or another. That is, the decisions and actions of the developer/investor can produce advantageous changes in the marketplace.

Systematic Simplification and Standardization. The feasibility analysis must be limited to the elements that have the most bearing on increasing or decreasing the success of a given program. Irrelevant detail increases the possibility of error. The findings can be no more specific than the credibility and suitability of the information on which the findings are based. Oversimplification of a problem is designed to identify priorities and to concentrate energies on those priorities in order to make the problem manageable.

However, because problems in land development can be as diverse as the circumstances associated with any individual property, problem identification and the structuring of objectives require resourcefulness and creative thought. For these reasons it is not always feasible for the analyst to work from standardized models or formats.

Standardized models or formats are a great tool for reducing the costs of analysis and stabilizing output. However, such models can only be used as general guides. If the analyst attempts to use a standardized model as a detailed guide for handling a wide range of problems and objectives, he will shape the problems and objectives to the model rather than developing a model to handle specific objectives related to specific problems. The best a model can do is to show how a specific problem can generally be approached and how objectives and procedures can generally be formulated. A feasibility program can benefit greatly from an underlying standardized approach but the feasibility analyst is required to custom-fit his program to the specific needs of the given investment situation.

The Control Program—An Important Criterion in Evaluating Feasibility. The feasibility of a specific project for a specific sponsor is clearly tied to the maintenance of a schedule of events and to the controlling of expenses, and cash flow during the implementation of the project. Indeed, financial projections are based on the occurrence of a certain sequence of events at specifically prescribed times. The plans, schedules and, controls which underlie the financial projections cannot be taken for granted, for they are the essence of the venture. The numbers in the financial projections represent the reliability and the outcome of the plans, schedules, and contents.

The value of any plan, no matter how brilliantly conceived, is ultimately measured by the effectiveness of its implementation. Since effective implementation requires a system of review, measurement, analysis, and timely corrective action, scheduling and controls must be an integral part of a plan. The plan and its controls are both inseparable parts of a continuous management process. To expect a plan to be executed without proper schedules and controls is to trust to chance and therefore to stray from objectives.

When an adequate control procedure is built into a plan, the effectiveness of the plan in achieving objectives can be measured consistently. The orderly feedback provided by an organized control procedure improves management's day-to-day implementation of the plan and allows for timely corrective action when results fail to achieve objectives.

Since the control program largely determines the outcome of an objective or strategy, it is an important criterion for success of the plan. *To evaluate the feasibility and practicality of a plan, management must also evaluate its control program.*

Most company failures arise from insufficient planning (not having information to plan with), overexpenditure (failure to control costs), unrealistic pricing (due to failure to control costs), and insufficient sales (poor value offered in relation to the price). The potential for flexibility and a quick response is realized only when management is operating on reliable information. Managers of small businesses often rely on their intuitive feel for how things are going in general, and as a result they are usually handicapped by a chronic lack of specific information on which to act. Both small and large companies owe their ultimate success or failure to the quality of management, the quality of the information available to management, and the effectiveness of the control program.

Pitfalls and Limitations of Feasibility Analysis. The typical feasibility analysis is characterized by a number of limitations. For one thing, imaginative audacity may be lacking. Researchers are often irresponsible about their findings in that they do not adequately explain what the findings mean and how the company can improve its position by making use of the findings.

Many feasibility reports are mediocre because researchers do not want to present what they cannot readily verify with statistics. When enough statistics are available to make a position ironclad, that position will assuredly be mediocre because it will be readily apparent. Researchers often focus emphasis on the path that is most readily documented and away from the opportunity that has not yet had a path worn to its door. Methods which rely on full and complete documentation can be the organization's worst enemy when it comes to attaining market leadership, because such data may simply not exist.

Expert analysts sometimes make recommendations that go beyond data. Technicians do not have the sensitivity that is required for such probing. It takes the broad understanding of the expert to see what makes sense even where there is not enough information to make this obvious.

Forecasts are often projections of what has already happened. It is difficult for the researcher to predict when a trend will break or when a cycle will top or bottom out, to forecast how long an opportunity will remain viable. Demand may drop sharply due to unforeseen economic events or the entry of unanticipated competition. Since local forecasts are dependent on regional, statewide, national, and international events, any major shifts can have a profound impact on the local market. Projections can help plan only for the likely events, but unlikely events may dominate. And when they do, it makes a big difference to feasibility.

Even though a manager may be intellectually aware that his industry is cyclic and that substantial risks are associated with a failure to take this into account, he may become emotionally committed to continued nonstop growth. Visualizing the rewards that are to be had if present favorable trends can be maintained until his firm has exhausted the opportunities they present, the manager may allow his emotions to overrule his intellect. He may disregard information that is inconsistant with his current emotional posture.

To survive violent cyclic change it may be necessary to alter management concepts as well as product lines; when the conditions require it, management must change its emphasis from growth to the preservation of capital. This can be a difficult feat because the management style tends to become part of the manager's personality, and thus may be more difficult to change than the product lines or the production volume. In some instances, radical change in the economic environment may require radical change in management style. The reception that a feasibility analysis receives will depend in part on the style of management.

All too often a company will be so preoccupied with the success of its own programs that it will fail to see that these programs suffer from deficiencies or that they are becoming obsolete. It is all too easy to become dominated by the economics of standardization and production and thus to develop a dangerously lopsided product or investment orientation.

The Value of Expertness. Management must appreciate the value and the use of expertness, which is more than the application of formal techniques and statistical analysis. In its essence, expertness is thorough understanding. It is the ability to assimilate and interpret events in order to synthesize them and determine the likely outcomes and, from that point, to recommend action-oriented policies for management to follow.

Expertness cannot verify or substantiate everything it says, but it does have to explain what it says in credible terms. The expert has a skill which can cut through mountainous drudgery to see trends that mere technicians cannot identify. The trick is to know what to look for and to use data and analyses to find it.

FINANCIAL FEASIBILITY ANALYSES

John L. Hysom

*J*OHN *L. HYSOM, PhD, Professor in charge of the Real Estate and Urban Development Program, at George Mason University, Fairfax, Virginia, and President of J. L. Hysom & Associates, Consultants in Land Development.*

Consultant in real estate and development to developers, investors, government agencies, consulting firms, trade associations, and nonprofit organizations, including the Educational Testing Service, Princeton, New Jersey. Speaker appearing before national convention audiences of the National Association of Home Builders, the Urban Land Institute, the Urban Regional Information System Association, and the National Association of Counties. Adjunct professor at The American University and the University of Maryland. Coauthor, Apartment Communities: The Next Big Market *(Washington, D.C.; Urban Land Institute, 1968); and* A Handbook for Creating an Urban Development Information System *(Fairfax County Court, Fairfax, Va., 1974). Author of numerous articles in professional journals.*

An important real estate development lesson of the early 1970s is that careful market research planning, and financial feasibility analysis may be more important today than ever before. Many real estate projects went into bankruptcy during the 1974–75 recession because their developers and lenders had failed to devote sufficient time and attention to evaluating the market feasibility or the financial feasibility of the projects. Few planners of real estate projects made any downside vacancy projections or interest rate escalation analyses. Most of the projects that failed might have been successful if the recession of 1974–75 had not dampened the demand for new space and increased the cost of financing. As a result of that experience, many lenders and developers have become much more conservative in their forward estimates and much more careful in their assessment of market and financial feasibility.

Will Feasibility Work?

In a broader context, feasibility includes the noneconomic aspects of a project, including legal, physical, and market feasibility. A number of questions have to be asked and answered:

Is the land zoned properly for the proposed project, and can the developer obtain all of the necessary governmental approvals to build?

Do the designs and the architectural and engineering plans satisfy the functional needs of the project?

Is there an adequate and durable market demand for the space that will be created by the project?

Assuming that these and related questions have been satisfactorily resolved, then the key test of project feasibility is whether the income, cash flow, and earning potential will be sufficient to meet the owners' and lenders' financial goals. Our discussion will consider how a project's financial feasibility or profitability is determined and how it is measured.

Financial feasibility criteria can be applied to any real estate property—whether it is an existing structure or a proposed project; an income-producing property or real estate for sale; residential, commercial, or industrial real estate; a multipurpose, a general-purpose, or a special-purpose structure; and finally, whether it is for a specific user or for a speculative user.

The basic principles are the same for all real estate purchases or developments, and a financial feasibility analysis of some sort is always conducted, regardless of what it is called, even if it be only on the back of an envelope. This review will focus on income-producing properties proposed for construction and will examine some of the sophisticated newer ways to evaluate and measure long-term, mid-term, and short-term profitability potential.

Criteria for Financial Feasibility

Both borrowers and lenders establish their own special criteria for financial feasibility in project evaluation. These criteria may vary among lenders and borrowers, and may also vary for different types of projects. Each lender, for example, takes a slightly different approach to evaluating the feasibility of commercial or income-producing properties. Some lenders depend on appraisals to establish property values; others arrive at their own estimates based on projected income streams, comparable properties, and construction costs.

Lenders are legally constrained as to the ratio of a property's value they can legally lend to a real estate borrower.[1] All lenders have written policies about loan-to-value ratios. Although each lender may vary his focus, virtually all lenders examine the debt service coverage ratios, the expense ratios, and the capitalization rates, but they may set different limits.

When a lender becomes interested in making a particular loan, but the numbers do not exactly fit this criteria, there are frequently opportunities for adjustment on three key factors:

1. Vacancy rates.
2. Management fees.
3. Capitalization rates.

These factors are far more flexible than gross income and expenses, which are well documented and well established in practice.

If, for example, a borrower needs a loan of $3,150,000 to complete a project comfortably, but the legal limits only justify a loan of $3 million, it may be possible to increase the project value by $200,000 or more in order to permit an increase of $150,000 in the loan amount. This is accomplished by changing one or more of the three factors in the loan submission package. Reducing the vacancy rate and the management fee, for example, increases the net operating income, thereby increasing the estimated project value. Reducing the capitalization rate also increases the project value. Relatively small changes in one or more of the three factors can produce substantial increases in project value— approximately ten times the change, assuming that the capitalization rate is about 10 percent.[2] Thus, an increase of $20,000 in income or a reduction of $20,000 in operating expenses will purport to increase the project value by $200,000.

Four Major Safety Ratios for Lenders. Lenders and mortgage bankers seeking to safeguard mortgage funds base their feasibility criteria on the borrower's ability to repay the loan and on the relationship between the value of the project and the loan amount. Lenders apply commonly four financial ratios to income-producing properties in order to evaluate the capacity of the properties to meet the operating and financial obligations.

The first ratio is the *debt service coverage ratio,* which is the primary financial criterion used by large institutional lenders.[3] This ratio measures the amount of cushion, income protection, or safety from legal

---

[1] For example, federally chartered savings and loan associations can lend up to 95% of the value of a single-family home if 15 percent of the value is covered by private mortgage insurance. Federally chartered commercial banks are limited to an 80 percent loan-to-value ratio on first trust mortgages and to a 90 percent ratio for commercial loans, either for construction or permanent lending.

[2] The capitalization rate for any real estate project or investment refers to that rate expressed as a percentage which includes provision for earning a rate of return and for recovering the investment.

[3] Halbert C. Smith, Carl J. Tschappat, and Ronald L. Racster, *Real Estate and Urban Development,* (Homewood, Ill.: Richard D. Irwin, 1977), p. 99. © 1977 by Richard D. Irwin, Inc.

default, should the revenues fall below projections. It is arrived at by dividing the net operating income (NOI) by the annual mortgage payment. The NOI is the income after direct expenses but before debt service. The coverage ratio indicates how many times the mortgage loan payment can be made from the NOI. A minimum acceptable debt service coverage ratio is generally 1.25 to 1.30 for projects with normal risk, such as apartment or office buildings. The ratio could be as high as 1.5 for a motel property, which is considered riskier.

$$\text{Debt service coverage ratio} = \frac{\text{Net operating income}}{\text{Annual mortgage payment}}$$

The second ratio of importance to institutional lenders is the *cash break-even point,* the *default point,* or the *break-even cash throw-off.*[4] This ratio indicates the relationship of all cash charges to gross income. It is computed by dividing the total of all expenses and debt service by the gross income for one year. A ratio of 75 percent indicates that three fourths of all income will be paid out in expenses and debt service, leaving 25 percent for income before taxes for the owners as well as safety for the lender. Typical ratios range from 60 percent to 80 percent.

$$\text{Cash break-even point} = \frac{\text{Expenses and debt service}}{\text{Gross income}}$$

The other two ratios that are usually computed in evaluations for financial feasibility are the *operating ratio*[5] and the *loan-to-value ratio.* The *operating ratio* is the annual operating expenses divided by the gross annual income. This ratio measures how much of the potential total income will be absorbed by the operating expenses. Operating ratios typically range from 25 percent to 50 percent. They may be even higher for older properties.

$$\text{Operating ratio} = \frac{\text{Annual operating expenses}}{\text{Gross annual income}}$$

The *loan-to-value ratio* is the amount of the permanent mortgage divided by the total price or the estimated project value. Loan-to-value ratios for newly financed properties are normally from 60 percent to 90 percent, but some institutions are limited by law to lend no more than 80 percent or 90 percent on real estate loans.

$$\text{Loan-to-value ratio} = \frac{\text{Amount of the loan}}{\text{Project price or estimated value}}$$

Profitability Ratios. Developers and owners apply profitability criteria to determine whether a project will provide a return that justifies financial investment and risk. The acid test of a project's desirability is its ability to produce income after all expenses and debt service, or more specifically, the relationship of that income to the equity capital required to obtain it.

---

[4] Ibid.

[5] Ibid.

The first measure of profitability in financial feasibility is called the *payback period.*[6] This ratio is calculated by dividing the equity capital, or owner's investment, by one year's cash flow (before income taxes). It is a crude or thumbnail measurement. It fails to account for such things as the value of money over time, the effects of income taxes or the benefits of tax shelter, project appreciation, or mortgage amortization. It is, however, the one measure used by some unsophisticated investors because it is fairly easy to compute. Investors frequently look for a payback period of five to seven years more or less as an important criterion for a real estate investment.

$$\text{Payback period} = \frac{\text{Equity capital}}{\text{Annual cash flow before taxes}}$$

A second frequently used and equally simplistic measure of return on a real estate investment is the *cash-on-cash return* or *equity dividend rate.*[7] It is arrived at by dividing the spendable income or cash flow before income taxes by the equity investment of the owners. This measure is the exact opposite, or reciprocal, of the *payback period,* and it shows the investors what percentage of their equity investment will be returned to them in cash in one year before income taxes. This method has the same weaknesses as the *payback period* measure. It fails to account for the time value of money, the effects of income taxes or the benefits of tax shelter, amortization, or project appreciation.

$$\text{Equity dividend rate} = \frac{\text{Annual cash flow before income taxes}}{\text{Equity investment}}$$

A third measure of the owner's rate of return is the *equity buildup rate.*[8] This method is a modification of the *equity dividend rate* to include the loan amortization (i.e., the principal buildup). It is arrived at by dividing spendable income plus amortization by equity.

$$\text{Equity build up rate} = \frac{\text{Annual cash flow and loan amortization}}{\text{Equity investment}}$$

A fourth measure is the *aftertax dividend rate*[9] or *aftertax equity dividend rate,* which is arrived at by dividing the aftertax cash flow by the equity investment. This measure can also be modified to include the loan amortization, which expands its scope somewhat.

$$\text{Aftertax dividend rate} = \frac{\text{Annual aftertax cash flow}}{\text{Equity investment}}$$

These last three measures of rate of return are first-year, second-year, or individual annual indicators of return to investors. They are relatively simple to compute, but they crudely treat both the value of money over

---

[6] Ibid., p. 100.

[7] Ibid., p. 100.

[8] Ibid., p. 100.

[9] William R. Beaten and Terry Robertson, *Real Estate Investment* (Englewood Cliffs, N.J.: Prentice-Hall, 1977), p. 169.

time and the impact of the eventual property disposition to the owners.

Finally, the most complete and comprehensive measurement of return to the owners, the one that accounts for *all* elements of return, is the *internal rate of return* (IRR). The IRR is the rate of interest that equates the present worth of the cash inflows over the estimated life of the ownership to the original investment or cash outflows required to obtain ownership. It includes the cash from its disposition related to the present worth of the equity investment. The IRR can be computed with before-tax cash flows or aftertax cash flows, but to be truly comprehensive it should be computed with the aftertax figures. The IRR formula or method of calculating rate of return on an investment assumes that the cash inflows during the ownership period can be and are reinvested at the internal rate of return.

Other Significant Questions

Good financial feasibility analyses always address a number of questions for the developer and owners and for the lenders. These questions vary according to the roles involved.

Questions for the Developer and the Owners

1. What is the short- and long-term economic viability othe community and the property?
2. What will the rate of return on the investment be during the period of ownership and after the sale is completed and all of the income taxes are paid?
   a. Does the return meet the investor objectives?
   b. Is it commensurate with the risk?
3. What is the margin of safety in the cash flow? (E.g., what level of rental and other income losses can the project stand and still be able to carry the expenses and debt service?)
4. What is likely to be the value of the property after a number of years? (E.g., is it likely to appreciate, and if so, how much?)
5. How does this investment opportunity compare with others that are available?

Questions for the Banker and the Mortgage Lender

1. Is the project economically viable at that location, in that community, and with that plan, design, or configuration?
2. Is the cash flow sufficient to provide an adequate margin of safety for this type of project?
3. If it is a new project, what is the probability that the developer will complete the construction on time, within the cost estimates, and according to plans and specifications?
4. How experienced is the developer in the construction business and with this type of property?
5. Do the owners have sufficient liquid assets to safely survive periods of economic difficulty? (E.g., are they investing enough cash or land or equivalent value in the project to survive periods of economic difficulty?)

An Example of a Financial Feasibility Analysis

It would be worthwhile now to walk through a typical example of financial feasibility analysis—say, a financial feasibility analysis of an apartment project.

Let us assume in our example that the local government approvals for our project are likely or have been granted, that mortgage money is available on terms acceptable to the developer, that the market study shows sufficient demand for the facility at acceptable rental levels, that the owners have sufficient financial strength and experience to complete and operate the project, and that the owners are properly organized and want to proceed. They are now ready to devote the necessary time and resources for a detailed financial feasibility analysis.

Six steps are involved in financial investigation of the apartment project or any other real estate project:

1. Delineate carefully all items of construction costs and rent-up expenses. These are to be put into a cash flow analysis statement by month and by year during the construction and rent-up period.
2. Estimate the projected income and operating expenses for up to ten years in the future, to begin immediately after rent-up.
3. Prepare a year-by-year pretax cash flow projection for the first eight to ten years of full operation.
4. Compute the income tax liability for each year and estimate the aftertax cash flow year by year for the eight to ten years of full operation.
5. Estimate the sale price for the project at a specifically set time in the future and compute the capital gains tax and the cash reversion to the owners.
6. Calculate the various measures of profitability before paying income taxes, after paying income taxes, and after selling the project.

In evaluations of feasibility, the borrower (that is, the developer or owner) should prepare several sets of figures using different assumptions. Whatever projections are made for rent levels, vacancy rates, expenses, construction costs, inflation rates, or financing costs and terms, the actual numbers will almost always be different when the project starts.

The borrower should test different assumptions about the values by preparing optimistic (high), pessimistic (low), and most probable (mid-level) projections. If the project is still attractive after the feasibility under the best and the worst of circumstances has been examined, then one may proceed to obtain financing from even the most prudent lenders.

One efficient method of assembling most of the financial data needed for a financial feasibility analysis is to prepare a cash flow and income tax analysis for up to ten years or longer. The number of years depends on the size of the project and one how long the owners plan to own it. A ten-year period of operating income and expenses is sometimes required, and always welcomed, by the mortgage lender.

The cash flow and income tax analysis can be prepared on an accounting spread sheet using a hand calculator, or a computer if the project is complex. The owners will always have use for the data. Using an *apartment project* as our example, we will present the data required for and the method of preparing the cash flow and income tax analysis.

Estimating Construction and Rent-Up Costs. Construction costs include both "hard" and "soft" costs. Hard costs are those that are directly related to the "brick and mortar" construction process. These costs include site preparation or development costs, planting and seeding, building labor and materials, and sometimes the cost of land. Soft costs are external to the construction process, but are needed to support construction. Architectural and engineering drawings, for example, construction loan interest and fees, appraisal expenses, legal and accounting costs, and construction fees are soft costs. Soft costs can account for 30 percent or more of any total construction budget.[10]

Several cautions should be considered when computing construction costs.

First, it is essential to be realistic and include everything. Do not think that you will be able to get everything done for the least cost.

Second, be realistic about how long it may take to construct the project and complete the rent-up. When the building is completed one year from start-up or later, the market may be completely different than it is today. Allow for unexpected difficulties.

Third, a frequent area of potential underestimating has been the cost of financing, particularly during the wide fluctuation of interest rates and the money market in recent years. The feasibility of any project depends on both the availability and the cost of financing, which includes construction financing as well as permanent mortgage financing. During the 1974–75 recession, developers were paying interest rates several percentage points higher than they had paid during the years 1971 to 73. This contributed to the failure of a number of widely publicized real estate projects.

A fourth factor critical to construction cost analyses is the architectural and engineering plans.[11] Plans are the bases for estimating hard construction costs. Using rules of thumb based on past experience is never sufficient. The construction costs for two buildings of identical size can vary by 10 percent or more, depending on the design and the materials called for in the plans. Careful cost estimating of the plans must be done by someone with extensive experience. It is even better to have contractors and subcontractors provide estimates or bids to complete the work.

Finally, the design and layout of the structure must meet the specifications of the current market analyses. An apartment project with only efficiency and one-bedroom units is not appropriate in a market which consists primarily of families. In the late 1970s on the other hand, the increased number of singles has made many apartment project developers reduce the two-bedroom units, increase the one-bedroom units—and

---

[10] John B., Bailey, Peter F. Spies, and Marilyn W. Weitzman, "Market Study and Financial Analysis = Feasibility Report," *Appraisal Journal,* October 1977, p. 568.

[11] Ibid., p. 570.

increase the amenities for single individuals.[12] Luxury apartments may not be suitable in a blue-collar suburb of an industrial city. The market analyst and marketing and sales officers of the company which will handle the rentals should be consulted before, during, and after the designs and plans are prepared.

A proposed 100-unit luxury high-rise apartment project is used as our example to illustrate the feasibility analysis procedure. These assumptions apply to our example:

1. The total project cost is estimated to be $3.6 million—$900,000 for land and $2.7 million for improvements.
2. The $2.7 million building costs are further broken down into hard costs and soft costs. The hard costs for labor and materials—($1,850,000)—comprise about 68 percent of the total building costs. The soft costs of interest on the construction loan, fees, rent-up costs, and other nonconstruction costs total $850,000, or 32 percent of the total building costs.
3. The construction and permanent loans are for the full $2.7 million construction and rent-up costs.
4. Land is purchase with 50 percent down, or $450,000, and the remainder is paid just prior to the start of construction.
5. The effective gross income during the rent-up period will be equal to half of the first year's rents.

Table 1 shows a typical cost pro forma for the 100-unit apartment project during the construction and rent-up period, which in this case is three years. One year is devoted to ground acquisition, plan preparation and securing local government approvals; one year to construction; and one year to rent-up. Three years, then, are needed from project initiation to full rental income.

The Projected Before-Tax Cash Flow The first task in preparing a cash flow statement is to estimate the projected rental and other income for a period of eight to ten years. Some of this data may come from the market study.

One source of information on rental income and other income is an inventory of what competing, comparable, nearby projects are offering and what they are charging. Total income includes revenue from all sources, including rents, governmental assistance (if applicable), and nonrental sources, such as parking fees, laundry service, and pool fees. To arrive at the effective gross income, an allowance must be made for vacancies and other rental losses.

The second task in preparing a projected cash flow analysis is to estimate the operating expenses. Although it may not be difficult to determine such expenses as real estate taxes and insurance, management, maintenance, and other costs, it may be difficult to know how much these expenses will increase over eight to ten years. Utility rates, for example, have skyrocketed in recent years, and many current projects

---

[12] "The Booming Singles Market," *Newsweek,* September 11, 1978.

TABLE 1
Projected Cash Flow Analysis during Construction and Rent-Up
(000 omitted)

Item	Year 1	Year 2	Year 3
Gross scheduled income	—	—	$285
Vacancy and rent loss	—	—	20
Effective gross income	—	—	$265
Equity investment	$677	$ 223	—
Financing proceeds	—	2,600	100
Land and development costs			
Land	$450	$ 450	—
Architect and engineer	50	100	—
Construction loan interest and fees	27	188	$232
Accounting, legal, and supervisory	75	110	—
Real estate taxes and other costs	75	125	—
Labor and materials	—	1850	—
Total	$677	$2,823	$232
Operating expenses			
Payroll	—	—	$ 12
Repair, Maintenance, and Utilities	—	—	$ 14
Administration and insurance	—	—	37
Management fee and overhead	—	—	14
Replacement reserve	—	—	2
Property taxes	—	—	54
Total	—	—	$133
Net operating income	—	—	$ 0
Cash flow before taxes	—	—	$ 0

Note: This analysis would normally be prepared on a month-by-month basis. It is summarized by year for this example.

are losing profits because of heavy fuel cost increases during hard winters.

The following assumptions apply to the case example:

1. The permanent mortgage loan of $2.7 million will be for 30 years at an interest rate of 9½ percent, and it will have a constant of 10.10.[13]
2. The gross scheduled income and the effective gross income figures are to increase at the annual rate of 5 percent.
3. Most expense items are to increase by 7 percent per year.
4. The expense ratio increases gradually over the eight-year period, and it ranges from 34 percent to 38 percent of the effective gross income.
5. All income and expense figures are computed in current dollars.
6. The project is to be sold after the eighth year of full operation.

Table 2 shows the pro forma operating income and pretax cash flow statement for the eight years of operation. This cash flow analysis is

---

[13] The mortgage constant refers to the ratio of the annual mortgage payment (principal and interest) to the amount of the mortgage.

TABLE 2
Projected Cash Flow Analysis after Rent-Up (000 omitted)

Item					Year			
	1	2	3	4	5	6	7	8
Income								
Gross scheduled income	$610	$639	$669	$700	$733	$767	$804	$843
Vacancy and rent loss	40	42	45	47	49	51	54	57
Effective gross income	$570	$597	$624	$653	$684	$716	$750	$786
Operating Expenses								
Payroll	$ 51	$ 55	$ 58	$ 62	$ 66	$ 70	$ 74	$ 78
Repair, maintenance, and utilities	27	30	32	34	36	39	42	45
Administration and insurance	32	34	35	36	38	39	42	43
Management fee and overhead	28	30	31	32	34	36	38	40
Replacement reserve	5	6	7	8	9	10	11	12
Property taxes	54	57	60	63	66	69	72	75
Total	$197	$212	$223	$235	$249	$263	$279	$293
Net Operating Income	$373	$385	$401	$418	$435	$453	$471	$493
Debt Service	273	273	273	273	273	273	273	273
Cash flow before taxes	$100	$112	$128	$145	$162	$180	$198	$220

based on careful estimates of increases in both income and expense items, which are shown in current dollars to reflect reality as closely as possible. Consequently, the cash flow before taxes should continue to increase over the life of the project. In the case example, the cash flow before taxes ranges from a low of $100,000 in the first complete year to $220,000 in the eighth year.

The Projected Aftertax Cash Flow. It is very important to compute the aftertax cash flow for each year because most real estate equity owners and investors look to their aftertax return as the most important measure of yield on their investment.

The tax liability is computed by subtracting the interest expense on the permanent mortage and depreciation from the net operating income figures for each year. The case example uses 200 percent declining balance depreciation to obtain the most favorable tax shelter for the owners and other investors.

The assumptions which apply to the case example are:

1. The owner's marginal income tax rate is 50 percent.
2. The building is depreciated over a 33-year life using the 200 percent declining balance method.
3. The tax loss benefits during the first two years are added to the before-tax cash flow to derive the aftertax cash flow.

The Estimated Return from the Sale of the Project. To estimate the total return from owning a property, the aftertax profit from the sale must be calculated. This involves selecting a probable estimated sale price and date of sale. From these projections, the capital gains tax liability, the pretax proceeds from the sale, and the aftertax proceeds from the sale can be estimated.

The following assumptions apply to the sale of the project in the case example:

1. The project will be sold at the end of the eighth full year of operations and the sale price will be $5.0 million after all the expenses of the sale, assuming that the project appreciates in value at the annual rate of 5 percent.
2. The remaining balance of the mortgage loan will be $2,450,000 at the time of the sale.
3. Capital gains taxes are computed on the basis of 40 percent of the capital gain, except for the recaptured portion of the depreciation, which is taxed at the full 50 percent income tax rate.[14]

To compute the return to the owners project, first calculate the tax liability at the time of sale.

The total tax liability incurred upon sale of the property is a function of four items: (1) the tax basis of the property when it was acquired, (2) the sale price after all selling expenses are deducted, (3) the method

---

[14] The capital gains computations are based on gains incurred after October 31, 1978, the date set by the 1978 Reform Act, after which a 60 percent deduction applies to capital gains.

TABLE 3
Projected Income Tax Liability and Aftertax Cash Flow (000 omitted)

Item				Year				
	1	2	3	4	5	6	7	8
Income								
Effective gross income	$570	$597	$624	$653	$684	$716	$750	$786
Less operating expenses	197	212	223	235	249	263	279	293
Net operating income	$373	$385	$401	$418	$435	$453	$471	$493
Less interest expenses	254	252	250	248	245	242	239	237
Less depreciation	162	152	143	135	126	119	112	105
Taxable income (loss)	$ (43)	$ (19)	$ 8	$ 35	$ 64	$ 92	$120	$151
Income tax liability	$ (21.5)	$ (9.5)	4	$ 17.5	$ 32	$ 46	$ 60	75.5
Before-tax cash flow	$100	$112	$128	$145	$162	$180	$198	$220
Less income tax liability	$ (21.5)	(9.5)	4	17.5	32	46	60	75.5
Aftertax cash flow	$121.5	$121.5	$124	$127.5	$130	$134	$138	$144.5

and amount of depreciation taken during the period of ownership, and (4) the marginal income tax rate of the owners at the time of sale.

The tax basis upon acquisition is the total of the land cost, which was $900,000 in the example, and the building cost, which was $2,700,000, for a total of $3,600,000. The depreciation taken was $1,054,000 based upon the 200 percent declining balance method. Thus, the adjusted basis of the property at the time of sale was:

Original tax basis	$3,600,000
Less accumulated depreciation	1,054,000
Adjusted basis at time of sale	$2,546,000

The taxable gain is based upon the difference between the adjusted sale price and the adjusted basis:

Adjusted sale price (after expenses)	$5,000,000
Less adjusted basis at time of sale	2,546,000
Taxable gain	$2,454,000

Had straight-line depreciation been taken, the total amount of the depreciation would have been taxed as a long-term capital gain. But since accelerated depreciation was taken, the difference between the straight-line and the accelerated depreciation is subject to recapture and is taxed as ordinary income.

Accelerated depreciation taken	$1,054,000
Less straight-line computation	654,000
Depreciation subject to recapture	$ 400,000

The amount that is then taxed as long-term capital gain is the amount that would have been declared as straight-line depreciation plus the difference between the acquisition basis and the sale price after the expenses of sale. The federal income tax code permits an exclusion of 60 percent of the long-term capital gain. The remaining 40 percent is taxed at the ordinary marginal income tax rate.

The taxable gain is computed as follows:

Adjusted sale price (after expenses)	$5,000,000
Less acquisition basis	3,600,000
Appreciation during ownership period	$1,400,000
Plus straight-line depreciation	654,000
Long-term capital gain	$2,054,000
Less the 60 percent exclusion	1,232,400
Taxable capital gain	$ 821,600

Adding the recaptured portion of the depreciation, which is taxed at the ordinary marginal income tax rate, to the 40 percent of the long-term capital gain, which is also taxed at the marginal income tax rate, and assuming a marginal tax rate of 50 percent at the time of sale, the capital gains tax liability is:

Recaptured depreciation	$400,000
Taxable capital gain	821,600
Total taxable income	$1,221,600
Taxed at the 50 percent rate	50%
Total tax liability upon sale	$ 610,800

The aforementioned shows only the calculation of the tax liability, not the proceeds of sale. The pretax proceeds of sale is the sales price after all selling expenses, less the mortgage balance:

Sales price after expenses	$5,000,000
Less mortgage balance	2,450,000
Pretax proceeds of sale	$2,550,000

The aftertax proceeds of sale is computed by subtracting the income tax liability from the pretax proceeds of sale:

Pretax proceeds of sale	$2,550,000
Less income tax liability	610,800
Aftertax proceeds of sale	$1,939,200

This series of calculations does not show what the owner's profit is. The calculation of a profit includes adjustments for the cash flow from owning the property; and, of course, a return of the initial investment.

The pretax profit from the sale of the property is the pretax proceeds of sale less the initial investment of $900,000. Subtract the income tax liability from the pretax profit to derive the aftertax profit from the sale of the property as follows:

Pretax proceeds of sale	$2,550,000
Less initial investment	900,000
Pretax profit from sale of property	$1,650,000
Less income tax liability	610,800
Aftertax profit from sale of property	$1,039,200

The other element of profit, the element which is not accounted for in this series of calculations, is the annual pretax and aftertax profit figures received during the two year construction and the eight year operating ownership periods. These are discussed in some detail below.

The Lender's Evaluation of Financial Feasibility. After the lender has confirmed that the projected income and expense factors are reasonable and accurately computed, he or she will calculate at least four ratios to check financial feasibility: the *operating ratio,* the *break-even cash throw-off,* the *loan-to-value ratio,* and the *debt service coverage ratio.*

$$\text{Operating ratio} = \frac{\text{Annual operating expenses}}{\text{Annual gross income}}$$

Using figures from the projections for the second year of operation, the operating ratio is $212,000/$639,000, or 33.2 percent. An operating ratio of 33.2 percent is very reasonable for a new apartment complex. The ratios for new projects are sometimes as high as 40 percent.

$$\text{Break-even cash throw-off} = \frac{\text{Expenses} + \text{Debt service}}{\text{Gross income}}$$

The break-even cash throw-off for the second full year of operation is $485,000/$639,000, or 75.9 percent. Thus, an estimated 75.9 percent of the total gross income will be needed to pay for the expenses and debt service. This is very near the top of the acceptable range for many conservative lenders, which is 80 percent.

$$\text{Loan-to-value ratio} = \frac{\text{Permanent mortgage}}{\text{Project value}}$$

Assuming that the estimated value at completion of the projects equals the cost of the land and building, the loan-to-value ratio is $2.7 million/$3.6 million, or 75 percent. A loan-to-value ratio is fairly common for new commercial projects.

$$\text{Debt service coverage ratio} = \frac{\text{Net operating income}}{\text{Debt service}}$$

For the second full year of operation, the debt service coverage ratio is $385,000/$273,000, or 1.41. A debt service coverage ratio of 1.41 is within the safe range for many lenders, most of which require 1.25 to 1.3 as their minimum.

Borrower's Evaluation of Financial Feasibility. There are several methods that are used to measure financial feasibility or rate of return to the owners or borrowers, some of which were discussed earlier in this chapter. The more frequently used ones will be demonstrated here: the payback period, cash-on-cash return before income taxes (the equity dividend rate), the equity buildup rate, the cash-on-cash return after income taxes (the aftertax dividend rate), and the internal rate of return.

$$\text{Payback period} = \frac{\text{Equity capital}}{\text{Cash flow before income taxes}}$$

This method shows how many years of operation will be required for the equity investment to be returned to the owners in before-tax dollars. It can be computed by using the cash flow figures for a typical year or if the projected figures change from year to year, as in this case example, the cash flow figures can be totaled cumulatively until they equal the original equity investment. Starting with the first full year of operation:

Year	Cash Flow before Taxes (000)	Cumulative Total (000)	
1	$100	$ 100	
2	$112	$ 212	
3	$128	$ 340	
4	$145	$ 485	
5	$162	$ 647	
6	$180	$ 827	$900,000
7	$198	$1,025	

The original owner's investment of $900,000 was projected to be returned to the owners sometime during the first half of the seventh year.

$$\text{Cash-on-cash return before income taxes} = \frac{\text{Cash flow before income taxes}}{\text{Equity}}$$

This measure is a simple division of the annual before-tax cash flow by the initial equity investment, which is $900,000 in this case example. The measure can be shown for each year, on a typical year basis or for an average of several years over time. From our example starting with the first full year of operation, we see:

Year	Before-Tax Cash Flow (000)	Rate of Return
1	$ 100	11.1%
2	112	12.4
3	128	14.2
4	145	16.1
5	162	18.0
6	180	20.0
7	198	22.0
8	220	24.4
Total	$1,245	

Typical year (fourth year) 16.1%
Average annual yield ($1,245,000 ÷ 8) 15.6%

The projected rates of return during the early years are reasonably attractive at 11.1 percent to 16.1 percent, but the return after the fourth year rises substantially.

The cash investment often represents actual dollars put up by the investor. The annual cash distribution represents spendable income which is usually tax free during the early years of ownership. This method of measuring return strips away some of the complexities. The weakness of the method, however, is that it fails to include the return to the owners from the loan amortization, the tax shelter, or potential project value appreciation. Further, it does not account for the profit made after selling the project at some time in the future, or the time value of money.

$$\text{Equity build-up rate} = \frac{\text{Spendable income} + \text{Amortization}}{\text{Equity}}$$

Since spendable income is cash flow before income taxes, this method simply adds the loan amortization for the year to the cash flow in computing the return. Taking figures from the second full year of operation, we have ($112,000 + $19,000)/$90,000, or 14.6 percent. This is 2.2 percent higher than the cash-on-cash return before income taxes, reflecting the value of the mortgage principal payment for that year.

$$\text{Cash-on-cash return after income taxes} = \frac{\text{Cash flow after taxes}}{\text{Equity}}$$

The aftertax return is more meaningful to most substantial investors because of the tremendous impact of the income tax code for investors in the 50 percent income tax bracket or higher. The tax shelter aspects of a real estate investment can make a very big difference to such investors. This case example shows the attractiveness of the tax shelter aspects in the early years of ownership.

During years 1 and 2, not only is the cash flow totally tax sheltered, but there is excess tax shelter which can be applied to the individual's other income. This is equivalent to giving the investor more than one dollar for each dollar that he or she receives before taxes.

The aftertax return for our 100-unit apartment project example for each of the eight years of full operation is shown as follows:

Year	Aftertax Cash Flow	Rate of Return
1	$ 121,500	13.5%
2	121,500	13.5
3	124,000	13.8
4	127,000	14.1
5	130,000	14.4
6	134,000	14.9
7	138,000	15.3
8	144,500	16.1
Total	$1,040,500	

Typical year (fourth year) 14.1%
Average annual yield ($1,040,500 ÷ 8) 13.0%

The aftertax project yield to the owner for a typical year of 14.2 percent and the average annual yield of 14.5 percent are both attractive returns when most investors are receiving less than 8.0 percent aftertax return on other investments.

$$\text{Aftertax buildup rate} = \frac{\text{Cash flow after taxes} + \text{Amortization}}{\text{Equity}}$$

Again taking the figures for the second year of operation, we get ($121,500 + $21,000)/$900,000, or 15.8 percent.

Although these methods of computing yield or rate of return account for the federal income tax impact on the investor, they still do not provide for the equity buildup from amortization and appreciation, the time value of money, or the aftertax return on the sale of the project. We therefore turn to the internal rate of return method to include the other benefits of real estate ownership.

The Internal Rate of Return Method. The internal rate of return (IRR) method of investment analysis is one of the most complete and comprehensive methods in use today. The IRR approach gives weight to the time value of money committed to one project that could have been earning a return elsewhere.

The IRR method holds that the profits received today are more valuable than profits received in the future. In addition, it shows that between two investments that may provide the same total return over a period of years, the one that provides the profits earlier may be better.[15]

The internal rate of return is that rate of discount which, when applied to a future income stream, will produce a total "present value" equal to the initial investment outlay.

One way of using the IRR to measure investment potential is to select a rate of return which would be satisfactory to the owners or investors and to work the formula to derive the present value of the future income stream. This present value of the future income is then compared with the initial investment. If the present value is larger than the actual required investment, the project would be considered sufficiently attractive to justify the investment.

For purposes of our case example, we will use an IRR of 12 percent as an acceptable yield and derive the present value of the income stream. This will be compared with the $900,000 initial equity investment made over a period of two years and adjusted to reflect its value at the beginning year 1. By using an imputed rate of return of 12 percent, the initial investment amounts to $1,018,830.[16] These values are shown below:

Year	12 Percent Present Value Factor	Aftertax Cash Flow	Present Value
1	0.893	$121,500	$ 108,500
2	0.797	121,500	96,835
3	0.712	124,000	88,290
4	0.636	127,500	81,090
5	0.567	130,000	73,710
6	0.507	134,000	67,940
7	0.452	138,000	62,375
8	0.404	144,500	58,380
Sale	0.404	1,039,200	419,835
Total			$1,056,955

Since $1,056,955 is more than the initial investment of $1,018,830 the investment meets the criteria of acceptability, assuming that it can be

---

[15] Smolkin, William R. *Building For Investors* (Washington, D.C.: National Association of Home Builders, 1973), p. 21.

[16] The owners' investment was made in two increments of $677,000 and $223,000 in the first and second years of construction (see Table 1). Since the computation of the IRR assumes that the first year of full operation is year 1, this equity investment is compounded by 12 percent per year to adjust it to year 1, assuming that the investors expected a 12 percent return per year on their investment. This increases the equity invested to $1,018,830.

financed under the terms specified, that it can be sold for 5.0 million after eight years, and that the projected income and expenses are reasonably close to actual experience.

Conclusion and Summary: "What If?"   The financial analysis portion of a feasibility study follows six basic steps:

1. A projection of effective gross income or total revenues.
2. A complete understanding of the construction budget and the annual operating budget for up to ten years.
3. A year-by-year pretax cash flow projection.
4. A year-by-year aftertax cash flow projection.
5. A computation of the aftertax effects of selling the project.
6. The computation of several measurements of yield or rate of return on the owners' initial investment.

Each step must be completed with care and precision. The major caveat is reiterated here for emphasis: *a single set of projections is not sufficient.*

Several sets should be prepared, each one answering a "What if conditions were different?" question. The "what if" questions should cover all of the major variables, including the amount and terms of financing, rental rates, vacancy rates, construction costs, operating expenses, and final sale price and sale date. *If,* after testing the feasibility with figures derived for several possible conditions, the project still looks attractive to the owners, then it may be undertaken.

All real estate projects are risky. The purpose of a financial feasibility analysis is to accurately assess and measure the risk. This provides a better understanding of what may happen and what will be the various outcomes should one or more of the basic financial assumptions turn out otherwise than anticipated. "Good luck" applies just as much to real estate investment as to any other entrepreneurial risk venture.

RISK AND SENSITIVITY ANALYSES

Richard T. Garrigan

Leon T. Kendall

*R*ICHARD T. GARRIGAN, PhD, Associate Professor of Real Estate
and Finance, Graduate School of Business, DePaul University,
Chicago, Illinois.

Formerly presidential interchange executive, Federal Home
Loan Bank Board; vice president–research, Real Estate Research
Corporation (Chicago); Associate Professor of Real Estate and
Finance, University of Wisconsin—Whitewater; Ford Founda-
tion fellow, University of Wisconsin—Madison. Member, Ameri-
can Finance Association, American Real Estate and Urban Eco-
nomics Association, and National Association of Corporate Real
Estate Executives. Author, "The Case for Rising Residential
Rents," Real Estate Review, Fall 1978; "How Much of a Down-
payment Should You Make on that Single-Family House?"
Federal Home Loan Bank Board Journal, July 1978; and "High
Loan-to-Value Ratio Lending by S&L's," Federal Home Loan
Bank Board Journal, March 1978.

LEON T. KENDALL, MBA, DBA, President, Mortgage Guaranty
Insurance Corporation, Milwaukee, Wisconsin.

Executive vice president, MGIC Investment Corporation.
Member, Board of Directors, MGIC and MGIC Investment Corporation, Commercial Loan Insurance Corporation, MGIC Indemnity Corporation, and AMBAC Insurance Corporation. Past
president, Securities Industry Association. First full-time president, Association of Stock Exchange Firms. Former vice president and economist, New York Stock Exchange; Economist of
the United States Savings and Loan League, and Economist,
Federal Reserve Bank of Atlanta. Council member, National Association of Business Economists.

Author of numerous articles, columns, and speeches. Author,
The Savings and Loan Business: Its Purposes, Functions, and
Economic Justification, *(Englewood Cliffs, N.J.: Prentice-Hall,
1962); and* The Exchange Community in 1975, *(New York Stock
Exchange, 1965). Coauthor* Who Buys the Houses *(1958). Editor,*
Thrift and Home Ownership: Writings of Fred T. *Green (1962);
Contributor,* American Enterprise: The Next Ten Years *(New
York: Macmillan, 1961); and* Readings in Financial Institutions
(Boston: Houghton Mifflin, 1965).

Most human activities present some forms of risk, and real estate
investment is no exception. In general, risk exists when there is the
possibility that physical or financial loss will occur. It is with the latter
kind of risk—financial risk—that we will deal in this chapter. Our concern is the risk associated with the investment returns on the ownership
of real estate.

We shall distinguish between *real estate risk* and *business risk.* Real
estate risk is defined as risk attributable to factors inherent in the ownership of real property itself. Business risk, on the other hand, is concerned
with factors which are part of the external business environment and
their effect on the productivity of a property. Both real estate and business risk are first dealt with conceptually. This treatment provides the
framework for introducing sensitivity analysis, a formal technique for
determining the risks which variations in key revenue and expense
items have upon the income flow and the value of a property. Our initial
focus is on real estate risk.

The Real Estate Risk

In evaluating a real estate investment, one of the first concerns is
to consider those intrinsic characteristics of the property which influence the size and the stability of its net operating income. The most
obvious are the characteristics related to the gross income that the property can produce.

In new construction, for instance, the largest unknown factor facing
the investor is whether or not his project will meet with market acceptance during the initial rent-up stages. At this time the physical appearance of the real estate itself can be critical to the project's overall success.
The investor should also understand that while buildings, like humans,
may be subject to cosmetic plastic surgery, the underlying "skeletal
structure" cannot be easily changed. He needs to gauge the likelihood
that the physical appearance of the real estate will create problems
initially or later on. Thus, the external physical attributes of the real
estate have a substantial effect on the overall risk of the transaction.
Another factor inherent in the real estate which can have a direct impact
on the gross income that the property earns is its functional utility and
whether or not this will attract and keep tenants. The investor may

find that if the property does not fit the tenants' needs, they will soon move on to locations which do.

Perhaps not as apparent, but just as deeply embedded in the real estate, are the expenses related to the maintenance of the property. For example, luxurious interiors in office buildings may lure superior tenants initially, but substantial expenditures may be required to maintain such features. Another item which can have an impact on the net income of real estate (and one which is directly related to physical and locational attributes) is property taxes, present and prospective.

Factors such as those that have been cited can increase the risk to a real estate investor on any given transaction. They may prevent the investor from obtaining the anticipated cash flow from the property, and may therefore impair the value of the property. Such factors may also impair the investor's ability to obtain reasonable financing for the investment.

The basic goal of our investor should be to minimize the amount of inherent real estate risk that he must assume. His basic strategy should be to invest in "quality" real estate. Let us assume that our model investor is a purely economic creature who measures the value of a property by the income that it can produce through rental to others. His first test of quality will probably be financial feasibility. This topic has been aptly discussed in the preceding chapter. However, it is worth restating here that a proper analysis of financial feasibility must encompass the entire cycle over which real estate should be successful, not just projections which apply under ideal operating conditions. A real estate investor who determines the existence of positive financial feasibility does not assure himself that the risk is minimal. Such a conclusion in itself is not sufficient cause for him to invest in a property. The financial feasibility test is merely one of the hurdles that the transaction must clear before he will even consider further analysis.

Assuming that a transaction demonstrates financial feasibility, our investor can then proceed to other measures of real estate "quality" which have an impact on risk and reward. The location and cost of proposed or existing structures or additions are the next difficult hurdles that the transaction must clear successfully (see Chapters 19 and 20). At this point, the investor knows where the property is and why it is there, and he believes in his own mind that the location is one of the best he can obtain. The key variable, of course, is the strength of market demand for the kind of space that is provided at a specific location. The character of such demand should be carefully documented through the intelligent use of rental and market price data for comparable space. All too many investors discovered in the 1975–77 real estate downturn that they insufficiently analyzed the basic demand for new facilities at the locations they had selected.

After the investor has determined that the site is appropriate to the real estate use, he must concern himself with the plant, equipment, and other structural components which constitute improvement of the real estate. To properly analyze this measure of real estate quality, the investor must have available a working knowledge of construction methods. Whether this knowledge is his own or that of trusted and respected associates, it is essential, for the type of improvements can have a definite impact on the income stream of the property and therefore on the real estate risk that the property presents. The investor's working knowledge of construction can also serve him well in assuring that the aesthetics set forth in the architect's elevations and blueprints are faithfully translated into brick and mortar. Many prospective tenants can be lost by properties which lose appeal when inappropriate materials are substituted during construction.

The Business Risk

In analyzing real estate risk, we have defined our risk-taker as an investor who seeks an adequate reward from real estate arising from rentals of the property. This economic orientation makes the investor also subject to business risk. In fact, the investor is probably more vulnerable to business risk than to real estate risk. The business risk in a real estate transaction flows from those factors in the business environment which may affect the ability of a property to generate net rental income. Some enterprises are more susceptible to business cycle risks than others, and less value should be attached to projects of less certainty.

Long-term secular changes can alter the economics of an investment. For example, an investor who owns an otherwise viable motel operation faces uncontrollable business risk from an energy crisis. The owner of a nursing home may see his lease-income stream diminish or even disappear due to licensing problems or to changes in the reimbursement methods of government programs. Similarly, an investor owning a property in a single-industry community may find that any disruption in the well-being of the primary employer results in widespread negative effects on tenants and on income flows.

The real estate investor can limit his exposure to business risk in two ways: first, by attempting to identify the most critical business risk factors; second, by subjecting those same factors to intensive analysis.

In order to identify the critical business risk factors, the investor must obtain an intelligent answer to the question "What factors, moving how much in which direction, will adversely affect the ability of the tenant to pay its rent and meet any other financial obligations?" Although not comprehensive, the following examples for a manufacturing firm illustrate an approach to answering this question:

1. *Supplies:* Are they available in the quantities required by the business and at reasonable prices, with adequate quality to permit ready production of the product?
2. *Employees:* Are qualified people available at reasonable wage rates, and are they likely to continue with the business?
3. *Customers:* Does the business properly serve its defined market segment? If so, does its customer group have sufficient breadth so that change will not adversely affect the overall business?

4. *Licensing and regulation:* How well can the business cope with the growing multitude of government regulations affecting its operations?
5. *Competitive position in the industry:* What share of the market is held by the business? Is the market position of the business strengthening or weakening? Are the prices of the business competitive? Are its products attracting new customers and markets?
6. *Sources of funds:* Not all of the initial resources needed by a business will come from its own capital. The appropriate use of credit is a proper measure of the chances of success. The key question is this: Does the potential tenant have sufficient resources to meet its immediate seasonal and cyclic operating needs?

These examples are not meant to imply that the investor must become an industry analyst for every type of tenant to which he rents. Rather they suggest that he should set down explicitly and examine the critical factors in the business risk facing his tenant. The investor may look to qualified experts to provide answers to the issues raised. Sensitivity analysis can help focus investors on the key variables that can most adversely effect a property's cash flow.

Sensitivity Analysis

Sensitivity analysis is an analytic technique which assigns alternative single values to the variables affecting a specific financial decision. Through the successive application of differing values to a specific variable, it is possible to determine how sensitive the financial outcome is to varying degrees of change. In real estate investment, the financial outcome being forecast is pretax cash flow.[1] The variables typically would be gross income, vacancy and bad debt expense, and selected individual categories of operating expenses. The advantages of using sensitivity analysis can best be demonstrated through the use of an example.

A Hypothetical 24-Unit Garden Apartment Investment. The information for this hypothetical investment is as follows:

1. Cost: $380,000
2. Mortgage financing
   Amount: $304,000 (80 percent)
   Interest rate: 9.5 percent
   Amortization term: 25 years
   Payments: Monthly
3. Equity investment: $76,000 (20 percent)
4. Gross income: $64,800 and $58,320
5. Vacancy and bad debt expense: $1,944 and $9,720
6. Operating expenses: $22,628 and $28,285.

---

[1] Alternatively, one could use aftertax cash flow. This, however, would require specific judgments as to both depreciation policies and the tax status of the ownership entity, judgments which we have chosen to exclude from the scope of this chapter.

The property is to be mortgaged for 80 percent of its cost. Two esti-mates are shown for each of three variables: gross income, vacancy and bad debt expense (hereafter called vacancy expense), and operating expenses. This financial information is set forth in Table 1 to demon-strate the potential impact of the selected variations in these amounts on the property's pretax cash flow.[2] Four separate cases are presented. Case 1 is based on the most favorable relationship among the variables. The projected gross income of $64,800 is reduced by an anticipated 3 percent vacancy expense ($1,944) and estimated operating expenses of $22,628, or 36 percent of the effective gross income. The net operating income is $40,228. After mortgage debt service of $31,872, the pretax cash flow is $8,356, for an 11 percent return on the $76,000 equity invest-ment.

TABLE 1
Variations in Pretax Cash Flow for a Hypothetical 24-Unit Garden Apartment Investment

	Case 1	*Case 2*	*Case 3*	*Case 4*
Gross income	$64,800	$58,320	$64,800	$64,800
Less vacancy and bad debt expense	1,944	1,944	9,720	1,944
Effective gross income	$62,856	$56,376	$55,080	$62,856
Less operating expenses	22,628	22,628	22,628	28,285
Net operating income	$40,228	$33,748	$32,452	$34,571
Less mortgage debt service	31,872	31,872	31,872	31,872
Pretax cash flow	$ 8,356	$ 1,876	$ 580	$ 2,699

Clearly, the estimates for gross income, vacancy expense, and operat-ing expenses can vary greatly. Thus, risk exists that the amount of cash flow will be less than the $8,356 being forecast. This point will be further illustrated through successive consideration of Cases 2, 3, and 4.

In Case 2, the gross income is estimated as $58,320, 10 percent less than in Case 1. Were gross income to decline by this percentage with no change occurring in either of the other two estimates, pretax cash flow would decline by 78 percent, to $1,876.

The sensitivity of pretax cash flow to 5 percent variations in the amount of gross income is presented in Table 2. As shown, pretax cash flow is extremely sensitive to changes in gross income; a specified per-centage change in gross income has a multiplier of about 7.8 times as great a change in the pretax cash flow associated with it. Thus, as re-vealed in Table 2, an increase in gross income of 25 percent would in-crease the pretax cash flow by 194 percent, to $24,556. Alternatively, were gross income to decline by 15 percent, pretax cash flow would decline by 116 percent, to a *negative* $1,364.

---

[2] The financial projections shown in Table 1 are for one year only. As riskiness over time is an important financial concept, the use of sensitivity analysis for actual investments would be expanded to include multiple-year projections.

TABLE 2
Sensitivity of Pretax Cash Flow to 5 Percent Variations in the Amount of Gross Income

Amount of Gross Income	Variation in Percent	Amount of Pretax Cash Flow	Variation in Percent
$81,000	25%	$24,556	194%
77,760	20	21,316	155
74,520	15	18,076	116
71,280	10	14,836	78
68,040	5	11,596	39
64,800	0	8,356	0
61,560	−5	5,116	−39
58,320	−10	1,876	−78
55,080	−15	−1,364	−116
51,840	−20	−4,604	−155
48,600	−25	−7,844	−194

The implications of this relationship are highly significant. The investor should very carefully determine whether the gross income being forecast is realistic. If the property exists, what are the probabilities that the forecast rentals will actually be achieved? If new units are to be constructed, how realistic are the rent projections based on existing comparables? How many units are currently being constructed in the competitive rental market? Will the potential supply of new competing units lead to either a reduction of rents or an unfavorable climate for future rent increases? Similarly, are projections of rent increases based on proven patterns of income growth among the residents of the area? And is the legal and political climate such that rent control is a likely occurrence?

Having considered the sensitivity of variations in gross income, let us turn to the potential impact of variations in the level of vacancy expense. Case 3 shows the impact of increasing vacancy expense from 3 percent to 15 percent of estimated gross income. So large an increase would reduce pretax cash flow by 93 percent, to $580.

Table 3 shows that pretax cash flow is far less sensitive to variations in vacancy expense than to variations in gross income. A 100 percent increase in vacancy expense results in only a 23 percent decline in pretax cash flow. A reduction of vacancy expense to zero would produce a 23 percent improvement in pretax cash flow.

Case 4 adds further perspective by applying sensitivity analysis to operating expenses. It shows the effect of increasing operating expenses by 25 percent. An increase of this magnitude would reduce pretax cash flow by 68 percent, to $2,699. Operating expenses thus comprise a middle ground. Pretax cash flow proves to be less sensitive to variations in operating expenses than to variations in gross income, but more sensitive to variations in operating expenses than to variations in vacancy ex-

TABLE 3
Sensitivity of Pretax Cash Flow to 33 Percent Variations in the Amount of Vacancy Expense

Amount of Vacancy Expense	Variation in Percent	Amount of Pretax Cash Flow	Variation in Percent
$9,720	400	$ 580	−93%
9,072	367	1,227	−85
8,424	333	1,876	−78
7,776	300	2,524	−70
7,128	267	3,172	−62
6,480	233	3,820	−54
5,832	200	4,468	−47
5,184	167	5,116	−39
4,536	133	5,764	−31
3,888	100	6,412	−23
3,240	67	7,060	−16
2,592	33	7,708	−8
1,944	0	8,356	0
1,296	−33	9,004	8
648	−67	9,652	16
0	−100	10,300	23

pense. Table 4 shows that a 35 percent increase in operating expenses would all but eliminate pretax cash flow. On the other hand, a 15 percent decrease in operating expenses would result in a 41 percent increase in pretax cash flow.

Given this degree of sensitivity, an investor would be well advised to evaluate closely the major components of operating expenses. For example, let us assume that the basic $22,628 projection for operating expenses included estimates of $6,100 and $8,275 for real estate taxes and utilities, respectively. These elements are volatile, and the investor would be well advised to determine the assessment policies of the taxing district as well as the likelihood of any increase in the mill rate. Specifically, he should determine whether the purchase of the property would trigger a reassessment with a consequent increase in the tax load. Analysis should also be made of the prospect for significant increases in real estate taxes due to changes in federal or state revenue sharing, rising personnel costs, and projections for capital expenditures. A fundamental question is whether the individual apartment units are designed so that tenants can absorb the cost of utilities. If not, the investor would be well advised to determine the likely future cost of fuel and electricity and to evaluate the likelihood that such costs could be passed on as additional rent. The importance of such analysis is underscored by the recent experience of investors whose apartment properties were fully occupied at projected rentals but were not breaking even due to huge increases in the cost of utilities.

TABLE 4
Sensitivity of Pretax Cash Flow to 5 Percent Variations in the Amount of Operating Expenses

Amount of Operating Expenses	Variation in Percent	Amount of Pretax Cash Flow	Variation in Percent
$30,548	35	$ 436	−95%
29,416	30	1,568	−81
28,285	25	2,699	−68
27,154	20	3,830	−54
26,022	15	4,962	−41
24,891	10	6,093	−27
23,759	5	7,225	−14
22,658	0	8,356	0
21,497	−5	9,487	14
20,365	−10	10,619	27
19,234	−15	11,750	41
18,102	−20	12,882	54
16,971	−25	14,013	68
15,840	−30	15,144	81
14,708	−35	16,276	95

Adding Probability to Sensitivity Analysis. As a risk evaluation technique, sensitivity analysis has several advantages. It is easy to understand and apply, and it will generally lead to correct conclusions in identifying those variables which are especially important to the financial success of an investment. With such knowledge, the investor can concentrate on analyzing the risks affecting those variables. A limitation of sensitivity analysis, however, is that it does not provide probability estimates of variations in financial outcomes. Such estimates, however, can be derived from the use of a companion technique, Monte Carlo simulation analysis.

In that technique, probability distributions must be assigned to the range of values specified for each variable affecting the financial outcome. Using vacancy expense as an example, the $9,720 vacancy expense shown in Table 3 might be assigned a probability of 5 out of 100 while the 3 percent vacancy rate and a vacancy expense of $1,944 might be assigned a probability of 20 out of 100. Appropriate probabilities would be assigned to each value appearing in the table. Collectively, all probabilities would sum to 100. This process would be repeated for the other variables in our example, gross income and operating expenses.

Following development of a simple computer program, values could be selected at random from the probability distributions specified for each variable.[3] The individual computer-selected variables would then

---

[3] Should the variables not be independent, this fact would affect the procedures for assigning probabilities. For example, the vacancy rate might affect the level of operating expenses likely to be incurred. This problem is dealt with through employing conditional probability distributions.

be combined in a manner like that used to provide the pretax cash flow for Cases 1 through 4. This process would be repeated over and over again, the outcome being a frequency distribution of the pretax cash flow. Using statistical procedures, it would be possible to judge the riskiness, that is, the degree of variability, associated with the pretax cash flow. Were this set of procedures performed in a consistent manner for a number of alternative real estate investments, it would be possible to rank each potential investment according to its estimated risk.

Summary

In this chapter we have attempted to apply sensitivity analysis to the risk associated with real estate investment in income-producing properties. We have demonstrated that real estate risk can be thoroughly analyzed by (1) identifying the possible causes of variations in the gross and net income streams and (2) evaluating the "quality" of real estate in terms of feasibility, location, and improvements. We have also attempted to describe the impact of business risk on the real estate investor and to suggest ways to identify and evaluate that risk. Finally, we have explored the use of a companion technique, as a means for placing probabilities on specific kinds of real estate and business risk. Through this exercise we hope that the investor will become a little more confident in dealing with the admittedly disturbing concept of risk.

INVESTMENT PROPERTY ANALYSES*

Byrl N. Boyce

Stephen D. Messner

*B*YRL N. BOYCE, PhD, SRPA, Professor of Finance and Real Estate, School of Business Administration, University of Connecticut, Storrs, Connecticut.

Director, School for Executive Development, Institute for Financial Education. President, American Real Estate and Urban Economics Association; Chairman, faculty subcommittee, Society of Real Estate Appraisers. Formerly editor, AREUEA Journal; and director, AREUEA. Acting director, CREUES. Author of numerous articles for various professional journals, including Land Economics, Right of Way, Appraisal Journal, Real Estate Today, and Real Estate Appraiser. Editor, Real Estate Appraisal Terminology (Cambridge, Mass.: Ballinger 1975). Coauthor, Management of an Appraisal Firm (Chicago: Society of Real Estate Appraisers, 1973); Analyzing Real Estate Opportunities (Chicago: Realtors National Marketing Institute, 1977); and Industrial Real Estate, 3d. ed. (Washington, D.C.: Society of Industrial Realtors, 1979).

STEPHEN D. MESSNER, DBA, SRPA, Head, Finance Department, School of Business Administration, University of Connecticut, Storrs, Connecticut.

Formerly director, Center for Real Estate and Urban Economic Studies; president, American Real Estate and Urban Economics Association; Co-editor, AREUEA Journal; director, AREUEA. Author of numerous articles for various professional journals, including Journal of Regional Science, Appraisal Jour-

---

* The authors drew heavily from their recent book, *Analyzing Real Estate Opportunities*, in writing this chapter.

nal, Real Estate Today, Real Estate Appraiser, AREUEA Journal, *and* Journal of Small Business Management. *Coauthor,* Effective Business Relocation *(Lexington: D.C. Heath and Company, 1970);* Industrial Real Estate *(Washington, D.C.: Society of Industrial Realtors, 1971 and 1979);* Management of an Appraisal Firm *(Chicago: Society of Real Estate Appraisers, 1973);* Marketing Investment Real Estate, *(Chicago: Realtors National Marketing Institute, 1975); and* Analyzing Real Estate Opportunities *(Chicago: Realtors National Marketing Institute, 1977).*

Overview of Market/Feasibility Analysis

All too often, traditional market analysis has involved collecting large masses of data, placing them in tabular form, and then ignoring them. Conclusions have then been stated which, for the most part, were arrived at before the data were even collected. Even more devastating, developers and investors have often committed themselves to projects whose long-run prospects or forecasted economic life they assumed without having undertaken any form of market analysis. Through the early 1970s it was not uncommon to see the effect of undertaking real estate investments on the basis of whim and unsubstantiated judgment about the market.

A large number of highly publicized recent real estate development failures have had one common feature—they were large-scale investment projects which had a significant impact on the local market area. Less clearly documented and less widely publicized has been the even larger volume of small individual properties that also failed. Both the smaller properties and the large-scale projects failed for same reason—lack of proper market analysis.

Small-scale developments may not have the economic or market impact or the visibility of large-scale developments, yet they still face the same investment problem—balancing the risk of losing venture capital and maintaining liquidity in the early stages of development. Small-scale developments require the same general framework of market analysis as large-scale developments.

Existing real estate developments also require a market analysis, especially when their disposition is being considered. Existing improvements are in reality a constraint on the use of a site. A market analysis is necessary to determine whether its present use should be continued, altered, or completely converted by demolition and replacement. A well-constructed market analysis is the key to real estate investment decisions, whether they involve existing properties or new development proposals.

A properly conducted market analysis can achieve the following: (1) identify market opportunity, that is, market shortages in the entire market area or locational deficiencies in specific sectors of the market area; (2) aid in the design of marketing strategies and plans; (3) serve as a guide in formulating development proposals for new properties or improved properties where conversion or rehabilitation is being considered; and (4) establish rent levels. Feasibility studies emanate from market analyses. Such studies cannot be conducted in a vacuum, and they often proceed under the presumption that existing markets can support the venture under consideration (see Chapters 16 and 17).

The Hierarchy of Studies/Analyses

We contend that there is a logical order in which studies/analyses are conducted and information flows or is refined so as to serve as an input into some subsequent form of analysis in the hierarchy of studies/analyses. The flowchart in Figure 1 identifies some of the more important forms of analysis that are needed in the evaluation of real estate investments and in the decision process associated with buying, selling, leasing, exchanging, and so on.

Broadly interpreted, the analysis of highest and best use would either incorporate or provide the necessary data to conduct an investment analysis. Appraisal analysis falls somewhere between feasibility studies, on the one hand, and highest and best use studies, on the other, incorporating at least some statement regarding the latter in the appraisal. All too often, however, what should have been analyzed before the valuation process or should receive more rigorous treatment in the appraisal report is assumed away, ignored, or given lip service.

Definitions

Below are a list of definitions that appear in the order in which they are most likely to be encountered in the analysis of a real estate investment potential. Each form of study or analysis provides some insight into the determination of a specific real estate investment decision. In some instances a broader study or analysis may include other studies or analyses that are conducted concurrently or separately as inputs to the broader study. In any event, it is felt that there is a logical sequence in which studies/analyses are conducted, and the definitions listed below follow that sequence.

1. *Market study*—The comparison of market analysis projections with the supply of space for a specified activity in an effort to identify market opportunities.
   a. *Market analysis*—a dynamic process involving the projection and analysis of the components of demand.
   b. *Economic base study*—an analysis of the employment and income-generating activities in an economically defined area.
2. *Marketability study*—determines to what extent a particular piece of property can be marketed under various development concepts; more generally, determines the ability of a market to absorb space with a specific use.
   a. *Strategy study*—determines the best location and marketing ad-

vantages for entrance into new, unexplored metropolitan market
areas, such as retail chains.

b.   *Volume expectancy study*—determines total sales volume for department store trade merchandise and comparison goods at shopping centers.

FIGURE 1

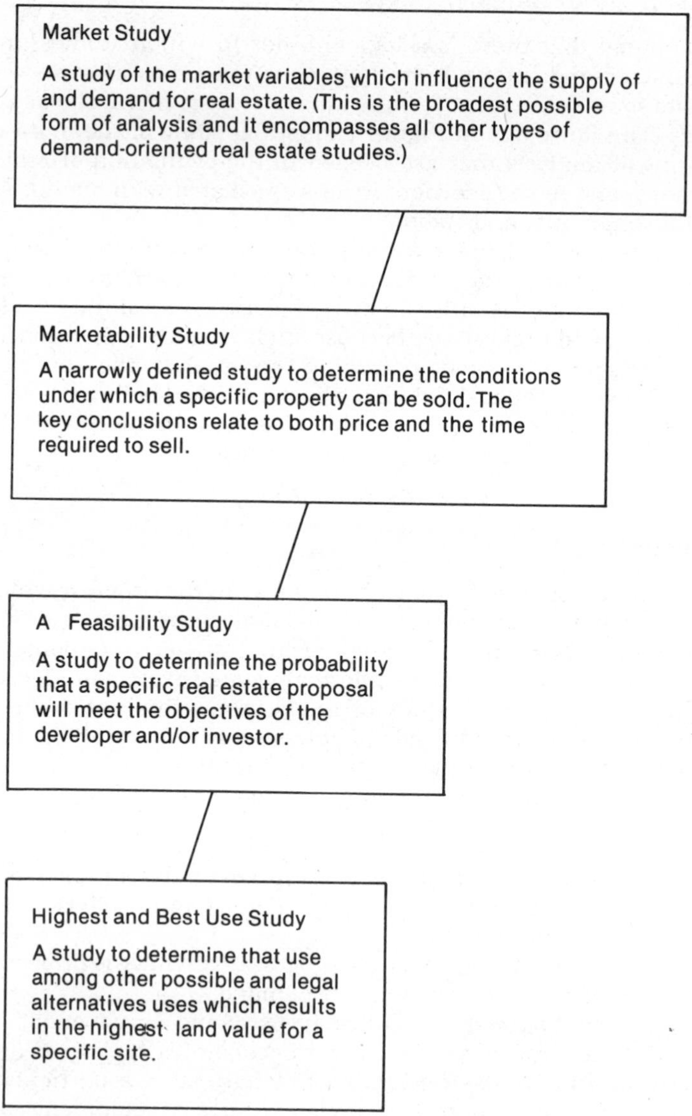

Market Study

A study of the market variables which influence the supply of
and demand for real estate. (This is the broadest possible
form of analysis and it encompasses all other types of
demand-oriented real estate studies.)

Marketability Study

A narrowly defined study to determine the conditions
under which a specific property can be sold. The
key conclusions relate to both price and the time
required to sell.

A   Feasibility Study

A study to determine the probability
that a specific real estate proposal
will meet the objectives of the
developer and/or investor.

Highest and Best Use Study

A study to determine that use
among other possible and legal
alternatives uses which results
in the highest land value for a
specific site.

Source: Stephen D. Messner, Byrl N. Boyce, Harold G. Trimble, and Robert
L. Ward, *Analyzing Real Estate Opportunities* (Chicago: Realtors National Marketing
Institute, 1977), p. 14. Reprinted with permission of Realtors National Marketing
Institute.

    c. *Branch bank application study*—determines potential deposits from a service area.

3. *Feasibility study*—determines whether a project or use is a "go" or "no-go" situation at a specific site, given certain financial criteria and client objectives. Conducted on either a before-tax (preliminary feasibility) or an aftertax basis.

4. *Highest and best use study*—determines which physically possible, reasonably probable, appropriately supportive, financially feasible, and legally permissible use results in the highest land value.

5. *Investment analysis*—determines the attractiveness of an investment by analyzing the costs and benefits utilizing time, the value of money and various ratios; an aftertax analysis.

Figures 2 and 3 point up not only the order in which certain phases of an analysis of real estate investment opportunities are conducted, but also indicate differences in that order which depend on what information is known at the outset. Although there may be variations on these themes, we consider two points of departure in the market/feasibil-

FIGURE 2
Use Known/Site to Be Determined

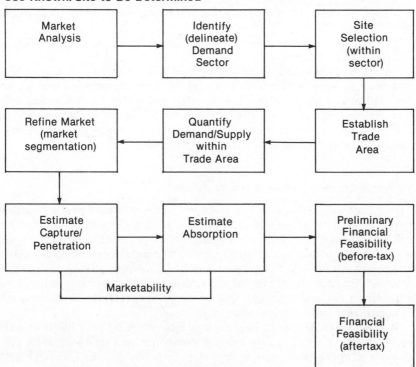

Source: Stephen D. Messner, Byrl N. Boyce, Harold G. Trimble, and Robert L. Ward, *Analyzing Real Estate Opportunities* (Chicago: Realtors National Marketing Institute, 1977), p. 17. Reprinted with permission of Realtors National Marketing Institute.

FIGURE 3
Site Known/Use to Be Determined

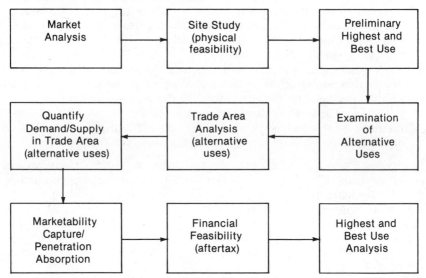

Source: Stephen D. Messner, Byrl N. Boyce, Harold G. Trimble, and Robert L. Ward, *Analyzing Real Estate Opportunities* (Chicago: Realtors National Marketing Institute, 1977), p. 18. Reprinted with permission of Realtors National Marketing Institute.

ity analysis framework: (1) a site or building in search of a user and (2) a user in search of a site and certain improvements. Further, we also explicitly recognize that a feasibility study can be conducted only after the market has been fully investigated and analyzed and consideration has been given to the marketability of the space or activity over some representative and realistic time frame.

The Importance of Market Analysis

As indicated above, real estate investment decisions are a function of an evolutionary process involving various forms of analysis or studies, with market analysis serving as the initial point of departure in all cases. Successful real estate development depends upon the relationship of three elements: (1) the physical entity (the property in its market environment), (2) the financial structure, and (3) the people involved in development and management. Only by successfully combining all three can real estate developments succeed.

Of these three elements, the weakest has been and very likely continues to be the property in its market environment. An analysis of past problem properties indicates that although the people involved may have had considerable developmental successes, the development concept was approved and funds were extended without even so much as a cursory examination of local real estate markets. The office building market in New York City in the late 60s is a prime example of this problem. The extraordinary boom in white-collar employment from 1965–69 was assumed by both interim and permanent lenders to signal high demand for new space even though existing and potential tenants had not been vocal about needing new space and had not been specifically identified by some form of market analysis. As a result of the presumed demand for new space, lending institutions threw caution to the winds in competing for the right to finance new buildings. Funds were extended on these new buildings without the traditional precautions.

Obviously, problems in the real estate market stem from a variety of causes, but the central cause is undoubtedly poor market research or perhaps no research at all. All too often, development takes place only on the basis of hunch, intuition, availability of money from lending sources and a whole host of less than scientific means of judging the demand for space.

The most significant reason for poor-quality market research is optimistic projections that result from boom periods in real estate development. Although a boom may be experienced in another part of the country or even in a use of space that is different from that being considered in the market being analyzed, there has been and there continues to be a tendency to transfer the euphoria of success rather indiscriminately. However, the emphasis placed upon the "bandwagon effect" must be rejected, and markets must be assessed on the basis of relevant statistical data compiled from primary and secondary sources.

Another reason for poor-quality market research is definitional in nature. Often it is not clear what type or form of study or analysis is needed. For example, institutional lenders often ask for an appraisal report for a construction loan when, in fact, a feasibility study would be more suitable for their purposes. Clients have difficulty in precisely articulating their objectives, and consultants therefore have trouble in precisely identifying the purpose of a study or an analysis. Thus, substantial imprecision has been built into terminology. It is not uncommon for the terms *market, marketability,* and *feasibility* to be used interchangeably. But these terms are not interchangeable. These terms represent types of studies which have precise requirements; they apply to distinct critical decision points within the framework of the development process.

In addition to these difficulties, inflexibility in projected results leads to a development plan that remains inflexible even in the face of changing market conditions. The precision of the mathematical processes by which data are manipulated often leads analysts or clients to the unwarranted conclusion that projected results are accurate. The narrowness of the data used to make such forecasts leads to rather sterile projections.

The Market Analysis Framework

The following framework is offered as a suggestion only. For example, the first step indicates the need to identify the problem and establish the client's goals and objectives. Problem identification requires, in part, identifying the point of departure indicated earlier, that is, to determine whether the problem involves (1) a site or building in search of a user or (2) a user in search of a site and certain improvements. Depending on how the problem is defined, subsequent steps in the framework may require alteration. If in defining the problem it is established that the use is known and the site is to be determined, step 2 in the framework would obviously appear after the market has been delineated and some basis for determining location has been identified. In any event, there is a need for flexibility in light of problem definition.

1. Problem identification—establishment of client's goals and objectives.
2. Site inspection and identification of physical locational factors, both external and internal to the site, relying heavily on engineering inputs to establish criteria of development.
3. Begin demographic analyses with cursory overview of regional and metropolitan historic patterns and trends.
4. Define the market area which impacts upon the subject property.
5. Identify supply and demand conditions within the market area for competitive developments similar to the one proposed by the client.
6. Estimate market penetration of the competition in relationship to the overall market within the larger region or metropolitan area.
7. In conjunction with the engineer, environmental specialists, and the architect, prepare a general development concept which would capitalize upon the inadequate supply in relationship to the demand within the area of impact.
8. Once the design has been created, determine the share which can be attributed to the site because of its location, access, or monopolistic position in the marketplace.
9. Design advertising or amenity packages which can skew absorption in favor of the client's position.
10. Restructure meetings with the client to reaffirm the satisfaction of goals and objectives as outlined previously.
11. Begin the financial analysis, which more than likely will include a discounted cash flow and result in some statement concerning the feasibility of the project.

The Analysis and Projection of Market Variables

Market analysis is demand oriented, that is, it involves the projection and analysis of the determinants of demand (income, population, employment, retail sales, etc.). Market analysis is concerned with the existing economic health of a specified market area (region, city, community, neighborhood, etc.) and with the potential for new, rehabilitated, or converted spatial units within that area. It is important to note that although market analysis is demand oriented, it would be meaningless to project demand determinants without making some provision to match those projections with information on the spatial activities in the area under consideration. Supply is not simply an enumeration of the existing spatial activity but also takes into consideration current or potential changes in that stock.

A given market analysis can rarely be handled by complete objective and quantifiable data that supports each of its elements. Measurement and analysis tasks can at times be so lengthy and costly that substantial reliance on judgment is needed. A distinction should be provided, therefore, between the use of technique and the use of judgment. Techniques such as statistical analyses (linear regression) or the gravity or retail allocation models for determining demand are to a large extent objective and free from bias. The application of techniques, however, involves the acceptance of a set of assumptions about the conditions in which the techniques may be employed. This requires judgment.

Forecasts using demand models represent a matter of judgment which is inescapable. Simple linear regression (SLR) is a highly objective technique (any two users will obtain the same results from the same data assuming no mathematical error). SLR results in a *projection,* a statement of what will happen if certain conditions prevail. The acceptance of the likelihood of these conditions is a matter of judgment, and only after that acceptance may the projection be properly called a forecast.

The techniques for arriving at demand forecasts are far more complex than presented here. The more accurate the forecast required by the client, the more complex and costly the process is likely to become. Similarly the less readily available the data, the greater is the cost of obtaining them. In all cases, the analyst must determine the degree of accuracy that is required to complete the assignment, given the budgeted estimate and the client's objectives.

Projection and Forecasting Methods

Forecasting is, at best, an inexact science. Most often, we are dealing with the extension of historic trends or assuming that the past will persist into the future—that observed relationships will extend beyond the range of data inputs. Projections are extremely useful, but in looking at the results of any projection, one must be reminded constantly that although the trend may now be a fact, extrapolations represent no more than an educated guess. The presumption is that all factors influencing what is being projected will continue to act in the same way and in the same magnitude.

There are, however, methods of forecasting that allow us to identify measures of reliability associated with the forecast. Thus, more sophisticated techniques of projection enable us to make more reliable forecasts, that is, to identify errors associated with forecasts.

No attempt is made here to provide complete coverage of the topic and tools of statistics as they relate to market analysis. The applications illustrated here utilize standard and conventional statistical techniques which are more fully developed and explained in any basic statistics text.

Trend Analysis (Linear). Measures of change over time (employment/ unemployment, population, household income) are relatively meaningless in and of themselves. To be meaningful for purposes of analysis, such changes must be compared to measures in other markets for the same time period or to previous levels in the same market. Growth or change can be measured in a variety of ways—its direction influences spatial resources and their allocation.

Within a particular market, trends over time may be measured in absolutes, in percentages, or in average or compound rates of change. Although the mathematical computations in trend analysis are rather simplistic, there are some serious practical limitations to their use. The initial difficulty with this means of projection is the implicit assumption that the average absolute change per year (or the average rate of change) will continue in the future. Further, if we are projecting unemployment as a function of employment, for example, then we are implicitly assuming that the relationship between employment and unemployment remains unchanged over time. Moreover, though we may have developed a model for projection purposes, we have no measures of reliability associated with either the model or the projection. Although it cannot resolve all of these limitations (because we are still dealing with averages), regression analysis certainly provides us with a means of testing the reliability both of the model and of the projections made from it.

Simple Linear Regression Analysis. Regression analysis is used primarily for forecasting or predicting the value of a dependent variable, given the values of one or more independent variables. The reliability of the forecast and the extent to which variation in the dependent variable is "explained" by variations in the independent variables can be tested and measured.

Regression and correlation analysis can never "prove" anything. They merely demonstrate association between or among variables, the closeness of that association, and the reliability of forecasts based upon the analysis.

In the simple linear regression, the first thing we ask ourselves is: What are we trying to do? We have two sets of data; we think there may be some relationship between the two sets, and we would like to know just what that relationship is. The first thing we do is plot the data. If it appears to be linear, we would like to identify the line that best fits the data.

If the curve fitted to the data were a straight line, it would be possible to express its formula as $Y_c = b_0 + b_1X$, where: $b_0 = Y$ intercept, or the value of Y where the line crosses the Y axis; $b_1 =$ slope of line, or $\Delta Y/\Delta X$, or the change in Y for a given unit change in X; and $Y_c =$ the computed value of Y at a given level of X. Any number of lines or curves could be fitted by eye to a given scatter diagram. A practical method exists to determine a unique line for a given set of data with certain desirable statistical properties. It is these statistical properties which provide the basis for tests of significance and reliability and thus make SLR preferable to simple trend analysis as a forecasting tool.

Multiple Linear Regression Analysis. Since a single independent variable often does not serve as an adequate basis for forecasting or predicting, forecasts or projections are usually a function of two or more independent variables. In such cases, multiple regression analysis is frequently more effective. The general equation is:

$$Y_c = b_0 + b_1 X_1 + b_2 X_2 \ldots b_n X_n$$

Multiple regression analysis is a process of separating the dependent variable into its several components or influencing factors and assigning a value or quantity to each. Conceptually, multiple regression is no more complex than simple regression. It does, however, require many more steps in the solution of several simultaneous equations. It is more complicated and time consuming, and its effective use really dictates the availability of either a computer or a programmable calculator with adequate storage capacity.

Multiple regression still indicates only association between the value of the dependent variable and those of the independent variables. Causation is not indicated nor implied; it is only inferred from the analyst's substantive knowledge or judgments about the relationships between the variables.

The coefficients derived in a given multiple regression equation are valid only for the data, variables, and limits of the data that go into the makeup of that specific equation. It is possible to include a variety of characteristics or predictor variables in the multiple regression equation as measurable influences on the dependent variable.

Location Quotients. The L.Q. method provides us with a means for determining which of the industries in a community are basic (export) and which are nonbasic (service). The representative (for a particular employment category) numerical and percentage distribution calculations for the metropolitan economic base area are compared with those for the United States as a whole on a percentage basis. The U.S. percentage distribution (though easily computed) is not shown. The location quotient (L.Q.) is the ratio of the percentage of local employment in an industry to that of national employment in the same industry. Uniform productivity within each industry group throughout the nation is assumed by the technique. Although the technique is not foolproof, it is a strong indicator of the industries which provide the underlying strength of an economy. The formula for the location quotient is as follows:

$$\text{Location quotient} = \frac{\text{Local employment in industry M}}{\text{Total local employment}}$$
$$\div \frac{\text{National employment in industry M}}{\text{Total national employment}}$$

An L.Q. of 1.00 for an industry group in an area indicates that the industry group has the same proportion of employment locally as it has nationally. This ratio implies that the area just takes care of its own needs (or could) for whatever goods or services the industry group provides. An L.Q. of less than 1.00 implies that the area must import a portion of its needs for the type of goods or services involved; and, of course, an L.Q. of more than 1.00 indicates that the area exports those goods or services. However, judgment must be exercised in interpreting the

L.Q. For example, an L.Q. of either 0.98 or 1.05 indicates that the area is probably self-supporting for all practical purposes and that an industry is nonbasic; but an L.Q. of 1.45 indicates substantial exports and marks an industry as overwhelmingly basic. At the other extreme, an L.Q. of 0.73 implies imports of goods and services and labels an industry nonbasic.

The L.Q. analysis is a very simple and short method for determining those industries which are basic and those which are nonbasic for the local economy. By virtue of its simplicity, the L.Q. is subject to interpretative analysis. It has been shown that L.Q.'s exceeding 1.00 are generally conservative in their nature. L.Q.'s below 1.00, however, are generally liberal. The disadvantage in the use of the L.Q. is that it is difficult to measure the nature and causes of changes which have occurred over a ten-year period.

Analysis of Marketability

Market analysis is an ongoing process concerned with the components of demand without any necessary regard to specific use at the outset (although specific use may at some subsequent point in the analysis determine the form in which the variables are projected or forecast). A study of marketability provides the basis for determining whether forecasted market forces will support specific development proposals and the rate at which such development could take place. A marketability study identifies precisely each use type or offering, income projections, and density or land requirements and absorption rates for each use, and it is conducted within the framework of the broader market analysis of past, current, and potential patterns of metropolitan area development. Development patterns and trends in the project market area (and the competitive strengths of the site, if known) with regard to other competitive offerings are evaluated to determine the specific use potentials and development timing.

The marketability of spatial activity (typically identified in such units as square feet, apartments, number of beds, and number of motel rooms) implies the ability of the market to accept the transference, salability, or exchange of some or all of the rights in that spatial activity. The marketability study usually considers a specific use or uses of spatial activity. This activity may not represent the highest and best use since the marketability study considers marketable use rather than optimal use.

Once the determinants of demand have been identified and have been contrasted with supply, the marketability study carries the analysis one step farther by identifying the number of units that can most probably be absorbed within a market over some specified time period.

As indicated previously, studies are often mistitled. This is particularly true of marketability studies which are frequently confused with feasibility studies. The purpose of a marketability study is to establish the relative rentability or salability of a project by estimating the rate at which the space in that project will be absorbed by the market over a specified period of time at specified rent or sale levels. The marketability study does not involve the consideration of the development costs or profitability.

The marketability study is sandwiched between the market study, on the one hand, and the feasibility study, on the other. The complexity of analysis increases in the progression from one form of analysis or study to another in the hierarchy of studies. To emphasize the point that a project may be marketable but not feasible, consider new three-bedroom, two-bath houses for $20,000. Obviously, these are most marketable commodities, but they are not feasible in most markets in today's economy.

The usual conclusions of a marketability study are three: (1) quality, which in economic terms means the price or rent levels at which the market might accept the spatial units; (2) quantity, or absorption scheduled by time periods; and (3) specific conditions, such as terms of financing, sales techniques, and amenities, that will enhance the acceptance of the property or encourage its acceptance by the market.

Methods of Market Delineation

Up to this point in market analysis, we have concentrated on projecting change in the various components of demand without consideration of specific location within a market. Feasibility analysis requires, however, the determination of a specific site as a condition of proceeding with the analysis. To the extent, then, that there is a gap to be filled in an existing market (as determined by market analysis) and in the absence of a predetermined location, the location of spatial activity is critical to the analysis of feasibility. Market delineation either implies a known location as a starting point or provides the means by which to determine the most effective location in light of existing or proposed competition.

Even if location is a given (a site in search of a use), it can be tested for effectiveness in comparison to alternative locations. Although we are dealing primarily with either a site in search of a use or a use in search of a site, it does not necessarily follow that we confine ourselves to a single method of market delineation. Rather, in instances where the site is unknown, market delineation is at least a two-step process which first identifies location and then the market for that location and the proposed use or uses. In those circumstances where site is given, in addition to testing for effectiveness, the demands of practical methodology strongly suggest the use of more than a single approach.

Geographic Delineation of Market Areas. Market areas can be delineated in geographic terms (physical areas or distances) or in competitive terms. Although the former terms are perhaps more familiar, the existence of competing firms will impose obvious economic constraints on geographic boundaries. In a geographic sense, a market area may also be defined in terms of the political boundaries of a given community or group of communities, while a retail trade area may be defined by a census tract. School districts may also form a housing market area or at least a segment of a housing market.

Time-Distance Boundaries. Traveling time to a spatial activity is quite important. The cost of travel (commutation) is usually measured in time, which is what the commuter must give up in order to get to work, shop, or attend civic, cultural, or social events.

Time "cost" is usually calculated as distance multiplied by the average rate of speed. Time-distance boundaries can be drawn as circles from the center of employment, or shopping, or other activity, but this simplified approach overlooks the fixed locations of transportation corridors over which travel may be possible at different speeds. The preferred approach would be to locate the major transportation corridors on a map, and then survey average speeds to and from major centers of employment or other activities along these corridors. Distances representing the prescribed travel time are then plotted, and the points connected. The result is a map of the specified market area.

Reilly's Law of Retail Gravitation. Reilly's "law" is based upon Newton's law of gravity. It substitutes population (or another size variable such as square footage of retail space, dollar retail sales, or average bank deposits) for mass, and it measures distance in miles or in driving time. Reilly's original formula reflects a generally held and readily acceptable axiom that the relative drawing power of two competing spheres of dominance from intermediate areas is in direct proportion to their population and in inverse proportion to the square of the distance from the intermediate areas to each sphere of dominance. The exponent of the distance was determined by an empirical study of some 225 cases of various-sized cities in Texas. From this study, a clear modal value for the exponent of the distance occurred in the range 1.51–2.5.

The formula in its original form identifies the proportion of the trade attracted by City A from an intermediate town relative to the proportion of the trade attracted by City B from that same intermediate town. In effect, then, the formula provides an index number which requires further "adjustment" to determine the proportions of the trade from an intermediate point or an intermediate market area two competing spheres of dominance can expect to enjoy.

Reilly's law represents a melding of two extremes that requires careful consideration before any wholesale application of the law is attempted. On the one hand, the law is represented by a mathematical formula producing a mathematical result which would be approximately correct, all other things, save distance and size, being equal. On the other hand, the formula requires considerable prudence and judgment in its application according to the particular circumstances that arise in specific cases. In other words, Reilly's law may provide the analyst with a good "first approximation" of the delineation of trade areas, but it should be utilized in conjunction with, not exclusive of, other methodology.

Estimating Market Penetration

The method for estimating the market penetration of a real estate development within the bounds of a market area and within the framework of a dynamic population depends greatly on quantified experience (analogues) and partly on subjective judgment. The more the quantified experience that is available, the less the dependence on subjective judgment. Similarly, the better the quantified experience and the subjective judgment, the greater the accuracy of the prediction.

Since no two sites are exactly alike, and since the market factors in one situation are never exactly like those in another situation, subjective judgment prevades throughout the use of competitive property statistics of analogues. Furthermore, market factors, such as the price levels obtained previously for certain projects (for example, the pace of condominiums sales), will change over time. Competitive property files on previously developed market characteristics may not be completely valid today or tomorrow. This, once again, requires subjective judgment in the use and projection of earlier quantifiable experience.

A firm's public acceptance or image can, and generally does, vary from one region to another. Tishman's success in New York City office building construction is not identical with its market penetration in Los Angeles nor in Philadelphia. In a similar manner, competitive condominium developments may differ drastically in price level and absorption for identical projects simply because of the differences in the corporate entities or images associated with the developments. This is especially true in Washington, D.C., where the team sponsored by the Watergate construction firm will generally outpull competitive developments in price level and sale pace simply because of its heavily publicized previous successes. Essentially, then, given equal locational and recreational amenities, a Watergate condominium development will take a larger share of the market than will competitive condominium projects. In a similar manner, the industrial development firm of Cabot, Cabot, and Forbes will have, in almost all cases, a faster selling pace than like firms.

Once the overall picture has been attained and the appropriate forecasts regarding the market behavior for a total area have been made, a decision must be reached as to the subject site's share of the overall market demand. This is commonly referred to as market penetration (capture), market share, or site share.

The Feasibility Study

The Nature of the Feasibility Study. As indicated above, real estate *market analysis* represents a broad form of study that may be used to forecast the size and composition of the demand for and supply of a variety of land uses. This type of analysis may be conducted without respect to a specific investor or even without specific investment objectives. The related and more refined *feasibility analysis* is a framework within which the results of the market analysis are used in determining which, if any, of a variety of alternative uses meets the investment requirements of a specific investor or group of investors.

More specifically, a feasibility study generally involves the analysis of a specific site for a single use or a combination of uses to answer the basic question: Will this proposed use of the site be successful from the standpoint of the investor? For example, a proposed apartment complex at a specific location is financially feasible when:

1. The location is zoned such that the proposed use may be legally constructed at the selected site.
2. The site is physically suited for construction of the apartment complex.
3. An analysis of forecast rentals and operating expenses indicates that the project produces sufficient cash flows to attract debt financing in a sufficient quantity and with interest costs and amortization terms that provide both a "satisfactory" safety margin between net operating income (NOI) and annual debt service (ADS) and an "adequate" cash-on-cash return (before-tax cash flows divided by the initial equity investment).
4. The aftertax cash flows, including the proceeds from sale, meet the safety, liquidity, and return criteria of the investors.

Note that this does *not* suggest that a project proposal for a specific land use which meets the test outlined above necessarily represents the "highest and best use" of the site, for a number of other alternative development plans may meet this same test of feasibility. The concept of *highest and best use analysis* encompasses much broader social considerations in which the most probable use is identified from among several feasible uses: "Specifically, highest and best use is that use which contributes to community environment or development goals as well as maximizing the wealth of the individual property owner. In more practical terms, the concept of highest and best use analysis involves the selection of those land uses with favorable economic potential for site development."[1]

Specific Questions to Be Answered. Within the context of a feasibility study, the investor's objectives must be carefully identified at the outset in order to answer the most fundamental of all questions: Will it work? In addition, other questions must be raised and answered in order to assess the likelihood that the proposal will produce the results desired by the investor. The following checklist is suggestive of the type of information that is needed or the questions that must be answered:

1. What are the investor's objectives? How are they to be measured or quantified? Are any of the objectives in potential conflict with each other?
2. What resources are available to the investor to achieve those objectives?
3. What concept or plan is proposed to achieve the objectives, within the limitations established by the available resources?
4. What constraints (external and internal) exist to influence or limit the achievement of the objectives?
5. What is the probability that the objectives can be achieved by the proposed actions within the framework of the given resources and constraints? (Will the plan work?)

[1] Stephen D. Messner, Byrl N. Boyce, Harold G. Trimble and Robert L. Ward, *Analyzing Real Estate Opportunities* (Chicago: Realtors National Marketing Institute, 1977), p. 15.

6. If the answer to the preceding question is no, what changes in constraints, resources, or proposed actions are required to make the objectives achievable? (What can be done to make the plan work?)
7. Can some or all of the changes identified above be accomplished? If so, which ones and at what cost?
8. What alternative courses of action are potentially available to meet the investor's objectives?
9. What are the expected outcomes of the alternative courses of actions? Do any of them meet the investor's objectives?
10. What is the relative attractiveness or ranking of the alternative courses of action (including the original proposal) which appear to meet the investor's objectives?[2]

The final product of a feasibility study is likely to be "more reportorial than evaluative or action oriented."[3] That is, although feasibility analysis identifies the probable outcomes of one or more investment proposals and compares these results with the investor's objectives, it does not deal with the actual selection process or concern itself with investment strategy. These final considerations are the focus of what is commonly called investment analysis.

Measures of Acceptability. Obviously the real estate analyst must somehow translate the objectives of the investor into measurable or quantifiable results so that the investor may compare the forecast outcomes against some standard of acceptability. Although it is possible to include qualitative objective standards, such as the appearance of the structure or neighborhood acceptance of the project, the analyst is much better able to deal with objectives whose standards can be quantified.

Since the primary objective of most investors may be expressed as a rate of return, an investment value, or some other comparative measure of investment desirability, the present section will consider the most commonly used standards of investment acceptability: (1) net present value (2) the profitability index, (3) the payback period, and (4) rates of return.

Net Present Value (NPV). Discounted cash flow (DCF) techniques are the most common means for converting future cash flows into a measure of investment acceptability. The most straightforward application of DCF techniques is the net present value approach. This is perhaps the most logical approach, since it simply involves finding the present value of all cash flows related to the investment proposed and subtracting from this sum the amount of the initial investment outlay. In essence, NPV may be defined as:

$$NPV = \sum_{t=0}^{n} \frac{C_t}{(1+i)^t},$$

---

[2] Adapted from William N. Kinnard, Jr., Stephen D. Messner, and Byrl N. Boyce, *Special Applications of Appraisal Analysis* (Chicago: Society of Real Estate Appraisers, 1972), pp. 1–2. This material was also drawn from a discussion in James A. Graaskamp, *A Guide to Feasibility Analysis* (Chicago: Society of Real Estate Appraisers, 1970), pp. 2–7.

[3] Kinnard, Messner, and Boyce, *Special Applications of Appraisal Analysis*, p. 5.

where C_t is the cash flow in period t, and i is the discount rate. Since the present value of all cash flows from time period 0 to time period t are summed, all cash outlays and cash receipts are included together. The discount rate i represents an opportunity rate or the minimum rate of return that is acceptable to the investor. Thus, the decision rule for the use of this measure is: "Accept any investment proposal where the net present value is zero or greater."

The Profitability Index (PI). Closely related to the NPV test of acceptability is the profitability index, which provides a measure of the present value of future cash inflows per dollar of outflow. This is calculated as:

$$PI = \frac{\sum_{t=1}^{n} \frac{C_t}{(1+i)^t}}{\text{Initial outlay}}$$

The NPV may be converted to a PI by adding the initial outlay to the NPV and then dividing this sum by the same initial outlay. As a test of acceptability, the PI criterion is: "Accept any investment proposal where the PI is 1 or greater."

The Payback Period (PP). This is the simplest method, but it suffers from the fact that it does not take into account the pattern of cash flows and thus fails to accurately reflect the time value of money. In essence, this criterion asks the question, How long will it take for the estimated cash flows from the investment to pay back the initial outlay? When the annual cash flows (C) are equal,

$$PP = \frac{\text{Initial outlay}}{C}$$

When the cash flows are not equal, the necessary recovery period must be measured by summing the annual cash flows up to the point at which the sum is equal to the amount of the initial outlay and counting the number of periods (years).

The Rate of Return. The most comprehensive measure of the yield of an investment is the internal rate of return (IRR). This may be defined as that rate of discount at which the sum of the present values of all future cash flows is exactly equal to the initial outlay. Thus, $i = $ IRR when:

$$\text{Initial outlay} = \sum_{t=1}^{n} \frac{C_t}{(1+i)^t}$$

Although widely discussed, the IRR does present some problems as a criterion of investment desirability, especially for real estate development projects which have future cash flows containing both receipts and outflows.[4] An alternative rate of return measure called the financial management rate of return (FMRR) was designed to overcome most

---

[4] See Stephen D. Messner, Irving Schreiber, and Victor L. Lyon, *Marketing Investment Real Estate* (Chicago: Realtors National Marketing Institute, 1975), pp. 46–52, for a more complete discussion of the problems associated with the use of the IRR.

of the shortcomings of the IRR. The FMRR is a specialized form of the geometric mean rate of return in which market rates are used to simulate the actions of a rational financial manager who sets aside cash flows to meet future obligations and reinvests excess funds at rate schedules obtainable in the market. Once all cash flows are treated appropriately, the resulting investment calculations are reduced to:

$$\text{FMRR} = \sqrt[n]{\frac{T_n^*}{D_0^*}} - 1,$$

where T_n^* is the terminal value of all future cash flows and D_0^* is the modified initial outlay.[5]

The Feasibility Framework. The general analytic framework for a feasibility study may be summarized in terms of a series of steps to be accomplished. These steps typically involve the inputs of a variety of specialists other than the analyst who is conducting and coordinating the overall feasibility study.[6] The real estate analyst uses his skills in looking at the financial feasibility or economic capability of the site for use within the context of its present and estimated future market environment. Other experts may be called in to provide data that relate to the physical nature of the site, the construction of the proposed improvement on that site, and so on. Architects, lawyers, engineers, planners, transportation consultants, ecologists, demographers, appraisers, and the like, may be needed to assemble the information required for the complete feasibility study. The feasibility study then incorporates information provided by such experts as it relates to estimates or forecasts of future revenue flows and cost data on the original construction costs and future operating expenses. The complete analysis also requires information on the present and most likely future financing terms in the marketplace, and tax counsel may be needed to provide early advice on the specific tax treatment that would be afforded this type of construction/investment project.

Step 1. The first step in the feasibility process is to assess the physical capabilities of the site. Various outside specialists will be needed in this initial undertaking since it deals with such matters as the quality and nature of the topsoil and subsoil; the availability and cost of water, sewerage, transportation, and utilities; zoning and code enforcement.

Step 2. The second step in establishing the feasibility of a project is to define its initial concept. This is most directly accomplished through discussions with the developer, investor, or owner. At this stage the analyst obtains information on the client's goals and financial capabilities as well as information explicitly defining the development plan.

Step 3. The third step in the feasibility process is to analyze the demand for the services provided by the property and to translate previously acquired market data into "spatial activities" and "spatial units."

---

[5] Stephen D. Messner and M. Chapman Findlay III, "Real Estate Investment Analysis: IRR versus FMRR," *Real Estate Appraiser,* July–August 1975, pp. 13–17.

[6] The following discussion has been adapted from Messner, Boyce, Trimble, and Ward, *Analyzing Real Estate Opportunities,* pp. 82–84.

Within the context of this discussion, spatial activities refer to the specific use to which the property is to be devoted rather than the use generally classified through zoning or other forms of use classification. In the same context, spatial units refer to the manner in which the space is being used or absorbed in the market. This is a crucial distinction, since market data are generally collected on a broad base that must be refined so that they relate to the specific spatial activities proposed for the site. For example, market data concerning the overall demand for housing may be available, but these data must be refined further if the proposed use for the site is residential condominiums for the elderly.

Once the spatial activities and the spatial units have been sufficiently defined, the analyst must develop a detailed profile of the most likely user at the site. Important ingredients in the overall analysis include such information as the general levels of consumption and patterns which may be observed over time. In the example of residential condominiums for the elderly, the analyst would be concerned with ability to pay, and thus both income and wealth levels would be required for the estimate of housing demand. Amenity requirements of this consumer group would have to be identified. Such things as public transportation, parks, room sizes, layouts, closets, and special facilities for the elderly would all provide useful guidelines in the analysis of demand. The consumer profile should consider when consumers will require the property and over what time periods they expect to use it. Although the housing market is traditionally studied in terms of a local market, condominiums for the elderly in Florida must consider a potential universe of users that spans the entire United States. Questions concerning the size and the stability of this universe and both local and extralocal competition must all be incorporated into the estimate of demand.

Step 4. The supply side of the market equation must then be studied in terms of the most likely competition for this spatial activity. The market area must be delineated, using locational criteria that are relevant to the specific spatial activity, and the competition must be inventoried and evaluated once the market area has been mapped sufficiently. Although the primary focus here is on current competition, the probable future expansion of competitive space must be estimated in terms of volume, size, and type. The main emphasis here is on how future expansion may help or hurt the proposed use at the subject site.

Step 5. The final development plan must be articulated in view of the market information acquired.

Step 6. All capital and operating costs must be estimated for the project in terms of the final version of the development plan.

Step 7. The financing information relevant to the project must now enter the overall equation, and it may be appropriate to develop the financial package for the proposed development. The financial effect of both construction costs and long-term financing must be analyzed. The physical data on the site should be considered in terms of construction time and the phasing of monies advanced and repaid. This is a liquidity consideration. In addition, the impact of leverage on the equity return must be analyzed in the final step.

Step 8. As with the financial analysis, the construction time and absorption rates should be considered in refining final demand estimates. For example, if a major apartment complex is being analyzed, the stages of development and the time required to rent the complex to anticipated normal market levels should be imputed in the analysis.

Step 9. This is the final phase of the analysis. It is at this point that income estimates, operating expenses, financing, and other considerations are brought together to a bottom line estimate of the project. This is the step that provides the go or no-go information.

In summary, the steps outlined above follow the logical progression which ties together and further refines data from a variety of sources and compares those data with the desired outcome or the objectives of the investor. (For additional information on feasibility analysis, see Chapters 16 and 17.)

HOUSING MARKET ANALYSES*

Michael Sumichrast

*M*ICHAEL SUMICHRAST, PhD, Vice President and Chief Economist, National Association of Home Builders, Washington, D.C.
Advisory Board member, The Real Estate Handbook (Dow Jones-Irwin). Director, Homer Hoyt Institute. Visiting professor of urban studies, The American University. Was U.S. delegate to the Fifth Triennial Congress of the International Council for Building Studies in Paris and was a United Nations Delegate for the United States at a Geneva building conference. Author, The Complete Book of Home Buying (Dow Jones Book Co., 1979). Coauthor, Housing Markets (Homewood, Ill.: Dow Jones-Irwin, 1975).

Forecasting Housing Demand

The loan application packages typically supplied by builder-developers to mortgage lenders usually include some statement of demand, based on analyses of the strength of the local economy and population projections. Indeed, if there is not an optimistic outlook for local growth in population and income, and hence in housing demand, there is no point in submitting the application.

The difficulty is that lenders may believe the projections without examining the foundation on which the whole structure of analysis is built or that they may not carefully examine the analyses themselves. There is the tendency for builders to build anything they can mortgage out of, or produce with little or no equity. Thus a builder-developer will commit himself to a parcel of land, possibly subject to getting the financing, get a research study–mortgage package on a project, and then

---

* This chapter is a condensed version of several chapters from Michael Sumichrast and Maury Seldin, *Housing Markets; The Complete Guide to Analysis and Strategy for Builders, Lenders, and Other Investors* (Homewood, Ill.: Dow Jones-Irwin, 1977). © 1977 by Dow Jones-Irwin.

submit it to a lender. It is then up to the lender to determine whether the local market really needs more of what the builder-developer or equity investor wants to build.

In looking for a place of strong demand, builders and lenders alike want local economies which have growth potential. They also want a viable community, able to respond to the forces of growth, so that the construction will be feasible. If the community also has stability, so much the better.

The Economic Outlook. The questions asked about the economic outlook consider employment, income, and construction. Naturally, the cost and availability of money are of a particular concern. The first question concerns the national outlook; the second concerns the local economy.

A variety of national outlook services are readily available from various sources. DRI, Wharton, and Chase provide the most prestigious national models. A daily reading of *The Wall Street Journal,* or a weekly reading of *Business Week, Newsweek,* or *Time,* provide information on the latest developments.

A regional and state model of housing starts is available at the National Association of Home Builders.

Economic-Base and Other Employment Analyses. An analysis of the local economy starts with a determination of its employment base, using the categories of the standard industrial classification (SIC) codes. An economic-base forecast uses employment rates at a given time to forecast employment changes, which are the basis for a projected change in population.

Other employment analyses can be as simple as identifying the major employers and assessing their future.

The employment opportunity analyses are useful for judging the character and stability of the community and for assessing the potential for development. In essence, both lenders and developers need to be able to judge the quality of the community. Some numbers are usually available for this purpose; the thing to do is look to the numbers and form an independent judgment as to whether there will be jobs in the community, what kind of income they will generate, and what the character and the extent of the demand for housing will be. Exhibit 1 gives a summary of where to obtain various types of employment-based information.

Population Projections and Forecasts. Typically, analysts will accept population forecasts done by demographers, which are usually supplied by planning bodies of local political bodies. States also make attempts to forecast population, as do private individuals. No single method of estimating population has shown consistently greater accuracy. Evidence also shows that a lower average error can be obtained by averaging several estimates made by different methods.

Methods. There are probably as many as two dozen methods for small-area population forecasting. Of these, four are the most consistently recommended (see Exhibit 2).

The summary of forecasts is a very important step in housing analysis, but it should not be an overwhelming issue. The analyst need not become

a demographer and go into the great detail which accompanies population forecasting. The methods described in Exhibit 2 should serve more
as a reminder that such methods are available. There are many others
than those described, some of which are very complicated.

Before accepting the forecast, the forecaster should:

1. Review the numbers for consistency. Do they make sense? Is this
   forecast possible? What is the record of the forecasting agency?

EXHIBIT 1
The Economic Base: What Facts to Get and Where to Get Them

Type of Information	How It Is Measured	Where to Get the Facts
Employment and unemployment	Number of people Number of men Number of women	State employment agencies Bureau of the Census State departments of economic development Manpower commissions and FHA
New industries	Type of industries Number of people to be employed Wages and salaries	Department of Commerce Employment agencies Newspapers Utility companies Council of government
Business conditions	Retail sales Department store sales Bank conditions	State tax office *Sales Management* magazine Federal Reserve Board (national and regional) Chamber of commerce

What to look for. Economic-base analysis must not be a static collection
of data. The analyst is looking for:

1. Trends influencing the demand for homes.
2. Changes in spending patterns.
3. Changes in employment levels.
4. Changes in economic levels.
5. Changes in the mix of employment opportunities.

What data to consider:

1. General business conditions.
   a. Bank debits.
   b. Department store sales.
   c. Opening or closing of facilities providing employment.
2. Employment trends by industry.
3. Trends in unemployment.

Where to get it. The chamber of commerce is a good place to start—but
not to stop. *Go for primary source materials* (see the table above).

EXHIBIT 2
Housing Market Data and Sources for Population Forecasts

Method of Estimating		*How Measured*	*Where to Get Data*
Housing inventory method	1.	Census of Housing	Bureau of the Census
	2.	Update by:	HUD annual metro surveys
		a. Completed units by type	Building permit office
			Lagged relations of permits to
		b. Adjust for net removals	completion if completions
			not available
		c. Adjust for change in vacancies	Permit office for removals; check census for trends
	3.	Determine housing by:	Census of Population
		a. Home ownership	Building owner's association
		b. Renters	for vacancies
	4.	Apply average number of persons per:	
		a. Owner	
		b. Renter	
Labor participation rates	1.	Employment by industries	State employment service
	2.	Projection of employment	Planning boards
	3.	Trends of employment, men and women	Local economists at banks, industries, etc.
	4.	Develop participation rates and trend	Chamber of commerce Utility companies
	5.	Translate into population	*Sales Management*
School enrollment participation rates	1.	School population, past	School boards
	2.	School population, present and expected in future	Parochial schools Individual private schools
	3.	Translate into population using census school enrollment techniques for population 4 through 15 years old	Bureau of the Census
Vital rates	1.	Trends in birth and death rates for small area; to estimate, follow trends of the state, or metro area, or region	Bureau of the Census State health departments County clerk Utility companies Planning boards
	2.	Get actual birth and death rates to obtain separate population estimate	
	3.	Average both methods	
	4.	Deduct or add military personnel	
	5.	Allow for in- and out-migration by using census techniques	

2. Make sure he is getting the same data from various sources. Some-times the data base in various forecasts is quite different.
3. No data should be accepted as fact. The data should be verified, and the validity of the source assessed.

Household Projections.   Population estimates such as those discussed can be translated into demand for new homes. Using an estimated number of persons per household, the raw population data can be translated into a forecast of new household formations (see Exhibit 3).

EXHIBIT 3
Population and Household Growth in Montgomery, Maryland,
1960–1990

Year	Population	Household Size	Households
1960	340,900	3.65	92,400
1970	522,800	3.30	156,700
1975	572,100	3.05	185,600
1980	600,000	2.86	206,000
1985	635,000	2.73	230,400
1990	686,000	2.70	250,000
Increase			
1960–70	181,900	—	64,300
1970–80	77,200	—	49,300
1980–90	86,000	—	44,000
1980–85	35,000	—	24,400
1985–90	51,000	—	19,600
1970–90	103,200	—	93,300

Source: U.S. Census of Population, 1960, 1970; U.S. Department of Commerce, Bureau of Economic Analysis; and the Metropolitan Washington Council of Governments.

Quantitative Housing Demand.   Effective quantitative housing demand uses the household projections as a base from which an annual demand for housing is derived. This procedure is presented in Exhibit 4.

Constraints Affecting Housing Demand.   The arithmetic presented in Exhibit 4 shows a demand for 4,600 new units for 1974. This is substantially below the levels of production in 1971, when 10,554 units were given building permits, or in 1972, when permits accounted for 10,380 units. Even production in 1973 was considerably higher, at 7,625 units.

Under normal conditions, the 4,600 units does not seem out of line. But examining the numbers clearly suggests a great deal of overbuilding, slow-moving inventory, and erosion of the economic base. The booming economy was just about to bust.

In addition, Montgomery County had started to experience the impact of a sewer moratorium which began in 1970. This sharply curtailed production and caused builders to move their new-housing efforts to nearby Virginia. Too, the expectation of a tapering of the economic boom

EXHIBIT 4
Forecast of Quantitative Housing Demand, Montgomery County, Maryland, 1974

Step	Item	Total	For Sale	For Rent
1.	Projected household increase*	6,365	3,820	2,545
2.	Net removals (0.68% of the standing inventory of 182,128)†	+1,236	+136	+1,100
3.	Gross demand (1 + 2)	7,601	3,956	3,645
4.	Available vacancies‡	5,040	810	4,230
5.	Normal vacancies (0.8% ownership; 5.4% rental)§	4,040	780	3,260
6.	Excess of vacancies (4 − 5)	1,000	30	970
7.	Quantitative demand (3 − 6)	6,601	3,926	2,675
8.	Units under consruction‖	7,500	3,600	3,900
9.	Normal rate of construction#	5,500	3,000	2,500
	Sales 10 months (4,500 units)			
	Rentals 12 months (2,500 units)			
10.	Excess of new construction (8 − 9)	2,000	600	1,400
11.	Net demand (7 − 10).............................	4,600	3,326	1,275
12.	Annual demand	4,600	3,326	1,275

* Between 1960 and 1970, Montgomery County past production activity shows that 46 percent of all units were single-family units and 64 percent were multifamily units. During that time 85,388 units were produced, of which 39,054 were single-family units. The high ratio of multiples was due to two years of unusually heavy multifamily activity. In 1966 and 1967, because of redefinition of zoning for apartment hotels, activity—just before the cutoff date—soared to record levels. These two years, therefore, are not typical. More in line with past activity are the years 1968, 1969, and 1970, when single-family units accounted for about 60 percent of the total. This share was expected to continue and was used in this table.

† Net removals have been estimated at 0.68 percent of the average annual inventory (midpoint in a year). Most of the removals occurred in multifamily units.

‡ Vacancies were derived from updating the 1970 census. When the census was taken on April 1, 1970, the data showed a relatively low number of vacancies. The census data were updated for the balance of 1970 and through 1974. There have been rapid increases in vacancies since the April date.

§ The high mobility rate in Montgomery County puts the "normal" vacancy rate at 0.8 percent for homeowners and at 5.4 percent for renters.

‖ Units under construction derived from FHA Unsold Inventory Survey. Data were adjusted to reflect all inventory, not only inventory in projects as defined by FHA.

Normal rate of construction is an estimate derived from past historical relations as well as what the rate of absorption was in the period 1970–73.

Source: Michael Sumichrast and Maury Seldin, *Housing Markets* (Homewood, Ill.: Dow Jones-Irwin, 1977). © 1977, Dow Jones-Irwin.

brought about a fear of changes in interest rates and a decrease in mortgage funds. This has always had an immediate impact on housing production.

Net demand should be adjusted to such interference with market forces. This, of course, is easier said than done, since to a large extent it involves judgment on how severe an impact these variables may have on production. To put the impacts in a model using regression analysis is not practicable, because some of the impacts are difficult to quantify. In addition, not enough experience has been accumulated to come up with a good impact measure as far as sewer moratoriums are concerned. The impact varies from place to place, depending on the enforcement in any particular area.

What is needed is a line item which would translate net demand into net effective demand, or units which will be absorbed, given the local economy and allowing for adjustments in supply. One way of doing this is presented in Exhibit 5.

EXHIBIT 5
Net Effective Demand, Montgomery County, Maryland, 1974

Item	Total	For Sale	For Rent
	Number of Units		
Net demand	4,600	3,326	1,275
Adjust for 1 percent increase in mortgage rates ...	−500	−400	−100
Adjustment for changes in employment, 4,100 × 88 percent index	3,610	2,575	1,035
Adjust for sewer moratorium, 45 percent	1,620	1,160	460
Net effective demand for 1974	1,990	1,415	575

Source: Michael Sumichrast and Maury Seldin, *Housing Markets* (Homewood, Ill.: Dow Jones-Irwin, 1977). © 1977, Dow Jones-Irwin.

A Short Method for Determining the Strength or Weakness of Housing Demand. Suppose that an investor wants to quickly verify whether there is a market for, say, 500 new homes, with construction starting in the next three months and spread over the next two years. A few numbers could give him a clue to the situation. The quick answer could strongly suggest that a more thorough examination should be made before proceeding, or it may verify that he already knows: that the market is viable and that he should proceed.

For single-family (for-sale) housing, a short method of demand analysis is shown in Exhibit 6.

Segmented Analysis

This section breaks down the housing market into *site and product analysis.* It is designed as a practical application of a market analysis to a specific problem and is illustrated with examples.

Segmented Demand by Income. Housing needs are not synonymous with housing demand. A poor area may have great needs but little demand for the housing which can be supplied. Much demand for new housing is caused by upgrading and mobility.

Incomes determine the price level of the units which can be absorbed. Combining data on incomes with the price ranges of the new homes being built and the homes being sold should give sufficient detail as to the potential price ranges of the houses that are likely to be in demand. The nine steps below illustrate how this can be done.

Step 1. Get the income distribution of the families of the area under investigation. This can be in the form presented in Exhibit 7 or another similar form.

EXHIBIT 6
Example of the Short Method for Determining the Market Situation of New For-Sale Housing, Fairfax County, Virginia, January 1, 1975

Ratios	Units	Current Ratio	Ratio Signifying Overbuilding Market	Rating
1. Unsold completed new homes	2,220			
as a percentage of:				
a. For-sale units, annual production	5,328	42%	25%	Too high
b. Houses currently under construction ...	2,640	119%	100%	Too high
c. Annual starts (not available)			250%	
d. Unsold units under construction	2,297	103%	100%	Too high
2. Unsold houses under construction	2,297			
as a percentage of:				
e. Total houses under construction	2,640	87%	75%	Too high
3. All unsold houses	4,517			
Completed	2,220			
Under construction	2,297			
as a percentage of:				
f. For-sale annual production	5,328	85%	40%	Too high
4. Presold units as a percentage of:				
g. All completed new units. (Sample only: 817 presold to 4,628 completed.)		17%	30% or below	Too low

Source: Michael Sumichrast and Maury Seldin, *Housing Markets* (Homewood, Ill.: Dow Jones-Irwin, 1977). © 1977, Dow Jones-Irwin.

ALL RATINGS ARE NEGATIVE, SIGNIFYING A SEVERE OVERBUILDING SITUATION.

How to interpret the data:

1. There was a significant drop in the number of families with incomes under $9,999. This income group decreased from 55,274 in 1970 to 30,600 in 1974—a drop of 45 percent.
2. The major growth was in the income categories of over $25,000, from 9,888 families in 1970 to 22,400 families in 1974—an increase of 126 percent.
3. The largest single income category remained between $15,000 and $24,999, 32.1 percent, or 53,600 families, in 1974. But even this category increased 16 percent since 1970.
4. Overall, there was a significant improvement in incomes, suggesting a better support for housing purchases in the future.

Step 2. Get a reading on what is being built, by price ranges. This is shown in the first two columns of Exhibit 8.

Step 3. Get a reading on how well the price ranges of new homes are selling, by price range. This is illustrated in the last two columns of Exhibit 8.

EXHIBIT 7

Distribution of Family Income, Prince George's County, Maryland

	1960		1970		1974		Average Annual Change, 1960–1970		Average Annual Change, 1970–1974	
	Number	Percent	Number	Percent	Number	Percent	Number	Percent	Number*	Percent
Total families	87,453	100.0%	163,400	100.0%	166,700	100.0%	7,595	8.7%	700	0.4%
Family income										
Under $4,000	10,848	12.4	9,820	6.0	4,700	2.8	−103	−1.0	−1,100	−11.2
$4,000–4,999	7,276	8.3	4,108	2.5	3,400	2.0	−317	−4.4	−200	−4.9
$5,000–7,999	30,921	35.4	21,224	13.0	9,900	5.9	−970	−3.2	−2,500	−11.8
$8,000–9,999	15,962	18.3	20,122	12.3	12,600	7.6	416	2.6	−1,700	−8.5
$10,000–11,999	{17,853	20.4	21,925	13.4	16,800	10.1	{3,410	19.1	−1,100	−5.0
$12,000–14,999			30,028	18.4	24,400	14.6			−1,300	−4.3
$15,000–24,999	3,918	4.5	46,285	28.3	53,600	32.1	4,237	108.1	1,600	3.5
$25,000–34,999	{675	0.8	{9,173	5.6	17,200	10.3	{921	136.5	{2,700	29.4
$35,000–49,999					4,200	2.5				
$50,000 and over			715	0.4	1,000	0.6			60	8.4
Not reported	—		—		18,900	11.3	—		—	
Median income	$7,344		$12,450		$15,400		—		—	

Note: Family income not adjusted for inflation. Data in boxes are used in Exhibit 9.

* Rounded to the nearest 100. Figures under 100 rounded to the nearest 10.

Source: Department of Commerce, Bureau of the Census, 1960, 1970, *Census of the Population;* Washington Center for Metropolitan Studies; Metro Metrics, Inc.

EXHIBIT 8

Completed New Single-Family Units, Washington SMSA and Prince George's County, Maryland (percentage by price range)

Price Ranges	Washington SMSA	Prince George's Co., Md.	Prince George's Co. Unsold Units	Interpretation
$25,000–27,499	1.1%			
$27,500–29,999	5.6			
$30,000–34,999	7.9	13.9 ⎫ 30.8%	72%	Very slow sales
$35,000–39,999	11.1	16.9 ⎭	65	Slow sales
$40,000–44,999	14.5	22.2 ⎫ 41.7	55	Slow sales
$45,000–49,999	9.9	19.5 ⎭	67	Very slow sales
$50,000–59,999	19.9	15.0 ⎫ 27.5	53	Slow sales
$60,000–69,999	17.0	8.0 ⎬	45	Mediocre sales
$70,000 and over	13.0	4.5 ⎭	40	Reasonably good sales
Total	100.0%	100.0%	60% (average)	Bad sale situation in all categories

Source: FHA, Washington, D.C. Insuring Office, Form 2398S, 1975.

How to interpret steps 2 and 3 for Prince George's County:

1. Over 40 percent of all new single-family units built were in the middle price range, between $40,000 and $50,000.
2. About 30 percent of all units built were priced under $40,000.
3. More than 27 percent of the units were over $50,000.
4. *The cheapest units did not sell as well as the most expensive units.*
5. *No single price range was selling well.* This was a strong indication of a bad market.

Step 4. Recap the changes in families from income groups (extract the data from the boxes in Exhibit 7), as shown in Exhibit 9.

EXHIBIT 9
Number of Families with Income over $15,000, Prince George's County, Maryland, 1974

| | Families | | Average Annual Change in Families, |
Income Bracket	Number	Percent	1970–1974
$15,000–24,999	53,600	32.1%	+1,600
$25,000–34,999	17,200	10.3	} +2,700
$35,000–49,999	4,200	2.5	
$50,000 and over	1,000	0.6	+ 60
Total	76,000	45.5%	+4,360

Source: U.S. Bureau of the Census, 1960, 1970 *Census of the Population:* Washington Center for Metropolitan Studies; Metro Metrics, Inc.

How to interpret the data: The income distribution indicates that the lower end of the single-family detached housing market is by far the strongest. At $20,000 income, the midpoint of the $15,000–$24,999 range, with a 2.5 price/income ratio, the market for $50,000 units has the greatest potential. The strong market ranges down to $40,000, if it can be built, and up to $60,000, which is thinning out and approaching the next category.

Step 5. Match incomes to loans (using a ratio of either 2 or 2½ times the family income). This is shown in Exhibit 10.

EXHIBIT 10
Conventional Mortgage Loan Ranges, Prince George's County, Maryland, 1974

Income Bracket	Debt-Free Loan Range @ 2 Times Income	Debt-Free Loan Range @ 2½ Times Income
$15,000–24,999	$ 30,000–50,000	$ 37,500–62,500
$25,000–34,999	$ 50,000–70,000	$ 62,500–87,500
$35,000–49,999	$ 70,000–100,000	$ 87,500–125,000
$50,000 and over	$100,000+	$125,000+

How to interpret the data: Family incomes in the ranges shown in Exhibit 10 are considered viable potential new-home purchasers. Most lenders operate within the following guidelines in accepting mortgage loan applicants:

1. Conventional loans are made at two times gross income.
2. FNMA and FHLMC set the guidelines in their underwriting, and 80 to 90 percent of the lenders use these guidelines so that they can package and sell loans to these two agencies.
3. Another measure used for conventional loans is that 33 percent of gross family income can be used for PITI (principal, interest, property taxes, insurance) and outstanding debts that have more than six months of payment remaining to be made.
4. FHA and VA loans are handled under more liberal terms. Loans can be made at 2½ to 3 times gross income.
5. At a $15,400 median family income, a family without debts could qualify for a $31,000 conventional mortgage loan or a $46,000 VA mortgage.

Step 6. Blow up the 45.5 percent total of income groups considered in Exhibit 9 to 100 percent. Table 9 shows that 32.1 percent of all families in Prince George's County had incomes of between $15,000 and $24,999. Altogether, about 45.5 percent of all families in the county have income high enough to be potential home buyers. Thus, more than one half of all families do not have income high enough to be considered potential home buyers. Using a universe of families with incomes over $15,000, or 76,000 families (Exhibit 9), the 45.5 percent income group is increased to 100 percent, as shown in Exhibit 11.

Step 7. Using *Sales Management* data or a finer breakdown of incomes from a county office (or an update from the decennial census), a more detailed breakdown of each income group is derived. The income group and home price (or home loan) ranges have been identified in Exhibit 10 for either 2 or 2½ times the family income. When the largest group, families making between $15,000 and

EXHIBIT 11
Conversion of Percentages of Four Categories of Incomes to 100 percent

Income	Percent of All Families		Converted to Percent
$15,000–24,999	32.1%	=	70%
$25,000–34,999	10.3	=	22
$35,000–49,999	2.5	=	6
$50,000 and over	0.6	=	2
Total	45.5%	=	100.0%

Source: Michael Sumichrast and Maury Seldin, *Housing Markets* (Homewood, Ill.: Dow Jones-Irwin, 1977). © 1977, Dow Jones-Irwin.

$24,999 annual income, is broken down, it is found that the 70 percent of families in this price range have the potential to qualify for the price range of homes shown in Exhibit 12.

EXHIBIT 12
Breakdown of $15,000–$24,999 Income Group to
Qualify Families for Certain Price Ranges of Homes
(using two times income ratio)

Price Range of Homes	Percent of Families in Group Who Could Qualify for These Homes
$30,000–34,999	23%
$35,000–39,999	20
$40,000–44,999	15
$45,000–49,999	12
Total	70%

Source: Michael Sumichrast and Maury Seldin, *Housing Markets* (Homewood, Ill.: Dow Jones-Irwin, 1977). © 1977, Dow Jones-Irwin.

Step 8. Break down the remaining income groups into various price ranges of homes. The distribution of the price ranges of the homes that the balance of the income groups could qualify for is indicated in Exhibit 13.

EXHIBIT 13
Percentage of Families Who Could Qualify for Homes in Price Ranges over
$50,000 (using two times income ratio)

Income Bracket	Price Range of Homes	Families Who Could Qualify for Homes
$25,000–34,999	$50,000–59,999	12%
$35,000–49,999	$60,000–69,999	10
$50,000 and over	$70,000 and over	8
Total		30%
Grand total, Exhibit 12 and Exhibit 13 totals		100%

Source: Michael Sumichrast and Maury Seldin, *Housing Markets* (Homewood, Ill.: Dow Jones-Irwin, 1977). © 1977, Dow Jones-Irwin.

Step 9. Recap the average annual demand and the price ranges. The annual demand for Prince George's County between 1976 and 1980 was estimated at 5,860, or a total of 29,300 for the period. Of this total, the demand for single-family homes was estimated at 19,000, or 3,800 annually. The demand for single-family homes by price ranges is shown in Exhibit 14.

Segmenting the Housing Market by Location. These are the major steps one should undertake to determine the demand for housing in a narrow geographic area.

EXHIBIT 14
Projected Demand for Single-Family Homes by Price Ranges, Prince George's County, Maryland, 1976–1980

Price Range	Percent	Number
$30,000–34,999	23%	870
$35,000–39,999	20	760
$40,000–44,999	15	570
$45,000–49,999	12	460
$50,000–59,999	12	460
$60,000–69,999	10	380
$70,000 and over	8	300
Total	100%	3,800

Source: Michael Sumichrast and Maury Seldin, *Housing Markets* (Homewood, Ill.: Dow Jones-Irwin, 1977). © 1977, Dow Jones-Irwin.

Step 1. Determine whether or not the market is in balance in the general area in which construction will take place.

Step 2. Determine what types of units are being built and are selling (see Exhibit 15).

EXHIBIT 15
Types of Units Built and Monthly Sale Rates, 26 Subdivisions, Suburban Township, January 1976

Type of Unit	Percentage Breakdown of Units Built	Cost per Square Foot	Monthly Sale Rates per Subdivision
Two story	28%	$31.64	4.55
Split foyer	44	37.36	3.50
Split level	18	38.59	2.80
Ranch	14	39.78	1.80
Total	100%	$36.36 (average)	3.16 (average)

Source: Michael Sumichrast and Maury Seldin, *Housing Market* (Homewood Ill.: Dow Jones-Irwin 1977.) © 1977, Dow Jones-Irwin.

Step 3. Identify the price range selling (see Exhibit 16).

Escalating Potential Supply

Analysis of the supply side of the housing market is less complicated than analysis of the demand side. It is not, however, confined simply to the enumeration of the existing structures and their occupancy. Rather, this analysis involves finding out what commitments have been made to development, what constraints thare are on future commitments, and what the current market situation is. In analyzing supply, consideration must be given to the general conditions and characteristics

EXHIBIT 16
Identification of Price Range Selling, 26 Subdivisions,
Suburban Township, January 1976

Average Price	Square Feet in Unit	Cost per Square Foot	Monthly Rate of Sales per Subdivision	Interpretation
$46,933 ...	1,000–1,300	$39.95	4.90	Excellent
$52,200 ...	1,300–1,600	38.58	3.30	Very good
$60,725 ...	1,600–2,000	34.52	4.20	Excellent
$67,740 ...	2,000–2,500	30.48	1.75	Satisfactory
$97,900 ...	2,500 and over	35.92	1.32	Slow

Source: Michael Sumichrast and Maury Seldin, *Housing Markets* (Homewood, Ill.: Dow Jones-Irwin, 1977). © 1977, Dow Jones-Irwin.

of housing and land availability, and to the aspects of supply. Many of these critical components are often ignored in making supply decisions, causing numerous failures.

Most of the information dealing with the general characteristics of housing in a given area is readily available, either through the federal censuses of housing or through local surveys. Overall changes in the total inventory are slow, and the location, size, age, type, and materials used are generally known. As to physical conditions, a personal survey of an area will reveal the degree of deterioration, the condition of streets and public walks, and the appearance of new housing developments.

Housing Starts and Units in the Housing Pipeline. In order to analyze the situation in housing, it is important to have data on the existing inventory. However, it is of little value to know the *exact* status of this inventory. It would also be impracticable; it is too expensive to establish an information system which would continually monitor the exact status of housing. In its Annual Housing surveys the Bureau of the Census now provides information on a sample basis of some 75,000 households.

There are many counties in the United States which, through their planning boards or statistical services, provide some degree of detailed information on the housing inventory. But this still does not answer the question that an investor or a developer must face: What are the chances of being successful in selling or renting new space when the housing to be produced hits the market?

Information on the supply of new housing and on the competition is therefore important. Such information is not shown in either building permits or housing starts. Important as they are, these data represent only a fraction of the actual and projected activity. An excellent illustration of why this is so can be found in Exhibit 17.

Of the 133,551 proposed housing units, 13,925 were committed construction (8,820 already started and 5,105 in outstanding permits). Another 39,000 could be classified as anticipated production. They fell into the category of the plan review process, had already been approved, or were eligible for sewer and water permits as well as building permits.

EXHIBIT 17
Proposed New Housing Units, Fairfax County, Virginia, January 1975

A. STAGE OF COMPLETION

Stage of Completion	No. of Units	Percentage Distribution of Proposed Units
Under construction	8,820	7.0%
Outstanding building permits, not started	5,105	4.0
Plans approved	12,118	9.0
Plans under review	27,475	21.0
Rezoned recently	7,155	5.0
Rezoning: Likely		0.0
Rezoning: Likelihood uncertain	67,545	50.0
Rezoning: Unlikely		0.0
Rezoning: Recently denied or withdrawn	5,333	4.0
Total units proposed	133,551	100.0%

B. COMPARISON OF PERMIT DATA

	No. of Units
Permits issued, January 1975	104
Permits issued, 1974	4,834
Permits issued, 1975	3,157

Source: A. Fairfax County, Office of Research and Statistics, *Standard Reports,* May 1975, pp. 1–2. Compiled from the files of the Urban Development Information System, May 1975. B. National Association of Home Builders, Economics Department.

Compare this to the permits actually issued in January 1975 in Fairfax County: 104 single-family units. Or to the 3,157 permits issued for the year 1975, or the 4,834 permits issued for the year 1974.

Thus there is much more in the housing pipeline than the permits or starts data indicate. What the analyst wants to know is what housing can and will be forthcoming, and when.

Supply Determinants and Constraints. The best statistical series of supply information comes from the building permits office. This, however, is already *past* information, focusing on very near-term construction. The best forward-looking information comes from planning offices, including the county court records of sold land, zoning and rezoning applications, and preliminary submissions of plans for engineering land development work. All of these data are related to future activity and as such are immensely important. They are hard to get and expensive to collect, and they are generally not readily available. But they are valuable.

The market provides a good deal of solid information on what is happening. The most important information is the information on the vacancy of rental units and the inventory of unsold homes. These are the residuals of market forces.

Total Completions versus Unsold Inventory. Another quick look at the current situation uses only two types of data: total completions and unsold new units. These data can be matched up to various parts of a metropolitan area or compared to the data for other areas (see Exhibit 18).

EXHIBIT 18
Completed and Unsold Units by Geographic Areas, Washington, D.C., SMSA, January 1, 1975

County	Completed Units	Unsold	Percent Unsold	Rating
Fairfax	4,628	1,707	36.8%	High
Loudoun	1,193	573	48.0	Very high
Prince William	760	579	76.2	Extremely high
Prince George's	1,274	609	47.8	Very high
Montgomery	1,551	417	26.8	About normal
Total	9,406	3,885	41.3% (average)	High (average)

Source: Michael Sumichrast and Maury Seldin, *Housing Markets* (Homewood, Ill.: Dow Jones-Irwin, 1977). © 1977, Dow Jones-Irwin.

Yet another way of looking at the picture of completed and unsold units is to break down these units by type: single family, town houses, and condominiums. This is shown in Exhibit 19.

EXHIBIT 19
Percentage of Unsold Units to Completed Units, Washington, D.C., SMSA, January 1, 1976

Type	Completed Units	Unsold	Percent Unsold	Rating
Single-family detached units	3,756	164	4.4%	Excellent market
Attached units	2,627	473	18.0	Excellent market
Attached condos	750	244	32.5	Medium to bad
Multicondos	3,686	1,689	45.8	Very bad— overbuilding

Source: Michael Sumichrast and Maury Seldin, *Housing Markets* (Homewood, Ill.: Dow Jones-Irwin, 1977). © 1977, Dow Jones-Irwin.

The condo market data can be misleading, however. A field examination made it clear that this market was concentrated largely in Alexandria, Virginia (about 80 percent), but that there was little surplus of condos in Montgomery County.

Another good way of measuring the strength or weakness of the for-sale market is to examine the time period in which the new unsold inventory has been on the market, as in Exhibit 20.

Measure of the Market by Price Ranges. An analysis of various types of units by price range is presented in Exhibit 21, which shows the

EXHIBIT 20
Unsold Inventory of New Single-Family Detached Homes, Washington, D.C., SMSA, 1974–1976

Date	Completions	Unsold Completions	Under 30 Days	30–90 Days	90–180 Days	180–365 Days	Over One Year
1/74	9,284	1,843	375	244	172	542	510
1/75	9,406	4,368	958	814	1,239	874	483
1/76	3,756	(235)	23	29	64	48	71
Unsold units as a percent of completions							
1/74	19.9%		4.1%	2.6%	1.8%	5.8%	5.5%
1/75	46.7		10.2	8.6	13.2	9.3	5.2
1/76	(6.2)		0.6	0.8	1.7	1.3	1.9

▢ Very weak market.
○ Strong market.
Source: FHA *Unsold Inventory Survey*, Washington, D.C., January, 1976.

EXHIBIT 21
Unsold Units, Actual and as a Percentage of Speculatively Built Homes, Washington, D.C., SMSA, January 1975

Price Range	Units			Percent		
	Singles	Town Houses	Condos	Singles	Town Houses	Condos
Under $17,500						
$17,500–19,999			1			3%
$20,000–22,499			10			42
$22,500–24,999			236			92
$25,000–27,499	4		320	9%		70
$27,500–29,999	254	30	654	48	22%	72
$30,000–34,999	279	258	969	44	50	76
$35,000–39,999	600	421	714	60	62	81
$40,000–44,999	298	281	234	(27)	(33)	67
$45,000–49,999	356	120	138	53	35	48
$50,000–59,999	2,094	423	269	52	66	33
$60,000 and over		193	(145)		46	(24)
Total	3,885	1,726	2,680	49% (average)	48% (average)	63% (average)

○ = Good market. ▢ = Weak market.
▣ = Very weak market.
Source: Federal Home Administration, January 1, 1975.

distribution of unsold units by single-family detached units, town houses, and condominiums. The condo market in general was in real trouble at the time of the survey, especially in the price categories $27,500–29,999 and $35,000–39,999, with a total of 1,368 unsold units. The $22,500–24,999 category was also very weak, but at least the number of unsold units (236) was relatively low. Even among condos, however, the most expensive ones, selling at over $60,000, did quite well.

The single-family market was also overbuilt: 49 percent of all speculatively built units were unsold. However, the $40,000–44,999 price range was doing quite well, with only 27 percent of all single-family units unsold. Compare this to the cheaper price range of $35,000–39,999, which had 60 percent, or 600, single-family units unsold.

Such a price distribution also gives the analyst a glimpse of the price distribution in the overall market. The absorption rate by price range is a pretty good indication of what should or should not be built. It shows the residual of all market forces.

Pipeline Projections.   The projection of units in the pipeline is simply an extension of land-committed analysis. It means getting together in one form all there is to know about the construction and development activity already under way, or in the pipeline.

Units Authorized.   Part of this projection shows the number of units permitted in building permits by months, or cumulative for a calendar year. The projection should also show the number of units projected. This information can be presented graphically, perhaps combined with the number of units permitted but outstanding (not used), as shown in Exhibit 22 for Fairfax County, Virginia.

EXHIBIT 22
Building Permit Activity by Planning District, Dwelling Units Authorized and Outstanding, Fairfax County, Virginia, April 1975

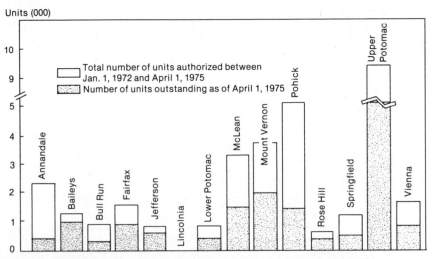

Source: Urban Development Information System, series no. 7, vol. 11–13, May 1975.

Permits Outstanding. The number of permits authorized but not used is very important in the determination of the total pipeline figure. Exhibit 22 includes this information, and Exhibit 23 shows a monthly average of outstanding permits issued in Fairfax County.

EXHIBIT 23
Monthly Average of Outstanding Units,
Fairfax County, Virginia, 1972–1975

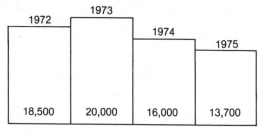

Source: Urban Development Information System, October 9, 1975, p. 2–2.

Site Plans and Subdivision Plats. Pipeline figures include the number of units in submitted plans. These are going to be competing with the proposed development.

Rezoning Cases Granted and Pending. To round up the total pipeline figure, the rezoning granted must be known, as well as what has been already submitted for rezoning.

Other Pipeline Indicators. When an area is subject to local, state, or federal restrictions, the whole of future development may be altered. Zoned land cannot be used as an indication of the future, since it may be unusable due to sewer moratoriums or no-growth policies.

Some More Tips on How to Analyze Housing Markets

This section offers some down-to-earth, practical suggestions on what to do and what not to do in undertaking a housing market analysis.

What to Do before Undertaking a Housing Market Analysis

1. *Set up an objective.* Spell out what it is you are trying to accomplish. This objective must be definite, factual, and to the point.
2. *Make a detailed outline.* This outline must be very specific and must include all of the thinking that has gone into setting the objective.
3. *Decide on the scope of the research project.* Here you must decide what data you should get, what information to collect, and what information to leave out.
4. *Determine the time needed to finish the research.* Obviously, time is usually the determining factor in any analysis. If you have only one week, then the outline will reflect that, the amount of data to be collected will depend on it, and so on.

5. *Determine the methodology to be used.* Pick up one or more that you will feel comfortable with. Do you need a "red flag" approach or a full-blown analysis?
6. *Decide who will be doing what.* The distribution of certain tasks is essential. Do not try to do it all yourself. Get some other people to serve as your eyes and ears. This is usually cheaper, and it is many times more fruitful.
7. *Before you start, decide on the format of presentation.* This decision early in the game will save you a lot of headaches later on. You will collect the material with an eye to how it will look in the final paper—instead of deciding on a format at the last minute. Get the information you need, not the information that is easiest to find.

What Kind of Market Analysis to Conduct

Minimum data requirements include:

1. What is selling by type and location.
2. What price ranges are selling.
3. What is unsold.
4. What is head in the pipeline.

Time needed to collect: two to four weeks.

This data collection can be done by:

1. Relying solely on internal company personnel.
2. Using company people plus hiring "scouts" to comparison-shop.
3. Hiring a consultant to do it all.

When done by the company staff, the cost will involve few, if any, cash outlays. The cost for scouts ranges from under $1,000 to $3,000, and the cost for consultants ranges from $4,000 to $8,000 (both in 1980 dollars). These rates are for relatively typical areas with good public records on pipeline projects. Large or problem projects could double the cost.

Other *essential data* include:

1. Economic trends—local.
2. Employment opportunities and changes.
3. Household formations.
4. Income distribution.
5. Sale characteristics.
6. Buyer characteristics.

Time needed: three to six weeks.

The company can collect these data itself, but only if it is already set up to do housing market analysis. If not, a competent analyst should be hired. The cost for a consultant will be $6,000 to $12,000. However, once a basic study has been completed, it is adaptable to other projects, and the cost to update it may be only about half of the initial cost.

Some Points to Remember

1. Do not flood the study with a lot of data.
2. Do not accept any data without checking them. Question all data.

3. Ask: Is the source of data questionable? What were the reasons behind the publication?
4. Do not accept press releases without checking further.
5. As a rule, do not accept interpretations of politically oriented groups. If possible, talk to professionals, not politicians.
6. Develop sources that you can trust. Select balanced sources of data.
7. Make sure that the supply, demand, and absorption analyses get a fair share of the study.
8. Use few data rather than many. Make sure that you use key information.
9. It is important to get all the critical data. Concentrate efforts on what is really needed, not on what is readily available.

What to Avoid in a Market Research Study

1. Do not attempt to gather more data than you can comfortably digest.
2. Avoid generalities. Do not use flowery words. Make your point clearly and concisely.
3. Do not write a master's thesis. This is not a school exercise.
4. Do not get too ambitious; decide in advance what you really need. It is easy to go on and on without adding to the substance of the report. The researcher does not get paid by the weight of the document; neither do houses sell or investors get their money back because of a weighty document.
5. Do not spend more than has been budgeted. Keep costs down and under control.
6. Avoid repetitions. Avoid repetitions. Avoid repetitions.
7. Avoid foldout tables—they are costly and hard to read.
8. Spell out the proper source of the data, with clear identification for further reference. Give credit to the people who supply you with information.
9. Avoid personal references and prejudices.
10. Ask yourself this about the information:
    a. Does it make sense?
    b. Does it fit a pattern?
    c. Is it complete?
    d. Is it a part of an established trend?
    e. Do other data verify this trend?

What to Watch Out for in Collecting Housing Data

1. Permits
   a. Are permits issued for one unit or for one structure with several units?
   b. Are permits issued for residential or nonresidential purposes?
   c. What is the type of housing: single-family detached, attached (town house), condominium, rental?
   d. What is the type of structure: low rise, midrise, high rise?
   e. For a large project, was the permit actually used, or is it still outstanding? If it was not used, determine why, and estimate when it will be used.

    f. Check the indicated price. Typically, price figures are *not* correct; there is a tendency to underestimate the actual sale price by 30 to 40 percent.

2. Production.
   a. Starts data can be accepted from the U.S. census or from state or local governments.
   b. The only *real* way of knowing starts data, however, is by checking the excavations or foundations poured or possibly the clearing of the site or demolition.
   c. Data on units under construction—national and regional—can be accepted as supplied by the Bureau of the Census.
   d. FHA surveys cover only medium and large projects—not total units.
   e. Utility companies may have the best information on both starts and units under construction—as well as completions.
   f. For data on completions, use utility company installations of meters for gas, electric, or water hookups.

3. Vacant units.
   a. Sold signs in the windows may not indicate that the unit has actually been sold. Pins in the sales office indicating sold units may or may not represent the true picture.
   b. Check unsold inventory with the FHA office or lenders—get a feel for the market.
   c. Do *not* trust the FHA post office vacancy survey. Check with FHA personnel, and let them explain the problems and pitfalls. Check previous surveys: Do they make sense?
   d. Check with local home builders' associations concerning unsold homes.
   e. Check with builder-owner management assocations for information on rental vacancies. Also, large management companies *know* what the situation is.

4. Pipeline figures.
   a. Make sure you know what the "pipeline" means—units which will be coming on the market and competing when a project get under way and runs through sellout.
   b. Check with a planning board or a county housing expert.
   c. Do not accept generalities such as "X number of units ready to get under construction." Ask for specific names, location, types, and dates.
   d. Check with financial institutions: applications for loans, FHA loan activity, and subdivision plans.

5. Costs and prices.
   a. Check local cost data with local home builders' associations or with the National Association of Home Builders in Washington. NAHB provides cost information broken down to 25 basic cost items for some 400 cities.
   b. The FHA has a great deal of cost information, as does the Farmers Home Administration and the VA.

   c. Know whether you are getting an average price or a median price. There is quite a bit of difference.

   d. Multiple listings and sales figures provide a good information source for the sale of existing homes. Distinguish between offered price, accepted price, and closing price. They are generally all different.

   e. Get price ranges rather than averages. The price distribution is more important than the average or the median, which really mean little to your work. If you need it, figure the median yourself, or make sure that your number is right.

   f. Other cost information is available from the American Appraisal Company, E. H. Boeckh, the FHA, the VA, and others.

Conclusion

These tips on how to analyze housing markets are based on substantial experience and a theoretical framework for understanding how the housing system works. The best advice that can be given to those who have housing decisions to make is to get the proper analyses conducted and to thoroughly understand how these analyses fit into the decision-making strategy. This requires:

1. An understanding of how the housing system works. The decision makers and analysts should have a sound understanding of the theoretical framework.

2. An understanding of one's own experience. Why did things work out well in the past, or why were there difficulties? Understanding past experience is important if one is to benefit from it.

3. An application of both the experience and the theoretical framework to the new situation. New situations require getting new facts. *Do not stint on getting the data;* it is expensive not to know what is really happening. But in addition to having the facts, it is important to relate them to the current situation and the rapidly changing environment.

Finally, watch the housing market environment. This is best done by forecasting changing conditions and having something to gauge events by. If you have a good idea of what to expect, you will have ample opportunity to make money by serving housing needs. If you watch events as they materialize and compare them with your plans, a proper strategy will keep you from losing your assets.

LOCATION ANALYSES

Robert O. Harvey

*R*OBERT O. HARVEY, DBA, Professor and Chairman, Real Estate
and Regional Science, School of Business Administration, Southern Methodist University, Dallas, Texas.

Director, Costa Institute of Real Estate Finance, Southern
Methodist University, Professor of business emeritus, University
of Connecticut. Director, American National Insurance Com-
pany, Galveston, Texas. Trustee, Heitman Mortgage Investors,
Chicago. Member, Separate Account Committee, Hartford Vari-
able Annuity Life Insurance Company. Educational consultant,
National Association of Realtors. Consultant, Dallas Federal
Savings. Formerly dean, School of Business Administration,
University of Connecticut. Past national president, Beta
Gamma Sigma.

Everything has to be at some place; the goal of location analysis is
to find the "right" place. Location uncertainties are at the heart of the
risk in real estate decisions. The ultimate question is, Will what I have
in mind work at that spot? The typical real estate investment involves
the commitment of a large sum of money for a long period of time at
a specific site which is at the mercy of events over which the investor
has scarcely any control.

Location analysis proceeds from macro to micro decisions: What part
of the world or country is appropriate? What urban environment is economically viable? And just where within an urban environment is the
proper place for a particular activity? Thus, analysis for a location decision includes three levels of review: a region, an urban area, and a
neighborhood or district.

This chapter treats each decision level in sequence, beginning with
regional analysis.

Regional Analysis

Some sections of the world offer greater growth potential than others? Can one know in advance where booms or major growth will occur? It is easier to describe why some regions are stronger than others than to predict with accuracy which areas will excel in economic development.

The Concept of a Region. A region is an arbitrarily defined area which is in some ways homogeneous. Regional boundaries may be geographic, topographic, political, functional, resource related, or just plain arbitrary. Boundaries may be precise or inexact. For example, a census region, say New England, is precise; but the Sun Belt is an inexact general description of an area. Readily recognized examples of regions are: the Midwest, the Dallas/Forth Worth Metropolitan Area, the Manufacturing Belt, the Cotton Belt, the census regions, a watershed, a trading area for a major shopping center, and a viewing area for a major television station.

The Concept of Comparative Advantage. The prosperity of a region and its potential are dependent on what that region can do best in the way of producing goods or services for buyers outside the region and on what it can produce for internal consumption that will not have to be imported. A region's prospects are related to economic activities that produce income flows to and within the region.

Regional analysis reduces to identifying a region's comparative advantage, that is, "what it can produce more effectively and efficiently than any directly competing region." A region will generate those economic activities through which it can earn the greatest returns relative to those that can be earned from all other realistic options. The key to analyzing a region is to identify its comparative advantage and to measure the extent, depth, and duration of that advantage.

An entrepreneur making a location decision frequently risks looking ahead of current reality. By the time published data are available on regional changes, it is already too late to "be the first" in an area. The issue, then, is, will an area start or continue to grow?

Information about regions is more commonly available in the form of data on population, employment, income, housing starts, building permits, and consumer expenditures.[1] The principal sources include the population reports of the Bureau of the Census, which are issued periodically and are available through the Department of Commerce field offices and the U.S. Government Printing Office. The Department of Labor publishes employment information; the Commerce Department's Bureau of Economic Analysis estimates and publishes data on incomes. Most of the population, employment, and income data are monitored by leading business magazines such as *Business Week* and *U.S. News & World Report,* both of which carry sections on regional change and material on major population and income data.

Each of the 12 Federal Reserve banks publishes a periodic newsletter which is frequently devoted to the economics of the region that the

---

[1] See Exhibit 1.

EXHIBIT 1
Selected Important U.S. Information Sources

U.S. Department of Commerce Publications
  Construction Review
  County Business Patterns
  Current Industrial Reports
  Current Population Reports
  Statistical Abstract of the United States
  Survey of Current Business
  U.S. Industrial Outlook
  Census of:
    Construction Industries
    Housing
    Manufactures
    Mineral Industries
    Population
    Retail Trade
    Selected Service Industries
    Transportation
    Wholesale Trade
  Foreign Direct Investment in the United States, eight-volume report to
Congress, April 1976
U.S. Department of Labor publications
  Area Wage Surveys
  Handbook of Labor Statistics
  Monthly Labor Review
Trade Association publications
  Automobile Facts and Figures (Automobile Manufacturers Association)
  Electronic Market Data Book (Electronic Industries Association)
  Annual Statistical Report (American Iron and Steel Institute)
  Statistics of Paper (American Paper Institute)
  Wood Pulp Statistics
  Textile Hi-Lights (American Textile Manufacturers Institute)
Others
  Federal Reserve Bulletin and monthly reviews from the 12 Federal Re-
serve district banks
  Standard & Poor's Industry Survey
  Conference Board publications
  State Employment Commission bulletins
  Sales & Marketing Management (special issues focus on "Surveys of
Buying Power" in cities, counties, and regions)

Source: Adapted from *Information for Foreign Investors Considering Operations in the United States,*
Peat, Marwick, Mitchell & Co., 1977.

bank serves. Major financial institutions in metropolitan areas, particularly large banks, report economic trends in their areas. Area development organizations such as chambers of commerce, special industrial development groups, or state development commissions, maintain information about opportunities in their areas. Research centers and consulting firms often publish reports on trends in particular areas. *Sales Management* magazine publishes an "Annual Survey of Buying Power" which also reports spendable income in states, major metropolitan areas, and major cities. Investment banking houses frequently publish research studies on areas and industries in which they have an interest. Travel magazines often carry stories about area developments; the major business publications, such as *Fortune,* carry special reports on areas.

Common to all published data is an emphasis on what *has* happened. An analyst is left with the task of interpreting whether the trends of the future will be an extension of the trends of the past. In making regional analyses, as with almost all economic analysis, one is compelled to rely on the terribly naive assumption that the future will resemble the past unless there are good reasons to believe otherwise.

Analysis of a region should focus on those activities which influence its comparative advantage.

Forces and Factors Which Alter the Comparative Advantage of Regions. The strength and potential of regions change as a result of the interaction of many factors. Several factors are listed below, but these must not be thought of as being mutually exclusive. They interact, and they can be separated from one another only in the artifical environment of a list.

1. *Alterations in agricultural production.* Agricultural production patterns change if new land is put under cultivation because water becomes available, because the land becomes accessible, or because a new kind of production machinery makes working the land profitable. They also change if land is withdrawn from cultivation because of soil depletion or diversion to urban uses.

2. *A major change in resources.* The most obvious changes in resources are the exhaustion of extractable resources and the discovery of new resources. Recognition of the utility of heretofore unutilized resources and the emergence of technological innovations that make resource recovery economically feasible also affect a region's comparative advantage. Shifts in the demands for products derived from a region's resources tend to alter the quality levels of economically recoverable raw materials.

3. *Governmental influences on regional economies.* Governments at all levels may affect the economy of a region through decisions relating to taxation, labor laws, subsidies, environmental regulations, or military installations. The economies of the U.S. regions may be altered as a result of decisions to open or close military installations, change agricultural subsidies, support or not support shipbuilding, launch electric power projects, regulate imports, alter tariffs, or manage exchange rates. Aid to foreign countries impacts unevenly on the U.S. regions.

4. *The industrialization of nonindustrial or less industrial areas.* Following World War II, the economic climate of the world changed very greatly as West Germany, Japan, and the countries of Eastern Europe rebuilt their industrial centers and entered world competition. As capital formation occurs in the less industrialized nations of the world, the comparative advantage of the various regions of the world will change markedly.

5. *Transport changes.* Changes in transportation technology and in government policy with respect to assigned routes, highway building, and carrier rates alter regional strengths. Changes in the rate structure at the ports or of competing carriers result in sharp shifts in the economic strength of areas. For example, a reduction in shipping rates on the Mississippi River may work to the great advantage of the Port of New Orleans and to the great disadvantage of, say, Philadelphia. The development of the Southeast relative to that of New England was in large measure a product of changes in railroad rates that gave a comparative advantage to industrial activities in the South.

Altering highway and air networks clearly influences the economic potential of the affected areas.

6. *New priorities relative to recreation and retirement amenities.* As incomes have increased and outlays for recreation and retirement have expanded, areas blessed with sunlight, water, and special recreation and retirement amenities have flourished.

7. *General improvements in the state of technology.* The character of regions may change very greatly simply as a result of technological breakthroughs which allow the production of materials or products at sites which were previously not economically competitive.

In summary, analysis of a region includes a review of what has happened in that region. Evidence is most likely to be found in the form of data on population, employment, income, housing starts, building permits, and household spending. A second element of regional analysis is making estimates regarding changes in the comparative advantage of the region. This is a far more difficult task.

The Potential of a Particular Urban Area

Once a region has been selected as a possible place for new economic activity, the question becomes, in what part of that region? Most location decisions relate to a particular urban area. An urban place exists because it functions for the people who live there. An urban place also exists because some group in it is able to attract income from people who do not live there. Estimating the potential of a particular city involves identifying that city's primary income-producing activities and measuring the interrelationships between and among them.

Activities that draw income from beyond the borders of the city are presumed to be a building or growth force for the city. Activities that service the people who live in the city are presumed to be maintainers of the city itself and to exist because they serve those who are primary income producers.

Economic-Base Analyses. Economic-base analysis is a way of looking at what a city does, at the principal sources of income drawn to the city, and at how those activities spawn other activities which are primarily local in character. Economic-base analysis is typically conducted through the measurement of basic and nonbasic jobs. Basic jobs (also called primary, export, or town-building jobs) are those involved in the creation of income through sales of goods and services to persons outside the city. In contrast, nonbasic jobs (also called service, secondary, or town-filling jobs) are concerned with the production of locally consumed goods and services. None of the designations for basic and nonbasic jobs are absolutely accurate, for these designations do not easily accommodate the primary income source of satellite or retirement communities. Retirees are to a retirement community what factory workers in a plant that exports everything it makes are to an industrial community. Both the factory workers and the retirees attract income to the community. A city that is a satellite of a major metropolitan center may have only two kinds of jobs: those held by people who commute to work outside the city, and thus bring income back to the city, and those who work in the city and provide services to others in the city. Out-commuters and most retirees are treated as primary or basic workers in economic-basic analysis.

Economic-base analysis proceeds by looking at the job categories in a particular city, such as agriculture, mining, construction, manufacturing, transportation, wholesale and retail trade, business and repair services, personal services, entertainment and recreation, professional and related public administration, education, and all income sources not otherwise accounted for.[2] It is possible to divide jobholders in each category into basic jobholders (those whose efforts are devoted primarily to attracting income from beyond the borders of the city) and nonbasic jobholders (those who provide primary service within the city itself). The ratio of the basic to the nonbasic totals becomes a tool for predicting growth. It is assumed that if growth occurs in the basic activities, additional growth will occur in the nonbasic activities. The basic-nonbasic ratio becomes an instrument of some importance.

The basic-nonbasic ratio is not something which is predictable for a particular city, and it is certainly not stable. There are forces at work all the time which change the ratio between basic and nonbasic categories. These forces are:

1. *The size of the city.* The larger a city, the larger the relative size of the nonbasic component of jobs will be. The larger the city, the greater the number of people that will be required to help those who live there get along. The larger the city, the greater the complexity of the city's bureaucracy. As city size increases, the number of persons involved in nonbasic or service activities tends to grow relative to the number of people involved in basic activities.

2. *The level of income in the city.* The higher the general distribution of incomes, the higher the service or nonbasic job component of the city is likely to be. If the household units of a city have large discretionary

---

[2] An illustration of an economic-base study is presented in Exhibit 4.

incomes, there is likely to be relatively greater nonrequired spending in that city, and thus more nonbasic jobs, than in a city where incomes are relatively low.

3. *Interrelationships between the city and other producing areas.* The ratio of basic to nonbasic jobs in a city is dependent upon the inclination of people within the city to import the goods and services they need as opposed to buying those locally. For example, as an illustration, a city of population that is near a major metropolitan center in which there are a number of shopping opportunities may have a relatively lower nonbasic number of jobs than a city of 50,000 population in the middle of a vast plain with no easy access to major metropolitan center. The latter city would have fewer opportunities to imports its goods and services, and for that reason alone it would tend to be self-supporting and to minimize its imports.

4. *The traditions, attitudes, and general life-styles of the people in the city.* If the people of a city tend to be gregarious, outgoing, and highly devoted to sports and recreational activities, the service, or nonbasic, job component may be high. If, in contrast, the people of a city are somewhat more introspective, then the service job component may be low.

It is not possible to say what the ratio between export and service jobs ought to be. The point is that all of the foregoing factors operate simultaneously. There are generalizations based on size which may not be useful in specific decisions. Once a city has a population of around 100,000 persons, it is not unusual for its basic-nonbasic ratio to be around 1-1. The larger the population is above 100,000, the more likely it is that the ratios will be from 1-2.5 to 1-3 or higher. Cities with a population below 100,000 are likely to import a share of their products and services. A city of 10,000 might very well have a basic-nonbasic ratio of 1-0.3 or 1-0.4. Of course, as the city of 10,000 grows to 20,000, 25,000, and 30,000, the expectation is that the basic-nonbasic ratio will rise from, say, 1-0.3 to 1-0.5 or 1-0.6.

The Use of the Basic–Nonbasic Ratio in Projecting Growth. Consider a very simple and crude example. Suppose that we are looking at a one-company town in which everything manufactured in the only factory is shipped outside the city. Suppose that the company announces that it will hire an additional 1,000 persons. An economic-base study of the city shows that the ratio of basic to nonbasic jobs is 1 to 0.8. If the factory will hire 1,000 persons, the full potential for growth and employment is not just the 1,000 basic jobs but the 1,000 basic jobs plus 800 nonbasic jobs. If it is assumed that there is no unemployment, that the report of the 1,000 new jobs is accurate, that the ratio of 1-0.8 is approximately correct, then the total increase in jobs will be 1,800.

The employment information is useful in helping us determine population growth. If we assume that the people who move to the town do so immediately and that they have family profiles very much like those of the people who already live there, then the new jobholders will have about the same numerical relationship to the new population that the present jobholders have to the present population. Since it is known that 35 percent of the people who live in the town currently are employed, we can therefore conclude that the 1,800 new jobholders will represent 35 percent of the total population generated by the new jobs. Eighteen hundred new jobholders will therefore represent a population growth of 5,143 persons. A less precise but more plausible estimate is that over whatever time it takes the new jobholders to move into the town and fill those jobs, the total population of the town will increase somewhat over 5,100.

The population growth projections allow us to make crude estimates about the land use needs that will be generated. Again, we will rely on the premise that the family household pattern of the new population will be similar to that of the present population. Assume that in this community, the average household size is relatively large, say 3.7 persons per household as compared to the 3.2 national average in 1970. Household size may be determined from the most recent Census of Population data or from school census information. If each household has 3.7 persons on the average, dividing then 5,143 by 3.7 reveals that 1,390 households, give or take a few, will be created by the increase of 1,000 basic jobs. Extension of the analysis permits speculation about the housing needs of the new households. It is reasonable to assume that the same proportion will want single-family, owner-occupied houses as was previously the case and that the same proportion will want rental houses, mobile homes, apartments, and condominiums. These calculations are summarized in Exhibit 2.

This simple example is meant only to illustrate that data generated through economic-base analysis, basic-nonbasic employment categories become a tool for projecting growth. The example included a number of ridiculous assumptions. An analyst may base projections upon any assumptions which seem to be reasonably realistic. If unemployment in a town could produce job takers of the kind needed by the factory, then the thousand new jobs would not be taken by people from outside the city. It is unusual to assume that all newcomers to a community work force would in fact move into town immediately. It is not prudent

EXHIBIT 2
Projecting Growth Using a Basic–Nonbasic Ratio

The ratio: Basic 1—nonbasic 0.8

Basic employment growth	1,000
Nonbasic employment growth	800
Total	1,800

Population growth
  Percent of population currently employed—35%
  Then, $1,800/0.35 = 5,143$ growth of population

Household growth
  Average number of persons per household—3.7
  Then, $4,143/3.7 = 1,390$ growth of households

---

to assume that the 800 new jobs in the nonbasic category would be filled by people moving into town, so most analysts working with basic-nonbasic data make assumptions about the minimum and maximum possibilities for growth in both the basic and nonbasic categories. These minimums and maximums are paired to make a range of potential projections. The projections for the future are typically matched with trend lines based on history and are compared with projections through straight extrapolation or linear regression.

Allocating Jobs between Basic and Nonbasic Categories. There are two fundamental methods for allocating jobs between basic and nonbasic categories. They are the survey method and the comparison with benchmark areas. The survey method involves sampling or taking a census of employers in a city and asking what share of their business is conducted locally and what share is conducted outside the city. At best the answers will be approximate, but the projection results are likely to be good enough for land use planning.

For example, a company reports that 40 percent of its business is done with local people and that 60 percent is done with people outside of town. Thus the total employment at that company would be divided into 60 percent basic and 40 percent nonbasic. The survey method would proceed to evaluate allocations in every category. Some are less difficult to do. The local fire department, the local grocery store, and the grade school and high school teachers deal only with people who live in the community and may be classified as nonbasic on the basis of their clientele. It is the department store or the manufacturing plant or the entertainment centers with both a local and a nonlocal clientele which cause allocation problems. Once a survey has been completed, the total number of jobs in the basic and the nonbasic categories and the ratio is established.

Another way of classifying jobs as basic or nonbasic compares of local employment in particular categories as a percentage of total local employment with employment in those categories as a percentage of total employment in a benchmark area, such as the United States, the state in which the city is located, or even a group of states or a combination of counties. One technique for using comparisons employs *location quotients,* which are derived from a fraction whose numerator is itself a fraction (local employment in a job category over the total local labor force) and whose denominator is also a fraction (employment in the same job category in a benchmark area over the total labor force in the benchmark area). For example, suppose that 10,000 persons were employed in job category X in a city and that there were 20,000 persons in the city's labor force.[3] The numerator would then be 0.50. Suppose further that in the benchmark area 200,000 persons were employed in job category X and that the total labor force of the benchmark area was 1 million. The denominator then proves to be 0.20. Dividing 0.50 by 0.20 produces the location quotient for job category X, or 2.5. The

---

[3] The location quotient calculations are shown in Exhibit 3.

EXHIBIT 3
Location Quotients

Calculating Location Quotients:

$$\dfrac{\dfrac{\text{Local jobs in category X}}{\text{Total jobs in local labor force}}}{\dfrac{\text{Jobs in category X in benchmark area}}{\text{Total labor force in benchmark area}}} = \dfrac{\dfrac{10,000}{20,000}}{\dfrac{20,000}{1,000,000}} = \dfrac{0.50}{0.20} = 2.5$$

Dividing employment into basic-nonbasic categories using location quotients:

$$\dfrac{1}{\text{Location quotient}} = \text{Percent in category in nonbasic employment}$$

$$\dfrac{\text{Location quotient} - 1}{\text{Location quotient}} = \text{Percent in category in basic employment}$$

Example: Location quotient = 2.5

$\dfrac{1}{2.5} = 0.40$ means 40 percent of jobs in Category X are nonbasic

$\dfrac{1.5}{2.5} = 0.60$ means 60 percent of jobs in Category X are basic

value of the location quotient is that it indicates which job categories are relatively heavily concentrated in a local area and therefore which industries have a high probability of including basic jobs. If the location quotient for a job category is greater than one, it is presumed that that job category includes basic workers. If the location quotient is one or less, it is presumed that the job category is nonbasic. Is the location quotient a reliable indicator of which categories are basic and which are not? Not necessarily, for the benchmark area chosen for comparison influences the location quotient. Anytime that the location quotient approaches one, it is reasonable to suspect that that job category may include basic employment. To illustrate, suppose that a town of 10,000 population with a labor force of 3,000 has a manufacturing plant which employs 200 people. All of the plant's products are exported from the city. Also assume that manufacturing employment in the United States, the benchmark, was 15 percent of the labor force. The location quotient for manufacturing in this little town would be 0.667, yet the entire manufacturing category would, in fact, comprise basic jobs. The classification of a category is very much dependent upon the selection of an appropriate benchmark.

One of the more difficult aspects of conducting an economic-base analysis is finding information on employment.[4] The U.S. population censuses include employment by occupation and are conducted during the first year of each decade—1960, 1970, and so on. The census of popula-

---

[4] See Exhibit 1 for information sources.

EXHIBIT 4
Employment and Location Quotients of Industries in Metropolitan Atlanta, 1970 (employment in 000)

Industry	Total Employment	Location Quotient	"Excess" Employment
Contract construction	31.4	1.09N	2.6
Lumber	2.7	0.54N	—
Furniture and fixtures	3.6	0.91N	—
Stone, clay, and glass products	4.5	0.82N	—
Primary metal industries	2.8	0.80	—
Fabricated metal products	5.7	0.80	—
Machinery, except electrical	5.1	0.89	—
Electrical machinery	3.9	0.79	—
Transportation equipment	34.3	4.25	26.2
Other durables	3.0	0.72	—
Food and kindred products	15.1	0.98N	—
Textile mill products	5.9	0.71N	—
Apparel and other textile products	8.1	0.68N	—
Paper and allied products	7.3	1.19N	1.2
Printing and publishing	9.3	2.38	5.4
Chemicals and allied products	5.5	1.07	0.4
Leather and leather products	1.7	0.84	—
Other nondurables	1.9	0.30	—
Transportation and public utilities	59.2	1.92	28.3
Wholesale trade	65.8	3.15	44.9
Retail trade	101.1	1.18	15.3
Finance, insurance, and real estate	44.2	2.04	22.5
Service, miscellaneous, and mining	92.4	1.40	26.2
Federal government	26.8	1.15N	3.5
State and local government	68.0	0.78N	—
Total	609.3		176.5

N = Based on national benchmark. The location quotient used is the greater of the quotients based on both national and state data.

The basic-nonbasic ratio is 1–2.45.

Source: Lawrence S. Davidson and William A. Schaffer, "An Economic-Base Multiplier for Atlanta, 1961–1970," *Atlanta Economic Review,* July–August 1973, p. 53.

tion lists people by where they live. Censuses conducted every five years include the censuses of business, wholesaling, retailing, manufacturing, and selective services. These censuses list people according to where they work, so they are not comparable to the data from the census of population.

One very important source of information on employment is the employment commissions of the several states. The employment commissions supply data to the U.S. Department of Commerce for use in national publications. An employment commission report typically lists only wage and salary employment by job category and does not include self-employed persons. The data are comparable to the monthly employment data in the *Survey of Current Business,* published by the U.S. Department of Commerce.

Unfortunately, all sources of information on employment but the *Survey of Current Business* and the employment commission bulletins are outdated before they are available. It is not easy to obtain current data on wage and salary workers or on independent contractors and other self-employed persons.

Dividing employment between basic and nonbasic categories allows identification of the areas which are responsible for a community's growth or decline. An interpreter may focus on the prospects for employment in particular categories. A basic-nonbasic ratio is useful in projecting employment trends and the resulting population changes.

An economic-base study is similar to a stop-action camera shot of a dynamic process. It is not apparent from a basic-nonbasic ratio whether a community is in a stable or an expanding state. For example, if one were to study the employment in a community just after a major expansion in basic activities, it is likely that the nonbasic employment would have reached its expected levels, so nonbasic employment would be understated. The recent history of employment in a particular city is an important facet of economic-base analysis.

Another hazard of economic-base analysis is classification errors. The failure to classify basic activities as basic tends to exaggerate the nonbasic component and makes for a lopsided ratio. If growth were projected using an exaggerated nonbasic component in the ratio, there is the probability of overstating the growth in employment and population that would follow from an increase in basic employment.

Input-Output Analysis. Another technique that is used in analyzing both local economies and regions is input-output analysis. An input-output table is a matrix of the money flows between economic categories in a particular area. Input-output analysis is complex and difficult to create and use. Input-output analysis suffers from a flaw that was popularly attributed to weather forecasting a few years back. The computer program for the 48-hour weather forecast was alleged to have taken 55 hours to prepare and run. The input-output approach is cumbersome, and it suffers from data limitations, as does the basic-nonbasic approach.

Input-output models have been created for the United States, several states, and a few cities. Each model is a table in which industries or economic activities are listed both as sellers and buyers of products and services. In an input-output matrix, all sectors are listed at both the side and the top of the table. The same groups are listed as sellers at the side and as buyers at the top. If trade is the first category in each case, the amount in the trade-to-trade box represents the amount that trading companies sold to each other. Exhibit 5 shows an input-output table for transactions in Colorado in 1972. Trade sold $256 million in products and services to trade. In contrast, trade sold $65 million in products and services to construction. The totals for rows equal the totals for columns. Most input-output tables have an adjustment column to take care of errors, for it simply isn't possible to be totally accurate in creating an input-output matrix.

EXHIBIT 5
Colorado Transactions Table: 1972 ($ millions)

	Trade	Construction	Services	Transpor-tation	Agri-culture	Mining	Finance	Manu-facturing	Final Use	Total Transactions
Trade	256	65	92	0	14	0	83	182	12,088	12,780
Construction	0	0	31	0	28	0	83	0	934	1,076
Services	767	75	184	147	28	0	124	182	1,558	3,065
Transportation	383	65	245	343	71	12	41	61	1,228	2,449
Agriculture	0	0	0	0	469	0	103	243	605	1,420
Mining	0	11	0	147	0	11	0	61	154	384
Finance	895	11	276	0	43	73	186	61	523	2,068
Manufacturing	1,278	334	153	0	270	0	41	2,976	1,021	6,073

Source: Peter H. Niehoff and Constantine E. Sotiriou, *Input-Output in Colorado for the Last Decade*, Occasional Studies no. 12 (Denver: Division of Research, College of Business Administration, University of Denver, March 1973), p. 5.

The input-output table is more sensitive to interactions between economic sectors in a particular area than is economic-base analysis. If manufacturing were to expand and the volume of purchases in the manufacturing sector could be identified, it would then be possible to have a reading on the potential increases in the sales of other sectors to manufacturers. The translation of increases from sales to jobs to population is intricate, but it can be accomplished.

Summary on the Analyzing of Local Economies. The true purpose of both economic-base analysis and input-output analysis is to help an analyst pierce the opaque veil of the future—to project what may happen. In either approach, the basic questions are: To what extent will economic activities already in the areas grow and prosper? To what extent will new activities grow and prosper?

Implicit in all location decisions involving economic activities is the *tendency* to seek a least cost place for doing business. The traditional business cost categories are: (1) procuring raw materials or components; (2) processing the materials or components; and (3) distributing the final product. The elements of procurement processing and distribution are most readily identified in manufacturing, but they are applicable to almost any kind of economic activity. Procurement and distribution costs are strongly related to transportation charges. Processing costs tend to be locally oriented and are closely related to labor costs, taxes, and energy charges.

In assessing the possibilities for growth in an area, it is vital to recognize that some kinds of business activity are unsuitable in some places. The acquisition of materials or of certain quantities of energy or water may not be possible. A needed labor skill may not be available, or processing costs may be prohibitive. The key to analyzing the future is to discover and focus upon the potential for economic activities which could exist and have a comparative advantage at a particular location.

For many economic activities in the United States there are several places which could approximate least cost circumstances. Accordingly, the final decision on locating economic activity is often related to personal considerations and to personal interpretations of the quality of life in a particular area.

Location Decisions within the Urban Area. Once a decision has been made to locate in a particular area, the final choice has to do with picking an appropriate spot within that area. Obviously, what place is picked is very much dependent upon what is to be done. The fundamental question in selecting a particular site is: How important is site location to the economic activity involved? To answer that question, three other questions must be answered: First, who needs to get to the site—employees, suppliers, customers? Second, how do they get there—public transportation, automobiles, trucks, airplane, rail? Third, where do users of the site need to get in other parts of the city, and with whom do they need to be associated? That is, do the operations at the site call for access to the flexible resource pool of a central city? does the user of the site require proximity to competitors in order to be a part of a critical mass? what other urban uses is it vital to have in proximity to the site? Once those questions have been answered, it is possible to make a determination of what attributes are necessary and desirable in terms of size, topography, character of subsoil, shape, and ingress and egress, and to compare those attributes with the physical attributes of a particular site.

Explanation of Urban Patterns

Two theories of how urban areas are put together and how they change are worth consideration. These are the multiple nuclei theory and the sector theory. The multiple nuclei theory is a static theory with dynamic implications.[5] A city is composed of several nuclei that fall into four distinct patterns: (1) Some uses are located at sites which have special considerations for them, and they are located at those sites because they must be there. (2) Some uses are located where they are in order to have proximity to other uses which are beneficial to them. (3) Some uses are located where they are in order to avoid hostile influences from other uses which would be detrimental to them. (4) Some uses simply take the best of whatever is left over because they have no particular requirements.

Industrial uses frequently require access to water, port, rail, and even truck facilities. Department stores tend to be located in the center of population patterns so that the greatest number of customers have access. Small retail outlets tend to cluster around powerful retail outlets. Historically, light manufacturing has been near to the center of cities, where operators could have rapid face-to-face communication with competitors, suppliers, and customers and access to the flexible resource pool and the economies of scale of the central city. High-value residential uses have most often developed in areas remote from manufacturing or other uses that are ordinarily hostile to them. Governmental units have tended to locate in central areas where there could be maximum access. Middle to lower income housing has tended to take space in areas with the least deficiencies, but simply accepting whatever was left over from other uses.

The ideas of the multiple nuclei theory are very useful in assessing the general configuration of a city and in making general judgments about where to locate a particular use.

The Sector Theory. The sector theory was developed by Homer Hoyt in the middle 1930s through the process of plotting land uses in 56 American cities.[6] After studying the uses, values, and rents, Hoyt evolved a theory which focuses mainly on the residential areas and especially the high value residential sectors. Underlying the sector theory are three premises: the greater part of the growth of cities occurs at their periphery; the highest income groups tend to live in houses of the highest

[5] See Chauncey D. Harris and Edward L. Ullman, "The Nature of Cities," *Annals* of *the American Academy,* November 1945.

[6] See Homer Hoyt, *The Structure and Growth of Residential Neighborhoods in American Cities* (Washington, D.C.: Federal Housing Administration, 1939).

values; and the movements of the high-value residential sector are highly instrumental in shaping where other land use patterns develop.

According to the sector theory, eight premises describe the behavior of high-value residential areas and the influence of those areas on the rest of the city: (1) High-value areas rarely overlook a freeway or a railroad line, but they are rarely remote from access to principal fast-transport arteries. (2) High-value areas seek out high ground where there are views and where the risks of flood are at least minimized. (3) High-value areas seek out and develop in free, open-ended sections of a city where there is no immediate, obvious threat to confinement in the form of a dead end. (4) High-value areas invariably contain the homes of the leaders of the community. The selection of an area by leaders often stamps it as "the" growth area. (5) Once established, a high-value area does not tend to relocate. Instead it grows generally outward, and it continues to grow generally outward until some major forces are encountered which compel the growth pattern to be stopped or altered. (6) Real estate promoters can bend the direction of growth of the high-value areas, but they cannot through their own efforts compel the high-value areas to be relocated. (7) The direction of growth of the high-value residential areas and the central business district tends to be the same. There is a strong possibility that the outward direction of growth of high-value residential sector pulls the growth of the central business areas with it. (8) High-value residential areas may be found near the central business district as well as the periphery of the city. High-rise, high-value residential districts tend to develop near the center of cities, usually in areas which had once been high-value residential and had gone through successions of uses.

The analytic strength of both the multiple nuclei theory and the sector theory is enhanced if the analyst employs generalized time interval land use maps.

City growth patterns tend to be self-fulfilling. Once the patterns are set they are difficult to change. If a city can be classified on topographic maps into current residential uses of high, middle, and low value and into current commercial, industrial, institutional, religious, and political uses, and if those uses can then be compared with the uses of a period 10 or 15 years earlier and if possible with the uses another 10 or 15 years before that, then it is relatively simple to project a rate and pattern of growth and to determine where growth can and probably will occur.

Area Dynamics. Any site is inevitably benefited or victimized by the dynamics of the areas surrounding it. In selecting a particular location, one has to be sensitive to the long-term prospects of the given area and to ask what its possible futures are.

The causes and catalysts of changes in areas are reviewed:

1. *Technological developments.* Changes in the technology of transportation, including both vehicles and surface facilities, and in the technology of construction encourage changes in areas.

2. *The family cycle.* A given household has a variety of housing needs, starting perhaps with a small house, then a larger house, then perhaps even a mansion, and ultimately a somewhat less commodious structure.

The key question is, What happens to the structures and the areas in which families are located as these families move through the family cycle? Will the families that move in maintain the structures in the style in which they were originally intended to be maintained? Areas with relatively small houses or apartments may suffer over time and offer fewer amenities, but these are areas into which it is difficult to introduce land use changes. The larger the houses in an area, the more likely it is that the area's units will be converted to something other than single-family residential use, even if this is only multiple-family use. The mansions have the greatest long-run potential for being converted into non-single-family uses.

3. *The introduction of nonconforming uses.* What are the prospects that uses hostile to present ones may ultimately be introduced into an area? Well-designed zoning and deed restrictions retard the introduction of different uses, but they cannot guarantee that no changes in uses will occur. Areas which are well designed, have been built at one time, are harmoniously related internally, and have an identity separate from that of the rest of the city tend to have long, stable lives and are ordinarily resistant to land use changes. Areas on the edge of a zoning border, where hostile uses can be developed "across the street," and areas which were partially built and then left idle, say during a recession, are areas in which different classes of uses are possible or probable.

4. *The introduction of nonconforming users.* This is a topic about which there is a great deal of confusion. Much has been said about racial problems, but the heart of the conflicts among residential users is class, not race. Residential users like to enjoy a homogeneity of class, culture, economics, and general life-style. To the extent that people perceive that those around them are relatively similar in culture, income, lifestyle, pattern of behavior, and jobs, race tends not to be a factor. However, whenever there are conflicts in class and culture, there tends to be a change in the occupancy of an area. Race need not be involved at all in such conflicts. If low-income, lower-class whites invade an area of middle-income, middle-class whites, there is likely to be a shift in the occupancy of the area, and the same is true if an area of middle-income, middle-class blacks is invaded by low-income, lower-class blacks.

5. *Physical deterioration and obsolescence.* Once structures in an area show signs of deterioration, the decay tends to feed upon itself. Efforts to clean up, fix up, and repair are retarded. If structures in an area are perceived to be obsolete in terms of architectural style, function, or equipment, the obsolescence exaggerates the tendency of the area to decline.

6. *The availability of competitive alternatives.* Some areas are unique, and no close substitutes to them are available in the marketplace. Such neighborhoods as Beacon Hill in Boston, Queen Ann Hill in Seattle, Telegraph Hill in San Francisco, and Mount Adams in Cincinnati are unique, and each of these neighborhoods has had a history of private rehabilitation.

Areas with rapidly expanding economic bases tend to develop new residential alternatives. The more rapid the growth of basic activities, the more likely it is that new direct competitors to old areas will be introduced. Given the presence of new alternatives to old areas, the old areas tend to become susceptible to decline in value and to the introduction of nonconforming uses and noncomforming users.

7. *Change in density.* There is no such thing as a correct density for an area. Areas and structures can be designed to accommodate any density. The hazard to stability of value occurs when increases in intensity are far beyond what either the area or the structures were ever intended to accommodate. Once increased densities occur, the change feeds upon itself. Amenities tend to disappear. Sometimes values rise, but over the long run, unless there are major modifications of the structures and the area to accommodate high-density land uses, old structures with increasing densities tend to fall in favor and usually in values.

8. *Public sector administrative decisions.* The public sector can alter tax burdens and introduce or permit the land use changes mentioned above by altering transportation routes and by changing zoning and building codes. The public sector can be responsible for both positive and negative influences on areas.

The comments in this section on picking a particular site in the urban area have been restricted to the general structural trends, patterns, and characteristics of particular areas. However, location decisions, though are complex in themselves, cannot be made independently of analyses of the market for whatever products and services might be offered at the site selected. Nothing has been said about measuring the market potential for the site. The topic is covered elsewhere in this book.

SELECTED REFERENCES

General

Heilbrun, James. *Urban Economics and Public Policy.* New York: St. Martin's Press, 1974. Chapters 2, 4, and 7 in particular

Weimer, Arthur M.; Hoyt, Homer; and Bloom, George F. *Real Estate.* 7th ed. New York: John Wiley, 1978. Chapters 5, 6, and 8 in particular

Regional and Economic-Base Analyses

Isard, Walter. *Introduction to Regional Science.* Englewood Cliffs, N.J.: Prentice-Hall, 1975. Chapters 1, 6, and 7 in particular

Miernyk, William H. *The Elements of Input-Output Analysis.* New York: Random House, 1965.

Perloff, Harvey S., with Vera W. Dodds. *How a Region Grows.* Supplementary Paper no. 17. New York: Committee for Economic Development, 1963.

Tiebout, Charles I. *The Community Economic Base Study.* Supplementary Paper no. 16. New York: Committee for Economic Development, 1962.

Urban Patterns

Bourne, Larry S. *Internal Structure of the City.* New York: Oxford University Press, 1971. Sections 2, 3, and 5 in particular

Hoyt, Homer. *According to Hoyt.* Washington, D.C.: Author, 1966. Sections 5, 8, and 9 in particular

ENVIRONMENTAL IMPACT ANALYSES

Lawrence S. Banks

*L*AWRENCE S. BANKS, MAI, SREA, Appraiser–Real Estate Analyst, Dallas, Texas.

Professional Recognition Award, American Institute of Real Estate Appraisers. Past President, North Texas chapter, American Institute of Real Estate Appraisers. Author, "Counseling with the Straight Line Recapture Premise," Appraisal Journal; and "Profit as a Unit of Production," Appraisal Journal.

This chapter explains how real estate appraisers and analysts can acquire an adequate understanding for the preparation or review of environmental impact statements.

Real estate specialists are familiar with the economic and political ingredients of regional, city, and neighborhood analyses. The process of environmental analysis is the same as the process of analysis for other areas of real estate decision making (i.e., defining the problem, planning a work program, and acquiring pertinent data which is then classified, analyzed, interpreted, and related in a conclusion). The study of environmental problems often relates several disciplines in the social and physical sciences. Much of the physical science data can be obtained with interpretation from such federal and state agencies as the Corps of Engineers, the Federal Aeronautics Administration, and fish and wildlife departments. These data are not always adequate, and supplementary private research or consultation may be necessary. The appraiser-analyst will need to exercise judgment as to the depth of research and analysis required. In order to meet the requirements of environmental impact analysis, the appraiser-analyst must consider not only the well-being of individual and corporate clients but also economic and ecological factors. Thus, the practicality of an environmental proposal must be considered.

Initial impact is measured in environmental analysis as it is measured in classical appraising. Ideally and most simply, the social and physical aspects of comparable market activities should be weighed against the value change on a before and after basis for the purpose of direct comparison with the proposed activity.

More frequently perhaps, a cost-benefit analysis may prove helpful. What is society's profit or loss if action A, B, or C is taken? What is the user's profit or loss? Such an analysis may resemble a series of highest and best use studies to select the optimum program, keeping in mind not only the economic results but also the social consequences.

The results of environmental action may not all be immediate. In fact, environmental action may not be a one-time effort but a continuing effort requiring a discounted analysis set against the social benefits or detriments over some period of time.

Various types of economic analysis that are described in other chapters of this handbook are readily adaptable to economic analysis in environmental studies. The difference is not necessarily in methodology per se, but in scope and inherent purpose. The inherent purpose of market value and highest and best use studies is to ascertain the optimum economic use of the given parcels of land. Appraising is strongly oriented toward a free enterprise economy.

The ethics of free enterprise have not been all bad, the individual worker in America being the richest, freest person the world has ever known. Nevertheless, having satisfied most human wants, society is now very much concerned with the remaining human indignities and with indignities to the environment. Today our concern is not with bread alone but with the quality of life as well.

In a sense the real estate appraiser-analyst has always been concerned with environment. His concern has been from the standpoint of beneficial or adverse extraneous influences, such as benefits of the view, and with the social environment of transportation, education, religion and services from the standpoint of quality and availability. Now in the environmental impact analysis the real estate practitioner must consider not only the economics of return on investment but return to the investor and to society in a much broader sense. The economics of return on investment need not be in conflict with environmental action. In fact, investors may benefit from environmental action. Waterfront lots on a nonpolluted lake may be worth more than waterfront lots on an otherwise comparable polluted lake.

There is a price to pay for engaging in or neglecting to engage in environmental endeavors, and the question is whether the benefits received are worth less than, as much as, or more than the price. This question may not be easy to answer in an area which requires the simultaneous consideration of nonmonetary and monetary rewards.

The National Environmental Policy Act of 1969

Described in its heading as "an Act to establish a national policy for the environment, to provide for the establishment of a Council on Environmental Quality, and for other purposes," the National Environmental Protection Act of 1969 was enacted as Public Law 91–190 by the 91st Congress. In describing its purpose, the act states that it is intended to "encourage productive and enjoyable harmony between man and his environment; to promote efforts which will prevent or eliminate damage to the environment and biosphere and stimulate the health and welfare of man; to enrich the understanding of the ecological systems and natural resources important to the Nation."

The act contains two titles. Title I continues the theme of balance and says that the act seeks "to create and maintain conditions under which man and nature can exist in productive harmony, and fulfill the social, economic, and other requirements of present and future generations of Americans." Title II says that the three members of the Council on Environmental Quality which is created in the Executive Office of the President shall be "conscious of and responsive to the scientific, economic, social, esthetic, and cultural needs and interests of the Nation."

The directions for implementing the act state in part that "it is the continuing policy of the Federal Government, in cooperation with State and local governments, and other concerned public and private organizations, to use all practicable means and measures" to achieve the goals of the law.

The Requirement of Environmental Impact Statements.   In defining methods of analysis, the act says that "all agencies of the Federal Government shall" make proposals after consultation with other federal agencies and state and local agencies which are authorized to develop and enforce environmental standards. Thus governmental bodies originate environmental impact statements or environmental assessments. Even in the case of a private nongovernment-insured residential subdivision, the Department of Housing and Urban Development prepares the environmental impact statement with assistance from the developer. When a state agency such as a park, wildlife, highways, or public transportation department is involved, the state agency generally prepares the statement for review by the appropriate federal agency or agencies. Municipal governments may also prepare environmental impact statements, subject to review by state and federal agencies. There is no provision in the National Environmental Policy Act for individuals to prepare a statement or to respond. On the other hand, the act does not prohibit reaction from private organizations, and it calls for "cooperation with . . . concerned public and private organizations."

The Council on Environmental Quality has provided for public hearings. Private consultants may be hired to prepare a study, but in all cases the final decision, short of appeal action, rests with a governmental agency. In the *Federal Register* for August 1, 1973, the Council on Environmental Quality issued guidelines for the preparation of environmental impact statements. The council commented, "Where an agency relies on an applicant to submit initial environmental information, the agency should assist the applicant by outlining the types of information required. In all cases the agency should make its own evaluation of the environmental issues and take responsibility for the scope and content of draft and final environmental statements." New regulations effective July 30, 1979, are substantially the same on this subject.

Implementing Regulations. Effective July 30, 1979, the Council on Environmental Quality has issued final regulations to establish uniform procedural provisions for the NEPA. These regulations were drafted at the direction of President Carter, who had indicated that they should be "designed to make the environmental impact statement process more useful to decision makers and the public; and to reduce paperwork and the accumulation of extraneous background data."

The table of contents of the regulations is divided into nine sections as follows:

Purpose, policy, and mandate.

NEPA and agency planning.

Environmental impact statements.

Commenting.

Predecision referrals to the Council on Environmental Quality of proposed federal actions found to be environmentally unsatisfactory.

NEPA and agency decision making.

Other requirements of NEPA.

Agency compliance.

Terminology and index.

Implementation of the National Environmental Policy Act is the purpose of the Draft Regulations.

> NEPA procedures must insure that environmental information is available to public officials and citizens before decisions are made and before action is taken. The information must be of high quality. Accurate scientific analysis, expert agency comments, and public scrutiny are essential to implementing NEPA. Most important, NEPA documents must concentrate on the issues that are truly significant to the action in question, rather than amassing needless detail. . . . NEPA's purpose is not to generate paperwork—even excellent paperwork—but to foster excellent action.

Policy statements reflect that purpose: "Environmental impact statements shall be concise, clear, and to the point, and shall be supported by evidence that agencies have made the necessary environmental analysis."

Guidelines for the Preparation of Environmental Impact Statements. The identification and assessment of "all reasonable alternatives to proposed actions that will avoid or minimize adverse effects . . . upon the human environment" is called for. The policy statement is strong, stating that "all practicable means" consistent with NEPA and other essential considerations of national policy shall be used "to achieve the purpose of the act."

The "Mandate" of the Draft Regulations states the legal requirements for the guidelines, and the interested appraiser-analyst can refer to section 1500–3 of the Draft Regulations for legal citations. Two additional sections titled "Reducing Paperwork" and "Reducing Delay" refer to material covered elsewhere in the guidelines and are discussed elsewhere in this chapter.

The guidelines prescribe early consideration of the environmental impact analysis in planning, cooperative consultation in the preparation of reports, and quick identification of significant issues, thus narrowing the scope of what might otherwise be an unnecessarily wordy analysis. Agencies are to "utilize a systematic, interdisciplinary approach which will insure the integrated use of the natural and social sciences and the environmental design arts in planning and in decisionmaking."

Appropriate alternatives to unresolved conflicts are to be studied, developed, and described.

If no significant environmental impact is found to exist, then a statement to that effect with adequate discussion is to be made available to interested parties and for public review for 30 days if the proposed action normally requires an impact statement or if the nature of that action is without precedent.

Determining the scope of a report, called "scoping," consists of identifying "significant issues to be analyzed in depth in the environmental impact statement." Scoping may also include the establishment of page and time limits for the report. It is hoped that scoping will also eliminate unnecessary detail and superfluous discussion.

Items to be considered in setting the time limit for a report include *(a)* the potential for environmental harm, *(b)* the size of the project, *(c)* the state of the art of analytic techniques, *(d)* the degree of public need, *(e)* the number of people involved, *(f)* the availability of relevant information, *(g)* the degree to which the action is controversial, and *(h)* legal and other regulatory restrictions.

Steps in the overall planning process include:

1. The decision to prepare or not prepare an environmental impact statement.
2. Scoping the proposed report.
3. Preparation of a draft environmental impact statement.
4. Public and agency review of the draft statement.
5. Preparation of the final statement.
6. Review of and comment on the final statement.
7. Decision on the action based in part on the environmental impact statement.

Environmental impact statements are action-forcing devices that "provide full and fair discussion of environmental impacts and shall inform decisionmakers and the public of all reasonable alternatives available for achieving Federal goals and shall compare the impacts of those alternatives on the human environment."

Significant environmental issues and alternatives are to be focused on and paperwork and the accumulation of extraneous background data is to be reduced. "Statements shall be concise, clear, and to the point, and shall be supported by evidence that the agency has made the necessary environmental analysis. It shall be used by Federal officials in conjunction with other relevant material to plan actions and make decisions."

An environmental impact statement is required to relate to the National Environmental Policy Act and other environmental laws and policies and to say how the alternatives and decisions of the statement will or will not implement those laws and policies. "Environmental impact statements are to serve as the means of assessing the environmental impact of proposed agency actions, rather than justifying decisions already made."

Normally the text of final environmental impact statements should not exceed 150 to 300 pages. Such statements "shall be written in plain language and may use appropriate graphics so that decisionmakers and the public can readily understand them." The statements may be supplemented when appropriate."

The Contents of Environmental Impact Statements. "Agencies shall use a format for environmental impact statements which will encourage good analysis and clear presentation. . . ." The following standard format is to be followed unless there is a compelling reason to do otherwise.

(a) Cover sheet.
(b) Summary.
(c) Table of contents.
(d) Purpose of and need for action.
(e) Alternatives, including proposed action.
(f) Affected environment.
(g) Environmental consequences.
(h) List of preparers.
(i) List of agencies, organizations, and persons to whom copies of statements are sent.
(j) Index.
(k) Appendices (if any).

"If a different format is used, it shall include paragraphs (a), (b), (c), (h), (i), (j) and shall include the substance of paragraphs (d), (e), (f), (g), and (k) . . . in an appropriate format."

The Cover Sheet. The cover sheet is not to exceed one page. It should state:

(a) A list of the responsible agencies, including the lead agency and any cooperating agencies.
(b) The title of the proposed action that is the subject of the statement (and, if appropriate, the titles of related cooperating agency actions), together with the state(s) and county(ies) (or other jurisdictions, if applicable) where the action is located.
(c) The name, address, and telephone number of the person at the agency who can supply further information.
(d) A designation of the statement as a draft, final, or draft or final supplement.
(e) A one-paragraph abstract of the statement.
(f) The date by which comments must be received.

Summary. Each environmental impact statement is to contain a summary which adequately and accurately summarizes the statement. The summary should stress the major conclusions, the areas of controversy (including issues raised by agencies and the public), and the issues to be resolved (including the choice among alternatives). The summary will normally be 5 to 15 pages long.

Purpose and Need. The statement is to briefly specify the underlying purpose and need to which the agency is responding in proposing the alternatives including the proposed action.

Alternatives, including the Proposed Action. This section is the heart of the environmental impact statement. Based on the information and analysis presented in the sections on the affected environment . . . and the environmental consequences . . . , it should present the environmental impacts of the proposed action and the alternatives in comparative form, thus sharpening the issues and providing a clear basis for choice among options by the decision maker and the public. Agencies should:

(a) Rigorously explore and objectively evaluate all reasonable alternatives. . . .
(b) Devote substantially equal treatment to each alternative considered in detail, including the proposed action. . . .
(c) Include reasonable alternatives not within the jurisdiction of the lead agency.
(d) Include the alternative of no action.
(e) Identify the agency's preferred alternative or alternatives, if one or more exists, in the draft statement and identify such alternative(s) in the final statement unless another law prohibits the expression of such a preference.
(f) Include appropriate mitigation measures not already included in the proposed action or alternatives.

Affected Environment. The environmental impact statement shall succinctly describe the environment of the area(s) to be affected or created by the alternatives under consideration. The descriptions shall be no longer than is necessary to understand the effects of the alternatives. Data and analyses in a statement shall be commensurate with the importance of the impact, with less important material summarized, consolidated, or simply referenced.

Environmental Consequences. This section should consolidate the discussions of the elements of an environmental impact statement required by NEPA. It forms the scientific and analytic basis for the comparisons. This includes the environmental impact of the proposed action and the alternatives, any adverse environmental effects which cannot be avoided should the proposed action be implemented, the relationship between short-term uses of the environment and the maintenance and enhancement of long-term productivity, and any irreversible or irretrievable commitments of resources which would be involved in the proposed action should it be implemented. The section should include discussions of:

(a) Direct effects and their significance.
(b) Indirect effects and their significance. Indirect effects may include

health effects, growth-inducing effects, and other effects related to induced changes in the pattern of land use, population density, or growth rate, and related effects on air and water or other natural resources, including ecological systems.

(c) Possible conflicts between the proposed action and the objectives of federal, regional, state, and local land use plans, policies, and controls for the area concerned.

(d) The environmental effects of both the proposed action and other alternatives.

(e) Energy requirements and conservation potential of various alternatives and mitigation measures.

(f) Natural or depletable resource requirements and conservation potentials of various alternatives and mitigation measures.

(g) Urban quality, history, and cultural resources, and the design of the built environment, including the reuse and conservation potential of various alternatives and mitigation measures.

(h) Means to mitigate adverse environmental impacts.

The List of Preparers. The environmental impact statement should briefly state the disciplines and qualifications of the individuals who have contributed to the preparation of the statement or who have contributed background papers for the statement. Where possible, the name of the preparer who assumes professional responsibility for a particular analysis should be identified. Normally the list will not exceed two pages.

Appendix. An appendix to an environmental impact statement:

(a) Consists of material prepared in connection with an environmental impact statement (as distinct from material which is not so prepared and which is incorporated by reference).

(b) Normally consists of material that substantiates any analysis which is fundamental to the impact statement.

(c) Should be analytic and relevant to the decision to be made.

(d) Shall be circulated with the environmental impact statement or be readily available on request.

Incorporation by Reference. Agencies are to incorporate material into an environmental impact statement by reference when doing so will reduce the bulk of the statement without impeding agency and public review of the proposed action. The incorporated material is to be cited in the statement and its content briefly described. Material based on proprietary data which is unavailable for review and comment should not be incorporated by reference.

When there are gaps in relevant information, including scientific uncertainty, it should be made clear that such circumstances exist. If the missing data are particularly significant a worst case analysis is to be included with appropriate probability analysis.

Cost-Benefit Analysis. Any cost-benefit analysis that is being considered with respect to the proposed action should be incorporated by reference or appended to the environmental impact statement. When a cost-benefit analysis is prepared, the agency should discuss the relationship between that analysis and any analyses of unquantified environmental impacts, values, and amenities. To comply with the act, "the weighing of the merits and drawbacks of the various alternatives need not be displayed in a monetary cost-benefit analysis and should not be when there are important qualitative considerations. . . . Agencies shall insure the professional integrity, including scientific integrity, of the discussions and analyses in environmental impact statements." Unfortunately, this statement lacks balance since there are normally monetary consequences as a result of environmental action.

Methodological Requirements. The environmental impact statement "shall identify any methodologies used and shall make explicit reference by footnote to the scientific and other sources relied upon for conclusions in the statements."

Analysis related to NEPA is to be integrated with "the Fish and Wildlife Coordination Act, the National Historic Preservation Act of 1966, the Endangered Species Act of 1973, and other environmental review laws and executive orders."

Further Provisions of the Draft Regulations. Comments by agencies and the public may or may not involve the independent analyst. The independent analyst could, of course, become very much involved in the review if his data or conclusions are challenged, and the analyst should exercise utmost care to ensure the collection of pertinent data and its evaluation in an unbiased manner.

The section on predecision referrals to the Council on Environmental Quality of proposed federal actions found to be environmentally unsatisfactory deals primarily with disagreements between agencies and their resolution.

The section on NEPA and agency decision making addresses itself to internal agency functions. It requires that the environmental impact statement be used in making decisions, that alternatives considered by the decision maker be considered in the environmental impact statement, "that the environmentally preferable alternatives be specified and that all alternatives be identified. A degree of preference may be established and discussed." It also requires a statement indicating whether "all practicable means to avoid or minimize environmental harm have been adopted and if not why not." For any mitigation adopted, a monitoring and enforcement program should be adopted and specified.

"Other requirements" of NEPA include administrative safeguards to the environment. This section also calls for cooperation among authorities and joint environmental research and studies that could benefit the analyst. If environmental impact statements are integrated, "such statements shall discuss any inconsistency of a proposed action with any approved state or local plan and laws (whether or not federally sanctioned)."

A document that meets NEPA requirements, from whatever source, may be combined with the environmental impact statement to reduce duplication of effort and volume of material.

Environmental impact statements are to be prepared directly by or under contract to the lead agency. The lead agency is the federal agency selected to be the primary sponsor. "Contractors shall execute a disclosure statement prepared by the lead agency "specifying that they have no financial interest in the outcome of the project." A contractor performing an agency function may expect to be required to comply with NEPA and related acts and policies that are not inconsistent with the integrity of the contractor's independence.

The Terminology of National Environmental Policy. The terminology of NEPA, as defined in the Draft Regulations, is required to be uniform throughout the federal government.

"Act" means the National Environmental Policy Act, as amended (42 U.S.C. 4321 et seq.), which is also referred to as NEPA.

"Affecting" means will or may have an effect on.

"Categorical exclusion" means a category of actions which do not individually or cumulatively have a significant effect on the human environment.

"Council" means the Council on Environmental Quality established by Title II of the National Environmental Policy Act.

"Cumulative impact" is the impact on the environment which results from the incremental impact of the proposed action when added to other past, present, and reasonably foreseeable future actions, regardless of what agency . . . or person undertakes such other actions. Cumulative impacts can result from individually minor but collectively significant actions taking place over a period of time.

"Effects" include direct effects and indirect effects.

(a) Direct effects are effects caused by taking the proposed action which occur at the same time and place.

(b) Indirect effects are effects caused by taking the proposed action which occur later in time or farther removed in distance but are still reasonably foreseeable. The terms *effects* and *impacts* are used synonymously. Effects includes ecological effects (such as effects on natural resources and on the components, structures, and functioning of affected ecosystems), aesthetic effects, economic effects, social effects, and health effects, whether direct, indirect, or cumulative. Effects may also include actions which have both beneficial and detrimental effects, even if the concerned agency believes that on balance the effects will be beneficial.

"Environmental assessment"

(a) Means a document by a federal agency which serves to:
  (1) Briefly provide sufficient evidence and analysis for the determination whether to prepare an environmental impact statement or a finding of no significant impact.
  (2) Aid an agency's compliance with the act when no environmental impact statement is necessary.
  (3) Facilitate preparation of such a statement when one is necessary.

(b) Shall include brief discussions of the need for the proposal, of alternatives as required by NEPA, of the environmental impact of the proposed action and alternatives, and a listing of agencies and persons consulted.

"Environmental impact statement" means a detailed written statement as required by NEPA.

"Finding of no significant impact" means a statement by a federal agency briefly presenting the reasons why a proposed action, not otherwise excluded . . . will not have a significant effect on the human environment and therefore will not require the preparation of an environmental impact statement. The statement "shall include the environmental assessment or a summary . . . and shall note any other environmental documents related to it.

"Human environment" should be "interpreted comprehensively to include the natural and physical environment and the interaction of people with that environment."

"Lead agency" means the federal agency or agencies which have prepared or have taken primary responsibility among federal agencies to prepare the environmental impact statement.

"Major federal action" includes action whose effects may be major and are potentially subject to federal control and responsibility. "Major" reinforces but does not have a meaning independent of "significantly."

"Mitigation" includes:

(a) Avoiding an environmental impact altogether by not taking a certain action or parts of an action.
(b) Minimizing environmental impacts by limiting the degree or the magnitude of an action and its implementation.
(c) Rectifying an environmental impact by repairing, rehabilitating, or restoring the impacted environment.
(d) Reducing or eliminating an environmental impact over time by preservation and maintenance operations during the life of an action.
(e) Compensating for an environmental impact by replacing resources or by providing substitute resources or environments.

"NEPA process" means all measures necessary for compliance with the requirements of NEPA.

"Scope" is the range of actions, alternatives, and impacts that are to be considered in an environmental impact statement. In scoping environmental impact statements, agencies should consider three types of actions, three types of alternatives, and three types of impacts.

(a) Actions may be:
　　(1) Connected, which means that they are closely related and should therefore be discussed in the same impact statement. Actions are connected if they:
　　　　(i)   Automatically trigger other actions that may require environmental impact statements.
　　　　(ii) Cannot or will not proceed unless other actions have been taken previously or are taken simultaneously,
　　　　(iii) Are interdependent parts of a larger action and depend on the larger action for their justification.
　　(2) Cumulative, which means that when taken together with other proposed actions they have cumulatively significant impacts and that they should therefore be discussed together with the other proposed actions in the same impact statement.
　　(3) Similar, which means that they have similarities when with other reasonably foreseeable or proposed agency actions, such as a common timing or a common geography, and that these similarities provide a basis for evaluating their environmental consequences together with those actions. An agency may wish to analyze similar actions in the same impact statement, and it should do so

when the combined impacts of similar actions or the availability of a reasonable alternative to such actions can be adequately assessed only by treating the actions in a single impact statement.
(b) Alternatives include:
   (1) No-action alternatives.
   (2) Other reasonable courses of action.
   (3) Mitigation measures (not in the proposed action).
(c) Impacts may be:
   (1) Direct.
   (2) Indirect.
   (3) Cumulative.

"Significantly" as used in NEPA requires considerations of both context and intensity.

(a) Context means that the significance of a proposed action must be analyzed in such settings as society as a whole (human, national), the affected region, the affected interests, and the locality. The significance of the proposed action varies with its setting. For instance, the significance of a site-specific action would usually be a function of the action's effects in the locality rather than in the world as a whole.
(b) Intensity refers to the severity of impact. The following should be considered in evaluating intensity:
   (1) Impacts that may be both beneficial and adverse. A significant effect may exist even if the federal agency believes that on balance the effect will be beneficial.
   (2) The degree to which the proposed action threatens public health or safety.
   (3) Unique characteristics of the geographic area, such as proximity to historic or cultural resources, parklands, prime farmlands, wetlands, wild and scenic rivers, or ecologically critical areas.
   (4) The degree to which the effects on the quality of the human environment are likely to be highly controversial.
   (5) The degree to which the possible effects on the human environment are highly uncertain or involve unique or unknown risks.
   (6) The degree to which the action may establish a precedent for future actions with significant effects or may represent a decision in principle about a future consideration.
   (7) Whether the action is related to other actions with individually insignificant but cumulatively significant impacts. Significance exists if it is reasonable to anticipate a cumulatively significant impact on the environment. Significance cannot be avoided by terming an action temporary or by breaking it down into small component parts.
   (8) The degree to which the action may adversely effect districts, sites, highways, structures, or objects listed in or eligible for listing in the National Register of Historic Places or may cause loss or destruction of significant scientific, cultural, or historical resources.
   (9) The degree to which the action may adversely affect an endangered species or its habitat has been determined to be critical under the Endangered Species Act of 1973.
   (10) Whether the action threatens a violation of federal, state, or local law or requirements that have been imposed for the protection of the environment.

"Tiering" refers to the coverage of general matters in broader environmental impact statements (such as national program or policy statements) and following these statements with narrower statements (such as regional or basinwide program statements or, ultimately, site-specific statements) that incorporate by reference the general discussions and concentrate solely on the issues specific to the statements subsequently prepared. The purpose of tiering is to eliminate repetitive discussions of the same issues and to focus on the issues ripe for decision.

Environmental Assessments. An environmental assessment, as defined above, is a brief report that precedes the preparation of an environmental impact statement and may show that there is no need for a complete statement. The assessment should be prepared so that the data in the brief analysis can readily be used in a complete statement if one becomes necessary. An outline for an environmental assessment might be as follows:

1. Cover sheet.
2. Introduction: cites the authority for the study and states the obligations of the law.
3. Summary of findings.
4. The purpose and scope of the study.
5. The environmental review process: cites the necessary publication dates, states the interdisciplinary basis of the assessment, and reports the extent of citizen participation, including specific hearing dates.
6. The assessment statement.
   a. Project identification and description—includes costs.
   b. Degree of conformity of project with local and regional plans and federal and state environmental policies and standards.
   c. The existing social and environmental setting.
      (1) The man-made environment.
      (2) The natural environment.
   d. Predicting environmental impacts.
      (1) On the natural environment.
      (2) On community facilities.
      (3) On energy uses.
   e. Evaluation of environmental impacts.
      (1) Individually.
      (2) In the aggregate.
   f. Consideration of alternative action.
   g. Statement of findings and conclusions.
   h. Appendices: copies of public notices, etc.

A statement of no significant impact is not a separate document but a brief conclusion to either an environmental assessment or an environmental impact statement.

Other Environmental Legislation

The Clean Air Amendments Act of 1970 (as Amended). This legislation defines areas of the United States which have the potential for failing to meet minimum air quality standards as defined by the act. Estimates issued by the U.S. Environmental Protection Agency have established that 187 areas might fail to meet the government's clean air standards, and a list of the areas is available from the agency. The time frame of the estimates is 20 years from the inception of the act.

Each state is required to analyze and report to the Environmental Protection Agency the effect that anticipated population changes is expected to have on air quality. By court decision in the District of Columbia (*NRDC* v. *EPA,* 475F., 2d 968, D.C. Cir. 1973), air quality standards must not only be achieved but must also be maintained.

To record its intent, a state must provide a written Air Quality Maintenance Plan. The plan must include five steps:

1. Obtain and update growth projections and information on how growth will contribute to air pollution.
2. Project future air pollution levels based on air pollution emission data and growth projections.
3. Evaluate and if necessary revise transportation controls, land use plans, and pollution abatement schedules so that air standards will not be violated.
4. Adopt and implement regulatory procedures and planning measures to ensure that air quality standards will be maintained.
5. Monitor air quality, pollution emissions, and growth patterns to determine whether more stringent steps will be necessary.

The Federal Water Pollution Control Act Amendments of 1972. Section 208 of these amendments mandates area-wide waste treatment plans to eliminate the discharge of pollutants into navigable waters by 1985 and to provide water whose quality meets the needs of fish and wildlife by July 1, 1983. Section 208 of the act also affects land planning in that it requires that a program be established to regulate the "location, modification, and construction of any facility . . . which may contribute to water pollutions." Pollutants discharged directly into navigable waters (sometimes referred to as point sources) and pollutants run off from land (often referred to as nonpoint sources) are covered by the amendments.

The Federal Water Pollution Control Act is administered by the Environmental Protection Agency through the National Pollutant Discharge Elimination System, which requires a permit to discharge a pollutant into the nation's waters. State agencies work with federal agencies in the enforcement of the act.

The act requires the "best practicable" or the "best available" pollution-control technology. The presence of a major new source of pollution, whether point or nonpoint, requires the filing of an environmental impact statement.

The Coastal Zone Management Act of 1972 and Its Amendment in 1976. Administered by the National Oceanic and Atmospheric Administration of the Department of Commerce this act requires that a land and resources management program for coastal zones be developed by states adjoining the Great Lakes; the Atlantic, Pacific, and Arctic oceans; the

Gulf of Mexico; and Long Island Sound. Coastal zones include inner tidal areas, wetlands, salt marshes, beaches, and land in sufficient proximity to the shoreline to control the shoreline.

The act provides for administrative grants, and in order to become eligible for such grants a satisfactory report covering the following items must be submitted:

1. Identification of the boundaries of the coastal zone.
2. A determination of permissible land and water uses which have a direct and significant impact on coastal waters, and the development of authorities to control those uses.
3. An inventory and designation of areas of particular geographic and environmental concern.
4. The means by which the public and local governments are involved.
5. A determination of how the program interacts with the federal government and addresses the national interest.
6. The organizational structure which would implement the management program.

In connection with the Coastal Zone Management Act and other environmental regulations, a Dredge and Fill Permit may be required from the Army Corps of Engineers. All navigable waters of the United States are covered, and a permit is required before dredging or filling that may affect these waters is undertaken. To use the terminology of another act, both "point" and "nonpoint" dredging and filling are covered.

Activities that require a permit include the following:

1. Site development fills for recreational, industrial, or commercial purposes.
2. Courseways, roadfills, dams and dikes, and artificial islands.
3. Property protection and reclamation devices (i.e., riprap, groins, seawalls, breakwaters, bulkheads, and fills.
4. Beach nourishment and levees.
5. Sanitary landfill and backfill.

A permit is requested from the district engineer responsible for the area in which the project is located. The request must include these topics:

1. A complete description of the proposed activity, including drawings, sketches, or plans.
2. The location, purpose, and intended use of the proposed activity.
3. The scheduling of the proposed activity.
4. The names and addresses of adjoining property owners and the location and dimensions of adjacent structures.
5. Approvals required by other federal, interstate, state, or local agencies for the work, including approvals or denials already made.

The Housing and Community Development Act of 1974. Community development block grants are a part of this legislation. Such funds may be used with some discretion by a local government that is successful in obtaining them. Among the uses which are closely related to the public sector of real estate is the acquisition of property which is inappropriately developed, blighted, or needed for rehabilitation, historic preservation, conservation, open space, or scenic areas. Funds may also be made available for the development of comprehensive land plans and other use-related activities.

The local government must submit a satisfactory report which includes the following:

1. A summary of its comprehensive three-year community development/land use plan.
2. A community development program which includes the activities to be undertaken with the grant.
3. A housing assistance plan which:
   a. Accurately surveys the condition of the community's housing stock.
   b. Estimates the housing assistance needs of lower income persons.
   c. Specifies a realistic goal for the number of units or persons to be assisted.
   d. Indicates the general locations of proposed lower income housing (to avoid undue concentration of low-income persons).

Comprehensive planning grants are available through The Department of Housing and Urban Development's 701 Comprehensive Planning Assistance Program. The purpose of the program is to financially assist local governments which wish to:

1. Develop and carry out a comprehensive plan.
2. Improve management capability to implement the plan.
3. Develop a policy planning capacity to determine needs and goals and evaluate programs.

The Noise Pollution and Abatement Act of 1970. This act established an Office of Noise Abatement and Control within the Environmental Protection Agency. The act provides that the Department of Housing and Urban Development must withhold assistance for dwellings that are subject to high noise levels and that the environment surrounding residential uses must be free of noise.

Reports relating to this act contain these topics:

1. The effects of various noise levels on the subject under study.
2. The projected growth of noise levels in urban areas to the year 2000.
3. The psychological and physiological effects of noise on humans.
4. The effects of sporadic extreme noise (such as the noise of jets near airports) as compared with constant noise.
5. The effects of noise on wildlife and property (including property values).
6. The effects of sonic boom on property (including property values).
7. Such other matters as may concern the public welfare.

The Federal Flood Insurance Program of 1968 and the Flood Disaster Protection Act of 1973 (with Amendments). The purposes of this legislation are to discourage unwise development in flood hazard areas, to lower insurance rates through proper building techniques, and to replace tax dollars for flood relief with insurance dollars. The Federal Insurance Administration in the Department of Housing and Urban Development administers the Federal Flood Insurance Program. The flood hazard boundary maps familiar to many appraisers are a result of this program.

Under the Flood Disaster Protection Act, new structures must be elevated above the 100-year flood level or be protected by floodproofing measures such as adequate berms. It is generally mandatory that structures in a flood-prone area be in the flood insurance program. However, existing housing, small business properties, and some farm buildings are exempted from this requirement. The act also requires that a lender disclose to a borrower that the dwelling on which a loan is made is in a flood hazard area and therefore requires flood insurance.

The extracted material from the various acts in this chapter is necessarily brief and additional understanding may be acquired by reading the acts or by consultation with government employees or private persons including sociologists, engineers, economists, attorneys, biologists, and others.

THE ECOLOGICAL AND ECONOMIC ENVIRONMENT

Environmental impact analysis, like economic analysis, occurs within the framework of society, most often domestic, but again like economic analysis, with a strong potential for international considerations. The occurrence is not new either domestically or internationally but the awareness is new. The strongest awareness as evidenced by law is domestic and the law leaves open the degree of most beneficial action. The law does not and probably cannot define the proper balance between optimum ecological and economic environment. The state of the art of recognition for both physical and economic realities are constantly changing and the occurrences themselves tend to be unique.

REAL PROPERTY
TAX ANALYSES

Ronald E. Gettel

*R*ONALD E. GETTEL, MAI, SREA, CRE, ASA, Real Estate Appraiser and Consultant, Fort Wayne, Indiana.
  Property tax counselor to numerous firms. Past president,
chapters of American Institute of Real Estate Appraisers and
Society of Real Estate Appraisers. Taught SREA appraisal
courses cosponsored by Indiana University and Purdue University. Author, Real Estate Guidelines and Rules of Thumb *(New
York: McGraw-Hill, 1976); and* You *Can* Get Your Real Estate
Taxes Reduced *(New York: McGraw-Hill, 1977).*

It is small wonder that knowledgeable real estate professionals pay
a lot of attention to property taxes. For many income properties, the
real estate tax burden is the largest single item of expense. A tax bill
may jump 40 percent—even 400 percent—in one bound. It is not unusual
for a property owner to pay twice as much tax as he or she should
without even being aware that the tax burden is out of line.
  There are numerous ways in which property taxes can be legally
reduced. In order to minimize property taxes (and thus increase cash
flow and property value), one should have a clear picture of how property
taxes work.

How Property Taxes Work

The Ad Valorem Concept. You sometimes hear property taxes referred
to as ad valorem taxes. "Ad valorem" is a Latin phrase which means
"to value" or "at value." In the most basic theory, real estate taxes are
supposed to be ad valorem taxes; that is, the amount of tax burden on
any property is supposed to be based on the value of that property. Not
on who owns the property. Not on how the property is used. Only on
how much that property is worth.

However, the ad valorem concept has been modified somewhat in every part of the United States. Some of the modifications are lawful. Some are not.

Classified Property Taxes and Other Modifications of the Ad Valorem Concept. One way in which the ad valorem concept is modified is to legally treat different types of properties differently. Six states have classified property tax systems, which simply means that certain types of properties are made to bear a share of the tax burden that is out of proportion to value. If the law is to be obeyed in Arizona, for example, a public utility *must* be valued at 50 percent of its "full cash value," a store at 27 percent, a farm at 18 percent, and a home at 15 percent. Since such classifications are essentially politically motivated, it is hardly surprising that homes and farms are valued at the lowest levels relative to their "full cash value."

There are so many ways in which the "to value" concept is altered that it would require a sizable book to discuss the specific laws and practices. Every state and many local jurisdictions have modified the ad valorem principle in order to help groups of people who are needy or politically potent and to affect the design and use of properties. For example, Louisiana's State Board of Commerce and Industry can enter into contracts to exempt new manufacturing enterprises from ad valorem taxes. Nevada exempts any increase in value for improvements to the property of a handicapped person which remove architectural barriers to that person. In Alaska, homeowners aged 65 and over are exempted from paying taxes on their dwellings. Localities in New Hampshire have been authorized to grant tax exemptions on homes that are equipped with solar heating or cooling devices. A San Francisco assessor prepared a lengthy list of repairs and improvements that would not normally result in an increased assessment. An Indiana statute provides that land devoted to agricultural use will be assessed as agricultural land as long as it is in that use. There are literally thousands of such modifications, and the list is constantly being changed and added to.

Inconsistent Appraisals. Except for the differences provided for by such laws, every property within a taxing jurisdiction should be valued at exactly the same percentage of its market value as every other property in that jurisdiction. Because property values are not subject to exact measurement and because these values change over time, we would naturally expect to see some variations from this ideal standard in actual day-to-day assessment practice. Regrettably, what we often do see in jurisdiction after jurisdiction are variations so gross as to challenge belief.

Legal Assessment Standards. In every state, there is a legal basis (or set of bases) for taxable property. In less than half of the states, including New York, assessed value is to be at essentially 100 percent of market value. (Euphemisms for market value abound. These include "true cash value," "fair cash value," "full value," "true value in money," and "actual value.") In the rest of the states, including California, assessed values are to be set at some fraction of market value (for example,

25 percent in California, 30 percent in Kansas, 35 percent in Nebraska, 40 percent in Georgia, 50 percent in Michigan, and 60 percent in South Dakota).

De Facto Levels of Assessment. However, for a variety of reasons, most assessments are substantially below the legal standards. According to a study conducted by the Bureau of the Census, it is not unusual to find that the typical assessment-to-value ratio in a particular state is just a fraction of the legal standard in that state. (Thus, if a store building in South Carolina is supposed to be assessed at 100 percent of its market value and is actually assessed at 50 percent of its market value, it may still be assessed several times as high as it should be in relation to the typical level of assessments on other store buildings.) Other studies have shown assessments ranging from far below to far above legal standards. The author has found assessed valuations ranging from less than one tenth of the legal standard to more than ten times the legal standard.

In real property tax analyses, the single most important principle is that—except for the operation of laws which give relief to certain properties and certain owners—every property within a jurisdiction should receive *equal treatment.* If one is to have the full protection of this equal treatment principle, it is essential to know the level—the typical percentage of market value—at which other properties in the given jurisdiction are assessed. This typical assessment level is commonly called the de facto level. How the de facto level is found and used will be discussed shortly.

Property Tax Administration. Property tax administration is a crazy quilt. There are 51 sets of laws—one for each state and the District of Columbia. These 51 areas are further subdivided into more than 13,000 separate property tax districts. The laws are not applied uniformly from one district to another and may not even be applied uniformly throughout a single district.

Deciding on assessed valuations is usually the responsibility of a local tax assessor. Most assessors are elected, and professional requirements are either nonexistent or meager in most areas. Most assessors are parttimers who do not have the equipment, staff, and budget to do their jobs properly. They are subjected to numerous pressures. There are some well-qualified assessors and other property tax officials who are doing a commendable job, but they are far too few and they are often inadequately supported. A survey of members of the International Association of Assessing Officers revealed how assessment officials themselves viewed the quality of assessment administration in the country as a whole: 62 percent of the respondents rated it as relatively poor. Incomplete ("horseback") property inspections, inaccurate property data, egregious arithmetic errors, and improper appraisal procedures are common.

There is a misconception that is too often repeated in the literature of this field. It is often stated or implied that appraising for property tax purposes is a highly specialized field, somehow different from other appraising, a field whose special problems call for special methods. The simple fact is this: if the appraiser disregards sound appraisal principles and practices because he or she has a large number of parcels to value and very limited time, money, and expertise, the resultant work is likely to be grossly unfair to many taxpayers and is unlikely to stand up if challenged.

Several statistical methods are used to measure the evenness of assessed values. Probably the best-known procedure is to:

1. Select a representative (random) sampling of numerous properties in a jurisdiction which have been involved in recent arm's-length sales.
2. Divide the assessed valuation of each property by its actual sale price in order to determine the indicated assessment-to-value percentage.
3. Find the average of these assessment-to-value percentages (this figure may be taken as the de facto level of assessment).
4. Calculate how much (usually in percentage terms) each individual assessment-to-value percentage varies from this de facto level.
5. Find the *average* variance from the de facto level.

An often-quoted rule of thumb in this field is that the average dispersion from the de facto assessment level should not exceed 20 percent. If one accepts 20 percent as an acceptable average dispersion, then one is accepting the proposition that charging one taxpayer half again as much as another is really quite acceptable. It appears that the 20 percent rule of thumb may have come into being because that was often found to be about the average dispersion for assessments on single-family dwellings. This occurred despite the fact that single-family dwellings, as a property class, are considered among the easier properties to value accurately in mass appraisal procedures. What, then, is the experience with properties that are harder to value evenly? Detailed studies in several parts of the country have often shown the dispersion of assessments on nonresidential properties to be awesome. One of the obvious implications is that those who pay property taxes must be on their guard. Although many properties are assessed for a small fraction of what they should be, many others are assessed at several times as much as they should be.

Appeal Processes. With so many objectionable assessments, it is important for each taxpayer to be able to check the fairness of an assessment and to be able to appeal an assessment if he or she believes it to be too high. Sometimes the taxpayer can gain a suitable reduction simply by having an informal talk with the assessor. Often, however, the taxpayer must ask for a formal review. (In several jurisdictions, assessors have short forms which taxpayers may sign to request the right to tell their objections to a review board.) The procedures vary from state to state, but most states have a local review board plus a state-level review board for taxpayers who may not be satisfied with the decision of the local review board. Further appeals are occasionally made to courts.

The Success of Appeals. Probably no more than 1 or 2 percent of assessments are challenged before review boards. The overwhelming majority of the assessments that are appealed are reduced. In a study of property taxes in ten major U.S. cities, Arthur D. Little, Inc., checked a sample of appeals and found that four out of five assessments were reduced. Interestingly, Arthur D. Little found that although owners of large income properties were much more apt to use the appeal procedure, "Success on appeal was quite evenly distributed by investor size."

Checking an Assessment for Fairness

The Availability of Records. In most jurisdictions, assessors recognize that they are public employees and that most of their assessment records are public records. With reasonable limitations (for example, records cannot be taken out of the assessor's office and no more than so many record cards will be shown at one time), most assessors show taxpayers certain records without foot-dragging. Unfortunately, some assessors are understandably not thrilled to have their work checked and will resist showing the assessment records. In such instances, the taxpayer (or the taxpayer's representative) who is quietly insistent or who raises his voice may have a better chance of seeing what he wants to see than the more timid visitor to the assessor's office.

Most taxpayers are reluctant to visit an assessor's office and would be unwilling to argue with the assessor over their right to see how their taxes were figured. This reluctance to see whether a public employee has figured one's tax fairly or unfairly is one reason why assessment administration has not improved very fast.

Grounds for Reduction. If an assessment is too high in any respect, grounds for reduction are usually found in the answer to one or more of the following questions, the first two of which merit your special attention.[1]

1. *Did the assessor make mechanical errors?* Finding a mistake in a building size or in simple computations—and there seem to be lots of mistakes—can put you in line for a sizable reduction.

2. *Is the assessment on your property out of line with assessments on similar properties in your area?* Now here is where you want to avoid making the mistake that so many taxpayers make. Do not assume that you are probably getting a bargain just because your assessed value is well below market value. If assessments are low, then the tax rate must be increased in order to collect any given amount of tax; the same amount of tax is collected, but taxpayers are deluded.

The most important test of the fairness of your assessment is *not* its relation to market value. It is this: *Is it fair in relation to assessments on other properties in your area?* If you have farmland worth $800 per acre and your assessment is based on an "appraisal" of $600 per acre, you may think that you are getting away with something and you may have no idea you may really be a victim. If nearby farmland comparable to yours is typically "appraised" at $200 per acre, *you are paying three times as much real estate tax as you should.*

---

[1] Ronald E. Gettel, *You Can Get Your Real Estate Taxes Reduced* (New York: McGraw-Hill, 1977).

3. *Is the assessor's work in accord with valuation guidelines he is supposed to follow?* Many assessors follow an official valuation manual issued by a state agency—or at least are *supposed* to unless they have a valid reason to depart from it. Copies of these manuals can usually be purchased from the state, but the manuals can be rather opaque reading for the inexpert taxpayer (and, alas, for the inexpert assessor).

4. *Has the property been appraised for more than its market value?* If it has, techniques discussed shortly should be helpful.

5. *Is the assessment on your property a legal one?* Perhaps part of the assessed property is supposed to be excluded from the property tax because of the type of property it is. Perhaps part is supposed to be exempted because of its ownership or use.

Preparing to Challenge an Unfair Assessment

Should you challenge an assessed value or not? The answer normally depends on answers to these two questions: Are there clear-cut grounds for a reduction in the assessment? Does the probable reduction in the tax burden justify the trouble and expense of pursuing the matter? Sometimes the answers to the questions will be obvious. Sometimes the taxpayer will want expert help in answering them.

Assuming that there are clear grounds for reducing an assessment, whoever is going to argue for the reduction should prepare thoroughly, tell the truth, limit the presentation to a few telling points, and use visual aids. It is usually wise to prepare a very brief summary of important points in writing to leave with whoever is hearing the arguments, because hours, days, or even months may pass before a decision is made. It is also usually wise to make a specific recommendation on what the assessment *should* be.

Of the many types of arguments that have been used to gain substantial reductions, the following four are perhaps the most common.

Assessment Comparables. If one finds that the assessment on a particular property is badly out of step with assessments on similar properties in the same jurisdiction, and this can be clearly shown, as in Exhibit 1, the chances for a sizable reduction are excellent.

Cost versus Value. If the assessor's estimate of building cost is much higher than the actual recent construction cost, one can show this in a simple, straightforward way. (See Exhibit 2.)

Market Data Comparisons. In some cases, recent arm's-length sales of similar properties can be used to demonstrate convincingly that a property is worth much less than the assessor's value estimate. A recent arm's-length sale of the subject property itself can be particularly useful, but one should not rely on any one sale—even a sale of the subject property itself—to make the whole case. It is better to be able to prove that this one sale was not a fluke.

Remember that the de facto level of the assessments in a jurisdiction is usually substantially below the legal basis for assessments. So, if your market data comparables indicate that your subject property is worth $1 million, but the de facto levels of assessments on other properties

EXHIBIT 1
How the Assessment on This Dwelling Compares

Location of Comparable Dwelling	Grade Factor	Square Foot Cost (assigned to dwelling)	Depreciation Allowed	Land Valuation per Front Foot
317 Windsor Drive	C	$10.35	20%	$40
325 Windsor Drive	C	10.65	20	40
452 Windsor Drive	C + 5	11.35	20	40
1723 Robinwood Court ...	C	10.35	25	45
1747 Robinwood Court ...	C − 5	9.85	25	45
1753 Robinwood Court ...	C	10.65	25	45
1760 Robinwood Court ...	C	10.65	25	45
340 Dover Road	C	10.35	20	40
346 Dover Road	C	10.65	20	35
417 Lawton Circle	C	10.15	25	40
420 Lawton Circle	C	10.65	25	40
443 Lawton Circle	C + 5	11.35	25	40
Subject	B + 5	$15.25	10%	$60

Selected items in the assessment on the subject property compared with those on similar dwellings (all trilevels built since 1965) in the same neighborhood.
Source: Ronald E. Gettel, *You Can Get Your Real Estate Taxes Reduced* (New York: McGraw-Hill, 1977). Reprinted with permission.

in the same jurisdiction is 40 percent, you can make a convincing argument for a proper assessment on the order of $400,000.

The Income Approach. In most jurisdictions, income properties form a large percentage of the property tax base and the people who own income properties are apt to be the ones who use the appeal procedures most often. Nevertheless, not one assessment worker in ten has a thorough understanding of the income approach, and most of the people who hear appeals have not mastered it. Therefore, even if a detailed demonstration of the income approach might be convincing to experts, it may not work well with some appeal boards. The simplified compari-

EXHIBIT 2

	Actual Cost	Assessor's Estimate of Reproduction Cost
Building	$215,350	$257,390
Carports	14,227	16,740
Paving	2,850	2,100
Fencing	740	600
Improvements	$233,167	$276,830
Land	30,000	37,500
Total	$263,167	$314,330

These cost figures include allowance for contractor's profit and indirect costs.
Source: Ronald E. Gettel, *You Can Get Your Real Estate Taxes Reduced* (New York: McGraw-Hill, 1977). Reprinted with permission.

EXHIBIT 3
Sundown Apartments: How Fair Is the Real Estate Tax Burden as a Percentage of Rents?

| | Six Competitive Apartment Projects | | | | | | Subject: |
	Colonial Square	Williamsburg Apartments	Woodcrest Villas	Brookwood Manor	Forest Hills Apartments	Kensington Apartments	Sundown Apartments
Gross rent roll	$157,500	$120,000	$117,360	$337,020	$225,000	$189,000	$234,960
Less adjustments for different rental bases :							
Heat included				22,020			
Golf course membership included						9,000	
Furnishings in units		48,000		9,000			
Gross rent roll on comparable basis	$157,500	$ 72,000	$117,360	$306,000	$225,000	$180,000	$234,960
Real estate taxes (actual, as of 9/1)	$ 19,367	$ 9,362	$ 11,490	$ 36,725	$ 24,623	$ 19,440	$ 46,530
Taxes as percentage of adjusted gross rent roll	12.3%	13.0%	9.8%	12.0%	10.9%	10.8%	19.8%

Notes on this comparison: All seven projects are garden apartment projects located in Cascade County. All were completed since 1968. In these projects, rents per unit per month range from $165 to $250. Most are rented unfurnished, without heat, and without unusual recreational facilities. (Adjustments were for the exceptions after interviews with the managers.) As a percentage of the rent roll, the real estate tax burden on the Sundown Apartments is clearly unusual and excessive.
Source: Ronald E. Gettel, *You Can Get Your Real Estate Taxes Reduced* (New York: McGraw-Hill, 1977). Reprinted with permission.

son in Exhibit 3 is a useful technique for showing that the property tax burden on a particular property is clearly excessive vis-à-vis the burdens imposed on other properties with which it competes.

Nonappeal Methods of Getting Taxes Reduced

Making sure that your assessed value is fair is, of course, a very important step in minimizing property taxes. However, there are others.

Find out about all of the forms of exemptions and relief which may be available. Familiarity with the way that assessors work can suggest other ways to save. For example, simply rewriting a legal description (from a gross to a net basis) or merging two or more parcels into a single parcel can lead to substantial savings in some jurisdictions. Important changes in a property which might justify a reduction in its assessed value after that property has been assessed (examples: the razing of a structure, a partial taking, or substantial damage by fire or weather) should be brought to the assessor's attention promptly. (It is risky to assume that an assessor knows about such changes. Some taxpayers continue to pay taxes on improvements for years after those improvements have been removed.) Increasingly, taxpayers are lobbying for changes in this badly administered system.

Forecasting Future Assessments

It is often important for a developer, a lender, a chain store operator, or some other type of property investor to be able to predict future assessments as accurately as possible. Two types of methods are most commonly used by real estate professionals. First, the assessments on the existing properties which are most similar to the subject property are studied, and adjustments are made for important differences. Familiarity with the official manual to be used by the assessor, if there is one, can be helpful in adjusting the assessment comparables to the subject property. A second method, which is less well known but is very useful in projecting tax assessments for new income properties, is illustrated in Exhibit 4. In this variation of the income approach to value, the analyst:

1. Makes a projection of income and expenses as usual, with the exception that the real estate tax burden is not deducted.
2. Selects an overall capitalization rate as usual, and to this adds the effective tax rate. (The effective tax rate is figured by multiplying the official tax rate by the assessment ratio.)
3. Divides the stabilized (net) income estimated in the first step by the composite rate developed in the second step.

A very important point: in computing the effective tax rate, it is usually better to use the de facto level of assessment rather than the level of assessment that is specified by law.

EXHIBIT 4
Using the Income Approach to Estimate the Fair Assessment

Method		Example
Effective gross income		
Start with the possible gross income that a well-informed person would anticipate in a typical year in the near future		$121,000
Deduct an allowance for anticipated vacancy and rent loss		6,000
Balance, total operating receipts		$115,000
Less operating expenses (except for real estate taxes)		
Insurance	$2,500	
Maintenance and housekeeping	9,000	
Administrative and miscellaneous	6,500	
		18,000
Balance: net operating income (except for real estate taxes)		$ 97,000
The final step: translate (capitalize) this stabilized income figure into an estimate of market value by adding two rates		
Overall capitalization rate indicated by market data	(0.1050 × 50%)	11.00%
The effective tax rate (official tax rate × assessment ratio)		5.25
Sum		16.25%
Then one divides the net operating income figure by this sum.	($97,000 ÷ 16.25%)	$596,923
Round the value estimate to a figure that does not tend to overstate the order of precision in your work.		$600,000
Check.		

If assessor used this value, then tax burden would drop to $31,500 per annum, operating balance (after payment of this tax) would increase to $65,500, and the value estimate would increase to ($65,500 ÷ 11% = $595,455, say) $600,000.

Then, any assessment substantially over this amount would appear too high.

Estimated market value × assessment ratio = estimated fair assessment $600,000 × 50% = $300,000

Source: Ronald E. Gettel. *You Can Get Your Real Estate Taxes Reduced* (New York: McGraw-Hill, 1977). Reprinted with permission.

Monitoring the Tax Burden

Unfortunately, one cannot simply do these things and then forget about them. Assessments change from time to time. De facto levels of assessment are continually changing. Even legal assessment levels are subject to change. New forms of relief are added, and others are modified or dropped. Real estate markets and submarkets are dynamic; property values do not remain constant. Assessors come and go, and their methods and mind-sets change.

Under these circumstances, an adequate program of monitoring the tax burden on sizable properties will normally include at least these steps:

1. First, a thorough check of the property tax burden.
2. Then, scrutiny of any substantial change.
3. Periodic sampling of assessment comparables and review of the results of appeals on generally similar properties.

Major U.S. corporations often have property tax departments, full-time staffs whose primary job is monitoring and minimizing property tax burdens. In some of these companies, the property tax department even maintains regional offices. Some of the staffers in such departments are recruited from the ranks of former assessors, and their qualifications may vary widely.

Many other corporations rely on independent consultants. Several firms undertake to get property tax burdens reduced for a percentage of the savings. (A common formula is that the fee will be equivalent to one fourth of the saving each year for four years.) Attorneys, appraisers, and others also often work to reduce assessed values for clients for a fixed fee or for a percentage of the reduction. Here again, experience and abilities vary widely.

Some property owners monitor their own tax burdens. Unfortunately, most property owners grumble but do nothing effective. They assume that their assessments were probably fixed by people who knew what they were doing, that the assessments were figured accurately, and that probably nothing could be done about it even if the assessments were too high. Most of the time such property owners are wrong on all three counts.

PART III
Real Estate Marketing

THE REGULATION OF COMPETITION

Charles M. Hewitt

*C*HARLES M. HEWITT, MBA, DBA, LLB, Professor of Business Law, Graduate School of Business, Indiana University, Bloomington, Indiana.

Lawyer and consultant to various firms and associations. Member, American Bar Association. Formerly editor in chief, American Business Law Journal. Author of numerous articles and chapters in professional journals and books. Author, Automobile Franchise Agreements (Homewood, Ill.: Richard D. Irwin, Inc., 1956); and CPA Law Manual. Coauthor, Readings and Cases in Business Law; Business Law: Principles and Cases (Homewood, Ill.: Richard D. Irwin, Inc., 1978); and Management and Finance Controls for Oil Jobbers.

The September 30, 1977, issue of *The Wall Street Journal* contained an item headlined "Conviction of Firms in Realty-Pricing Case Seen Having Impact." The first few paragraphs were as follows:

> Elated by their victory in a major price-fixing suit against real-estate firms, Justice Department prosecutors believe the outcome will make professionals a "lot more sensitive" to the perils of discussing fees among themselves.
>
> A jury in Baltimore, after deliberating two days, convicted six Washington-area real-estate brokerage firms and three of their presidents of conspiring to raise commissions on home sales to 7% from 6% in September 1974. The dependants are expected to appeal the verdict.
>
> As a result of the felony convictions Wednesday, the companies face fines of up to $1 million each, while the executives could each receive a maximum three-year prison term and a $100,000 fine. Sentencing was set for Oct. 28.

The threat of antitrust lawsuits against those engaged in the real estate field (and in other service areas) is a very real and growing source of concern. Since 1969, the Justice Department has filed antitrust law-suits against real estate boards and multiple listing services in Atlanta, Cleveland, Memphis, Pittsburgh, Portland, Los Angeles, and a host of smaller cities.

Although the federal antitrust laws are clearly the most important laws regulating and attempting to promote and protect competition, other federal and state legislation and common-law rules relating to various competitive activities are also important. The principal focus of this chapter will be directed at possible application of the Sherman Act (particularly Section 1) to the real estate industry. In addition, some other important areas of law having relation to competitive practices are identified and briefly discussed.

At least five general trends or circumstances are likely to increase litigation relating to competitive activities in the real estate and other services oriented industries:

1. The increasing relative importance of the service area in the total economy.
2. Growing public concern over the persistent and seemingly insoluble inflation problem.
3. Evidence that the high inflation rate in the services area has been a major contributing cause of the inflation problem.
4. "Consumerist" trends, manifested in part by the strengthening and stepped-up enforcement of state and federal antitrust laws.
5. Virtual abandonment of the historic public policy which has permitted most trade and professional associations maximum leeway in self-regulation even where some of the "ethical" rules adopted and enforced produced anticompetitive consequences.

In addition, as will be discussed subsequently, the increasing interdependence of all parts of the modern economy means that virtually all business activities are now subject to regulation under federal law.

The Passage of the Sherman Act

With the development of national markets following the Civil War, large industrial combines and trusts engaged in monopolistic practices that soon led to a public outcry for regulation. In 1890, Congress enacted the Sherman Act (26 Stat. 209 [1890] as amended, 15 U.S.C. §§1–7), thereby adopting a public policy that called for the preservation and promotion of free competition within the American economy. Although a number of important exceptions or exemptions have been made, and although the antitrust laws have been amended and expanded in coverage, this basic competitive policy has been maintained since 1890. The Supreme Court summarized the basis for this belief in competition when it said:

> Basic to the faith that a free economy best promotes the public weal is that goods must stand the cold test of competition; that the public, acting

through the market's impersonal judgment, shall allocate the Nation's resources and thus direct the course its economic development will take.[1]

Penalty and Enforcement Provisions of the Sherman Act

Criminal and Civil Proceedings. Violators of either Section 1 or Section 2 of the Sherman Act are subject to criminal prosecution for a felony and, upon conviction, to a fine not exceeding $1 million in the case of a corporation or $100,000 for a person, or imprisonment for three years, or both a fine and imprisonment. The Department of Justice may also institute civil proceedings to restrain conduct in violation of the act and may ask the court for various remedies, including decrees of divorcement, divestiture, or, in extreme cases, dissolution.[2]

Any person injured as a result of violations of the Sherman Act may bring a suit for treble damages against the violators and also recover reasonable attorney's fees. Once private treble-damage claimants have proven violation of the antitrust laws by the defendants, the plaintiffs then prove that the violation was the proximate cause of economic injuries to their businesses and properties in terms of dollars and cents. (The actual damages approximated are multiplied by three to produce the final damages awarded.)

While the government typically seeks injunctive relief, private individuals usually seek money damages. The recent rash of private antitrust lawsuits has been due in some measure to increasing awareness of the possibilities for recovering large treble-damage awards plus reasonable attorney's fees.

Consent Decrees. In seeking injunctive relief, the government relies heavily on the "consent decree." An important element in the field of antitrust administration and enforcement, the consent decree is a compromise; its terms are fixed by negotiation between the parties and approved by a federal judge. A consent decree has the same legal effect as a court-rendered judgment.

For the defendant, the consent decree offers three advantages: less publicity, less expense, and the safeguard that consent decrees cannot be used as proof of violation of the Sherman Act by private litigants subsequently bringing treble-damage suits.

For the government, the consent decree is an efficient and inexpensive method for securing results. Uncertainty is eliminated, as is the need for proving the factual basis for the complaint. The government's purposes for securing a consent decree are to punish past illegal activities,

---

[1] *Times-Picayune Co.* v. *U.S.,* 594, 605 (1953). Some of this general descriptive material is borrowed with the permission of the publisher from: Harold F. Lusk, Charles M. Hewitt, John D. Donnell, and A. James Barnes, *Business Law: Principles and Cases,* 4th ed. (Homewood, Ill.: Richard D. Irwin, 1978) © 1978 by Richard D. Irwin, Inc.

[2] Divorcement means that the company is separated from some operating function. For example, the meat-packers were divorced from owning or controlling retail outlets. A company may be ordered to divest itself of assets or stock. Thus, Du Pont was ordered to divest itself of GM stock. Dissolution means that a company must liquidate its assets and go out of business.

to prevent future violations, to encourage competitive environments, and to recover past illegal profits from the defendants.

In the real estate field, the case of *United States* v. *Prince George's County Board of Realtors, Inc.* (1971 Trade Cases para. 89,603), provides a typical example of the terms included in a consent decree.

> The Board, whether acting unilaterally or in concert or agreement with any other person, is enjoined and restrained from:
>
> (A) Fixing, establishing, or maintaining any commission rates for the sale, lease, or management of real estate;
>
> (B) Urging, recommending, or suggesting that any of the members of the Board adhere to any schedule or other recommendation concerning the amount of commissions or fees for the sale, lease, or management of real estate;
>
> (C) Adopting suggesting, publishing, or distributing any schedule or other recommendation concerning the amount of commissions or other fees for the sale, lease, or management of real estate; . . .
>
> (E) Taking any punitive action against any of its members where such action is based upon the member's failure or refusal to adhere to any schedule or other recommendation concerning fees;
>
> (F) Fixing, maintaining, suggesting, or enforcing any percentage division of commissions between the selling and listing broker;
>
> (G) Boycotting or otherwise refusing to do business with any person; . . .
>
> The defendant is ordered to insert in all . . . forms which previously contain a set commission rate, a provision that commission rates for the sale, lease, or management of property shall be negotiable between the broker and his client.

The consent decree is a powerful tool for government action. Its use has substantially increased in recent years.

Main Regulatory Provisions of the Sherman Act

Section 1. *Section 1 of the Sherman Act provides: Every contract, combination in the form of trust or otherwise, or conspiracy, in restraint of trade or commerce among the several states, or with foreign nations, is declared to be illegal.*

The "contract" is the agreement to restrain competition. A "combination" occurs when two or more persons join together for the purpose of carrying out united action. A "conspiracy" is a continuing partnership in restraint of trade. At least two persons are required under all of these forms of joint activity. The departments or divisions of a company are viewed as being parts of one company, and intracompany conduct not directed against a competitor does not violate Section 1. A principal corporation, however, may be found in violation of Section 1 where it conspires with a subsidiary.

Section 2. *Section 2 of the Sherman Act provides: Every person who shall monopolize, or attempt to monopolize, or combine or conspire with any other person or persons to monopolize any part of the trade or commerce among the several states, or with foreign nations, shall be deemed guilty of a felony.*

A single firm (or person) may monopolize or attempt to monopolize.

Two or more firms are required in order to combine or conspire to monopolize.

Monopolizing. Monopolizing takes place where a firm acting singly, or a group of firms acting together, have the power to control prices or to exclude competitors from a market. The power to monopolize must be coupled with a deliberate purpose or intent to exercise that power. Where monopolization is charged, the required element of intent is established if monopoly is the *probable* result of what is done.

Illegal power to control prices or to exclude competitors is measured in relation to the relevant market. The relevant market is determined by defining the product or service line being monopolized and then by fixing the geographic market for the defined product or service line. The product line is determined by including those products (or services) which are competitive substitutes for the defendant's products. The geographic scope of the market is measured in terms of the area where the products are customarily made available for purchases. A similar determination of the relevant market is made where services are monopolized rather than products.

It is doubtful that individual real estate firms or even combinations of several firms ordinarily will possess the economic *power* required to prove a violation of Section 2. On the other hand, real estate associations, multiple listing services, and franchising operations might acquire enough power within local or regional "relevant" markets so that Section 2 monopolizing violations might occur. Assuming that sufficient monopoly power within a relevant local or regional market is established, proof of exclusionary practices, such as denying competitors market access, would be sufficient to establish intent to monopolize.

Elements Necessary to Prove a Violation of the Sherman Act

Jurisdiction and Violation. To succeed in proving a violation of the Sherman Act, the complainant must prove three elements: (1) that the activities of the defendants constitute "trade" activities, (2) that the activities fall within the scope of "interstate commerce," and (3) that the activities are in violation of Section 1 or Section 2, or both. In addition, if the complainant is a private party seeking treble damages he must prove that the illegal activities caused him losses and, within reasonable bounds, he must prove the extent of such losses.

The first two elements are of a jurisdictional nature and must be resolved prior to determining whether an activity restrains trade. The Sherman Act gives a broad definitional meaning to activities that can qualify as "trade." The definition is so encompassing that the services of a single real estate broker can qualify as trade.

Application to "Local" Activities. "Interstate commerce" is the critical factor in limiting the jurisdiction or application of the Sherman Act. The issue of whether the activities of real estate brokerage have the necessary minimal connection with interstate commerce has not been conclusively resolved; but decisions of lower courts have suggested that this connection need be only tenuous at best.

Although real estate operations are generally considered to be local in nature, the concept of interstate commerce has been given a very expansive reading since the 1930s. Under the "in commerce," or *qualitative,* test, if the activities are a functional part, however small, of an interstate network of activities, the Sherman Act applies to those activities. The "substantial effect," or *quantitative,* test, is even broader in its possible application. Under this doctrine even local activities with no direct interstate connections may be subject to the Sherman Act if they substantially affect interstate market either directly or through their interplay with or relationship to any other commerce-related business activities.

One authority has stated the jurisdictional issue as follows:

> Thus, it appears settled that only those activities are beyond the reach of the Sherman Act which are "purely local" in the double sense that they (1) are not within the flow of interstate commerce and (2) have no significant effect on that flow. This result appears to accord with the generally expansive view taken of the "commerce clause" by the Supreme Court.[3]

In the Maryland case that was mentioned at the beginning of this chapter, the judge found that the Sherman Act applied, noting that the defendant real estate firms "conduct multimillion dollar operations and are located in an expanding metropolitan area," that their services "are used by buyers and sellers moving into and out of Maryland," that they "assist in arranging financing of residential properties sold with governmental and lending agencies outside of Maryland," and that they "attract purchasers through the use of multistate referred services, and advertise their brokerage services interstate."

Activities in Restraint of Trade. The third element necessary in a Sherman Act violation is a determination that the activities restrain or attempt to restrain, or that there is an agreement, combination, or conspiracy to restrain competition. For this determination, the Supreme Court has developed two alternative approaches: the *per se rule* and the *rule of reason.* Violation of either rule is sufficient for conviction.

Per Se Violations of the Sherman Act. A per se violation is one that is so reprehensible to the policies of the Sherman Act that adverse competitive consequences are presumed. To win the case, the government only has to prove that particular activities took place and need not prove injury to competition or to competitors. In a private treble-damage suit by an injured competitor, proof of per se activities plus reasonable proof of approximate losses suffered as a result of the illegal restraints is all that is required. The defendant is precluded from introducing any defense. Specifically irrelevant as defenses to the case are the defendant's "good" motives, arguments that the illegal activities had no significant effect on competition, or arguments that price-cutters were destroying the industry or confusing or defrauding the public.

Per se violations include price-fixing, boycotts, "black listings," market divisions, tie-in arrangements, sabotage of competitors, and virtually

---

[3] *Antitrust Developments, 1955–1968* (Supplemental Report Attorney General's National Committee to Study the Antitrust Laws, American Bar Association 1968), p. 39.

all forms of coercion exerted to accomplish anticompetitive purposes.

Price-Fixing. Price-fixing (including rate fixing, discount fixing, or fee fixing) is considered the most serious and reprehensible of all Sherman Act violations. Although price-fixing techniques vary in sophistication, proof of any joint activity among competitors which causes or *may tend* to affect price behavior is suspect.

In the real estate field, employment of the standardized fee schedule is a per se violation. The lending case, *United States* v. *National Association of Real Estate Boards,* 339 U.S. 485 (1950), specifically prohibits both imposed and recommended fee schedules. Whether deviations from fee schedules are sanctioned or punished is completely irrelevant. Nor does it matter whether the fee schedule eliminates cutthroat competition or maintains prices at an artifically low level. Regardless of motive, competitors are not allowed to engage in any form of *joint* action which has the effect of creating or perpetuating price uniformity, stability, or movement in any direction. Under the antitrust laws, markets are to control businessmanagers and businessmanagers are never to control markets.

One writer argues that the impact of recent antitrust actions taken against associations utilizing standardized fee schedules has been to raise real estate commission rates rather than to lower them.[4] The antitrust laws, however, are not concerned with what happens to specific prices (or rates) so long as the prices are set by competitive market forces, and not by competitors.

The cases clearly demonstrate that any form of discussion, or certainly understanding, concerning prices is extremely risky. Ten years ago the Supreme Court condemned an agreement among competitors whereby each simply agreed to share his price lists on request. There was no evidence of any agreement or understanding concerning any of the prices exchanged. The Court stated:

> The exchange of price data tends toward price uniformity. . . . Stabilizing prices as well as raising them is within the ban of . . . the Sherman Act. . . . The inferences are irresistible that the exchange of price information has had an anticompetitive effect in the industry, chilling the vigor of price competition. (*United States* v. *Container Corp. of America,* 393 U.S. 333 [1969])

In general, however, where there is no evidence of express or tacit agreement or understanding, and no other conduct which might support an inference of collusion, the fact that there are pricing similarities among competitors is not of itself evidence of illegal conduct. One rationale for substantial similarity in price levels and price shifts is that smaller or less efficient firms often have no practical choice except to follow the prices charged by the industry leaders. Vigorous competition can, of course, lead to price similarities; but according to economic theory, effective competition should result in price diversities over time.

---

[4] C. Barasch, "How Antitrust Actions Have Affected Real Estate Brokers' Commissions," *Real Estate Law Journal,* vol. 3 (1975), pp. 227–40.

Horizontal Market Divisions. When competitors divide the market on a geographic basis, with each agreeing not to sell in a particular area, a per se violation of the Sherman Act occurs. Market divisions effectively eliminate all semblance of competition. Rivals thereby do not compete on the basis of price, quality, or service. Consequently, the anticompetitive impact of territorial allocation agreements may be greater than that of price-fixing. The courts have uniformly condemned such horizonal market division practices, and it is apparent that any market allocation agreement in the real estate field would be given the same unfavorable consideration.

Tie-In Agreements. Tying exists when a company has two products or two services to sell—one in high demand, the other in low demand. When the sale of the high-demand product or service to a customer is made contingent upon the customer's purchase of the less desired product or service, an illegal tie-in agreement may exist. Tie-in agreements restrict competition in the market for the less desired product, as competitors are forced to overcome the artificial sales obstacles created by the tying arrangement.

A tie-in agreement usually constitutes a per se violation of the Sherman Act—at least where the firm utilizing the tie-in is in a dominant position in the relevant market for the tying product and a substantial volume of business is being tied up in the market for the tied product. This type of agreement is a unique method for discouraging competition.

Illegal agreements of this type are probably rare in the real estate field. Typically, there is but one product to offer—the brokerage of property. If an agency expands into other businesses, an illegal agreement of this type might occur. For example, an illegal tie-in arrangement might be effectuated if a dominant agency in a relevant market offered to underwrite the financing at very low interest rates of all property purchased through the agency. In this example, the desired service is the low-interest loan; the less desired service is the brokerage service.

Keep in mind that even upon a satisfactory showing that a tie-in arrangement exists, a second determination must be made to sustain a violation of the Sherman Act. This determination must conclude that the seller had sufficient economic power in the market for the desired product or service to actually restrict competition for the less desired product or service. Sufficient economic power generally necessitates control or dominance in the market for the desired product or service—a rare circumstance in the real estate business.

Association Exclusion Practices. Real estate associations establish ethical standards, police trade abuses, and generally improve the efficiency of real estate operations. One of the typical problems facing associations is that of exclusionary practices. When there is a deliberate attempt to injure or destroy a nonmember rival, a per se violation of the Sherman Act occurs.

A frequent issue facing many associations is the arbitrary exclusion of a licensed broker. Arbitrary membership denial has been judged a per se violation in at least two states (New Jersey and Pennsylvania).

Membership denial has also been judged under the *rule of reason* analysis (Illinois).

The Rule of Reason Approach. The *"rule of reason"* test is utilized for determining the reasonableness of restraints of trade which are not classed as per se illegal. What is reasonable is based upon the practical business needs of the industry, the purposes behind the restraint, and the competitive environments prior to and after the restraint of trade. Each case is judged on its own merits. The defenses and justifications that are appropriate in one situation may not be appropriate in other situations.

Justice Brandeis described the rule of reason as follows:

> The true test of legality is whether the restraint imposed is such as merely regulates and perhaps thereby promotes competition or whether it is such as may suppress or even destroy competition. To determine that question the court must ordinarily consider the facts peculiar to the business to which the restraint is applied; its condition before and after the restraint was imposed; the nature of the restraint and its effect, actual or probable. The history of the restraint, the evil believed to exist, the reason for adopting the particular remedy, the purpose or end sought to be attained are all relevant facts.[5]

The rule of reason articulates a standard for judging whether the societal benefits of a particular activity outweigh its anticompetitive influences. If society benefits more from the activity than it is harmed by it, the activity is not considered to be an unreasonable restraint of trade.

The rule of reason test has been employed to determine the legality of many real estate activities. Among them are association information exchanges and multiple and exclusive listing arrangements.

Multiple Listing Services. A multiple listing service functions to reduce market imperfections by providing a common collection and dissemination point for information. The service expands the sales potential of each member. Consequently, nonmembers are placed at a competitive disadvantage. As multiple listing services provide economic benefits to offset possible adverse effects on competition, they are not illegal per se.

In 1945 the Supreme Court ruled that bylaws similar to those of many real estate associations were an unreasonable restraint of trade (*Associated Press* v. *United States,* 326 U.S. 1 [1945]). In the *Associated Press* case, members were required to use the news service regularly, were required to supply AP with any news gathered, and were prohibited from selling AP news to nonmembers. Admission requirements were difficult to meet. The Court, in declaring the bylaws an unreasonable restraint of trade, premised its decision upon the significant competitive disadvantages of exclusion.

The *Associated Press* analysis was applied to real estate associations in *Grillo* v. *Board of Realtors,* 219 A. 2d 635 N.J. (1966). In that case, a

---

[5] *Chicago Board of Trade* v. *U.S.,* 246 U.S. 231–238 (1918).

real estate association having functionally the same bylaws as the Associated Press excluded a licensed broker from membership. Access to the multiple listing service was denied.

In resolving the lawsuit, the court ordered the association to grant the plaintiff access to the multiple listing service. The court stated:

> His knowledge of available properties is the broker's chief stock in trade. . . . Without goods to sell the businessman cannot survive. The restrictions placed in the way of a nonmember obtaining and using listings may drive that nonmember from the field of real estate listings.

The more an association controls and dominates the field of property listings, the more imperative it is to have access to the service. Under such circumstances, exclusion of a qualified broker can be an unreasonable restraint of trade.

Although a real estate board can set standards for competence and ethical conduct, such standards do not supersede those legislated by the state. Most state courts have declared that when there are state standards governing competence, association standards are unnecessary and superfluous. The conclusion is that once a broker is certified by the state, an association cannot deny membership on the basis of its own standards of competence.

Real estate associations can impose some admission requirements. The catch is that the requirements have to be "reasonable," and what is reasonable varies from state to state. An Illinois court has approved an association initiation fee of $1,000 and association requirements that members not employ part-time salespersons or have more than one office.

If an admission requirement is arbitrary or is designed to exclude an individual or a group of individuals, the courts would most likely declare the requirement to be an unreasonable restraint of trade.

Exclusive Dealing. An exclusive dealing agreement gives the broker the exclusive right to market property for a particular period. Such agreements can provide economic and social benefits to all parties: the broker gains some degree of protection for the time he spends selling the property; the owner is more likely to receive a good faith sales effort; and the buyer, too, may gain from the concentrated attention that the broker gives to the transaction.

Despite these economic benefits, exclusive dealing agreements can restrict competition and are judged under the rule of reason analysis. The antitrust problems with exclusive dealing agreements develop where competition is being substantially impaired. When competition is eliminated from a substantial share of a relevant market by a dominant broker group, courts tend to take a hard look at any exclusive dealing arrangements that may be involved. In numerous consent decrees, real estate associations have been enjoined from insisting that members must contract for the "exclusive right to sell." If these "dominant group" and "pressuring to conform" factors are absent, an exclusive dealing arrangement is likely to be upheld.

Other Important Areas of Law Related to Competition

Tort Law. Tort law protecting economic relations from unreasonable interference exists in three main categories. First, business firms are protected against the diversion of patronage or injury to their goodwill resulting from falsehoods or other deceitful practices by competitors. Second, by the law protects ideas relating to trade secrets, patents, and copyrights. Third, the law gives protection against certain unjustifiable interferences with contracts or economic expectations. To an important extent, the rights in these areas are now governed by federal and state statutes creating special procedures, rules, and remedies.

Trademarks. Trademark law arose out of unfair competition. The *Lanham Trade-Mark Act* now provides the basic protection for those having registered trademarks (including service marks) by prohibiting any person from employing a word, symbol, or device that is deceptively similar to an existing trademark registration. More particularly, the law prohibits marks or sales practices that could confuse the public as to the origin of a product or service. Infringement of a registered trademark is a form of unfair competition. Remedies include the recovery of damages, profits, and court costs and the confiscation and destruction of infringing materials. The Lanham Act provides a limited monopoly to the owners of registered trademarks.

Interference with Contracts. In a sizable number of cases, real estate brokers have recovered damages because third parties interfered with their sale contracts and commissions. Although the cases are not in complete agreement they seem to make a distinction between those situations in which the defendant actively induced the breach of a contract and those in which the defendant's conduct simply caused the breach. For example, Able contracts to sell a house to Baker, and Baker then contracts to sell the house through a broker to Carl. The broker cannot recover his lost commission from Able if Able then breaches his contract with Baker. Able may have *caused* the collapse of the Baker-Carl sale, but he did not *induce* it.[6]

Even where a person directly induces the breach, his conduct might be privileged or justifiable on some ground. For example, it was held that a mother who induced a school to exclude a diseased child from her child's private school was not liable to the parents of the diseased child for having induced the school to breach its contract. Business competition affords only a limited justification for interference with contracts. As Prosser states:

> The courts have held that the sanctity of the existing contract relation takes precedence over any interest in unrestricted competition, and have enforced as law the ethical precept that one competitor must keep his hands off of the contracts of another. This is true of contracts of employment,

---

[6] Of course, under normal circumstances the broker would have earned his commission by producing a ready, willing, and able buyer and could collect from Baker despite the collapse of the contract.

where workmen are hired away from an employer, as well as competitive business dealings in general; and it has found particular application in cases of offers of better terms to induce the breach of a contract, and of the violation of exclusive agency agreements and the purchase of goods in derogation of a contract limiting their resale.[7]

Interference with Economic Expectations. The early cases of interference with economic expectations usually involved situations in which physical violence was employed to drive off customers or workers. Liability was later extended to cover nonviolent malicious interference, and then to unjustifiable intentional interference. Where the intent to interfere is present, the liability depends upon the motives and purposes of the defendant and upon the means that he utilizes. For example, a broker shows a potential customer property and the customer agrees to sign the purchase agreement the next day. That evening another broker learns of the pending deal and persuades the customer to call off the purchase. If the interfering broker acted out of pure spite (malice) or used deceitful methods of persuasion, the first broker could recover. In general, however, actions taken out of self-interest in pursuit of legitimate competitive objectives are not illegal, even though such actions interfere with the economic expectations of competitors.

Ancillary Restraint Contracts. Agreements in direct restraint of trade are illegal. For example, an agreement between city brokers and suburban brokers never to compete in each other's markets would directly restrain competition and would probably be illegal under both state and federal antitrust laws.

Agreements which only indirectly restrain competition are legal and enforceable in the courts, provided that the restraints imposed are reasonable and that valid economic interests are being protected by the restraints. For example, a contract for the sale of a real estate business will frequently contain a provision which provides that the seller agrees not to compete with the buyer for a certain period of time within a certain distance from the business sold. Such a provision is legal, provided that the time and space limitations are reasonable in light of the competitive market factors involved. A contract selling a real estate firm in Chicago which prohibits the seller from competing for ten years in the Chicago metropolitan area would probably be illegal and unenforceable. A similar contract restricting competition within three miles of the firm sold for a period of three years could probably be enforced. Real estate firms occasionally require that employees agree not to solicit customers on termination of the employment relationship. The courts do not agree on the validity of such employee restraint clauses, but the clauses will generally be upheld if they are limited and reasonable.

As has been stated, there are many other state and federal statues and laws relating to competition; but those discussed would seem to be the most important ones that apply to the real estate business.

---

[7] William L. Prosser, *Torts,* 4th ed. (St. Paul, Minn.: West, 1971), p. 945.

SELECTED REFERENCES

"Antitrust Law: An Emerging Problem for Florida Realtors." *University of Florida Law Review,* vol. 24 (1972), p. 266.

Astin, Arthur D.   "The Antitrust Threat to Real Estate Brokerage." *Real Estate Review,* vol. 2 (1973), p. 9.

Astin, Arthur D.   "Real Estate Boards and Multiple Listing Systems as Restraints of Trade." *Columbia Law Review,* vol. 70 (1970), p. 1325.

FEDERAL CONSUMER PROTECTION

Charles G. Field

*C*HARLES G. FIELD, PhD, JD, Associate, Troy, Malin & Pottinger, Washington, D.C.

Formerly Director, Real Estate Practices, Office of the Assistant Secretary for Neighborhoods, Voluntary Associations, and Consumer Protection, Department of Housing and Urban Development, Washington, D.C. Responsible for the Real Estate Settlement Procedures and the Energy Conservation Standards for New Buildings programs and for the Interagency Task Force on Condominiums. Author of numerous articles. Coauthor, The Building Code Burden *(Lexington, Mass., Lexington Books, 1975).*

Two basic facts have characterized the real estate market. Laissez-faire has been the framework of the real estate transaction, and caveat emptor has been the doctrinal thread tying seller and buyer. This means that the market has been unregulated and that the buyer has had to watch out for himself. The trend has shifted, however. A shift toward consumer protection has become increasingly apparent with the passage of recent federal laws. This chapter describes the major federal consumer protection programs.

The late arrival of federal programs has been due in part to the assumption that real estate markets are sufficiently competitive to be self-regulating and thus work to benefit the consumer. In truly competitive markets all parties are well informed. However, the real world does not conform with such assumptions. Many consumers are ill informed about the real estate sale transaction and about the services they are required to obtain. Title insurance, title opinions, appraisals, financing, and surveys are only a few of these technical requirements. Moreover, consumers have to deal with complex legal documents and make major financial decisions. Add to this cauldron of legal and financial complexities the ladle of great emotional stress that people experience when purchasing a home, and the mixture is ripe for abuse.

Buying or selling a house is an adversarial process, for the interests of the principal parties—purchasers, sellers, lenders, and brokers—naturally conflict. Although all parties share the common interest of completing the sale, the interests of the different parties diverge at that point. Purchasers want their "dream house" at the lowest possible cost. Sellers often seek the highest possible sale price to maximize equity for their next home. Lenders, in turn, want security and a return on their financial investments. Brokers want to close the sale so that they can earn their commissions.

These factors have contributed to the abuses that have occurred. Unsophisticated buyers and sellers obligate themselves to major payments in real estate as in other areas. This may be done through a listing agreement with the broker or a contract of sale between the buyer and the seller. In many cases, consumers lack legal advice prior to making such binding and enforceable commitments, entrusting themselves to the advice of the broker or the friend next door. This reliance sometimes returns to haunt consumers depended on those who were ostensibly there to serve them.

Federal involvement with consumer protection in the real estate market started in 1966 with the Truth-in-Lending Act. In 1968, Congress passed the Interstate Land Sales Full Disclosure Act (OILSR) in response to fraudulent and abusive sales of unimproved property to consumers. Between 1968 and 1974, congressional attention was focused on real estate settlement abuses, but little legislative action was taken. In 1970, as part of the Emergency Home Finance Act, Congress mandated the Department of Housing and Urban Development and the Veterans Administration to undertake a study of real estate settlement charges and to set maximum settlement charges on FHA-insured and VA-guaranteed loans. The study was released in 1972, but no final action was ever taken on the rate-setting authority.[1] In response to mounting allegations of abuses, Congress in 1974 passed the Real Estate Settlement Procedures Act (RESPA).

These three federal consumer protection laws emphasize disclosure on the premise that informed consumers can best protect their own interests. Both the Truth-in-Lending and the Interstate Land Sales programs provide consumers with time in which to evaluate the disclosure information and to exercise a rescission power should a deal not look good. RESPA, though not providing for rescission, prohibits kickbacks and denies sellers the right to require purchasers to use particular title insurance companies.

By the mid-1970s a new trend in consumer protection began to emerge—namely, protecting the consumer by regulating the quality of the product. The Mobile Home Construction and Safety Standards Act of 1974 and the Energy Conservation Standards for New Buildings Act of 1976 reflect this trend. Instead of relying on disclosure to the consumer, these two programs bypassed the consumer to control the product. The Mobile Home Act establishes national standards to be met by all mobile

---

[1] See U.S. Department of Housing and Urban Development and the Veterans Administration, *Report on Mortgage Settlement Costs* (January 1972).

homes, regardless of the state in which they are produced. The Energy Standards Act will sepcify minimum energy conservation performance standards for all new construction. The political judgment was (1) that the issues involved in mobile home quality and energy conservation techology are too complex and technical for consumers to effectively influence the decisions of manufacturers and builders, (2) that governmental regulation in these areas was needed, and (3) that federal action was needed.

THE REGULATION OF INFORMATIVE CONTENT

The Truth-in-Lending Act

Purpose. The Truth-in-Lending Act was designed to give consumers meaningful information about credit and leasing terms to facilitate informed credit selection. Prior to its passage, consumers were faced with a bewildering array of explanations and terms, the net effect of which was to make impossible any meaningful comparison of credit offers. Moreover, varying terminology in itself resulted in consumer confusion as to exactly what they were obtaining, the effective cost of their loans, and their obligations to the creditor. To aid consumers, Congress required the use of a common credit terminology and of common methods of expressing the effective interest rate.

Prior to Truth-in-Lending, the true or effective interest rate was an elusive concept to everyone but the lender. The simple interest rate almost never reflected the true financing cost. Consumers had to pay service fees, transaction charges, loan fees, points, finder's fees, appraisal fees, discounts, and investigation or credit charges whose effect on the true financing cost was unclear to them. If knowledgeable consumer choice is the key to a healthy competitive market, this condition was absent prior to Truth-in-Lending.

Truth-in-Lending was also designed to impose substantive limitations and requirements upon creditors. For purposes of real estate transactions, the major consumer right was a rescission power in limited situations. In addition, Truth-in-Lending set substantive limitations in the areas of advertising, credit cards, and bank credit billing. These last items are not discussed in this chapter.

Scope. Truth-in-Lending covers all consumer credit transactions involving debtors who are natural persons; it does not apply to transactions in which the debtors are corporations, partnerships, trusts, joint ventures, governments, or other organizations. Jurisdiction extends to amounts less than $25,000 except where real property is used as security.

The disclosure of required material must be made before the transaction is consummated. This often occurs at the time of the loan commitment. Lenders must disclose all finance charges payable directly or indirectly as an incident to or a condition of the extension of credit. Such charges include interest, discounts, loan fees, points, and finance fees. Where credit is extended for real property, certain closing costs are excluded, the costs for namely the title examination, the preparation of legal documents, escrows, notary fees, appraisal fees, credit reports, and termite inspections.

In limited situations, consumers are provided a right of rescission. If a credit transaction other than a first lien creates a lien on the mortgagor's principal residence, the consumer can rescind the transaction within three days of its signing. (This right covers second mortgages and many refinancing and nonpurchase money first liens.) If the consumer rescinds by mail, the effective date of rescission is the time of mailing. The creditor is required to wait a reasonable period of time after midnight of the third business day to receive notice of such rescission. Upon rescission, the consumer is relieved of all liability for finance or other charges under the financing agreement and any lien created on the property is automatically void.

Rescission applies solely to the financing agreement and not to an underlying purchase agreement between a buyer and a seller. Truth-in-Lending does not protect buyers from making unwise purchase decisions.

Enforcement. Truth-in-Lending compliance by regulated creditors is enforced by various federal regulatory agencies (e.g., the Federal Reserve Board, the Federal Deposit Insurance Corporation, the comptroller of the currency, and the Federal Home Loan Bank Board); compliance by nonregulated creditors is enforced by the Federal Trade Commission. The Federal Reserve Board issues regulations and clarifying interpretations which are given great weight by the courts.[2]

There are civil and criminal sanctions. Consumers may sue lenders for failure to comply with Truth-in-Lending and can recover actual damages, legal costs, and either the amount of the financing charge involved (but not less than $100 nor more than $1,000) or amounts that the court would permit in a class action suit (not to exceed $500,000 or 1 percent of the net worth of the lender, whichever is less). The lender can defend against suit either by correcting an error within 15 days of its discovery or by demonstrating in court that the violation was unintentional and had resulted from a bona fide clerical error. In the latter case, the lender must show that there were adequate procedures to avoid such errors.

Lenders are subject to criminal sanctions (a fine of not more than $5,000 or imprisonment for not more than one year, or both) if they willingly or knowingly fail to comply.

Information. Truth-in-Lending inquiries should be sent to the Federal Reserve Board, Fair Credit Practices Section, 20th and C Streets, NW, Washington, D.C. 20551.

The Interstate Land Sales Full Disclosure Act

Purpose. The Interstate Land Sales Full Disclosure Act was passed in 1968 by a Congress deeply concerned about fraudulent land sale practices. Slick promotion and deceptive pictures were tools used by owners of unimproved land to trap consumers into signing installment sale con-

---

[2] *Philbeck* v. *Timmers Chevrolet, Inc.,* 449 F2d 971, 977, (5th Cir. 1974).

tracts for the purchase of lands which often were swamps, or inaccessible by transportation, or unserviced by public facilities. Like Truth-in-Lending, the act sought to provide consumers with full disclosure of all pertinent information to enable prudent purchase decisions and to provide adequate consumer remedies when proper disclosure was not forthcoming. The Act, though, does not establish substantive requirements governing the nature of the development or the timing of promised construction.

Scope.   Under the Act the Office of Interstate Land Sales Registration covers all developers offering through interstate commerce 50 or more unimproved lots for sale or lease under a common promotional scheme. Unless exempted,[3] the developer is required to file a Statement of Record with the Department of Housing and Urban Development (HUD).

The Statement of Record covers, but is not limited to, information concerning the identity of parties having an interest in the subdivision and the extent of such interest; a legal description of the subdivision that includes topographical maps; a statement as to the condition of the title to the land; a statement of the general terms and conditions under which the lots are being offered; a statement of the present condition of access to the property, with indications of any unusual conditions relating to noise or safety; information on the availability of public utilities; copies of the deed showing the developer's title to the property; and copies of other legal or contractual documents. The developer is obligated to make timely amendments to the Statement of Record to reflect material changes.

At least three days prior to the signing of the agreement for the purchase or lease of property, the developer is also required to provide purchasers a printed Property Report which contains pertinent extracts from the Statement of Record.

Enforcement.   OILSR establishes civil and criminal liability. It is unlawful for a developer or an agent to sell or lease land covered by this act unless a Statement of Record has been filed and a printed Property Report is provided to purchasers. Fraud also gives rise to liability. Violations subject the developer or his agent to criminal penalties of imprisonment for not more than five years or to a fine of not more than $5,000, or both.

Consumers can sue developers in federal district courts and may collect in damages the difference between the amount paid for the lot plus for reasonable costs of improvement and the lesser of (1) the value of the lot at the time of the suit or (2) the bona fide sale price if the lot was sold before or during the court proceedings. In no case may the penalty exceed the purchase price, reasonable costs of improvements, and reasonable court costs.

Purchasers who have been given a copy of the Property Report within 48 hours of the signing of the contract or agreement can rescind up to

---

[3] Interstate Land Sales Full Disclosure Act, 15 U.S.C. Section 1702 (Supp. 1979). Specific exemptions include sales of lots with complete buildings on them; sales to builders; sales of lots which are free and clear of liens, encumbrances, and adverse claims; and situations in which purchasers have made an on-site inspection.

three days after the signing. A purchaser may waive this right only if he receives the Property Report prior to purchase or if he visits the site and then signs a separate waiver. If no Property Report is provided, the purchaser may void the contract at any time. There is no right of rescission if the Property Report was provided more than 48 hours prior to the signing.

HUD is authorized to conduct all necessary investigations and to seek injunctions in a federal district court for violations of the act. If HUD suspends a developer's Statement of Record because of noncompliance with the act, he cannot sell or lease lots.

Information. For information on the Interstate Land Sales Program, write to the Office of Interstate Land Sales Registration, U.S. Department of Housing and Urban Development, Room 4130, 451 7th Street, SW, Washington, D.C. 20410.

The Real Estate Settlement Procedures Act

Purpose. The Real Estate Settlement Procedures Act (RESPA) was passed by a Congress that was greatly concerned about abuses in real estate settlements and the high costs of such settlements. In passing RESPA, Congress intended that consumers be given timely and sufficient information to facilitate shopping for the best settlement services and costs. Advance disclosure of costs and a special information booklet were the principal mechanisms for providing this information. In addition, Congress sought to curb abusive practices. It prohibited kickbacks; limited the amount that a lender could hold in escrow for property taxes, insurance, and so on; and prohibited sellers from requiring buyers to use specific title insurance companies.

Scope. RESPA covers most loans secured by a first mortgage on one–four-family residential properties. The act has a regulatory and a research dimension. On the regulatory side, it requires the following disclosures:

1. The lenders is to provide the loan applicant with a copy of the settlement booklet within three working days after the loan application has been received.
2. The lender is to provide the loan applicant with good faith estimates of likely settlement charges within three working days after the loan application has been received.
3. Upon request, purchasers are entitled to receive a statement of known costs from settlement agents on the day before settlement.
4. Purchasers and sellers are entitled to receive at or before closing a Uniform Settlement Statement which itemizes all settlement costs.

The act also establishes the following prohibitions or limitations:

1. Persons are prohibited from giving or receiving kickbacks and unearned fees. In its regulations, HUD has published a series of fact-comment patterns to serve as guidance. To clarify an admittedly murky area HUD has issued illustrations of the more typical kickback schemes.

In the absence of any litigation to date, the HUD illustrations are repro-
duced as guidance to the reader.[4]

The following illustrations provide additional guidance on the meaning
and coverage of Section 8 of RESPA. While particular illustrations may
refer to particular providers of settlement services, such illustrations are
applicable by analogy to providers of settlement services other than those
specifically mentioned. It should be noted that other provisions of Federal
or state law may be applicable to the practices and payments discussed
in the following illustrations.

1. *Facts.* A, a provider of settlement services, maintains an abnormally
large balance in a non-interest-bearing account with B, a mortgage lender,
pursuant to an understanding that B will refer borrowers of Federally Related Mortgage Loans to A for the purchase of settlement services in connection with the settlement of such loans.

Comments. Allowing B to use the deposited funds at no interest appears
to be a thing of value given by A to B pursuant to an agreement or understanding that business incident to a real estate settlement shall be referred
to A in violation of Section 8 of RESPA. The maintenance of any accounts
reasonably needed by A in the normal course of its business would not
be a violation of Section 8.

2. *Facts.* B, a lender of Federally Related Mortgage Loans, pays A, a
real estate agent, a fee of $25 per transaction purportedly for services per-
formed such as arranging for B's appraiser to visit the property. The purported services for which the fee is paid are services that real estate agents
frequently perform as part of their services and the fee is really intended
to enable B to compensate A for referring potential borrowers to B.

Comments. Both A and B are in violation of Section 8 of RESPA, since
the fee is being paid in compensation for the referral of business rather
than for legitimate services actually rendered by B on behalf of A.

3. *Facts.* A, a provider of settlement services, provides settlement services at abnormally low rates or at no charge at all to B, a builder, in
connection with a subdivision being developed by B. B agrees to refer purchasers of the completed homes in the subdivision to A for the purchase
of settlement services in connection with the sale of individual lots by B.

Comments. The rendering of services by A to B at little or no charge
constitutes a thing of value given by A to B in return for the referral of
settlement business and both A and B are in violation of Section 8 of RESPA.

4. *Facts.* B, a Lender, encourages persons who receive Federally Related
Mortgage Loans from it to employ A, an attorney, to search title and perform
related settlement services in connection with their transaction. B and A
have an understanding that in return for the referral of this business A
will provide legal services to B or B's officers or employees at abnormally
low rates or for no charge.

Comments. Both A and B are in violation of Section 8 of RESPA.

5. *Facts.* A, a provider of settlement services, pays referral fees to persons
who refer settlement business on commercial real estate to A.

Comments. While commercial transactions are not covered by RESPA,
the payment of such referral fees would be a violation of Section 8 if they
involve indirect compensation for the referral of settlement business covered by RESPA.

6. *Facts.* A, a real estate broker, obtains all necessary licenses under

---

[4] RESPA Regulation X, 24 CFR 3500 App.B.

state law to act as a title insurance agent. A refers individuals who are purchasing homes in transactions in which A participates as a broker to B, a title company, for the purchase of title insurance services. A fills out a simple form but performs no other services in connection with the issuance of the title insurance policy. B pays A a commission for the transaction.

Comments. The payment of a commission by B to A under circumstances where no substantial services are being provided by A to B is a violation of Section 8 of RESPA.

7. *Facts.* A, a "mortgage originator" or "mortgage broker," receives loan applications and refers borrowers to lenders for a fee.

Comments. If A performs services such as obtaining credit and appraisal information or preparing an application for mortgage insurance or guarantee which are of value to the lender paying the fee, without reference to the referral value of such services, and the fee paid bears a reasonable relationship to the value of such services, the payment of such a fee would not be in violation of Section 8 of RESPA.

8. *Facts.* A, a title insurance company, provides among its other services an "Insured Closing Service Letter." Under this letter, for which no separate or additional charge is made, the company agrees to provide indemnity against loss due to certain fraudulent or negligent acts of the company's policy-issuing agents or approved attorneys in complying with closing instructions and in conducting the closing of any transaction in connection with which a policy of title insurance is to be issued by A

Comments. Where A has provided such an Insured Closing Service Letter to a specified person and the protection afforded thereby is effective without regard to whether the particular case was referred to A by the person receiving protection under such letter, the provision of the letter would not be pursuant to an agreement or understanding that settlement services be referred, and therefore not in violation of Section 8.

9. *Facts.* A, a service corporation, is a title insurance agent for B, a title insurance company. The search and examination of title, in connection with applications for title insurance policies prepared by A, are performed by employees of B. Employees of B also make any determinations as to the insurability of title. A issues title insurance policies on behalf of B and receives a commission equal to the amount paid other title insurance agents in the community, including other agents of B, who perform the title search and examination as well as prepare and issue the title insurance policy.

Comments. While A may be performing some real service for B, the fact that the amount of the commission received by A is equal to the commissions customarily paid to full-service title insurance agents who perform substantially greater and more valuable services indicates that the commission paid by B to A is really intended to compensate A for the referral of business. The amount by which the commission exceeds the reasonable value of the services rendered by A to B would be a referral fee prohibited by Section 8 of RESPA. Section 8 does not prohibit variations in the amount of commissions that may be paid, nor does it require that the quantum of services rendered be identical in all cases, so long as services significant to the issuance of a title insurance policy are rendered and the amount of the commission bears a reasonable relationship to the services rendered.

10. *Facts.* A, a real estate broker, refers title business to B, a company that is a licensed title agent for C, a title insurance company. A is part owner of B. B performs the title search and examination, makes determina-

tions of insurability, and issues a policy of title insurance on behalf of C, for which C pays B a commission. B pays annual dividends to its owners, including A, based on the relative amount of business each of its owners refers to B.

Comments. While the payments of a commission by C to B is not a violation of Section 8 of RESPA, if the amount of the commission constitutes reasonable compensation for the services performed by B for C, the payment of a dividend or the giving of any other thing of value by B to A that is based on the amount of business referred to B by A constitutes a violation of Section 8. Similarly, if the amount of stock held by A in B (or, if B were a partnership, the distribution of partnership profits by B to A) varied in proportion to the amount of business referred or expected to be referred, or if B retained any funds for subsequent distribution to A where such funds were generally in proportion to the amount of business A referred to B, such arrangements would constitute violations of Section 8.

2. Sellers are prohibited from requiring purchasers to use specified title insurance companies.

3. Lenders are limited as to the amount of escrow deposits for taxes, insurance, and other items they can require from mortgagors. A simple rule of thumb is that the amount to be escrowed at the time of settlement equals the pro rata amount that would have been ascribed to the period between the date taxes were last paid and the date of the first mortgage payment plus an additional two months. Thus if taxes were last due on January 1, and the first mortgage payment occurred on July 1, the maximum escrows would be eight months. With each monthly mortgage payment, the lender could require one twelfth of the annual amount for taxes, insurance, and so on. The amount could be adjusted for increases in costs.

The second important dimension of RESPA is research and evaluation. HUD has initiated a multiyear analysis and demonstration of improved land recordation procedures. This research will cover public land recordation procedures, private title plant techniques, and legal impediments to more efficient title searches and examinations. The department will also evaluate RESPA and report to Congress no later than June 1980. New research issues to be included in the research for possible recommendation to Congress include using a "lender-pay" approach wherein lenders secure all settlement services and pass the cost on to the mortgagor; directly regulating settlement services; and providing loan applicants with estimates of settlement service costs in the form of ranges at the time of the loan application.

Enforcement. Unlike the Truth-in-Lending Act and OILSR, RESPA provides no expressed civil right of action for the failure of a settlement service provider to make the necessary disclosures. Civil damages are specified for violations of the kickback provision and the provision prohibiting sellers from requiring the purchaser to use specific title insurance companies. Criminal penalties are established for the kickback provision, with fines up to $5,000 or imprisonment for not more than five years, or both.

HUD lacks any express powers to assure compliance with the law. This lack has led the Department to secure the cooperation of the federal financial regulatory agencies (the Comptroller of the Currency, the Federal Reserve Board, the Federal Deposit Insurance Corporation, the Federal Home Loan Bank Board, and the National Credit Union Administration) to assure compliance through their supervisory responsibilities over member lenders.

Information. For information write to RESPA, U.S. Department of Housing and Urban Development, Room 4108, 451 7th Street, SW, Washington, D.C. 20410.

REGULATION OF THE PRODUCT

Although the Truth-in-Lending, Interstate Land Sales, and Real Estate Settlement Procedures acts build on disclosure, federal policy has also focused directly on the project itself. Major illustrations of this approach are the Mobile Home Construction and Safety Standards Act and the Energy Conservation Standards for New Buildings Act. In these two instances, but for different reasons, Congress deemed it necessary to control the construction quality of the product. These programs are briefly described below.

Mobile Homes Construction and Safety Standards

Purpose. The Mobile Home Act was passed by a Congress which was concerned that mobile homes were not effectively regulated by state laws to assure a minimum level of occupant safety. Congress sought to reduce "the number of personal injuries and deaths and the amount of insurance costs and property damage resulting from mobile homes accidents and to improve the quality and durability of mobile homes." Unlike most other residential construction, mobile homes were not subject to local building codes because these structures were considered personalty not realty. Industry had developed a minimum standards code, but the adoption and enforcement of that code were irregular across the United States. Because mobile homes are easily shipped from one state to another, Congress established one set of federal standards which preempted state and local codes.

Scope. The Mobile Home Act applies to all mobile homes built after June 1976. A mobile home is any transportable structure which is at least 8 feet wide and 32 feet long and includes plumbing, heating, air conditioning, and electrical systems. Initially, modular units were included under the definition, but these were subsequently exempted.

Enforcement. The Department of Housing and Urban Development has developed a collaborative enforcement procedure with state governments. If HUD approves, a state may be the primary enforcement agency for mobile homes built within the state. The state would approve designs, conduct quality control of manufacturer programs and manufacturing processes, and conduct in-plant inspections of mobile homes. Where a state does not undertake these functions, HUD can contract to have private engineering and inspection agencies perform them.

As for quality control, HUD monitors the activities of states through the National Conference of States on Building Codes and Standards. This is principally accomplished by a team of federal and state officials who spot-check the state inspection programs.

If a consumer feels that an imminent safety hazard exists or that the manufacturer has failed to build a mobile home to standards, he can immediately bring this fact to the attention of the manufacturer. The manufacturer is obligated either to repurchase the mobile home or to remedy the defects or the nonconformance. If a consumer is not satisfied with the manufacturer's actions, he may bring the matter to the attention of the state authority or of HUD. Consumers may also bring suit in a federal district court to require compliance with the Mobile Home Standards Act.

The Department of Housing and Urban Development has civil authority to subpoena information, seek injunctions in federal court, inspect manufacturers' plants and records, and seek civil fines against manufacturers for failure to comply. Where HUD determines that mobile homes constitute an imminent safety hazard or do not comply with its standards, HUD may, after presenting the evidence, require the manufacturer to issue notices to purchasers concerning the defects. HUD may also require the manufacturer to replace mobile homes whose defects present an unreasonable risk of injury or death or relate to an error in design. The secretary of HUD has the authority to require recalls of defective parts.

Information.   To secure more information concerning the Mobile Home Construction and Safety Act, inquiries can be sent to Mobile Home Construction and Safety Act, Office of the Assistant Secretary for Neighborhoods, Voluntary Associations and Consumer Protection, 451 7th Street, SW, Washington, D.C. 20410.

Energy Performance Standards for New Buildings

Purpose.   The Energy Conservation Standards for New Buildings Act was passed in 1976 by a Congress concerned that buildings were being constructed without due consideration for energy consumption. The Act authorizes the Department of Energy to develop and promulgate performance standards for all types of new buildings, and it authorizes Department of Housing and Urban Development to enforce those standards.

Scope.   All new buildings are covered by this act after the standards become effective. The federal government is to publish minimum standards by 1980, and the states are to adopt those standards or standards which equal or exceed the federal minimums within one year after the issuance of the final federal standards. No federal financial assistance would be made available for use in a locality (1) lacking certified standards, (2) not exempted by the Department of Housing and Urban Development, or (3) not having an established approval process (which would qualify a building as having met the federal standards). For all practical purposes, this would stop all institutional lending for buildings except for private financing or financing by state-chartered lending institutions which are not members of the Federal Deposit Insurance Corporation. The act requires that both houses of Congress pass a resolution to trigger the withholding of funds sanction. The sanction would not apply to localities not covered by appropriate standards but having an approved testing procedure or officially exempted by HUD from compliance.

Builders will be required to secure design approval to demonstrate that their projects meet the energy performance standards. Those standards are expected to vary by geographic location and building type and to provide appropriate adjustments for the use of nondepletable energy sources (e.g., solar heating).

Enforcement. There are no explicit criminal or civil penalties under this act. Since the energy standards will be included within local building codes, the civil and criminal enforcement actions would be those normally attendant on local building codes. The major enforcement mechanism under the act, as has been mentioned above, is the termination of federal financial assistance.

Information. While this program has yet to be developed, information is available through the Assistant Secretary for Conservation and Solar Applications, Department of Energy, Forrestal Building, Washington, D. C. 20585.

CONDOMINIUMS: A NEW AREA OF CONCERN

During the years 1975–77, condominium consumer protection actions took a variety of shapes which suggested the possibility of broad reforms in the future. The need for consumer protection in this area became politically visible in the mid-70s, as explosive condominium activity occurred in such states as Florida.

Condominium ownership—fee simple in the dwelling unit and an undivided interest in the common elements among unit owners—has been highly attractive, combining the privacy and tax advantages of ownership along with the care and maintenance of the common areas (hallways, parking, major utility systems, recreational facilities) by a unit owners' association. The developer of a condominium would create a unit owners' association to govern the common areas of the condominium and would retain control over the association until most of the units were sold, at which time control would be transferred to the association. The association would then enter into contracts for necessary services—professional management, recreation services, parking, and so on.

In some instances, most visible in Florida, the developer retained ownership of the recreational facilities and leased them to the unit owners' association on a net-net lease. The association carried all the costs of operating and maintaining the recreational facilities, the developer having no obligations except to receive a fee. This fee was often tied to an automatic escalator clause (the escalator perhaps being the consumer price index), with the result that unit owners were locked into a lease arrangement whereby they shouldered all costs and risks and faced automatic rent increases. This abusive practice varied in form. For example, a developer might own a strip of land between the condominium units and the beach and impose a charge to unit owners for the right to cross the strip.

As a result of flagrant abuses, Congress mandated the Department of Housing and Urban Development to undertake a study of condominium problems and to report whether legislation was needed. This study was completed in 1975. It identified the following types of concerns: abusive use of long-term recreation leases, poor construction quality, complex legal documents beyond the comprehension of average purchasers, displacement of tenants where condominiums were created by conversions from rental units, management of the homeowners' association, problems of community living, misuse of purchaser deposits, nonpayment of fees by the developer, lack of warranties and engineering reports, and misleading disclosures of expected operating costs to potential purchasers.[5]

Consumer protection activities have occurred in several forms. Several states, among them Florida and Virginia, have enacted progressive condominium legislation. At the same time, the National Conference of Commissioners on Uniform State Laws has developed the Uniform Condominium Act for state adoption. At the Federal level, bills have been introduced into Congress that would provide substantive minimum protections to purchasers and owners of condominium units. Thus far, no federal legislation has been enacted.

CONCLUDING OBSERVATIONS

The federal consumer protection programs discussed above represent the major federal regulatory activities affecting real estate to date. In addition, there is growing federal antitrust activity as evidenced by recent Federal Trade Commission investigations into title insurance and real estate broker activities and by the criminal convictions for price-fixing which the Department of Justice won against leading Maryland real estate brokers in 1977. A variety of state regulatory programs also affect real estate, such as the licensing requirements for real estate brokers or legislation concerning rate setting or approving, as in title insurance. Many of these programs, however, do not have substantial consumer protection measures.

Given our interdependent economy and our tightening housing market, the opportunities for the abuse of consumers will increase. Consumers will experience many problems that they will be unable to control. As a consequence, the pace of federal and state consumer protection activities will probably increase.

---

[5] *HUD Condominium/Cooperative Study*, vols. 1–2 (Washington, D.C.: U.S. Government Printing Office, July 1975).

LICENSURE AND SELF-REGULATION

David Sachs

Donald H. Treadwell

Bruce Grewell

Robert J. Reid

*D*AVID SACHS, MBA, MAI, Partner, George S. King Co., Real Estate, Washington, D.C.

   Appraiser, Anacostia Federal Savings and Loan Association, Washington, D.C. Past Member, panel of approved appraisers, General Services Administration, Region 3. Formerly professional lecturer in real estate, School of Business Administration, The American University, Washington, D.C. Member, Washington Board of Realtors®; American Institute of Real Estate Appraisers; and Real Estate Commission, Washington, D.C.

DONALD H. TREADWELL, JD, MAI, CRE, President, Treadwell Real Estate Company, Southgate, Michigan.

   Director and member, Executive Committee, National Association of Realtors®. Member, state bar of Michigan. Certified instructor, American Institute of Real Estate Appraisers and University of Michigan Extension Service. Past president, Michigan Association of Realtors® and Downriver Board of Realtors®. Formerly chairman, National Association of Realtors® Professional Standards Committee and Ad Hoc Committee to Revise Code of Ethics. Contributor to Appraisal Journal.

BRUCE GREWELL, BS, JD, CPA, Attorney and Real Estate Broker, Gulledge Corp., Alexandria, Virginia.

   Lawyer and financial consultant to various firms. Consultant on home warranties to National Association of Realtors® and various insurance companies. Member, American Bar Association, American Institute of Certified Public Accountants, and various state professional societies.

ROBERT J. REID, President Home Owners Warranty Corporation, National Housing Center, Washington, D.C.
Formerly president and chief executive officer Charter American Insurance Co. and vice president and assistant treasurer American Investment Company.

REAL ESTATE LICENSURE

Types of Licenses

Every state and the District of Columbia has a real estate licensing act. Each of these acts includes a provision which establishes at least two types of licenses: broker and salesperson.

The broker's license is required of any party who is engaged in exchanging, leasing, or selling real estate. The salesperson's license is required of any party who engages in these activities but is associated with, licensed under, and responsible to a broker.

A third type of license, that of associate broker, has been designed for corporations and partnerships in which more than one member or officer engages in the acts of a broker. In some jurisdictions, the associate broker may be a broker who is working for another broker.

Leasing and selling are the most common activities of persons who hold real estate licenses, but a state may include other real estate pursuits within the scope of its real estate licensing act. Here are some examples of such pursuits and of jurisdictions in which they are subject to licensure:

Apartment condominium management	Florida
Appraising	Nebraska
Auctioneering	Louisiana
Erecting houses for sale	District of Columbia
Mortgage loan negotiation	California
Selling used mobile homes together with land	Washington
Subdividing and selling land in building lots	Maryland

Activities closely associated with real estate but not covered by real estate licensing acts include those of title insurance companies, escrow agents, counselors, and sellers of cemetery lots. There are approximately 1.9 million real estate licencees in the United States.

Application for Licenses

The minimum requirements for obtaining a real estate license are a formal application, a passing grade on the written examination, and in some cases the successful completion of courses.

The application includes questions on such matters as the following:

Form of business organization
  Individual
  Partnership
  Corporation
    Type of license sought
  Associate broker
  Broker
  Salesperson
    Residency status
  nonresident
  resident
    Personal information
  Name, trade name, social security number, date and place of birth
  Home address and telephone
  Business address and telephone
  Previous and present employment
  Previous real estate or other business or professional applications and licenses
  Present real estate or other business or professional licenses
  Revocations, suspensions of real estate or other business or professional licenses
  Surety bond—declinations and recoveries
  Real estate experience
  Charges or convictions of forgery, embezzlement, obtaining money under false pretenses, extortion, criminal conspiracy to defraud, or other like offenses
  Ability to read, write, understand the English language
    Miscellaneous
  Broker's certificate of occupancy
  Broker's bank escrow account number
  Broker's endorsement of salesperson
  Property owner's recommendation
  Irrevocable consent for service in suits (nonresidents)
  Notarization

The Real Estate Commission

The real estate commission, to which the application is forwarded, is established by the real estate licensing act. The commission generally consists of four to six public members plus a chairperson who may be a full-time state employee. The public members are licensed real estate brokers who have been appointed by the governor or some other state executive. There also may be a "law" member and possibly a "consumer" member (a person who is neither an attorney nor a licensed broker).

The basic obligations of the real estate commission are:

(1) to define, regulate, and license brokers and salespersons; and (2) to protect the public against fraud in real estate transactions. By virtue of these obligations, the commission's functions are administrative and regulatory.

Administration

The administrative functions of the real estate commission entail determining the qualifications of applicants for licenses, approving applications, supervising examinations, and renewing and issuing licenses.

Upon receiving a completed application, the commission's staff checks and verifies the answers. The commission then considers the application. If it is approved, the applicant is scheduled for examination or is issued a nonresident license based upon a reciprocal agreement between the state issuing the license and the applicant's state of residence or licensure.

Examination

Although the examination may be prepared, administered, and graded by state representatives, it is more likely that the test preparation and grading will be done by a professional testing company. Two of the best-known concerns of this type are the Educational Testing Service and the American College Testing Program.

The applicant's preparation for the licensing examination may follow several routes.

1. Study a real estate text and the state's real estate law. Three recent books especially written to help in preparing for the examination are:
   Fillmore W. Galaty, Wellington J. Allaway, and Robert C. Kyle, *Modern Real Estate Practice.*
   Jack C. Estes and John W. Kokus, Jr., *Real Estate License Preparation Course for Salespersons and Brokers.*
   William B. French, Stephen J. Martin, and Thomas E. Battle III, *Real Estate Review's Guide to Real Estate Licensing Examination for Salespersons and Brokers.*
2. Study the manual provided by the state and/or the information bulletin provided by the outside testing bureau.
3. Enroll in a formal class in real estate. State-approved and state-required courses are typically given by degree-granting colleges or universities.
4. On-the-job training may provide a valuable adjunct to the above.

The examinations for salespersons and for brokers take about four hours each and are divided into two parts. Part I is called the "uniform" test because it contains questions required by all of the states. The subjects covered in Part I include:

The real estate business	The law of agency
Definition of real estate terms	Property management
The law of contracts	Settlements
Financing real estate transactions	Elements of appraisal
Real estate estates and interests	Real estate arithmetic

Part II is called the "state" test because it deals with the given state's real estate act. Obviously, the examination for brokers is more detailed than the examination for salespersons. Most of the questions are multiple choice but there are problems for which blank contract, listing, and settlement forms are provided.

Although the real estate commission's administrative responsibilities may appear routine, numerous problems in connection with licensing require decisions. For example:

What shall the passing grades on examinations be? Shall they be the same or different for brokers and for salespersons?

Where only one part of the examination is passed, must the applicant be required to retake both parts?

Will licenses be granted by "reciprocity" (waiver of examination requirement) to applicants from states which refuse "reciprocity" to applicants from the given state?

Are real estate franchisers subject to the real estate licensing act and therefore required to be licensed?

Do apartment or house referral services engage in activities covered by the real estate licensing act and therefore require licensing?

May a salesperson be licensed simultaneously with different brokers who operate in different states.

Regulation

The real estate commission's regulatory function involves the investigation and disposition of complaints. The commission does not have legal jurisdiction over matters involving disputes between licensees but only over disputes between the public and licensees and only on behalf of the public.

There are no available statistics showing complaints by cause. In urban centers, however, it is likely that most grievances fall under one of the following headings:

1. Failure to account for or to remit money.
2. Substantial misrepresentation (in most instances as a consequence of poorly drawn contracts).
3. Ignorance of the agent's obligation to his principal.

The following excerpts are paraphrased excerpts from typical letters of complaint:

I am unable to get settlement on rental accounts and security deposits. The last two rent checks, for the months of March and April, were returned because of insufficient funds.

Broker A sold a house for me. I paid her fee and trusted her completely to take care of my interest, but she lied and she cheated me out of $800.87. She told me that in order to have a binding contract, she had to put in a clause stating that I would pay all settlement charges over $1,000. I didn't want to, but she assured me it was necessary.

I was told that settlement would not take place because my broker refused to bring the purchaser to settlement unless I agreed to pay him a greater commission.

Generally, a complaint is assigned to a commissioner, who determines whether it should be investigated or dropped. Only complaints over which the real estate commission has jurisdiction under the real estate act are investigated. If an investigation is conducted, then the findings are attached to the complaint and returned to the commissioner. He may recommend that an informal meeting be held with the licensee in order to obtain satisfaction of the complaint or that a formal hearing be held. The suspension or revocation of the broker's license and or the salesperson's license may result under certain circumstances.

Real estate commissions are ordinarily reluctant to seek out violations of the real estate act. In part, this is due to limitations in help and funds. But the larger explanation is that the commissioners are highly visible to the public and receive many complaints. With the possible exception of the board which deals with alcoholic beverages, the real estate commission may be the busiest of the local public bodies overseeing occupations and professions.

Real estate license applicants and licensees frequently challenge the administrative and regulatory decisions of real estate commissions in the courts. Such cases may result in judicial clarifications of the real estate acts and in the passage of further real estate legislation.

Changes

The protection that real estate regulation gives the public has long been recognized. But now there is an awareness that the public interest may be even better served if real estate licensees are subjected to higher educational standards. In response to that awareness, the more advanced states have increased the experience and educational requirements for real estate licensing and are instituting courses of continuing education. Florida, for example, has passed a law which may require the completion of a 14-hour update course prior to license renewal every four years. In Colorado, even inactive licensees must meet educational and/or active practice requirements.

A contrary movement emphasizes experience rather than education as a requirement for licensure. This movement, a throwback to the age of apprenticeship, is a response to the need to provide employment opportunities for the less advantaged.

The public insists that licensees be knowledgeable in all laws, federal and local, which are in any way related to real estate. Antitrust legislation, the Equal Credit Opportunity Act, the Fair Housing Act, the Interstate Land Sales Full Disclosure Act, and the Truth-in-Lending Act are representative of the increasing number of pertinent federal regulations (see Chapters 22, 24, and 25). In response to an inquiry, the librarian of the National Association of Realtors® wrote, "Unfortunately, we do not know of any one publication that compiles or even cites all federal legislation bearing on real estate matters." The office of one senator estimated that two persons working full time would require two months to make such a compilation.

Numerous laws related to real estate have also been enacted at the local level. For example, in some communities rent control acts have limited the landlord's rights to possess and dispossess. It is questionable whether the average licensee, no matter how capable and honest, will be able to advise the client regarding the application of *all* of these federal and local laws to an individual transaction.

Narello

The National Association of Real Estate Licensing Law Officials (NARELLO) was established in 1929. Its primary purpose is to improve the administration and enforcement of real estate licensing laws in the states, districts, territories, possessions, and provinces of the United States and Canada. The real estate licensing officials of all 50 states, the District of Columbia, and four Canadian provinces, are members of the association.

NARELLO's accomplishments and activities include the preparation of a model licensing law; a proposal for a real estate educational curriculum; an exchange for samples of licenses, examinations, and licensee data; and the publication of *Narello News,* which includes reports on significant court decisions.

SELF-REGULATION OF THE REAL ESTATE INDUSTRY

Self-regulation of the real estate industry in the United States has expressed itself in three ways: first, the articulation of standards of practice or codes of ethics to better define the standards to which individual real estate practitioners might aspire; second, the requirement that others joining in association conform to certain minimum standards and be subject to formal hearings and sanctions in the event of failure to meet those standards; and third, the encouragement and promulgation of licensing laws providing for the regulation of real estate practitioners by governmental authorities. The third way has been covered in the preceding section of this chapter; in this section attention will be confined to the first two ways.

Self-regulation was a dominant factor in the formation of real estate boards throughout the United States in the last two decades of the 19th century and the first decade of the 20th century. Although the aims and objectives of these boards were diverse, their leaders were in general agreement on three issues. The priorities of the founders of the National Association of Real Estate Exchanges, set forth at their meeting in Chicago in 1908, were: (1) to pool existing skills and information and to expand knowledge through education and research; (2) to establish ethical standards; and (3) to muster effective support for sound public policies on matters affecting real estate. Through a succession of name changes this organization became the National Association of Realtors® (NAR) and despite its growth to more than 700,000 members by 1979, its principal objectives have remained remarkably constant. Because of its dominant position in the real estate industry, the National Association of Realtors® has been associated with all of the most significant developments in industry self-regulation.

Evolution of the Code of Ethics

The original bylaws which were adopted by the National Association of Real Estate Exchanges in 1909 made mandatory a standing committee on the Code of Ethics. In 1913, the National Association adopted its first code. It was based almost entirely upon codes which the real estate boards in Kansas City and Omaha had adopted, and it provided standards in many areas for judgment by oneself and one's peers. In 1915 the first major revision was submitted to the local real estate boards for their voluntary adoption.

These early codes reflected the disorganized condition of the prevailing real estate market. Specific articles sought to discourage practices which were not considered in the best interests of either the client or the broker. The broker's responsibility toward his client was specifically set forth, and exclusive written listings were urged as a means of clearly defining that responsibility. Net listings were generally discouraged, and the broker was required to make full disclosure whenever he was not acting in complete accordance with the agency relationship. The broker was obligated to work toward eliminating fraudulent misrepresentation by others. Continuing education was urged, and the broker was enjoined against accepting assignments for which he was less well qualified than competing brokers. In the event of disputes among brokers, voluntary arbitration conducted by the real estate board was encouraged.

Not yet resolved was the fundamental question of whether the Code of Ethics was to be a standard to which the members should aspire or a code of minimum conduct which the members would be required to meet. The draft of the 1915 revision proposed a disciplinary procedure which was optional with each board adopting the code. The procedure provided for hearings and discipline in the event of violations. Disciplinary action included censure, fines in amounts of up to $200, suspension for periods of up to one year, and expulsion from the board.

Since 1915 there have been nine additional revisions of the code. During those years, adoption of the Code of Ethics by each board and agreement to adhere to its standard by each individual member have become the unifying threads in the relationship between the National Association of Realtors® and individual Realtors®. The local boards are considered autonomous within the exclusive territory awarded by their charter, subject only to the payment of dues and some limitations designed to promote open memberships and access to board services. Their single specific charge is that they must enforce the Code of Ethics within their assigned territories. Failure to do this is cause for revocation of their charter.

The Code of Ethics and Licensing Laws

Although the membership of the National Association of Realtors®
now includes most of the more active brokers and salespersons, a large
number of people engaged in the real estate business have not been
associated with the National Association and therefore have not come
under the Code of Ethics. Parallel with the development of the Code
of Ethics, the National Association has promulgated and urged the adoption of state license laws which are similarly designed to protect the
public. Realtors® have been in the forefront of this drive, and in some
states the licensing statutes have virtually adopted the then existing
Code of Ethics. In many instances local boards have utilized the authority of the state licensing officials to prevent actions contrary to both
the license law and the Code of Ethics.

The Code of 1924

By the time of the second major revision of the Code of Ethics, in
1924, the bylaws of the National Association of Real Estate Boards required each member board to adopt the Code of Ethics as a part of its
rules and regulations. Any board which neglected or refused to enforce
the Code of Ethics became subject to expulsion from the National Association.

The code remained virtually intact from 1928 through 1949. The new
conditions of the post–World War II era were reflected in the controversy
over the changes that were made in 1950, 1951, and 1952, when changes
were made in articles that dealt with standard fee schedules and viewed
the introduction of people of diverse races into a neighborhood as an
inharmonious use. As a result of these debates, the code eliminated any
reference to segregation by race and thus established the National Association as being in the forefront of those who maintained that the right
to own property should not be determined by race. This principle was
adopted by the U.S. Congress in the Civil Rights Act of 1964.

Concerning fees, Realtors® were enjoined to charge "only such fees
as are fair and reasonable and in accordance with local practice in
similar transactions." The reference to fees was completely eliminated
in the revision of 1961.

The Success of the Realtor®

The decade of the '60s brought demands for social change and an
increased public awareness of the importance of property ownership,
particularly home ownership. Public expectations as to competence and
service rose sharply as the consumerist movement spread.

During the decade of the '60s the role and motives of Realtors®, as
members of the National Association of Realtors® were called, also
changed. As has been indicated, the founders of the association were
motivated in large measure by a desire for self-improvement and for

the improvement of conditions in their industry. They were well-established business leaders who viewed the Code of Ethics primarily as a commitment by themselves to principles which could be held up as an example to others, and which could improve their image in the community and their self-esteem in their chosen work.

The success of the Realtor® movement, however, introduced strong economic motives for membership in the association. The spread of multiple listing services, offered in most sections of the country as an additional service of the real estate boards, resulted in widespread recognition that participation in such services was an essential condition for success in the real estate business. This view was supported by the courts in several decisions.

The growth of multiple listing also resulted in an explosion of cooperative transactions. In such transactions, one broker lists a property, the information is widely disseminated, and other brokers are invited to submit the property to their clients. Testimony to the obvious benefits of such a broad market is provided by the expansion of multiple listing systems throughout the country. At the same time, however, cooperation among vast numbers of Realtors® and salespeople has created many friction points for potential controversy which have tended to impede the free flow of information in the real estate market.

The Code Revision of 1974

During the 1950s and '60s the boards occasionally met with resistance to the enforcement of the Code of Ethics. Members who had been disciplined resorted to the courts to enjoin the enforcement of sanctions, particularly expulsion. Nonmember brokers sued for access to the multiple listing system or for the board membership which would entitle them to the benefits of the system. As a consequence, a committee was appointed in 1972 to review the entire Code of Ethics. The committee's charge was to make certain that the code did not encourage any anticompetitive actions and that it was consistent with federal and state law. The subsequent revision of 1974 was the most sweeping revision since that of 1915.

The committee viewed the code as having a three-fold function. First, it provided a framework establishing the relationships among brokers. The Code and interpretations issued by the Professional Standards Committee would enable Realtors® and Realtor®-Associates to ascertain what standards of conduct they would be expected to meet and what standards of conduct they could expect from cooperating brokers. Second, the code provided a similar framework governing the relationship of brokers and salespeople to their clients and customers. In some instances it restated the law of the land, but in many other instances it set a considerably higher standard. Third, it provided a method of settling disputes through arbitration rather than expensive and time-consuming litigation.

The thrust of the first six articles of the code revision of 1974 is primarily aspirational. These articles set forth the duty of the Realtor®

Code of Ethics, National Association of Realtors®: As Approved by the Delegate Body of the Association at Its 67th Annual Convention, November 14, 1974

Preamble

Under all is the land. Upon its wise utilization and widely allocated ownership depend the survival and growth of free institutions and of our civilization. The Realtor® should recognize that the interests of the nation and its citizens require the highest and best use of the land and the widest distribution of land ownership. They require the creation of adequate housing, the building of functioning cities, the development of productive industries and farms, and the preservation of a healthful environment.

Such interests impose obligations beyond those of ordinary commerce. They impose grave social responsibility and a patriotic duty to which the Realtor® should dedicate himself, and for which he should be diligent in preparing himself. The Realtor®, therefore, is zealous to maintain and improve the standards of his calling and shares with his fellow-Realtors® a common responsibility for its integrity and honor. The term Realtor® has come to connote competency, fairness, and high integrity resulting from adherence to a lofty ideal of moral conduct in business relations. No inducement of profit and no instruction from clients ever can justify departure from this ideal.

In the interpretation of his obligation, a Realtor® can take no safer guide than that which has been handed down through the centuries, embodied in the Golden Rule, "Whatsoever ye would that men should do to you, do ye even so to them."

Accepting this standard as his own, every Realtor® pledges himself to observe its spirit in all of his activities and to conduct his business in accordance with the tenets set forth below.

Article 1

The Realtor® should keep himself informed on matters affecting real estate in his community, the state, and nation so that he may be able to contribute responsibly to public thinking on such matters.

Article 2

In justice to those who place their interests in his care, the Realtor® should endeavor always to be informed regarding laws, proposed legislation, governmental regulations, public policies, and current market conditions in order to be in a position to advise his clients properly.

Article 3

It is the duty of the Realtor® to protect the public against fraud, misrepresentation, and unethical practices in real estate transactions. He should endeavor to eliminate in his community any practices which could be damaging to the public or bring discredit to the real estate profession. The Realtor® should assist the governmental agency charged with regulating the practices of brokers and salesmen in his state.

Article 4

The Realtor® should seek no unfair advantage over other Realtors® and should conduct his business so as to avoid controversies with other Realtors®.

Article 5

In the best interests of society, of his associates, and his own business, the Realtor® should willingly share with other Realtors® the lessons of his experience and study for the benefit of the public, and should be loyal to the Board of Realtors® of his community and active in its work.

Article 6

To prevent dissension and misunderstanding and to assure better service to the owner, the Realtor® should urge the exclusive listing of property unless contrary to the best interest of the owner.

Article 7

In accepting employment as an agent, the Realtor® pledges himself to protect and promote the interests of the client. This obligation of absolute fidelity to the client's interests is primary, but it does not relieve the Realtor® of the obligation to treat fairly all parties to the transaction.

Article 8

The Realtor® shall not accept compensation from more than one party, even if permitted by law, without the full knowledge of all parties to the transaction.

Article 9

The Realtor® shall avoid exaggeration, misrepresentation, or concealment of pertinent facts. He has an affirmative obligation to discover adverse factors that a reasonably competent and diligent investigation would disclose.

Article 10

The Realtor® shall not deny equal professional services to any person for reasons of race, creed, sex, or country of national origin. The Realtor® shall not be a party to any plan or agreement to discriminate against a person or persons on the basis of race, creed, sex, or country of national origin.

Article 11

A Realtor® is expected to provide a level of competent service in keeping with the Standards of Practice in those fields in which the Realtor® customarily engages.

The Realtor® shall not undertake to provide specialized professional services concerning a type of property or service that is outside his field of competence unless he engages the assistance of one who is competent on such types of property or service, or unless the facts are fully disclosed to the client. Any person engaged to provide such assistance shall be so identified to the client and his contribution to the assignment should be set forth.

The Realtor® shall refer to the Standards of Practice of the National Association as to the degree of competence that a client has a right to expect the Realtor® to possess, taking into consideration the complexity of the problem, the availability of expert assistance, and the opportunities for experience available to the Realtor®.

Article 12

The Realtor® shall not undertake to provide professional services concerning a property or its value where he has a present or contemplated interest unless such interest is specifically disclosed to all affected parties.

Article 13

The Realtor® shall not acquire an interest in or buy for himself, any member of his immediate family, his firm or any member thereof, or any entity in which he has a substantial ownership interest, property listed with him, without making the true position known to the listing owner. In selling property owned by himself, or in which he has any interest, the Realtor® shall reveal the facts of his ownership or interest to the purchaser.

Article 14

In the event of a controversy between Realtors® associated with different firms, arising out of their relationship as Realtors®, the Realtors® shall submit the dispute to arbitration in accordance with the regulations of their board or boards rather than litigate the matter.

Article 15

If a Realtor® is charged with unethical practice or is asked to present evidence in any disciplinary proceeding or investigation, he shall place all pertinent facts before the proper tribunal of the member board or affiliated institute, society, or council of which he is a member.

Article 16

When acting as agent, the Realtor® shall not accept any commission, rebate, or profit on expenditures made for his principal-owner, without the principal's knowledge and consent.

Article 17

The Realtor® shall not engage in activities that constitute the unauthorized practice of law and shall recommend that legal counsel be obtained when the interest of any party to the transaction requires it.

Article 18

The Realtor® shall keep in a special account in an appropriate financial institution, separated from his own funds, monies coming into his possession in trust for other persons, such as escrows, trust funds, clients' monies, and other like items.

Article 19

The Realtor® shall be careful at all times to present a true picture in his advertising and representations to the public. He shall neither advertise

426 Part III. Real Estate Marketing

without disclosing his name nor permit any person associated with him to use individual names or telephone numbers, unless such person's connection with the Realtor® is obvious in the advertisement.

Article 20

The Realtor®, for the protection of all parties, shall see that financial obligations and commitments regarding real estate transactions are in writing, expressing the exact agreement of the parties. A copy of each agreement shall be furnished to each party upon his signing such agreement.

Article 21

The Realtor® shall not engage in any practice or take any action inconsistent with the agency of another Realtor®.

Article 22

In the sale of property which is exclusively listed with a Realtor®, the Realtor® shall utilize the services of other brokers upon mutually agreed upon terms when it is in the best interests of the client.

Negotiations concerning property which is listed exclusively shall be carried on with the listing broker, not with the owner, except with the consent of the listing broker.

Article 23

The Realtor® shall not publicly disparage the business practice of a competitor nor volunteer an opinion of a competitor's transaction. If his opinion is sought and if the Realtor® deems it appropriate to respond, such opinion shall be rendered with strict professional integrity and courtesy.

Article 24

The Realtor® shall not directly or indirectly solicit the services or affiliation of an employee or independent contractor in the organization of another Realtor® without prior notice to said Realtor®.

Note: Where the word Realtor® is used in this Code and Preamble, it shall be deemed to include Realtor®-Associate. Pronouns shall be considered to include Realtors® and Realtor®-Associates of both genders.

The Code of Ethics was adopted in 1913. Amended at the Annual Convention in 1924, 1928, 1950, 1951, 1952, 1955, 1956, 1961, 1962, and 1974.

Source: National Association of Realtors®. Copyright© National Association of Realtors®, 1974. All rights reserved.

to keep informed on real estate matters, to protect the public against fraud and misrepresentation, to work fairly and willingly with other Realtors® in promoting the public welfare, and to promote the use of exclusive listings in order to minimize misunderstandings and dissension between Realtors® and their clients and among Realtors®. These objectives would have been applauded by those who had assumed the obligations of the first code more than 60 years earlier.

The remaining 18 articles set minimum standards of conduct which all Realtors® and Realtor-Associates are required to meet. These articles require persons whose primary interest is in the economic advantages of Realtor® and Realtor-Associate membership to conduct themselves responsibly in their relationships with the public, their clients, and fellow professionals. The articles reaffirm the position of the Realtor® as agent and enjoin the Realtor® to promote the interests of the client, bound only by an obligation to treat fairly all parties to the transaction. Misrepresentation of any kind is prohibited. Full disclosure is required where there is any possibility of a conflict of interest. A new Article 10 affirms the Realtors® and Realtor-Associates are obligated to provide equal professional services, regardless of race, creed, sex, or country of national origin. The new code also contained an expanded statement concerning the obligation of the Realtor® and Realtor-Associate to provide competent service and to confine his efforts to the areas in which he is competent.

Article 14 in the current Code of Ethics provides for the resolution of controversies among Realtors® and Realtor-Associates by arbitration rather than litigation. The implementation of this article depends on the laws of the various states, some of which prohibit agreements to arbitrate in advance of a controversy or will not enforce an arbitration award. These matters are resolved by appropriate regulations in the bylaws of individual boards and state associations.

Implementation of the Code of Ethics

As with the previous codes, member boards are required to enforce the terms within their own jurisdictions. To assist them in this effort, interpretations of the code have been prepared by the Professional Standards Committee and Standards of Practice setting forth the application of articles to specific situations have been adopted.

Because of the interest of the courts in protecting the economic benefits of association with a Realtor® board, enforcement of the Code of Ethics has required a careful adherence to rules of due process. Most boards have developed manuals of procedure which provide for adequate notice and hearing as well as review. Local boards are enjoined to follow these procedures carefully in order to assure the equitable resolution of complaints against the membership. In matters of considerable consequence, the boards in many states resort to declaratory judgments to ensure that the code has been enforced in a manner consistent with state laws.

Court reviews of the procedures involved in the enforcement of the code have reduced the ability of the real estate industry to police itself. Although the need to do this has been lessened somewhat by the universal adoption of license laws, license laws tend to establish bare minimum standards of conduct and even such standards can be enforced only where there is an easily proved technical violation or overwhelming evidence of misfeasance. Of far greater significance in maintaining the higher standards of the Code of Ethics is the response to peer pressure and the educational programs provided for the membership. The same desire to improve the image of the real estate profession and their position in it which motivated the founders of the National Association in

1908 persists among many of its members today. Improvement in quality of service and standards of conduct has been recognized as in the best self-interest of the membership generally.

Parallel Developments

While this development of ethical standards has proceeded within the National Association of Realtors®, somewhat parallel developments have occurred among other real estate groups. Groups affiliated with the National Association are, of course, bound by its Code of Ethics. Many of these groups have supplemented the code with articles that bear on their particular problems.

The American Institute of Real Estate Appraisers, in particular, has set forth detailed requirements with regard to competence, experience, and work standards. It has made provision for the review of members' work by a special Appraisal Review Committee, which may refer issues to the Ethics Committee when a suspicion of advocacy or incompetence exists.

The Society of Real Estate Appraisers has developed a somewhat similar system of review procedures. Following these leads, most of the other specialty real estate associations have adopted codes of ethics which cover to some degree matters which are included in the more detailed and extensive code of the National Association of Realtors®.

Throughout almost a century of organized real estate activity, the primary motivating force behind the regulation of the real estate industry has been the industry itself. The promulgation of and adherence to a higher standard of conduct than that generally found in the real estate industry has been a crucial function of the National Association of Realtors®. The association has been in the forefront of efforts to enact ever higher licensing standards. Although the distinction between voluntary and compulsory regulation has become blurred in many respects, in many other respects the boards are urging and in some cases insisting that their members adhere to ever higher standards.

WARRANTIES ON RESALE HOUSING

Background

Since the early 1970s, there has been a steadily increasing availability of protection against the cost of mechanical repairs (and sometimes structural repairs) that may be required after the purchase of used homes. Such protection has evolved into two basic forms which differ in their legal characterization (warranty versus insurance) but have the same effects in application. Basically, certain real estate brokers and real estate franchise organizations (such as Century 21), the National Association of Realtors® (NAR), and various insurance companies have all begun to promote and/or provide contracts which undertake either to pay for the cost of repairing a resale home or to provide the repairs per se.

Such contracts are commonly referred to as "home warranties." However, that title is technically impermissible according to the Magnuson-Moss Federal Warranty Act, which distinguishes between warranty and service contracts. Technically, these "home warranties" are service contracts and not warranties.

Due to the embryonic status of the home warranty industry and the multiple approaches currently being taken by the companies in the field, it is impossible to generalize concerning the industry except at the most basic levels. In addition, state licensing does not yet exist, so that, depending upon which state is involved, a "home warranty" company may be regulated by the contractor's licensing bureau, the state insurance department, the real estate commission, or no special authority whatsoever. The availability and legality of a home warranty or insurance contract must therefore be evaluated on an individual basis.

The home warranty industry developed from a related new industry, the home inspection industry. In the late 1960s, a number of firms were created which specialized in inspecting older housing for potential purchasers. Some of these firms began to offer to repair any undisclosed defect that had been omitted from the inspection report. This, in turn, led to the development of an insured home inspection/warranty program by the NAR in 1974–75.

The NAR program, which involves the preinspection of a property, is available on a very limited scale through real estate brokers in most states. After the preinspection a service contract is obtainable on acceptable structural and mechanical components. In general, this program has been offered by insurance organizations. It is the only program available which provides coverage against structural defects. If a structural warranty is desired, the local Board of Realtors® should be contacted to find out what company, if any, in a particular area is offering it.

At the same time that the NAR began to promote its inspection/warranty program, several private companies began to market service contracts on mechanical systems without inspection. These programs have been much more successful than the NAR program. The contract is usually purchased by the seller of a home when the property is listed for sale, and it is given to the buyer upon settlement. However, home buyers can also purchase a service contract directly. It is this type of noninspection operation which is now commonly referred to as the "home warranty industry." In 1979 about 300,000 such contracts are expected to be sold in the United States, and the number of homes being marketed with "Warranties" appears to be doubling every six months. At present, most of the homes that are being sold under such contracts are in California. However, the contracts are being offered in all 50 states.

Available Coverage

As mentioned, in addition to the companies offering noninspection service contracts, certain companies offer inspection/warranties according to the guidelines set forth by the NAR. Generally, both types of contracts provide coverage for a house buyer against the cost of repairing specified mechanical parts during the first year of ownership; both types are priced between $180 and $300, depending upon coverage; and both types are subject to a deductible of between $20 and $100. The typical noninspection contract provides coverage against failure in the central heating system, the cooling system, the plumbing system, the electrical system, and in some cases built-in appliances. Under an inspection warranty, if the house passes inspection, the roof, walls, ceilings, and floors are covered as well.

Since inspection/warranty programs are generally unavailable, the balance of this discussion is confined to noninspection warranty contracts. The availability of inspection programs can be determined by looking up "Building Inspection" in the Yellow Pages.

Under noninspection programs, the buyer of a home is typically provided with a contract which entitles him to repairs of defective mechanical items that are discovered within one year after settlement for a service call fee of between $20 and $100 per call. (In some cases, the contracts can be renewed from year to year.)

If the buyer of the home discovers a defective component he calls the service company, which usually sends a repairer out to fix the defect. The company then pays the repairer directly. In some instances, however, the homeowner can utilize a contractor of his choice and seek reimbursement from the warranty company.

Legal Restrictions on Home Warranties

A number of states, such as Florida, California, Arizona, Washington, Wisconsin, and New York, have examined the home warranty industry in order to determine whether the type of service it provides falls within the province of insurance. In most cases, the state insurance departments have taken the position that the service does constitute insurance, although a few, such as the Ohio Insurance Department, have demarcated the inspection warranty programs from the noninspection programs, holding that the former do not constitute insurance, whereas the latter do. In any event, most of the companies providing noninspection warranty contracts are not licensed insurance companies, and the question of whether they must qualify as insurance underwriters is as yet unresolved. Home warranty contracts may be contracts of insurance in some states, contracts of warranty in other states, and general service agreements in still other states. However, the prevailing trend is to treat them as insurance contracts.

At present, only a few states, such as Florida and California, have specific statutes dealing with the regulation of the home warranty industry, and the Florida and California statutes place the industry under the jurisdiction of the insurance department. Under these circumstances, the prospective purchaser of a home warranty contract is cautioned to thoroughly examine the company, its assets, and its business history in order to be sure that the company is capable of meeting its service obligations. Several small home warranty companies have gone bankrupt in recent years, leaving their contract holders without recourse.

The Department of Housing and Urban Development, on order of the U.S. Congress, conducted a survey and study of the home warranty industry in 1977. The results can be obtained from the department. Basically, the study indicates that the industry is too new to warrant federal regulation. In addition, the Federal Trade Commission has studied the industry to determine whether or not its service contracts must comply with the warranty contract provisions of the Magnuson-Moss Act. The FTC concluded that compliance was not necessary because these were service contracts, not warranties.

In addition to express warranties or service agreements, an implied warranty of habitability may be available with a home. Beginning in the late 1960s, the courts in various states have begun to recognize a doctrine called the "implied warranty of habitability." This implied warranty is similar to the implied warranty of fitness for a particular purpose that is recognized under the Uniform Commercial Code. The implied warranty has generally been found to apply between the builder of a home and its first buyer. Each state's decisions must be consulted to determine the potential applicability of this implied warranty because the doctrine is new and not universally recognized. For instance, recent legislation in New Jersey clearly recognizes the doctrine and even appears to create an implied warranty between the seller of a used home and the buyer. However, in other states, such as Georgia, even the builder of a new home is apparently not subject to an implied warranty.

HOME BUILDER WARRANTIES

In 1974 the housing industry decided to police itself, offering the consumer a protection plan. It had recognized the growing strength of the consumer movement and the increasingly insistent agitation for federal controls of the industry. Turning its gaze inward under the visionary leadership of then President George Martin, the National Association of Home Builders brought the Home Owners Warranty (HOW) Corporation into being, the nation's first ten-year buyer protection plan.

HOW was patterned on the British system of home warranties, which effectively provide protection for 99 percent of new home construction. Savings and loan associations, which finance virtually all British housing, refuse to finance new homes unless the builder offers a warranty backed by the National House Building Council, which is England's version of NAHB.

The American HOW program is a voluntary one, based on the establishment of regional and/or statewide councils which are licensed by the national headquarters and are responsible for screening each builder-applicant for his technical competence, financial stability, and integrity in dealing with customers and for administering the program and the dispute-settlement mechanisms.

The program fulfilled a real need, and it has grown rapidly.

The Ten-Year Warranty/Insurance Program

This HOW policy cannot be bought by the consumer, as it is "built into" the house. It is divided into three segments:

1. First year: The warranty covers all major structural defects, all systems, and faulty workmanship as outlined in the HOW standards of construction.
2. Second year: The warranty covers all major structural defects and the performance of the electrical, plumbing, and heating/air conditioning systems.
3. Third through tenth years: The home is insured against all major structural defects by INA Underwriters Insurance Co.

The builder's warranty is insured by HOW's national insurance carrier during the first two years. If the builder should be unable to perform for any reason, the home is brought up to standard under the carrier's agreement with HOW.

The HOW policy is transferable. It is written on the home itself, and it therefore transfers to each subsequent buyer during the ten-year period. This is an enormous selling tool, as the buyer can feel secure in knowing that the house will be protected.

Dispute Settlement by Conciliation-Arbitration

The conciliation-arbitration mechanism provided by HOW is a significant step forward in the housing industry. Most problems are resolved by the builder and the buyer. However, problems of personality and understanding always arise. Prior to the advent of HOW, when this happened, neither the buyer nor the builder had recourse short of the courts. Since the time and the expense of litigation is so great, this meant that both parties were often rendered helpless. The ceiling on the amounts that small claims courts allow are too often below the desired figure.

HOW has been pioneering the third-party informal dispute-settlement procedure with extraordinary success through its conciliation and arbitration procedures. In conciliation, the disputant notifies the local HOW council of the complaint. The council then brings the buyer and the builder together to discuss their problems in the presence of a third, impartial party. In 79 percent of the conciliation cases handled so far, agreement has been reached at this stage. The general understanding and goodwill between the consumer and the builder are improved by this procedure too, a consideration all of us should be conscious of.

If no agreement is reached, then the American Arbitration Association is called in. The arbitrator's decision is binding on the builder, although the buyer may reject it and proceed with litigation.

On the rare occasions in which the buyer has bypassed these steps and gone directly into court, the judge has thrown the case out and referred the litigant back to the available HOW procedures.

HOW National Construction Standards

HOW builders must enroll each home they build and must pledge that it will be built according to the HOW standards. Where the local building codes are of sufficient quality, these prevail. However, HOW reserves the right to inspect construction in progress. A builder who fails to meet the required standards is dismissed from the program. Builders pay $2 per $1,000 of the selling cost of the home for the HOW coverage as a one-time premium.

Spelling out quality standards of performance has proved advantageous for both the builder and the buyer, since this clears up any questions in the builder's mind and explains to the buyer just what may be expected. In addition, the procedure serves as an educational tool for buyers who have little or no understanding of the fundamentals of home building.

HOW coverage is available on single-family housing, condominiums, and town houses.

The *Approved Standards* booklet is attached to each warranty agreement. These standards consist of two parts:

1. Standards regulating the structural, mechanical-plumbing, and electrical systems which apply during the applicable initial warranty period.
2. Quality standards which establish minimum performance standards relating to specific deficiencies which apply during the applicable initial warranty period.

The codes under which HOW builders work are those contained in the building code, the mechanical-plumbing code, and the electrical code regulating construction in the given area. Inspection by the governmental jurisdiction will provide evidence of compliance.

Where no codes exist or where the existing codes are not completely acceptable, one of the following will apply:

1. The Minimum Property Standards of the U.S. Department of Housing and Urban Development with inspection by HUD, VA, or FmHA personnel.
2. A combination of the following model codes to cover building, mechanical-plumbing, and electrical work.

Building Codes

Boca Basic Building Code
Building Official and Code Administrators International, Inc.
National Building Code
American Insurance Association
Southern Standard Building Code
Southern Building Code Congress
Uniform Building Code
International Conference of Building Officials
One and Two Family Dwelling Code
    under the National Recognized Model Codes

Mechanical Codes

Uniform Building Code, vol. 2: *Mechanical*
International Conference of Building Officials

Boca Basic Mechanical Code
Building Official and Code Administrators International, Inc.

Southern Standard Mechanical Code
Southern Building Code Congress

Plumbing Codes

Southern Standard Plumbing Code
Southern Building Code Congress

Uniform Plumbing Code
International Association of Plumbing and Mechanical Officials

Boca Plumbing Code
Building Official and Code Administration International, Inc.

Electrical Codes

Electrical Code for One and Two Family Dwellings
National Fire Protection Association

National Electrical Code
National Fire Protection Association

The Relationship between HOW and the Federal Government

HOW has worked closely with federal housing agencies and has been gratified to have its standards recognized by several.

In order to make Veterans Administration financing more readily available, HOW homes at the trim stage or beyond are eligible for financing although no conditional CRV was issued. This has proved an enormous boon to the veteran purchaser, who is thus given a much broader opportunity to find a suitable home, and it has been a time and money saver for the builder.

The Federal Housing Administration has made a similar move in waiving its first and intermediate inspections of HOW-built homes. Normal HOW-approved inspections suffice.

The Federal Trade Commission has given HOW a special exemption under the Magnuson-Moss Act, permitting the use of industry experts during a 20-day conciliation period for the settlement of buyer-builder disputes without rendering a binding decision. HOW is the only warrantor in the country that is given this exemption.

MARKETING PROPERTY THROUGH AN AGENT

Howard L. Chertkof

*H*OWARD L. CHERTKOF, SIR, *Howard L. Chertkof & Company, Real Estate Broker and Developer, Baltimore, Maryland.*
Specializes in commercial and industrial real estate. His experience encompasses all phases of real estate brokerage, management, and development. He has negotiated pipeline rights-of-way, managed railroad properties, and leased land for many unusual purposes. His most recent development project is Port Capital Center, an office and industrial park in the Baltimore-Washington corridor. Instructor for the Society of Industrial Realtors® at various cities across the country.

In recent years, real estate sales have been increasing substantially. As the volume of sales has increased, seller's choice as to the use of professional assistance has grown markedly. Nevertheless, the great majority of homes and nonresidential properties in the United States are sold through brokers. The reasons are many, and they vary with the type of property that is sold. Insights into those reasons are provided in this chapter as part of a discussion of how the real estate industry performs its role of bringing buyers and sellers together and getting sales consummated.

To arrive at those reasons we might begin by viewing the process of creating a sale from the buyer's point of view. Most participants view the real estate buying process as one of selection. Actually, however, it is a process of rejection. The procedure consists of applying a set of standards or criteria to a total population of properties—houses, for example—and thus gradually whittling down the total population to a manageable number of candidate properties which are then inspected.

This whittling process is difficult to accomplish without the help of a broker. It requires professional guidance to suggest what the buyer should look for and what the buyer can and cannot afford. In addition, the agent must perform a function known as qualifying the buyer. This consists of determining the earning capabilities and projecting the income potential of the husband and wife, ascertaining how much money they have readily available for their equity contribution, and thus arriving at the mortgage funds that will be required. Armed with this information, the agent can assess what price range of housing is within the buyer's reach and can anticipate what type of financing (VA, FHA, or conventional) will best suit the buyer's wants and needs. It would be unfair to show buyers houses priced upward of $100,000 if they can only afford houses in the $50,000 to $60,000 range, and it would be equally unfair to waste the time of sellers by showing their homes to prospects who obviously lack the means to buy them.

The performance of the functions discussed above give a listed property better exposure to qualified buyers than is obtained by an unlisted property, and usually enables a well-trained agent to produce a better offer to buy in a shorter period of time than would be obtainable by the property owner without his assistance.

This chapter will not attempt to discuss the techniques of selling or leasing real properties. It is intended to give an overview of the functions performed by the brokerage firm and to describe the responsibilities of the agent. The techniques of selling and leasing are discussed in detail in the chapters that follow.

The most common real estate transaction, by far, is buying or selling a house for family residence. The broker plays a very necessary role in this situation, particularly in large urban areas where the number of possible choices is so great. In the Washington, D.C., metropolitan area, for example, the number of homes offered for sale or lease in the typical Sunday classified section of the *Washington Post* is between 15,000 and 16,000. The process of reviewing all these possibilities is mind-boggling. No wonder that the prospective buyer soon wearies and seeks the professional guidance of a broker. This holds true particularly if the buyer is a newcomer to an area and is completely unfamiliar with the local housing market.

The buyer is further motivated to seek the guidance of an agent because he feels that the service is furnished without cost to him. The seller pays the broker's commission, and the fact that this is done with the buyer's money is usually overlooked. The buyer reasons that he will pay a fair market price for the house he buys, whether or not a brokerage fee is involved.

It should also be noted that the purchase of a house is an emotional experience. The purchase often constitutes the culmination of a buyer's dream, the fruition of a long search. The experienced agent knows how to learn what the buyer is seeking and to help the buyer in his search. The agent is a skillful guide who finds the one right house for the buyer.

When the one right house is finally found and it becomes necessary to prepare a contract of sale, the agent will prove knowledgeable as to local usage and general contract provisions. He will know who pays the transfer tax, whether the house should be inspected for termites, and that a contingency clause should be included for the buyer's protection. He advises not as a legal counselor but as a practical professional who knows in general what is and is not done in his locality.

Brokerage Functions

Residential. He must list the property that is for sale or rent. In essence, the broker who accepts a listing contract commits himself to seek a buyer. He must advertise at his cost, submit the listing to other brokers, and expend substantial amounts of his time and energy in showing the property. When a buyer is found, he must negotiate the sale and obtain the best price and terms possible. The listing agent must apprise the seller of what is expected of him; of what price the seller can achieve; of what points the seller may have to pay if a federally guaranteed mortgage is sought. The listing agent should advise the seller to put his house in good repair prior to offering and should inform the seller that he will have to allow his life to be interrupted so that the house can be shown. The listing agent should assemble information in anticipation of questions that may be posed by prospective buyers, for example, information on schools, transportation, houses of worship, employment centers, job opportunities, recreational facilities, and access to interstate highways.

The agent must know what types and terms of financing are available, and usually maintains rapport with local thrift institutions, banks, insurance companies, and mortgage brokerage firms. He knows who is eligible to get a VA or an FHA mortgage, and he can provide assistance in making the proper applications.

Some sale contracts contain contingencies that must be satisfied by a stated time for the sale to close. The agent must see that all of the stipulated milestones are reached in a timely manner. Thus, if the buyer has 30 days to obtain a suitable mortgage, the agent must see to it that the buyer applies for a mortgage and that the lending institution processes the application in time. If inspections are required, the agent must see that they are made. The agent may also help in arranging for a title search and the preparation of a deed.

The other side of the coin is for the agent to perform the role of procuring broker—to work with and represent the buyer.

As the procuring broker, the agent must qualify the buyer—to determine what the buyer needs, what the buyer wants, and what the buyer can afford. After interviewing the buyer in depth, the agent may seek the services of the multiple listing bureau or some other source for the purpose of narrowing down the selection process. Eventually, the buyers are shown houses which seem to meet their needs, their desires, and their circumstances. Just as the listing broker advises the seller on contract terms, so the procuring broker advises the buyer. The procuring broker is present at the closing to make sure that there are no slipups and that a smooth transfer is accomplished. He does all of this because he is a trained professional and because he knows that his future sales will be based on the reputation that he builds in the community he serves.

Nonresidential. The functions of the nonresidential broker resemble the residential broker's functions in many respects. However, there are differences which should be noted. Whereas residential properties (i.e., houses) are traded in a largely local market, commercial, industrial, and income-producing properties tend to be traded in a national market. For example, if an automobile assembly factory in the Maryland area were vacated, an industrial broker would offer the facility to automobile manufacturers all over the country and, for that matter, all over the world. A group with special justifications in the industrial field is the Society of Industrial Realtors®, a division of the National Association of Realtors®. This group, through an information exchange network, expedites the marketing of industrial properties and can usually find the right buyers for highly specialized commodities.

Income-producing property is bought for cash flow and for equity growth via debt reduction and inflationary appreciation, as well as the tax benefits from depreciation and long term capital gains rates. A knowledgeable agent knows what benefits investors expect, and can advise his sellers how to price and market their properties accordingly.

Commercial and industrial brokers must be able to assemble thorough, concise, well-documented information, including such things as maps, aerial photographs, plats, surveys, and feasibility studies, if they are to procure a buyer. In one situation, a broker listed a parcel of land whose highest and best use seemed to be as a site for a motel. The site enjoyed a large frontage at a cloverleaf on a major interstate highway. At the broker's suggestion a motel feasibility study and a detailed topographic survey were undertaken. The study, conducted by a leading firm of motel market analysts, strongly recommended that a motel be erected at the site. Armed with the study, the broker was able to attract the attention of several national motel chains and eventually to effect a lucrative sale.

The Role of the Agent. When the subject of marketing real estate through a broker is mentioned, the thought usually conjured up is that of an agent selling a house and earning a fee, as either a listing or a procuring broker. An equally important area that tends to be overlooked is the leasing of space.

The successful negotiation of a lease requires the skills and acumen of a seasoned professional. Each situation must be hand-tailored to the needs and comforts of the two parties to the lease—the landlord (lessor) and the tenant (lessee). Each situation involves unique goals and unique personalities. Impasses are frequently encountered, and when this happens it is the agent's job to get the negotiations moving again.

We are speaking now of leasing mercantile buildings (i.e., factories, stores, warehouses, and offices), not apartments. In general, there are three categories of leases: leases of unimproved land, leases of a structure that is to be built, and leases of a structure that is to be remodeled. (Seldom are existing structures leased as is.)

Let us look at the leasing of an existing structure first. The listing broker must first inspect the property and develop a detailed analysis of its physical characteristics, together with information as to taxes, the availability of rail and truck service, utilities, and zoning. He must then determine the highest and best use for the property and decide what categories of business are most likely to be candidates for the premises. (In the case of unimproved land, he must also ascertain the highest and best use and he should catalog the land's physical characteristics for future reference. Just the land may be leased, or the land may be used as a host site for a structure that is to be built to suit.) The next step is to advertise and show the property. When a suitable tenant has been found, the negotiation phase begins.

Let us say that the prospect wants a structure built to suit. His goals will be to get the longest term lease at the lowest possible rent, without any increases in rent during his term, and to negotiate sufficient flexibility into the lease so that he can vacate the premises at specific times if they no longer serve his purposes. On the other hand, the lessor's goals are to obtain maximum net rental, ensure stability of income, increase the income stream over time, and safeguard the property against abuse or damage. In a multitenant building, the lessor will want to make sure that all of the occupants are compatible.

In addition to satisfying the objectives of each party, the lease must provide for contingencies. For example, what happens in the event of a fire? What happens if the property is condemned under eminent domain? Who maintains the roof and parking lots? And who maintains the interior?

It should also be noted that because of income tax constraints the U.S. government is, to all intents and purposes, an adverse party to all other parties to a lease (or, for that matter, any other business negotiation). Often, for example, an owner of real property will lease a property even though he would prefer to sell it because the tax consequences of leasing may be far less severe than the tax consequences of selling.

A lease, simply put, can be considered to consist of a negotiated portion and a language portion. The negotiated portion is the basic agreement whereby the principals agree on the lease term and on the amount of rent to be paid. The language portion is usually negotiated by attorneys, and at this point matters can really get sticky. To further complicate the situation, it is not unusual for each party to have a tax adviser who suggests the most advantageous format for minimizing his client's income taxes. (For additional information on lease arrangements, see Chapters 7 and 32.)

In this scenario, the broker is cast in the role of referee, and he must prod and cajole all of the parties in order to reach the common goal of a completed lease. When an impasse is reached, the broker should be able to come up with a fresh suggestion that will resolve it. In order to accomplish this end, the broker must have a practical knowledge of income taxes, real estate law, and basic business, and most important, he must understand his client's goals and needs.

The Organization of an Independent Agency

The simplest type of brokerage firm is the single office, staffed by a licensed broker and one or more salespeople, or by agents under the broker's direction. The broker is the responsible party with respect to the client, and in most states he has a fiduciary responsibility to the seller-client. In addition to performing the functions enumerated earlier, the broker often provides contract forms that are used in preparing the written memorandum of sale between the parties and holds earnest money or escrow deposits in safekeeping.

The Multiple-Office Operation. A more complicated type of brokerage operation is the specialized multiple office operation. Typically, the firm specializes in the sale of residential properties, and it establishes more than one office simply because the geographic area being served is too large to be handled by one office. Multiple offices are especially common in large urban areas. In essence, they break up such areas for the purpose of facilitating buyer selection.

The Diversified Office. A third type of brokerage operation is the diversified office, either single or multiple. Such an office provides services that are adjuncts to residential, such as providing casualty insurance or performing the mortgage brokerage function. In addition, a diversified office may have commercial, industrial, and investment departments. The marketplace for such departments is entirely different from the marketplace for the residential department; the clientele is different; even the hours of operation are different. For example, whereas Sunday is the most important day in residential sales, commercial and industrial selling is done during the normal workweek.

The Franchised Office. In recent years, there has emerged a new form of brokerage office organization known as the franchised office. Under a franchise arrangement, the local broker enters into an agreement with a national company, the franchisor, and in return for paying an initial and continuing fee is given the privilege of using a nationally known name in a specified area. Thus the local broker benefits from national advertising which he could not otherwise afford; acquires access to training programs, sales aids, and business forms that are prepared and supplied by the franchisor; and obtains clients that other francisees throughout the country refer to him. These are the advantages of being part of a franchise operation. The disadvantages are that the broker must pay for all the services he receives from the franchisor and, thus, his operating costs are higher, and in some cases his profits diminished. More important, his identity is subordinated to that of the franchisor. Many brokers feel that their relationship with the public has evolved through years of social contact and community service, and they set a high value on their own good name. Such brokers may prefer not to be a part of a large organization—a small cog in a big wheel.

Staff. The single office and the multiple office have a similar staff makeup. First, there is the broker. A license from the state or some other licensing authority enables him to accept a fee for introducing a buyer to a seller and consummating a sale. The broker is officially responsible for the acts of his agents and employees, and in the event of fraud his license could be suspended or revoked.

The agents, or salespersons, are the direct contact of the brokerage firm with the buying and selling public. In most instances, the public has contact only with the agent and judges the performance of the brokerage firm and the brokerage industry from that contact.

A large office will also have a sales manager. His function is to supervise the agents and other office personnel. Secretaries, bookkeepers, and file clerks work in support of the agents, and there may be specialists who handle insurance or finance correspondence.

Public Ownership

In addition to the franchise, a form of national brokerage organization that is prominent in the United States is the publicly held corporation. These companies have sufficient resources to penetrate any market they decide to enter. Their modus operandi is to preselect a major urban areas, such as Atlanta, Chicago, or Washington, D.C., to set up an office, and to hire a large number of agents on a salaried basis until the office starts to produce. The cost of financing an operation of this size until it turns a profit may run into millions of dollars. To date, however, the smaller firms have been able to compete against the publicly held brokerage corporations, primarily because of the personal services rendered by the smaller firms and the reputation of these firms in the communities they serve.

Broker Associations

Broker associations communicate and cooperate in many ways. These associations are designed to better serve the public. In recent years, the U.S. Justice Department has kept a watchful eye on them to make sure that their purpose is not to fix prices but in fact to improve service to the public.

The National Association of Realtors® (NAR) is, by far, the largest brokers' organization in this country. The overriding goal of NAR is to promote excellence in the profession of real estate brokerage. The association is broken up into many subgroups, some operating almost autonomously. These include the Farm and Land Institute, the Society of Industrial Realtors®, and groups dealing with property management, property appraisal, and myriad related real estate functions. These groups seek to achieve excellence through continuous education, to maintain good public relations, and to stay well informed about new legislative developments affecting the real estate marketplace. Courses of study are offered regularly. The completion of educational requirements, coupled with a demonstration of skill and experience in a particular speciality, leads to the award of a formal designation. These designations guide clients in their choice of the proper professional for the job at hand. For example, a holder of the designation MAI (Member Appraisal Institute) is usually recognized by lending institutions as a person who has achieved excellence in appraising. Similarly, the CPM (Certified Property Manager) is recognized as well qualified to handle the management of income-producing property, and the SIR (Society of Industrial Realtors®) is recognized as a specialist in factory and warehouse locations. (See appendix for further information on these and other associations.)

Training is a constant function of the brokerage industry. There are always new people who take an interest in the real estate profession, and these people must be taught. In addition to having his agents obtain the formalized education that each state may require, the broker is interested in seeing that those agents acquire certain skills and techniques of listing and selling properties. There are companies which produce audiovisual and other training aids for this purpose. The broker buys or rents these aids and uses with new recruits.

Communication among brokers throughout the country is often a practical necessity. For example, a California executive who is being relocated to Texas may ask his California broker not only to sell his house but also to guide him choosing a broker who will help to find a home at his new location. There is a national network of broker groups which has been established to handle such situations. Typically, the originating broker will contact the service group and the service group will put him in touch with a cooperating broker in the new state. In a situation of this sort, the originating broker receives a percentage of the commission earned by the broker at the new location.

Multiple Listing Services

No discussion of marketing property through a broker would be complete without a discussion of the multiple listing service (MLS). A multiple listing service can be found in most urban areas. The MLS serves as a clearinghouse through which brokers can exchange listings. It enables each member firm to acquire knowledge about the listings of every other member firm.

For example, the Central Maryland MLS serves 475 member firms in a metropolitan area covering the city of Balitmore, Balitmore County, and the three adjoining counties of Carroll, Harford, and Howard. This MLS covers territory under the jurisdictions of four separate real estate boards. It handles more than 40,000 listings and more than $1 billion in sales per year.

Each member firm pays a quarterly flat rate membership fee and an additional fee for each lising that it sends to the MLS for dissemination to the other member firms. The MLS reproduces the listing it receives and uses its own fleet of vehicles to deliver the listings to each office on a daily basis.

In addition, the MLS categorizes listing information in its central computer by neighborhood, price, and size. Member firms can purchase or rent a computer terminal linked by telephone to the central computer, and use the terminal to extract information from the central computer. For example, an agent at a member office can ask what three-bedroom houses under $80,000 are available in Columbia, Maryland, and instantly receive a printout of candidates. Each listing has a reference number, and for more detailed information the agent can pull the listing form (Exhibit 1) from the office file. The MLS also extracts from the computer monthly sales data reports showing pertinent information of interest to the brokerage community, including the monthly sales volume for houses by neighborhood, by price category, and by size—two-bedroom, three-bedroom, and so on (see Exhibit 2).

EXHIBIT 1

| DATE OF LISTING CONTRACT _____ | EXPIRATION DATE _____ |
| M / D / Y | M / D / Y |

For M.L.S. Use Only	Broker No.	Zip Code	Neighborhood	Design	List Price	Ground Rent

No. Floors	No. Baths	Dining Room	Base-ment	Fire-place	Garage	Public? Water	Sdw.	Bed-rooms	Age	Taxes	K Box		Lot Size	Water Sit.	Features

RESIDENTIAL - SALE ONLY PUBLISHED BY THE CENTRAL MARYLAND MULTIPLE LISTING SERVICE, INC.   FORM LD 1
THIS DESCRIPTIVE INFORMATION, THOUGH BELIEVED ACCURATE, IS NOT GUARANTEED.

ADDRESS _____ LIST NO. _____ ZIP _____ PRICE $ _____
NEIGHBORHOOD _____ COUNTY _____ LOT SIZE _____ GR. RT. _____
IMPROVEMENT _____ CONSTRUCT _____ CONDITION _____ WHEN RED. _____
DIRECTIONS _____
                                                                    Age _____
                                                                    Key Box

BASEMENT	1ST FLOOR	2ND FLOOR	EQUIPMENT	YES	NO	SITUATIONS
NONE _____	ENT. HALL _____	BEDROOMS _____	CENTRAL AIR			POSSESSION _____
CRAWL SPACE _____	HALF BATH _____		DISHWASHER			GAS -PUB: _____ PRV: __
HALF _____	BATH _____		GARBAGE DIS.			WATER -PUB: _____ PRV: __
FULL _____	LIV. RM _____		SHADES			SEWER -PUB: _____ PRV: __
PANELED _____	DIN. RM. _____		STORM DR.			FIREPLACE -YES _____ NO: __
HALF BATH _____	KITCHEN _____	BATHS _____	STORM WIN.			GARAGE -YES _____ NO: __
FULL BATH _____	FAMILY RM. _____		SCREENS			CARPORT -YES _____ NO: __
BEDROOMS _____	BEDROOMS _____	3RD FLOOR	T.V. ANT.			HEAT TYPE _____
CLUBROOM _____		BEDROOMS _____	STOVE			HEAT COST $ _____
LAUNDRY _____			CURTAIN RODS			TAXES $ _____
		BATHS				MET. DIST. $ _____
EXTRAS INCLUDED _____						MAINT. FEE $ _____

EXCLUDED FROM SALE _____
MORTGAGEE _____ INS. AGENT _____ TITLE LIBER _____ FOLIO _____
LOAN TYPE _____ BALANCE _____ PAYMENT _____ INTEREST _____ YRS. TO GO _____
REMARKS _____ OCCUPIED BY _____

                                                                    POST SIGN
                                                                    FOR M.L.S. USE ONLY
LA. _____ PHONE _____ RATE _____
REALTOR _____ NO. _____ PHONE _____ LR __ SR __ DATE: _____

THIS PROPERTY IS OFFERED WITHOUT REGARD TO RACE, COLOR, CREED, SEX OR NATIONAL ORIGIN

REALTOR® MLS MULTIPLE LISTING SERVICE

CENTRAL MARYLAND
MULTIPLE LISTING SERVICE, Inc.
1501 MOUNT ROYAL AVENUE / BALTIMORE, MARYLAND 21217
(301)462-5100

C BENNETT ROSE
EXECUTIVE SECRETARY

Your property has been multiple listed as shown above. All members of the service have been sent a copy of this information. All communications regarding your contract should be with your Realtor. Please be sure to read "How to make your house more saleable" enclosed herewith.

The MLS computer is also programmed to perform a large variety of other functions. For example, a prime tool for selling income-producing property is the income investment analysis. This is a projection showing the gross income less vacancy, operating costs, debt service, and income taxes, and the net spendable income in dollars and as a percentage of investment. The computer instantly computes this from a predesigned program, and can make printed projections for years 1 through 20, or longer if need be (see Exhibit 3). It can also take the

EXHIBIT 2

CENTRAL MARYLAND MULTIPLE LISTING SERVICE
SALES DATA REPORT OF HOMES SOLD
BY PRICE RANGE AND NUMBER OF BEDROOMS

PRICE RANGE	THIS YEAR MAY 1978					LAST YEAR MAY 1977				THIS YEAR TO DATE 1-1-78 thru 5-31-78					LAST YEAR TO DATE 1-1-77 thru 5-31-77			
	2BR	3BR	4BR	TOTAL	%+or-	2BR	3BR	4BR	TOTAL	2BR	3BR	4BR	TOTAL	%+or-	2BR	3BR	4BR	TOTAL
up to 9,999	17	22	7	46	+24	10	23	4	37	53	97	37	187	-11	59	117	33	209
10,000 to 12,499	13	11	4	28	+40	4	13	3	20	27	48	14	89	-28	34	71	19	124
12,500 to 14,999	7	8	4	19	-35	11	16	2	29	20	56	27	103	-36	56	87	17	160
15,000 to 17,499	6	17	10	33	+03	10	18	4	32	35	77	32	144	-30	59	119	29	207
17,500 to 19,999	10	24	10	44	+05	8	25	9	42	38	93	29	160	-57	111	217	45	373
20,000 to 22,499	8	23	4	35	-17	12	25	5	42	53	98	16	167	-55	78	256	37	371
22,500 to 24,999	14	15	8	37	-51	20	49	7	76	66	105	33	204	-55	96	310	42	448
25,000 to 29,999	61	93	19	173	-24	64	145	19	228	229	478	87	794	-26	191	750	132	1073
30,000 to 39,999	75	308	48	431	+01	69	284	73	426	316	1331	221	1868	+07	211	1199	330	1740
40,000 to 49,999	35	261	60	356	+05	14	259	66	339	142	1025	273	1440	+14	88	852	327	1267
50,000 to 59,999	20	199	71	290	+44	7	126	69	202	57	742	298	1097	+66	29	354	278	661
60,000 to 69,999	3	116	69	188	+30	2	80	63	145	17	415	293	725	+73	9	181	228	418
70,000 to 79,999	3	42	57	102	+42	-	21	51	72	10	164	242	416	+101	8	51	148	207
80,000 to 89,999	3	24	63	90	+50	2	13	45	60	7	89	197	293	+111	2	34	103	139
90,000 to 99,999	1	10	23	34	-06	-	6	30	36	5	26	110	141	-13	11	22	129	162
100,000 to 124,999	1	6	32	39	+39	-	5	23	28	5	33	130	168	+211	.	10	44	54
125,000 to 149,999	0	2	14	16	+60	-	2	8	10	1	10	55	66	+313	1	2	13	16
150,000 & over *	1	1	19	21	+91	2	-	9	11	7	5	51	63	+215	2	1	17	20
TOTAL	278	1182	522	1982	+08	235	1110	490	1835	1088	4892	2145	8125	+06	1045	4633	971	7649

NOTE - 2BR means 2 or less bedrooms - 4BR means 4 or more bedrooms

EXHIBIT 3

```
++ INCOME PROJECTION ++
```

						GROSS				
END	GROSS		OPER.	NET OPER	LOAN	SPEND.	INCOME		NET SPEND.	
YR	INCOME	-VACANCY-	COSTS=	INCOME-	PAYMENT=	INCOME-	TAX	= INCOME	RATE
1	150000	7500	50000	92500	76331	16169	4600-	20769	6.92
2	165000	8250	55000	101750	76331	25419	373	25046	8.35
3	181500	9075	60500	111925	76331	35594	5844	29750	9.92
4	199650	9983	66550	123117	76331	46786	11864	34922	11.64
5	219615	10981	73205	135429	76331	59098	18488	40610	13.54
6	241577	12079	80526	148972	76331	72641	25777	46864	15.62
7	265735	13287	88579	163869	76331	87538	33796	53742	17.91
8	292309	14615	97437	180257	76331	103926	42622	61304	20.43
9	321540	16077	107181	198282	76331	121951	52331	69620	23.21
10	353694	17685	117899	218110	76331	141779	63015	78764	26.25

```
++ TOTALS ++
   2390620  119532  796877 1474211   763310  710901  249510  461391

C-CONTINUE Y/N :        Y
D -ANY CHANGES : Y
E -ENTER FIELD : A
A -PRINT OPTION: B
D -ANY CHANGES : N
```

```
++ TAX DATA ++
```

END	NET OPER.	LOAN		TAXABLE	INCOME TAX	NET EQUITY	
YR	INCOME-	INTEREST-	DEPREC. =	INCOME +	DUE	+ INCOME	RATE
1	92,500	69,699	32,000	9,199-	4,600-	27,401	9.13
2	101,750	69,004	32,000	746	373	32,373	10.79
3	111,925	68,237	32,000	11,688	5,844	37,844	12.61
4	123,117	67,390	32,000	23,727	11,864	43,863	14.62
5	135,429	66,453	32,000	36,976	18,488	50,488	16.83
6	148,972	65,419	32,000	51,553	25,777	57,776	19.26
7	163,869	64,277	32,000	67,592	33,796	65,796	21.93
8	180,257	63,014	32,000	85,243	42,622	74,621	24.87
9	198,282	61,620	32,000	104,662	52,331	84,331	28.11
10	218,110	60,080	32,000	126,030	63,015	95,015	31.67

```
++ TOTALS ++
  1,474,211  655,193  320,000  499,018   249,510  569,508

C-CONTINUE Y/N :        Y
D -ANY CHANGES : Y
E -ENTER FIELD : A
A -PRINT OPTION: C
D -ANY CHANGES : N
```

```
++ MARKET DATA ++
```

END						TAX ON	CAP		I.R.R.	
	MARKET	LOAN		SALES	SALES RECAP.	GAINS	NET SALE	BEFORE	AFTER
YR	VALUE -	BAL. =	EQUITY -	COMM.-	COST -DEPREC.-	TAX =PROCEEDS+	TAX	TAX
1	1000000	693368	306632	60000	30000			216632	5.55-	5.15-
2	1000000	686041	313958	60000	30000			223958	10.55-	10.19-
3	1000000	677948	322052	60000	30000		1500	230552	14.65-	15.06-
4	1000000	669007	330993	60000	30000		9500	231493	17.80-	20.78-
5	1000000	659129	340870	60000	30000		17500	233370	19.67-	27.03-
6	1000000	648218	351782	60000	30000		25500	236282	19.86-	33.86-
7	1000000	636163	363836	60000	30000		33500	240336	18.20-	40.96-
8	1000000	622847	377153	60000	30000		41500	245263	14.97-	47.45-
9	1000000	608136	391863	60000	30000		49500	252363	10.87-	51.78-
10	1000000	591885	408114	60000	30000		57500	260614	13.78-	91.98-

```
C-CONTINUE Y/N :        N


 6-08-78
PROG.?
```

same information, and prepare a tax data study showing the effective rate of return after taxes. The computer is very versatile, and it can be adapted to any task.

The Organization of Brokerage Operations

A brokerage organization must perform many functions. The most basic function is the procuring of a listing. Listings are the broker's merchandise. Listings may be solicited with mailings of literature or phone calls, though these practices are frowned upon by some, and they are prohibited in many areas. The agent gets leads on listings principally through social contact. He may also get leads by being stationed at an open house. An open house is a listed property which may be inspected by all who are interested. While on duty at the open house, the agent may find persons who are willing to list their present house for sale in order to facilitate the purchase of a new home. In similar fashion, agents will take on the sale of newly constructed houses because of the possible stimulation of brokerage of the purchasers' former houses.

Not only must the agent find properties for sale, he must also find buyers. Prospecting is the term used for looking for possible buyers. This is accomplished in large measure through advertising. The most important form of advertising for the broker is the on-premises sign. This silent sentry produces a large response at a very low cost. Second in importance to the on-premises sign is the newspaper ad, particularly in the Sunday paper. However, whereas an inquiry generated by a sign pertains to a specific property, an inquiry generated by a newspaper ad tends to be less specific. Other forms of advertising may include direct mail (prohibited in some localities) and advertising in programs or magazines which promotes the broker rather than specific properties for sale. Radio, television, and billboards are also used, though to a lesser extent.

Licensure

Every state requires that agents and brokers trading in real property be licensed. Although the requirements vary from state to state, they are very similar in nature. Some states require residency as a requirement for licensure. Other states allow reciprocity. For example, in the metropolitan Washington, D.C., area, it is common for a broker or an agent to maintain three licenses, one for Maryland, one for the District of Columbia, and one for Virginia. However, a broker who trades in various states throughout the country may find that if he does not maintain a license in the state where the property being sold is situated, the seller may not be legally bound to pay the commission or it may not be legal for the broker to receive the commission even though the seller has agreed to pay it. In such a situation, the broker may be well advised to obtain a license even for a single sale or to work through a broker who maintains an active license in the given state.

The requirements for licensure usually include attendance at a college-level curriculum for about one year on a part-time basis. The course of study covers real estate law, fiduciary responsibility, financing, and how to hold a closing for transferred property. In many states, another requirement of licensure is the furnishing of a bond guaranteeing to the public that the broker will not act in a fraudulent manner and will keep earnest money deposits in a separate bank account not commingled with his business or private funds. In addition, a candidate for a broker's license must usually have held a license as an active agent for three to five years. The trend today in many states is to make continuing education on the part of the broker and the agent a prerequisite for license renewal. (For additional information on licensure, see Chapter 26.)

Relationships with Agents

The relationship between the agent and the broker can be handled in two different ways. Either the agent is an employee of the broker, or else the agent is treated as an independent contractor. The latter approach seems to be the more popular today. That approach is also handled in two different ways.

The more common method is for the agent to pay his personal business expenses, such as automobile, home phone, license fees, and club membership dues, and for disability and hospitalization insurance. Under this arrangement, the agent gets 50 percent of the commissions and fees he generates up to a certain amount and, usually, a larger portion of the commissions and fees over that amount. Example: After the agent generates a total of $40,000 in commissions (of which he receives 50 percent, or $20,000), he may receive 70 percent of all the additional commissions he generates. The rationale for this is that the $20,000 received by the broker is sufficient to cover the broker's overhead and expenses with respect to that agent, plus a reasonable profit. Beyond that sum, the portion that goes to the broker is largely profit, so that the broker can afford to adjust the split.

Under this method, the broker furnishes and pays for general office overhead and advertising, and receives a larger share of the commissions generated by the agent. The alternative method is for the agent to pay the broker a specified monthly sum that fully covers the agent's portion of the office overhead. Since the broker has no risk and no expense under this arrangement, he is entitled to only a small percentage of the commissions earned by the agent. The usual split is 90 percent for the agent and 10 percent for the broker. Again, the agent pays for all personal expenses, as well as contributing to the office overhead.

Where the agent is an employee of the broker, the broker pays for all overhead and may even pay certain personal expenses, such as fuel for the agent's automobile. Commissions earned are divided between the broker and the agent, either on a 50–50 basis or in some other fixed proportion. In this instance, the agent rarely gets more than a 50 percent share, no matter how productive he may be, because the broker is taking the entire financial risk.

Finally, the agent may be on salary, and in that case the broker usually pays all office and personal business expenses and keeps all the commissions earned. Under this arrangement, the agent is usually offered a bonus or some type of participation in profits as an inducement to produce more. This arrangement is characteristic of the large publicly owned real estate brokerage firms.

Selecting the Firm and the Agent

Once the potential client understands the value of marketing property through a broker, the question becomes how to select the right agent and broker when the need arises. It is entirely possible that social contact will be the decisive consideration. For example, a person who is ready to sell his house, may know that a friend will do a good job.

But let us assume that the prospective client is coming into a new city, has no recommendations, and wants to buy a house. In this instance, he should ask around and pick the brokerage firm with the best reputation. Size is not a criterion. He should also pick a broker who maintains an office in the area in which he is most interested in locating a house.

On the other hand, let us assume that the prospective client wishes to sell his house. Then in addition to reputation, he should consider the broker's track record for sales. How many houses has the broker sold in the seller's neighborhood lately? The seller should also select a broker who cooperates on listings with other brokers in the area. The seller should ask the agent what he will do to market the property. He should judge the agent on appearance, personality, and character, as the agent will be the person most directly responsible for selling the home.

Real estate is big business, and brokers play an important role in it. They provide a service to the community, and they are entitled to earn a fee or commission for that service. The following chapters will discuss in more detail how agents sell and lease various categories of properties.

SELLING THE RESALE HOUSE

Bruce T. Mulhearn

*B*RUCE T. MULHEARN, GRI, CRB, Bruce Mulhearn, Inc., Realtor
Bellflower, California.
*Master instructor for GRI in California and senior member
of NAR faculty. Chairman of CAR (California Board of Real-
tors®) and formerly chairman for education, CAR. Author of
the following CAR books:* In Search of Agreement; You Gotta
Work the Territory; Closing the Sale; *and* Creative Real Estate
Financing. *Coauthor,* Real Estate Office Management People
Function Systems.

Although the principal purpose of this chapter is to present the techniques of listing and selling the resale house, the chapter would be incomplete if it did not mention the qualities that are required for success
in real estate selling. The successful real estate salesperson is able to
set goals and to meet them, to begin his or her day at a regular time
and to work on a regular schedule. He has the courage to work steadily
and eagerly, regardless of success or failure. His confidence in himself
and his clients enables him to build trust and rapport. He is generous
in his appreciation and his praise. He maintains the highest ethical
standards in his transactions. He knows his community intimately, and
he is totally involved in his work. He regards his profession as a worthy
one, and he seeks to be worthy of it.

Sellers and Listings

Sources. "Listing is the name of the game." This adage summarizes
the basis of success in the real estate business. Because without an inventory there is nothing to sell. Listings are the inventory of the real estate
business. That inventory derives from contacts; the contacts come from
sources.

There are two kinds of listing sources: active and passive. Active listing sources accrue from prospecting, from attacking. Passive listing sources are referrals from past clients, friends, or relatives, or calls that come into the office, such as responses to ads and signs. Exhibit 1 enumerates listing sources.

Prospecting is essential in securing active sources. The For Sale by Owner, former sellers, and would-be sellers whose listings have expired require a search and close approach.

1. For Sale by Owner. This source, known as the "Fisbo," provides a rare advantage to an agent. The prospect wants to sell, but he doesn't want help. The agent must develop a technique for obtaining a hearing from the Fisbo.

First, the agent must overcome his fear of the Fisbo. Fear prevents sales. One Fisbo put a For Sale sign on his lawn. Not one agent called on the first day, but on the second day an agent came to the door. The owner said, "I don't know a broker in this area, so I put up the sign to see which one was aggressive enough to want to handle my house. You ready to write up the listing?"

Second, the agent must get an appointment to see the home. He may seek to obtain one by visiting the home or calling from the office. If the owner refuses, the agent might try to overcome the owner's objection by asking for permission to work on the property while the owner is selling it himself, by suggesting that the property might be worth more than comparable properties in the neighborhood, and by hinting that

EXHIBIT 1
Where to Look for Listings

Advertising	Divorce	Janitors
Affiliations	Door-to-door canvass	Joints
Announcements		Joke
Anybody	Effort	Judges
Appraisals	Enthusiasm	Junior league
Asking	Executors	Junior partners
Associations	Factories	
Attorneys	Financial institution	Key clubs
	Floor duty	Kids
Banks	Foreclosures	Knowledge
Barbershops	Former buyers	
Beauty Shops		Lawyers
Births	Gas stations	Leases
Brochures	Generosity	Letters
Brokers	Get-up-and-go	
Builders	Golf club	Mailman
Building and loan associ-	Gossip	Management
ation	Graduates	Marriages
	Grocer	Milkman
Center of influence	Ground	Ministers
Change of business		Motels
Church activities	Hospitals	
Civic activities	Hotel managers	Neglected property
Clubs	House-to-house canvass	Neighbors
Cops	Illness	Newspapers
Courtesy	Index	Notaries
Death notices	Influence	Old listings
Direct mail	Institutional advertising	Organizations

EXHIBIT 1 *(continued)*

Owner ads
Owner "for sale" signs
Owners of adjacent prop-
   erties
Parties
Partners
Phone calls
Pregnancy
Problems
Public sales
Quarrels
Quest

Questions
Quintuplets
Real estate board
Real estate–minded rela-
   tives
Rentals
Sales
Satisfied customers
School boards
Servicemen
Sincerity
Sitters

Telephone calls
Thankfulness
Transfers
Trustees
Union activities
United appeal
Universities
Urban renewal
Van lines
Veterans
Window Displays

Thirty Sources of Listings

Referrals: Satisfied clients.

Advertising: Classified, institutional, direct mail; For Sale and Sold signs.

For sale by owner: "I was wondering if you'd be offended if I looked at your home."

Choose and meet your new neighbor cards: Delivered in area of new listings; carry a Sold sign with you.

Public relations: Cards on anniversaries, birthdays, special holidays.

Be a neighborhood broker: Stick to a specific area "farm"; know it.

Canvassing on weekends: Stop and chat with people who are out watering lawns, etc.

Telephone: Stop, take a deep breath, and begin; use a criss-cross directory.

Newspaper notices: Divorces, births, deaths, promotions, transfers.

Civic organizations/service clubs: Gain recognition in community.

Be a specialist: Single-family homes, income property.

Open houses: All lookers are prospective sellers.

Home trade-ins—Literature and promotions: Our Equity Purchase department.

Leads from business people: Your barber, waitress, doctor, banker.

Leads from friends/relatives: Keep passing out cards.

Publicity: News releases to local papers, church papers, about you and your company, special projects (e.g., your recruitment seminar).

Follow-up of old clients: Contact them for one hour each day.

Other departments in firm: Escrow, mortgage, accounting.

Builders: The buyers often have homes to sell.

Owners of listed property: Keep in touch with your sellers.

Expired listings: Watch board limitations; call early in the morning.

Out-of-town owners: Use tax books for names and addresses.

Advertising for special properties: Ads asking for specific types of properties.

Furniture for sale ads: This can be a tip for possible sales of properties.

Personnel managers: Of small and large businesses—contact them.

Previous seller clients: Revisit them for one or two hours each week.

Market bulletin boards: How about putting up a bulletin board that says, "Compliments of _____, Realtor®"?

Moving companies: Give and take leads on people who are moving.

Bird dogs: Milkman, mail carrier, gardener—they know your neighborhood.

Other valuable sources: Mortgage handlers, tract salespersons.

through the broker's efforts it might be possible to sell the property for the owner's asking price plus the broker's commission.

2. *New Listing—Call Around.* Whenever you list a home, prospect around it. Visit neighbors of the person whose home is listed to find out whether they know of people who might be interested in purchasing the home or whether they would also be interested in listing their homes.

3. *Farming.* Farming is door-to-door canvassing in a specific area. But it is more than that. It is selecting an area where homes are selling and devoting all your door-to-door canvassing to learning about every owner in the area. The number of homes you can handle depends on you. Don't take more than you can properly service, because you should visit every owner in your farm at least once a month during the first year. Your goal is to make every owner think of you whenever he thinks of real estate.

A farm should be large enough to create 50 listings annually. If people move every five to seven years, as they do in California, 300 to 500 homes is a large enough farm.

The first visit is "cold." Knock on the door, introduce yourself and your company, and ask the owner whether he's planning to sell. If you get no for an answer, ask the owner if he knows anyone in the neighborhood who's considering moving. Build rapport by asking the owner for an opinion of the area. Then say, "Would you take my card in case you have any real estate questions."

Keep records. Get to know your owners. Offer something unique: a free market analysis certificate, pumpkins at Halloween, Santa Claus on a truck at Christmas with free photos of kids on his lap. Put out a monthly newsletter with items of interest in your farm: baby-sitters, garage sales, services available.

Every item you use for advertising in your farm must have your name, your company's name and logo, and your picture on it.

Finally, let your homeowners know about your listings. They can find buyers for you. As your farm is cultivated and planted, you will reap the harvest when your homeowners begin to call you to say that they want to sell and that they want you to handle the transaction.

4. *Telephone Prospecting.* Cold canvassing on the phone requires the ability to accept rejection because you know that you will eventually get the desired response. A telephone criss-cross directory, which lists telephones according to streets, and a prospect card are your tools.

5. *Expired Listings.* These can also be cold-canvassed by telephone. Ask the owner for an appointment to discuss why the house didn't sell. However, some boards have strict requirements regarding soliciting from sellers whose listings have just expired, and these rules must be observed.

Appointments. The first step in a real estate listing or sales transaction is the appointment. Getting an appointment is itself an act of selling.

Incoming calls on ads and signs provide the best opportunities for making appointments. To handle such calls properly requires preparation, tools, a procedure, and a purpose: to make an appointment.

To be prepared you must know your ads, know the properties, and know the prices and terms.

Your tools are a copy of all ads, a list of sign properties, prospect cards, a list of company listings (sometimes called the "hot sheet"), copies of ad and sign listings, message forms (for calls that are not ad or sign calls), a clear desk, a work plan to follow while you're not on the phone, and a register for incoming calls.

Ad and sign calls are handled very simply. You answer. You listen. You wait for a couple of questions. You answer them. Then you ask for a telephone number. Then you ask for an appointment.

Appointment for Listing. After getting an appointment, the agent must be sure that the time is convenient. The best time is when both the husband and wife are at home.

A kit of listing tools is necessary. These tools include a competitive market analysis form (showing the selling prices of currently listed homes, of homes sold during the past year, and of expired listings), a clipboard, pencils, listing forms, a ball-point pen, seller's net forms, a schedule of escrow fees, a schedule of title policy fees, a 50-foot measuring tape, business cards, and a visual aid presentation book containing information about you and your company.

Other items that an associate should have in his listing kit are: a realty blue book (mortgage rates), a phone book, a city map guide, rubber cement, a hole punch, a flashlight, a stapler, paper clips, an open house guest book, a For Sale sign, deposit receipts, and copies of an action plan stating what the agent will do for the client after his home is listed.

Be exactly on time. Too early makes sellers nervous; too late loses points for you. When entering the home, give the sellers your business card. After being seated, ask to tour the property. On your clipboard have a blank sheet of paper on which to make notes of things that interest you. Ask questions about the home. Get data regarding the room sizes, built-ins, the water heater, and special features.

Following the tour, suggest that you sit with the sellers at the dining room table. Give the sellers your visual aid book so that they can see what your company and you have done and what you can offer: escrow, insurance, financing, and so on. Encourage questions. *A good lister is a better listener, and vice versa.* Show the sellers your listing kit. Don't rush. You want rapport, and you want the sellers to have a feeling of comfortable assurance.

Ask the sellers about their mortgage: interest rate, terms, and taxes. You need their loan number. Present your competitive market analysis, turning it so that the sellers can read it together. Answer all questions, for this analysis determines the selling price.

Next, prepare an estimated seller's net sheet, which breaks down all the seller's costs and fees and estimates the proceeds that the seller will realize. Discuss points, prepayment penalties, title insurance and escrow fees, transfer taxes, reconveyance fees, and forwarding fees. This will accomplish two things: first, it will demonstrate what it will cost the sellers to sell their home; second, it will emphasize why the sellers should list with a Realtor®. Remember to explain that the net is only an estimate, based on a fair market price minus the costs of selling. Use maximum charges. Be sure to include estimated costs for corrective work that may be required by the building department, various agencies, or the buyer.

From the seller's net sheet it is easy to proceed to the listing agreement, which is known in the profession as the Exclusive Authorization and Right to Sell form. Know the form well. As you fill it out, you may request copies of desired documents. (Exhibit 2 shows a standard form used by the California Association of Realtors, and Exhibit 3 shows how to employ the order blank close, which consists of filling out the listing form item by item.)

When the listing agreement is being solicited, various objections are often put forward by the sellers. Exhibit 4 suggests how some typical objections might be dealt with by the agent.

After the listing agreement has been signed, the agent should review all of the steps that he will take to merchandise the sellers' house: disseminate the listing facts to all of the company's offices; provide details to the Board of Realtors®; give all local realty offices advance notice; publicize the listing at board meetings and at company meetings; advertise; conduct an open house; caravan (this means taking all of the agents from your office in a group to see the home); invite other offices to caravan; publish fliers; keep the house before agents and buyers until it is sold.

The Open House.   The open house is the best way to service a listing. It serves two purposes: first, it gives the home exposure; second, it gives the agent exposure. Proper preparation and publicity can start a wave of events that never seem to end.

The open house should be planned on a six-day plan. Day 1: Select house for Sunday; ask owner's permission; write ad (with owner); prepare flier. Day 2: Submit ad; knock on doors and pass out 50 fliers in neighborhood; secure permission to put up arrow signs. Day 3: Canvass 50 additional homes with fliers. Day 4: Canvass 50 more homes. Day 5: Get owner's permission to use phone to invite prospects and brokers; give phone number of open house to associates in your office. Day 6: Open house—one to six P.M.; set up open house; place arrow signs and flags; call clients; get thank-you notes.

Give the owner a preparation sheet: clean up the house; trim and mow yard; clean garage; turn on soft music and lights; turn on air conditioning if it's a hot day; open draperies and curtains; make cardboard signs indicating points of interest; make (or buy) cookies, tea, coffee; take valuables; take pets. The agent should check everything on Sunday at noon to be sure that the open house is ready.

The agent's checklist should include: a guest register, business cards, a chalkboard, a credit application, a deposit receipt, a multiple listing book, a criss-cross directory (for calling neighbors in the area), fliers, flags and arrows, and signs (Welcome, Come In).

As a part of his preparation the agent should review the facts about the school district, taxes, and other homes of the same price range in

EXHIBIT 2

EXCLUSIVE AUTHORIZATION AND RIGHT TO SELL

THIS IS INTENDED TO BE A LEGALLY BINDING AGREEMENT — READ IT CAREFULLY.
CALIFORNIA ASSOCIATION OF REALTORS® STANDARD FORM

1. **Right to Sell.** I hereby employ and grant _____
hereinafter called "Agent," the exclusive and irrevocable right commencing on _____ , 19 ____ , and expiring at
midnight on _____ , 19 ____ , to sell or exchange the real property situated in _____ ,
County of _____ , California described as follows:

_____

_____

_____

_____

2. **Terms of Sale.** The purchase price shall be $ _____ , to be paid in the following terms:

_____

_____

    (a) The following items of personal property are to be included in the above-stated price:

_____

_____

    (b) Agent is hereby authorized to accept and hold on my behalf a deposit upon the purchase price.
    (c) Evidence of title to the property shall be in the form of a California Land Title Association Standard Coverage
Policy of Title Insurance in the amount of the selling price to be paid for by _____ .
    (d) I warrant that I am the owner of the property or have the authority to execute this agreement. I hereby authorize
a FOR SALE sign to be placed on my property by Agent.
3. **Compensation to Agent.** I hereby agree to compensate Agent as follows:
    (a)_____ % of the selling price if the property is sold during the term hereof, or any extension thereof, by Agent,
on the terms herein set forth or any other price and terms I may accept, or through any other person, or by me, or _____ %
of the price shown in 2, if said property is withdrawn from sale, transferred, conveyed, leased without the consent of Agent, or
made unmarketable by my voluntary act during the term hereof or any extension thereof.
    (b) the compensation provided for in subparagraph (a) above if property is sold, conveyed or otherwise transferred
within _____ days after the termination of this authority or any extension thereof to anyone with whom Agent has had
negotiations prior to final termination, provided I have received notice in writing, including the names of the prospective
purchasers, before or upon termination of this agreement or any extension thereof. However, I shall not be obligated to pay
the compensation provided for in subparagraph (a) if a valid listing agreement is entered into during the term of said protection
period with another licensed real estate broker and a sale, lease or exchange of the property is made during the term of said
valid listing agreement.
4. If action be instituted to enforce this agreement, the prevailing party shall receive reasonable attorney's fees and costs
as fixed by the Court.
5. I authorize the Agent named herein to cooperate with sub-agents.
6. This property is offered in compliance with state and federal anti-discrimination laws.
7. In the event of an exchange, permission is hereby given Agent to represent all parties and collect compensation or
commissions from them, provided there is full disclosure to all principals of such agency. Agent is authorized to divide with
other agents such compensation or commissions in any manner acceptable to them.
8. I agree to save and hold Agent harmless from all claims, disputes, litigation, and/or judgments arising from any
incorrect information supplied by me, or from any material fact known by me concerning the property which I fail to disclose.
9. Other provisions:

_____

_____

10. I acknowledge that I have read and understand this Agreement, and that I have received a copy hereof.
Dated _____ , 19 ____   _____ , California

         OWNER   OWNER

       ADDRESS   CITY—STATE—PHONE

11. In consideration of the above, Agent agrees to use diligence in procuring a purchaser.

       AGENT   ADDRESS—CITY
By _____
                                PHONE   DATE

NO REPRESENTATION IS MADE AS TO THE LEGAL VALIDITY OF ANY PROVISION OR THE ADEQUACY OF ANY PROVISION IN ANY
SPECIFIC TRANSACTION. IF YOU DESIRE LEGAL ADVICE, CONSULT YOUR ATTORNEY.

Reprinted by permission of the California Association of Realtors.®

EXHIBIT 3
The Listing Order Blank Close

1. *Complete description* (use physical action close by touring property and filling out listing)
   "Would you please hold the tape? Then we could measure the house."
2. *Date* (alternative close)
   "Is today the 14th or the 15th?"
3. *Company name* (verbalize)
   "_____ Realtors® "
4. *Expiration date* (length of listing: *don't* verbalize; assume and write in 180 days; if the sellers object, at first ignore; if objections continue, compromise)
5. *Title policy and loan statement* (trial close)
   "If you'll get me your policy of title insurance, I can get the legal description more accurately. Then, when we go to escrow, we'll have the correct information."
6. *Address* (verbalize)
7. *Existing liens* (verbalize onto the listing form)
8. *Possession*
   "We will have your money at the close of escrow, but we'll try to arrange to give you an additional three days to move."
9. *Co-op split*
   "I'm going to do everything I can to sell your home. I'm going to give 50 percent of the commission to any other broker who brings us a contract. This will ensure the sale of your property."
10. *Terms* (net sheet information should be filled out now; then verbalized onto listing form; net sheet should be initialed by sellers)
11. *Commission* (do *not* verbalize: write in and assume 7 percent)
12. *Sale price*
    "Based on the competitive market analysis I've shown you, what would seem like a fair price to you?"
13. *Agent's signature* (write in your name)
    "I'm going to make a total commitment to market your property and create the best possible sale for you."
14. *Sellers' signatures* (turn listing to sellers)
    "If you will approve this, I'll be in contact with other brokers to move your property."

the same area; he should also review the list of his potential prospects—motivated sellers, interested neighbors (and their friends and relatives), sellers who are buyers, buyers for other homes—and call other brokers to let them know he's holding an open house.

Follow-up on an open house is imperative. It should be done within three days of the initial contact. Ask the prospect whether he has seen any other homes. Set up an appointment to see his present home. Get an appointment to show him homes comparable to the one that was held open. Send personal notes thanking guests for having visited your house.

Contact the owner immediately after holding the open house—before he contacts you—and report on your success or failure. Have suggestions

EXHIBIT 4
Answering Sellers' Objections

Objection: "I don't want a lockbox on my home.

Response:

Mr. Seller, our company has been in business since _____, and I have never heard of any instance where a problem of any kind occurred because the home was shown by using a lockbox to gain entrance.

We understand our responsibility in this regard, and are careful to lock every door when we leave. We give evidence of our visit by leaving a business card. There is nothing we would do to jeopardize the safety of your home. I say this to give you assurance that there is no danger in putting a lockbox on your door.

Even if you say you are always home, there could be a time when you would leave for a short period, perhaps to visit a neighbor. That could be the time a salesperson would be phoning to ask permission to show your home. It might ultimately be your buyer. If there is no response to a phone call, and no lockbox on your door, the salesperson has no other course but to show other property. We could lose your buyer this way.

I ask you to reconsider and permit me to put a lockbox on your door.

Objection: I'll give you an open listing.

Response:

Mr. Seller, an open listing is everybody's listing and no one's responsibility. Our offices sell more homes in one month than a lot of brokers sell in a year. We do this only because we put the full effort of our merchandising program behind our exclusive listings.

This means expenditures in advertising and mail-outs, plus a concentrated effort by a truly experienced sales staff in canvassing the neighborhood for buyers. We will be holding open house and literally leaving no place for a buyer to hide.

This is all in an attempt to sell your home at the best possible price. Mr. Seller, I ask you to list your home exclusively for 120 days, and you can be assured that we will do everything possible to provide a quick sale.

Objection: I don't want a sign in front of my house.

Response:

Mr. Seller, approximately 5 percent of home sales are made because someone drove by a specific home and called in on the sign. I'm certain that you don't want to miss the opportunity to find your buyer, no matter how small the percentage. It's possible that he may be somewhere in that 5 percent.

I'll leave you some of my business cards, and if anyone should drop by to make inquiries, you can simply refer him to me.

If it's questions from your neighbors that you are concerned about, please keep in mind that one of your neighbors may have a relative or friend who wants to live near him. Without a For Sale sign, that neighbor may never know your home is for sale.

Objection: I'll list with you, but I'll only give you a 30-day listing.

Response:

Mr. Seller, in a 30-day listing there are only four weekends . . . only eight days in which your property will receive maximum activity. Most

EXHIBIT 4 *(continued)*

real property is sold on the weekend. Eight days just isn't sufficient time
to expose your property to enough potential buyers.

Unless, of course, you are willing to establish a "quick sale" price. This
competitive market analysis form shows it takes an average of
_____ days to sell a well-priced home in your area. In 30 days there
just wouldn't be enough time to obtain results from our merchandising
program. That program includes processing, inspecting, advertising, open
houses, and mail-outs.

Objection: I want to buy a new home before I sell.

Response:

(If the seller wants to purchase another home in your area, you can
present him with a plan for the purchase of another home subject to the
sale of his present home or you can persuade him to list and sell his present
home first to assure a smooth transition from his present home to the next
one.

You should stress that his home must be listed at a competitive market
price if he is to accomplish his objective, and you should point out that
by selling before buying, sellers are certain of an equity which might otherwise fluctuate according to points, loan charges, interest, and so on. You
should also point out that he will be a stronger buyer if he can look for a
new home knowing that he has cash from the sale of his existing home
to work with.)

Objection: I don't want to pay the points.

Response:

You don't have to, Mr. Seller, . . . if you are willing to wait a considerable
length of time to find a buyer with the cash necessary to purchase your
home. You see, the majority of homes in this area are being sold under
new government financing. These programs require that a seller pay the
discount points. This means, Mr. Seller, that if you aren't willing to pay
the points you will lose about 70 percent of the purchasing market.

I want to sell your home—and the best way to do that is by making it
available to the greatest number of potential buyers. Believe me, the number of buyers who have sufficient cash to purchase your home any other
way are few and far between.

Let me ask you a question. If you had only $10,000 in cash, would you
put it all down to purchase a home? Then how can you expect a buyer to
be willing to do that?

Doesn't it make good sense to make your home available to as many
buyers as possible?

Objection: Couldn't we start at a higher price and come down?

Response:

Mr. Seller, I realize that sounds logical to you, but let's really look at
it. You could price yourself out of the market, so that no offers will be
made and you will have no opportunity to lower the sale price.

I am going to be taking the listing back to my office and then place it
on the multiple listing service. I want to be able to brag about this listing
to other salespeople. When they ask me the listed price, I don't want to
have to tell them a price that is high.

Good salespeople know the market, and they have a backlog of qualified

EXHIBIT 4 *(concluded)*

buyers. But they will not even bother showing their clients overpriced property.

The best time for a listing to sell is when it is first placed on the market. Our salespeople will caravan it, and if it is priced right, they will really try to sell it.

If we start too high, the other salespeople won't be interested and the property will sit. Later on, if you decide to adjust the price, the property will be "shopworn" and new listings will be on the market. Then it will be hard to generate new enthusiasm for your home.

to make, particularly with respect to a price revision if this should prove necessary. Outline to the owner your next plan for promoting the sale of his home. If you sell during an open house, canvass at least 60 of the homes nearby and tell the owners that you found a number of people who were interested in the area because of its amenities.

Meeting Sales Targets

Until an agent has built up a clientele from which he can derive sufficient referrals, he will get most of his buyers from incoming ad calls, incoming calls about signs, rent option calls, free rental service ad calls, and renters. As has been indicated in the discussion of listings, the agent's first step is to get an appointment.

The form shown in Exhibit 5 is a functional instrument for optimizing

EXHIBIT 5

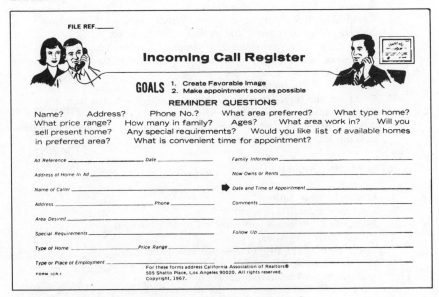

FILE REF. _____

Incoming Call Register

GOALS
1. Create Favorable Image
2. Make appointment soon as possible

REMINDER QUESTIONS

Name?   Address?   Phone No.?   What area preferred?   What type home? What price range?   How many in family?   Ages?   What area work in?   Will you sell present home?   Any special requirements?   Would you like list of available homes in preferred area?   What is convenient time for appointment?

Ad Reference _____ Date _____

Address of Home In Ad _____

Name of Caller _____

Address _____ Phone _____

Area Desired _____

Special Requirements _____

Type of Home _____ Price Range _____

Type or Place of Employment _____

Family Information _____

Now Owns or Rents _____

➤ Date and Time of Appointment _____

Comments _____

Follow Up _____

_____

FORM ICR-1   For these forms address California Association of Realtors® 505 Shatto Place, Los Angeles 90020. All rights reserved. Copyright, 1967.

Reprinted by permission of the California Association of Realtors.®

the use of office space and handling incoming calls. It makes provision for facts that constitute a preliminary qualifying of the buyer, and it lists suggested responses to typical buyers' objections.

Qualifying the Buyer. Qualifying the buyer requires the agent to be familiar with financing, especially with eligibility requirements for all types of loans (FHA, VA, FHA–VA, and conventional) and for FHA and VA repossessions. The agent should know the basic monthly income necessary to qualify, the current interest rates, the maximum loan allowed, and the down payment, guarantees, and insurance required.

It is necessary to get all the information you can about a buyer and to put it down on a credit application. Often you will sell one of your own listings to one of your buyers, so you have to be sure that your seller's property is not tied up (and your seller's hopes and plans built up) only to have the buyer's credit fail to qualify him for a loan. Many buyers do not give agents all the facts. Frequently judgments against a buyer do not surface until a preliminary title report comes into escrow. Credit bureaus pick up many items, but it takes the credit bureaus and the title company to dig out every item of credit information.

Showing the Property. Assume that you have qualified the buyer in your own mind. (This should be done prior to showing property—simply to save time and embarrassment.) If the buyer has called in, and you have given him an appointment at the office, you should be prepared to show him the property.

It is recommended that you go through the following checklist prior to showing the property:

1. Check your car to be sure it's clean and neat.
2. Check yourself to be sure you're clean and neat.
3. Review and know your inventory.
4. Check with the seller for an appointment to show (if necessary).
5. Ask the seller to prepare the property for showing.
6. Show only three properties at a time. This saves time, does not tire the buyer, and forces you to match the buyer with the house more carefully.
7. Show last the home most suited to the buyer's needs.
8. Don't tell the buyer how many homes he will see that day.
9. Give the buyer a pad and pencil.
10. Ask the buyer whether there is anything that would prevent him from making a decision if he found a home that met all his needs.

In going to the property:

1. Select the best route.
2. Continue to qualify the buyer.
3. Point out other properties that you may have sold.
4. Cite comparable sales.
5. Don't oversell the property—let it sell itself.
6. Sell the buyer on the neighborhood (schools, parks, shopping, etc.).
7. Sell the buyer on other property owners.
8. Park across the street from the property—*never park in the seller's driveway.*

After arriving at the property:

1. Slow down your pace.
2. Don't defend the property.
3. Listen to the buyer's objections—they are buying signals.
4. Observe.
5. Save the best for last.
6. Show the property to the husband and wife together.
7. Find the right home for the buyer

Closing the Sale. After showing three homes, you are prepared to close. Knowing when the buyer is ready to be closed is the mark of a good salesperson. He always knows. He knows because of his ability to observe, to sense, to feel, to identify, to assert. Even getting the buyer into the closing room back at the office takes skill. One of the best ways is to refer to a question that the buyer asked about taxes or zoning while the property was being shown.

You may find that the deposit receipt close is the most effective of the scores of closes available. In this close, you start filling out the deposit receipt, verbalizing each item as you write—the date, the terms you've already discussed (write in the full sale price unless a different price has been established), the buyer's name, the escrow period, the title of vesting, and the amount of the deposit. Then say, "If you approve this, I will be in touch with the seller this evening, and I promise that I will try to get it accepted so that you can own your own home."

Objections. When a buyer raises an objection for the first time, ignore the objection. When he repeats the objection, say, "I understand how you feel. Many people feel the same way. In order for you to think it over properly, let me jot down all the information. When I'm finished, you may take the agreement home with you if you wish." (Hand the buyers a credit application or statement of identification to complete.)

After your buyer has given his approval, you should prepare him for what is called "buyer's remorse." Be frank and explain the causes: increasing interest rates, escrow delays (because of loan shopping, verification of out-of-town credit, the appraisal being too low, or repairs not being made to the lender's satisfaction), negative reactions to the purchase by friends and relatives, marriage problems, transfer of the buyer, death in the family, and so on. (These possibilities should be explained to the seller too, so that he will be forewarned.)

This is also the time to give the buyer a copy of the Estimated Buyer's Costs. As has been indicated earlier, from the moment you begin to qualify the buyer you apprise him of the approximate amount of the monthly payment that he will have to invest in his new home. Although this is not precisely accurate because of the wide differences in property taxes and the fluctuating interest rate, you can figure that the monthly payment for principal, interest, taxes, and insurance will be about 1 percent of the loan amount. Thus, a $50,000 mortgage will require about a $500 per month payment. (Exhibit 6 shows an Estimated Buyer's Cost sheet.)

Presenting the Offer. Preparation is required to present the offer properly. A good agent goes over each of the following items prior to the

EXHIBIT 6

Estimated Buyer's Costs

☐ CTL
☐ FHA _____
☐ VA
☐ conventional
☐ 90% conventional
☐ 95% conventional

Property Address _____

WORK SHEET ONLY—exact figures cannot be known until transaction is set to close escrow.

Selling price .... $_____
Loan amount .... $_____
Down payment.................................. $_____

Estimated closing costs
  Nonrecurring costs
    Origination fee (FHA and VA) .... $_____
    Points _____% of new loan (conventional) ... $_____
    Appraisal .... $_____
    30 days' interest proration .... $_____
    One-month MMI (FHA only) .... $_____
    Title policy .... $_____
    Tax service .... $_____
    Credit report .... $_____
    Escrow fee .... $_____
    Miscellaneous .... $_____
  Recurring Costs
    Fire insurance policy (one year) .... $_____
    Impounds (_____ months at $____) .... $_____
      Total estimated closing costs .... $_____
      Total cash investment from buyer .... $_____

Estimated monthly payment
  Principal and interest .... $_____
  One-tenth annual taxes .... $_____
  One-twelfth annual insurance premium .... $_____
    Total estimated monthly payment .... $_____

Prepared for _____   Prepared by _____
         Buyer's name   Salesperson's name

presentation: the signed deposit receipt, the deposit (personal check, cash, cashier's check, or promissory note), the loan application (completely filled out), the buyer's statement of information, and a competitive market analysis. (The listing agent also prepares a seller's net sheet.) Allow yourself plenty of time for preparation.

Then either call the listing agent and tell him you have a deposit or have someone in your office make the call. Do not divulge any part of the contract to the listing agent. Ask him to make an appointment with his seller so that an offer can be presented. Do not approach the seller directly. (If, however, you are the listing agent, contact your seller—again, do not divulge the terms on the phone—and set up an appointment to present your offer.) Do not take your buyer with you to make the offer.

The listing agent must be present while the buyer's agent presents the deposit to the seller. Present your buyer's offer clearly and courteously. Point out the good credit status of your buyer, and emphasize his sincerity. (You have the loan application to prove your points.) But remember never to argue with the listing agent or the seller—doing so damages the business relationship.

Get in touch with your buyer immediately after you have presented the deposit to the seller. According to real estate law, there is no sale until communication between all parties is complete.

The Counteroffer. Often buyers will submit an offer that is below the listing price. Consequently, the seller may make a counteroffer that will fall between the buyer's offer and the listing price. The agent is obligated to present the counteroffer to the buyer, whom, by the way, the agent should have forewarned of this possibility from the moment that the buyer decided to make the low offer. Having been forewarned, the buyer will not be surprised or resentful if the agent comes back with a counteroffer.

The agent should call the buyer and tell him that he would like to drop by to discuss the details of the new home. Even though the agent has forewarned the buyer of the possibility of a counteroffer, he does not discuss it on the phone. When the agent meets the buyer, he advises the buyer that the seller has accepted the buyer's requests that the draperies and carpet be left and that the buyer be given possession on the desired date. Then he explains the seller's counter-proposals and the reasons for them—financing a new home, house underpriced, and so on. The agent doesn't present arguments in favor of acceptance. Rather, he sits back and keeps quiet. The buyer may approve the counter without question.

If the buyer resists the counteroffer, the agent explains that the seller has compromised and has given the buyer an exclusive option on the home. He also points out that if the buyer doesn't accept, someone else will receive an investment benefit from the buyer's efforts. The agent explains that a $500 increase in sale price means less than $5 per month on the mortgage payment. The professional salesperson gives a second effort at this point to help the buyer and the seller satisfy their needs.

Contingency Offers. Often the sale of a house is contingent on the sale of another property. The following guidelines are set forth to enable the agent to make a sale possible while still acting in the best interests of both the buyer and the seller.

1. The contingency must be fully explained to all parties.
2. The contingent property must be priced at market value.

3. An appraisal must be ordered one week after listing.
4. The contingent property must be sold and in escrow within 30 days.
5. Normal deposits and all policies must apply to the sale of the contingent property.
6. The contingent property must include the financing terms predominant in the area.
7. If FHA and/or VA terms are included, all parties must be aware of the time problem—and other problems.
8. The listing agent must inspect the property and advise his seller as to its market potential.
9. It is best not to accept contingencies unless they are put in escrow.

After a sale, the real selling begins. Your buyers and your sellers are your best sources. They know you; they trust you; they like you; they believe in you. Keep in touch with them. Show a genuine interest in them. Make them feel that you are not only their real estate agent but their friend. If you keep in touch, you will soon find that 90 percent or more of your business is "referral business."

Escrow

To open an escrow the agent should take the following documents: the deposit receipt, signed by all parties and indicating the exact terms of the transaction (the receipt must be explicit, legible, and complete, or it will serve no purpose); a copy of the listing; the loan application; the deed or title policy with a legal description of the property; information regarding commission and board fees; and all loan applications, permits, certifications, and the like. All loan documents are sent to the escrow office before they are signed and go back to the lender.

Send deposits to escrow. The initial deposit is placed in the broker's trust account. Escrow will call for funds as they are needed to pay fees for credit reports, appraisals, and so on. Do not put rent money in escrow.

The deposit for closing costs must be in cash or certified funds. An escrow cannot be closed if the buyer's closing costs are in the form of a personal check.

Finally, always put repair bills in escrow prior to closing. Otherwise, you, as the agent, will have to pay them yourself.

Be sure to allow sufficient time in escrow for your clients. An escrow cannot be extended automatically—all parties must agree to the extension.

In localities where settlement is conducted by attorneys or title companies, a somewhat different procedure is used. There is a "closing" at which the papers are passed and signed by all parties or their representatives.

Time Management

A real estate agent needs time to prospect and time to service his clients. Time management is an absolute necessity for the successful real estate agent. Exhibit 7 presents a "daily planner" that has been

EXHIBIT 7

DAY: _____ DATE: _____
GOALS: *Today—* _____
This Month— _____
Long Term— _____

APPOINTMENTS TO KEEP	PRIORITIES BETWEEN APPOINTMENTS
7:30	○
7:45	○
8:00	○
8:15	○
8:30	○
8:45	○
9:00	○
9:15	○
9:30	○
9:45	○
10:00	○
10:15	○
10:30	○
10:45	○
11:00	○
11:15	○
11:30	○
11:45	○
12:00	○
12:15	○
12:30	○
12:45	○
1:00	○
:15	○
1:30	○
1:45	
2:00	**PHONE CALLS TO MAKE**
2:15	○
2:30	○
2:45	○
3:00	○
3:15	○
3:30	○
3:45	○
4:00	○
4:15	○
4:30	○
4:45	○
5:00	○
5:15	○
5:30	○
5:45	○
6:00	○
6:15	○
6:30	○
6:45	○
7:00	○
7:15	○
/:30	○
7:45	○
8:00	○
8:15	○
8:30	○
8:45	○
9:00	

used with tremendous success by associates in a real estate office. Although the daily planner is self-explanatory, it should be emphasized that one of its features reflects an important tenet of time management, namely, that a person must keep his goals constantly in view. At the top of the daily planner is a place for the agent to write down his goals each day.

The following is a "typical day" for the real estate agent who invests his time to achieve optimum productivity.

Time	Activity
6:00 A.M.	Get up, jog, shower, etc.
6:45 A.M.	Breakfast. Read newspaper For Sale by Owner ads and ads of competition.
7:30 A.M.	Leave for office; listen to motivation tapes on the way to work.
8:00 A.M.	Arrive at office.
8:05–9:30 A.M.	Review daily plan; check message box; address direct mailings; match buyers with property; prepare multiple listings and office listings for inspection; call other brokers regarding their listings; plug your listings to associates; check escrow status; review production sheets; analyze callbacks; review listing checklist, lockboxes in an out, For Sale and Sold signs; prepare expired listings for evening calls; make five calls from criss-cross.
9:30–11:00 A.M.	After completing above items, call escrow office to handle any problems that your checklist showed; call back on your listing progress; take out For Sale and Sold signs and pick up lockboxes; call five For Sale by Owners; call three expired listings; call potential buyers and set up appointments to show property.
11:00–12:00 A.M.	Inspect new listings, new repossession listings.

(On alternate mornings, go door knocking 10 to 12.)

Time	Activity
12:00–1:00 P.M.	Lunch. Get out of office.
1:00–2:30 P.M.	Canvass five For Sale by Owners; view available listings.
2:30–3:30 P.M.	Return all phone calls; take care of messages.

(If you work the alternate plan of door knocking in the morning, from 1:30–3:30 P.M. follow the 9:30–11:00 A.M. schedule shown above.)

Time	Activity
3:30–5:30 P.M.	Work defaults; show property.
5:30–6:00 P.M.	Prepare and confirm evening appointments.
6:00–7:00 P.M.	Dinner.
7:00–9:00 P.M.	Call clients who were not home during the day; set up daily plan for the next day; list and sell property; do real estate reading.
9:00 P.M.	Go home for the evening.

Obviously there will be conflicts. Priorities will have to be set up. The first priority should be to present an offer. Each agent will learn that the other priorities involve contacts with buyers and sellers. As we noted at the beginning of this chapter, selling the resale house is ultimately contacts. An agent should talk to no less than 50 people every day about real estate. Any agent who does that will be successful.

SELLING NEW HOUSES

Milton E. Kettler

*M*ILTON E. KETTLER, BA, Director and Chairman of the Board, Kettler Brothers, Inc., Gaithersburg, Maryland.

Life director, National Association of Home Builders. Director and past president, Metropolitan Washington Builders Association. Director, Union First National Bank of Washington. Director and Executive Committee member, C&P Telephone Company of Maryland. Member, Institute of Residential Marketing. Member, Board of Trustees, The American University, Washington, D.C.

For the builder, selling new houses is a long, carefully calculated process which begins before the land is purchased and ends long after the customers have moved into their new homes. Properly executed, the process results in a successful venture which has met the myriad challenges that must be faced. This chapter highlights the stages of the process, with particular emphasis on the builder's standpoint. Some additional comment is provided to assist brokerage firms in understanding how their selling service can become part of the builder's marketing function.

The Purpose of a Housing Business

The Creation of Customers. Creating customers is the essential purpose of a housing business. From this essential is derived the need to create an entire marketing program, which is infinitely more complex than developing a sales program alone. Thus, the purpose evolves into a product that, in effect, creates a customer. It is important to recognize here that profit is a by-product—an inherent goal, of course, but not the purpose itself. The by-product of profit is related to a home-building company's effectiveness and efficiency in identifying, seeking out, and serving the customer. Therefore, our discussion of new-house selling will cover the whole field that is often referred to as marketing.

Home building is a retail business in which selling out the product means selling the "store." A primary difference between a housing project and a large retail store is that when all of the houses are sold and occupied, the "store" (i.e., the building company) moves.

There is another major difference. While a Neiman-Marcus probably offers up to 150,000 retail items (the bulk of which are inventory stock), the builder of new homes will seldom have more than five samples of his wares. Most of what he sells, therefore, will be special order—that is, homes built (or at least completed) on contract for specific customers. (Even in very large housing projects, a particular grouping seldom offers more than five sample types.) The days of mass speculative building are long gone, for the most part: very little is sold "off the rack." The lesson that conservatism pays off has been learned all too often in the home-building industry. The builders who don't get stuck with a lot of inventory are the ones who survive. The failure to realize profits because insufficient products are on hand in a boom market is a minimal problem when compared to the disaster of losing everything because too much inventory is on hand in a down cycle.

Thus, a housing business should be governed by many of the same sound marketing principles that govern other retail businesses. It should be remembered, however, that although home building is a retail business, it is also one of the few retail businesses in which the retailer is also the designer and the manufacturer.

Selling and the Marketing Framework.   Selling as a function cannot be isolated from the chain of marketing actions which define, create, and properly present the product. This means that there is a need for continued input into the marketing effort, including an ongoing quest for up-to-date information.

Marketing is an operating system which has many ramifications, for it is, in essence, (or at least it should be) *the way a building company conducts its business.* Marketing includes research: the investigations that are necessary to discover the available markets and the analysis of those markets to see what should be done to cater to them in every detail—price, location, style, amenities, and the units themselves.

Discovering available markets often requires sensitive research which goes beyond the obvious evidence of need markets to ferret out less obvious subsurface markets that can be created by targeted appeals. Inherent in such investigations is the recognition of the design and costing which fall within the constraints of the markets.

Selling is a function within the marketing framework. After the research conducted by the builder's company has been reflected in the appropriate product planning and design, it continues to be reflected in the company's communication system for the market the company has defined: merchandising, advertising, public relations, promotion, product presentation, selling, postsale selling, and service.

Selling is but one link in the marketing chain. It is not done in a vacuum; it is the end result of masses of thought, actions, and expenditures. It is in the marketing efforts which precede selling and in the subsequent follow-through that principles which are crucial to successful selling may be found. And for the building company, unlike most other retail businesses, it's a matter of relatively few customers with an attendant high dollar value per customer for a product which cannot be moved. The fact that the product cannot be moved is another critical element in the marketing process. The building company has no retailing parallel to the process of shipping unsold swimsuits to the South in winter.

Only the sales department brings in money; every other department spends money. How that money is spent is the essence of the company marketing—that is, operating—system which is supportive of the end goal: creating a customer and thereby making a sale. Thus, how a company spends its money is dictated by a specific marketing program which is related to all expenditures.

The Effect of Spending Priorities on Sales

From the thesis that marketing is the operating system by which a company conducts its business, it is obvious that money is going to be spent for marketing purposes. Historically, the allocation percentages varied little from project to project. In more recent times, however, a heavy emphasis has often been placed on a particular category for a particular marketing focus. Thus, to talk about the selling aspect alone would be to put the subject out of context. Rather, it is necessary to consider how selling fits into a total marketing program and how selling relates to the essential elements of that program.

Land Acquisition. The acquisition of well-located land is the first element, and it can come about in a number of ways. The ideal approach is to find a hole in the market that needs filling and then to acquire appropriate land—meaning land at a good location with proper zoning, topography, soils, utilities, convenient transportation and facilities, and so on—at a price (naturally!) that is compatible with the market. Frequently somewhat less than ideal is land that is acquired through inheritance, specific "deals" from friends or family, or unique opportunity purchases. The location of such land—which is often acquired because the financing is relatively easy—is sometimes significantly less than ideal.

In making any land choice or marketing decision, it is wise to recall that the value of real estate is a state of mind. In the development of the marketing program this means, among other things, that expensive land in an area of high activity and desirability will require lower advertising expenditures than remote, inexpensive land in a pioneering location.

Market Research. Professionally developed market research and market knowledge have already been referred to as the primary basis for determining expenditures, identifying the available markets, and determining how to satisfy those markets with the right types of products and how to communicate with them.

The need for professional research cannot be overemphasized. Such research must reveal the facts as they are rather than as the builder wishes them to be. Tailoring research conclusions to the unfounded beliefs of the builder has been the cause of many a needless disaster in the home-building industry.

A buyer profile should be developed in great detail, because this will influence decisions about land acquisition and land development. The details of the buyer profile should include all of the aspects which work to narrow the market: these are the constraints which must be reckoned with throughout the marketing program.

The lender should have enough experience with the builder to know that the builder's market targets are correct; and if not, he should obtain assurance from the builder that the necessary facts have been made known and properly interpreted. (This is particularly true when the builder is venturing into unknown territories and unknown markets.)

The Land Plan. The best possible land plan goes far beyond the simplicities of an engineer's grid. A new house is a retail product that comes with the land—and this means that the land plan must suit the consumer as well as the house itself. Working in concert with a professional land planner, an engineer, an architect, and even a landscape architect, the builder develops a land plan which is compatible with the established buyer profile and the housing units which are to be produced.

The best possible land plan must not only suit the consumer but must also conform to a great many regulatory constraints. All too often, unfortunately, codes and regulations impose such severe problems and costs, so many adjustments and compromises, that the result seems to be something less than "the best possible land plan."

The Housing Designs. The best possible housing designs require the talents of the best possible architect. This does not imply a need for the most expensive architect. Rather, it implies the hiring of the architect who has the most experience and the best proven track record in designing the particular type of product that is being offered. The best possible architect for a project will also be able to work within the established marketing constraints—he will design the housing products for the groups of people who have been targeted in the buyer profiles.

The Standard of Quality. Balanced material quality incorporates a consistent standard of quality which is related to the income and preferences of the markets being sought. That standard is best developed by a team. The sales staff should be represented on the team, for salespeople are often the most well informed on what consumers are seeking in the way of materials, equipment, accessories, and the like.

There's an equally important benefit in having sales department participation. The discussions at this stage make the salespeople aware of the need for give-and-take. They acquire a good understanding of why certain products are selected and others are not. If a salesperson asks for an additional item of kitchen equipment, is he willing to reduce the quality of another product or to eliminate something altogether in order to make room in the budget for the new item? Or perhaps the salesperson hasn't heard (as the builder has) about the high-service callback problem on the item he asked for.

Give-and-take has a double meaning in this situation. It's a give-and-take discussion about what is to be given to the house and what is to be taken out. And when the process has been completed, the salespeople will feel more confident in their sales encounters because they will understand the basis for product selection.

The Landscaping Budget. A sufficient landscaping budget is one which not only permits the enhancement of the model area but also the enhancement of the entire community, which thus becomes an influential selling factor. Landscaping is not something that should be given a last-minute allowance for a bush tossed in here and there. Landscaping is an important element in building on single lots as well as building on a larger scale.

The Model Home Presentation. The best possible model home presentation can cause a prospective buyer to want a particular house. If models are furnished, the furnishings should suit the taste of the prospective buyer and be within his means.

Avoid cuteness and excessive cleverness in decorated models. Builders aren't trying to win decorating contests—they are merely trying to have their products demonstrated to the best possible advantage. Professionally decorated models should not be deceptive. They should demonstrate how people are actually going to live in a house. Utilizing a bedroom's only closet for a built-in desk merely tricks people into thinking that a room is larger than it is.

Every effort should be made to have at least one furnished model. It is the "store" that attracts people; it shows off the company and its abilities in the best possible way; it provides a base of operations; and it implies a permanence of operation to prospects who may be leery about a company's stability.

It is economically sound to furnish a model if it can be projected that 12 to 15 houses will be sold from it in a year's time. This means that it is feasible for even a small building company to exhibit a furnished model.

The Merchandising Tools. The best possible merchandising tools are necessary *to unify* the entire process of communicating with the markets being sought. All graphics, signs, brochures, sale displays, and advertising should communicate the quality and value of the housing in terms which the designated markets will understand and appreciate. Professional market research should indicate the means for relating the products to the market profiles.

At all price levels, a house is a lot of money for the prospective purchaser, and its value will be more easily recognizable if appropriate communication tools are used. A subdivision logo should be carefully designed to suitably represent the housing product—and it should be utilized whenever the name of the product is shown. The same, of course, holds true for the company logo.

The budget for merchandising tools works far better if it is predetermined. Market research will provide an idea of how much money may be needed for this purpose.

The Sales Staff. The best possible sales staff means having sincere, knowledgeable, energetic people who are and regard themselves as professionals—that is, men and women who look upon their sales job as worthy and valuable.

A builder should try to get his own sales staff as early as possible. With all due respect for general realty agents, it is my view that a builder needs a full-time, full-team sales contribution. A salesperson can be brought into a building company's operation at a much earlier stage than most small builders seem to believe possible. It can be proven that a salesperson is appropriate for a builder with an annual gross volume of between $200,000 and $400,000. A professional salesperson can handle many things in addition to selling, such as scouting up new ground or individual lots, advertising, placing signs, and literature, settlements and perhaps financing, community relations (which is a very important phase of prospecting), and even customer service.

Despite all the advantages of a "kept" staff, there are serious disadvantages. Furthermore, most small builders would find it impossible to afford a first-class agent with a yearly sales volume of less than $1 million. What, then, are some of the advantages of outside brokerage?

1. Generally the broker has a more-rounded experience, having worked for several different building operations over a period of time.
2. The independence derived from outside employment usually permits more objective counsel and advice.
3. The larger or franchised brokerage offices provide excellent formal training which may not be readily obtainable elsewhere.
4. Since most brokerage offices are staffed by professionals who are on a commission basis, the builder is relieved of the need to pay salesperson's salaries and benefits, such as social security, and health insurance.
5. Name identity is never a problem when an established broker is hired. Few new-home builders have successful reputations on which to trade, so that the use of the nationwide franchises names will assist most builders in establishing familiarity with their trade names.
6. The economic overhead of maintaining a satisfactory sales staff cannot easily be borne by most builders.

Which is better—brokers or a builder's sales staff—will depend upon a number of factors, including size, stability of volume, and the management of the building enterprise.

Advertising. Advertising has but one goal: to bring qualified prospects to the sales location. It is an aspect of merchandising, but one that must stand on its own. It is the final element of the marketing budget, and if everything else is accomplished properly, it will most likely have a surplus at the end of the project.

Because its sole goal is to provide qualified prospects, advertising must accurately reflect the quality of the company and the character of the product if the prospects are to qualify themselves. Otherwise, advertising costs and sales time and costs are wasted.

The Development of a Marketing/Sales Budget

In preparing a marketing/sales budget, it is mandatory that everything that should be considered be considered at the outset. The marketing/sales budget is, of course, different for each building company. But realistic budgeting requires a realistic appraisal of what it is going to cost to sell all the units—that is, a realistic appraisal of the costs that will be incurred by/or will be directly related to the sales process. Some companies begin the marketing/sales budget with the cost of market research, whereas others charge market research to up-front "seed monies," and still others to product planning/design.

These are the primary marketing and sales categories which may be considered in a projected budget:

1. All costs of the model home except those which will be recaptured upon its ultimate sale.
2. Model home utilities.
3. Telephone.
4. Stationery and postage.
5. Merchandising aids—signs, literature, displays.
6. Advertising—production and media.
7. Model furnishings, including depreciation.
8. Cleaning and maintenance (including yard care and snow removal).
9. Financing (including insurance and taxes).
10. Promotions.
11. Public relations and publicity.
12. Security.
13. Compensation/commissions.
14. Miscellaneous items, such as licenses, fees, and clerical help.

It is true that controls can be exercised on these costs; but the best way to control them is to recognize at the beginning that they are (or will be) part of the cost of doing business.

It is impossible to be precise about the percentage relationship between the marketing/sales budget and the sales volume. Depending upon myriad circumstances, the percentage *generally ranges from a low* of 3 percent to a high of 7½ percent. There is no "right" figure. The owner of the business must ultimately decide as to whether or not he is getting recognizable value for marketing/sales expenses. In the meantime, there are two ways in which the marketing/sales budget might be reduced:

1. By greater efficiency, which may well mean improved proficiency.
2. By increasing the emphasis in one area of expenditure and decreasing the emphasis in another in order to obtain more effective results. For example, beefing-up postsale selling and service in order to improve referrals could result in reduced advertising costs and a noticeable increase in benefits to the company.

The most important point is best represented by the Boy Scout motto: Be prepared! Having to suddenly cut back a needed advertising schedule in order to clear the model home parking lot and walkways after a January blizzard may seriously affect early spring sales.

Model homes and decorating can be an expensive item in the marketing/sales budget. It has certainly been proven that proper product presentation is a major factor in building industry sales. Often, however, money is spent needlessly for this purpose—even to the detriment of the house itself.

If there is more than one model, money might be saved by furnishing only the one which offers the most possible room uses. Carpeting and draperies are a big help. Vignettes—particularly in bedrooms—will often set a room's mood. A grouping of pictures or posters will also serve this purpose.

Merchandising tools range from total inadequacy to excessive elaborateness. Striking the effective means requires careful analysis of the product being sold and the market being sought. (All merchandising communications should properly reflect the product being sold and the people for whom it was designed.) Here again, market research should establish the appropriate guidelines.

Differences between Selling New Houses and Selling Used Houses

The limitation of products may make a difference between the functions of an outside realty sales agent and the salesperson who devotes himself to new houses exclusively. There may be a difference in the manner of handling objections. The salesperson of a single company or project must answer objections by being able to sell only the limited product line he has to sell: he cannot put his prospects in his car and drive them to another site and product somewhere across town. An outside brokerage firm, unless it is very large and has a policy of restricting new-house sales agents to one project, can handle objections by showing other products.

A housing community is a group of people—not a bunch of houses or buildings—who have a common interest. Thus, there is the need to sell the community and its immediate environment and general location, as well as the individual structure. The salesperson who becomes deeply involved with a project of new homes does so by working with each of the buyers and developing a common thread which builds up a supportive group of referrals. This contributes significantly to the sales pace of a project.

Builder reputation is important in new-house selling, and it is something that should be given more than lip service. In used housing, no promises can be made: the neighborhood is already there. However, the new-house salesperson can sell promises. What the community will become depends upon what the builder plans to put into it for the types of people who have been targeted as his markets.

Newness is an advantage that most salespeople don't fully utilize. From a purely practical standpoint (and this too is tied in with builder reputation), the new products carry warranties and the more recent assurance of the HOW (Home Owners Warranty) program for most reputable building companies (see Chapter 26).

There is often an opportunity to cater to individual tastes (depending on how the builder operates) with the customizing of many details or at least in color selections and product choices and options. Even though the astute salesperson may be restricted in these areas, he does have some tools that, if well handled, can be used to help close deals. It's a matter of suggesting to the customer that she can "create" her own house and not have to compromise her desires, tastes, and personality in order to live in someone else's used house.

The New-House Salesperson

The selection and training of salespersons is a continuing process, the training being a joint effort of the employer and the salesperson. Intelligence, verbal ability, curiosity, poise, energy, and self-motivation are necessary characteristics, and these characteristics are not limited to either sex or to a specific age group.

There is no satisfactory substitute for training as a continuing process. Training is not something that, once done, can be considered finished. It is an ongoing development of salespeople: the salespeople who are the most successful are the ones who never stop training. The truly successful salespeople know that training does pay off—in a manner similar to that of professional persons in any field, be they doctors, teachers, engineers, or athletes.

Formal Training. If available, formal training should be taken advantage of as often as time and budgeting will allow. The National Association of Home Builders and its local associations have done a fine job of providing sales seminars for members throughout the country. Sales course records/tapes and books provide an opportunity for training by a company sales manager or for self-training by each salesperson.

Informal Training. This is a matter of reading and studying such things as the NAHB's *Salesman's Handbook,* industry publications, newspapers, and other publications which have some relationship to the salesperson's job. Salespeople should "shop" housing projects in other areas. This offers a good chance to "see how the other person does it." Informal training is often left up to the individual.

Status within the Company. A salesperson is the company's principal representative. To the consumer, the salesperson is "the firm," or at least its principal voice. He must therefore be well informed by his company so that he can at all times be accurate.

For the most part, the salesperson is a loner. His hours are odd, and he is generally out of the mainstream of the company's day-to-day activities and operations, so that he doesn't experience the same degree of camaraderie as do other employees. His time is his customer's time, not his company's time. Nevertheless, the rest of the company should constantly think in terms of supporting the salespeople and keeping them informed. There is nothing more embarrassing to a salesperson than to be asked by an acquaintance or prospect, "What kind of houses are *you* planning to build on *your* new property?" when the salesperson doesn't even know that the property has been bought by the builder.

Although the sales department has the sole responsibility for bringing in signed contracts (that is, money), it should be recognized that the company as a whole is selling too. This includes every employee and function: telephone contacts, correspondence, bookkeepers, on-site workers, and customer service, including on-site trucks. Some builders hide their service department behind unpainted trucks, but service departments should do a good job and get credit for it. Prospects and resident customers alike are favorably impressed when they see that the service department isn't "hiding."

Relationship to the Community.   The best community relationships are developed by the salesperson who is compatible with the buyers' profile. As the voice of the builder, the salesperson who tries to be a part of the life of the community finds a real payoff in referrals. Enforced residency is generally not a prerequisite to doing a good job, but it certainly provides a solid foundation for one-upmanship. The builder who helps make it easy for a salesperson's family to move from one completed project to another recognizes the contributions that can result.

When a salesperson is the catalyst for getting a new community rolling (this may require some reimbursement from the builder), he can be in on the ground floor of helping to organize the community—all to the builder's advantage. For example, the salesperson can sponsor get-acquainted parties, which can range from small coffee klatches to cocktail parties. If a specialized prospect list has been developed, a certain exclusivity can be encouraged by inviting the prospects to a cocktail party to review the plans and offer comments—and make deposits which are subject to refund after the prices are announced.

A community bulletin board in the sales office can provide helpful information on matters ranging from baby-sitters to new move-ins. Prospects will be impressed too.

It's a philosophy of selling: it's selling a community, not selling a house and then another house. Involvement with the people means that selling is an ongoing process of helping to create customers—which goes back to the essential purpose of a housing business.

Hours and Compensation.   These must vary from situation to situation. Certainly, model homes must be open (as the store must be in any retail business) at stated hours, and there can be no deviation. In some manner, the compensation should recognize the unique duties and the taxing requirements in order to attract superior sales talent.

Self-motivation is a necessary ingredient in the makeup of the truly good house salesperson. He or she should be expected to be a self-starter. At the same time, however, the company owner or sales manager should continually consider extra possibilities for sales motivation. It's not just a matter of dollars: it's also a matter of goals; it's a matter of recognizing achievement, remembering the person on the firing line who is responsible for bringing in the money to all the others in the company who are responsible for spending it.

The three basic means of compensation are salary with no commission, commission with no salary, and a combination of the two. From time to time it may be necessary to alter the arrangement. The change is a delicate matter, and it should be made only for good reasons. The reason should not be that the salesperson has suddenly made too much money. A good salesperson should not be penalized for doing a good job. By the same token, care should be taken to make sure that the salesperson doesn't get too fat too quickly, because then his motivation for bringing in "extra" sales may wane. This is an area that bears careful and continual consideration.

A minimum base salary augmented by commissions on actual sales has two basic advantages. (1) Paying a salary—even a low one—gives management more control over a person's activities, such as his use of time, his hours, and his adherence to company policies and practices. (2) A minimum salary can free a person to think about selling in a well-motivated manner rather than worrying about whether or not he is going to be able to feed his family in the coming week.

On the other hand, some people don't really "scratch and dig" as hard as they might if they know that there will be a paycheck every week. This can result in the loss of insufficiently developed sales.

The fully commissioned, unsalaried person must be a consistently strong self-starter who is not easily overwhelmed by discouragement or slow spells. He must be a good personal money manager in order to handle the peaks and valleys that may occur.

Demonstrators.   Whether demonstrators are used depends upon a company's size, method of operation, and sales theories. For a relatively low expenditure, model home hours can easily be extended, thus also extending the salesperson's possibilities.

Quite often, residents of the community or nearby areas, or from a builder's houses in a previous community, can be excellent demonstrators. Such people are often enthusiastic and loyal believers in the product. Their primary purpose is to persuade the prospect to make an appointment with the salesperson. Demonstrators (usually women) can often establish rapport even more quickly than salespersons, because prospects somehow seem to know that demonstrators are not permitted to sell houses. (State and municipal laws should be researched to determine just what services demonstrators can and cannot perform.)

In addition, demonstrators can be a great source of future sales personnel. It's like the baseball farm system of having players train and work in the minor leagues and then perhaps getting called up for a crack at the big time.

Selling

Prospecting.   Every company employee is a sales representative wherever he or she goes. That's being an integral part of the building company team. But the bulk of prospecting is done through advertising, direct sales prospecting, and postsale selling.

Advertising should not be depended upon as the sole method of prospecting.

Personal prospecting is related to a salesperson's ability to do more than merely wait to sign up the prospects that are brought in by advertising. The self-starter will go out into the marketplace and develop his own prospects.

Phone calls will enable the salesperson to get many prospects and to keep in touch with them. Introductory letters will reach people who haven't seen the ads and heard the commercials. Even more important, phone calls and letters can be utilized to develop referrals from earlier, satisfied customers. Some salespeople think this is a waste of time: many *successful* salespeople believe otherwise.

The effectiveness of membership in civic organizations and community clubs is hard to measure, but this is another means of communication which builds referrals and sales. Public relations is far more than getting a few stories in the newspapers.

A good salesperson is a thought leader. People respect his judgments, ideas, and recommendations. Such a salesperson's exposure to public activities can evolve into selling opportunities. This is professionalism in selling at its best. This type of salesperson takes pride in his vocation.

Face-to-Face Selling.   Entire books and sales training courses have been built around the subject of face-to-face selling. There are a few essentials, however, that top producers develop as almost second nature.

The language of the top producers is benefit talk developed through a thorough knowledge and appreciation of the facts regarding every aspect of the builder, community, product, location, and environment they are selling. The top producers see communication as a two-way street, which means that a sales pitch cannot be canned but must be a response to the particular prospect's interests, needs, desires, and personality.

Listening and questioning is selling by learning what the prospects are contemplating and then trying to satisfy their needs. If it can be worked in, politely, shortly after a prospect enters the model home—your place of business—*one key question* is: "When will you be needing your new home?" This will usually evoke an informative, qualifying response about employment (transfer, promotion, etc.), ages of children (the desire and timing for new schools), present living arrangements (lease termination, sale of present house), changing size of family, and so on.

Another key question is: "What type of home do you live in now?" or "Where do you live now?" The answer will probably be extremely informative because it will probably indicate urgent needs and areas of satisfaction and dissatisfaction.

Demonstrating the house is something that many salespersons believe in, whereas some tend to ignore this sales technique. For the most part, those in the latter group are not sales professionals. They are order-takers who believe in letting the house sell itself and thereby miss many opportunities to generate sales. Demonstrating is a "must" in new-house selling. It is a totally preplanned and prerouted "show and tell" program which can convert a model home to a personal home for a particular prospect. Professional selling requires energy, enthusiasm, and empathy—the three *e*'s of *excellent* salespeople. Order-taking requires only sales clerks (who don't get paid as well).

Motivating the second visit involves selling the idea of the next interview. Few people make up their minds to buy during the first visit to a model, but this should not discourage the professional. Keeping in mind the prospect's attitude of "What's in it for me?" will help maintain the prospect's interest and desire to return.

Sale closings can be generated by some cinchers of developing key assurances about newness. These include warranties (HOW), the community, investment augmentation, builder reputation, and service. Facts which are converted to benefits for the buyer are sold by example and information that will relieve the prospect's spoken and unspoken concerns. It's a big decision for the prospect. The prospect needs to have his desires reinforced by logical reasoning which will provide the justifications he needs.

Follow-up and follow-through are necessary characteristics of a strong sales posture. Promising to get additional information about a prospect's question (even though you may already know the answer) creates an opportunity for obtaining the prospect's phone number and address so that a follow-up contact can keep the prospect's interest at a high level. Again, the follow-through information should be in terms of benefit to the customer.

Postsale Selling. Postsale selling starts when the sale contract is signed, by making sure that the customer fully understands the company's service policy so that there are no misunderstandings at a later date. The company's authority, together with its sincere desire to please its customers, should be established very early, by "educating" the buyer about exactly what he can rightfully expect. Properly presented, the service policy will be a positive sale-clinching tool.

The salesperson's job is by no means completed with the signing of the contract. The prospect has been converted to a customer through the selling process. But he remains a prospect in one sense: at this point and for some time to come, he is a prospective source of referrals for new business.

Although the procedure is time consuming and its productiveness is not readily apparent, it is truly worthwhile to stay in touch with all postcontract customers. They are now particularly receptive to detailed information. Keeping such customers posted on the construction progress of *their* houses will prevent them from feeling left out. If feasible, help the postcontract customer to visit his home during construction or send him a Polaroid of his house every week or so.

Postsettlement Selling. Moving into a new home is a hectic experience for most buyers. Eager anticipation soon gives way to a terrible letdown of crates and confusion. The salesperson should recognize this and respond to the buyers' mood with empathy and understanding. Be the first friend to stop by. Tell the buyers about some new neighbors who are also moving in. Remind them about school enrollment procedures.

Be your own special welcome wagon. Thus, the pattern will be instantly set for remaining friends with the buyers. This will enable you to help them get involved in neighborhood activities in which you too may be involved.

However, it takes the company's service department to make all of this really work. The best sales staff in the business can function successfully only if its commitments to customers are backed up by the company's products and service.

The service department and the sales department should function well together, each understanding the needs and the importance of the other. Appropriate service policies and attitudes can pay off for the entire company, for there is no better sales representative than a satisfied customer whose referrals will convert new prospects to new customers.

Since the purpose of a housing business is to create customers, the selling process has come full circle when the sales staff can keep in touch with customers who have been truly satisfied by products and promises. Enthusiastic customers bring referrals—and sales.

SELLING APARTMENT HOUSES*

Norman L. Jacobson

*N*ORMAN L. JACOBSON, Secretary/Treasurer, Wagner-Jacobson
Co., Inc., Realtors®, Los Angeles, California.
　　Lecturer on apartment house marketing at Los Angeles and
Irvine Campuses, University of California. Formerly regional
vice president and director of the California Association of Real-
tors®, and vice chairman of the Syndication Division. Formerly
president, Los Angeles Board of Realtors®. Author of numerous
articles for real estate trade publications and of the specialized
text, Real Estate Exchange Techniques with Tax Implications.
Founding editor of The California Syndicator.

Motivations for Selling

It is crucial that there be a motivation on the part of the seller, that
the seller be able to define that motivation, and that the broker be able
to recognize it. If the wheels are set in motion to market a piece of
property when the seller has no clear-cut motivation for parting with
it, a substantial amount of time is going to be wasted by a number of
individuals, including the seller, the broker, the prospective buyer, and
the lender.

Even an established brokerage operation will obtain no more than
one third of its prospective apartment house sellers on an unsolicited
basis. The typical prospective seller is obtained through public seminars
and educational programs or through an extensive direct mail program
followed up by random telephoning and doorbell ringing of apartment
house owners on the basis of such sources as specially designed owner
directories and for Sale by Owner ads. It doesn't matter how the commu-

---

*From Norman L. Jacobson, *Apartment Houses . . . How to Invest, How to Sell* (Los
Angeles: California Association of Realtors®, 1978). © 1978 by California Association of
Realtors®.

nication with the apartment owner is first made. Even if he walks into the office and says he wants to sell, it is absolutely critical that he be qualified as a bona fide seller and that he have an honest-to-goodness reason for selling now or in the very near future. An owner cannot be talked into selling his property with so-called good salesmanship. The sky may be falling in, the mortgage market may be collapsing, and vacancies may be on the upswing. But it is still up to the owner to decide whether or not he is ready to sell, and it is up to the broker to realize that he cannot create a motivation for selling where none exists.

As a Realtor® specializing in income property, you should know how to prepare an analysis of an apartment house which presents factual information showing the benefits of the sale to both the seller and the buyer. However, before committing yourself to prepare such an analysis, you should determine whether the owner is motivated to sell. If the owner is willing to divulge a substantial amount of information on the status of his property, you may interpret this as an indication that the owner may be motivated to sell.

Many apartment house owners are eager to pick the brains of a Realtor® in order to receive free advice. After they obtain the advice, they may try to sell the property without the Realtor® or they may choose not to sell at all. It is therefore important for you to determine conclusively the owner's motivation for selling a property before you proceed with an analysis. You need not be reticent about asking owners why they are interested in selling their property.

There are a number of motivations for selling an apartment house. If none of these exists for a particular owner, it probably won't be wise for you to waste much time on an analysis of the property, even if the necessary information is readily obtainable from the owner. The following are among the most common motivations for selling an apartment house.

Divorce.   In this instance, it is essential that both partners agree on the price and terms at which the property is going to sell. It is also essential that both parties sign the exclusive listing contract or other agreements relating to the sale of the property.

You should never accept only one party's word, because the two parties to a divorce are usually fighting each other. The first thing to do is find out whether both parties are in accord on the price. Even that may not be enough, since it is always possible that one party will pull the rug from under the other party by refusing to sign a document when the sale is made. If there is any doubt at all, it's essential to determine whether or not there is a written agreement, signed by both the husband and the wife, to sell that property at a given price and terms. The broker may find it beneficial to ask the husband and wife for the names of the attorneys who represent them. He should then obtain the necessary documentation from the attorney to assure himself that he is obtaining a valid listing which, when sold at the stipulated price and terms, will be signed by all parties so that the sale can be consummated.

Poor Health.   Poor health is one of the most frequent reasons behind the sale of smaller properties which are personally managed by the owner.

Old Age.   A very frequent motivation for selling even a prime property is old age. The usual reasons given are that the owners want to be relieved of the on-site or off-site management duties involved in the ownership of the property so that they can take it easy, do a little traveling, and so on.

Because some attorneys advise clients to hold their property and let their heirs dispose of it, you should suggest to owners of advanced age that they check with their tax attorney or their CPA before they sell their property. A tax attorney may have a certain kind of tax plan set up for the sellers, and he may be instrumental in determining the terms and the timing of the sale.

Recent changes in the law affecting taxes on real property paid by the heirs may influence owners to sell before death. It is important for you to know about tax law changes that may create an advantage or a disadvantage in selling an apartment house. However, no matter how knowledgeable you may be, it is dangerous for you to get involved in giving tax advice or interpreting recent tax law changes. In order to stay clear of any problems that may arise from your giving inaccurate advice, you should urge the prospective seller to see an attorney for the proper advice. This will make your job substantially easier and a lot safer.

Partnership Problems.   A partnership problem may arise because one partner complains that he is doing all the work while the other partner is sitting around and simply collecting the spendable income from a property. As with divorce, it is essential that both partners agree in writing to the terms and conditions of the sale. It is also essential that you get both partners to sign the final listing agreement.

If a general partner is acting for various limited partners, or if one partner is empowered to act for the others, you should accept that partner's signature to a listing only if you have been given a copy of the document showing that the partner signing the listing is authorized to act on behalf of the other partners. In the case of a limited partnership, it is senseless to market a property unless the general partner has first received a written authorization from the required percentage of ownership interests to sell the property at the agreed-upon price and terms.

Owner's Need for Cash.   If an owner's present loan is small in relationship to the amount he can raise from a new loan, he may be able to raise cash immediately by refinancing. On the other hand, a property which has been purchased recently and is heavily mortgaged may not be capable of generating enough cash to meet the owner's needs through refinancing.

A sale may therefore be the most practical means of generating cash, especially if the property can be sold for a high down payment. Highly sophisticated property owners are usually well informed about the cash-raising potentials of selling their property, but it is your responsibility to be extremely explicit with a cash-hungry seller who wants to market his property. You should not mislead the seller. You should lay your cards on the table and tell the seller the price and terms at which the property can be marketed quickly, especially if the owner is selling because he needs cash in a hurry. In addition to any listing forms or analyses that you present to the seller, you should have a form showing what the approximate net proceeds will be at the close of escrow. This enables the owner to know exactly how much cash he will receive after he pays the expenses involved in the transaction and pays off existing loans.

Death. The surviving spouse may need to sell a property for a number of reasons. The seller, however, should be able to tell you what information he needs concerning any complications that might arise in the event of such a sale. You have to determine whether the property can be freely listed and sold by the surviving spouse or whether the estate must approve the sale. If the property can be sold, you should determine whether or not there might be a long delay in closing the sale in order to satisfy requirements of the estate as to the distribution of assets.

Evidence of authorization to sell the property must be made available before the property is shown to prospective buyers. Prospective buyers must be told about any complications which may affect the ultimate consummation of the transaction. Given a complex probate, the loan market may have changed substantially or mortgage money may be unavailable by the time the transaction can be consummated.

Management Problems. If there are management problems, the seller may simply want to sell in order to be relieved of the responsibilities of operating the property.

Owner's Relocation. A move from one city to another may be an important enough reason for a seller to want to dispose of his property, especially if it is a small building which he would be unable to manage from a great distance.

Exchange for Commercial Property. Some owners are unhappy with apartment house management and want a property which requires less supervision. They may be willing to accept a smaller return by acquiring a commercial property or a small shopping center with all tenants on net-net leases.

In many cases, however, a broker will get involved with an owner who wants to exchange his property for a prime piece of commercial property located at the most prestigious corner in the city. Such properties are rarely available, and when they are available, the prices are very high and the terms inflexible.

Many brokers chase things they can never catch. When you are involved with an owner who wants to dispose of his apartment house for geographic reasons or wants to trade up, you must set him straight in the beginning as to what is actually available in an exchange transaction. Many good salespeople have left the business because they lost months of production in an effort to put an impossible exchange together. The multimillion-dollar "dream" exchange is rarely consummated.

Owners who are motivated to exchange can be good prospects for selling their property and buying another property. You can work out all the costs of selling the property, paying whatever tax is involved, and then buying another property. The owner may discover that even after paying the costs of the sale, he can acquire a property which will produce a good income and will appreciate over the years.

This is a simple procedure that many owners and brokers overlook because they have been overly influenced by the tax consequences of a straight sale and by bits and pieces of information about tax-free exchanges. They have heard that exchanging is the only way to minimize taxes. Many brokers don't seem to realize that some owners simply want to minimize their taxes in the most practical way possible.

You should make a thorough study of installment sales and of all-inclusive trust deeds and land contracts, and you should understand the seller's current motivations. Knowing an owner's present tax basis and his present income from all sources will enable you to determine what the tax burden would be in the year of sale if an installment sale was executed. An owner may be surprised to find that in his present tax bracket the amount of tax he has to pay on the sale of his property will be substantially lower in the year of sale than he thought. Thus, he will proceed with a straight sale rather than insist that you locate an exchange property for him.

Minimizing Taxes. This often occurs when the owner retires from regular employment and is no longer in a high tax bracket. Look for retired owners; they are better prospects for selling now than they were before they retired. There are many complications because the tax laws have changed substantially, but at the same time property values have skyrocketed in recent years. Quite frequently an owner has an apartment house that he bought many years ago for, say, $100,000. He has depreciated it down to, say, $50,000. He has a $50,000 tax basis, and his property is worth $250,000. Naturally he is concerned about the possibility of paying the taxes on a gain of $200,000. One method of minimizing the taxes is to combine an installment sale with the use of a wraparound instrument—either an all-inclusive trust deed or a land contract, depending upon which is more appropriate at the time.

> *Example:* A property is worth $250,000, and the tax basis is $50,000. To qualify for an installment sale under the federal tax laws, the owner may not take an initial payment of more than 30 percent of the purchase price in the year of sale—$75,000 in this case. The 30 percent—or 29 percent as it is commonly referred to—includes the down payment, the excess of any existing mortgage over the tax basis, and the principal payments in the year of sale.
>
> In this case, let's assume that the property was refinanced recently for $150,000. Thus, the excess of the mortgage over the basis ($150,000 loan amount less $50,000 tax basis = $100,000) exceeds the $75,000 maximum which the owner may receive as an initial payment. All of the gain on the sale of the property would therefore be subject to taxes, and the potential for minimizing and deferring such taxes would be eliminated.
>
> You might arrange the transaction to have the seller carry a wraparound all-inclusive trust deed or land contract, which would work out as follows: sale price $250,000, $50,000 down, and a $200,000 wraparound loan. The owner remains liable for the underlying first trust deed of $150,000, and the excess of the mortgage over the basis is not calculated in the determination of the initial payment (the maximum 30 percent in the year of sale). Depending upon the term of the wraparound contract, he could defer the gain on the rest of the sale for a long time.

Although you may be armed with adequate information, you must make certain that the seller checks with a tax attorney and that you are not responsible for giving any kind of legal or accounting advice.

Analysis Procedures

Before you proceed to inspect and appraise an apartment house property and spend substantial time making an analysis, you should obtain significant pertinent information. Obtain the address of the property, survey the neighborhood, and mentally grade the area on some kind of arbitrary scale (such as a scale of one to ten—one being the best, ten the worst).

Characteristics of the Property. Your first obligation, obviously, is to the seller. You are obligated to appraise the property at the highest price it will bring on the market. You must not quote an unreasonably high price to secure the listing. After taking all factors into consideration, you should determine the highest obtainable price. In looking at an area, for example, you should evaluate the property trends and the quality of the apartment house tenancy. If the area and the property are both "number one" on a scale of one to ten, you will recommend the highest possible price and the highest possible down payment because buyers react favorably to a number one property in a number one area. However, if the seller owns a number ten property in a number ten area, he will understand that his property cannot be sold on such favorable terms.

You have to obtain the listing at a price and terms that will make it attractive to an investor. If buyers had their choice, they would prefer properties in such glamorous locations as Beverly Hills. Then why do people buy properties in far less glamorous areas? They buy them because the broker establishes prices and terms which produce substantially higher returns than does investment in property located in a number one area.

Your first step in filling out the analysis form (see Exhibit 1) is to determine the authorized number of units in the building (item 1). If the owner is uncertain, check with the local building department. This information will enter into your final estimate of price, and it must be disclosed to the prospective buyer. If a 12-unit was converted from an 8-unit, or if a 15-unit is indeed a 12-unit, this must be disclosed, and the disclosure will affect the price.

The age of the property is very important, but some owners do not know the *exact* age of their property. One simple way to find out the approximate age is to lift up the top of the water closet and look at the date stamped on the lid. Some properties, however, may have had their toilets replaced, so you cannot always depend on this method. Again, you may have to check with the building department.

You should indicate on your analysis form the number of parking spaces and whether they are covered or open. You should also specify the type of construction—frame, frame and stucco, brick, or whatever. You should also show the lot size and the zoning of the property. Al-

EXHIBIT 1

UPON RECEIPT OF THIS <u>FULLY COMPLETED FORM</u>
YOU WILL BE PROVIDED WITH A FREE

COMPUTERIZED APARTMENT HOUSE ANALYSIS
Prepared by **Wagner/Jacobson Co., Inc.** *Realtors*

Number One in Apartment House Sales and Exchanges
CORPORATE OFFICES: 5858 WILSHIRE BOULEVARD, LOS ANGELES, CALIFORNIA 90036 • CR-4-6688 • 937-3731

1 PROPERTY ADDRESS: ___12704 COLTON AVENUE, LOS ANGELES___

Number of units: __12__ Parking covered: __7__ Exterior: __Stucco__ Lot size: __60 X 150__
Property age: __20__ Parking open: __5__ Alley: __Rear__ Zone: __R-3__

2 FEATURES: Carpets ☒ Built-ins ☒ Pool ☐ Rec.room ☐ _____☐
Drapes ☒ Air cond. ☐ Elevator ☐ F.A. heat ☐ _____☐

3 EXISTING FINANCING (CURRENT BALANCES):

				Payable		Holder		Final due date
1st TD:	88,000	at	7.75 % Int.	801	/month	Home S/L		16 years
2nd TD:	None	at	% Int.		/month			

4 PROPERTY VALUE/DEPRECIATION:
(Copy this information
from you current
property tax bill.)

Improvements .... $ __30,000__
Furnishings ...... $ __1,000__
Land .... $ __7,500__
TOTAL .... $ __38,500__

5 FIXED ANNUAL EXPENSES:

Taxes .... $ __4,467 (18%)__
Insurance .... $ __400(1)__
Utilities .... $ __1,584(2)__
Trash .... $ __180__
Gardener .... $ __300__
Manager .... $ __864(3)__
Pool .... $ _____
Elevator .... $ _____
License/Permits ... $ __43__
Work Comp. Ins.... $ __200(Est)__
Other .... $ __120__
Other .... $ _____
TOTAL .... $ __8,158(32.86%)__

6 HOW LONG OWNED?
Since 1967

7 TAX BASIS: $ __102,000__

8 REASON FOR SELLING:
Getting Divorced

9 LOCATION, DIRECTIONS:
__3__ blocks __East__ of
La Brea
__1__ blocks __North__ of
Third Street

0 REMARKS: (1) New Policy; (2) $11 per unit per month; (3) Est. at $6/Unit-
owner lives O/P and manages.

1 OWNERS: __Mr. & Mrs. Harold Lewis__ Address: __O/P Apartment 12__ Phone: __937-2147__
_____ Address: _____ Phone: _____
To show: Manager's name: __Owner__ Apt. # __12__ Phone: __937-2147__

2 FILL OUT THE REVERSE SIDE OF THIS FORM WITH YOUR
"RENT AND MISCELLANEOUS INCOME SCHEDULE"
**IT IS VERY IMPORTANT THAT YOU FILL OUT BOTH SIDES OF
THIS FORM COMPLETELY AND ACCURATELY**

RETURN TO ►

CONFIDENTIAL

though this is not necessarily going to affect the price substantially, it is information that has to be placed on a listing.

You should become totally familiar with the features and amenities of the property (item 2 of Exhibit 1). The features can be quite basic, such as carpets and drapes and built-in ovens and ranges, but a building may also have air conditioners, a swimming pool, elevators, a recreation room, a roof garden, or whatever. These features will influence your ultimate appraisal, especially your determination of whether the rent levels reflect the amenities.

The Existing Financing. Next, you should find out the status of the existing financing. (item 3 of Exhibit 1). This involves obtaining the outstanding balance and the interest rate and payments of the first trust deed as well as the name of the lender, and also finding out whether the lender is in the market for refinancing. This factor is important both for your final price estimate and for the net proceeds sheet that you prepare for the seller. If a loan cannot be obtained through the existing lender, a prepayment penalty will probably be involved and a new lender must be used for the ultimate refinancing of the property.

Your analysis should show the seller's costs involved in two types of selling arrangements. One type uses the existing lender and involves a lesser loan and the possible acceleration of the interest rate up to the current levels. The other type involves paying off the present loan, with a prepayment penalty charged to the seller, and obtaining a larger loan through a new lender. Analyze both types, and then show the owner how the property can be marketed either way.

For example, assume that the present loan on an apartment house is $50,000 and that the present lender will increase the loan to only $100,000, in which event there would be no prepayment penalty. Assume further that a loan from a competing lender is available at $130,000. Given these assumptions, the broker should make two analyses and prepare two net proceeds sheets showing the net result of both options to the seller.

Most lenders will not send out an appraisal crew to a building simply on the strength of a phone call from a broker who says that he is making an analysis of a property and hopes to get a listing. However, if you have good rapport with various savings and loan sources, you can briefly describe the property to them and ask them what criteria they would use in determining the loan and on what factors the loan would be based if such a property were presented to them for refinancing. After being given the appropriate information, a lender might say, "Well, based upon what you have told me, with the given rent schedule and the condition, location, and type of tenancy, we would lend an amount whose annual debt service does not exceed 55 percent of today's scheduled gross income." This gives you a yardstick on which to base your loan projections.

When the prices of apartment houses are inflated, the lender is careful not to make a loan that will put a property in a negative cash flow position. The lender may only be concerned with the payments on his first trust deed loans, *not* second trust deed loans. He looks at the property this way: "We want to be able to at least break even on the property if we have to foreclose. What the buyer pays for the property is his problem. We want to protect our loan."

It is essential for the broker to understand the lender's problem and not to delude himself into believing that he can get a loan that is not obtainable. This makes the seller believe that he can receive more cash than he really can, and it makes the net proceeds sheet erroneous, showing an incorrect amount of cash as being generated from a down payment and new financing. If the new financing is fictitious, the listing is not worth the paper it is written on. Also, if the property is placed on the market predicated upon a loan that is $30,000 more than the amount that is really obtainable, and an offer is obtained at the exact price and terms of the listing, the sale will be invalid because the broker and the seller will not be able to comply with the terms of the listing.

With a listing that shows inaccurate financing information, you are just spinning your wheels and creating ill will with the seller and the buyer. In some cases, the seller may be unsophisticated and may convince the broker that a 70 percent loan is obtainable. But 70 percent of what? Is it 70 percent of the selling price or 70 percent of the lender's appraisal, which may be substantially less than the selling price? If the seller does a good sales job on the broker and the broker yields to the seller's suggestion that the listing should be predicated upon the obtaining of a 70 percent loan based on the specified price, then the broker is eventually going to be in trouble with his buyer. The loan is not going to be obtainable, and the sale will probably never be consummated.

It is important to research the financing and to check with the savings and loan institution before the analysis is made, so that a factual presentation can be given to the seller for the purpose of obtaining the listing. If secondary financing exists on the property, it should be determined whether the holder of the second trust deed is available for discussion. He may elect not to be paid and may continue to carry all or part of his loan at a renegotiated rate and terms, or with a partial payoff behind a substantially higher first trust deed. Some holders of second trust deeds carry them in order to obtain income which they may not be able to obtain at the bank, and thus may want to keep the second trust deed and note intact. This is a source of additional financing that is often overlooked because the broker automatically assumes that all secondary financing must be paid off. Sometimes a lock-in clause in the secondary financing provides that it may not be paid off for another several years. In this event, the broker may have to go into wraparound types of financing to make the transaction.

You should obtain a copy of the seller's present property tax bill (item 4 in Exhibit 1) for a number of reasons. First of all, you need to look at the tax bill to evaluate the property. You can compare that evaluation with like kinds of property that you may have analyzed recently.

Frequently the assessor doesn't get around to reappraising a given piece of property for three, four, or five years. If the property taxes are low in relationship to the scheduled gross income or to the square footage, you should be able to recognize this so that you can call the local county assessor's office and find out whether the area in which the property is located is due to be reassessed during the coming year. It may be that the assessed valuations will increase sharply. Armed with this information, you are in a position to make a more objective analysis and to present the seller with the possibility of a property tax increase.

The property tax bill will also give you information about the improvements, personal property, and land in relationship to the total assessed valuation of the property. This information will be useful in establishing the recommended depreciation schedule for the property if you obtain the listing.

Expenses. The next item of the analysis (item 5 of Exhibit 1) involves the expenses category. You should divide this into two subcategories: fixed expenses (inevitable expenses that cannot be changed, such as property taxes, insurance, and utilities); and variable expenses (such as allowances for vacancies, maintenance, repairs, and replacements).

There are several "usual" categories of fixed expenses, and each of these should be verified with the owner and analyzed in terms of how realistic it is in today's market. First, consider property taxes. Are the property taxes realistic, or is it possible that they will increase substantially? You should become familiar with the relationship between property taxes and scheduled gross income for like properties in the area. For example, in California, property taxes upon change of ownership are adjusted to equal about 1.25 percent of the selling price.

Insurance is a variable item. The easy way out is to simply look at the owner's present comprehensive insurance bill, which covers fire insurance, liability, loss of rents, and other multiperil coverage. However, insurance rates increase almost annually, and you should determine whether the insurance policy premium now being paid by the seller would be the same for the buyer. A simple way to do this is to call up your own apartment house insurance specialist. Describe the building, and be prepared to give him the approximate square footage. The insurance agent will be able to come up with a rough estimate of what a new premium will be this year. Insurance policies that were established three years ago may be due to expire, and the insurance cost which should be placed on the analysis form should be the new premium, not what the owner is paying.

Your analysis serves two objectives. It enables you to see the true picture so that the listing price is what it really should be, and it enables you to eliminate a lot of figures that a prospective buyer would recognize as inaccurate. Apartment house buyers are knowledgeable about costs and would recognize immediately whether the taxes on your analysis form were too low or the insurance understated. They know about what these figures should be because they have been looking at other properties or perhaps because they already own other properties.

This is a big problem for many brokers. For example, a broker may obtain a listing and include the seller's figure for insurance at $400 a year. Then the property receives a new fire rating because it has reached a new age level, and the new policy costs $1,000 a year. The broker should have found out about this when he obtained the listing. Instead, the sale is ready to close and the insurance carrier sends in a bill for $1,000. The buyer can then claim that the cost of the insurance was misrepresented and that the $600 differential effectively reduces the spendable income from the building. He probably has a good case for backing out of the transaction, even though a lot of time and money has been spent to put it together.

The same holds true for utilities. It is quite simple to take a seller's word for the utility bills that he claims to have paid during the preceding year. Utilities can vary considerably among buildings with an equal number of units. For example, one ten-unit apartment house may have separate utility meters for each apartment, and those meters may be connected to the porch lights of the apartments and to the gas that heats individual hot water tanks in the apartments. In this case, the owner of the property need only pay for the water used in the building and the utilities may cost him as little as $5 or $6 per unit per month in the state of California. Another ten-unit property may have a master hot water tank, so that the owner is required to pay for the water and for the gas to heat it. The porch lights too may be paid for by the owner. In addition, there may be a central hallway which is serviced by a central air conditioning unit whose operating costs are borne by the owner and the building may have a swimming pool whose water and gas costs are also paid for by the owner.

Miscellaneous Information. Unless you are a recognized expert on capital gains tax rates and installment sales you should consult a certified public accountant on these matters. We discussed motivations for selling and you should include on your analysis sheet (item 8 of Exhibit 1) the real reason why the owner is selling his property—old age, divorce, a partnership dissolution, and so on. You should attach a map of the area to the analysis, pinpointing the location of the property. Finally you should ask the owner whether there are others who share in the ownership. The owner you are working with may own 60 percent of the property, and another party may own 40 percent. There may be a limited partnership situation, and the owner who is seeking the appraisal may simply be the general partner. It is essential to find out the correct vesting. If there is more than one owner, you should present your ultimate appraisal when all of the parties to the transaction are present.

You should also have the manager's name, and you should know how the property can be shown. Owners are often reluctant to allow brokers to disturb tenants or to upset the manager. In such a case, you should explain to the owner that you must inspect several apartments in order to make an objective appraisal. If the owner thinks that your doing so will cause the manager to quit or to be worried about selling the property, you might suggest that he tell the manager that he is sending over an appraiser because he is considering the possibility of refinancing.

Income. You are now ready to verify the rent and miscellaneous income from the building (Exhibit 2). Many brokers and salespeople take the easy way out, accepting a very general statement of the rental

EXHIBIT 2

RENT AND MISCELLANEOUS INCOME SCHEDULE

APT. #	# BDRMS.	# BATHS	MONTHLY RENTS UNFURN.	MONTHLY RENTS FURN.	VACANT?	LEASED TO (DATE)	MISC. INFORMATION	TENANT STAY
1	1	1	150				Widow	8 yrs.
2	1	1	155				Account. (age 55)	1 yr.
3	2	1 1/2	190				Shoe Store Owner	New
4	1	1		175			Sec/t, Texaco	1 1/2 yrs.
5	2	1 1/2	200				2 Brothers	1 yr.
6	Sngl	1		140			Retired Announcer	4 yrs.
7	1	1	160		X		Last Tenant there	3 1/3 yrs.
8	1	1	155				Belly Dancer	1 yr.
9	2	1 1/2	195				Engineer & Wife	3 yrs.
10	1	1		180			Architect	2 yrs.
11	2	1 1/2	190				Salesman (age 60)	1 yr.
12	Sngl	1		145			Retired Couple (owner)	9 yrs.
					#10 Has new furniture			

MONTHLY GARAGE INCOME $ -0-

MONTHLY TOTAL RENTS $ 2,035

ANNUAL TOTAL RENTS $ 24,420

ANNUAL LAUNDRY INCOME $ 400 (Equipment owned by building)

ANNUAL TOTAL INCOME $ 24,820

income. The seller may say, "My building has ten one-bedrooms at a price range of $190 to $235 per month and ten two-bedrooms at a range of $225 to $275 per month." This very general rental information will then appear on the listing, and this is the way it is given to the prospective seller.

However, whether the subject property is a 20-unit building or a 220-unit building, each and every rental should be itemized. You should make a list of all the apartments, and the list should show the number of bedrooms, the number of baths, and the rental rate for each apartment, unfurnished or furnished. If an apartment is partially furnished, the list should indicate whether a refrigerator or a range is included. It is also important to know whether an apartment is subject to an unexpired lease and when the lease expires. In order to establish the character of a building, you should take time to determine what kinds of tenants reside in it. For example, a building which has as long-term tenants three accountants, two department store managers, an oil company executive, and a college professor, all of whom are between 45 and 60 years old, has a character which is entirely different from that of an apartment house whose residents are cocktail waitresses, artists, motorcycle repairers, and sign painters with an average tenancy of between four and six months.

Itemize the occupations of the tenants, possibly the ages and the number of children in the building, and any other information that may be pertinent in establishing the character of the property. Information on each tenant's length of stay will enable you to determine the stability of the property. You may also wish to note which apartments have new furniture or new carpeting and drapes or other amenities which are not common to all of the apartments. If a one-bedroom apartment which rents for $250 is next door to another that rents for substantially less, you should state why the differential exists.

Be sure to include miscellaneous income, such as that obtained from laundry equipment. It is important to know whether the laundry income is generated by laundry equipment that is owned by an outside company or by laundry equipment that belongs to the building.

Establishing the Price. In order to enable you and your prospective buyer to compare one apartment house with another, it is important to use the same method of analysis and the same form. If your prospective buyer is considering another property and has an analysis of it on a different form, you should take the time to analyze that property and to make any changes that are needed to enable the two properties to compete on an equal basis. Because of the great variety in the ways that properties are presented to buyers, the buyers often look at the bottom line only, and the figures on that line can be misleading if a complete analysis of all expenses has not been made.

When you are taking a listing, do not set a price on the apartment house until you have made a thorough analysis of the property. Take the needed time, and make an appointment with the owner for presenting your analysis.

Now that your analysis of income and expenses has been completed, how do you establish the price? In some unusual times and markets, buyers are confronted with an analysis which reveals that an apartment house will have a zero return or even a negative cash flow. They purchase the property anyhow because they are anxious to own real estate that they believe will increase in value so long as inflation continues. Even in such a case, the more thorough analysis is valuable because it will show in exact terms what the monthly cost of owning the property will be.

Fear of competition frequently motivates brokers to give owners rough estimates of price in an effort to list a property before someone else does. You should explain to the owner that you cannot give him a determination of value until you have completed an area survey and other background work and have made a number of mathematical computations, and that it will take a day or so before you can get back to the owner with an honest appraisal based upon fact rather than fancy. You may also tell the owner that this kind of information is going to be required by the prospective buyer and that if it is not obtained in advance, the chances of selling quickly and at the listed price and terms become more difficult. Indicate that this is a free professional service that you provide in marketing apartment houses.

Physical Examination of the Property.   Make a thorough physical examination of the property and grade it as excellent, average, or poor. This grade will be considered in the evaluation of the property. Determine what maintenance has been deferred and how much it will cost. Quite often, you can find experts in the area who, for a very reasonable fee, will provide you with estimates for such work as repairing broken staircases, painting the trim or the building, repairing or replacing the roof, and replacing carpeting and drapes. You need this information so that you can present the seller with documented evidence when you give him your estimate of present value.

You should examine the rental rates of the subject property in relationship to at least four or five comparable buildings in the immediate area. You will find that resident managers or owner-occupants are very willing to offer information concerning their rentals and their apartments in exchange for information that you have acquired in your research. From your survey you will be able to determine whether the rentals of the subject property are at the average market rates, at the top market rates, or at rates somewhat or substantially below those that could be obtained with modest improvements to the property, such as recarpeting, repainting, landscaping, and so on. If the subject property is not located in a city subject to rent control, and you plan to suggest improving the property and increasing rents, you must determine whether the new rents will be competitive. You may also take into consideration the vacancy rate, the quality of the tenancy, and the effectiveness of the present on-site management. You should be prepared to say whether or not a change of manager will result in a more efficient operation.

Establishing a Value.   Unfortunately, an age-old tendency of real estate brokers, especially those who spend most of their time selling single-family residences, is to multiply the scheduled gross income of the property by some arbitrary figure and to arrive at the estimated value on this basis. Income properties are not sold on gross income; they are sold on net income or potential net income. Thus, gross multipliers are useful only in comparing the selling prices of similar buildings. The gross multiplier estimate is misleading because one building may cost more to operate than another. For example, a major differential in the cost of operation exists when the utilities are paid entirely by the tenants in one building and entirely by the owner in another.

The first questions you must ask yourself in making your appraisal are: What return will a buyer of this particular property expect as a percentage of his down payment? What down payment will a buyer make for this building? What kind of financing can be obtained, and at what interest rate and payment schedule?

Some apartment houses, depending upon their rental levels and their potential, can be sold with net spendables that are barely above the break-even point. Some properties with negative cash flows may be sold when property values are increasing and the property is not subject to rent control. However, sophisticated investors will buy a building with a negative cash flow only if they think that the negative cash flow can soon be changed to a positive cash flow which will give them the expected return on the investment.

A property in a number one area can usually be sold for a cash-to-the-loan down payment, with no need for the seller to carry secondary financing. Properties in marginal locations, properties with substantial deferred maintenance, and properties with some major physical problem may at best be salable at down payments of only 10 to 15 percent of the selling price. Buyers purchase such properties because the price and terms are attractive and the down payment meets their budget. The down payment in a number one area may be way beyond what a buyer can afford to pay at present.

The Band of Investment Type of Approach. One means for determining the value of property is the "band of investment" type of approach. This is a simple technique for determining a capitalization rate and arriving at a price. A specific example is shown in Exhibit 3. In evaluating the information supplied by the seller of this property, the broker determined from a rent survey of neighboring apartment houses that the current scheduled gross rental income of $39,420 could be increased by at least 5 percent, to $41,391. The broker also determined that the owner's fixed annual expenses had to be adjusted in accordance with the notations in Exhibit 3.

Your first task in this example is to determine the net income before debt service, after which you can arrive at a capitalization rate. From this rate you can determine the price on the basis of certain assumptions. Your next task is to determine what the traffic will bear in the way of down payment and return on investment, as well as the maximum first trust deed that is obtainable at the prevailing rate and terms. We'll assume that you evaluate the area and grade it in the six–seven category— not the worst but not the best. You determine that a buyer would not

EXHIBIT 3
Band of Investment Type of Approach for Arriving at Capitalization Rate

Facts

Current scheduled gross income		$39,420
But can be increased by 10 percent		1,971
Projected scheduled gross income		$41,391
Adjusted fixed expenses	$8,927	
Vacancies/maintenance/replacement (11% of projected SGI)	4,553	
Total expenses (32.6% of projected SGI)		$13,480
Net income before debt service		$27,911

Assumptions

Down payment	20%	
Maximun first trust deed	65%	At 11.57%, 30-year amortization
Maximum second trust deed	15%	(11.88 constant/$100)
Return on down payment	6%	

Band of investment calculations

	A Proportion of Sale Price	B Annual Constant	A × B
Down payment	0.20	6*	1.20%
First trust deed	0.65	11.88†	7.72
Second trust deed	0.15	9‡	1.35
	1.00		10.27%
			(or 0.1027 capitalization rate)

* Return on down payment.
† Annual payment per $100 of loan amount at 11.5 percent for 30 years.
‡ Interest only at 9 percent.

place more than 20 percent down on this type of property in this area, that the buyer would require a minimum return of 6 percent on his down payment, that the maximum first trust deed obtainable would be 65 percent of the appraisal at 11.5 percent amortized for 30 years (the payments per $100 per year would be $11.88), and that the maximum first trust deed to be carried by the owner would equal 15 percent of the selling price.

Arriving at a Capitalization Rate. With this information in hand you can now use a band of investment type of approach to arrive at a capitalization rate (Exhibit 3). The purpose is to divide the selling price into segments, which you have already done. Each of the components has been weighted in relationship to the total selling price of the property, and the weighted percentages are multiplied by the annual constants which apply to the down payment and the first and second trust deeds. For example, in Exhibit 3 the numeral 6 is used as the annual constant for the down payment because this is the required percentage return on the down payment. For the first trust deed the annual constant of 11.88 is used. This is the payment per $100 of loan amount with 11.5 percent loan amortized for 30 years. The assumption is made that the seller of the property will carry the second trust deed at a 9 percent annual interest rate, with monthly payments of interest only. Here the annual constant is simply 9. Each figure in column A is multiplied by the accompanying figure in column B to arrive at the various components of the capitalization rate on a weighted basis. In this case, as you will note, the 20 percent down payment is multiplied by 6 for a total of 1.20; the first trust deed amount of 65 percent of the selling price is multiplied by its annual constant per $100 of 11.88 for a total of 7.72; and the second trust deed amount of 15 percent of the selling price is multiplied by the annual constant of 9 for a total of 1.35. When the components are added, you arrive at a 10.27 percent capitalization rate, which when converted from a percentage to a decimal would be .1027.

Arriving at the Sale Price from the Capitalization Rate. You previously arrived at a net income before debt service of $27,911. Divide $27,911 by the established capitalization rate of 0.1027, and you have a selling price of $271,272 (Exhibit 4). This is equal to 6.5% times the gross; but keep in mind that gross multipliers are not necessarily the correct means of determining values. In some areas apartment houses sell for multipliers of up to ten times the gross or better, depending upon how eager investors are to obtain income property. Here the reference to the gross

EXHIBIT 4
Arriving at Sale Price with Band of Investment Capitalization Rate

$$\frac{\text{Net before debt service}}{\text{Capitalization rate}} = \text{Selling price}$$

$$\frac{\$27,911}{0.1027} = \$271,772$$

Projected scheduled gross income of $41,391 = 6.57 × Gross

Price	$271,800
Down (20%)	54,400
	$217,400
First trust deed (65%)	176,700($1,750 mo—11.5%, 30 yr)
Second trust deed (15%)	$ 40,700($305.25/mo—9% interest only)
Projected scheduled gross income	$ 41,391
Expenses (fixed, vacancies/ maintenance/replacement)	13,480
	$ 27,911
Annual first trust deed payments ..	21,000
	$ 6,911
Annual second trust deed payments	3,663
Projected net spendable income ...	$ 3,248
Net spendable income as percentage of down payment	5.97%

multiplier is simply a statement of fact. If you carry these calculations through and work out a simple pro forma, the ultimate return of 6 percent will be achieved as shown in Exhibit 4.

If you experiment with the band of investment calculations for this property (see Exhibit 3), you will find that when the annual constants are lowered the ultimate capitalization rates are also lowered. The lower the capitalization rate, the higher the price. If the annual constants are increased, the capitalization rate will increase and the price will be lower.

For example, what would the price be on this example if you projected a zero return on the down payment? In this case you would assume that it would still be possible to obtain a 65 percent first trust deed (in ordinary circumstances the first trust deed amount would probably be somewhat less). You originally arrived at a 10.27 percent capitalization rate which included a 1.20 weighted figure in the down payment column. To arrive at a capitalization rate and price at a zero return you would multiply .20 by zero and arrive at zero, so your capitalization rate of 10.27 would be reduced by the 1.20, resulting in a capitalization rate of 9.07 percent. Converting this to the decimal 0.907 and dividing that decimal into the net income before debt service of $27,911, we arrive at a projected selling price of $307,728. The gross multiplier in this case is 7.43.

The price is affected by a change in any of the constants. If the interest rate in your area increases, the annual constant for the first trust deed would go up and the price would go down. If the interest rate goes down, the annual constant would be reduced and the price would go up. If your seller will carry the second trust deed at 7 percent rather than 9 percent for the first couple of years, the capitalization rate would be lowered and the price could be increased.

There are numerous variations on this theme. If the rents have not reached their full potential and only a modest increase is projected in order not to disrupt the operation of a building, an owner may be willing to carry a second trust deed at an interest rate of only 6 percent or 7 percent for the first year or two, with the understanding that the rate will be increased to 8 percent during the third year and perhaps to 9 percent during the fourth or fifth year. This requires a bit of creative thinking and the ability to convey your analysis to the seller in a logical and systematic fashion.

There is no simple formula for appraising apartment houses that can be applied to every city and community. Expense ratios and income potential vary from area to area. Operating expenses may be entirely different in one part of the country than in another. In the Northeast, for example, there's a fuel expense to heat furnaces during the winter which is not a factor in states with more moderate climates. Moreover, some apartment houses sell purely on their emotional appeal. Thus, it is dangerous to use rules of thumb.

Negative Cash Flow Sales. If an owner wants an unrealistic price for his property and you think it will sell at that price, you must still provide an honest estimate of the expenses and of the maintenance and repair costs, and if there is to be a negative cash flow, this should be indicated on the pro forma statement so that there is no misunderstanding between the broker and the buyer.

If the buyer wants to buy a property with a $3,000 a year negative cash flow, that is up to him. But it is your responsibility to analyze the property for him and to tell him in no uncertain terms that there will be a $3,000 per year negative cash flow. The important thing is to be factual about your projections and not to be concerned about whether the figures are favorable or unfavorable.

SELLING COMMERCIAL AND INDUSTRIAL REAL ESTATE

Stanley D. Greenblatt

*S*TANLEY D. GREENBLATT, BS, SIR, Partner in the firm of Stanley D. & Alan L. Greenblatt, t/a Chas Greenblatt specializing in Industrial and Commercial Real Estate Sales, Rentals, Appraisal and Management, Baltimore, Maryland.

Past president, Industrial Real Estate Council of Baltimore. Member, Education Committee, Society of Industrial Realtors®. Member, Review Committee, Real Estate Today. *Author of various articles in* Real Estate Today.

Buyers and sellers of commercial and industrial real estate are constantly changing roles. A party that is selling one piece of real estate often contemplates purchasing another. It is this continuous reversal of roles that forms the lifeblood of the commercial and industrial real estate business and makes it so fascinating.

This chapter will set forth guidelines for locating and qualifying buyers, presenting the offering, and closing the deal in a professional manner. In evaluating these guidelines, the reader must bear in mind that real estate selling is a 10 percent proposition. That is, we spend 90 percent of our time and energy to make the other 10 percent pay off.

Finding Buyers

In general, the nature, size, and value of the property will dictate where to look for prospects. However, certain broad sources apply to all types of real estate.

Indirect Methods. The first such source can be called "personal contact." This is one of the most difficult and time-consuming ways to seek prospects. In connection with commercial and industrial property, personal contact is best accomplished by being a "doer"—and if you have the ability, a leader—in civic, charitable, and religious organizations. Your purpose should be to do a good job in each assignment given you and thereby to gain exposure, contacts, and eventually business. You should be very selective in the organizations you join, and you should not take on more than you can handle.

Your newspaper is another source of prospects. By reading the local news section and the financial pages on a regular basis, you can glean much information about who is doing what in the business world. With practice and experience, you can put two and two together to come up with likely prospects for your offerings.

Still another source is your prospect file. It is most important to keep that file current and usable. Each prospect's needs—stores, land, warehouses, and so on—should be spelled out in as much detail as possible. To facilitate matching prospects to properties and to lessen the likelihood of your overlooking the obvious, the information on prospects should be filed by the type of real estate requested and within each type by the size or the dollar value of the real estate.

Referrals and repeats are very satisfying sources of prospects, as these represent rewards for past services well done. They are the clients' way of saying, "Thank you—I appreciate what you did for me." Unfortunately for the beginner, such sources can be developed only through years of hard work and dedicated service. Attention to detail, consideration, and understanding of the prospect's problems, as well as an intelligent knowledge of the local real estate market and a willing attitude, all contribute to the so-called luck that we thank for our success.

The weekly sales meeting is yet another means for opening up new avenues to potential buyers.

Direct Methods. In addition to these indirect methods of seeking prospects, a number of direct approaches can be used. As a general rule, direct approaches usually require an initial cash outlay without any guarantee of cash return. The danger lies in overspending before these approaches bear fruit. This danger is especially great for persons who are just entering the real estate field. For such persons a tightly structured budget is most important. In fact, if a seller insists that the Realtor® spend more on promotion that is prudent, then the Realtor® should refuse to accept the listing unless the seller bears a share of the costs.

One of the most widely used direct selling tools is media advertising. This is an expensive way to seek a buyer. However, when all else fails, it can be the only way. Depending on the type of offering, national publications, local newspapers, trade journals, and even radio and television can be used. Bear in mind that there is no quicker way to go bankrupt than by letting media advertising get out of hand. Those who survive in the real estate field have learned how to get the most out of their advertising dollars.

Another widely used direct approach is direct mail. This is an expensive and time-consuming method. However, it has the decided advantage of being a one-shot operation whose costs can be predetermined. Moreover, it places the sales story in the prospect's hands in a permanent written form and it serves as institutional advertising.

Direct mail is no more effective than the mailing list you use. A poorly designed flier that is sent to a well-chosen list will produce far better results than will a beautiful, expensive, eye-catching brochure that is sent to a misdirected list. Mailing lists can be purchased from various sources, but the most effective mailing lists may prove to be those which you develop yourself. Your prospect file can be an excellent source of potential buyers. The Yellow Pages are a good source. However, the best sources for mailing lists are the directories sold by state and local economic development commissions and by trade organizations. These include such directories as:

> *American Motor Carrier Directory,* national edition. Published by Guide Services, Inc., for the American Trucking Association, Inc., 2161 Monroe Drive, N.E., P.O. Box 1344, Atlanta, Georgia 30324.
>
> *Directory of Maryland Manufacturers.* Published by the Maryland Department of Economic and Community Development.
>
> *Directory of Leading Chain Stores in the United States.* Published by Chain Store Business Guide, Inc., 425 Park Avenue, New York, New York 10022.
>
> *Dun & Bradstreet Million Dollar Directory.*
>
> *Tourist Court Journal,* with offices in Chicago, New York and Pasadena, California.
>
> Society of Industrial Realtors® annual roster of members and associates, 925 15th Street, N.W., Washington, D.C. 20005.
>
> *American Industrial Properties Report,* September 1977, listing 650 office/industrial parks. Published by Indprop Publishing Co., Inc., P.O. Box 2060, Red Bank, New Jersey 07701.
>
> *The National Real Estate Investor.* Published by Communications Channels, Inc., 461 Eighth Avenue, New York, New York 10001.
>
> *The Shopping Center Directory.* Published by the National Research Bureau, 104 South Michigan Avenue, Chicago, Illinois 60606.
>
> *The Baltimore City Criss-Cross Directory,* 1977 edition. Published by Stewart Directories, Inc., 304 West Chesapeake Avenue, Towson, Maryland 21204.

Directories of this kind give you not only the company name, address, and telephone number, but often tell you which company official to seek and provide useful information about the size and nature of the company's operation. The more you know about the potential prospect, the more effective your mailing list will be.

Then, of course, we can ring doorbells. Often the buyer is just across the street, so that a little time spent in this way at the very beginning may save much money and energy. Moreover, neighbors are curious about everything that is going on in their area, and if you take them into your confidence you may obtain a world of information and a prospect or two.

For the timid and for those in a hurry there is a shortcut for ringing doorbells. Let's call it ringing telephones. Handled skillfully, this method can be very productive. Here such directories as those mentioned above, which give a little history of the business and an official's name, can get you past the overprotective secretary, put the call on a personal basis, and permit you to present your offering with an eye to the possible needs of the prospect.

Let's not forget about the silent seller, namely the For Sale sign. It is on duty 24 hours a day, rain or shine. It is a lot cheaper than media advertising and direct mail, and if properly placed and carefully worded, it serves to tell the viewer an enticing story. The posted sign is especially helpful in attracting the prospect who prefers anonymity until he sees what he wants. It should be big enough to be readily seen, but it should not be out of proportion to the size of the offering. Since the passerby is not seeking out the sign, the message must be bold and brief in order to get across.

A most important tool that is used in marketing real estate is the cooperative listing association. The day of the loner is long past. Today many deals are cooperative transactions involving a number of brokers.

Qualifying Buyers

Once we have a prospect, we must make certain that he is likely to make the purchase. This stage of the sale is referred to as qualifying the buyer.

Financial Considerations. The first and foremost question is whether prospect is financially capable of handling the deal. A certified financial statement from a CPA is an excellent way to find out, but such information is seldom available at the early stages of the negotiations, if at all. A Dun & Bradstreet report can be helpful, but often Dun & Bradstreet is able to say little more than that the prospect pays his bills promptly and maintains a modest balance in a commercial bank.

Fortunately, there are other ways of getting a feel for the financial strength of the prospect. Asking the prospect where he banks, with whom he does business, and whether he currently owns any real estate can often lead the knowledgeable broker to sources from which he can discreetly obtain some meaningful answers.

Physical Considerations. Another important method is to visit the prospect at his place of business and to see for yourself the size and nature of his organization. This visit will not only indicate the prospect's financial strength to you but will indicate whether or not the property in question meets his needs. If you have any doubts, do not hesitate to ask questions. This point brings us to the next step in qualifying the prospect, namely, determining whether he can use the property.

The Investment Buyer. In the case of an investment buyer, we will have to know his goals. Is he looking for cash flow, or for a tax shelter, or for capital gains and retirement income? Often the investor wants an immediate tax shelter and future appreciation and retirement income. The broker's ability to discover the needs of the investor can make or break a sale, as the broker must structure his presentation and select the investment to fit the prospect's requirements.

The User-Buyer. In the case of a user-buyer, the problems are more evident. They boil down to whether the prospect can use a property or whether the property can be adapted to the prospect's needs within his budget. The first factor to consider is location. This is one item which neither words nor money can change. However, there is a way to make a wrong location look right, and that is a low price.

Once the location has been accepted, the improvements thereon must be evaluated. Do they meet the prospect's needs? If not, how much will it cost to improve them? The better informed the broker is as to the prospect's needs, the better able he will be to respond to those needs.

Psychological Considerations. Even if the Realtor® has a good location with suitable improvements at a price that the prospect can afford, he is still faced with the psychological aspect of qualifying the buyer. "Seller's or buyer's fright" can occur in the sale of a corner grocery store or a major plant relocation of a large corporation. Spotting this problem early in the game gives the Realtor® an opportunity to overcome it in easy stages before it becomes an uncontrollable monster. In short, the Realtor® must not only be sure that the prospect has the necessary financial wherewithal and that the prospect needs and wants the property—the broker must also be sure that the prospect is in a decision-making frame of mind.

Legal Pitfalls. The Realtor® should also be aware of the legal pitfalls involved in a deal. He should know whether or not the property is properly zoned for the intended use, and if not, what is involved in obtaining a zoning change or variance. If extensive improvements or additions will be required, the Realtor® must know whether they conform with the zoning and building code requirements. He should also know whether any rights-of-way or easements through the property can interfere with the buyer's use of the building or the land. (Such problems sometimes show up during a title search, and by that time there may be the makings of a lawsuit.) In other words, not only must the prospect be qualified with respect to the property but the property must be qualified with respect to the prospect.

Presenting the Property to the Buyer

Physical Appearance. Whether the offering be a large office complex or a one-story concrete block warehouse, a well-kept building is usually indicative of an improvement whose regular repairs and maintenance have not been neglected. A few carefully spent dollars prior to marketing a property can start a sale off in a positive direction. Words just do not seem to overcome that first bad impression. The grass should be cut; trash and debris should be removed, holes in the walls should be repaired, and even painting the walls and above all, the roof should be kept in good repair. Leaving the electricity and even the heat turned on can help with the showing of a property. These items represent out-of-pocket expenses on the owner's part, but such expenses are insignificant when compared to the value of the product being offered.

Descriptive Materials. When first showing the listing to a prospect, it is important to furnish him with a written reminder of the inspection. For a user property, this reminder can be an information sheet. For an investment property, it can be a simple operating statement, with or without a list of tenants and lease expirations, depending on how far negotiations have progressed. The statement can be expanded to include detailed income and expense statements and a detailed analysis of lease information and landlord/tenant responsibilities. If the size and value of the property warrant it, the broker can prepare a brochure containing aerial and ground-level pictures, plot plans, floor plans, topographical studies, and other material on the offering.

In general, the initial flow of information should be simple and to the point and then the information package should be built up as the prospect's interest increases. Some properties will almost sell themselves, and here the Realtor® should tread lightly. Most offerings require a certain degree of persuasion, and this is where the salesperson is separated from the order-taker. Leading a buyer toward a decision rather than trying to push him into a sale is more likely to produce repeat business and referrals. This approach takes patience and persistence, with attention to details, but in the long run it pays off.

At the end of each contact with the prospect, the Realtor® should ask him whether he needs any additional information. If not, the Realtor® might say that he will call the prospect in a week to see whether any questions have arisen.

Case Studies

A Small Industrial Building in an Urban Environment. The following case study will show how the techniques discussed in this chapter were applied to the sale of a 9,000-square-foot, one-story warehouse in an urban environment. The property had a limited but adequate land-to-building ratio, and it was being offered for sale for $75,000 in fee simple. An inspection of the property revealed it to be in good physical condition. At the time of the inspection the information sheet was completed (Exhibit 1). Upon returning to the office, the broker compiled a list of comparable sales and obtained a plot plan from the owners (Exhibit 2). We are now ready to market the property.

A direct mailing to a selected list of small manufacturing firms plus names selected from the prospect file was considered advisable. Since the list contained fewer than 300 firms, an in-house flier was run off (Exhibit 3). Such fliers are inexpensive and easy to prepare. At the same time, this three-foot by four-foot sign was ordered for the property:

```
SALE
9,000 SQ FT

CHAS. GREENBLATT
REALTOR® 889-9000
2211 Maryland Ave.
```

The office decided on a weekly newspaper promotion in the classified section of the local Sunday newspaper under Warehouses/Factories for Sale. The following ad was used:

```
┌─────────────────────────────────────┐
│                                     │
│           9,000 SQ FT               │
│       MODERN ONE-STORY BLDG         │
│                                     │
│        LARGE LOADING DOCK           │
│         AIR-COND. OFFICES           │
│         NEAR "X"WAY RAMP            │
│                                     │
│          CHAS. GREENBLATT           │
│        REALTOR® 889-9000            │
│                                     │
└─────────────────────────────────────┘
```

EXHIBIT 1

STANLEY D. GREENBLATT AND ALAN L. GREENBLATT
Trading as

Chas. Greenblatt
2211 Maryland Avenue   •   Suite 200
Baltimore, Md. 21218
(301) 889-9000

I N F O R M A T I O N   S H E E T

Location: One Unknown Avenue, Baltimore, Maryland

Zoning: M-1-1 (Light Industrial)

Utilities:
           Gas   : Yes
           Water   : Yes
           San. Sewer : Yes
           Storm Sewer : Yes

Rail: No

Area of lot   : 12,000 sq. ft.
Dimension of lot : Approx. 120x100
Grade of lot   :

Area of bldg.   : 9,000 sq.ft. + conc. loading platform 480 sq.ft.
Dimensions of bldg. : 60x117 plus 50x40
Description of bldg. :

           Stories   : One

           Exterior Construction: Brick and masonry block

           Loading Facilities   : 2-8x8 OH doors from loading platform

           Ceiling Height   : 13 feet

           Column Spacing   : 60' clear span-2 columns in entire building

           Floor Construction   : Concrete

           Sprinkler   : No

           Electricity   : 110-220V

           Heat   : Gas blowers, whse; gas hot air ducts, office

           Air Conditioning   : Offices

           Offices   : Approximately 1,000 square feet

           Lavatories   : Two

           Elevator   : No

Possession:
Public Transportation: One long block
Remarks: Building has attractive brick and moziac tile front, off-street
         parking and loading at front
The above information was given us by a reliable source yet we make
no warranty as to its accuracy.

EXHIBIT 2

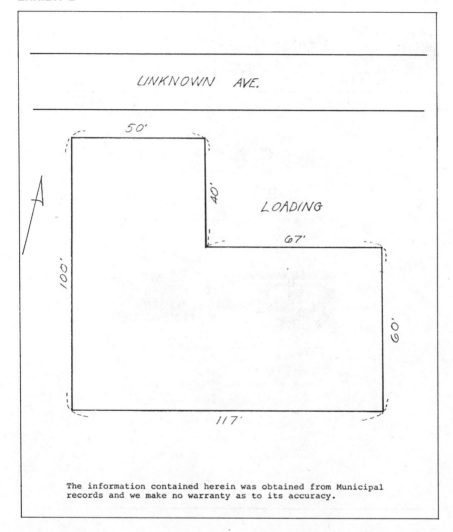

UNKNOWN AVE.

50'

40'

LOADING

67'

100'

60'

117'

The information contained herein was obtained from Municipal
records and we make no warranty as to its accuracy.

Meanwhile, the listing agent was busy preparing the information
to be sent out to the cooperative listing association, checking through
the prospect file and his personal contacts for firms to call on, and checking with the neighbors.

A Sizable Facility in an Industrial Park. Let us take now the case of a
50,000-square-foot one-story factory building located on a 2.8-acre site
and selling for $850,000. First, a personal inspection of the offering was
made, and at the same time the information sheet was completed and
the necessary pictures taken. Back at the office, leads from the broker's
personal contact file and the prospect file were reviewed.

A factory of this size had to be marketed through media advertising

EXHIBIT 3

STANLEY D. GREENBLATT AND ALAN L. GREENBLATT
Trading as

Chas. Greenblatt

INDUSTRIAL AND COMMERCIAL REAL ESTATE
APPRAISAL AND MANAGEMENT

Suite 200 • 2211 Maryland Avenue
Baltimore, Maryland 21218

SALE
9,000 SQ. FT

BALTIMORE, MARYLAND

*   MODERN ONESTORY INDUSTRIAL BUILDING

*   LARGE COVERED LOADING DOCK

*   1000 SQ. FT. OF MODERN AIRCONDITIONED OFFICE

*   ZONED FOR LIGHT MANUFACTURING

*   JUST OFF THE DOWNTOWN "X" WAY RAMP

as well as direct mailings. The Warehouses/Factories for Sale section of the local Sunday newspaper and the financial pages and the local news page of the Wednesday morning edition were used. This promotion was planned and repetitive.

A direct mailing for an offering of this size required a brochure. The data and photographs were assembled at the broker's office and reviewed by the broker's advertising agency, which prepared a suggested brochure for the broker's comments and approval. The finished product is illustrated in Exhibit 4.

The mailing list had to be tailored to the offering. This problem was approached by first determining the highest and best use of the property.

A review of the information sheet indicated that a manufacturing operation requiring the use of bridge cranes represented the ideal user. In addition, the listing provided for the sale of the property at a price that precluded the speculative investor. The broker's office mailing list was color-coded for manufacturing firms, and within this classification it was further coded by the number of employees in each firm listed, making it easy to pinpoint the firms to be included in the mailing list. The

EXHIBIT 4

50,847 Sq. Ft.
ONE STORY BUILDING
ON **2.8±** Acres
IN BALTIMORE, MD.

THIS BLDG. MUST BE SOLD

FOR SALE
MANUFACTURING FACILITY AND WAREHOUSE

BUILDING APPROXIMATELY 1½ YEARS OLD

Ideally located — convenient to I-95 and 695 with easy access to all major highways and routes.

IMMEDIATE POSSESSION

STANLEY D. GREENBLATT AND ALAN L. GREENBLATT
Trading as

Chas. Greenblatt
2211 Maryland Avenue   •   Suite 200
Baltimore, Md. 21218
(301) 889-9000

EXHIBIT 4 *(continued)*

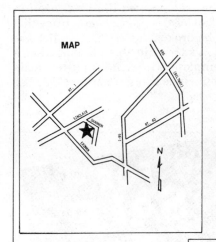

MAP

LOCATION

- Sinclair Lane Industrial Park, Balto., Md.

- Zoning M-1-1 (Manufacturing)

- Public Utilities

- Public Transportation

- Convenient to I-95, 695 and all Major Highways

FEATURES

- Building approximately 1½ years old

- Electric — 3 Phase — 1,000 Amps — 277-480 Volts

- 21 Ft. Ceiling in Shop Area

- Compressed Air Lines in Factory

- Columns 28′ x 34′ C. C.

- 3 — Five Ton Bridge Cranes

- Heated Throughout

- 4,676 Sq. Ft. Air Conditioned Offices

- Locker Room & Shower Facilities

- Xenon Vapor Lighting & Skylites in Shop

- Paved Parking & Fenced Yard

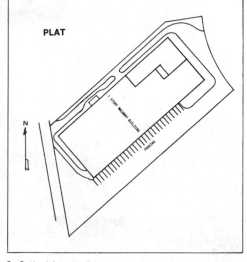

PLAT

For Further Information Call

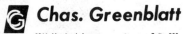

INFORMATION CONTAINED HEREIN WAS OBTAINED FROM RELIABLE SOURCES, HOWEVER, WE MAKE NO WARRANTY AS TO ITS ACCURACY.

Chas. Greenblatt

2211 Maryland Avenue   •   Suite 200
Baltimore, Md. 21218

information and the brochure on the property were also mailed to the broker's cooperative listing association and to a selected list of out-of-town members of the Society of Industrial Realtors®.

Meanwhile, the neighbors were contacted, and selected leads were telephoned and visited. A sign was not posted as the building was occupied and the occupant preferred to delay posting a sign.

Once a prospective buyer is in hand, the qualifying process begins. The first and foremost question is, Can he handle a deal of this size? When dealing with established business firms, this question is easily and directly approached by simply asking what type of financing is required. In most cases the buyer of larger commercial and industrial property is able to arrange his own financing. However, at times the Realtor® can be extremely helpful in this matter, especially if the seller's cooperation is needed for primary or secondary financing or if the prospect is an out-of-town buyer who is unfamiliar with the local money market.

In this type of sale it is also important to qualify the buyer with respect to the physical and legal features of the offering. Major considerations are zoning, the adaptability of the offering to the buyer's current business and anticipated growth, and the desirability of the location in relation to the buyer's customers and the buyer's delivery and receiving requirements. If the property is in the wrong area for the buyer's customers and materials deliveries, then as a rule only reducing the price can affect his decision. In our case study this could not be done. A buyer who needs a large loading dock and yard space for many trucks can be eliminated. A buyer who finds a rail siding desirable will consider a facility without rail only if the price is right. Zoning can sometimes be changed to fit the buyer's needs, but this takes time and requires patient from both the buyer and the seller. If the buyer requires extensive improvements, the Realtor® can be most helpful in obtaining the necessary estimates.

In preparing the contract of sale, rights-of-way, easements, and restrictions should be spelled out. In deals of this type, it often helps to insert a time limit for acceptance by the owner. This holds especially true for deals with large corporations and out-of-town buyers. These are reluctant to commit themselves in writing prior to the seller's acceptance of their offer. When an offer below the asking price is submitted to the owner, a time limit for the owner's acceptance should be included.

A Small Retail Service Center.   Now let us examine the marketing of a small retail service center containing five stores and seven second-floor walk-up offices. The center was fully rented and was being offered for sale at a price of $525,000 in fee. A personal inspection of the property was made, and an information sheet was prepared. At the same time a plot plan was obtained from the owners (Exhibit 5). This plan showed a more than adequate land-to-building ratio and served as an occupancy map for the center.

Before the marketing program could begin, all of the legal and financial data pertaining to the offering. The legal data was obtained from the owner's deed and the various outstanding leases. This information was compiled in an easy-to-understand form (Exhibits 6 and 7). Since the income and expense statement was used to attract buyers, it was kept general in nature so as not to divulge any information that could be detrimental to the center if it fell into the wrong hands.

In dealing with an investment, care must be exercised to avoid promotion that gives the impression of a going out of business sale. The posting

EXHIBIT 5

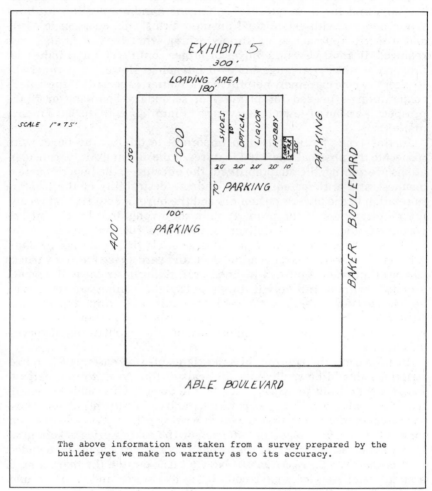

The above information was taken from a survey prepared by the builder yet we make no warranty as to its accuracy.

of a For Sale sign on the property was precluded, as was any large-scale advertising program broadcasting the fact that the "center" is on the market. Although an investment package was being offered, it had to be marketed as if it were a highly successful going business.

Leads for this type of offering usually come from personal contacts, repeat business, and the prospect file. Here too, it never hurts to discreetly approach the neighbors and, with the owner's permission, the tenants in the center. Telephone calls are also very important. Additional names can be selected from the Yellow Pages. Lawyers, accountants, and doctors are good prospects for this type of property. Certain lawyers and accountants are in constant contact with buyers seeking investments, and this also holds true for key bank officials. Newspaper advertising

EXHIBIT 6

TENANT	SIZE SQ.FT.	LEASE EXPIRATION	RENEWAL OPTION	RENT	OPTION RENT	PERCENT CLAUSE
Food	15,000	12/31/88	5 yrs	$3/sq.ft.	½ CPI	Yes
Shoes	1,600	12/31/80	3 yrs	$4/sq.ft.	½ CPI	Yes
Optical	1,600	7/01/79	3 yrs	$4/sq.ft.	20% incr.	Yes
Liquor	1,600	12/31/85	5 yrs	$4/sq.ft.	½ CPI	Yes
Hobby	1,600	8/01/78	none	$4/sq.ft.	none	Yes
Office A	2,000	12/31/82	none	$3/sq.ft.	none	no
Office B	1,000	7/01/85	none	$3/sq.ft.	none	no
Office C	1,000	6/15/79	none	$3/sq.ft.	none	no
Offices	2,400	monthly	none	$4/sq.ft.	none	no

The above information was furnished us by the owner. We make no warranty as to its accuracy as we have not personally verified the information.

also plays a part in the marketing program. The financial page and the local news page of the Wednesday morning edition have been found to be productive. A typical advertisement would read as follows:

INVESTORS
SEEKING 15% NET
RETURN

*Suburban retail center
*Fully rented—modern
*Room for growth

CHAS. GREENBLATT
REALTOR®   889-9000

EXHIBIT 7

```
                        IMAGINATION CENTER
                 INCOME AND EXPENSE STATEMENT
                      December 31, 1977


Base Rent - $71,000.00

Percentage Overages:   1974-$3,500.00
                       1975-$5,000.00
                       1976-$9,000.00

Annual Gross Income-Stores      $ 80,000.00

Average Gross Income-Offices      21,600.00

  Total Average Gross Income    $101,600.00

Less Vacancy Factor (3%)           3,000.00

Average Gross Effective Income  $ 98,600.00
                                                    $98,600.00


EXPENSES

Real Estate Taxes (77-78) $10,200.00
  Reimbursed                2,000.00
                                      $8,000.00
Insurance                              2,000.00
Repairs (estimated)                    3,000.00
Common Area Maintenance
  and utilities            9,000.00
  Reimbursed               5,000.00
                                       4,000.00
Management                             3,000.00

Total Actual & Estimated Expenses                   $20,000.00
  (rounded)

NET INCOME                                          $78,600.00




This information was furnished us by the owner, yet we make no
warranty as to its accuracy as we have not personally verified it.
```

Once a potential buyer is in hand, he must be qualified before the broker discloses all of the financial details of the investment. The broker should be reasonably sure that the prospect has the necessary cash or credit to handle the transaction. The Realtor® should also satisfy himself that the buyer is suited to the property, that he understands the management problems involved and is in a position to assume them or to hire the necessary personnel. Investors whose professions are very demanding of their time want the high return of an investment property but are often reluctant to accept the responsibilities that go with it. A limited partnership type of arrangement can solve their problem and offer the Realtor® a constant source of buyers for quality investment property.

Now the lawyers and the financial advisers scrutinize the broker's facts and figures. The broker's presentations should state his sources. The deal will move along smoothly if the Realtor® has the confidence of the buyer and seller as well as their advisers. This can be attained only through careful attention to details; forthright, honest answers; and a willingness to seek out answers to all reasonable questions. If the broker is looking for referrals and repeat business, this is the time and place to prove himself.

A Large Investment Property. The problems of selling a very large investment property are similar to but far more complex than those just discussed. Here even before seeking a buyer, the Realtor® must fully understand the physical, legal, and financial nature of the offering. The Realtor® can spend hours upon hours with attorneys, accountants, project managers, and owners, just assembling the facts and figures. Buyers of such a property usually work through financial advisers as well as attorneys and accountants, so that the initial presentation must be in a very technical and legal form in order to attract their interest. Experts deal with experts, and the Realtor® must exercise patient persistence once the prospect is in hand. As with the small retail service center, personal contacts and the prospect file represent the first place to look for leads. Buyers for a large investment property are usually large corporations, wealthy individuals, and syndications seeking to improve their investment portfolio through diversification, inflation protection, and growth potential as well as a higher return on their capital invested. A check of local real estate tax records and *The Directory of Shopping Centers* will reveal who owns or is an agent for similar investment properties. Such buyers can also be reached through advertising in the financial pages of local newspapers as well as such national publications as *The Wall Street Journal* and *The National Real Estate Investor*. This type of promotion is very expensive, but again, the amount involved is insignificant as compared to the value of the property. When handling this type of property, the broker has to be prepared to spend considerable money for travel as well as promotion. General economic conditions and the money market dictate when the time is ripe to go all-out in promoting the really big investment property.

A Single-Purpose Commercial or Industrial Property. The single-purpose commercial or industrial property presents another interesting and difficult marketing problem. As an example of this type of problem, we will examine the sale of a one-story truck terminal facility, 50 feet wide by 200 feet long, with 18 cross-dock doors and a general office. This terminal was located on a three-acre site and was being offered at a price of $300,000. As always, the broker began by inspecting the offering, completing the information sheet, and taking the needed pictures.

Considered in light of the asking price, the long and narrow shape of the improvements, the lack of facilities in the dock area, and the high ratio of land to building severely limited potential users of the property. In fact, in numerous instances a well-rated tenant must be obtained for a single-purpose building before the building can be sold as an investment.

Local newspaper advertising may or may not produce a prospect. However, it serves to keep the owner happy while the broker seeks out more productive approaches. Posting a sign on the property and calling on the neighbors are recommended here. Persons in the broker's prospect file and in the Motor Freight section of the Yellow Pages can be telephoned. A list of the trucking companies that have terminal facilities in the area or that have rights to operate in the area can be compiled from the *American Motor Carrier Directory.* A one-page flier similar to the one shown in Exhibit 3 can then be mailed to these companies. In addition, advertisements in the motor freight trade publication *Transport Topics* have produced leads for similar properties. Timing, luck, and a well-directed marketing effort over a considerable period of time will usually prove successful.

Unimproved Commercial or Industrial Acreage. Before offering unimproved commercial or industrial acreage for sale, the Realtor® should make sure that he has a marketable product or he can wind up with a loss of time and money, an irate buyer, and perhaps even a lawsuit. Building moratoriums and moratoriums on sewer and water hookups can be deadly. A lack of utilities has stymied many a project. Zoning is a force to be reckoned with. Access roads, rights-of-way, subdivision requirements, and required off-site improvements should all be investigated beforehand. Federal, state and local regulations governing the development of raw land can not only delay sales but preclude otherwise feasible projects.

Once the Realtor® has satisfied himself as to the marketability of his product, he should proceed to secure the listing. A listing of at least six months—and in the case of a large tract of at least a year—is essential. At this time the Realtor® should reach a complete understanding as to what is expected of him in connection with the promotion of the property. If large sums of money are involved, the Realtor® should not hesitate to ask the seller to make a sizable contribution toward the marketing program. If the seller is truly anxious to move the property, this request will usually prove acceptable, and if the request is presented together with a viable marketing program, it will enhance the image of the broker's firm in the client's eyes.

The next step is to obtain plats, topographical studies, aerial photographs, and cost and time estimates for utilities if they are not at the property line. It is also important to check out the neighbors. In this way a possible buyer may be obtained and the broker can find out what other acreage is available and at what price. In promoting one 250-acre industrial site, a broker learned from a check with the neighbors that a contiguous land area of over 500 acres could be assembled if the need arose.

Now one or more large signs are placed on the property. A typical sign would read as follows:

```
┌─────────────────────────────────────────┐
│                                         │
│                 SALE                    │
│               250 ACRES                 │
│        Zoned Industrial-All Utilities   │
│                                         │
│            CHAS. GREENBLATT             │
│        REALTOR®     (301) 889-9000      │
│        2211 Maryland Ave. Balto., Md.   │
│                                         │
└─────────────────────────────────────────┘
```

Such signs should be simple and informative.

Up to this point a mass of data has been collected; now the question is how to get this information into the hands of interested prospects. The development of unimproved land is for the most part a slow process requiring a continuous effort over a long period of time. Consequently, the advertising program must both reach the right people and be funded for the long haul. The prime purpose of promotion should be to give the site as broad an exposure to interested prospects as prudently spent dollars permit.

Just who are those interested prospects? They are, for the most part, developers, large industrial corporations seeking expansion, local and state economic development commissions seeking sites for industry, industrial Realtors® with clients in mind, and land speculators. A mailing list can be compiled from such sources as the list of office and industrial parks in the September 1977 issue of *American Industrial Properties Report,* the *Dun & Bradstreet Million Dollar Directory,* and the Society of Industrial Realtors® annual roster and list of leading industrial firms. A check of local land records will reveal who the local developers and land speculators are. The directory of state and local commissions, personal contacts, and the prospect file should yield additional names. An attractive brochure complete with aerial photographs, a plot plan, a location plan, and zoning and utility information should be sent to the mailing list periodically. If the follow-up mailings contain an eye-catching insert, so much the better.

Occasional inserts in the classified and financial sections of the local paper remind local developers and speculators of the availability of the site. Advertising in papers enjoying national circulation, such as *The Wall Street Journal* and the *New York Times,* is expensive, but it can attract interested eyes. If a property has a broad appeal, inserts in such trade journals as *Area Development Sites and Facility Planning* (published by Halcyon Business Publications, Inc., New York, New York) can be productive.

News items in the local papers, especially in the financial and local news sections, can afford the trained observer productive leads. Items on such matters as the relocation of a major highway, building moratoriums, the relocation plans of a major industry, the awarding of a large contract requiring a new facility, labor problems in other areas, the development of a new port facility, and the zoning problems of a major industry in a nearby area are examples of the kind of information that can lead to prospects.

Once a serious buyer has been found, a new set of challenges arises. At this stage, cooperation between the seller and the broker is the key to success. Options are required while development plans are being prepared and permits obtained. Interim financing can prove expensive and difficult to obtain. In such situations, owner-assisted financing is essential. Where the situation warrants it, or the profit margin is great, or the seller wants a deal badly, long-term financing by the seller is not unusual. This is especially true in a tight money market. Land speculation is not for those who lack patience and financial staying power.

The Role of the Realtor®

What is the role of the Realtor® in the sale process? Legally, he is the agent of the party who hires him and pays his commissions, and as such he is subject to all the laws, rules, and regulations governing an agency relationship. It is of utmost importance that the Realtor® know and understand the laws and regulations that control this highly confidential relationship (see Chapter 8). However, the agency relationship does not relieve the Realtor® of the obligation to be honest and forthright in dealing with other parties to the transaction, particularly with regard to hidden defects.

The experienced Realtor® knows where to look for buyers. He has all the tools of his trade at hand, and he knows how to use them to best advantage. He can best advise the seller on improvements that should be made before the property is placed on the open market. He can advise the seller as to the market value of the offering and as to the prevailing market conditions with respect to the offering. In marketing the property, the Realtor® usually offers not only his own services but also those of his cooperative listing association. In most instances he risks the front money required to promote the sale without any guarantee of recovering it in the process. The experienced Realtor® knows how to weed out the information seeker and the unqualified prospect. He is knowledgeable in sensing the presence of seller's or buyer's fright and in the ways of overcoming it. Most important, he acts as a buffer between the buyer and the seller. He prevents misunderstandings and opposing points of view from hardening into insurmountable obstacles. The owner who wants the best possible results in the shortest possible time stands the best chance of success when he places his real estate problems in the hands of a real estate professional.

COMMERCIAL LEASING

Herbert D. Weitzman

Joe J. Lancaster, Jr.

*H*ERBERT D. WEITZMAN, CSM, CMB, SIR, President, Commercial Retail Division, Henry S. Miller Company, Realtors®, Dallas, Texas.

Member, Dallas Board of Realtors®, Texas Association of Realtors®, National Association of Corporate Real Estate Executives, and Urban Land Institute. Formerly State Director, Texas region, International Council of Shopping Centers. President, North Texas chapter, Society of Industrial Realtors®, 1978–80. Coauthor, The Percentage Lease Manual, *(National Institute of Real Estate Boards).*

JOE J. LANCASTER, JR., BBA, President, Henry S. Miller Management Corporation, Dallas, Texas.

President, Henry S. Miller Management Corporation, which manages about 80 shopping centers, primarily within the state of Texas. Senior vice president of the parent organization, Henry S. Miller Co. Member, International Council of Shopping Centers; Urban Land Institute; Texas Association of Realtors®; and Commercial Investment Division, Dallas Board of Realtors®.

This chapter will deal with the specialized marketing techniques that are required to lease commercial properties. The marketing efforts of the developer and the project leasing agent will be discussed, and the skills and techniques employed by the commercial broker in negotiating leases will be considered. The main focus will be on the leasing of office buildings, shopping centers, industrial parks, free-standing retail and warehouse properties, and unimproved sites.

Before the specialized areas involved in commercial leasing are discussed, it will be necessary to define certain terms and relationships involved in a lease transaction. The lease itself is a legal document that is designed to create a landlord-tenant relationship. In most instances it covers both real property (i.e., the land and major improvements) and personal property (i.e., movable fixtures and equipment). The landlord is the owner of the property that is being leased by the tenant, who is the user. The modern commercial lease is a sophisticated legal document which sets out varied performance requirements for both the landlord and the tenant. However, except for very specialized situations that are described later in the chapter, this discussion will involve situations in which the landlord is required to provide the initial improvements and to maintain structural integrity throughout the term of the lease, with the tenant being responsible for the maintenance and repair of leasehold improvements throughout the occupancy. The property being leased is often referred to as the demised premises (especially in leases for multitenant projects).

Lease Provisions by Type of Space

In recent years the leases utilized by major developers (landlords) and large companies (tenants) have involved very specialized types of property (shopping centers, office buildings, etc.). This chapter will not deal with the legal aspects and requirements of a lease agreement, but an understanding of the unique characteristics of the commercial leases designed for different types of commercial properties is necessary in order to appreciate the complexities involved in a landlord-tenant relationship and the difficulties involved in completing a successful commercial leasing effort.

The "Standard" Commercial Lease. In most major metropolitan areas the local Board of Realtors® chapter or a similar trade organization for the commercial real estate brokerage community has a "standard" lease form that has been designed to provide for the leasing of many different types of property. Although this generalized form may be acceptable in some instances (it usually requires the addition of a significant number of provisions that are not covered in the printed form), it is suggested that the parties to a transaction utilize a form that has been designed for the particular type of property under consideration. Our discussion of the more specialized leases will take up the unique characteristics that are required to fulfill the landlord's or tenant's needs in specific areas.

A prudent landlord will require that a commercial lease include provisions to protect the landlord against future increases in the cost of operating the property, especially when the primary lease term is for a significant period of time (five years or more). Such provisions cover three basic areas of concern.

1. *Maintenance requirements.* The lease should clearly define the maintenance responsibilities of the landlord and the tenant. Either the tenant or the landlord may bear all the responsibility for physical maintenance. However, most leases divide this responsibility between the

landlord and the tenant, and the landlord is usually held responsible for the structural integrity of the leased premises (i.e., the foundation, the roof, and the exterior walls), with the tenant assuming responsibility for maintenance and repair within the leased premises (usually referred to as the leasehold improvements).

2. *Real estate taxes.* The landlord requires protection against future increases in real estate taxes. This operating expense item has increased substantially in recent years. As with all other expense items, the lease may be structured on a net basis, so that the tenant is responsible for all real estate taxes and other assessments levied by governmental bodies. However, the typical commercial lease makes the landlord responsible for "base year" taxes (usually the taxes for the first full calendar year of the lease), with the tenant assuming the burden of all tax increases above the base year level. For multitenant properties in which the tenant's building or leased area is not assessed separately, each tenant's share of the real estate tax increase is prorated, usually on the basis of the size of the tenant's leased area as compared to the size of the entire property.

3. *Casualty insurance.* Although casualty insurance premiums are a less significant expense item than real estate taxes, the prudent landlord will demand protection against increases. The lease may allocate the entire burden of casualty insurance to the tenant, but the usual format is to make the tenant responsible for a pro rata share of increases over the base year premium.

The three areas discussed above should be covered in all commercial leases. The lease forms designed for specific types of commercial properties will contain additional provisions covering unique aspects of the property involved.

The Office Lease. A modern, multitenant office building must provide many services to its tenants. The nature of the tenancy involved (i.e., most of the space is leased to relatively small users for comparatively short primary terms) requires the landlord to bear the expense of the basic services. The landlord must establish a significant operating budget (including salaries and overhead expenses for an on-site staff) in order to meet the requirements for heating, air conditioning, and lighting; janitorial services; trash removal; maintenance and repair of mechanical equipment, the parking lot, and landscaped areas; and the numerous other services that must be provided to the tenants. The most common form of "inflation protection" for the landlord in an office lease is a provision which requires each tenant to pay an increased rental at certain intervals (at least on an annual basis) in accordance with the increase in certain stated expense items over the preceding period. The operational expenses that are utilized to determine the increase in rental generally include real estate taxes and insurance in addition to the items mentioned above. Due to the nature of the property and of the tenancy, the typical office building lease will include a provision combining all expense factors into one rental escalation clause to make certain that the income stream generated by the project will increase by an amount that is at least equal to the increase in operating expenses. The tenant must be persuaded of the need for this clause during the leasing process.

The Shopping Center Lease. The large, multitenant retail development probably has more characteristics that are unique to it than do the other types of commercial property. The goal of each tenant and of the landlord is to maximize the retail sales generated by each tenant and by the entire project. Many factors critical to the success of a shopping center are not requirements for an office building, a warehouse, or other types of commercial property, and accordingly the shopping center lease will contain numerous provisions that do not appear in other types of specialized commercial leases. Among the more important are the following.

1. *Percentage rental.* A sophisticated shopping center developer or owner of existing retail properties will require that each tenant pay, in addition to the fixed rent and other charges, a percentage of gross sales, usually on a monthly basis, after the tenant's sales have reached a predetermined level. The exact percentage will range from less than 1 percent to 10 percent or more, depending on the use involved. This provision gives the landlord protection against inflation and serves as a source of additional revenue that is not available in other types of commercial properties.

2. *Continuous occupancy and hours of operation.* It is critical to the success of a shopping center that all tenants be open for business during normal operating hours and that they continuously provide their product or service throughout the term of their lease so that customers are given the proper variety of shopping opportunities and the gross sales of the shopping center are maximized. In contrast, it makes little, if any, difference to the landlord or the tenants in an office building or an industrial property whether tenants occupy or do not occupy their space.

3. *Merchants' association.* Many successful shopping centers have established a merchants' association, whose membership consists of the tenants in the shopping center, to sponsor advertising and promotional events that are designed to increase sales. The knowledgeable shopping center owner will require each tenant to join such an association if there is one.

4. *Other escalation clauses.* A shopping center lease will require the tenant to pay a pro rata share of increases in real estate taxes, insurance, and common area maintenance. Generally the tenant pays a pro rata share of the common area maintenance charges (for the parking lot, landscaping, sidewalks, exterior lighting, etc.). Except for projects with enclosed malls, the utilities for each tenant are metered separately and the landlord absorbs no utility expenses.

The Warehouse (Industrial) Lease. The lease utilized for industrial and warehouse properties is generally less complicated than an office building lease or a shopping center lease because the tenant is generally responsible for all building maintenance and on-site requirements. Also, a far greater percentage of warehouse leases than of leases for other types of properties provide for the payment of real estate taxes and insurance on a net basis.

The Net Lease. As has been noted, the word *net* is used to describe the complete assumption of a particular responsibility by the tenant. If a lease is net of real estate taxes, the tenant pays all of the real estate taxes. Net leases are more attractive to a landlord than nonnet leases, but they are usually more difficult to negotiate. However, the base rental for a nonnet lease is higher than that for a net lease since a prudent landlord will require a higher rental to offset the higher expense burden of the nonnet lease.

The Ground Lease. Tenants often lease unimproved or partially improved tracts of land and proceed to construct their own improvements. Since a ground lease requires a larger capital expenditure by the tenant, the primary lease term is generally longer in duration than that of other commercial bases (to provide sufficient time for the tenant to amortize the investment) and the tenant usually pays for all operating expenses relating to the improved site.

The preceding discussion of several specialized leases only illustrates some of the complexities involved in leasing commercial property. The person responsible for leasing should be intimately familiar with the potential economic consequences of each provision in a lease and should impart this information to the prospective tenant during the lease negotiation process. Knowledge of the economic consequences of lease provisions is very useful in qualifying tenant prospects and in avoiding expenditures of time and effort on prospects whose financial resources are not adequate to meet the required tenant obligations. The time saved in this way can be used to locate viable tenants. (For additional information on lease arrangements, see Chapter 7.)

Market Analyses

Before any real property can be leased, there has to be a need for it. Understanding the needs of prospective tenants, and the extent to which such needs exist, is vital to the success of any income-producing real property development. The prudent developer will conduct or underwrite a market analysis that is designed to measure the existing supply of space versus the current demand, or the expected demand in the near term. However, such an analysis will, at best, only indicate the probable success of a given project. What will determine its success will be the demand for the completed space by potential tenants. A project's ability to meet the current demand will depend on economic considerations (for example, rental and other occupancy charges), location, design, and other factors. The problem is to accurately determine that demand does exist or will soon exist, and then tailoring the project to meet that demand.

Any proposed development can be made to perform well on paper. The purpose of market analysis is to ensure that what works well on paper during the pro forma stage will be an economically viable project when the bricks and mortar have been put in place. A knowledgeable leasing agent can provide invaluable input to a market analysis. The leasing agent will know whether the projected rents are obtainable; whether the projected sizes of the various tenant spaces are adequate to meet current needs; whether the projected amenities are competitive with the amenities provided by other developments; and indeed, whether there is sufficient demand to justify the scope of the project.

The Leasing Program

If a market analysis determines that there is a demand for a proposed new development or a proposed renovation of an existing property, the commercial leasing program is ready to begin. One of the most difficult, time-consuming, and challenging tasks in the real estate industry is leasing commercial space (office, retail, industrial, or a hybrid) to the unknown tenant. It is less difficult and risky to plan a new project with the tenants already lined up and ready to go (which seldom occurs except for single-user developments) than it is to plan a project on a speculative basis and then to proceed with a significant portion of the space unleased. The rest of this chapter will be devoted to a discussion of the steps that should be taken to achieve 100 percent occupancy. A succinct description of the process is "wearing out shoe leather."

The developer, the leasing agent, the commercial real estate broker or the owner who sits back and waits for tenant prospects to come to him will lag far behind the person who pursues potential tenants in order to lease a project. The measures outlined below are by no means the only techniques that a leasing agent should employ, but they are requirement to a successful leasing effort:

Making Cold Calls. The leasing agent who visits prospective tenants has a better chance of turning potential occupants into rent-paying customers than does the leasing agent who is content to sit back and wait for tenants to call on him.

Prospecting in Competitive Projects. Although the recently completed development down the street may seem to contain only satisfied tenants, perhaps one or two of those tenants need additional space that is unavailable at their current location or may find a move to another location desirable for one of many other reasons. How do you know unless you ask?

Approaching Manufacturers, Suppliers, and Wholesalers. These sources can provide information about companies that are entering an area for the first time (or about companies in an area that are interested in an alternative or second location). Such sources are probably more productive for shopping center and industrial projects than for other types, but any source that might produce a lead is worth pursuing. Trade organizations and chambers of commerce are also good sources of tenant prospects.

Advertising. A project sign, mailings, and institutional advertising can be effective means of generating prospects, but these means are productive only when they are followed up with personal contact—and when a prospective tenant responds to them, the follow-up must be immediate. If the potential space user is interested enough to make the response, this usually means that the decision to relocate or to lease additional space has already been made and that unless contact is established quickly the prospect will probably become the tenant of another landlord.

Closing. If the location and the physical characteristics of the available space meet the tenant's needs, the factors involved in consummating the transaction will be mostly economic in nature. The lease provisions discussed above illustrate several areas in addition to the base rent that are of economic consequence to both the landlord and the tenant, and the successful leasing agent will have to be innovative in negotiating the lease. The leasing agent should not assume that "the deal will not make" after one or two seemingly insurmountable problems arise. For example, perhaps the landlord may have set a limit on the improvements to the space that is considerably less than the tenant requires, and the tenant may not be willing to make the necessary capital expenditure. One potential solution to this problem is to give the tenant a certain amount of free rent in return for providing the additional funds required to complete the leasehold improvements. If the duration of the free rent period is not too great (the space would undoubtedly remain vacant for some time unless a new prospect were found), this arrangement might be advantageous to both parties. The point is that the obstacles to the negotiation of a lease should be identified and an attempt should be made to find a solution acceptable to both parties.

The marketing effort that results in a fully executed commercial lease requires specialized knowledge, persistence, and dedication. The individual responsible for leasing a commercial property must make personal contact with as many potential tenants as possible, and the true professional will seek out the prospective tenants by every means available. The time that the prospect requires to digest the information presented, make a decision, and enter into a lease agreement may be only a few days or it may be many months. However, once a prospect indicates an interest in leasing, the follow-up must be immediate and consistent in order to maximize the probability of completing the lease.

Commercial leasing is a challenging, demanding, and rewarding vocation. Excellent opportunities for the enterprising commercial real estate broker who elects to specialize in the leasing of commercial space arise from the considerable amount of commercial space that is available for lease, particularly in the major metropolitan areas of the United States, and from the fact that a multitenant property will realize its economic potential only if it is fully leased (and the occupancy maintained over the life of the property). Current information concerning the rental rates of comparable properties is vital to the landlord who wishes to maintain rental rates "at the top of the market," and the commercial leasing specialist will have this information. The developer of a new project needs accurate estimates of the obtainable rental rates in order to make an accurate income projection (which determines loan values, cash flow, and basic economic feasibility). These estimates may be more important than estimates of the capital costs (construction costs, professional fees, etc.) of the new development. The commercial leasing specialist can provide such rental estimates as well as a knowledgeable opinion concerning the anticipated tenant demand (at any price) for the project.

Commercial leasing is becoming an increasingly specialized endeavor within the real estate industry. It offers challenging opportunities, coupled with commensurate financial rewards, to persons who are considering real estate as a career. Such persons may serve as project leasing agents for major developers or as independent contractors who work within the framework of a total market area. Their opportunities, within reason, will be limited only by their desire to succeed.

PROPERTY MANAGEMENT

W. Donald Calomiris

W. *DONALD CALOMIRIS, CPM, Executive Property Manager and Treasurer, William Calomiris Investment Company, Washington, D.C.*

Advisory Board Member, The Real Estate Handbook, (Dow Jones-Irwin). Director, Central National Bank of Maryland. Past national president, Institute of Real Estate Management. Past supreme president, Rho Epsilon, professional real estate fraternity. Member, Board of Trustees, The American University, Washington, D.C.

The objectives of professional property management are to provide informed supervision of the real estate investment so as to ensure its highest and best use over as long a period as possible, with the highest reasonable net return that is obtainable without prejudice to the original capital investment. To accomplish these objectives, the professional property manager must be able to forecast. For example, he is forecasting when he decides whether leases should be long term or short term. He is forecasting when he recommends whether leases should have a high minimum guarantee or a percentage clause. He is forecasting when he advises his client to buy property or to sell it, to borrow or to pay off loans, to remodel, to raise rents, or to make capital improvements.

In order to be able to forecast with good results, a property manager must be research oriented. He must keep abreast of the international and national political and economic developments that affect his industry. He must be able to determine how government housing programs affect the real estate market. On the local level, he must be aware of the trends in residential occupancy, rental price levels, purchasing power, evictions, employment, family formations, and a host of other factors which affect the local real estate market. To keep abreast of such developments his office must maintain a wide variety of statistics.

Such sources as *Newsweek, Time, Forbes, House and Home, The Wall Street Journal,* and the Institute of Real Estate Management will help the professional property manager accomplish these research objectives. The *Journal of Property Management,* the *Apartment Building Income and Expense Analysis,* and the many other publications of the Institute of Real Estate Management, the property management arm of the National Association of Realtors®, would serve as a good nucleus of source materials for the research-oriented office.

The Professional Management Agreements

It is the understanding between the property owner and the managing agent that determines their mutual duties and obligations throughout the existence of the agency relationship. A written contract serves a number of purposes. It avoids misunderstanding. It provides a basis for settling disputes. It is a permanent record of the relationship between the parties. It gains respect for the agent and the industry.

The length of the contract should be determined by the work of the property manager and by the transition time that is required to get involved with a property. The most common length is one year, with a 30-day cancellation fee after the first year. Many property managers now feel that a two- or three-year contract is needed to fulfill the objectives of professional management. However, the length of the contract should be determined by the requirements of the given situation. (See Figure 1 for sample agreement.)

A number of items should be covered in the management contract. All of the owners and the agent should be named, and they or their authorized representatives should sign the agreement. The commencement date and the term of the agreement should be stated. There should be a clause pertaining to the signing of leases and other documents. If the agent is authorized to sign, the length of time for which he can commit all parties should be stated. There should be a clause pertaining to repairs. The agreement should provide for authorization to advertise and should state who pays for advertising. The duties of the agent should be stated. The agreement should contain a statement holding the agent harmless for liability arising out of his operations. This hold harmless clause should require that the agent be named in the owner's contract of liability insurance as an additional insured. An insurance clause should contain all of the information pertaining to the insurance coverage of the property. There should be a bank account clause. Usually the agent selects the bank. A cancellation clause should state how, by whom, and when the agreement may be terminated; how much notice should be given; and what form the notice should take. An employees clause should state that the property employees are the employees of the owner and not the agent, although they will be under the direction and control of the agent and will be paid by the agent out of the owner's funds. There should also be a clause that gives the agent the exclusive right to sell and to lease and a clause that sets forth the agent's fee or renumeration. The agreement should state what records will be kept and what, if any, accounting will be done by the owners. There should be a clause concerning the reserves—reserves for

FIGURE 1
Sample Management Agreement

Between

OWNER_____

and

AGENT_____

for Property located at_____

Beginning_____19_____

Ending_____19_____

MANAGEMENT
AGREEMENT

In consideration of the covenants herein contained,_____

_____ (hereinafter called

"OWNER"), and_____(hereinafter called "AGENT"),
agree as follows:

1. The OWNER hereby employs the AGENT exclusively to rent and
manage the property (hereinafter called the "Premises") known as_____

_____

_____

upon the terms hereinafter set forth, for a period of_____years beginning

on the_____day of_____, 19_____, and ending on

the_____day of_____,19_____, and there-
after for yearly periods from time to time, unless on or before _____ days
prior to the date last above mentioned or on or before _____ days prior
to the expiration of any such renewal period, either party hereto shall notify
the other in writing that it elects to terminate this Agreement, in which case
this Agreement shall be thereby terminated on said last mentioned date.
(See also Paragraph 6(c) below.)

FIGURE 1 *(continued)*

2. THE AGENT AGREES:

(a) To accept the management of the Premises, to the extent, for the period, and upon the terms herein provided and agrees to furnish the services of its organization for the rental operation and management of the Premises.

(b) To render a monthly statement of receipts, disbursements and charges to the following person at the address shown:

Name   Address

_____   _____

_____   _____

and to remit each month the net proceeds (provided Agent is not required to make any mortgage, escrow or tax payment on the first day of the following month). Agent will remit the net proceeds or the balance thereof after making allowance for such payments to the following persons, in the percentages specified and at the addresses shown:

Name   Percentage   Address

_____   _____   _____

_____   _____   _____

_____   _____   _____

In case the disbursements and charges shall be in excess of the receipts, the OWNER agrees to pay such excess promptly, but nothing herein contained shall obligate the AGENT to advance its own funds on behalf of the OWNER.

(c) To cause all employees of the AGENT who handle or are responsible for the safekeeping of any monies of the OWNER to be covered by a fidelity bond in an amount and with a company determined by the AGENT at no cost to the OWNER.

3. THE OWNER AGREES:

To give the AGENT the following authority and powers (all or any of which may be exercised in the name of the OWNER) and agrees to assume all expenses in connection therewith:

(a) To advertise the Premises or any part thereof, to display signs thereon and to rent the same; to cause references of prospective tenants to be investigated; to sign leases for terms not in excess of_____years and to renew and/or cancel the existing leases and prepare and execute the new lease without additional charge to the OWNER; provided, however, that the AGENT may collect from tenants all or any of the following: a late rent administrative charge, a non-negotiable check charge, credit report fee, a subleasing administrative charge and/or broker's commission and need not account for such charges and/or commission to the OWNER; to terminate tenancies and to sign and serve such notices as are deemed needful by the AGENT; to institute and prosecute actions to oust tenants and to recover possession of the Premises; to sue for and recover rent; and, when expedient, to settle, compromise and release such actions or suits, or reinstate such tenancies.

FIGURE 1 *(continued)*

(b) To hire, discharge and pay all engineers, janitors and other employees; to make or cause to be made all ordinary repairs and replacements necessary to preserve the Premises in its present condition and for the operating efficiency thereof and all alterations required to comply with lease requirements, and to do decorating on the Premises; to negotiate contracts for non-recurring items not exceeding $_____ and to enter into agreements for all necessary repairs, maintenance, minor alterations and utility services; and to purchase supplies and pay all bills.

(c) To collect rents and/or assessments and other items due or to become due and give receipts therefor and to deposit all funds collected hereunder in the Agent's custodial account.

(d) To refund tenants' security deposits at the expiration of leases and, only if required to do so by law, to pay interest upon such security deposits.

(e) To execute and file all returns and other instruments and do and perform all acts required of the OWNER as an employer with respect to the Premises under the Federal Insurance Contributions Acts, the Federal Unemployment Tax Act and Subtitle C of the Internal Revenue Code of 1954 with respect to wages paid by the AGENT on behalf of the OWNER and under any similar Federal or State law now or hereafter in force (and in connection therewith the OWNER agrees upon request to promptly execute and deliver to the AGENT all necessary powers of attorney, notices of appointment and the like).

4. THE OWNER FURTHER AGREES:

(a) To indemnify, defend and save the AGENT harmless from all suits in connection with the Premises and from liability for damage to property and injuries to or death of any employee or other person whomsoever, and to carry at his (its) own expense public liability, elevator liability (if elevators are part of the equipment of the Premises), and workmen's compensation insurance naming the OWNER and the AGENT and adequate to protect their interests and in form, substance and amounts reasonably satisfactory to the AGENT, and to furnish to the AGENT certificates evidencing the existence of such insurance. Unless the OWNER shall provide such insurance and furnish such certificate within _____ days from the date of this Agreement, the AGENT may, but shall not be obligated to, place said insurance and charge the cost thereof to the account of the OWNER.

(b) To pay all expenses incurred by the AGENT, including, without limitation, attorney's fees for counsel employed to represent the AGENT or the OWNER in any proceeding or suit involving an alleged violation by the AGENT or the OWNER, or both, of any constitutional provision, statute, ordinance, law or regulation of any governmental body pertaining to fair employment, Federal Fair Credit Reporting Act, environmental protection, or fair housing, including, without limitation, those prohibiting or making illegal discrimination on the basis of race, creed, color, religion or national origin in the sale, rental or other disposition of housing or any services rendered in connection therewith (unless the AGENT is finally adjudicated to have personally and not in a representative capacity violated such constitutional provision, statute, ordinance, law or regulation), but nothing herein contained shall require the AGENT to employ counsel to represent the OWNER in any such proceeding or suit.

(c) To indemnify, defend and save the AGENT harmless from all claims, investigations and suits with respect to any alleged or actual violation of state or federal labor laws, it being expressly agreed and understood that as between the OWNER and the AGENT, all persons employed in connection

FIGURE 1 *(continued)*

with the Premises are employees of the OWNER not the AGENT. The OWNER's obligation under this paragraph 4(c) shall include the payment of all settlements, judgments, damages, liquidated damages, penalties, forfeitures, back pay awards, court costs, litigation expense and attorneys' fees.

(d) To give adequate advance written notice to the AGENT if payment of mortgage indebtedness, general taxes or special assessments or the placing of fire, steam boiler or any other insurance is desired.

5. TO PAY THE AGENT EACH MONTH:

(a) FOR MANAGEMENT:_____per month or_____

percent (_____%) of the monthly gross receipts from the operation of the Premises during the period this Agreement remains in full force and effect, whichever is the greater amount.

(b) APARTMENT LEASING_____

_____

_____

(c) FOR MODERNIZATION (REHABILITATION/CONSTRUCTION)

_____

_____

(d) FIRE RESTORATION_____

_____

_____

_____

(e) OTHER ITEMS OF MUTUAL AGREEMENT_____

_____

_____

_____

_____

6. IT IS MUTUALLY AGREED THAT:

(a) The OWNER expressly withholds from the AGENT any power or authority to make any structural changes in any building or to make any other major alterations or additions in or to any such building or equipment therein, or to incur any expense chargeable to the OWNER other than expenses related to exercising the express powers above vested in the AGENT without the prior written direction of the following person:

Name   Address

_____   _____

FIGURE 1 *(continued)*

except such emergency repairs as may be required because of danger to life or property or which are immediately necessary for the preservation and safety of the Premises or the safety of the tenants and occupants thereof or are required to avoid the suspension of any necessary service to the Premises.

(b) The AGENT does not assume and is given no responsibility for compliance of any building on the Premises or any equipment therein with the requirements of any statute, ordinance, law or regulation of any governmental body or of any public authority or official thereof having jurisdiction, except to notify the OWNER promptly or forward to the OWNER promptly any complaints, warnings, notices or summonses received by it relating to such matters. The OWNER represents that to the best of his (its) knowledge the Premises and such equipment comply with all such requirements and authorizes the AGENT to disclose the ownership of the Premises to any such officials and agrees to indemnify and hold harmless the AGENT, its representatives, servants and employees, of and from all loss, cost, expense and liability whatsoever which may be imposed on them or any of them by reason of any present or future violation or alleged violation of such laws, ordinances, statutes or regulations.

(c) In the event it is alleged or charged that any building on the Premises or any equipment therein or any act or failure to act by the OWNER with respect to the Premises or the sale, rental or other disposition thereof fails to comply with, or is in violation·of, any of the requirements of any consititutional provision, statute, ordinance, law or regulation of any governmental body or any order or ruling of any public authority or official thereof having or claiming to have jurisdiction thereover, and the AGENT, in its sole and absolute discretion, considers that the action or position of the OWNER or registered managing agent with respect thereto may result in damage or liability to the AGENT, the AGENT shall have the right to cancel this Agreement at any time by written notice to the OWNER of its election so to do, which cancellation shall be effective upon the service of such notice. Such notice may be served personally or by registered mail, on or to the person named to receive the AGENT's monthly statement at the address designated for such person as provided in Paragraph 2(b) above, and if served by mail shall be deemed to have been served when deposited in the mails. Such cancellation shall not release the indemnities of the OWNER set forth in Paragraphs 4 and 6(b) above and shall not terminate any liability or obligation of the OWNER to the AGENT for any payment, reimbursement or other sum of money then due and payable to the AGENT hereunder.

7. This Agreement may be cancelled by OWNER before the termination date specified in paragraph 1 on not less than __ days prior written notice to the AGENT, provided that such notice is accompanied by payment to the AGENT of a cancellation fee in an amount equal to __ % of the management fee that would accrue over the remainder of the stated term of the Agreement. For this purpose the monthly management fee for the remainder of the stated term shall be presumed to be the same as that of the last month prior to service of the notice of cancellation.

This Agreement shall be binding upon the successors and assigns of the AGENT and their heirs, administrators, executors, successors and assigns of the OWNER.

FIGURE 1 *(continued)*

IN WITNESS WHEREOF, the parties hereto have affixed or caused to be affixed their respective signatures this_____day of_____, 19_____

WITNESSES: OWNER:

_____   _____

_____   _____

_____   _____

                                              _____

                                              AGENT:

                                              Firm_____

                                              By_____

Submitted by _____

POWER OF ATTORNEY

KNOW ALL MEN BY THESE PRESENTS, THAT

_____
                          (Name)

_____located at
(State whether individual, partnership or corporation, etc.)

_____has made,
                          (Address)

constituted and appointed, and, by these presents does hereby make, constitute and appoint, _____ , a resident of the United States, whose address is _____, (its) true and lawful attorney for (it) (me) in (its) (my) name, place and stead to

execute and to file any Tax Returns due on and after _____

_____

under the provisions of the Social Security Act, now in force or future amendments thereto.

Dated at _____this _____day of_____, 19_____

                                    _____
                                    Signature of Taxpayer

                                    _____
                                    Title

Executed in presence of: _____
                                    Signature of Taxpayer

                                    _____
                                    Title

_____   _____
Witness   Signature of Taxpayer

_____   _____
Witness   Title

Acknowledged before me this_____day of_____, 19_____
NOTARIAL
SEAL

_____

This is a Standard Form of the Institute of Real Estate Management of the National Association of Realtors, 155 East Superior, Chicago, Illinois 60611. When placing order specify Form No. 7-11.)
© Copyright 1974, Institute of Real Estate Management of the National Association of Realtors, Chicago, Illinois.

FIGURE 1 *(continued)*

IREM
MANAGEMENT AGREEMENT
A SHORT EXPLANATION

The **IREM MANAGEMENT AGREEMENT** is another service of the Institute of Real Estate Management of the National Association of Realtors? As with any form agreement, it should be carefully reviewed to be certain that all of the various blanks are completed and that this form agreement fully and completely sets forth the understanding between you, as the manager of the property, and the owner, your client. It may also be desirable to discuss this with competent legal counsel. The following explanation should be of some assistance to you in filling in the blanks as well as understanding the basic format of the agreement so, if necessary, proper modification may be made.

Introductory Clauses
This sets forth by and with whom the agreement is made, and the blanks should be so completed.

Section 1. In this section, you should set forth the specific address of the property which you are to manage, as well as the effective term of the agreement. You will note that you should insert additionally, the time for notification in the event that there is a termination. You should also be sure that you check paragraph 6 (c) to be sure that it comports with your understanding.

Section 2. This section sets forth your responsibilities as manager. Subparagraphs (a) through (c) should be reviewed carefully to be sure that they are in accordance with the understanding between you and your client. Note that subparagraph (b) obligates you to provide monthly statements of receipts, disbursements and charges against the property to the person whose name and adress you should insert in the blanks. Furthermore, you are obligated under this section to remit the net proceeds of any rent payment to the person whose name and address you should insert in the next series of blanks in the next paragraph. In the event of multiple ownership, the percentage of the net rent should also be set forth. In the case of disbursements for charges in excess of receipts, you should, of course, send a monthly bill. Note also that you must obtain a bond, at your own expense, for your employees who will be handling money.

Section 3. This section sets forth the obligations of the owner. Here, too, you should be certain that subparagraphs (a) through (e) properly reflect the agreement between you and your client. Subparagraph (a) obligates the owner, among other things, to sign leases for terms not in excess of the period of time that you should set forth in the blank in that section. This subparagraph allows you, as the manager, to collect late rent charges and other charges which may result from your activities as manager without having to account to the owner. Subparagraph (b) requires the owner to undertake the negotiation of contracts and nonrecurring items not to exceed a certain dollar amount which you should insert in the blank. You should inform the owner that he is required by subparagraph (d) to refund tenants' security deposits at the expiration of the lease and, if required to do so by law, to pay interest on such security deposits. Many states now require the payment of interest on such security deposits. You should consult with your legal counsel to determine what other obligations may be required by state or local laws.

FIGURE 1 *(concluded)*

Section 4. By this section, the owner further agrees to idemnify the agent and to provide adequate insurance for the property. The blank in subparagraph (a) should be completed to set forth the period of time within which the owner is to provide insurance. Subparagraphs (b) through (d) set forth other indemnification requirements. Review these carefully also.

Section 5. This section should be filled in to set forth your fees. Subparagraph (e) should be completed if there are other areas for which you are to be compensated.

Section 6. This section sets forth various matters relative to the property. Subparagraph (a) requires that you obtain permission before making any structural changes and then only in accordance with the specific power and direction given by the person whose name and address should be inserted in the blank in that subparagraph. Each of these subparagraphs should be reviewed to be sure they are in accordance with your understanding and that they comport with your state or local laws.

Section 7. This section provides for cancellation. You should insert the time period for written notice that is required for cancellation as well as the percentage amount that you will receive in the event of such termination.

NOTE

Care should be taken in using any form agreement so as to be sure that it does completely comport with your undertsanding with your client and that it is in compliance with state and local laws. If in doubt, competent legal counsel should be consulted.

This is short explanation for Standard Form No. 7-11, The Management Agreement prepared by the Institute of Real Estate Management, 155 East Superior, Chicago, Illinois 60611.
© Copyright 1974. Institute of Real Estate Management of the National Association of Realtors, Chicago, Illinois.

taxes, repairs, or other items. A clause might also list other items of expense. Such a clause might state whether the agent is to be paid for additional services—for example, services pertaining to alterations and remodeling.

Management Fees

The management fees are usually governed by local custom. They should be high enough to produce a fair profit, for otherwise neither the agent nor the owner is likely to be well served. The agent should not set his fees until he has inspected the property and cost-accounted the amount of work that he and his staff will have to do in order to fulfill his objectives as a professional property manager. The fees are usually either flat fees or percentage fees. In addition to flat fees and percentage fees, many contracts have charged fees. Sometimes these are extra fees for extraordinary services, such as keeping the corporate books in addition to doing the regular accounting or providing neighborhood surveys, appraisals, and consultation services in addition to carrying out the normal property management work.

Selecting a Manager

The profession of property management is becoming so complex and sophisticated that the task of seeking out firms to manage a real estate portfolio should be done thoroughly and meticulously.

Management Firms. All professions have specialties within their respective fields, and this holds true for the real estate profession. Property management is a specialty within the real estate profession.

The fact that a real estate firm claims to be competent in property management does not necessarily qualify it to manage your property. Each firm that you consider should be asked to show how qualified it is to implement a comprehensive management program for you. It should be asked how large its management portfolio is and what types of property it manages—single-family dwellings, small or large low-rise apartment houses, nonluxury or luxury elevator apartment houses, large or small office buildings, large or small shopping centers, strip commercial stores, cooperative condominiums, or government-subsidized properties. Although many real estate management firms are specialized to manage all of these types of real estate, some are not. Therefore, when a firm to manage a real estate property or a real estate portfolio is being sought, the firm selected should be one which specializes in the management of property and is experienced in managing the type of property for which a property management firm is needed.

Professional Qualifications. Some time ago Realtors® became convinced that property management by trial and error was not only nonprofessional, but also very costly. They decided, therefore, to qualify individuals for the management of a property portfolio by having them complete various educational courses satisfactorily and by having them acquire a certain amount of experience.

The Institute of Real Estate Management of the National Association of Realtors® was formed to qualify Realtors® who specialized in property management (see Appendix). The association states:

> For over 40 years the Institute of Real Estate Management (IREM) has been awarding professional recognition to those property managers who have achieved standards of excellence through education and experience. Today its members, Certified Property Managers (CPM), who manage more than 77 billion dollars worth of the nation's real estate assets, continue to elevate the prestige of the property management profession.

The Building Owners and Managers Institute International was also formed to qualify real estate personnel who specialized in property management. It states:

> That service to the public continuously may be improved, the Building Owners and Managers Institute International, Inc., presents an education program for adults associated with the ownership, management or operation of real property. Those who successfully pass the seven examinations of the program will receive the professional designation Real Property Administrator (RPA). For those who seek to improve their skills in specialties within the industry, the program offers a wide vareity of subject matters.

The Council of Shopping Centers, the International Council of Shopping Centers New York, and the Realtors® National Marketing Institute also qualify individuals who specialize in property management.

Evaluating Management Performance.   A property owner should evaluate the performance of his management firm at least once a year. This is not too difficult to do, because the Institute of Real Estate Management publishes its *Apartment Building Income and Expense Analysis* yearly. That publication shows the income and expense performance of each type of property in most cities. The owner can determine how well his property is doing by comparing its performance with these data.

Each year the Building Owners and Managers Institute International publishes performance data on office buildings. Again, an owner can use these data to determine how well his individual building is doing.

Moreover, many local Boards of Realtors® and other real estate organizations also publish income and expense data which can be used by an owner to evaluate the performance of his management firm.

Property Service Programs

Maintenance.   The professional property manager should have an adequate maintenance program and should be able to supervise personnel who are charged with maintenance responsibilities. These qualifications are necessary if he is to fulfill his objectives of ensuring the highest and best use of the property for as long as possible without prejudice to the original capital investment.

There are two types of maintenance: *preventive maintenance* and *corrective maintenance.*

Preventive maintenance is nothing more than taking care of an item before it needs repair or breaks down. Preventive maintenance anticipates the wear and the changes that systems undergo during the operation and management of a property and makes continuous corrections to minimize loss in income from deterioration. A good preventive maintenance program is one of the most important programs that a professional property manager must establish to operate a property successfully. Such a program will ensure the long-range success of a property and will save maintenance dollars. It involves a planned and controlled program of inspections, adjustments, repairs, and performance analysis that is designed to keep an operation at peak efficiency relative to cost.

Corrective maintenance is nothing more than making repairs after items have already broken down or are already in need of repair. Corrective maintenance can never be eliminated, for it is really maintenance by demand. It is usually more costly than preventive maintenance, as the damage involved tends to be greater and the work is often done at overtime rates. A leaky roof and leaky plumbing are good examples of situations that require corrective maintenance.

A professional property manager should know what each trade does, and be able to analyze competitive bids and specifications. He makes sure that the physical integrity and economic viability of his structures are maintained.

Purchasing.   As with maintenance, the property manager can be a great influence in controlling purchasing expenses and thus enhancing the profitability of properties. There are basically two types of purchasing by property management firms. A firm which handles larger projects and buildings usually employs centralized purchasing, if possible on a building basis. The purchasing agent makes it his full-time business to get the lowest prices, the best quality, the best service, and the most responsible vendors. By organizing a bill control system, he is assured of getting discounts for prompt payment. In such an operation, all requisitions and purchase orders reach the purchasing agent through the resident manager, the building superintendent, or the property manager. The purchasing agent phones the order to the proper vendor, giving an order number. He has the original copy of the purchase order filed in the property file and a carbon copy filed in the vendor's file, alphabetically awaiting the invoice. The invoice is matched against the purchase order and is verified for performance and price by the property manager, the building superintendent, or the resident manager. Then it is charged to the proper account and category and forwarded to accounting.

In the smaller firms, the property manager usually performs the functions of the purchasing agent. He recommends vendors to the resident manager or the building superintendent. The purchase order is filled out in the property manager's office, and the purchase order number is given to the resident manager or the building superintendent. This method requires training in standard policies and procedures for handling unidentified bills that come in.

Service Contracts.   These contracts usually cover items that the building or the management staff cannot handle. They usually include elevator service contracts, cleaning contracts, and service contracts for exterminating, for trash removal, and for maintaining certain mechanical equipment, the swimming pool, and the landscaping. The contracts should be reviewed periodically for coverage, term, exclusions, and the cost and quality of the service that is being given. The workmanship should be checked periodically, and communication lines should be open.

Financial Management

Accounting. The two most important obligations of the professional property manager are the physical maintenance of the property, which we discussed earlier, and the maintenance of the fiscal records of the property. The most important fiscal items of concern to the property manager are the annual budget and the monthly operating statement, which he usually submits to the owner at the end of each month. The property manager must be able to prepare a meaningful annual budget which includes all anticipated income expense items for his property. All of the professional property manager's knowledge and all of his source materials play a part in the thinking that goes into his budget. Once the property manager has obtained approval for his budget, he should be careful to operate within it.

Reporting. The professional property manager usually submits monthly operating statements to the property owner. These statements include all operating income, the bulk of which comes from rents, and any nonoperating income, such as the income from parking, the swimming pool, washing machines, dryers, and vending machines. The statements also show all operating expenses, which normally include the debt service. The operating statements give the owner an idea of how his property is working on a cash basis. They can include the yearly budget and the percentage of that budget which has been spent to date, thus providing a budgetary control as well as a cash control.

Insurance. The protection of real property is a major reason for the use of professional property managers. Insurance is, of course, an important means for protecting property. Although the professional property manager is not required to be an insurance expert, he must be familiar with the various types of coverages so that he can adequately protect the property owner and his property. Among the insurance coverages of concern to the professional property manager are fire insurance, liability insurance, workers' compensation, fidelity bonds, boiler insurance, rental insurance, and plate glass insurance. He must also be familiar with deductible items and with rates, and he must be able to use judgment in increasing or reducing insurance costs. About 1½ to 2 percent of rental income goes to insurance, and the amount spent for insurance is continually rising.

Generating Rental Income

If we were to list the phases involved in the development of a project in chronological order, we would begin with the research that gives us all the data pertaining to the property. Then we would go on to design, which is normally done by the architect; to financing, which is normally done by the thrift and mortgage institutions; and to construction, which is done by the builder. The next phase, the one we are now examining, is marketing, putting the property up for leasing or renting. The final phase would be management, which we will examine later.

What are the general considerations of the professional property manager when he merchandises rental property? First, he must know his bargaining position—whether the property will be easy to merchandise or difficult to merchandise. Again, we get back to the research orientation of the professional property manager. He is abreast of the pertinent international, national, and local trends and puts all of his knowledge to work when he is determining his bargaining position. Second, he is involved with advertising and tries to make every advertising dollar count. He measures the success of his advertising by keeping statistics on the responses. He will usually budget between 1 and 2 percent of his income for advertising. He compares his results with those achieved by his competitors. He shows good taste in maintaining the image he is trying to project of himself as a professional property manager, and of the building he is managing. He wants to be original but not cute, and he avoids being overly critical of others.

Merchandising Rental Space. It is very important to make the rental unit presentable before showing it to prospective tenants, who may be unable to visualize how the unit will look after it is completely redecorated. Therefore, all of the rehabilitation and redecorating should be done before the unit is shown.

Rental markets are sometimes very competitive. To hold his own, the professional property manager must keep abreast of the amenities that are needed and wanted by prospective tenants. He should be familiar with all of the details of his unit before he or his personnel merchandise it.

Apartments. With apartment houses, the best advertising results come from a proper sign on the property. It is estimated that 50 to 75 percent of apartment merchandising is done by signs. The next best results come from classified advertising in the newspapers. The most natural place for a prospect to look for an apartment is in the classified advertising section of the newspaper. Display advertising is sometimes effective for apartment houses. Many times, however, the agent places too much emphasis on such advertising. Nevertheless, display advertising does confer prestige. Magazine ads are usually unwarranted for apartment advertising because they are too expensive and not very effective. TV and radio advertising is sometimes effective, but it is generally prohibitive because of its cost. However, a large project can achieve a great deal of success from radio and TV advertising. Direct mail advertising of apartments is very expensive but not very effective.

Showing the apartment is one of the most important aspects of merchandising. You cannot rent an apartment to someone whom you cannot get to look at it. You must show it. The professional property manager should make certain to teach his resident manager and his office personnel good showing techniques. Otherwise he will spend a lot of money in getting prospects to a property but will be unable to sell them when they get there. He should make certain that his resident manager and other staff members point out important features and avoid superfluous remarks, such as "this is the bedroom," that they sell the amenities of the building and the caliber of its tenants. The apartment being shown should be rehabilitated, decorated, and clean. It is also important to have the public areas look attractive. Many tenants are lost because the public areas create a poor impression before the unit is inspected.

A model apartment can be very helpful if a significant number of vacancies exist. It should be done in good taste and near the rental office.

Office Buildings. Although classified ads are effective with apartment buildings, they are not very effective with office buildings. Signs are very important. As with apartments, 50 to 75 percent of the merchandising of office space is done by proper signs. The use of brochures on office buildings in direct mail advertising is very effective. Follow-up is necessary if such mailings are to achieve their maximum potential. The advertising of office buildings in trade or professional magazines can be effective. Radio and television are very expensive and not very productive.

In apartment merchandising a model apartment is used; in merchandising office space a tenant's plush offices are exhibited or an office model is set up. Sometimes the professional property manager throws a cocktail party for the tenants and business guests. He provides layout and decorating service without charge.

When you show space for office buildings, you never let the prospect go alone and you never let the janitor or the elevator operator show the space. The space should be shown by a qualified leasing specialist who knows the competition and is familiar with the tenants in the building. The leasing specialist should know the market for the competition's space and should know how the competition merchandises its space. The space should, of course, be shown only after it has been made ready for merchandising by being completely rehabilitated. The clean space demonstrates the efficiency of the building staff.

Negotiating is perhaps the most important phase of merchandising office buildings. This function should be performed by the professional property manager or his leasing agent.

Merchandising Industrial Space. As with apartment and office buildings the sign on the building is the most productive advertising medium. Brochures or direct mailers are very effective, as is advertising in trade publications. The same techniques are used in showing industrial space as are used in showing office space.

Merchandising Commercial Stores. Again, the sign is the most important advertising medium, and it may be worthwhile for the property manager to explain its importance to the owner. Brochures are also effective.

Property Analysis

Depreciation. The professional property manager needs to understand depreciation for several reasons. He must make a physical inspection of the property and determine which items are in need of immediate attention and which items can have their maintenance deferred. He must determine what amount should be budgeted for repairs and for replacement reserves. He is expected to explain to the owner why items depreciate and how an appraiser treats depreciated items if the owner needs an appraisal to obtain financing or for other purposes. The depreciation survey gives the professional manager an opportunity to make a comprehensive examination of a property and to make an analysis of its financial status.

Depreciation is the difference between the cost new of a property and its market value as of a given date, assuming that the market value is less than the cost new. It is a loss in value due to certain causes. Accrued depreciation is depreciation which has already taken place. Recapture is the provision that is made to recoup the losses of future depreciation, either in periodic amounts or in a lump sum. Recapture is the provision that is made for future depreciation—the depreciation that is expected to take place.

Physical Deterioration and Functional Obsolescence. Physical deterioration is caused by wear and tear and the action of the elements. It is measured by the cost that the professional property manager requires to cure the defects. For example, if a roof costs $100 to repair, a window costs $15 to repair, these items are the measure of the physical deterioration that has occurred.

Functional obsolescence is caused by poor planning, design, and utilities. It is measured by the loss of rent. For example, if a unit in an apartment building with narrow hallways, small rooms, and a poorly designed bath rents for $50 a month less than a unit in a new building which has adequate hallways, large enough rooms, and a properly designed bath, functional obsolescence is causing a loss of $50 per unit per month, or $600 per year. If you capitalize it at a proper rate and if the capitalization rate is assumed to be 8 percent, the loss in value due to functional obsolescence would be $7,500.

Economic Depreciation. The economic depreciation of a property is caused by such external factors as changes in zoning, in the surrounding property, in traffic patterns, and in population. Like functional obsolescence, economic obsolescence is measured by the increase in rent that would be obtainable if the condition did not exist. For example, the vacancies in an office building increased 10 percent a year for three successive years because of numerous violent crimes within a block of the building.

A professional property manager must be able to estimate future depreciation because this is an ingredient in the projections that he is expected to make as to the future income of a property. He is the specialist in assessing the future net income of a property, a figure which he arrives at by estimating the future gross income (the income from rents and other sources, less the anticipated rental loss) and subtracting the future estimated expenses from it.

Neighborhood Analysis. What factors is the professional property manager concerned with when he analyzes a neighborhood? First, he defines the neighborhood. It is an area within which there are common characteristics in *population* and land use.

The size of a neighborhood varies. Farm neighborhoods may be several square miles in area; city neighborhoods may be as small as a single block. A neighborhood usually has natural boundaries. For instance, it may be adjacent to a lake, a river, a hill, or a ravine. Sometimes, the boundaries of a neighborhood are set by man-made barriers, such as highways, freeways, railroads, commercial districts, industrial areas, parks, airports, and golf courses. Population characteristics often determine the boundary of a particular neighborhood.

It is important for the professional property manager to ascertain the boundaries of the neighborhood in which a property is situated because he cannot study his market until he knows who and what the market comprises. He doesn't want to include real estate or people that belong to another market because this will distort his findings.

Having defined the boundaries of the neighborhood, the professional property manager evaluates the accessibility, the shopping areas, and the educational, recreational, and transportation facilities of the neighborhood.

He also evaluates the physical improvements of the neighborhood. How old are the improvements? What is their physical condition? What types of improvements are there? Are they single-family homes, office buildings, apartments, commercial stores? He is interested in the new construction and in construction trends. Is the neighborhood completely built up? Is there vacant land? Where does the land value exceed the value of the improvements? What construction is planned? Are the improvements homogeneous? How popular are they? What is the social standing of the neighborhood? Is the climate suitable for the type of people he is seeking as tenants? He is interested in the physical trends in the neighborhood—he wants to know whether the neighborhood is improving, remaining stationary, or declining.

The professional property manager is also interested in the population. It was noted earlier that people create real estate values. Therefore, a most important characteristic of a neighborhood is its population trends. The professional property manager determines which segments of the overall population occupy the real estate in a neighborhood— the unmarried employed, divorced, the married employed without children, the retired, and so on. Such information provides important indications of the economic potential of his product. The divorced and the retired, for example, are increasing in number, and the married employees without children tend to be able to afford higher priced units.

The professional property manager wants to know the economic status of the population because this is a key to rent-paying ability. The relative economic stability of a neighborhood may be measured in part by the adequacy and the permanence of the income sources of its inhabitants. Information on family income, family size, and the movement of people into the neighborhood and out of it help the professional property manager to provide effective advice on the disposition of a given property.

Property Analysis. Having analyzed the neighborhood, the professional property manager proceeds to the property analysis. This is one of the studies that he must make in order to arrive at a proper management plan. It includes an inspection of the building to determine its physical condition, its layout, its design, and other qualities. It includes an investigation of the facilities and conveniences which are offered to the tenants. It includes an appraisal of the site. It includes a determination of the relationship between the subject property and its neighborhood and market. It includes an income and expense projection. After this analysis has been made, a management program can be suggested.

In making his analysis of the property, the professional property manager wants to know what the depreciation is. He wants to know what the deferred maintenance costs are. He lists the items that must be repaired if the building is to operate properly. He wants to know what the functional obsolescence is. In studying functional obsolescence, he takes note of curable and noncurable items. With this distinction in mind he examines the baths, the archways, the high ceilings, the French doors, or the arched doors. Noncurable functional obsolescence is the biggest source of losses in real estate income. He is interested in finding out what the economic obsolescence is—what factors outside the building are causing it to become obsolescent.

He takes a walk through the building and near it and makes a checklist of the physical items that are to be studied for deferred maintenance, functional obsolescence, and economic obsolescence. He begins with the public areas—the lobby, the elevator, the halls. He checks the roof, the exterior. Does the exterior need painting, sandblasting, or cleaning? He checks the windows. Do they need painting or screens? He checks the downspouts, the landscaping, the basement—are they in good condition? Then he wants to know about the equipment. He is careful to check the plumbing and the heating systems. Does the building have the proper equipment, and what condition is it in?

Then he analyzes the rental unit. He wants to know the size and the layout. He wants to note the traffic pattern of the unit. Is it functional? He wants to know how many people the rental unit can accommodate comfortably. What is the condition of the unit? How long will it be before it has to be refurbished? Then he considers each room of the unit. What about the kitchen? What about the bath? What about the dressing room and the closet? What about the bedrooms? What about the living room? What facilities are there? Is there a laundry space? Is there a pool? Is there a patio? Is there a yard? Is there a recreation room? And is there parking?

Now the professional property manager is ready for his site analysis. How is the site set? Is it level or hilly? Are there steps? Does it have light? What about the neighbors?

Then the manager wants to note the desirability of the location. He indicates what items might improve the atmospheric qualities of the building and its location.

Income Analysis. The professional property manager has made a neighborhood analysis. He has made a property analysis. He has made a physical inspection of the property that has even included each room or suite. Now he is ready for an income analysis. He wants to get a copy of all the leases and rent schedules. He wants to know what services are included in the rent. He wants to know how the rents compare with rents that are being charged elsewhere. He wants to know about the tenants.

Then he wants to know how to go about stabilizing the income from the property. He wants to know what the vacancy and collection losses are. He establishes what vacancy factor is expected. This becomes the first item of expense. He wants to know what the vacancy trends and what the seasonal fluctuations in vacancies are.

Now he is ready to analyze his expenses. He wants to know about the payroll, the utilities, and the *sundry expenses,* such as the expenses for advertising, extermination, supplies, licenses and fees, and trash removal. Then he wants to know the expenses for normal maintenance—for the elevators, the air conditioning, the plumbing, building repair, the pool, the furniture and equipment, painting, and landscaping. Finally, he wants to know the insurance and tax charges and the management fee.

Now he correlates all of his information concerning income and expenses with the information that he obtained from his market analysis of similar buildings in the neighborhood. He stabilizes the income and the expenses by making the adjustments that are necessary to bring his property to its highest and best use.

The property manager is now ready for conclusions and recommendations. He studied the neighborhood population data and population trends. He studied the physical improvements of the neighborhood. When he completed his neighborhood analysis he made a thorough property analysis. He made a market analysis of the neighborhood and the property. He made certain that the stabilized income of the property was in keeping with that of similar units in similar property in the neighborhood. He is ready to made recommendations for necessary repairs or remodeling to ensure the continuance or the increase of the income from the building. He is ready to make recommendations for the lease or rental terms that will fit the neighborhood patterns. He seeks to maintain neighborhood stability by giving a detailed tenancy potential and selection. When he stabilizes his expenses he uses the Institute of Real Estate Management *Apartment Building Income and Expense Analysis* as a guide. He details the expense data and stabilizes them after increasing or decreasing each expense item. He makes recommendations relative to operating expenses, perhaps eliminating some services. He analyzes the financial structure. He calculates stabilized net income, and he compares the present net income with the stabilized net income.

Based on his findings, the professional property manager recommends a course of action and a management program.

The Professional Property Manager

The professional property manager can accomplish perhaps half of what the appraiser needs to do in order to arrive at a valuation of an income-producing property. Take the appraiser's formula in determining the valuation of an income-producing property. The formula is:

$$\text{Value} = \frac{\text{Net income}}{\text{Rate}}$$

The professional property manager is the individual who is most capable of determining net income. This is one half of the appraiser's work in arriving at a valuation. Although the professional property manager isn't competent at determining the capitalization rate (the appraiser is), he is competent at determining net income.

When he assumes responsibility for the physical management of a particular property the professional property manager is ready to put into effect all of the preliminary work that he has done up to that point. You will recall that before he was ready to assume the management he made a neighborhood analysis (an analysis of the population and the capital improvements of the neighborhood), a property analysis, a site analysis, an income and expense analysis of the building, and a market analysis of comparable properties in the neighborhood. Since he now knew the building's price levels, expense levels, and amenities and had comparable data for similar neighborhood properties, he was able to stabilize the income and the expenses of the building, by making provision for the necessary additions or subtractions. He did all of this before he began his first minute of managing the building, and he is now able to assume the management of the building because he has done the preliminary work in a professional manner.

His research orientation and the data he compiles also enable him to manage the building completely.

He makes needed changes in personnel. He knows what personnel are required to make his building comparable and competitive with other buildings in the neighborhood. He trains his personnel in his way of managing a building. He sets up a system for apprasing the supervision and the efficiency of the building's operation. He determines how much authority each employee needs. He sees that the employees understand the entire management program as it affects his building. He may institute incentives and merit raises in order to fulfill his management plan. He makes certain that his personnel are adequately prepared, and he imparts a sense of pride to them by taking their problems into consideration.

He is ready to put his management program into effect, and he is ready to plan the operation of the property on a day-to-day basis, a week-to-week basis, a month-to-month basis, and a year-to-year basis. He establishes a program of inspections and preventive maintenance.

He prepares an annual budget, and he is ready to administer it, to cross-compare his budget with that of comparable properties. He evaluates the performance of the property against his budget. He has budget controls and an effective preventive maintenance program. He is ready to check the performance of assigned work and the effectiveness of merchandising. He knows the vacancy level, and he knows how quickly vacant apartments are renovated and rented. Being competent in leasing, he knows what the lease terms and the rentals should be, and what his subletting policy should be. He knows whether security deposits are necessary, and how large they should be. He knows how much is involved in credit and collections.

He is able to institute an adequate inventory and purchasing program. He knows his sources of supply. He knows what materials are needed to complete the jobs that have to be done. He has control over the acquisition care of materials and equipment. He knows who is authorized to make purchases authority and what measures are being taken to ensure the security of the storage area.

He is able to select and to adequately supervise service contractors. He is ready to review their charges periodically. He is involved in the training of the building superintendent, and through the building superintendent he can verify on an hourly basis the amount and the quality of contractual work, the condition of the supplies used by contractors, and contractors' charges for working time.

And finally, in his operation of the building the professional property manager is involved with tenant relations. He knows that he must be courteous but not too formal. He knows that there should be no close social relationships. He knows that he must provide prompt service. And he knows that he must be completely impartial in his treatment of the tenants.

When the professional property manager assumes the management of a building, he has spent a good deal of time in acquiring the necessary competence. His many hours of preparation enable him to perform his functions properly and professionally.

EXCHANGING
INVESTMENTS

Victor L. Lyon

VICTOR L. LYON, MAI, SRPA, CRE, CCIM, President, Victor L. Lyon, Inc., Tacoma, Washington.

President, Conifer Developments, Inc. Director, Pierce County Escrow Co., Inc.; and Land Title Company. President in 1977 of Realtors® National Marketing Institute. Director, National Association of Realtors®. Past president of Multiple Listing Service, Tacoma Board of Realtors®, Washington Association of Realtors®, and Washington Real Estate Educational Foundation. Coauthor Marketing Investment Real Estate (Chicago, Ill.: Realtors National Marketing Institute, 1975).

The phrase "exchanging real estate" is greatly misunderstood because it describes two totally different types of real estate transactions.

First, it can describe a bartering process, in which one or more properties are exchanged for one or more properties, primarily because none of the properties are readily salable. This type of exchange process can also be used to hide true values by emphasizing differences of equities. Many brokers have established reputations for excellence in this field, though much exchanging of this nature is highly questionable. Because of this, many property owners add 25–100 percent to what they assume to be their highest price in order to allow for "excess" in a property that is to be acquired by them in the exchange process.

Second, "exchanging real estate" can mean the structuring of a transaction in such a manner that it qualifies for special tax treatment under the Internal Revenue Code. This chapter will consider the latter type of exchange transaction. It will discuss the pertinent code section and interpret it so that a real estate broker may easily recognize the circumstances that are favorable for an exchange of this type, and how to estimate the tax impact of an exchange against the sale of a property.

The "how to" will be demonstrated by examples that will permit the reader to analyze his own possibilities for exchanges.

The chapter has been written for the practicing real estate person, and the language used is for that person and not the accountant or the attorney. Because of this approach, some of the language and calculations depart from the usage of the Internal Revenue Code, but it is hoped that the language and calculations used here will have more meaning for the reader.

Finally it should be understood that the material as presented is an introduction to the basic concepts and calculations of the tax-deferred exchange. Not covered are the many and varied complications that can occur in the exchange process. Therefore, although the material presented here is designed to teach the real estate practitioner how to estimate the tax consequences of exchanges, the author strongly recommends the use of knowledgeable accountants and attorneys for the final calculations and the drafting of exchange agreements.

Advantages of 1031 Exchanges

There is only one reason to take advantage of Section 1031 of the Internal Revenue Code, and that reason is to defer the payment of income taxes normally due upon the sale of a parcel of real estate.

Let us assume that in 1960 Mr. Green purchased a vacant property at a cost of $20,000. In 1978, because of increased population, increased traffic in the area, inflation, and many other factors, the property is valued at $200,000 and Mr. Brown wishes to acquire the vacant property as the site for an office building (ignore sale costs). If Green sells, his aftertax proceeds are as follows:

Sale price net	$200,000
Basis of property	$ 20,000
Gain on sale	$180,000
Taxable (40%)	$ 72,000
Tax at maximum rate 70%	$ 50,400
Net proceeds ($200,000 − $50,400)	$149,600

But if the property qualifies for a Section 1031 exchange, the seller pays no tax on the increased valuation and his equity in new property is $200,000. Assuming a 9 percent yield on equity:

Income after sale and purchase (9 percent of $164,000)	$14,760 annual income
Income after exchange (9 percent of $200,000)	$18,000 annual income

It can readily be seen that under these conditions the exchange not only defers the taxes but also increases the annual yield before income taxes from *$13,464* to *$18,000.* Is it not fair to say that in *11* years the extra income will "pay" the tax deferred?

$50,400 (estimated taxes on sale) ÷ $4,536 (annual extra income) =
11.1 years

Because the proper use of Section 1031 not only defers the payment of income taxes due upon a sale but also provides a larger equity "at work," it is imperative that all practitioners dealing in investment property understand how to apply the section to each potential transaction. This can best be accomplished by examining each important phrase of Section 1031 and by showing what procedures to follow so as to be able to analyze most potential exchange transactions.

Section 1031 states, "No gain or loss is recognized upon the exchange of property held for productive use in a trade or business, or for investment, solely for property of a like kind to be held either for productive use in a business or for investment."

Qualified Types. The practitioner must understand that the only types of properties that can qualify for a tax-deferred exchange are properties that are used in a trade or a business or as investment properties.

The former include the doctor's clinic, the manufacturer's warehouse, the grocer's retail building, the broker's office. They also include properties that are held for rental income, such as apartment houses or office buildings.

An investment property is a property that is held for appreciation and is not held for resale. Since rental property is classified as business property, basically the only real estate "held for investment" is vacant land.

It should be emphasized that real estate acquired for development, rehabilitation, or remodeling with intent to resell does not qualify for a 1031 exchange. Neither does vacant land acquired for the purpose of subdivision and resale. All of these may be profitable "investments," but none of them qualify as investment property under this section of the Internal Revenue Code.

"Like Kind." This phrase refers to the types of property described above rather than the kind or grade of property. "Like for like" does not mean land for land, apartment for apartment. It means business property for business property, investment property for investment property, or investment property for business property. Leaseholds that have 30 years or more to run and are used in a trade or a business or are held for investment also qualify.

The following are examples of like for like properties that can be exchanged: motel for office building, lot for lot, land for apartment; 40-year fast-food lease for warehouse to be used in a trade or a business.

Unlike Properties. It is possible to have an exchange under Section 1031 that involves properties other than like properties. For instance, one party can add cash, notes, personal property, or other nonqualifying property without destroying the tax-deferred feature of the exchange. However, the *receipt* of unlike property can cause the exchange to be partially or totally taxable for the party receiving the unlike property.

"Must Be Exchanged." Finally, it is important to understand that to qualify under Section 1031, a property must actually be exchanged for another property and the property received in the exchange must be acquired to hold for use in a trade or a business or as an investment.

The property must be exchanged rather than sold so that the funds can be used to purchase another property. It is especially important to make certain that the filing order of documents is correct when more than two parties are involved in an exchange. This will be discussed in greater detail later.

The tax-deferred exchange can be disallowed if the party claiming the deferment resells the property received in the exchange soon after it has been acquired. The property acquired in the exchange must be held. However, it can be exchanged on a tax deferred basis as often as desired so long as the basic requirements of Section 1031 are met.

Analysis of an Exchange Transaction

Making an exchange is not simple, and an exchange should normally be made only if there are significant tax savings. Therefore, the real estate practitioner will find it helpful to go through a series of simple steps to analyze a potential exchange transaction and to estimate the tax advantages of the exchange as opposed to a sale.

These steps include:

1. Identifying the property as qualified (as previously discussed).
2. Calculating the tax consequences if the property were to be sold (the indicated gain).
3. Balancing the equities.
4. Identifying and qualifying unlike properties.
5. Calculating the recognized gain from the exchange.

It is logical to assume that if substantial tax savings can be effected by substituting an exchange for a sale, the practitioner will take the necessary steps to structure the transaction so that an exchange takes place.

To convey an understanding of the process the following example is used.

> Mr. A owns an apartment house valued at $500,000. He has owned it for 15 years, and his basis (book value) is $300,000. He has encumbrances on the property for $250,000. He wants to get out of the problems of management and would like to get into a long-term leased commercial property. In the event of sale or exchange A's transaction costs would be $30,000, which he would pay in cash.
>
> You, the broker, have:
>
> a. A warehouse owned by Mr. B that Mr. A would like to acquire. The property is priced at $700,000 with a $300,000 encumbrance under a long-term lease. B's basis is $500,000.
> b. A buyer for Mr. A's property.

Let us go step by step to determine the feasibility of a 1031 exchange.

Step 1. Does the property quality?

Yes. Mr. A holds the apartment as a trade or business property. The warehouse would serve the same purpose, and A plans to hold it, not resell.

Step 2. What would the tax consequences be in the event of a sale (the indicated gain)?

Sale price (apartment house)		$500,000
Less		
Basis (book value)	$300,000	
Transaction costs	30,000	
	330,000	
Indicated gain		$170,000
Income tax on sale (assume 28%		
capital gain rate)		47,600

Step 3. Balance the equities.

	Mr. A (apartment house)	Mr. B (warehouse)
Value	$500,000	$700,000
Encumbrance	250,000	300,000
Equity	250,000	400,000
To balance	$150,000	
	$400,000	

Assume that Mr. A will pay the difference with $100,000 in cash and $50,000 on a note secured by a second mortgage on Mr. B's property.

Step 4. Determine the unlike properties.

In order to do this we ask ourselves three questions about the party to the exchange *whom we are studying.* Let us consider Mr. A for the moment. If he makes the exchange will he *receive:*

Any cash?	No, he will *pay* cash—$30,000 for transaction costs and $100,000 for the equity difference.
Any boot?	No, he is not receiving any notes or personal property. In fact, he is giving a $50,000 note.
Any net loan relief?	Prior to the exchange Mr. A's encumbrances were $250,000. After the exchange he would owe the $300,000 first mortgage and a $50,000 note and second mortgage. He has *no* net loan relief.

Summarizing Mr. A's position after the exchange as to unlike properties:

Cash	$0
Boot	0
Net loan relief	0
Total unlike	
properties	$0

Step 5. Calculate the recognized gain.

To calculate the recognized gain we *compare* A's indicated gain and the sum of the unlike properties.

> Indicated gain $170,000
> Sum of the unlike properties . . .   0

The *lesser* of the two is the recognized gain in the exchange. Therefore, we can see that if A makes the exchange, his recognized gain (and tax liability at this time) is zero; thus it makes sense for A to exchange rather than to sell and buy.

Before we leave the example, let us consider the effect of the exchange versus sale on Mr. B, assuming that his transaction costs are $45,000.

In the event of a sale, B's indicated gain is:

> Sale price $700,000
> Less
> > Adjusted basis $500,000
> > Transaction costs   45,000
> >   545,000
> Indicated gain $155,000

Step 4. Determine the unlike properties received by B.

Any cash?   Yes—$100,000 from A, less $45,000 transaction costs, or $55,000.

Any boot?   Yes—the $50,000 note and the second mortgage

Any net loan relief?   Yes—B had a $300,000 encumbrance and will acquire a $250,000 encumbrance. Therefore, he has a net loan relief of $50,000.

Total unlike properties $155,000

Step 5. Calculate the recognized gain.

> Indicated gain $155,000
> Sum of unlike properties $155,000

Therefore, the recognized gain is $155,000 and the exchange has no advantage for Mr. B.

Implementing the Exchange

You meet with Mr. A to show him your estimates of taxes due in the event of a sale or exchange. You also point out to him that if he sells, his aftertax proceeds are estimated at:

Sale price		$500,000
Less		
Encumbrance	$250,000	
Income tax	47,600	
	297,400	
Net proceeds		$202,400
Therefore, if he applied		
the proceeds to the purchase		700,000
Assume loan...........................	$300,000	
Down payment	$202,400	
Cash added	$100,000	
	602,400	
To be carried by		
seller on note		$ 97,600

It is readily seen that A's purchasing power is $47,600 less after a sale than with the exchange where only $50,000 was needed by note.

Mr. A elects to exchange and requests that you ask B whether if he will exchange. You tell Mr. A that's not the way to proceed and get him (and his wife if necessary) to sign an exchange agreement covering the following:

> A will exchange his equity in Property A subject to a mortgage not to exceed $250,000 for Property B with a mortgage not to exceed $300,000. In addition, A will pay the following to balance equities:
>
> $100,000 in cash.
>
> A $50,000 note secured by a second mortgage on Property B.
>
> A will also pay $30,000 in cash for transaction costs. Any difference in equities due to a difference in encumbrances at the time of closing will be adjusted in cash by the property owner affected. Also, all rents, taxes, and the like, will be prorated as of the closing date.

As a practitioner you must now understand the realities of the market. It is 99 percent probable that Mr. B does not need and does not want Mr. A's property. If you will only believe that statement you will then do what has to be done. You will *not* go to Mr. B to convince him that he should take Mr. A's property. You will inform him that A wants his property and *must* acquire it by exchange because of the tax consequences of the sale of A's property and the subsequent purchase of B's property. "Mr. B, my job as broker is to inform you that I have a person who wants your property and that I am now in the process of marketing his property—if you want it you can have it." Mr. B's reply is that he wants no other property and that he agrees to give you time to sell the A property.

You then go to Mr. C, your potential customer (or you find a Mr. "C"), who wants A's property and you get him to sign an earnest money receipt (or offer, or purchase contract, whatever you use) to acquire the property.

Mr. C will not overpay for the property because A is going to exchange—he will only buy it at market. Because it is rare for A and B to exchange and because in most cases of 1031 exchanging it is necessary to have a cash-out buyer "in the wings," it is important to take properties for exchange at market value, not an inflated "exchange" price.

Now with an exchange agreement executed by A on B's property and a purchase agreement executed by C on A's property, the agent goes to *B*, who will sign the exchange agreement providing that the A property will be sold to a third party prior to or during closing and B also signs the purchase agreement subject to acquiring the property in the exchange. By this method the exchange of properties will take place in such a manner as to qualify under Section 1031.

Step 1.   A and B will exchange properties.
Step 2.   B will sell A's property to C.

An attempt to save recording fees or other transaction costs by conveying A to C, conveying B to A, and paying B his proceeds can jeopardize the exchange upon IRS examination.

The Exchange Client

Before we leave the exchange process, it would be well to describe some of the characteristics that are needed by the exchange client:

The client must understand or be taught the rudiments of the 1031 exchange. Even more important, the client's advisers must understand or be willing to understand the law *and* the exchange process. It is much better to get the client, his lawyer, and his accountant to approve the process long before a property is found for exchange. The client and his advisers must understand as a minimum:

1. The tax consequences of sale or exchange.
2. The 99 percent probability that when a property is located, its owner will not want the client's property.
3. The necessity of selling the client's property to someone and the costs of sale.
4. The necessity of pricing the exchange property at market value so that a sale can be effected.
5. The need to incur extra costs by reconveying from B to C and to have A, who is receiving the tax advantage, pay these double costs.
6. The time involved in finding an exchange property and then finding a buyer for the client's property.
7. The need for cash in the transaction, either added by the client or available from resale or refinancing the client's property.
8. The need of the client and his advisers to have confidence in the broker.

It is necessary for such a foundation of information and confidence to be erected so that the exchange will close. It is well to create the foundation before the transaction is attempted.

The "Cost" of a 1031 Exchange

For the benefit of deferring the gain normally due on a sale, the parties to the exchange generally carry their basis in the old property to the new property. Adjustments are made to reflect some of the elements in the exchange.

The old basis is increased by any new loans, cash paid, the fair market value of any boot paid, and any recognized gain in the transaction. From this new amount are subtracted any loans given up and any cash or boot received, to calculate the basis after the exchange.

An examination of the effects of a sale and purchase or an exchange on basis can be compared.

New Basis on Warehouse Acquired by:

	Exchange	Purchase
Old basis (including transaction costs)	$330,000	$330,000
New loan	$300,000	$300,000
Cash paid.....................................	100,000	100,000
Boot paid	50,000	50,000
Recognized gain	0	170,000
Total	$780,000	$950,000
Less old loan.................................	250,000	250,000
Less cash/boot received......................	0	0
New basis..............................	$530,000	$700,000

Calculation of Annual Depreciation

	Exchange	Purchase
Assume 20 percent land	$106,000	$140,000
Available for depreciation (assume 25-year straight-line depreciation—4 percent)	$424,000	$560,000
Annual depreciation	$ 16,960	$ 22,400

The "penalty" or cost of the exchange is having a smaller basis for depreciation. In the example, if Mr. A sold, then purchased, his annual depreciation would be $5,440 greater than on the exchange. This could or could not be significant. That determination is not considered here.

Summary

Exchanging under Section 1031 is an important tool for the investment broker. It not only permits deferring tax payment; it also keeps more equity working, and it moves the acquisition date of the property exchanged to the property acquired, thereby increasing the holding period of the second property.

But the advantages of the tax deferment must be weighed against the effects of the exchange in other areas. There are some disadvantages. The new property will have a lower basis and therefore less annual depreciation, which will increase annual income taxes. Moreover, under certain circumstances excess depreciation taken in the first property can be recaptured at the time of the exchange and cause a tax liability at that time. Finally, the 1976 Tax Act made a significant change in the tax-deferred exchange. It used to be said that the tax was deferred but could be escaped entirely by dying. This was because under the previous law at the time of death (or six months later) property was valued at market value. This meant that the low basis carried forward because of the tax deferment feature of the exchange was stepped up automatically at the time of death. This permitted heirs to sell the property at market value and have no gain upon which to pay taxes. Under the 1976 law the low basis is carried forward to the heirs and they face the tax consequences previously deferred.[1]

On the one hand, it might be concluded that the 1976 Tax Act makes exchanging less profitable and less important. On the other hand, the exact opposite might be true. Under the 1976 act, properties will be valued on a "fresh start basis," which will generally be less than market value at the time of death.[1] Now, not only "exchange properties" but almost all properties upon resale by heirs will create increased tax liabilities. This could create an even greater need for 1031 exchanges.

There is another unstudied aspect of tax deferred exchanging that needs greater exploration. As the real estate industry increases its understanding and use of calculating present values from future benefits, more consideration will be given to understanding the alternatives of immediate tax savings by exchanging as opposed to paying the tax now and getting greater income because of greater depreciation write-offs.

Notwithstanding these more challenging aspects, property owners, needless to say, are more impressed with the immediate savings afforded by the 1031 exchange. Therefore, the practitioner must be aware of this important tool.

Finally, it would be well to point out the need to have the broker, the accountant, and the attorney work as an investment team on behalf of the client. If those three advisers cannot work as a team, only the client will suffer, especially in the field of tax-deferred exchanging.

---

[1] At the time this manuscript went to press these provisions have been delayed until after 1979. It is speculation as to when and what implementation will take place after 1979.

REAL ESTATE AUCTIONS

Sheldon F. Good

SHELDON F. GOOD, BA, President, Sheldon F. Good & Company, Chicago, Illinois.

Member, mayor's advisory committee to rewrite the Chicago Building Code. Past vice president and chairman, Commerical and Investment Division, National Institute of Real Estate Brokers; past director, Chicago Real Estate Board; and past member, Editorial Board, Realtors® National Marketing Institute. Recipient of National Association of Realtors® Snyder Trophy. Author of such articles as "How to Sell Apartment Buildings," "Techniques of Investment Property Exchanging," "Trading— The Key to Success," "An Approach to Creating Value in the Marketing of Investment Property," "Merchandising Investment Property," and "From the Opening Bid."

The dictionary defines an auction as "a public sale at which a thing is sold to the person who offers the most money." Tobacco auctions, cattle auctions, machinery auctions, and all kinds of personal property auctions are familiar in many communities. In some Western and rural communities, the auction method is a common real estate marketing device. Farm and ranch auctions are a regular occurrence, and even an occasional house or industrial property may be sold at public auction. I am told that in Australia almost every residence is sold by posting a "For Sale Bill," which states when the owner will sell his home. A crowd of interested prospects gathers at the house, an auctioneer calls for the bids and a sale is consummated.

Our company, a real estate brokerage firm in the Chicago area, specializes in the sale of commercial and industrial real estate. Sales of office and apartment buildings, shopping facilities, factories and loft buildings, vacant land, and special-purpose real estate are an everyday occurrence at our office. We are brokers only. We do not buy or sell real estate. We do not manage, insure, syndicate, or develop real estate.

All our efforts are directed at counseling owners about real estate matters and real estate sales.

Over the years, I have attended many personal property public auctions, some liquidations, special merchandise sales, and an occasional charity auction. The general mood of the audience and the auctioneers' ability to stir up the interest, anxiety, and desire of the bidding participants have always interested me. The greed, competition, and desire of the bidders are readily seen. The relief and disappointment of the losers are also evident.

During my real estate career, I have experienced situations in which I felt that the owners of real property could not solve their problems by the usual private sale method of marketing. I think we all agree that the toughest listing is sometimes the most anxious seller. Time is important to such sellers, and they demand quick results. I felt that the public auction method might well be actively and aggressively used to sell real estate. I decided to research my idea by speaking and meeting with as many auctioneers as possible. I went from California to New York and spoke with as many experienced auctioneers as possible. As always happens in such situations, some agreed and some disagreed with my ideas. But I knew that only a few auctioneers were selling real estate publicly and that no real estate companies were offering the auction method as a sales service.

Most of the auctions being held were auctions of personal property, and the auctioneers were liquidators who were unfamiliar with modern real estate merchandising methods. They wanted to conduct a sale as cheaply and quickly as possible. The few auctioneers who were involved with real estate obtained poor results. I attended some real estate auctions that were held by these auctioneers and immediately recognized that they were selling improperly because they were not familiar with real estate. In order to sell real estate properly, you have to sell and market its amenities; you have to package and merchandise it properly; you have to collect information regarding its physical condition, income, and expenses; you have to make arrangements for financing. The marketing program is different. Not everyone is a prospect, and getting the best price demands a thorough knowledge of real estate. These auctioneers couldn't sell what they didn't know.

My marketing research disclosed that there were several "auction schools" in various parts of the United States. I selected the one I thought best and attended its program. The entire curriculum was intended to provide a working knowledge of selling personal property at public auction. There were sessions for those who were interested in real estate. Farm and ranch auctioneers discussed their experiences and their auctioneering techniques. Overall, I thought the school excellent, as it provided a practical working knowledge about the sale of all kinds of property at public auction. Catalog research, the how of calling bids, preparing the inventory, the use of ring men, and the psychology of the auction were all reviewed and discussed. However, using the auction properly to sell real estate was another matter.

I reached the conclusion that there was a need for the auction service in real estate but that very few, if any, professional real estate firms were providing such a service. I felt that I was capable of conducting real estate auctions and that their use could solve real estate problems— for some owners. Upon my return from the auction school, our company released some promotional material offering our services as real estate auctioneers.

Within a month, we were approached by a major corporation located in California. It had to sell a number of new fast-food buildings in Illinois immediately. Did we think we could handle the sale at public auction? We reviewed the properties and reported our conclusions to the owners. Sixty days later we had sold over $1,500,000 worth of Minnie Pearl free-standing buildings throughout the state of Illinois. I was now convinced that under the proper circumstances the public auction could serve as a fine tool for marketing real estate.

That was about eight years ago. Since then, Real Estate Auctions, Inc., our auction subsidiary, has conducted over 80 auctions of property valued at over $15 million. Our sale success has been better than 90 percent.

The Reasons for Real Estate Auctions

As has been noted, certain circumstances of owners create the need for a sale at public auction. Frankly, although there are various reasons for real estate auctions, our experience has revealed that the primary reason is the need for an immediate sale.

1. *Time demands.* The owners no longer have a need for the real estate and they want it sold now.
   a. The owners need cash.
   b. The property must be managed or supervised; the property is unoccupied and requires guard service; and so on.
   c. The owners cannot absorb the high costs of ownership—heating costs, the costs of guard service, real estate taxes, mortgage payments, and so on.
2. *Partition suits, partnership arguments, and estate planning.* Sometimes a group of owners—partners or family members—cannot agree. The multiple owners of estates may have different desires and goals. Arguments over management develop, and cash payouts create problems. A public sale gives everyone the chance to bid, buy, or sell with full disclosure.
3. *Bankruptcy and corporation planning.* Companies sometimes have excess real estate that can provide cash to pay off debts or reorganization costs. Excess real estate can create problems on financial statements.
4. *Income tax planning.* A capital gain or loss from a rapid sale can offer tax benefits. The sale of a property before death, new tax laws, corporate expansion, or corporate liquidation could save tax dollars.

There are probably many other reasons. Most of the reasons are inter-related. In any case, time, people, and money problems are the most easily recognizable reasons, and a negotiated sale may take too long to solve the problems at hand.

Kinds of Properties that Are Salable at Auction

All kinds of real estate can be sold at public auction. Industrial buildings, land, apartment buildings, office buildings, shopping centers, nursing homes, and just about any other type of property are auctionable. An auction *will always* ensure the successful sale of an attractive property. However, a property that is not salable privately is not salable publicly. Junk property, slum buildings, overmortgaged nonequity properties will not sell at auction.

Property of any size can be sold at auction. However, the advertising and promotional costs of an auction, not including commission, can range from $5,000 to $50,000. The amount depends upon the market for the property (local, national, international) and on the exposure that you plan to give the property. Obviously, you can't spend $50,000 to sell a $30,000 building.

Normally, we will not list a property for sale at auction if it does not have a value of more than $150,000. Sometimes we err in our judgment of value, and the property sells for less than we thought it would. In such instances, the percentage cost of the sale is high and this sometimes upsets the seller.

How to Obtain Auction Listings

There are opportunities to list properties for sale at public auction in every community. There are a number of ways in which you can avail yourself of those opportunities.

1. *Public relations.* You must inform the public of your qualification as a real estate auctioneer. Send notices to trade and local publications stating that you are a qualified auctioneer. Articles about real estate auctions or activities help. This type of publicity is free and somewhat newsworthy, and free PR is the best PR.
2. *Display and classified advertising.* You can use professionally prepared classified and display ads in your local newspapers and magazines and in trade publications. These ads should be well designed and informative.
3. *Logos.* The business cards, stationery, and any other printed material distributed by your firm should include the words *Realtors®* and *Auctioneers.*
4. *Institutional brochures.* This material should be professionally prepared and should contain information on the need for auctions and on the problems your service can solve. It can be mailed, delivered personally, and displayed.
5. *Banks, savings and loans associations, lawyers, and corporations.* These are all good auction prospects. Personal letters, personal calls, and brochures may produce business from them.

6. *Other Realtors® and auctioneers.* These are an excellent source of business. People refer business to people they know and like. Expose your unusual services, and you'll get calls. We pay referral fees to other Realtors®, and this helps develop business.

Kinds of Auctions

There are two kinds of auctions.

1. *Auctions with reservation.* The owner offers the property for sale at public auction but reserves the right to accept or reject the highest bid.
2. *Auctions without reservation, or absolute auctions.* The owner offers the property for public sale and agrees to accept the highest bid.

Getting the Listing

Having convinced a potential customer that he needs real estate auction service, how are you going to get his business? The first meeting with the owner is very important.

1. At the first meeting you must find out why the owner thinks he needs an auction, what the property is, what the existing financing is, and the location of the property. You advise the owner that you would like all the pertinent data, and you make an inspection. You must determine whether the owner really needs an auction, whether the property has any equity, and whether the property is salable.

2. Then you must provide the owner with a written report outlining your findings—that the need for an auction exists, that the property is salable, and that you will market it. You recommend a marketing program. Sample ads, brochures, signs, and the like, should be included. You should tell the owner what the total advertising and promotional costs will be. The report serves as your tool to "sell the seller" on the auction method and on his use of your firm to do the job.

Auction Costs and Preparation

Obviously, you will charge some fee or commission for your services. You must determine what your services are worth and what the costs of conducting the auction will be. Some firms pay costs of conducting the auction themselves and some pass them on to the seller. Your reputation, your need for business, your anxiety for the listing will determine which method you adopt. The auction costs are for the following items:

1. *Special pictures, maps, and drawings of the property and of the area in which it is located.* These will be used for your special auction "bill" or "brochure."
2. *The special auction bill or brochure.* This piece tells the story of the auction—who, what, and where; the terms of sale; the open for inspection dates; broker cooperation; the financing terms; and so on.
3. *The special auction sign.* This sign announcing that the property

is "For Sale At Public Auction," should be placed on the property immediately. The sign should give your phone number and the date of the auction. It is not necessary to say where the auction will be conducted, but this sometimes helps.

4. *The direct mail program.* You describe the who and what of the auction to prospective bidders—banks, buyers, corporations, owners of adjoining property, speculators, and so on. This is one of your most important buyer contact methods.

5. *Display and classified ads.* You recommend an advertising program for the marketing period—what publication to advertise in and how often; advertising for the local, national, or international market.

6. *Room guards, and miscellaneous legal charges.* All of these costs must be budgeted and presented to the seller. These are costs of the sale, and they must be paid by someone. Surveys, title reports, and contracts must be prepared prior to the auction.

We prepare this information on costs in a report that includes samples from other auctions, and we usually mail this material to the owner. The last page of the report asks that upon completing his review of the material the owner call to arrange a personal meeting to discuss any questions he has regarding the auction procedures and costs.

When we have our second meeting with the owner, we have inspected the property and the income and expense information that he has provided, and the owner has seen our auction marketing reports and various samples of the material that will be used to auction his property. At the second meeting, the questions most commonly raised by the owner are as follows:

1. *Is this an absolute auction, or can I turn the highest bid down?* We review the types of auctions and help the owner decide. Most of our auctions are with reservation. However, the auctions costs are very high and most owners are very anxious to make a sale.

2. *Can we trim down the advertising and marketing costs?* Our entire sale and its success are dependent upon drawing a crowd. Usually, the more people, the more bidders and the higher the price. We are very careful about our preliminary budget and about how we present it to the seller. The auction must be advertised and promoted aggressively. In some communities, however, classified advertising may be as effective as expensive display ads. The frequency of an ad is sometimes more important than its size. The auctioneer must decide how much exposure the sale will require and deal with the seller and these costs as he deems necessary.

3. *How soon can we have the sale?* We like to have eight to ten weeks from the signing of the auction listing agreement to the date of the auction. However, the determining factor for us is how long it will take to get pictures, surveys, and other required information for our auction bill or brochure and to gather lists for mailings and personal calls? We find that the shorter the sale time, the more active a classified and display advertising program we must have. The time requirements of the seller and your auction team will decide how soon you conduct the

sale. But be careful. It takes some time to expose a property to the market.

4. *Can I get cash?* Almost every auction sale is a sale of improved property, with owner or outside financing provided before a buyer is obtained. If the mortgage money market is difficult or if money for financing is not available and the seller must have cash, cash is always available. But all-cash sales are more difficult than sales in which terms are offered and all-cash sales usually result in a reduced price. Still, the seller can achieve his all-cash goal.

5. *Where should we have the sale?* Some auctioneers like to hold the auction on the property. We find this difficult. If the property is vacant land, there may be weather problems. If the property is an unoccupied building, there may be communication problems.

Our best auctions have been held in the meeting rooms of motels, hotels, banks, or title companies. Coffee, rest rooms, secretarial assistance, and general office facilities are available. We feel that this makes things easier.

6. *Have you your listing agreement with you for this review?* We ask the seller to provide his attorney's name and number, and we arrange a meeting with the attorney to review our listing agreement and to discuss the legalities involved in an auction sale.

At our third meeting with the owners, his attorney is usually present. We have prepared and delivered some type of auction listing agreement, and the attorney wants to discuss the entire matter with us. The attorney may have sent the client to us. We discuss the listing in detail, the costs involved, and the attorney's obligations. These include:

1. Providing a current survey and a current preliminary report on title. We want to be sure that the title is in order and that the seller can deliver a clear and merchantable title to the buyer.
2. Obtaining copies of mortgages, trust deeds, or notes that relate to existing financing.
3. Preparing the sale contract for review by prospective bidders prior to the auction. With the attorney, we prepare a real estate sale contract which we expect the seller and highest bidder to sign at the auction. This agreement follows the "terms of sale" of the auction bill or brochure. Everything is in the contract except for the price and the exact mortgage balance if this is an other than cash sale.

The auction listing is signed, and we now have the responsibility of conducting a real estate sale at public auction. We have a room and a date, and we must now start to gather and review the material for our auction marketing program.

Ordering a special "For Auction" sign is an art in itself. The size, location, color, and letter size of the sign are all very important. We use professional sign painters, and together with them we pick the exact location for placement.

Our auction bill or brochure varies from sale to sale. We might use a one-, two-, four-, or six-page brochure, depending upon the type of property upon the photographs, surveys, and other descriptive material that are needed. Our brochure is a major sales piece. It must interest the prospect in investigating the auction further.

Most of our brochures are self-mailers. The front page of a brochure has a return mail section and a first-class mail designation, and it boldly announces "AN IMPORTANT REAL ESTATE AUCTION ANNOUNCE-MENT," We want whoever receives a brochure to read it and act. Sometimes we include a photo and general information on the front page.

If a property is vacant, we would have an aerial photograph and survey on the interior pages; if it is improved, we would have interior and exterior photos. All of these photographs are taken by professionals. The interior pages also contain information regarding the lot size, building size, improvements, income and expenses, and taxes, as well as descriptive matter about the property and its environment. These pages could also include complete mortgage and financing information.

The most important page of the auction bill or brochure is devoted to the terms of sale. These tell interested parties *all* the facts about how, when, and where the auction will take place. Among those facts are:

1. Where surveys, the legal description, the escrow agreement, contracts, and similar material will be available for inspection.
2. The amount of the earnest money required and how, where, and when the closing will take place.
3. The financing terms, if any.
4. The fee of cooperating brokers.
5. Open house information and information on inspection procedures.

Our brochure is useful only if it is made available to the logical prospects. We review the property, try to determine the possible prospects, and then try to develop a good direct mail list. We usually prepare about 7,500 brochures, and we make a great effort to compile a good mailing list. *All* of our brochures are mailed first class, as we want the returns.

Obviously, the type of property will determine the type of list. Industrial buildings have different types of users and investors than do apartment buildings. There are, however, people whom we place on all our mailing lists. These are:

1. Members of our real estate board and in particular brokers and Realtors in the community in which the property is situated.
2. Officers of banks and savings and loan associations in the community.
3. Owners of property in the entire neighborhood.
4. Tenants of similar properties in the area.
5. Speculators who have been obtained as prospects at other auctions.

We think that our advertising copy must be well written and attractively designed. Again, it must attract readership and bring the reader to action. We usually headline our ads "REAL ESTATE AUCTION!" Then we give the what, where, and when of the auction and state who is to be called for our special sale brochure. All of our display ads are heavily blocked and bordered, and even the classified ads have our corporate logo.

We use about three classified ads a week during the first several weeks of the auction campaign and then a daily classified ad during the last two weeks. Depending on the value, location, and construction of the property, we might use only one major newspaper or several newspapers.

We use our display ads once a week during the first several weeks and then step them up to an almost daily basis toward the end. We use *The Wall Street Journal* and the financial pages of neighborhood and city-wide newspapers for display ads. If a property has a national market, we might advertise in the *New York Times,* the *Los Angeles Times,* and similar publications. We sometimes promote specialized properties in industry-type periodicals.

We have tried television and radio promotions, but have found that just the preparation cost can exceed the entire auction budget. (See Exhibit 1 for an estimate of the advertising costs for a typical real estate auction.)

We send news releases accompanied by pictures of the property to all local periodicals and radio and television stations. We announce that the owners have selected our firm to conduct a public real estate sale

EXHIBIT 1
Budget of Estimated Advertising Costs

1.	Special "For Sale at Auction" signs	$ 5,000
2.	Photographs and reproduction of plans, etc.	2,000
3.	Layout, production, artwork—10,000 brochures, mailing list costs	10,000
4.	Addressing, stuffing, postage—10,000 brochures, mailing list costs	2,000
5.	Classified ads in state, regional, and national daily periodicals	6,500
6.	Preparation of a special display ad by agency	750
7.	Actual cost of display ads in *The Wall Street Journal,* state regional, and national publications	23,500
8.	Miscellaneous auction room costs and materials	500
9.	Public relations	1,500
10.	Travel, telephone, housing, and miscellaneous expenses	2,500

We anticipate these costs to total between $50,000 and $55,000. The variable is the cost of display advertising. However, because of the nature and the size of the properties, maximum exposure in local and national markets is dictated.

or auction on this particular property. We describe the real estate and say where and when the sale will take place. We have had some kind of free coverage with every sale. If you use some imagination in writing your release, it will get the attention of your local real estate editor and generate some action and interest.

We send an associate into the community and have him call on banks, savings and loan officers, and other real estate officers. He promotes our auction and looks for logical prospects. We visit prospects on our direct mail list. We follow up ad responses and sign inquiries personally. Throughout the auction campaign, we try to expand our market by using "imagineering" sessions—who might buy, and how do we get to them? All of our efforts are directed at advising prospects that the property "must be sold" and that the owner will "sell at the best bid obtained." We stimulate and encourage all prospects to "buy at their price" and not to pass up this bargain. We do everything possible to get as many prospects as possible to attend our public real estate sale.

The open house is generally held on the premises the day before the sale. Surveys, title reports, and mortgage and contract documents are available for review. The auction team has some idea of the public interest in the sale from the requests for information and from attendance at the open house. However, vacant property can be inspected without your knowledge and many bidders don't want their identity disclosed. They avoid showing any interest until they bid. We have received bids from undisclosed buyers through attorneys or brokers.

Conducting the Auction

All of your work has been completed. You have mailed your fliers, placed your classified and display ads, and made hundreds of personal and telephone calls. The open house is over, and you are ready for the auction. You have little or no idea whether you will have 1 bidder or 20. You go forward.

You have selected a large conference room or ballroom at a local hotel to conduct your auction. The management announces that you are conducting the sale, and it has an obvious, well-designed, printed sign directing prospects to the room. The room has facilities for about 60 to 100 people. There is a podium and a microphone, and you have a private room in which you will sign the contract with the highest bidder. On the walls are blow-ups of surveys, photos, and other material regarding the sale. Contracts, title reports, and escrow agreements are all available for review.

You have the entrance to the auction room blocked by a table containing "sign-in books" and supervised by a member of the auction team. You review this book reviewed prior to the sale, and that gives you some idea of who is in attendance and of who the possible bidders might be.

The room is full. You step up to the mike, introduce yourself, and;

1. You call the crowd to order. You tell those present your name and company, and you welcome them to the auction sale of the property. You ask them to review the documents and the display material.
2. You introduce the guests in the crowd—the owners, the representative from the bank, the escrow officer, and so on. Then you introduce your auction team.
3. You read the terms of sale and ask for questions.
4. You call the bid. "What'll you pay, what am I bid for this property."

The results of all your work will now be apparent. If you have done your job well, then a sale will probably be made. If not, there may be no one in attendance and a "bust-out" auction.

PART IV
Real Estate Financing

OVERVIEW OF FINANCING: HOME OWNERSHIP

John P. Wiedemer

*J*OHN P. WIEDEMER, BS, Lecturer, Real Estate Finance, College of Continuing Education, University of Houston, Houston, Texas.

Senior partner, Greenwood Realty Company. Investment consultant. Adviser, Texas Real Estate Research Center. Member, Houston Board of Realtors®. Author, Real Estate Finance, 2d ed. (Reston, Va.: Reston Publishing). Author, Real Estate Investment, (Reston, Va., Reston Publishing, 1979). Coauthor, California Real Estate Finance (Reston, Va.: Reston Publishing, 1978).

Of the approximately $900 billion in mortgage debt outstanding in this country, 60 percent represents one–four-family housing. The requirement for new money to fund the increase in home ownership fluctuates, but it has been averaging about $40 billion per year. It comprises the largest segment of all private demand for loanable funds in our financial system. Only the government exceeds this requirement—in years when it funds heavy deficit spending.

Where does the money for long-term loans to finance homes come from? And what reasons induce the lender to make 30-year loans? Like all types of loans, mortgages have their own special requirements. The long-term lender must have a substantial pool of lendable funds with a reasonably controlled inflow and outflow. The lender must also have personnel who are knowledgeable in the field of mortgage loans and possess the legal qualifications to make long-term loans. The institutions best able to meet these special requirements are listed in the accompanying table along with the percentage of home loans that each category of lenders now holds, based on the total mortgage debt outstanding in one–four-family houses. The following is a brief description of the activities in home mortgages that are undertaken by each of these lender categories.

Categories of Lenders

Category of Lenders	Percent of Home Loans
Savings and loan associations	50%
Mutual savings banks	11
Commercial banks	17
Life insurance companies	4
Federal and related agencies	13
Miscellaneous others	5

Savings and Loan Associations. As the percentages of all mortgage loans outstanding in the one–4-family category indicate, savings associations are far ahead of the other types of lenders in making loans to home buyers. As a major depository for the nation's savers, they hold over $400 billion in assets and have been averaging increases in assets of nearly $30 billion per year. So the savings associations represent a major pool of loanable funds. Their control of the inflow and outflow of funds, which is an important requirement for a long-term lender, has been limited. Depositors may freely withdraw their cash. To improve this situation and provide backup liquidity for member savings associations, the Federal Home Loan Bank will lend money against mortgage notes pledged by the savings associations. In 1970, a further step was taken with the establishment of the Federal Home Loan Mortgage Corporation for the purpose of purchasing mortgage notes from members and nonmembers.

Two basic reasons place savings associations in their position of dominance as primary lenders for home buyers: (1) they are chartered for that purpose; and (2) an income tax benefit is derived from making residential loans. More specifically:

1. *The chartered purpose.* Savings associations date back to colonial America and the formation of local groups of people for the purpose of accumulating capital that might be used in building homes. Subsequently, government charters specified home loans as the purpose of savings associations. As a form of thrift institution, their purpose remains the same today.

2. *The income tax benefit.* As an encouragement of thrift as an aid to the building of homes, federal income tax rules provide that a savings association will receive favorable treatment if otherwise taxable funds are placed in a surplus account and made available for additional home

loans. In order to qualify, according to IRS rules, an association may carry only 18 percent of its assets in commercial loans. The balance must be held in residential loans and reserves. (See Chapter 40.)

Mutual Savings Banks. Another type of lender that is included in the category of thrift institutions is the mutual savings bank. Such banks were formed initially as a means of protecting their members' savings, and they had no designated purpose for the investment of the accumulated funds. Mutual savings banks are state chartered, are mutually owned by the depositors, and are found primarily in the Northeastern and Northwestern states. As a group, they represent about $135 billion in total assets and carry 11 percent of the outstanding home mortgage debt. A clearer indication of their attraction to home loans is that they hold about 60 percent of their assets in this type of loan.

Mutual savings banks find mortgage loans to be sound and profitable investments. Because such banks are located mostly in the Northeast (predominantly in New York and Massachusetts), which enjoys substantial cash deposits relative to the growth of housing demand, the mutual savings banks have provided cash for many growth areas of the country. Their home loans used to be predominantly in FHA–VA types because of the minimal lender risk and the absence of limitations on the amounts that could be loaned out-of-state. (See Chapter 41.)

Commercial Banks. The largest lenders of all types of loans are the commercial banks. With total assets exceeding $800 billion, they keep about 19 percent of their loans in mortgages. This represents 17 percent of the total outstanding mortgage debt. But the figures can be a bit misleading to the potential home buyer who is seeking mortgage money. The largest commercial banks make a very small number of long-term loans to home buyers. A few of the medium-sized regional banks will make such loans, and a number of the smaller localized banks may do so. The reasons for limiting these loans are primarily the need for liquidity in the loan portfolio, compliance with the requirements of demand deposits, and the greater yields that can be earned on business loans and consumer installment loans. Such long-term loans as a commercial bank does make are based on the amount of savings, or time, deposits that are held by the bank.

In the approximately $150 billion of outstanding mortgage debt that is held by commercial banks there is a substantial portion of short-term mortgage loans. These are loans that are made to developers or builders as construction loans or to mortgage bankers as warehouse lines of credit to fund their lending activities. One type of direct mortgage loan that is made by commercial banks is the intermediate-term commercial loan. Typically, such loans are 10–15-year loans for a plant addition (perhaps a warehouse), a service station, or a small owner-occupied office building.

Although the home buyer benefits from the construction loans of the commercial banks and from their warehousing of mortgage loans, commercial banks are not a prime source of mortgage money for the home buyer. (See Chapter 42.)

Life Insurance Companies. Historically, life insurance companies have been very active in making real estate loans, but more recently they have been decreasing their investments in home loans. Although life insurance companies hold almost 30 percent of their more than $300 billion in assets in mortgages, only 19 percent of that $90 billion portfolio represents one–four-family houses. The bulk of their mortgage loans, amounting to 73 percent of their $90 billion portfolio, are in commercial real estate, with 8 percent in farm loans.

A number of factors have shifted the direction of the investments made by life insurance company. One is the need for greater yields to compete with other forms of investment that are available to their potential policyholders, such as investment in mutual funds. The ownership of real estate can provide greater returns than a fixed interest mortgage loan, so the larger insurance companies have substantially increased their participation interests in real estate ventures. This has included their own major urban developments, joint ventures with local developers, and the building of such properties as hotels and motels for lease to major operators. Like the smaller commercial banks, many of the smaller life insurance companies actively participate in the local home loan market. (See Chapter 43.)

Federal and Related Agencies.   The best-known government agencies for promoting home ownership—the FHA and the VA—encourage private lenders to make mortgage loans rather than making loans directly. This is done through the FHA insurance program and the VA guarantee program. However, several government agencies do make primary loans to home buyers, and three other government agencies are also authorized to generate loanable funds that flow into the secondary market for home loans. (See Chapters 49 and 50.) Altogether, the government agencies hold 13 percent of the outstanding mortgage debt on one–four-family houses.

If the prospective home buyer meets the requirements of the government agency, he or she may apply to any of the following as a primary source for a home loan:

1. *Farmers Home Administration.* If the applicant has an adjusted family income of less than $15,600 per year, lives in a rural area or a town of less than 10,000 population, and is seeking a house of less than 1,300 square feet of living area, he or she would be eligible to make application to FmHA for a loan.

2. *Federal Land Bank.* Loans are made for farms and ranch property only up to 85 percent of the bank's appraisal for a term of 35 years.

3. *Federal Housing Administration* and *Veterans Administration.* Many of the properties which have been acquired by the government through foreclosure action on an underwritten loan are rehabilitated and sold by these agencies, with a government loan as a part of the deal.

Although the funds are not directly available to the home buyer, three government, or quasi-government, agencies sell bonds and use the proceeds to purchase mortgage loans from originators. The originators are mortgage companies and savings associations which handle the processing and servicing of the loans. The agencies are:

1. *Federal National Mortgage Association* (Fannie Mae). This is no

longer a federal agency, but it is still classed as such in mortgage terminology and statistical reports. In 1968 FNMA became a publicly owned corporation with stock listed on the New York Stock Exchange. Every other Monday, FNMA holds an auction for forward commitments called the Free Market System. Mortgage companies submit most of the bids for the loan commitments, but any FNMA-approved lender may participate. In loans listed under government agencies, FNMA holds almost one half of the one–four-family mortgages.

2. *Federal Home Loan Mortgage Corporation* (Freddy Mac, also known as the Mortgage Corporation). This is a newcomer to the secondary market, having been created by Congress in 1970. FHLMC is a part of the Federal Home Loan Bank System and was established for the purpose of purchasing mortgage loans primarily from member savings associations. It is growing rapidly, and at the end of 1976 it held 7 percent of the total government direct home loans.

3. *Government National Mortgage Association* (Ginnie Mae). This agency, which operates under the Department of Housing and Urban Development, was partitioned from the Federal National Mortgage Association in 1968. GNMA implements government subsidy programs for home buyers by participating in the mortgage loan market.

Miscellaneous Other Sources. The list of other sources for mortgage loans is a broad one. Although not all of these sources operate in all areas of the country, the list should provide suggestions of possible alternatives to the major lenders:

1. Pension and trust funds.
2. Individuals.
3. Real estate investment trusts.
4. Title companies.
5. Endowment funds.
6. Foundations.
7. Fraternal and religious associations.
8. Credit unions.

The mortgage participation certificate is a newcomer to the field of mortgage money. It is not so much a new source as a new method to increase the loan capability of existing sources. Banks and savings associations have started to enter the field formerly dominated by GNMA, and more recently by FHLMC. The new certificates offer participating interests in a pool of mortgages. Unlike the government agencies, the private institutions have not added a guarantee of payments to the buyer.

Access to the Markets

Lenders have long played down the role of selling in the loan underwriting decision. Yet in order to operate efficiently the system requires persons who are knowledgeable of the borrowers' needs and the lenders' requirements. Mortgage bankers and the mortgage brokers fit this role. (See Chapter 47.)

The Mortgage Broker.   The mortgage loan broker may be an individual broker, a well-organized company operating in the mortgage loan field, or an institutional lender performing an extra service for one of its customers. The essential element in loan brokerage is knowing which lenders are making what types of loans—and being able to prepare loan packages that meet the lenders' special requirements. Loan brokers handle the collection of necessary information on the borrower and on the property to be mortgaged. They then submit it to a lender who is interested in that particular type of loan and consider their work complete when the lender and the borrower have agreed on the loan terms. The funding and servicing of the brokered loan are handled by the lender. The brokerage fee, which is negotiable, ranges from one-half point to two points of the loan amount.

The residential loan industry is broad based and has less need for loan brokers than does the commercial lending field. In the commercial field the requirements have many variations and the need for specific knowledge of the lenders' requirements is greater. Also, larger loans than home loans are generally needed to provide adequate fees.

The Mortgage Banker.   Mortgage bankers offer more services than a broker. Basically, the banker can (1) prepare the package of information necessary on the borrower and the property, (2) fund the loan at closing, and (3) service the loan during the repayment period. Mortgage bankers have the capability of handling both home loans and commercial loans.

Mortgage bankers may also undertake loan brokerage work, particularly for the larger commercial borrowers. Commercial loans cannot often be grouped together as an easily described category of house loans would be packaged. So the commercial loans tend to be handled as brokerage operations, whereas home loans are more suited to the mortgage bankers' procedures.

The Secondary Market.   Secondary market purchasers (those who do not originate loans) buy loans in multimillion-dollar blocks and seldom have access to a physical inspection of the property or a face-to-face meeting with the borrower. To obtain accurate information, these lenders look to correspondents, agents, and individual brokers. Further, there is a need for a "common denominator" to assist the secondary market underwriter.

The first such common denominator was an FHA-insured commitment which was established in 1934. This was followed in 1944 by the Veterans Administration certificate of guaranty. Later still, private mortgage insurance expanded to provide a very acceptable form of default insurance for conventional loans. All of these programs provided the lender with a standard—a basis for comparing the package of loans—and substantially reduced the risk of loan default.

In the beginning, only house loans could be insured (FHA) or guaranteed (VA). As private mortgage insurance grew, coverage was provided for the more popular forms of commercial loans—apartments, office buildings, mobile home parks, and others, but these have waned. An insured commercial loan would have greater acceptability for a lender than a noninsured in the secondary market.

The growth of the secondary market since 1970 has provided a large increase in the funds available for all types of mortgage loans. Major increases in loan purchases have resulted from the establishment of the Federal Home Loan Mortgage Corporation, which purchases home loans mostly from member savings associations, and the expansion of the Federal National Mortgage Association's Free Market System to include conventional loans.

FHLMC and FNMA, plus some private institutional investors, have increased the acceptability of mortgage loans by offering various forms of participation certificates. These certificates represent fractional interests in a diversified pool of mortgage loans and are often guaranteed by the issuer.

Life insurance companies at one time did a great deal of direct lending. However, they moved away from mortgage servicing. More recently they have shown a resurgence of interest in single-family loans through the use of participation certificates. (See Chapters 48 and 52.)

Types of Mortgage Loans

Depending on the home buyer's qualifications, he or she may apply for several alternative types of loans. Three types dominate the field— FHA, VA, and conventional.

The FHA-Insured Commitment. Since 1934 the Federal Housing Administration has been insuring home loans with various programs (identified under title and section numbers) plus a number of assistance programs that Congress has authorized from time to time. The detailed requirements for the borrower and the lender, the forms and procedures that are used, and the limitations that have been established have placed FHA-type loans in a category by themselves. Explaining the FHA requirements has long been a duty of the real estate broker. Implementing the loan procedures is a large portion of the mortgage banker's work.

The insurance policy sold by the FHA is a federal agency guarantee for repayment of the balance due on the loan in case of default by the borrower. For this insurance coverage, the FHA charges a standard fee of one half of 1 percent of the loan balance, calculated on an annual basis.

One of the more publicized features of an FHA commitment is the requirement that the interest rate charged for the loan cannot exceed a limit that is set by the secretary of HUD. Historically the FHA interest rate has been held slightly under the market rate for conventional loans. Since the FHA makes no loans itself for this purpose, the lendable funds must come from the private sector, which must weigh the advantages of an insured commitment against the yields obtainable from other forms of investment. The result is that lenders discount an FHA loan sufficiently to produce a yield that is competitive with conventional loans. The FHA responds to this procedure by forbidding the borrower to pay any discount points—that is, the discount cost falls on the seller. Then the seller raises the price to whatever extent he can.

Congress grants the authorization for FHA programs each year in a national housing act. Changes are made to reflect housing needs. The most commonly used programs and the limitations on them are detailed in Chapter 49.

The VA Guaranty Certification. As a part of the GI Bill passed in 1944 to assist returning veterans, a grateful country established a federal program under the Veterans Administration to guarantee a portion of a loan that would enable a veteran to purchase a residence. The amount of the loan that is guaranteed for the veteran is not a gift—any default in payment that the VA has to make good can be assessed against the veteran obligor along with any government benefits that may belong to that veteran. The service of providing the guaranty is a gift to the veteran, who pays no additional service fee, as is required with the FHA commitment.

The amount of the guaranty is termed the veteran's "entitlement." That entitlement has been adjusted upward periodically to meet the rising cost of home ownership. The entitlement is now a continuing right for a veteran who qualifies by service time, and the right can be renewed by paying off the existing loan or by substituting another veteran's entitlement in an assumption sale. However, the veteran is entitled to only one guaranty at a time, and that must apply to the place of residence.

The thrust of the VA requirements and procedures is to protect and assist the veteran. Loan payments must not overburden the veteran financially. The property to be purchased must be appraised and the veteran informed of any major defects. The lender must be a government-supervised institution or an institution specifically approved by the VA. The maximum interest rate that may be charged is set by the administrator of veterans affairs, but as with the FHA rate, lenders are not prohibited from adjusting the yield to meet market rates through discounting the loan.

The distinctive requirements of the Veterans Administration guarantee are well known to lenders and provide a solid category of loan identification. (See Chapter 49.)

Conventional Loans. By far the largest category of home loans are the conventional loans. The term *conventional loan* simply means a loan that is not underwritten by an agency of the federal government. In the absence of specific government guidelines to set standards, many forms of conventional loan have developed. Each lender has had some freedom to establish its own policies within the framework of regulations established by the state or federal regulatory authorities.

Beginning in the early 1970s, conventional lending patterns have been changed to conform with new incentives and new requirements:

1. Major incentives to conform.
   a. The establishment by FNMA and FHLMC of standard forms for mortgage instruments, appraisals, and loan applications.
   b. The acceptance of private mortgage insurance with its own list of requirements.

2. Major requirements to conform.
   a. The passage of the Equal Credit Opportunity Act.
   b. The passage of the Real Estate Settlement Procedures Act.

The result of the above-listed actions has been to reduce the variations formerly found in conventional loans. Lenders are now less free to set their own guidelines. The use of more standardized practices in conventional loans gives the lender more flexibility in dealing with secondary market sources. It also gives the lender some assurance that its loan officers will not be in violation of the new laws while uncertainties are being clarified.

Private Mortgage Insurance. Private mortgage insurance has become so much a part of the higher ratio conventional loans in the 1970s that it should be considered here. A few insurance companies have offered insurance against loan default since the 1950s. But the premiums were rather high initially, so that such insurance found little lender acceptance. Prior to 1970, the word *insured* as used in mortgage terminology meant an FHA or VA loan. The big change came in 1971, when the Federal Home Loan Bank raised the limits on permissible home loans for its members from 90 percent LTVR (loan-to-value ratio) to 95 percent LTVR. The added proviso that any loan with an LTVR of over 90 percent must carry insurance against default set off the boom in private mortgage insurance.

Private mortgage insurance is a specialized form of insurance, and relatively few companies have gained prominence in the field. The types of policies offered give the purchaser some choice of policy term and manner of payment. The lender usually specifies the term, which may be five, seven, or perhaps ten years. The borrower may elect to pay the cost in a single premium payment at the loan closing or in annual installments. The coverage is limited to the top portion of the loan amount, usually 25 percent. The reasoning is that in the first five or ten years, depending on the term of the loan, the principal balance due would be reduced sufficiently to eliminate the need for further insurance coverage.

Lenders were quick to see the advantages of mortgage insurance when it became available at a reasonable cost. Borrowers have also found an advantage in purchasing private mortgage insurance. They are thus able to qualify for higher ratio loans than would otherwise be available to them and to conserve cash that would otherwise be needed for a down payment. (See Chapter 48.)

Mortgage Terms

In real estate finance, a background of mortgage law is most helpful. The security for a mortgage loan is a pledge of rights to real property. Although real estate brokers and loan officers are usually not qualified to give legal advice, a basic knowledge of terminology and procedures is an important part of the expertise needed to work in the field. The rights to real property and their conveyance are dependent on state laws. So there can be considerable differences among the various states. The information presented here gives generally established patterns and definitions. The preparation of any legal instrument or the giving of legal advice can be considered the practice of law and should be handled only by a qualified attorney.

Obligations of the Borrower.   The assumption by business people that anyone who borrows money certainly knows that it must be repaid is not always a safe one. Some of the publicity associated with federal subsidized housing programs, plus the equation of rent with a mortgage payment by a minority of people, should signal the broker and the lender to make certain that a borrower understands the obligations of a mortgage agreement. Most of the more recent laws and regulations affecting housing and credit—such as those on fair housing, equal credit opportunity, and settlement procedures—have stressed the individual's rights. This might be a good time to reemphasize the obligations that a borrower undertakes:

1. *Loan repayment.* A loan must be repaid in a timely manner—there is no right to use someone else's money unless there is full compliance with the conditions agreed to for repayment.
2. *Payment of property taxes and hazard insurance.* The borrower is required to meet the cost of taxes and insurance on the mortgaged property, either by direct payment when due or, more commonly, by monthly additions to the mortgage payment for escrow and payment by the lender.
3. *Maintenance of property.* The borrower is responsible for the repair and maintenance of the property either as an individual owner or as a member of a condominium type of maintenance association.
4. *Prevention of liens.* No act can be permitted by or against the borrower that would tend to diminish the lender's security interest in the property. This includes such actions as insolvency, eminent domain, or the enforcement of a city code.
5. *Inspection.* The borrower must permit the lender to make reasonable inspections of the property if given a reasonable cause related to the lender's interest therein.

Obligations of the Lender.   Once the lender has funded a loan for a house, the lender's further obligations revolve around compliance with the contract terms and the laws, and permitting peaceable enjoyment of the property by the borrower. More specifically, the lender's obligations may be listed as follows:

1. *Notification of nonpayment.* Although the lender has a right to receive timely repayments, there is an obligation to notify the borrower of any failure to receive a payment. The borrower's rights to the mortgaged property are placed in jeopardy if a payment is not made. Proper notification protects the rights of both the borrower and the lender.
2. *Accounting records.* The lender must maintain the payment and

escrow records accurately. Periodic reports, normally once a year, should be made to the borrower as to the status of the loan, the amount of interest that has been paid, the principal reduction, and the condition of the escrow accounts.

3. *Escrow accounts.* The Real Estate Settlement Procedures Act placed limitations on the amount that a lender may require to be held in escrow for tax and insurance payments on a house loan. The lender must use the escrow money to make timely payments for insurance and taxes.

4. *Peaceable possession.* The borrower in possession of the property has the right to its peaceable use. The lender's right to inspect the pledged property is limited to reasonable times, and such inspection must be for a reasonable cause.

The Promissory Note and the Mortgage Instrument. The promissory note is the evidence of the obligation. It is often called a mortgage note because of its relation to a mortgage instrument. However, the note is an obligation to repay a debt—with or without a valid mortgage.

The mortgage instrument, whether it is in the deed of trust form, the standard form, or any other form, is the security pledge. The mortgage provides the collateral in the form of a pledge of real property to secure the promissory note. If there is no note—no debt to secure—there can be no valid mortgage. Without a debt to secure, the mortgage becomes, as its French derivation indicates, a "dead pledge."

A mortgage instrument may fail for some legal or technical reason, such as an incorrect property description; but such failure does not invalidate the obligation of the note. The mortgage failure may leave the note as a simple unsecured promise to pay. But once the money is borrowed, it is the note that promises the repayment.

The Property as Collateral. The property pledged as collateral for a mortgage loan must be clearly and accurately described. Since residential loans other than the condominium type pledge a tract of land as the basis of the security, it is customary for a survey prepared by a registered surveyor to be a part of the loan package. In the case of a condominium, a legal description made in accordance with the applicable state laws would be sufficient identification of the property.

It almost goes without saying, but the property pledged must be pledged by the rightful owner. And the owner must have proper legal authority to make such a pledge. Property owned by estates, trusts, minor children, or legally incapacitated persons requires proper legal counsel to assure the lender that a mortgage signed by the owner is a binding pledge.

Mortgage Clauses. The covenants used in any mortgage instrument must, first of all, comply with the state laws in which the property is located. Within the parameters of these laws, there is no mandatory form of mortgage terms. The conditions under which money is loaned and how the collateral is pledged are matters that are subject to negotiation between the borrower and the lender. The lender has an obligation to include terms that will help to protect its investment in case of default by the borrower. And the borrower may want certain clarifying phrases included or certain inapplicable clauses eliminated. Under the present laws, neither the borrower nor the lender can be required to accept or to make a specific loan. The lender is obligated by the Equal Credit Opportunity Act to apply uniform credit standards for borrowers in a nondiscriminatory manner.

The growth of the secondary market standardized mortgage forms, and the pressures of federal regulations have encouraged more uniform instruments in the field of residential loans. But even the FNMA–FHLMC standard note and mortgage forms are issued for the various states. So it is difficult to list specific terminology except by separate states. The following discussion identifies the principal clauses found in mortgage instruments.

1. *Payment and conveyance.* The key clause in any mortgage instrument is the acknowledgment of a debt, the agreement to repay the debt or, upon failure to do so, to make or permit the conveyance of the property in satisfaction of the specified debt.

2. *Acceleration.* In case of a default in the mortgage terms, the lender has the right to demand payment of the full amount of the unpaid balance immediately. The alternative might be a foreclosure procedure each month that a payment would come due.

3. *Prepayment.* Lenders value their contractual rights to the substantial amount of interest that may be earned during the life of a long-term mortgage loan. Permitting an early payment of the principal could mean a forfeiture of that right to the interest. So lenders often require some form of compensation to partially offset the loss of interest. Lenders refer to the prepayment fee as a premium; homeowners most commonly call it a penalty. Prepayment fees vary with lenders' policies. A common feature of residential loans is a clause that requires an additional 1 percent to 3 percent of the unpaid balance to be paid when the loan is paid off. Another clause often found is one that permits the borrower to prepay a certain percentage of the loan, usually 20 percent, in any one year without additional prepayment charges.

When FNMA introduced its standard mortgage forms in 1972, the prepayment charges had been eliminated as a condition for the loan. The FHA shortly thereafter dropped prepayment charges from its permissible conditions for lenders. The VA has never permitted a prepayment charge in a loan to a veteran.

4. *Right to sell.* Mortgaged property can be sold anytime and the loan paid off. But the lender can and does restrict the conditions under which mortgaged property can be conveyed when the loan is to be assumed. Older mortgages often limited this requirement to a simple notification to the lender—the original borrower remained fully liable for the debt, and the property was still subject to the mortgage lien. More recently, lenders have required that any sale with an assumption of the existing mortgage loan be subject to the lender's specific approval. Quite often, the lender's approval of the loan assumption has entailed an adjustment of the interest rate upward to a near-market level.

5. *Taxes and insurance.* Unpaid property taxes can take precedence

to a first-mortgage lien, and an uninsured building can be destroyed through fire or other hazard. So to protect the lender's interest in the mortgaged property, the mortgage terms usually require an escrow account held by the lender, with monthly payments into it of one twelfth of the annual taxes and insurance premiums. The lender thus assures funds for the timely payment of these annual charges.

6. *Foreclosure.* In the case of default on any of the contractual terms of the mortgage agreement, the lender can demand that the property be offered for sale, with the proceeds of such sale going toward payment of the mortgage debt. Each state has some variations on the steps that must be taken to protect the rights of both the borrower and the lender in a foreclosure action. But the results are rather similar—under foreclosure proceedings the mortgaged property is sold to the highest bidder and the proceeds are distributed by the court or its agents in accordance with the lien priorities on the property.

Forms of Mortgages

Again, state laws determine how real property can be pledged as collateral, so that the forms used vary across the country. The principal forms that may be found can be described under the following headings.

1. *The standard mortgage.* The definition of a standard mortgage applies mostly to the manner in which the collateral shall be conveyed in case of a default. The rights of the lender may be expressed as a lien right that must be converted to a title or as a limited conveyance of the title which must be approved by a court. The conveyance clause in a standard mortgage would specify the lender as the grantee. A conveyance of this type would be expressed in such terms as "Borrower does hereby mortgage, grant, and convey to Lender, with power of sale, the following described property. . . ."

2. *The deed of trust.* The mortgage form found most often in community property states introduces a third party, a trustee, to hold the mortgaged property for the benefit of the lender. The conveyance would be stated in terms like these: "Borrower, in consideration of the indebtedness herein recited and the trust herein created, irrevocably grants and conveys to Trustee, in trust, with power to sell, the following described property. . . ."

3. *The blanket mortgage.* Although most mortgages pledge a single piece of property as security, a blanket mortgage pledges more than one parcel of real estate.

4. *The open-end mortgage.* The right of a lender to increase the amount of the mortgage obligation during the life of the mortgage is usually limited to advances made by the lender that become necessary to protect the lender's lien rights. An example would be the payment of a special tax assessment. An open-end mortgage allows a lender to make additional advances to the same borrower for other purposes, such as an improvement to the property. The new advance carries the same lien priority as the original loan. This form is often used in farm and ranch loans.

5. *The package mortgage.* The term *package mortgage* is used to identify a mortgage that contains some personal property along with the real property as a part of the collateral. Mortgages of this type are used in residential loans in order to include such appliances as dishwashers, ranges, or other equipment that is commonly found in newer houses but may not be part of the real estate.

6. *The junior mortgage.* A junior mortgage denotes a claim of lower priority than that of another claim. Second and third mortgages are sometimes referred to as "junior."

7. *The purchase money mortgage.* When the seller of a property agrees to assist in its financing by accepting a note and mortgage as a part, or all, of the consideration, such a mortgage can be identified as a "purchase money mortgage." (For additional information on mortgage instruments, see Chapter 6.)

The Loan Application

Legislation passed in 1974 and mostly amended in 1976 has established some new rules for lending practices that begin with the loan application. The new laws are the Equal Credit Opportunity Act and the Real Estate Settlement Procedures Act. In an effort to comply with the regulations and their subsequent clarifications, many lenders have opted to use or be guided by the standard application forms released as FHLMC-65 and FNMA-1003.

The Equal Credit Opportunity Act. In order to reduce the possibility of discrimination in the extension of credit, Congress passed the Equal Credit Opportunity Act in 1974, then amended and expanded the coverage of the act in 1976. Essentially, the act prohibits discrimination in credit transactions because of race, color, religion, national origin, sex, marital status, age, the receipt of public assistance income, and the exercise of rights under the Consumer Credit Protection Act, of which ECOA is a part.

The information that a lender may request from an applicant for a loan is now somewhat restricted. The lender may not question all sources of income—only those that an applicant expects to use for loan repayment. Questions on race and sex were at first dropped from the loan application, but this created difficulties for enforcement officials who were trying to determine whether or not the law was being complied with. Now this information can be requested, but it may only be used for statistical purposes. It is illegal to require a social security number as a condition for making a loan, as this has been determined to be an invasion of privacy.

The thrust of the new law is to require that the same standards be applied to all loan applicants. The law does not attempt to set any credit standards: that is still the clear responsibility of the lender. But it does require that the standards be applied to each applicant as an individual and without discrimination. An applicant with a credit history tied to a married name has the right to provide evidence showing that the facts in a joint credit report do not accurately reflect his or her creditworthiness. A wife's credit record may now be established in her own name if she so desires. If a loan applicant is rejected, the lender is now required to furnish the specific reasons for the rejection. But the applicant must make a request for reasons.

The act supersedes state laws that are inconsistent with the federal law, but it allows the states to add their own requirements. However, any action undertaken by a creditor in accordance with state property laws which affect creditworthiness does not constitute discrimination.

The Real Estate Settlement Procedures Act.   The Real Estate Settlement Procedures Act (RESPA) is directed toward the regulation of loan closing procedures and the full disclosure of settlement costs on all residential sales. And it places several additional burdens on the lender.

First, a loan applicant must be given a copy of the *Settlement Costs Guide,* a pamphlet prepared by the Department of Housing and Urban Development. The guide explains a number of real estate practices and lists the borrower's rights and obligations. Second, the loan applicant must be furnished with a "good faith estimate" of the settlement service charges that can be expected if the loan is consummated. This information must be given to the applicant within three business days of the application date.

RESPA further prohibits a lender from designating the use of any service agent as a condition for making a loan. The borrower may select the agent from a list acceptable to the lender. The act forbids kickbacks of any kind, but it does permit fees to be paid to any broker or agent for actual services rendered.

The Application Form.   Lenders may still prepare their own loan application forms so long as they comply with the federal requirements. The wording of the new laws, the complex nature of the regulations, the mixed and changing interpretations of the laws, and the lack of court rulings have made lenders approach the handling of loan applications more cautiously. Many have adopted the standard FNMA–FHLMC Residential Loan Application form as a prudent procedure. With the potential for liability that just taking a loan application involves, loan officers are very careful with the questions they ask and even the phraseology of asking.

OVERVIEW OF FINANCING: INVESTMENT PROPERTIES

John P. Wiedemer

*J*OHN P. WIEDEMER, BS, Lecturer, Real Estate Finance, College *of Continuing Education, University of Houston, Houston, Texas.*

Senior partner, Greenwood Realty Company. Investment consultant. Adviser, Texas Real Estate Research Center. Member, Houston Board of Realtors®. Author, Real Estate Finance, 2d ed. (Reston, Va.: Reston Publishing): Coauthor, California Real Estate Finance (Reston, Va.: Reston Publishing, 1978). Author, Real Estate Investment, (Reston, Va. Reston Publishing 1979).

Sources for Commercial Loans

An analysis of the Federal Reserve Bank figures on mortgage debt outstanding shows that 33 percent of over $900 billion total mortgage debt is classified as multifamily and commercial loans. (Of the remaining 67 percent, 60 percent is in residential loans and 7 percent is in farm loans.) Of this percentage, 12 percent is in multifamily loans and 21 percent is in commercial loans. The accompanying breakdown shows what percentages of the mortgage holdings in multifamily, or apartment, loans and in commercial loans are held by the various major sources of these loans.

In apartment and commercial lending, unlike residential lending, no one source dominates the field. Apartment loans vary substantially in size, but they present the lender with a fairly uniform base for comparison. Commercial loans, on the other hand, are much more diverse

Source	Percent of Apartment Loans	Percent of Commercial Loans
Commercial banks	6	32
Mutual savings banks	14	10
Savings associations	26	20
Life insurance companies	21	31
Federal and related agencies	13	0
Individuals and others	20	7
	100%	100%

since they include all other forms of income property, ranging from raw land to huge office building–shopping center complexes.

General Characteristics

Commercial loans are difficult to categorize. Their size can range from a few thousand dollars to several hundred million dollars. They can run from less than 3 years to as long as 40 years. The interest cost is usually higher for a commercial loan than for a residential loan. One common characteristic of commercial loans is that the property on which the loans are made is expected to produce income—from rentals or resale, or both. A commercial loan analysis therefore focuses attention on the property and its income potential rather than on the borrower's income, which is so important in residential loans.

The lending officer has few guidelines to assist him in the analysis of commercial loans. There is no broad secondary market for commercial loans to provide detailed parameters for acceptable loans. The variations in the quality of commercial loans make them more difficult to sell. The result is that commercial loans are made on a more selective basis than residential loans, mostly by lenders who expect to retain the loans in their own portfolios.

Commercial Income Properties

In commercial lending there is a specialization among sources that are more interested in and better qualified to handle particular types of properties. There is also a selectivity that results from the size of loans and from the lenders' specific portfolio needs.

Types of Properties. Certain commercial lenders favor particular types of properties because they have gained experience with them. Such specialization can result from a local business growth or a successful pattern of loans. For example, the expansion of the Holiday Inns motel chain based in Memphis has made that city a center for motel loans. Mobile home park loans are more easily financed through California and Florida lenders who are better acquainted with the particular problems involved. Other lenders are more familiar with office building loans and can more quickly analyze potential success or failure with them. Knowing which institution favors what type of loan is the special expertise of the mortgage banker and the mortgage broker.

The Size of Loans. Most residential loans fall between $35,000 and $60,000, but commercial loans are considerably larger. Most commercial lenders would consider anything under $250,000 to be a rather small loan. Which loans are defined as "large" or "small" in this field depends very much on who is doing the defining. A multibillion dollar insurance company would have a perspective different from that of a savings association with, say, $5 million in total assets. The $1 million loan still seems to draw a rather vague line between the large loan and the small one. Usually the larger loans must be obtained from the larger lenders. However, many aggressive smaller lenders have working relationships with larger companies as agents or correspondents and work as participants in the loans of the larger companies. Even the largest lenders set limits on the size of any one loan and prefer participation interests that will spread the risk of the bigger loans. Some lenders work with two parameters of loan limits—one insurance company has a lower limit of $250,000 to $750,000 and an upper range of from $1.5 million to $2.5 million. The smaller category of loans is kept 100 percent in its own portfolio, and the larger category is open to participations.

Portfolio Requirements. All lenders, large or small, strive to maintain a balance of investments in the overall distribution of the assets they hold and within each major category of assets. The percentage of a lender's portfolio that is allocated to mortgage loans may be further divided among various types of real estate investments. At any one time, a given lender may be overloaded with apartment loans and may be looking for something good in a shopping center loan to recover a desired balance. This internal requirement of the lender is a bit of information that a mortgage company might be able to use to good advantage.

Residential Income Properties

Apartment Properties. Apartment loans account for one eighth of all mortgage loans outstanding. This was the only category of mortgage loans that actually declined in total volume from 1975 to 1976. The decline was a direct result of the shakeout of real estate developments in 1973 and 1974, when interest and inflation rates soared to unprecedented levels. It also indicated the rather volatile nature of apartment building. Growth has returned to the apartment loan category, and that category of loans may be expected to continue upward in the foreseeable future.

In the large urban areas where apartments provide a sizable portion of the available housing, there is enough trading of properties to develop some market value data that can help guide the lender and investor. However, any analysis of income property centers on the investment return. And the available operating figures on apartment houses that are under competent management will permit the lender to make sound comparative analyses. With these figures available, the major question becomes that of potential income or—more simply stated—occupancy.

Lenders examine apartment occupancy data in any given region, city, or neighborhood, and from this information they can quickly determine whether further loans are advisable. A common cutoff point is 90 percent occupancy. If the occupancy in a market area falls under that rate, lenders may refuse to look at additional loan applications from that area.

Single-Family Rental Properties. Many families have found good profit and security in retaining an older house when buying a newer one, and thus securing future rental income. The purchase of two–four-family units is another common means by which a family both provides itself with suitable housing and earns rental income. A few entrepreneurs have made a solid business of buying older homes, renovating them, and renting or selling them for profit.

In some areas of the country, speculative buying of houses has distorted the market and brought more stringent lender limitations on rented houses than on owner-occupied houses. Loans for rental housing are usually handled as commercial loans commanding higher interest rates and larger down payments than required for owner-occupied house loans. There are more sources for this type of loan than for either commercial loans or residential loans because the loans are classified as both residential and commercial. Savings associations and the commercial lenders are good sources for such loans.

Both the FHA and the VA have programs that permit them to underwrite two to four-family housing. The FHA allows higher loan limits on two to four-family housing than on single-family housing, and it requires larger down payments. The VA has an additional requirement—the veteran borrower must use one of the units as a residence.

Commercial Features of Loans

Statistical information often separates multifamily or apartment loans from other types of commercial loans. However, the general requirements for both multifamily and commercial loans are very similar and for our purposes can be discussed together. The information necessary to prepare a commercial loan package is discussed next, followed by a brief outline of the costs and obligations involved.

When a loan package for a commercial loan is prepared for presentation to the selected lender, considerably more detail is required on both the property and the borrower than is generally needed for a residential loan. Lenders vary somewhat in the emphasis that they place on the extent and the kinds of information that they require. Often, the initial package of information will trigger a request from the lender for more specific data on one or more parts of the package. It is the collection of information as presented by the borrower, the verifications and substantiations that may be added by the lender, and the commentary and conclusions of the lending officer that make up the loan package. The loan package, carefully indexed and bound in one or more file folders, is a permanent history of the loan that can be examined by regulatory authorities. It also contains the complete reference information that would be needed in case of default or foreclosure. A basic list of the information needed to process a commercial loan follows.

The Application. A standard form required by the lender is generally used, but the borrower may wish to expand on the information presented. Essentially, the application calls for information on the identity and location of the borrower and the type of loan that is requested, a description of the property that is being offered as collateral, and answers to a series of questions regarding the background of the borrower, the purpose of the loan, and legal matters pertinent to state requirements.

The Financial Statement. In making a business loan, the commercial borrower can be expected to furnish a detailed financial statement. A requirement for the larger loans would be a statement made from a full audit and so certified. A lesser requirement would be a statement prepared by an independent certified public accountant, but without a full audit. Seldom does the lender permit the borrower to prepare its own financial statement. The statements that may be required include:

1. Balance sheets on all individuals and companies acting as principals requesting the loan.
2. Profit and loss statements on the company's operations, preferably for the last five to ten years.
3. A pro forma statement showing the effects of the loan on the company's future earnings.

The Appraisal. Most lenders have lists of appraisers who are acceptable to them for evaluating certain types of properties. As an alternative to specific names, the lender may state minimum qualification requirements for the appraiser. The important point is that the borrower should determine in advance what the lender's requirements are for appraisals. The appraised value is a key element in the lender's decision on the amount of money that can be approved for a loan. Almost all lending regulations forbid a mortgage loan to be in excess of the appraised value of the property, and usually mortgage loans are restricted to 80 percent of the appraisal or less.

The Property Survey. To properly identify the land and buildings that are being offered as collateral, a survey prepared by a registered surveyor is often required. The survey may not be required for a preliminary screening of the loan application, but it would be needed before the loan can be approved.

Title Information. Customs vary in different parts of the country, but some form of title report or title information letter is always advisable, so that the lender will know what the legal status of the property is. This information can also be helpful to the borrower, who may discover title defects that were not previously known. This type of preliminary report is a takeoff of the county records that relate to the subject property, with an advisory review by a qualified attorney.

Additional Requirements. If the application is for a loan that is to be used on land that has not yet been purchased, the lender will want some evidence that the applicant holds an element of control on the land, such as an option contract. If the project is a new development of speculative rental property, the lender may ask for a market study or a feasibility analysis on the project. If the loan is for the construction of a building, the lender will expect to see the bids of responsible contractors covering the work to be done. The lender may add its own requirements after the preliminary discussion of the proposed loan. These requirements may be in the form of a request for additional information, or as a firm condition that must be met before the loan is funded.

The Costs of Commercial Loans

Interest and Discount. The cost of borrowing money is often defined as "interest." There are other costs. But interest is the largest and most important one. It is somewhat negotiable within the lenders' parameters for loan quality and current capital market conditions. In addition to the interest cost, commercial loans are often discounted a point or two (one point is equal to 1 percent of the loan amount). This discount amounts to a prepayment of interest and is also negotiable. A higher discount may buy a slightly lower interest rate, and vice versa. A rule of thumb that is sometimes used within the industry is that one point of discount is worth ⅛ percent of interest. The comparison is a rough one, as the discount point is a one-time charge "up front," whereas interest is charged as long as the loan is being amortized. The accompanying table compares the value of a discount versus an interest payment over a period of 12 years. The comparison clearly indicates that for the 6 percent interest rate, a loan paid off in less than 11 years would provide a greater yield for the investor on a one-point discount than would a ⅛ percent increase in the interest rate.

Yield Comparison—Discount to Interest (on $10,000)

At End of Year	Yield from One Point	Yield from ⅛ Percent Interest
1	$106.00	$ 12.50
2	112.36	25.75
3	119.10	39.80
4	126.25	54.69
5	133.83	70.47
6	141.86	87.20
7	150.37	104.93
8	159.39	123.73
9	168.95	143.65
10	179.09	164.77
11	189.03	187.16
12	201.23	211.09

One point = $100.
⅛ percent interest = $12.50 annually.
Yield calculated at 6 percent compound interest.

Service Charges. The applicant for a loan may expect to pay various service charges. These charges are usually, but not always, related to the amount of services performed. The Real Estate Settlement Procedures Act places some limitations on the handling of service charges that are made in connection with residential loans. But the act does not apply to commercial loans.

The Application Fee. It costs money for a lender to review the package of information submitted in a loan application, and if the loan is rejected, there is no income for the lender. Therefore, many lenders collect a nonrefundable fee for reviewing a loan application.

The Finance Charge. In residential lending this charge would probably be called an origination fee. This term is also used in commercial lending, as is the term *brokerage fee.* The charge varies from one to two points, and it is usually paid at closing from the loan proceeds. The fee is paid to the mortgage company, the loan broker, or some other loan originator for processing the loan package. A part of the value of this service lies in the loan originator's expertise in knowing where to place the loan for most favorable consideration.

The Commitment Fee. If the loan agreement calls for the delivery of the loan proceeds at some future date, the lender will issue a letter of commitment, that is, a letter promising to lend the money at a specified time, contingent upon the completion of certain stipulated requirements. For this commitment of money, the lender asks a fee that can vary from one to five points. The fee is payable when the commitment letter is accepted by the borrower. A commitment fee is normally nonrefundable, but some or all of it may be applied against the finance or brokerage charge when the loan is funded.

A loan commitment may be mandatory or nonmandatory. As a part of the commitment agreement, the lender may require that the borrower accept the loan when and as specified, regardless of any change in capital market conditions. A nonmandatory commitment would permit the borrower to forfeit the commitment should a better loan become available. Forfeiture of the commitment would include forfeiture of the commitment fee.

The Funding Fee. Some lenders prefer a procedure that calls for the payment of a commitment fee when the loan is promised plus the payment of an additional fee when the loan is actually funded. The funding fee is normally deducted from the loan proceeds at closing.

The Renewal Fee. The renewal fee is used mostly in construction loans to home builders. The charge can vary from ⅛ to 1½ points, payable at the time a mortgage note is renewed. The initial term for the construction loan may call for repayment in six months. If the house has not been completed and sold at the time of maturity, the builder-borrower may ask for a three to six months' extension. As a condition for granting such a renewal, the lender may charge a renewal fee.

Legal Fees. With commercial loans the borrower can be expected to pay not only the costs of its own attorneys but also the costs of the attorneys employed by the lender. Legal fees vary greatly, even within local areas. Some lawyers base their fee on the size of the deal—that is, the larger the loan, the higher the fee. Other lawyers relate the fee more closely to the amount of work required—that is, the number of hours necessary to prepare legal instruments and to provide the proper legal guidance to the client. In residential loans, legal fees are subject to the provisions of the Real Estate Settlement Procedures Act and are expected to be based on the amount of services performed. The provisions of this act do not apply to commercial loans.

Accounting Fees. Lenders prefer that financial statements presented with a loan application be prepared by independent certified accountants. The cost varies with the amount of service required and with the person or firm furnishing the service.

Appraisal Costs. Appraisers who have achieved professional recognition are the ones most acceptable to a lender. Appraisers are usually willing to quote a total charge in advance of the work performed, or to give a "not to exceed" limit on their services. Many appraisers are qualified to furnish market studies and feasibility analyses which may be charged at a flat fee or on a per diem basis.

Survey Costs. Sometimes land surveys are already in the hands of owners and need only a simple updating to provide the preliminary data that are required for a loan application. If a new survey is required, and the cost would appear to be high, a lender may temporarily waive the requirement for this piece of information until the other qualifications for the loan have been approved. But a survey by a registered surveyor is a very necessary part of the loan package. The attorney preparing mortgage instruments expects to have a survey on hand with which to verify the identity of the property being mortgaged.

If the loan is for a building that is to be constructed, the lender will require an initial survey to identify the tract of land and a final survey that shows the exact location of the new building after it has been built. The final location is not always where the owner or the architect originally intended it to be.

The cost for a survey is usually based on the time required to perform the necessary fieldwork and drafting. Some surveyors will quote a flat fee in advance of the work performed.

Title Information. A preliminary title report is often furnished by a title company at no charge for regular customers. But a fee for the information is justified, and it would certainly be owed if the title insurance or title guarantee is not purchased from the same insurance company. In many states the fee charged is set on a sliding scale by the state insurance commission.

Obligations on a Commercial Mortgage Loan

Repayment Terms. The number one obligation on a mortgage loan is to repay it. Commercial mortgage loans normally require a monthly amortization payment that is calculated on the basis of a constant monthly payment for the term of the loan. This is the method that is used for most residential mortgage loans. However, there can be a number of variations in commercial loans. For example, the payments can be made quarterly, semiannually, or annually. In another variation, the interest payments may be required at specific intervals during the year and a reduction in principal may be required once a year. Taxes and insurance may be a part of the payments made to the mortgage for escrow, or they may be paid directly by the borrower when due, with receipts furnished to the lender. The repayment terms are generally a matter of negotiation between the borrower and the lender to best suit the circumstances.

Two features of the repayment requirements should be examined carefully, as they can prove costly in future years. These are lock-ins and prepayment fees.

Lock-ins. The loan contract provides a consistent return to the lender, as the interest is paid over a number of years. A good loan is an income-producing asset for the lender, and repayment stops that income. There-fore, some lenders add to the mortgage terms provisions that will prevent early payment of the loan. Such a provision might prohibit any prepay-ment of the principal for, say, the first ten years of the loan, or even for the full term of the loan. The borrower could conceivably be placed in the position of having to pay off the full amount of the loan with interest to maturity in order to sell or refinance the property during the term of the loan.

Prepayment Fees. A lesser, more common requirement than a lock-in is to stipulate an extra fee for any early payment of the loan principal. Such a provision might call for an addition of 3 percent to the unpaid balance to require the lender accept a payoff of the loan. Or an additional two years of interest charges might be required for the prepaid amount. Another method of restricting prepayment is to permit, say, up to 20 percent of the initial loan amount to be repaid in any one year with no additional fee charged, but to call for a fee of, say, 5 percent on any amount over 20 percent paid in any one year.

Restrictive Covenants. *The Loan Agreement.* In addition to the two basic legal instruments that are involved in residential loans—promis-sory note, which evidences the debt, and the mortgage, which provides the collateral security for the debt—the commercial loan may also in-clude a third legal instrument, namely, the loan agreement. The restric-tive covenants in the mortgage instrument relate to the mortgagor's use and protection of the property (see Chapter 36). The loan agreement that is made as a part of a commercial loan concerns the borrower's business operations. The lender does not want to see the loan placed in jeopardy by potentially detrimental actions of the borrower or changes in the borrower's operations. Therefore, a typical loan agreement could prohibit any or all of the following actions from being taken without the express permission of the lender:

1. The sale of company stock by an officer or a director or the sale of a partnership interest.
2. Any increase in compensation to the principals in the company.
3. Company loans made to officers, directors, or stockholders.

4. The sale of any company assets, patents, or royalties.
5. Additional borrowing.

Asset-to-Liability Ratios.   In a financial statement analysis, the ratio of current assets to current liabilities represents the degree of liquidity in the assets held by a company. A solid ratio of, say, two to one ($2 in current assets for each $1 of current liabilities) could be made an initial requirement for funding a loan and a ratio that must be maintained. If a ratio requirement is a part of a loan agreement, the failure of the company borrower to maintain the required ratio would be an act in default. The lender may view the declining ratio as signaling a weakening of the company and may demand the right to step in to protect its interest before the company becomes a distress case.

Personal Liability.   On a commercial loan the addition of personal liability for the principals is a negotiable item. With smaller loans for smaller companies, the principals are almost always expected to endorse the note. For larger loans, the lender tends to look more to the property and its income potential than to individuals. The feeling is that a company default on a large loan would only mean personal bankruptcy for the endorsing principals and no help toward repayment. Construction loans are a major exception. Even the large construction loans usually require some principal's personal endorsement. A principal can make changes in the plans during construction and substantially increase the cost of a building.

Assignment.   A borrower's rights to a mortgage loan commitment are generally not assignable. Approval of the borrower is a condition of the loan. If a loan has been consummated and the property is then sold, the loan may be assumed. But assumption of the loan obligation usually requires the consent of the lender and does not relieve the original borrower of its obligations. The lender, on the other hand, normally has the right to sell the loan and to assign the mortgage lien to the note purchaser without the consent of the borrower.

Foreclosure.   Rights in foreclosure are determined by the laws of the state in which a property is located, but normally an act by the borrower that comprises a default on the mortgage terms gives the lenders a right to ask that the property be sold to satisfy their claims. Under the foreclosure procedure the property is offered for sale to the highest bidder and the proceeds of the sale are disbursed to the various claimants against the property. The proceeds from the foreclosure sale are usually disbursed in this order of priority: first, the costs of the foreclosure action; second, taxes; third, claimants in the order of the priority of their valid liens; fourth, the former owner-borrower, who receives any remainder. If the sale of a property yields insufficient cash to cover the mortgage claims, the lender may ask the court for a deficiency judgment against the borrower for the difference. In the foreclosure sale, a lender may use the amount of the balance due on the mortgage note as part or all of the consideration. Other bidders at such a sale must pay in cash. (For additional information on mortgages, see Chapter 60).

Federal Income Tax Considerations

This overview is intended to point out the relation of tax procedures to real estate investments. Real estate investors need expert advice to guide them on the continually changing tax requirements and on the impact of a particular investment on their other income.

Since the passage of the Tax Reform Act of 1969, there have been numerous changes in the tax benefits of real estate investment. These changes relate to the use of lower capital gains taxes, the write-off of advance interest payments, and accelerated depreciation and associated recapture provisions. Some income property tax benefits to the owner are discussed below.

Appreciation. In an inflationary economy, appreciation is a big benefit because the increase in asset value during the holding period is not taxed immediately. In addition, in comparison with such other forms of investment as savings accounts, stocks, and bonds, real estate has enjoyed favorable increases in asset value over the past ten years. Since the tax on this value growth does not have to be paid until the real estate is sold, and then at capital gain rates, the owner can exercise some control over the tax liability during his or her lifetime and can provide for the postponement of tax payment through changes.

Depreciation. The tax code permits the cost of a building that is used for business to be deducted in equal increments spread over the anticipated life of the building as an expense. Since this cost is not a direct annual cash outlay, the deduction of depreciation from income provides a cash benefit in taxes saved. The rate at which buildings can be depreciated is controlled under Internal Revenue Service rules which serve as guidelines. Variations from the rules are permitted if they are reasonable and if they can be justified to the IRS. Land cannot be depreciated.

To encourage residential construction, the IRS has long permitted an accelerated form of depreciation of rental housing units. The highest depreciation rate, under the double declining balance schedule, is given to the first owner of a newly constructed housing project. However, more recent tax laws have classified any depreciation taken in excess of straight-line schedules as a form of tax preference income which may be subject to additional taxes. Further, the tax law has a recapture provision which requires that upon the sale of a property income taxes be paid on any tax preference type of deductions taken during the term of ownership.

Passing by Will or Descent. Real estate that passed upon death to an heir was formerly subject only to inheritance taxes based on the market value of the property at the time of death. Thus the appreciated value of property could be passed on to a beneficiary without the payment of income taxes. These rules are in the process of being changed, and such property will be subject to a capital gains tax when it is sold by the beneficiary.

Refinancing. Some studies of the tax considerations that relate to real estate list as an advantage the tax-free cash that can be obtained from refinancing or from adding a second-mortgage loan. To illustrate, take a property originally valued at, say, $1 million with a mortgage loan of $750,000. After ten years of payments, the loan has been reduced to $500,000 and the value of the property has increased to $1,400,000, giving the owner an equity interest of $900,000. If a new loan for $1 million is arranged, the owner will receive $500,000 in cash and pay no income taxes on it. But a loan is a debt, and it cannot realistically be classed as income or profit. It is cash from refinancing without an immediate tax liability. There are, however, tax consequences if there is a foreclosure and the debt exceeds the tax basis. (See also Chapters 9 and 10 for information on the relationship between tax considerations and real estate investment.)

Methods of Financing Other than Mortgage Loans

Because of the dominant use of mortgage loans in financing real estate, most of the information presented here on real estate financing relates to mortgage loans. However, many other methods and procedures are used to obtain financing for the acquisition and development of real estate. Some of the methods, such as the wraparound mortgage, are largely a repackaging of older concepts; others, such as supplier participation, are highly imaginative ideas; still others are assorted methods of strengthening mortgage collateral. The following discussion takes up several of the more widely used procedures which might be shaped or adjusted to better accomplish the financing of real estate.

Seller Financing. In acquiring real estate, one obvious source of financing is the present owner. If a property is being sold because an estate needs cash or because of some other form of financial stress, seller financing is probably not possible. But if a property is being acquired from a source that is interested in a continuing income with good security, there are at least two procedures that can be offered to attract seller financing.

The Second Mortgage. Most commercial properties already have a mortgage loan outstanding. And if the existing mortgage terms are favorable, it might be wise for the buyer to assume the existing loan and to ask the seller to finance at least a portion of the equity interest, secured by a second mortgage. The seller is familiar with the property and would know its income and expense structure. A second mortgage would command a higher interest rate than a first mortgage, and this rate might be an attractive return for the seller. For the buyer, the cash requirement would be reduced substantially.

The Wraparound Mortgage. The wraparound mortgage is a variation of the second-mortgage procedure. The "wrap" consists of the amount of the seller's financing plus the amount of the existing first-mortgage loan. The buyer thus agrees to make payments to the seller that include both the new financing and the existing financing at an interest rate higher than that of the existing loan, thus giving the seller a margin of profit on the old loan. The idea of making a 1 percent or 2 percent margin of interest on the old loan has an attraction for some sellers. To protect the buyer, the mortgage payment is usually made to a bank or some other trustee that is responsible for dividing the proceeds between the mortgage holders.

Supplier Financing. For various sales-motivating reasons, it is possible that a material supplier, or even a labor contractor, will assist a building project with financial support. Two principal methods are used.

Direct Loans. Only the largest suppliers, such as General Electric or Ford, are in a strong enough cash position to make direct loans. The purpose of such help is to encourage the use of the vendor's product. In some areas, even smaller suppliers can be helpful with assistance in arranging a bank loan.

Extended Terms. A more common method of supplier financing is to permit repayment over an extended period of time. Lumber dealers and ready-mixed concrete firms are two types of suppliers that may participate in such a financing arrangement. A home builder might use such an agreement to obtain construction materials for which it would pay with interest, plus probably a small premium on the price, when the house is sold.

Balloon Notes. A balloon note is a note that is set up with repayments that are too small to amortize the loan. At maturity, the full balance becomes payable. There are several reasons for such an arrangement. One is to allow the lender to class the loan as "short term" without overtaxing the borrower immediately. The borrower may prefer to make the lower payments while he is building up his financial strength. There are three common forms of balloon-type notes.

Reduced Principal Payments. For a short-term loan, the note could call for periodic interest payments along with a principal payment that would be less than was needed to amortize the loan. At maturity, the full balance would become due. Often, timely payments will induce the lender to grant a renewal for another short term, but renewal is not mandatory.

The Sliding Amortization Schedule. With a longer term loan of, say, 15 years, the lender might set up a payment schedule that would call for having the first five years of payments made at the rate of a 30-year amortization schedule, the next five years made at a 20-year rate, and the last five years made at a 10-year rate. At the end of the 15 years of payments, the remaining principal balance would fall due. Many variations can be made on this pattern, borrower and lender willing.

Interest Only. Another variation of the balloon note is one which calls for no principal payment for the first two or three years, at which time only the interest would be payable. At maturity, the entire principal might become due. Or at the end of two or three years of paying interest only, the note might call for full amortization in monthly payments over the next, say, five years. This form of financing is sometimes used in the sale of raw land near urban centers. The seller receives a high market price for the land but agrees to take interest payments only for the first few years. During this period, the buyer may be conserving its cash for development work or may simply be holding the land for speculative resale by making a tax-deductible interest payment during the holding period.

Endorsement. A third-party endorsement or guarantee can be very helpful in strengthening the security for a loan. In a house loan this is sometimes asked of a parent or another person with a continuing interest in the buyer's welfare. In commercial loans, endorsement is used where it promotes a business objective of the endorser. From time to time, automobile manufacturers will assist a dealer to build a new sales and service facility. A large retailer, such as Sears, may find it beneficial to provide a form of guarantee that will enable a valued supplier to increase its production. A restaurant may assist a small dairy; a large farm may underwrite a food processor. The help to the borrower could take the form of a straight endorsement of a note for the banker, a letter of guaranty addressed to the lender, or a long-term purchase agreement.

Reappraisal. Continuing inflation has created another source of possible financing help. A potential borrower might look at its own inventory of buildings and equipment for possible reappraisal. The escalation of prices has effected most assets, and it is possible that the increased value would provide additional collateral for a new loan.

Purchase and Leaseback. A purchase and leaseback arrangement is a method of freeing invested capital for better uses. For example, an owner-occupied building could be sold to an investor who, in turn, leases the property back to the seller. Thus a hotel that has been substantially depreciated for tax purposes might be sold to an insurance company which leases it back to the previous owner under a long-term operating agreement. Or an oil company might elect to buy one of its operator-owned service stations and to lease the service station back to the same operator. Here the incentive might be an investment plus the protection of a good marketing outlet. Many purchase and leaseback arrangements are possible. Essentially the idea is to provide the purchaser with a secure investment and a proven tenant and to provide the seller with a release of cash that can be used to better advantage in the expansion of its business.

Syndication. The "syndication" of property has become so popular in parts of the country that it has been considered more a sales technique than a method of financing. It is a method of raising money through the sale of participating interests, and it is not confined to real estate ventures. A syndicate is a partnership that is organized to accomplish a single project. The partnership may be formed with individuals, other partnerships, or corporations, depending on state laws. The partnership may be a general partnership, or it may be a limited form requiring state approval. A large project that is mostly owned by companies rather than individuals is often called a joint venture.

The most popular form of syndicate is a group of individuals who are joined together as a limited partnership to share a risk and enjoy the benefits of a particular endeavor. The project might be cattle feeding, movie making, or oil exploration. In a real estate syndicate, the general partner usually locates the project to be developed or operated, prepares the necessary data, sells a percentage to the limited partners, and takes the responsibility for the management. So much depends on the integrity and the ability of the general partner that an analysis by the prospective investor should focus as much on that individual's operating record as on the property itself.

The theory of syndication is sound. It is a method that permits a smaller investor to participate in the ownership benefits of an income-producing property without bearing the responsibility of day-to-day management. (See Chapters 44 and 66.)

FINANCIAL LEVERAGE

William B. Brueggeman

*W*ILLIAM B. BRUEGGEMAN, PhD, Corrigan Professor in Real Estate, School of Business Administration, Southern Methodist University, Dallas, Texas.

Faculty instructor, National School of Real Estate Finance, American Bankers Association, Real Estate Institute, and Ohio Association of Realtors®. Consultant, Office of Policy Development and Research, U.S. Department of Housing and Urban Development. Member, Board of Directors, American Real Estate and Urban Economics Association. Member, editorial review board, Journal of the American Real Estate and Urban Economics Association. Author of numerous articles on real estate finance and taxation in Journal of Finance, Real Estate Review, Appraisal Journal, Land Economics, and other publications. Coauthor, Real Estate Finance, 6th ed. (Homewood, Ill.: Richard D. Irwin, 1977).

Favorable Financial Leverage

The term *financial leverage* generally refers to the case in which an investor can borrow funds at a rate of interest (after tax) below the rate of return (after tax) on total asset investment. To the extent that an investor can borrow on such favorable terms, the return on the equity invested increases as borrowing increases. This situation is usually referred to as *favorable* financial leverage. To illustrate:

Assume that a building costs $100,000 to construct and that the investor can either purchase the building outright or finance it with an $80,000, or 80 percent, loan at 8 percent for 25 years. Assume further that the building is owned for one year and then sold for $100,000. The operating statement and the return from the sale of the asset are compiled in Exhibit 1.

Note from Exhibit 1 that if the owner of the building purchased it outright, the aftertax return on equity in the first year would be 5.7 percent, as compared to the 12.5 percent return if the building were

EXHIBIT 1
Favorable Financial Leverage

Operating Statement	Without Financing	With 80 Percent Financing
Revenue	$ 15,500	$ 15,500
Less		
Expenses	5,400	5,400
Net operating income (NOI)	$ 10,100	$ 10,100
Depreciation	2,500*	2,500*
Interest	—	6,363†
Taxable income (Loss)	$ 7,600	$ 1,237
Taxes	3,800	619
Net income after tax	$ 3,800	$ 618
Statement of Cash Flow:		
Net operating income	10,100	10,100
Less		
Debt service	—	7,411†
Taxes (savings)	3,800	619‡
Aftertax cash flow (ATCF)	$ 6,300	$ 2,070

Return from Sale:

Sale

Price	$100,000	$100,000
Book value	97,500	97,500
Gain	$ 2,500	$ 2,500
Tax at 25 percent	$ 625	$ 625

Net Proceeds:

Sale price	$100,000	$100,000
Less		
Mortgage balance	—	78,952
Tax	625	625
Cash from sale	$ 99,375	$ 20,423
Return on equity, first year	$6,300 + $99,375 − $100,000 / $100,000	$2,070 + $20,423 − $20,000 / $20,000
Percent return	5.7%	12.5%

* Straight-line depreciation over 40 years—building only.
† Monthly payments based on loan constant 0.00772.
‡ Federal tax rate, 50 percent; capital gains rate, 25 percent.

financed with an 80 percent mortgage. It is clear that in this case "borrowing" gives the investor a higher return on the equity actually invested than would be earned if the building were purchased outright.

Given "favorable financial leverage," the return on equity will increase as long as the aftertax cost of debt, or $r \times (1 - t)$, where $r =$ interest rate and $t =$ tax rate, is less than the return on equity when the building is purchased outright. In our example, 8 percent $\times$ $(1 - 0.50) = 4$ percent where leverage is used, and the return on equity is 5.7 percent where leverage is not used. Since 5.7 percent is greater than 4 percent, the investor can increase the return on equity by borrowing. This relationship will hold true until the aftertax cost of debt equals the aftertax return when no leverage is used, or when both are 5.7 percent.

Unfavorable Financial Leverage

Just as there are cases in which favorable financial leverage may occur, so there are also cases in which unfavorable financial leverage may occur. Unfavorable leverage occurs if the aftertax returns on equity when no leverage is used is *greater* than the aftertax cost of borrowing. Exhibit 2 shows the effect of unfavorable leverage on investor returns. If we assume, for example, that rents do not reach the amount shown in Exhibit 1 due to unfavorable economic conditions but that operating expenses remain at the previous level, the return on equity when no borrowing occurs falls to 3.8 precent after the building is sold. Since the aftertax cost of borrowing is 4 percent, it is clearly greater than the aftertax return on equity when no leverage is used. In this case, the return on equity when leverage is used, or 3.2 percent, is lower than the return when no leverage is used, or 3.8 percent. Unfavorable leverage will continue in this case regardless of the amount borrowed. Since the average is unfavorable in this case, the investor is better off with *no borrowing*.

How Much Should Be Borrowed?

Based on the above example, it is clear that favorable financial leverage can be employed to the investor's advantage whenever the aftertax cost of borrowing is below the aftertax return on investment before financing. However, that example assumed an 80 percent loan. Another question has to do with whether to borrow beyond 80 percent, particularly if the cost of borrowing increases when we do so. For example, if the aftertax cost of borrowing is less than the aftertax return on investment before financing, would we be better off with an 80 percent loan at 8 percent or with a 90 percent loan at 9 percent? Clearly we might be able to increase the financial leverage to 90 percent advantageously even if the financing cost of doing so is higher.

To analyze the influence of the 90 percent alternative we can return to the basic example used in Exhibit 1, changing only the financial data. This is done in Exhibit 3.

EXHIBIT 2
Unfavorable Financial Leverage

Operating Statement:	Without Financing	With 80 Percent Financing
Revenue	$11,800	$11,800
Less		
Expenses	5,400	5,400
Net operating income (NOI)	$ 6,400	$ 6,400
Depreciation	2,500*	2,500*
Interest	—	6,363†
Taxable income (loss)	$ 3,900	$ (2,463)
Taxes (Savings)	$ 1,950	$ (1,232)‡
Net income (loss) after tax	$ 1,950	$ (1,231)
Statement of Cash Flow:		
NOI	6,400	6,400
Less		
Debt service	—	7,411†
Taxes (Savings)	1,950	(1,231)
Aftertax cash flow (ATCF)	$ 4,450	$ 220
Return on equity	$4,450 + $99,375§ − $100,000	$220 + $20,423§ − $20,000
	$100,000	$20,000
Percent return	3.8%	3.2%

* Straight-line depreciation over 40 years.
†Monthly payments based on loan constant 0.00772.
‡ Federal tax rate, 50 percent; capital gains rate, 25 percent.
§ From Exhibit 1.

EXHIBIT 3

Operating Statement	90 Percent Financing
Revenue	$ 15,500
Less: Expenses	5,400
Net operating income	$ 10,100
Depreciation	2,500
Interest	8,053†
Taxable income (loss)	(453)
Taxes (Savings)	(227)
Net income after tax	$ (226)
Statement of Cash Flow:	
Net operating income	$ 10,100
Less: Debt service	9,061†
Add: Tax savings	226
Aftertax cash flow (ATCF)	$ 1,265
Proceeds from Sale:	
Sale price	$100,000
Less mortgage balance	88,992
	$ 11,008
Less taxes (Exhibits 1 and 2)	625
Cash from sale	$ 10,383
Return on Equity	$\dfrac{\$1,265 + \$10,383 - \$10,000}{\$10,000}$
Percent return	16.5%

* Monthly payments based on loan constant 0.00839.

From the results shown in Exhibit 3, it is clear that the percentage return on equity increases from 12.5 percent when the 80 percent loan is used, shown in Exhibit 1, to 16.5 percent when the 90 percent loan is used. This result is obtained even though the interest rate on the loan rises from 8 percent to 9 percent. (We should note that the aftertax cost of borrowing, or 9 percent $\times (1 - 0.50) = 4.5$ percent, is still less than the 5.7 percent return when no borrowing is used.) Hence, not only is financial leverage favorable in this case, but it remains favorable even though the interest rate is increased.

However, the analysis presented in Exhibits 1 and 3 must be extended slightly in order to place the investment in proper perspective. For example, in Exhibit 1 the amount borrowed was $80,000 at 8 percent and in Exhibit 3 the amount borrowed increased to $90,000 at 9 percent. The cost of borrowing the additional $10,000 has increased significantly. Not only must the investor pay 9 percent to borrow the additional $10,000, but he must pay an *additional* 1 percent interest on the *first* $80,000 in order to make the $90,000 loan. Looked at in terms of simple interest, the interest on the 80 percent loan would be 8 percent $\times$ $80,000, or $6,400, and the interest on the 90 percent loan would be $90,000 $\times$ 9 percent, or $8,100. Hence the difference in interest or $8,100 − $6,400 = $1,700 in relation to the additional amount borrowed, or $10,000, represents 17 percent. Hence the *marginal cost* of borrowing the additional $10,000 would be 17 percent.

At this point the investor must ask whether or not the 17 percent should be paid to acquire the additional $10,000. Based on the results shown in Exhibits 1 and 3, it is clear that return on equity increases as long as the leverage is favorable. However, even though the leverage may be favorable, the relevant question to ask is: "What will the investor do with the $10,000 reduction in equity if he takes the $90,000 loan rather than the $80,000 loan?" Clearly this question must be considered before choosing the appropriate leverage alternative.

The answer in this case is that if the additional $10,000 can be reinvested at a rate greater than 17 percent, then the 90 percent loan alternative should be chosen. If the investor cannot earn a rate in excess of 17 percent, then the 80 percent alternative should be chosen.[1] Hence the question of favorable and unfavorable leverage must be coupled with an analysis of the marginal cost of borrowing and reinvestment opportunities before making decisions on which loan alternative provides the investor with maximum returns.

Leverage and Value Appreciation over Time

The analysis to this point has been limited to a consideration of leverage and operating results for only one year. To provide a more complete example of leverage and a situation in which the income, expenses, and value of a building increase over a number of years, we extend, in Exhibits 4 and 5, the example presented in Exhibit 1. In this case we assume that revenues grow at an annual rate of 5 percent and that expenses remain at a constant 34.8 percent of revenue. The property appreciates 10 percent during the five-year period, at which point it is sold. Exhibit 4 contains the operating results, and Exhibit 5 contains the results from the sale after five years.

It should be noted that the aftertax rate of return where no leverage is used is still considerably below the aftertax rate of return where leverage is used. The discounted return on equity where no borrowing occurs is 7.5 percent, which increases to over 19 percent when the 80 percent loan at 8 percent interest is considered.[2] Hence, the pattern described in connection with Exhibit 1 holds true even where revenues and property value increase over time. That is, when the aftertax cost of borrowing (4 percent in our example) is lower than the overall return on equity in any period (12.5 percent in Exhibit 1), the return on equity will be *greater* with leverage than without it and the return on equity will increase at a faster rate when the property appreciates in value. It should be pointed out, however, that the opposite result also holds true. That

---

[1] For a more detailed analysis, see H. Hoagland, L. Stone, and W. Brueggeman, *Real Estate Finance*, 6th ed. (Homewood, Ill.: Richard D. Irwin, 1977), especially chap. 10.

[2] For a more detailed discussion of discounted returns, see ibid., especially chaps. 8 and 11.

EXHIBIT 4
Multiperiod Operating Statement: Favorable Financial Leverage

	Without Financing		Year		
	1	2	3	4	5
Revenue	$15,500*	$16,275	$17,090	$17,940	$18,840
Expenses	5,400†	5,670	5,950	6,190	6,550
Net operating income	$10,100	$10,605	$11,140	$11,750	$12,290
Depreciation	2,500	2,500	2,500	2,500	2,500
Interest	—	—	—	—	—
Taxable income	$ 7,600	$ 8,105	$ 8,640	$ 9,250	$ 9,790
Taxes	3,800	4,052	4,320	4,625	4,895
Net income after taxes	$ 3,800	$ 4,053	$ 4,320	$ 4,625	$ 4,895
Cash Flow					
Net operating income	$10,100	$10,605	$11,140	$11,750	$12,290
Debt service	—	—	—	—	—
Tax	3,800	4,053	4,320	4,625	4,895
Aftertax cash flow	$ 6,300	$ 6,552	$ 6,820	$ 7,125	$ 7,395

With Financing

	Year				
	1	2	3	4	5
Net operating income	$10,100	$10,605	$11,140	$11,750	$12,290
Depreciation	2,500	2,500	2,500	2,500	2,500
Interest	6,363	6,275	6,187	6,075	5,971
Taxable income	$ 1,237	$ 1,830	$ 2,453	$ 3,175	$ 3,819
Tax	619	915	1,227	1,588	1,910
Net income after taxes	$ 618	$ 915	$ 1,226	$ 1,587	$ 1,909
Cash Flow					
Net operating income	$10,100	$10,605	$11,140	$11,750	$12,280
Debt service	7,411	7,411	7,411	7,411	7,411
Tax	619	915	1,227	1,588	1,910
Aftertax cash flow	$ 2,070	$ 2,279	$ 2,502	$ 2,751	$ 2,959

* Income growing at 5 percent per year.
† Expenses 34.8 percent of income in each year.

EXHIBIT 5
Returns in Year of Sale

	Without Financing	With Financing
Sale price	$110,000	$110,000
Less: Mortgage balance	—	73,816
Cash from sale	$110,000	$ 36,184
Taxes on sale		
Cost	$100,000	$100,000
Depreciation	12,500	12,500
Tax basis	$ 87,500	$ 87,500
Sale price	$110,000	$110,000
Basis	87,500	87,500
Taxable gain	$ 22,500	$ 22,500
Tax at 25 percent	$ 5,625	$ 5,625
Cash from sale	$110,000	$ 36,184
Less taxes	5,625	5,625
Aftertax cash flow from sale	$104,375	$ 30,559

A. Return on equity—without financing

$$\$100,000 = \$6,300 \frac{1}{(1+i)^1} + \$6,552 \frac{1}{(1+i)^2} + \$6,820 \frac{1}{(1+i)^3}$$

$$+ \$7,125 \frac{1}{(1+i)^4} + \$7,395 \frac{1}{(1+i)^5} + \$104,375 \frac{1}{(1+i)^5}$$

$$i = 7.5\%$$

B. Return on equity—with financing

$$\$200,000 = \$2,070 \frac{1}{(1+i)^1} + \$2,279 \frac{1}{(1+i)^2} + \$2,502 \frac{1}{(1+i)^3}$$

$$+ \$2,751 \frac{1}{(1+i)^4} + \$2,959 \frac{1}{(1+i)^5} + \$30,559 \frac{1}{(1+i)^5}$$

$$i = 19.5\%$$

is, if the income and the value of a property decline over time, the decline in the rate of return on equity will be *faster* in cases where financial leverage is used as compared to the decline in the rate of return on investments with no financial leverage.

Summary and Conclusion

As shown above, as long as the aftertax borrowing rate is favorable in relation to (lower than) the return on equity with no borrowing, then financial leverage can be used successfully. The opposite holds when the aftertax borrowing rate is not favorable in relation to the return with no borrowing. Also, to the extent that income and property value increase or decrease over time, returns or losses on equity will be magnified by a greater amount when leverage is used than when no leverage is used. Finally, even when opportunities for favorable leverage exist, the investor must decide how much to borrow. As more leverage is used, the marginal cost of borrowing increases; hence the investor must judge the increased cost of financing against the investment alternatives for capital that are made available by lower equity requirements. This is true regardless of how long a property is held, how much it appreciates in value, or how much income rises.

JUNIOR MORTGAGE FINANCING

David F. Seiders

William R. Beaton

*D*AVID F. SEIDERS, PhD, Senior Economist, Division of Research
and Statistics, Board of Governors of the Federal Reserve System,
Washington, D.C.
   Currently doing research in household sector finances and
mortgage and real estate markets. Author, "Household Sector
Economic Accounts," Federal Reserve Staff Economic Study no.
83, January 1975; and "Mortgage Borrowing against Equity in
Existing Homes: Measurement, Generation, and Implications
for Economic Activity," Federal Reserve Staff Economic Study
no. 96, May 1978. Author, "Credit-Card and Check-Credit Plans
at Commercial Banks," Federal Reserve Bulletin, September
1973; "Housing in the Recovery," Federal Reserve Bulletin,
March 1977; and "Recent Developments in Mortgage and Housing Markets," Federal Reserve Bulletin, March 1979. Coauthor,
"The Impact of Inflation on the Distribution of Income and
Wealth," American Economic Review, May 1971; and "Household Borrowing in the Recovery," Federal Reserve Bulletin,
March 1978.

   WILLIAM R. BEATON, PhD, Professor of Real Estate, School
of Business and Organization Sciences, Florida International
University, Miami, Florida.
   Author of numerous articles in such trade and professional
periodicals as Appraisal Journal, Real Estate Appraiser, Journal
of Property Management, Valuation, Urban Land, and Journal
of Retailing. Author, Real Estate Finance (Englewood Cliffs, N.J.:
Prentice-Hall, 1975). Coauthor, Real Estate Investment, 2d ed.;
and Real Estate.

A junior mortgage (also known as a second encumbrance, a second lien, a junior lien, a second mortgage, junior financing, and secondary financing) is any mortgage which is subordinate, or junior, in priority of claim or rights to an existing first mortgage, or senior lien, on a property. The concept includes not only second mortgages but any mortgages on a property (such as third, fourth, and fifth mortgages) which are subordinate to an existing first, or senior, mortgage. This discussion is confined to the use of a single second mortgage. The basic legal instrument used in secondary financing is a deed of trust; a contract for deed, or land contract; or a mortgage. The mortgage is probably the most commonly used of these three instruments. Unusual financing arrangements involving the use of second mortgages have sometimes been described as "creative financing."[1]

Reasons for Use

Second mortgages can be used to solve special needs or situations and to make possible real estate transactions which might not have been possible otherwise. Second-mortgage financing is usually employed for one of three purposes: (1) to enable a seller and buyer to complete a transaction by means of a purchase-money second mortgage; (2) to enable a property owner to use the equity in his property as collateral to obtain funds for a number of possible uses; or (3) to enable a developer or an investor to raise funds for the development or acquisition of a project and to utilize maximum leverage.

To Buy and Sell Property. A buyer may not have sufficient funds to make the needed down payment on a property or may be unable to obtain other financing. The seller may be willing to take a purchase-money second mortgage as part of the purchase price. This assumes that there is already a first mortgage on the property which the buyer is going to take over ("assume" or take "subject to"), or that the buyer is going to obtain a new first mortgage from an institutional lender (which will permit secondary financing). The seller is then holding a second purchase-money mortgage, and the buyer makes payments on the mortgage directly to the seller. The seller is helping to finance the buyer's acquisition of the property. (The buyer also, of course, makes payments on the first mortgage directly to the institutional lender.) Individual sellers thus become a source of funds for second mortgages.

There can be five benefits to the seller: (1) He may be able to dispose of property which he might otherwise have to hold longer. (2) He may be able to earn a good rate of interest on the second mortgage. (3) Since the seller is doing a part of the financing for the buyer, he is in a better position to negotiate price and terms—the second mortgage can help the seller obtain his desired price. (4) The seller may be able to reach a larger number of prospective buyers since less cash is needed for a down payment. (5) The seller may obtain a higher price for the property

---

[1] William R. Beaton, *Real Estate Finance* (Englewood Cliffs, N.J.: Prentice-Hall, 1975, pp. 203-4.

and the buyer may be willing to pay the higher price since with the purchase-money second mortgage he is putting less cash into the property and since the resulting leverage could give him a higher rate of return on his equity.

The buyer can also benefit in five ways from secondary financing: (1) He may acquire a property that he might not otherwise be able to purchase because of the large downpayment; or because the buyer or the property, or both, do not meet the requirements of other lenders; or because the seller is not willing to wait the necessary time for the buyer to qualify and receive loan approval from other lenders; or because money is tight and funds are not available for second mortgages; or because the cost of second mortgages in terms of interest rate is high. (2) Interest on the second mortgage, like interest on the first mortgage, is deductible from the buyer's income in computing his income taxes. (3) The seller may be willing to give the buyer more favorable or more flexible terms on the purchase-money second mortgage than would be available to the buyer if he went to other sources for the funds. (4) It is relatively simple and economical for the buyer and seller to set up a direct relationship as borrower and lender since they are not restricted by laws and regulations governing institutional lenders. (5) The reduced cash down payment that is made possible by secondary financing may give the buyer a higher rate of return on his cash investment.

To Borrow Funds against Equity.   Property owners, and particularly homeowners, may have accumulated a substantial amount of equity in their property through mortgage amortization or inflation, or both. Inflation has caused a rapid rise in the market value of most existing properties. This equity may serve as collateral for mortgage loans, especially for second mortgages where an existing first mortgage is to remain on the property. The first mortgage may not provide for the lending of additional funds under the same mortgage (the "open-end" provision), or the second mortgage may be available at a lower interest rate than is available on a consumer finance installment loan. The proceeds from such loans may be used for numerous business and personal purposes: home repair, remodeling, or improvement or a structural addition to the home; the acquisition of investment property; the purchase of appliances and other durable consumer goods; the paying of bills, taxes, and educational and medical expenses; and the paying off of debts that may have a high interest rate as compared with present market rates. Second mortgages against home equity are usually less risky and more secure for both the borrower and the lender than are other uses of second mortgages. A proper improvement should result in a higher market value for the property and thereby increase the security behind such a loan.

It is clear that inflation in the market value of homes provides individuals with large amounts of collateral for mortgage borrowing. However, the homeowner should consider carefully the pros and cons of borrowing against that collateral, and the relative costs of the alternative ways of raising such mortgage funds.

When a homeowner considers borrowing against inflated housing equity, he should recognize that a rise in house values need not imply any increase in the real value of his net worth as it affects his standard of living. Even if the price of his house has risen at a faster rate than the prices of consumer goods and services, it may not have risen relative to the cost of equivalent housing. The major effect of inflation on house prices, as far as most homeowners are concerned, has simply been to provide collateral for borrowing at the going mortgage rates and terms—ordinarily lower rates and longer terms than are available on other types of household debt. However, it should be stressed that the ability to repay debts incurred has not necessarily been enhanced by the accrued capital gains on homes.

The homeowner may wish to use mortgage funds raised against housing equity not only to purchase tangible assets, such as consumer durables and real estate, but also to increase the liquidity of his balance sheet through the acquisition of financial assets. The net costs and benefits of converting illiquid housing equity to liquid financial asset balances through mortgage borrowing will depend primarily on the spread between long- and short-term interest rates and future income growth.

Borrowing against housing equity, particularly in connection with transactions in homes, and the simultaneous acquisition of financial assets need not imply irrationality on the part of the homeowner, even if the mortgage rates paid are above the yields on the assets acquired. In a world of uncertainty and imperfect capital markets, it is not necessarily economical to minimize debts by holding no financial assets. Indeed, survey data reveal that a majority of households have debts and hold financial asset balances at the same time, even when the borrowing costs are higher than the yields on the financial assets.

The aftertax net interest cost of borrowing mortgage funds and investing these funds in financial assets may be approximated as:

$$(1 - t)(m - r),$$

where t is the individual's marginal income tax rate, m is the mortgage rate paid, and r is the yield on the financial assets acquired.

Thus, 1 minus a marginal tax rate of 40 percent, or 60 percent, times the difference between the mortgage rate paid, say 10 percent, and the interest earned, say 9 percent (which is 1 percent), amounts to only 0.6 percent. Thus, for six tenths of 1 percent the homeowner can get the liquidity of shorter term assets yielding 9 percent against longer term mortgage debt of 10 percent. This net aftertax interest cost may be compared by the homeowner with the perceived opportunity cost of holding illiquid assets (equity in homes or consumer durables) in an uncertain world, an opportunity cost which varies directly with the probability of future financial difficulties. If the household balance sheet were highly illiquid, income shortfalls would have to be met by the sale of durable assets in highly imperfect capital markets, by borrowing at high interest rates (since the borrowing would be done when the homeowner was in financial difficulty), or by a drop in consumption, none of which are attractive alternatives. Some homeowners will pay substantial differentials in order to get liquidity.

Other individuals sell homes on which they have accrued substantial capital gains in order to raise large amounts of funds at relatively low costs. The new tax law facilitates this for homeowners who are approaching retirement. But, selling might not meet their personal objectives.

The marginal costs of borrowing against accumulated equity through new first mortgages for households already engaged in selling and buying homes are quite low, per dollar raised, relative to the costs of other forms of household borrowing, including junior mortgage borrowing or refinancing for homeowners who have not moved. The transaction costs associated with new first mortgages will have been incurred by the home buyers, regardless of the size of the mortgages received. Moreover, the relatively low interest rates on first mortgages, which averaged about 9 percent during 1977, are ordinarily not highly sensitive to increases in the loan/value ratio, except at high levels of this ratio. The available data suggest, for example, that the interest rate differential on new conventional first mortgages with 50 percent and 75 percent loan/price ratios is typically only about ten basis points.

The effective marginal interest rate on mortgage funds raised against accumulated equity by an individual engaged in selling and buying homes is dependent upon the amount of money borrowed in order to make the new purchase, the amount of unreinvested cash which is taken out of the sale of the house sold, and the difference in the interest rate paid in order to get a higher loan which permits taking the cash out. It may be calculated as:

$$r_m{}^{me} = r_m{}^1 + (r_m{}^1 - r_m{}^s)\left(\frac{L}{ME} - 1\right),$$

where:

$r_m{}^1 =$ Rate on mortgage loan acquired for purchase of home
$r_m{}^s =$ Rate available on mortgage loan if all equity accumulated in previous home were reinvested in home purchased
$L =$ Size of mortgage loan acquired for purchase of home
$ME =$ Amount of equity in previous home that is "monetized" in process of selling and buying (accumulated equity in the home sold less the down payment on the home purchased)

If $ME = 0$, then $(r_m{}^1 - r_m{}^s) = 0$, since $r_m{}^1 = r_m{}^s$. Also, if $L/ME = 1$, then $r_m{}^s = 0$. Ordinarily $L > ME > 0$ and $r_m{}^1$ will vary directly with the size of ME. For example, assume that the buyer of a house priced at $100,000 has accumulated $50,000 equity in the home he is selling and that mortgages for the purchase of the new home are available with interest rates of 9.00, 9.10, and 9.20 for loan/value ratios of 50, 70, and 80 percent, respectively. Using the above formula, the effective marginal rate paid for funds raised against accumulated equity would be 9.35 percent if $20,000 of equity were monetized (choosing the 70 percent loan/value ratio, rather than 50 percent) and 9.53 percent if $30,000 of equity were monetized (choosing the 80 percent loan/value ratio).

A homeowner not engaged in selling his home who wishes to borrow funds for some investment or consumption purpose has several major alternatives: (1) take out a consumer loan, either unsecured or secured by the consumer durables purchased; (2) take out a junior mortgage against accumulated equity in his home; (3) refinance an outstanding first mortgage, increasing the size of his first-mortgage debt in the process; and (4) take out a new first mortgage if there is no outstanding mortgage debt.

If a small amount of funds is sought, a consumer loan is an economical option. Large transaction costs on mortgage loans, particularly first mortgages, make mortgages relatively expensive for small loans even when interest rates on consumer loans are higher. Moreover, for small loans, the monthly payments required on the consumer loans of relatively short maturity may not be unduly burdensome, relative to current income.

Mortgage loans are clearly preferable to consumer loans when a homeowner wishes to borrow relatively large amounts of funds at intermediate- or long-term maturity. For homeowners with some outstanding mortgage debt, a choice must be made between junior mortgage borrowing and the refinancing of outstanding first mortgages. The transaction costs for these two alternatives may differ greatly, since the requirements of various lenders with regard to title search, appraisal, credit reports, and the like, can be quite different. It should also be noted that the transaction costs paid by borrowers are ordinarily smaller with second mortgages than with first mortgages, partly because the lenders promoting such loans often absorb whatever closing costs are involved since they expect to recoup these costs through interest income.

A summary of typical terms on junior mortgages made by a sample of commercial banks in 1977 is provided in Table 1. Generally, the junior

TABLE 1
Typical Terms Offered by Banks on Junior Mortgage Loans to Individuals, 1977

	High	Low	Average
Amount financed	$80,000	$4,000	$14,757
Percent of appraised value	100%	20%	79%
Maturity	15 yr	5 yr	9 yr
Interest rate	15%	6%	11.63%
Total closing costs	$850	$16	$138.55

Source: Consumer Bankers Association.

mortgages offered by the respondent banks to individuals were large as compared with consumer loans, had intermediate-term maturities, and had interest rates ranging between 10 percent and 15 percent. Most banks write junior mortgages for no more than 80 percent of the appraised value of a property, less any outstanding mortgages.

To Develop Land and Acquire Investment Property.   Second mortgages are used by land developers and by buyers and sellers of income-producing investment property. Home builders are able to broaden the market for their houses by taking purchase-money second mortgages from buyers as part of the down payment on a house. Further, through second mortgages land developers are able to obtain funds for the installation of streets, sewers, utility lines, and other expenses of making land ready for building. The lender takes a second mortgage for these funds since the developer has already given a first mortgage to buy the land. Both the second mortgage and the first will be paid off as the developed land is sold to site and house purchasers, who obtain their own individual mortgages. The developer uses the payments for these sales to pay off his mortgages.

Purchasers of income-producing property use second mortgages as a means of acquiring more property and increasing their return on equity through leverage. A second mortgage reduces the amount of his own money that an investor needs in order to acquire a property, thereby enabling him to acquire more property with a given amount of cash. The second mortgage may be taken by the seller as a part of the transaction.

One authority on the subject writes of several ways in which second mortgages may be used. Four of these ways are as follows:

1. To liquify real estate investments without any tax consequences; in effect, to trade cash flow for instant dollars. For property that has appreciated considerably in value, the appreciation may be pulled out in cash by using a three- or five-year second mortgage. The rate on the second mortgage will be higher than on the existing first mortgage, but the total interest cost will be less than if the entire first mortgage is refinanced at a higher rate. The amortization on the second mortgage will be small during its life, so the investor must be prepared to refinance the loan at its maturity. A higher interest rate may, of course, have to be paid at that time. However, second mortgages can often be prepaid at any time without penalty and as a result they may be refinanced if rates decline during their duration.

2. The investor or developer may want to refinance his existing first mortgage to obtain cash but prefer to delay it for a year or two until long-term rates are lower. Second mortgages can provide interim financing. The slightly higher cost during the interim period can be more than offset by interest saved on a refinanced long-term mortgage.

3. One partner in a real estate business may desire to buy out another. The cash may be raised by a second mortgage which provides the cash for an immediate buyout and which can be repaid from anticipated future income that will belong solely to the remaining partner.

4. The second mortgage may be used to increase the leverage return to the investor. Large interest payments on the second mortgage are tax deductible and have a substantially lower net cost to the investor. It must be pointed out, however, that second mortgage financing can increase the risk assumed by the investor substantially. Any significant decline in net operating income could wipe out his cushion and require him to put up additional cash to avoid a default. Periodically, he must refinance the second mortgage, possibly at higher rates. This type of financing, therefore,

should be limited to sound, stable properties where income fluctuations should be minimal.[2]

The Market for Junior Mortgages

Junior mortgages have been used for many years. The extent of their use tends to increase and decrease with the availability of money for real estate lending. When mortgage money is readily available, the need for junior mortgages tends to fall, particularly among home buyers when high-ratio first mortgages are available and down payment requirements are lower. Buyers of income-producing property frequently use junior mortgages to generate leverage and a higher rate of return on their equity in a property.

Junior mortgages are speculative, and they usually carry a large element of risk, though the degree of risk can vary with the given situation. Junior mortgages usually carry a higher interest rate than do first mortgages because of the additional risk. That risk arises primarily from the fact that if the first mortgage is foreclosed and the sale does not bring in enough to pay anything on the second mortgage, the second mortgage holder is wiped out. He could, however, sue on any promissory note which accompanied the second mortgage. Another source of risk is the lack of an organized institutional market for second mortgages. Second mortgages are usually for a shorter duration than first mortgages, with terms of three to five years being common, and they carry a higher rate of interest. They may or may not be amortized.

Funds for second mortgages are available through a variety of sources, such as individuals, real estate investment trusts, mortgage bankers, and institutional lenders if they are permitted by law and regulation to lend on second mortgages. Real estate brokers, mortgage brokers, and loan officers of financial institutions can usually supply the names of individuals and companies that specialize in making or buying second mortgages. The potentially high return or yield on these mortgages and the comparatively small cost and effort of handling them attract individual investors to the second-mortgage market.

Individual lenders and investors who specialize in second mortgages know the risks involved in this type of lending and take steps to minimize those risks. Such steps can include one or more of the following: (1) have the buyer sign a promissory note and thereby become personally liable for repayment of the debt; (2) carefully evaluate present and future market conditions for the type of real estate which is to serve as security for the second mortgage; (3) carefully select borrowers who not only have the financial capacity to repay the mortgages but have demonstrated a willingness to repay obligations; (4) carefully analyze the financing needs of the borrower; (5) analyze the specific property to determine its ability to generate sufficient income to carry two mortgages;

---

[2] "How to Use Second Mortgages in Today's Real Estate Market," *The Mortgage and Real Estate Executives Report,* April 16, 1973, pp. 1–3. Quoting Jerome J. Hoffman, managing partner of Atlantic Continental Co. of New York City. This quotation and footnote credit appear in Beaton, *Real Estate Finance,* pp. 203–4.

(6) analyze the local market conditions for second mortgages; (7) require that the borrower have equity in the property; and (8) include special provisions or clauses in the second mortgage that are designed to protect the borrower or the lender, or both. Three such provisions are discussed below.

Special Provisions of Junior Mortgages

In addition to having the usual provisions of any mortgage, junior mortgages may have clauses that are designed to serve a special purpose for either the lender or the borrower, or both. Three such clauses are the *lifting or waiver clause,* the *default in prior mortgage clause,* and the *sales clause.*

The lifting clause permits the borrower to lift the first mortgage and replace it with another mortgage without changing the junior status of the second mortgage. The clause protects the borrower by keeping the second mortgage in a junior position of priority; otherwise, when the senior mortgage is fully amortized, paid off, or refinanced, the junior mortgage would be raised to the senior position. The borrower not only waives his priority to the senior lien but also to any new mortgage that may replace the senior lien. It may be difficult or impossible for the owner to obtain new financing if the junior mortgage becomes a first mortgage, since most institutional lenders are legally required to lend only on first mortgages. The junior mortgage should also provide that the amount of a new first mortgage cannot exceed the amount of the original first mortgage.

The default in prior mortgage clause protects the lender on the second mortgage. It provides that if the borrower defaults on the senior lien, the junior mortgage holder may pay the defaulted items and take over the payments or reinstate the first mortgage, add the amount to the second mortgage, and foreclose on the junior mortgage. The senior mortgage is of importance to the junior mortgage holder since the latter may be wiped out if the senior loan is foreclosed and the sale does not realize an amount sufficient to pay both mortgages.

Another protection for the second-mortgage holder is to have a provision in the mortgage prohibiting the property owner from selling the property without fully paying off the second mortgage. Even though the original mortgagor would remain liable on the second mortgage if the property were sold and a new owner assumed the existing second mortgage, the lender might not have as much trust in the new owner as he had in the original owner.

The senior mortgage holder has an interest in the actions of the junior borrower. If the junior borrower gets into financial difficulty, this may affect his paying habits on the senior mortgage. The obligations on the junior mortgage can have an adverse effect on the senior mortgage.

Institutional Junior Mortgage Lenders on Home Equity

Junior mortgages may be the most economical way in which home-owners who do not wish to sell can get cash based upon their equity.

They do this through borrowing, particularly when interest rates have been trending upward. Some junior mortgages are also acquired by homeowners who sell their houses, particularly during periods of tight money. The buyer takes over the outstanding first mortgage, and the seller takes back a second purchase-money mortgage as partial payment. However, this type of junior mortgage financing is not discussed in this section.

A wide variety of financial institutions have traditionally invested in junior mortgages. Moreover, in recent years the junior mortgage lending powers of federally chartered depository institutions have been expanded and in many areas restrictions on junior mortgage lending by state-chartered depository institutions and finance companies have been eased. On the other hand, approximately half of the states still prohibit certain institutions from making loans that are secured primarily by junior liens on homes, and restrictions on the use of funds by households as well as on maximum interest rates, loan sizes, and/or loan maturities, may limit junior mortgage lending even where it is permitted by law.

Junior Mortgage Lending by Financial Institutions. Current data on the amounts of junior mortgages are not available from trade associations, federal credit agencies, or federal and state regulatory agencies. Fragmentary data from 1971 and 1975 indicate that a variety of financial institutions have traditionally engaged in junior mortgage lending, and data from recent surveys of consumer finances confirm this fact. There are, however, a number of legal and regulatory constraints on the supply of funds to this market. The various types of institutions that make junior mortgages have differing degrees of lending power, as defined by federal or state regulations. Although there has been a definite trend toward broader lending powers, significant constraints still exist for some types of institutions.

National Banks. Until August 1974, national banks were permitted to make junior mortgages only in "abundance of caution" situations. The loans were to be based primarily on the creditworthiness of the borrower rather than on the value of the collateral. Currently, national banks may invest in loans that are secured primarily by junior liens on homes, and the holdings of national banks in such loans may amount to as much as 10 percent of the maximum amount that national banks are permitted to invest in conventional real estate loans. (In practice, this maximum is usually equal to the bank's time and savings deposits.) There are no restrictions on the use of funds by borrowers.

Federal S&Ls. Until 1975, federally chartered savings and loan associations could acquire junior mortgages only if they also held the first mortgages on the same properties. Currently, federal S&Ls may invest from 2 to 5 percent of their total assets in junior mortgage in cases where they do not hold the first mortgages. (The exact percentage will depend on the net worth position of the given association.) There are no regulatory restrictions on the use of funds by borrowers.

Federal Credit Unions. Until recently, federally chartered credit unions were permitted to make first or junior home mortgages with maturities of up to ten years, with no percent-of-asset or use-of-funds restrictions. Regulations which became effective in May 1978 permit federal credit unions to make first mortgages with maturities of up to 30 years and junior mortgages with maturities of up to 12 years (the change in maturity was authorized by the Depository Institutions Act of 1977). Under the revised regulations there are no percent-of-asset, use-of-funds, or loan-to-value ratio restrictions on junior mortgage lending. However, the interest rates on such loans may not exceed 1 percent per month, inclusive of all prepaid interest, processing fees, and other service charges.

State-Chartered Depository Institutions. The junior mortgage powers of state-chartered depository institutions vary from state to state and often differ for different types of institutions within a state. Table 2 provides a summary of current state regulations. Some of the highlights are as follows:

TABLE 2
Powers of State-Chartered Depository Institutions to Make Junior Mortgages Secured by Homes, 1978

State	Commercial Banks	Mutual Savings Banks	Savings and Loan Associations	Credit Unions
Alabama	A, F, Q		A, E	D
Alaska	A, I	A, E, I		
Arizona	A, F, G		A, F, G	A
Arkansas	A, F		A	C
California	A, F		A, J	B
Colorado	A, H, Q		A, E, I	D
Connecticut	A, I, J	A, F	A, F, J	B
Delaware	A, I	A, I	A, I	
Florida	A, I		A, F, G, Q	A
Georgia	A, F		A, Q	D
Hawaii	A, F		A, F	C
Idaho	A		A, G, J	A
Illinois	A, I, Q		A, F, G	B
Indiana	A, F	A, F	A, F	P
Iowa	A		A	P
Kansas	A		A, E	B
Kentucky	R		A, G	C
Louisiana	A		A, G	C
Maine	A	A	A	C
Maryland	A, I	A	A, E, I	C
Massachusetts	A	A	A	A
Michigan	A, G, I		A, G, I	D
Minnesota	A, F, Q	A, E	A, F	C
Mississippi	A		A, E	D
Missouri	A		A, E	D
Montana	A, E		A, E	D
Nebraska	A		A, E	D
Nevada	A, H		A, E	D
New Hampshire	A, F	A, F	A, F	B
New Jersey	A, E, F, Q	A, E, F, Q	A, E, F, Q	D
New Mexico	A, I		A, E, F	D
New York	A	A	A	B
North Carolina	A		A, E	D

TABLE 2 *(continued)*

State	Commercial Banks	Mutual Savings Banks	Savings and Loan Associations	Credit Unions
North Dakota	A, F		A, F	B
Ohio	A, E, F		A	C
Oklahoma	A, F, I		A, E, G	D
Oregon	A	A	A, E	D
Pennsylvania	A, E	A, E	A, E	C
Rhode Island	A, E, G, I	A, E, G, I	A, E, G, I	B
South Carolina	A		A, E	B
South Dakota	A, E, F		A, E	
Tennessee	A		A, E	D
Texas	A, E, F		A, E, F	C
Utah	A		A, E	D
Vermont	C, Q	C, Q	C, Q	D
Virginia	A		A, E	D
Washington	A, F	A, F	A, E, I	C
West Virginia	A		A	D
Wisconsin	A	A	A, E	B
Wyoming	A, F		A, F	

Note: Blank cells indicate that the state has no state-chartered depository institutions of the given type.

Key:
A. The law specifically authorizes junior mortgages.
B. The law authorizes real estate loans generally, and it does not limit such loans to first-mortgage loans.
C. The law specifically authorizes first-mortgage loans, but it is silent as to junior mortgage loans.
D. The law is silent as to mortgage loans of any type.
E. The depository institution may hold a junior mortgage only if it also holds the first mortgage.
F. The junior mortgage may not be the primary security for a loan. The junior mortgage may be taken only as excess collateral. It may be granted only in "abundance of caution" situations, only to cover "debts previously classified," etc.
G. Junior mortgages may be the primary security only if they are used for home improvements.
H. The depository institution has the same junior mortgage powers as do national banks.
I. The sum of the first and junior mortgages cannot exceed a specified percentage of the appraised value.
J. The junior mortgages may not exceed a specified percentage of the total assets or of capital plus surplus.
P. The law specifically prohibits second-mortgage loans.
Q. The regulatory agency discourages junior mortgage lending.
R. The depository institution which holds a junior mortgage cannot also hold the first mortgage. The first mortgages granted in the state include a clause allowing extensions to be made for home improvements.

Sources: An informal survey of the appropriate state regulatory commissions; and the National Credit Union Administration.

1. *Commercial banks.* Restrictions on junior mortgage lending by state-chartered commercial banks have been eased in some areas in recent years. In Colorado and Nevada, for example, state-chartered banks have recently been given the same powers as national banks. However, although no state specifically prohibits state-chartered banks from making junior mortgages, in one third of the states such banks are currently prohibited from making loans that are secured primarily

by junior liens on real estate. Most states that permit their banks to take junior mortgages as primary or secondary collateral place some restrictions on the size of junior mortgage loans, their maturity, the proportion of the property value that may be mortgaged, and/or the proportion of the bank portfolio that may be invested in such assets. In a few states, commercial banks may make junior mortgages only for the purpose of home improvement.

2. *Savings and loan associations.* About a dozen states prohibit state-chartered S&Ls from making loans that are secured primarily by junior liens, and in about 25 states such institutions may hold a junior mortgage only if they also hold the first mortgage. Nine states allow their S&Ls to make loans that are secured primarily by second mortgages only if the proceeds of such loans are to be used for home improvement.

3. *Mutual savings banks.* Of the 17 states with mutual savings banks, 12 states permit these institutions to make loans that are secured primarily by junior liens on real estate. However, in four of these states a mutual savings bank may make a junior mortgage loan only if it also holds the first mortgage.

4. *Credit unions.* Only two states specifically prohibit state-chartered credit unions from making junior mortgages, and in Florida and Massachusetts provisions were enacted in 1977 in order to specifically authorize junior mortgage lending. Still, in 19 states the credit union statutes are silent as to mortgage loans of any type, and in 11 other states the statutes authorize credit unions to make first-mortgage loans but are silent as to junior mortgages. Thus, in these 30 states the junior mortgage lending powers of state-chartered credit unions are unclear.

Junior Mortgage Lending by Finance Companies. Finance companies in 38 states are permitted to make loans that are secured by real estate (Table 3). However, trade sources indicate that in seven of these states—Arizona, Florida, Georgia, Nebraska, New Mexico, North Dakota, and Washington—restrictions on loan size or maximum maturity render most junior mortgage loans less profitable than unsecured personal loans. In only one state, Missouri, are finance company junior mortgages restricted as to purpose; in that state, the proceeds of such loans may not be used for home improvement. (In Missouri, home improvement loans are subject to a lower interest rate ceiling than are junior mortgages.)

Junior Mortgage Lending by Mortgage Companies. The lending activities of mortgage companies are not regulated in any formal way, and such companies may make junior mortgages without lending restrictions. (State-imposed usury ceilings may restrict lending by all institutions when market interest rates are high.) However, mortgage companies ordinarily sell the mortgage loans they originate. (In some cases, of course, the mortgage company subsidiary of a bank holding company will retain the loans it makes.) Since junior mortgages are of limited marketability, mortgage banker participation in the junior mortgage market is rather limited and junior mortgages have been accounting for less than one half of 1 percent of the total loans closed by mortgage companies in recent years.

TABLE 3
States Permitting Finance Company Loans Secured by Real Estate, 1978

State	Maximum Loan Size	Maximum Maturity
Alabama	None	None over $1,000
Arizona	$2,500	36½ months
California	None	84½ months to $10,000; none over $10,000
Colorado	None	None over $1,000
Connecticut	$5,000	None over $1,800
Delaware	10 percent of net worth of lender	84 months
Florida	$2,500	36½ months
Georgia	$3,000	36½ months
Hawaii	None	72 months
Idaho	None	None over $1,600
Illinois	$10,000	121 months
Indiana	None	None over $1,300
Iowa	20 percent of net worth of lender	None over $1,000
Kansas	None	None over $1,000
Kentucky	$7,500	61 months
Louisiana	$25,000	None over $1,000
Maryland	$6,000	72½ months
Massachusetts	None	None
Mississippi	None	None
Missouri	None	None
Montana	$7,500	None over $2,500
Nebraska	$3,000	36 months
New Hampshire	None	None
New Jersey	None	None
New Mexico	$2,500	None
North Carolina	$7,500	None
North Dakota	$2,500	None
Ohio	$15,000	60 months
Oklahoma	None	None over $1,000
Oregon	$50,000	None
Pennsylvania	$5,000	60½ months
Rhode Island	None	None
South Carolina	None	None over $1,000
Utah	None	None over $1,600
Virginia	None	None
Washington	2 percent of capital of lender	24 months
Wisconsin	None	None over $3,000
Wyoming	None	None over $1,000

Source: Household Finance Corporation.

Discounts

Junior mortgages are speculative, and the holders of such mortgages sometimes sell the completed mortgages to investors at a substantial discount from their face amount. Such sales free the lenders' capital for other ventures.

A discount may also be charged to the borrower when the loan is originated by the lender. The discount becomes a source of income to the lender, and along with the higher interest rate it is a form of compensation for the risk he takes in making the loan.

Discounts are sometimes used to enable property owners to sell their property and obtain the full price they want for it. For example, assume that a seller wants $60,000 for a property and that a buyer can obtain an 80 percent first mortgage of $48,000, leaving a down payment of $12,000. Assume further that the buyer has only $8,000, leaving $4,000 still needed to buy the property. The seller can take back a second mortgage of, say, $5,000 or more and then sell the mortgage at a discount which will net him the desired price for his property. Another alternative is for the seller to increase the price of the property sufficiently to cover any discount that he may have to pay in selling the second mortgage. In either case, the buyer is paying more for the property than he would pay if second-mortgage financing were not used. The buyer, however, has acquired a property which he might not have been able to acquire otherwise.

A borrower may have to pay discounts whenever he wants to renew his second mortgage. When such a borrower's second mortgage is about to come due, it may be desirable for him to consider refinancing the first mortgage. The balance on the first mortgage may be low; the value of the property may have risen; and refinancing may raise funds sufficient to pay off the second mortgage. The borrower must, of course, be financially capable of making the payments on the new first mortgage. This alternative frees the borrower from having to pay a discount each time he renews the second mortgage.

Default Remedies

The holder of a junior mortgage has a legal right to foreclose on it in the event of a default by the borrower. The decision to exercise this right can depend upon one or more of the following considerations: (1) the current value of the property; (2) the remaining balance on the first mortgage; (3) the market outlook for real estate values; (4) the borrower's present and prospective financial situation and his willingness to meet his obligations; (5) the reasons for the default; (6) whether there are other junior mortgages on the property; and (7) the desirability of working out something with the senior mortgage holder, assuming the latter's willingness to cooperate with the junior mortgage holder.

Foreclosure is expensive and time consuming, and lenders try to avoid it if possible. It is a measure of last resort. There are several alternative measures that a lender might pursue, depending upon the status of the above seven considerations: (1) negotiate with the borrower for a voluntary deed in lieu of foreclosure; (2) purchase or pay off the senior mortgage; (3) negotiate with the borrower for a grace period, during which the lender will not seek to enforce his claim; (4) negotiate with the borrower to renew the second mortgage and possibly make an adjustment in its terms to better suit the borrower's financial situation; (5) negotiate with the borrower and the holder of the first mortgage to refinance the first mortgage and possibly merge the two mortgages; and (6) negotiate with the holder of the first mortgage, if it is in default, to have him exercise forbearance and give the borrower time to cure the default.

If none of the above remedies are feasible, the second-mortgage holder may decide to foreclose on the second mortgage. He will join in the suit any subsequent junior lien holders and have the property sold at public auction. The purchaser of the property will take the property with the existing senior mortgage on it.

Usury Ceilings and Junior Mortgage Financing

State-imposed interest ceilings may make junior mortgage lending unprofitable for some lenders. (There are no federal junior mortgage programs or rate ceilings.) Also, a given state may subject different types of institutions to different usury ceilings. Maximum interest rates permitted under state consumer loan laws ordinarily pose no serious constraints to junior mortgage lending by finance companies in states that permit these institutions to make loans secured by real estate. However, junior mortgage lending by other types of institutions may be constrained by interest rate ceilings.

Table 4 provides a summary of state usury ceilings on junior mortgage loans made by institutions other than finance companies. Only 12 states and the District of Columbia have special usury ceilings for junior mort-

TABLE 4
State Interest Rate Ceilings on Junior Mortgage Loans to Individuals, 1978

State	Rate Ceiling	State	Rate Ceiling
Delaware	14%	Ohio	8%
Georgia	6	Rhode Island	15
Maryland	12	Texas	8
Massachusetts	18	Virginia	8
New Hampshire	18	West Virginia	6
New Jersey	15	Washington, D.C.	11½
North Carolina	12		

Note: Ceilings are defined in terms of actuarial rates, except by: *(a)* Georgia, North Dakota, Texas, Virginia, West Virginia—add-on-rates; *(b)* Delaware and Maryland—constant-ratio rates. The statutes generally define and limit fees for such items as credit reports, appraisals, and title examinations.

Source: Financial Publishing Company, *The Cost of Personal Borrowing in the United States.*

gages, permitting annual percentage rates ranging from 11½ percent to 18 percent (West Virginia's 6 percent add-on rate ceiling translates into nearly 12 percent on an annual-percentage-rate basis). In the seven states which have adopted the Uniform Consumer Credit Code (UCCC)—Colorado, Idaho, Indiana, Kansas, Utah, and Wyoming—depository institutions and finance companies are subject to the same interest rate ceilings. These ceilings are high enough to impose little constraint on junior mortgage lending.

The usury laws are unfavorable or unclear in many of the remaining 31 states. In some states, lending institutions must make junior mortgages under the same usury ceilings that apply to first mortgages. The ceilings on mortgage rates are set at 10 percent or less in 18 states which have neither junior mortgage statutes nor UCCC provisions, and these maximums may render junior mortgage lending unprofitable. In New York, for example, all loans to individuals which are secured primarily by real estate are subject to a ceiling of 8.5 percent.

In a number of states, it is not clear which statute governing usury ceilings applies to junior mortgages. In Pennsylvania, for example, there is no special second-mortgage ceiling, and it is not clear whether junior mortgages should fall under the consumer loan limit (12 percent) or the first-mortgage limit (a floating ceiling tied to a long-term Treasury bond rate). In such situations, lenders have become reluctant to grant junior mortgages at the consumer loan limit, while lending at the first-mortgage ceiling may not be economically feasible.

SAVINGS AND LOAN ASSOCIATIONS

Norman Strunk

James N. Kendall

*N*ORMAN STRUNK, MBA, Executive Vice President, United States
League of Savings Associations, Chicago, Illinois.

Member, Board of Directors, Institute of Financial Education;
Financial Managers Society for Savings Institutions; Savings
Institutions Marketing Society of America; Advertising Divi-
sion, Inc.; American Savings and Accounting Supply, Inc. Au-
thor of numerous articles and monographs, including "Know
Your Competition," Savings & Loan News, May 1977; "Is Your
Concept of 'Directorship' Up to Date?" Directors Digest, Jan-
uary 1977; "Real Estate Taxes: Can We Afford Not to Pay as
We Go?" monograph, 1973; and The Quiet Revolution in Latin
America, monograph, 1973.

JAMES N. KENDALL, BS, Director, Public Information, United
States League of Savings Associations, Chicago, Illinois.

Editor, Consumer Soundings, quarterly newsletter. Editorial
consultant, Public Relations: A Handbook for Savings Association (Institute of Financial Education, 1977). Formerly senior
editor, Savings & Loan News; editor, IGA Grocergram; and news
director, WEER, Warrenton, Virginia.

More than any other industrialized country, the United States is a
nation of homeowners. Home ownership has become so much a part
of the American way of life that the words *family* and *home* are often
used interchangeably, and the typical family desires a home of its own.
Nearly two out of three American families own their homes, and the
savings and loan business has had a lot to do with making that possible.
Savings associations provide more mortgage credit to American families
than is provided by any other type of lender.

By both charter and preference, savings associations are residential mortgage lending institutions. Thus, while the interest of other types of lenders in mortgage lending varies with the relationship between mortgage investment rates and other long-term investment rates, the provision of home financing for American families is an unvarying objective of savings associations. More mortgage money is available at some times than at others, but even in so-called tight money periods, savings associations remain the nation's chief source of home mortgage loans.

Landownership and Home Ownership: An American Tradition

The American tradition of landownership and home ownership is an old one. Perhaps the first "official" act expressing that tradition came in 1785, when the Continental Congress passed a law permitting anyone to acquire 640 acres of unclaimed land at $1 an acre. Ever since, Congress has continued to encourage landownership and home ownership as a national policy. That encouragement is exemplified in such legislation as the Homestead Act of 1862, which helped open the Western United States to family settlement; the Home Owner's Loan Act of 1933, which fostered the modern savings and loan business; the laws which created the loan guarantee and insurance programs of the Veterans Administration and the Federal Housing Administration; and the tax deduction of mortgage interest payments. Congress has also encouraged the growth of the specialized savings and loan business. One way in which Congress has done this is by allowing savings associations to pay a slightly higher rate to savers than commercial banks can pay.

The savings and loan business dates back to 1831, when the need for specialized financial institutions for savers and home buyers first became apparent. (At that time, commercial banks and other financial institutions had no desire to attract small savings accounts or to make home mortgages.) Despite the considerable changes that have occurred since then, the savings and loan business still places its emphasis on thrift and home ownership.

Savings associations finance the purchase of both new homes and existing housing.

The most common type of loan made by savings associations is mortgage loans for families that buy existing homes. But savings associations often provide the construction and permanent financing for new homes and new housing developments, and many associations also provide the construction financing or permanent financing for multifamily rental projects. Some savings associations write mortgage loans on commercial and industrial properties, although regulatory restrictions tend to limit the number and size of such commercial lending projects.

The Housing Market

The housing market is much broader than is generally realized. Newspaper real estate sections tend to concentrate on new homes, and many of the economists who are quoted in the newsweeklies and in business publications base their projections on new housing starts. However, far more existing homes are sold than new homes. In the best of times, the number of housing starts construction by homebuilders in the United States, including multifamily starts, can top 2 million. Rarely have as many as 1.5 million new single-family homes been built in a calendar year. In contrast, the sales of existing homes recently passed 4 million houses a year.

There are several reasons why more families buy used homes than new ones. One reason is price. Existing homes generally sell for less money than new homes. The difference can often be as much as $5,000 or $10,000. That difference is especially important for younger families that are buying their first homes.

Critics have claimed that first-time buyers are being excluded from the housing market by rising prices for new homes. But those critics fail to recognize that most new homes are built to meet the requirements of second- and third-time buyers—and that existing homes offer excellent housing bargains for families and individuals that are just entering their home-buying years.

In addition, many families buy the less expensive existing homes, then in a few years use their equity to help finance a new home. In fact, nearly two thirds of all the new homes built are purchased by families that use the accumulated equity and appreciated value of their existing homes to purchase new housing.

Furthermore, a look at the increased size and the increased number of amenities in new houses indicates that people who are making new-home purchases are looking for some things that they probably could not afford in their first homes. For example, 52 percent more new homes in 1976 had at least one fireplace than did new homes built in 1972, the most recent years for which comparative figures are available. In addition, 40 percent more had a two-car garage; 26 percent more had at least two bathrooms; and almost 29 percent more had at least 1,600 square feet of living space.

An increasing number of families have been discovering that homes in formerly almost forgotten older city neighborhoods often have many advantages. One, of course, is price; but many families are purchasing older homes in older neighborhoods because they find in these houses that hard-to-define something called "character." Perhaps it is the mahogany woodwork, or the spacious rooms, or the ornate trim. Moreover, the homes in older neighborhoods often have the additional advantages of being close to jobs, shopping, and public transportation. Whatever the reason, the older neighborhoods in many cities are being "discovered" by a growing number of families.

Nevertheless, most of the used homes bought and sold every year are not in the cities. Roughly two thirds of all the housing units in the United States are located in the suburbs and smaller towns of our nation.

But new homes have advantages, too. There is a certain satisfaction in being the first family to live in a particular house, and being able to tailor the house to the family's special needs and desires confers many practical benefits. Then, too, many of today's homes are being constructed with a particular concern for energy efficiency.

From the above it can be seen that the "housing market" comprises various segments—new homes and used homes; housing for young families and for older families; homes in the cities and homes in the suburbs and smaller towns. Each segment of that housing market has special needs that must be met.

Families and Savings Associations

Most families finance their housing needs with mortgage loans from savings and loan associations. It is important, then, to understand the relationship between the typical family and its savings association.

The typical family opens a savings account at a nearby savings association in order to set some money aside for emergency use and to save enough for a down payment on a home. When the family has put aside enough for a down payment, typically a savings and loan association provides the mortgage it needs for the purchase of its home. When the family grows and a larger home is needed, the equity built up in the first home by mortgage payments and the gain realized from the sale of the first home help the family to purchase its next home. Later in the life cycle—after retirement—savings association regular and certificate savings accounts may be a source of income. In fact, 21 percent of all savings association savers are retired persons.

Savings account deposits provide much of the money that savings and loan associations lend to home buyers. The four basic sources that savings associations tap for mortgage loan funds are: savings deposits; monthly loan repayments from current borrowers; money borrowed from the Federal Home Loan Bank System; and money gained by the sale of mortgage loans to federal secondary mortgage market agencies.

Where Mortgage Money Comes From

One of the most important sources of home mortgage money is the deposits that savers make to their accounts in savings and loan associations. In fact, the availability and the cost of home mortgage money are directly related to savings flows. Associations pay savers a stated interest rate on their deposits and lend that money to borrowers, who, in turn, pay for its use. The interest borrowers are charged provides the savings association with funds that are used to pay savings interest rates and the association's operating expenses or are set aside in reserve accounts.

Because of their almost exclusive support of the nation's housing market, savings associations are allowed to offer savers a slightly higher savings rate than can commercial banks. That rate differential is currently one fourth of 1 percent. The higher savings rate has been mandated by Congress because savings and loan associations are not able to offer the full financial services package that commercial banks can offer to savers—checking accounts, consumer loans, credit cards, family trust services, and the like. The savings rate differential is especially important to home buyers because without it savings associations would be unable to attract the money needed to finance home purchases. Thus if savings associations could not attract savings deposits, new-home construction and sales of existing homes would slow drastically.

The relationship between savings inflows at savings and loan associations and the home mortgage market can be seen in everyday mortgage market activities. When savings deposits are strong, there is ample mortgage money and mortgage rates are generally at the lower end of the market. But when savers are putting less money into their savings accounts—or perhaps withdrawing savings money to put it into other investments—less mortgage money is available and mortgage rates are higher.

That is why mortgage lenders—and all the other people in the real estate business—remain concerned about continuing high rates of inflation. As inflation drives up costs, more and more demands are made on the nation's credit markets. These increasing demands tend to drive up the cost of the money that is available.

When the demand for both business loans and mortgages is high, and the Treasury must go to the money markets in order to finance the government debt, then the rates that all of these borrowers must pay for their money tends to rise. Those money cost increases directly affect the home mortgage market.

The most significant effect occurs when the Treasury is faced with the need to finance a large federal deficit. When increased Treasury borrowings are added to the normal demands upon the nation's credit markets, money market rates go up and the interest rates paid by the Treasury go up, too. When the rates on short-term Treasury issues begin to reach past 6 percent, savings flows at savings and loan associations are often affected.

The people who would normally be depositing money into savings accounts increasingly tend to take that money and buy Treasury bills. Less money is going into savings accounts. Sometimes savers take money out of their savings accounts and buy higher-rate Treasury issues—a situation known as "disintermediation."

Since its first bout with disintermediation and tight money back in the mid-1960s, the savings and loan business has developed longer-term savings accounts that help combat the drain on savings dollars. Long-term savings certificates, which carry terms of from one to eight or more years and savings rate maximums of 6.5 percent to 8 percent, help assure that savings deposits remain in savings associations. Federal regulations require an interest rate penalty when a certificate is cashed in by a saver prior to the certificate's expiration date. More than half of the savings dollars in savings associations are currently in savings certificates, a fact which helps ease the drain on savings money during tight money periods.

Other savings account plans that are intended to help provide longer-term money that savings associations can count upon are the IRA and

Keogh retirement savings plans. These savings plans offer self-employed persons and individuals not covered by corporate pension plans a way to set aside money for their retirement years. Up to predetermined limits, deposits to IRA and Keogh plans are tax deferred—as is the interest those deposits earn.

In mid-1978 an innovative savings certificate was inaugurated in order to reduce the extent of disintermediation when interest rates rise. For savings association this certificate, known as a money market certificate, bore an interest rate one quarter of 1 percent higher than that of six-month U.S. government bills. On March 15, 1979, that differential was eliminated when certificate rates are 9 percent or more. And in mid-1979, a four-year "money market" certificate was authorized by federal regulators. Rates on the new certificate are tied to rates on four-year Treasury issues, with savings associations allowed to pay a higher rate to savers than banks can pay. The regulators also increased passbook savings rates at all financial institutions.

In spite of these newer types of savings plans, the home mortgage market still is adversely affected by tight money periods. However, payments received from each association's current borrowers make a significant amount of money available for mortgage loans each month. But mortgage loan repayments cannot make up for the drain on savings funds that inevitably occurs during tight money periods. It is at this point that the Federal Home Bank System comes into play.

Virtually all savings associations are members of the Federal Home Loan Bank System. The System is an important source of regulation and supervision in the public interest; it is also a source of funds when savings money is scarce. When money is tight, the Federal Home Loan Bank System can draw upon its own resources to make money available to member savings and loan associations. If savings inflows are insufficient to enable an association to meet local home mortgage demands, the association can, if it chooses, borrow funds from its regional Federal Home Loan Bank and use those funds to help provide mortgage loan dollars.

The secondary mortgage market offers still another alternative source of funds. The secondary market is a little understood but very effective mechanism for transferring funds from areas where capital is abundant to areas where capital is in short supply.

Typically, savings associations located in markets where even strong savings flows may be inadequate to meet exceptionally heavy mortgage demand make use of the secondary mortgage market to obtain additional funds. Associations make mortgage loans, then sell them to other investors—most often savings associations in other parts of the country where mortgage demand is somewhat lower and savings flows are more than adequate. The originating association normally continues to service such a loan—but it uses the proceeds from the sale of a mortgage loan package to fund more mortgages in its local market. Insurance companies, pension funds, and other institutional investors often buy mortgages in this way.

In tight money periods when mortgage funds are scarce nationally, such federally chartered agencies as the Federal Home Mortgage Corporation (known as FHLMC, Freddie Mac, or the Mortgage Corporation) and the Federal National Mortgage Association (FNMA, or Fannie Mae) come more directly into play in secondary market activities. These agencies purchase mortgage loans made by savings associations, thus funneling additional dollars back into the mortgage market.

In spite of active use of secondary market facilities, increased use of Federal Home Loan Bank System advances, and the mortgage loan repayments made by borrowers every month, the savings and loan business is dependent upon its continued ability to attract savings dollars to support the home mortgage market. And the ability of the business to attract savers and their deposits rests upon continuation of that important one fourth of 1 percent interest rate differential.

Financing the Home: Budgetary Considerations

In many ways, the financing of a home is the simplest part of the home-buying process. The key is the down payment. The typical down payment runs about 25 percent of the purchase price of the home. This means, of course, that many down payments are larger—and that many are smaller, especially for younger families that are buying their first home.

Lender practices vary, but most lenders suggest that the price of the home should not exceed 2½ or 3 times a family's gross annual income. To put it another way, a family's monthly mortgage obligation should run between 25 percent and 35 percent of its gross monthly income.

Obviously, those numbers are important to families that are trying to determine how much house they can buy. Most families, particularly families that are buying their first home, use savings money for their down payment. Very often, families that already own a home use the equity in their present house as a down payment on a newer and, typically, more expensive home.

The amount of the down payment has a direct bearing on the amount of each borrower's monthly payment. The two essential elements of the monthly payment are principal and interest. Usually, funds to build a real estate tax reserve and a property insurance reserve are added to the monthly principal and interest payments. Thus a typical $500 monthly mortgage loan payment might include $400 as a principal and interest payment to the savings and loan association, an $80 payment to the tax reserve, and a $20 payment to the homeowner's insurance reserve.

Although the total dollars earmarked for the monthly principal and interest repayment will remain unchanged over the life of the loan—assuming that the mortgage loan is a fixed rate, fully amortized loan—the amount allocated to both principal and interest will change monthly because each month the borrower pays interest only on the amount of money still owed. For example, let's assume that $50 of the borrower's first $400 principal and interest payment is applied to a $50,000 mortgage loan. That leaves $350 for interest charges. The second month's payment will include interest on the $49,950 principal that the borrower now owes. The total $400 principal and interest payment will remain unchanged, but slightly less will be used for interest charges—because the borrower now owes slightly less money. Therefore, slightly more will be allocated to reduce the outstanding mortgage debt.

This is not to say that the borrower's monthly payment will never go up. If the home buyer escrows his real estate tax and his homeowner's insurance bills—that is, pays one twelfth of the estimated annual cost each month—the monthly payment is destined to inch upward. The persistent rise in real estate taxes and the upward trend in insurance coverage and costs make rising payments seem inevitable.

Energy costs are also becoming increasingly important budgetary considerations of the home buyer—and of those in the real estate business who counsel families about the amount of home that their dollars can purchase. Location (Will a second car be needed? Is there a long commute from home to job?) and the home's energy efficiency (Is more insulation needed? How about storm windows and weather stripping?) are becoming factors in more and more buying decisions, and mortgage loan appraisers and officers are taking a closer look at energy cost data as they make creditworthiness and value judgments.

Mortgage lenders also look closely at the number and the amount of a family's outstanding debts. Although there is no hard-and-fast rule, the family's income must be enough so that mortgage lenders can be assured of the loan repayment. Of course, a number of things enter into a family's buying decision—for example, the quality of local schools, the proximity of local shopping facilities, and the quality of local municipal services, such as police and fire protection, garbage collection, and street lighting. But it is the financial aspect that we are concerned with here: the amount of the monthly mortgage payment, utility costs, and the family's monthly income and expense pattern.

Once each family has made its necessary budget considerations—often with the help of a local Realtor®—it is ready to shop for a home. Once a purchase agreement is signed, it is time to get down to the nitty-gritty of obtaining a home mortgage loan.

Financing the Home: The Mortgage Loan

Many Realtors® are able to help home buyers obtain mortgage financing. When a mortgage lender comes to know that a Realtor® sends mortgage loan applicants who are truly qualified, a natural working relationship often arises between the Realtor® and the mortgage lender. Therefore, the Realtor®—or some other individual who counsels home buyers—often has up-to-the-moment information about mortgage loan rates and charges at local lending institutions.

Even so, many buyers will check the local mortgage market themselves—comparing various home loan rates and charges. It may be, for instance, that one lender will have a 10 percent mortgage rate and a 2 percent service fee, while another lender will have a 10.25 percent mortgage rate and a 1 percent service fee. The service—or closing cost—fee is intended to reimburse the lender for the time and expense involved in processing a mortgage loan and its accompanying documents. The fee is expressed as a percentage of the total loan amount. Thus a 1 percent charge on a $50,000 mortgage would be $500. Borrowers pay this fee at the mortgage closing, the final step in obtaining a home loan. (The fee is also known as "points." Two percentage points is a one-time fee of 2 percent of the amount of the loan.) The point to remember is that the mortgage package that best suits the individual borrower's needs is not always the package with the lowest rate.

The buying and financing of a home involves a lot of important paperwork, and at this point it would be worthwhile to see just what details are likely to be handled by the savings and loan association which makes a customer's mortgage loan. The savings association will make an appraisal which will help establish the value of the home and, consequently, the amount of money that the association is willing to lend on it. Some associations use staff appraisers for this purpose; many use outside appraisers. A survey of the land or lot may be required to make certain that the property fits its legal description and that there are no encroachments. The association will arrange for the examination of the title to the property, check the borrower's ability to carry the loan, and make a proper notification to the many local government agencies that change and update public records. Finally, the association assembles the various mortgage and legal documents and reviews them with both the buyer and the seller—or their representatives—at the closing.

Most lenders charge for these services. Buyers pay the charges, as we noted earlier, at the loan closing. There is a great variety in the way the closing costs are assessed, however, and sometimes even in what they are called. Some of the closing costs are part of the mortgage transaction and are paid to the lending institution, but most are usually fees and charges which the lender simply collects and passes on to others for services rendered. Title search and credit reporting fees are examples of the latter.

Regardless, the mortgage lender is required by law to give the borrower an estimate of the charges prior to the actual closing date. The lender is also required to make full disclosure to the borrower of all costs, fees, and other charges involved in the mortgage loan transaction.

Sometimes mortgage lenders will require that conventional mortgage loans be covered by private mortgage insurance. This is often the case for loans with low down payments—generally those loans in which the borrower puts only 5 percent or 10 percent down. Because loans with smaller down payments are somewhat riskier, many lenders prefer to have a private mortgage insurance company insure part of the additional lending risk. If the borrower defaults and the lender suffers a loss, the insurance company will reimburse the lender for the portion of the loan that is covered by the mortgage insurance. In many instances, private mortgage insurance can enable home buyers to qualify for a conventional mortgage loan. The cost of private mortgage insurance is included in the borrower's monthly mortgage payment. Typically, private mortgage insurance is dropped once the borrower's equity in the home has increased to a predetermined level.

The federal government makes loan guarantee and insurance programs available through the Veterans Administration and the Federal Housing Administration. These plans allow the government to assume part of the mortgage lender's risk and help assure that loans can be made to families who might not otherwise qualify for home ownership. Like the mortgage loans backed by private mortgage insurance, the FHA-insured and the VA-guaranteed loans are usually loans with small down payments. Like the conventional mortgage loan, they are paid off on a monthly basis.

The fully amortized, fixed-rate conventional mortgage loan has helped tens of millions of families buy homes since savings associations pioneered the concept back in the 1930s. But changing economic conditions have caused mortgage lenders to conclude that it is not the best instrument for all borrowers. Therefore, savings and loan associations have sought to develop new types of mortgage loans that will fit differing borrower needs. Although at this writing many details remain to be worked out in each of the new types of mortgage loans, it seems likely that home buyers soon may have a choice of mortgage loan repayment plans—picking the one that best suits their individual needs.

Alternative Mortgage Plans

It is highly unlikely that alternative mortgage plans will ever totally replace the standard, conventional mortgage loan. For many families the conventional mortgage loan will remain the best financing tool.

Yet some inadequacies of the the conventional loan have been manifested—particularly in the economic conditions that have characterized the late 1960s and the 1970s. For example, the conventional mortgage instrument is unable to accommodate changing patterns of family income. It ignores, for instance, the fact that young families seeking to buy their first home can expect to see a rise in their income. Perhaps such families could best be served by a so-called graduated mortgage payment plan which starts with lower-than-normal payments that then rise to predetermined levels at about the same pace that family income rises.

The standard mortgage loan also makes it virtually impossible for older families, many of them retired, to tap the equity that many of them have in their home. Many older families are discovering that their retirement budgets are inadequate to meet the rising costs of living. Yet many of those families have debt-free homes that are worth thousands of dollars. The "reverse" mortgage loan might enable such families to tap the equity in their homes. With a reverse mortgage, an older family could take out a mortgage loan which would be disbursed to it by the lender in regular monthly payments over a period of years. The loan proceeds could be used to supplement the family's retirement income. Settlement of the loan would be made when the family or its estate finally sells the house.

To see how a reverse mortgage loan might work, assume that a retired couple are living in a home that they purchased many years ago and that the home, now worth $50,000, is fully paid for. Assume further that the couple want to tap the equity in their home without selling it—and moving. They go to their savings and loan association and inquire about a reverse mortgage. They have already figured that they would like another $150 per month. Working with their mortgage loan officer, they decide that they would like that $150 a month for the next five years. At this point, the savings association proceeds as if a typical mortgage loan were being granted.

This means that the home is appraised to make certain of its value. Once all is in order—appraisal, title, and so on—the savings association agrees to make a reverse mortgage loan. But instead of paying out the loan proceeds to the couple in a lump sum, the association will send them $150 a month for five years. The settlement of the mortgage loan will come at the end of the five-year period—or when the couple or their heirs sell the home, if that happens first. Alternatively, the reverse mortgage loan could be extended at the end of the five-year period—assuming, of course, that the home has continued to appreciate in value.

These two examples indicate how changes in the mortgage loan instrument might benefit families at opposite ends of the life cycle. Other types of alternative mortgage instruments might benefit other home-buying families. Consequently, the savings and loan business has been carefully looking at different types of mortgage instruments. In several states, savings associations have authority to experiment with some of the new plans. However, many legal and regulatory restraints must be overcome before many of the new plans can be adopted widely. Nonetheless, it seems likely that there will be changes in the typical mortgage plan. Therefore, let's take a look at some of the most widely used plans.

Perhaps surprisingly, one plan that has been popular with borrowers is the variable rate mortgage. Although many consumer leaders have attacked the variable rate concept, in California, where both variable rate and fixed-rate plans have long been available, a large number of borrowers have opted for the variable rate mortgage.

The popularity of the variable rate mortgage in California is one reason the Federal Home Loan Bank Board authorized all federally chartered savings associations throughout the country to issue VRMs, effective in mid-1979. Because of "tie-in" provisions, state-chartered associations received a companion VRM authority at the same time.

The variable rate mortgage is a mortgage whose interest rate can vary over the life of the loan in accordance with a predetermined index. The mortgage loan rate can go up or down—but within rather tight limits. Under the new regulations, for instance, it cannot go up more than 2.5 percent over the life of the loan. Thus a borrower with a 9 percent mortgage loan would never pay more than 11.5 percent. Because of the controls on the mortgage loan rate, the typical home buyer's monthly mortgage payment would probably change no more than $25 or $30 over the life of a variable mortgage loan. Alternatively, the term of the loan might be extended—or shortened.

The index upon which changes in the VRM are based is a national savings and loan cost-of-funds index published by the Federal Home Loan Bank Board. Within the limits set, lenders have the option of raising loan interest rates when the cost of funds increases, but they must reduce those rates if the cost of funds declines. The fact that interest rates must fall if the cost index falls is apparently one reason why many borrowers opt for the variable rate mortgage plan. There are also other reasons.

Some variable rate mortgage plans offer a "portable" variable rate loan which permits the borrower to take the present mortgage at its current rate to a new house. Thus a borrower who has a variable rate mortgage at 9 percent could transfer that mortgage to another home even when market rates on new loans are higher. Sometimes the new buyer of the family's home is permitted to assume the variable rate mortgage at its current rate.

Other types of variable rate plans often include an open-end feature which allows families to borrow against the equity they have built up in their homes—and to use that new loan money for whatever purposes they desire. In most instances, families find that borrowing at a mortgage rate against the equity in their homes is far cheaper than taking out short-term consumer loans.

Borrowers typically have the right to prepay their loan if the variable loan rate goes up. In those instances, the variable rate loan is prepaid with no prepayment fee.

Other mortgage lenders are experimenting with what is called a "rollover" mortgage loan. Especially popular in Canada, the rollover mortgage plan features a loan rate which is set for a specific period—normally three or five years—and then renegotiated at the current mortgage loan rates. The monthly repayments are figured on a longer-term amortization schedule, however.

In effect, the rollover mortgage plan is a five-year loan—with monthly repayments figured on a 25- or 30-year basis. At the end of the five-year period, the borrower and the lender renegotiate the loan rate. If the two parties cannot agree on new loan terms, the borrower normally has the option of finding new financing. In that case, the borrower has the privilege of paying off his current obligation without a prepayment fee.

It seems likely that the conventional mortgage loan will remain the staple of the mortgage lending business. There is little doubt, however, that some changes in the mortgage repayment plan are both desirable and necessary; and the savings and loan business is working with Congress, regulatory agencies, and state legislatures to effect the changes in laws and regulations that are needed in order to make the mortgage loan a more flexible and more useful instrument.

Special Urban Loan Programs

An increasing number of families are returning to the once grand older neighborhoods that so many Americans at one time called home. The revitalization of America's cities has begun. The revitalization process is one virtually everybody in the real estate business must get to know, but it is a process that requires more than home buyers and mortgage money.

Action to address all of the nation's urban problems is essential if revitalization is to succeed. The outlook for revitalizing our cities will remain dim, for instance, if unemployment rates for young people continue to exceed 40 percent in some cities; or if crime and violence remain a way of life in large areas of some cities; or if some urban school systems remain so inadequate that children simply do not learn.

Nearly every older city in the United States faces profound social and economic difficulties: the flight of families and businesses, loss of tax revenue, an increase in crime and violence, insufficient health services, deteriorating public works and school systems. Unless effective action is taken on the broadest possible scale, many of our older cities will continue to decay—and that will mean more deterioration in many of today's neighborhoods.

The private sector is capable of creating new housing and rehabilitating older housing, but so many diverse forces are involved that addressing urban problems requires a comprehensive neighborhood approach—one which includes not only lending institutions but also Realtors®, appraisers, and all other segments of the housing business.

However, the housing business cannot solve basic urban problems alone, either. In dealing with the quality of neighborhoods—the total economic, social, and cultural environment in which housing exists—many participants must work together:

Neighborhood residents must make an effort to upgrade and improve their environment.

City governments must make an honest commitment to older neighborhoods. Schools must be improved. Parks must be cleaned and created. Police and fire protection and other municipal services must often be upgraded.

Insurance underwriters must be willing to extend fire and casualty insurance coverage to property owners.

Business and industry must create places in or near a neighborhood where people can work and shop.

Many urban revitalization programs already exist, and a description of some of those programs follows. However, it should be borne in mind that each city and each neighborhood has its own unique set of circumstances and that the challenge for real estate professionals is to adapt general programs to specific local needs.

One of the most successful urban lending programs of the savings and loan business is the Neighborhood Housing Services (NHS) plan. This plan has been successful in large part because it requires the cooperation of three important groups: residents, city officials, and the real estate business.

The plan has five basic ingredients: (1) residents who are concerned about the quality of life in their neighborhood and are willing to work within the NHS framework to improve conditions; (2) local government officials who will make necessary changes in, for example, school, sanitation, and police protection programs and who will coordinate housing code compliance and inspection programs with the NHS effort; (3) financial institutions which will voluntarily underwrite the cost of the local

NHS program and agree to make market rate mortgage and home improvement loans to qualified borrowers in the neighborhood; (4) foundations, private institutions, or government bodies which will underwrite a high-risk revolving loan fund to make money available to local residents who cannot meet normal loan underwriting standards; and (5) a local, nonprofit state-chartered NHS corporation which administers the local NHS program. The local NHS corporation typically has a three-number paid staff and is governed by a local board of directors. A majority of the directors must be community residents, and a significant number of directors must represent cooperating financial institutions.

Establishing the necessary close working relationships among community activists, lenders, and city officials can take several months. Once established, however, NHS programs have shown outstanding results. Such programs currently exist in more than 50 cities. Local savings associations generally know whether or not NHS programs are operating in their cities. Mortgage lenders are also good sources of information about these and other urban revitalization projects.

In many large cities, savings and loan associations have banded together with community organizations to create urban mortgage review boards. The purpose of a mortgage review board is to make certain that families seeking to purchase a home have every opportunity to obtain a mortgage loan. The mortgage review board is intended to serve as an impartial observer for borrowers who feel that their mortgage loan applications have been unfairly treated. Such borrowers may go to the board for a review of their mortgage loan case. Typically, both the mortgage lending and the public interest communities are represented on a mortgage review board. In instances in which borrowers seeking to purchase single-family housing bring their cases to a review board, both the public interest and the mortgage lending representatives must agree on the final disposition of the mortgage loan.

The Department of Housing and Urban Development has an urban homesteading plan, under which families can purchase "as is" homes in certain neighborhoods for a minimum amount of money, but with a pledge to bring the homes to local code standards within a certain amount of time. Typically, conventional financing is available from mortgage lenders for the necessary upgrading.

In many cities, FHA mortgage loans are also available to families purchasing older homes in older neighborhoods.

And in scores of older neighborhoods, private revitalization projects are under way. Many of these projects are financed by savings and loan associations. This means that local savings associations can often help home buyers and real estate professionals who are seeking information about special urban housing efforts.

The problem of urban revitalization stems from a vast range of social and economic factors. Simplistic attempts to explain or solve the nation's complex urban problems will fail. Americans in the housing and real estate businesses have an enormous stake in the solution of those problems. As the nation's primary mortgage lenders, savings and loan associations have a strong commitment to the survival—and revival—of urban neighborhoods.

EXHIBIT 1

181242

INSTRUCTIONS

1. Detach worksheet and complete before typing.   2. At Final Settlement combine respective copies of sets A and B and distribute as indicated.

Form Approved OMB NO. 63-R-1501

A. U.S. DEPARTMENT OF HOUSING AND URBAN DEVELOPMENT **SETTLEMENT STATEMENT** **NAME OF FINANCIAL INSTITUTION** 1234 MAIN STREET ANYWHERE, U. S. A.	B. TYPE OF LOAN

B. TYPE OF LOAN

1. ☐ FHA   2. ☐ FMHA   3. ☐ CONV. UNINS.

4. ☐ VA   5. ☐ CONV. INS.

6. FILE NUMBER: 7. LOAN NUMBER:

8. MORT. INS. CASE NO.:

C. NOTE: This form is furnished to give you a statement of actual settlement costs. Amounts paid to and by the settlement agent are shown. Items marked "(p.o.c.)" were paid outside the closing; they are shown here for informational purposes and are not included in the totals.

D. NAME OF BORROWER: E. NAME OF SELLER: F. NAME OF LENDER:

G. PROPERTY LOCATION: H. SETTLEMENT AGENT: I. SETTLEMENT DATE:

PLACE OF SETTLEMENT:

J. SUMMARY OF BORROWER'S TRANSACTION:		K. SUMMARY OF SELLER'S TRANSACTION:	
100. GROSS AMOUNT DUE FROM BORROWER		**400. GROSS AMOUNT DUE TO SELLER**	
101. Contract sales price		401. Contract sales price	
102. Personal property		402. Personal property	
103. Settlement charges to borrower (line 1400)		403.	
104.		404.	
105.		405.	
Adjustments for items paid by seller in advance		*Adjustments for items paid by seller in advance*	
106. City/town taxes to		406. City/town taxes to	
107. County taxes to		407. County taxes to	
108. Assessments to		408. Assessments to	
109.		409.	
110.		410.	
111.		411.	
112.		412.	
120. GROSS AMOUNT DUE FROM BORROWER		**420. GROSS AMOUNT DUE TO SELLER**	
200. AMOUNTS PAID BY OR IN BEHALF OF BORROWER		**500. REDUCTIONS IN AMOUNT DUE TO SELLER**	
201. Deposit or earnest money		501. Excess deposit (see instructions)	
202. Principal amount of new loan(s)		502. Settlement charges to seller (line 1400)	
203. Existing loan(s) taken subject to		503. Existing loan(s) taken subject to	
204.		504. Payoff of first mortgage loan	
205.		505. Payoff of second mortgage loan	
206.		506.	
207.		507.	
208.		508.	
209.		509.	
Adjustments for items unpaid by seller		*Adjustments for items unpaid by seller*	
210. City/town taxes to		510. City/town taxes to	
211. County taxes to		511. County taxes to	
212. Assessments to		512. Assessments to	
213.		513.	
214.		514.	
215.		515.	
216.		516.	
217.		517.	
218.		518.	
219.		519.	
220. TOTAL PAID BY/FOR BORROWER		**520. TOTAL REDUCTION AMOUNT DUE SELLER**	
300. CASH AT SETTLEMENT FROM OR TO BORROWER		**600. CASH AT SETTLEMENT TO OR FROM SELLER**	
301. Gross amount due from borrower (line 120)		601. Gross amount due to seller (line 420)	
302. Less amounts paid by/for borrower (line 220)	( )	602. Less reduction amount due seller (line 520)	( )
303. CASH (☐ FROM) (☐ TO) BORROWER		**603. CASH (☐ TO) (☐ FROM) SELLER**	

HUD 1A REV. 5/76 AS & AS (1323)   **LENDER'S COPY**

EXHIBIT 1 *(continued)*

INSTRUCTIONS

1. Detach worksheet and complete before typing. 2. At Final Settlement combine respective copies of sets A and B and distribute as indicated.

NAME OF FINANCIAL INSTITUTION
1234 MAIN STREET
ANYWHERE, U. S. A.

U.S. DEPARTMENT OF HOUSING AND URBAN DEVELOPMENT
SETTLEMENT STATEMENT
PAGE 2

L. SETTLEMENT CHARGES		PAID FROM BORROWER'S FUNDS AT SETTLEMENT	PAID FROM SELLER'S FUNDS AT SETTLEMENT
700.	**TOTAL SALES/BROKER'S COMMISSION based on price** $ @ %		
	Division of commission (line 700) as follows:		
701.	$ to		
702.	$ to		
703.	Commission paid at Settlement		
704.			
800.	**ITEMS PAYABLE IN CONNECTION WITH LOAN**		
801.	Loan Origination Fee %		
802.	Loan Discount %		
803.	Appraisal Fee to		
804.	Credit Report to		
805.	Lender's Inspection Fee		
806.	Mortgage Insurance Application Fee to		
807.	Assumption Fee		
808.			
809.			
810.			
811.			
900.	**ITEMS REQUIRED BY LENDER TO BE PAID IN ADVANCE**		
901.	Interest from to @ $ /day		
902.	Mortgage Insurance Premium for mo. to		
903.	Hazard Insurance Premium for yrs. to		
904.	yrs. to		
905.			
1000.	**RESERVES DEPOSITED WITH LENDER FOR**		
1001.	Hazard insurance mo. @ $ /mo.		
1002.	Mortgage insurance mo. @ $ /mo.		
1003.	City property taxes mo. @ $ /mo.		
1004.	County property taxes mo. @ $ /mo.		
1005.	Annual assessments mo. @ $ /mo.		
1006.	mo. @ $ /mo.		
1007.	mo. @ $ /mo.		
1008.	mo. @ $ /mo.		
1100.	**TITLE CHARGES**		
1101.	Settlement or closing fee to		
1102.	Abstract or title search to		
1103.	Title examination to		
1104.	Title insurance binder to		
1105.	Document preparation to		
1106.	Notary fees to		
1107.	Attorney's fees to		
	(includes above items No.:)		
1108.	Title insurance to		
	(includes above items No.:)		
1109.	Lender's coverage $		
1110.	Owner's coverage $		
1111.			
1112.			
1113.			
1200.	**GOVERNMENT RECORDING AND TRANSFER CHARGES**		
1201.	Recording fees: Deed $; Mortgage $; Releases $		
1202.	City/county tax/stamps: Deed $; Mortgage $		
1203.	State tax/stamps: Deed $; Mortgage $		
1204.			
1205.			
1300.	**ADDITIONAL SETTLEMENT CHARGES**		
1301.	Survey to		
1302.	Pest inspection to		
1303.			
1304.			
1305.			
1400.	**TOTAL SETTLEMENT CHARGES** (enter on lines 103 and 502, Sections J and K)		

The Undersigned Acknowledges Receipt of This Settlement Statement and Agrees to the Correctness Thereof.

_____
Buyer

_____
Seller

HUD 1B REV. 5/76 AS & AS (1324)

LENDER'S COPY

EXHIBIT 2

LOAN COST DISCLOSURE STATEMENT
as required by Federal Reserve Regulation "Z"
Real Property Purchase Transaction Secured By First Lien on a Dwelling

NAME OF FINANCIAL INSTITUTION
1234 MAIN STREET
ANYTOWN, U. S. A. 00000

Loan No. _____ Date _____

1. The **AMOUNT OF THE LOAN** in this transaction is $ _____

2. The **FINANCE CHARGE** on this transaction will begin to accrue on _____

3. The **ANNUAL PERCENTAGE RATE** on this transaction is _____ %. The Interest component of the Finance Charge will be computed at the annual contractual rate of _____ % on the outstanding balance of the loan from time to time.

4. Payments of principal and Finance Charge shall number _____ and shall be in the numbers and amounts shown below, with the first such payment due on the _____ day of _____ 19 __, and all subsequent payments due on the _____ day of every month thereafter.

NUMBER OF PAYMENTS	AMOUNT	BEGINNING	NUMBER OF PAYMENTS	AMOUNT	BEGINNING	NUMBER OF PAYMENTS	AMOUNT	BEGINNING

SAMPLE

5. The **PREPAID FINANCE CHARGE** includes:
Loan Origination Fee . . . . $ _____
Assumption Fee . . . . $ _____
Interest From Date of Settlement Till
 Amortized Interest Begins . . . . $ _____
Initial Mortgage/F.H.A. Insurance
 Premium . . . . $ _____
_____ $ _____
_____ $ _____
_____ $ _____

5a. Total **PREPAID FINANCE CHARGE** . . . . $ _____

6. The **AMOUNT FINANCED** in this transaction (Subtract 5a from Amount of Loan) $ _____

7. Itemized Charges Excludable from **FINANCE CHARGE**:

	7a Paid By Cash	7b Paid From Loan Proceeds
Title Examination/Insurance	$ _____	$ _____
Appraisal Fee	$ _____	$ _____
Credit Report Fee	$ _____	$ _____
Survey	$ _____	$ _____
Initial Hazard Insurance Premium	$ _____	$ _____
Insurance Reserve/Escrow	$ _____	$ _____
Tax Reserve/Escrow	$ _____	$ _____
Recording Fees	$ _____	$ _____
	$ _____	$ _____

Total Itemized Charges **Paid From Loan Proceeds** (7b) . . . $ _____
and included in the **Amount Financed**

8. **NET PROCEEDS** (Subtract Total 7b from Line 6) $ _____

9. This institution's security interest in this transaction is a _____ on property located at _____ also specifically described in the documents furnished for this loan. The documents executed in connection with this transaction cover all after-acquired property and also stand as security for future advances, the terms for which are described in the documents.

10. Late payment formula:

11. Prepayment formula:

12. Miscellaneous disclosures:

13. **PROPERTY INSURANCE:** Hazard insurance, if written in connection with this loan, may be obtained by borrower through any person of his choice, provided however, the creditor reserves the right to refuse, for reasonable cause, to accept an insurer offered by the borrower. If borrower desires hazard insurance to be obtained from or through the creditor, the cost will be:
$ _____ for the _____ year term of the initial policy.

14. **OTHER INSURANCE:** Credit life, accident, health or loss of income insurance is not required to obtain this loan. No charge is made for such insurance and no such insurance may be provided unless the borrower signs the appropriate statement below.
_____ is available at a cost of $ _____ for the _____ year term of the initial policy.

I desire _____ insurance coverage.

_____   _____
Signature   Date

I hereby acknowledge receipt of the disclosures made in this notice.

_____   _____
Lender   Borrower   Date

_____   _____
Authorized Signature   Date   Borrower   Date

TIL DISCLOSURE - PURCHASE TRANSACTION

7/77 (1307-8)
SAF (American Savings & Accounting Supply, Inc.)

LENDER'S COPY

EXHIBIT 3

This instrument was prepared by:

. . . .
(Name)

. . . .
(Address)

MORTGAGE

THIS MORTGAGE is made this . . . . day of . . : . . . . ,
19 . . . , between the Mortgagor, ...
NAME OF FINANCIAL INSTITUTION . . . . (herein "Borrower"), and the Mortgagee, ...
. . . . , a corporation organized and
existing under the laws of . . . . , whose address is . . . .
1234 Your Street   Your City, Your State . . . . (herein "Lender").

WHEREAS, Borrower is indebted to Lender in the principal sum of . . . .
. . . . Dollars, which indebtedness is evidenced by Borrower's
note dated . . . . (herein "Note") providing for monthly installments of principal and
interest, with the balance of the indebtedness, if not sooner paid, due and payable on . . . .
. . . . ;

To SECURE to Lender (a) the repayment of the indebtedness evidenced by the Note, with interest thereon, the
payment of all other sums, with interest thereon, advanced in accordance herewith to protect the security of this
Mortgage, and the performance of the covenants and agreements of Borrower herein contained, and (b) the repayment
of any future advances, with interest thereon, made to Borrower by Lender pursuant to paragraph 21 hereof (herein
"Future Advances"), Borrower does hereby mortgage, grant and convey to Lender the following described property
located in the County of . . . . , State of Illinois:

which has the address of . . . . , ... '. . ,
                                                           [Street]   [City]
. . . . (herein "Property Address");
[State and Zip Code]

TOGETHER with all the improvements now or hereafter erected on the property, and all easements, rights,
appurtenances, rents, royalties, mineral, oil and gas rights and profits, water, water rights, and water stock, and all
fixtures now or hereafter attached to the property, all of which, including replacements and additions thereto, shall be
deemed to be and remain a part of the property covered by this Mortgage; and all of the foregoing, together with said
property (or the leasehold estate if this Mortgage is on a leasehold) are herein referred to as the "Property".

Borrower covenants that Borrower is lawfully seised of the estate hereby conveyed and has the right to mortgage,
grant and convey the Property, that the Property is unencumbered, and that Borrower will warrant and defend
generally the title to the Property against all claims and demands, subject to any declarations, easements or restrictions
listed in a schedule of exceptions to coverage in any title insurance policy insuring Lender's interest in the Property.

ILLINOIS—1 to 4 Family—6/77—FNMA/FHLMC UNIFORM INSTRUMENT   (2627-8)
                                                                   SAF (American Savings and Accounting Supply, Inc.)

EXHIBIT 3 *(continued)*

Uniform Covenants. Borrower and Lender covenant and agree as follows:

1. Payment of Principal and Interest. Borrower shall promptly pay when due the principal of and interest on the indebtedness evidenced by the Note, prepayment and late charges as provided in the Note, and the principal of and interest on any Future Advances secured by this Mortgage.

2. Funds for Taxes and Insurance. Subject to applicable law or to a written waiver by Lender, Borrower shall pay to Lender on the day monthly installments of principal and interest are payable under the Note, until the Note is paid in full, a sum (herein "Funds") equal to one-twelfth of the yearly taxes and assessments which may attain priority over this Mortgage, and ground rents on the Property, if any, plus one-twelfth of yearly premium installments for hazard insurance, plus one-twelfth of yearly premium installments for mortgage insurance, if any, all as reasonably estimated initially and from time to time by Lender on the basis of assessments and bills and reasonable estimates thereof.

The Funds shall be held in an institution the deposits or accounts of which are insured or guaranteed by a Federal or state agency (including Lender if Lender is such an institution). Lender shall apply the Funds to pay said taxes, assessments, insurance premiums and ground rents. Lender may not charge for so holding and applying the Funds, analyzing said account, or verifying and compiling said assessments and bills, unless Lender pays Borrower interest on the Funds and applicable law permits Lender to make such a charge. Borrower and Lender may agree in writing at the time of execution of this Mortgage that interest on the Funds shall be paid to Borrower, and unless such agreement is made or applicable law requires such interest to be paid, Lender shall not be required to pay Borrower any interest or earnings on the Funds. Lender shall give to Borrower, without charge, an annual accounting of the Funds showing credits and debits to the Funds and the purpose for which each debit to the Funds was made. The Funds are pledged as additional security for the sums secured by this Mortgage.

If the amount of the Funds held by Lender, together with the future monthly installments of Funds payable prior to the due dates of taxes, assessments, insurance premiums and ground rents, shall exceed the amount required to pay said taxes, assessments, insurance premiums and ground rents as they fall due, such excess shall be, at Borrower's option, either promptly repaid to Borrower or credited to Borrower on monthly installments of Funds. If the amount of the Funds held by Lender shall not be sufficient to pay taxes, assessments, insurance premiums and ground rents as they fall due, Borrower shall pay to Lender any amount necessary to make up the deficiency within 30 days from the date notice is mailed by Lender to Borrower requesting payment thereof.

Upon payment in full of all sums secured by this Mortgage, Lender shall promptly refund to Borrower any Funds held by Lender. If under paragraph 18 hereof the Property is sold or the Property is otherwise acquired by Lender, Lender shall apply, no later than immediately prior to the sale of the Property or its acquisition by Lender, any Funds held by Lender at the time of application as a credit against the sums secured by this Mortgage.

3. Application of Payments. Unless applicable law provides otherwise, all payments received by Lender under the Note and paragraphs 1 and 2 hereof shall be applied by Lender first in payment of amounts payable to Lender by Borrower under paragraph 2 hereof, then to interest payable on the Note, then to the principal of the Note, and then to interest and principal on any Future Advances.

4. Charges; Liens. Borrower shall pay all taxes, assessments and other charges, fines and impositions attributable to the Property which may attain a priority over this Mortgage, and leasehold payments or ground rents, if any, in the manner provided under paragraph 2 hereof or, if not paid in such manner, by Borrower making payment, when due, directly to the payee thereof. Borrower shall promptly furnish to Lender all notices of amounts due under this paragraph, and in the event Borrower shall make payment directly, Borrower shall promptly furnish to Lender receipts evidencing such payments. Borrower shall promptly discharge any lien which has priority over this Mortgage; provided, that Borrower shall not be required to discharge any such lien so long as Borrower shall agree in writing to the payment of the obligation secured by such lien in a manner acceptable to Lender, or shall in good faith contest such lien by, or defend enforcement of such lien in, legal proceedings which operate to prevent the enforcement of the lien or forfeiture of the Property or any part thereof.

5. Hazard Insurance. Borrower shall keep the improvements now existing or hereafter erected on the Property insured against loss by fire, hazards included within the term "extended coverage", and such other hazards as Lender may require and in such amounts and for such periods as Lender may require; provided, that Lender shall not require that the amount of such coverage exceed that amount of coverage required to pay the sums secured by this Mortgage.

The insurance carrier providing the insurance shall be chosen by Borrower subject to approval by Lender; provided, that such approval shall not be unreasonably withheld. All premiums on insurance policies shall be paid in the manner provided under paragraph 2 hereof or, if not paid in such manner, by Borrower making payment, when due, directly to the insurance carrier.

All insurance policies and renewals thereof shall be in form acceptable to Lender and shall include a standard mortgage clause in favor of and in form acceptable to Lender. Lender shall have the right to hold the policies and renewals thereof, and Borrower shall promptly furnish to Lender all renewal notices and all receipts of paid premiums. In the event of loss, Borrower shall give prompt notice to the insurance carrier and Lender. Lender may make proof of loss if not made promptly by Borrower.

Unless Lender and Borrower otherwise agree in writing, insurance proceeds shall be applied to restoration or repair of the Property damaged, provided such restoration or repair is economically feasible and the security of this Mortgage is not thereby impaired. If such restoration or repair is not economically feasible or if the security of this Mortgage would be impaired, the insurance proceeds shall be applied to the sums secured by this Mortgage, with the excess, if any, paid to Borrower. If the Property is abandoned by Borrower, or if Borrower fails to respond to Lender within 30 days from the date notice is mailed by Lender to Borrower that the insurance carrier offers to settle a claim for insurance benefits, Lender is authorized to collect and apply the insurance proceeds at Lender's option either to restoration or repair of the Property or to the sums secured by this Mortgage.

Unless Lender and Borrower otherwise agree in writing, any such application of proceeds to principal shall not extend or postpone the due date of the monthly installments referred to in paragraphs 1 and 2 hereof or change the amount of such installments. If under paragraph 18 hereof the Property is acquired by Lender, all right, title and interest of Borrower in and to any insurance policies and in and to the proceeds thereof resulting from damage to the Property prior to the sale or acquisition shall pass to Lender to the extent of the sums secured by this Mortgage immediately prior to such sale or acquisition.

6. Preservation and Maintenance of Property; Leaseholds; Condominiums; Planned Unit Developments. Borrower shall keep the Property in good repair and shall not commit waste or permit impairment or deterioration of the Property and shall comply with the provisions of any lease if this Mortgage is on a leasehold. If this Mortgage is on a unit in a condominium or a planned unit development, Borrower shall perform all of Borrower's obligations under the declaration or covenants creating or governing the condominium or planned unit development, the by-laws and regulations of the condominium or planned unit development, and constituent documents. If a condominium or planned unit development rider is executed by Borrower and recorded together with this Mortgage, the covenants and agreements of such rider shall be incorporated into and shall amend and supplement the covenants and agreements of this Mortgage as if the rider were a part hereof.

7. Protection of Lender's Security. If Borrower fails to perform the covenants and agreements contained in this Mortgage, or if any action or proceeding is commenced which materially affects Lender's interest in the Property, including, but not limited to, eminent domain, insolvency, code enforcement, or arrangements or proceedings involving a bankrupt or decedent, then Lender at Lender's option, upon notice to Borrower, may make such appearances, disburse such sums and take such action as is necessary to protect Lender's interest, including, but not limited to, disbursement of reasonable attorney's fees and entry upon the Property to make repairs. If Lender required mortgage insurance as a condition of making the loan secured by this Mortgage, Borrower shall pay the premiums required to maintain such insurance in effect until such time as the requirement for such insurance terminates in accordance with Borrower's and

EXHIBIT 3 *(continued)*

Lender's written agreement or applicable law. Borrower shall pay the amount of all mortgage insurance premiums in the manner provided under paragraph 2 hereof.

Any amounts disbursed by Lender pursuant to this paragraph 7, with interest thereon, shall become additional indebtedness of Borrower secured by this Mortgage. Unless Borrower and Lender agree to other terms of payment, such amounts shall be payable upon notice from Lender to Borrower requesting payment thereof, and shall bear interest from the date of disbursement at the rate payable from time to time on outstanding principal under the Note unless payment of interest at such rate would be contrary to applicable law, in which event such amounts shall bear interest at the highest rate permissible under applicable law. Nothing contained in this paragraph 7 shall require Lender to incur any expense or take any action hereunder.

8. Inspection. Lender may make or cause to be made reasonable entries upon and inspections of the Property, provided that Lender shall give Borrower notice prior to any such inspection specifying reasonable cause therefor related to Lender's interest in the Property.

9. Condemnation. The proceeds of any award or claim for damages, direct or consequential, in connection with any condemnation or other taking of the Property, or part thereof, or for conveyance in lieu of condemnation, are hereby assigned and shall be paid to Lender.

In the event of a total taking of the Property, the proceeds shall be applied to the sums secured by this Mortgage, with the excess, if any, paid to Borrower. In the event of a partial taking of the Property, unless Borrower and Lender otherwise agree in writing, there shall be applied to the sums secured by this Mortgage such proportion of the proceeds as is equal to that proportion which the amount of the sums secured by this Mortgage immediately prior to the date of taking bears to the fair market value of the Property immediately prior to the date of taking, with the balance of the proceeds paid to Borrower.

If the Property is abandoned by Borrower, or if, after notice by Lender to Borrower that the condemnor offers to make an award or settle a claim for damages, Borrower fails to respond to Lender within 30 days after the date such notice is mailed, Lender is authorized to collect and apply the proceeds, at Lender's option, either to restoration or repair of the Property or to the sums secured by this Mortgage.

Unless Lender and Borrower otherwise agree in writing, any such application of proceeds to principal shall not extend or postpone the due date of the monthly installments referred to in paragraphs 1 and 2 hereof or change the amount of such installments.

10. Borrower Not Released. Extension of the time for payment or modification of amortization of the sums secured by this Mortgage granted by Lender to any successor in interest of Borrower shall not operate to release, in any manner, the liability of the original Borrower and Borrower's successors in interest. Lender shall not be required to commence proceedings against such successor or refuse to extend time for payment or otherwise modify amortization of the sums secured by this Mortgage by reason of any demand made by the original Borrower and Borrower's successors in interest.

11. Forbearance by Lender Not a Waiver. Any forbearance by Lender in exercising any right or remedy hereunder, or otherwise afforded by applicable law, shall not be a waiver of or preclude the exercise of any such right or remedy. The procurement of insurance or the payment of taxes or other liens or charges by Lender shall not be a waiver of Lender's right to accelerate the maturity of the indebtedness secured by this Mortgage.

12. Remedies Cumulative. All remedies provided in this Mortgage are distinct and cumulative to any other right or remedy under this Mortgage or afforded by law or equity, and may be exercised concurrently, independently or successively.

13. Successors and Assigns Bound; Joint and Several Liability; Captions. The covenants and agreements herein contained shall bind, and the rights hereunder shall inure to, the respective successors and assigns of Lender and Borrower, subject to the provisions of paragraph 17 hereof. All covenants and agreements of Borrower shall be joint and several. The captions and headings of the paragraphs of this Mortgage are for convenience only and are not to be used to interpret or define the provisions hereof.

14. Notice. Except for any notice required under applicable law to be given in another manner, (a) any notice to Borrower provided for in this Mortgage shall be given by mailing such notice by certified mail addressed to Borrower at the Property Address or at such other address as Borrower may designate by notice to Lender as provided herein, and (b) any notice to Lender shall be given by certified mail, return receipt requested, to Lender's address stated herein or to such other address as Lender may designate by notice to Borrower as provided herein. Any notice provided for in this Mortgage shall be deemed to have been given to Borrower or Lender when given in the manner designated herein.

15. Uniform Mortgage; Governing Law; Severability. This form of mortgage combines uniform covenants for national use and non-uniform covenants with limited variations by jurisdiction to constitute a uniform security instrument covering real property. This Mortgage shall be governed by the law of the jurisdiction in which the Property is located. In the event that any provision or clause of this Mortgage or the Note conflicts with applicable law, such conflict shall not affect other provisions of this Mortgage or the Note which can be given effect without the conflicting provision, and to this end the provisions of the Mortgage and the Note are declared to be severable.

16. Borrower's Copy. Borrower shall be furnished a conformed copy of the Note and of this Mortgage at the time of execution or after recordation hereof.

17. Transfer of the Property; Assumption. If all or any part of the Property or an interest therein is sold or transferred by Borrower without Lender's prior written consent, excluding (a) the creation of a lien or encumbrance subordinate to this Mortgage, (b) the creation of a purchase money security interest for household appliances, (c) a transfer by devise, descent or by operation of law upon the death of a joint tenant or (d) the grant of any leasehold interest of three years or less not containing an option to purchase, Lender may, at Lender's option, declare all the sums secured by this Mortgage to be immediately due and payable. Lender shall have waived such option to accelerate if, prior to the sale or transfer, Lender and the person to whom the Property is to be sold or transferred reach agreement in writing that the credit of such person is satisfactory to Lender and that the interest payable on the sums secured by this Mortgage shall be at such rate as Lender shall request. If Lender has waived the option to accelerate provided in this paragraph 17, and if Borrower's successor in interest has executed a written assumption agreement accepted in writing by Lender, Lender shall release Borrower from all obligations under this Mortgage and the Note.

If Lender exercises such option to accelerate, Lender shall mail Borrower notice of acceleration in accordance with paragraph 14 hereof. Such notice shall provide a period of not less than 30 days from the date the notice is mailed within which Borrower may pay the sums declared due. If Borrower fails to pay such sums prior to the expiration of such period, Lender may, without further notice or demand on Borrower, invoke any remedies permitted by paragraph 18 hereof.

NON-UNIFORM COVENANTS. Borrower and Lender further covenant and agree as follows:

18. Acceleration; Remedies. Except as provided in paragraph 17 hereof, upon Borrower's breach of any covenant or agreement of Borrower in this Mortgage, including the covenants to pay when due any sums secured by this Mortgage, Lender prior to acceleration shall mail notice to Borrower as provided in paragraph 14 hereof specifying: (1) the breach; (2) the action required to cure such breach; (3) a date, not less than 30 days from the date the notice is mailed to Borrower, by which such breach must be cured; and (4) that failure to cure such breach on or before the date specified in the notice may result in acceleration of the sums secured by this Mortgage, foreclosure by judicial proceeding and sale of the Property. The notice shall further inform Borrower of the right to reinstate after acceleration and the right to assert in the foreclosure proceeding the non-existence of a default or any other defense of Borrower to acceleration and foreclosure. If the breach is not cured on or before the date specified in the notice, Lender at Lender's option may declare all of the sums secured by this Mortgage to be immediately due and payable without further demand and may foreclose this Mortgage by judicial proceeding. Lender shall be entitled to collect in such proceeding all expenses of foreclosure, including, but not limited to, reasonable attorney's fees, and costs of documentary evidence, abstracts and title reports.

19. Borrower's Right to Reinstate. Notwithstanding Lender's acceleration of the sums secured by this Mortgage, Borrower shall have the right to have any proceedings begun by Lender to enforce this Mortgage discontinued at any time

EXHIBIT 3 *(concluded)*

prior to entry of a judgment enforcing this Mortgage if: (a) Borrower pays Lender all sums which would be then due under this Mortgage, the Note and notes securing Future Advances, if any, had no acceleration occurred; (b) Borrower cures all breaches of any other covenants or agreements of Borrower contained in this Mortgage; (c) Borrower pays all reasonable expenses incurred by Lender in enforcing the covenants and agreements of Borrower contained in this Mortgage and in enforcing Lender's remedies as provided in paragraph 18 hereof, including, but not limited to, reasonable attorney's fees; and (d) Borrower takes such action as Lender may reasonably require to assure that the lien of this Mortgage, Lender's interest in the Property and Borrower's obligation to pay the sums secured by this Mortgage shall continue unimpaired. Upon such payment and cure by Borrower, this Mortgage and the obligations secured hereby shall remain in full force and effect as if no acceleration had occurred.

20. Assignment of Rents; Appointment of Receiver; Lender in Possession. As additional security hereunder, Borrower hereby assigns to Lender the rents of the Property, provided that Borrower shall, prior to acceleration under paragraph 18 hereof or abandonment of the Property, have the right to collect and retain such rents as they become due and payable.

Upon acceleration under paragraph 18 hereof or abandonment of the Property, and at any time prior to the expiration of any period of redemption following judicial sale, Lender, in person, by agent or by judicially appointed receiver, shall be entitled to enter upon, take possession of and manage the Property and to collect the rents of the Property including those past due. All rents collected by Lender or the receiver shall be applied first to payment of the costs of management of the Property and collection of rents, including, but not limited to, receiver's fees, premiums on receiver's bonds and reasonable attorney's fees, and then to the sums secured by this Mortgage. Lender and the receiver shall be liable to account only for those rents actually received.

21. Future Advances. Upon request of Borrower, Lender, at Lender's option prior to release of this Mortgage, may make Future Advances to Borrower. Such Future Advances, with interest thereon, shall be secured by this Mortgage when evidenced by promissory notes stating that said notes are secured hereby. At no time shall the principal amount of the indebtedness secured by this Mortgage, not including sums advanced in accordance herewith to protect the security of this Mortgage, exceed the original amount of the Note plus US $. . . . .

22. Release. Upon payment of all sums secured by this Mortgage, Lender shall release this Mortgage without charge to Borrower. Borrower shall pay all costs of recordation, if any.

23. Waiver of Homestead. Borrower hereby waives all right of homestead exemption in the Property.

In Witness Whereof, Borrower has executed this Mortgage.

. . . .
—Borrower

. . . .
—Borrower

State of Illinois, ... County ss:

I, ... a Notary Public in and for said county and state,

do hereby certify that . . . .

. . . . personally known to me to be the same person(s) whose name(s) . . . .

subscribed to the foregoing instrument, appeared before me this day in person, and acknowledged that . . . . he . . . .

signed and delivered the said instrument as . . . . free and voluntary act, for the uses and purposes therein

set forth.

Given under my hand and official seal, this . . . . day of . . . . , 19 . . . . . .

My Commission expires:

. . . .
Notary Public

——————— (Space Below This Line Reserved For Lender and Recorder) ———————

EXHIBIT 4

NOTE

US $.......................... ...., Illinois

City

.........................., 19....

FOR VALUE RECEIVED, the undersigned ("Borrower") promise(s) to pay..........................
..... Name of Financial Institution..., or order, the principal sum of
....Dollars, with
interest on the unpaid principal balance from the date of this Note, until paid, at the rate of....................
.....................percent per annum. Principal and interest shall be payable at..........................
.... 1234 Your Street................. Your City, Your State ......, or such other place as the Note holder may
designate, in consecutive monthly installments of..
..........................Dollars (US $.........................), on the...................
............day of each month beginning.........................., 19.... Such monthly installments
shall continue until the entire indebtedness evidenced by this Note is fully paid, except that any remaining indebtedness, if not sooner paid, shall be due and payable on..

If any monthly installment under this Note is not paid when due and remains unpaid after a date specified by a
notice to Borrower, the entire principal amount outstanding and accrued interest thereon shall at once become due
and payable at the option of the Note holder. The date specified shall not be less than thirty days from the date such
notice is mailed. The Note holder may exercise this option to accelerate during any default by Borrower regardless of
any prior forbearance. If suit is brought to collect this Note, the Note holder shall be entitled to collect all reasonable
costs and expenses of suit, including, but not limited to, reasonable attorney's fees.

Borrower shall pay to the Note holder a late charge of..........................percent of any monthly
installment not received by the Note holder within..........................days after the installment is due.

Borrower may prepay the principal amount outstanding in whole or in part. The Note holder may require that
any partial prepayments (i) be made on the date monthly installments are due and (ii) be in the amount of that
part of one or more monthly installments which would be applicable to principal. Any partial prepayment shall be
applied against the principal amount outstanding and shall not postpone the due date of any subsequent monthly
installments or change the amount of such installments, unless the Note holder shall otherwise agree in writing.

Presentment, notice of dishonor, and protest are hereby waived by all makers, sureties, guarantors and endorsers
hereof. This Note shall be the joint and several obligation of all makers, sureties, guarantors and endorsers, and shall
be binding upon them and their successors and assigns.

Any notice to Borrower provided for in this Note shall be given by mailing such notice by certified mail addressed
to Borrower at the Property Address stated below, or to such other address as Borrower may designate by notice to
the Note holder. Any notice to the Note holder shall be given by mailing such notice by certified mail, return receipt
requested, to the Note holder at the address stated in the first paragraph of this Note, or at such other address as may
have been designated by notice to Borrower.

The indebtedness evidenced by this Note is secured by a Mortgage, dated..........................
........................, and reference is made to the Mortgage for rights as to acceleration of the indebtedness
evidenced by this Note.

....

....

....

Property Address   *(Execute Original Only)*

ILLINOIS —1 to 4 Family—6/75—FNMA/FHLMC UNIFORM INSTRUMENT

SAF (2628-6)
American Savings & Accounting Supply, Inc.

MUTUAL SAVINGS BANKS*

Maurice E. Kinkade

MAURICE E. KINKADE, PhD, Senior Vice President, Poughkeepsie Savings Bank, Poughkeepsie, New York.

Senior vice president, Poughkeepsie Savings Bank. Member, Board of Directors, Institutional Investors Mutual Fund. Member, Board of Directors, Rehabilitation Programs, Inc. Member, NAMSB Committee on Asset and Liability Management. Member, SBANYS Committee on Urban Affairs. Faculty member, NAMSB Graduate School of Savings Banking. Member, Planning Board, United Way. Formerly assistant professor of finance, University of Wisconsin—Oshkosh. Consultant to Fox Valley Water Quality Planning Agency. Author of articles on mortgage cash flows and corporate bond investment.

Characteristics

Mutual savings banks serve as intermediaries in the flow of funds to convert small short-term deposits into larger and longer-term investment funds. Savings banks were founded by philanthropic individuals who wished to promote thrift among the working class. The use of such words as *five cents, dime, dollar,* and *savings society* in the names of many savings banks captures the essence of the industry's original purpose.

In theory, the ownership of a savings bank rests with the depositors. However, actual control is vested in the self-perpetuating boards that were originally elected by the founders of the bank. Profit from bank operations could be distributed to the depositors, the same as with other mutual organizations, except for the regulations limiting interest rates.

---

* Data for this chapter were obtained from the *1978 National Fact Book of Mutual Savings Banks,* National Association of Mutual Savings Banks, 200 Park Avenue, New York, New York.

In fact, profits are retained by the bank to provide the capital base for deposit growth.

Mutual savings banks are currently located in 17 states, with approximately 90 percent of them located in New York, Massachusetts, Connecticut, Maine, New Hampshire, and New Jersey. The number of savings banks has been steadily decreasing due to intraindustry mergers. It decreased from 532 in 1945 to 467 in 1977. The average size of assets, however, increased from $32 to $315 million during the same period.

Asset-Liability Structure

Mutual savings banks have broad investment powers. They are authorized to invest in diverse instruments, ranging from common stocks and foreign bonds to personal lines of credit.

The distribution of savings bank assets has varied since 1900, when most savings bank investments were corporate securities and mortgages. In 1945 most savings bank investments were government securities and mortgages, and by 1977 there had been a return to corporate securities and mortgages. As Chart 1 shows, mutual savings banks have always been mortgage investors, but in 1977 the proportion of their assets in mortgages and mortgage-backed securities had risen to more than 65 percent. This increase in mortgage investment by mutual savings banks corresponds to the expansion of mortgage debt in the economy. As shown in Chart 2, in 1955 the ratio of mortgage credit to total credit outstanding was less than 30 percent. By 1976 it rose to more than 40 percent.

CHART 1
Percentage Distribution of Assets of Mutual Savings Banks, Selected Years, 1900–1977

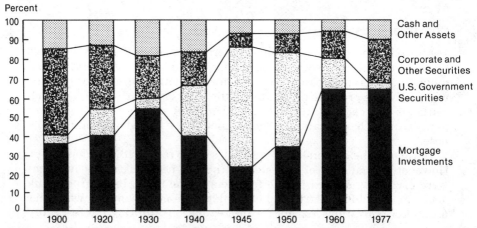

Note: End-of-year data except for 1900 to 1930, which are as of midyear. Corporate and other securities include state and municipal obligations for all years shown, and cash and other assets include nonmortgage loans. Mortgage investments for 1977 include GNMAs.

Sources: FRB, NAMSB, and state banking departments; *1978 National Fact Book of Mutual Savings Banks.*

CHART 2
Percentage Distribution of Selected Types of Capital
Market Debt Outstanding, Year-End Dates, 1955–1976

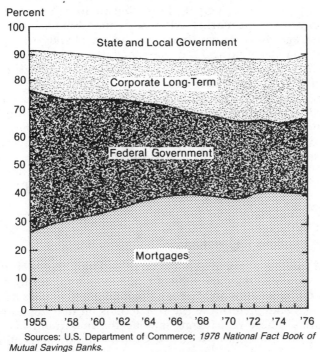

Sources: U.S. Department of Commerce; *1978 National Fact Book of Mutual Savings Banks.*

The liabilities of mutual savings banks have always consisted predominantly of deposits. As mutuals, savings banks have only borrowed capital and retained earnings as sources of funds, with 91 percent of their funds derived from deposits in 1977. These deposits were divided between short-term regular savings accounts (59 percent of deposits) and time savings accounts (41 percent of deposits).

Mortgage Portfolio

Mutual savings banks have generally preferred mortgages to other types of investment. Mortgage investment has permitted savings banks to lend money to borrowers within the bank market area where demand for funds is high, while simultaneously investing in instruments with favorable yields and medium maturity. Mortgages have returned a competitive yield and have provided an asset whose maturity more closely matches the liability structure of mutual savings banks than do other assets. The self-liquidating feature of the fully amortizing postdepression mortgage has reduced the adverse impact that results from borrowing short and lending long in periods of rising interest rates. Although savings banks have not been as successful as other types of financial institutions in adjusting yields on assets to costs on liabilities when interest rates are rising, the amortizing mortgage has provided a partial adjustment without loss of principal. Since the monthly mortgage payment includes a portion of principal, the savings bank is able to receive at par and to reinvest at market principal which was earning below the current market rate of return. In contrast to most bonds, mortgages provide a mandatory sinking fund via scheduled amortization over the mortgage life. The scheduled amortization reduces, though it does not eliminate, the risk of a fixed return on investment.

Because mutual savings banks serve a primarily local market, mortgages tend to be the predominant type of asset, since within the local market there is a greater demand for mortgage money than for other financial instruments. Supplying money for local mortgages provides savings banks with the ability to invest in desirable assets, to serve the borrowers within the communities where the banks draw deposits, and to provide the funds for the support of a major segment of local economies.

Mortgage Lending Restrictions

Mutual savings banks are chartered by the state in which they operate, and as a result they are subject to the laws and regulations of the given state's legislature and banking regulators. The laws and regulations of each state determine the restrictions on mortgage investment by the banks. These restrictions include the maximum loan-to-value ratios for in-state and out-of-state loans, the maximum percentage which may be invested in mortgages, and the maximum interest rates which may be charged. Because mutual savings banks are chartered in 17 states, there are 17 different sets of restrictions, ranging from few limitations in Washington to a variable usury ceiling in New York.

Mortgage Lending Operations

Savings banks are primary suppliers of mortgage money in their respective locations. In New York, Connecticut, and Massachusetts, which comprise 74 percent of all savings banks and 77 percent of savings bank assets, savings banks held more mortgages than did commercial banks and savings and loans combined at the end of 1977.

Savings banks are organized for full-service mortgage lending, beginning with the mortgage interview and counseling session and continuing to the final closing of the mortgage agreement and the disbursal of funds. Many borrowers are referred to banks by real estate agents. These agents frequently prescreen the borrowers to determine their qualifications for a loan.

Bank policies with regard to loan underwriting vary from placing total emphasis on the borrower's credit qualifications to placing total emphasis on the quality of the mortgaged property. The attitude of a bank's management determines the degree to which mortgage loans are underwritten on a credit basis or on a collateral basis, with most banks including both considerations and emphasizing one.

In addition to originating mortgages in their local markets, mutual savings banks purchase mortgages from other financial institutions and from brokers and mortgage bankers. The number of mortgages purchased varies by state and by bank, depending upon demand and interest rate limits. Savings banks in small cities and suburban and rural areas where the demand for mortgage money is high rely on local originations rather than the secondary mortgage market. Savings banks in larger metropolitan areas with limited mortgage demand rely more on the secondary mortgage market than on local originations.

In those areas where mortgage demand is sufficient and the usury laws do not impose low interest rate limitations, savings banks originate mortgages in order to generate earnings. In areas with insufficient demand or with interest rate restrictions, savings banks place a greater reliance on mortgage purchases as a source of earnings. Because most savings banks are located in the Northeastern United States, where the supply of capital exceeds the demand for capital, from 1951 to 1976, a period of rapid population and economic growth in regions outside the Northeast, the proportion of out-of-state mortgage holdings increased from 14.8 percent to 34.1 percent.

Prior to the late 1960s, savings banks relied on FHA/VA loans for out-of-state purchases because of their uniform document, their uniform insurance or guaranty, and their plentiful supply. Since 1968, conventional mortgages have become the primary type of mortgage purchased by savings banks, and since 1972, savings bank net holdings of nonconventional mortgages have decreased, whereas savings bank holdings of conventional mortgages have increased dramatically. Whereas in the years 1964–66 FHA/VA mortgages constituted 81.7 percent of the total out-of-state mortgage flows of savings banks, they accounted for just over 11 percent in 1970–72 and for a minus 99.8 percent by 1974–76. Conversely, conventional mortgage flows rose from 18.3 percent in 1964–66 to slightly less than 200 percent in 1974–76.

Because government insurance, underwriting, and uniform document standards do not apply to conventional mortgages, savings banks carefully examine the quality of the originator, servicer, and mortgagor when purchasing conventional loans. The higher costs engendered by this more detailed examination of mortgage purchases necessitates larger investments from a given seller in order to realize the higher effective yield that is obtainable from conventional mortgages. Savings bankers closely examine the strength of the local economies in the out-of-state areas where they purchase mortgages as well as the strength and the expertise of the originators of the conventional mortgages they purchase.

The originators of the conventional mortgages purchased by savings banks are primarily savings and loan associations in Texas, California, Florida, and Virginia, and it is the strength of these economies and the expertise of their savings and loan associations that savings bankers carefully examine to determine the risk of the mortgages they acquire.

Having made such an examination, savings banks have committed sums as large as $250 million for one large savings bank to a single originator for the acquisition of conventional mortgages. Allocating large amounts to a single originator allows the savings bank to realize the economies of scale in order to take effective advantage of the higher yields of conventional mortgages at an assessed and acceptable level of risk. If conventional mortgages with private mortgage insurance continue to replace FHA/VA in the flow of one–four-family mortgage funds, as they have since 1959 when today's private mortgage insurance companies began their operations, mutual savings banks will continue to turn to conventional mortgages as a source of out-of-state mortgage investment.

Savings banks, like many other participants in the secondary mortgage market, rely on forward commitments for most out-of-state mortgage acquisitions. The terms of such commitments require either firm or standby delivery for a specified amount, interest rate, and delivery time. Both types of commitments are accompanied by a fee from the seller of ½ to 2 percent of the amount of committed, depending upon the terms, but the standby gives the seller the option of delivering mortgages to another buyer if a better price can be obtained elsewhere.

The Supply of Mortgage Funds

Mutual savings banks, like other depository financial intermediaries, are affected by the availability of deposits when they make investments or commitments for investments. Prior to 1978, savings banks were particularly vulnerable to disintermediation during periods when the monetary authorities tightened credit and interest rates rose above the regulatory limits allowed on deposits. Depositors withdrew their money in order to take advantage of the higher rates of return that were available on government and other securities in the open market. This forced savings banks to use all available funds in order to meet the demand for deposit withdrawals.

Beginning in June 1978, savings banks and other depository institutions were permitted to offer a six-month savings certificate whose interest rate ceiling was linked to rates in the open market. This new account was designed to allow depository institutions to compete with other short-term open market investments. It appears to have reduced the outflow of deposits from thrift institutions and to have enabled savings banks and other thrift institutions to make investments and commitments for investments in a period of the economic cycle when they had heretofore been liquidators rather than investors. The new short-term savings account may provide greater stability and continuity to the housing market by reducing the variability in the flow of deposits to the financial institutions that supply the bulk of the funds that finance the output of the housing industry. Thus mutual savings banks may become a more stable source of mortgage funds.

Although the new six-month certificate appears to have reduced the effects of high short-term interest rates, savings banks in some states are still restricted by usury laws that set mortgage interest limits at below-market rates. In New York, where until recently the usury laws limited mortgage rates to 8½ percent, savings banks have been placed in a particularly difficult situation. The desire of these banks to originate mortgages in the local market and to support the local housing market has been mitigated by the need to pay rates on deposits which are competitive with open market rates while local mortgage investment has had to be made at below-market rates imposed by the state's usury laws. As a result these banks have imposed restrictions on local mortgage investment which range from requiring high down payments and short amortization periods to eliminating intrastate mortgage lending altogether. The usury laws, whose purpose was to limit borrowing costs in the event that competition was unable to do so, have become responsible for the export of mortgage money to states where supply and demand forces have produced a mortgage rate well in excess of those statutory limits. Where the cost of money approaches the return on investment, the investor is unable to make sufficient provision for operating costs and profits and must therefore seek alternative investments in order to remain competitive in bidding for deposits.

Variations in Mortgage Lending among Different Types of Financial Institutions

Mutual savings banks are located primarily in regions that are characterized by capital surplus. These regions have lower economic growth rates than do other areas of the country and a level of savings that is higher than the level of investment demand. The result of this capital surplus is reflected in Table 1, which shows that savings banks receive lower interest rates and lower fees on conventional home mortgages than do other lenders, whereas they extend approximately equal maturities. Slightly lower loan-to-value ratios partially compensate for the reduced effective rate. However, because of the low risk reflected in the low delinquency and foreclosure rates in conventional mortgages since the depression, the reduction in rate probably exceeds the reduction in risk.

The four major types of mortgage lenders are commercial banks, savings and loan associations, insurance companies, and mutual savings banks. At the end of 1977 the proportion of FHA/VA mortgages to the total mortgage investment of savings banks was approximately 3.6 times more than the average of the other three major mortgage lenders. As of December 1977 savings banks held 35 percent of the total federally underwritten mortgage debt. The greater reliance of mutual savings banks on FHA/VA loans probably reflects the need of savings banks to purchase out-of-state mortgages, the ease of buying FHA/VA loans, and the conservative attitude of the management of savings banks.

Mutual savings banks continue to be the dominant mortgage lenders in the states in which they are chartered as well as significant lenders in the national mortgage markets.

TABLE 1

Average Interest Rates and Other Terms on Conventional First-Mortgage Loans on Single-Family Homes Originated by Major Lenders, 1976 and 1977

Type of Home Purchased and Institution	Contract Interest Rate (percent)		Fees and Charges (percent)		Effective Interest Rate (percent)		Maturity (years)		Loan-to-Price Ratio (percent)	
	1976	1977	1976	1977	1976	1977	1976	1977	1976	1977
New-home purchase										
All institutions	8.76	8.80	1.44	1.33	8.99	9.01	27.2	27.9	75.8	76.3
Mutual savings banks	8.69	8.53	0.43	0.54	8.76	8.62	26.5	27.9	68.7	71.5
Commercial banks	8.79	8.81	0.68	0.80	8.90	8.94	21.9	23.5	68.8	70.9
Savings and loan associations	8.79	8.81	1.55	1.43	9.04	9.04	28.1	28.4	76.8	77.0
Mortgage companies	8.50	8.82	2.54	1.75	8.91	9.10	29.8	29.5	83.3	83.0
Existing home purchase										
All institutions	8.92	8.83	1.17	1.17	9.11	9.02	24.5	25.8	73.8	75.1
Mutual savings banks	8.75	8.57	0.51	0.47	8.83	8.65	24.1	25.4	69.1	71.0
Commercial banks	8.90	8.77	0.80	0.81	9.03	8.91	20.1	21.9	66.6	67.6
Savings and loan associations	8.94	8.86	1.34	1.32	9.16	9.08	25.6	26.6	76.2	76.8
Mortgage companies	9.01	8.90	1.76	1.45	9.30	9.13	29.4	29.6	86.0	86.4

Note: Data are unweighted averages of monthly loan terms approved during 1976 and 1977 by the four major types of lenders. Coverage is confined to loans originated directly and excludes loans acquired through correspondents. Fees and charges refer to discounts and initial payments that provide income to the lender and are expressed as a percentage of the principal amount of the mortgage. Effective interest rate includes, in addition to the contract interest rate, fees and charges amortized over a ten-year period. Loan-to-price ratio is the amount of mortgage credit extended as a percentage of the purchase price of the home.

Sources: FHLBB and NAMSB; *1978 National Fact Book of Mutual Savings Banks.*

Trends in Mortgage Financing by Mutual Savings Banks

Mutual savings banks can be expected to continue to be major suppliers of mortgage credit in their local markets as well as in the secondary mortgage markets. Savings banks have continually participated in new developments in mortgage financing. Among the better known developments are their use of private mortgage insurance and their increased use of FHA-insured mortgages for redevelopment, low-income housing, and housing for the elderly, as well as their use of the more traditional FHA loans and GNMA securities. Less well known developments include the formation of regional groups of savings banks in order to share the risk of privately financing urban renewal efforts by pooling the mortgages for renewal and financing the mortgages through participations.

Savings banks are also assisting a new development in mortgage lending which is designed to process FHA lending more efficiently. The new program, which is operated as a Section 244 FHA loan, shifts many of the functions performed by FHA personnel to the mortgage originator. The 244 mortgage is similar to the standard FHA 203 mortgage, except that the inspection, appraisal, underwriting, and approval functions are completed by the originator. The originator is able to process the 244 application for a mortgage in much the same way as a conventional mortgage application is processed, thus reducing the time required from application to the dispersal of funds from as long as four months to two or three weeks. In order to ensure the use of careful underwriting standards, FHA requires the originator to complete special training, inspects each of the first 50 mortgages approved by the originator, spot-checks subsequent approved mortgages, and requires the originator to coinsure 10 percent of the mortgage.

The 244 program will result in improved efficiency in originating FHA mortgages and will thus overcome borrowers' reluctance to use FHA. Mortgages insured by the FHA under Section 244 will remain as coinsured mortgages for the first five years following origination, after which FHA will assume full insurance. Such mortgages can be sold in the secondary market or pooled for the issuance of a GNMA security. Savings banks will probably find Section 244 mortgages advantageous because of the efficiency with which they are originated, because of their marketability, and, for savings banks in New York, because they are not constrained by the state usury law. New York savings banks will be able to offer mortgages in their local markets which will be at market rates and acceptable to mortgagors.

Savings banks have begun issuing various alternative mortgage instruments, subject to the restrictions of the different states, in an effort to reduce the interest rate risk inherent in long-term fixed-interest mortgages. The alternative instruments used by savings banks have taken the same forms as those used by other financial intermediaries, including the variable rate mortgage, the graduated payment mortgage, and the rollover mortgage. It seems evident that savings banks, like other thrift intermediaries, must find alternatives to current long-term fixed-rate mortgages financed by short-term deposits so long as inflation continues to contribute to an upward trend in interest rates.

In addition to taking steps to reduce interest rate risk arising from their assets, savings banks have made changes in their liability structure. Recently, mutual savings banks have begun using debt capital other than deposits as a source of funds. They have been borrowing primarily in order to meet regulatory requirements by making additions to their capital positions as capital ratios dropped due to the rapid growth of deposits. More recently, they have used borrowing in order to acquire funds to meet increased loan demand. The funds have been raised through borrowing from the Federal Home Loan Banks and through mortgage-backed securities. These two relatively new sources of funds have given the mutual savings banks increased access to the capital markets and have added a new device which can be used for liability management. For most savings banks located in the Northeast, the mortgage-backed bond is probably the more viable of the two types of mortgage-backed securities because of the lower yields on their mortgage pass-through. In mid-1978, Washington Mutual Savings Bank in Seattle, Washington, became the first savings bank to issue a pass-through. Both the bond and the pass-through will provide savings banks with additional sources of capital, and will allow closer matching of their asset and liability maturities.

A development suggested by the Hunt Commission report of 1972 and enacted by Congress in late 1978 is the federal charter option for mutual savings banks.[1] The most immediate effects of this option will be felt by state legislatures and banking departments which previously represented the only regulatory option for mutual savings banks. The federal charter option will probably result in competition between state and federal regulators who are attempting to provide an efficient yet sound mutual savings bank system in the same way that regulatory competition has created an efficient yet sound system of commercial banks and savings and loan associations.

The federal charter option is almost certain to produce a significant number of conversions by state-chartered savings banks in the 17 states where they are permitted and in the other states in the event that enabling legislation is passed. Savings banks in these 33 states will probably be created by the formation of new institutions as well as by conversions of commercial banks and savings and loan associations. The conversions will, of course, be dependent on the powers and restrictions of the federal charter option vis-à-vis the powers and restrictions embodied in existing charters.

---

[1] *The Report of the President's Commission on Financial Structure and Regulation* (Washington, D.C.: U.S. Government Printing Office, 1973).

COMMERCIAL BANKS

Willis W. Alexander

*W*ILLIS W. ALEXANDER, MBA, Executive Vice President, American Bankers Association, Washington, D.C.
   As chief staff executive of American Bankers Association, heads a staff of more than 300 at the Washington headquarters. President, Trenton (Mo.) Trust Company, 1960; chairman since 1974. Past president, Missouri Bankers Association.

The Scope of Commercial Banking

A bank is a business which makes its profits by attracting funds from customers and lending those funds to other persons. Its basic function is to serve as a financial intermediary for those who want to put idle funds to work earning more money and those who want to borrow funds for personal or business needs. Most of the money that banks use for loans and investment comes from demand deposits (checking accounts) and time deposits (savings accounts), whose combined total came to $838 billion at the end of 1976. The rest, which brought the 1976 total of U.S. bank assets to over $1 trillion, comes from shareholders and from the banks' own borrowings. In 1976 America's banks earned $80.4 billion in revenues, mostly from loans and investments, against $70.4 billion in expenses, including savings account interest, taxes, and salaries. Their net operating earnings totaled $10 billion ($12.1 billion before taxes).

The "price" that banks charge for lending or investing their deposits is interest. Although the payment of interest on checking accounts is illegal for banks, a growing number of banks do give customers an implicit return on those funds by not charging a service fee. In some states, banks and other financial institutions can offer NOW (Negotiable Order of Withdrawal) accounts, in which a savings account withdrawal ticket is a transferable instrument—and, in effect, the account becomes an interest-bearing checking account.

Although other kinds of institutions attract and lend savings money, in most states banks are unique in their right under law to establish checking accounts. Moreover, the nation's 14,500 banks offer an unrivaled "department store" variety of financial services. These range from reconciling a depositor's checkbook balance to handling complex international transactions for corporate customers, from managing an inheritance to serving as bankers for other banks. In the area of real estate lending, it is generally recognized that savings and loan institutions were created expressly for home mortgage lending, whereas commercial banks serve as *all-purpose real estate lenders.*

Major Banking Functions of Commercial Banks

Loans. *Business Loans.* Comprising the largest share (50 percent) of all bank loans, business loans are used primarily by commercial and industrial firms to invest in business expansion. They also help other financial enterprises, for instance, mortgage bankers, to carry out their business. The classic business loan is short term, meaning that it is repaid within one year and that it usually serves to meet seasonal needs.

Mortgages. Mortgages account for about one fourth of all bank loans. They are extended to help people and businesses buy real estate. More than half of all bank mortgages underwrite home purchases. Second in importance are purchases of business properties, such as factories and office buildings, apartment houses, and farm property. Banks rank second to savings and loan associations in mortgage holdings. Banks, however, account for nearly half of all home construction loans, more than half of all home improvement loans, and the bulk of all lending for mobile home purchases. Banks hold more in municipal securities—$105 billion—than does any other group of lenders. About $80 billion of that amount was issued to finance residential support facilities, such as transportation, utilities, schools, and public services.

Consumer Installment Loans. Eighteen percent of all bank loans are in the form of consumer loans. Banks now lead all other lenders in this area, with nearly half of the market. Most consumer loans are for cars, boats, furniture, and other expensive durable goods. In 1976, automobile loans accounted for 42 percent of all bank installment loans, and home improvement loans were fourth in loan volume.

Farm Loans. At the end of 1976, almost 12,000 of the more than 14,500 banks in the United States held $28 billion in outstanding farm debt—more than one fourth of the nation's total farm debt of $93 billion. Banks accounted for $7 billion in farm real estate loans and for $21 billion in agricultural operating loans. An estimated two thirds of the nation's 2.8 million farmers make short-term loans to pay expenses before crops are harvested or cattle sold or long-term loans to buy heavy-duty equipment.

Investments. After loans, the next biggest source of banking assets, making up about 20 percent, is investments. All of these investments are in state, local, and federal government securities. Nearly half of all bank-held securities are long-term state and municipal bonds that local governments sell, usually to finance schools, roads, sewage, and other expensive construction projects that direct tax assessments cannot cover. The net result is a wide, ready market for government securities and means for improving municipal facilities while keeping local tax assessments down.

Trust Management. Banks receive less than 5 percent of their income from trust fees for managing other people's assets for their benefit or for the benefit of their heirs, friends, or employees. Trust investments are an important source of funds for real estate. The mortgage-backed security, for example, is an instrument that has found great popularity among trust fund managers. In addition, commercial banks are the prime custodians for the mortgages which back GNMA securities.

Real Estate Loan Policies and Practices of Commercial Banks

Construction Loans. Without the necessary experience and skill, financing construction can be one of the riskiest lending activities of a commercial bank. A construction loan can be described as a short-term loan that is made to an owner of real property, the funds of which are used to construct an improvement upon the property. The loan is secured by a mortgage lien on the property itself.

Few residential or commercial buildings are purchased outright. In almost every case, the potential owner applies for a long-term mortgage through a financial institution and agrees to repay the debt over a long period of time. However, the original contractor or developer, that is, the individual or organization responsible for the actual construction of the home, office building, apartment building, condominium, shopping center complex, and so on, requires funds to erect the structure long before the permanent mortgage money is needed. As a result, interim or construction financing is necessary; this need is filled by the commercial lender. The commercial lender provides the developer with the financial assistance that is necessary to erect the structure.

During construction, the funds are advanced gradually at a predetermined schedule and in amounts commensurate with the amount of construction that has been completed to date. When the project is completed, the funds advanced through the construction loan are repaid to the lender, generally by the long-term lender. In most cases, the developer has previously secured a commitment from the long-term lender to replace the short-term construction loan.

At Community Commercial Banks. Community banks rarely make construction loans beyond the boundaries of their local banking areas. The loans are often combination construction and long-term mortgages that are given to individuals for new homes or to small businesses for new buildings. Relative to their size, community banks finance more residential dwelling construction—both for local tract builders and individuals—than do larger banks.

The rate on construction loans at smaller banks is often identical to the permanent mortgage rate, or at most a percentage point above it. When making construction loans, community banks normally rely on outside specialists for assistance in legal matters, document preparation, and fact-finding, whereas large banks maintain in-house staff capabilities for these matters.

At Large Commercial Banks. Large commercial banks, which have traditionally favored short-term loans and investments, most often make only the construction loan on a project, leaving the long-term mortgage to a life insurance company, a pension fund, a savings institution, or some other type of lender. Large banks finance developers who intend to construct sizable residential projects, mostly multifamily, and large commercial projects. Many of these developers are given construction loans on projects that are outside the home state of the lending bank.

Because of the highly specialized nature of construction lending, large banks are more active than small banks in construction lending for large projects. However, large banks hold widely different proportions of their portfolios—from 1 to 10 percent of total deposits—in construction loans. In addition to originating construction loans, many large banks are active in the purchase and sale of construction loan participations. Large banks will often purchase a participation in a construction loan originated by a smaller bank when the size of the original loan is beyond the legal lending limits of the smaller bank.

The Analysis of a Construction Loan Application. Although a construction loan is secured primarily by real estate, the analysis of an application begins with the applicant himself—the developer. If a lender has had no previous experience with a developer, a dossier is prepared to arrive at an informed opinion of the developer's ability and reputation. The important components of the analysis include net worth, completion assurance, feasibility, and source of repayment.

1. *Net worth.* Typically, the balance sheet of an experienced developer will show a net worth composed principally of real estate investments in the form of direct ownership of real estate, stock ownership of real estate corporations, and mortgages. A lender is interested in the liquidity of the assets and the developer's net income from them, and hence the cash flow available for the contemplated construction. It is assumed, of course, that there will be no diversion of these funds into other projects.

2. *Completion assurance.* Although the net worth and the capability of a developer are important, the lender's main goal is to determine whether the developer will have sufficient funds available to complete the job, over and above the amount of the construction loan. When the source of these funds is not readily apparent from an analysis of the figures shown on the developer's financial statements, the lender may insist on the additional protection of a corporate surety bond. Generally this takes the form of two documents, a "Performance Bond" and a "Labor and Material Payment Bond," each written for the total contract price. Taken together, these bonds ensure that the contractor will fulfill his contract and pay all amounts owing for labor and materials. The bonds are usually drawn in favor of the owner. If the lender wants to be included as an insured party, it is necessary to make a specific request to the underwriter.

3. *Feasibility.* After determining what assurances of completion are

available or required, the next step in considering an application is to analyze the feasibility of the project. Often, especially on a large commercial project, a developer will submit with his application a feasibility report which shows the projected gross income and operating expenses of a project. When these figures can be ascertained with a fair degree of accuracy, it will be possible to arrive at a tentative value for the property, based on the net income capitalized at an acceptable rate. When the appraised value exceeds the costs, the lender may issue a commitment for the loan, conditioned upon the fulfillment of other requirements.

4. *The source of repayment.* Another primary concern of a construction lender is the source of repayment for his loan. In many cases a construction loan will not be granted unless a suitable financial institution has given the borrower a prior written commitment to purchase the construction loan or to disburse a new loan upon the completion of the project. This commitment is examined very carefully by the construction lender, since it sets forth the conditions for "taking out" the construction loan. For purposes of his preliminary analysis, a lender will determine whether there is any condition that the developer may be unable to fulfill and whether the expiration date set forth in the commitment will give the developer sufficient time to complete the job. The possibilities of delay caused by strikes, weather, shortages, or tenants' requirements are kept in mind.

5. *Other aspects.* The lender will also pay very close attention to location, plans and specifications, design features, and local amenities, since these affect the ability of the developer to sell or rent the property. Zoning, the reputation of subcontractors, environmental issues, the source and cost of utilities, topography, and the cost of land preparation will also be considered. Construction lending can be very risky business for nonprofessionals. In summary, there is every reason to thoroughly analyze the project, the builder, and the long-term commitment.

The Permanent Takeout Commitment. When the permanent lender does not also make the construction loan, he usually obtains his permanent mortgage on a new income-earning property through a takeout commitment. Through such a commitment, the permanent lender, in consideration of a fee, agrees to become the permanent mortgagee on the property in question, provided that certain conditions are met by the borrower. Should the borrower fail to meet those conditions, then the permanent lender is, of course, not obligated to meet his commitment.

Construction lenders carefully examine the terms of the takeout commitment, and carefully weigh the reputation of the takeout lender, when they are considering whether or not to extend a construction loan on a particular project. Most high-volume bank construction lenders and many low- and intermediate-volume lenders may be willing to make construction loans without takeouts to developers with superior financial strength who have demonstrated their ability to market their product and whose property enjoys a prime location.

Construction Loan Servicing. After the underwriting and the negotiating have been completed, and the commitment has actually been accepted, the initial settlement of the loan occurs. The necessary documentation is executed and recorded, and funds are set aside to pay construction expenses.

Internal bank record keeping is set in motion by placing a checkoff sheet into the loan file. The terms and conditions of the commitment and loan agreement are reviewed, and a tickler system is used if necessary.

Administering a construction loan is not confined to the supervisory responsibility of making advances. Periodic inspections of the project are usually made by a designated individual from the construction loan department of the lending institution. Periodic advances are made from the loan fund on the inspector's approval. It is not unusual for developers to make changes in plans and specifications from time to time. These change orders must receive approvals from both the construction lender and the long-term lender.

Holding back a portion of the amounts due subcontractors and materials suppliers to ensure loan repayment is a common practice in the building industry. A general rule followed is that holdbacks, agreements for deferment of payments, acceptance of notes, and the like, should not be for an amount greater than the portion of the contract price that represents the profit of the subcontractor or the materials supplier. In any event, the developer must satisfy the lender that he will be able to meet all of the costs, both direct and indirect, that are necessary to complete the project.

Long-Term Loans

Residential. Commercial banks recognize that residential home mortgages are a major means of meeting community needs. For most community banks, the residential home mortgage is the most important type of real estate lending. At the end of 1976, banks held $94 billion in residential loans and were the second largest originators of such loans on a nationwide basis.

Four main types of residential loans are extended by commercial banks: conventional loans, FHA loans, VA loans, and construction loans. A *conventional real estate loan* is any loan secured by real estate that the lender makes without benefit of government insurance or guaranty. The term *conventional* includes loans insured by private insuring agencies, where the loan-to-value ratio exceeds the limitations set by banking laws or policies. An *FHA real estate loan* is any loan secured by residential real estate in which the lender is insured by the Federal Housing Administration. The borrower, the property, and the loan must comply with requirements that have been established by FHA. A *VA real estate loan* is any loan secured by real estate and made to an eligible veteran in which a portion of the loan is guaranteed by the Veterans Administration. The veteran, the property, and the loan must meet the requirements of the VA. A *real estate construction loan* is any loan secured by real estate on which partial disbursements are made during the construction period. Such a loan may be arranged on a long-term conventional basis, on an FHA or VA basis, or on a short-term loan basis.

The two main elements that affect the mortgage risks for a single-family dwelling are the real estate that has been placed as security for the loan and the credit of the borrower. Some authorities contend that the uncertainties of the market for single-family dwellings justifies placing greater weight on the credit of the borrower as security for the loan. The alternative view holds that the possible deterioration in the borrower's financial status over the life of a mortgage justifies paying greater attention to the marketability of the real estate. Both of these views receive full consideration from the bank lending officer.

Industrial. Financing industrial property is more complex than financing residential or commercial property. In this type of financing, judging the mortgage pattern calls for special knowledge of industrial location and industrial technology and for a more intensive review of borrower credit.

The borrower of funds secured by industrial real estate generally has three options. First, he may negotiate a conventional mortgage. Here the alternatives include combinations of conventional financing and subsidies granted by federal, state, and local organizations. A desire to increase local employment leads to subsidies that are not available to nonindustrial borrowers. Second, he may place a direct loan. Loans granted on this basis are secured by the credit of the borrower and not merely by the real estate. Third, he may make use of a sale leaseback. In each of these options, credit analysis follows the same general pattern.

The mortgage risks associated with industrial properties, many of which are highly specialized, require more than the usual care in judging the credit of the borrower. This is where a bank capitalizes on its technical industrial knowledge. Its review of borrower credit starts with an analysis of the company and its financial capacity. Related information covers the history of management, including the background of company leaders, the effect of mergers, subsidiaries, the location of branch plants and their degree of modernization. Banks rely not only on written statements from the company but on the reports of Standard & Poor's and of Dun and Bradstreet. Location and building design analysis are also considered. Special care is taken in reviewing financial statements. Great importance is placed on historical analysis, since financial ratios may change quite rapidly. However, financial ratios are reviewed to determine a loan applicant's ability to service the mortgage. Ideally, balance sheets and profit- and loss statements should cover a minimum of five years.

Shopping Centers. Leading authorities regard the professionally developed shopping center as a superior investment. The rent schedule compensates for inflation, and shopping center investments create cash flow. The economics of shopping centers favor their continued growth.

For this type of property, bankers reduce risk by detailed financial analysis. In most respects, the criteria applied to shopping centers rest on objective income and expense data that are not always available for single-family dwellings or industrial properties. Shopping center analysis is unusually complex, and the expert in this field possesses some knowledge of shopping center architecture and planning. The economics of retailing, forecasting techniques, and mortgage finance are part of the typical analysis.

Errors on shopping center mortgages can be minimized by a careful review of four items: (1) retail sales forecasting, (2) site characteristics, (3) shopping center management, and (4) tenant selection. Although the bank loan officer ordinarily does not undertake these detailed studies, a review of the data will help the loan officer to judge the competence of feasibility studies.

Shopping center financing may vary significantly from conventional, first-mortgage financing. At the outset, interim financing and long-term permanent loans are unlikely without provision of a key tenant lease. By the same token, letters of commitment are withheld until legal fees, architectural fees, and land controls have been arranged. Financing a shopping center requires land acquisition, the presentation of the loan proposal, and special financing techniques.

Other Types of Real Estate Loans

Mortgage Warehousing Loans. Interim loans by commercial banks to nonbank lenders are often designated as "mortgage inventory" loans. Bankers commonly identify as "inventory loans" the loans they make on securities that are being underwritten by an investment banker while the securities are being prepared for sale and distribution to individuals and financial institutions that buy them for investment portfolios. The mortgage inventory loans made by banks serve exactly the same purpose for the mortgage banker, as he requires financing to expedite the origination, sale, and distribution of his mortgages to permanent investors. The practice of granting such loans has been called "mortgage warehousing." The notion of warehousing arises from the temporary nature of the advance as the mortgage passes from its originator to the ultimate lender.

There are two general types of warehousing loans that are made directly to mortgage bankers: the committed-technical and the uncommitted-technical. The more common type is the "committed-technical" warehousing loan. Under this arrangement, the commercial bank simply makes a loan to the mortgage banker to provide financing between the time of payment for construction and the time when he can deliver perfected mortgages to the permanent investor. This loan is supported by a prior commitment of the investor to purchase the mortgages when completed. Numerous procedural details must be handled before the mortgage is ready for purchase. The time required, including the time needed to assemble mortgages in the proper amounts, is usually five to six months. The amount of the warehousing loan is usually based upon the commitment of the permanent investor. The lending bank limits its loan to the amount of the commitment or slightly less than that amount.

The uncommitted-technical warehousing loan, differs from the committed-technical loan only in that there is no prior commitment of a permanent investor to take up the loan from the mortgage banker.

Land Development Loans.   In earlier times, landowners had a virtually unrestricted right to use and dispose of their property as they saw fit. Today, although the institution of private property in land remains strong, landowners must observe a wide range of land use controls that are administered by federal, state, and local officials. In addition to the relatively new public restrictions on the use of vacant land, the financing techniques that are applied to the development of vacant land differ from the financial techniques that are applied to dwellings and income-producing property.

The risks arising from land development stem from (1) the heavy cost of carrying vacant land, (2) the large sums required for streets and utilities, (3) the lag between the conception of a project and the actual sales. Although other investments may be equally large, money invested in land development is returned only over a relatively long period. Profits may not be realized until a substantial portion of the land has been sold.

In addition, feasibility analyses of subdivisions sometimes rests on shaky grounds. The optimistic projections of developers may lead to new projects, each of which would be highly marketable if it were the only one of its kind under way, but if ten developers reach the same conclusion and proceed with identical projects, the supply may soon outrun even the most optimistic projections of demand. To avoid this danger, developers should check with the local planning office to see what other projects are in process. Even though it may not be possible to forecast the change of supply with reasonable certainty, accurate estimates of demand can be made by analyzing observed trends that affect the real estate market. Such estimates of the demand for land tend to minimize at least part of the risk of land development.

Producers must supply goods to satisfy consumer demands. So, too, must the subdivider produce residential space to meet local demands. Like the producer, he must make sure that he is providing what is actually in demand. For example, he must guard against developing a subdivision of $60,000 lots if the existing demand is for $30,000 lots. Because of the immediate investment that is required to develop a subdivision and because receipts from the sale of subdivided lots are stretched over several years, developers devote considerable attention to judging the site potential. If a site seems adapted to local demand, the next step requires a pro forma income and cost estimate, which is then converted to a projected cash flow over the marketing period.

Though the financial plans for land development may assume many different forms, most such plans could probably be classified into one of four categories: The land contract, the purchase-money mortgage, the option to purchase, and the conventional first mortgage. A separate discussion of the first three of these plans shows how they vary.

1. The land contract is a device that is sometimes used to finance a subdivision. The seller retains title, and the buyer makes a very small downpayment. This device is most likely to be employed if the land is

undergoing a change in use, for example, from farm use to subdivision use; and if subdivision lots may be sold within three or four years. There are certain dangers that arise from the contractual relations between the buyer and the seller. Since the seller retains title, liens placed against the title may prevent the seller from granting free and clear title when the contract is fulfilled. However, the seller also assumes a certain risk in enforcing the terms of the contract if the builder is unsuccessful in disposing of subdivided lots. Given a favorable market, land contracts are a useful means for financing land that is adapted to development.

2. The purchase-money mortgage serves as a substitute for cash—that is, the selling landowner normally agrees to a nominal down payment and accepts a purchase-money mortgage for the balance of the purchase price. Since in most states the purchase-money mortgage does not include a promissory note, the seller is secured only by the value of the real estate pledged. The difference between this arrangement and the land contract lies in the transfer of title. In accepting an equity payment and a purchase-money mortgage, the seller transfers title to the buyer.

3. An option is a right to purchase something within a specified time on stated terms in return for a specified price. The land development option allows the developer to commit land to a project without committing equity funds. It should be noted that under an option the seller does not sell the land immediately. By the same token, the person holding the option has no legal obligation to purchase the land. However, the option gives the buyer time to acquire or develop adjoining property, allowing him to commit the land covered by the option as development progress recommends.

Loans on Farm Real Estate. Commercial banks play a leading role in financing farm real estate. Not only is this an expanding market, but trends in agricultural finance favor farms as long-term security. To see why this is so, we will examine trends in agricultural production, marketing, and processing techniques; land value trends; and the role of banks in agricultural real estate.

Technological changes have created a favorable market for farm real estate credit. A recent study revealed that farmers produced 20 percent more on 56 percent fewer acres than they did ten years earlier and that farm output per worker-hour had increased 82 percent in ten years. The data further showed that farms were becoming larger and more complex. Farm mortgages outstanding increased from $18.8 billion in 1965 to $46.8 billion at the end of the second quarter of 1975—an increase of 148.9 percent. The volume of long-term farm real estate credit will continue to grow primarily because:

1. Farms will continue to substitute capital for labor.
2. Increased farm operating inputs require more capital in herbicides, pesticides, and custom-purchased services (such as crop dusting) that substitute for purchases of machinery.
3. Higher operating expenses, including the high cost of credit, are expected to continue.

4. As farms continue to grow larger, more farm credit will be demanded, since larger farms require more credit than do smaller farms.
5. Farmers are becoming more business minded, and they accept long-term debt as a necessary part of farm operations.

Commercial banks are attracted to farm mortgages because commercial banks have a long-run interest in promoting loans that stimulate local economic growth. To the extent that time deposits continue to grow relative to demand deposits, banks will have a greater supply of credit available for farm mortgages. The participation of commercial banks with federal and intermediate-credit banks acts as a further incentive to invest in long-term farm mortgages. Thus, commercial banks hold $7 billion in farm mortgages directly and provide assistance in the placement of farm mortgages with other investors. To be sure, commercial banks must serve the total capital and credit needs of the community. Consequently, in farming communities the primary thrust is directed toward local short-term and intermediate-term credit needs.

Home Improvement Loans. The commercial banking industry held $4.8 billion of the nation's total of $8.3 billion in home improvement loans in 1975. The typical 1975 home improvement loan averaged $3,000 and required no collateral. Interest rates ran from 10 to 14 percent, with a payback period of five to seven years.

Such loans are generally handled by the commercial bank's installment lending division on a conventional basis. Many banks also offer FHA Title I guaranteed loans at an annual rate fixed by FHA, a fixed maximum of $10,000, and a payback period of up to 12 years. Amounts under $7,000 require no collateral.

Second Mortgages. Another loan type which has been increasing in frequency is the second mortgage. In the 1960s, banks did not favor this type of loan. However, during 1977 such loans were not only acceptable to banks but were being encouraged by them. By and large, a bank making a second-mortgage loan will provide the borrower with the difference between the first-mortgage balance and about 75 percent of the value of the property. Borrowers can use the money to consolidate existing debts, to put children through college, or to undertake home improvement projects. In short, second-mortgage lending is a useful service when families badly need cash for important purposes.

LIFE INSURANCE COMPANIES

• **Thomas F. Murray**

*T*HOMAS F. MURRAY, CRE, Financial and Real Estate Consultant, New York, New York.

Trustee and past president, Urban Land Institute. Formerly executive vice president and chief investment officer, Equitable Life Assurance Society of the United States. Member, Board of Directors, Rockefeller Center, Inc.; Olentangy Management Co.; Allied Stores Corporation; Bank of Tokyo Trust Company, Inc.; and Paine Webber Cashfund, Inc. Chairman, Board of Directors, New York City Public Development Corporation. Trustee, Franklin Savings Bank of New York. Author of numerous articles on transportation and financing.

Availability of Mortgage Money

A typical life insurance company may allocate a portion of its available mortgage investment funds for the current year—and often two to three years ahead—because of the time that is required to complete the construction and leasing that are necessary to qualify for the mortgage advances. These life company investments are normally for the takeout of construction loans by other lenders, since many life companies do not have the facilities to handle construction loans and since life companies often prefer to have other lenders undertake the higher risks of making advances during construction.

The funds available for investment by a life company are those funds that are left after all operating expenses, mortality claims, pension payments under long-term contracts, and previous loan commitments have been provided for. If a life company's existing loan commitments are at a high level, the company tends to be restrictive in its requirements for the approval of new loans, whereas if its loan commitments are low, it tends to seek out new loans. Life company loan commitments are usually lowest after a period of rapid economic growth and high interest rates. During such a period, money tends to get tight and life companies often withdraw from the market until their existing commitments are sharply reduced and money is in better supply. The level of life company commitments may also influence the level of interest rates that are acceptable to such companies, since there is usually some pressure to keep fully invested—especially when the rates available on short-term investments that are made pending advances on long-term mortgages are much lower than the long-term rates.

In allocating overall investment funds, life company investment officers tend to emphasize loans that will provide the best investment yield in relation to appropriate risks. Some companies establish minimum rates, and this often causes them to consider higher-risk loans than they might consider otherwise. There is no clear-cut pattern among the national lenders whose flow of funds tends to keep them in the market at the best rates obtainable.

If mortgage rates are higher than direct placement rates (the rates for corporate debt placed privately, which are usually higher than the rates for public issues of debt securities), then mortgage allocations receive preferred treatment. If the differential is narrow—or nonexistent—then a minimum level of allocation will be set, probably aimed at keeping the organization "in the market" until greater funds are available for it. This is especially true for life companies that have mortgage department employees in the field as well as the home office. Sometimes the need to use up allocations at the year-end will cause a life company to "reach" for loans that might have been unattractive earlier in the year or to lower interest rates in order to attract loans.

In recent years, life company mortgage departments have had difficulty in obtaining interest rates which, after the deduction of operating and servicing expenses, would equal those available from bonds and direct placements. In addition, business corporations have had such great need for borrowings to finance capital and expansion requirements that the interest rates for such loans have often exceeded the rates available on good mortgages. Evidence of shifts in fund allocations can be perceived by following the interest rates for industrial or utility issues as compared to the interest rates for FHA mortgages, GNMA issues, or the mortgage-backed securities issued by lending institutions. The best time to seek mortgage refinancing is when the rates for AA utilities or AAA industrial hit new lows or are sharply depressed from previous levels. It is usually desirable to accomplish refinancing *whenever* additional borrowing is required, since current prepayment terms are designed to restrict refinancing solely for the purpose of obtaining a lower interest rate.

Another reason why life companies have curbed their mortgage fund allocations is that the constant payment plan for the amortization of mortgages does not return funds to the lender nearly as fast as do the fixed principal payments customary for bonds and direct placements. In a period of relatively high inflation, such as we have experienced recently, the lender will seek to get his loans amortized faster to offset the anticipated declining value of the dollar. During recent years many lenders have been unwilling to make a loan for longer than 10 or 15 years without a call provision at 10 or 15 years. (The amortization plan for such loans may, however, be based on a term of 25 years or longer.) More demand for good mortgage investments could easily overcome this lending requirement. It remains to be seen how these call provisions will work out, since they can only be met by refinancing with the same lender or another lender.

The level of prepayment of existing loans has a strong influence on the amount of money that life companies make available for mortgages. When interest rates are rising, there are likely to be few prepayments of loans, whereas when interest rates are falling, the borrower will often refinance the outstanding amount on his mortgage with another lender. During a "tight money" market, such as existed in 1973, prepayments are largely nonexistent, thereby greatly reducing the amount of money that is available for new investment by all long-term lenders.

For most life companies, policy loans (loans by policyholders on their policies) have become a way of life. During "easy money" periods, such loans are not a disturbing factor. However, in "tight money" markets, policy loans can interfere with the supply of funds that is available for other investments. For example, the volume of policy loans for 15 of the major life insurance companies increased from $2.04 billion in 1972 to $2.83 billion in 1973 and to $3.29 billion in 1974. Thus in two years there was a decrease of $1.25 billion in the funds that these companies had available for other investments. Some insurance companies used up their entire cash flow to meet policy loan requirements. Since the right to borrow against the cash surrender value of a life insurance policy is contractual, all life companies provide these funds as a number one priority. The growing demand for policy loans has been especially disheartening to investment officers, since the bulk of such loans are at 5 or 6 percent, or much less than the market rates that have been available on other investments in recent years.

Much of the money that life companies invested in mortgages in recent years was used to fund construction loans by other interim lenders. For sizable projects, this usually meant that the commitment to invest was made two to three years in advance of the actual investment. This is necessary because interim lenders usually require a permanent loan commitment before they will advance a construction loan. The system can hamper mortgage investment when a life insurance company has an unusually heavy inflow of investment funds. That occurred during 1975–76, when the insurance companies received substantial pension funds because many pension fund managers had become disenchanted with their investments in common stock. Since pension funds must be invested promptly, long-term mortgage commitments were not the way. Such funds will be directed to mortgages only if the funds can be advanced quickly. Otherwise the money will flow into the bond and direct placement market (where the investment can be advanced and start earning within a few months) or into publicly marketed bonds (where the investment can be advanced and start earning immediately upon approval). This situation did result in lower interest rates on mortgages that were available for immediate delivery, as compared to the interest rates on long-term mortgage commitments.

Over the years, however, the growth in the total assets of life insurance companies has been a steady source of new money for investment. As Table 1 shows, the total assets of U.S. life insurance companies increased more than sevenfold from 1945 to 1976. This great growth in assets has produced substantial growth in the various investment classifications. Table 2 shows that growth by type of assets from 1966 to 1976.

TABLE 1
Assets of U.S. Life Insurance Companies

1945	$ 44,497,000,000
1950	64,020,000,000
1955	90,432,000,000
1960	119,000,000,000
1965	158,000,000,000
1970	207,254,000,000
1975	289,304,000,000
1976	321,552,000,000

Source: American Council of Life Insurance.

The net growth (advances less repayments) of the major investment classifications during the same years is shown in Table 3, and the new mortgage investments mode by life insurance companies during those years are shown in Table 4.

The results shown in Table 4 include an increasing emphasis of life insurance companies on commercial mortgages, because of the better yields available, at the expense of a declining emphasis on home mortgages. The state usury statutes and the aggressive attitude of savings and loan associations and mutual savings banks have practically eliminated insurance companies as a source of home financing. It will be further noted from Tables 2 and 3 that the bond classification leads both in absolute dollars and in percentage growth. At the same time bonds barely increased as a percentage of total assets, from 36.32 percent to 37.53 percent, whereas mortgages declined from 38.58 percent to 28.47 percent of total assets.

A comment on the growth of the real estate held by life insurance companies is warranted by the concerns that are often expressed that insurance companies will soon own all of the real estate in America. During the period covered by Table 2—a very strong development period for commercial real estate—the growth in the real estate holdings of insurance companies was $5.591 billion. Although this is a large sum, it is really only a "token" part of the total growth in real estate holdings, and it is an even smaller part of the total value of real estate.

TABLE 2
Distribution of Assets of U.S. Life Insurance Companies (000,000 omitted)

Year	Government Securities	Corporate Securities		Mortgages	Real Estate	Policy Loans	Miscellaneous	Total
		Bonds	Stocks					
1966	$11,396	$ 60,819	$ 8,832	$64,609	$ 4,885	$ 9,117	$ 7,797	$167,455
1967	11,079	64,487	10,877	67,516	5,187	10,059	8,427	177,832
1968	11,096	68,310	13,230	69,973	5,571	11,406	9,150	188,636
1969	10,914	70,859	13,707	72,027	5,912	13,825	9,964	197,208
1970	11,068	73,098	15,420	74,375	6,320	16,064	10,909	207,254
1971	11,000	79,198	20,607	75,496	6,904	17,065	11,832	222,102
1972	11,372	86,140	26,845	76,948	7,295	18,003	13,127	239,730
1973	11,403	92,796	25,919	81,369	7,693	20,199	14,057	252,436
1974	11,956	96,652	21,920	86,234	8,331	22,862	15,385	263,349
1975	15,177	105,837	28,061	89,167	9,621	24,467	16,974	289,304
1976	20,260	120,666	34,262	91,552	10,476	25,834	18,502	321,552

Source: American Council of Life Insurance.

TABLE 3
Net Increase in Assets of U.S. Life Insurance Companies, 1966–1976 (000,000 omitted)

Government securities . . .	$ 8,864	5.75%
Bonds	59,847	48.84
Stocks	25,430	16.50
Mortgages	26,943	17.48
Real estate	5,591	3.63
Policy loans	16,717	10.85
Miscellaneous assets	10,705	6.95
Total	$154,097	100.00%

TABLE 4
New Mortgage Investment of U.S. Life Insurance Companies (000,000 omitted)

1966	$10,217
1967	8,470
1968	7,925
1970	7,531
1971	7,181
1972	7,573
1973	8,696
1974	11,463
1975	11,339
1976	9,801

Mortgage Loan Policies

Mortgage loan approvals by a life insurance company reflect the investment policies adopted by that company. Although there is a thread of similarity among the investment policies of life insurance companies, the investment policies of an individual life company are influenced by a number of factors, which include:

1. The location of the home office.
2. The relative size of the company.
3. The portion of the company's assets that is identified with pensions and annuities.
4. The portion of the company's assets that is identified with casualty insurance operations.
5. The states in which life insurance sales are important.

Insurance companies are strongly conscious of their role in their community and region. As a result, a regional company might show a greater interest in a local proposal than might be shown by a more distant national company. As a potential borrower, you can identify your local insurance companies by writing to the state insurance department. Usually your local bank can advise you of the names of life insurance companies that are active in your area.

The size of the life company often determines how large a loan it can consider. For example, a life company with $1 billion in assets might limit its maximum loan to $5–$7½ million, whereas the five largest companies could accommodate loans of almost any size. Although the largest life companies can and do seek loans smaller than a million dollars, such loans are almost sure to receive greater attention from the smaller life companies.

Life company mortgage policies usually recognize four main types of properties:

1. Homes.
2. Farms
3. Income or commercial properties.
4. Special-purpose properties.

For many years, home mortgage loans were a fundamental part of the investment plans of all life companies. FHA and VA loans as well as conventional loans were important and attractive outlets for life company investment funds. In recent years, however, when mortgage rates rose strongly, along with bond and direct placement rates, residential rates were limited by usury ceilings in most states. (New York State at this writing still has an 8½ percent usury limit for home mortgages despite the higher level that is permitted for other mortgages.) As a result, many insurance companies abandoned the home mortgage market during the years when other mortgage rates rose to 8, 9, and 10 percent, or higher. This has not seriously hampered home-financing, for this has long been provided largely by S&Ls, mutual savings banks, and some commercial banks.

Farm loans are made by some insurance companies, but because of the wide variety of farm properties—grain farms; cattle ranches; cotton, peanut, cranberry, and other food-producing acreages; citrus farms; timber farms; and many other types—a specially trained organization is required to originate and service such loans. Many life companies tend to concentrate on other types of property, especially since farm loans are usually made to individuals and are accordingly subject to the limitations of usury statutes. Those life companies which have farm investments have found that the sharply escalating acreage values have provided them with larger and larger margins and often default-free portfolios in recent years.

Most life companies emphasize investment in income or commercial properties. These include apartment houses, retail stores and shopping centers, office buildings, hotels, and industrial plants and warehouses. Such properties lend themselves to the appraisal approach to value in which the predictable net income is capitalized. Many of these properties have tenant leases for 5–10 years, and often up to 20–25 years or longer. The loan underwriting, therefore, often utilizes the credit of the tenant in addition to the property itself. If the leases contain escalation clauses for operating expenses and taxes, then the loan risks may be further minimized. Hotels and motels are popular with some life companies and unacceptable to others. However, a lease, or possibly a management contract with a national hotel chain, will often help to obtain financing acceptance.

Some life companies will consider investment in special-purpose properties. Such properties are usually constructed to meet a specific need—with little possibility of alternative use. Hospitals, some manufacturing plants, most mart buildings, and truck terminals are illustrative of properties in this class. Such properties are usually financeable only if they are occupied by a user who has adequate credit strength to overcome the handicap of a low "alternative use" value.

There are no clear-cut life company sources for financing specialty properties—such as retirement homes, automobile agencies, and truck terminals. At any given time, what life-company sources are available depends on the lending experience of the life company—both recent and long term—and on its appetite for mortgage investment.

Most insurance companies do not routinely make construction loans (though a few of the larger insurance companies are advisers to real estate investment trusts, which would ordinarily be interested in construction financing)—only loans based on the completion of construction. Construction loans require a source—typically a commercial bank—that is willing to make the construction advances if there is a firm takeout permanent loan commitment. Many long-term life company lenders utilize a three-party agreement which requires the interim lender to deliver the mortgage to the permanent lender upon meeting the requirements contained in the permanent commitment. Often the same mortgage papers can be used for both lenders, which provides a savings in legal expenses. Takeout commitments are usually drawn by the attorneys for the lender, and the forms are generally similar for the different lenders. Variations are designed to meet the specific conditions of each loan.

In addition to conventional life company mortgage loans, where the loan-to-value ratio is generally 75 percent, higher loan ratios may be achieved if the property is leased on a net basis to a tenant with strong credit. For such loans, the credit of the tenant must be strong enough to meet prescribed earnings tests. This is equivalent to the strength that is adequate to qualify him for unsecured debenture borrowing from a life company. For these limited cases, financing of 90 percent or higher may be attainable if the borrower is willing to absorb additional legal expenses.

To comply with statutory requirements, commercial mortgage loans must meet the loan-to-value ratio (typically not in excess of 75 percent) prescribed by the state law that is applicable for the property. Some life companies have their own appraisal staff—others require the borrower to absorb the cost of an appraisal made by an independent appraiser selected by the lender. The property must be improved (not vacant) land, and it must be income producing. The mortgage must be for the first lien on the property, and clear title acceptable to the lender is called for. Most life company lenders require the assignment of important leases to the lender. Fire and other casualty insurance in amounts acceptable to the lender must be provided. In recent years, some life company lenders are requiring proof that the property meets environmental and zoning requirements.

Most life company lenders require a signed application in which the applicant agrees to stated terms if, the application is approved by the lender's investment committee. Often a "good faith" deposit is required. This is forfeited if the lender approves the application but the applicant decides not to go through with the loan. The applicant usually agrees to absorb the legal costs for having the loan closed by counsel selected by the lender. There may be a standby fee to compensate the lender for earmarking the closing funds until the loan can be advanced. Key items in the application are the terms of repayment and the borrower's options for full or partial prepayment.

One other development is worth mentioning. As project construction costs have soared, it has become more difficult for developers to obtain large enough loans to supplement their often meager supply of "hard dollar" equity. This has resulted in joint ventures in which the lender receives an agreed-upon percentage of the net income of the property as well as part ownership of the property. Usually the developer continues to manage the property for an agreed-upon fee. Sometimes the lender receives a preferred share of the income and the balance is split between the parties.

In the negotiation of a joint venture, the life company will usually provide most of the cash dollars needed for a project in excess of a normal mortgage amount. In exchange for this additional risk exposure, it expects a higher rate of return than that for the mortgage on the property. The developer, on his part, contributes his know-how and experience in putting the project together so that tenants secured by him help assure the success of the project. He must deal with local zoning and other problems, including environmental and construction hazards. These entitle him to a part of the earnings even though his cash investment may be minimal. The split of the earnings, and of ownership and tax benefits too, are usually agreed upon after intense bargaining.

Obtaining a Mortgage Loan

Financing for home loans is usually obtained in the local market—in many cases the broker who sells the home helps the purchaser to obtain mortgage financing if he does not have his own preferred source. This procedure is followed to a limited extent for small farm loans.

For larger loans in the farm and income property classifications, consideration must be given to selecting the proper lenders—often lenders that are located far away from a property. It is, however, usually desirable to consider regional life companies because these typically will have a greater interest in financing properties in their service territory than will distant lenders.

At this point it may be desirable to point out that insurance companies differ from one another in how they originate and service mortgage loans. Some companies concentrate their mortgage staff in headquarters—whereas others have dispersed branch offices which process all mortgage applications in their assigned territories. Some companies operate through the correspondent system. In this system the company selects real estate firms to represent it and to originate and service loans for it in the areas where it is desirous of obtaining mortgage investments. Some of these correspondent firms often represent a number of insurance companies; others may be retained on an exclusive basis.

In all of the above systems, most life companies will accept applications that meet their requirements from any of the local, regional, and national real estate brokers and investment bankers. When such an application is filed, complete information about the property that is to be security for the loan should be provided. The names of architects, contractors, engineers, and leasing agents will lend credence to the application. Any previous experience that the applicant has had with similar or other properties should be stated. Good photos help. It can be most helpful if the application is submitted to the life company office which has jurisdiction over the area in which the property is located.

Whether or not an intermediary is engaged to assist the owner in obtaining an acceptable mortgage, the first step is to select a life company lender that is most likely to be interested in the offering. Most applicants do not want their application to be widely "shopped" simultaneously, but informal inquiries can be discreetly made before a formal presentation or application is made to a lender that has been identified as a most likely source.

Once an application has been filed and accepted by an insurance company, it is processed. The processing usually includes: inspection of the site; a review of the plans and specifications, an appraisal of the property, which would include a review of competitive properties; and an analysis of the offering versus similar properties. If the application meets these tests it will be presented for approval to the investment committee of the life company having jurisdiction over this type and size of loan. Many life companies have delegated authority to approve loans up to a maximum amount, for example, to a department or qualified person who can act for the company. The delegated amount will vary with the size of the company and the importance of the office. One major life company delegates to its field offices the authority to approve loans of up to $2 million—provided that the loan has no unusual features and that the category is one which has a good volume potential—usually throughout all the states. Examples of such categories are apartment houses, retail stores, and industrial properties. It is not unusual for a life company to renegotiate the applied-for amount or terms anywhere in the processing operation. The applicant must then decide whether the offered amount and terms are satisfactory or whether he should seek his loan at another institution.

If an acceptable loan is approved by a life company, the file is turned over to a lawyer so that he can issue a commitment to the applicant. Sometimes the applicant finds that the commitment contains require-

TABLE 5
Money and Capital Markets (in $ billions)

	1966	1973	1974	1975	1976*
Life insurance companies	$ 8.4	$ 15.9	$ 15.6	$ 19.0	$ 25.9
Private nonlife insurance company pension funds	6.3	7.8	8.1	13.8	13.4
State and local retirement funds	4.2	9.1	9.0	11.1	13.5
Savings and loan associations	4.2	27.5	20.8	35.3	53.1
Mutual savings banks	2.7	5.4	3.0	10.8	13.1
Commercial banks	18.2	83.4	62.2	29.4	46.9
Federal Reserve banks	3.5	9.2	6.2	8.5	9.8
Federal loan agencies	8.3	13.3	27.1	31.0	28.9
Nonfinancial corporations	0.8	15.7	12.1	16.6	29.0
Fire and casualty companies	2.5	5.7	4.4	4.7	7.7
Real estate investment trusts	—	5.6	0.7	−5.4	−3.4
Mutual funds	2.5	−2.5	−0.8	−0.5	−1.8
Foreigners	−1.9	3.5	11.7	10.8	16.2
Individuals and others	16.0	36.8	41.6	40.5	30.0
Total	$75.7	$236.4	$221.7	$225.6	$282.3

* Preliminary.
Source: American Council of Life Insurance.

ments that he had not expected to find in it or that he cannot accept—though this is rarely the case, since most key points have probably been covered in negotiating and processing the application.

Upon the issuance of a commitment and its acceptance by the applicant, the life company usually instructs local counsel to prepare the mortgage papers, order a title search, and submit all papers for its approval. It is important that the applicant keep the life company informed of the date on which he will be prepared to close the mortgage so that the closing can be properly scheduled by all concerned.

Role in U.S. Money and Capital Markets

Life insurance companies, because of their continued growth in assets and because of their ability to study and analyze unusual as well as routine applications for financing, have become increasingly important as a source of capital for mortgages and other financing. This role is indicated in Table 5.

Although life insurance companies are not the largest source of funds in the capital markets, they are increasingly important in the financing of both unusual and large projects. They have staffs with national experience, and they are usually interested in new outlets for their steadily increasing supply of funds.

REAL ESTATE INVESTMENT TRUSTS

Gary Alan Brown

GARY ALAN BROWN, BA, JD, Associate Counsel, National Association of Real Estate Investment Trusts, Inc., Washington, D.C. Managing editor of Middle East Executive Reports, *assistant editor,* Securities Regulation and Law Reports, *published by BNA, and research assistant for the Commission on the Revision of the Federal Appellate System. Member, Colorado and District of Columbia bar. Author, weekly articles in* Securities Regulation and Law Reports *and numerous articles for the American Enterprise Institute,* Boulder Camera, Denver Post, *and* National VFW Magazine. *Author,* For REITs–Corporate Conversion: What's Involved? *(Washington, D.C.: NAREIT).*

REITs represent one of the newest of the major American financial institutions to specialize in real estate investment in response to special tax privileges. By issuing shares, bonds, and commercial paper and by borrowing from other financial institutions, REITs serve as an intermediary for funds from financial markets to income-producing real estate, thereby offering an investment medium which pools funds in a professionally managed portfolio of properties and loans secured by real estate. Earnings are passed through to shareholders without taxation at the corporate (or trust) level due to conduit tax treatment similar to that for mutual funds.

To qualify for exemption from state and federal taxes, a REIT must first elect to be nontaxed and then must meet various tests. At least 90 percent (95 percent as of 1980) of the trust's net taxable income must be paid out to shareholders. More than 75 percent of the trust's assets must be in investments related to real estate (including mortgages), in cash, or in government securities, and more than 75 percent of its income must be derived from real estate investments. REITs do not seek only tax-sheltered investments; they also seek real estate investments that provide maximum cash return with potential long-term appreciation.

Within the confines of these basic requirements, REITs exhibit wide differences in structure, portfolio management, and investment objectives. Perhaps the most extreme difference is in their investment strategies—REITs hold portfolios whose composition varies widely between property ownership and mortgage loans. Trusts specializing in property ownership are often referred to as equity trusts, whereas those at the other extreme are called mortgage trusts, even though most own some properties. Portfolio composition is a matter of choice, and in many instances the choice depends upon a trust's perception of what sort of investment offers the greatest profit at the time that it has money to invest. Between extremes are a large number of combination, or hybrid, trusts that hold both mortgage and properties.

Beyond this simple distinction, trusts often specialize within these broad investment categories. For mortgage trusts, there has traditionally been a preference for short-run construction and development loans (C&D loans). Other trusts have a mixture of interim loans, wraparound loans, long-term mortgages, and junior mortgages as well as C&D loans. Some trusts choose to lend only on certain types of properties (e.g., shopping centers, office buildings, etc.) and may further specialize in terms of geographic areas. Equally diverse investment preferences characterize those trusts that concentrate on property ownership or on a combination of ownership and lending.

REIT Management and Organization

There are three important entities to be considered in analyzing REIT management and organizations: (1) trustees, (2) investment advisers, and (3) independent contractors.

All REITs have trustees who are elected by, and are responsible to, the shareholders of the REIT, in a manner similar to that of a corporate board of directors. The trustees determine the trust's investment policies, oversee the trust's asset and liability management, and approve trust loans and investments. To accomplish their tasks, the trustees often organize into one or more specialized committees, such as an investment committee or an executive committee.

Many REITs contract with an investment adviser to run the trust's day-to-day operations and to present investment opportunities to it. The investment advisers are often affiliates of banks, mortgage banking firms, insurance companies, or real estate organizations, and they are usually part of the management group that originally set up the trust. Although the adviser is organizationally separate from the trust, trusts frequently derive their names from those of advisers or parent organizations. Thus, the ABC Realty Investors is run by the ABC Advisory Company, which is a subsidiary of the ABC Bank or Insurance Company.

The role and the fees of the adviser vary from trust to trust. Some trust advisers, for example, prefer to deal directly with borrowers or with purchasers and sellers of property, and thus have large nationwide staffs to do so. Others deal with borrowers, purchasers, and sellers solely through correspondent relationships with other firms. Advisory services typically include administering the daily operations of the REIT, serving as the REIT's agent in purchases and sales and other dispositions of the trust's investments, and obtaining or providing the services for property management, mortgage servicing, construction loan disbursement, and other activities related to the investment portfolio.

Management by an investment adviser is not a prerequisite of REIT status. A number of smaller trusts (primarily equity trusts) have not had advisers since their inception. Other trusts began their existence with advisers but later elected to terminate their advisory agreements and to operate without advisers. In such cases, the advisory functions are performed by employees of the trust where possible.

The activities of trust personnel—whether on the adviser's staff or on the trust's payroll—are limited by the requirement in the Internal Revenue Code that a REIT not manage or operate properties directly. Thus, if a REIT owns properties, it can either lease out the properties to others who will operate them or it can hire an independent contractor to manage the properties. The management of properties by an independent contractor includes general maintenance activities, such as supplying utilities, cleaning, and repair work. The independent contractor may also solicit and screen prospective tenants, but the trustees still have the authority to approve tenants or to establish rental terms. The important point is that trustees are not required to contract out their fiduciary duty to manage the trust itself, as distinguished from furnishing services to the tenants of properties.

An investment adviser cannot serve as the independent contractor

EXHIBIT 1
REIT Assets by Type of Adviser

Category	Number of REITs	Total Assets ($ millions)	Percentage of Industry Assets
Commercial bank	32	$ 3,412.6	23.4%
Independent mortgage banker, broker, or real estate–oriented company	35	1,938.9	13.3
Adviser owned by individuals	23	880.2	6.0
Conglomerate	10	856.2	5.9
Life insurance company	9	1,679.3	11.5
No adviser	87	5,200.5	35.7
Other, including unknown	23	590.1	4.1
Totals	219	$14,557.8	100.0%

In many instances, indirect ties, overlaps, and partial ownership of the adviser impede efforts to place an adviser in any one category. Any REIT whose adviser was at least 50 percent owned by a bank; a bank holding company, or a bank holding company subsidiary was considered to fall into the "commercial bank" category. Similar yardsticks were employed in classifying REITs into the other categories of adviser affiliation.

to manage the REIT properties, although under certain circumstances the adviser can set up an affiliate to serve in this capacity. (See Exhibit 1 for a breakdown of REIT assets by type of adviser.)

The Recent History of REITs

Much of the earlier growth of REITs (total REIT assets nearly doubled each year between 1968 and 1973) was attributable to increases in land development and construction loans and in the number of trusts that specialized in such loans. However, the combination of overbuilding, recession, high interest rates, and inflation that characterized the real estate market from 1974 to 1976 had a marked impact upon REITs; short-term mortgage loans outstanding have since declined to less than half of the 1973 level.

At this writing, the industry is still in the process of working its way out of the recession, and if anything, the diversity within the industry is greater than it was in the past. Many trusts have ceased making new commitments for lending altogether and are concentrating their efforts and resources toward restoring existing assets to an earnings status. A number of trusts continued to make investments during the real estate recession of 1974–75, and these have since been joined by other trusts that are now back in the market in response to the real estate recovery that began in 1976. Currently, between 40 and 50 trusts are investing in real estate loans and properties.

The investment patterns are, however, somewhat different from those of the past, with many trusts now orienting their future growth toward property ownership. Nonetheless, more than 20 trusts are now making mortgage loans. The number of trusts that are actively lending should continue to grow in the future as the problems of the past few years are resolved. (See Exhibit 2 for financial data on the leading REITs.)

REIT Investment Patterns

Property Ownership. REIT property holdings center on such structures as apartment houses, shopping centers, office buildings, warehouses, and light industrial centers. In evaluating possible investments, REITs look for high rental income as well as appreciation of property values or possibilities for increased future rental income. (See Exhibit 3 for a breakdown of REIT assets.)

REIT property holdings tend to be on a long-term basis. If a trust buys and sells property in a short period, as a dealer instead of an investor, it faces a tax of 100 percent on any gain realized. This 100 percent tax is designed to discourage REITs from developing properties and selling them shortly after completion, as real estate developers might. The sale of property held for long-term investment is not subject to the 100 percent tax, but to the usual taxes on long-term capital gains.

An exception to this rule applies where a REIT acquires properties by foreclosing on a mortgage or by receiving a deed in lieu of foreclosure. The REIT may then characterize such property as foreclosure property

EXHIBIT 2

REIT Industry Investment Review

March, 1979

Compiled by the Research Department of NAREIT

In February—

REIT Share Price Index Shows Slight Decline

The NAREIT share price index declined by less than 1% to 28.04 during February from the previous month's value. The February index remains some 4.9% above the corresponding 1978 level. During the month, 68 shares declined, 57 advanced and 37 remained unchanged.

Included in the decline were San Francisco Real Estate, down 1%; Connecticut General Mortgage and Realty, −1¼; Hotel Investors, −1¼; and U.S. BanTrust, −1.

Shares advancing during the month included C.I. Realty Investors, up 2%; General Growth, +1¾; Baird and Warner, +1½; Franklin Realty, +1½; H.S. Miller Trust +1½; and U.S. Equity, +1.

Total first quarter distributions are estimated to be $42.5 million for the 75 dividend-paying trusts, up 6% from the previous quarter. The first quarter total reflects announced increases in the regular dividends of 21 trusts so far. Total distributions have reached their highest level since early 1975.

NAREIT Share Price Index

(January, 1972 = 100)

	1976	1977	1978	1979
January	21.04	24.36	26.39	28.21
February	22.93	24.13	26.72	28.04
March	21.58	24.03	28.00	
April	21.15	24.73	28.36	
May	20.29	24.29	27.60	
June	20.40	25.03	27.35	
July	20.74	26.03	28.13	
August	20.89	26.28	30.42	
September	21.05	25.94	30.60	
October	20.81	25.20	25.90	
November	21.89	27.81	25.60	
December	24.30	27.46	26.00	

Source: The month-end price of REITs traded on the New York Stock Exchange, the American Stock Exchange and the national O-T-C market.

Most Recent Financial Data of 50 Largest Trusts by Market Value

Market Value Ranking	Asset Ranking	Trust Name	Date of Data	Assets	Shareholders' Equity	Market Value	MV/SE	Share Price Last Month 2/28/79	Annualized Distribution*	Market Yield*
					($ mil)					
1	4	GENERAL GROWTH	9/78	$363.8	$ 37.3	$179.1	4.80	$28.875	$ 1.56	5.40%
2	2	EQUITABLE LIFE	1/79	$400.8	$132.5	$101.2	0.76	$17.875	$ 2.00	11.19%
3	5	CONN GENERAL	12/78	$339.1	$108.1	$ 98.7	0.91	$17.250	$ 1.80	10.43%
4	7	CONT ILL PROP	10/78	$283.4	$ 94.0	$ 78.6	0.84	$16.375	$ 1.36	8.31%
5	13	MONY MTG INV	11/78	$236.8	$ 87.4	$ 71.6	0.82	$ 8.000	$ 0.92	11.50%
6	32	HUBBARD REAL EST	10/78	$102.4	$ 99.1	$ 67.1	0.68	$15.750	$ 1.60	9.55%
7	18	MASSMUTUAL MTG	10/78	$191.2	$ 92.7	$ 53.6	0.69	$13.625	$ 1.36	9.98%
8	6	LOMAS & NETTLETON	12/78	$284.4	$103.0	$ 62.0	0.60	$16.750	$ 1.96	11.70%
9	21	CONSOLIDATED CAP	11/78	$135.4	$ 34.4	$ 53.7	1.54	$27.000	$ 2.06	7.63%
10	17	FIRST UNION	10/78	$205.7	$ 48.0	$ 47.7	0.99	$11.125	$ 1.08	9.71%

#	#	Company	Date							
11	15	WELLS FARGO	12/78	$217.2	$69.4	$47.0	0.68	$12.000	$1.20	10.00%
12	12	NTHWSTN MTL LIFE	12/78	$239.8	$90.7	$45.8	0.50	$9.625	$1.00	10.39%
13	11	SAIL,B F REIT	12/78	$252.1	$29.3	$42.0	1.43	$7.125	N.A.	N.A.
14	25	C I REALTY	11/78	$117.1	$43.3	$40.8	0.94	$15.625	$0.10	0.54%
15	19	BANKAMERICA	10/78	$171.0	$60.3	$40.3	0.67	$11.375	$1.00	8.79%
16	89	WASH REIT	9/78	$44.6	$17.3	$34.2	1.97	$22.500	$1.88	8.36%
17	53	UNITED REALTY TR	8/78	$77.6	$63.6	$31.6	0.50	$8.750	$0.80	9.14%
18	28	DIVERSIFIED MTG	9/78	$108.9	$61.8	$31.1	0.50	$4.250	N.A.	N.A.
19	82	REAL EST INV TR AM	11/78	$48.0	$35.5	$26.3	0.74	$15.125	$1.40	8.56%
20	60	MTG TRUST AMER	8/78	$71.7	$49.8	$26.1	0.52	$5.750	N.A.	N.A.
21	50	HOTEL INVESTORS	11/78	$81.7	$27.3	$25.9	0.95	$16.500	$1.80	10.91%
22	65	SAN FRANCISCO REI	12/78	$64.8	$27.4	$25.6	0.93	$18.625	$1.60	8.59%
23	34	REALTY & MTG PAC	11/78	$100.2	$34.5	$25.3	0.73	$13.375	$1.40	10.47%
24	54	ICM REALTY	8/78	$77.3	$45.5	$24.8	0.55	$9.250	$0.50	6.10%
25	121	NEW PLAN REALTY	7/78	$24.7	$6.8	$24.4	3.59	$9.625	$0.78	8.10%
26	59	PENNSYLVANIA REIT	8/78	$74.1	$20.0	$24.3	1.21	$16.000	$1.45	9.06%
27	27	SECURITY MTG	9/78	$109.4	$40.4	$23.5	0.58	$3.625	N.A.	N.A.
28	39	PNB MORTGAGE	12/78	$95.7	$46.7	$23.5	0.50	$9.625	$1.08	11.22%
29	79	PROPERTY CAPITAL	10/78	$48.8	$28.2	$22.5	0.80	$10.875	$1.32	12.14%
30	68	SUTRO MTG INV	12/78	$42.3	$37.3	$21.5	0.58	$9.250	$1.00	10.81%
31	80	UNIVERSITY REAL	9/78	$48.5	$20.5	$21.4	1.04	$8.500	$0.72	8.47%
32	62	REALTY REFUND	10/78	$66.6	$25.2	$21.2	0.84	$15.375	$1.68	10.93%
33	99	FEDERAL RLTY INV	9/78	$39.2	$14.1	$21.1	1.49	$15.250	$1.36	8.92%
34	87	MTG GROWTH INV	8/78	$45.5	$28.0	$20.9	0.75	$7.875	$0.72	9.14%
35	63	AMER EQUITY	9/78	$65.9	$16.3	$20.0	1.23	$8.000	$1.60	20.00%
36	49	REALTY INCOME TR	10/78	$82.2	$19.5	$18.1	0.93	$11.500	$1.40	12.17%
37	75	FIRST CONT REIT	11/78	$52.7	$21.8	$17.1	0.78	$9.125	$0.80	9.85%
38	44	U S REALTY INV	9/78	$86.4	$13.6	$16.7	1.23	$4.875	N.A.	N.A.
39	95	USP REIT	9/78	$41.6	$20.0	$16.6	0.83	$5.625	$0.76	11.47%
40	14	C I MORTGAGE GR	10/78	$217.7	$-16.1	$16.2	---	$3.375	N.A.	N.A.
41	102	VIRGINIA REIT	9/78	$37.2	$12.5	$15.3	1.22	$12.000	$0.80	6.67%
42	74	M & T MORTGAGE	11/78	$53.0	$15.3	$14.6	0.96	$9.875	$1.20	12.15%
43	112	NATIONWIDE RE INV	12/78	$32.6	$26.2	$14.4	0.55	$13.750	$0.48	3.49%
44	94	PRUDENT	8/78	$41.9	$7.6	$14.3	1.88	$4.250	$0.28	6.59%
45	81	STATE MUTUAL	12/78	$48.3	$22.9	$13.2	0.58	$4.750	N.A.	N.A.
46	71	DENVER REIA	9/78	$54.8	$9.3	$13.2	1.42	$12.000	$0.72	6.00%
47	22	NORTH AMER MTG	8/78	$134.3	$38.7	$13.2	0.34	$3.000	N.A.	N.A.
48	109	INV REALTY TRUST	8/78	$34.2	$16.4	$13.0	0.79	$8.250	$0.60	7.27%
49	115	NTRWSTN FIN INV	9/78	$30.9	$21.7	$13.0	0.60	$8.625	N.A.	N.A.
50	88	U S BANTRUST	11/78	$45.4	$14.5	$13.0	0.90	$15.500	$0.80	5.16%

*"Annualized Distribution" is based upon the most recently announced or paid regular distribution, whether characterized as a dividend, capital gain, return of capital or some combination thereof. "Market Yield" is obtained by dividing Annualized Distribution by the most recent share price. "Market Value" is the share price times the outstanding shares. Share prices are bid quotes on the last trading day of the prior month. "MV/SE" is the market-to-book ratio obtained by dividing the latest recorded Shareholders Equity into Market Value. All information has been compiled from REITs public financial reports, as well as from financial periodicals. Although information has been obtained from sources believed to be reliable and reasonable care has been exercised in compiling data, accuracy or completeness cannot be guaranteed.

EXHIBIT 3
REIT Industry Balance Sheet ($ millions)

Assets	3d Quarter 1977	2d Quarter 1977	Liabilities	3d Quarter 1977	2d Quarter 1977
First mortgages			Commercial paper	$ 523.0	$ 585.2
Land and development	$ 1,351.6	$ 1,529.5	Bank borrowings	6,616.6	7,237.2
Construction	1,710.0	2,016.6	Senior nonconvertible debt	336.	323.2
Completed properties:			Subordinate nonconvertible debt	875.1	901.9
0–10 years	974.5	951.8	Convertible debt	626.7	624.3
10 + years	1,853.4	1,838.0	Mortgages on property owned	2,454.0	2,437.6
Junior mortgages	842.7	849.5	Other liabilities	370.3	346.6
Loan loss allowance	(1,876.6)	(2,101.1)		$11,801.9	$12,456.0
Property owned	8,839.3	9,134.6			
Cash and other assets	862.9	988.1	Shareholders' equity	2,755.9	2,751.0
Total	$14,557.8	$15,207.0	Total	$14,557.8	$15,207.0

Source: The published financial statements of all REITs of which the National Association of Real Estate Investment Trusts, Inc., has any record, including trusts which are not currently qualifying as REITs for federal tax purposes. For the third quarter 219 trusts are included. Due to rounding, the totals in this table do not necessarily equal the sum of their parts. "Property owned" includes $5.2 billion of property acquired by or in lieu of foreclosure. Joint venture and partnership interests are also included in "property owned" at the amounts reported on REIT balance sheets.

and may sell it as a dealer within as much as four years after acquiring it, in which case it pays taxes at the corporate rate on ordinary income.

In some cases, the tax peculiarities of a REIT may enable it to purchase property which might not be of interest to other investors. Many non-REIT purchasers of real property are concerned about the tax shelter implications of the deal. This may cause such purchasers to seek property where high leverage and low amortization can be arranged.

Often it is not possible to find such financing. For example, a property may be sold with the purchaser assuming or taking the property subject to an existing mortgage. If much of the mortgage has been repaid, the purchaser may be required to make a large down payment to acquire the seller's equity in the project, and the mortgage payments may represent largely payments of principal, which is not tax deductible. Although such a project would not interest a tax-oriented investor, a REIT with its dividends-paid deductions is less concerned about the tax implications of its mortgage payments and it may have the cash to buy out the seller's accumulated equity in the project. Thus a low-leverage–high-amortization deal may interest a REIT.

Property Acquisition. REITs acquire properties through several methods. They may purchase existing improved properties for their portfolios; they may hire independent contractors to construct improvements on land that they own; or they may invest in a joint venture with developers. They may also acquire properties by foreclosing on mortgages or by receiving deeds in lieu of foreclosure.

Properties may be purchased with cash or in some instances with trust shares. The latter would constitute a tax-free exchange for the seller. In some cases, REITs have acquired properties in exchange for properties in their portfolios. This may also save the seller taxes.

Ownership positions by REITs vary from 100 percent ownership in properties to joint ownership in the form of partnerships or joint ventures. In a joint venture involving new construction, the REIT usually becomes a passive partner with a developer. The developer contributes expertise and possibly some capital, and the REIT typically contributes most of the capital to the joint venture.

In another type of joint venture, the REIT may be a passive holder of rental units which will be converted into condominium units and marketed by the developer/partner. Sometimes the REIT may take back the long-term financing on the units sold.

Another popular combination is the purchase-leaseback transaction. The most frequent form here is for the REIT to own the land under buildings that are owned by others. The REIT leases this land on a long-term basis to the owners of the buildings.

Regional Preferences. There is considerable diversity within the REIT industry regarding project location. Some REITs prefer to work only in areas near their headquarters. Others prefer regional diversity and may own projects nationwide. For housing and apartment development, REITs have looked to areas where there is no rent control.

California, Georgia, Florida and Texas have the heaviest concentration of REIT investments. As suppliers of capital for growth, the REITs can be expected to continue financing in the Sun Belt areas.

Mortgage Lending. For those trusts that are now actively lending, construction loans continue to be the favored investment. Very few trusts are offering land acquisition loans, largely because of the relatively large losses that have been experienced on such loans in the recent past and because the long-term required holding period is inconsistent with the availability of short-term funds to the REIT. Those REITs that do lend on land usually expect to provide construction and development funds for the land soon after acquisition. Intermediate and gap loans are available at several trusts, particularly those that do not require a takeout for construction lending. Some trusts specialize in such loans because competitors (banks) refuse to do so. Some trusts specialize in wraparound mortgages, and a few trusts are taking junior mortgages with equity kickers. Very few trusts are now providing long-term mortgage loans; the cost and availability of trust funds are such that the profit opportunities are limited in the long-term sector.

Preferred Projects. REIT investment preferences vary widely. Some trusts will make loans only on income-producing properties, to the exclusion of single-family developments and condominiums. Other trusts will invest in single-family projects but not in condominiums. Most trusts are now avoiding condominium construction financing; those few that lend money to finance condominium construction do so only in a few areas and for builders with established track records.

One trust will not lend for hotels, whereas another trust considers hotel loans a preferred investment. Generally, shopping centers rank high as a favored type of investment.

Most REITs prefer to originate their loans independently. A wall plaque often found in REIT offices proclaims: "Beware of brokers bearing deals."

Regional Preferences. Again, there is considerable diversity within the REIT industry regarding the location of loans. In general, trusts have shown a preference for regions and cities that are experiencing above-average growth in population, employment, and income.

Another key concern is state usury limits. For example, the California 10 percent usury limit, which is applicable to loans made by out-of-state lenders and nonbank entities such as REITs, has acted to discourage REIT lending activity in that state. Ease of foreclosure under the various state laws is also taken into account.

Some REITs are willing to lend nationally and even internationally (though most trusts avoid lending in Canada and Mexico because of local foreclosure laws). Others concentrate their lending in the states in which they are located. Contiguous states are sometimes included. Still other trusts prefer to lend in areas where they have lent previously, inasmuch as they have built up expertise in those areas.

Loan Mechanics

Construction Loans. The selection of a REIT by a developer who is seeking a construction loan depends on the risk of the project and the REIT's cost of funds. The REIT's cost of funds tends to be higher than that of traditional real estate lending institutions, such as savings and loan associations and commercial banks, because these traditional lenders are able to obtain relatively low-cost (and usually government-insured) deposits. This means that REITs have to charge more for lending than these institutions in order to cover their higher cost of funds. As a result, REITs seek higher-risk projects where the higher price is justified.

The degree of risk acceptable to a REIT depends on the REIT's sources of money. REITs which are able to sell commercial paper or which have substantial shareholders' equity, bonds, or other nonbank sources of construction money have a lower cost of funds and can lend at lower risk. Some REITs in this category even assert that they use almost the same criteria and accept the same risk as banks do. Trusts in this category tend to deal largely with established developers who have good track records.

REITs which must pay more for their money because they must borrow from banks are more flexible about builder experience and the risk involved and, accordingly, charge higher rates. Usually such REITs pay their own lenders a percentage of prime (such as 115–130 percent) and charge between 3 and 4.5 points above prime. REITs with nonbank sources will sometimes charge a fixed rate or, more commonly, a floating rate of as low as 2 percent above prime.

Some trusts require a permanent loan takeout, whereas others do not. In part due to the recent experiences, long-term mortgage lenders tend to write the so-called takeout with so many restrictions and release clauses that many borrowers recognize that some takeouts are not worth the cost. A few REITs even prefer to lend on projects without takeouts, because the rates are generally higher and they anticipate being able to obtain long-term financing later on. Other REITs are flexible, depending upon developer experience. A few trusts are now seeking joint ventures in conjunction with construction loans, but other trusts have no interest in an equity participation.

Lending limits vary from trust to trust, with the large trusts and the trusts that have strong institutional sponsorship willing to lend the greatest amount. For the latter, minimum/maximum loan limits are $1.5 million to $10 million. Some trusts will participate with the sponsor on larger loans. Smaller trusts without such sponsorship typically provide loans in the $0.5 million to $4 million range. During the REIT growth period, REITs often participated with banks or other REITs in big loan transactions—but the recent experiences of trying to unravel participants in a foreclosure situation have led most REITs to spurn such participations.

Applications. In the past, prospective loans were brought to the attention of the REIT by mortgage brokers who tended to charge between 1 and 1½ points or more to shop the borrowers' loan application around to various lenders. Although this fee was paid up front by the borrower, it ultimately became funded as part of the REIT loan. Brokered loans are no longer common.

Other loan applications may be referred to the REIT by its own bank lenders, who may be unable to take the loan themselves or may be seeking participations in the loan. Sometimes the REIT sponsor will refer loans. One REIT sponsored by an insurance company, for example, has the automatic right to fund half of any loan application submitted to the insurance company. In some cases, the borrower will make direct contact with the REIT, without the use of any intermediary; most often, once the REIT has established a working understanding, this non-brokered relationship continues.

The loan application will be reviewed initially by a loan officer to determine whether it meets the trust's investment objectives. The loan officer may be an employee of the trust or of the adviser. After an initial screening has been made of the loan, the trust may require a good faith deposit of perhaps one-half point before completing its loan analysis or underwriting. If a loan commitment is made by the REIT and accepted by the borrower, this good faith deposit will be applied as payment to the loan. If a commitment to fund the loan is made by the REIT and is not accepted by the borrower, the REIT will keep the deposit to cover the cost of its underwriting analysis.

Approval of the loan is usually made by an investment committee of the trustees; sometimes the full board of trustees must approve. Exhibit 4 is a checklist of the data that one trust required before it would approve a loan to a condominium project.

In general, REITs will want to know about the following:

1. *The characteristics of the property and the plan for its development.* The REIT will be interested in the topography of the proposed building site and in the cost of land preparation. Zoning, the source and cost of utilities, and local amenities will be considered. Sketches, models, and architectural plans will be reviewed.

2. *The feasibility of the project.* This requires the preparation of a financial pro forma statement. Trusts vary as to whether they will require a formal appraisal; obviously, the closer the data come to an appraisal, the better. This requires that all projected income sources, such as rents, be itemized. Construction costs and other development expenses should be included, together with supporting documentation from architects or general contractors. Operating expenses, especially taxes, insurance, maintenance, management, and anticipated assessments, also need to be itemized. The purpose of these data is to arrive at a tentative value of the project when it is completed (in case the REIT is required to foreclose). A separate feasibility study analyzing the competition and the probable success of the business proposed on the land site may also be required.

3. *The experience, integrity, and financial responsibility of the developer.* The REIT is concerned about the track record and the reputation of the developer. Information will be sought from other creditors who have financed the developer. The balance sheet and cash flow of the developer will be studied to determine whether the developer will have sufficient funds available, over and above the amount of the construction loan, to complete the job and to carry the project through the rent-up period.

EXHIBIT 4
Loan Application Data Required for Condominium Project

1. Application fee _____
2. Appraisal _____
3. Feasibility market analysis _____
4. Survey _____
5. Plans/specs _____
6. Engineering analysis of construction costs _____
7. Use of proceeds statement _____
8. Projected cash flows _____
9. Cash requirement schedules _____
10. Schedule of proposed sales prices _____
11. Sales promotion program _____
12. Financial statements _____
13. Income statements (from sales) _____
14. Credit reports _____
15. Bank references _____
16. Personal résumés _____
17. Proof of zoning _____
18. Public health department compliance _____
19. Pollution control letter/permit _____
20. Availability of utilities (water, electric) _____
21. Soil test borings _____
22. Water/sewer plant facilities _____
23. Building permits _____
24. General contractor's construction contract _____
25. Land purchase contract _____
26. Deed _____
27. Title insurance binder/policy _____
28. Performance bond _____
29. All-inclusive risk hazard insurance _____
30. Estoppel letters _____
31. Corporate resolution
    or partnership agreement of borrower _____
32. Letter of credit _____

4. *Takeout and standby commitments.* The REIT will review such commitments, which involve purchasing the construction loan or making a new loan upon completion of the project, to determine whether there are any conditions that the developer may be unable to fulfill.

Servicing. This will be done by either adviser personnel or trust personnel, and essentially it involves the taking of precautions by the REIT to ensure that at every stage of construction the improvements are valued at an amount greater than the outstanding balance of the construction loan. A schedule of advances is almost universally employed to this end.

An inspection is normally made prior to each advance in order to confirm that the work claimed to have been done has actually been done. In addition, holdback schedules requiring that payments not exceed costs for a given period and other precautions, such as direct payments by the REIT to the developer, general contractor, subcontractors, and other parties, may be employed, depending· on the size and type of project.

Standby or Gap Financing. As has been indicated earlier, many REITs will issue takeout commitments for "gap" or "standby" loans in lieu of long-term takeouts. In the case of REITs sponsored by insurance companies, the REIT will sometimes make the construction loan and the sponsor the takeout commitment. A developer seeks a standby commitment if he is unable to obtain a permanent loan or if he does not want a permanent loan because he believes that long-term interest rates are currently too high or that a larger loan or better terms may be available after the structure has been completed and rented.

A standby commitment is issued for a fee, and such a commitment requires the REIT to provide a takeout if at the end of the construction period a permanent loan has not been secured. Normally a standby is not funded, because its terms and rate tend to be more onerous than those of a normal permanent loan. If it is funded, it is usually a standing or nonamortizing loan.

The need for "gap" financing usually occurs when permanent lenders issue a "two-tiered" takeout commitment. The lower-tier permanent mortgage will be issued no matter what the rent achievement of the property is, provided that all of the other conditions of the takeout are met. If a stipulated level of rentals is achieved and if all other conditions of the takeout are met, the permanent lender will issue a mortgage for the upper-tier amount. The size of the gap between the two tiers is usually 15 to 20 percent of the larger amount.

The difference between the partial amount that a permanent lender would advance and the amount of the full mortgage is supplied by the REIT for a fee—hence the term *gap financing.* Some REITs will offer this accommodation only if they have supplied the construction financing; others have no such restrictions.

The terms of a gap or standby loan are often similar to the conditions necessary for a long-term takeout, such as:

1. *A requirement that the construction must be completed by a specific date.*

2. *Approval of all leases by the lender.* In the event that the construction is, for example, an office building or a shopping center, the permanent lender often relies heavily on the existence of long-term, high-quality leases as evidence that the project is likely to be a financial success. The interim lender normally approves the leases as well, realizing that only after full occupancy will a long-term lender be interested.

3. *A certificate of occupancy.* The lender may require that a certain minimum percentage of the construction be leased before it will honor the gap commitment. In verifying that this percentage has been met, the lender may require a certificate of occupancy which ensures that the developer's obligations to the lessee have been met. When the higher limit of the gap has been reached, such certificates may be needed to have the long-term commitment take place.

4. *Approval of all plans and specifications by the lender.* This requires that all changes made during the construction period be approved

by the lender. An independent architect must certify that the building was completed in accordance with the plans.

It is clear from the foregoing that REITs are characterized by diversity. Some REITs emphasize ownership positions in real estate, some are in the mortgage-lending business, and some are hybrids, involved in both types of real estate business. Within the mortgage-lending sector, construction loans appear to be the favored investment. REITs also make standby loans, gap commitments, and on occasion, long-term mortgages and junior mortgages.

PENSION FUNDS

Joseph P. Clancy

*J*OSEPH P. CLANCY, JD, Manager, Real Estate Division, Rauen-
horst Corporation, Chicago.
  Formerly Manager of Fund F for the First National Bank of
Chicago. Member, Urban Land Institute, Chicago Bar Association, New York State Bar Association, and American Bar Association. Author, "Real Estate Investing," Commerce, May 1978.

Pension Funds as Organizations

What Are Pension Funds? Pension funds are the most significant retirement assets of many corporate employees, whether they are salaried
or hourly and whether they are employed by large or small corporations.
When the employer contributes monies to the pension fund it sponsors,
those monies become the responsibility of the fund's trustees. Sometimes
the trustees themselves will undertake to manage the monies by making
investments, but more frequently they will hire professional money
managers, such as bank trust departments or insurance companies, that
will make investments on behalf of the trustees. The investment manager is often given a large measure of discretion by the trustees, so
long as it maintains the required level of prudence in investing and
can itself determine whether to invest in stocks, bonds, or real estate.
In other instances, the trustees will direct the manager to invest in certain asset types, such as stocks, and the manager will then decide in
which stocks to invest, always maintaining the necessary level of prudence. In some cases, the money manager itself, if it has trust powers,
will be appointed trustee by the corporate plan sponsor.

Pension funds have grown dramatically to become the largest pool
of private capital in the world, with assets estimated to currently approach $280 billion. Investing this pool of funds is an incredibly complex
task. In his excellent book *The Unseen Revolution*, published in 1976,
Peter Drucker estimated that at the end of 1974 the market value of
all securities listed on U.S. stock markets approached $500 billion and
that pension funds owned 30 percent of the total value of the securities

listed. Drucker predicted that by 1985 pension funds would own as much as 60 percent of the value of listed securities and that the percentage would increase further by the year 2000. It is generally estimated that real estate, including mortgages and equities, accounts for only 1–2 percent of the total assets held by pension funds. Trustees and managers are concerned about how to invest the ever-growing pool of pension fund capital, and real estate is one obvious solution.

The most significant piece of legislation that has been enacted with respect to pension funds is the Employee Retirement Income Security Act of 1974, commonly referred to as ERISA. Although it initially raised more questions than it answered, ERISA has nevertheless clearly admonished trustees who for many years thought only in terms of stocks and bonds to diversify their assets. The consistent, stable returns generated by investments in carefully purchased equity real estate provide elements of the diversification being sought. Many plan sponsors and trustees are now looking to real estate for 5–10 percent of their asset placement, others for as much as 20 percent, at some undetermined future date. With this degree of anticipated involvement, it is no wonder that pension funds are termed "the sleeping giant of the real estate industry."

Pension Funds and Real Estate—The Past. Since pension plans were started in the early 1950s, the investment managers have generally sought to invest some money in real estate. However, at no time could it be said that real estate was an important part of the total assets of pension funds. Much of the early pension fund investing in real estate was done through the purchase of individual mortgages or packages of mortgages which were brought to the managers by mortgage bankers. These 20-, 30- and even 40-year debt instruments were private placements that were analyzed by the managers as they would have analyzed bonds of similar maturities. The mortgages were considered attractive because the yield on cost was generally one eighth to one half of 1 percent greater than the yield on a bond of similar maturity. It was not important that the returns under these instruments were fixed, because inflation was then insignificant. In disposing of these mortgages, the pension funds have sold many of them at substantial discounts from their cost. The mortgages that have been retained are, of course, carried at reductions in value that reflect today's higher interest rates.

A second real estate vehicle that pension funds have utilized is the sale-leaseback arrangement. Under this traditional vehicle, a pension fund would purchase a property that was owned by a seller whose credit was highly rated and would lease it back to the seller for an extended period of time, often 40 years or more. The tenant paid rent to the owner under an absolutely net lease in which the tenant was responsible for every expense, including structural items such as roofs, sidewalls, and parking lots. Some of these leases also required the tenant to return the premises to whatever condition they were in at the beginning of the lease. The writer has seen some leases in which even "normal wear and tear" is not excepted. Many of the improvements which are the subject of these leases are very special purpose and of limited value to a substitute tenant. Also, many sale-leasebacks contained purchase options which gave the tenant the right to repurchase the property at its original selling price at the end of the lease term. Finally, some corporations sold buildings that they themselves were occupying to pension funds that they sponsored, believing that if the corporation was going to pay rent to an owner that owner could be the corporation's own pension fund. ERISA would seem to prohibit such transactions due to the possibility of a conflict of interest in establishing the selling price and setting the rentals.

Although it is tempting to apply the benefits of hindsight to some of those past transactions and to wonder why investors would enter into transactions that did not provide with either a right of reappraisal or escalations in rent during a 40-year lease term, it is important to recall that the investment climate was substantially different 25 years ago—and even 10 years ago—than it is today. At that time, inflation was not regarded as a significant element of investment decision making. Today, many investment managers feel that a long-term flat-rate mortgage or sale-leaseback would violate the prudent man doctrine described in ERISA.

Pension Funds and Real Estate—The Present. Although, as has been noted, pension trustees and investment managers were aware that real estate existed, it was not a significant part of their thinking prior to 1970. The investments they made in real estate were placed privately. Some managers purchased land for some of their funds or went into joint ventures with developers, but that was an exceptional practice, and it was done on as passive a basis as possible. For the most part, trustees and managers did not have the staffs or the expertise to purchase, lease, operate, manage, administer, and sell real estate. They were unfamiliar with the analysis of properties. They did not know how to tell a good property or location from a bad one, and they felt uncomfortable about negotiating the purchase price of real estate or even about monitoring the performance of a managing agent.

In the late 1960s and early 1970s, this began to change. Trustees and managers were concerned about inflation and about the all too apparent fact that it was becoming the largest component in the total return expected from any given type of prudent investment. In looking for investment vehicles that would keep ahead of inflation, they began to consider real estate. Equity real estate appeared to be the most realistic way to keep ahead, as leases, if not too long, would allow an owner to reflect increasing operating costs, construction costs, and desired return on investment in the tenants' new lease rates.

However, a very limited number of vehicles existed to allow trustees to invest in equity real estate. The real estate investment trusts (REITs) were beginning to become a factor in real estate finance and ownership, but they were still too new and they did not have the years of investment experience, the stature, the "marble columns" that the trustees wanted. Therefore, many trustees looked to the more traditional managers, the insurance companies and bank trust departments. These managers, in conjunction with some of their larger pension fund clients, started commingled real estate funds. Other trustees, a much more limited number, decided to use in-house people to purchase what are perhaps best described as mortgage equities—mortgages with equity participations (for example, a mortgage with a 30-year amortization, which balloons in 20 years and in which the mortgagee receives a percentage of the project's gross revenues).

Commingled Funds. As of September 30, 1978, the three largest commingled funds were managed by two life insurance companies, the Prudential Insurance Company of America and the Equitable Life Assurance Society of America, and by a bank trust department, the First National Bank of Chicago. Other insurance companies and banks with commingled funds were the Aetna Insurance Company, the John Hancock Mutual Life Insurance Company, the Travelers Insurance Companies, the Continental Illinois National Bank, the First National Bank of Boston, the Crocker National Bank and the Wells Fargo National Bank. Two noninstitutional funds are managed by Coldwell Banker and Rosenberg Capital Management.

A number of banks and insurance companies are contemplating forming such funds, and the investment requirements of the established funds tend to change as the market changes. Because the real estate market is relatively inefficient in disseminating information, it is not possible to keep fully current with the changes in the acquisition criteria of each fund. Two publications that follow pension funds closely are *The Institutional Investor* and *Pensions and Investments*. A broker or a developer who expects to be working regularly with pension funds should consult these excellent publications at least periodically.

Pension Fund Operations in Real Estate

Acquisition Criteria. In general, the pension funds seek to purchase income-producing properties of four types—office buildings, industrial buildings, shopping centers and apartment buildings—and to purchase these properties free and clear of all mortgages, including construction loans and permanent loans, and free of land leases. Some pension funds will purchase properties which are subject to mortgages that the funds consider to have favorable rates, whereas other funds require that any mortgages be retired at or prior to purchase. Some of the funds purchase hotels and motels, unimproved land, and farms. However, the funds seem to prefer operating commercial properties.

The "free and clear" requirement of most pension funds is attributable to the Internal Revenue Code, which expressly grants tax-exempt status to qualified retirement plans and then effectively limits it. The limitation arises because the code imposes income tax liability if a retirement plan purchases a property that is subject to mortgages or debt. Although some commingled funds will purchase properties that are subject to mortgages, taking the viewpoint that any taxable income will be eliminated by depreciation or other deductible items, even those funds will not purchase heavily leveraged properties. No specific rule of thumb applies, though leverage in excess of 75 percent would probably be rejected.

As to more specific investment criteria, commingled funds tend to be extremely conscious of the quality of construction. They will have architects and engineers review plans and specifications and as-built plans, if available, and they will see that detailed physical inspections are made. They are conscious of local market variations and of the subject property's position within a particular market. They will analyze competing projects for comparable rents and levels of expense. Before purchase, all leases will be read and analyzed and the seller will be asked to obtain estoppel letters from no fewer than the major tenants and in some cases from substantially all of the tenants. Of course, surveys and title insurance policies will also be required before a transaction is closed.

Experience indicates that commingled funds will not agree to "as is" transactions. The seller who has developed the property will be required to give certain warranties having to do with its construction and operation. The seller who has not himself developed the property will be required to give many of the same warranties, to describe problems of which he has notice or knowledge, and to review his files for pertinent information prior to sale. Because pension fund managers are charged with fiduciary responsibility, they must be extremely careful. Although the legal documentation of a sale to a pension fund is perhaps more difficult than that of a sale to a nonfiduciary purchaser, the knowledgeable seller takes comfort in the fact that the purchaser is sophisticated, well capitalized, and able to make a decision.

Most funds have an acquisitions staff that solicits submissions locally or regionally. Others request all submissions be sent to a central office. To determine which approach is preferred, a broker or developer should consult the central office. The funds have varying requirements as to what a submission should contain. In general, it should contain photographs of the improvements; the most recent annual operating statement and a pro forma operating statement; a complete physical description; a complete current rent roll; relevant data on the community in question; and a map showing the property, the central business district, and major highways. The fund managers receive numerous property submissions every week, many of which contain inadequate information. They will tend to fully consider those that contain a substantial amount of useful information and to quickly reject those that do not.

As has been indicated, the pension funds buy similar types of properties, but they differ in the range of properties that they will buy. As a general requirement, office buildings should be at least 50,000–60,000 square feet in size and industrial properties should be multipurpose and 80,000–300,000 square feet in size. Neither type of property should be special purpose unless the special improvements required by the tenant are amortized over the lease term. Shopping centers, whether regional, miniregional, or strip community centers, should be large enough to justify professional management. Thus, strip centers should be at least 75,000–80,000 square feet in size. Further, the funds tend to avoid free-standing, single-tenant retail stores.

Those funds that will consider residential properties seem to restrict themselves to projects that have at least 250 units, so that they will be large enough to justify the expenditure of time that is required to manage them.

The commingled funds do not generally prefer to enter into joint ventures or partnerships, though some insurance companies have made investments in certain large hotels and regional malls that, to the developer or seller, have the characteristics of joint ventures. The funds want to have absolute control over the property, to lease and operate it as they wish, and to sell or retain it without having to be concerned about any partners. A simple business rationale for this approach is that most partners would be taxpaying entities and would have substantial income tax considerations prior to selling a property. Such considerations could upset the delicate complexities of a transaction and effectively reduce the control that the fund requires over a property. A legal rationale for this approach is that a fiduciary should not delegate control of the investment-making role to a third party, and that since any taxpaying partner is likely to require some control over disposition, the fund should avoid partnership vehicles.

The funds generally avoid involvement in construction. In most cases, the risks of cost overruns and materials shortages, together with the clear necessity of joint venture construction with a developer or a contractor, are too great to justify the return that may result. The funds may possess the development and the construction expertise to build their own properties, but as fiduciaries they do not believe that the risk of doing so is justified. In certain instances, the funds may take a leasing risk and purchase a property that is partially occupied or even vacant, because the market risk is considered justifiable.[1]

Management.   Most pension funds choose to manage their properties through local fee managers. Such funds have staffs of supervisory or executive property managers whose role is to review the leasing and operating activities of the fee manager. The supervisory managers participate in the preparation of budgets, capital improvements to the properties, and major lease negotiations.

In structuring a purchase, the funds seem willing to hire the seller's management division to provide fee management. Close supervision over the fee management is then provided by the management staff of the fund.

Direct Investment.   A small number of pension funds seem to be making direct investments in real estate. Those that are doing so are utilizing joint ventures or partnerships or are purchasing first or second mort-

---

[1] The above criteria reflect the preferences and requirements of Fund F, the commingled fund managed by the First National Bank of Chicago, of which the writer was portfolio manager. The criteria are general, however, and in the writer's opinion they apply to most institutional funds.

gages. The latter are often purchased through mortgage bankers after a completed package has been put together, or the trustees or investment managers will negotiate and structure the investment itself.

It is difficult to determine which individual pension funds, trustees, or investment managers are making direct investments and what their criteria may be. The developer looking for financing or the broker seeking an investor may consider contacting them directly.

The Future. As has been noted, pension funds have control over the largest private pool of capital in the world and that pool is continuing to grow dramatically. Most corporate plan sponsors have considered real estate as an alternative only in the last few years. Much of the credit for this interest results from the efforts of a few vigorous pension consultants whose analysis of real estate has indicated that it has the characteristics of stability and consistency of return that are sought by most plan sponsors. The sponsors with whom the writer is acquainted have indicated a desire for real estate to be as little as 2 percent or as much as 20 percent of their portfolios, with most considering approximately 10 percent, depending upon the availability of quality properties. The total real estate investment of today's commingled funds does not exceed $2 billion, far short of the $28 billion that 10 percent of the total pension pool would represent. It is therefore important to consider how trustees and investment managers will meet the tremendous real estate needs of the increasing pension pool.

The competition for income properties in the United States is keen. The large life insurance companies are quite active on behalf of their own accounts, and many of them, as has been noted, are also seeking properties for the commingled funds they sponsor. Foreign investors are investing in the more stable U.S. economy by purchasing real estate with "cheap dollars." Accustomed to the relatively higher inflation within their own countries and to the protection that real estate equities afford, they are driving up prices and driving down initial yields. And despite the great demand, the supply of newer, high-quality properties has not kept up due to a lack of building as the United States emerged from the 1973–74 recession.

This scenario makes it likely that as pension trustees and investment managers gain experience and a better understanding of real estate risks, they will get closer to the initial stages of development, though remaining short of undertaking the construction risk. One way to do this is to commit to purchase a property at the completion of construction, with normal escrows and holdbacks for tenant improvements and finish work. The investment manager will have already had its architects and engineers review the project's plans and specifications, and it will have analyzed the market to determine that the project will be readily acceptable at projected rents and operating expenses and that the lease form will be readily acceptable to prospective tenants. Because the fund's architects will review and oversee construction, and because no monies will be funded until construction has been completed, construction risk will be avoided. At completion the investment manager will be able to purchase the property at a price as much as 20 percent lower than it would have been if the manager had waited until the property was both constructed and leased. The risk that the manager takes is a market risk, as the manager may have to purchase a property that is not fully leased. However, from experience most managers have learned that any multitenant building will have leases that expire and vacant space that must be leased. The key element is the price at which space is being offered. If the manager's analysis has been done properly, it will be able to offer the partially leased building at rental rates that are well under the market for competitive space.

An advantage of this approach is that it enables the investment manager to avoid competing with all the other buyers for existing cash flow on every proposed transaction. Today, capitalization rates are advertised to be anywhere from 6 percent to 11 percent, depending upon location, property type, and leasing level. The competition for cash flow is extreme, driving down the capitalization rates. Therefore, although many of the investments that a manager makes will continue to involve the purchase of existing cash flow, once a portfolio has been established, it can be attractively augmented by a number of relatively low risk predevelopment transactions.

Pension funds have been called the sleeping giants of the real estate business. They obviously have great resources. They have only recently begun to use those resources for the purchase of real estate, and the activities of commingled funds represent the initial steps. This pool of capital is conservative due to its fiduciary obligation to its owners. As the established funds continue to have favorable experience with real estate, and as the attractive returns of real estate are proven over a period of time, new investment structures will be undertaken. There is every reason to believe that real estate will become a significant part of pension fund investment portfolios. As pension funds move to increase the real estate share of their portfolios to 10 percent and even 20 percent, it is obvious that their activity in real estate will be great.

Chapter

46

UNCONVENTIONAL
SOURCES

Samuel K. Freshman

SAMUEL K. FRESHMAN, JD, Freshman, Marantz, Comsky & Deutsch Law Corporation, Beverly Hills, California.

Vice chairman, American Bar Association Real Property Finance Committee, in charge of Subcommittee on Trade Associations and Subcommittee on Real Estate Investment Trusts. Adjunct professor of real estate, Graduate School of Business, University of Southern California. Member, Construction Industry Panel, American Arbitration Association; and American Right of Way Association. Formerly chairman, Legal Committee, California Real Estate Association, Syndicate Division; secretary, National Real Estate Securities Institute; member, Board of Governors, Beverly Hills Bar Association; and chairman, Real Property Committee, Beverly Hills Bar Association. Author of numerous articles on real estate subjects in Los Angeles Bar Journal, Beverly Hills Bar Journal, University of West Los Angeles Law Review, *and* American Land Development Journal. *Author,* Principles of Real Estate Syndication, *2d ed. (Los Angeles: Parker, 1973).*

Conventional lenders, such as commercial banks, savings and loan associations, mutual savings banks, life insurance companies, real estate investment trusts, and pension trusts, are referred to by the real estate industry as "institutional loan sources." The number of unconventional lenders is far greater than the number of conventional lenders. The wide diversity of noninstitutional lenders as well as the broad range of terms that are available from such lenders make them a primary tool of successful real estate entrepreneurs.

Unconventional lenders are less well known than conventional lenders because they do not normally solicit borrowers as aggressively as do conventional lenders and because they are characterized by a lack of formality and by greater flexibility in the types of loans that they will consider.

Unconventional Sources of Financing

Conventional Loans Unavailable. In certain circumstances, institutional lenders may be unwilling or unable to consider a particular loan request because *(a)* the loan exceeds the loan-to-value ratios that are generally required by institutional lenders, which normally limit their loans to from 66⅔ percent to 80 percent of value; *(b)* the geographic locale may be one in which no institutional lenders are operating or one which institutional lenders shun because of past foreclosure experience; *(c)* during periods of tight money, institutional lenders may be prohibited by governmental regulations from making the loan; or *(d)* the security may not be of the kind that institutional lenders are authorized to lend upon.

Most conventional lenders are limited to first mortgages and in certain cases to secondary positions. The equity available for loan purposes may be a third position or even a fourth position behind various senior encumbrances. Federal or state tax regulations may preclude an institutional lender from participating in a project. For example, real estate investment trusts, as has been pointed out in Chapter 44, cannot take an active position or role in a project.

More Favorable Terms Available from Unconventional Sources. The cash flow of a project may be such that the terms available from conventional lenders would not be suitable for the project. This would be particularly true for a project that may have a negative cash flow for a time and would therefore be unable to service an amortizing loan of the type that is normally made by institutional lenders. The cash flow projection of such a project might be highly speculative, although substantial, and therefore the payment for the use of the loan funds would be more heavily weighted toward a participatory interest in the project or toward future profits than toward customary interest charges. The circumstances may be such that an unconventional lender may desire benefits other than a charge for the use of money, so that the "constant" or the interest rate or the loan charges obtainable from the unconventional lender may be more favorable than those obtainable from institutional lenders.

Property-Related Sources of Unconventional Loans

Purchase-Money Loans. Purchase-money loans are generally described as loans that are provided by the seller of a property and are secured in whole or in part by the property being sold. Before the buyer resorts to financing from other sources, he should always consider using the seller as the lender because the terms available from the seller may be more favorable than those available from any other source. The seller knows the property being sold, and he demonstrated a preference for that property when he bought it. Tax considerations may make a purchase-money loan transaction advantageous to the seller (for example, through the use of the installment sale method). Price concessions to the seller may result in more favorable loan terms, such as a lower interest rate, a lower constant, a longer maturity date, and most important, a higher loan-to-value ratio (requiring a smaller equity investment) than may be available from other sources.

The Terms of Sale. Sale terms are an excellent source of financing. Two different prices are paid for real property, the stated price and the actual price after prorations and adjustments.

When the seller is carrying back financing, this technique is used to reduce the actual cash required at the close and to increase the amount carried by the seller: where the net prorations are determined to be in the buyer's favor, the purchase contract calls for the adjustment of all prorations in cash at the close; where the net prorations are determined to be in the seller's favor, the contract provides for the adjustment of net prorations by adding them to the purchase-money financing being carried by the seller.[1]

Tenants and Concessionaires. Tenants and concessionaires are excellent sources of financing. They supply financing in two ways.

First, they supply financing through advance rentals or "key money" (money paid for the right to lease the premises) and through substantial security deposits. A true security deposit is refundable at the conclusion of the lease term. If such a deposit is not segregated, it is in a sense a loan to the lessor as well as security for the tenant's obligations. Many tenants who are desirous of obtaining a location are willing to pay a more than normal security deposit if the landlord will pay a reasonable rate of interest on it. Where security deposits are substantial, they may be secured by a junior mortgage. Most security deposits do not have to be segregated, and so long as interest is paid on them and the landlord is personally liable for the return of the funds, such deposits will be given the same tax treatment as any other loan.

Second, for a premium location or for a location which creates a "monopoly position," tenants and concessionaires will make substantial direct loans on very favorable terms to the landlord. Examples of such locations are the parking lot concession in a large office building; special leased departments in hospitals, medical buildings, and clinics (such as pharmacies and laboratories); departments and concessions in large hotels (many major gasoline companies have financed large motels and resort operations in exchange for the exclusive right to operate the service station); and high-street-traffic locations for various kind of retailers.

Professionals, Contractors, and Materials Suppliers. Professionals, contractors, and materials suppliers are a common source of construction financing. There are two ways of using this source. The first way is to secure deferred payment terms. Quite often, the architect, the engineer, the attorney, and other professional people who are working on a construction project will take a nominal retainer fee and either a participating interest in the project or deferred payment for their services. In

---

[1] For details on this technique, see Samuel K. Freshman, *Principles of Real Estate Syndication,* 2d ed. Los Angeles: Parker, 1973), chap. 7, "How To Negotiate Financing," pp. 121–37.

construction projects, personal services rendered by professionals constitute as much as 12 percent to 20 percent of the overall costs. Thus, getting extended payment terms from these professionals may enable the developer to finance out the rest of the cost of the project from conventional sources without having to put up a substantial amount of equity.

Deferring payments to the general contractor, the subcontractors, and the materials suppliers, particularly if this can be done past the time that cash flow is expected to begin, may enable the developer to put together a large project with a rather nominal outlay of funds. If an 80 percent loan is available from conventional loan sources and payments to the professionals, the contractors, and the materials suppliers can be deferred, the amount that needs to be deferred will only be 20 percent of the cost of the project. If the professionals represent 20 percent of the cost of the project and will defer 50 percent of their billings for payment after the completion of the project, and if the labor and materials suppliers will defer 10 percent of their billings, these sources will have contributed 18 percent of the cost of the project, or 90 percent of the equity required. This will enable the developer to proceed with only 2 percent of the total project cost as "front money." If, upon completion, he is able to sell all or a portion of the equity to meet the deferred payments, the percentage return on his actual cash outlay can be astronomical.

It is this ability to "leverage" the equity required that enables thinly capitalized, highly experienced developers to put together and build projects that cost many times as much as their working capital.

Equipment leasing on a subordinated basis and the financing of component parts is an excellent source of "equity" to support a conventional loan. In order to secure the bid for their product, suppliers of elevators, escalators, and other electrical components have often provided secondary financing for a substantial part of the price of their products. This financing may be subordinated to the conventional first-mortgage financing, and it would have to be if the component part were an integral part of the building.

If the electrical systems constitute 10 percent of the cost of a project and they can be bought for 20 percent down and 80 percent financed over a five- to ten-year period, then 8 percent of the project cost can be generated by applying this method to the electrical systems. Plumbing and air conditioning systems are also commonly financed in this way.

Where furnishings and fixtures constitute a substantial portion of a project's value, as is true for hospitals, hotels, bowling alleys, and restaurants, the primary mortgage lender may require a first lien on "personal property" required for operation and the seller of the "personal property" may be willing to take a subordinate position in order to secure the contract for its product.

If the suppliers of the personal property or of some structural components have a sufficient profit motivation, they may be willing to supply not only secondary financing for their own product but a portion of the cash required for other building components as well. If their component happens to be substantial, they may even become the primary financing source for the entire project. For example, where hospital supply companies were selling personal property whose price exceeded the cost of the hospital land and building, in order to make the sale they would supply the primary financing for the land and the building, either directly or through the use of their credit line. Such "tie-in arrangements," however, must be carefully analyzed to make sure that they do not violate any state or federal restrictions on the supplier providing credit as a sale inducement. Title insurers have supplied interim financing and lines of credit to major builders in return for their title insurance business, but many states now prohibit this practice.

Service Companies.   Organizations which supply services to a project can also be a source of financing. The most obvious way of assistance would be delayed billing. Once a project is completed, it may need janitorial services, guard services, property management services, insurance, accounting, and other services. If a service company will delay its billings from 60 to 90 days, the landlord has (as long as he continues to use that company) the cash flow which is generated from the tenants for that period without having to pay the underlying proportion of operating expense, which in a sense helps provide working capital for the project. The working capital generated by delayed billings from service companies can be used to discharge short-term gap construction loans which may have been made from other sources in order to cover the difference between the total construction costs and the funds which were being supplied by the primary lender. Service companies may also be willing to make direct loans in order to secure the business that a construction project generates.

Outside Agencies and Companies

Junior Financing Prohibition.   Where a lien must be given on a project in order to secure secondary and unconventional financing, the borrower must make sure that there is no prohibition in the senior financing against the pledging of personal property. Many first-mortgage lenders prohibit such a pledge even though it is subordinated to their position on the ground that they want the borrower to maintain a substantial cash equity.

Government Agencies.   A number of federal, state, and local governmental agencies can be direct sources of loans or loan guarantees. These are agencies which have been set up to foster certain types of business enterprises or certain objectives which the particular segment of government has found to be in the public interest. The most widely known is the federal Small Business Administration, which has a large number of programs to assist small businesses. These include direct loans and loan guarantees as well as other forms of assistance. In some cases, a lease guarantee will enable the landlord to secure financing from a conventional lender. (Lease guarantees are available from private companies as well as government agencies.)

Other departments of government, such as the Department of Agriculture and the Department of Commerce have programs and material which may be of assistance to developers. Such specialized government agencies as the Federal Land Bank and the Bank for Cooperatives assist rural development. State and local development agencies have been organized to provide loan programs, tax moratoriums, the supplying of off-site improvements, and other assistance to the developer which can defray all or a portion of the equity cost required in development.

Although there is considerable delay and additional "red tape" involved in processing loans with government agencies, they are often very attractive alternatives to conventional loan sources.

Finance Companies. A substantial number of major finance companies supply funds for real estate development and acquisition. They are not considered conventional lenders in that their interest rates and terms are generally less attractive than those of such conventional lenders as banks, insurance companies, and savings and loan associations. They will, however, lend on property which does not necessarily meet the underwriting criteria of the institutional lenders and they will make loans with a larger loan-to-value ratio than the loans of the institutional lenders. Their response time is often quicker than that of the conventional lenders, and they are an excellent source of interim short-term financing until a project establishes an earnings record that would justify longer-term financing from the conventional lenders.

Finance companies fall into two categories: (1) those that are strictly in the business of lending money and are independent of any manufacturer; and (2) those that are affiliated with a major manufacturer and were formed to assist in the sale of that manufacturer's products by providing financing that would enable dealers, customers, and the public to purchase those products.

In addition to the major companies in this field, there are a number of regional and local companies which work either independently or in conjunction with local commercial banks. Your local commercial banker will generally be able to put you in touch with one of these companies.

Public Utility Companies. Before the present power shortage, gas and electric utilities competed aggressively for customers and offered advantageous financing to encourage the use of gas or electric appliances. In some cases, this financing extended to outright grants, subsidies for advertising, and favorable terms for the purchase of gas or electric appliances and mechanical systems. If the present power shortage should be solved, there will undoubtedly be a return to this type of competition.

Industrial developers can look to competing transportation forms, particularly railroads, for land subsidies, trackage subsidies, and other forms of assistance if they are heavy users of transportation services.

In areas of underemployment, developments that will produce jobs for a substantial number of people, may receive the support of a wide range of local industries and services. Such support can include outright grants, tax moratoriums, and revenue bond financing.

Various Investor Types

Unconventional Loans from Conventional Sources. Some conventional lenders are authorized to make unconventional loans with a portion of their funds. These are often called "basket loans" because the portion of funds which is available for unconventional loans is referred to as a "basket." These loans may take the form of junior mortgages, joint venture equity participations, subordinated ground leases, trust participations, or other types of advances which are secured or structured in a manner different from that of a conventional first mortgage.

Many major insurance companies will purchase the entire equity of a property subject to an existing or new first-mortgage loan in favor of another institution and then lease the property back to the developer. Commercial banks will make working capital and turnaround loans to on which interest alone has to be paid and in some cases even with interest payments deferred. To qualify for such loans, a high degree of creditability is required, as well as a good financial statement and a showing that repayment can be made from sources other than the project itself.

Private Individuals. In communities throughout the United States there are private individuals who have accumulated substantial funds that they would like to place at higher interest rates than those offered by savings accounts at commercial banks or other conventional financial institutions. Such persons can be reached through classified and display ads in local newspapers, through mortgage brokers and mortgage bankers (see Chapter 47), and through the special advisers that these persons rely upon.

Persons who have funds available for investment often look to their attorney, insurance broker, accountant, business adviser, local banker, stockbroker, or real estate broker for advice on where and how to invest the funds. These professionals are excellent sources for leads to secondary financing and to unconventional first loans. Other sources may be found among relatives, business associates, friends, neighbors, and acquaintances.

In dealing with private individuals, the lender should be aware that local usury laws place restrictions on the effective interest rate which private individuals can charge. Private individuals are often not familiar with these laws, and it is incumbent upon those who resort to this segment of the "unconventional loan market" to know how a transaction may be structured to meet both the lender's and the borrower's objectives. Many carefully negotiated and well-documented private loans fail at the last minute when a lender is informed by his advisers that a loan cannot be made under the usury laws of the given jurisdiction. In dealings with private lenders, the usury laws are an issue which must be faced squarely at an early stage of the negotiations.

Structure of Ownership and Other Debt

Time Sharing, Licenses, Condominiumizing, Membership Sales, and Undivided Interests. The facilities of many projects lend themselves to use by many persons at the same time or at different times. Although this phenomenon is most common for recreational properties, such as summer homes, athletic facilities, guest ranches, and hotels, it may also characterize other types of properties. For example, a beach home could be owned by a number of families each of which would own it for a particular "time slot," such as specified weeks or months during the year. Thus the cost to each coowner would be merely a fraction of what owning the entire facility would be. The technique of common ownership and interim recreational use has been used successfully as a method of financing the development, acquisition, and ownership of such properties and also as a means for overcoming environmental objections to subdividing large recreational projects.

Bonds and Notes. In the 1920s it was quite common to issue mortgage participation bonds on projects that required substantial financing. These bonds represented a participating interest in a mortgage and were sold directly to the public in much the same way as stocks or corporate bonds are sold today. During the depression many of these bonds defaulted, causing this form of investment to fall into disrepute. The selling of participations, however, should be considered where appropriate. For example, mortgage participation in a first-mortgage position rather than various levels of junior financing might be offered to materials suppliers and others who are desirous of seeing a project built. This has been a popular method of building hotels, convention centers, and other public facilities in local communities where conventional financing was unavailable.

Revenue bonds are another unconventional source of financing. These bonds are issued by local authorities, and the interest upon them may be exempt from state and federal taxation under certain circumstances, but the sole obligation for repayment is the revenue from the specific project. Revenue bonds are in the nature of mortgages, and they do not bear the full faith and credit of the local agency. They may be used not only for the project itself but also for the project "infrastructure," such as streets, street lighting, curbs, road signs, sewers, and ornamental landscaping.

Public and Private Placement Syndication and Joint Venture. A portion of the equity in a project can be sold to private or public investors through a syndication or a joint venture. Combining equity syndication or the securing of a joint venture partner—either to obtain cash equity investment or to enable the developer to use the partner's established lines of credit—with the techniques discussed previously generally results in a financing of 100 percent of the total cost of a project.

In times of high interest rates and capital shortages, it is more feasible to raise funds by selling equity than by borrowing. The choice can be made by considering whether the available loan constant will be higher than the loan constant that investors require for equity investment. By raising equity capital for a portion of the investment, a loan can often be secured at lower interest rates and longer terms, thus reducing the loan constant and increasing the cash flow. By increasing the return on his retained interest, this may more than compensate the developer for the fact that he has to surrender a portion of the equity, a portion of the future appreciation, and some of his tax benefits in order to secure investor participation.

On the other hand, during times of high fund availability and low interest rates the developer is able to secure maximum loans at loan constants which, together with the other techniques set forth, will enable him to retain all of the tax benefits and all of the future appreciation and to avoid the costs of syndication.

Conclusion

Consideration of the opportunities to leverage equity and improve cash flow by utilizing noninstitutional investment alternatives enhances the developer's ability to take on new projects and maximize profit opportunities. Loans from a combination of unconventional and conventional sources can result in the magic 100 percent financing that all real estate developers seek. The techniques required involve complex legal, accounting, and investor considerations, but those techniques have saved many an otherwise "unfinanceable" project.

MORTGAGE COMPANIES

Phillip E. Kidd

Oliver H. Jones

*P*HILLIP E. KIDD, PhD, Director of Economic Research, McGraw-Hill Information Systems Company, New York, New York.
   Working on annual and five-year construction forecasts and helping extend McGraw-Hill economic analyses into new industries. Formerly economist, Mortgage Bankers Association of America. Past vice president, National Capital Chapter, National Association of Business Economists. Author of articles on mortgage banking operations, structural changes in the mortgage market, and alternative systems of allocating mortgage market funds. Author, Mortgage Banking, 1963 to 1972: A Financial Intermediary in Transition.

OLIVER H. JONES, PhD, Oliver Jones & Associates, Consulting Economist, Manns Choice, Pennsylvania.
   Author, Oliver Jones Report. Formerly executive vice president, Mortgage Bankers Association of America; expert adviser to secretary of housing and urban development and president of Federal National Mortgage Association; and professorial lecturer, The American University, Washington, D.C. Past member, Board of Directors, American Finance Association; past president, George Washington Chapter, National Association of Business Economists; and past president, International Fraternity of Lambda Alpha. Formerly author of a column for 30 newspapers. Coauthor, The Secondary Mortgage Market.

Mortgage companies are a unique member of the family of institutions that finance real estate transactions. Unlike mortgage brokers, they originate mortgage loans with their own funds and credit resources. Unlike other financial institutions, they sell the mortgage loans they originate to other investors and they service those loans for these investors. As a result, mortgage companies are the intermediaries of the mortgage market, the focal point of the nationwide secondary market for mortgages and the fulcrum that balances its needs.

As a group, mortgage companies are the most diversified of all the financial institutions that serve the real estate market (see Table 1). One mortgage company may specialize in financing single-family residences; another may specialize in commercial lending; and still another may combine the two. Most mortgage companies are also active in a variety of other functions related to real estate.

In total, mortgage companies provide financing for every type of real estate, from land development and construction to the long-term mortgage. They sell mortgages to and service mortgages for every type of lender, from individuals to other financial institutions to federal agencies. They engage in every type of activity related to real estate—provid-

TABLE 1
Diversity of Mortgage Company Industry, 1976 ($ millions)

Type of loan closed			
First-mortgage loans			$23,579
One-family		$18,986	
FHA	$5,938		
VA	9,051		
Conventional	3,997		
Multifamily		1,446	
Nonresidential*		3,147	
Servicing retained	$21,448		
Servicing not retained	2,132		
Home improvement loans			36
Construction loans			
Face amount		4,439	
Amount disbursed	$ 2,979		
Land development loans			451
Second-mortgage loans			96
Other nonmortgage loans†			164
Total loans closed			$28,766
Type of purchaser			
Life insurance companies			$ 3,001
Mutual savings banks			1,181
Savings and loan associations			3,154
Commercial banks (trust departments included in trusteed funds)			694
Trusteed funds			287
FNMA..............................			2,334
GNMA			1,629
REITs			89
Mortgage pools for GNMA securities ...			9,454
State finance agencies			317
Others			865
Inventory without commitment			574
Totals			$23,579

* Includes farm and ranch loans.
† Principally mobile home and consumer loans.
Source: Mortgage Bankers Association of America.

ing insurance, purchasing land, development, construction, sales, and property management. As active participants in federal housing programs, they are specialists in the paperwork and the regulatory requirements prescribed by federal agencies. Not regulated by any one agency, they must comply with the regulations that are imposed on the private and public financial institutions that purchase their products and that insure or guarantee the loans they produce and the securities they issue.

Economic Functions

The Allocation of Resources. Through loan originations and sales, mortgage companies make a significant contribution to the nation's economic efficiency by allocating an essential but limited resource—savings—through the nationwide mortgage market.

The nationwide mortgage market is a complex of interrelated, but separate, local markets. It is localized by the fixed site of the building, and it is interrelated by the movement of funds. Local markets seldom enjoy a balanced supply of and demand for mortgage credit. Growing markets are always short of savings, and old established communities are always long on savings. In most areas, needs for houses and other buildings are constantly changing.

Prior to the development of a nationwide secondary market, local borrowers depended upon local lenders to meet their mortgage credit needs. Marked variances in mortgage interest rates and the availability of mortgage credit were common, as these were determined by the balance between savings and credit demands at the local level. Differences in the cost and the availability of credit varied over a wide range prior to 1945, and such variations have recurred in periods when the nationwide market was unable to work effectively because of state usury laws or nationwide monetary crises.

Inasmuch as credit is a highly liquid commodity and investors seek the highest yield available for comparable risks, one might assume that mortgage credit always moved across the nation with ease. This has not been the case, because savings and loan associations and mutual savings banks were not permitted to extend mortgage credit on properties located outside lending areas that were prescribed by law and regulation. Commercial banks and life insurance companies were largely free from such restrictions, but they did not have the vehicles necessary to lend on properties that were located beyond the areas they knew and understood.

In the early postwar years, the mortgage company provided long-distance lenders with the local knowledge they needed in order to make mortgage investments and with on-site facilities for looking after their interests once the loans were on the books. The Federal Housing Administration (FHA) and the Veterans Administration (VA) provided loan insurance and guarantees, respectively, as well as underwriting and building requirements that generated a standard of negotiability and acceptability for mortgages. The Federal National Mortgage Association (FNMA) provided the backstop that mortgage companies needed by supplementing the private secondary market and maintaining a ready market for FHA and VA mortgages.

In the years that followed, these proven vehicles were supplemented by laws that permitted savings and loan associations and mutual savings banks to purchase mortgages on properties in other areas, by the creation of the Federal Home Loan Mortgage Corporation and the Government National Mortgage Association, and by the extension of the scope of the Federal National Mortgage Association to include the purchase of mortgage loans on residences and apartments that were not federally insured or guaranteed. Private mortgage insurers were established. And without any of these supports the growth of mortgage companies and the confidence of investors in their performance made it possible to finance commercial and industrial properties on a nationwide basis.

There are still numerous impediments to the development of a totally free market in mortgages over state lines, but considerable progress has been made and the mortgage company has played a central role in the advances that have taken place. Today the nationwide mortgage market enables mortgage borrowers in Texas to obtain funds from Massachusetts at a cost that is about the same as that paid by borrowers in Massachusetts and enables savers in Connecticut to earn interest at a rate that is about the same as that earned by savers in California.

A Buffer against Cyclic Change.   Mortgage companies also function as a buffer against dramatic changes in interest rates and the availability of mortgage credit. By giving builders and borrowers commitments to provide mortgage credit at a fixed yield before funds are actually needed, mortgage companies enable the construction and lending markets to continue their activities even when the markets are severely disrupted. When a given group of institutions, say commercial banks, contract their mortgage lending because consumer and business demands for credit command a greater use of their resources, mortgage companies find funds for mortgage borrowers by turning to other investors, federal agencies, or the securities markets.

The ability of mortgage companies to smooth the adjustment process is, of course, limited by the extent of the forces that are contracting the market and by the length of time that those forces are in place. Nevertheless, mortgage companies and the commitment process that grew out of their activities have played a significant role in enhancing the economy's ability to adjust to change.

Local Service for Long-Distance Lenders.   In a narrower scope, mortgage companies function as intermediaries whose knowledge of local real estate markets makes it possible for portfolio investors to extend credit over wide geographic areas. Over the life of the loans that mortgage companies sell to portfolio investors, these companies also perform the loan management functions, commonly referred to as mortgage servicing, that can be performed only by local contact with the borrower.

This arrangment enables long-distance lenders to avoid the overhead expense of maintaining branch offices, whether they need mortgage investments or not. The mortgage company, in turn, meets its obligations by serving a number of investors and by shifting its sales to those who remain in the market for mortgages. If all investors are out of the market, the mortgage company can sell only to federal agencies and must absorb the cost of any overhead that is not fully utilized.

Originating Mortgage Loans

Single-Family Residential. Loan origination is the process that leads up to and includes closing, when funds are disbursed to the borrower. Commonly referred to as production, the loan origination process typically begins with the loan application. Few residential borrowers contact the mortgage company directly. Most residential loans are produced by regular mortgage company contacts with builders and real estate brokers. A builder may already have a mortgage company's commitment to make a loan and, particularly in a rising market, may be able to offer better terms than are currently available. The real estate salesperson knows the terms that are currently available from the mortgage company and from local investors as well as the time that it will take to close a loan. Accordingly, he advises the buyer, typically a buyer of an existing property, where he can best be served and he may assist the buyer in obtaining the mortgage loan.

Once an application is in hand, it is the mortgage company's responsibility to prepare the loan package, that is, to take all the steps necessary to prepare the loan for final closing—make credit checks and appraisals, obtain FHA insurances or VA guaranty, check the site and the structure, negotiate terms, and fulfill other underwriting requirements.

For this service, the mortgage company typically earns an origination fee of 1 percent of the loan amount which is paid by the home buyer. The FHA and the VA limit this origination fee to 1 percent, and competition often forces the mortgage company to charge the same fee for conventional home loans. Even so, the company typically loses one or more percent in loan originations. The loss is absorbed in order to develop servicing income.

During the production process, the mortgage company must see that the loan finally produced will meet the requirements of one or more of its investors and to see that it has a sufficient volume of commitments from permanent investors to purchase its production. Keep in mind that the mortgage company closes the loans with its own funds.

Commercial. Because of the size of large commercial loans and because of the wide differences in types, the production of such loans follows a different pattern. Developers do make direct contacts with mortgage companies, because mortgage companies maintain a staff of specialists in commercial lending who regularly seek out developers for new business.

The investor is typically brought into the process early. As soon as the loan package has been prepared, it is presented to the investor who is most likely to purchase the loan. The investor often seeks to negotiate special terms in the loan arrangement and often specifies requirements that must be met before he will make the mortgage loan. He will assuredly require that construction be completed according to plans and specifications. He may also require that leases be signed by good credit risks for 80 percent of the space. Such negotiations have generated a wide variety of investor requirements and financing arrangements— from sale-leaseback loans to gap loans—all of which the mortgage company arranges.

Once the mortgage company has completed these negotiations and has a commitment to purchase—when the specified requirements are met—it is the mortgage company's job to prepare the loan for closing. Typically, the commercial loan is closed on the committed lender's forms in accordance with its preestablished requirements, originated in the committed lender's name, and closed with the committed lender's funds.

Origination fees vary on large commercial loans, but they are often as much as 2 percent of the loan amount. Origination costs are seldom absorbed by the mortgage company, because the investor may service the mortgage and the servicing fee is often a small percentage of the loan balance.

Marketing Mortgage Loans

Marketing cannot be described separately from the origination process, and the above discussion noted the necessity to produce loans that meet the needs of particular investors, that are, in fact, marketable.

Normally, commercial loan producers market their production well before final closing. Single-family loan marketing follows a quite different pattern. Here, the individual responsible for selling the loans wants to avoid having closed loans for sale with no buyer in sight. The objective is to obtain a volume of commitments from investors that is sufficient to cover anticipated loan production.

Warehousing. This is the marketers' first line of defense. Mortgage companies must arrange sufficient lines of credit with their commercial banks to cover their residential loan production until the loans can be closed and packages of mortgages, usually amounting to $1 million or more, are ready for delivery to investors. Banks have been willing to establish lines of credit for mortgage companies because: (1) mortgage companies usually have commitments from permanent investors to purchase the loans in inventory and the construction loans that they are funding; (2) the single-family mortgages in inventory are mostly insured or guaranteed by the government; (3) single-family loans are usually rolled over every 90 to 120 days; and (4) single-family construction loans also roll over fairly quickly since repayments to disbursements average 85 to 90 percent each year.

The cost of warehousing lines varies from the bank prime rate to the prime rate plus one or two points. Since the early 1970s, however, mortgage companies have expanded their short-term borrowing options to improve earnings when money market rates are below the prime rates charged by banks. Many mortgage companies issue commercial paper, either through their parent holding companies, which are financially stronger, or in their own names, but backed by lines of credit from their commercial banks. Large issuers of GNMA securities also obtain funds by arranging repurchase agreements in which they sell GNMA securities to investment bankers and buy the securities back 60 to 90 days later at a higher price, usually about half a point higher.

Mortgage companies maintain strong relationships with their banks. These institutions act as trustees for pool documentation when mortgage companies issue GNMA securities. Banks also frequently support the commercial paper issues of mortgage companies. They remain the most important source of short-term credit for mortgage companies.

The Commitment Process. This is clearly an important aspect of a mortgage company's success or failure in single-family lending. The process came into existence in the early postwar years, when life insurance companies, eager to invest in FHA and VA mortgages, provided advance commitments to purchase mortgages. From this simple agreement to purchase a fixed volume of mortgages that met the investor's specifications, at a fixed and sometimes negotiable yield, the commitment has become a highly flexible vehicle.

Three major types of investor commitments are used—firm or mandatory delivery, optional delivery, and standbys. Each type has its strengths and weaknesses, so mortgage companies use the three types in combination to protect their position.

Under a firm commitment, mortgage companies agree to deliver a specified volume of loans at stated prices or yields by a set date, usually one to four months in the future. If the loans meet the agreed-upon conditions, the investor must purchase them. Generally, the commitment fees, if any, are small. The major risk for mortgage companies is in originating, processing, and delivering the appropriate volume of loans. Steep penalties, including possible legal actions, exist if loan delivery is not made.

Under optional delivery commitments, such as those auctioned by FNMA, mortgage companies have the choice of delivering or not delivering the loans. Such commitments permit mortgage companies to hold loans in inventory while searching the market for better prices from other investors. If other investors offer higher prices, mortgage companies sell them the loans and use the optional delivery commitments to protect other loans or allow the commitments to expire. If no better offers exist, mortgage companies deliver under the optional commitments and if the loans fit the conditions of the commitments, the investors must purchase them.

Mortgage companies usually pay a fee for optional delivery commitments. It may be a flat fee for a predetermined number of months (e.g., FNMA auction commitments), or it may be a fee that increases one eighth of 1 percent per month (e.g., investment banker commitments for GNMA securities).

Usually, optional delivery commitments are for less than six months. Consequently, mortgage companies can use them only to cover loans that are nearly closed or are actually closed and in inventory.

Under standby commitments, mortgage companies are seeking long-term protection, primarily for their commitments to builders. Standbys are optional delivery commitments carrying a fixed yield for which mortgage companies pay fees, but usually standbys have a much longer life than optional delivery commitments, frequently extending six months to a year, and often longer.

Investors establish their standby yields according to their expectations about the direction and the level of interest rates throughout the life of the standbys. The yields are set well above the market rate to discourage mortgage companies from delivering loans.

Investors issue standby commitments because of the fee income, not because they want mortgages. However, if prices should fall suddenly, or if mortgage funds should become unavailable, standby commitments allow mortgage companies to deliver loans, especially loans that are being produced from commitments issued to builders.

New Sources of Commitments. In recent years, several changes have added important new sources of commitments to those provided by institutional investors.

FNMA Commitments. FNMA maintains a biweekly auction for 4-month optional commitments and an open window for 12-month standby and convertible standby commitments. The latter can be converted into four-month optional commitments at any time during the period of the original commitment.

The FNMA auction system provides an important degree of flexibility to the residential mortgage market. Because financial institutions, especially thrift institutions, can adjust their loan purchases from mortgage companies to cover any imbalances, they no longer have to match their originations perfectly with their savings inflows. On the other hand, mortgage companies with FNMA commitments can hold mortgages in inventory and search the market for better prices. If there are no better offers from private investors, the loans can be sold to FNMA.

GNMA Securities. Another action that improved liquidity in the mortgage market was the development of the GNMA mortgage-backed, pass-through security. The concept of a mortgage-backed security rests on pooling mortgages, issuing a security, and using the income from the underlying pool of mortgages to pay off the security. Although an old concept, the security adds a significant new feature in the guaranty of the Government National Mortgage Association (GNMA). Security holders are now assured of the timely payment of principal and interest by the "full faith and credit of the United States Treasury," which stands behind the GNMA guaranty.

Even though Farmers Home Administration loans are eligible to back GNMA securities, nearly all of the pools to date have been made up of FHA and VA loans. Mortgage companies are the largest originators of FHA and VA home loans, originating about three out of every four of the loans closed. Thus, it is not surprising that mortgage companies are the largest issuers of GNMA securities.

GNMA securities are highly standardized financial instruments in which secondary market trading has developed. The ability to originate new GNMA securities or to buy outstanding GNMA securities to fill investors' commitments has substantially improved the operating flexibility of mortgage companies. If their loan production falls short of projections, they can fill their outstanding investor commitments for GNMA securities through security purchases in the secondary market.

Equally important, mortgage companies, which relied on their own sales personnel to market mortgage loans, have found it much more efficient to market GNMA securities through investment bankers. These companies have sales staffs that are in constant touch with a wide range of financial and nonfinancial investors, from which they obtain commitments to buy GNMA securities. In turn, they use these commitments to set the prices at which they will buy GNMA securities from mortgage companies. Moreover, since the different types of investors have unique needs, investment bankers tailor GNMA transactions to specific investor requirements. Consequently, investment bankers have a mixture of firm, optional delivery, and standby commitments that they can offer mortgage companies.

Because GNMA securities are standardized financial instruments, the Chicago Board of Trade has developed a GNMA futures contract in which trading began in October 1975. Trading in futures is another tool that mortgage companies now have for minimizing their risks from interest rate changes between the date of their commitment to the builder-borrower and the date they sell a mortgage to an investor. For instance, if mortgage bankers have issued commitments to builders and borrowers for loan financing in four months at a fixed price (long in the cash market), they can hedge their position by selling an equal amount of four-month GNMA futures contracts (short in the futures market). If interest rates rise, mortgage companies would suffer a loss in the cash market because they will have to discount the loans being produced from their commitments to sell them. However, rising yields would lower prices in the futures market. Therefore, as the date of the mortgage closing approached, the mortgage companies would offset their short position in the futures market by buying lower-priced futures contracts. Thus, the gains in their futures transactions would theoretically offset the losses they incurred in the cash market.

The GNMA futures market represents an important means of adding liquidity to the mortgage market because it attracts institutions, companies, and individuals that are not usually involved in mortgage finance. Still, there are costs for mortgage companies in buying, selling, and holding GNMA futures contracts. Moreover, the futures market is not a delivery market, even though recent developments have eased the barriers against delivery. Consequently, mortgage companies can use the futures market to hedge their activity position, but they must still find investors that will buy the loans.

Servicing Mortgage Loans. After selling loans to investors, mortgage companies usually service the loans for them. Servicing consists principally of collecting and accounting for the monthly payment, maintaining an escrow account for the payment of property taxes and insurance premiums, checking insurance coverage, examining the property periodically, and handling foreclosures when necessary.

In loan servicing, mortgage companies are on-the-spot agents for investors. They see that mortgagors' payment are current; they credit the principal and interest payments to investor accounts; they use the tax and insurance escrows that they collect from mortgagors to pay these bills for the mortgagors. If mortgagors become delinquent in their mortgage payments, loan servicers work with them to solve the problem. Payment extensions may be granted, and loan terms may be recast. If loans continue to be delinquent, loan servicers institute foreclosure proceedings and, if necessary, after foreclosure has been completed, they sell the properties in order to recover their investors' money.

For these services, mortgage companies collect a servicing fee which is commonly three eighths of 1 percent of the principal balance for single-family loans and considerably less for large commercial loans. This steady source of income enables mortgage companies to weather the vicissitudes of the market. Obviously, the size of the loans put on the books is a principal factor in determining the level of servicing income.

Mortgage Companies and Federal Housing Programs

Mortgage companies are major catalysts in translating federal housing programs into products. They are the principal originators of mortgages under federal social housing programs.

In the late 1960s and early 1970s, mortgage companies were major originators of FHA 235 loans (a subsidy program designed to assist low- and moderate-income families in purchasing new homes) and FHA 236 loans (a rent subsidy program for low- and moderate-income families). Currently, they are major originators of Section 221(d)(3) and (4) rental housing loans (subsidy programs that help house low- and moderate-income families and families displaced by urban renewal).

The contribution of mortgage companies to federal social housing programs has been twofold. First, they have worked aggressively to attract private funds to these programs. For instance, they actively sold subsidized loans to GNMA and then bought these loans back for resale to private investors under various GNMA tandem plans.

Since the first GNMA tandem plan was initiated in 1970, the plan has had many forms. The basic concept, however, is for GNMA to establish above-market prices at which it will buy eligible FHA, VA, and Farmers Home Administrations mortgages and then to offer these mortgages for sale at market prices. In this way, GNMA increases the number of units that are funded through its limited appropriations and mortgage investors obtain mortgages at current market yields. At first, GNMA arbitrarily set both its purchase and sale prices. Later it established the purchase prices but auctioned the loans, so that market forces established the sale prices.

Currently, mortgage companies oriented toward FHA projects are aggressively trying to package section 221(d)(3) and 221(d)(4) multifamily loans in GNMA securities. These securities will greatly expand the marketability of such loans, thus attracting more private funds to the FHA programs.

Second, because of their multiplicity of real estate skills, mortgage companies are better able than other originators to cope with the problems posed by the complex and frequently contradictory regulations of HUD. Consequently, mortgage companies have become the chief private explainers of federally sponsored housing programs to builder-developers and investors, including nonprofit sponsors that have little knowledge of construction and mortgage practices and procedures. It is the knowledge capital and real estate skills of the mortgage companies that keep these diverse interests together until projects are completed.

Mortgage Company Activities Related to Real Estate Lending

The modern mortgage company developed in the postwar years, although its predecessors date back to the middle of the 19th century. Many firms that began in other businesses in the postwar years now retain those activities as an adjunct to their mortgage company business. These activities include, most notably, real estate sales, construction, and land development.

Other related activities have grown out of the mortgage-lending activity of various firms, either as supplements to that business or a means of producing mortgage loans. Most mortgage companies, for example, make insurance available to their borrowers. This may go no further than fire and hazard insurance, but it may also include mortgage life insurance or a full complement of insurance.

Some mortgage companies purchase and hold land for builder-developers; others are engaged in joint ventures with builders and land developers. A number of the real estate investment trusts of the late 60s were established by mortgage companies which functioned as advisers to the trusts.

Mortgage companies provide a range of real estate services to both builder-developers and investors. Three of the most important services are construction financing, sales and leases, and property management.

Being able to make construction loans is extremely important to mortgage companies because this satisfies a need of builder-developers and because it leads to the production of the mortgages that are required by the investor clients of the mortgage companies. Mortgage companies fund their construction lending through borrowings from their commercial banks. Commercial banks support this activity because they may not be interested in funding the construction projects or because they may lack the necessary in-house expertise to be construction lenders themselves. Moreover, in this way the banks can obtain a high interest rate, usually several points above their prime rates, while minimizing their risks. Moreover, mortgage companies normally have investor commitments, assuring the banks that the construction loans will be repaid once the projects are completed. Mortgage companies are known customers with an established credit history, whereas builder-developers may lack these credentials. In effect, commercial banks substitute the credit rating of mortgage companies for that of the builder-developers.

Permanent investors frequently require that significant portions of the space be preleased once construction has been completed before they will extend permanent mortgage funds. Builder-developers often lack the people to arrange such leases. Consequently, many mortgage companies have established property management and sales and leasing departments. Personnel from these departments find potential tenants and negotiate leases. Such leases indicate that a project is not speculative and provide a measure of the cash flow that will be generated by the project.

Altogether, mortgage companies combine the skills that are needed to take project proposals from the development stage through construction and beyond. They can help builder-developers obtain permanent financing commitments, and they can arrange construction financing, either directly or through other interim lenders, such as commercial banks and real estate investment trusts. If developers lack leasing expertise, mortgage companies can find the tenants. Furthermore, they provide both developers and lenders with on-the-spot supervision of projects under construction. Then, when construction has been completed, their property managers work to keep properties profitable.

The Structure of the Mortgage Company Industry

The number of mortgage companies is small when compared with the number of other financial institutions. The data provided here relate to 735 mortgage companies which are members of the Mortgage Bankers Association of America (MBA) (see Table 2). In 1963, when there were 880 MBA member firms, a special study estimated that there were 1,200 firms in the mortgage company business. However, the nonmember firms were relatively small, accounting for less than 20 percent of the total activity of mortgage companies.

TABLE 2
Structure of Mortgage Company Industry, 1976

Size of Servicing Portfolio ($ millions)	Number of Firms	Volume Serviced ($ millions)	Volume Closed ($ millions)
Under $20	176	$ 1,588	$ 1,559
$ 20– 50	114	3,695	1,451
$ 50–100	133	9,900	2,843
$100–200	134	19,643	4,031
$200–400	92	26,366	4,959
$400–800	43	24,847	4,667
$800 or More	43	60,809	9,256
Totals	735	$146,848	$28,766

Source: Mortgage Bankers Association of America, Trends Report Number 21.

As with other financial institutions, the number of mortgage companies has dwindled as a result of mergers and acquisitions and a relatively small number of firms account for a major share of the business. Over the past two decades, many mortgages companies have been purchased by commercial banks, bank holding companies, and business corporations. Some mortgage companies have been absorbed into banks, but many operate as subsidiaries of the parent company. This process has strengthened the credit of the industry and enhanced its ability to serve the market. As an industry, mortgage companies provide other market participants, including home buyers, builder-developers, investors, and federal agencies, with a flexibility which helps them adapt to changing economic and social conditions.

SELECTED REFERENCES

Books

Jones, Oliver H., and Grebler, Leo. *The Secondary Mortgage Market, Its Performance and Its Potential.* Los Angeles: Real Estate Research Program, University of California at Los Angeles, 1961.

Kidd, Phillip E. *Mortgage Banking 1963 to 1972: A Financial Intermediary in Transition.* West Lafayette, Indiana: Krannert Graduate School of Management, Purdue University, Monograph No. 5, 1977.

Klaman, Saul B. *The Postwar Rise of Mortgage Companies.* National Bureau of Economic Research, Occasional Paper 60. New York: National Bureau of Economic Research, Inc. 1959.

Periodical

Colean, Miles, L. "Challenge to the Correspondent System." *Quarterly Economic Report,* August 1972, pp. 1–4.

PRIVATE MORTGAGE INSURANCE

Chester Rapkin

C*HESTER RAPKIN, PhD, Professor of Urban Planning, School of Architecture and Urban Planning, Princeton University, Princeton, New Jersey.*

Consultant to municipal, state, and foreign governments and to the U.S. government; to planning commissions, civic associations, and banking institutions; to builders, developers, and architects. Formerly commissioner, New York City Planning Commission; and staff director, Presidential Task Force, The White House. Author of many articles for various professional journals. Author, An Evaluation of the Urban Renewal Experience in the United States *(Haifa: Center for Urban and Regional Studies, Nieman Institute for Policy Research, The Technion—Israel Institute of Technology, 1979). Coauthor,* The Private Insurance of Home Mortgages: A Study of the Mortgage Guaranty Insurance Corporation *(Institute for Urban Studies, University of Pennsylvania, 1967; rev. 1973);* The Demand for Housing in Racially Mixed Areas *(University of Pennsylvania Press, 1960);* The Mutual Mortgage Insurance Fund *(New York: Columbia University Press, 1956);* Housing Market Analysis *(Washington, D.C.: U.S. Government Printing Office, 1953).*

Real estate mortgage guarantee insurance indemnifies mortgage-lending institutions for the direct and consequential losses that these institutions incur because of nonpayment of first-mortgage loans. Such indemnification is provided both by government agencies (the Federal Housing Administration and the Veterans Administration) and by private mortgage insurance companies. Mortgage insurance, public or private, permits regulated lenders (such as banks and savings and loan associations) to make a loan greater than the percentage of value of the secured property that is stipulated in their controlling statutes or regulations, because in addition to being secured by the property, the loan is secured (in part or in full) by the insurance guarantee.

When mortgage insurance is written by a government agency, it usually covers the entire outstanding amount of the loan; private mortgage insurance, on the other hand, guarantees only the top 20 to 25 percent of the outstanding balance of the mortgage. There are other significant distinctions between private and governmental mortgage insurance. Private mortgage insurance is a business whose operating companies are owned by stockholders. The FHA and the VA are arms of government that are designed to meet social as well as business objectives. Interest rates on FHA and VA loans are set by federal regulation, whereas the private mortgage insurer accepts the interest rate agreed upon by the lender and the borrower. When the FHA and VA rates are out of phase with the market rates, they are brought into reasonable balance by discounting an appropriate number of points.

Mortgage insurance itself does not necessarily reduce the aggregate amount of actual or potential loss. In fact, it may tend to increase losses by encouraging mortgages that ordinarily might not be made. As long as revenue continues to exceed losses with the enlargement of the mortgage market, however, mortgage insurance is beneficial both to the lender and to the family whose mortgage application might fall just short of acceptance without it. Conversely, there is always the danger that under these circumstances the lender will make loans as long as there is an opportunity to increase income, even in the face of a disproportionate rise in risk. There are several important safeguards against this contingency. One safeguard is the separation of the insurance and lending functions, placing each in independent institutions that deal with each other at arm's length. Another is the establishment by the insurer of a review procedure that makes certain that the appraised value of the property and the loan-to-value ratio are as certified by the lender. A third safeguard is the assurance that there is no adverse selection—that is, that the lender insures not only the poor risks but a reasonable cross section of the loans in the insured class. A fourth safeguard is the establishment, on an actuarial basis, of a reserve system that will enable the insurer to cope with a foreclosure and loss experience commensurate with a major reversal in the economy.

In addition to these safeguards, there are criteria for a sound mortgage guarantee insurance operation. The mortgage insurance company must be large enough to be able to avoid the concentration of a risk in any one state or geographic area, any one type of property, or any one type of borrower, in order to minimize the possibility of a loss experience substantially in excess of the average. The company must have sufficient capitalization (and surplus) in the first stages of operation to meet early claims and high initial costs. It must analyze experience in order to compute appropriate and useful measures of the incidence of delinquency, foreclosure, and loss. It must establish an actuarial basis for the computation of reserves, not only in order to cope with anticipated losses, but also in order to define legal and economic solvency with precision. It should also provide for sufficient flexibility of investment policy to be able to capitalize on periods of economic expansion and to reduce the impact of economic contraction.

Private mortgage insurance performs many useful functions. First, it is instrumental in augmenting the flow of funds into home construction which supports a considerable amount of on- and off-site construction employment and also enlarges the housing stock by adding new units to the supply. This, in turn, provides shelter for families, improves the average quality of the housing supply, and helps force substandard units out of the market. Second, mortgage insurance increases the fluidity of credit. By shouldering much of the risk of home mortgage lending, it provides home mortgage credit with a competitive advantage in the financial markets. It also allows a variety of public and private sources of funds to be tapped, because an insured mortgage is salable throughout the country. Private mortgage insurance facilitates the marketing of a mortgage by an investor or an intermediary. Private mortgage insurance not only makes the mortgage more attractive to the investor, but it is required before a conventional mortgage can be purchased by the Federal Home Loan Mortgage Corporation (FHLMC, or "Freddie Mac") or the Federal National Mortgage Association (FNMA, or "Fannie Mae"). Third, mortgage insurance helps bolster demand for home purchase by enabling the lender to accept a larger proportion of mortgage applications than would otherwise be feasible. This is particularly true in the case of high-ratio mortgages, which usually cannot be made without insurance. More households with lower incomes and assets are thus eligible for home ownership than would ordinarily be the case. In general, then, mortgage insurance has helped to support the volume of new construction with its attendant economic benefits, to elevate the quantity and quality of the housing supply, to increase home ownership, and to foster growth and stability in the mortgage market by opening sources of funds that would ordinarily not be available to it.

Since the late 1950s, private mortgage insurance has grown from a modest experiment to a major dynamic force in the home mortgage market. This development is all the more astonishing because of the unfortunate experience of real estate title and mortgage guarantee companies during the Great Depression of the 1930s. In addition, during the two ensuing decades, mortgage insurance was taken to be the exclusive domain of government. Following the entrance of the Mortgage Guaranty Insurance Corporation (MGIC) into the field in 1957, private mortgage insurance surged ahead, attracting a number of other companies and expanding its market. By the end of 1977, private mortgage insurance in force stood behind one out of every three dollars of total mortgage insurance, public or private, on the outstanding mortgage debt on one–four-family nonfarm homes, and behind one out of every two new insured mortgages made.

Some Early History

The revival of private mortgage insurance was inhibited by the memory of the disastrous collapse of the mortgage guarantee companies in the early 1930s. Most of these companies were bank affiliated, and the most active of them were located in New York. Originally, the mortgage guarantee companies could only guarantee the payment of mortgages that were owned by an applicant for insurance, though such an applicant could be (and often was) an affiliated company. The insurance law was amended in 1911 to permit the companies to buy and sell mortgages, thus enabling them to acquire mortgages and then to sell them with a guarantee attached. In fact, the origination or the purchase and sale of mortgages became their primary business, the guarantee being added to make their product more attractive to financial institutions and the investing public. Delinquent or foreclosed mortgages were often substituted at face value for sound mortgages, which could then be sold to more knowledgeable or careful investors. The Bank Holiday of 1933 forced the closing of these firms.

The failure of the mortgage guarantee companies led to the appointment of a New York State investigatory committee, headed by George W. Alger, to service existing mortgages and to liquidate the assets of the mortgage guarantee companies with the least possible loss to both the mortgagor and the mortgagee. The insurance activities of the mortgage guarantee companies were not restored, and they never resumed business again, their function being taken over in essence by the federal government under the National Housing Act of 1934.

The Alger Committee made a number of recommendations for legislation to correct the then existing legal flaws, including: the separation of the mortgage insurance companies from the banking institutions; the requirement of paid-in capital and surplus minima; limitations on the ratio of the amount of the outstanding guarantee to the aggregate of capital and surplus; the requirement that the investment of the guarantee fund be in U.S. bonds or New York State bonds; and the stipulation that guarantees be of first mortgages only. Many of the Alger Committee's recommendations later formed the basis of the legal requirements in current state law governing private mortgage insurance. The Alger Committee's report, however, viewed the combination of the lender and the insurer as a major reason, if not *the* major reason, for the collapse of the industry. In fact, the Alger Committee's report concluded, in part, that

> the business of guaranteeing mortgages is not an ordinary banking function, and the public would have been better off if none of the companies had owned or been affiliated with banking institutions, or in turn had not been owned by them.
>
> I think that the above illustrations make it abundantly clear, if it were not too obvious to require illustration, that banking affiliates or subsidiaries should be no part of the business of a mortgage guarantee company, and that the practice has proved injurious to the public and to the holders of guarantees.

An additional flaw that had substantial impact on the dissolution of the "pre-Crash" private insurers and, indeed, was the death knell for many of these firms, was that these early insurers covered the entire mortgage amount, not merely the top 20–25 percent. The liability of the mortgage guarantee companies was complete and, in many cases, fatal, as the growing number of delinquencies and foreclosures depleted reserves beyond financial solvency. Thus, the private mortgage insurance industry of the pre-Crash period went out of existence during the Great Depression and, in fact, became an impermissible activity for some years in certain jurisdictions.

But mortgage insurance itself was too useful a device to remain submerged for long. By the mid-1930s the federal government recognized that it could be employed as a powerful instrument to implement federal policy throughout the vast constellation of social and economic objectives and institutions that constitute the housing market. During the depression, the establishment of the FHA helped revive the construction industry by generating confidence among mortgage lenders and thus increasing the flow of funds. During World War II, FHA mortgage insurance was the primary means that the U.S. government used to keep housing construction in the private sector of the economy, and thus making sure that the industry would be viable when it was needed for postwar building. After the war, the FHA and the VA aided the returning veteran in acquiring a home. In the following decades, mortgage insurance was used to support the housing components of urban renewal as well as to provide for the construction, rehabilitation, or acquisition of housing for the elderly, for low- and middle-income families, and for housing cooperators.

The Rise in Residential Mortgage Debt

Since the end of World War II, a striking rise in long-term residential mortgage debt has been fed by a continually increasing number of new residential structures, a rise in market values, and a greater use of borrowed funds to support ownership. These have resulted from fundamental demographic forces, as well as from changes in attitude toward home ownership and consumer debt which have combined to alter the predominant residential tenure from rental to owner-occupancy, based on greatly expanded mortgage finance. The proportion of households residing in their own structures has increased from less than one half to almost two thirds; and the percentage of owner-occupied structures financed with mortgages has risen to over 60 percent. In addition, the number of dwelling units has more than doubled since World War II. As a consequence of these changes, total outstanding mortgage debt on one–four-family nonfarm houses grew from $19 billion in 1945 to $652 billion in 1977.

The governmental insurance programs have had a significant (if incalculable) effect on the growth of the mortgage debt, both directly, through the mortgages issued under their aegis, and indirectly, through their influence on mortgage terms generally. Between 1934 and 1976, almost 10 million housing units with mortgage face amounts of over $120 billion were insured by the Mutual Mortgage Insurance Fund (MMIF), the insurance reserve established for FHA Section 203(b) loans. By the end of 1976, the MMIF had acquired 412,000 properties at a cost of $5 billion, or an average of $12,150 per property, on which an average loss of $3,560, or 29 percent, was incurred. Between 1934 and 1976, the MMIF had routinely met all claims, had accumulated reserves of $2.0 billion, or 5 percent in excess of actuarial requirements, and had returned to the U.S. Treasury all of the funds that had been advanced for its establishment, plus interest.

In general (largely under the influence of the governmental programs), there has been a shift from unamortized or partially amortized mortgages to mortgages that are completely repaid in a systematic manner over the life of the loan; from low loan-to-value ratios to much smaller equity requirements; from mortgages with relatively short terms to long-term mortgages; and until recently, from higher interest rates to lower interest rates. Further, the standardization of mortgage terms and the relatively uniform property evaluations of the FHA and the VA have served to promote a secondary mortgage market which facilitates the distribution of mortgage funds from capital-rich areas to areas in which capital funds for mortgages have been relatively scarce.

The Reemergence of Private Mortgage Insurance

Despite its significant influence, government mortgage insurance reached a maximum of only 44 percent of the home mortgage debt in the mid-1950s, and in recent years it has declined to roughly one fifth of the total home mortgage debt. The rigidity of the application form, a fixed interest rate that often stood below the market level, the lengthy and complicated procedures, and the restrictions on the kind and quality of housing led many types of lending institutions (notably savings and loan associations) to remain with or to return to the conventional mortgage. In 1957 the first private mortgage insurance company, the Mortgage Guaranty Insurance Corporation, was organized to provide mortgage insurance on a somewhat different basis from that offered by the FHA. Whereas the FHA insured the total outstanding balance of the loan, private mortgage insurance covered only a portion of the outstanding mortgage amount. Today private mortgage insurers have the option of paying the lending institution the outstanding balance of the mortgage loan and receiving the title to the mortgaged property or of satisfying the claim by paying the lending institution a fixed percentage of the outstanding balance of the mortgage loan. This percentage is usually 20 percent, but it may be 25 percent for higher-ratio loans, that is, loans having a ratio to value of up to 95 percent. Of course, the 25 percent option carries a higher premium than the 20 percent option.

The Growth of Private Mortgage Insurance

Measured in terms of insurance in force, that is, in terms of the amount of first-mortgage indebtedness subject to insurance, the private mortgage insurance industry grew from its inception in the late 1950s to $7.3 billion in 1970 and then surged ahead, reaching $63.0 billion in 1977 (see Table 1). As one would expect from these figures, the rise in

TABLE 1
Key Statistics of the Private Mortgage Insurance Industry

Year	Insurance in Force ($ millions)	Premiums Written ($ thousands)	Premiums Earned ($ thousands)	Losses and Loss Expenses ($ thousands)	Loss Ratio (percent)	Assets ($ thousands)	Unearned Premium Reserve ($ thousands)	Loss Reserve ($ thousands)	Contingency Reserve ($ thousands)
1965	$ 3,256	12,951	10,438	3,261	31.2	58,383	16,440	2,401	15,155
1970	7,312	21,425	20,318	1,746	8.6	159,124	27,568	2,604	56,048
1971	9,643	46,731	26,589	2,295	8.6	245,044	48,869	3,044	68,436
1972	17,454	113,442	55,102	5,373	7.8	408,956	106,760	4,369	91,974
1973	27,430	154,317	92,807	18,709	20.2	502,906	145,603	10,401	138,329
1974	33,975	130,274	115,230	31,533	27.4	552,248	153,671	18,037	192,354
1975	39,925	140,849	125,734	39,737	31.6	677,928	165,654	27,424	251,350
1976	49,296	181,396	168,685	50,325	29.8	828,606	182,092	35,182	326,622
1977	63,030	234,222	207,400	39,000	18.8	1,038,859	211,000	38,598	383,307

Source: Mortgage Insurance Companies of America.

new private insurance written has been even more rapid. This amount rose from $162 million in 1960 to $1.4 billion in 1970, and it reached $21.6 billion in 1977, a 15-fold increase in seven years. In the late 1970s, approximately two decades after their reestablishment, private mortgage insurance companies had attained a high level of operation and had become a major force in the mortgage market.

This conclusion is confirmed by the fact that private mortgage insurance in force represented 0.2 percent of the total mortgage debt in one–four-family nonfarm homes in 1960 and 9.7 percent in 1977. Private mortgage insurance has also enlarged its share of the total market for mortgage insurance, public and private. In 1960, private mortgage insurance constituted 0.5 percent of the total mortgage insurance in force, including FHA Section 203(b) and VA loans. By 1970 this proportion had risen to 7.0 percent of the insured indebtedness, and by 1977 it had reached 30.8 percent. Even more impressive is the fact that by the early 1970s new insurance written by private mortgage companies exceeded the share of the market represented by FHA mortgage insurance and the VA home loan program combined, thus placing the private mortgage companies ahead of the major government mortgage insurance programs.

The Market Served by Private Mortgage Insurance

Since the market for insured and guaranteed mortgages has become evenly divided between private companies and government agencies, the sectors of the market served by each, although still retaining some measure of difference, tend to overlap to a considerable degree. Private firms in the period 1976–77 insured larger mortgages and dealt with higher priced homes than did the FHA or the VA. Families whose mortgages are insured by private firms tend to have higher income and to spend less of their income for housing than do those families whose mortgages are insured or guaranteed by the FHA or the VA. Private mortgage insurers tended to take mortgages with somewhat lower loan-to-value ratios—89.3 percent—than did the FHA, with 94.8 percent, and the VA, with 97.2 percent.

The difference in the loan-to-value ratio is due in considerable measure to the FHA's current mortgage limits for single-family houses. For loans up to $25,000, a loan-to-value ratio of 97 percent is permissible; for loans of $35,000, the loan ratio can go to 95 percent; and for loans of $45,000, the FHA maximum, the limit is set at 92 percent. Private mortgage insurers (PMIs), on the other hand, cannot insure loans that represent more than 95 percent of value, but there is no legal maximum on the loan amount. Thus, legal eligibility may indeed account for the differences in the loan-to-value ratio of FHA- and PMI-insured loans.

In contrast with the FHA and the PMIs, the VA wrote guarantees for loans representing 100 percent of value in 72 percent of its new business in 1976. There is no limit on the loan amount of a GI home mortgage, even if it constitutes 100 percent of value. The VA guarantee, however, covers 60 percent of the outstanding amount of the loan or

$25,000, whichever is less. Thus, the guarantee is 60 percent of the outstanding balance on loans with an original face amount of up to $41,666. On a larger loan, say one of $100,000, the guarantee will be $25,000, or 25 percent of the original amount. As such a loan is amortized, the guarantee will remain at $25,000 until it reaches $41,666, after which it is reduced commensurately, maintaining a constant 60 percent as the remainder of the loan is entirely repaid.

Both the FHA and the VA tend to write more of their business on existing properties (as opposed to new construction) than do private insurers. But although the ratio for the two government agencies remained virtually unchanged between 1972 and 1973, MGIC tended to write more of its insurance on mortgages secured by existing properties. The MGIC ratio was 58.1 percent of the total in 1972 and 62.0 percent of the total in 1973.

The experience of the past few years indicates that the differences in market coverage have diminished considerably and that in some places they have disappeared. There is little doubt, for example, that the FHA and the private mortgage insurers deal with substantially the same family income distribution, whereas the lower-income market has fallen to the VA, where it is likely to remain as long as 100 percent loans are made available to young veterans. The difference between the market of the private mortgage insurance companies and the VA market is reduced, however, when the average mortgage amounts covered by each are examined. The 100 percent VA loan compensates in the mortgage market for whatever difficulties young veterans may experience because of deficiencies in their earning capacity. The VA guarantee carries no premium, and it is backed by the U.S. Treasury. Its remarkable rise in the 1970s indicates that it is prepared to fill any gaps that may arise in the availability of mortgage guarantee insurance, thus increasing the overlap and minimizing the segmentation.

Competition in the Private Mortgage Insurance Industry

Private mortgage insurance did not remain a single-company industry for very long. Within a few years after MGIC demonstrated its ability to operate profitably, other private mortgage insurance firms began to be formed. By the end of 1977, 14 companies were actively engaged in the business. In actuality, a greater number of firms were established during this period, but the number was reduced as the result of mergers.

The companies that followed MGIC have made substantial inroads into the market. Prior to 1960, MGIC was the sole private mortgage insurance operation and it accounted for 100 percent of the net premiums written. As more firms entered the market, the proportion of premiums written by MGIC dropped. By 1977 the MGIC proportion of premiums was 43.4 percent, with United Guaranty Corporation and Verex Assurance accounting for 11.2 and 10.7 percent, respectively. Four of the remaining companies wrote between 6.8 and 8.2 percent, and the seven companies in the lower half shared 5.9 percent among themselves. Very similar figures characterize the distribution of private mortgage insurance in force at the end of 1977.

The growth of the private mortgage insurance industry is also revealed in the aggregation of total policyholders' reserves. At the end of 1977 this figure exceeded $753 million, of which MGIC accounted for 49.1 percent, down from 100 percent two decades earlier. A considerable proportion of the total sum for the industry is represented by contributed capital or by stock or flotations developed with the financial support of Wall Street. These sources of capital provide funds for entry by competitive enterprises, thereby making it possible for new companies to organize and begin operation without depending entirely on the capital contributions of their principals. The ease with which new firms have entered the field has served to extend the market by providing private mortgage insurance in areas of the country which were not fully served or by offering a choice of insurers in areas in which such coverage was available. Thus competition was not only a response to the growth of the private mortgage insurance industry; it was also instrumental in generating that growth.

As the market for private mortgage insurance expanded in volume and in geographic coverage, changes occurred in the sources of business. Savings and loan associations declined in importance, though they still maintain a major position. This source, which provided 84 percent of premiums written in 1968, had declined to 66 percent by 1978. Commercial banks dropped from 10 to 8 percent, and credit unions and others remained unchanged at about 1 percent. The most marked shift occurred among mortgage bankers, whose share dropped from 6 percent in 1968 to 3 percent in 1970 and then rose rapidly, reaching 21 percent in 1978.

The Legal Framework and the Legal Safeguards of Private Mortgage Insurance

Private mortgage insurance is currently regulated by the insurance departments of the individual states, and the insurer is subject to the restrictions imposed both by its home state and by other states in which it does business. In general, state laws and regulations set minimum requirements for paid-in capital and surplus; stipulate that insurance exposure be limited to 25 times the value of the capital, surplus, and contingency reserves; and restrict private mortgage insurance to amortized first liens that do not exceed 95 percent of fair market value on one–four-family houses. To meet severe and unusual demands, state authorities require the establishment of a contingency reserve into which half of the earned premiums are paid each year to remain for ten years, and against which claims may be paid only when the annual losses exceed a certain percentage (typically 35 percent) of the annual earned premiums.

Two federal layers of regulation are represented by the Federal Home Loan Mortgage Corporation (FHLMC) and the quasi-federal Federal National Mortgage Association (FNMA), since as a practical matter any private mortgage insurer intending to do business on a nationwide basis must secure their approval. Both are a secondary market for conventional loans. The FHLMC sets the "qualifications" for private mortgage insurers that may be used by financial institutions regulated by the

FHLBB. For a private insurer to have the loans it insures eligible for purchase by these two agencies, the private insurer must: (1) conform with a number of restrictions, including a prohibition of compensation to lenders as an inducement to do business with the insurer; (2) have a total of capital surplus and contingency reserve that is not less than $5 million for firms doing business with FHLMC and $2 million for firms during business with FNMA; (3) have no more than 20 percent of its insurance in force in any one standard metropolitan statistical area and no more than 60 percent in any one state (according to FHLMC); and (4) audit the evaluation practices of the lender seeking insurance (according to FHLMC). The FHLBB also holds that only FHLMC-approved insurers may be used by federal associations for the insurance of loans exceeding 90 percent of value.

Potential conflict of interest, a subject that warrants greater attention than it has received, is one of the most important issues currently facing the private mortgage insurance industry. The history of the collapse of mortgage guarantee companies during the depression of the 1930s, the Alger Committee recommendations which followed, and the FHLBB inquiry on conflicts of interest in 1964 indicate that a lender's decisions as to whether or not a loan should be insured and a lender's selection of a private mortgage insurer should be free of such conflict. They also indicate that lenders availing themselves of a particular private mortgage insurer should be prevented from controlling that insurer.

It is possible to enumerate a wide variety of situations in which the lender can control the purchase of private mortgage insurance, or can use private mortgage insurance to clear its liabilities at the expense of an affiliated underwriter, or can be subject to pressure to underwrite private mortgage insurance, or in which lender-affiliated insurers could trade risks that each is forbidden to underwrite. The separation of the lender and the insurer is essential to avoid conflicts in the liquidity and capital needs of lending and insuring institutions. There may indeed be circumstances in which a mortgage insurer is threatened with seizure by an insurance department or faces an order to cease writing insurance at the same time that a Federal Reserve Board directive requires a bank to produce additional capital resources. Since both the mortgage insurer and the bank would be calling on the same capital pool (the holding company or other subsidiaries), their simultaneous demands could produce a manifest conflict between the requirements of two sets of regulatory government agencies. If the demand for capital on the part of the bank occurs while the private mortgage insurer that it controls is still legally solvent (although the mortgage insurer's position may be financially precarious), the bank will be tempted to strip cash from the mortgage insurer by having it pay the full claim, rather than exercising the 20 percent (or 25 percent) settlement option. In all likelihood, such a contingency would require the mortgage insurer to take title to the property when its market value is below the outstanding mortgage debt.

The separation of the lender from the insurer is also necessary to implement the basic banking precept embedded in government regulations: the lender should minimize the risk of a loan default. Limiting the loan-to-value ratio is one of the most important devices that is used to carry out this principle. It underlines the point that banks do not engage in credit extension to seek profit by taking the risk of default, though some risk is present even in the most judiciously selected loan. Seeking profit from default risk is the business of mortgage insurance. Lenders are allowed to make higher-ratio loans when all or part of the outstanding amount is insured by an independent entity, public or private. To the extent that insurance is extended by essentially the same financial body, the basic principle is ignored and the regulation circumvented.

It is equally important that private mortgage insurers be prohibited from inducing mortgage insurance business from lenders through tie-in practices, such as paying larger than customary commissions on other seemingly unrelated insurance products or services or by placing on deposit inordinately large sums of money. Such circumvention may occur because of statutory prohibitions against the payment of commissions to lenders purchasing mortgage insurance. In addition to the concerns expressed above, the prohibition of tie-in practices serves to prevent lenders from imposing unnecessary insurance on borrowers that may not require it, merely to earn the commission.

Although there is no indication that these or similar practices currently exist among private mortgage insurers, in view of the likelihood of more intense competition in the future, it is essential that all possible steps be taken to prevent these potential conflicts of interest.

The Ability of the Private Mortgage Insurance Industry to Withstand Economic Reversal

An assessment of the ability of the private mortgage insurance industry to withstand increasingly severe economic conditions was made by Arthur D. Little, Inc., in a study prepared for FNMA and FHLMC in 1975. The test was based on a simulation of a typical mortgage insurance company faced with several assumed future conditions. The design was made up of a number of modules that simulated all insurance operations and the composition and alteration of the asset portfolio, and that provided for variations in policy data. The estimated values of 14 simulator parameters were based on an analysis of 1.5 million policies and claims for the period 1964–73. The resultant data were used to develop functions describing policy volume, underwriting expenses, claim and delinquency rates, claim settlement rates, stock market and interest rate indexes, and other items.

In order to gauge the performance of the hypothetical mortgage insurance company, the variables that affect its financial operations were specified over a decade (1974–83). The functioning of a mortgage insurance company is a product of operating revenues (premiums and fees) and expenses (selling, satisfying claims, and ordinary business operations), investment income, and financial assets.

Tests were then run to examine the mortgage insurance company's performance under three different types of future economic climate.

An optimistic scenario postulated recovery from a depressed housing market and subsequent vigorous economic growth, followed by moderate levels of economic activity and a subsidence of inflation. It was further assumed that loan-to-value ratios would dip and rise again, that cancellation rates would decline in the first few years and then rise again, as do nonrenewal rates, that carrying and disposal costs would increase from 10 percent to 11–12 percent of property value, and that property value at the end of the period would be 25 percent above the historical levels.

The pessimistic scenario postulated a housing decline in the first three years of the decade, with a business contraction leading to bond defaults and high interest rates for long-term money. The beginning of an expansion phase of the economy was postulated for the end of the decade. The pessimistic scenario further assumed the same policy mix by loan-to-value ratios as was assumed in the optimistic scenario, a smaller decline in cancellation rates in the first two years, followed by an increase thereafter, a similar pattern for nonreversal rates, a sharp increase in carrying and disposal costs to 10 percent of property value, and property value in 1983 of about 40 percent above the historical levels.

The results of the optimistic scenario indicate that the simulated mortgage insurance company would show no serious profitability problems during the test period of 1974–83. If the simulated company purchases tax and loss bonds to defer taxes, surplus would increase rapidly; if the company does not, then surplus would increase more slowly. In either event, the simulated company would not suffer operating losses and there would be no need to raise capital.

Under the assumptions of the pessimistic scenario, the simulated company that purchases tax and loss bonds would have a little change in surplus during the first years, followed by a rise thereafter. If tax and loss bonds are not purchased, surplus would dip in the first half of the period and subsequently increase. Here, as in the optimistic scenario, no losses would occur, but if tax and loss bonds are not purchased, the position of the company would become precarious.

Since the simulated company survived the circumstances of the pessimistic scenario, a catastrophic forecast was introduced which assumed that default rates were five times as large as they were in that scenario. If the company purchases tax and loss bonds, it would still maintain a positive surplus. Its contingency reserve, however, would be exhausted shortly, then revive and disappear again at the end of the test period. If the company does not purchase tax and loss bonds, the minimum surplus would exceed tax refunds. If tax refunds are not available, the company would have a negative surplus three years before the end of the test period on a statement as well as a market value basis.

Since the hypothetical mortgage company seemed to be so impervious to reversal, the Arthur D. Little group postulated a "Doomsday" forecast which revealed that it would take a 14-fold increase in claim rates to throw the company into insolvency, a rate of increase higher than that experienced during the depression of the 1930s. In view of the built-in strengthening of the economic and financial system since that time, it was concluded that a typical mortgage insurance company could weather an economic reversal as severe as that of the 1930s.

A similar study was undertaken by the author in 1973 and reported in a volume entitled *The Private Insurance of Home Mortgages.* In it, a computer simulation model of the Mortgage Guaranty Insurance Corporation, the oldest and largest company in this field, demonstrated that with its then current premiums and reserves MGIC could withstand catastrophic and unprecedented losses. In general, it was found that the MGIC reserve was equivalent to that held by the Mutual Mortgage Insurance Fund of the FHA and was adequate to meet contingencies as severe as those for which the FHA was preparing itself.

New Directions

The mortgage insurance companies have been responsive to new programs that are designed to facilitate or enlarge the home financing market. A new type of mortgage insurance policy has been written on a Bank of America pass-through issue, in which the insurer pays the entire loss on loans up to 5 percent of the original principal in the mortgage pool. Since state regulators forbid mortgage insurance companies to offer full coverage, a company that writes this type of policy will have to reinsure a minimum of 75 percent of the coverage with other companies. The primary company underwriting the loans, however, remains contingently liable for all claims.

In a variant of the pass-through certificate, the mortgages carry a variable rate in which the debt service is subject to a possible change in the interest rate. By mid-1978, the aggregate amount of the public offering of these instruments reached $675 million, and this type of vehicle appears to have considerable growth potential. To this total must be added the considerable volume of state housing finance agency bonds that require or accept private mortgage insurance on the underlying individual mortgages. It is this type of receptivity to productive methods of operation and to innovational activity in a complex market that has placed the private mortgage insurance companies in a position of prominence in the home financing industry, which is one of the most vital economic activities in the United States.

FHA AND VA FINANCING*

Nicholas R. Monte, Jr.

*N*ICHOLAS R. MONTE, JR., CRB, President, L & M Realty of New Jersey, Edison, New Jersey.

President and owner, L & M Realty of New Jersey; L & M Agency of New Jersey; Kare-Kris Investment; Chip n Dale Associates; and Longstreth & Monte, Inc. Education chairman, Middlesex County Board of Realtors®. Instructor for 11 state graduate Realtor® Institutes; Rutgers University; and Middlesex County College of New Jersey. Past chairman, RNMI Membership Committee for New Jersey. Author of several articles in Real Estate Today.

The Advantages of FHA Financing

As compared with the real estate purchaser who uses conventional financing, the real estate purchaser who uses FHA financing enjoys the advantages of such favorable financing terms as a minimum down payment, maximum mortgage amounts, low interest rates, and an absence of prepayment penalties. Moreover, as a condition of FHA financing, certification is required as to the physical condition of the roofing, the plumbing, and the electrical systems, as well as the standards of water and sewer service.

Qualifying the FHA or VA Applicant

Qualifying the applicant is one of the most important tasks in real estate sales that require FHA or VA financing just as it is in real estate

---

* All figures pertaining to down payment and interest rates contained in this chapter are current as of this writing. However, pending legislation in Congress may change the figures.

The author wishes to acknowledge that some of the reference matter and facts in this chapter were obtained from J. I. Kislak Mortgage Corporation, Newark, N.J., and the Larson Mortgage Corporation, Plainfield, N.J.

sales generally. It is therefore necessary to have a working knowledge of the factors that determine whether a mortgage risk is acceptable to the FHA or the VA.

Net Effective Monthly Income.   This is income which the applicant can reasonably expect to receive during the early years of the mortgage obligation. It represents the applicant's take-home pay, any anticipated rental income, and other income (for example, a VA pension, social security, etc.). Income from part-time jobs, overtime, and the like, is rarely considered to be effective income, unless it can be proven that such income will continue for a period of five years and that it has been received for the past two years. A steadily employed wife's income is considered. However, information should be furnished as to who takes care of the children and the costs involved. Income for child support, alimony, and unemployment is rarely considered to be effective income. However, verification should be submitted.

After net effective monthly income has been arrived at, the prospective housing expense should be calculated. The prospective housing expense should not be greater than about 35 percent of net effective monthly income.

Prospective Housing Expense.   The percentage of income paid for housing expense varies. That percentage is generally higher for lower-income persons than for upper-income persons.

Housing expense consists of the following:

Mortgage principal and interest.

Taxes.

Hazard insurance premium.

Flood insurance premium, if applicable.

Maintenance and repairs (estimated on a 12-month basis).

Utilities (estimated on a 12-month basis).

FHA mortgage insurance premium on FHA loans (not applicable to VA loans).

Fixed Monthly Expenses.   Fixed obligations which extend for a period of 11 months or more will be added to the prospective housing expense. The total of the prospective housing expense, social security and retirement deductions, income tax withholding, installment obligations which extend for more than 11 months, and the operational expenses of other real estate should not exceed 50 percent of "net effective monthly income." (See Exhibit 1.)

Credit History.   Prospective mortgagors with a poor credit history may be rejected. There are, of course, legitimate reasons why a mortgage applicant may have failed to meet payments. Sickness, accidents, involuntary unemployment, and disputed accounts are a few such reasons. The applicant must furnish a written explanation of any adverse account which appears on his credit report and proof that the adverse account has been brought up to date or paid off. This written explanation is an essential part of his application to the FHA or the VA.

In case of bankruptcy the applicant must supply a "Discharge of

EXHIBIT 1
Mortgage Qualification Formulas for FHA/VA

Buyer: _____

Address: _____

A. Mortgage amount _____   Principal and interest $_____

Mortgage insurance
premium $_____

Taxes $_____

Hazard insurance $_____

Flood insurance $_____
Total

Heat and utilities $_____

Maintenance and repairs $_____

A-1 Total   _____

(This is the total monthly
housing expense.)

Plus other fixed
monthly expenses $_____

A-2 total fixed
expenses $_____

B. Income   Gross monthly income $_____

Less income tax $_____

B-1 net monthly income

C. Ratios
   1. Income ratio: A-1 ÷ B-1 = _____ %
      If this does not exceed 35 percent, income is OK.
   2. Total expense ratio: A-2 ÷ B-1 = _____ %
      If this does not exceed 50 percent, your buyer qualifies.

Bankruptcy" statement containing a complete list of all creditors satisfied.

Additional Factors Affecting Qualification. Complete submission of the following will further determine the applicant's qualifications for FHA or VA financing:

1. Appropriate mortgage company or lending institution forms (see Exhibit 2).
2. Ownership certification—required when property is unoccupied by the owner or when title has been held less than two years (also required by RESPA).
3. Description of property (see Exhibit 3).
4. Application for conditional commitment (FHA Form 2800).
5. Application for mortgagor approval (FHA Form 2900) (see Exhibit 4).
6. Copies of sale contracts.
7. Verification of employment forms see Exhibit 5.
8. Verification of deposit forms.
9. Verification of stocks and bonds.

EXHIBIT 2

BROKER:

1. Property address | Sales Price | Mtg. amt. | No. of months

2. Mortgagors: Husband   Age   Wife   Age   Telephone
Name
Address .... Zip Code ....

If at present address less than 5 years, complete item 12

Married   Years   ☐ Divorced   ☐ Single   ☐ Widow   No. of Children   Ages

3. Purpose of Loan: ☐ Finance New Constr.   ☐ Finance Purchase   ☐ Refinance Exist. Loan   ☐
Mortgagor will be: ☐ Occupant   ☐ Landlord

4. Other Real Estate: To be sold ☐ Yes ☐ No.   Type Mtg.   VA ☐ FHA ☐ Conv. ☐   Original Mtg. Amt. $..........
Address ....   Unpaid Balance $..........
Name and Address of Lender: ....

5. EMPLOYMENT Social Security No. ....
Husband's occupation.................years employed.........
Employer......................
Employer's address & phone no. ....

Social Security No. ....
Wife's occupation.................years employed.........
Employer......................
Employer's address ....

Part Time Employer......................
Address......................
Position.................years employed.........
Days of Week.................Hours of Day.........

7.   PREVIOUS MONTHLY HOUSING EXPENSE
Mortgage Payment or rent..................... $.........
Hazard Insurance......................
Taxes, special assessments......................
Maintenance, Heat & Utilities......................
                              TOTAL $...............

VA Claim No. ....Amount of Pension $........
6.   MONTHLY INCOME
Husband's base pay...................... $.........
Other earnings (source)......................
Wife's base pay......................
Other earnings (source)......................
Gross income, other Real Estate......................
Other income......................
                              TOTAL $........

8.   LIABILITIES
Automobile...................... $......... $.........
Debts, other Real Estate P & I only ....
Life Insurance Loans......................
Notes payable ....
Retail ....
Stores ....
                              TOTAL $........

9. ASSETS
(a) Savings Bank (Name, Add. & Acct.)........................... $...........
   Checking Bank (Name, Add. & Acct.)........................... $...........
(b) U. S. Savings Bond No. and Denomination...................... $...........
(c) Cash on Hand...................... $...........
(d) Stocks and other Bonds, Name and No. .... $...........
(e) TOTAL ASSETS FOR CLOSING...................... $...........
(f) Cash Deposit on Purchase...................... $...........
(g) Est. Resale Value, other Real Estate .... $...........
(h) Est. Resale Value of Automobile $............Furniture and Personal $.... $...........
(i) Life Ins. (Amt.) $............ Premium $............ Cash Value $.... $...........
                              TOTAL $...........

10. List 3 Trade References: (name and address)

11. Previous Employment (name and address)...........................years employed........
   If Item 5 Less Than 2 Years ....years employed........

12. Previous Home Address
The purpose of this proposed loan is to finance the purchase of the residential property identified herein which I intend to move into and occupy as my home within a reasonable period of time after the closing.

MORTGAGOR'S CERTIFICATE (FHA ONLY)

13. "I hereby authorize Larson Mortgage Company to release the information contained in this application and all information disclosed in any credit report ordered by Larson Mortgage Company, to the Real Estate Broker, if any, who has assisted me in preparing this mortgage loan application."

14. Have you sold property within the last 2 years which had an FHA mortgage? ☐ Yes ☐ No. If "Yes" give FHA Case No. ....
Buyer's Name........................... Did buyer intend to occupy ☐ Yes ☐ No   Property Address...............
...........................Orig. Mtg. Amt. $............... Unpd. Bal. when sold $...............

Have you ever been obligated on a home loan, or a home improvement loan which resulted in foreclosure, deed in lieu of foreclosure, or judgment? ☐ Yes ☐ No
If "Yes" give   Property Address........................... Name & address of Lender...............

If dwelling to be covered by the mortgage is to be for rent - is it a part of, adjacent or continguous to any project subdivision or group of rental properties involving eight or more dwelling units in which you have any financial interest ☐ Yes ☐ No. If "Yes" give details. Do you own four or more dwelling units insured under any title of the National Housing Act ☐ Yes ☐ No. If "Yes" submit Form 2561. The mortgagor certifies that all information in this application is given for the purpose of obtaining a loan to be insured under the National Housing Act and is true and complete to the best of his knowledge and belief. Verification may be obtained from any source named herein.

It is understood and agreed by all parties that the mortgage described herein will close with interest at the maximum rate and/or service charge permitted by the Government Agency at the time of closing. (Not less than ....%.)

The undersigned applies to LARSON MORTGAGE COMPANY for a mortgage loan in the amount and upon the terms stated herein, and authorizes you to use the information for application to the appropriate Government Agency.

It is understood that I am obliged to advise you of any changes in my Employment or Financial Status before Closing.

The undersigned has funds available for closing costs of the above transaction.

....   Date: ....

PURCHASER   SPOUSE
THIS APPLICATION MUST BE SIGNED BY PURCHASERS

This is the most important part of the application. Please complete in detail with all names, addresses, zip codes and account numbers.

EXHIBIT 3

Property Description

THIS FORM MUST BE COMPLETED ACCURATELY
IN DETAIL IN ORDER TO OBTAIN AN APPRAISAL

1. PROPERTY ADDRESS (including zip code) _____ County _____ | 2. SALE PRICE OF PROPERTY

3.   LOT DIMENSIONS _____ Front x _____ x _____ x _____ x _____ x _____

4. MONTH AND YEAR BUILT	5. STATUS OF PROPERTY
	☐ NEVER OCCUPIED ☐ OCCUPIED ☐ PRESENTLY VACANT ☐ UNFURNISHED ☐ FURNISHED

6A. OCCUPANT'S NAME	6B. TELEPHONE NO.	7A. BROKER'S NAME	7B. TELEPHONE NO.

8 NAME OF OWNER—IF OTHER THAN OCCUPANT	9. DATE AND TIME AVAILABLE FOR INSPECTION A.M. P.M.	10. KEYS AT (Name, Address and Phone No.) IF VACANT, KEYS MUST BE ATTACHED

11. NO. BLDGS.	12. NO. LIVING UNITS	13. RENTAL 2nd APT.	14. RENTAL 3rd APT.	15. UTILITIES	PUBLIC	COMM.	INDIV.	TYPE OF STREET PAVING
				WATER				
				GAS				CURBS
				ELECT.				SIDEWALK
				SANIT. SEWER				STORM SEWER

16. DESCRIPTION

☐ DETACHED   ☐ WOOD SIDING   ☐ ASB. SHINGLE   ☐ STONE   ☐ BRICK   ___ % CRAWL SPACE   ☐ SPLIT LEVEL
☐ SEMI-DET.   ☐ WOOD SHINGLE   ☐ BRICK VENEER   ☐ BRICK & BLOCK ☐ COMB. TYPES   ___ % BASEMENT
☐ ROW   ☐ ALUM. SIDING   ☐ C. BLOCK   ☐ STUCCO   ___ STORIES   ☐ SLAB

___ NO. ROOMS   ___ 1/2 BATHS   ☐ KITCHEN   ☐ STORAGE RM.   ☐ FIREPLACE   ☐ BUILT-IN   ☐ CENT. AIR COND.
☐ BEDROOMS   ☐ LIVING RM.   ☐ FAMILY RM.   ☐ UTILITY RM.   ___ CAR GARAGE   ☐ ATTACHED   TYPE OF HEATING
___ BATHS   ☐ DINING RM.   ☐ REC. ROOM   ☐   RM.   ___ CAR CARPT.   ☐ DETACHED   AND FUEL _____

ROOFING MATERIAL   ☐ SLATE   ☐ ASPHALT   ☐ WOOD   ☐ OTHER _____

17. OTHER FEATURES

☐ ENCLOSED PORCH   ☐ EXPANDABLE ATTIC   ☐ BREEZEWAY   ___ # COMB. STM. DOOR   ☐ DEHUMIDIFIER   ☐ PATIO
☐ OPEN PORCH   ☐ FINISHED ATTIC   ☐ SWIMMING POOL   ___ # COMB. STM. SASH   ☐ FENCE

18. NON-REAL ESTATE ITEMS WILL HELP TO INCREASE VALUE.
CHECK ALL THAT ARE INCLUDED IN THE SALE.

☐ RANGE OR COUNTERTOP UNIT   ☐ REFRIG.   ☐ GARB. DISPOSAL   ☐ PERMANENT BLENDERS
☐ DISHWASHER   ☐ AUTO. WASHER   ☐ DRYER   ☐ VENT FAN   ☐ PERMANENT FIRE ALARM
___ VENETIAN BLINDS   ☐ BUILT-IN VACUUM CLEANER   ☐ PERMANENT AIR CONDITIONER
☐ INTER-COM SYSTEM (with or without radio attachments)   ☐ WALL TO WALL CARPETING

19. DIRECTIONS TO PROPERTY FROM NEAREST MAIN ARTERY	20. SHOW BELOW: Shape, location, distance from nearest intersection and street names. Mark N at North point.	21. TAX INFORMATION (if existing construction)

	ASSESSED VALUATION	ANNUAL TAXES
LAND	$	$
IMPROVEMENTS		
OTHER		
TOTAL	$	$

NAME, ADDRESS AND PHONE NUMBER OF SELLER'S ATTORNEY _____

SPECIAL INSTRUCTIONS: _____

GOVERNMENT AGENCIES REQUIRE A SURVEY AND LEGAL DESCRIPTION FOR APPRAISAL
SURVEY MUST SHOW HOUSE AND ALL BUILDINGS

FOR OFFICE USE ONLY

Inspector's Comments: _____

GRADE _____

PLEASE COMPLETE FROM YOUR LISTING.

EXHIBIT 4

U.S. DEPARTMENT OF HOUSING AND URBAN DEVELOPMENT FEDERAL HOUSING ADMINISTRATION	2. FHA Case No.

1. MORTGAGEE'S APPLICATION FOR MORTGAGOR APPROVAL AND COMMITMENT FOR MORTGAGE INSURANCE UNDER THE NATIONAL HOUSING ACT

☐ SEC. 203(b) ☐ SEC.

(NOTE: See reverse for Privacy Act Statement)

5. MORTGAGEE - Name, Address & Zip Code   *(Please Type)*

(Please locate address within corner marks)

3. PROPERTY ADDRESS

4. MORTGAGORS/BORROWERS:

Mtgor. _____ Sex ___ Age ___

Co-Mtgor. _____ Sex ___ Age ___

Address _____

Married ___ Yrs. No. of Dependents ___ Ages ___

Co-Mortgagor(s) ___ Sex ___ Age(s) ___

(Check one)
☐ White, not of Hispanic origin   ☐ Asian or Pacific Islander
☐ Black, not of Hispanic origin   ☐ Hispanic
☐ American Indian or Alaskan Native   ☐ Other

6. MORTGAGE APPLIED FOR →

	Mortgage Amount	*Interest Rate	No. of Months	Monthly Payment Principal & Interest
	$	%		$

7. PURPOSE OF LOAN: . . .   MORTGAGOR WILL BE: .

☐ Finance Constr. on Own Land   ☐ Finance Purchase   ☐ Refinance Exist. Loan   ☐ Finance Impr. to Exist. Prop.   ☐ Other
☐ Occupant   ☐ Landlord   ☐ Builder   ☐ Escrow Commit. Mortgagor

8. ASSETS

Cash accounts _____ $ _____

Marketable securities _____

Other (explain) _____

OTHER ASSETS   (A) TOTAL $ _____

Cash deposit on purchase . . . . _____

Other (explain) _____

(B) TOTAL $ _____

9. LIABILITIES   Monthly Payt.   Unpd. Bal.

Automobile . . . . $ _____ $ _____

Debts, other Real Estate . . . . _____ _____

Life Insurance Loans . . . . _____ _____

Notes payable . . . . _____ _____

Credit Union . . . . _____ _____

Retail accounts . . . . . _____ _____

NAME   ACCOUNT NO.

If more space is needed, attach schedule.   TOTAL $ _____ $ _____

10. EMPLOYMENT

Mortgagor's occupation _____

Employer's name & address _____

_____ years employed _____

Co-Mtgor. occupation _____

Employer's name & address _____

_____ years employed _____

11. MONTHLY INCOME

Mortgagor's base pay . . . . $ _____

Other Earnings (explain) . . . . _____

Co-Mtgor. base pay . . . . _____

Other Earnings (explain) . . . . _____

Gross Income, Real Estate . . . . _____

Other (explain) . . . . _____

TOTAL $ _____

Alimony, child support or separate maintenance income need not be revealed if you do not wish to have it considered as a basis for repaying this obligation.

12. SETTLEMENT REQUIREMENTS

(a) Existing debt (Refinancing only) . . . . $ _____

(b) Sale price (Realty only) . . . . _____

(c) Repairs & Improvements . . . . _____

(d) Closing Costs . . . . _____

(e) **TOTAL** (a + b + c + d) Acquisition cost . . . . _____

(f) Mortgage amount . . . . _____

(g) Mortgagor's required investment(e-f) . . . . _____

(h) Prepayable expenses . . . . _____

(i) Non-realty & other items . . . . _____

(j) **TOTAL REQUIREMENTS** (g + h + i) . . . . _____

(k) Amt. pd. ☐ cash ☐ Other (explain) . . . . _____

(l) Amt. to be pd. ☐ cash ☐ Other (explain) . . . . . _____

(m) Tot. assets available for closing (B)(A) . . . . . . $ _____

13. FUTURE MONTHLY PAYMENTS

(a) Principal & Interest . . . . $ _____

(b) FHA Mortgage Insurance Premium . . . . _____

(c) Ground rent (Leasehold only) . . . . _____

(d) **TOTAL DEBT SERVICE** (a + b + c) . . . . _____

(e) Hazard Insurance . . . . _____

(f) Taxes, special assessments . . . . _____

(g) **TOTAL MTG. PAYT.** (d + e + f) . . . . _____

(h) Maintenance & Common Expense . . . . _____

(i) Heat & utilities . . . . _____

(j) **TOTAL HSG. EXPENSE** (g + h + i) . . . . _____

(k) Other recurring charges (explain) . . . . _____

(l) **TOTAL FIXED PAYT.** (j + k) . . . . $ _____

14. PREVIOUS MONTHLY HOUSING EXPENSE

Mortgage payment or rent . . . . $ _____

Hazard Insurance . . . . _____

Taxes, special assessments . . . . _____

Maintenance . . . . _____

Heat & Utilities . . . . _____

Other (explain) . . . . _____

TOTAL $ _____

15. PREVIOUS MONTHLY FIXED CHARGES

Federal, State & Local income taxes . . . . $ _____

Prem. for $ _____ Life Insurance . . . . . . _____

Social Security & Retirement Payments . . . . _____

Installment account payments . . . . _____

Operating Expenses, other Real Estate . . . . _____

Other (explain) . . . . _____

TOTAL $ _____

16. Do you own other Real Estate? ☐ Yes ☐ No   Is it to be sold? ☐ Yes ☐ No   FHA mortgage ☐ Yes ☐ No   Sales Price $ _____   Orig-Mtg. Amt. $ _____
Unpaid Bal. $ _____   Address _____   Lender _____

17. MORTGAGOR'S CERTIFICATE -- I ☐ have ☐ have not received a copy of the FHA Statement of Value (FHA Form 2800-6) or Veterans Administration Certificate of Reasonable Value (VA Form 26-1843) showing the estimated value of the property described in this application. Have you sold a property within the last year which had an FHA mortgage? ☐ Yes ☐ No. If "Yes" was the mortgage paid in full? ☐ Yes ☐ No. If "No" give FHA Case Number _____ , buyer's name _____ property address _____ date of transfer _____ lender's name and address _____ original mortgage amount $ _____ unpaid balance when sold $ _____ Did buyer intend to occupy? ☐ Yes ☐ No. Have you ever been obligated on a home loan, home improvement loan or a mobile home which resulted in foreclosure, transfer of title in lieu of foreclosure or judgement? ☐ Yes ☐ No. If "Yes" attach statement giving full details including date, property address, name and address of lender, FHA or VA Case Number, if any, and reasons for the action. If dwelling to be covered by this mortgage is to be rented, is it a part of, adjacent or contiguous to any project, subdivision, or group of rental properties involving eight or more dwelling units in which you have any financial interest? ☐ Yes ☐ No. Not to be rented. If "Yes" give details. Do you own four or more dwelling units with mortgages insured under any title of the National Housing Act? ☐ Yes ☐ No. If "Yes" submit FHA Form 2561. The Mortgagor certifies that all information in this application is given for the purpose of obtaining a loan to be insured under the National Housing Act and is true and complete to the best of his knowledge and belief. Verification may be obtained from any source named herein. *NOTE: The interest rate shown in item 6 is the FHA-VA maximum rate in effect on the date of this commitment and may increase prior to closing unless buyer and lender agree otherwise.

Signature(s) _____   Date: _____ 19__

18. MORTGAGEE'S CERTIFICATE - The mortgagee certifies that all information in this application is true and complete to the best of its knowledge and belief.

Signature _____   Date: _____ 19__

FHA-2900-1 (4-78)

FHA COPY - FILE IN CASE BINDER

EXHIBIT 5

FHA FORM NO. 2004-G Rev. 5/75 VA FORM NO. 26-8497 Rev. 5/75	VETERANS ADMINISTRATION and U. S. DEPARTMENT OF HOUSING AND URBAN DEVELOPMENT FEDERAL HOUSING ADMINISTRATION	FORM APPROVED OMB NO. 63-R1288

REQUEST FOR VERIFICATION OF EMPLOYMENT

INSTRUCTIONS: Lender – Complete Items 1 through 6. Have applicant complete Items 7 and 8. Forward the completed
form directly to the employer named in Item 1.
Employer – Complete Items 9A through 15 and return form directly to lender named in Item 2.

PART I   REQUEST

1. TO: (Name and Address of Employer):	2. FROM: (Name and Address of Lender): JORDAN MORTGAGE CORPORATION 554 Bloomfield Avenue Bloomfield, New Jersey 07003

3. Signature of Lender:	4. Title of Lender:	5. Date:	6. HUD-FHA or VA Number:

I certify that this verification has been sent directly to the employer and has not passed through the hands of the applicant or any other interested party.	I have applied for a mortgage loan and stated that I am employed by you. My signature below authorizes verification of this information.
7. Name and Address of Applicant:	8. Employee's Identification Number: _____ Signature of applicant

PART II   VERIFICATION

9 A . Is applicant now employed by you? ☐ Yes ☐ No	10A. Position or Job Title:	11. TO BE COMPLETED BY MILITARY PERSONNEL ONLY.	
9B. Present Base Pay is $ _____ This amount is paid: ☐ Annually ☐ Hourly ☐ Monthly ☐ Other (Specify) ☐ Weekly	10B. Length of Applicant's employment:	Pay Grade:	
		Base Pay	$
		Rations	$
9C. EARNINGS LAST 12 MONTHS Amount $	10C. Probability of continued employment:	Flight or Hazard	$
Basic Earnings $ Normal Hours worked per Week:	10D. Date Applicant left:	Clothing	$
Overtime Earnings $ _____ ☐ Regular ☐ Temporary	10E. Reason for leaving:	Quarters	$
Other Income $ _____ ☐ Regular ☐ Temporary		Pro-Pay	$
		Overseas or Combat	$

12. REMARKS:

13. Signature of Employer:	14. Title of Employer:	15. Date:

RETURN DIRECTLY TO LENDER

HAVE THIS FORM SIGNED BY APPLICANT IN BLOCK # 8 ONLY

10. Character and credit statement.
11. Checks for appropriate amounts to cover credit report and appraisal.

FHA Appraisals

FHA conditional commitment appraisals are issued on existing properties and proposed construction as follows:

1. Existing construction over one year old or built under FHA or VA.

> Term of appraisal—six months.
> Cost of appraisal—$55 for one-, two-, three-, or four-family houses.
> Term of loan—30 years maximum.

2. Existing construction less than one year old and not built under FHA or VA.[1]

> Term of appraisal—six months.
> Cost of appraisal—$50 for one-, two-, three-, or four-family houses.
> Term of loan—30 years maximum.
>   If the property has a well or a septic tank and the property has not been occupied for at least 12 months, the FHA requires certain information to be submitted with the appraisal request.

3. Proposed construction.

> Term of appraisal—one year.
> Cost of appraisal—$55.
> Term of loan—30 years maximum.

FHA/VA-Proposed Construction Exhibits Required to Request Appraisal

1. Plans and specifications signed by the builder and the applicant (three sets).
2. The plot plan (three sets)—must show the location of the house, well, septic tank, drain field, and percolation test holes.
3. The legal description—should include a copy of the deed description.
4. A property location map (three copies).
5. FHA Form 2800, "Mortgagee's Application for Property Appraisal," or VA Form 26–1805, "Request for Determination of Reasonable Value," must be signed by the builder.
6. A check in the amount of $50 (FHA) or $50 (VA) for one- and two-family homes and $50 (VA) for three- and four-family homes made payable to the lender. Mileage may be charged by the VA on properties located at distant points.

The plans should include the following:

A. Specifications—Form 2005.
B. Foundation or basement details.

---

[1] The loan amount is reduced. The FHA requires 10 percent down on the first $35,000 of the sale price; the VA still requires no down payment.

C. Floor plans (all floors).
D. Exterior elevations.
E. Kitchen cabinet details.
F. Roof detail and wall section.
G. The heating layout and heat cost calculation.
H. The plumbing layout.
I. Window schedules.
J. Fireplace details (when applicable).
K. Plans of optional extras.

FHA Loans

FHA Section 203(b) Loans. Section 203(b) is the most commonly used section of the National Housing Act. This section covers home mortgages to finance one–four-family dwellings.

Loan-to-Value Ratio—Occupant Mortgagor's Minimum Investment.[2] For houses over one year old or houses built under FHA or VA inspections, loans can be 97 percent of the value to $25,000 plus 90 percent of the value between $25,000 and $35,000 plus 80 percent of the value over $35,000. The maximum loan amount for a single-family dwelling is $60,000.

For houses less than one year old and not built under FHA or VA inspection, loans can be 90 percent of the value to $35,000 plus 80 percent of the value above $35,000. Maximum loans on multifamily dwellings are as follows:

$65,000—two-family dwelling.

$65,000—three-family dwelling.

$75,000—four-family dwelling.

The maximum term of loans is 30 years.

Loan-to-Value Ratio—Nonoccupant Mortgagor and Refinances. The limits here are 85 percent of the limits for owner-occupants.

FHA "Veteran" Loans. This program is designed for veterans who have had a minimum of 90 days of active duty with the armed services. The program is open to certain other veterans who may not be eligible under the VA program or who have obtained a VA loan that has not been paid off.

Although this is an FHA program, it is necessary for the veteran to obtain a "Certificate of Veteran Status" (VA Form 26–8261a) from the VA. This certificate must accompany the application to the FHA for a

---

[2] The term *value* as defined by the FHA is the appraised price or the sale price, whichever is less, plus an estimate of the closing costs to be paid by the purchaser.
Example:

Sales price or appraised price	$30,000
Estimated closing costs	1,000
Total *value* to determine maximum loan	$31,000

Here the maximum loan for an owner-occupant for a house over one year old or a house built under FHA or VA inspections is $29,650 for a $30,000 sale price.

home loan. All that is needed to obtain a "Certificate of Veteran Status" is a copy of a DD-214 form showing that the applicant has had 90 days of active duty and a signed copy of VA Form 26–8261a.

This program has the advantage of lower down payment requirements, and there is no limit to the number of times that this benefit can be used by the veteran. The maximum loan is $60,000; the maximum term is 30 years; and the loans are limited to single-family dwellings occupied by the mortgagor. The minimum investment requirements (which may include prepaid items) are $200 down for the value up to $25,000 plus 10 percent of the value from $25,000 to $35,000 plus 15 percent of the value from $35,000 to $45,000.

FHA Section 222 "In-Service Loans." These loans are made to active duty service personnel who have not achieved veteran status and have been on active duty for a period of two years or more.

The advantage of this program is that the person in service does not pay the ½ percent FHA mortgage insurance premium so long as he or she remains in service and retains ownership of the property. The FHA insurance premium is paid by the government.

The person in service must obtain four copies of Form DD 802 from his duty station personnel office in order to obtain this type of loan. These forms certify that the person is eligible for an "in-service loan."

The maximum loan is $65,000. The maximum term is 30 years. The minimum investment requirements are:

New construction built under FHA or VA inspections or existing construction over one year old: 3 percent of value to $25,000 plus 10 percent of value from $25,000 to $35,000 plus 15 percent of value over $35,000.

Existing construction less than one year old and not approved before construction began: 20 percent of value to $35,000 plus 20 percent of value over $35,000.

FHA Section 221(d)2 Loans. This section is designed to finance low-cost homes for low- and moderate-income families and families displaced by urban renewal or other governmental action. The mortgagor must be married or the head of the household and cannot own any other residential property.

For one-family homes approved by the FHA prior to construction or more than one year old, the amount insurable by an occupant mortgagor is $36,000 if there are three bedrooms or less and $42,000 for a family of five or more if the house has four or more bedrooms.

For a displaced person (displaced by a board of health, urban renewal, or other governmental action) with a Certificate of Displacement, the amount insurable by an occupant mortgagor in a two-family house is $65,000; in a three-family house, $65,000; in a four-family house, $75,000.

The *loan-to-value ratio* for a displaced family is a $200 down payment (includes escrow). The maximum mortgage term is 30 years.

The Appealing of FHA Loan Rejections. To appeal an FHA loan rejection, the applicant must submit a proposal from a contractor stating what work will be completed to correct the "deficiencies." A letter from the purchaser requesting the waiver of certain requirements will be considered. In some cases, however, the FHA will stand firm on its rejections, regardless of the purchasers' requests.

Repairs. Either the buyer or the seller can elect to do required repairs. However, if the buyer does the repairs, he must show enough assets on the mortgage application to cover the cost of those repairs.

FHA Underappraisals. Under the FHA amendatory clause, the buyer has the right to proceed with the purchase, regardless of the appraisal amount. However, the FHA will only insure the amount on the appraisal. The buyer must make up the difference in his cash down payment.

The seller may choose to reduce the contract price to coincide with the appraisal amount. However, he is not obligated to do so. If the buyer and the seller cannot reach agreement, then the contracts are no longer binding on either party.

Closing Costs. The closing costs consist of attorney's fees; search and survey fees; the cost of the mortgage title insurance policy; recording fees; the loan organization fee; and the cost of prepaid items. The closing costs can be paid by either the seller or the purchaser. On FHA loans the prepaid items must be paid by the purchaser and the FHA will reduce the loan amount if this is not done.

Prepaid Items

1. The first year's hazard insurance premium, together with two months' additional premium, which is held in escrow.
2. A sum sufficient to pay the current year's taxes when they become due is placed in escrow with the lender. Taxes are prorated between the buyer and the seller at closing.
3. One month's FHA insurance premium (no charge on VA loans).
4. Interest from the day of closing through the remaining days in the month is either prepaid or adjusted in the first monthly mortgage payment.

The Seller's Costs

1. Sales commission.
2. Deed and affidavit of title—the cost of preparation. (State stamps on the deed or some other form of state transfer tax will also be required from the seller.)
3. Taxes—actually assessed city and/or county taxes.
4. Discount—subject to money market conditions.
5. Repairs—if necessary.
6. Prepayment penalty—on the present mortgage, if applicable.

The Advantages of VA Financing

The two biggest advantages of the VA loan are that no down payment is required and that the loan is guaranteed by the U.S. government, so that there is no mortgage insurance premium. In addition, VA loans have no prepayment penalty, and a low interest rate. VA loans require certification of physical quality similiar to those required for FHA loans.

Eligibility for VA Loans

A veteran's eligibility is good for his lifetime, but he may have only one outstanding VA-guaranteed loan at a time.

World War II Veterans and Korean War Veterans. To establish eligibility for a VA loan based upon active military duty during World War II or the Korean War, the veteran must have been discharged or released from active duty under conditions other than dishonorable:

1. After active duty of 90 days or more, any part of which was during the period September 16, 1940, to July 25, 1947, or during the period June 27, 1950, to January 31, 1955; or
2. By reason of a service-connected disability from a period of active duty, any part of which occurred during either of the above two wartime periods.

Cold War Veterans. To establish eligibility for a VA loan based upon active duty after January 31, 1955, the veteran must have been discharged or released from active duty under conditions other than dishonorable:

1. From a period of continuous active duty of 181 days or more, any part of which occurred after January 31, 1955; or
2. From active duty after such date for a service-connected disability.

In the absence of a discharge or a release, the veteran must have served on continuous active duty at least 181 days in active duty status.

Unremarried Widows. Such a widow may be eligible for a VA loan if her husband died in service or as a result of a service-connected injury or disability.

Exhibits Required to Obtain a Certificate of Eligibility. VA Form 1880 and separation papers (DD-214's) for all periods of active duty are needed to request the certificate of eligibility. If such papers have been misplaced, they can be obtained by filing form DD-1108. The VA should be contacted if assistance is needed to obtain lost forms. A "Statement of Service" is required if the veteran is currently on active duty. This can be obtained from his or her personnel officer.

Entitlement derived from service during the post-Korean period cancels any unused entitlement derived from service during the Korean War.

Reinstatement of Eligibility. Eligibility can be restored under the following conditions:

1. *If the prior VA loan has been repaid in full, and if evidence of such payment is submitted to the VA.*
2. *If the prior VA loan has not been repaid in full.* A World War II veteran or a Korean War veteran who has purchased a home under his World War II or Korean War eligibility prior to becoming eligible under the post-Korean period and who sells that home on an assumption basis can purchase another home using his post-Korean increase in eligibility if that assumption is in good order. A veteran's eligibility will be restored if a veteran-transferee has agreed to assume the

outstanding balance on the loan and consented to the use of his or her eligibility to the same extent as was done by the veteran who originally made the loan.

Exhibits Necessary for Approval of VA Loan

Exhibits which may be necessary for buyer approval on a VA loan include the following:

1. An application for a VA appraisal, which is the Certificate of Reasonable Value (CRV).
2. An initial interview form, which includes personal data, especially employment history.
3. An application for a home loan guarantee (see Exhibit 6).
4. A copy of the sale contract indicating the terms, especially the down payment, if any.
5. *Certificate of Eligibility*—A certificate noting that the applicant is eligible for the purchase (see Exhibit 7).
6. A verification of employment form, showing employment and income for at least the past two years.
7. A verification of deposit form, required if the applicant has a bank account.
8. An appraisal fee ($50 for a one- and two-family house, $55 for a three- and four-family house) and a credit report fee ($15).
9. If the veteran or his spouse was previously divorced, a copy of the divorce decree nisi.
10. If the veteran is in the service, a letter from his commanding office authorizing him to live off the post.
11. One character and credit statement for each credit reference and each individual account listed on the application.

The Terms and Requirements of VA Loans

A Property cannot be sold to the veteran at a price higher than the value shown on the CRV unless the veteran acknowledges same on VA Form 1802a. If the price is being reduced to conform with the CRV, an amendment to the contract must reflect the reduced sale price. There is no maximum amount on VA loans. However, most lenders will not make a VA loan in excess of $70,000 in some areas.

A VA loans does not require a down payment, though such a loan is more desirable if a down payment is made. Closing costs and prepaid items can be paid by either the veteran or the seller. A veteran can obtain a loan on a one–four-family residence. He is required to occupy one of the units. VA loans are made for terms of up to 30 years.

A CRV is valid for a period of six months on existing properties and for a period of one year on proposed construction. However, if the CRV is issued on behalf of a specific veteran, it will be valid until the specific transaction is either consummated or terminated.

If repairs are required, they must be completed before the loan is closed. An escrow can be established only with VA approval prior to

EXHIBIT 6

VETERANS ADMINISTRATION **APPLICATION FOR HOME LOAN GUARANTY**	1. VA LOAN NUMBER	2. LENDER'S LOAN NO.

3. NAME AND PRESENT ADDRESS OF VETERAN *(Include ZIP Code)*

5A. VETERAN. *If you do not wish to complete Items 5B or 5C, please initial here* ▶ | INITIALS

5B. RACE/NATIONAL ORIGIN | **5C. SEX**

☐ AMERICAN INDIAN ALASKAN NATIVE   ☐ ASIAN, PACIFIC ISLANDER   ☐ FEMALE
☐ BLACK   ☐ HISPANIC
☐ WHITE   ☐ OTHER *(Specify)*   ☐ MALE

4. NAME AND ADDRESS OF LENDER *(Include No., street or rural route, city, P.O., State and ZIP Code.)*

6A. SPOUSE OR OTHER CO-BORROWER. *If you do not wish to complete Items 6B or 6C, please initial here* ▶ | INITIALS

6B. RACE/NATIONAL ORIGIN | **6C. SEX**

☐ AMERICAN INDIAN ALASKAN NATIVE   ☐ ASIAN, PACIFIC ISLANDER   ☐ FEMALE
☐ BLACK   ☐ HISPANIC
☐ WHITE   ☐ OTHER *(Specify)*   ☐ MALE

7. PROPERTY ADDRESS INCLUDING NAME OF SUBDIVISION, LOT AND BLOCK NO., AND ZIP CODE

8A. LOAN AMOUNT | **8B. INTEREST RATE** | **8C. PROPOSED MATURITY**

$ | % | YRS.   MOS.

DISCOUNT: *(Only if veteran to pay under 38 U.S.C. 1803 (c) (3) (C) or (D))* ▶ | **8D. PERCENT** % | **8E. AMOUNT** $

The undersigned veteran and lender hereby apply to the Administrator of Veterans' Affairs for Guaranty of the loan described here under Section 1810, Chapter 37, Title 38, United States Code to the full extent permitted by the veteran's available entitlement and severally agree that the Regulations promulgated pursuant to Chapter 37, and in effect on the date of the loan shall govern the rights, duties, and liabilities of the parties.

SECTION I—PURPOSE, AMOUNT, TERMS OF AND SECURITY FOR PROPOSED LOAN

9. PURPOSE OF LOAN-TO:
☐ PURCHASE EXISTING HOME PREVIOUSLY OCCUPIED   ☐ CONSTRUCT A HOME-PROCEEDS TO BE PAID OUT DURING CONSTRUCTION   ☐ PURCHASE EXISTING HOME NOT PREVIOUSLY OCCUPIED   ☐ PURCHASE NEW CONDOMINIUM UNIT   ☐ PURCHASE EXISTING CONDOMINIUM UNIT

10. TITLE WILL BE VESTED IN:
☐ VETERAN   ☐ VETERAN AND SPOUSE   ☐ OTHER *(Specify)*

11. LIEN
☐ 1ST MORTGAGE   ☐ OTHER *(Specify)*

12. ESTATE WILL BE
☐ FEE SIMPLE   ☐ LEASEHOLD *(Show expiration date)*

13. IS THERE A MANDATORY HOMEOWNERS ASSOCIATION?
☐ YES   ☐ NO *(If "YES", complete Item 14F)*

14. ESTIMATED TAXES, INSURANCE AND ASSESSMENTS		**15. ESTIMATED MONTHLY PAYMENT**	
A. ANNUAL TAXES	$	A. PRINCIPAL AND INTEREST	$
B. AMOUNT OF HAZARD INSURANCE ON SECURITY		B. TAXES AND INSURANCE DEPOSITS	
C. ANNUAL HAZARD INSURANCE PREMIUMS		C. OTHER	
D. ANNUAL SPECIAL ASSESSMENT PAYMENT			
E. UNPAID SPECIAL ASSESSMENT BALANCE			
F. ANNUAL MAINTENANCE ASSESSMENT		D.	
		TOTAL	$

SECTION II—PERSONAL AND FINANCIAL STATUS OF VETERAN

16. PLEASE CHECK THE APPROPRIATE BOXES). IF ONE OR MORE ARE CHECKED, ITEMS 18B, 21, 22 AND 23 MUST INCLUDE INFORMATION CONCERNING THE VETERAN'S SPOUSE (OR FORMER SPOUSE IF BOX "D" IS CHECKED). IF NO BOXES ARE CHECKED, NO INFORMATION CONCERNING THE SPOUSE NEED BE FURNISHED.

☐ A. THE SPOUSE WILL BE JOINTLY OBLIGATED WITH THE VETERAN ON THE LOAN
☐ B. THE VETERAN IS RELYING ON THE SPOUSE'S INCOME AS A BASIS FOR REPAYMENT OF THE LOAN
☐ C. THE VETERAN IS MARRIED AND THE PROPERTY TO SECURE THE LOAN IS LOCATED IN A COMMUNITY PROPERTY STATE
☐ D. THE VETERAN IS RELYING ON ALIMONY, CHILD SUPPORT, OR SEPARATE MAINTENANCE PAYMENTS FROM A SPOUSE OR FORMER SPOUSE AS A BASIS FOR REPAYMENT OF THE LOAN

17A. MARITAL STATUS OF VETERAN	17B. MARITAL STATUS OF CO-BORROWER OTHER THAN VETERAN'S SPOUSE	17C. MONTHLY CHILD SUPPORT OBLIGATION	17D. MONTHLY ALIMONY OBLIGATION	18A. AGE OF VETERAN	18B. AGE OF SPOUSE	18C. AGE(S) OF DEPENDENT(S)
☐ MARRIED ☐ UNMARRIED ☐ SEPARATED	☐ MARRIED ☐ UNMARRIED ☐ SEPARATED	$	$			

19. NAME AND ADDRESS OF NEAREST LIVING RELATIVE *(Include telephone number, if available)*

20A. MONTHLY PAYMENT ON RENTED PREMISES VETERAN NOW OCCUPIES $ | **20B. UTILITIES INCLUDED?** ☐ YES ☐ NO

21. ASSETS		**22. LIABILITIES** *(Itemize all debts)*		
A. CASH *(Including deposit on purchase)*	$	NAME OF CREDITOR	MO. PAYMENT	BALANCE
B. SAVINGS BONDS-OTHER SECURITIES			$	$
C. REAL ESTATE OWNED				
D. AUTO				
E. FURNITURE AND HOUSEHOLD GOODS				
F. OTHER *(Use separate sheet, if necessary)*				
G. TOTAL	$	JOB-RELATED EXPENSE *(Specify)*		
		TOTAL	$	$

23. INCOME AND OCCUPATIONAL STATUS			**24. ESTIMATED TOTAL COST**	
ITEM	VETERAN	SPOUSE	ITEM	AMOUNT
A. OCCUPATION			A. PURCHASE EXISTING HOME	$
			B. ALTERATIONS, IMPROVEMENTS, REPAIRS	
			C. CONSTRUCTION	
B. NAME OF EMPLOYER			D. LAND *(If acquired separately)*	
			E. PURCHASE OF CONDOMINIUM UNIT	
			F. PREPAID ITEMS	
C. NUMBER OF YEARS EMPLOYED			G. ESTIMATED CLOSING COST	
			H. DISCOUNT *(Only if veteran permitted to pay)*	
D. GROSS PAY	MONTHLY $ HOURLY $	MONTHLY $ HOURLY $	I. TOTAL COST *(Add Items 24A through 24H)*	
			J. LESS CASH FROM VETERAN	
E. OTHER INCOME *(Disclosure of child support, alimony and separate maintenance income is optional)* $		$	K. LESS OTHER CREDITS	
			L. AMOUNT OF LOAN	$

NOTE - IF LAND ACQUIRED BY SEPARATE TRANSACTION, COMPLETE ITEMS 25A AND 25B.
25A. DATE ACQUIRED | **25B. UNPAID BALANCE** $

READ CERTIFICATIONS ON REVERSE CAREFULLY

VA FORM JUN 1977 **26-1802a** | SUPERSEDES VA FORM 26-1802a, DEC 1975, WHICH WILL NOT BE USED | LENDER   8

EXHIBIT 7

Form Approved
OMB No. 76-R0371

VETERANS ADMINISTRATION **REQUEST FOR DETERMINATION OF ELIGIBILITY AND AVAILABLE LOAN GUARANTY ENTITLEMENT**	TO	VETERANS ADMINISTRATION ATTN: Loan Guaranty Division

NOTE   Please read instructions on reverse before completing this form. If additional space is required, attach separate sheet.

1. FIRST-MIDDLE-LAST NAME OF VETERAN	2. ADDRESS OF VETERAN (No., street or rural route, city or P.O., State and ZIP code)

3. DATE OF BIRTH

4. MILITARY SERVICE DATA—I request the Veterans Administration to determine my eligibility and the amount of entitlement based on the following period(s) of active military duty: (Start with latest period of service and list all periods of active duty since September 16, 1940.)

PERIOD OF ACTIVE SERVICE		NAME (Show your name exactly as it appears on your separation papers (DD Form 214) or statement of service)	SERVICE NUMBER	BRANCH OF SERVICE
DATE FROM	DATE TO			
4A.				
4B.				
4C.				
4D.				

5A. WERE YOU DISCHARGED, RETIRED, OR SEPARATED FROM SERVICE BECAUSE OF DISABILITY, OR DO YOU NOW HAVE ANY SERVICE-CONNECTED DISABILITIES? ☐ YES ☐ NO (If "Yes," complete Item 5B)	5B. VA FILE NUMBER C-	6. IS THERE A CERTIFICATE OF ELIGIBILITY FOR LOAN GUARANTY OR DIRECT LOAN PURPOSES ENCLOSED? ☐ YES ☐ NO (If "No," complete Items 7A and 7B)

7A. HAVE YOU PREVIOUSLY APPLIED FOR A CERTIFICATE OF ELIGIBILITY FOR LOAN GUARANTY OR DIRECT LOAN PURPOSES? ☐ YES ☐ NO (If "Yes," give location of VA office(s) involved)	7B. HAVE YOU PREVIOUSLY RECEIVED SUCH A CERTIFICATE OF ELIGIBILITY? ☐ YES ☐ NO (If "Yes," give location of VA office(s) involved)

8A. HAVE YOU PREVIOUSLY SECURED A VA DIRECT HOME LOAN? ☐ YES ☐ NO (If "Yes," give location of VA office(s) involved and complete Items 9 through 18)	8B. HAVE YOU PREVIOUSLY OBTAINED HOME, FARM, CONDOMINIUM OR BUSINESS LOAN(S) WHICH WERE GUARANTEED OR INSURED BY VA? ☐ YES ☐ NO (If "Yes," give location of VA office(s) involved and complete Items 9 through 18)	8C. HAVE YOU PREVIOUSLY OBTAINED A VA MOBILE HOME AND/OR LOT LOAN(S)? ☐ YES ☐ NO (If "Yes," give location of VA office(s) involved)

NOTE. Complete Items 9 through 18 only if you have previously acquired property with the assistance of a GI Loan.	9. ADDRESS OF PROPERTY PREVIOUSLY PURCHASED WITH GUARANTY ENTITLEMENT	10. DATE YOU PURCHASED PROPERTY
		11. DO YOU NOW OWN THE REAL PROPERTY DESCRIBED IN ITEM 9? ☐ YES ☐ NO (If "Yes," do not complete Items 12 through 18)

12. CHECK WHETHER YOU ☐ ENTERED INTO AN INSTALLMENT SALE CONTRACT WITH THE PURCHASER, OR ☐ EXECUTED AND DELIVERED A DEED TO THE PURCHASER CONVEYING ALL YOUR RIGHTS, TITLE, AND INTEREST IN THE PROPERTY	13. NAMES OF PERSONS TO WHOM YOU SOLD THE PROPERTY	14. DATE THE DEED, IF ANY, WAS DELIVERED TO PURCHASER
		15. IS THERE ANY UNDERSTANDING OR AGREEMENT WRITTEN OR ORAL BETWEEN YOU AND THE PURCHASERS THAT THEY WILL RECONVEY THE PROPERTY TO YOU? ☐ YES ☐ NO

NOTE. It will speed processing if you can furnish the information in Items 16, 17, and 18.	16. NAME AND ADDRESS OF LENDER TO WHOM LOAN PAYMENTS WERE MADE	17. LENDER'S LOAN OR ACCOUNT NO.
		18. VA LOAN NO. (LH)

19. Check only if this is a request for a DUPLICATE Certificate of Eligibility ▶	☐ PLEASE ISSUE A DUPLICATE CERTIFICATE OF ELIGIBILITY IN MY NAME. THE CERTIFICATE PREVIOUSLY ISSUED TO ME IS NOT AVAILABLE BECAUSE IT HAS BEEN LOST, DESTROYED OR STOLEN. IF IT IS RECOVERED, IT WILL BE RETURNED TO THE VA FOR CANCELLATION.

I certify that the statements herein are true to the best of my knowledge and belief.	20. SIGNATURE OF VETERAN	21. DATE

FEDERAL STATUTES PROVIDE SEVERE PENALTIES FOR FRAUD, INTENTIONAL MISREPRESENTATION, CRIMINAL CONNIVANCE, OR CONSPIRACY PURPOSED TO INFLUENCE THE ISSUANCE OF ANY GUARANTY OR INSURANCE BY THE ADMINISTRATOR.

THIS SECTION FOR VA USE ONLY

DATE CERTIFICATE ISSUED AND DISCHARGE OR SEPARATION PAPERS AND VA PAMPHLETS GIVEN TO VETERAN OR MAILED TO ADDRESS SHOWN BELOW	TYPE OF DISCHARGE OR SEPARATION PAPERS RETURNED	SIGNATURE AND TITLE OF APPROPRIATE OFFICIAL (If applicable)	STATION NUMBER
			CERTIFICATE NUMBER

VA FORM 26-1880, JAN 1977   DO NOT DETACH

IMPORTANT—You must complete Item 22, since the certificate of eligibility together with all discharge and separation papers will be mailed to the address shown in Item 22 immediately below. If they are to be sent to you, your current mailing address should be indicated, or if they are to be sent elsewhere, the name and address of such person or firm should be shown in Item 22.

The amount of loan guaranty entitlement available for use is endorsed on the reverse of the enclosed Certificate of Eligibility. This certificate must be returned to the VA at the time a loan application or loan report is submitted.

22. RETURN TO (Enter name and address below dots)

[PLEASE DELIVER THE ENCLOSED PAMPHLETS AND DISCHARGE OR SEPARATION PAPERS TO THE VETERAN PROMPTLY. THANK YOU.]

Must be enclosed with the veteran's separation papers

VA FORM JAN 1977 **26-1880**

closing. A termite inspection report prepared by an approved exterminating company must be obtained on all VA loans, and the veteran must
acknowledge receipt of the report in writing. This report has to be forwarded to the lender before closing.

VA Refinances

Public Law 91–506 revived the previously expired loan guarantee entitlement of World War II and Korean War veterans. Because of the phase
out, many otherwise eligible veterans had not been able to use their
entitlement and therefore had made FHA or conventional loans. The
new authority granted under Public Law 91–506 gave these veterans
an opportunity to utilize their loan guarantee entitlement. They were
given the full statutory entitlement of $25,000.

Where a portion of the entitlement has been used, the balance still
available may be sufficient for refinancing. In addition, the veteran must
be an owner/occupant and the purpose of the loan must be: (1) to refinance a sum due the holder of a mortgage or other lien indebtedness;
or (2) to refinance a sum due the holder of a mortgage or other lien
indebtedness and to provide the veteran with funds for a purpose acceptable to the lender. In other words, the loan may include the amount
needed to satisfy mortgages or liens of record, including accrued interest
and a contractual prepayment penalty, plus any amount in cash, provided that the total amount does not exceed the reasonable value of
the property, in which case a statement from the veteran outlining the
purposes to which the cash will be put must accompany the application.
The VA expects the lender to encourage only "cash fund" applications
that are for "meritorious" purposes such as repairs, alterations, or improvements to the property.

Exhibits Required to Appeal a Low FHA or VA Appraisal

For an appeal of a low FHA or VA appraisal, the broker is required
to secure all of the written exhibits. The mortgagee is required to submit
those exhibits to the appropriate government agency. The exhibits
should include market data on three recent sales of comparable properties that have closed in the immediate neighborhood. The data should
include the following information on each property:

1. Address.
2. Type—two-story, ranch, split-level, etc.
3. Construction—frame, brick, etc.
4. Date built.
5. Number of rooms, baths, etc.
6. Garage—number of cars; attached, built-in, etc.
7. Date of closing.
8. Sale price obtained.
9. Manner of financing—cash, conventional, assumption, FHA, VA.

On VA loans, the appeal must be accompanied by a letter from the
veteran requesting the increase in appraised value.

Discounts on FHA and VA Loans

Discounts on FHA and VA loans are based primarily on the following three factors:

1. *The property*—loan amount, age, condition, location, and area.
2. *The mortgagor*—income, length and type of employment, credit rating. Comortgagors other than a husband and wife are acceptable but less desirable. Loans to such comortgagors are harder to place and generally require a higher discount.)
3. *The prevailing money market.* During periods of tight money, discounts are always higher. FHA and VA interest rates are set by Congress and unlike interest rates on conventional loans, they cannot be adjusted upward or downward. FHA and VA interest rates are usually set at levels below those of conventional mortgages. Due to the lower interest rate, lenders usually require a discount in order to increase the return on their investment in such mortgages. Since the borrower cannot pay more than one point, the seller must pay whatever amount is necessary to make an FHA or VA loan salable to a lender.

Loans covering older and less desirable properties and loans covering mortgagors with low income, poor credit, and unstable employment histories will require higher discounts. Consequently, consideration should be given to these factors when listing properties and qualifying prospective purchasers. Although many borderline cases are approved by the FHA and the VA, such loans always carry a higher discount, FHA and VA regulations generally require that the discount be paid by the seller. The only exception to this is on FHA refinancing, on which the mortgagor pays all of the points. However, it should be noted that the discount is not an unreimbursed expense to the seller since the discount is reflected in FHA and VA appraisals based on the recent market prices of comparable homes.

Important Points to Remember about FHA and VA Loans

1. The down payment and the closing costs cannot be borrowed funds unless the purchaser is 60 years of age or older.
2. The mortgage amounts are reduced to the nearest $50 multiple.
3. A house can be sold for more than the FHA or VA appraisal. However, the maximum loan is based on that appraisal or the contract price, whichever is less.
4. A gift for the down payment should come from someone related by blood, marriage, or an act of law. A gift letter should show the address of the donor and the donor's relationship to the applicant. The letter should state that there is no obligation of repayment by money or services, and it must be accompanied by proof of the gift giver's ability to give the gift.
5. The FHA mortgage insurance premium (MIP) is a ½ percent charge paid by the mortgagor in his monthly mortgage payment to the mortgagee, who in turn remits it to the FHA. This fee is pooled by areas and used to defray the cost of foreclosures by the lending

institution and the FHA. It may be used by the FHA in the event that it has to purchase properties after foreclosure.

6. The FHA or the VA may find properties unacceptable for a number of reasons. The following are the most frequent:
   a. Unsatisfactory septic tank areas, wet basements.
   b. An unapproved subdivision.
   c. An unacceptable drainage system.
   d. Economically unfeasible repairs.
   e. Marketing instability due to a transition to commercial use.
   f. An unacceptable water supply.
   g. Unsound construction.
   h. A lack of privacy due to poor room arrangement.

7. Non–real estate items should be covered by a separate bill of sale and paid for separately. If non–real estate items are included in the real estate contract, their value will be deducted from the FHA/VA appraisal or the sale price, whichever is less, and the insurable loan reduced accordingly.

8. If the FHA or VA appraisal indicates that certain repairs are to be made to the property, then these repairs must be made and inspected prior to closing. A request for an escrow amount to complete repairs after closing will be considered only on repairs that cannot be completed due to weather or hardship, and such a request must be approved by the FHA or the VA.

9. An individual can be an approved mortgagor on no more than four outstanding FHA-insured mortgages at a time.

10. There is no maximum age limit on VA or FHA loans. However, if there is a question as to the minority of the applicant, an attorney should be consulted.

11. When applying for an FHA or VA appraisal, an old survey should be submitted whenever possible. This will reduce the chances of problems at closing.

12. Contracts must have original signatures.

13. All conditions appearing on FHA, VA, or LMC commitments must be complied with before a closing date is set.

14. Flood insurance is required on all homes in designated floodplain areas in approved towns. There is a mandatory 14-day waiting period from the date of application for flood insurance to the time that it becomes effective, and the flood insurance must be effective by the date of settlement.

Special Problems in Connection with Veterans' Loans

1. *Property excluded.*
   a. Property with space heaters.
   b. Property with ceilings lower than seven feet in height.
   c. New construction not built under VA specifications.

2. *Buyers excluded.* Dishonorably discharged veterans or nonveterans.

3. *Interest rates lowered or raised.* Should the interest rate increase when a mortgage application is in process, the buyer will continue

to pay the old interest rate provided that his approval was granted before the interest rate increased. However, should the interest rate go down after the buyer obtained his approval, then the buyer will close the loan at the older, higher interest rate.

4. *Tight money.* This generally occurs because of an increase in the interest rate charged by the Federal Reserve Bank to its member banks. Generally, VA interest rates will rise accordingly.

5. *Undesirably discharged veterans.* Under special conditions, undesirably discharged veterans have received VA financing. However, each such case must be submitted to the Veterans Administration Special Panel for adjudication, and eight weeks should be allowed for this process at the outset of the transaction.

6. *Assets that matter.* All assets of monetary value should be listed on the veteran's mortgage application. Many times, veterans are deprived of mortgage financing due to the omission of valuable assets other than cash and savings.

OTHER GOVERNMENT PROGRAMS

Arthur E. Warner

*A*RTHUR E. WARNER, DBA, Chairprofessor of Real Estate, Property Finance, and Urban Development, College of Business Administration, University of South Carolina, Columbia, South
Carolina.

*Director, Center for Real Estate and Urban Economic Studies,
University of South Carolina. Formerly director, programs for
the doctoral degree in business administration, Michigan State
University; dean and professor, College of Business Administra-
tion, University of Tennessee; dean and professor of real estate
and urban development studies, The American University,
Washington, D.C. Member, Committee on Education, National
Association of Realtors®, and Board of Directors, Realtors®
Education Foundation of South Carolina. Author of articles in*
South Carolina Realtor, Tennessee Survey of Business, Business
Topics *(Michigan State University),* Appraisal Journal, Michi-
gan Economic Record, *and* Land Economics, *and numerous
monographs.*

The Legislative Background of the Farmers Home Administration

The Farmers Home Administration (FmHA) supposedly views itself
as a "lender of last resort," although this may not be what it is in practice.
Under the Consolidated Farmers Home Administration Act, an applicant
for a Farmers Home administration loan must agree that when the secretary of agriculture (through FmHA) determines that he is able to obtain
suitable credit from other sources to refinance his loan, he will do so.
This requirement has been identified as the "graduation" requirement.

The Farmers Home Administration grew out of the emergency measures that were taken by Franklin D. Roosevelt when he took office as
president in 1933. A primary function of the Resettlement Administra-

tion, which Roosevelt created by executive order in 1935, was to make loans that would assist farm families in remaining on their farms. In 1937 the Bankhead-Jones Farm Tenant Act created a program that gave farmers who could not obtain credit elsewhere 40-year loans to purchase farms and make improvements in farm housing. Soon afterward, the Resettlement Administration, which was responsible for implementing the act, was renamed the Farm Security Administration and placed in the Department of Agriculture.

In 1946 the Farmers Home Administration Act created the FmHA, assigning it the functions of the Farm Security Administration and giving it authority to make direct loans to farmers and to insure loans made to farmers. The Housing Act of 1949 authorized FmHA to make housing loans to farmers as part of a program to provide a decent home and a suitable living environment for all Americans. The Consolidated Farmers Home Administration Act of 1961 pointed toward FmHA loans to provide for water, sewer, waste disposal, and other facilities in rural America. The Federal Housing Act, passed in the same year, made non-farm rural residents eligible for FmHA housing loans.

In 1962 FmHA rural housing services were expanded further by the Senior Citizens Housing Act, which provided loans to finance low-rent apartment projects for older persons living in rural areas. Under the Housing and Redevelopment Act of 1968, the FmHA was assigned responsibility for about 1½ million of 6 million federally subsidized housing units that were targeted for production during the years 1969–78. "Rural areas," which had been defined to include towns with populations up to 2,500 in the Federal Housing Act of 1961 and up to 5,500 in the Housing Act of 1965, were increased to a ceiling of 10,000 by the Housing Act of 1970.

The Rural Development Act of 1972 authorized FmHA to guarantee loans made by commercial lenders for farming, rural housing, and rural business and industry. The 1974 Housing and Community Development Act authorized it to include loans on mobile homes and condominiums and to include cities of up to 20,000 persons outside standard metropolitan statistical areas that the secretary of agriculture in consultation with the secretary of HUD designated as deficient in credit facilities. Thus the FmHA has become the primary housing agency for nonmetropolitan America.

The Farmers Home Administration Rural Housing Lending Programs

During the more than 40 years that it has functioned under its present name, the Farmers Home Administration (FmHA) has been actively involved in large-scale lending programs on rural housing only since 1961. In earlier years most FmHA loans on rural housing were made to farmers and were tied directly to farm ownership and farm operations. The authorization for these loans came primarily from the Farmers Home Administration Act as amended. At the end of 1962 farm mortgages of over $637 million were held by FmHA.

Under authorization provided by the Housing Act of 1949, FmHA rural lending activities advanced sharply in 1961, largely as a result of the provision in the Housing Act of 1961 which gave FmHA the authority to make housing loans to nonfarm families in towns with populations of up to 2,500 persons. Rural housing loans amounting to $46 million were made in fiscal year 1962, and a total of $317 million in rural housing loans was outstanding at the end of the year.

The years 1969–71 represent the period of greatest expansion in FmHA's rural housing programs. During those years the major FmHA home ownership loan program (Section 502) more than doubled, from 48,000 in 1969 to nearly 104,000 in 1971. This increase can be attributed in part to the increase in the size of eligible communities to 10,000 persons and in part to an increase in congressional appropriations.

Since 1971, the number of rural home ownership loans made annually has remained fairly steady in the range of 90,000 to 100,000. During the past six years the FmHA has provided rural housing loans with a total mortgage amount of $13 billion to more than 800,000 persons. Approximately three fourths of the total number of loans made during the 1970s were in Section 502 loans. The remainder were made for home repair, rural rental, farm labor loans and grants, site loans, and self-help and technical assistance.

The Home Ownership Loan Program. The largest and most significant FmHA-administered program in rural housing is based on the Section 502 authority to make funds available for home ownership. Loans can be secured to purchase new or existing structures or to build, rehabilitate, or relocate owner-occupied single-family dwellings. Where appropriate, the loans include funds to cover the cost of adequate building sites. Low- and moderate-income families are eligible if they cannot obtain credit on reasonable terms elsewhere.

The Section 502 Interest Credit Program provides a reduction to as low as 1 percent in the interest rate paid by borrowers, or 20 percent of the family's adjusted income, whichever is less. Such loans are made for the most part to families with adjusted annual incomes of less than $8,000 and are restricted to houses not exceeding 1,200 square feet of living space.

Other FmHA Programs. Under Section 504, loans are made to install inside plumbing, cooking facilities, toilets, screens, storm windows, and insulation, and to finance other construction to improve the quality of housing. Sections 514 and 516 make farm labor housing loans and grants available for buying, building, or repairing housing for domestic farm labor. The rural housing rental program of Section 515 makes direct loans to finance rental housing and related facilities for occupancy by low-income to moderate-income rural families and by persons 62 years of age or older. Under the provisions of Sections 523 and 524, short-term loans enable public bodies and nonprofit organizations to buy and develop building sites for use by low-income and moderate-income families. Section 523 TA makes funds available to endeavors involving cooperating groups of families that will provide a major portion of the labor required to construct their own homes. Grants enable public and private nonprofit groups to organize and assist families in using the self-help approach by making equipment available to those families, by training family members in construction techniques, and by hiring construction supervisors to work with the families.

Obtaining FmHA Loans

The lending policies and practices of FmHA have been consistent throughout the years. Credit has been extended to eligible borrowers without racial or ethnic discrimination. These general eligibility requirements apply to all types of rural housing loans:

1. The income of the family must be in the low or moderate range.
2. The family must reside in a rural community with a population of under 10,000. The family may reside in a town or a city with a population of between 10,000 and 20,000 that is located outside a standard metropolitan statistical area if the secretaries of agriculture and housing and urban development certify that a serious lack of mortgage credit exists in that town or city.
3. The family must be without decent, safe, and sanitary housing.
4. The family must be unable to obtain a loan from private lenders on terms and conditions that it can be reasonably expected to meet.

Single-Family Home Ownership Loans (Section 502). Home ownership loans may be used to buy, build, improve, repair, or rehabilitate rural homes and related facilities, including water and waste disposal systems. The homes may be located on individual sites or in subdivisions.

Loans may be made for up to 100 percent of the FmHA-appraised value of a property if construction inspections are made by the FmHA, the FHA, or the VA. Homes over one year old and improvements may also be financed with 100 percent loans. The maximum maturity of these loans is 33 years.

The local FmHA field staff determines the eligibility of all applicants. Applicants must provide data on total family income, obtain evidence of inability to obtain credit elsewhere, live in a rural area, and be citizens of the United States or be legally admitted as permanent residents.

The FmHA Loan Package Concept. In making residential loans to persons living in rural areas, FmHA has developed a set of guidelines to assist builders, developers, real estate brokers, and others who may wish to package applications on behalf of prospective eligible borrowers. Loan packagers are required to work directly with applicant families in completing all forms and required information.

FmHA Forms Provided to Packager. The FmHA county supervisor will provide assistance and guidance to all packagers in obtaining the required information. No one, however, should attempt to package applications unless he can work directly with the applicant family in completing all the forms, provide all of the necessary information about the completed home, and assure the delivery of the home at a specified price.

The FmHA county supervisor will provide the packager with the following forms as needed:

Form FmHA 444–12   Check Sheet for Rural Housing Loan Package

Form FmHA 410–4[1]   Application for Rural Housing Loan (Nonfarm Tract)

Form FmHA 410–5   Request for Verification of Employment

Form FmHA 444–10   Information on Property (Rural Housing Nonfarm Tract)

Form FmHA 424–2   Dwelling Specification

Form FmHA 440–32   Option to Purchase Real Property

Information That the Packager Must Provide. 1. *Information to be submitted for all applicants.* The applicant family should complete the appropriate application form. If the applicant already has a pending application on file in the FmHA county office, another application need not be included in the package unless it is specifically requested by the FmHA county supervisor. If the applicant obtains income from his own business other than farming, the most recent operating statement must be attached to the application.

The packager will use Form FmHA 410–5, "Request for Verification of Employment," to check the employment and income of the applicant. The form will be mailed to the employer to be completed and returned directly by the employer to the FmHA county office.

If it appears that the applicant has sufficient income or assets to qualify for housing credit from another source, he must make a diligent effort to obtain such credit from at least two lenders who customarily make long-term housing loans in the area. If he is unable to obtain credit from these lenders, the loan package should include letters stating why they cannot assist the applicant.

Although the packager may obtain a credit report on the applicant, he is not required to do so. FmHA will not pay for or collect fees from an applicant to pay for a report ordered by a packager. If a report is ordered by a packager in the expectation that the information obtained will be used by the FmHA in processing the rural housing loan, the report should be mailed by the reporting bureau directly to the FmHA county officer rather than a third party.

Information specified in either item 2 or item 3 below will be submitted. If FmHA has already issued a conditional commitment on the property, information on the house will be on file in the county office and need not be resubmitted. If a house to be purchased is under construction, the loan will not be closed until the house is completed. In such a case the information in item 3 below will be submitted.

2. *Information to be submitted for homes that are to be built or reha-*

---

[1] If the applicant depends primarily on farm income, the following forms should be used instead of Form FmHA 410–4:

Form FmHA 410–1, "Application for FmHA Services."

Form FmHA 410–2, "Supplement to Application for FmHA Services" (to be used if family also has off-farm income).

bilitated. The information and materials described on the front page of Form FmHA 444–10, "Information on Property," will be submitted along with the completed form. This applies whether or not a conditional commitment is being requested in connection with the package.

3. *Information to be submitted for loans to buy existing homes.* A signed or certified copy of an option on the property must be submitted. The option must provide that any deposits or down payments made by the applicant will be refunded if a loan is not made by FmHA and cannot be obtained from another source. Form FmHA 440–34, "Option to Purchase Real Property," may be used for this purpose.

The specifications of the house and site, including individual water and waste disposal systems, when applicable, will be submitted, along with the plans if the house has not been occupied or, whenever possible, if the house has been occupied but is less than one year old. In either case, the builder, if available, will provide a statement certifying that the house has been built and the site developed according to the plans and specifications and the local building codes.

If major improvements are involved, three sets of complete plans and specifications of the work to be done and reliable cost estimates or a contractor's bid will be provided. A termite certification will be provided whenever required.

When an individual well or waste disposal system is involved, the loan will not be closed until evidence is furnished by the seller that the water or the septic system meets health department requirements. Written evidence of inspection or testing indicating that a water system is acceptable must be received from the health department or a reliable laboratory; written evidence of the acceptability of a waste disposal system must be received from a reliable and competent firm that can determine whether the system is functioning properly. If either system is determined to be unacceptable, the deficiency must be corrected before the loan is closed, and written evidence furnished showing acceptance by the state health department or a determination by the county supervisor that it meets FmHA requirements.

Form FmHA 444–10, "Information on Property," must be completed, as must a direction map to the property and a plot plan drawn to scale showing the location of the house and related facilities.

Review and Acceptance of a Complete Package. The packager will deliver completed rural housing loan packages to the county office assembled in the order shown on Form FmHA 444–12, "Check Sheet for Rural Housing Loan Package," which should be attached. Whenever possible, the applicant and the applicant's spouse will be present when the application is presented. The FmHA county supervisor will review the package to determine whether it contains all of the necessary information in acceptable form to process the loan. If information is missing or incomplete, he will request that the packager or the applicant provide additional information. If the applicant is not present when the application is submitted, the FmHA county supervisor will ordinarily not proceed until the applicant visits the county office for an interview.

After a loan package is received, the FmHA county supervisor:

1. Interviews the applicant family.
2. Works with the applicant or the packager to obtain any additional information that may be needed to evaluate the application.
3. Checks the applicant's credit and character references.
4. Makes an appraisal of the property.
5. Presents the application to the FmHA county committee for a determination of the applicant's eligibility.
6. Approves the loan.
7. Notifies the applicant of the loan approval.
8. Requests the applicant to order preliminary title work if this has not been ordered previously.
9. Closes the loan. (The family must meet with the FmHA employee who is authorized to close the loan.)
10. Assists with the preparation of a construction contract if one is involved.
11. Authorizes any planned construction to start. (Before doing so, the county supervisor may require a preconstruction conference with the family and the contractor.)
12. Makes the required inspection of the construction.

If for any reason the loan cannot be made, the FmHA county supervisor will notify the applicant and the packager.

Other Requirements.

1. The FmHA county supervisor will inform the applicant of any special loan approval conditions that must be met before the loan is closed.
2. Loan checks will be deposited in a supervised bank account which requires the countersignature of the FmHA county supervisor for disbursements unless all funds are to be used immediately and paid to one payee.
3. Fire and extended insurance coverage must be provided on all insurable buildings on the property on the date that the loan is closed or not later than the date on which construction starts if the construction work is to be paid for with loan funds.
4. Construction work that is to be paid for with loan funds may not be started until authorization to do so is given by the FmHA county supervisor.

Conditional Commitments for Rural Housing Loans.

Conditional commitments are issued to home builders or sellers. These commitments provide assurance that homes to be built or rehabilitated and offered for sale will be suitable for purchase with an FmHA loan by eligible loan applicants at a price not above a specified maximum amount. The commitments are not reservations of funds or assurances that eligible applicants will be available.

Packagers may obtain a commitment if they are able to deliver a house that meets all FmHA requirements. If information on the house and the applicant family is submitted at the same time, the following conditions will be met to avoid any misunderstanding of FmHA's obligation to either the rural housing applicant or the packager requesting the conditional commitment:

1. The rural housing loan will be approved before the conditional commitment is issued.
2. Loan funds will be obligated before construction is started.
3. The dwelling will be built and final inspection made before the rural housing loan is closed.

The Farm Credit System

American agriculture consists of a tremendously complex set of organizations, including farms, farm supply firms, product marketing firms, and public agriculture services. The application of modern techniques and management principles have been responsible for an increasing capital investment in agriculture and the consolidation of many small units—causing agricultural employment to decline sharply and capital requirements per farm to increase much more rapidly than aggregate requirements. In addition, farm managers are now using credit to finance a larger proportion of their total investment. Consequently, the use of credit has increased much more rapidly than the use of capital from retained earnings.

The Farm Credit System is designed to help the farmer meet this growing need for credit. Its primary purpose is to furnish sound, adequate, and constructive credit and closely related services to farmers and ranchers. It also makes credit available to farm cooperatives and to farm-related businesses that are necessary for efficient farm operations. The system also supplies credit for rural homes to qualified borrowers as described above.

Farm assets increased from less than $52 billion in 1950 to over $350 billion in 1974. During the same period Farm Credit System loans outstanding increased from $2 billion to $22 billion.

The Farm Credit System operates in 12 farm districts. In each of the districts there is a Federal Land Bank, a Federal Intermediate Credit Bank, and a Bank for Cooperatives. There is also a Central Bank for Cooperatives in Denver, Colorado. The Federal Land banks make long-term loans secured by first mortgages on farm real estate through 566 local Federal Land Bank associations. The Federal Intermediate Credit banks make loans to and discount farmer's notes for 434 Production Credit associations and discount notes for about 100 other financing institutions serving farmers. The Banks for Cooperatives make loans to farmers' marketing, supply, and business service cooperatives. The Central Bank for Cooperatives participates with these banks on larger loans. These banks and associations are supervised and examined by the Farm Credit Administration, an independent agency in the executive branch of the U.S. government.

The Farm Credit Act of 1971 provides the present authority for the activities of the banks and associations of the Farm Credit System. The act supersedes all previous acts and resolutions governing the system.

However, the various units of the system came into being at different times to fill different needs.

After the turn of the century, larger farms, the increased use of fertilizers, more intensive labor, and growing mechanization created a need for a system of agricultural financing and credit. The Federal Farm Loan Act of 1916 was intended to cope with that need. It provided for the establishment of Federal Land banks and local Federal Land Bank associations (then called National Farm Loan Associations) through which the banks would make loans. It also provided a means by which the Land Bank stock was eventually acquired by the associations from the U.S. Treasury through stock subscriptions by borrowers in the associations.

The decade of the 1920s was a period of worsening agricultural depression. In order to provide agriculture with short- and intermediate-term credit, Congress passed the Agricultural Credits Act of 1923, which provided for the establishment and the capitalization of 12 Federal Intermediate Credit banks. These banks were intended to discount the notes that agricultural producers had given to other financing institutions. However, financial institutions did not use the services of the credit banks to the extent expected and the credit needs of farmers remained unfilled. In 1933 the Farm Credit Act of 1933 authorized the establishment of local Production Credit associations which could discount farmers' notes with the credit banks. It also provided for the initial capitalization and staffing of these institutions, and it brought credit service closer to borrowers. The Federal Intermediate Credit banks were entirely owned by the government until 1957. Then, as a result of passage of the Farm Credit Act of 1956, the Production Credit associations began to acquire stock in the credit banks. The ultimate goal, as expressed in the act, was the ownership of the credit banks by the associations. Complete ownership of the Banks by the Associations was achieved in 1968.

The Farm Credit Act of 1933 also recognized the need that farmers' marketing, supply, and business service cooperatives had for credit. It provided for the establishment and initial capitalization of 13 Banks for Cooperatives. The Farm Credit Act of 1955 paved the way for the ultimate ownership of the banks by the cooperatives which borrowed from them. The Banks for Cooperatives became completely owned by their borrowers in 1968.

The Farm Credit Act of 1971 recodified all the prior laws governing the Farm Credit System, modernized the functions of the system, broadened its lending authorities, and brought decision making closer to the borrowers. That act now governs the entire Farm Credit System.

The Federal Land Banks. The Federal Land banks make loans ranging from 5 to 40 years on primary security consisting of the equivalency of a first lien on real estate through local Federal Land Bank associations to farmers or ranchers. These may be organized as partnerships, corporations, trusts, or other types of organizations that are legally authorized to conduct a business. Loans may also be made to rural residents, secured by first liens on single family, moderate-priced conventional homes, modular homes, or mobile homes in rural areas. No borrower may have more than one loan outstanding on a rural home at any one time, and loans are not made for the purpose of renting or reselling a home. A rural area is primarily agricultural open country. It may, however, include towns or villages whose population does not exceed 2,500 persons. In rural home lending, each Bank is limited to 15 percent of its total loan volume outstanding.

The banks may make loans to farmers or ranchers for other than agricultural requirements. However, they are primarily agricultural lenders, and the amount they advance for other than agricultural purposes is dependent on the agricultural assets of the borrower. Loans may be made to rural residents to build, buy, remodel, improve, refinance, or repair a home. The loan total may include closing costs and participation certificates purchased as a condition of the loan.

Owners of farm-related businesses may borrow to purchase or refinance necessary sites, capital structures, and equipment, and for initial working capital. The banks are authorized to make sound loans that do not exceed 85 percent of the appraised value of the real estate security. The actual percentage loaned is dependent upon all credit factors, and additional collateral may be required to supplement the real estate security.

The Federal Land banks obtain most of their loan funds through the sale of securities, Consolidated Federal Land Bank bonds, and system-wide discount notes to investors in the nation's money markets and through the sale of farm credit investment bonds to their own borrowers. These securities are backed by the mortgages held by the banks. They are sold through a fiscal agency in New York City with the aid of a nationwide group of securities dealers. Temporary loan funds, between security issues, are obtained through borrowings from other Farm Credit banks and from commercial banks and other financial institutions.

TABLE 1
Federal Land Banks and Associations

	12/31/74	*12/31/75*
Number of loans outstanding	447,001	467,039
Amount of loans outstanding	$13.9 billion	$16.6 billion
Number of loans made during year	74,450	66,609
Amount farmers borrowed during year	$4.2 billion	$4.4 billion
Bonds outstanding	$12.2 billion	$14.8 billion
Average cost of bonds outstanding	7.36%	7.60%
Average cost of bonds issued during year . . .	8.41%	7.98%
Average interest on loans outstanding	7.83%	8.24%
Total net worth of land banks	$1,314 million	$1,575 million
Capital invested by associations	$793 million	$950 million
Accumulated savings	$521 million	$625 million
Total net worth of associations	$949 million	$1,098 million
Capital invested by members	$789 million	$941 million
Accumulated savings	$160 million	$157 million

Note: All percentage-of-change figures are based on rounded data.
Source: Farm Credit Administration.

The Federal Intermediate Credit Banks and Production Credit Association.   In each of the 12 Farm Credit districts, there is a Federal Intermediate Credit Bank. These banks are the chief source of loan funds for the Production Credit Associations (PCAs), and they may participate with the associations on some loans. Their primary functions, however, are to provide loan funds to the PCAs and to supervise some of their operations. They also discount the notes that farmers give to certain other financing institutions serving agriculture. The Federal Intermediate Credit Banks (FICBs) obtain their loan funds through the sale of securities to investors in the nation's money markets. These securities are marketed through a fiscal agent in New York City with the assistance of a nationwide group of securities dealers. The cost of loan funds depends largely on the rates that the banks have to pay on their securities.

Production Credit Associations may make loans with terms of up to seven years to legal entities engaged in the production of agricultural products, producers or harvesters of aquatic products, rural residents, farm-related businesses, and operations that combine farming, producing or harvesting aquatic products, or a farm-related business.

The Banks for Cooperatives.   The Banks for Cooperatives are themselves cooperatives. They are financial institutions whose business is to improve the income and well-being of producers of food and fiber by providing credit and related services to the agricultural and aquatic cooperatives of such producers. A principal objective of the Banks for Cooperatives is to furnish those cooperatives with loan funds. The Banks for Cooperatives provide about two thirds of the credit used by agricultural cooperatives.

Any association of farmers, ranchers, or producers or harvesters of aquatic products or any federation of such associations which is operated on a cooperative basis may be eligible to borrow from a Bank for Cooperatives if it is engaged in one or more of the following functions:

1. Storing, packing, processing, or marketing farm or aquatic products.
2. Purchasing, testing, grading, processing, furnishing, or distributing farm or aquatic supplies.
3. Furnishing business services to farmers, producers or harvesters of aquatic products, or other eligible cooperatives.

To be eligible to borrow from a Bank for Cooperatives, a cooperative must also meet the following requirements:

1. At least 80 percent of the voting control of the cooperative must be held by farmers, ranchers, or producers or harvesters of aquatic products.
2. The cooperative must do at least 50 percent of its business with or for its members.
3. No member of the cooperative shall have more than one vote because of the amount of stock or membership capital he owns, or the cooperative must restrict dividends on its stock or membership capital to either 10 percent per year or the maximum allowed by state law, whichever is less.

FIGURE 1
The Farm Credit System

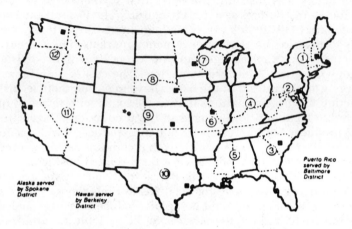

FARM CREDIT SYSTEM

Alaska served
by Spokane
District

Hawaii served
by Berkeley
District

Puerto Rico
served by
Baltimore
District

■ The United States is divided into 12 Farm Credit Districts.

Farm Credit Administration   Phone (202) 755-2195   490 L'Enfant Plaza East, S.W.   Washington, D.C. 20578
★ Central Bank for Cooperatives   Phone (303) 534-1313   Suite 2201, First National Bank Building
                                                    621 - 17th Street   Denver, Colorado 80202
● Farmbank Services   Phone (303) 373-0180   Suite 520, 12075 E. 45th Ave.   Denver, Colorado 80239

1. **Farm Credit Banks of Springfield**
   Farm Credit Building
   Phone (413) 737-1481
   Box 141
   Springfield, Massachusetts 01101

2. **Farm Credit Banks of Baltimore**
   Farm Credit Building
   Phone (301) 235-9100
   Box 1555
   Baltimore, Maryland 21203

3. **Farm Credit Banks of Columbia**
   Federal Land Bank Building
   Phone (803) 253-3361
   Box 1499
   Columbia, South Carolina 20202

4. **Farm Credit Banks of Louisville**
   Farm Credit Building
   Phone (502) 587-9621
   Box 239
   Louisville, Kentucky 40201

5. **Farm Credit Banks of New Orleans**
   Federal Land Bank Building
   Phone (504) 586-8101
   Box 50590
   New Orleans, Louisiana 70150

6. **Farm Credit Banks of St. Louis**
   Phone (314) 342-3200
   Box 504
   St. Louis, Missouri 63166

7. **Farm Credit Banks of St. Paul**
   Phone (612) 725-7722
   375 Jackson Street
   St. Paul, Minnesota 55101

8. **Farm Credit Banks of Omaha**
   Farm Credit Building
   Phone (402) 341-2904
   (402) 444-3333 after May 3, 1976
   206 South 19th Street
   Omaha, Nebraska 68102

9. **Farm Credit Banks of Wichita**
   Farm Credit Banks Building
   Phone (316) 264-5371
   151 North Main
   Wichita, Kansas 67202

10. **Farm Credit Banks of Houston**
    Federal Land Bank Building
    Phone (713) 227-6111
    430 Lamar Avenue
    Houston, Texas 77002

11. **Farm Credit Banks of Berkeley**
    Farm Credit Building
    Phone (415) 841-4701
    2180 Milvia Street
    Berkeley, California 94704

12. **Farm Credit Banks of Spokane**
    Phone (509) 747-7141
    W. 705 First Avenue
    Spokane, Washington 99204

Source: Directory, Farm Credit Banks of Omaha

The Banks for Cooperatives may make loans to meet any credit need which will enable an eligible cooperative to perform its marketing, supply, or business service function. They may also make loans for purposes not directly related to the primary function of a cooperative if the amount is relatively modest in relation to the total credit extended and the loan will enhance the well-being of their members and patrons.

The Banks for Cooperatives are designed to provide a complete credit service to cooperatives. To accomplish this, they offer loans that are tailored to meet the specialized needs of their borrowers.

Term loans are generally made to finance long-term assets or working capital. These may include loans for constructing, remodeling, or expanding facilities, or for purchasing land, buildings, or equipment. Such loans are ordinarily made on an amortized basis, and they may be secured or unsecured, depending on the purpose, the repayment period, and other credit factors. Loans scheduled for payment over an extended time are usually secured.

Seasonal loans are made primarily to finance current or seasonal assets. They mature within 18 months, and they may be secured or unsecured. Loans secured by merchandise or goods (except for live animals) which are in acceptable storage, are transportable, can be accurately classified by standards of quality and quantity, and enjoy broad markets may receive special consideration, especially if such loans are hedged or covered by warehouse receipts or other title documents. Loans of this type are generally called commodity loans. Established borrowers frequently maintain lines of credit from a Bank for Cooperatives which they use for seasonal needs. An established line of credit assures the borrowing cooperative that money will be available when required.

TABLE 2
The Banks for Cooperatives

	12/31/74	12/31/75
Cooperatives having loans outstanding	3,028	3,171
Amount of loans outstanding	$3.6 billion	$4.0 billion
Borrowing by cooperatives during year	2,587	2,768
Amount loaned during year	$8.4 billion	$8.9 billion
Consolidated bonds outstanding	$3.6 billion	$3.6 billion
Average cost of consolidated bonds outstanding ..	9.01%	7.03%
Total net worth	$416 million	$464 million
Capital invested by cooperatives	$246 million	$286 million
Accumulated savings	$170 million	$177 million

Note: All percentage-of-change figures are based on rounded data.
Source: Farm Credit Administration.

Table 2 gives an indication of the recent activity of the Banks for Cooperatives.

Lending Policies of the Farm Credit System. The banks and associations of the Farm Credit System are authorized to make only sound loans. In determining what constitutes a sound loan, the following factors are considered:

1. *The individual or entity.* The applicant must be of established integrity, and responsible and cooperative management must be evident.
2. *Financial position and progress.* Financial responsibility reflects the applicant's ability to meet obligations, continue business operations, and protect the lender against undue risk. The total assets controlled by the applicant and the history of the applicant's earnings to date are significant measures of financial responsibility.
3. *Repayment capacity.* This is determined by an analysis of cash flow history and a projection of cash flow. A cash flow projection reflects the cash generated from the applicant's operation and all other sources. Generally, the cash flow must be sufficient to meet all obligations and provide a remainder for contingencies.
4. *Basis of approval.* The amount of the loan, the use of funds, and the loan terms are the principal factors over which the lender has direct control. Therefore, the loan must be constructive in amount and purpose and the repayment terms must be practical for both the borrower and the lender. Loan conditions such as loan agreements, personal liability, additional collateral, insurance, and the like, are required as conditions warrant.
5. *Collateral offered or available as security.* Collateral needs are contingent upon the requirements of the law and upon the strengths and weaknesses of all credit factors. The requirement of collateral and the collateral taken must reasonably protect the lender, provide the necessary control of equity and repayment, and leave the borrower in a position to manage his business constructively.

The Borrowers and the Controllers. Agricultural producers control the local Federal Land Bank associations, Production Credit associations, and Banks for Cooperatives by directly electing their boards of directors. The boards of the local Land Bank associations and Production Credit associations and stockholders of the local Bank for Cooperatives each elect two members to the district Farm Credit Board for three-year terms. A seventh member is appointed by the governor of the Farm Credit Administration. This board sets the policies for the district Bank for Cooperatives, Federal Land Bank, and Federal Intermediate Credit Bank. The board of directors of the Central Bank for Cooperatives is composed of one director elected by each district Farm Credit Board and a 13th member appointed by the governor of the Farm Credit Administration.

Borrowers also have a voice at the national level through their representatives on the Federal Farm Credit Board. This board, which serves part time, consists of one member from each of the 12 Farm Credit districts, appointed by the president of the United States to six-year terms, and one member who represents the secretary of agriculture. The Federal Farm Credit Board sets policies for the Farm Credit Administration. The board appoints the governor, who is the chief executive of the Farm Credit Administration. The Farm Credit Administration is an independent agency within the executive branch of the U.S. government. Its purpose is to coordinate, supervise, and examine the 37 district banks, the Land Bank associations, and the Production Credit associations. This agency, the district banks, the Central Bank for Cooperatives, and the local associations are known collectively as the Farm Credit System.

The Future Sources of Funds for Farm Financing. In 1975, the Economic Research Service of the Department of Agriculture conducted a nationwide survey of farm lenders regarding the risk associated with farm real estate loans: 61 percent of the respondents believed that the risks had increased significantly; 33 percent believed that the risks were about the same as they had been in previous years; only 5 percent believed that the risks had decreased. If lenders continue to view farm loans as risky, they will tend to reduce the funds they make available for such loans, to increase the interest rates on the loans, or to decrease the term of the loans. It seems likely that farm borrowers will increase their lending demands upon both the nonprofit Federal Land Bank and the federal government, more specifically the Farmers Home Administration. Further, if the capital requirements for land continue to increase, more funds will be needed, causing the above sources to increase their market share of lending even more.

Government action with regard to such measures as price supports will determine whether farming risks will be shifted more onto the government or onto farmers. A reduction in the risks taken on by farmers will, in turn, reduce the risks taken by their lenders. At this time, however, it is unclear what action the government will take with regard to reducing farm risks.

The Section 8 Housing Assistance Payments Program

The federal government first assumed responsibility for the administration of public housing programs under the Housing Act of 1937. Under this act the federal government provided financial aid for housing owned and operated by local housing authorities for the benefit of low-income families, disabled persons, and elderly persons who are not able to afford decent housing.

Until recently, each local community was responsible for constructing and operating housing projects under this section of the federal government's public housing program, with administration left in the hands of local housing authorities. With the passage of the Housing and Community Development Act of 1974, however, a new low-income housing subsidy program was authorized under Section 8 of the Housing Act of 1937 as amended.

The new program authorizes the Department of Housing and Urban Development to render financial aid through assistance payment contracts. These contracts are made on behalf of eligible families and individuals occupying new, substantially rehabilitated, or existing rental units. HUD is now authorized to contract directly with private owners as well as public housing agencies to construct new housing units or rehabilitate existing units.

Assistance payment contracts may run for as long as 15 years for an existing unit and for as long as 20 years for a new or rehabilitated unit. Longer terms are available if a given project is owned or financed by a loan or a loan guarantee from a state or local agency or if it is financed by an FHA-insured loan.

The amount of assistance is equal to the difference between the established maximum rent for a unit and the occupant's required contribution to monthly rent. Aided families are required to contribute between 15 and 20 percent of their monthly income to rent, as prescribed by the secretary of HUD. For some families a 15 percent maximum is established.

In general, eligible families are those which have incomes not in excess of 80 percent of the median income in the area at the time of the initial renting of units. Also, at least 30 percent of the families assisted must be families with gross income not in excess of 50 percent of the area median income. These rules are subject to adjustment by the secretary of HUD, to take into account local construction cost variations, unusually high or low family incomes, and other relevant factors.

All private owners and public housing authority (PHA) owners must make several stipulations and assurances to participate in the revised Section 8 program. The certification includes assurances that the private owner, the PHA owner, or the private owner and the PHA will

1. Comply with Title VI of the Civil Rights Act of 1964 (P.L. 88–353) and regulations pursuant thereto (Title 24 CFR Part I) which states that no person in the United States shall, on the ground of race, color, or national origin, be excluded from participation in, be denied the benefits of, or be otherwise subjected to discrimination under any program or activity for which the applicant receives financial assistance; and will immediately take any measures necessary to effectuate this agreement. With reference to the real property and structure(s) thereon which are provided or improved with the aid of Federal financial assistance extended to the PHA or the Owner, this assurance shall obligate the PHA or owner, or in the case of any transfer, the transferee, for the period during which the real property and structures(s) are used for a purpose(s) for which the Federal financial assistance is extended or for another purpose involving the provision of similar services or benefits.

2. Comply with Title VIII of the Civil Rights Act of 1968 (P.L. 90–284), as amended, which prohibits discrimination in housing on the basis of race, color, religion, sex or national origin, and administer its programs and activities relating to housing in a manner to affirmatively further fair housing.

3. Comply with the Executive Order 11063 on Equal Opportunity in Housing which prohibits discrimination because of race, color, creed, or national origin in housing and related facilities provided with Federal financial assistance.

4. If the proposed project is to be located within the area of a local Housing Assistance Plan (HAP), the PHA or owner will take affirmative action to provide opportunities to apply for units in the proposed project to the class of persons identified in the local HAP as expected to reside in the community as a result of current or planned employment.

5. In establishing the criteria for the selection of tenants, the PHA or owner will not utilize preferences or priorities which are based upon the length of time the applicant has resided in the jurisdiction. The PHA or

owner shall treat non-resident applicants who are working, or have been notified that they are hired to work in the jurisdiction, as residents of the jurisdiction.

6. It will comply with Executive Order 11246 and all regulations pursuant thereto (41 CFR Chapter 60–1) which states that no person shall be discriminated against on the basis of race, color, religion, sex or national origin in all phases of employment during the performance of Federal contracts and shall take affirmative action to insure equal employment opportunity. The PHA or owner will incorporate, or cause to be incorporated, into any contract for construction work, as defined in Section 130.5 of HUD regulations, the equal opportunity clause required by Section 130.15(b) of the HUD regulations.

7. It will comply with Section 3 of the Housing and Urban Development Act of 1968, as amended (12 U.C. 170 lu) and regulations pursuant thereto (24 CFR Part 135), which requires that, to the greatest extent feasible, opportunities for training and employment be given lower-income residents of the project area and contracts for work in connection with the project be awarded to business concerns which are located in, or owned in substantial part by persons residing in, the area of the project.

Miscellaneous FHA Programs

The Federal Housing Administration was created in 1934 with the passage of the National Housing Act. The primary goal of the act was to revitalize the construction industry and provide employment in the building trades. The FHA was designed as a temporary agency. Its most important tool for contributing to the recovery program of the Roosevelt Administration was an insurance scheme that encouraged financial institutions and other fundholders to invest in mortgages on residential properties.

The most significant insurance programs administered by the FHA and embodied in the FHA array of financial supports are Title I, which provides insurance for home improvement loans, and Title II, which provides insurance for loans granted for the construction or purchase of a home and for the refinancing of an existing mortgage debt. Section 203 of Title II covers insurance for mortgages on one–four-family homes. It is the most popular and widely used FHA program, accounting for about 70 percent of all FHA insurance.

Other programs under Title II, including the following, have been added by Congress through the years.

Section 207 authorizes the insurance of mortgages, including construction advances, on rental housing projects of eight or more family units. It also covers mobile home courts and projects undertaken by nonprofit corporations for occupation by the elderly.

Section 213 authorizes the insurance of mortgages on cooperative housing projects of eight or more family units. The section provides for two types of FHA-insured cooperative housing projects—the management type and the sales type. The mortgagor of the management type must be a nonprofit ownership housing corporation or trust, with permanent occupancy of the housing facility restricted to members. In a sales-type project, each individual member is a stockholder of the cooperative corporation, or a beneficiary of the trust, undertaking the construction of the housing project. Upon the completion of the sales-type project, provision is made for the acquisition of title to an individual housing unit by each member and the insurance of an individual mortgage thereon.

Section 220 permits insurance in connection with the financing of the rehabilitation of existing salable housing and the replacement of slums with new housing.

Section 221 authorizes mortgage insurance on low-cost housing for the relocation of families in connection with urban renewal and slum clearance programs. Its benefits are also extended to any family of low or moderate income, to handicapped persons, and to persons aged 62 or over.

Section 221d, as amended in 1968, provides for the insurance of mortgages for single homes, permits a mortgagor to contribute the value of his labor to the acquisition of his dwelling, and authorizes the secretary of HUD to reimburse the mortgagee for its expenses in handling the mortgage. The loan-to-value ratio can be 100 percent for an owner-occupant, except if the home was not constructed under FHA or VA inspection or if over a year has passed since its completion. In the latter case, the maximum ratio is 90 percent. The minimum cash investment is $200 for a displaced family and 3 percent of the acquisition cost for other families. Normal FHA ceiling interest rates apply, and a ½ percent mortgage insurance premium is charged. In the case of displaced families, the term of the mortgage can be up to 40 years. For other families, it is generally 30 years.

Section 221(d)(3) provides special terms for the construction or rehabilitation of housing located in approved urban renewal areas for mortgagors approved by the federal housing commissioner. Where the mortgagor accepts regulation in regard to rents, charges, and methods of operation in a manner designed to effectuate the purposes of the program, a below-market interest rate will be allowed. Under those conditions, construction financing is charged at the FHA market rate, but when construction has been completed and the final endorsement of the mortgage insurance has been made, the rate can be reduced to 3 percent. On mortgages carrying this rate, the FHA waives its mortgage insurance premium and the mortgages will be purchased by the Federal National Mortgage Association.

A rent supplement program was also established by Section 221(d)(3). By this authority, low-income individuals or families that are either elderly, handicapped, displaced by government action, occupants of substandard housing, or occupants or former occupants of homes damaged by acts of God are eligible for admission as tenants to new or rehabilitated housing owned by a nonprofit organization participating in the below-market interest rate (BMIR) program. The housing owner contracts with the secretary of HUD for federal rent supplement payments. The contracts run for terms of up to 40 years. The rent supplement payments are limited to the excess of the fair rental value of the unit over one fourth of the tenant's income. When the tenant can afford to pay the whole rent by this standard he may continue to live in the unit without a rent supplement payment.

The Housing and Urban Development Act of 1968 extended the rent supplement program to owners of housing projects financed under a state or local program which provided assistance through loans, loan insurance, or tax abatements, provided that the projects meet the approval of the secretary of HUD for rent supplement benefits before the completion of construction or rehabilitation. Rent supplement benefits may also be extended to housing financed by direct loans under Section 202 of the Housing Act of 1959.

Section 221(h) of the Federal Housing Act was added in 1966 to establish a program to promote home ownership for low-income families with the assistance of FHA mortgage insurance. Under this authority, the FHA insures mortgages of nonprofit organizations to finance the purchase and rehabilitation of deteriorating and substandard housing. Mortgages may also be insured to finance the resale of housing to low-income individuals or families that are eligible for rent supplements under the rent supplement program.

The mortgage of the nonprofit organization may be insured for an amount equal to the appraised value of the property plus estimated rehabilitation costs. Its maturity is set by the FHA. Under legislation enacted in 1968, the regular FHA ceiling interest rate was prescribed until the final endorsement of the mortgage for insurance, then 3 percent. Under the 1968 amendment, the interest rate may be as low as 1 percent for purchasers whose income is low enough to warrant the lower rate. As a result, individual mortgages insured under this section may bear interest between 1 and 3 percent, depending on the individual income and needs of the homeowner. The mortgage of the homeowner in any individual case can be an amount equal to the unpaid balance of the mortgage of the nonprofit corporation selling the property that is allocable to the dwelling being sold. The minimum down payment required is $200, but this may be applied to closing costs. The maximum mortgage term is 25 years. The mortgage must contain a provision that the interest rate will increase to the highest rate permitted by the FHA if the mortgagor does not continue to occupy the property. However, this provision is not applicable to a resale to the nonprofit organization from which the property was originally purchased, or to a sale to a local housing authority or another low-income purchaser approved by the FHA.

Section 222 authorizes FHA insurance for mortgages on dwellings owned by members of the armed forces or the Coast Guard upon proper certification by the Department of Defense, or by the Treasury Department as to Coast Guard personnel. The national security objectives of such a program are apparent.

Section 231 provides insurance for the construction or rehabilitation of rental housing for the elderly or the handicapped. The facility constructed must contain at least eight units.

Section 232 authorizes FHA insurance of mortgages on urgently needed nursing homes. The insurance is applicable to convalescents who do not require hospitalization but do need nursing care. To qualify a nursing home for such insurance, the appropriate state agency charged with licensing and regulating such establishments must certify that the nursing home is needed and that minimum operating standards will be enforced in it. The property may be new or rehabilitated, but it must have at least 20 beds.

Section 233 gives the FHA authority to insure mortgages on experimental housing. This insurance is available for mortgages or home-improvement loans meeting the requirements of any of FHA's Title II programs. The program extends to all types of operations. The experimentation may involve the utilization or testing of new design, materials, construction methods, or experimental property standards for neighborhood design. Major effort is directed toward improving low-income housing construction.

Section 234 authorizes the FHA to insure a mortgage covering a family unit in a multifamily building of five or more units and an undivided interest in common areas and facilities serving the structure. This is known as condominium ownership. Under the 1961 Housing Act, the insurance was limited to a mortgage on a structure carrying mortgage insurance under one of the FHA multifamily insurance programs other than Section 213. By the Housing Act of 1964, insurance was authorized for blanket mortgages to finance the construction or rehabilitation of multifamily projects to be sold as condominiums, provided that the mortgagor certifies that it intends to sell the project as a condominium and will make all reasonable efforts to sell the family units to FHA-approved purchasers.

Section 235 (added in 1968) was designed to establish a home ownership assistance program for the purchase of new, single-family homes by families with low and moderate incomes, handicapped persons, or single persons 62 years of age or older. The assistance takes the form of periodic payments to the mortgagee by the secretary of HUD to make up the difference between 20 percent of the family's monthly income and the required monthly payment under the mortgage for principal, interest, taxes, insurance, and the mortgage insurance premium. The amount of the subsidy varies according to the income of the homeowner.

Because of shoddy construction by developers under this program, further funding was halted in January 1973. The program was restarted in 1976. Changes were made to prevent some of the earlier abuses. The average incomes of participants in the program were raised somewhat by the new formula adopted for establishing eligibility. Further, to preclude the possibility of more subsidized slums, regulations were revised to require that HUD insure no more than 30 percent of the homes built in a subdivision. Higher down payments were required. They must now equal at least 3 percent of the first $25,000 of the acquisition cost, plus 10 percent of all acquisition costs over $25,000.

To illustrate how a subsidy works, the revised Section 235 is described in greater detail and by example. This section provides assistance in the form of a monthly payment to the mortgagee from HUD, reducing the interest cost to as low as 5 percent of the loan balance but to not less than 20 percent of the homeowner's adjusted monthly family income. To be eligible for assistance, the family must have an adjusted income not exceeding 80 percent of the median income for the area, with appropriate adjustments for family size. A deduction of $300 is made for each family member under 21 years of age, and the earnings of such minors are not included.

An assistance payment computation is made to determine the lesser of:

(a) The difference between the total monthly payment under the mortgage for principal, interest at the market rate, mortgage insurance (0.7 percent), taxes, and hazard insurance and 20 percent of the mortgagor's adjusted monthly income; or

(b) The difference between the monthly payment of principal, interest at the market rate, and mortgage insurance premium (MIP) under the mortgage and the monthly payment that would be required at a 5 percent interest rate, excluding the monthly insurance premium (MIP).

For example, assume that a family has an adjusted annual income of $8,088, or a monthly income of $674. Other transaction items are as follows:

Sale price: $25,600
Down payment: $1,400
Mortgage amount: $24,200
Term in months: 360

Computation of monthly mortgage payment:

Principal and interest	$190.40
MIP (0.007 × $24,200) ÷ 12	14.12
Taxes and hazard insurance	31.00
Total	$235.52

Assistance calculation:

1.	Monthly mortgage payment as above	$235.52
2.	20 percent of adjusted monthly income	134.80
1–2.	Monthly subsidy per formula *(a)* above	$100.72
3.	Monthly payment (principal + market interest + MIP, excluding taxes and hazard insurance)	$204.52
4.	Monthly payment (principal + interest at 5 percent)	129.95
3–4.	Monthly subsidy under formula *(b)* above	$ 74.57

Since formula *(b)* provides the lesser subsidy, the amount computed by that method is the authorized assistance payment. The mortgagor's monthly payment, therefore, is $235.52 − $74.57 = $160.95.

Section 236 (added in 1968) was established to provide the counterpart of Section 235 for rental and cooperative housing for families with low and moderate incomes. This section emerged from the below-market interest rate program authorized under Section 221(d)(3), which has been successful in providing needed rental and cooperative housing for families whose incomes are too high for public housing and too low for standard housing available in the competitive market.

Section 221(d)(3) has suffered from the limitation of depending on direct federal lending from the special assistance funds of FNMA to support its 3 percent mortgages. The limited availability of these funds greatly restricted the activity. The new subsidy program made it possible to obtain funds from the private mortgage market.

Under the Section 236 program the mortgagor-owner of the housing must make a monthly payment for principal and interest under the mortgage as though it bore a 1 percent interest rate. The difference between this amount and the monthly payment due under the mortgage, which bears the market rate of interest, for principal, interest, and mortgage insurance premium is paid to the mortgagee on behalf of the mortgagor by the federal government.

From the standpoint of the tenant, a basic rental charge is established on the basis of a 1 percent mortgage interest rate. The tenant is then required to pay either the basic rental charge or 25 percent of his income, whichever is greater.

Funding for construction under Section 236 was frozen in January 1973 for the same reason that funding for construction under Section 235 was halted—the creation of "instant slums" by loose practices. Future operations under Section 236 are contingent upon the further availability of government funds.

Section 237 was added in 1968 to extend FHA mortgage insurance to families of low or moderate income with impaired credit histories or irregular income patterns. Such families may become eligible if the secretary of HUD finds them to be reasonably satisfactory credit risks and capable of home ownership with proper financial counseling. Mortgages insured under this program must generally meet the requirements of the specific FHA financing program under which the applicant seeks assistance. The credit and income requirements do not apply, however. Insurance will not be authorized under Section 237 unless the monthly mortgage payments for principal and interest, plus real estate taxes, can be paid with 25 percent or less of the mortgagor's monthly income, based on his income for the past year or on his average income for the past three years, whichever is greater.

In addition to relaxing credit restrictions, the 1968 legislation gave the FHA more flexible authority to accept insurance on properties in declining urban areas. Insurance may now be accepted in areas that do not meet normal eligibility requirements. Acceptance of these mortgages is permitted when the FHA is able to establish that the area is "reasonably viable," giving consideration to the need to provide adequate housing for families of low or moderate income in the area, and that the property is a reasonably acceptable risk in view of such consideration. This authority enlarges upon the 1966 amendment to Section 203 of the National Housing Act, whereby the secretary of HUD was authorized to insure one–four-family dwellings in areas fraught with riots or other disorders, without regard to economic soundness, in view of the urgent need for adequate housing for families with low and moderate incomes who lived in the area.

Section 238 established a "Special Risk Insurance Fund" to receive premiums from and pay claims under programs that are not intended to be actuarially sound. These include mortgages insured under the new Sections 235, 236, and 237, as these relate to properties in declining areas that do not pass minimum standard tests for economic soundness. Also included in this fund are mortgages issued under Section 233, which is primarily oriented to the development of new technologies for lower-income housing.

National Housing Act.   Among other titles of the National Housing Act that should be mentioned are Title VII, Title X, and Title XI. Title VII, Section 701, provides for insurance of the yield from investment in rental housing projects for moderate-income families. This insurance extends to commercial space and community facilities. Title X relates to land development and new communities, allowing insurance to back the financing to purchase land and develop building sites, including streets, water and sewer systems, and similar costs. Title XI authorizes mortgage insurance for financing the construction and equipment of local group practice facilities for doctors, dentists, and optometrists. In certain localities, one practitioner will be sufficient to qualify.

SELECTED REFERENCES

Hoagland, H. E.; Stone, L. D.; and Brueggeman, W. B. *Real Estate Finance.* 6th ed. Homewood, Ill.: Richard D. Irwin, 1977.

Warner, Arthur E. *Rural Housing Loan Programs of the Farmers Home Administration.* Chicago: U.S. League of Savings Associations, 1977.

Federal Register. Selected volumes and dates, 1976–78.

Packaging Applications for Rural Housing Loans. Farmers Home Administration, Department of Agriculture, Washington, D.C., 1971.

Duggan and Battles. *Financing the Farm Business.* New York: John Wiley, 1950.

National Housing Act of 1934, as amended.

Section 8 Housing Assistance Payments Program Developer's Packet, Department of Housing and Urban Development, Washington, D.C., 1978.

Chapter

51

THE COST AND AVAILABILITY OF MORTGAGE MONEY

Richard L. Haney, Jr.

*R*ICHARD L. HANEY, Jr., DBA, Associate Professor of Real Estate
and Finance, Texas A&M University, College Station, Texas.
Formerly Assistant Professor of Real Estate and Urban Devel-
opment, University of Georgia (received University of Georgia
citation for superior teaching in 1977). Instructor, for Graduate
Realtor® Institutes, Mortgage Bankers Association's Case Study
Seminar in Income Property Financing, U.S. League's Executive
Development Program, and Southeastern Credit Union School.
Member, American Real Estate and Urban Economics Associa-
tion, American Finance Association, Western Finance Associa-
tion, American Economic Association, and Southern Finance
Association. Author of articles in numerous professional jour-
nals, including American Real Estate and Urban Economics
Association Journal, Quarterly Review of Economics and Busi-
ness, Financial Management, Appraisal Journal, Business Hori-
zons, Journal of Portfolio Management, California Management
Review, Atlanta Real Estate Journal, and Real Estate Today.
Author of forthcoming book describing the latest laws governing
Real Estate Investment and Taxes.

Earlier chapters in Part IV have provided excellent descriptions of
the most important financial institutions that make mortgage loans. This
chapter examines those same institutions, but from the perspective of
a borrower who is most concerned with the answers to two questions.
First, he wants to know whether mortgage money is going to be available
when he needs it. Second, he wants to know what the financing is going
to cost him. In order to help the borrower answer these questions, this
chapter explains why the cost and the availability of mortgage money

change, so that he may develop a strategy for obtaining the needed financing at the lowest possible cost.

The first section of the chapter examines the single-family residential mortgage market. The section briefly describes the various financial institutions that are active in that market, identifies the sources of the money they use to make mortgage loans, and isolates the determinants of that money's cost and availability and, consequently, of the cost and availability of the mortgage loans made by those financial institutions. The second section provides the same information for the income property mortgage market. As a result of this analysis, we find that the mortgage markets are closely interrelated with both the money market and the capital market. The third section examines in more detail the money markets and their influence on the availability of mortgage money, and the fourth section examines the capital markets' impact on the cost of mortgage money. The final section summarizes the preceding analysis by providing the borrower with four scenarios for predicting the cost and availability of mortgage money (1) for construction loans, (2) for conventional loans on residential properties, (3) for FHA and VA loans, and (4) for income property loans.

THE SINGLE-FAMILY RESIDENTIAL MORTGAGE MARKET

The "mortgage market" occupies a very prominent position in the U.S. capital markets. Table 1 shows that the size of the mortgage market varied from $26.4 billion in 1970 to $129.7 billion in 1977. During each of these years, more money was raised in the mortgage market than in either the corporate bond market or the common stock market.

Although it is easy to speak of the "mortgage market," that "market" is not a homogeneous one. Two parts of it, the market for single-family mortgage loans and the market for income property loans, operate very differently and thus will be dealt with separately. Even within the single-family residential mortgage market, there are pronounced differences in the cost and availability of money, depending upon whether the loans

TABLE 1
Funds Raised in U.S. Capital Markets, 1970–1977 ($ billions)

	1970	1971	1972	1973	1974	1975	1976	1977
Federal government debt	21.1	30.9	23.6	28.3	34.3	98.2	88.1	84.2
Mortgage debt	26.4	52.6	77.0	79.9	60.5	57.2	86.8	129.7
Corporate debt	23.8	23.5	18.4	13.6	23.9	36.3	37.0	31.7
Consumer debt	6.0	13.1	18.9	22.0	10.2	9.4	23.6	35.6
State and local government debt	11.2	17.4	14.7	14.7	17.1	13.6	15.1	28.1
Corporate equities	7.7	13.7	13.8	10.4	4.8	10.2	12.2	9.9
All others	14.5	17.7	39.8	84.7	78.2	(5.3)	34.0	79.4
Total funds	110.7	168.9	206.2	253.6	229.0	219.6	296.8	398.6

Source: *Federal Reserve Bulletin.*

TABLE 2
Long-Term Mortgage Loan Originations, 1970–1977 ($ billions)

	1970	1971	1972	1973	1974	1975	1976	1977
Income property loans	21.275	31.808	39.959	41.419	36.226	34.897	37.452	48.777
Single-family loans—conventional	22.972	39.964	59.659	66.364	55.088	62.350	93.098	128.211
Single-family loans—FHA/VA	12.615	17.824	16.205	12.762	12.425	15.592	16.974	29.136
Farm Loans	2.970	4.143	5.803	7.128	7.663	7.876	9.767	12.068
Total long-term mortgage loans	59.832	93.739	121.625	127.673	111.402	120.715	157.290	218.192

Source: U.S. Department of Housing and Urban Development.

are conventional or government insured (FHA) or guaranteed (VA). Table 2 shows the size of the single family mortgage market as compared to the income property mortgage market and the relatively greater importance of the conventional single-family market than the FHA-insured and VA-guaranteed market.

Conventional Mortgage Loans

The crucial factor as far as the cost and availability of money for conventional mortgage loans are concerned is that *the lender who originates these mortgage loans holds them in his own portfolio.* Most often, such a loan is a conventional loan. However, this lender may also sell conventional loans that he has originated, as well as keep some FHA and VA loans in his portfolio.

Mortgage Lenders. What lenders typically originate single-family mortgage loans and then hold them in their portfolios? The major lender in this category is the savings and loan association (S&L). A specialist in single-family mortgage loans, the S&L holds approximately half of the outstanding single-family mortgage debt.[1] Table 3 indicates that S&L holdings ranged from a low of 46.0 percent of the single-family debt in 1970 to a high of 52.0 percent of the single-family debt in 1977. The table also indicates how important single-family loans are to savings and loan associations as they have kept approximately two thirds of their assets in single-family loans during each of the years covered.

Whereas Table 3 gives us a snapshot picture of the S&Ls' mortgage portfolios at the end of each year, Table 4 gives us a moving picture of single-family originations during the years 1970–77. Table 4 shows that S&Ls originated only $14.8 billion of single-family loans in 1970, but increased that amount sixfold to $86.3 billion in 1977. Moreover, Table 4 indicates that in 1977 S&Ls sold only 15 percent of the single-family loans they originated; the other 85 percent they held in their portfolios.[2]

In terms of single-family mortgage debt outstanding, the second largest lender is the commercial bank, though Table 3 shows that commercial banks held no more than about one sixth of the single-family debt during each of the years 1970–77. Because a bank's primary lending orientation is toward short-term business loans, Table 3 also shows that only about 7 percent of bank assets are invested in single-family mortgage loans. Moreover, Table 4 indicates that commercial bank sales as a percentage of originations are typically two to four times those of the S&Ls, an action which is consistent with the banks' short-term, commercial loan orientation.

The next most important lender that originates and then holds mortgage loans in its portfolio is the mutual savings bank. Geographically concentrated in the Middle Atlantic and New England states and commonly grouped together with savings and loan associations into a cate-

---

[1] The federal government defines *single family* to include one–four-family dwelling units.

[2] This ignores lags between originations and subsequent sales of those mortgage loans.

TABLE 3
Single-Family Mortgage Debt Outstanding at Year-End, 1970–1977

	1970	1971	1972	1973	1974	1975	1976	1977
Savings and loan associations								
Amount (in billions of dollars)	122.3	138.4	161.7	182.3	196.5	218.5	253.5	300.2
Percentage of U.S. single-family debt	46.0	47.5	49.5	50.2	49.9	50.6	51.6	52.0
Percentage of savings and loan assets	69.4	67.2	66.5	67.1	66.5	64.6	64.7	65.4
Commercial banks								
Amount (in billions of dollars)	39.4	43.7	50.8	59.6	66.6	68.8	78.1	93.9
Percentage of U.S. single-family debt	14.8	15.0	15.6	16.4	16.9	15.9	15.9	16.3
Percentage of commercial bank assets	6.8	6.8	6.9	7.1	7.2	7.1	7.6	8.1
Mutual savings banks								
Amount (in billions of dollars)	41.9	43.2	45.8	48.4	48.8	49.7	52.5	57.4
Percentage of U.S. single-family debt	15.8	14.8	14.0	13.3	12.4	11.5	10.7	9.9
Percentage of savings bank assets	53.1	48.3	45.5	45.4	44.5	41.0	38.9	39.0

Source: U.S. Department of Housing and Urban Development.

TABLE 4
Single-Family Mortgage Originations and Sales, 1970–1977

	1970	1971	1972	1973	1974	1975	1976	1977
Savings and loan associations								
Originations (in billions of dollars)	14.8	26.6	36.7	38.4	30.9	41.2	61.9	86.3
Sales (in billions of dollars)	0.8	1.7	2.9	2.8	3.1	4.7	7.7	13.0
Sales as a percentage of originations	5.4	6.2	7.9	7.2	10.0	11.5	12.5	15.0
Commercial banks								
Originations (in billions of dollars)	7.8	12.6	17.7	18.8	16.1	14.5	22.1	36.4
Sales (in billions of dollars)	1.7	2.0	2.2	2.0	1.6	2.9	3.7	5.9
Sales as a percentage of originations	21.5	15.6	12.7	10.7	10.0	20.2	16.8	16.1
Mutual savings banks								
Originations (in billions of dollars)	2.2	3.5	5.1	5.9	3.9	4.3	6.4	8.8
Sales (in billions of dollars)	0.3	0.2	0.2	0.2	0.2	0.2	0.5	0.2
Sales as a percentage of originations	13.6	5.0	4.0	2.7	5.8	5.4	7.1	2.5

Source: U.S. Department of Housing and Urban Development.

TABLE 5
Mortgage Loans Outstanding at Credit Unions, 1974

	Mortgage Loans Outstanding ($ billions)	Percent of Assets	Percent of All Single-Family Loans
State-chartered credit unions	1.3	8.8	0.3
Federally chartered credit unions	0.7	4.1	0.2

Source: Credit Union National Administration.

gory called thrift institutions, savings banks hold approximately one eighth of the outstanding single-family mortgage debt. They allocate less than half of their assets to single-family homes. On the other hand, they generally sell about 5 percent of the single-family loans they make, as is shown in the last row of Table 4.

A lender whose impact on the mortgage market is so small that it does not appear in federal government mortgage statistics is the credit union. In fact, a 1974 trade association survey, the results of which are highlighted in Table 5, showed that credit unions held only 0.5 percent of all single-family mortgage debt outstanding. In 1977, however, federally chartered credit unions were given substantially broader powers which will enable them to become a major factor in the single-family mortgage market. Moreover, this additional competition may serve to prod state-chartered credit unions, which generally operate under more liberal rules and regulations, into making more mortgage loans. Credit union members should now look to their organizations as a potential source of mortgage credit.

Thus, the major lenders that originate mortgage loans and then hold those loans in their portfolios are the savings and loan associations, commercial banks, and mutual savings banks.

Money Sources for Mortgage Lenders. It is important to determine where savings and loan associations, commercial banks, and mutual savings banks obtain the money they use to make single-family mortgage loans, because that affects the cost and the availability of mortgage money.

Customer deposits are one of the two major money sources. These may be either "short term" deposits, commonly called passbook accounts, which the depositor may withdraw whenever he wishes, or "longer term" accounts, commonly called savings certificates, which the customer agrees to leave with the financial institution for periods of time ranging from 90 days up to eight years. Table 6 shows, for each of the types of financial institutions, the percentage of liabilities that are funded with the passbook savings accounts as opposed to the longer term savings certificates. Notice how the thrift institutions have been attempting to lock in their sources of mortgage money by shifting their liabilities to a longer term basis.

TABLE 6
Year-End Savings Deposits at Financial Institutions, 1966–1977

	1966	1967	1968	1969	1970	1971	1972	1973	1974	1975	1976	1977
Savings and loan associations												
Savings deposits (in billions of dollars)	n.a.	n.a.	127.2	131.0	141.8	170.0	200.9	220.9	236.7	278.8	328.2	378.8
Percentage in passbook accounts	n.a.	n.a.	77.0	68.7	59.4	54.9	50.6	46.7	44.1	42.7	40.3	37.9
Percentage in savings certificates	n.a.	n.a.	23.0	31.3	40.6	45.1	49.4	53.3	55.9	57.3	59.7	62.1
Commercial banks												
Savings deposits (in billions of dollars)	141.7	162.2	180.1	175.9	205.0	238.5	272.9	313.9	360.3	393.1	430.3	556.5
Percentage in passbook accounts	63.8	58.5	53.6	53.5	48.3	47.2	45.6	40.8	37.9	41.0	46.1	39.4
Percentage in savings certificates	36.2	41.5	46.4	46.5	51.7	52.8	54.4	59.2	62.1	59.0	53.9	60.6
Mutual savings banks												
Savings deposits (in billions of dollars)	54.9	60.1	64.4	67.0	71.5	81.2	91.4	96.3	98.4	109.5	122.6	133.3
Percentage in passbook accounts	100.0	99.8	99.6	99.1	94.1	81.2	75.8	68.6	66.2	64.2	61.5	59.1
Percentage in savings certificates	0.0	0.2	0.4	0.9	5.9	18.8	24.2	31.4	33.8	35.8	38.5	40.9

Sources: Federal Home Loan Bank Board; and Federal Deposit Insurance Corporation.

TABLE 7
Financial Institutions' Sources of Mortgage Funds, 1970–1977 ($ billions)

	1970	1971	1972	1973	1974	1975	1976	1977
Savings and loan associations								
Net new savings	5.3	20.7	23.9	10.5	4.7	29.3	34.4	32.0
Mortgage repayments	12.2	18.5	23.9	25.1	21.4	25.6	35.5	47.3
Investment income	9.8	11.6	13.8	16.7	20.1	21.3	24.9	28.9
Total	27.3	50.8	61.6	52.3	46.2	76.2	94.8	108.2
Commercial banks								
Net new savings*	22.4	32.3	28.7	25.7	24.6	45.9	29.0	54.9
Mortgage repayments	12.2	14.8	16.8	17.1	16.0	18.3	20.5	28.2
Investment income	30.5	31.6	35.0	47.0	61.2	57.9	67.9	82.3
Total	65.1	78.7	80.5	89.8	101.8	122.1	117.4	165.4
Mutual savings banks								
Net new savings	0.9	5.7	5.5	(0.4)	(2.8)	4.8	5.3	2.9
Mortgage repayments	4.0	5.5	7.0	7.2	6.2	6.3	7.2	8.7
Investment income	3.9	4.4	5.1	5.8	6.2	6.9	8.0	9.2
Total	8.8	15.6	17.6	12.6	9.6	18.0	20.5	20.8

* Includes interest credited to savings accounts.
Sources: Federal Home Loan Bank Board; U. S. Department of Housing and Urban Development; and Federal Deposit Insurance Corporation.

The other major source of the money that financial institutions have available for mortgage lending is their investments, which yield interest and are repaid, thus producing funds for reinvestment. Although the interest and the *scheduled* repayments are fairly predictable sources of mortgage money, the investments are often mortgage loans which are paid ahead of schedule as the mortgagor sells his house and the purchaser for one reason or another does not assume the existing loan. Such relatively unpredictable sources, as well as the significantly less reliable inflow of new savings deposits, make future planning by the financial institutions somewhat hazardous. The variability in net new savings, shown in Table 7, is the major reason why the thrift institutions are attempting to shift their deposits into the longer term, more stable savings certificates.

Determinants of Availability. Of the three determinants of availability, the most important is the relationship between the interest rates financial institutions are allowed to pay on their customer deposits and the interest rates available in the money and capital markets. Prior to the 1966 credit crunch, thrift institutions relied upon passbook accounts, which could then pay no more than 4.75 percent interest per year. On the other hand, unconstrained money market interest rates, such as the 90-day Treasury bill rate, increased rapidly during 1966, at one point reaching 5.36 percent. What happened? Many savers withdrew their thrift institution deposits and invested in the relatively high yielding Treasury bills. Some intermediate-term capital market instruments, such as three-year Treasury notes, were paying even higher interest. Because their yields were attractive to investors, even more of the traditional savings deposits were withdrawn and invested in these instruments. This phenomenon, in which depositors withdraw their savings from relatively low yielding savings accounts and invest them directly in higher yielding government instruments, is known as *disintermediation.* It is caused by the government placing a ceiling on the interest rates that financial intermediaries can pay to savers while market interest rates, primarily those on equally secure government instruments, rise rapidly.

After the 1966 experience, government regulators provided financial institutions with some new instruments which they could use to combat disintermediation, that is, savings certificates. Although these certificates also carried interest rate ceilings, the ceilings were higher than the passbook ceilings because the saver had to agree to leave his money on deposit for a longer period of time. During the 1970 credit crunch, for example, savings and loan associations were able to offer depositors rates of up to 6 percent on two-year certificates, a full percentage point higher than the 5 percent passbook rate. Table 8 shows the maximum interest rates that the savings and loan associations were able to offer on the various types of customer deposits during the 1966, 1969–70, and 1973–75 recessions.

As has been shown in Table 6 in order to protect themselves against disintermediation the financial institutions placed increasing emphasis on longer term savings certificates as opposed to passbook accounts. Nevertheless, Table 9 demonstrates the close relationship between

TABLE 8
Maximum Interest Rates Payable on Savings and Loan Association Deposits, 1966–1977 (percent)

Type of Account	9/26/66	1/21/70	7/6/73	11/1/73	12/23/74	6/1/78
			Effective Date and Percentage Rates			
Regular	4.75	5.00	5.25	5.25	5.25	5.25
90-day notice	N/P	5.25	5.75	5.75	5.75	5.75
Certificates with minimum terms						
Balance less than $100,000						
90 days to 6 months	N/P	5.25	5.75	5.75	5.75	5.75
6 months to 1 year	5.25	5.25	5.75	5.75	5.75	5.75
1 year to 2 years	5.25	5.75	6.50	6.50	6.50	6.50
2 years to 2½ years	5.25	6.00	6.50	6.50	6.50	6.50
2½ years to 4 years	5.25	6.00	6.75	6.75	6.75	6.75
4 years to 6 years	5.25	6.00	N/MR	7.50	7.50	7.50
6 years to 8 years	5.25	6.00	N/MR	7.50	7.75	7.75
8 years or more	5.25	6.00	N/MR	7.50	7.75	8.00
Balance $100,000 or more	5.25	6.5–7.5	N/MR	N/MR	N/MR	N/MR
Money market certificate with a $10,000 minimum denomination and a six-month term	N/P	N/P	N/P	N/P	N/P	0.25 above average weekly yield on six-month Treasury bills

N/P = Not permitted.
N/MR = No maximum rate.
Source: Federal Home Loan Bank Board.

TABLE 9

Relationship between Money Market Interest Rates and Savings Inflows, 1970–1977

	1970	1971	1972	1973	1974	1975	1976	1977
Interest rates on one-year Treasury bills (percent)	6.49	4.67	4.77	7.01	7.71	6.30	5.52	5.71
Net new savings at thrift institutions (in billions of dollars)	6.24	26.35	29.34	10.07	1.85	34.06	39.64	34.87

Sources: Federal Reserve Bulletin; and Federal Home Loan Bank Board.

money market interest rates and savings inflows. Note that as money market interest rates decrease, savings inflows rise, and that as money market interest rates rise, savings inflows tumble. It is expected, however, that disintermediation will be a less severe problem for the financial intermediaries as they are able to shift more of their customer deposits into the relatively high yielding, longer term savings certificates when interest rates are generally low, and into the market-sensitive money market certificates when interest rates are generally high. Because the financial institutions were forced to dramatically constrict their mortgage lending during past periods of disintermediation, this bodes well for a more stable supply of mortgage money during future periods of high market interest rates.

A second, but substantially less important, factor affecting the availability of single-family mortgage money is the relationship between the rates that financial institutions can earn on single-family mortgages and the interest rates on income property mortgages. This is an important consideration for mutual savings banks and commercial banks, which make a substantial amount of income property loans. For savings and loan associations, it is becoming an important factor because their government regulators are granting them additional lending flexibility, part of which is taking the form of less stringent restrictions on income property loans. Among other rate comparisons, Table 10 shows the relationship between single-family mortgage market rates and rates on income property loans. Note how the high-interest-rate years of 1970 and 1975 found income property mortgage rates rising substantially higher than single-family rates as the usury limits on single-family mortgages inhibited their reaction to market pressures. This also suggests another reason for the diminished availability of single-family mortgage loans during those years.

The third determinant of the availability of single-family mortgage money, also illustrated in Table 10, is the relationship between mortgage rates and commercial loan rates. This is not generally considered to be an important determinant, because it compares the interest rates available on long-term lending opportunities with those available on short-term loans. Indeed, for most thrift institutions it *is* unimportant, as their regulatory and policy orientation is toward the long-term markets. However, the comparison with short-term commercial loan rates and, by implication, with the demand for short-term funds is an extraordinarily important mortgage availability determinant for commercial banks. If business loan demand is soft and rates are low, commercial banks expand their mortgage lending. On the other hand, if a strong real estate market occurs at the same time as a weak commercial loan market, banks are often able to channel a greater portion of their excess funds into short-term acquisition, development, and construction loans. Because the short-term, high-return loans are more closely related to the banks' typical commercial loan business, the banks generally prefer such loans to the long-term mortgage loans.

The consumer loan market is also a very important one for both commercial banks and credit unions. As Table 11 shows, commercial banks

TABLE 10
Mortgage, Commercial, and Consumer Loan Rates, 1966–1977 (percent)

	1966	1967	1968	1969	1970	1971	1972	1973	1974	1975	1976	1977
Single-family residential mortgage interest rate	6.41	6.52	7.03	7.82	8.36	7.67	7.51	8.01	9.02	9.21	9.11	9.02
Income-producing property mortgage interest rate	6.42	6.97	7.66	8.69	9.93	9.07	8.57	8.76	9.47	10.22	9.83	9.34
Commercial loan rate	6.00	6.00	6.68	8.21	8.48	6.32	5.82	8.30	11.28	8.65	7.52	7.85
Consumer loan rate	n.a.	n.a.	n.a.	n.a.	n.a.	n.a.	12.45	12.60	13.02	13.11	13.02	12.98

Sources: Federal Home Loan Bank Board; American Council of Life Insurance; and Federal Reserve Board.

TABLE 11
Selected Commercial Bank Loans Outstanding at Year-End, 1970–1977

	1970	1971	1972	1973	1974	1975	1976	1977
Commercial loans								
Amount (in billions								
of dollars)	124.6	118.5	132.7	159.4	186.8	179.0	182.9	195.5
Percent of loans	47.2	43.2	41.7	42.2	44.4	42.7	40.6	38.1
Real estate loans								
Amount (in billions								
of dollars)	73.3	81.6	98.4	118.0	130.6	134.8	149.5	176.9
Percent of loans	27.7	29.7	30.9	31.3	31.0	32.0	33.2	34.5
Consumer loans								
Amount (in billions								
of dollars)	66.3	74.5	87.2	99.9	103.2	106.7	118.4	140.3
Percent of loans	25.1	27.1	27.4	26.5	24.6	25.3	26.2	27.4

Source: Federal Reserve Bulletin.

have lent substantial sums in this market. Because the rates they can obtain there generally exceed those in the mortgage markets (see Table 10), these institutions often meet consumer loan demand before considering investing excess funds in the mortgage markets. However, with the passage of recent legislation, both commercial banks and credit unions are striving to fill a role as full-service institutions. This means that credit unions in particular will be adding funds to the single-family mortgage market in the foreseeable future.

In summary, by far the most important determinant of the availability of single-family mortgage money is the relationship between interest rates on deposits and money market interest rates. As the latter increases above deposit rate ceilings, the lenders have less money available for single-family mortgages. Conversely, higher deposit rates at financial institutions usually cause lenders to be flush with funds for such mortgages.

Determinants of Cost. A number of factors interact to determine the cost of single-family mortgage loans. Although these factors differ slightly for each of the three major types of financial institutions, we shall examine them from the perspective of the savings and loan association because of its major role in the single-family mortgage market. Most S&L costs increase at relatively slow and predictable rates. But Table 12 indicates that their major cost, the average interest rate on customer deposits, has increased substantially since 1966 as they have shifted their liabilities from passbook accounts into savings certificates. Because S&Ls try to maintain a spread ranging from about 1.5 to 1.75 percentage points between the average rate that they pay on customer deposits and the average rate that they earn on outstanding mortgages, increases in their deposit costs due to greater use of the more stable savings certificates often result in higher mortgage rates. Thus, the new customer is paying for the greater stability in the availability of mortgage money by having to pay the higher mortgage interest rates shown in the first row of Table 12. In fact, during weak mortgage markets the increase in S&L deposit costs serves as a floor for mortgage interest rates.

Another important piece of information in Table 12 is the S&Ls' net income. Notice how the profits of the S&Ls increase during periods of strong demand when they are able to raise mortgages rates, then shrink during periods of disintermediation when they are forced to rely heavily on high-cost savings certificates to attract deposits. Moreover, because their average deposit costs have increased 3.5 percent per year during the past decade while their average mortgage rates have risen only 3.0 percent per year, S&Ls have turned increasingly to other sources of income. Table 12 suggests that they now rely on nonmortgage interest receipts for one out of every five dollars of income, whereas the "other income" accounted for only one out of eight dollars back in the mid-'60s. Thus, not only are the increasing deposit costs placing even higher floors under mortgage rates, but they are also forcing S&Ls to turn away from the politically constrained mortgage rates in their primary lending area.

A second major factor affecting the cost of single-family mortgage

TABLE 12
Savings and Loan Association Operating Data, 1966–1977

	1966	1967	1968	1969	1970	1971	1972	1973	1974	1975	1976	1977
						Percent						
Effective single-family mortgage rate on loans for newly built homes	6.35	6.53	7.02	7.84	8.51	7.79	7.63	7.96	8.92	9.05	9.04	9.04
Average interest rate on outstanding mortgages	5.94	6.01	6.13	6.32	6.56	6.81	6.98	7.17	7.43	7.66	7.95	8.21
Average interest rate on customer deposits.........	4.48	4.68	4.71	4.81	5.14	5.30	5.37	5.51	5.96	6.21	6.31	6.39
					Percent of Gross Income							
Mortgage loan interest	87.4	86.2	85.1	84.9	83.9	82.6	83.4	83.5	82.3	81.6	80.5	79.8
+ Other income	12.6	13.8	14.9	15.1	16.1	17.4	16.6	16.5	17.7	18.4	19.5	20.2
= Gross income	100.0	100.0	100.0	100.0	100.0	100.0	100.0	100.0	100.0	100.0	100.0	100.0
– Interest charges	70.9	72.6	70.4	69.4	71.4	70.0	69.0	69.3	73.3	74.7	72.6	70.1
– Labor compensation	8.7	8.5	8.3	8.0	8.1	7.8	7.6	7.5	7.6	7.7	7.6	7.1
– Other operating expenses	10.1	9.7	9.7	9.8	9.7	8.8	8.6	8.7	8.7	8.8	8.7	8.5
– Income taxes	1.4	1.4	1.7	2.2	2.2	3.4	4.2	4.2	3.2	2.7	3.4	4.1
– Nonoperating expenses	0.5	0.4	0.5	0.5	0.7	0.8	0.7	1.0	1.1	1.3	1.1	0.9
= Net income	8.4	7.4	9.4	10.1	7.9	9.2	9.9	9.3	6.1	4.8	6.6	9.3

Source: Federal Home Loan Bank Board.

money is its supply. During times of limited availability, mortgage lenders use the interest rate as a rationing device. In order to allocate their scarce funds to the customers who are most able to repay the loans, they raise interest rates. As shown in Table 13, the years 1973 and 1974 are good examples of this. Then, during periods when they are flush with funds (1971, 1972, and 1976), their rates tend to fall, the extent of the decrease being limited by their cost-of-deposits floor.

The cost of single-family mortgage money is also affected by the strength of demand from the mortgage borrower. The stronger the housing markets, the greater the demand for mortgage money. During these periods, mortgage lenders tend to keep rates steady, or perhaps to increase them slightly. This helps explain the 1976 and 1977 rate behavior illustrated in Table 13. However, any rise in rates, whether due to increased demand or to a restricted supply of lendable funds, is moderated in many states by the existence of usury ceilings. Although this restrains mortgage rates from rising as high as competitive pressures would dictate, it also means that lenders reallocate their available funds to other markets or to states where they can obtain a better return on their customers' deposits.

The last major factor affecting the cost of single-family mortgage money is the competition from other mortgage lenders. Because mortgage markets are closely tied to housing markets, which exhibit strong local characteristics, the competitive influence of other *local* lenders is most important. On the other hand, national mortgage market conditions are at least partially reflected in the local market, although sometimes the local market will lead and other times lag national market changes. (The national market will be discussed in greater detail below.) In Table 14 a comparison between the national market rate and several local market rates indicates the diversity evident throughout the country.

Another important competitive factor is the widespread lack of mortgage market information among borrowers. Because borrowers obtain loans relatively infrequently, they are usually poorly informed. They do little rate shopping, usually accepting the real estate broker's suggested mortgage lender. Because of this, sometimes rates, and often fees, vary widely within a local market. As consumers become more informed borrowers, price differentials among local mortgage lenders are expected to narrow.

The Key Factor. This section has suggested that the major determinant of the availability of single-family mortgage money is the difference between money market interest rates and the ceiling rates that financial institutions are allowed to offer on customer deposits. The higher the ceiling rates are relative to the money market rates, the greater is the availability of mortgage money. In addition, the major cost determinants are the same customer deposit rates. In order to avoid the effects of disintermediation, financial institutions have been shifting their liabilities from passbook accounts into longer term, but more costly, savings certificates. This has improved mortgage availability, but at a cost of higher rates as institutions are forced to pay more for their raw material, customer deposits. This strongly suggests that the key factor

TABLE 13
Single-Family Mortgage Lending and Interest Rates, 1970–1977

	1970	1971	1972	1973	1974	1975	1976	1977
Single-family home sales (in millions of units)	2.10	2.68	2.97	2.95	2.77	3.00	3.64	4.39
Single-family home loans (in billions of dollars)	35.59	57.79	75.86	79.13	67.51	77.20	110.07	158.62
Single-family mortgage loan rates (percent)	8.36	7.67	7.51	8.01	9.02	9.21	9.11	9.02

Sources: National Association of Realtors®; U.S. Department of Commerce; U.S. Department of Housing and Urban Development; and Federal Home Loan Bank Board.

TABLE 14
National versus Local Single-Family Mortgage Rates,
January 1978

	Effective Interest Rate on Conventional Loans for Newly Built Homes (percent)
United States	9.15
Boston	8.60
Washington, D.C.	9.18
Atlanta..............................	9.23
Louisville	8.95
Chicago.............................	8.92
Minneapolis	9.10
Denver	9.33
Houston	9.45
Los Angeles	9.39
Seattle..............................	9.57

Source: Federal Home Loan Bank Board.

in both the cost and the availability of mortgage money from the financial institutions that originate mortgages and then hold them in their portfolios is *the level of money market interest rates.*

FHA and VA Mortgage Loans

In the preceding section we examined the cost and availability of loans held in the mortgage originator's own portfolio. Although we called those conventional loans, we recognized that this was just a convenient label because some conventional loans are sold to investors and some FHA and VA loans are held in the originator's portfolio. Similarly, we are not necessarily concerned with FHA and VA loans in this section. Rather, our interest is in *the lender who originates mortgage loans and then sells them to an investor* instead of holding them in his own portfolio.

When a borrower obtains a mortgage loan from his lender, that is commonly called the primary mortgage market; if the loan is subsequently sold to an investor, that is referred to as the secondary mortgage market. Table 15 indicates that most primary market loan originations are conventional loans and that an increasing percentage of all secondary market sales in recent years have also been conventional loans.

Mortgage Lenders. There are mortgage lenders that specialize in originating loans in the primary market and then selling those loans to investors in the secondary market. These lenders, called mortgage bankers or mortgage companies, hold only 1 percent of the outstanding single-family mortgage debt yet originate approximately one sixth of all single-family mortgage loans (see Table 16). In addition, as Table 16 also suggests, mortgage bankers typically sell all of the mortgage loans that

TABLE 15
Primary versus Seconary Mortgage Markets, 1970–1977

	1970	1971	1972	1973	1974	1975	1976	1977
Primary mortgage market originations (in billions of dollars)	35.6	57.8	75.8	79.1	67.5	77.9	110.1	158.6
Conventional loans as a percentage	64.6	69.2	78.6	83.9	81.6	80.0	84.6	80.8
FHA/VA loans as a percentage	35.4	30.8	21.4	16.1	18.4	20.0	15.4	19.2
Secondary mortgage market sales (in billions of dollars)	13.6	18.5	24.1	23.8	23.1	29.6	40.4	51.3
Conventional loans as a percentage	20.2	19.6	29.1	37.9	44.4	46.6	52.5	55.0
FHA/VA loans as a percentage	79.8	80.4	70.9	62.1	55.6	53.4	47.5	45.0
Percentage of FHA/VA loan originations sold in secondary market	85.9	83.6	105.5	115.7	103.4	101.5	113.0	75.8

Source: U.S. Department of Housing and Urban Development.

TABLE 16
Mortgage Banker Single-Family Activity, 1970–1977

	1970	1971	1972	1973	1974	1975	1976	1977
Mortgage debt outstanding at year-end								
(in billions of dollars)	4.5	4.6	4.2	4.8	3.5	3.7	4.2	6.3
Percentage of U.S. single-family								
debt outstanding..............	1.7	1.6	1.3	1.3	0.9	0.8	0.9	1.1
FHA and VA mortgage originations								
(in billions of dollars)	8.5	11.9	11.2	8.6	9.4	10.9	12.3	17.2
Share of market (percent)	67.3	66.5	68.9	67.2	75.4	70.1	72.4	59.1
Conventional mortgage originations								
(in billions of dollars)	0.4	0.6	2.2	4.1	3.7	3.1	3.1	5.2
Share of market (percent)	1.8	1.6	3.6	6.2	6.6	4.9	3.4	4.1
Total originations								
(in billions of dollars)	8.9	12.5	13.4	12.7	13.1	14.0	15.4	22.5
Share of market (percent)	25.0	21.6	17.6	16.0	19.3	18.0	14.0	14.2
Sales (in billions of dollars)	9.0	12.4	14.3	13.9	14.9	14.4	17.1	23.3
Sales as percentage of originations	101.1	99.2	107.5	109.5	114.3	103.3	110.9	103.6

Source: U.S. Department of Housing and Urban Development.

they originate, as well as some additional loans that they have purchased.

Mortgage banking firms, which typically are either moderate to small-sized independent companies or subsidiaries of commercial bank holding companies, have traditionally been the major originators of FHA and VA loans. A further examination of Table 16 indicates that approximately 70 percent of the mortgage companies' originations are FHA/VA loans. Note, however, that they expanded their conventional loan origination program in the mid-1970s, when the total FHA/VA market did not keep pace with housing market growth.

Savings and loan associations, commercial banks, mutual savings banks, and, potentially, credit unions are other financial institutions that must be considered, although they are much smaller factors in this market. Recall from Table 4 that S&Ls usually sell only about 8 percent of their originations, commercial banks about 15 percent, and savings banks about 5 percent. Although credit unions are more interested in entering the originate-and-sell market than the previously described originate-and-hold market, they have yet to make a major impact in either of the single-family mortgage markets.

Money Sources for Mortgage Lenders. It is extremely important to clearly distinguish between the primary and the secondary mortgage markets. A primary mortgage market transaction occurs when a lender originates a mortgage loan for a borrower. If the lender holds the mortgage in his own portfolio, then there is no secondary market transaction. On the other hand, if the originating lender were to sell that loan to some other lender or investor, then the sale would occur in the secondary market. In examining the money sources in this section, we are concentrating upon those lenders or investors who purchase mortgage loans in the secondary market, as they are the penultimate sources of the mortgage funds.

In the past few years, up to 81 percent of the FHA and VA primary market originations have been sold to investors via Government National Mortgage Association–guaranteed, mortgage-backed, pass-through securities, commonly called Ginnie Maes or GNMA pass-throughs (see Table 17). The Ginnie Maes are not issued by the Government National Mortgage Association, as their name might imply. Instead, they are issued by FHA-approved mortgagees (primarily mortgage bankers), while the Government National Mortgage Association provides a guarantee to the security purchaser that the issuer will "pass through" to the purchaser the monthly interest and principal amortization *scheduled* to be collected on the FHA-insured and VA-guaranteed mortgages backing up the Ginnie Maes, as well as any additional amounts actually collected due to foreclosure, loan prepayment, or the receipt of hazard insurance proceeds. Furthermore, the GNMA guarantee is backed by the full faith and credit of the U.S. government. The creation of this instrument in 1970 enabled many nontraditional mortgage investors to place a portion of their funds in the mortgage market by purchasing Ginnie Maes. Not only do these instruments have the same security as Treasury issues, but the purchaser is able to obtain

TABLE 17
Ginnie Mae Pass-Throughs at Year-End, 1970–1977

	1970	1971	1972	1973	1974	1975	1976	1977
Amount issued								
In billions of dollars	0.5	3.2	5.8	8.8	13.3	20.8	34.5	52.0
As a percentage of yearly								
FHA/VA originations	3.6	15.2	16.4	23.1	36.6	47.8	81.1	59.9
Percentage ownership								
Savings and loan								
associations	46.9	49.2	41.7	33.3	30.4	27.3	19.6	14.8
Mutual saving banks	19.0	19.2	20.9	21.6	18.0	14.7	13.0	11.7
Commercial banks	0.9	4.0	5.2	5.7	5.9	4.8	5.3	6.0
Credit unions	*	6.7	6.1	5.1	4.0	3.2	2.6	2.6
Individuals	0.6	0.6	1.3	1.9	1.6	1.2	1.1	1.2
Mortgage and investment								
bankers	4.1	7.5	9.4	10.1	10.6	18.9	20.3	17.3
Retirement and pension funds	14.9	5.1	5.0	7.1	7.7	7.9	10.0	11.4
All others, including								
nominees	4.4	7.7	10.4	15.3	21.7	22.1	28.1	35.0

* Included in savings and loan association category.
Sources: Government National Mortgage Association; and U.S. Department of Housing and Urban Development.

the higher mortgage yield without accepting the default, administrative, legal, and servicing risks that are typically associated with purchasing mortgages directly.

The market for the Ginnie Mae pass-through has grown extremely rapidly since 1970. Table 17 shows that the amount of Ginnie Maes issued increased from $0.5 billion at the end of 1970 to $52.0 billion at the end of 1977. It is interesting to note that in the early years of the security's existence, the thrift institutions were the major holders of pass-throughs. This has changed dramatically over the years as the thrifts have continued to reduce their proportional ownership while pension funds, mortgage and investment bankers, and "all others" have increased their shares. Because it is generally considered that between one third and one half of the "all other" group is composed of pension funds, this would make them the largest investor group at approximately 20 to 25 percent of the total amount issued. Thus, a large part of the secondary market funds are coming from company- and union-sponsored retirement accounts.[3]

A major purchaser of mortgage loans, as opposed to securities which are backed by pools of loans, is the Federal National Mortgage Association (FNMA), commonly called Fannie Mae, which has assumed a much greater role in the secondary mortgage markets since it was converted from government to private ownership in 1968. Fannie Mae purchases primarily FHA and VA mortgages from mortgage bankers, although it has recently expanded its purchases of conventional loans. Using a biweekly auction system to obtain market prices, Fannie Mae issues commitments which obligate it to purchase a certain amount of mortgages at the auction price within the four-month commitment term. As mortgage money becomes scarcer and interest rates rise, FNMA greatly expands the volume of purchase commitments that it agrees to make; conversely, it contracts its activity during times of relative mortgage money abundancy. Table 18 illustrates how its commitments have fluctuated in recent years, as well as its orientation toward the FHA/VA market. The table also indicates Fannie Mae's smaller FHA/VA role during 1976 and 1977, as mortgage bankers sold most of their loans via Ginnie Mae pass-throughs. This reduced role is even more noticeable in the Table 19 comparison of FNMA auction volume with GNMA pass-through volume.

Where does the Federal National Mortgage Association obtain the money to buy loans? It purchases primarily with borrowings from the money and capital markets, via discount notes and debentures, respectively, but also with the proceeds from the sale of its common stock.

A third money source is the thrift institution. There are times during the business cycle when S&Ls and savings banks receive more deposits than they are able to invest in their local mortgage markets. They then turn to the secondary market and buy mortgage loans originated by

---

[3] While both mortgage bankers and investment bankers, who purchase many of the pass-throughs from mortgage bankers for ultimate resale to investors, hold large inventories, neither can realistically be considered permanent investors. This percentage most likely represents securities which are in various stages of distribution.

TABLE 18
Federal National Mortgage Association Activity, 1970–1977

	1970	1971	1972	1973	1974	1975	1976	1977
FNMA commitments (in billions of dollars)								
FHA/VA mortgages	5.2	3.6	2.8	3.1	2.4	3.8	2.8	4.8
Conventional mortgages	0	0	0.3	1.3	0.7	0.8	1.9	3.9
FNMA purchases (in billions of dollars)								
FHA/VA mortgages	4.8*	2.7*	2.5*	3.2*	3.8	3.1	0.8	2.4
As a percentage of FHA/VA originations	37.9*	15.4*	15.7*	25.3*	30.5	20.2	4.9	8.1
Conventional mortgages	0	0	0.1	0.9	1.1	0.5	2.5	2.4
As a percentage of conventional originations	0	0	0.1	1.4	2.0	0.9	2.7	1.8

* Excludes FHA 235 mortgages.
Sources: Federal National Mortgage Association; and U.S. Department of Housing and Urban Development.

TABLE 19

Single-Family Secondary Mortgage Market Volume, 1970–1977 ($ millions)

	1970	1971	1972	1973	1974	1975	1976	1977
GNMA pass-through securities issued	452	2,702	2,662	2,952	4,553	7,447	13,764	17,440
FNMA mortgage purchases	8,849	3,499	3,699	6,160	6,953	4,262	3,606	4,724
FHLMC mortgage purchases	325	778	1,297	1,334	2,190	1,173	1,127	4,124
S&L mortgage purchases	3,397	6,635	9,502	5,862	4,824	7,165	11,104	13,155
Savings bank mortgage purchases	1,408	1,874	2,708	1,928	1,039	1,103	2,127	2,918
Commercial bank mortgage purchases	521	1,130	1,046	925	372	236	816	1,945

Sources: Government National Mortgage Association; Federal National Mortgage Association; Federal Home Loan Mortgage Corporation; and U.S Department of Housing and Urban Development.

mortgage bankers or other thrift institutions in local markets where there is a strong demand for mortgage money. Their purchases often take one of three forms. As has been noted, they sometimes buy Ginnie Mae pass-throughs. At other times, they will purchase an 80 or 90 percent ownership in a package of mortgages, while the originating institution retains the other 10 or 20 percent. This is called purchasing a "participation." Finally, they may buy 100 percent of a mortgage loan, a "whole loan" purchase instead of just a part of it. The latter two categories are combined and shown as "S&L mortgage purchases" in Table 19.

The Federal Home Loan Mortgage Corporation (FHLMC, commonly called Freddie Mac or the Mortgage Corporation), the fourth secondary market money source, is similar to Fannie Mae. Because Fannie Mae purchased primarily FHA and VA mortgages from mortgage bankers, Congress in 1970 created Freddie Mac to purchase conventional loans from S&Ls. Although the conventional-FHA/VA distinction between Freddie Mac and Fannie Mae was fairly well maintained through the mid-1970s, the legislation creating the Mortgage Corporation also gave it the right to purchase FHA and VA loans, and gave Fannie Mae the right to purchase conventional mortgages. Table 19 illustrates the Mortgage Corporation's role of expanding purchases during times of credit stringency, for example in 1974 and 1975.

Freddie Mac obtains the money to fund its mortgage loan purchases primarily from two sources. First, it issues guaranteed mortgage certificates to nontraditional mortgage investors, such as pension funds, that demand a bond-type instrument which pays interest semiannually, returns the principal at maturity, and is fully collateralized with mortgages. Second, it issues participation certificates (PCs), which are similar to Ginnie Mae pass-throughs except that (1) they are issued only by Freddie Mac and (2) they do not carry the full faith and credit guarantee of the U.S. Treasury. Prior to 1976, most PCs were purchased by thrift institutions. Recently, however, the nontraditional mortgage investors have been buying substanital quantities because a group of securities dealers began making a secondary market in the PCs. As Table 20 indi-

TABLE 20
Federal Home Loan Mortgage Corporation
Issues, 1970–1977 ($ millions)

Year	Guaranteed Mortgage Certificates	Participation Certificates
1970	0	0
1971	0	67
1972	0	494
1973	0	317
1974	0	52
1975	500	526
1976	400	1,456
1977	400	4,834

Source: Federal Home Loan Mortgage Corporation.

cates, FHLMC sales of participation certificates rose sharply during the past two years.

The final secondary mortgage market instrument, a conventional mortgage-backed pass-through security, is of relatively recent origin. It is similar to a Ginnie Mae pass-through, except that it does not carry a government guarantee and that it is backed by conventional mortgages instead of FHA and VA loans. First issued by the Bank of America in 1977, this instrument is expected to find great favor with both savings and loan associations and commercial banks because of its pass-through nature. In part because Standard and Poor's is now rating these issues, the investment community also appears to be viewing them favorably, as evidenced by its acceptance of relatively lower yields which enable the financial institutions to sell the instruments at correspondingly higher prices.

Mortgages are purchased in the secondary markets by a number of other institutions, including commercial banks, state and local credit agencies, state and local retirement funds, and life insurance companies, but the impact of these institutions is generally small and that impact is not expected to expand appreciably in the near future.

In summary, the largest secondary mortgage market purchasers are thrift institutions, which purchase both loan packages and mortgage-backed securities, Fannie Mae and Freddie Mac, which only purchase loan packages, and pension funds, which primarily purchase mortgage-backed securities.

Availability and Cost Determinants. It is impossible to separate the availability and cost determinants for the secondary mortgage markets because of the interaction between the two: the availability of mortgage money depends upon the yield that the mortgage originators are able to offer investors, and vice versa. Generally, the higher the yield that the lender must offer, the larger the interest rate that it must charge in the primary mortgage market.

Because single-family mortgage loans sold in the secondary market are often FHA-insured and VA-guaranteed, one of the factors that influence the cost of those loans is borrower demand for FHA and VA mortgages. Recall from Table 2 that FHA and VA loans have fallen from 35 percent to 15 percent of loan originations as conventional single-family mortgages have grown in popularity. This has happened in part because of borrower preference for conventional loans due to their lower costs. Although the interest rate on FHA/VA mortgages is almost always below the conventional single-family rate, the discount points often indirectly result in a buyer paying more in a down payment than he would have to pay on a high-ratio conventional loan. The cost of that additional equity capital may be substantial. In addition, the FHA insurance premium is higher than private mortgage insurance company premiums on mortgage loans requiring similar down payments.

The primary demand impediment, however, comes not from the cost of the mortgages which are to be sold in the secondary market but from the extra builder and lender costs which those mortgages must often absorb. The restrictive FHA/VA building standards impose additional and frequently unrecoverable costs on the builder. Similarly, the FHA/VA's paperwork requirements usually cost the lender more than the 1 percent origination fee that he is allowed to charge. Thus, both the builder and the lender have monetary incentives to stress conventional loans instead of FHA and VA mortgages. Moreover, mortgage bankers, the primary originators of FHA and VA loans, often do not operate aggressively in small- and medium-sized communities. Due to the interaction of these three factors, the borrower is frequently not even aware of the FHA or VA alternative, thus leading to a lower demand.

Another important demand factor is the level of discount points. Although the seller ostensibly pays the points, he usually increases the price of the property by the amount of points involved. Because the number of points are related to the spread between the ceiling interest rate on FHA and VA mortgages and the capital market interest rates, the higher the market rates rise above the ceiling rate, the greater the discount points. In the past borrowers have generally avoided FHA and VA mortgages when the level of discount points exceeded four. The government authorities would usually let the points rise even higher, to approximately 5.5, thus further reducing buyer demand for the FHA/VA mortgages, before they would increase the ceiling interest rate sufficiently to reduce the discount points to approximately two. At that point, buyer resistance would disappear and FHA/VA mortgages would again become more attractive.

However, it is not primarily the relatively unvarying demand factors that determine the cost and the availability of mortgages that are intended to be sold in the secondary markets. Instead, the investors who buy those mortgages play a much more important role. The combination of mortgage originator preference for conventional loans (except for the mortgage bankers, who specialize in FHA and VA loans), the frequent unavailability of properties which meet the FHA and VA construction standards, and widespread buyer resistance due to a high level of discount points suggests that the more important cost and availability determinants are associated with the supply factors examined in the following paragraphs.

Recall that the ultimate sources of secondary mortgage market money are the investors that purchase loans from the mortgage originators. Because the availability and cost of money are of key importance to them, each of the major types of investors is isolated in order to examine their investment decisions. As indicated in Table 19, S&Ls are the largest secondary market purchasers because they must invest most of their customer deposits in mortgage instruments. If there is sufficient demand, they will usually invest most, if not all, of their funds in the local mortgage market. On the other hand, if they have more money to invest than there are local investment opportunities, or if the usury limit is holding the local mortgage interest rates below the free market rate available elsewhere, they will typically invest a portion of their funds in the secondary mortgage market instruments that give them the highest return. Thus, their choice of investment options (and, consequently, the availability of secondary market funds) depends upon the relative returns in the different mortgage markets.

Because the return that must be paid to attract savings and loan association money determines the cost of mortgages in the primary market, the cost determinants are closely linked to the availability determinants. If S&Ls face weak local market demand, the mortgage originators will not have to offer them as high a yield in order to entice them to invest in the secondary market. That lower yield is then passed along to the borrower in terms of a lower mortgage interest rate, or fewer discount points. Conversely, higher mortgage rates prevail if money is scarce and the mortgage originators must offer a high yield in order to attract S&L money into the secondary market.

The mutual savings banks, the other type of thrift institution, operate similarly to the S&Ls, except that they have corporate and government bonds as additional investment options. This is highly significant because it means that mortgages must not only compete with one another for investment dollars but that they must also compete with other capital market instruments, such as bonds. Thus, the secondary mortgage market rate must move in the same direction as the bond rates if mortgage originators wish to attract mutual savings bank investment funds.

The third major secondary market investor group includes three kinds of trust funds: private pension funds, state and local retirement funds, and trust company and commercial bank trust funds. The investment options for these organizations, however, are substantially broader than those available to S&Ls and savings banks. For example, Table 21 indicates that private pension funds, with assets of approximately $175 billion at the end of 1976, have traditionally invested approximately two thirds of their assets in stocks and another fifth in corporate bonds. State and local retirement funds, on the other hand, have followed the opposite investment policy, with 60 percent of their assets in corporate bonds and 20 percent in stocks. A few trust funds have achieved equity positions in the real estate area by purchasing income-producing properties. Most, however, have limited their real estate exposure to long-term mortgage loans on income properties, with the retirement funds adopting a more aggressive posture than the pension funds. If trust funds invest in single-family mortgages, most often it is through a purchase of Ginnie Mae pass-throughs, Mortgage Corporation PCs, mortgage-backed bonds, or conventional mortgage-backed securities.

What determines the investment strategy of the trust funds is usually a combination of two factors, the more important one being the relative returns available on the different investment vehicles. After adjusting the returns in order to compensate for the relative riskiness of the various investments, the fund managers choose those investments that they expect to give them the highest returns. During the early and mid-1970s, they generally expected the highest returns from common stocks, and consequently they invested substantial amounts in them. When the stock markets failed to perform as well as the managers expected, they diversified into the safer government securities markets. However, an invest-

TABLE 21
Retirement Fund Assets at Year-End, 1970–1976

	1970	1971	1972	1973	1974	1975	1976
Private pension fund							
assets (in billions of dollars)*	104.7	126.9	154.4	132.2	111.7	145.6	173.9
Mortgages (percent)	3.3	2.5	1.6	1.6	1.8	1.5	1.2
Stocks (percent)	64.1	69.8	74.7	68.5	56.6	60.8	63.1
Corporate bonds (percent)	23.8	20.6	17.0	20.9	27.6	23.7	21.8
U.S. government securities (percent)	2.9	2.2	2.4	3.4	5.0	7.6	8.6
Other assets (percent)	5.9	4.9	4.4	5.7	8.9	6.4	5.3
State and local retirement fund							
assets (in billions of dollars)†	57.7	64.5	71.8	81.6	93.5	102.4	117.2
Mortgages (percent)	11.8	11.0	9.7	8.2	7.2	8.1	7.2
Stocks (percent)	13.9	17.4	19.7	22.8	22.8	22.7	22.2
Corporate bonds (percent)	58.6	59.9	60.5	60.5	62.5	59.5	57.7
U.S. government securities (percent)	11.1	8.1	7.0	5.7	5.5	5.7	7.5
Other assets (percent)	4.6	3.7	3.0	2.9	2.1	4.1	5.4

* Market value.
† Book value.
Source: Securities and Exchange Commission.

ment with excellent future potential is the GNMA pass-through security because it offers even better risk-adjusted returns than those available in the government securities markets. Providing impetus for this development was the passage of the Employee Retirement Income Security Act (ERISA) in 1974. Because ERISA strongly encouraged fund managers to diversify their investments to a greater extent than they had been accustomed to doing, many managers are finding the relatively high yielding mortgage investment a good way to comply with the act's diversification requirements.

The other factor which influences trust fund investment strategy is the expertise of the fund manager. Most fund managers are familiar with stock and bond analysis. Because mortgage underwriting requires substantially different skills, the fund managers have been reluctant to take their funds into areas where their lack of expertise might adversely affect fund performance. However, the dismal performance of the stock market during the past decade, the relatively high returns available on mortgage investments, the ERISA diversification requirements, and the development of such new mortgage instruments as the mortgage-backed pass-through security and the mortgage-backed bond, instruments which more closely resemble corporate bonds than mortgages, combine to heighten expectations that trust funds will become significant investors in the secondary mortgage markets.

The next investor group includes the Federal National Mortgage Association and the Federal Home Loan Mortgage Corporation. As was pointed out above, the former funds its investments by borrowing in the money and capital markets and the latter sells mortgage-related securities in the capital markets. The key cost and availability factors for Fannie Mae and Freddie Mac are the conditions in the money and capital markets. As funds in these markets become scarce and Fannie Mae and Freddie Mac have to raise the yield they offer in order to attract those scarce funds, the yields on the mortgages they purchase must likewise increase. Of course, lower primary market interest rates occur during times of relative monetary ease, when funds competition is not as strong.

The Key Factor.   There are a number of other investors, including life insurance companies, which purchase a relatively small amount of single-family mortgages, primarily because they can obtain higher capital market yields elsewhere. That appears to be the common thread running throughout this section: the key factor in the single-family secondary mortgage market is *the rate on competing capital market investments.* The primary market mortgage rate (the cost) depends upon the yields available on other capital market instruments, and the availability of mortgage money is determined by the willingness of the residential mortgage market to pay a high enough interest rate to attract the necessary funds.

THE INCOME PROPERTY MORTGAGE MARKET

The income property mortgage market operates quite differently from the single-family market. The loan amounts are substantially greater, the construction period is much longer, the construction lenders and the permanent lenders are usually different, and the security for the permanent loan is typically *not* the equity investor's income but the rental income from the property.

Single-family construction loans were not described in the preceding section because such loans are treated either as commercial loans by the banks or as partial advances on permanent loans by the thrifts. On the other hand, the cost and the availability of income property construction loans deserve special attention because of their unique characteristics.

Construction Loans on Income Properties

In addition to the security of a mortgage, the income property construction lender typically requires a permanent loan commitment, that is, a written agreement by the permanent lender to fund his loan upon the satisfactory completion and rental of the income-producing property. Because the funding of the permanent loan provides the money to repay the construction loan, the two are inextricably linked by the commitment. Often it is a mortgage banker or a mortgage broker[4] who arranges both the construction loan and the permanent loan commitment for the equity investor or the developer.

Construction Lenders. There are six types of financial institutions that the mortgage banker might look to for construction financing. As shown in Table 22, commercial banks typically make about 25 percent of multifamily and 55 percent of nonresidential construction loans. Although these short-term, high-return loans are a significant source of income for many banks, the commercial banks made some unwise construction lending decisions in the early 1970s. When the real estate market went into a tailspin in 1974, commercial banks were forced to foreclose on many construction projects that were either completed and unrentable or were uncompleted because the developer had declared bankruptcy. After an extended real estate recession, most markets recovered sufficiently for the lender to sell the projects and thus remove the foreclosed properties from its balance sheet. Although this resulted in some losses and in a corresponding hesitancy of the banks to reenter the construction lending market, most commercial banks are once again active as construction lenders.

The table indicates that the second most important lender group are the thrift institutions. Although these typically have between 20 percent and 45 percent of the outstanding construction loans, depending upon the type of project, most of the lending that is done by the thrift institutions takes place on smaller projects that are significant in their local markets. An individual institution's financial base is usually too small to enable it to make such loans on large developments even if it wanted to. In addition, the thrift institutions are particularly active construction lenders in the single-family market, where the loan is often a combination construction-permanent mortgage.

---

[4] The distinction between the two is generally recognized to be that the former has a servicing capability whereas the latter is unable to service the loan for the permanent lender.

TABLE 22
Construction Loans Outstanding at Year-End, 1970–1977 (market share in percent)

	1970	1971	1972	1973	1974	1975	1976	1977
Commercial banks								
Single-family loans	33.4	34.6	36.3	40.1	39.0	38.8	29.4	35.4
Multifamily loans	23.5	19.8	22.0	22.8	28.3	26.2	35.1	38.7
Nonresidential loans	59.5	52.2	50.5	48.5	51.9	52.7	58.4	59.1
Savings and loans								
Single-family loans	49.5	49.0	45.0	37.5	38.8	45.3	57.3	55.7
Multifamily loans	37.8	36.9	29.4	19.2	13.7	18.1	23.3	28.1
Nonresidential loans	12.7	15.9	16.3	14.5	12.9	14.9	19.6	20.5
Savings banks								
Single-family loans	2.7	2.4	2.3	2.2	1.7	2.0	2.5	2.0
Multifamily loans	4.3	5.0	4.9	4.1	3.5	3.3	2.6	3.8
Nonresidential loans	3.3	3.3	3.0	2.4	1.6	2.0	2.1	2.7
Mortgage trusts								
Single-family loans	5.2	4.6	5.0	8.6	8.9	6.2	4.1	2.0
Multifamily loans	15.2	16.6	22.6	26.9	30.1	24.4	14.1	9.0
Nonresidential loans	18.4	19.7	21.7	25.3	23.1	18.3	9.8	7.1
Mortgage companies								
Single-family loans	9.2	9.4	11.2	11.1	11.0	7.1	6.1	4.7
Multifamily loans	11.2	14.9	12.7	18.2	11.7	10.5	7.9	7.3
Nonresidential loans	4.5	6.3	5.0	6.9	8.2	8.8	6.5	7.2
State and local credit agencies								
Single-family loans	—	0.0	0.2	0.3	0.5	0.5	0.4	0.0
Multifamily loans	3.9	4.6	7.3	8.1	12.0	16.9	16.5	11.6
Nonresidential loans	—	—	0.0	0.0	0.0	0.0	0.1	—
Life insurance companies								
Single-family loans	0.0	0.0	0.1	0.1	0.0	0.0	0.1	0.0
Multifamily loans	0.7	0.5	0.3	0.4	0.4	0.3	0.3	0.6
Nonresidential loans	1.1	2.5	3.2	2.2	1.8	2.6	2.4	2.2

Source: U.S. Department of Housing and Urban Development.

Another potential source of construction money is the mortgage-oriented real estate investment trust. Although the REITs were very important lenders in the early 1970s, they suffered many of the same underwriting problems as the commercial banks. However, the REITs lacked the necessary staying power to readily ride out the bad times. Instead, some went bankrupt, others converted from trust status, and most are still trying to cope with their problem loans. It appears that it will be some time before the mortgage trusts are able to play more than a minor role in the construction lending area.

Mortgage bankers themselves are the fourth source of construction funds. Although dwarfed by the commercial banks and the S&Ls, mortgage bankers do provide a small amount of construction loans as part of their financing package (see Table 22). However, due to the limited capital base of most mortgage companies, such loans are typically restricted to relatively small projects.

A fifth source of construction funds, identified as state and local credit agencies, includes state housing finance agencies and local public housing authorities. As Table 22 indicates, these credit agencies are most active in the multifamily area, primarily for low- and moderate-income rental dwelling units, and do little construction lending in the two other categories.

Life insurance companies, the last source of construction money, are introduced in order to call attention to their potentially larger role. Because permanent mortgage loans on income-producing properties are a significant part of their portfolios, the life insurance companies have developed a substantial expertise in real estate loan underwriting. In 1975, when the banks did not provide the interim financing which enabled the construction of improvements upon which life companies could ultimately make permanent mortgage loans, the life insurance companies debated the merits of substantially expanding their construction lending exposure. This was, however, an uncomfortable role for them to fill at that time. Nevertheless, the life insurance companies are *potentially* an important income property construction lender.

In summary, the commercial banks and the savings and loan associations make most of the construction loans, though the state and local credit agencies hold a significant share of the primarily low-income multifamily loans.

Determinants of Availability. The most important factor influencing the availability of construction money is the permanent loan commitment. Although exceptions were made in the early 1970s, most construction lenders require the commitment before they will advance the construction funds. Because permanent lenders do not grant commitments until they are satisfied that sufficient market demand exists to enable the developer to profitably operate the property and repay the permanent loan, the fundamental availability factor is market demand for the property's services.

Examining availability on a short-term basis suggests that monetary policy also plays a role. If the Fed reduces the growth of the money supply, commercial banks have fewer lendable funds available. At the same time, the high interest rates that often accompany the restrictive Fed policy lead to disintermediation from the thrift institutions. Both effects result in a reduction of the funds that are available for construction lending.

Finally, the availability of construction funds depends in part upon the rate that borrowers are willing to pay, that is, availability depends upon cost. Furthermore, the rate is more important for the commercial banks because they have many short-term lending opportunities that the other lenders do not have. If they are able to charge a higher rate on one type of loan than on another type, after adjusting for the differences in riskiness between the two loans, they would rather make the loan that yields them a greater risk-adjusted return. On the other hand, the banks sometimes neglect to adjust the lending rates adequately for differences in risks, and consequently they commit more of their funds to relatively high yield construction lending than they would otherwise do. Such myopic analysis was one cause of the banks' disastrous experiences in the mid-1970s.

Determinants of Cost. As shown in Table 23, many income property construction loans are variable rate loans whose interest rate is tied to another money market rate. Often this indexing rate is the prime interest rate, the one that commercial banks ostensibly charge their most creditworthy customers. For example, the builder/developer may have to pay a construction loan interest rate which is 2 percentage points above the prime rate. As the prime rate increases from 9 percent to 10 percent, the construction loan rate would increase from 11 percent to 12 percent.[5] As a result of this pricing mechanism, the cost of income property construction loans depends heavily upon money market interest rates.

Because commercial banks make such a large proprotion of the construction loans, their commercial loan rates, which are tied to their prime rate, are the primary determinants of the cost of construction loans. Even when construction loans are issued at a fixed interest rate, that rate is determined by the other short-term lending opportunities available to the bank. Thus, the real estate market must compete with other money market users, and the rates that those users are willing to pay, in order to attract commercial bank funds. In addition, the construction loan rate is often used as a rationing device as the availability of money decreases. It takes only a short period of time at very high interest rates for an otherwise profitable development project to become uneconomic. Given such interest rates, builders, especially builders of the smaller income properties, will tend to postpone their developments until the rates fall.

The construction loans of both savings and loan associations and mutual savings banks are usually at rates competitive with the market rates determined by the commercial banks. However, when the thrifts have an excess of funds that would encourage them to become active

---

[5] During times of rapidly changing interest rates, commercial bankers try to protect themselves with construction loan rate floors, while builder/developers seek ceilings above which the variable rate will not rise.

TABLE 23
Fixed versus Variable Rate Construction Loans, November 1977

			Size of Loan		
	$1,000–$24,999	$25,000–$49,999	$50,000–$99,999	$100,000–$499,999	$500,000 and Up
Percentage of dollars lent at a variable interest rate	8.8	17.0	24.8	57.1	86.7
Type of construction as a percentage					
Single-family	61.9	57.8	70.9	29.3	2.7
Multifamily	1.0	2.2	6.4	16.7	18.3
Nonresidential	37.1	39.9	22.8	54.0	79.0

Source: Federal Reserve Board.

construction lenders, the market rate is usually lower than the rate available on long-term mortgage loans. Conversely, when the construction rate is higher than the long-term rate, the thrifts generally do not have funds to commit to construction lending due to the disintermediation effect.

Finally, construction loan demand plays a relatively small role in determining construction loan rates. The other lending opportunities of commercial banks are usually sufficient to keep the banks from significantly lowering rates in order to attract developers. This is partly because the developers are rather rate insensitive and partly because the lenders frequently compete on nonrate terms.

The Key Factor. The key factor affecting both the cost and the availability of construction funds is other *money market interest rates*. As those rates increase or decrease, construction rates usually move in the same direction. Moreover, as money market rates increase and funds become less available, the lenders curtail their construction lending. This is partly due to decreased lending opportunities as permanent loan commitments become scarcer, and partly due to the rationing effect of very high interest rates on the economic viability of construction projects. Of course, the opposite occurs as money market rates fall.

Permanent Mortgages on Income Properties

Long-term loans on income-producing properties are often originated by mortgage bankers. As part of their total package of financing services, mortgage bankers typically maintain correspondent relationships with a number of income property lenders. After assembling all of the information about a property, the mortgage banker approaches one of his correspondent lenders and asks for its permanent loan commitment. If the project has not yet been built, he then uses the commitment to secure construction funds, as explained in the previous section. After the permanent loan is funded, the mortgage banker will continue to service it for the lender, forwarding a monthly check covering interest and principal amortization.

The second group of financial institutions that originate income property mortgage loans, the mortgage brokers, are similar to the mortgage bankers. There are, however, some important differences. First, mortgage brokers do not usually maintain correspondent relationships with individual lenders. Instead, they will circulate a property information package as widely as practicable until a lender agrees to provide the commitment. Second, because they do not service mortgage loans, the lender must do that himself. Third, mortgage brokers concentrate on very large loans because it is often not economic for the lender to service a loan unless it is a very large one. Fourth, most mortgage brokerage companies are relatively small, privately owned firms. During the 1970s, however, many Wall Street investment houses have purchased or established their own mortgage brokerage operations. It is these firms that are beginning to dominate the brokerage industry.

The third group of financial institutions that originate income property mortgage loans consists of the life insurance companies that originate, fund, and service their own loans on income-producing properties. Although the majority of life companies use mortgage bankers as correspondents, several of the larger companies maintain mortgage branch offices that are scattered throughout the country. From these offices, they seek out lending opportunities, performing the mortgage banking function because their lending volume enables them to handle that function more economically themselves.

Permanent Lenders. The largest source of long-term mortgage money on income-producing properties is the life insurance company. Since their reorientation from the single-family market in the late 1950s, the life companies have been very aggressive lenders in this area. Table 24 shows that they hold approximately 30 percent of all outstanding income property debt. Although they contracted their multifamily lending volume slightly in the mid-1970s, as the real estate market worked off its excess supply of previously constructed properties (see Tables 24 and 25), in 1977 they increased their lending substantially. This will continue at an advanced rate for at least the next few years, based upon their large amount of outstanding commitments for future lending.

The next largest group of permanent lenders includes the thrift institutions. As shown in Table 24, the S&Ls and the savings banks combined hold approximately 45 percent of the multifamily loans and 27 percent of the outstanding nonresidential loans. As indicated in the previous section, however, they tend to specialize in smaller projects which have an impact within the communities they serve. Moreover, due to their residential orientation most of their income property loans have been made on multifamily residential developments, especially those upon which they granted the combined construction-permanent financing. Table 25 demonstrates their cyclic lending pattern. During 1973 and 1974, as rising money market interest rates increased the disintermediation pressures on the thrifts, they reduced their income property lending.

The commercial banks are the third largest source of permanent loan money. Like the thrift institutions, they specialize in the smaller, local projects, except in rural areas where the commercial bank is often the only financial institution. There the banks engage in a much broader diversity of lending projects, including all types of real estate loans. As Table 25 suggests, bank activity in income property lending has also been cyclic. When the banks have a surplus of funds due to weak business demand, they tend to look to the real estate markets for investment opportunities. Then, when commercial loan demand is strong, they tend to give the commercial loan market a higher priority than the real estate market. There is nothing wrong or immoral about this orientation, but it is a factor that borrowers must recognize.

Thus, the three most important lenders of long-term funds for income-producing properties are life insurance companies, commercial banks, and thrift institutions. The first two emphasize loans on nonresidential properties, whereas the thrifts concentrate more on multifamily property loans.

Determinants of Availability. As has been indicated in the construction loan section, the major determinant of loan availability for an income property is the anticipated market demand for the property's services.

TABLE 24
Income Property Mortgage Debt Outstanding at Year-End, 1970–1977

	1970		1971		1972	
	Multifamily Properties	Nonresidential Properties	Multifamily Properties	Nonresidential Properties	Multifamily Properties	Nonresidential Properties
Life insurance companies						
Amount (in billions of dollars)	15.4	25.0	16.1	27.3	16.7	30.2
Market share as a percentage	33.6	37.6	30.3	36.6	27.3	34.5
Percent of assets	7.4	12.1	7.3	12.3	7.0	12.6
Savings and loan associations						
Amount (in billions of dollars)	11.5	9.2	13.9	11.3	17.0	14.2
Market share as a percentage	25.0	13.9	26.1	15.2	27.8	16.2
Percent of assets	6.5	5.2	6.7	5.5	7.0	5.8
Mutual savings banks						
Amount (in billions of dollars)	7.5	7.6	9.1	8.6	10.3	10.0
Market share as a percentage	16.4	11.5	17.1	11.5	16.7	11.4
Percent of assets	9.5	9.7	10.2	9.6	10.2	9.9
Commercial banks						
Amount (in billions of dollars)	1.8	18.8	2.1	20.6	2.9	25.0
Market share as a percentage	3.9	28.2	3.9	27.6	4.7	28.6
Percent of assets	0.3	3.3	0.3	3.2	0.4	3.4

TABLE 24 (continued)

	1973 Multifamily Properties	1973 Nonresidential Properties	1974 Multifamily Properties	1974 Nonresidential Properties	1975 Multifamily Properties	1975 Nonresidential Properties
Life insurance companies						
Amount (in billions of dollars)	17.8	34.9	18.9	39.6	18.9	43.1
Market share as a percentage	26.0	33.9	24.6	34.2	23.3	33.4
Percent of assets	7.0	13.9	7.2	15.0	6.5	14.9
Savings and loan associations						
Amount (in billions of dollars)	19.5	16.7	21.7	19.1	23.0	23.1
Market share as a percentage	28.4	16.2	28.2	16.5	28.4	17.9
Percent of assets	8.0	6.1	7.3	6.5	6.8	6.8
Mutual savings banks						
Amount (in billions of dollars)	11.6	11.6	12.4	12.4	13.2	13.1
Market share as a percentage	17.0	11.3	16.2	10.7	16.3	10.1
Percent of assets	10.9	10.9	11.3	11.3	10.9	10.8
Commercial banks						
Amount (in billions of dollars)	3.1	30.2	3.3	34.0	2.9	37.7
Market share as a percentage	4.6	29.4	4.3	29.3	3.6	29.2
Percent of assets	0.4	3.6	0.4	3.7	0.3	3.9

TABLE 24 *(concluded)*

	1976 Multifamily Properties	1976 Nonresidential Properties	1977 Multifamily Properties	1977 Nonresidential Properties
Life insurance companies				
Amount (in billions of dollars)	18.4	46.7	18.0	52.0
Market share as a percentage	21.0	33.8	19.2	34.0
Percent of assets	5.7	14.5	5.1	14.8
Savings and loan associations				
Amount (in billions of dollars)	26.6	26.2	29.9	28.7
Market share as a percentage	30.3	18.9	31.9	18.7
Percent of assets	6.8	6.7	6.5	6.2
Mutual savings banks				
Amount (in billions of dollars)	13.8	13.9	14.6	14.6
Market share as a percentage	15.7	10.1	15.6	9.5
Percent of assets	10.3	10.3	9.9	9.9
Commercial banks				
Amount (in billions of dollars)	4.3	39.7	4.8	46.3
Market share as a percentage	4.9	28.7	5.1	30.3
Percent of assets	0.4	3.8	0.4	4.0

Sources: U.S. Department of Housing and Urban Development; and *Federal Reserve Bulletin.*

TABLE 25
Income Property Mortgage Acquisitions,* 1970–1977 ($ millions)*

	1970	1971	1972	1973	1974	1975	1976	1977
Life insurance companies	5,701	5,873	6,791	9,154	8,964	7,350	7,005	9,376
Savings and loan associations	3,514	7,536	9,745	8,693	7,447	9,252	11,155	13,189
Mutual savings banks	2,520	3,922	4,663	5,026	3,445	3,416	3,437	3,561
Commercial banks	4,579	7,668	11,162	12,136	10,523	10,464	12,044	18,645

* Acquisitions are defined as loan originations plus loan purchases less loan sales.
Source: U.S. Department of Housing and Urban Development.

For example, if the property is an apartment project, the lender's concern will be about the future market demand for those apartment units because the tenants' rents provide the funds to repay the loan. Similarly, the availability of permanent mortgage loan money for a shopping center development will depend upon the market demand for additional shopping facilities, which is often evidenced by the signed leases of major tenants for over half of the shopping center space. If a developer or a purchaser has an income-producing property in which financially strong tenants wish to rent space, it is highly likely that he can obtain the permanent loan commitment that he needs in order to initiate the project.

Specific factors affecting each of the three major types of lenders also influence the flow of funds into long-term mortgage loans. Life insurance companies depend primarily upon premium receipts to fund their loan commitments. Although such receipts are fairly predictable, the life companies must also face a situation similar to the disintermediation that affects thrift institutions. When market interest rates rise to high levels, people tend to borrow money from the life insurance companies, using the cash values of their insurance policies as security. This is attractive to policyholders because, until recently, most whole life policies allowed the policyholder to borrow the cash value at a 5 percent or 6 percent interest rate. The holder then invested that money at the high rate available in the market, thus leveraging his returns by the difference between the two rates. When people rapidly increase their policy loans, life insurance companies have fewer funds available for their investments, including long-term mortgage loans.

A second factor that affects the availability of permanent mortgage money from life insurance companies is the rate of return that the companies can obtain from alternative investment opportunities. Life companies invest in stocks, bonds, and real property as well as mortgages, and the expected risk-adjusted returns available from the other investments may be more attractive than those from mortgages. If so, the life insurance companies will tend to channel more of their funds into those investments and away from the income property loan market.

For thrift institutions, two factors influence the availability of income property mortgage money. The first is the disintermediation factor; when thrift institutions do not have money, they cannot lend it. The second is the regulatory environment of the savings and loan associations. Currently, no more than 20 percent of their assets can be invested in mortgages on commercial properties. Because of this, they cannot develop a high degree of expertise in income property lending. Moreover, unless a savings and loan association is quite large, its overhead is so great that it can obtain a better return by concentrating on single-family mortgage loans.

Although less severely affected than the thrift institutions, commercial banks are also subject to disintermediation pressures. Banks usually respond to periods of credit stringency and strong commercial loan demand by concentrating their lending in the short-term, business loan sector. Moreover, during those periods commercial loan rates are frequently higher than the rates of long-term income property mortgage loans, thus providing an extra incentive for the commercial banks to emphasize their traditional lending activities.

In summary, the availability of permanent loans for income properties depends upon the market demand for services of the properties, upon the disintermediation effect, and upon the rates obtainable from other investment opportunities that are available to the lenders.

Determinants of Cost. The major factor affecting the cost of permanent mortgage money is the rate of return that financial institutions can obtain on alternative investments. If mortgage loans are to compete with those investments, they must offer risk-adjusted rates that are at least as attractive as those that financial institutions are able to obtain by investing their funds elsewhere.

Table 26 shows how life insurance companies have allocated their investable funds each year among stocks, bonds, and mortgages. Notice how they flexibly shifted their investments from one medium to another as the *expected* returns in the different areas changed over time. However, Table 27 shows the returns that were actually available in the different markets. The insurance company investment managers clearly did not expect negative stock market returns in 1970 or 1974. In fact, due to the relatively poor performance of the stock market as a whole in recent years, the life insurance companies have been reemphasizing the bond markets as attractive investment opportunities.

Savings and loan associations, on the other hand, are generally restricted to mortgage investments. Most S&Ls are willing to offer income property loans at about the same rates as those of the life insurance companies because the borrower will turn to the life companies if the S&Ls require a higher rate. Conversely, if the S&Ls offer a lower rate, they will be swamped by more income property loan business than they are allowed to accept.

Mutual savings banks operate much like the S&Ls. However, because the savings banks do not have the asset restrictions of the S&Ls, long-term bonds are a viable investment alternative. Thus, mortgages must compete on a risk-adjusted rate basis with the yields available on bonds in order to attract savings bank money. For both types of thrift institutions, funds availability is also an important factor. As disintermediation restricts their investable funds position, they raise rates in order to ration the weaker borrowers out of their market.

Commercial banks are faced with a slightly different situation. They must decide whether to invest their money in long-term mortgages or in short-term commercial or construction loans. Table 28 compares the rates that were available in these markets from 1966 to 1977. Because the banks are oriented toward short-term loans, the long-term mortgage market usually receives only their excess funds. Even then, banks are reluctant to tie up their funds on a long-term basis due to the rising trend and the rapid fluctuations in interest rates since the mid-1960s. When the banks do make long-term loans, they tend to follow the rate structure set by the life insurance companies.

The Key Factor. It appears, then, that the life insurance companies dominate the rate structure on income property mortgages. The most important factor in their rate decision is the expected returns on their

TABLE 26
Percentage Distribution of Life Insurance Company Long-Term Investments, 1966–1977

	1966	1967	1968	1969	1970	1971	1972	1973	1974	1975	1976	1977
Mortgages	60.8	51.4	46.2	36.6	36.4	26.3	25.6	32.8	37.6	25.3	19.4	23.5
Real estate	3.0	4.1	4.8	3.9	4.4	3.6	2.9	3.4	4.3	5.6	3.6	3.3
Stocks	7.9	12.5	19.4*	19.9	20.7	23.6	24.9	23.4	16.0	15.7	15.2	11.8
Corporate bonds	21.9*	26.7*	24.1*	32.9	34.5	40.8	41.9	36.4	37.3	43.7	47.5	50.5
Government securities	6.4*	5.3*	5.5*	6.8	4.0	5.7	4.7	4.0	4.8	9.7	14.3	10.9

* Allocation to long-term category estimated by author.
Source: American Council of Life Insurance.

TABLE 27
Total Rates of Return in Different Investment Markets, 1966–1977 (percent)

	1966	1967	1968	1969	1970	1971	1972	1973	1974	1975	1976	1977
Income property mortgage market	3.64	2.68	1.61	−0.92	−2.18	14.77	11.76	5.93	1.80	1.63	10.67	11.56
Standard and Poor's Composite Stock Index	0.10	11.02	10.43	2.37	−11.11	21.25	13.94	1.41	−18.39	8.31	22.20	0.87
Moody's Corporate Bond Index	−0.21	2.29	0.29	−1.02	−3.31	13.25	10.66	5.81	−3.36	2.17	12.84	13.21
Long-term U.S. Treasury bonds	−3.12	0.35	−2.51	−7.84	−3.16	14.86	4.45	−5.60	−5.50	2.98	5.65	−0.51

Sources: American Council of Life Insurance; *Survey of Current Business;* Federal Reserve Bank of St. Louis; and author's calculations.

TABLE 28
Commercial Bank Rates on Selected Loan Types, 1966–1977 (percent)

	1966	1967	1968	1969	1970	1971	1972	1973	1974	1975	1976	1977
Long-term rates												
Single-family mortgages	6.55	6.24	6.74	7.52	7.99	7.39	7.30	7.77	8.84	8.88	8.79	8.81
Income property mortgages	6.42	6.97	7.66	8.69	9.93	9.07	8.57	8.76	9.47	10.22	9.83	9.34
Short-term rates												
Construction loans	n.a.	n.a.	n.a.	n.a.	n.a.	n.a.	n.a.	n.a.	n.a.	n.a.	n.a.	8.75
Commercial loans	6.00	6.00	6.68	8.21	8.48	6.32	5.82	8.30	11.28	8.65	7.52	7.85

Note: All rates are contract rates on commercial bank loans, except for the income property mortgage rate series, which, because of a lack of data, is the contract rate on life insurance company loans.

Sources: Federal Home Loan Bank Board; American Council of Life Insurance; and *Federal Reserve Bulletin*.

alternative investment opportunities. Those returns are, for the most part, the rates available in the capital markets. Thus, *capital market interest rates,* which play a key role in determining the rates on single-family mortgages sold in the secondary market, are also of primary importance in determining the rates on income property mortgage loans.

MONEY MARKET INTEREST RATES

The previous sections demonstrated the important role that money market interest rates play in the mortgage market. Not only are they key determinants of the cost and availability of construction loans, but they also play a major role in the cost and availability of single-family residential mortgages to be held in the originating lender's portfolio.

Money market interest rates are the rates on financial instruments with maturities of one year or less. These investment vehicles, which typically represent a portion of the borrowing needs of government and corporate issuers, are purchased by investors with short-term excess funds. U.S. Treasury bills, corporate commercial paper, bank certificates of deposit, and bank acceptances comprise most of this $310 billion market. Because of the importance of money market rates, this section explores some of the supply and demand factors that are involved in predicting them.

Demand Considerations

There are three broadly defined groups that demand short-term credit in the financial markets: consumers, businesses, and governments. Because each of the three groups influences the market in a different way, their impacts are examined separately.

Consumer Demand. Most short-term consumer credit originates when customers charge purchases to their accounts at individual establishments, or to their accounts at financial institutions via credit cards such as Visa or Master Charge. This borrowing is usually at nonnegotiable interest rates, with the individual having a predetermined credit limit. Individual demand for short-term credit appears to lag slightly behind changes in the economy as a whole. Consumers expand their demand for credit during economic upswings and attempt to reduce their obligations during recessionary periods. Because they frequently deposit their liquid assets with financial institutions, this retrenchment not only reduces consumer loan demand but also increases the institutions' lendable funds. Due to the relatively inflexible consumer loan rates, the result is often marginally lower consumer loan interest rates, as indicated in Table 29.

Business Demand. The demand of business firms for short-term credit also closely follows the economic cycle, though with a greater lag than consumer credit demand. Businesses use their short-term loans to finance raw material, work-in-progress, and finished goods inventories. Coming out of a recession, businesses wait for increased sales to reduce their inventories before they raise production rates and thus rebuild

TABLE 29
Market Rates on Short-Term Loans, 1966–1977 (percent)

	1966	1967	1968	1969	1970	1971	1972	1973	1974	1975	1976	1977
Consumer rates												
Automobiles	n.a.	n.a.	n.a.	n.a.	n.a.	n.a.	10.05	10.21	10.97	11.36	11.08	10.89
Other consumer goods	n.a.	n.a.	n.a.	n.a.	n.a.	n.a.	12.45	12.60	13.02	13.11	13.02	12.98
Business rates												
Commercial paper (prime, four–six month)	5.55	5.10	5.90	7.83	7.72	5.11	4.69	8.15	9.87	6.33	5.35	5.60
Bank acceptances (prime, 90-day)	5.36	4.75	5.75	7.61	7.31	4.85	4.47	8.08	9.92	6.30	5.19	5.59
Negotiable certificates of deposit (large, three-month)	5.47	5.02	5.86	7.77	7.56	5.02	4.64	8.39	10.27	6.43	5.26	5.58
Commercial banks' prime rate	5.62	5.61	6.28	7.95	7.91	5.69	4.77	8.02	10.80	7.86	6.84	6.82

Source: *Federal Reserve Bulletin.*

their inventories back to a normal level. On the other hand, when the economy moves into a recession and consumers curtail their purchases, businesses often temporarily continue their current production schedules, and thus build inventories above the normal level, before cutting production in response to the reduced consumer demand.

Table 29 lists some market indicators of business credit demand. The first three business loan rates—the commercial paper rate, the bank acceptance rate, and the negotiable certificate of deposit rate—are responsive to market demand conditions. The prime commercial paper rate is the money market rate that large corporations must pay for four–six-month loans from other corporations. Prime bank acceptances are short-term business borrowings that a commercial bank guarantees will be repaid, thus making the bank's credit the primary determinant of the instrument's riskiness. The 90-day certificate of deposit rates indicate what commercial banks must pay to borrow large amounts in the money markets for three-month periods.

On the other hand, the prime bank loan rate is typically an administratively determined rate that banks charge their highest-quality customers for short-term funds. As such, it does not necessarily reflect supply and demand conditions in the short-term credit markets. Consequently, one must rely most heavily on movements in the first three rates in order to assess changing money market conditions.

Government Demand. Government demand for short-term credit is most often associated with the fiscal policy of the federal government. Prior to the 1970s, when state and local government demand for funds increased at a moderate and predictable rate, this was a reasonable assumption. In recent years, however, state and local borrowing first rose, then diminished dramatically as the severe 1973–75 recession and the rapid economic rebound whipsawed their budgetary plans. As spending inevitably increases in order to use the "excess funds" currently available, the state and local government position is expected to return to a more normal pattern.

At the federal level, it is the U.S. Treasury Department that implements the financing arrangements dictated by the relationships between revenue and spending patterns that result from congressional decisions. In only 2 of the 12 years from 1966 to 1977 have those decisions left the federal government with a surplus of revenues over expenditures (see Table 30). Moreover, with deficits of between $50 and $75 billion per year during the last half of the 1970s, the Treasury has become a large and constant borrower in both the money market and the capital market.

Although the deficits have not drastically altered the cyclic nature of the money markets as dictated by business credit demands, they have caused three pronounced market changes. First, they have led to higher short-term interest rates than would have otherwise been the case as the Treasury, with its need to finance the government's deficit spending, expanded its role in the market. Table 31 shows 90-day and one-year Treasury bill rates since 1966. Second, the Treasury, which *must* borrow the money, will pay whatever rate is necessary to attract the needed

TABLE 30
Federal Government Surplus or Deficit, 1966–1977 ($ billions) (calendar years)

	1966	1967	1968	1969	1970	1971	1972	1973	1974	1975	1976	1977
Surplus (+) or deficit (−) on national income accounts basis	−7.3	−14.0	−16.1	+5.4	+21.9	−12.0	−17.4	−7.9	−10.9	−75.1	−56.6	−51.0

Source: *Federal Reserve Bulletin.*

TABLE 31
Selected Treasury Bill Rates, 1966–1977 (percent)

	1966	1967	1968	1969	1970	1971	1972	1973	1974	1975	1976	1977
90-day Treasury bills	4.86	4.29	5.34	6.67	6.39	4.33	4.07	7.03	7.84	5.80	4.98	5.27
One-year Treasury bills	5.07	4.71	5.46	6.79	6.49	4.67	4.77	7.01	7.71	6.30	5.52	5.71

Source: *Federal Reserve Bulletin.*

funds. This can lead to such high interest rates that businesses cannot afford to borrow in the money and capital markets, a phenomenon known as "crowding out." Third, there is the potential for "monetization of the debt" by the Federal Reserve. In order to keep interest rates down, the Federal Reserve may be tempted to increase the money supply enough to allow the Treasury to borrow its needed funds without raising interest rates. This strategy works in the short run, but in the long run, as we shall see below, the increased money supply frequently leads to greater inflation.

Supply Considerations

Interacting with the demand for short-term funds from consumers, business, and governments is the supply of those funds. As was indicated above, the supply of funds changes cyclically as the demand for liquidity, particularly by individuals and businesses, increases during periods of economic downturn.

Monetary Policy. In spite of this procyclic impact of business and consumer liquidity demands, the federal government can greatly influence supply conditions through its implementation of monetary policy. Although economists disagree over what is meant by monetary policy, this chapter adopts the longer run viewpoint which suggests that monetary policy is primarily concerned with controlling the money supply rather than interest rates. Thus, if the federal government is interested in restraining the economy through monetary policy, it would attempt to slow the growth rate of the money supply. On the other hand, short-run efforts to stimulate economic activity could be accomplished by increasing the growth rate of the money supply.

The federal government agency responsible for monetary policy is the Board of Governors of the Federal Reserve System, commonly called the Fed. The board, which is composed of seven members, each appointed to a 14-year term by the president with the advice and consent of the Senate, meets monthly in order to chart the nation's monetary policy.[6]

In order to implement its monetary policy decisions, the Fed relies upon three tools. First, it can change the percentage of a commercial bank's deposits that must be kept in a non-interest-bearing reserve account at a regional Federal Reserve bank.[7] For a commercial bank to be a member of the Federal Reserve System, and thus be able to utilize the system's check-clearing and credit reserve services, the bank must agree to keep a certain percentage of its deposits as reserves. If the Fed decreases its reserve requirement, that is, reduces the percentage of the bank's deposits that must be kept as reserves, then the bank has

---

[6] Because of monetary policy's crucial role in our economic system, the fourteen-year term was chosen to insure the Fed's independence from both administrative and congressional pressures. Although Congress has recently attempted to strengthen its control over the Fed, the existing procedures appear to be working fairly well.

[7] A current Federal Reserve proposal would institute the payment of interest on reserve accounts.

additional money that it can lend. Of course, the opposite occurs if the Fed increases its reserve requirement.

The second tool for carrying out the Fed's directives is called raising or lowering the discount window and changing the discount rate. If a commercial bank that is a member of the Federal Reserve System temporarily needs funds, it may borrow from its regional Federal Reserve bank. By raising or lowering the so-called discount window, the Federal Reserve banks can control the amount of money that they lend to the commercial banks. In addition, they can influence commercial bank borrowing by changing the interest rate that they charge the banks, that is, the discount rate. Together, the discount window and the discount rate operate to increase the money supply when the Fed makes discount window loans more attractive, and vice versa.

The most important monetary policy tool of the Fed is its open market operations. The Board of Governors and 5 of the 12 Federal Reserve bank presidents meet monthly as the Federal Open Market Committee (FOMC) in order to set appropriate money supply growth targets.[8] When the FOMC wants to reduce the money supply, it directs the Federal Reserve Bank of New York to sell government securities, usually Treasury bills, from the system's $108 billion portfolio. The dealer buying the securities pays for them through his commercial bank. Because the payment goes to the Federal Reserve, the Fed simply takes the money due it from the non-interest-bearing reserve account maintained by the dealer's bank. Because the reserve account no longer meets the Fed's reserve requirements, the bank must transfer some otherwise lendable funds into that account.[9] By reducing the commercial bank's available funds, the Fed has effectively reduced the money supply.

On the other hand, the Fed buys government securities when it wants to increase the money supply. When it pays for these, this time by adding the money to a commercial bank's reserve account, it increases the money that the bank can lend, thereby increasing the nation's money supply. Of the three tools, this is the most widely used because the Fed can quickly and directly control how much money it inserts or withdraws from the banking system.

Since money market interest rates are influenced by money supply changes, how can one determine whether the Fed is implementing its monetary policy decisions? One way would be to observe how the money supply changes in response to Fed actions. Unfortunately, this is difficult to do for a number of reasons. First, there are several definitions of "the" money supply, as shown in Table 32. The simplest definition, adjusted Federal Reserve credit, is a money supply component which consists mostly of the Federal Reserve's government securities portfolio. A broader component, the monetary base, can be derived by adding

---

[8] The five presidents are selected on a rotating basis.

[9] An alternative, and more likely, scenario would be for the commercial bank to borrow the needed reserves on a short-term basis from either a large corporate customer with excess demand deposits or from another bank that has an excess in its reserve account. The bank must then deposit its own funds when the customer or the other bank needs its excess, usually the next day.

the nation's gold stock to adjusted Federal Reserve credit. The second definition of the base in Table 32 is more consistent with the remaining money supply definitions. It is derived from the *uses* of the Federal Reserve's credit, thus dividing the monetary base into currency in circulation and commercial bank reserve accounts maintained with the regional Federal Reserve banks.

TABLE 32
Alternative Money Supply Definitions with an Example as of December 1977 ($ billions)

U.S. government securities held by the Federal Reserve	$ 108.3
+ Miscellaneous adjustments	2.5
= Adjusted Federal Reserve credit	$ 110.8
+ Gold stock	21.5
= Monetary base	$ 132.3
Currency in circulation	$ 90.0
+ Adjusted bank reserves	42.3
= Monetary base	$ 132.3
Currency in circulation	$ 90.0
+ Demand deposits at commercial banks	254.9
= M_1	$ 344.9
+ Savings and time deposits at commercial banks	466.8
= M_2	$ 811.7
+ Savings and time deposits at savings and loan associations, mutual savings banks, and credit unions	562.6
= M_3	$1,374.3

Source: Federal Reserve Bank of St. Louis; and *Federal Reserve Bulletin.*

A broader measure than the monetary base, and the first true money supply indicator, is called M_1. It also includes currency in circulation, but it substitutes demand deposits for bank reserves. Because banks must hold approximately one sixth of their deposits as reserves, the base and M_1 are closely related. Recall that if the Fed buys additional securities, it pays for them by increasing the dealer's bank reserve account. This raises the monetary base. As the bank uses the excess in its reserve account to make more loans, the money it lends is often deposited in the checking accounts of other commercial banks (demand deposits). The other banks can then use most of the deposit to make additional loans. This continues until approximately five times the amount of the original Fed purchase is lent, and thus appears as demand deposits in banks throughout the country. The increase in the monetary base consequently results in an increase in M_1. As Table 32 indicates, M_2 equals M_1 plus savings and time deposits at commercial banks, and M_3 adds savings accounts at savings and loan associations, mutual savings banks, and credit unions to M_2.

Table 32 demonstrates that the more encompassing the measure of "the" money supply, the less control the Fed has over it. Those who feel that the Fed should concentrate on controlling the money supply, rather than interest rates and credit market conditions, tend to emphasize the less inclusive measures, such as adjusted Federal Reserve credit and the monetary base, because the Fed has more direct control over these monetary aggregates. On the other hand, others argue that time lags cause the relationship between the monetary base and M_1 to be unpredictable. They feel that the Fed should control both interest rates and M_1, or perhaps M_2 or M_3 because M,'s usefulness is affected by seasonal adjustment problems as well as such financial innovations as NOW accounts and checking account credit lines.

Whatever the money supply measure chosen, analysts are faced with another major problem. It takes time to gather the raw money supply data, to compile those data into the different measures, and to release preliminary estimates to the public. Moreover, the preliminary data are subject to substantial revision. This means that there is a time lag in the availability of money supply information, a lag which may cause one to miss an important turning point in monetary policy.

To compensate for the problems created by different money supply measures and by time lags in the availability of money supply data, most analysts gauge short-run monetary policy by examining changes in the Fed funds rate. The Fed funds rate is an important indicator of monetary policy because it is the rate at which one commercial bank lends its excess reserves to another. Recall that the Fed purchases government securities from a dealer when it wishes to use open market operations to increase the money supply and that it then credits the reserve account of the dealer's commercial bank to pay for its purchase. Having more reserves than it needs, that bank can either withdraw the excess or, more likely, lend it on an overnight basis to a bank that is temporarily short of reserves. However, if this were the only transaction that occurred during the day, no other bank would need reserves, because the remaining banks would be in balance from the preceding day. In order to encourage another bank to borrow its excess reserves, the dealer's bank would have to charge a slightly lower Fed funds rate than the one which achieved yesterday's balance. Consequently, the money supply increase caused by the Fed's government securities purchase is frequently associated with a decrease in the Fed funds rate. On the other hand, an effort by the Fed to decrease the money supply typically causes the Fed funds rate to increase.

An Interaction of Supply and Demand

This section has shown that money market interest rates are key factors in the cost and availability both of construction loans and of single-family residential mortgages originated by the lender and then held in the lender's own portfolio. In addition, money market rates have been shown to be influenced by both demand and supply factors. Part of the demand by consumers, businesses, and governments for short-term loans was associated with the level of business activity, and the remainder was shown to be dependent upon the perceived liquidity needs of individuals and business firms. On the supply side, liquidity needs, as manifested by currency holdings and savings, were shown to influence most of the money supply measures too. However, the Fed implementation of its monetary policies was shown to have the largest individual impact on the monetary aggregates. Finally, the Fed funds rate was identified as a sensitive indicator of changes in those policies.

Note, however, that any short-term interest rate, whether it be the commercial paper rate, the Treasury bill rate, or the Fed funds rate, is determined by an interaction of *both* supply and demand factors. Because the Fed does not have complete control over the money supply and because the demand for loans and the supply of deposits also affect the reserve positions of commercial banks, the Fed funds rate is only an *indicator* of monetary policy. Nevertheless, persistent increases in the Fed funds rate suggest a tightening monetary policy, and persistent decreases suggest the opposite.

CAPITAL MARKET INTEREST RATES

Whereas *money* market interest rates are important determinants of the cost and availability of construction loans and of single-family residential mortgages which are originated by the lender and then held in the lender's own portfolio, *capital* market interest rates are important determinants of the cost and availability of single-family residential mortgages sold in the secondary markets and of mortgage loans on income-producing properties.

The determination of the capital market rate is easier to grasp if the interest rate is visualized as being composed of a number of components which sum to equal the rate. Of these components, the inflationary expectations component stands out as a highly variable determinant which accounts for most of the changes that take place in capital market interest rates.

The Real Rate of Return Component

The component embodying many of the previously described supply and demand influences is the "real rate of return," the rate that investors would demand, and that borrowers would be willing to supply, for a riskless asset. Of course, it is impossible to invest in such an asset, and economists must therefore use sophisticated statistical procedures to estimate the real rate of return. They have found that during recessionary periods, when business and consumer demand for funds decreases, the real rate of return is often at its low point. As economic recovery progresses, the demand for funds increases more rapidly than the supply, leading to a rise in the real rate of return. During the boom times that precede a recession, business demand is so large that the real rate of return normally reaches a cyclic high.

All capital market interest rates include a real rate of return component. However, these rates comprise a number of interest rates that correspond to instruments having different maturities. These instruments include intermediate-term instruments, with maturities ranging from two to nine years, and long-term instruments, with maturities of ten years or longer. The longer the maturity, the higher the real rate of return, as the lender must forgo the use of his money for a lengthening period of time.

Many financial instruments qualify as capital market instruments. It is impossible to list them all, but a few of the most common ones are Treasury notes and bonds issued by the federal government, intermediate- and long-term tax-exempt issues of local and state governments, intermediate- and long-term instruments issued by federal government agencies, and bonds issued by corporations. Table 33 shows some sample instruments in each of these categories.

Long-term mortgages are also capital market instruments that have a real rate of return component which varies both over the business cycle and according to maturity. However, an additional factor influences the return on mortgages. Most of the instruments in Table 33 return interest to the investors semiannually and the principal at maturity; mortgages return principal and interest monthly. Because the mortgage investor receives his money back in periodic payments during the life of the mortgage, a 30-year mortgage would have a lower real rate

TABLE 33
Sample Capital Market Instruments

Treasury notes and bonds
    8 percent Treasury note due May 15, 1982
    8¼ percent Treasury bond due May 15, 2005, but callable
        May 15, 2000

Tax-exempt issues
    6⅜ percent Houston Sports Arena first-mortgage revenue bond
        due December 1, 2003
    6.3 percent Georgia Residential Finance Authority term bonds
        due December 1, 2007

Agency issues
    7.6 percent Federal Home Loan Bank Board consolidated obligation due August 25, 1987
    7.4 percent Federal National Mortgage Association capital debenture due October 1, 1997

Corporate bonds
    7 percent Centex Corporation senior subordinated convertible debenture due February 11, 1986
    5½ percent Lomas & Nettleton Financial Corporation convertible subordinated debenture due June 1, 1991

Mortgage-related investments
    9⅛ percent California Federal Savings and Loan Association mortgage-backed bond due July 15, 1985
    8 percent GNMA-guaranteed mortgage-backed pass-through securities (Ginnie Maes)

of return than would a 30-year bond. This is so because the mortgage investor's money is outstanding for a shorter period of time.

The precise measurement of the real rate of return is not of major importance. What is crucial is that each capital market interest rate includes a real rate of return component, that the real rate varies over the business cycle because of different supply and demand considerations, and that its variability is usually restricted to a relatively narrow and predictable range.

Risk Components

In addition to the risk-free, or real, rate of return, capital market interest rates are composed of several other components that compensate the holders of financial instruments for a variety of risks. Each of these risks is discussed below.

Default Risk. The default risk component compensates the investor for accepting the risk that the issuer of the instrument may not pay him the interest or repay him the principal. This risk varies with the issuer's credit rating. For example, the default risk premium for federal government issues is negligible, whereas agency and most state and local issues carry some default risk. A few private companies have ratings almost as good as those of agencies and better than those of some state and local issues, although most private companies must pay a greater premium to induce investors to accept their default risk. As an aid to investors, many state and local government issues, as well as most corporate bonds, are rated by firms that specialize in assessing the default risk for particular issues. These firms, either Moody's or Standard and Poor's, then assign the issues to one of several risk categories, with the required interest rate closely related to the risk categories of the issues.

Because the rating of mortgage offerings has just begun, it will probably be some time until a generally accepted rating scheme is in widespread use. In the past, the most common classification scheme was based upon the insurance or guarantee of the mortgage instrument: the lowest default risk was associated with FHA-insured or VA-guaranteed mortgages, the next lowest with conventional mortgage loans having private mortgage insurance, and the greatest with conventional loans not having private mortgage insurance. For income property loans, those which relied for repayment on the rentals from highly rated tenents were considered more secure than those which were collateralized solely by the real estate.

Regardless of the default risk category, the default risk usually changes relatively little during the instrument's life, though it may increase during recessionary periods as the possibility of issuer default increases. Still, this is a relatively minor change compared to the changes in the inflationary risk component, which will be discussed later.

Callability Risk. The second risk component that must be paid in order to attract the investor is the callability risk component, which compensates him for assuming the risk that his invested monies will be returned prior to their scheduled repayment. Most capital market instruments contain a provision which allows the borrower to call the instrument and prepay the loan. Because the call feature frequently requires the borrower to pay a penalty fee, when a bond is called, the investor usually receives more money than he initially paid the borrower.

On the other hand, the investor usually does not want the bond called, even if the call provision includes a penalty payment, because bonds are most often called to take advantage of lower interest rates. For example, if a bond were issued during a period of high interest rates and the interest rate subsequently dropped considerably, the issuer may wish to call the high-rate bond and to refinance it with a new one carrying the lower current interest rate. Whether he does so depends upon the savings that he can achieve from the lower interest rate, including the call premium he must pay, as compared to the costs that he must incur to float a new bond issue.

The mortgage market has a similar feature, though it is commonly called prepayment instead of callability. The mortgage market differs from the bond market in that most single-family mortgages, which often have no prepayment penalty, are not prepaid to take advantage of lower interest rates but because the homeowner sells the house and the purchaser is unable or unwilling to assume the existing mortgage. On the other hand, income property mortgages, which frequently include a prepayment prohibition for the first ten years and prepayment penalties thereafter, are usually refinanced to obtain additional equity capital for other investments, not to achieve a lower interest rate. In either case, mortgage prepayments occur more often than other capital market instrument calls, leading to a greater callability risk premium for mortgages.

Marketability Risk. The marketability risk component compensates the investor for the potential difficulty he would have in selling the instrument due to its relatively poor secondary market. Marketability risk, which varies substantially among different financial instruments, is low for widely traded issues which have an extensive secondary market. On the other hand, because most mortgages have an extremely limited or a nonexistent secondary market, their interest rates must include a large marketability risk premium. The only mortgage-related instrument with excellent marketability is the Ginnie Mae pass-through, though the marketability of Mortgage Corporation participation certificates is rapidly improving.

Taxation Risk. The taxation risk component reflects the differential demand for capital market instruments due to the tax situations of the various investors. For example, commercial banks invest heavily in tax-exempt municipal bonds in order to earn tax-free income. Life insurance companies, on the other hand, generally do not pay income taxes on their investment income, and thus have little interest in tax-exempt bonds.

The major taxation risk factor associated with mortgages is favorable, thus tending to lower mortgage interest rates. If thrift institutions invest at least 82 percent of their assets in residential mortgage loans, they are eligible to place a substantial portion of their net income in a bad debt reserve account, thus sheltering it from income taxes. Because this account does not necessarily bear a close relationship to actual bad debt losses, thrifts are willing to make some mortgage loans at lower rates than other lenders just to maintain their tax shelter.

Inflationary Risk. The last risk component that is added to the real rate of return compensates the holders of financial instruments for inflationary risks. Because this component is based upon expectations of future inflation which often shift rapidly, extensively, and unpredictably, it holds the key to the successful determination of future capital market interest rates.

Table 34 shows the inflation rate from 1966 to 1977 and the interest rates on some long-term bond and mortgage series. Although inflation plays a major role in the determination of capital market interest rates, it does not affect long-term rates in any lockstep fashion. In most cases the effect of inflation is immediate and substantial, but in a few situations, where the increase or decrease in inflation is expected to be transitory, inflation has little impact. Even though no one-to-one relationship exists, there is a strong tendency for relatively "permanent" changes in inflationary expectations to be associated with similar changes in capital market rates.

Because of the major role that is ascribed to changes in inflationary expectations, inflation's two major causes will be examined here. The first cause is called demand-pull inflation. In this situation, there is a greater demand for goods and services than the economy's productive potential is able to satisfy. Consumers, whether they are individuals, businesses, or governments, then tend to bid up the prices of the relatively scarce goods and services in an effort to meet their wants.

Demand-pull inflation is caused by an excessively stimulative fiscal or monetary policy. In the former case, the government contributes to the excess demand that leads to price increases either by buying too many goods and services or by taxing the private sector inadequately and thus encouraging it to spend too much money. In the latter case, the government increases the money supply more rapidly than the economy can absorb it. Because consumers have too much money relative to the economy's productive capacity, the excess is used to bid up the prices of goods and services. The solution in the former case is to restrain government and consumer spending, and the solution in the latter case is a less rapid increase in the money supply. Although the Administration and the Fed ideally work in tandem to restrain inflationary influences, the political process often makes fiscal policy a less flexible inflationary deterrent, thereby leaving the Fed with the major role in controlling demand-pull inflation.

The second type of inflation, cost-push or structural inflation, was common in the United States during the mid- and late-1970s. Cost-push inflation refers, in part, to the tendency of businesses to raise their prices because of an increase in costs. For example, single-family home prices have been increasing rapidly in part because material, land, and labor

TABLE 34
The Relationship between Inflation and Interest Rates, 1966–1977 (percent)

	1966	1967	1968	1969	1970	1971	1972	1973	1974	1975	1976	1977
Inflation rate (percentage change in GNP implicit price deflator)	3.28	2.94	4.49	5.03	5.35	5.10	4.14	5.92	9.71	9.62	5.27	5.53
Long-term government bonds	4.66	4.85	5.25	6.10	6.59	5.82	5.63	6.30	6.98	6.78	6.39	7.06
New-issue Aaa utility bonds	5.43	5.82	6.50	7.71	8.68	7.62	7.31	7.74	9.33	9.40	8.48	8.19
Ginnie Mae pass-throughs	n.a.	n.a.	n.a.	n.a.	n.a.	7.32	7.09	7.80	8.82	8.62	8.24	8.04
Single-family mortgage loans	6.41	6.52	7.03	7.82	8.36	7.67	7.51	8.01	9.02	9.21	9.11	9.02
Income property mortgage loans	6.42	6.97	7.66	8.69	9.93	9.07	8.57	8.76	9.47	10.22	9.83	9.34

Sources: *Survey of Current Business; Federal Reserve Bulletin; Money Manager;* Federal Home Loan Bank Board; and American Council of Life Insurance.

costs have increased. At the same time, labor increases its price, the wage rate, as the costs that labor must pay, including housing costs, increase.

Cost-push inflation is reinforced by structural shifts in the economy. For example, when industries move out of an area, the workers who elect to remain behind often seek jobs that pay wages that are the same as or better than they received previously, even though there may now be less demand for their skills. Similarly, when the demand for construction workers dropped substantially during the real estate depression of the mid-1970s, instead of construction industry wage rates falling correspondingly, their rate of increase was only slowed, as our social welfare system provided extended unemployment benefits for the laid-off workers.

Inflation and the Money Supply

Whatever the cause of inflation the preceding analysis suggests two important conclusions. First, changes in inflationary expectations are closely related to the variability in capital market interest rates. Second, the Fed's monetary policy is being relied upon as the primary defense against inflation. For this purpose, it is not short-run money supply changes that are of prime importance, but substantial money supply changes over three–six-month periods. Changes of this duration influence the course of economic activity and thus may alter the inflation rate.

FOUR MORTGAGE MARKET SCENARIOS

The preceding sections of this chapter suggested that the cost and the availability of mortgage money are significantly affected by both money market and capital market interest rates. In this concluding section, these results are summarized by outlining four scenarios, one for construction loans, a second for single-family residential loans which are originated by the lender and then held in the lender's own portfolio, another for single-family residential loans which are sold to a third-party investor, and the last for income property loans.

Construction Loans

The cost of construction loans is influenced primarily by money market conditions. Because the construction lender typically depends upon the proceeds of the permanent loan for repayment of his construction loan, the availability of the permanent loan is a major consideration. Nevertheless, single-family construction loans are often made without any assurance of ultimate loan repayment. If the housing market appears strong to the lender, he will make a short-term construction loan at an interest rate somewhat above his prime lending rate.

For income property loans, the lender usually requires a permanent loan commitment before he will advance the construction funds. The availability of such a commitment depends upon competing capital market interest rates and upon the permanent lender's evaluation of the market for the property's services. The cost of the construction loan is related to the lender's prime rate, a money market interest rate. Consequently, forecasting construction loan interest rates involves forecasting money market interest rates. This is best done by using changes in the Fed funds rate and the monetary base to help predict growth rate variations in the money supply.

Single-Family Mortgages Held in Portfolio

To forecast the cost and availability of single-family mortgages which the originating lender holds in his own portfolio, one must predict both capital market and money market interest rates. The availability of money to fund such mortgages, usually conventional mortgages originated by thrift institutions, depends upon the relatively predictable debt service from the lender's portfolio of outstanding mortgage loans plus the lender's more variable net new savings inflow. The amount of new savings rests upon the relationship between money market rates and the deposit rate ceilings of the thrifts. If money market rates are expected to rise, as an increasing Fed funds rate would suggest, net new savings used to decrease, thus adversely affecting the availability of mortgage money. Now, however, the availability of money market certificates is helping to maintain adequate mortgage money availability, even during high interest rate periods, although it is adversely affecting the thrifts' cost of funds.

The cost of single-family mortgage money primarily reflects other capital market investment opportunities and the thrifts' own cost of funds, with one thrift institution charging rates similar to those of its competitors. If capital market rates are increasing, one can expect mortgage rates to rise as well, assuming that they are not artifically constrained by usury ceilings. If other capital market rates are decreasing, one can also expect mortgage rates to fall, though the thrifts' cost of funds usually provides a floor below which mortgage rates seldom drop.

Single-Family Mortgages Sold to Investors

The cost and availability of loans sold in the secondary mortgage market, frequently FHA and VA loans originated by mortgage bankers, are determined primarily by capital market interest rates. The cost of these loans, which can change daily as the number of discount points changes, depends upon the yield that mortgage bankers must offer secondary market investors. That yield, in turn, depends upon the rates on capital market investment opportunities that are available to those investors.

The availability of mortgage money, like its cost, is related to capital market rates. If mortgage bankers can provide an attractive rate in the secondary market, investors will purchase large volumes of mortgage loans. As long as mortgage bankers can persuade borrowers to pay the market interest rate for mortgage loans, availability is not a problem.

The key to forecasting mortgage market conditions is to accurately predict capital market rates by examining both the stage in the business cycle and the prospects for inflation. Because the prospects for inflation are most directly related to changes in the money supply, a projection of monetary policy shifts becomes most important.

Income Property Loans

The cost and availability of mortgage loans for income-producing properties depend upon capital market interest rates. Like FHA and VA loans, income property mortgages often reside in the portfolios of lenders with diversified capital market lending opportunities. Consequently, the loans must offer the investor an attractive yield to induce him to place his limited funds in particular income-producing properties rather than in some other capital market instrument. Forecasting these yields depends upon accurate predictions of the economy's progression through the business cycle as well as the changes in investors' inflationary expectations. Probably the best tool for both purposes is money supply changes over three–six-month periods.

The availability of an income property mortgage loan is keyed to the lender's evaluation of the market demand for the services of that property. If he judges that there is adequate market demand for the property and the borrower is willing to pay the market-determined interest rate, then the lender will advance the funds.

Regardless of the type of mortgage loan, whether it be a single-family, income property, or construction loan, *the key factors in the cost and availability of the mortgage money are money market and capital market interest rates.* Forecasting the former involves close attention to the Fed funds rate, and predicting the latter requires an examination of changes in the money supply over three six-month periods. Other factors also influence mortgage rates, but money market and capital market interest rates, along with changes in the business cycle, are the key determinants of the cost and availability of mortgage money.

THE SECONDARY MORTGAGE MARKET

Dennis J. Jacobe

*D*ENNIS J. JACOBE, PhD., Economist, United States League of Savings Associations, Chicago, Illinois.

Formerly associate professor of business and economics, New River Community College, Dublin, Virginia, and Arkansas College, Batesville, Arkansas. Author, Fact Book, 1975 *(Chicago: U.S. League of Savings Associations). Coauthor,* Tax Management for Savings and Loan Executives *(Institute of Financial Education, 1977);* Mortgage Portfolio Management *(U.S. League of Savings Associations, 1978); and* Economic Topics for Savings and Loan Management, *quarterly publication of Economics Department, United States League of Savings Associations, May 1975 to date. Author, "Money Market,"* Savings and Loan News, *monthly article, 1977 to date; "Federal Propensities to Spend and to Tax,"* Budgets and Bureaucrats, *1977; "Business and Real Estate,"* Savings and Loan News, *monthly article, 1974–77.*

The secondary *mortgage* market, like any other secondary market, is a place where loans—in this instance, mortgage loans—can be traded after they have been originated by primary lenders. In contrast, the primary mortgage market is a place where mortgage instruments are created and funds are provided to mortgage borrowers.

Mortgage trading has been a feature of our nation's mortgage market for many years. However, the development of what can truly be called a secondary mortgage market is a rather recent phenomenon. The objective of this chapter is to describe the operations and growth of the secondary mortgage market, the impact of the secondary mortgage market upon the primary mortgage market, and the role of the secondary mortgage market in national housing policy.

The Growth of the Secondary Mortgage Market

Few changes have had as significant an impact upon the mortgage market during recent years as has the growth of the secondary mortgage market. Exhibit 1 illustrates the spectacular nature of that growth. From 1970 to 1974, the secondary mortgage market grew at an average annual rate in excess of 16 percent; during the years 1974–78 it grew about twice as fast, an average annual increase of 32 percent.

EXHIBIT 1
Secondary Mortgage Market Growth, 1970–1978

Year	Total Purchases ($ billions)	Dollar Change ($ billions)	Annual Percent Increase	Cumulative Percent Increase
1970	$13.4			
1971	18.3	+$ 4.9	36.6%	36.6%
1972	25.1	+ 6.8	37.2	87.3
1973	22.6	− 2.5	−10.0	68.7
1974	23.0	+ 0.4	1.8	71.6
1975	31.9	+ 8.9	38.7	138.1
1976	42.8	+ 10.9	34.2	219.4
1977	55.0	+ 17.5	40.9	350.0
1978	62.0	+ 7.0	12.7	362.7

Sources: Federal Reserve Bank of Kansas City; U.S. Department of Housing and Urban Development; and U.S. League of Savings Associations.

The spectacular growth of the secondary mortgage market in the United States has its roots in the need for a mechanism to facilitate the transfer of funds from capital surplus to capital deficit areas of the country. During the past decade there has been a pronounced regionalism to economic growth. The so-called Sun Belt areas, such as the West and the South, have grown much more rapidly than other parts of the country.

Exhibit 2 shows two of the factors that are usually associated with economic growth: population growth and new housing starts. In each instance, the South and the West have been pronounced growth leaders. In contrast, the Northeast has clearly been lagging substantially.

EXHIBIT 2
Regional Economic Growth Rates

Growth Measure	South	West	Northeast	North Central
Population growth, 1970–78	9.2%	9.4%	1.0%	2.4%
Housing units built 1970–1978	21.0	20.0	8.6	11.4

Source: U.S. Department of Commerce.

As a result of these growth imbalances, some parts of the nation, such as California, often find themselves in a capital deficit position. Simultaneously, other parts, such as many of the New England states, have capital surpluses. This situation creates a need for the transfer of capital from some parts of the nation to other parts.

During the mid-1960s—prior to the imposition of savings rate ceilings which specify the maximum interest rates that commercial banks, savings and loan associations, and mutual savings banks can pay on savings accounts of less than $100,000—depository mortgage lenders that were unable to satisfy local mortgage demands could cure their funds deficit by increasing their interest rates on savings deposits. These institutions advertised in out-of-state markets to attract needed funds.

The California lending institutions were a well-known example of this process during the late 1950s and early 1960s. At that time, California was one of the fastest growing states in the country and the strongest building market. The local lending institutions, unable to satisfy the huge and growing demand for mortgage credit, advertised for out-of-state funds, offering interest rates on savings which were higher than those found in most other areas. As a result, a number of California lending institutions were able to attract out-of-state funds equal to 20 percent or more of their total savings balances. In this way, they were able to satisfy local mortgage market needs without massive sales of mortgages to out-of-state mortgage lenders.

The imposition of rate controls, however, effectively prevented financial institutions in capital deficit areas from paying higher rates for savings than were being paid in other parts of the country. As a result, significant pressures for increased mortgage trading developed.

Congress reacted to this pressure by providing major new inducements to the growth of the secondary mortgage market. Through the 1968 Housing and Urban Development Act, Congress privatized the Federal National Mortgage Association. In subsequent legislation it created the Federal Home Loan Mortgage Corporation and the Government National Mortgage Association. It also authorized new Farmers Home Administration mortgage programs. Most of these agencies are involved in purchasing mortgages from primary lenders. In addition, a number of these agencies created such new securities as the Government National Mortgage Association's pass-through security and the Federal Home Loan Mortgage Corporation's participation certificate. These actions increased the liquidity of mortgages and broadened the market for mortgage-related securities.

Actions by state governments also promoted the growth of the secondary mortgage market. By 1977, over 40 states had state housing authorities which purchased mortgages or provided funds for investment in mortgages by private institutions.

The Participants in the Secondary Mortgage Market

The major participants in the secondary mortgage market include savings and loan associations, mortgage bankers, mutual savings banks, commercial banks, life insurance companies, and federal credit agencies. Other investors, such as private pension funds, state and local credit agencies, and mortgage investment trusts, participate in the secondary mortgage market, but only in a small way.

Exhibit 3 shows that private sector participants have been the major secondary market purchasers during the 1970s. Over the period 1970–78, private sector purchases averaged $26.5 billion annually and represented 73.0 percent of total secondary mortgage market purchases. In contrast, purchases by federal credit agencies averaged $9.8 billion annually over the same period.

EXHIBIT 3
Mortgage Purchase, 1970–1978*

Year	Private Sector		Federal Credit Agency		Total Purchases
	$ Billions	Percent	$ Billions	Percent	
1970	$ 9.0	62.5%	$ 5.4	37.5%	$14.4
1971	15.6	79.6	4.0	20.4	19.6
1972	21.6	80.3	5.3	19.7	26.9
1973	16.6	67.2	8.1	32.8	24.7
1974	15.8	62.2	9.6	37.8	25.4
1975	22.4	65.1	12.0	34.9	34.4
1976	35.3	77.4	10.3	22.6	45.6
1977	52.0	82.0	11.4	18.0	63.4
1978	50.0	69.5	24.9	30.5	71.9
1970–78 average	$26.5	73.0%	$ 9.8	27.0%	$36.3

* Includes one–four-family and multifamily home mortgages.
Source: Department of Housing and Urban Development.

The Private Sector. Exhibit 4 shows that private participants accounted for 70 percent of all secondary market single-family mortgage loan purchases in 1978. The largest group of private purchasers were savings and loan associations, which accounted for $10.2 billion, or 16.6 percent, of single-family mortgage loan purchases in that year. Other active purchasers included mutual savings banks, with $2.8 billion in purchases, and mortgage bankers, with $3.1 billion in purchases. (Mortgage pools, which accounted for $23.2 billion of purchases, are mostly held by private market participants but are grouped together for statistical purposes.)

Private participants accounted for 85 percent of secondary mortgage market sales in 1978. The largest sellers were mortgage banking companies, whose sales totaled $27.8 billion. Other major sellers included savings and loan associations, with $15.0 billion in sales, and commercial banks, with $5.8 billion in sales.

Federal Credit Agencies. Several federal credit agencies participate in the secondary mortgage market. Exhibit 5 shows that over the period 1970–78 federal agencies as a group purchased single-family mortgages

EXHIBIT 4
Mortgage Purchases and Sales of Single-Family* Mortgage Loans for 1978

	Purchases		Sales	
Participants	$ Millions	Percent	$ Millions	Percent
Commercial banks	$ 1,481	2.4%	$ 5,819	9.8%
Mutual savings banks	2,802	4.5	290	0.5
Savings and loan associations	10,283	16.6	14,999	25.2
Life insurance companies...........	803	1.3	20	†
Private pension funds	177	0.3	15	†
Mortgage banking companies	3,130	5.0	27,846	46.7
Mortgage investment trusts	24	†	60	†
State and local retire- ment funds	390	0.6	49	†
Federal credit agencies	18,779	30.3	9,088	15.4
Mortgage pools	23,202	37.4	1,427	2.4
State and local credit agencies	945	1.6	9	†
Total	$62,015	100%	$59,622	100%

* One–four-family home mortgage loans.
† Less than 0.1 percent.
Source: Department of Housing and Urban Development.

totaling $11.7 billion annually and sold mortgages totaling $5.2 billion annually. The only year during this period that federal agencies were net sellers was 1976.

Of all the federal credit agencies the Federal National Mortgage Association (FNMA, or Fannie Mae) is the largest mortgage loan purchaser. Over the period 1970–78 this privately owned and sponsored institution made secondary market purchases averaging $4.8 billion annually. This represented 13 percent of the total secondary market mortgage purchases that were made during this period. At year-end 1978, 85 percent of Fannie Mae's mortgage holdings were federally insured.

Fannie Mae has the authority to sell the loans it purchases, but it

EXHIBIT 5
Federal Agency Purchases of Single Mortgage Loans: Yearly Average, 1970–1978

	Purchases		Sales		
Agency	$ Billions	Percent of Market	$ Billions	Percent of Market	Net Purchases (Sales) ($ billions)
FNMA	$ 4.8	13.2%	$0.0	0.0%	$4.8
GNMA	2.3	6.3	2.1	6.9	0.2
FHLMC..........	2.0	5.5	1.5	2.1	0.5
FmHA	0.6	1.6	1.6	8.1	(1.0)
Total	$11.7	32.2%	$5.2	21.1%	$6.5

Sources: Department of Housing and Urban Development; and Federal Reserve Board.

rarely does so. During the period 1970–78 its secondary market sales were insignificant.

The Federal Home Loan Mortgage Corporation (FHLMC, which is also known as Freddie Mac and as the Mortgage Corporation) is also active in the secondary mortgage market. Over the 1970–78 period Freddie Mac's single-family mortgage purchases averaged $2.0 billion annually and its single-family mortgage sales averaged $1.5 billion. Most FHLMC purchases involved conventional mortgages.

Two other federal agencies are active in the secondary mortgage market: the Government National Mortgage Association (GNMA, or Ginnie Mae) and the Farmers Home Administration (FmHA). Ginnie Mae had secondary market purchases averaging $2.3 billion and sales averaging $2.1 billion annually over the 1970–78 period. As a part of the Department of Housing and Urban Development, this agency has special secondary market functions which will be discussed later. The Farmers Home Administration uses the Federal Financing Bank for its secondary market activities.

Trading Instruments in the Secondary Mortgage Market

Exhibit 6 provides a summary of the primary participants in the secondary mortgage market and of the trading instruments used in that market. Essentially, three major types of transaction instruments exist in the secondary mortgage market: whole loans, mortgage-backed bonds, and mortgage pools. These transactions involve both federally insured mortgages (FHA/VA) and privately insured conventional loans.

Whole loan trades are usually made on a highly personal basis, and they frequently depend upon long- and well-established business relationships. Mortgage loan originators usually contact former customers or potential customers whom they have met informally. Trades are often conducted by telephone, with the potential buyer stating terms and the seller describing his loan. In many instances, buyers routinely review the loans they are buying, the underlying properties, and the seller's record keeping and servicing procedures.

Mortgage-backed bonds are more like typical bonds than are mortgage pools. They have set maturities, and they usually pay interest on a semi-annual basis. They are backed by a package of mortgages which provide the cash flow that supports bond interest payments. The underlying mortgage package provides the security base and the earning to support mortgage-backed bonds.

Of all the instruments traded in the secondary mortgage market, mortgage pools have been most responsible for the rapid growth of the secondary mortgage market during the 1970s. Because of the complexities of originating and servicing individual mortgage loans, many institutional investors, such as insurance companies and pension funds, found mortgage loan investments less appealing than the more marketable and more easily serviced corporate bonds, municipal bonds, stocks, and government bonds. As a result, efforts were made to develop securities backed or secured by mortgage loans which had the attributes of market-

EXHIBIT 6
Participants and Trading Instruments of the Secondary Mortgage Market

---

Participants

Private depository institutions
  Savings and loan associations
  Commercial banks
  Mutual savings banks
  Credit unions

Federal credit agencies
  Federal National Mortgage Association (FNMA)
  Federal Home Loan Mortgage Corporation (FHLMC)
  Government National Mortgage Association (GNMA)
  Farmers Home Administration (FmHA)

State agencies
  State housing finance agencies
  State mortgage finance agencies

Other private institutions
  Mortgage banking companies
  Life insurance companies
  Private and government pension funds
  Mortgage investment trusts
  Trust funds
  Bond brokerage firms

Trading Instruments

Whole mortgage loans
Private issue mortgage participations
GNMA pass-through securities
FHLMC participation certificates
FHLMC-guaranteed mortgage bonds
Private issue mortgage pass-through securities
Private issue Mortgage-backed bonds
Industrial development bonds

Source: *Mortgage Portfolio Management* (Chicago: U.S. League of Savings Associations, 1978).

ability, reinvestment ease, and minimal servicing requirements which appealed to such institutional lenders. Mortgage pools seem to be one generally accepted answer.

Mortgage pools are created by setting aside a group of mortgage loans and then selling shares in this group or pool of mortgages. Holders of pool securities receive the mortgage payments on the mortgages which the pool comprises. The pool originator generally handles the collecting and distributing of these mortgage payments as part of his mortgage-servicing function, for which he receives a fee.

A number of federal programs use federal credit agencies to sponsor mortgage pools. The most significant of these is the GNMA program which approves private originators who create a pool of FHA/VA mortgages totaling $1 million or more. The private originators do the servic-

EXHIBIT 7
The Dispersion of Major City Effective Mortgage Interest Rates on Newly Built Homes

	1965	1966	1967	1968*	1969*
National average (percent)	5.81	6.26	6.43	7.17	7.51
Average basis point difference between national average and 18 city averages	26	32	33	36	41
Average difference between the national average and each city average (percent)	4.5	5.1	5.1	5.0	5.5

Note: As of July of each year.
* The peaks in 1968–70 and 1974 were due mainly to usury law constraints in several states.
Source: Federal Home Loan Bank Board.

ing, and GNMA guarantees the payment of the interest and principal. As of year-end 1978 there were $41 billion of FNMA pass-throughs outstanding. The major holders of these securities were savings and loan associations, which held 25 percent, and mortgage and investment banks, which also held 25 percent.

The FHLMC also sponsors mortgage pools, its primary vehicle being the mortgage participation certificate (PC). With a participation the investor can purchase a percentage of a mortgage pool. Although this can range from 50 percent to 90 percent, the usual purchase is 85 percent of the outstanding mortgage pool principal balance. During the period 1971–78 almost $6 billion in participations were sold. More than 95 percent of these were purchased by savings and loan associations.

The Impact of the Secondary Mortgage Market on the Primary Mortgage Market

The rapid growth and the general acceptance of the secondary mortgage market has significantly influenced the way in which the primary mortgage market operates. The secondary market has had an impact on the mortgage instrument, the level and diversity of mortgage yields, and even the operating strategy of the mortgage lender. As a result of its impact on the primary mortgage market, the secondary mortgage market has proven highly beneficial to the mortgage borrower.

The Mortgage Instrument. One of the most important conditions for the development of a secondary mortgage market is that the credit instruments traded be very similar with respect to their risk characteristics and their other investment characteristics. Since the shares of common stock in any given company are identical, common stock meets this condition very well. Commercial and industrial bank loans, by contrast, do not generally satisfy this condition. As a result, the U.S. economy has a very efficient and active secondary market in common stocks and virtually no secondary market activity in commercial and industrial bank loans.

1970*	1971	1972	1973	1974*	1975	1976	1977	1978
8.49	7.66	7.56	7.87	8.96	8.89	8.99	8.80	9.30
50	26	24	21	31	20	19	22	18
5.9	3.4	3.2	2.7	3.5	2.2	2.1	2.3	1.9

On the surface, the typical mortgage contract would appear to be a less than satisfactory candidate for secondary market trading since the typical mortgage is secured by a unique piece of real property. The value of this security is a key determinant of the risk associated with any particular mortgage asset.

Initially, the problems created by the lack of mortgage loan homogeneity were overcome by the National Housing Act of 1934, which created the Federal Housing Administration (FHA). This government instrumentality provided an insurance service for certain types of mortgage loans. The Servicemen's Readjustment Act of 1944 created another homogeneous mortgage instrument, the Veterans Administration (VA)–guaranteed mortgage. The combination of a standard contract and federal insurance permitted FHA and VA mortgages to meet most of the standardization requirements of a secondary market. As a result, FHA and VA mortgages paved the way for widespread mortgage trading.

As the years passed, greater efforts were made to standardize the conventional mortgage contract. Both FNMA and FHLMC developed standard mortgage loan applications for the conventional mortgage. They also developed credit-screening guidelines for the purchase of conventional mortgages.

At the same time, private mortgage insurance (PMI) companies such as the Mortgage Guaranty Insurance Corporation (MGIC) developed. These companies provided the conventional mortgage with private insurance. The net result was the development of a nearly standardized privately insured conventional mortgage contract which met the needs of the secondary mortgage market.

In sum, the trading requirements of the secondary market have produced a virtually standardized set of mortgage contracts. This makes it much easier for the mortgage borrower to compare the contract terms offered by many different mortgage lenders.

The Mortgage Yield. The secondary mortgage market has also had a substantial impact on both the diversity and the level of mortgage rates across the United States. The increased tendency of lenders to buy and sell mortgages has produced a convergence of mortgage rates toward a national norm. This is evidenced by Exhibit 7, which shows

EXHIBIT 8
Yield Spreads among Home Mortgages, Income Property Mortgages, and Corporate Bonds

	(1) Effective Conventional Mortgage Rate on New Homes	(2) Contract Rate on Insurance Company Income Properties	(3) Yield on New Issues of High-Grade Corporate Bonds	Yield Spreads		
				Between Home Mortgage Rate and Income Property Rate (1)−(2)	Between Home Mortgage Rate and Bond Rate (1)−(3)	Between Income Property Rate and Bond Rate (2)−(3)
1963	5.84	5.90	4.34	−0.06	1.50	1.56
1964	5.78	5.90	4.47	−0.12	1.31	1.43
1965	5.74	5.94	4.61	−0.20	1.13	1.33
1966	6.25	6.54	5.67	−0.29	0.58	0.87
1967	6.46	6.97	6.08	−0.51	0.38	0.89
1968	6.97	7.68	6.84	−0.71	0.13	0.84
1969	7.81	8.79	8.06	−0.98	−0.25	0.73
1970	8.45	9.92	9.05	−1.47	−0.60	0.87
1971	7.74	9.08	7.85	−1.34	−0.11	1.24
1972	7.60	8.57	7.59	−0.97	0.01	0.99
1973	7.95	N/A	7.89	N/A	0.06	N/A
1974	8.92	10.30	9.42	−1.38	−0.50	0.88
1975	9.01	9.95	9.50	−0.94	−0.49	0.45
1976	8.99	9.20	8.59	−0.21	0.40	0.61
1977	9.01	9.90	8.23	−0.89	0.78	1.67
1978	9.54	10.20	9.11	−0.66	0.43	1.09

Source: Federal Home Loan Bank Board; American Life Insurance Association; and U.S. Department of Commerce.

the dispersion of effective mortgage interest rates on newly built homes in major cities from 1965 through 1978. It is obvious from the exhibit that the relative variance of mortgage rates arïnd the national average has decreased significantly in recent years. During the 1970s, mortgage rates throughout the country have conformed more closely than ever before to the national mortgage rate average. That is, the secondary market has made the mortgage market a more "national" market.

The impact of the secondary market on mortgage rates is also reflected in relative mortgage yields. The yields on single-family mortgages have declined over the past decade relative to the yields on other long-term interest rates. Exhibit 8 suggests that the heavy investment in single-family mortgages by government agencies has helped to decrease significantly the spread between corporate bonds and new single-family mortgages. In the early to mid-1960s the spread between corporate bond rates and mortgage rates was over 1 percent in favor of mortgages. In contrast, during the late 1960s and early 1970s that spread has actually been negative—that is, high-grade corporate bonds have at times yielded more than mortgages.

In sum, the secondary mortgage market has produced a relatively more uniform or national mortgage rate and the activities of federal credit agencies in the secondary market have kept mortgage rates relatively lower than they would have been otherwise. As a result, the mortgage borrower has benefited not only from a relatively lower mortgage rate but also from an absence of regional barriers to lower mortgage interest rates.

The Mortgage Lender. From the viewpoint of the mortgage portfolio manager, the growth of secondary mortgage market activity has significantly influenced the operating strategy of his institution and its role in its local markets. One of the more obvious aspects of that influence is the new willingness of financial intermediaries to act as mortgage bankers. Savings and loan associations, commercial banks, and mutual savings banks located in capital deficit areas respond to large local demands for credit by selling loans to government agencies or other investors. Thus these financial intermediaries benefit from the origination and servicing fees usually associated with the mortgage banking business. Frequently, the marginal cost of additional originations and servicing is sufficently low to produce a favorable return for the mortgage lender.

The growing willingness of mortgage lenders to participate in the secondary mortgage market is evidenced by Exhibit 9, which shows the total volume of loans closed and loans and participations purchased by insured savings and loan associations from 1960 through 1978. The exhibit shows that the proportion of mortgage loans acquired by savings and loan associations in the secondary mortgage market from 1970 through 1978 ranged between 13.0 percent and 17.5 percent of their total loans closed.

This new attitude on the part of mortgage lenders has greatly benefited mortgage borrowers in capital deficit areas. By means of their frequent use of the secondary mortgage market, mortgage lenders in such

EXHIBIT 9
Mortgage Loans Closed and Purchased by Insured Savings and Loan Associations
($ millions)

Year	Loans Closed	Loans and Participations Purchased	Total Loans Acquired	Purchases as Percent of Total Loans Acquired
1960	$ 13,802	$ 851	$ 14,653	5.8%
1961	16,835	1,377	18,212	7.6
1962	20,220	1,588	21,808	7.3
1963	24,180	2,326	26,506	8.8
1964	23,980	2,198	26,178	8.4
1965	23,309	2,385	25,694	9.3
1966	16,323	1,186	17,509	6.8
1967	19,448	2,112	21,560	9.8
1968	21,298	2,332	23,630	9.9
1969	21,169	2,331	23,500	9.9
1970	20,760	3,745	24,505	15.3
1971	38,341	7,529	45,870	16.4
1972	50,024	10,612	60,636	17.5
1973	48,193	7,229	55,422	13.0
1974	38,050	5,904	43,954	13.4
1975	53,799	8,544	62,343	13.7
1976	77,103	12,799	89,902	14.2
1977	105,287	14,497	119,784	12.1
1978	108,273	10,984	119,257	9.2

Source: Federal Home Loan Bank Board.

areas have been able to provide funds for many borrowers whom they would not have been able to serve otherwise.

The Role of the Secondary Mortgage Market in National Housing Policy

As was mentioned at the beginning of this chapter, the secondary mortgage market performs the same function as any other secondary market. That is, it provides a place in which investors can buy loans and originators can sell loans—mortgage loans. In this way, the secondary mortgage market permits mortgage money to flow freely from capital surplus areas to capital deficit areas.

The participation of federal credit agencies in the secondary mortgage market not only facilitates this flow of mortgage money, but also substantially broadens the role of the secondary mortgage market with respect to our nation's housing policy. Ideally, the participation of federal credit agencies in the secondary mortgage market could be utilized to stabilize the primary mortgage market. That is, federal credit agencies could buy loans during periods of tight money and sell loans as monetary conditions ease. During the 1970s, however, Congress showed a preference for using the secondary market participation of federal credit agencies to subsidize mortgage interest rates rather than promote housing stability.

Housing Goals. The 1949 Housing Act called for "a decent home and a suitable living environment for every American family." During the 1960s, that objective was translated into specific production goals. In 1969, the nation's housing production goal was set at approximately 26 million new units over the next decade and a production schedule was established. In 1970, the goal was revised to 25.5 million new units

EXHIBIT 10
Housing Goal Attainment

Units (000)

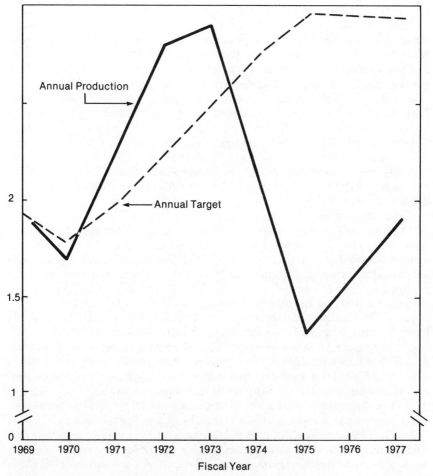

Fiscal Year

Source: Committee on Banking, Housing, and Urban Affairs, U.S. Senate; and Federal Reserve Board.

and 1.0 million publicly subsidized, rehabilitated units. Since then, a number of studies of our nation's housing needs have come up with estimates ranging from 22 million to 29 million new units over ten years.

On a cumulative basis, the attainment of the 1970 production schedule was fairly good between fiscal 1969 and 1975. The cumulative target for 1975 was 16.3 million new units, and 15.2 million new units were produced. As of fiscal 1975, the nation had achieved 93 percent of its target for the period 1969–75. Exhibit 10 shows, however, that this success was not achieved in a stable, healthy manner. In fiscal 1971, production was 13 percent over target, and this was followed by a 25 percent overshot in 1972 and a 15 percent overshot in 1973. Then, in 1974 production fell to 23 percent below the target set and in fiscal 1975 it fell to 55 percent below the target set. In 1976 and 1977, housing production increased substantially. In fact, by 1977, housing production had once again approached the 2.0 million new unit level. Still, even this high production rate left the nation far behind its housing goals.

The Activities of Federal Credit Agencies. The sharp fluctuations in housing market activity during the early 1970s clearly indicate that the secondary market activities of federal credit agencies have produced neither mortgage market stability nor housing market stability. Still, those activities have been aimed in a stabilizing direction. Exhibit 11 shows that the Federal Home Loan Mortgage Corporation and the Federal National Mortgage Association greatly increased their mortgage holdings during the poor housing year of 1973–74 and reduced those holdings drastically as housing improved during 1975–77. In other words, they acted countercyclically. As the private mortgage market contracts, stability requires that federal credit agencies increase their relative mortgage market share. Exhibit 12 shows that the FHLMC and FNMA did this during 1973–77.

Tandem Programs. During the early 1970s the federal government utilized several agencies to subsidize housing credit through its tandem programs. The tandem plan was originated during 1969 in response to a need to provide mortgage financing for the subsidized FHA 235 and 236 housing programs. Using the National Housing Act, the president authorized the Government National Mortgage Association to purchase subsidized housing mortgages at par or at modest discounts.

As GNMA issues a commitment to purchase a mortgage, it arranges a sale by simultaneously obtaining a commitment from the Federal National Mortgage Association to purchase the mortgage at the free market price. The loss (the difference between what GNMA pays and what it gets from FNMA) is absorbed by GNMA. The tandem or piggyback process acts to minimize the impact of tandem programs on the federal budget balance because the loss is absorbed by GNMA and is not classified as a federal budgetary item but rather as an off-budget item.

In 1971, the tandem program was extended to FHA mortgages insured under unsubsidized programs and to VA-guaranteed mortgages. During 1974, a further extension of the tandem concept permitted GNMA to purchase conventional mortgages. The tandem programs grew rapidly between 1971 and 1974. From 1971 to 1973, GNMA extended new-home

EXHIBIT 11
Net Changes in Mortgages Held by Federal Credit Agencies

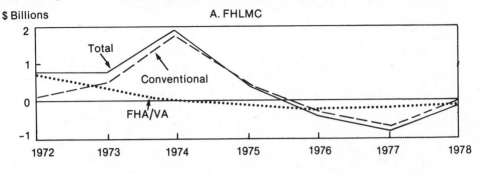

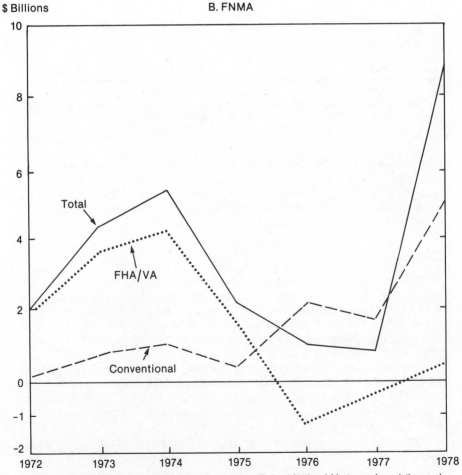

Sources: Federal Home Loan Mortgage Corporation; Federal National Mortgage Association; and Federal Reserve Board.

EXHIBIT 12
The Annual Change in FHLMC and FNMA Mortgage Holdings as a Percentage
of the Total Annual Increase in Residential Mortgages

Percent

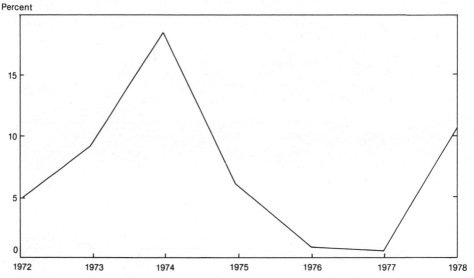

Source: Federal National Mortgage Association; Federal Home Loan Mortgage Corporation; Federal Home Loan Bank Board; Federal Reserve Board; and U.S. League of Savings Associations.

commitments of $0.8 billion. By contrast, GNMA made $7 billion in new commitments in 1974 alone.

The tandem programs have proven to be a favorite of Congress. They permit federal subsidization of mortgage rates without requiring federal budget expenditure increases.

Summary

The secondary mortgage market experienced spectacular growth during the 1970s. This was the result not only of a great need for a freer flow of mortgage money, but also of congressional actions in response to that need. The creation of new federal credit agencies and innovations in secondary market instruments have substantially increased the viability of the secondary mortgage market.

Major participants in the secondary mortgage market include savings and loan associations, mortgage bankers, mutual savings banks, commercial banks, life insurance companies, and federal credit agencies. The types of secondary mortgage transactions include whole loan trades, mortgage-backed bonds, and mortgage pools.

The secondary mortgage market has influenced the primary mortgage market significantly. It has increased the standardization of the mortgage contract, reduced the diversity of local mortgage rates, produced relatively lower mortgage rates, and made mortgage lenders willing to act as mortgage bankers. All of these changes have benefited the mortgage borrower.

Finally, the secondary mortgage market has played a role in national housing policy. Although the activities of federal mortgage credit agencies in the secondary mortgage market have not produced housing stability, those activities have been in the proper direction. Further, Congress has utilized those agencies to subsidize mortgage rates without increasing federal budget expenditures.

SELECTED REFERENCES

Brockschmidt, Peggy. "The Secondary Market for Home Mortgages." *Monthly Review,* Federal Reserve Bank of Kansas City, September–October 1977, pp. 11–20.

Department of Commerce. *Housing Starts.* Washington, D.C.: U.S. Government Printing Office, 1975. Pp. 4 and 6.

Estimates of Housing Needs, 1975–1980. Prepared for the use of the U.S. Senate Committee on Banking, Housing, and Urban Affairs. Washington, D.C.: U.S. Government Printing Office, 1975. Pp. 2–4.

Grebler, Leo. "The Role of the Public Sector in Residential Financing." In *Resources for Housing,* proceedings of the First Annual Conference. San Francisco: Federal Home Loan Bank of San Francisco, 1975. Pp. 67–116.

Jacobe, Dennis J., and Thygerson, Kenneth J. *Fiscal Policy and Housing.* Working Paper no. 8. Chicago: U.S. League of Savings Associations, 1975.

The Mortgage Corporation and the Secondary Mortgage Market. Monograph Series no. 5. Washington, D.C.: Mortgage Corporation, 1977.

Shenkel, William M. *Modern Real Estate Principles.* Dallas, Tex.: Business Publications, Inc., 1977. Pp. 306–31.

Thygerson, Kenneth J. *The Cost of Overspecialization in the Mortgage Market.* Working Paper no. 12. Chicago: U.S. League of Savings Associations, 1973. Pp. 11–13.

Thygerson, Kenneth J. and Jacobe, Dennis J. *Mortgage Portfolio Management.* Chicago: U.S. League of Savings Associations, 1978.

Von Furstenberg, George M. "The Economics of the $16 Billion Tandem Mortgages Committed in the Current Housing Slump." Unpublished. Bloomington: Indiana University (no date). P. 1.

SELLING MORTGAGES

Richard G. Marcis

*R*ICHARD G. MARCIS, PhD, Deputy Director, Office of Economic
Research, Federal Home Loan Bank Board, Washington, D.C.

Formerly senior economist, Federal National Mortgage Association, Washington, D.C.; associate professor of economics,
Bowling Green State University, Bowling Green, Ohio; staff co-director, Alternative Mortgage Instruments Research Study; instructor, School of Mortgage Banking, Notre Dame University;
and lecturer, Savings Institutions Marketing School, University
of Wisconsin. Author of articles on monetary policy and housing
and mortgage financing in such publications as Journal of Financial and Quantitative Analysis; Quarterly Review of Economics and Business; Metroeconomica; Journal of Finance;
Western Economic Association Journal; Journal of Money,
Credit and Banking; Review of Economics and Statistics; Journal
of Business; Journal of Regional Science; and Journal of Decision Sciences.

Selling mortgages is big business in the United States, and getting
bigger. In 1978, sales of residential mortgage loans in the United States
totaled approximately $64 billion, a more than four-fold increase in the
dollar volume of such transactions since 1970.

Activity in the secondary mortgage market (i.e., the resale market
for mortgages) is dependent to some extent on the volume of mortgages
originated in the primary market, which is, in turn, determined essentially by the flow of savings to mortgage-lending institutions. Thus, over
time changes in primary mortgage market activity have been reflected
in similar changes in secondary mortgage market activity.

The sensitivity of mortgage sales to primary market origination activity is due to the fact that depository thrift institutions are the largest
originator of mortgages as well as the largest purchaser of mortgages
in the secondary market. Although some progress has been made in

recent years in attracting non-mortgage-oriented investors to the mortgage market, depository thrift institutions remain the primary source of demand for mortgages in the secondary market, and their willingness and ability to purchase mortgages is, in the aggregate, determined to a large extent by the same set of conditions that influences their ability to originate mortgages.

Despite the dependence of mortgage sales on primary mortgage market activity, the two markets do not necessarily move in tandem and they have frequently diverged in terms of relative activity. For example, the ratio of sales of residential mortgages to originations declined between 1970 and 1973 as mortgage origination activity expanded rapidly and outpaced mortgage sales. This ratio began rising in 1974 as the volume of mortgage originations declined, and it continued to rise in 1975 even though home mortgage originations increased from 1974 levels. The ratio of mortgage sales to originations subsequently declined in 1976, and it continued to decline in 1977, as originations of residential mortgages increased substantially and outpaced the increase in residential mortgage sales.

Thus, although the general levels of sale activity and origination activity are related, the relative levels of activity will frequently diverge. These differences are attributable to differences in regional sources and uses of funds and regional mortgage rates and to changes in the attractiveness of mortgages and mortgage-related securities relative to the attractiveness of other investment alternatives.

Before examining the mechanisms available for selling home mortgage loans, it may be well to examine briefly why lenders sell mortgages. There are essentially two reasons: (1) profit motivation and (2) liquidity considerations. Many mortgage lenders find that they can commit for, originate, and sell mortgages profitably. Although some mortgage originators find it financially advantageous to sell mortgages only at particular points in the interest rate cycle, others, such as mortgage bankers, routinely originate mortgages not in order to add the mortgages to their portfolio but in order to sell the mortgages. The sources of profit from selling mortgages include the income derived from commissions and fees for originating mortgages, the income received for "servicing" sold mortgages, and the profits received from selling mortgages at yields that provide an excess over the total costs of extending the mortgage loan.

Mortgages are also sold because mortgage originators need cash. The secondary market enables mortgage holders to obtain cash by selling the mortgages to other investors.

This chapter will review and assess the procedures for selling residential mortgages and the market for such mortgages. Mortgage sales may be classified into three different categories: (1) private market transactions, (2) the transactions of federally assisted agencies and (3) transactions in mortgage-related securities. Each of these categories will be discussed below, and the discussion will be followed by a brief analysis of the factors which influence the alternative selected by a mortgage seller.

The Government-Assisted Secondary Mortgage Market

The three principal federally assisted agencies to which residential mortgages may be sold are the Federal National Mortgage Association (FNMA), the Federal Home Loan Mortgage Corporation (FHLMC), and the Government National Mortgage Association (GNMA). Sales of mortgages to these institutions account for 20 to 40 percent of all the residential mortgages sold in the United States in a given year. However, those mortgage sales have a distinctly cyclic flavor in that the mortgage-purchasing activity of the government-assisted agencies increases dramatically in periods of high interest rates and reduced credit availability, when there are fewer demands for residential mortgages from the private sector. Thus, the government-assisted agencies purchased approximately 40 percent of all residential mortgages sold in the United States in 1970 and 1974. On the other hand, purchases by the agencies generally diminish when interest rates are declining and credit is readily available, as was true in 1972, 1976, and 1977.

Each of the three agencies buys residential mortgages from lenders who have originated mortgages, so that none of the agencies lend directly to the general public. None of them do any servicing of the single-family mortgages they purchase (i.e., collect monthly payments from mortgagors, escrow insurance funds, taxes, etc.), but instead the agencies pay a fee for servicing by the originator (usually one half to three eighths of 1 percent of the principal mortgage amount outstanding).

Although all three agencies were created for the basic purpose of buying or facilitating the sale of mortgages, the commitment/purchase programs of GNMA may be differentiated from those of FNMA and FHLMC. GNMA is a federal agency, and the borrowings it uses to purchase residential mortgages are reflected in the federal budget. FNMA is a private stockholder-owned corporation, and FHLMC is under the direction of the Federal Home Loan Bank Board.

Thus, these institutions have different approaches to providing secondary mortgage market support which are reflected in their commitment, purchase, and sale programs. FNMA and FHLMC supplement the secondary market for residential mortgages by buying mortgages originated by primary lenders, especially in periods in which less credit is available for the purchase of mortgages from other private investors. They thereby improve the marketability of mortgage loans, improve the regional distribution of mortgage credit, and increase the availability of funds for financing the construction and sale of housing.

GNMA, on the other hand, purchases mortgages in order to provide support for types of housing for which financing is not readily available, such as housing for low-income families, and to counter declines in mortgage lending and housing construction. The GNMA commitment/purchase programs implement specific federal housing policy initiatives and budgetary funding authorization. Thus, the mortgages purchased by GNMA are subsidized to some extent in either the interest rate or the mortgagor's income and can therefore be treated differently from those of FNMA and FHLMC.

All three agencies have a variety of commitment/purchase programs for residential mortgages whose requirements have been altered in response to changing market conditions and requirements. The following dicusssion highlights the major commitment/purchase programs and the basic procedures of the agencies for committing for and purchasing residential mortgages.

Federal National Mortgage Association. FNMA is the oldest and largest of the federally assisted secondary market institutions. Primarily a purchaser of FHA/VA mortgages, it began to purchase conventional mortgages in 1972, under authorization granted by the Emergency Home Finance Act of 1970. At year-end 1978, FNMA had a mortgage portfolio of $43.3 billion, which consisted of $31.8 billion in FHA/VA loans and $11.5 billion in conventional loans.

FNMA is a federally chartered but privately owned and managed corporation. Originally organized in 1938 as a corporation wholly owned and administered by the federal government, under the Housing and Urban Development Act of 1968 FNMA assumed responsibility for its own management and became a stockholder-owned private corporation in 1970. FNMA finances its operations primarily through the issuance of debentures and short-term discount notes. In addition, FNMA has issued mortgage-backed bonds, capital debentures, and convertible capital debentures.

The basic FNMA commitment/purchase program is the free market system (FMS) commitment auction. Initiated in 1968, the FMS commitment auction has become FNMA's principal vehicle for the purchase of single-family mortgages. The auction originated from the idea that the prices or yields for mortgage purchases should be determined by a bidding and acceptance process. The successful bidders in the auction receive commitments from FNMA to purchase mortgages offered under those commitments for a four-month period. The delivery of the mortgages within the four-month commitment period is at the discretion of the seller. The auction of forward commitments assures a seller of a ready buyer for its mortgages at a specific yield. This enables home builders and mortgage originators to plan their future activities in the assurance that financing will be available.

In order to bid in the FMS auction, bidders must be qualified as eligible mortgage sellers and must have executed an appropriate selling agreement with FNMA. A qualified seller wishing to make a bid to sell mortgages telephones FNMA on the day of the auction and specifies its bid amount and the amount that it will accept on the package of loans it is offering.

At the close of the auction, FNMA determines the lowest yield that it will accept and every seller that has submitted a bid yield above this minimum is accepted. FMS auctions are usually held biweekly, and simultaneous but separate auctions are held for conventional mortgages and FHA/VA mortgages. Sellers that need to obtain commitments and do not want to take the chance that their bids will be rejected can make noncompetitive offers which are automatically accepted at the average yield of all accepted offers.

FNMA also buys mortgages on single-family properties outside the auction system via "convertible standby commitments." These are 12-month commitments to purchase mortgages which may involve proposed or existing construction. Because of the risk of interest rate changes during the 12-month term, the yield required on these mortgages is not determined through auction but through the posting of administratively determined yield requirements. These yield requirements are related to FMS auction yields, adjusted for future assumed interest rate risks.

After the first four months, the commitment can be converted by the holder to the yield obtained at the most recent FMS auction. Thus, the convertible standby commitment gives the lender the security of a firm 12-month commitment with the option of taking advantage of any improvements in market conditions as reflected in the FMS auction rates.

Other FNMA mortgage commitment/purchase programs have recently become available. The conventional multifamily program involves buying conventional mortgages on two–four-family dwellings. FNMA also has a program for purchasing individual units in condominiums and planned unit developments, and it has been streamlining its purchase requirements under this program to make approval of such projects less time consuming and less costly to sellers. FNMA also has an urban participation program involving 60–90 percent participation by FNMA in pools of one–four-family conventionally financed properties located in specifically designated urban areas.

FNMA purchases most of its mortgages from mortgage bankers. Of FNMA purchases in 1978, for example, 85 percent were from mortgage companies and about 6 percent from commerical banks and trust companies. Savings and loan associations, the primary originator of residential mortgage loans, only sold 6 percent of the mortgages purchased by FNMA.

FNMA finances its mortgage purchase programs through portfolio income and through the issuance of long- and short-term obligations in the money and capital markets. In this aspect of its operations, FNMA differs significantly from FHLMC, which finances its operations primarily through the sale of mortgages. Thus, although FNMA sells mortgages periodically, it is primarily an accumulator of mortgages. Its portfolio of mortgage holdings has grown steadily as it has continued to buy more mortgages than it has sold.

The Federal Home Loan Mortgage Corporation.   In July 1970, by an act of Congress, FHLMC was created as a corporation under the general direction of the Federal Home Loan Bank Board. FHLMC has attempted to improve the marketability of mortgage instruments so as to enable mortgage lenders to more easily sell loans and obtain additional funds to meet mortgage demand and to marshal and redirect funds from outside the thrift industry into mortgage lending.

Unlike FNMA, which emphasizes FHA/VA mortgage activity, FHLMC has focused almost exclusively on conventional mortgage loans in its recent secondary market operations. For example, in 1978, FHLMC committed to purchase $7.5 billion in mortgages, almost all of which was for conventional loans.

FHLMC encountered several obstacles in its attempts to foster development of a viable secondary market for conventional mortgages in the early 1970s. Unlike the terms and documentation of FHA/VA mortgages, conventional loan terms and documentation differ markedly among lenders, especially among lenders in different states. Moreover, since no standard procedure existed for underwriting conventional loans or for making appraisals of property, FHLMC could not purchase conventional loans on a volume basis. Consequently, FHLMC developed standardized documents for use by mortgage originators that intended to sell loans to it.

FHLMC also developed a computerized underwriting matrix to facilitate the purchase of single-family conventional loans. The underwriting matrix permits the evaluation of a large number of loans in a minimum amount of time while assuring that the loans purchased are of investment quality. This matrix was the first attempt to standardize underwriting guidelines and to develop a standard of quality for the purchase of conventional mortgages.

The mortgage commitment/purchase programs of FHLMC differ from those of FNMA in two significant respects. (1) Although FHLMC has recently implemented an auction process for the issuance of six- and eight-month commitments, most of the mortgages purchased by FHLMC are made via an immediate delivery program, with the delivery of loans mandatory for the seller, whereas FNMA purchases most of its mortgages through commitments issued at market-determined auction rates, with the delivery of mortgages at the option of the seller. (2) FHLMC purchases mortgages on a participation basis (as opposed to a "whole loan" basis), where the seller retains a percentage interest in the loans sold to FHLMC. With the few exceptions (such as its experimental urban purchase program), FNMA purchases only whole loans.

FHLMC commits for and purchases mortgages under a variety of programs that allow for delivery of whole loans or participations on an immediate or forward delivery basis. FHLMC purchases single family whole loans and participations primarily through its weekly auction, which requires mandatory delivery within sixty days. Noncompetitive offers are also available at the average weighted yield of the current week's auction.

Commitments to buy single family loans are also available through FHLMC's six month and eight month forward commitment programs. Delivery is optional under both programs, and sellers are required to pay a fee for the commitment. Auctions for both forward commitment programs are held monthly and minimum and maximum offer requirements are imposed. Under any of these single family programs, FHLMC will purchase either the entire loan, or a participation of between 50–95 percent of the outstanding principal balance.

FHLMC commits to purchase multifamily loans through an administered price program under which offers are received weekly. Whole loans and participations may be sold under the multifamily program, which requires mandatory delivery within sixty days. Prior approval is available for specifically approved sellers.

For both the whole loan and the participation programs, FHLMC periodically adjusts the yield at which the mortgages will be purchased. These yield requirements are published regularly in various newspapers and journals. For these programs, no commitment fees are charged sellers who are members of the Federal Home Loan Bank System.

In 1976, FHLMC introduced a forward commitment program that was similar in major respects to the FMS commitment auction of the FNMA. The forward commitment program offers lenders a six-month commitment for the purchase of mortgages, with delivery at the option of the commitment holder. As with the FMS auction, the commitment rate under this program is determined by an auction. The FHLMC program also resembles the FMS auction procedure in that FHLMC accepts noncompetitive bids to sell conventional home mortgages at yields equaling the weighted average of the offers accepted under competitive bidding, but only from sellers who do not participate in the competitive bidding.

FHLMC buys mortgages and mortgage participations from insured depository institutions, principally S&Ls. In 1978, FHLMC was authorized to purchase mortgages from mortgage bankers, effective June, 1979.

FHLMC operations are financed primarily through the sale of mortgages via mortgage-backed participation certificates (PCs) and, to a more limited extent, through the sales of guaranteed mortgage certificates (GMCs). In 1976 and 1977, FHLMC funded its mortgage purchase activity almost exclusively through the sale of PCs.

The Government National Mortgage Association. GNMA's background and history are closely intertwined with that of FNMA. Under the Housing and Urban Development Act of 1968, FNMA was partitioned into two separate corporations, each of which assumed a portion of the original FNMA's functions. One of the corporations retained the name FNMA and became a private institution owned and financed by stockholders. It continued to perform the secondary market operations that were designed to provide supplementary assistance to the private residential mortgage market by providing liquidity for residential mortgages.

The other corporation, which became known as GNMA, remained in the Department of Housing and Urban Development. It assumed those mortgage market activities of the original FNMA that could not be carried out economically by the private sector: (1) special assistance that was designed to provide financing for special housing programs and to ease the effects of unfavorable economic conditions on the housing markets; and (2) servicing and disposing of the then existing mortgage portfolio. The newly created GNMA became an agency of the federal government, operating within the Department of Housing and Urban Development, with the secretary of HUD determining its general policies.

The secondary mortgage market operations of GNMA involve two main functions: (1) committing for and purchasing at market prices mortgages with below-market interest rates and then selling those mortgages at competitive rates to investors in the private market; and (2) administering the GNMA mortgage-backed securities program of guaranteeing timely payment of principal and interest on privately issued securities backed by pools of FHA/VA mortgages.

The GNMA mortgage-backed pass-through securities program has been tremendously successful, with over $67 billion in such securities having been issued by year-end 1978. GNMA does not actually issue these securities, but merely acts as a guarantor of the timely payment of principal and interest on securities issued by private originators, primarily mortgage bankers. Since it is the private lender's responsibility to originate and service the mortgages, these securities will be discussed later.

GNMA's direct secondary market programs involve committing for and purchasing mortgages for certain special categories of low- to moderate-income housing during periods when credit is relatively less available from private sources. Mortgages at below-market interest rates are purchased by GNMA at market prices. GNMA then sells the loans purchased, generally at auction, to investors in the private market at competitive market rates. The discounts involved in these purchase/sale operations are borne by the federal government, which thereby furthers the construction of the type of housing being financed.

GNMA's commitments to purchase mortgages at market prices enable lenders to make commitments for permanent mortgage financing to builders and developers. The permanent financing (or takeout) commitment from GNMA enables lenders to obtain the interim funds necessary to finance construction.

GNMA's commitments for mortgage purchases are sufficiently long term to include the entire construction period. The GNMA commitment is one year for one–four-family programs and two or three years for multifamily programs. The commitments are optional delivery commitments, which means that lenders have the option of delivering or not delivering a mortgage to GNMA under an existing commitment. If a lender chooses not to deliver, his only liability is the payment of a commitment fee.

Before 1974, GNMA committed/purchased only FHA/VA mortgages. Subsequently GNMA initiated the purchase of conventional mortgages under authorization granted by the Emergency Home Purchase Assistance Act of 1974. Lenders participating in GNMA FHA/VA programs must be HUD/FHA-approved sellers, and lenders participating in GNMA's conventional mortgage programs must be FNMA- or FHLMC-approved sellers.

The specific mortgage purchase programs of GNMA change to reflect changes in federal housing policy objectives and budgetary funding authorizations. For each program, GNMA specifies requirements in terms of the mortgage type (FHA, VA, or conventional); the type of structure (single-family or multifamily); specific locational requirements, if any; and such other requirements as the maximum interest rates on the loans, the maximum dollar amount of mortgages, and the commitment period.

GNMA has provided substantial support to the housing market and has administered housing support programs which could not be carried out in the private market.

The Private Secondary Mortgage Market

This sector encompasses all mortgage transactions that do not involve a government-assisted institution as either a buyer or a seller of mortgages. In this sector, mortgages are sold to private investors, either in the open market, directly through "brokers," or directly through personal contacts determined by established business relationships.

Excluding sales of mortgages via mortgage-backed securities, about 50 percent of all mortgage sales involve private lenders and investors. However, as was indicated previously, this percentage can vary dramatically with changing interest rates and changing financial conditions. Transactions in the private secondary mortgage market decline sharply in periods of high interest rates and reduced credit availability (when activity by the federally assisted agencies increases) and increases in periods of low interest rates, when credit from private investors is generally available.

Although mortgage-backed securities, both GNMAs and conventional pass-through securities issued by private lenders, technically fall into the private secondary mortgage market, the techniques and procedures involved in the sale of mortgage assets via mortgage-related securities are sufficiently different from those involved in whole loan or participation transactions to merit separate treatment below.

The Efficiency of Private Sector Mortgage Transactions. As has been indicated, until recent years there was no private national secondary market of any depth and breadth for conventional mortgages. A national private secondary market for mortgages existed only for FHA/VA mortgages, with sales of conventional residential mortgages existing only on a very limited basis, primarily among sellers-investors in the same geographic area and among sellers-investors with long-established correspondent relationships.

Uniform documentation and underwriting standards and government insurance or guarantees facilitate the trading of FHA/VA loans. The greater standardization of FHA/VA mortgages facilitates the "pooling" of individual mortgages into packages of mortgages for sale to investors. The federal government guarantee or insurance on the mortgages enhances the marketability of FHA/VA mortgages, since it eliminates the need of investors to undertake an elaborate inquiry into the creditworthiness of the issuer and the instrument.

Despite the greater volume of conventional mortgages in the primary market, conventional loans have historically possessed more limited marketability than have FHA/VA loans. Because they lacked standardization—since they were originated by different lenders with different standards and procedures—conventional mortgages were relatively unmarketable until recently. There was no efficient method of evaluating the investment quality of individual mortgages, and trading in these instruments was therefore handicapped.

However, several recent developments have enhanced the marketability of conventional residential mortgages. There has been some increases in the standardization of conventional mortgage loan terms and conditions, primarily as a result of the initiatives of FNMA and FHLMC in developing a standardized mortgage loan document.

The growing use and acceptance of private mortgage insurance has also facilitated the marketability of conventional mortgages in the private secondary mortgage market. Insuring the investor against default losses up to a maximum of 20–25 percent of the loan amount enhances the marketability of the conventional mortgage instrument. The use of private mortgage insurance increased dramatically in the early 1970s, and with it the ability of S&Ls and other mortgage originators to originate high-ratio loans carrying private mortgage insurance (see Chapter 48).

The development of an information network that permits buyers and sellers of mortgages to evaluate prices, yields, and other characteristics of the conventional loans being offered for sale has been promoted by the establishment of the Automated Mortgage Market Information Network (AMMINET) by FHLMC in 1974. AMMINET assists secondary mortgage market participants by providing information on offers to buy and sell mortgages, thus reducing the cost of obtaining information on mortgage market activity.

The private mortgage insurers have also facilitated the development of the secondary mortgage market through their role in bringing together buyers and sellers in this informal market. Private mortgage insurers have frequent contact with both lenders and investors, and so have knowledge of what institutions have funds seeking investment and what lenders have mortgages for sale. By providing information on mortgage purchase/sale opportunities, the mortgage insurance companies have been responsible for a significant proportion all private secondary mortgage market transactions.

The Terms and Conditions of Private Sector Mortgage Transactions. The primary private sellers of mortgages include savings and loan associations, commercial banks and mortgage bankers. The primary private investors in mortgages are the depository institutions—savings and loan institutions, mutual savings banks, and commercial banks. A small but growing volume of mortgage loans is also being purchased by traditional non-mortgage-oriented investors, primarily pension funds and life insurance companies.

Despite the innovations which have increased the efficiency of secondary mortgage market transactions in recent years, the private sector of the secondary market still functions primarily through an informal, unstructured, and varying network of sellers and investors. Unlike the federally assisted agencies, the private sector functions on a highly personal basis, with the terms and conditions of many mortgage transactions tailored to meet the specific needs and requirements of particular investors.

Mortgage lenders who desire to sell some of their mortgages usually do so by contacting former customers or by going through brokers with whom they have done business previously. If a sale is consummated, the sale may be an over-the-counter sale or a spot sale, as opposed to a sale pursuant to forward commitments issued by investors. The delivery of mortgages under commitments may be either mandatory or optional, with delivery under optional (standby) commitments at the discretion of the seller.

On the other hand, a mortgage sale may be carried out via a correspondent relationship, in which loan volume and other terms and conditions of the sale are determined by previous agreement. Although such transactions are usually conducted by telephone, a buyer will usually insist upon a personal review of the mortgage loans as well as a review of the seller's servicing arrangements and procedures and a personal inspection of the property underlying the loan. The type of review is primarily a function of the investor's familiarity with the seller and of the track record of the loans purchased to date from that seller, with less intensive review required of loans from sellers with whom investors have previously done business.

Once the terms of the sale have been agreed upon, the seller sends the investor the necessary documentation and evidence of ownership. The investor then sends the seller an amount equal to the principal outstanding balance of the mortgages sold—plus or minus any premium or discounts. Since the buyer pays a price that will yield an agreed-upon rate of return, the loans may have to be sold at a discount (premium) to raise (lower) yields to the investor.

The loans may be sold on a whole loan or participation basis. With whole loans the investor purchases the entire outstanding principal balance of the loan, whereas with participations the investor purchases a percentage, usually from 50 to 90 percent, of the outstanding principal balance. Sales of mortgages on a participation basis may be easier to complete, since investors may feel more secure about purchasing mortgages when the seller retains an interest in the mortgage loans. Individual loans are rarely sold in the mortgage market. Typically, mortgages are traded in groups of loans known as pools or packages, in which the individual loans that the pool comprises have generally similar characteristics.

Generally, the seller (originator) of whole loans services the mortgages sold, with the principal and interest payments passed through, as received, to the investor on a regular basis. The seller is paid a fee for servicing the loans, usually one half to three eighths of 1 percent per year of the outstanding principal balance for single-family loans. Sellers of loans on a participation basis are generally not paid a separate fee for servicing, since they continue to own a share of the loans serviced.

The informal and unstructured nature of the private sector of the secondary mortgage market is both an advantage and a disadvantage to participants. It is a disadvantage because the lack of a central marketplace and the relative lack of standardization of conventional mortgage instruments have limited the marketability of these instruments. On the other hand, the unstructured nature of the market permits greater flexibility for participants, so that buyers and sellers are better able to negotiate arrangements that meet their particular needs and requirements. For many sellers, mortgage sales in the private sector can often be made at lower costs and at better prices than comparable sales to federally assisted institutions.

Mortgage-Backed Securities

In recent years new instruments called mortgage-backed pass-through securities have gained attention as an attractive alternative to selling mortgages as either whole loans or participations. Mortgage-backed pass-through securities are mortgages that are grouped into pools, fractional participations of which are sold to investors. All collections of interest and principal in a pool are "passed through" to the investors, whether or not those amounts are collected from the mortgages. Thus, the investor is assured a minimum yield in monthly payments of principal and interest. However, due to prepayments of some mortgages and possible foreclosure and delinquent payments, the cash flow from the pool may vary from payment to payment. It is primarily the uncertain nature of the periodic payment to the certificate holder that distinguishes pass-through instruments from "bond-type" instruments, which provide for periodic fixed payments.

Pass-through certificates permit the sale of mortgages in an orderly and efficent manner and give sellers direct access to major capital market sources of funds other than the thrift institutions that have dominated the private sector of the secondary mortgage market. Since mortgage-backed pass-through securities are not general obligations of the issuer, but rather constitute a sale of assets, it is the pool of mortgages behind the securities, and not the seller, that constitutes the source of repayment to the investor. As with any sale of mortgages, the lender's balance sheet shows a reduction in mortgages and an increase in cash. There are certain responsibilities for the pass-through certificate issuer, however. These relate to his obligation to service (for a fee) the mortgages in the pool, to advance funds to the investor whether or not they are received from the mortgages, and to maintain any required insurance policies on the pool of mortgages.

Two general categories of mortgage-backed pass-through certificates can be issued by private lenders: (1) GNMA pass-through certificates based on pools of FHA/VA mortgages whose principal and interest payments are guaranteed by GNMA; and (2) privately issued pass-through certificates based on pools of conventional mortgages. The primary difference between the two is the lack of a government guarantee on the mortgage payments for the private conventional mortgage-backed securities.

Initiated in 1970, the GNMA mortgage-backed security program first introduced non-mortgage-oriented investors to mortgage-related securities. A GNMA mortgage-backed pass-through security is an obligation collateralized by a pool of existing FHA or VA mortgages. The securities are issued by private institutions, and GNMA grants the pool its guarantee of timely payment of principal and interest on the underlying mortgages. Acting as guarantor, GNMA is required to assume responsibility for the monthly payments in the event that an issuer defaults on the obligation. In the event of default by the issuer or upon his request, GNMA will assign a pool to another issuer. (See also Chapter 54.)

By avoiding the loan origination and administration problems that are involved in handling individual mortgages, the GNMA pass-through securities program has been successful in attracting to mortgage-related investments investors who had not traditionally been investors in residential mortgages. Moreover, the high liquidity and marketability of GNMAs and their high investment quality, coupled with their relatively high yield for a government-guaranteed security, have increased their attractiveness to investors. Investor acceptance of pass-through securities has also been facilitated by FHLMC's issuance of participation certificates (PCs), which have become the agency's primary financing vehicle.

Interest in mortgage-backed pass-through securities has increased recently with the issuance of conventional mortgage-backed pass-through securities by major private mortgage lenders. By year-end 1978, approximately $700 million in private conventional pass-through certificates have been issued since the Bank of America marketed its first private conventional pass-through security offering in September 1977. Since then, conventional pass-through issuers have included savings and loan associations, mutual savings banks, and commercial banks. Mortgage-backed pass-through certificates offer a convenient and flexible means of selling mortgages and hold the potential for substantially altering the traditional process of selling mortgages.

The flexibility of a pass-through security enables a lender to structure a mortgage package that meets his own financial requirements and capabilities while providing investors with a yield package. Sale of mortgages via pass-through securities can open up many profitable loan origination and selling activities for lenders who have not thought in terms of originating and selling mortgages and profiting from the yield spreads.

Private conventional pass-through securities may be offered publicly or through a direct placement with an investor. A direct private placement is more advantageous to the issuer when the total amount of the issue is small—generally less than $50 million. Such a placement may be accomplished quickly, and it does not require registration with the Securities and Exchange Commission. On the other hand, greater liquidity and a broader market are the primary advantages of a public offering rated by a major investment rating agency.

The loan origination capacity of the lender and his desire for servicing income and yield spreads in the marketplace are factors that influence the decision to issue a pass-through security. The issuance of pass-through securities becomes profitable when the yield spread between the rates on available conventional mortgages and the rates that investors will pay on pass-through securities is sufficient to cover the full costs of issuing the pass-through securities. Thus, pass-through securities are most likely to be issued at times when current mortgage loan rates exceed intermediate- and long-term capital market rates.

The advantages of issuing pass-through securities must also be weighed against the rates available from alternative secondary market sources such as FNMA or FHLMC, as well as the rates available from sales of whole mortgage loans or mortgage participations to private investors.

Thus far, mortgage-backed pass-through securities appear to be making good progress in tapping institutional portfolio investors which heretofore were insignificant mortgage buyers. A significant volume of pass-through securities has been purchased by nondepository institutions such as life insurance companies and pension funds. By attracting non-mortgage-oriented investors, pass-through securities should make mortgage lenders less reliant on deposit funds as a source of mortgage credit and hence less vulnerable to periodic disruptions in the availability of mortgage credit.

Evaluating Alternatives

Previous sections of this chapter have described the programs available for selling residential mortgages and have analyzed some of the recent changes in the secondary mortgage market. This section will evaluate and compare the alternative sources of funds that are available to mortgage sellers. It will present the advantages and disadvantages of selling whole mortgage loans and participations to the private sector or to the federally assisted agencies and via mortgage-backed securities.

The federally assisted agencies have dramatically expanded the secondary mortgage market and have improved the flow of residential mortgage credit. A primary advantage of selling mortgages to either FHLMC or FNMA is that these investors are always in the market, particularly in periods of credit distress, whereas private investors may have to withdraw from the market in periods of credit distress. The primary investors in the private sector of the secondary mortgage market are thrift institutions, which are most likely to withdraw from the purchase of residential mortgages precisely in periods of high interest rates, when mortgage lenders are most desirous of selling mortgages.

FNMA and FHLMC also offer a rapid processing of loans submitted for purchase. FNMA offers prior approval of single-family loans to be originated for purchase by FNMA. FHLMC offers prior approval on multifamily mortgages submitted for purchase. The prior approval of mortgages permits the lender to originate mortgages knowing that a mortgage is acceptable for purchase under existing commitments. With many purchasers in the private market, mortgages must go on the books of the originator before they can be sold to the investor. In this case, mortgages must be originated without any assurance that the mortgages will meet the investor's requirements.

Both FNMA and FHLMC now offer optional delivery and forward commitments for the purchase of residential loans. Although investors in the private sector may offer optional delivery and forward commitments, not all do so. Because of their liquidity position, some investors will specify purchase on a "spot" basis, with delivery of the mortgages within a 30-day period.

The commitment/purchase requirements of FNMA and FHLMC differ in only minor respects. However, FHLMC does offer to purchase residential mortgages on a participation basis, whereas FNMA does not (except for certain programs designed for specific urban areas). Also, FHLMC does not charge members of the FHLB system a commitment fee, whereas FNMA's commitment fees apply to all commitment holders.

The commitment/purchase programs of GNMA differ from those of the other federally assisted agencies in that its mortgage purchase programs are more specialized. GNMA purchases mortgages only for specialized types of loans that are originated under specific terms and conditions. The mortgages are originated under GNMA commitments and are purchased by GNMA to carry out policy mandates regarding federally assisted housing. Consequently, its volume and activity are limited by budgetary restrictions and its purchase commitments have sometimes had to be rationed among available lenders.

The primary advantage of the private sector of the secondary mortgage market is the greater flexibility it accords participants. Buyers and sellers are better able to negotiate arrangements that meet their particular needs and requirements. For example, mortgages may be sold on a participation basis or a whole loan basis in the private sector, but these choices are not always available from the federally assisted agencies. Generally, a participation loan sale has simpler administrative requirements than a whole loan sale since fewer documents have to be reviewed by the investor. Moreover, a mix of loan sale opportunities involving sales on a "spot" basis and forward commitments is available in the private sector of the secondary market.

The efficiency of private secondary market transactions, as reflected in administrative burdens and costs imposed on buyers and sellers, varies from transaction to transaction, depending primarily upon the stability of established secondary market relations. Sellers who have established stable relations with investors and who are regularly active in the secondary market probably experience lower administrative expenses than do sellers who enter the secondary market on an irregular basis and without established investor contacts. For sellers in the former category, sales of mortgages in the private market at particular points in the interest rate cycle will often be more flexible, at lower costs, and at better prices than comparable sales to federally assisted agencies.

This is not necessarily the case for irregular mortgage sellers who lack established investor relationships. Despite improvements in the efficiency of secondary market transactions, the lack of a central marketplace means that occasional sellers have few guidelines for ferreting out sources of funds for the purchase of mortgages and for evaluating alternative prices and the particular requirements of investors.

However, even for established sellers funds are not always routinely available from investors in the private sector. Despite the recent improvements in tapping non-mortgage-oriented sources of funds in the capital market, depository thrift institutions still remain the primary source of funds for the purchase of mortgages. Their demands for mortgages are volatile, reflecting changes in their sources and uses of funds and shifts in money and capital market conditions. They have traditionally withdrawn from the secondary market in those periods in which sellers are most desirous of selling mortgages. This has been especially true for particular types of commitments, such as standby commitments, which are not always readily available from investors in all phases of the interest rate cycle.

Mortgage-backed securities increase the flexibility of sellers in that they present lenders with an alternative to the sale of whole loans or participations to private sector participants or the federally assisted agencies. The desirability of pass-through certificates is measured by comparing the prices at which loans can be sold to investors with a mortgage-backed security with the prices available from FNMA or FHLMC and with the prices available from private investors for whole loans or participations.

There is a broad and active market for GNMA mortgage-backed securities. GNMAs are highly liquid, with over $1 billion in GNMAs being issued each month. Thus, mortgage sellers have the alternative of combining FHA or VA loans originated for sale into pools of mortgages for sale to investors as GNMA mortgage-backed securities.

The conventional mortgage-backed security issued by private lenders is not as liquid as a GNMA security, since the private conventional mortgage-backed securities market lacks the depth and breadth of the GNMA market. However, a growing volume of conventional mortgage-backed securities is being offered in the marketplace and several securities dealers serve as "market-makers" for publicly offered conventional mortgage-backed securities.

Mortgage sellers who are not large enough to efficiently bring a mortgage-backed security to market in a public offering can sell mortgage-backed securities via a private placement with an institutional investor. Large numbers of conventional mortgage-backed securities have been sold on this basis. For example, in 1977 a $54 million East Coast lender privately placed $8.5 million in conventional pass-through certificates rated by Standard and Poor's with an investor. Lenders who do not have a retail distribution capacity can sell to dealers or can employ a broker to assist them in locating investors.

However, it is the larger lenders with deep origination capability, extensive mortgage portfolios, and established servicing operations that can take maximum advantage of the flexibility afforded by mortgage-backed securities. These lenders have maximum flexibility in their secondary market operations in that they can sell either whole loans or participations to private investors or to the federally assisted agencies or they can sell mortgages via mortgage-backed securities publicly or through direct placements. Which alternative they select will depend on the prices that the various alternatives will yield, and mortgage sellers are constantly altering their selling strategies on the basis of the changing price relationships of these alternatives in the marketplace. Small or infrequent mortgage sellers have fewer alternatives available to them.

Perhaps the primary disadvantage of the mortgage-backed securities market as a means of selling mortgages is the great volatility of yields and prices for GNMAs and private conventional pass-through securities. Yield/price relationships may be such that the sale of mortgages via pass-through securities is not a viable alternative. Because mortgage-backed securities are competitive with intermediate- and long-term capital market instruments, prices and yields on mortgage-backed securities vary more in response to changes in capital market conditions than to changes in housing and mortgage market conditions. Prices on mortgage-backed securities follow the rates on capital market instruments such as corporate and Treasury bonds more closely than they follow the rates on the individual mortgages comprising the mortgage-backed security pool. Consequently, sellers will find the yield requirements in the mortgage-backed securities marketplace to be much more volatile than the conditions in the housing and mortgage markets in which they originate mortgages. The greater volatility of yields on mortgage-backed securities as compared to mortgage yields means that the sale of mortgages via the mortgage-backed securities route may not be financially feasible to sellers in periods of high or rising rates of interest when capital market rates equal or exceed mortgage rates. In this event, other means of selling mortgages must be examined.

The sensitivity of mortgage-backed security offerings to capital market conditions is amply demonstrated by the limited number of conventional mortgage-backed security offerings that were brought to market in the second half of 1978, when market rates increased sharply, as compared to the number that were brought to market in the first half of 1978, when capital market rates were considerably lower.

Summary and Overview

The secondary mortgage market has undergone a number of significant changes in recent years. Among the more significant developments have been upgrading and facilitating improvements in secondary market processes and procedures. These improvements have included extensions of secondary market trading information networks and the evolution of standardized mortgage loan underwriting and documentation procedures.

New approaches to selling mortgages have also been developed. Perhaps the most significant innovation has been the growing use and acceptance of mortgage-backed pass-through securities. This includes the GNMA mortgage pass-through security program and the more recent and growing volume of privately issued pass-through securities utilizing conventional mortgages. These mortgage-related securities provide mortgage lenders with a means of selling mortgages which is in many respects more flexible and efficient than the traditional way of selling loans to investors. Of even greater importance, mortgage-backed securities have expanded the market for mortgage loans beyond the traditional sources of mortgage credit, which consists primarily of thrift institutions.

Opening up new sources of capital which are not dependent upon interest rate-sensitive deposit funds should make mortgage-lending institutions less vulnerable to the periodic disruptions in the availability of mortgage credit that have occurred in the post–World War II era. Moreover, by providing an efficient means through which mortgage lenders can sell the mortgages that they originate, mortgage-backed securities may induce some lenders, such as commercial banks and credit unions, to expand their mortgage-lending operations. As increasing numbers of financial institutions are finding that they can increase their earnings and their profitability not only through originating mortgages but also through selling and servicing mortgages.

INVESTING IN MORTGAGE-BACKED SECURITIES

Kenneth J. Thygerson

*K*ENNETH J. THYGERSON, PhD., *Chief Economist and Director, Economics Department, United States League of Savings Associations, Chicago, Illinois.*

Directs economic research activities of United States League of Savings Associations in the areas of legislative and regulatory impact, economic forecasting, and financial analysis. Instructor, Institute of Financial Education executive development and graduate school programs. Liaison between League of Savings Associations and economists in government, academia, and industry. Formerly director and president, Chicago chapter, American Statistical Association; director, American Real Estate and Urban Economic Association; and director, Savings Institutions Management Science, Inc.; Author, The Effects of Government Credit and Housing Programs on Savings and Loan Associations, *Occasional Paper (Chicago: United States Savings and Loan League, 1973). Coauthor,* Tax Management for Savings and Loan Executives *(Chicago: United States League of Savings Associations, 1977);* Mortgage Portfolio Management *(Chicago: United States League of Savings Associations, 1978); and* Economic Topics for Savings and Loan Management, *semimonthly publication of Economics Department, United States League of Savings Association, May 1975 to date. Author,* "Real Estate Finance," Savings and Loan News, *monthly article, 1970 to date. Author of ad hoc reviews for* Journal of Political Economy, Journal of Money, Credit and Banking, Journal of Economics and Business, *and* Management Science. *Author of numerous articles in* Journal of Finance, Journal of Financial and Quantitative Analysis, AREUEA Journal, *and* Savings and Loan News.

The mortgage market is the largest debt market in the United States. It is not surprising, therefore, that major innovations have been developed for the purpose of broadening the base for mortgage loan invest-ment. Although the secondary market has played a long-standing role as a means of shifting funds from capital surplus to capital deficit areas, major innovations in mortgage securities took place in the decade of the 1970s, when mortgage-backed and secured debt instruments were developed.

A basic objective of these mortgage instrument innovations has been to integrate the bond and mortgage markets. In this way, mortgage loan originators hope to tap the significant sources of investment funds con-trolled by pension funds, trusts, and insurance companies. Historically, mortgage and bond market participants have not communicated fre-quently or adequately understood each other's investment needs. The creation of new mortgage instruments in recent years, however, has strengthened the ties between the participants in these two major debt markets.

To the extent that traditional nonmortgage investors are attracted to these new mortgage instruments, the mortgage market is expected to be less vulnerable to cyclic disruptions in the flow of mortgage credit and the overall availability of residential mortgage credit is expected to be increased. In addition, the creation of these new mortgage instru-ments enhances the liquidity of the mortgage originator's mortgage hold-ings. This increased liquidity can translate into a freer flow of funds from capital surplus to capital deficit areas and can also bring about lower mortgage rates.

The innovations in mortgage instruments occurred, in large part, with the help of the U.S. government. The National Housing Act of 1968 au-thorized the creation of the Government National Mortgage Association (GNMA) pass-through security program. (The first GNMA pass-through was issued on February 19, 1970.) This program—to be discussed more fully later—represented the most significant single effort to broaden the base of investor interest in mortgage loans. Because of the complexities of originating and servicing individual mortgage loans, many institu-tional investors, such as insurance companies, pension funds, and other trusts, found mortgage loan investments less appealing than the more easily marketable and serviceable corporate bonds, municipal bonds, stocks, and government bonds. Thus, in order to broaden the investment base for mortgage investment, efforts had to be made to develop securi-ties backed or secured by mortgage loans which had investment attri-butes—marketability, reinvestment ease, and minimal servicing re-quirements—that were more appealing to the many institutional inves-tors who had not traditionally been attracted to mortgages but were very familiar with bonds. The GNMA pass-through security program was the first of numerous efforts which have proved to be a successful means of broadening the investment base for mortgage loans.

Since the inauguration of the GNMA pass-through security program in 1970, a number of other mortgage-backed securities have been devel-oped by quasi-governmental and private institutions servicing the mort-gage market. The economic motivation behind each of these mortgage security innovations is similar. It involves the creation of new mortgage-backed and -secured debt instruments with investment attributes that are more appealing than those found in the underlying mortgage loans. Generally speaking, mortgage-backed and -secured bonds are found to have higher liquidity, less default risk, and broader marketability than do the underlying mortgages.

Since 1970, at least six major types of mortgage-backed or secured debt instruments have been developed and offered in the credit markets. These are: (1) the government National Mortgage Association pass-through security, (2) the Federal Home Loan Mortgage Corporation (FHLMC) participation certificate, (3) the Federal Home Loan Mortgage Corporation guaranteed mortgage certificate, (4) the private issue mortgage-backed bond, (5) the private issue pass-through certificate, and (6) the industrial development mortgage bond. Four of these six types of mortgage-backed securities are sponsored by federal agencies or quasi-agencies or by state agencies. These include the GNMA pass-through security, the FHLMC participation certificate, the FHLMC guaranteed mortgage certificate, and the state agency–sponsored industrial development mortgage bond. Two of the six types, the mortgage-backed bond and the pass-through certificate, are issued by private mortgage lenders, such as savings and loan associations and commercial banks.

Like the sponsoring organizations, the underlying mortgages which act as security for the instruments differ significantly. The GNMA pass-through securities, for example, use FHA-insured and VA-guaranteed mortgages as collateral. The FHLMC participation certificates normally use conventional residential mortgages as collateral, as do the FHLMC guaranteed mortgage certificates. The private issue mortgage-backed bonds and pass-through certificates normally utilize conventional, FHA, and VA residential mortgages as collateral. The underlying security of the industrial development mortgage bonds, by contrast, is normally commercial mortgages on shopping centers, plants, and other commercial properties.

In addition, the marketability and yields on these securities differ substantially. This is because several of these securities are backed by various government and agency guarantees, whereas others are not.

The investor in mortgage-backed and -secured instruments is concerned with at least these seven major characteristics: (1) the denomination of the securities issued, (2) the marketability and liquidity of the issue, (3) the safety or the susceptibility to default risk of the issue, (4) the means of paying the principal and interest of the issue, (5) the expected average loan life or maturity of the issue, (6) the tax status of the issue, and (7) the relative yield of the issue.

The remainder of this chapter will discuss the background and the investment characteristics of the six major mortgage-backed securities.

Government National Mortgage Association Pass-Through Securities

The GNMA pass-through security was first issued in 1970 under Section 306(g) of Title III of the National Housing Act. The security represents a share in a pool of FHA and VA mortgages, all of which have the same interest rate and a similar term to maturity. GNMA pools are formed for mobile home loans and multifamily project loans as well as the more common single-family mortgage pools.

The GNMA pass-through security was conceived as a means of attracting institutional money into mortgage investments. By mid-1978, there were over $58 billion of GNMA pass-through securities outstanding. Over two thirds of these were held by investors other than the traditional mortgage-lending thrift institutions.

The major issuers of GNMA pass-throughs are mortgage bankers. Of the approximately 500 issuers, 90 percent are mortgage bankers, the rest mainly thrift institutions. Purchases can be made directly from the issuer, but they are normally made through a dealer. The Ginnie Mae Mortgage-Backed Securities Dealers Association has more than 60 members including most of the large Wall Street investment bankers. Though the minimum denomination certificate is $25,000 of principal at issue, Wall Street trades are usually in blocks of $250,000 or $1 million. Dealers do trade in amounts as small as $25,000, however.

On the GNMA issues backed by single-family mortgages, the contract rate of the underlying mortgages is 50 basis points higher than the coupon rate shown on a GNMA pass-through security. The additional 50 basis points are retained by the mortgage servicer, who receives 44 basis points and pays the Government National Mortgage Association 6 basis points as an insurance fee for the government guarantee. The servicer of the underlying mortgages receives a fee higher than is usual for servicing agreements in the secondary mortgage market because the servicer must pay the scheduled interest and principal payments on the underlying mortgages to the holders of the GNMA pass-through securities, whether or not he actually receives those funds from the pool in a timely manner.

The investor in the GNMA pass-through security receives his pro rata share of the principal and interest payments accruing to the underlying mortgages in the pool. Adding to the appeal of GNMA pass-through securities is the fact that the "full faith and credit" of the U.S. Treasury guarantees that the principal and interest on these securities will be paid to investors on a timely basis. Technically, the GNMA pass-through is referred to as a "modified pass-through" security because payment to security holders is made whether or not the issuer receives his payment from the individual mortgagor. As a result, for all practical purposes the GNMA pass-through security is as safe an investment as a U.S. Treasury bond.

In addition to possessing a high degree of safety, GNMA pass-through securities are characterized by high marketability. This results from the high volume of these issues that is available in the market—over $58 billion of GNMA pass-through securities were outstanding at mid-1978—and the substantial trading in these issues. In some respects, the GNMA pass-through security is the premier mortgage-backed security in the capital market. It has the highest marketability and the greatest safety of all the available types of mortgage-backed securities.

Another desirable feature of the GNMA pass-through is that there is now an organized futures market in GNMAs which allows investors to hedge forward purchases and sales of GNMAs. This market, which was established by the Chicago Board of Trade, is one of the more active futures markets that have been established in recent years. The basic contract unit is a principal balance of $100,000 with a stated interest

EXHIBIT 1

PROSECTUS

$ _____

_____% *Modified Pass-Through Mortgage-Backed Securities (Single-Family Mortgages)*

FULLY GUARANTEED AS TO PRINCIPAL AND INTEREST

by

GOVERNMENT NATIONAL MORTGAGE ASSOCIATION

(Backed by the Full Faith and Credit of the United States)
Issued by

GNMA POOL NO.:   ISSUE DATE:
CUSTODIAN: FIRST PAYMENT DUE:
MINIMUM CERTIFICATE AMOUNT: MATURITY DATE:

The above information has been provided by Issuer. Government National Mortgage Association has prepared the balance of the information contained in this Prospectus.

The securities to be issued under this Prospectus provide for timely payment to the registered holder of interest at the specified rate plus scheduled installments of principal. These installments of interest and principal (adjustable) will commence on the 15th day of the month following the month of issue and will continue every month thereafter over the life of the mortgage pool, whether or not such principal and interest shall be collected by the Issuer.

> Timely payment of principal of and interest on the Securities is guaranteed by GNMA pursuant to Section 306(g) of Title III of the National Housing Act. Section 306(g) provides that "The full faith and credit of the United States is pledged to the payment of all amounts which may be required to be paid under any guaranty under this subsection" and an opinion dated December 9, 1969, of an Assistant Attorney General of the United States states that such guarantees under Section 306(g) of mortgage-backed securities of the type offered hereby "constitute general obligations of the United States backed by its full faith and credit."

The Certificates have not been registered under the Securities Act of 1933 since they are exempt from registration.

HUD-1717 (8-71)

rate of 8 percent. GNMA pass-throughs with other face rates, however, are delivered in principal amounts which are equivalent to $100,000 of GNMA pass-throughs when calculated at par with an assumed 30-year amortization and a 12-year prepayment.

Prices are quoted as a percentage of par. Consequently, when the cash market yield is 8 percent, an expiring GNMA futures contract trades at about 100. As interest rates rise, the price of the contract falls, so that futures market yields tend to be in harmony with prevailing cash market yields. The minimum fluctuation in the contract price is $\frac{1}{32}$ of 1 percent of par, or $31.25 per contract. Traders can buy or sell contracts for any of four designated "delivery months"—March, July, September, and December.

The GNMA futures market enables mortgage investors to hedge their positions in the cash market. In so doing, they are able to guarantee the price yield of a GNMA pass-through that they contemplate buying or selling in the cash market.

The greatest problem associated with the GNMA pass-through security is the uncertainty regarding the prepayment experience of the underlying mortgages in the pool. It has become conventional in the secondary market for the yield on 30-year GNMA pass-through securities to be quoted as if they were prepaid in 12 years. That is, it is assumed that at the end of 12 years all unpaid principal will be fully paid off and that normal amortization of the mortgage will occur from the date of issue to the end of the 12-year period. Of course, these assumptions run counter to actual experience. Some of the underlying mortgages will prepay earlier than 12 years, thus negating the assumption of normal amortization during the first 12 years; and some of the mortgages will still be outstanding at the end of 12 years, thus negating the assumption of full prepayment of all mortgages at the end of 12 years. As a result, the yield obtained on GNMA pass-through securities can differ from the quoted yields to the extent that the actual prepayment experience does not conform to the assumed prepayment experience.

A copy of the first page of a GNMA pass-through prospectus is shown in Exhibit 1.

Federal Home Loan Mortgage Corporation Participation Certificates

The FHLMC participation certificate is a mortgage-backed pass-through security that has many of the same attributes as the GNMA pass-through security. The major difference is that the underlying securities in the participation certificate pool consist of conventional whole loans and conventional loan participations underwritten and purchased by the Federal Home Loan Mortgage Corporation. Over 95 percent of the principal consists of conventional single-family loans; less than 5 percent consists of conventional multifamily loans.

The other major difference is that the FHLMC participation certificate does not include the "full faith and credit" provision of the GNMA pass-through security. The timely payment of interest and the repayment of all principal on participation certificates are guaranteed by the Federal Home Loan Mortgage Corporation, which is not quite as strong a guarantee as the "full faith and credit" protection of the GNMA pass-through security.

Another limitation of the participation certificates is that they are less marketable than the GNMA pass-through securities. This is largely because of the substantially lower volume of participation certificates that is available in the marketplace. Through mid-1978, $10.7 billion in participation certificates had been issued overall since the initial offering in November 1971. Although the volume has grown significantly in recent years, the volume of participation certificates traded in the marketplace is not nearly as great as that of the GNMA pass-through securities.

To encourage a secondary market in participation certificates, the FHLMC stands ready to buy back participation certificates from any holder, provided that the certificates have been registered to that holder for at least 60 days and that the repurchase totals no more than $5 million on any one day. The interest of securities dealers in trading participation certificates has grown, and today a group of dealers distribute all new issues and make a resale market for secondary issues. As a result, a smaller percentage of participation certificates are bought directly from or sold directly to FHLMC.

Yield quotes are available continuously. If a purchase order is made over the phone, a mailed confirmation should arrive within three days. Deferred delivery at the option of FHLMC entitles the purchaser to a commitment fee, depending on how long the deferral period is. Delivery in up to 29 days is considered immediate. As with GNMA pass-throughs, the exact settlement amount is not known until a few days before actual delivery.

The yields of participation certificates, like the yields of GNMA pass-throughs, are quoted on the assumption that the average loan life will be 12 years, which may or may not be reasonable. Thus, uncertainty over the "time" yield and cash flows are present in these investments because the investor receives his pro rata share of mortgage prepayments which do not necessarily conform to the 12-year prepayment assumption.

Because of the lesser guarantee and liquidity of the FHLMC participation certificates as compared to the GNMA pass-throughs, the participation certificates yield slightly higher interest rates than the pass-throughs.

Federal Home Loan Mortgage Corporation Guaranteed Mortgage Certificates

In February 1975, the Federal Home Loan Mortgage Corporation created a new instrument called the guaranteed mortgage certificate. The purpose of the guaranteed mortgage certificate (GMC) is to encourage institutional investors in the capital markets to purchase mortgage-secured instruments. The GMC was specifically designed to appeal to pension funds, trusts, and insurance companies that find that cash flow certainty and greater freedom from reinvestment problems makes corporate bonds more appealing than the mortgages. Because of the complexity of the GMC, the total amount issued through mid-1978 was only $1.8 billion.

EXHIBIT 2

<u>PROSPECTUS</u>

$200,000,000

 Federal Home Loan Mortgage Corporation

Guaranteed Mortgage Certificates, Series B 1976

Dated: August 25, 1976   Certificate Rate: 8.375%

> **Any Certificate holder may, at his option, require The Mortgage Corporation to purchase his Certificate on September 15, 1996, at the then unpaid principal balance thereof, plus accrued interest, if any. Certificates as to which this option is exercised will have a maximum average weighted life of 10.2 years. Certificates as to which the option is not exercised will have a maximum average weighted life of 10.9 years.**

Interest payable semi-annually each March 15 and September 15, commencing March 15, 1977. Annual principal reduction payable September 15, 1977, and annually thereafter. Fully registered Certificates in initial principal amounts of $100,000, $500,000 and $1,000,000.

Price 99.125% plus accrued interest, if any, at the Certificate Rate from August 25, 1976

The Guaranteed Mortgage Certificates ("Mortgage Certificates" or "Certificates") offered hereby will represent undivided interests in specified conventional mortgages and/or participations therein presently owned by the Federal Home Loan Mortgage Corporation ("The Mortgage Corporation" or "FHLMC"). (The aggregate of the undivided interests in such mortgages and participations to be represented by the Certificates are referred to herein as the "Mortgages".)

FHLMC Guarantee: The Mortgage Corporation unconditionally guarantees payment of interest on the Mortgages to the extent of Certificate Rate and collection of principal on the Mortgages; unconditionally warrants return on the Mortgage Certificates at the Certificate Rate; and unconditionally warrants that until all principal on the Mortgages has been collected, payments of principal on the Mortgages will be sufficient to return to the holders of the Certificates the minimum annual principal reduction payments indicated below (expressed as percentages of the initial principal amounts of the Certificates):

SCHEDULE OF MINIMUM ANNUAL PRINCIPAL REDUCTION PAYMENTS

September 15	% of Initial Principal Amount	September 15	% of Initial Principal Amount	September 15	% of Initial Principal Amount	September 15	% of Initial Principal Amount	September 15	% of Initial Principal Amount
1977	7.5	1983	5.0	1989	3.0	1995	2.5	2001	1.5
1978	7.0	1984	4.5	1990	3.0	1996	2.0	2002	1.5
1979	6.5	1985	4.5	1991	2.5	1997	2.0	2003	1.5
1980	6.0	1986	4.5	1992	2.5	1998	2.0	2004	1.5
1981	6.0	1987	4.0	1993	2.5	1999	2.0	2005	1.0
1982	5.0	1988	3.5	1994	2.5	2000	1.5	2006	1.0

Since principal payments on the Mortgages could exceed scheduled amounts in a given year, notice of the amount of principal to be paid to each Certificate holder will be published not less than 25 days before each principal payment date.

Interest and principal reduction payments are payable by check to Certificate holders of record on the February 15 or August 15 next preceding the applicable payment date.

More complete information regarding the Certificates appears under "Description of Mortgage Certificates" in this Prospectus.

The Mortgage Certificates are not guaranteed by the United States and do not constitute a debt or obligation of the United States. Interest on the Certificates is not exempt from federal income taxes.

The Mortgage Certificates do not constitute "qualifying real property loans" within the meaning of Section 593(e) of the Internal Revenue Code.

The Certificates are not required to be registered under the Securities Act of 1933 and are "exempt securities" within the meaning of the Securities Exchange Act of 1934.

The Mortgage Corporation has authorized the Office of Finance, Federal Home Loan Banks (Michael Mickett, Acting Director), 320 First Street, N.W., Washington, D. C. 20552 (Telephone 202/376-3485) to act as agent to arrange for the sale of the Mortgage Certificates. It is expected that delivery of Certificates against payment in Federal Funds will be made on or about August 25, 1976.

The date of this Prospectus is August 23, 1976.

The GMC represents an undivided interest in specific mortgages tailored so as to meet the requirements of institutional investors that dislike the servicing and origination costs and the inconvenience of the monthly principal and interest payments associated with mortgage investments. To do this, the GMC includes these provisions: (1) semiannual payments of interest and annual repayments of principal; (2) minimum annual principal reduction payments according to a predetermined schedule; (3) an unconditional guarantee by the Federal Home Loan Mortgage Corporation of interest payments to the extent of the certificate rate and of the full payment of the principal; and (4) where principal payments—prepayments—exceed the scheduled minimum amounts in a given year, published notice of the amount of principal that will be paid must be given not less than 25 days before principal payment date.

The GMCs have been offered in registered certificate form with initial principal amounts of $100,000, $500,000, and $1,000,000. The maturity of a GMC depends on the maturity of the underlying mortgages in the pool, though FHLMC stands ready to redeem the certificates for the amount of the unpaid principal balance of the underlying mortgages prior to the longest maturity of the mortgages. This latter feature is very appealing to investors, since it gives them the option, usually after 15 to 20 years, to sell the certificates back to the Federal Home Loan Mortgage Corporation for the amount of the unpaid principal of the underlying pool. The investor would be expected to exercise this option if alternative market interest rates exceeded the coupon rate on the GMCs, and vice versa.

The GMC provides the institutional investor with many of the desirable attributes of corporate bonds and fewer of the undesirable attributes of mortgages. Security dealers make a secondary market in GMC public issues. A copy of the first page of the prospectus of a recently issued GMC is shown in Exhibit 2.

Private Issue Mortgage-Backed Bonds

Mortgage-backed and -secured debt instruments have been issued by private lending institutions, such as savings and loan associations and commercial banks. Savings and loan associations have been encouraged to do so by Federal Home Loan Bank Board regulations allowing them to issue mortgage-backed bonds.

A mortgage-backed bond is a debt security with fixed payments of interest and principal and a stated maturity. It differs from a corporate bond in that it is secured by the pledge of mortgage assets. It differs from a pass-through security in that it does not give its purchaser an undivided interest in the mortgage collateral. Unlike pass-through securities, mortgage-backed bonds pay interest twice yearly, and like corporate or government bonds, they return the principal in lump sums. Thus, the cash flow problem (and the problem of principal reinvestment) which falls on the holder of a pass-through security is transferred to the issuer.

Mortgage-backed bonds are a step further removed from the underlying mortgages than pass-through securities. A pool of mortgages serves as collateral, but the cash flow to the holder of the mortgage-backed bond does not depend on the cash flow from the mortgage pool. This is of some benefit to the issuer since older, lower-yielding mortgages can be used as collateral. On the other hand, since the market value of such mortgages is less than par, the pool must be overcollateralized. Because mortgages pay down, however, the pool must be overcollateralized in any event.

The Federal Home Loan Bank Board regulations stipulate that the mortgage-backed bond must have a minimum average life of five years and that the lenders cannot require that the borrowed money be repaid in amounts which exceed 20 percent of the original amount borrowed in any year. Any issue must call for at least five equal annual repayments of principal and must satisfy the average five-year requirement by having a final maturity that is not shorter than seven years. The bonds must have a minimum denomination of $100,000 unless they are sold through brokers and dealers registered with the Securities and Exchange Commission. In that case, they can be offered in denominations as low as $10,000.

The mortgage-backed bond differs from the other types of mortgage-backed securities in that the bondholder does not have a pro rata interest in the underlying mortgage assets. The safety of the mortgage-backed bond is determined in part by the quality and the type of the underlying collateral. The bond is an obligation of a regulated and insured financial institution, which also enhances its quality rating. The quality of the collateral is determined by the types of mortgage loans that make up the collateral—that is, commercial or apartment mortgages, one–four-family conventional mortgages, or one–four-family FHA/VA mortgages—and by the value of the collateral relative to the amount of the borrowing.

The bond-rating services frequently give ratings to mortgage-backed bonds which allow the purchaser to compare the safety of these bonds with that of corporate bonds. These ratings are a significant determinant of the relative interest cost on mortgage-backed bond issues. Standard and Poor's, a primary rating service for mortgage-backed bonds, regards the following as the most important criteria in its ratings: (1) the quality of the mortgages and the credit risk protection built into the pool, (2) the interest rate protection built into the pool, (3) the liquidity of the mortgages, (4) the general creditworthiness of the issuer and its ability to honor its commitment to the pool, and (5) the indenture terms. Most publicly issued mortgage-backed bonds have been granted the top AAA rating.

Mortgage-backed bonds may be offered by an institution through either public offerings or private placements. Large institutional investors are more likely to be interested in private placements, whereas small investors are more likely to be interested in public offerings. Clearly, the marketability of mortgage-backed bonds will be dictated by the size of the issue and the breadth of ownership. Dealers make a market in mortgage-backed bonds.

The popularity of mortgage-backed bonds increased significantly during the real estate recovery of 1975–78. Through mid-1978 an estimated $1.75 billion mortgage-backed bonds were publicly issued. During the same period, an estimated $650 million of mortgage-backed bonds were placed privately. A primary market for these issues has been pension funds, trusts, and insurance companies.

The marketability of mortgage-backed bonds varies significantly, since the size and type of offering for these securities is determined by the individual issuer's preferences. The overcollateralization of most mortgage-backed bonds and the fact that the issuer is a regulated and insured financial institution frequently results in high ratings by the rating services. Thus, yields on mortgage-backed bonds tend to be closer to higher grade corporate debt securities.

EXHIBIT 3
Mortgage-Backed Bonds

Offering Circular Summary

The Bonds

Issuer	California Federal Savings and Loan Association.
Type of Security	Mortgage-Backed Bonds.
Amount	$50,000,000.
Rate of Interest	9⅛% per annum.
Maturity	July 15, 1985.
Redemption	Redeemable in whole or in part at the option of the Association on or after July 15, 1982, at 100% plus accrued interest.
Collateral	Mortgage Notes, either FHA insured or VA guaranteed, secured by deeds of trust (mortgages) on 1 to 4 family dwellings in California. The initial collateral consist of approximately 4,600 such Mortgage Notes having an aggregate unpaid principal balance of approximately $110,000,-000, an average remaining term to maturity of 27 years and a nominal interest rate of 7% per annum.
Discounted Value of Collateral . .	Initially and at least semi-annually thereafter, the Mortgage Notes will be valued on a discounted basis using a discount rate related to certain prevailing mortgage market yields. The initial discount rate is 10.00%.

Exhibit 3 *(continued)*

Initial Amount of Collateral	The Discounted Value of the Mortgage Notes constituting the initial collateral will be not less than $87,-500,000, equal to 175% of the aggregate principal amount of the Series A Bonds to be outstanding.
Maintenance of Collateral	In the event the Discounted Value of the Mortgage Notes declines less than 135% of the principal amount of Series A Bonds outstanding on any semi-annual valuation date before June 30, 1983, the Association will deposit sufficient additional collateral (which may include Government Securities) to restore the Discounted Value thereof to the 135% level, subject to certain regulatory limitations. The required maintenance level will increase to 140% for the period beginning on June 30, 1983, and to 150% for the period beginning on June 30, 1984.
Use of Proceeds	Principally to make loans to finance the construction and purchase of residential properties.

Source: Printed with the permission of California Federal Savings and Loan Association.

A copy of the offering circular summary of a recent mortgage-backed bond issue is shown in Exhibit 3.

Private Issue Pass-Through Certificates

Unlike the private issue mortgage-backed bond, the private issue pass-through certificate involves pro rata ownership in a specific mortgage pool similar to that of the GNMA pass-through security and the FHLMC participation certificate. The principal difference between the private issue pass-through certificate and the GNMA pass-through or the FHLMC participation certificate is that the private issue pass-through involves no governmental "full faith and credit" or FHLMC guarantee. In some instances, however, the private issue pass-through certificate may include private mortgage insurance coverage on some of its underlying mortgages and/or a blanket private mortgage insurance coverage on some portion of the initial aggregate principal amount of the mortgage loans in the pool.

The safety of the pass-through certificate is directly related to the underlying mortgages represented in the mortgage pool. Here the investor will be concerned with the number of mortgages, the average size of the mortgages, the location of the mortgaged properties, the age of the mortgages, and the governmental jurisdiction within which the mortgaged properties are located. All of these factors will affect the default risk, the loan-life, and the prepayment characteristics of the underlying assets.

Apart from the differences noted above between the private issue pass-through certificate and the GNMA pass-through and FHLMC participation certificate, the attributes of private issue pass-through certificates are roughly comparable to those of the GNMA pass-through and the FHLMC participation certificate. Since the pass-through certificate is offered to the investor through a public offering or a private placement, the specific attributes of the issue (size, minimum investment, interest rate, and marketability) will all be dependent on the prospectus stipulations. As with the other pass-through securities, the actual maturity and cash flows will be uncertain, due to the uncertain prepayment experience of the underlying mortgages.

It is too early to assess the general marketability and the relative yields of private issue pass-through certificates. The first issue was offered in 1977. Through mid-1978, a total of $650 million were issued. Securities dealers can be expected to make markets in larger issues.

A summary of a prospectus for a recent public offering of a private issue mortgage-backed pass-through certificate is shown in Exhibit 4.

Industrial Development Mortgage Bonds

The industrial development mortgage bond is one of the most complicated and least known of the mortgage-backed securities. This bond is an adaptation of the industrial revenue bond. Revenue bonds are limited obligations of political subdivisions of states. They are not, however, backed by the taxing authority of a state or its subdivision. Rather, they are issued by a public body in order to finance private projects and they are secured exclusively by the revenues derived from these projects. Industrial development mortgage bonds involve close cooperation between the investor, the business or industrial issuer, and the state government agency. They are essentially nothing more than a commercial mortgage repackaged into a bond debt instrument.

The interest payments accruing to each type of mortgage-backed security that we have discussed thus far are subject to federal income taxes. The industrial development mortgage bond, by contrast, is tax exempt for federal tax purposes, much like any other state and municipal revenue bond. The tax-exempt status of the industrial development mortgage bond arises where the state has developed a municipal industrial development corporation and uses that corporation to promote commerce and industry and "serve a public purpose." This has generally been interpreted to include shopping centers, industrial parks, warehouses, hospitals, colleges, and arenas, all of which have been financed with industrial development mortgage bonds.

EXHIBIT 4

Summary of Prospectus

Title of Security . . . .
Mortgage-Backed Pass-Through Certificates, issuable in series.

Originator and Servicer of
Mortgage Loans . . . .
Bank of America National Trust and Savings Association.

Description of Security . . . .
Each Certificate represents a fractional undivided interest in one of a number of Mortgage Pools to be formed by the Bank from time to time. A single Certificate will initially represent a minimum investment of approximately $25,000. The Certificates will be offered in such minimum amounts, or integral multiples thereof, in fully registered form only.

Interest . . . .
Passed through monthly at the Pass-Through Rate applicable to each series of Certificates, commencing on the 25th day of the month following the month of initial issuance of such Certificates. See "Yield Considerations" and "Description of the Certificates."

Principal (including
prepayments) . . . .
Passed through monthly, commencing on the 25th day of the month following the month of initial issuance of each series of Certificates. See "Maturity and Prepayment Assumptions" and "Description of the Certificates."

The Mortgage Pools . . . .
Pools of conventional fixed-rate Mortgage Loans secured by single-family residential properties in California, with a loan-to-value ratio at origination (based on the Bank's appraisal of the mortgaged property) of 80% or less. Mortgage Pools may be formed from time to time in varying sizes, but no Mortgage Pool will contain less than $5,000,000 aggregate principal amount of Mortgage Loans. See "The Mortgage Pools."

EXHIBIT 4 *(continued)*

Mortgage Guaranty
    Insurance . . . .   Neither the Certificates nor the under-lying Mortgage Loans are insured or guaranteed by any governmental agency. The Bank will obtain a mortgage guaranty insurance policy for each Mortgage Pool, limited in scope, covering defaults on the underlying Mortgage Loans in such pool in an amount equal to 5% of the initial aggregate principal balances thereof. See "Description of Insurance."

Hazard Insurance . . . .   All of the Mortgage Loans will be covered by standard hazard insurance policies insuring against losses due to various causes, including fire, lightning, and windstorm. Certain other physical risks which are not otherwise insured against (including earthquakes, mud flows, and floods) will be covered by a special hazard insurance policy to be obtained with respect to each Mortgage Pool, limited in scope and amount. With respect to each Mortgage Pool, any hazard losses not covered by either the standard hazard policies or the special hazard insurance policy will not be insured against and will therefore be borne by the holders of Certificates of the series evidencing such Mortgage Pool. See "Description of Insurance."

Tax Status . . . .   Certificates owned by a "domestic building and loan association" will be considered to represent "loans secured by an interest in real property" within the meaning of Section 7701(a)(19)(C)(v) of the Internal Revenue Code and to represent "qualifying real property loans" within the meaning of Section 593(d) of the Code. See "Tax Aspects."

The foregoing summary is qualified in its entirety by reference to the detailed information appearing elsewhere in this Prospectus, and by reference to detailed information with respect to each Mortgage Pool contained in the Supplement to this Prospectus to be prepared in connection with each series of Certificates.

The industrial development mortgage bond is a revenue bond secured by a three-party mortgage. Normally, the mortgagee is the political subdivision which issues the bond, granting it tax-exempt status under Section 103 of the Internal Revenue Code. The commercial or industrial firm and the political subdivision enter into a long-term net lease agreement containing an option to purchase, or into a long-term installment sale contract. The issuer then sells its debt obligation to an underwriter or through a private placement. Typically, the bond is secured by an indenture of mortgage and trust and further secured by an assignment to the lender of the net lease or the installment purchase contract. Once the transaction is completed, the mortgage lender has a first lien on the real estate security.

It is virtually impossible to generalize as to the characteristics of industrial development mortgage bonds. The legal documents needed to perfect the tax-exempt transactions are extremely complex. Basically, the municipality acts initially as a funds conduit between the developer and the lender; and later it acts as a funds conduit between the tenants— under a net lease—and the lender. By performing this role, the municipality can shelter the transaction under its own tax exemption. As a result of this relationship between the municipality and the investor, the investor acquires Municipal Industrial Development Act bonds rather than the mortgage note. However, this difference is somewhat cosmetic since the municipality normally assigns the mortgage loan to the lender as security to cover the bonds. Thus, the holder of the industrial development mortgage bond receives first-lien protection on his investment.

Because the major advantage of the industrial development mortgage bond is its tax-exempt status, careful thought and study are essential before investments are made in such debt instruments. Investors in industrial development mortgage bonds normally require additional protection against the unforeseen elimination of the tax-exempt status of the bond. This can take the form of a clause requiring that in the event that tax-exempt status is lost, the return on the bond be increased to an acceptable taxable equivalent rate or that the bond be called.

The marketability of industrial development mortgage bonds suffers from the highly specialized status of these securities, their generally small issue amounts, and their lack of homogeneity. As a result, they are among the highest yielding tax-exempt securities.

Summary

Recent innovations in mortgage instruments have led to substantial integration of the mortgage and bond markets. These new mortgage instruments have been successful in attracting funds from investment sources not historically tapped by the mortgage borrower. This success dates back to the successful efforts of the federal government in developing the GNMA pass-through security. The specific investment attributes of this instrument provided the basis for other innovations.

The primary innovations of the GNMA pass-through program include

EXHIBIT 5
The Basic Investment Characteristics of Mortgage-Backed Securities

	GNMA Pass-Through Security	FHLMC Participation Certificate	FHLMC Guaranteed Mortgage Certificate
Issuer or originator	FHA-approved mortgagee with GNMA approval.	Federal Home Loan Mortgage Corporation.	Federal Home Loan Mortgage Corporation
Seller	Typically a securities dealer, mortgage banker, or financial institution.	Federal Home Loan Mortgage Corporation or any holder.	Federal Home Loan Mortgage Corporation. Public issues handled through investment banking companies.
Type of security	Share in a pool of FHA or VA mortgages—usually one–four-family loans of similar interest rate and maturity. Minimum pool size is $1 million for one–four-family pools.	Undivided interest in a pool of conventional whole loans or participations underwritten and purchased initially by FHLMC. A typical pool consists of 2,000 to 5,000 mortgages with unpaid principal of $100 million. At least 95 percent of the principal is in single-family loans.	Undivided interest in a pool of specified conventional mortgages and/or participations owned by FHLMC.
Term to maturity	Term of pool usually 30 years for one–four-family pools. Actual maturity subject to loan-life experience of underlying mortgages.	Term of pool determined by maturity of longest maturity mortgage in the pool, usually 30 years. Actual maturity subject to loan-life experience of underlying mortgages.	Term of pool is determined by maturity of longest maturity mortgages in pool, usually 30 years. FHLMC will redeem the GMC prior to maturity, usually after 20 years, at the then unpaid principal balance of the underlying mortgages.

Denomination or typical size	$25,000 minimum denomination in multiples of $5,000. Most securities dealer trades are $250,000 and up.	$100,000, $200,000, $500,000, and $1,000,000.	$100,000 $500,000, and $1,000,000.
Tax status	No preferred tax status.	No preferred tax status.	No preferred tax status.
Relative yield	Generally the highest yielding government security.	Set by FHLMC, generally above comparable GNMA yield.	Comparable to that of high-grade corporation bonds.
Guarantee and safety	Backed by the full faith and credit of the U.S. government. Prompt payment of principal and interest guaranteed even if not collected. Prepayments passed through to holders.	Mortgage Corporation guarantees timely payment of interest and repayment of all principal. Prepayments are passed through to holders.	Mortgage Corporation unconditionally guarantees collection of principal and payment of interest to the extent of the certificate rate; unconditionally warrants return on the mortgage certificates at the certificate rate; and unconditionally warrants that until all principal on the mortgages has been collected, payments of principal will be sufficient to return to the holders of the certificates the minimum annual principal reduction payments.
Marketability	Extremely liquid. Securities dealers make a market in GNMAs. More than $1 billion traded monthly.	Freely transferable, and securities dealers make a market in PCs. FHLMC will purchase PCs subject to certain conditions. Bid price typically one-half point or less below offer price.	Secondary market available for larger public issues through various securities dealers.

EXHIBIT 5 *(continued)*

	Private Issue Pass-Through Certificate	Private Issue Mortgage-Backed Bond	Industrial Development Mortgage Bond
Issuer or originator	Financial institutions or other holders of mortgages.	Savings and loan associations.	Municipal industrial development corporation.
Seller	For private placement, an investment banker. For a public offering, an SEC-registered dealer.	For private placement, investment banker. For public offering, SEC-registered broker.	Issuer sells its debt obligation to underwriter or privately places it with financial institution pursuant to a bond purchase agreement.
Type of security	Undivided interest in a pool of specified FHA/VA or conventional mortgages. Some conventional mortgages may be privately insured, or a blanket insurance coverage may be used.	Regular bond collateralized by mortgage pool whose principal normally exceeds by a significant amount the amount of the bond issue.	Municipal bond backed by first lien on real estate. Pays down like mortgage.
Term to maturity	Maturity will depend on the maturity of the underlying mortgages in the pool, usually 30 years.	Depends on issue. Usually noncallable for a period of time.	Coincides with mortgage life on underlying real estate.
Denomination or typical size	Depends on issue.	$10,000 minimum if sold via brokers; otherwise large institutional size.	Depends on issue.
Tax status	No preferred tax status.	Subject to all federal and state taxes.	Exempt from federal taxes.
Relative yield	Somewhat above GNMA pass-through securities and FHLMC participation certificates.	Dependent on bond rating.	Depends on issue.

Guarantee and safety	No guarantee. May include a blanket coverage of some proportion of principal by a private mortgage insurer.	No guarantee, but collateral usually FHA/VA guaranteed and sometimes privately issued conventional loans. Issuers are government-regulated and deposit-insured institutions.	None: not a general obligation of the municipality. This revenue bond is secured by an indenture of mortgage or trust and by an assignment of the net lease or the installment purchase contract by the commercial or industrial firm.
Marketability	Secondary market is available for larger public issues through various securities dealers.	Large public issues traded by securities dealers.	No organized market. Dealers may make markets in large issues.

the concept of mortgage pooling, the use of insurance and guarantees, the development of mortgage loan servicing arrangements, and the development of an active secondary market to enhance the liquidity of these instruments. Other innovations have built on these accomplishments.

Exhibit 5 summarizes the major investment information relating to mortgage-backed and -secured debt instruments. It is clear from the exhibit that these securities offer appealing investment possibilities for many institutional investors.

Looking to the future, it seems clear that the innovations of the last decade represent only the beginning of more far-reaching changes that can be expected to take place. Because mortgage-backed securities are relatively new to the investment markets, the investor must be aware of the likelihood that additional instruments will be developed and that modifications of the investment characteristics of the existing instruments will be made.

PART V
Real Estate Investments

HOME INVESTMENT

John Kokus, Jr.

*J*OHN KOKUS, JR., PhD, Associate Professor of Real Estate and Urban Development, School of Business Administration, The American University, Washington, D.C.

Real estate consultant to investors. Consultant to Educational Testing Service, Princeton, N.J., on Uniform Broker's and Salesperson's Licensing Examinations; consultant to American Council on Education, Washington, D.C. Expert witness and researcher on housing for U.S. Senate Subcommittee on Housing and Urban Affairs. Author of numerous articles in academic and professional journals. Author, Housing Requirements in the 70's and 80's *(NAHB);* Housing Requirements for 1975–1990 *(NAHB); and "Investor's Bookshelf," in* Real Estate Investment Strategy *(Wiley-Interscience). Coauthor,* Real Estate License Preparation Course for the Uniform Examinations for Salespersons and Brokers *(New York: McGraw-Hill). Consultant,* Housing Fact Book *(NAHB).*

The purpose of this chapter is to promote a better understanding of home ownership decisions. The chapter will begin by exploring the motivations that explain the initial step into home ownership. After the decision to buy has been made, the next matter that must be resolved is how much to pay. The discussion of home values and prices examines this question by identifying a set of related issues, including supply and demand, location, "the 1970s phenomenon," selection, mortgage money, qualification, and loans, rates, and terms.

However, the trade-off between renting and owning may be returned to as a final checkpoint before buying. This is a very personal psychological and financial review which can explain why homeowning is not for everyone. After the decision to buy has been made, the completion of a series of procedural steps results in the goal of home ownership. Finally, the chapter describes how the homeowner's role is played.

Why Home Ownership?

Basically, people have certain needs and desires that they wish to satisfy. These needs and desires may be oriented to the self and the family or to the group. Self- and family-oriented needs and desires include both psychological and economic motivations. Group-oriented needs and desires involve community-belonging and political participation. The following listing summarizes the needs and desires that motivate people to purchase homes.

1. Self- and family-oriented needs and desires
   a. Psychological motivations
      (1) Basic shelter — Some place to live
      (2) Family security — A safe place to live
      (3) Independence and freedom — Your own home and piece of earth, room for family growth
      (4) Adventure — Finding the right home
      (5) Creativity — Designing and using your property as you see fit
      (6) Personal growth — Learning about contracts, title/deeds, financing
      (7) Peace of mind — From eviction or rent raises, residence security
      (8) Emotional — Love of home, land, and residential location
   b. Economic motivations
      (1) Credit standing — Better borrowing terms, improved credit rating
      (2) Amortization — Loan repayment, principal recapture
      (3) Tax shelter — Mortgage interest and property tax deductions, tax-free loan refinancing proceeds, reduced capital gains at sale
      (4) Appreciation — Property value increase
      (5) Peace of mind — Asset grows in value, financial security
2. Group-oriented needs and desires
   a. Community-belonging
      (1) Responsible resident — An element of stability in the neighborhood
      (2) Shared interests — Home ownership thrift and savings, upkeep of neighborhood
      (3) Good standing — Interest in betterment or improvement of neighborhood
      (4) Tax base contributor — Property-tax payer
   b. Political participation
      (1) Responsible citizen — Stable voter, vested interest in good government
      (2) Constitution upholder — Right of private property
      (3) Public support — Local civic affairs, contributor to national wealth of housing inventory

From the above it can be seen that the reasons why people decide to buy homes constitute a rather large shopping list of motivators, comprising anything from consumer needs to investment goals, with personal and family needs mixed in with social needs. A number of the needs and desires listed above would probably play a prominent part in any home-buying decision, a decision which should not be undertaken casually, since the usual home-buying decision represents the largest financial commitment that most people will ever make. An examination of who buys homes will shed additional light on this subject.

Who Buys Homes?

Most studies have shown that a first home is usually purchased by a family household consisting of a husband, a wife, and preschool-age children. The growing children require more space, and by the time the children reach school age, the parents make a schooling decision as well as a decision to buy a home. The net result is that both apartment living and renting become unacceptable. The need for family space is combined with the desire for family stability, neighborhood permanence, and community-belonging. Home ownership begins extensively at about age 25, and it is greatest after age 45. Family assets or net worth do not reach a peak until after age 35.

Earlier, the cycle of apartment rental generally begins at adulthood or marriage. The modern social custom of postponing marriage has not reduced the quantity of shelter needed, but instead has resulted in a need for more rental units. A typical sequence of housing changes will upgrade the type of shelter (first rental and then ownership) with increases in personal or family needs and assets, and also with increases in individual and family ages.

Consequently, condominium and cooperative ownership has become a logical extension of apartment rental living, generally for young one- and two-person families that desire amenities other than space. Condominium and cooperative ownership also meets the needs of elderly persons whose children have grown and departed and who now desire reduced home ownership responsibilities. Such persons are willing to exchange reduced space and some reduction in privacy for newness of quarters and group-shared public areas. Condominium and cooperative forms of ownership account for about 1 percent of all owner-occupied units and for about six tenths of 1 percent of all occupied units. However, the "condo" and "co-op" forms of ownership were not even counted until the 1970 census. Prior to 1970, they were subsumed under the owner-occupied category.

The 1970 U.S. census reported that approximately 40 million housing units were occupied by their owners ("owner-occupied"). Almost 90 percent of these units, or 35.66 million, were one-family houses, the primary form of housing in the United States. In addition, about 65 percent of all occupied housing was owner occupied. Thus, about one out of three families in the United States rent their dwellings. Among the nation's homeowners, about two families out of three occupy property that is mortgaged or otherwise financed.

Table 1 reveals an increasing trend toward home ownership. Prior to 1930 the rate of home ownership remained in the 46–48 percent range,

TABLE 1
Number and Percentage of Owner-Occupied Dwelling Units,
1890–1974

Year	Number (000)	Percentage
1890	6,066	47.8
1900	7,205	46.7
1910	9,084	45.9
1920	10,867	45.6
1930	14,002	47.8
1940	15,196	43.6
1950	23,560	55.0
1960	32,797	61.9
1970	39,885	62.9
1974	45,785	64.6

Sources: U.S. Bureau of the Census, *The Statistical History of the United States from Colonial Times to the Present* (Stamford, Conn.: Fairfield, 1965), p. 395; U.S. Bureau of the Census, *Statistical Abstract of the United States* (Washington, D.C.: U.S. Government Printing Office, 1961), p. 761; U.S. Bureau of the Census, *Census of Housing, 1970*, vol. 1: *Housing Characteristics for States, Cities, and Counties*, part 1, "U.S. Summary" (Washington, D.C.: U.S. Government Printing Office, 1972), p. 16; and U.S. Bureau of the Census, *Current Housing Reports*, "Advance Report H-150-74, Annual Housing Survey, 1974," part B, "Indicators of Housing and Neighborhood Quality for the United States and Regions" (Washington, D.C.: U.S. Government Printing Office, 1976), p. 1.

but the rate had dropped to 44 percent by 1940, reflecting the hard times of the depression. Between 1940 and 1960 the rate of home ownership increased notably, to 62 percent, partly because of the availability of FHA-insured and VA-guaranteed low down payment home loans. Table 1 shows that the rate of home ownership continues to inch upward as the younger homeowners of the 1970s join the majority of older homeowners.

Home Values and Prices

How much should a home buyer pay for the home of his choice? The answer to this question comes most directly from the economics of supply and demand. However, an understanding of several interrelated forces will assist the buyer in arriving at his "set" of decisions, over a period of time, as to whether to rent, buy, hold on, or sell.

Supply and Demand. The price of housing depends upon the supply of and the demand for housing. In real estate, supply and demand relate to the local marketplace where homes already exist or are being built. On the one hand, there is an inventory (supply) of existing, older housing and of newly built homes, and on the other hand, a certain number of home buyers (demand) are out in the market looking for homes. Three out of every four homes sold are older homes. One out of every four homes sold is a new home.

The value of a home depends upon current and anticipated local economic conditions. That value is supported by many factors, including the strength and diversity of a community's economic base—its jobs market and the earnings level of its workers. The higher the earnings level, the higher the housing prices and the more likely it is that the level of housing values will increase over a period of time.

A locality that has a strong jobs market will attract nonlocal people, with a resultant demand for working space, living space, and recreational space. Thus, office buildings will be erected, and cultural and recreational opportunities will expand. Services to the local population will also grow, providing still more jobs. The growth and diversity of such a locality will attract industry, jobs, people, and housing. Demand will rise, prices will rise, and housing values will be enhanced.

Location. Any locality is composed of a number of living areas, or neighborhoods. A neighborhood has "location" if it evidences superior housing designs, well-groomed and -maintained houses and yards, trees and tranquillity, quality public services (e.g., schools, libraries, fire stations), and abundant private services, such as shopping, professional offices, theaters, and churches. When the home buyer wishes to "guarantee" the long-lasting value of his forthcoming home purchase, he buys "location" as well as his home.

In housing, the prime importance of location cannot be overstated. Residential location explains why certain homes in certain neighborhoods maintain higher (or lower) differential pricing than do other homes in other neighborhoods. In short, people want to live there and will pay a higher price to do so.

The 1970s Phenomenon. During the 1970s the stock of existing housing in America did not depreciate in value, as it is ordinarily expected to do. A house is a consumer product which should diminish in value with increasing age and use. Yet during the 1970s market prices of older houses went sky-high because of the rising costs of land and a lack of sufficient new construction.

There is a set of costs that are associated with the housing product, that includes the costs of the unimproved land, building materials, labor, short-term construction financing, long-term mortgage financing, marketing, and administration. And there is another set of costs that are not usually associated with the housing product, including the costs of sewerage, fuel and utility unavailability, construction moratorium delay, application and permit fees, and compliance with federal and local regulations. In various localities across the country the supply of new housing has been legislated, delayed, or constrained, with attendant effects on the prices of new homes. If demand is not restricted along with supply, price levels necessarily rise. Rising prices on both new and used homes, as well as rising energy costs, have caused a second glance at run-down inner-city properties as hidden values. As a result there has been a thriving urban rehabilitation market.

Selection. Basically, a home may be purchased either for the amenities that home ownership provides or for investment. Prior to severe inflation and the rapid price escalations of the 1970s, home buyers regarded their purchases as falling into the former category rather than the latter. Since home prices have been rising substantially, however, home purchases must not only provide "nice living" but be sound financially. Otherwise, when the homeowner has to sell his home he may be unable to do so on satisfactory terms.

As a result, the selection of a home—whether new, slightly used, or very much used; urban, suburban, or rural; condominium or cooperative apartment (in a garden, row house, or high-rise structural arrangement); semiattached town house or free-standing single-family house—should be predicated on its future resale probabilities. Today's home buyer must calculate more options and variables into his home ownership decision than existed only a few short years ago. His risk of financial loss is higher, not only because of the larger sums of money required but because of the larger number of shopping variables that have been introduced into the home-buying decision.

Mortgage Money.   As home prices have increased, so have the mortgage loans required. Higher loan-to-value ratios are widespread, with private mortgage insurance coverage on the top 20–25 percent of the loan limiting the conventional lender's topside risk. The size of monthly mortgage payments has also increased, so that two-person incomes are frequently required to meet them.

The availability and the cost of mortgage money in any locality depends largely on factors that go beyond the local scene. The prime determinant is the national monetary policy pursued by the Federal Reserve Board and the effects of that policy on interest rates.

Closely related to national monetary policy is national fiscal policy, or deficit spending as a result of unbalanced federal budgets. As the U.S. Treasury underwrites a rising national debt by competing for short- and intermediate-term loan funds in money markets, its competition forces interest rates to rise. As savings deposits are withdrawn from mortgage lenders, the available loan funds shrink and mortgage interest rates rise. This process of disintermediation acts as an obstacle to both the purchase of new homes and the sale of existing homes in order to trade up.

To the extent that the home buyer (or the home seller) reviews broad mortgage market conditions, his home ownership decision will be more soundly conceived. He will know when mortgage interest rates will be higher or lower and when it will be easier or harder to buy or sell his home. As he understands more and becomes more flexible, he will also be more willing to enter into creative financing and contractual arrangements that will facilitate his purchase or sale of a home.

Qualification.   Essentially, both the home and the home buyer must qualify. An appraisal report establishes the market value of the home for mortgage loan purposes. The lender may then issue a loan commitment to the buyer, so that the buyer knows how much loan he can get and at what cost. Loan terms and charges vary considerably from lender to lender, property to property, area to area, and neighborhood to neighborhood. Home buyers are well advised to shop around among lenders for the best rates and terms.

Second, the home buyer must qualify as to creditworthiness. Important determinants of creditworthiness include the stability of employment and the gross earnings of the husband and wife, assets and savings, prior contractual debt, and prior installment debt repayment. We live in a credit-oriented society in which debt payments have become a way of life. As long as one's income statement reflects proportional balance of debits over credits, and one's balance sheet shows a surplus of assets over liabilities and a resultant net worth, one becomes a viable candidate for home ownership. If one has shown responsibility in paying earlier, smaller bills, one moves upward to the responsibility for home ownership where the debt and the bills become larger.

Loans, Rates, and Terms.   New-home loans include private, conventional loans and loans that are guaranteed (VA) or insured (FHA) by the U.S. government. Loans on the sale of existing homes include these three categories plus assumptions (takeovers) of existing mortgages and junior financing (second mortgages, deeds of trust). Lending institutions make the new loans; private individuals such as home sellers grant loan assumptions; and various real estate investors grant secondary or junior loans.

Conventional home loans are made predominantly by savings and loan associations, at market rates of interest, for long terms with high loan-to-value ratios (between 70 percent and 95 percent). Buyers who wish to make low down payments need private mortgage insurance for the top part of the loan extended. In this way, down payments can be as low as 5 or 10 percent of a home's sale price.

FHA and VA "loans" are usually made not by the federal government but by lending institutions (mutual savings banks, mortgage bankers) which receive FHA insurance (up to $65,000) or a VA guarantee (up to $25,000). Historically, these "no (or low) down payment" loans with the highest loan-to-value ratio have been especially helpful to first-time home buyers. As home prices have climbed, the number of conventional loans that have been written has exceeded the number of FHA/VA loans.

The rate of interest on FHA and VA loans has been set by government action. Since the market rates of interest on mortgage loans are usually higher than the FHA/VA rates, lenders who process FHA and VA loans require that "points" be paid to bring those loans up to the market rate. One point equals 1 percent of the face amount of the loan, and a lender's charge (called the "discount") of one point raises the net yield on the loan by one eighth of 1 percent. The law requires that one point only be paid by the home buyer as a loan-processing fee, with all other points (discount points) being charged to the home seller. As a result many home sellers require buyers to qualify for conventional rather than FHA or VA loans.

The Ownership Decision

From our analysis thus far, the reader might reasonably surmise that the deck is stacked in favor of home ownership and against renting. Unfortunately—as further analysis will reveal—this is so, whether because of the concerted buying actions of numerous individuals and families, local community sentiment, or federal taxation policy. However, there are situations that favor renting over owning.

The Advantages of Renting.   Psychologically and emotionally, owning is not for everyone. The signing of contracts for large sums of money, both for the home purchase and for the mortgage loan, may be traumatic experiences. Moreover, the home-buying commitment is long term, involving personal responsibility for, say, 360 regular monthly payments over a 30-year period. On the other hand, the rental lease contract is short term, involves much lower sums, and leaves all housing options open.

Although it is generally believed that home ownership is a good investment, the numerous decisions about when, where, and what to buy and how much to commit to the purchase price and the down payment are often not too well recognized nor analyzed by home buyers, especially first-timers. Horror stories abound of home buyers who bought unwisely. By and large, buying a home is an emotional rather than an analytic experience.

Adding to the difficulties of home buying, there is much ignorance and confusion concerning the terms, the economics, the legalities, the procedures, and the alternatives available in the home-buying transaction. Since so much money is involved, many different and specialized real estate actors hover over the home-buying scene. Those who are in the business of handling the transitions from renter status to ownership, and beyond, must still do a great deal to dispel buyer ignorance and buyer fears.

High mobility needs present another justification for rental. Local and wider geographic movements necessitated by job changes and other factors are facilitated when only a lease needs to be broken rather than a house sold or rented. America's families move on average every five years. Given the scattered "extended" family and the shortening of distances by advances in transportation, social commentators feel that mobility will increase even further.

Moreover, ownership imposes such burdens as the care of landscaping, the knowledge and use of maintenance tools and equipment, and the handling of paperwork (insurance and tax forms, mortgage payments, repair and maintenance contracts and payments). Operating his home requires the homeowner to make more decisions and to allocate more time, money, and physical attention than he may realize. The renter may not wish to burden himself with these cares, choosing alternative ways to spend his time and money. Freedom from home management may give the renter time to increase his earnings, to travel, to engage in cultural or athletic pursuits, and so on.

The condominium and homeowner association responsibility for the shared common area, as in certain retirement villages, are seen as two life-style choices which reduce the physical burden of home ownership. Thus, by paying others to do the physical work, one can live to some extent as a "carefree renter," yet enjoy the advantages of home ownership.

The rental of a house rather than an apartment may be advisable where the homeowner-to-be wishes to learn firsthand of the varied responsibilities of ownership. Also, a rental/home ownership arrangement might be entered into through a lease with an option to purchase, perhaps with payments that accumulate toward the down payment. Certain absentee owners who live at great distances from their housing assets believe that such contractual arrangements will impel renters to exercise better care in maintaining the rented property. This reduces the worries of the absentee owner and increases the opportunities for the renter.

Some long-standing renters prefer regularized rental payments with reasonable rent increases factored in, to the risk of unexpected or hidden home ownership expenses, such as central air conditioning, heating system, and roof repairs and electrical, plumbing, and appliance replacements. Any monies saved in this way can be invested in non–real estate holdings to enhance a liquid, financial position.

The Costs of Owning versus the Costs of Renting. The previous section presented the rationale for home ownership and the rationale for renting. Here the dollars-and-cents choice between owning and renting is assessed.

Table 2 assumes the purchase of a $42,000 home for which the buyer paid $2,100 down (or a 5 percent down payment) and $1,400 in title closing charges and qualified for a $39,900 conventional mortgage that is to be amortized monthly over a 30-year period with interest at 9 percent per year. On those assumptions, the table shows typical monthly home ownership and rental costs.

The above calculation, or one like it, would have to be performed each and every year in order to compare the costs of owning with the costs of renting. For the first year as presented, the renter would pay only $430 while the owner would pay $578.37 out in cash. The owner would have tax advantages and loan amortization which would reduce his monthly costs to $472.31 without appreciation being considered. Appreciation would further reduce the monthly costs.

In succeeding years the rents would rise. The comparisons for later years should also consider changing property taxes, income tax brackets, and appreciation rates.

The Homeowner's Role

Should the decision be made to buy, the goal of home ownership can be attained by a series of identifiable steps. The "mystery" of buying a home is nothing more than understanding the sequence of steps involved.

How to Become a Homeowner. *1. Finding the Home.* Listings of available older houses for sale usually come on the market by way of listing agreements (contracts) between the home seller (the principal) and the broker (the agent) who represents the home seller. In addition, new homes in subdivisions may be handled by employees of the builder who sell at the site. Other homes are advertised for sale by their owners.

2. Selecting the Right Home. The choice of a home is made by means of two analyses: (1) inspecting the home and the lot for the soundness of the structural condition (quality of construction, basement, roof, insu-

TABLE 2
The Costs of Owning versus the Costs of Renting

Ownership Costs		*Rental Costs*	
Gross Housing Cost			
Monthly mortgage payment (principal and interest)	$321.06	Monthly rental	$350.00
Other monthly costs		Garage fee	30.00
Real estate taxes prorated	74.00	Utilities	50.00
Property insurance prorated	12.00		
Private mortgage insurance prorated ...	8.31		
FHA insurance prorated	0		
Second-mortgage payments	0		
Homeowners association/condominium	0		
Total (PITI)	$415.37		
Add maintenance costs (estimated at 1.5 percent of dwelling value)	53.00		
Add repair costs (to stabilize depreciation or maintain property value)	35.00		
Add utilities	75.00		
Total monthly housing cost	$578.37	Total rental	$430.00
Net Housing Cost			
Add monthly income lost on down payment plus closing costs ($2,100 plus $1,400) at 6.5 percent per year (rounded)	$ 19.00		

Subtract income tax deductions
Monthly mortgage interest,
first year (about $286)
times 25 percent income tax
bracket (assumed) 71.50
Monthly real estate taxes ($74)
times 25 percent income tax
bracket (assumed) 18.50
Total monthly tax savings ...... $ 90.00
Subtract monthly amortization
(principal repayment—$321.06
minus $286) .... $ 35.06

Net before Appreciation $472.31
Subtract monthly appreciation
of home ($42,000 times average
rate of price inflation of
6 percent per year) $201.65
Net after Appreciation $270.66

lation), the state of the various mechanical systems (electrical, plumbing, heating, and air conditioning), and drainage or settling (expert appraisals may be necessary to ascertain remedial deficiencies); and (2) establishing the "value soundness" of the price and the property. Then, if the buyer has to sell quickly, he will not have overpaid nor will he be unable to sell because of a poor house or location. Homeowner warranty insurance is now available for both new and used housing. Such insurance can cover structural components and mechanical systems. However, no guarantees of value soundness exist for the buyer. The "right" price must be paid for the "right" place.

3. *Making the Offer.* When the prospective buyer has selected the house he wants he makes an offer to the seller incorporating the inspection conditions noted above and a financing clause indicating how and at what terms he wishes to qualify, and stating the house-and-lot items that he wishes to be included in the sale. If the buyer needs assistance, he should seek out his own broker or agent to represent his interests. Should the buyer's offer be accepted by the seller, the buyer and seller would have a valid sale contract at that point, and contract modifications would require agreement from both parties. Thus, the buyer's first offer should be complete. Oral understandings cannot be enforced; everything must be in writing.

4. *Obtaining the Loan.* The home sale price minus the buyer's down payment equal the amount of loan necessary. The lender's appraisal will establish the fair market value for loan purposes. The lender's qualification of the buyer generally establishes *(a)* that the sale price should not exceed two to three times the buyer's annual income, or *(b)* that the total monthly mortgage payments (including principal, interest, taxes, and insurance) should not exceed 25 percent of the buyer's gross income, or *(c)* that all housing expenses (including utilities, maintenance and upkeep, association fees, sewerage, and special assessments) should not exceed one third of the buyer's gross income.

Sometimes the seller will provide loan money by carrying back all or a portion of the sale price (when this is done, the mortgage is called a purchase-money mortgage) or by permitting the buyer to assume the existing loan (this is usually subject to the lender's permission). Sometimes a private, third-party source of financing is obtained, so that a second mortgage (or a deed of trust) is used for a portion of the total loan.

5. *Getting Good Title.* Just as the lender wants to receive his money eventually, the buyer wants to receive his title. The lender will require a title examination, or the buyer will see that the public records are searched for the chain of title and outstanding liens against the property. An attorney's written opinion of title will report on the state of title. Even when these things are done, defects in title may exist which the search of the public records failed to disclose. Therefore, a mortgagee's title insurance policy is obtained in order to protect the lender's loan and an owner's title insurance policy is obtained in order to protect the buyer's equity (the down payment).

For recorded subdivisions, property descriptions pose no problem. The surveyor's plat establishes the boundary lines of the property. In the absence of a surveyor's plat, a survey may be necessary to establish a legal description of the property and to determine whether any encroachments exist. If encroachments do exist, they constitute a cloud on the title until they are removed or resolved. A deed with a legal description is the legally recognized document that evidences and conveys title to the property.

Transfer Costs. Transfer costs are the closing costs of the sale transaction. In that transaction, title is transfered from the seller to the buyer—or from one owner to another—and money is exchanged. Most of this is the lender's money, for the lender pays off the lien of the old loan, gives the remainder of the funds to the seller as owner's accumulated equity (the sale price minus outstanding loans and liens equals the owner's equity), and places his own mortgage lien on the property for the amount of the new loan that he grants.

Closing costs can be either the seller's costs or the buyer's costs, depending upon the terms of the sale contract. These can be split in various combinations. What usually determines how they are split is the customary practice of the given locality. Table 3 is a listing of typical closing costs payable by the buyer and the seller in the Washington area. As was noted earlier, the closing costs can differ—slightly or very greatly—for each sale transaction, since the contractual terms between the buyer and the seller are arrived by a process of negotiation.

"Closings" are sometimes performed with efficiency, usually with speed. At many closings, the buyer is entering new territory. He should feel free to request time to ask questions and to read the documents before he signs them. The federal Real Estate Settlement Procedures Act (RESPA) requires that buyers and sellers have access to the settlement charges one to three business days before the closing date—just so that they can read and understand these papers beforehand.

Playing and Ending the Homeowner's Role. As a condition of obtaining the mortgage loan, the new homeowner agrees to keep the property in good condition. The mortgage instrument is itself a pledge of property (by the debtor or borrower) as security for the payment of a debt. Thus, the property must be kept "whole" and not allowed to waste or deteriorate.

Also, the promissory note which accompanies the mortgage (or the deed of trust) is a formal document showing the existence of a debt and stating the terms of repayment. Should the homeowner fail to meet those terms or cause waste to the asset, the lender may initiate foreclosure action. The lender may also practice loan forbearance and the like if the homeowner has been reliable and reasonable in his earlier dealings with the lender and other creditors.

Home repairs may be necessary in the course of time. At this point, the homeowner's basic skills may be taxed to their limits. If the homeowner doesn't know what he is doing, he may be better advised to rely on warranties, guarantees, service agreements, and the like, than to at-

TABLE 3
Closing Costs Paid by the Buyer and the Seller in the Washington, D.C., Area

Buyer Pays

1. The down payment.
2. The appraisal fee.
3. The credit report fee.
4. The inspection fee.
5. The new mortgage.
6. The loan origination fee.
7. The private mortgage insurance fee (on a conventional loan with a high loan-to-value ratio).
8. The pro rata share of real estate taxes which the seller has paid in advance (from the date of closing through the end of the tax payment period).
9. Term life insurance to cover the total mortgage loan.
10. The fee for the preparation of loan documents (mortgage promissory note).
11. The notary's fee.
12. The title search and report fees.
13. The costs of title insurance for the lender's policy and the owner's policy.
14. Prepaid real estate taxes for the next payment period (six months or one year).
15. Prepaid hazard insurance for one to three years.
16. The deed-recording fees.
17. The documentary stamp tax.
18. The settlement attorney's legal fees (on VA loans, the buyer is not permitted to pay these fees).

Seller Pays

1. The commission to the real estate broker.
2. The balance of the existing mortgage.
3. Transfer taxes to the local government and the state government.
4. The survey fees.
5. His pro rata share of real estate taxes which have not been paid in advance (from January 1 to the date of the closing/title transfer).
6. For the agreed-upon repairs or replacements.
7. The discount points if the buyer has an FHA or a VA loan qualification.
8. The deed preparation fees.
9. The fees of the seller's attorney.
10. If the property is rented, his pro rata share of the rent he has received in advance (from the first of the month to the date of closing) plus the security deposit.

tempt to do repair work himself. In fact, should the homeowner botch a repair job, he may void whatever warranty may exist on the system or appliance that he attempted to repair.

It is more pleasant to contemplate the tax benefits of home ownership than the problems of home maintenance. Home ownership provides income tax deductions. The monthly interest payments are deductible from the annual income tax. Lenders usually furnish an annual principal and interest statement to the homeowner.

Real estate or property taxes are also deductible in the year that they are paid to the local government. Should an impound escrow account exist with the lender into which the buyer prepays his real estate taxes, the lender will furnish an annual statement showing the amount of real estate taxes paid.

The "loan origination fee" or "points" paid by the buyer in order to obtain a mortgage on the buyer's personal or principal residence are tax deductible as an itemized personal interest expense, if such charging of points constitutes established business practice in the given locality. These charges are compensation paid solely for the use of money and are deductible in full in the year they are paid. However, a VA or FHA "loan processing fee" is not tax deductible.

Other tax deductibles include the amount charged by a lender as penalty for the prepayment of a mortgage and the portion of interest paid by tenant-stockholders in cooperative apartments on the cooperative housing corporation's indebtedness.

As the years go by and the homeowner builds up sufficient equity in his residence, he may refinance his loan and "pull out" some of that equity for home improvement, investment, vacation expenses, college costs, and so on. The funds he receives are tax free—they are not treated as income received. Moreover, the new, larger loan now carries a larger interest cost, and all mortgage interest is tax deductible.

Profits from the sale of capital assets, including one's home, are called capital gains. Upon the sale of his home the homeowner pays taxes on only 40 percent of his gain. This is the long-term capital gain rate for assets owned 12 months and one day, or longer. The other 60 percent of his profit is untaxed.

Should the homeowner move up to higher priced housing, his capital gains tax is deferred until such time as he sells his house or trades down to less expensive housing. The residence replacement rule applies to the purchase of a more expensive replacement principal residence which is bought or built within 18 months of the time that the present residence is sold. If the homeowner buys or trades down to a less expensive replacement, his profit is taxed up to the difference in the two prices.

If the homeowner or the spouse is 55 or older, and they have lived in the principal residence at least three of the last five years, profit from the first $100,000 of the home sale price is tax exempt.

On an installment sale, if the homeowner elects to receive 30 percent or less of the home's sale price in the year of sale, from the buyer's down payment and principal payments on the mortgage or contract, the seller's tax is paid in the year that the installment payments are received. The advantage of an installment sale is that the home seller does not receive large sale profits all at once, placing him into a higher tax bracket. Also, the seller earns interest on the purchase-money mortgage loan, or the sale contract, which the seller has extended to a qualified buyer.

During the period of home ownership, money may be spent on capital home improvements which add to the value of the property. Such improvements include built-in appliances, kitchen or bathroom remodelings, air conditioning systems, room additions, improvements, roof, patios, and major driveway and garage repairs. The cost of these capital improvements is added to the home's original cost basis (the home's purchase price), to become part of the adjusted cost basis when the home is sold or transferred. The adjusted cost basis is subtracted from the adjusted sale price (the gross sale price minus the sale costs) to determine the capital gain.

Other items that may be added to the purchase price of the old home for purposes of capital gain computations when the owner sells his home include title search and insurance costs, survey, appraisal, and credit report fees; and attorney's fees. Good records of pertinent outlays should be kept for later reference and use from the date that a home is purchased.

Similarly, fix-up costs incurred in contemplation of a home sale and made within 90 days of the signing of a sale contract, are subtracted from the sale price to arrive at an adjusted sale price. Such costs can include painting and repair costs and cleanup costs. The broker's sale commission and other closing costs incurred by the home seller are also subtracted from the sale price to arrive at the adjusted sale price.

SECOND-HOME INVESTMENTS*

Ina S. Bechhoefer

*I*NA S. BECHHOEFER, *Bethesda, Maryland.*

Research associate, Homer Hoyt Institute and Metro Metrics, Inc. Consultant in real estate and urban development. Formerly instructor in real estate and urban development studies, School of Business Administration, The American University, Washington, D.C. Author of articles, book reviews, and annotated bibliographies on real estate and urban development for such publications as Growth and Change *and* Realtor.

During the 1960s and 1970s there has been a growing trend toward second-home ownership. As used in this chapter, the term *second homes* refers to vacation homes—units which are generally not intended to provide primary living space but rather are designed to serve or foster various types of leisure activities.[1]

In many cases, second homes are bought for investment purposes—second-home purchases often seek capital appreciation and rental income from their properties. In this regard, however, the results have been decidedly mixed. This chapter will focus on the financial aspects—the rewards and risks—of second-home ownership.

There are many types of second homes and second-home communities. Second homes may take the form of detached single-family houses, town houses, units in multifamily (apartment) houses, or farms. They may be located on lakes, rivers, or oceans or in the mountains. They may be located on scattered sites, in subdivisions, or in high-amenity

---

* The author would like to acknowledge the assistance of Charles Bechhoefer in the preparation of this chapter. Mr. Bechhoefer is an attorney and, with the author, a partner in a second-home condominium unit.

[1] Second homes are generally not retirement homes, though some are used for that purpose. Retirement homes present a host of their own unique problems and are beyond the scope of this discussion.

leisure home communities equipped with such attractions as swimming pools, golf courses, and tennis courts. (At the other extreme, what is purchased may be only a campsite or a campground or a lot for future second-home construction.) Second homes may be in locations that emphasize summer activities, such as swimming and boating, or they may be at winter-oriented ski resorts. Indeed, some second homes are in locations at which both summer and winter activities are stressed. Second homes may be new or used—custom built or prefabricated. Second-home units in multifamily dwellings may be condominiums or cooperatives. In fact, the number of possible configurations is endless. Because of this variety, if a financial analysis of second-home ownership is to be relevant to any particular investment, the characteristics of second-home units serving comparable purposes must be taken into account.

THE POTENTIALS AND PROBLEMS OF SECOND-HOME INVESTMENTS

Appreciation

As regards appreciation, whether a second-home investment makes sense depends both on the property involved and on the owner's investment objectives. The prices of second homes have been escalating rapidly: the price of an average second home is more than twice what it was five years ago. In fact, in many communities the prices of second homes have risen as much as 10 percent per year. However, the price performance of second homes has been uneven and, as will be shown, buying a second home for investment purposes may be rather risky.

Many real estate investments provide a greater—and more certain—rate of return than does second-home ownership, and hence represent superior investments. For example, primary residences in rapidly growing metropolitan areas have appreciated far more rapidly than have second homes. Similarly, the average rates of return on commercial and industrial properties have been higher than those on second homes.

Moreover, much of the average price rise in second homes has resulted from changing trends in second homes. These include trends toward increases in square footage, the upgrading of accommodations and amenities, and a growth in services. Whereas most second homes traditionally had no heat, a growing proportion of them now have not only heat but central air conditioning as well. In addition, many second homes now include such costly features as swimming pools and golf and tennis privileges. Many people desire to buy second homes in maintenance-free communities such as condominium or cooperative developments. The cost of the services rendered in such communities is reflected in (and in part a cause of) higher average second-home prices.

Moreover, the effects of inflation must be taken into consideration when evaluating the appreciation potential of second-home investments. After the annual inflation rate of recent years has been deducted, the real rate of appreciation of particular second-home prices may turn out to have been very small indeed.

Marketability

Not only has the appreciation rate of second-home units lagged behind that of primary housing, but the salability of "used" second-home units has fluctuated to a greater extent than has that of primary units. A good rule of thumb is that in marketing a vacation home property, one should be prepared to hold on to the property for a long time. Selling a second home is usually more difficult than selling a primary residence. The consummation of such sales is highly dependent upon the state of the economy—during economic downturns, the market for second homes can virtually disappear, as it did in many areas of the country during the 1974–75 recession. (This means that an investor who is forced to sell a second home quickly may pay a substantial price penalty in order to do so.)

Under normal economic conditions, a vacation home is usually more marketable in season than during off-season periods. Properties which feature such attractions as swimming and boating should be sold in the summer and—conversely—bought in the winter. The reverse is true for ski properties. Consequently, if one fails to sell a property during a given peak season, one should try to hold off selling until the following peak season. If the market has soured by that time, it may be necessary to wait out the poor market period or to take a substantial loss in order to sell the property.

Financing

Coupled with the risky appreciation potential of second-home units, and to some extent a cause of it, is the relatively poor financing that is available for such units. The financing of such units may be tight, with mortgage money often unavailable. As second homes have proliferated, however, this problem has lessened somewhat. Nevertheless, at certain times and for high-risk properties, the terms for second-home mortgages, particularly on resales, are poor in comparison with the terms for other real estate investments.

Second-home properties can be financed in several ways. In seeking financing for a second home, it is important to remember that the lender will seek to make sure that the second-home owner's sources of income will be sufficient to support the debt service *after* other expenses (such as the mortgage on a primary home) have been met.

Unimproved Property. Most sales of land for a second-home unit are made on a cash basis. However, the land can be used later as security for the building of the second home. Some land for second homes is sold through a land contract (or an installment contract) in which the purchaser makes a small down payment (often 10 percent or less) and pays off the balance in small monthly payments, at interest rates which are usually several points higher than the prevailing prime interest rate. Under such contracts, no title is passed until the contract is paid off; if as little as one payment is missed, the land can revert to the seller. Land for second homes may also be financed through purchase-money mortgages (under which the seller, in most cases, takes back a mortgage and thus helps finance the purchase).

Improved Property. Where improved properties are involved, additional alternatives are available.

Conventional Mortgages. The term of years of conventional mortgages on second homes is normally shorter than that of conventional mortgages on primary homes, and the interest rate is usually higher. Down payments on scattered-lot developments may range from 25 percent to 40 percent, and a term of as little as 15 years is not uncommon. In some cases, the use of private mortgage insurance may enable the buyer to purchase a second home with a down payment of 10–20 percent, but such insurance also has a cost. Only in large developments are second-home down payments in the 10 percent range common, but even there private mortgage insurance may be required in order to obtain such financing.

It is frequently difficult to find an institution that is willing to lend on second-home properties, particularly where a resale is involved. The best bet is a bank or a savings and loan association in the area of the property, rather than an institution in the area of the buyer's primary home. The local lending institution is more familiar with the values and the peculiarities of the area and with the subject property itself. Further, it will have a stake in the growth and development of the area.

In general, the larger a development or project, the easier it is to get financing for a second-home unit in it. But, in many high-risk areas, conventional mortgages for second homes may be unobtainable, leaving open only marginal means of financing.

Open-End Mortgages. In this type of mortgage, the amount borrowed can be increased after the mortgage has been issued. Such an arrangement is particularly attractive if the owner intends to remodel or add to an existing structure.

Package Mortgages. These mortgages cover not only the structure and the lot but also such items of personal property as appliances, carpeting, and draperies. Package mortgages are often used in second-home developments—particularly where items such as carpeting serve as a substitute for finished flooring. The advantage of this type of financing is that it lowers the initial investment costs. However, since many of the items included in a package mortgage may wear out or become functionally obsolescent before the mortgage is paid off, replacement items may have to be purchased while the owner is still paying for the original items.

Second Mortgages. These mortgages bear more risk than first mortgages, and for second homes the resulting cost may be so great that the buyer may have to seek alternative means of obtaining the funds he or she needs in addition to the amount of the first mortgage. The seller may, however, be willing to take back a second mortgage, particularly as an incentive for a sale. In such cases, the cost of a second mortgage may be more reasonable.

Personal Loans. Where other financing is unavailable, resort may have to be made to financing obtained personally by the second-home buyer. Personal unsecured loans usually carry high interest rates and are limited in term and amount. Some persons have used the equity on their primary homes to finance second homes (or have refinanced their primary homes to do so). Refinancing for primary homes is usually more available and more advantageous in terms of interest rate and repayment terms than is second-home financing. But refinancing a primary home in the current mortgage market normally results in the payment of a higher interest rate than the interest rate on the original primary-home mortgage. Moreover, many new risks may accompany this alternative. With a higher financial obligation on the primary home, adverse conditions could jeopardize the investment in the primary home, particularly if it is then difficult to sell the second home. A loan on the cash value of a life insurance policy is yet another way to obtain low-cost funds for the purchase of a second home.

Distress Areas. What might appear to be "bargains" in financing are among the incentives which may be offered to market distress properties. Ocean City, Maryland, was greatly overbuilt in 1976, and as a result it contained many such distress properties. At that time, reflecting the desire of owners to unload distress properties, signs in the overbuilt condominium area proclaimed terms of as low as 5 percent down; 6, 7, or 8 percent interest rates (considerably less than the otherwise prevailing 9½–10 percent rates); and no payments for over a year. In many instances these terms were coupled with lowered asking prices. Those "bargains," however, had to be balanced against the likelihood that a considerable number of years would have to elapse before returns could be generated in the distressed area and that second-home buyers would be faced with extreme difficulties if they wished to sell their properties in the interim.

Refinancing. At this writing, the refinancing of second homes remains an acute problem even in successful large-scale developments. Stiff prepayment penalties on existing mortgages are the rule rather than the exception. The assumption of a loan by a new purchaser is rarely permissible. Even where an institution has been the mortgagee on a property, the terms it offers a new purchaser are rarely as good as the terms it offered the existing owner.

Other Risks

It is important to bear in mind that second-home investments are susceptible to many risks besides the market, financial, liquidity, and inflation risks that have already been discussed. Indeed, those additional risks can be particularly threatening to second-home investments. The additional risks include legal risks, natural hazards, and developability risks.

Legal Risks. Potential legal risks can be a serious problem, particularly in rural areas. Second homes are often located in areas in which property boundaries are poorly delineated. Ascertaining property lines can involve lengthy and expensive legal hassles. In such areas zoning and building codes are commonly nonexistent or poorly enforced. Therefore, little protection is afforded the individual property owner. Frequently there is little that a homeowner can do to prevent the erection of nearby jerry-built structures or nonconforming structures that can adversely affect property values. At the other extreme, however, conservation groups and environmental protection agencies, particularly in coastal areas, may be able to prevent a second-home owner from using his property as he wishes.

Risks from Natural Hazards. Unfortunately, where great scenic amenities exist, there may also be a potential for natural disaster. At the seashore, there may be the threat of hurricanes. In the mountains, avalanches may be a problem. In still other areas, earthquakes may be a strong possibility. Other natural hazards—less dramatic but no less severe—must also be taken into consideration. For example, the risk of erosion is particularly great in mountain and seashore areas. In the mountains, erosion can affect the stability and the usability of a structure. At the seashore, it is not uncommon for several feet of land to be washed away in a season or even in a single storm. Barrier beaches, in particular, have constantly shifting coastlines. In desert areas, there are risks of sandstorms and dwindling water sources.

Developability. Developability problems may be more difficult to solve in second-home areas than in areas of primary-home development. The feasibility of developing a given property may be dependent upon a host of factors beyond the control of an individual property owner. To give but one example: in rural, sparsely developed areas, the cost of running utility lines to a property from the nearest juncture point may be so great as to render a project undevelopable.

RENTALS

Given the appreciation uncertainties inherent in second-home properties, many would-be investors have looked into vacation units for their rental potential. It has been estimated that over 40 percent of second-home owners have attempted to rent their units at one time or another. But the percentage of second homes that have actually been rented is much smaller. In areas where a variety of recreational opportunities are available throughout the year, only one fourth of the homes are actually rented. In areas where only seasonal activities are available, the proportion of rented homes is even lower. Given all-season developments with active rental management, however, the percentage could be higher. But, on average, the rewards of rentals have been uncertain and the risks high.

Perhaps the most important factor to be taken into account in determining the rental potential of a second-home property is the length of the rental season. In many Southern areas, the season may be virtually year-round, though there may be high and low subseasons. In Northern seaside resorts, the season covers roughly the summer months (with some rentals possible at lower rates in the spring and fall).

What occupancy does this lead to? The typical second home is occupied only about 50 days per year, including both rental and owner occupancy. The figure varies with the distance of the second home from the owner's primary home or from a major metropolitan area from which weekend clients may be drawn, with the length of the prime season in the second-home area, and with the extent to which the property is endowed with amenities. Amenities may serve to extend the season considerably—for example, such features as indoor swimming pools and indoor tennis courts give year-round attractiveness to summer resorts in northern climates.[2] But amenities are also reflected in the costs of a rental unit, and the investment worth of such a unit is dependent upon the relationship between the rental received and the costs—both capital costs and operating and marketing expenses.

Any claims by a seller as to a property's potential for rental income should be checked out very thoroughly. If purchasing a used property in a community with similar units, ask to see income statements covering several years. Compare these statements with the experience of other owners in the area. Extreme caution should be exercised in purchasing a property if your ability to carry the unit is dependent upon the rental income it produces.

Self-Rentals versus Rentals through an Agent

An owner contemplating the rental of a unit must first decide between self-rental and rental through an agent. Rental agents have been known to charge from 12 to 50 percent of rental income for their services. Like the fees the services which the agents provide are highly variable—with the extent and quality of the services not always proportional to the fee charged for them.

In considering whether to use an agent, an owner should carefully consider all of the services which that agent can offer, as well as the agent's reputation in performing those services, and then determine whether, in the given circumstances, the services are worth the cost.

An agent should provide access to a considerable number of prospective tenants, either through past dealings with those customers or through marketing efforts. A good agent may make use of a number of forms of marketing, such as newspaper advertising and long-distance toll-free telephone lines. The latter will help make the property available to out-of-state tenants, since it will enable them to call directly without charge to obtain information on the nature of the property, the furnishings and accommodations, and the dates for which the property is available for rental. An individual owner could not reasonably afford to provide such a service and would, therefore, be practically limited to potential rental clients from the primary-home area. Moreover, even newspaper advertising, which is often used by individual owners, is expensive. Far greater volume enables an agent to secure such advertis-

---

[2] Occasionally, off-season rentals can be negotiated at very reduced prices to people such as teachers or retirees who desire to remain for the entire off-season and are willing to move on during the high-rent prime season. Since the prices are so low for such rentals, their major advantage is security—an occupied property is less susceptible to vandalism.

ing at lower rates and hence to advertise a property more extensively than can an owner.

Aside from expense, the time required to locate tenants can be considerable and the process frustrating. If an owner advertises for weekly rentals (a very usual time period for renting), three or four potential clients may have to be interviewed for each rental week. Many prospective tenants may make inquiries about the most attractive time period (for example, August at the ocean), but several advertisements may have to be placed before the less attractive weeks are filled. Moreover, some potential clients may not be satisfied with the particular unit or with the price; and many potential clients may be unsatisfactory to an owner because of such considerations as the number of persons in a party, or the number of children, or the use that is likely to be made of the property. Thus, many condominium developments establish a maximum number of persons who are permitted to occupy a unit of a given size. This is desirable not only to protect the unit itself but to prevent facilities from being overloaded. And an owner is always well advised to avoid renting a unit when it appears that the prospective tenants intend to use the unit for certain undesirable purposes, such as drinking brawls. In general, tenants in vacation homes can be very destructive—they are on vacation, and they often "do not care." But when a unit is sought for undesirable purposes, the potential for destruction is accentuated. A wise owner will attempt to avoid such situations. An on-site agent will be better able than an absentee owner to enforce limitations as to number of persons. On the other hand, an owner may be in a better position to find out whether use of the unit for undesirable purposes is contemplated and may be more willing to try to find out.

Cleaning must be carried out to some degree after every tenancy—an incoming tenant expects a unit to be reasonably clean. Rental agents' fees do not usually include cleaning expenses, but a rental agent will invariably see that a cleaning service is obtained and carries out the work as ordered prior to occupancy by a new tenant whom the agent has obtained. An absentee owner can often obtain the same service, but is in a much less favorable position to see that it is carried out properly in a timely manner.

Relying on tenants to clean the units themselves—in return for a lower rental price—may be risky, particularly if the owner does not know the tenants personally. An unclean unit will, in the long run, be less rentable.

One of the chief benefits of using a rental agent is the availability of a representative to handle the on-site problems which inevitably arise. In an area where second homes are frequently equipped with numerous appliances—air conditioners, washers, dryers, dishwashers, garbage disposals, television sets and the like—it is important for tenants to be able to enjoy the appliances which they are paying for. An on-site agent can often help see that the necessary repairs are made. Moreover, an agent can see that unneeded utilities are turned off or that excessive temperature settings are avoided when a unit is not rented.

An owner who rents his or her own unit should be prepared for crises.

Irate tenants may call at any hour of the day or night about countless major and minor disasters—from broken appliances to leaky faucets to noisy neighbors—and an owner who is far away may find it difficult to appease such tenants.

For self-rentals, an owner should leave explicit instructions as to how appliances work, where and how to obtain repairs, billing procedures, and how to turn appliances off before vacating the premises. An owner might be well advised to purchase service contracts on certain appliances and to let tenants know how they can obtain services under those contracts.

Selecting an Agent

Assuming that an owner decides to use an agent, how should the agent be selected? In some situations, a development may require that only a specified agent be used. But if a choice is available, the agent chosen should, if possible, be one whose major business is second-home rentals. The agent should be willing to pay personal attention to renting the property in question and should offer the services discussed above. The agent's reputation for performance should always be checked. Finally, there are some specialized national second-home rental services, such as Creative Rentals, a San Francisco–based organization which takes listings for condominiums at the more luxurious resorts.

The Rental Agreement

If an owner lists with an agent, the rental agreement should make clear the owner's desires or rights with regard to the following matters.

1. The type of tenants preferred (families, children, singles, etc).
2. The maximum number of occupants.
3. Whether or not pets are acceptable and, if so, the types of pets and the tenant's responsibility for damage done by pets.
4. The dates available for rental (and, conversely, the dates on which the owner plans to use the unit). The agreement should clearly specify the amount and type of notice that the owner must give in order to withdraw the unit from the market for a specified period of time.
5. The asking rental price and the pricing policy that the agent is to follow if the unit cannot be rented at the asking price (in particular, whether the owner must be consulted in such situations).
6. The deposit amount required, whether the balance is payable in advance, and the policy that is to be followed in the event of cancellation (including the amount of rental commission that is payable to the agent under those circumstances).
7. The types of services to be performed by the agent.
8. The fee or commission to be paid for the agent's services, including the timing of payments and additional fees, if any, for services not included in the basic agreement.

9. The assignment of responsibility for cleaning the unit between ten-
    ancies (and perhaps at other times).

A Case Example

It is impossible to cite a typical situation that illustrates the potential
for rental returns on vacation properties—the variations are just too
great. But the author's own condominium might well illustrate the financial risks involved in renting even a most desirable and rentable property.

The condominium is part of a large and reasonably luxurious development, less than 130 miles from Washington, D.C. and Baltimore and
within easy access of Philadelphia and Wilmington, Delaware. The unit
is quite large (almost 1,300 square feet), and it includes a living room,
a dining room, a kitchen, two bedrooms, two baths, a laundry-utility
room, and a 26-foot balcony that overlooks the ocean. It is on the 12th
floor of a 14-floor high rise. Its purchase price in 1975 (including closing
costs) was in the mid-50,000s—somewhat less than average for a comparable unit, reflecting both the developer's need to generate cash to pay
off construction financing and the unit's 12th-floor location, a somewhat
undesirable characteristic, given the preference of many renters and
buyers to be as close to the ocean as possible. It is furnished with attractive, durable, color-coordinated furnishings.[3]

The unit is subject to approximately 80 percent financing, at 9 percent
for 25 years. In addition, the land is not owned but is subject to ground
rent (a tax advantage in this case, as will be shown in the section on
taxes). The unit has been rented at the going rate for virtually all of
the eight- or nine-week summer prime season, for a substantial number
of weeks in the spring and fall, and for occasional winter weekends.
The extended rental season results from the numerous all-season recreational facilities—the ocean, indoor and outdoor swimming pools, indoor
and outdoor tennis courts (more than in any other development in the
area), and health club facilities (whirlpool, sauna). Yet, even assuming
100 percent in-season rentals and substantial rentals at other seasons,
the income cannot cover out-of-pocket costs. An annual income statement can be briefly represented as shown in Exhibit 1.

It should be stressed that the condominium development of which
this unit is a part is one of the most desirable and most rentable on
the East Coast. The rental income it yields is higher and its effective
season is longer (because of indoor facilities) than the rentals and the
season of competitive units. Yet the units in the development do not
come close to covering their out-of-pocket costs, much less the earnings
allocable to the amount expended for the down payment and the costs
of furnishings. The costs listed in Exhibit 1 include no allowance for

---

[3] Attractively furnished units with such luxuries as air conditioning, dishwashers, washers, dryers, television, and telephone tend to draw more rental business than do Spartan,
uninviting units, particularly in competition for off-season rentals. Durability and ease of
maintenance are the primary criteria for furnishing and equipping second-home rental
units.

EXHIBIT 1
Year 2 Cash Flow before Taxes for a High-Amenity Oceanfront Condominium

Gross Income		
Nine weeks at $420	$3,780	
Four weeks at $275	$1,100	
Seven winter weekends at $120 average	840	
Total gross income		$5,720
Expenses		
Rental agency commission at 15%*	$ 858	
Real property taxes	244	
Ground rent interest	517	
Property insurance (portion not		
included in condo fee)	67	
Mortgage insurance†	105	
Condominium and recreation associa-		
tion fees	1,220	
Utilities (electricity and telephone)	600	
Cleaning service	400	
Miscellaneous	150	
Debt service		
Amortization	$ 538	
Interest (year 2, at 9 percent, 25 years)	3,804	
Total debt service	4,342	
Total expenses‡		8,503
Cash flow (before income tax		
considerations)		($2,783)

* Self-rentals would lower this expense. However, allowance must then be made for advertising and related expenses.
† It is anticipated that the mortgage insurance payment will be dropped when the amortization exceeds the amount covered by the mortgage insurance.
‡ No allowance has been made for such items as repainting and replacements. Further, the costs of inspection trips to property that are tax deductible if it is used as a business have not been included in expenses.

extraordinary expenses or depreciation. The commission is average, and it covers the cost of an agent who offers a toll-free telephone service and adequate services, such as cleaning services, for which an owner is usually billed extra. The rents shown were in effect in 1977; rental increases were scheduled for 1978, but only to cover increased utility costs. The market would probably bear no greater increases. There are potential tax benefits, which will be treated below. As will be seen, however, they are scarcely sufficient to rescue an otherwise marginal investment.

TAX IMPLICATIONS

The tax implications of real estate investments have been covered in detail in Chapters 9 and 10. Only the tax factors specific to second-home investment will be discussed here.

At the outset, it is important to note that interest and taxes are deductible for second-home owners as for primary-home owners. But owners who sell their second homes are not permitted to defer the taxes on the capital gains they obtain in this way if they reinvest the proceeds within a designated time—a tax benefit that is available to primary-home owners.

It is desirable for an owner to be able to write off unrecouped expenses against other income—that is, to create a "shelter" for that income. As a result of tax reforms enacted in 1976, however, the opportunity for doing so has been reduced significantly.

Non-Owner Occupancy versus Part-Time Owner Occupancy

In general, the tax treatment of expenses for a second home depends on two factors: the length of time that the property is rented and the length of time that it is occupied by the owner or his or her guests or associates (on other than a fair rental basis). For a property that is used entirely for business purposes, essentially all expenses (including depreciation) are deductible. For a property that is used entirely for private residential purposes, only interest and taxes are normally deductible. (Some forms of ground rent are regarded as interest and are deductible on that basis.) The question of proper tax treatment becomes more complicated when a property is used partly for business purposes, partly for personal purposes.

Prior to the 1976 revision of the Federal tax laws, the determination of whether a property was intended primarily for business use or primarily for personal use (and hence the tax treatment of expenses) depended upon the intent of the owner—or more precisely, upon the revenue agent's evaluation of the owner's intent. If the agent judged that a property was intended primarily for business use, an allocable proportion of various expenses could be attributed to business use, even if that produced a loss which could shelter other income. The only qualification was that in order to avoid the "hobby loss" prohibitions of Section 183 of the Internal Revenue Code, a property had to show a profit in two out of five years.

The new tax law is less flexible. If a property is rented for more than 15 days per year and is used personally for less than 14 days per year (or 10 percent of the number of days rented, whichever is greater), it is considered to be used primarily for business purposes. (The "hobby loss" requirement of a profit in two out of every five years is still in effect.) In these circumstances, expenses are allocated between business and personal use. All business expenses (including depreciation) are deductible. The portions of interest and taxes allocable to personal use are also deductible.

If property is rented for more than 15 days per year but is used for personal purposes for more than 14 days per year (or more than 10 percent of the rental time, whichever is greater), the expenses are still allocable to business and personal use. All interest and taxes allocable to both business and personal use are deductible. In addition, expenses attributable to the business use of the property (allocated on the basis of the number of days that the property is used for personal and business purposes, respectively) are deductible, but only to the extent that gross income exceeds the otherwise deductible interest and taxes. In other words, business losses are not recognized and expenses are deductible only in the following order of precedence: interest and taxes, operating expenses, and depreciation and other basis items. If the "hobby loss" limitations come into play and the property does not show a profit in two out of five years, similar (and indeed possibly more stringent) loss limitations are applicable. If the property is rented for less than 15 days annually, no income need be reported and no expenses (other than interest and taxes) are normally deductible.

Case Examples

To illustrate how second-home rental income is treated for tax purposes, Exhibit 2 shows a property that is used entirely for rental purposes and a property that is used 50 percent for business purposes and 50 percent for personal purposes. (The basic income and expense figures that were used in Exhibit 1 are also used here.)

It can be seen from Exhibit 2 that if the property were used entirely for business, there would be a tax loss of $3,955, which could be taken (and offset against other income), assuming that the "hobby loss" requirements were not invoked. But if the unit were used only 50 percent for business (with rental income amounting to 50 percent of that received from 100 percent rental usage), a loss of $1,987.50 would be incurred. But only $2,860 of the expenses allocable to business use of $4,847.50 could be taken ($2,282.50 interest and taxes plus $577.50 of the remaining operating expenses), leaving a net rent income of $0. In addition, the $2,282.50 interest and taxes allocable to personal use could be deducted.

Thus, the 1976 tax revision substantially lessens the potentials for tax shelters. Indeed, even with 100 percent business use, it is questionable whether most second-home properties can show a profit during any of the early years of their operation. It is therefore likely that an owner will wish to use part of the second-home investment for personal enjoyment, bringing into play severe limitations on the practical deductibility of most expenses. Even with the limitations, however, rental income will, in effect, amount to tax-free income (since it will probably be wholly offset by expenses) which can be used to reduce the burdens of ownership. That this feature has continued to be an incentive to second-home ownership is suggested by the large number of second-home owners who use it and by the lack of any current evidence that the Tax Reform Act of 1976 has had any meaningful impact on second-home markets.

Government officials have launched "trial balloons" to sound out sentiment toward proposals which would place further tax restraints on second-home ownership. Among the proposals mentioned have been

EXHIBIT 2
Year 2 Income Tax Flow for a High-Amenity Oceanfront Condominium*

	100 Percent Business Use	50 Percent Business Use	
Gross Income	$5,720.00	$2,860.00	
	All Expenses Allocable to Business Use	Expenses Allocable to Business Use	Allowable Business Expenses	Expenses Deductible as Personal Deductions
Expenses				
Real property taxes	$ 244.00	$ 122.00	$ 122.00	$ 122.00
Debt service (mortgage) interest	3,804.00	1,902.00	1,902.00	1,902.00
Ground rent (interest)	517.00	258.50	258.50	258.50
Rental agency commission	858.00	429.00		0
Regular homeowner's insurance	47.00	23.50		0
Extra insurance for renters	20.00	20.00		0
Mortgage insurance	105.00	52.50	577.50	0
Condominium and recreation association fees	1,220.00	610.00		0
Utilities (electricity and telephone)	600.00	300.00		0
Cleaning service	400.00	200.00		0
Miscellaneous	150.00	75.00		0
Depreciation	1,060.00	530.00	0	0
Building (50-year life, straight line)				
Furnishings (five year life, straight line)	650.00	325.00	0	0
Total expenses	9,675.00	4,847.50	2,860.00	2,282.50
Total income	5,720.00	2,860.00	2,860.00	0
Income tax flow	($3,955.00)	($1,987.50)	0	$2,282.50
	(loss)	(loss)		(deduction)

* This example has been based upon interpretations of the Tax Reform Act of 1976 as of spring 1978. However, future IRS rulings may necessitate modification of these calculations.

† The assumption of 50 percent business–50 percent personal use has been selected for illustrative purposes only. If business use were reduced to 25 percent (for example), personal deductions for mortgage interest, ground rent, and real property taxes would increase to $2853.00, $387.75, and $183.00, respectively (total $3423.75), but business deductions (and presumably income) would be reduced.

ceilings on deductible interest payments, using either a dollar limitation or a restriction of deductible interest to primary homes (and, presumably, second homes serving solely business or investment purposes).[4]

MAKING SECOND-HOME INVESTMENTS MORE AFFORDABLE AND ENJOYABLE

There are a number of arrangements which can make second homes more affordable and enjoyable. Several are reviewed here.

The Second-Home Partnership

Pooling assets with other parties via a partnership arrangement is one way to make a second-home investment more affordable. The advantages are obvious. The disadvantages are also obvious—disagreement as to the use, maintenance, and disposition of the property can lead to serious friction. However, the problems can be alleviated and even eliminated by careful planning and consideration of all the circumstances, including the needs of each partner. The objectives of a smooth-running second-home partnership arrangement are to avoid aggravation and the duplication of effort so that the investment and enjoyment potentials of the second home can be maximized.

It is highly recommended that the parties to a second-home partnership enter into a detailed partnership agreement outlining their rights and responsibilities. The agreement should also state what will happen if one or all of the parties decide to sell out or to terminate the partnership.

If the second home is to be occupied by any or all of the partners, the time of such occupancy should be divided equitably among the partners. Rental policies need to be established and rental arrangements monitored. One partner should be responsible for scheduling. Basic policies for handling furnishings, maintenance, and improvements need to be agreed upon by all of the partners. One partner can be responsible for supervising those functions. One partner should coordinate all bookkeeping activities. The jobs can be rotated, but the important point to remember is that a division of labor is timesaving and efficient.

If these matters are handled in a responsible yet unofficious manner with partners who share similar values, a vacation home partnership can work and work well.

---

[4] The following general Internal Revenue Service publications (available from your local IRS office) will be helpful in obtaining further tax information on various aspects of second-home investments:

Publication 523: *Tax Information on Selling or Purchasing Your Home.*

Publication 530: *Tax Information for Homeowners.*

Publication 534: *Tax Information on Depreciation.*

Publication 588: *Tax Information on Condominiums and Cooperative Apartments.*

See also Terry R. Nygaard, "Vacation Homes and TRA: A Grab Bag of Surprises," *Real Estate Review,* vol. 7, no. 4 (Winter 1978), pp. 78–82.

Time-Sharing

Time-sharing was devised as a marketing concept that could help developers survive the economic recession of the mid-70s. It has become a much-discussed technique for placing the ownership of vacation homes within the reach of many who could not otherwise afford them. However, time-sharing is a highly controversial and risky technique, and any potential investment in a time-sharing unit should be very carefully evaluated.

Under a time-sharing arrangement, a purchaser secures the right to use a unit for a specified period of time each year for a specified number of years. A unit may be divided into as many as 52 time-sharing intervals—one for each week of the year. An individual may purchase one or more of these intervals. In some cases, a purchaser is required to purchase some minimum number of intervals. The prices of time-sharing intervals usually vary by season and by the size and relative location of the unit itself—some seasons and units being more desirable than others. There are dozens of time-sharing plans and arrangements. However, they fall into two basic types:

1. *Fee simple interval ownership.* In this arrangement, one purchases title to a unit for a specified time interval over a specified time period, often the economic life of the building. The purchase can include a share in the land and the common facilities. One receives a title, a deed, and the right to resell.

2. *Lease or license plans.* Here, one obtains the guaranteed right to use a property for a specified period of time over a given number of years. Neither deed nor title is passed. This alternative is merchandised as a paid-in-advance vacation plan which enables the purchaser to buy future vacation usage rights at today's prices.

The major advantage of time-sharing is price. For as little as a couple of thousand dollars, it is possible to own a part of a vacation home, thus bringing the luxury of resort living within the reach of the middle-income purchaser. The inflation hedge of buying tomorrow's vacation at today's prices and the possibility of reciprocal use arrangements with other time-sharing operations around the world have been attractive incentives for many purchasers.

However, the merchandising costs for a time-sharing unit are very high—so high that price markups to cover these costs can be well over 100 percent higher than the price markups for a non-time-sharing unit. For example, if a 100-unit building is marketed in one-week segments, up to 5,000 buyers may be required. To find 5,000 purchasers, a massive and costly promotional program is required. In general, the shorter the time segments, the lower the price that an individual pays per unit but the higher the marketing costs are for that unit. It will also take a long time for such a development to be fully sold, so that the appreciation potential, in the short run at least, is very uncertain. The long-term appreciation potential may be equally questionable.

The financing of time-sharing units has been a real problem. Most lending institutions have been unwilling to commit conventional mortgage funds for this purpose. As a result, most time-sharing units are sold for cash. Alternatively, installment contracts have been used as a financing device for such units. Also, time-sharing units invariably have high expenses, especially for management and maintenance.

Thus, despite the many attractive features of time-sharing units, it is highly questionable whether such units sold at inflated prices can be an attractive investment compared to most other real estate investments.

Undivided Interest

This is another cost-cutting scheme that has recently become popular in the field of recreational land development. The undivided interest concept is a common ownership arrangement that permits one to purchase undivided shares of a piece of property. The arrangement may include recreational facilities that are reserved for the use of all shareholders. No title is passed for individual units, land, or common facilities. Suffice it to say that there are so many risks identified with this arrangement that other investment alternatives appear to be preferable.[5]

Vacation Home Exchange Programs

As has been suggested, the personal enjoyments that are realizable through second-home ownership are generally sufficient to offset the financial detriments to such ownership. In a relatively affluent yet stress-ridden society, the needs for rest and recreation are of substantial importance, and in many instances such needs are well satisfied through second-home ownership. In recent years, second-home ownership has conferred an additional potential benefit: the vacation home exchange program.

There are a number of vacation home services.[6] The typical service

---

[5] For a more detailed discussion of the problems inherent in the undivided interest concept, see D. E. Hanson and T. E. Dickinson, "Undivided Interests: Implications of a New Approach to Recreational Land Development," *Land Economics,* vol. 51, no. 2 (May 1975), pp. 124–32.

[6] The best-known service of this type is:

> Vacation Home Exchange Club, Inc.
> 350 Broadway
> New York, New York 10013

Other services include:

> Inquiline
> Box 208
> Katonah, New York 10536

> Holiday Homes Exchange Bureau, Inc.
> P.O. Box 555
> Grants, New Mexico 87020

In addition, as mentioned earlier, vacation home exchange programs have been included in, and promoted by, various time-sharing plans. An example of a time-sharing vacation home exchange program is:

> Interval International
> 6075 Sunset Drive
> South Miami, Florida 33143

works as follows. The owner of a second home pays a fee to have the property listed in a directory published by the service. The listing includes a basic description of the unit and its accommodations, its location, the facilities and amenities available in the development or the area, and the time periods when the unit is available. Often the listing also states where the owner wishes to swap. Armed with this information, owners can arrange trades of their units at mutually agreeable times. Some services will also list units for rent. The services usually publish directories twice a year.

Listing fees, from $10 to $25 per year, entitle an owner only to list a unit. From that point on, the services take no further responsibility. Members make their exchanges themselves. In this way, an owner may be able to enjoy a vacation away from home for little more than the cost of transportation. A maid or an auto is often a part of the swapping arrangement, lending additional touches of luxury to the arrangement. To minimize the chances of trouble, owners who wish to swap should exchange financial and character references.

ESTABLISHING AN INVESTMENT STRATEGY

Establishing an investment strategy for second-home ownership starts with clearly defining a set of investment objectives and subobjectives. Once these have been defined, one can proceed along a rational decision-making path. At each decision point, there are a number of choices whose advantages and disadvantages need to be evaluated.

At the outset, it is important to determine whether the primary objective is investment or usage, or both. The parameters already outlined in this chapter as well as other chapters on real estate investment (see, for example, Chapter 19) will be helpful in establishing an investment strategy. That, however, is not the end of the story, particularly if one decides to occupy the property for at least part of the time.

If one decides to occupy the property for at least part of the time, a new set of objectives and criteria must be established and evaluated. These involve the way in which the second home is to serve the investor—its functional utility. The functions of second homes are determined, at least in part, by the amount of time that is to be spent in them and by the way in which that time is to be used.

The amount of time that an owner plans to spend in a unit also influences the location of that unit. For example, if an owner wishes to use a unit routinely on weekends, it is important that the unit be located within an approximate three-hour commuting distance from the primary residence. However, if one plans to use a unit for only one or two weeks a year plus one or two of the longer weekends, the locational opportunities broaden to a national or even an international scope. The time of year that one intends to use a property (summer versus winter activities) will also influence its location.

How the time spent at the second home is to be used is associated with the second home's "place utility" for the individual investor. This "place utility" can be locational or situational, or both. It is clearly linked to socioeconomic status and to one's stage in the life cycle and one's life-style. Undoubtedly, a family with children will have requirements that are entirely different from those of a "swinging" single or a retiree. A few of the factors that should be considered in determining investment objectives that will take "place utility" into account might include:

1. The need for seclusion or isolation.
2. Ease of maintenance.
3. The amount of living space required inside and outside.
4. Proximity to scenic amenities.
5. The presence of planned recreational activities.
6. Security.
7. Proximity to area facilities, such as shopping, restaurants, entertainment, health services, and churches.

Moreover, since a second-home investment may be illiquid and long-term investment in a second home is advisable, it is important to decide that the second home selected will serve one's needs for the foreseeable future as well as the present.

Once these decisions have been made, the search for a specific community and property can begin. As with any real estate investment, before the purchase of a particular piece of property is negotiated, the site and structure and all foreseeable financial, legal, political, and environmental aspects of the transaction should be checked thoroughly.

It is highly recommended that one rent in a community before buying there. Ideally, one should be able to study the community under a variety of seasonal conditions. Renting gives one time to decide whether the life-styles and facilities of a community coincide with one's personal objectives.

Also, one cannot be too cautious in checking out a developer's or builder's reputation for honesty and reliability. The vacation home field has been rife with fly-by-night operations, perhaps more so than any other area of real estate. Check with local banks, the chamber of commerce, knowledgeable local attorneys, and people who have already purchased in the area. Make full use of federal and state consumer protection organizations.

Above all, allow adequate time for all negotiations. It is easy to get carried away by the atmosphere of a vacation environment. It may be well worth losing an apparently desirable property if you do not have all the facts.

CONCLUSIONS

In sum, second homes offer a new dimension to life. Although they may be poor investments, they meet important human needs. In the long run, their costs may be recoverable, assuming that one has bought wisely. In the short run, various rental arrangements or purchasing plans can reduce the costs of second-home ownership sufficiently to make second homes increasingly available to the middle class. Recreational property is a luxury whose future success depends on rising

consumer incomes and preferences. Over the long run, few seriously
question that these will occur.

Yet overall economic and demographic forces need to be continually
monitored with regard to second-home investments, especially in light
of the volatile market behavior of such investments. However, some
general trends have emerged. Escalating energy costs and other operating costs will tend to favor second-home communities that are within
125 miles (or three hours' distance) of major affluent metropolitan areas.
For these reasons, and because of national population shifts, Sun Belt
communities (particularly those in relatively unexploited areas) will
experience a continued growth of the second-home industry. High-
amenity projects seem to be the wave of the present and the future.
Their continued development is consistent with emerging life-styles in
this country. Also, assuming that working couples continue to provide
a large share of the second-home market, communities offering ease
of maintenance and security, such as condominium communities, will
continue to be popular.

CONDOMINIUM INVESTMENTS

John R. Lewis

*J*OHN R. LEWIS, MBA, PhD, CLU, CPCU, CRA Professor, Risk
Management and Real Estate, College of Business, Florida State
University, Tallahassee, Florida.

President, Value Analysts, Inc., (consulting and expert testimony), and Value Systems, Inc., (residential construction).
Member, American Real Estate and Urban Economics Association, American Risk and Insurance Association, National Association of Realtors®, and other professional associations. Past
president, Florida Association of Real Estate Professors. Author
of articles on risk management and real estate in such publications as Insurance Counsel Journal, Real Estate Review, Journal
of Risk and Insurance, and Real Estate Law Journal.

Condominium Ownership

The Condominium Concept. The condominium is a form of real property ownership. Most simply, a condominium provides for the fee ownership of a designated portion of a building and an undivided interest in the common elements. Sole ownership applies to designated portions of the building, known as "airspace," between the walls and between the floor and ceilings of a particular unit. In some instances, individual ownership may apply to the walls, the floor, and the ceiling. However, if the walls, the floor, or the ceiling are for the support of the building or are in common with another unit, they belong to the category called "common elements." The common elements of a condominium thus refer to the land beneath the buildings, the yard and parking areas, those parts of the building intended for common use (such as foundations and party walls), service installations (such as elevators, fire escapes, and central utility services), recreational facilities (such as swimming pools and handball courts), and community entrances and exits. The important point is that the unit owner owns his cubicle of space (his unit) individually, whereas he owns the common elements jointly with other unit owners in the project.

The condominium concept is not new. Its origin may be traced back to ancient Rome and earlier. The concept was invented primarily for the purpose of solving title and other legal problems that existed when individually owned spaces encroached upon each other vertically. The concept is most frequently applied in crowded areas with a scarcity of land for development. In Europe, the condominium has been a recognized form of ownership since medieval times and it has been a very popular form of middle-class housing since World War II. The condominium concept did not catch on big with developers in the United States until the 1970s because this country has long had an abundance of land for development and a preference for home ownership of detached dwellings. Although condominium development appeared to suffer a substantial setback during the tight money market of the mid-1970s, the concept appears to be here to stay. As a form of ownership, the condominium offers significant potential advantages and relatively few potential disadvantages to the investor.

The Potential Advantages of Condominium Ownership. Condominium ownership offers the investor the potential of (1) ownership enjoyment of amenities during the investment holding period and (2) financial gain. Unlike many non–real estate investments, condominiums may be purchased with a minimum of initial equity, thereby creating substantial leverage. Through loan amortization and probable capital appreciation, the investor in a sound condominium project should be constantly increasing his equity. In addition, the tax advantages of condominium ownership include mortgage interest and property tax deductions and the possibility of depreciation write-off if the condominium unit is held as an income property.

A primary appeal of residential condominium ownership is freedom from the chore of routine maintenance. This is particularly appealing to young executives, singles, and the elderly. The convenience of a pool, a clubhouse, and other recreational facilities that are often attendant upon a condominium project also add to the attractiveness of the investment. Due to denser vertical and horizontal development, the land and construction costs per square foot (given an established quality) are usually lower for condominiums for the traditional detached unit.

Condominium ownership potentially offers the investor the best of two worlds. Consider the residential condominium with the benefits of home ownership and the simplicity and ease of apartment living. Unlike the tenant, whose rent is "never seen again," the condominium owner builds up equity through mortgage amortization and may experience appreciation in the value of his unit. Also, the condominium owner's constant mortgage payments protect him against escalating rents, while he benefits from the tax deductibility of mortgage interest and property taxes.

Although somewhat simplified in its assumptions, Exhibit 1 provides an analysis of the "effective aftertax costs" of purchasing a condominium unit. Though the monthly figures provided are based on first-year data only and do not deduct for tax on realized capital gain due to capital appreciation, the tax advantages of ownership are readily apparent. After taxes, a total monthly housing payment of $419 (as in Exhibit 1) may be reduced to an effective cost of as low as $156.75. A potential investor in a condominium would be well advised to complete such an analysis for the unit considered for purchase with the aid of his accountant or financial adviser. Such an exercise provides desirable investment insights.

If the investor in the condominium unit is primarily interested in acquiring an income property, alternative analysis is required. Exhibit

EXHIBIT 1
Buying a Condominium versus Renting

Consider the purchase of a 2 bedroom, 1½ bath energy-efficient condominium for $39,900. With a 90 percent loan, 9 percent interest for 29 years, the expenses of ownership total:

		Monthly Average
1.	Principal and interest	$291.00
2.	Property taxes (estimate)	40.00
3.	Insurance expense (estimate)	13.00
4.	Utilities (with energy-saving features and reasonable care)	55.00
5.	Association fee	20.00
6.	Total monthly payment	$419.00

However, condominium ownership qualifies for the tax advantages of conventional home ownership. Assuming a 35 percent marginal tax bracket and a taxpayer who itemizes his deductions, 35 percent of the investor's monthly mortgage interest ($270.39) and property taxes ($40) should be deducted from the before-tax total monthly payment to calculate the monthly payment after taxes, as follows:

6.	Total monthly payment	$419.00
7.	Tax savings (interest and taxes)	−108.65
8.	Total monthly payment after taxes	$310.36

In addition, it is reasonable to assume that a quality condominium unit will appreciate at an annual rate of 4 percent, or $133 per month, with an equity increase of $20.61 per month due to partial monthly retirement of the original loan amount. Considering these figures as additions to the owner's net worth, the effective monthly payment after taxes is:

8.	Total monthly payment after taxes	$310.36
9.	Monthly appreciation	−133.00
10.	Monthly equity increase	20.61
11.	Effective monthly ownership cost after taxes	$156.75

It is this figure, $156.75 (effective monthly ownership cost after taxes), which should be compared to the combined monthly rent and utilities of a comparable rental home or apartment. Estimating the monthly rent of a hypothetical comparable apartment to be a minimum of $260 and the utilities to be $90, the monthly cost of a comparable rent unit totals a minimum of $350.

2 briefly presents some investment assumptions and pro forma operating results for a 2-bedroom, 1½-bath condominium renting for $345 per month. Although the calculations involved in generating the pro forma results and the aftertax return on equity figure are quite involved, the investment assumptions and results are fairly simple. On a condo-

EXHIBIT 2
Sample of the Investment Appeal of the
Income-Producing Condominium

Investment Assumptions

General
Purchase price of two-bed-
room unit $39,600
Holding period of investment .... 15 years
Average monthly rental income .... $ 345
Annual growth in rental income 3%
Initial equity investment (including
1.5 percent closing costs) .... $ 8,395
Marginal tax rate of investor 40%
Expense
Vacancy allowance 5%
Operating expenses as percentage
of gross income 24%
Depreciation method used .... 200% DB
Useful life for depreciation .... 35 years
Salvage value .... $ 1,500
Mortgage
Mortgage amount (at 80 percent
loan-to-value ratio $31,680
Interest rate... 8½%
Term of mortgage .... 29 years
Resale of Property
Gain on sale of property at end
of 15-year holding period $44,010

Pro Forma Operating Results

Years of Project	Cash Throw-off	Tax Shelter	Cash Flow after Taxes
1	($ 202)	$837	$ 630
2	93	656	749
3	191	560	751
4	292	465	757
5	397	371	768
6	504	276	780
7	615	181	796
8	729	85	815
9	847	0	836
10	969	0	860
11	1,094	0	887
12	1,223	0	916
13	1,356	0	946
14	1,493	0	979
15	1,635	0	45,023

Overall aftertax return on equity (internal rate of return) = 16.9 percent.

minium investment, it is possible to earn a return in excess of 15 percent after taxes. Of course, any investment analysis is only as good as the assumptions upon which it is based. Because of this, predictions of a high average yield or return on equity should be viewed cautiously.

The Condominium versus the Cooperative. Though the concepts are often confused by the lay person, the condominium and the cooperative are greatly differing forms of ownership. The condominium is a statutory estate combining one-person ownership with ownership in common. The cooperative is an ownership form (generally a nonprofit corporation) whose stockholders hold an undivided interest in all units and common areas, with a lease arrangement giving the tenant-shareholder the right to occupy a specific unit. Thus, the distinction between a shareholder in a cooperative and the owner of a condominium is material.

Exhibit 3 presents an abbreviated summary of the differences between the condominium and the cooperative. The differences are substantial. It should not, however, be assumed that there are no similarities between the two forms of ownership. In fact, there are. A cooperative shareholder, like the unit owner in a condominium, benefits from the elimination of the owner's profit on a conventional rental. Likewise, both the condominium unit owner and the cooperative shareholder ben-

EXHIBIT 3
The Condominium versus the Cooperative

	Condominium	Cooperative
Nature of ownership	Fee	Stock
Title vested in	Unit owner	Cooperative organization
Unit occupant's relationship to unit	Owner	Lessor
Ability to approve neighbors	Seldom	Usual
Property tax liability	On specific unit	Percentage of total
Financing	Individual	Corporation
Mortgage liability	On specific unit	Percentage on entire project
Refinancing possibility	Yes	Not by individual
Transfer costs on sale	Standard	Low

efit from the tax advantages of home or unit ownership—specifically, the deductibility of mortgage interest and property taxes. From an investment viewpoint, the differences are much more important than the similarities. In fact, a person purchasing a unit for investment purposes will be unlikely to become involved in a cooperative project unless it is his desire to actually occupy space within the project.

For example, it is noted in Exhibit 3 that the condominium unit owner has the title to his unit and an undivided interest in the common areas, whereas the stockholder in a cooperative simply owns stock in a nonprofit business organization and does not specifically own a unit within the project. In fact, unlike the condominium unit owner who actually takes title to his particular unit, the cooperative stockholder takes no such title. Title is held by the cooperative. The shareholder who wishes to occupy a unit in the cooperative must sign a proprietary lease with the cooperative in order to obtain the right to do so.

From an investment point of view, the condominium offers a substantial advantage over the cooperative in that condominium unit owners seldom retain any significant right to approve new unit occupants in the project. Although a condominium covenant may provide for such approval, cooperatives tend to be more restrictive in this respect.

The way in which property taxes are levied on the condominium differs from the way in which they are levied on the cooperative. Enabling legislation specifically recognizes the condominium unit as a separate legal ownership, and property taxes are assessed on each unit separately. Property taxes are based on the assessed value of the unit, which in most states is a function of market value. Because of this, it is not necessary for taxes to be levied specifically on the common elements, which theoretically are already accounted for in the market value of the individual unit. With respect to the cooperative, however, property taxes are levied on the entire project and the shareholder is responsible for a percentage of this total. Today, if 80 percent or more of a cooperative's income is derived from shareholder/tenant rentals, the individual cooperator may deduct his proportionate share of property taxes for income tax purposes.

Condominiums and cooperatives also differ substantially in the area of financing. One major difference is that the condominium unit owner obtains his own financing or takes over the developer's commitment, whereas the shareholders of a cooperative obtain cooperative financing on the entire project. Thus, the mortgage liability of the condominium relates to a specific unit and individual, whereas the mortgage liability of the cooperative relates in an undivided fashion to the entire project. As a result, the shareholder in a cooperative is unable to refinance his investment, as is possible for a condominium unit owner. Since the cooperative shareholder is not personally liable for the mortgage debt of the cooperative, but assumes his pro rata share of the mortgage according to the value of the unit he occupies, the refinancing of his individual unit is simply not a possibility.

The only investment advantage that ownership in a cooperative would have over the ownership of a condominium pertains to the transfer costs that are associated with the sale of one's interest. Since the mortgage financing on a cooperative is procured by the corporate body and ownership interests are transferred by a sale of stock in that corporate body, the need for an expensive title search, a loan origination fee, closing costs, and other financing costs is generally eliminated. However, such standard charges are incurred upon the sale of a condominium.

The Standard Condominium versus the Investment Condominium. The potential for applying the condominium concept is seemingly limited only by the imagination of the developer or the entrepreneur. Although owner-occupied residential condominiums are by far the most widely recognized form of condominium ownership, the income or investment condominium appears to be gaining in popularity.

As has been noted, even the residential condominium may be purchased as an investment, in order to rent it out to others. Such a purchase offers the investor the potential for receiving yield from appreciation in the unit's value, cash throw-off from the margin of rental revenue over expenses and debt service, depreciation or tax shelter, and amortization of the loan principal. The key advantage of the purchase is that it enables the investor to participate in a quality project of some magnitude without having to become involved in the financing of more than a single unit. In addition, the management problems associated with being a landlord for such a unit are generally minimal, due to the condominium association's agreement with the management firm. Before a residential condominium is acquired for investment purposes, however, it is important to determine whether the covenants of the condominium place any restrictions on leasing or subleasing.

The application of the condominium concept to U.S. commercial and industrial projects first became noticeable in the 1970s. Today, the condominium concept is frequently applied to commercial properties. In many municipalities one does not have to look very far to see an office condominium, a neighborhood shopping center set up on a condominium basis (with each merchant holding his own space and having an interest in the common areas, which generally include the parking and green areas surrounding the complex), or a condominium shopping mall. The condominium concept is also being widely applied to such industrial properties as warehouse facilities, industrial parks, and even miniwarehouse facilities and office-warehouse arrangements.

Great possibilities exist for involvement in income or investment property projects via the condominium ownership route. The advantages of having someone else develop the project and of minimum maintenance and repair responsibilities and minimum problems following development make the condominium a viable investment alternative.

The Legalities of the Condominium

The first condominium enabling legislation impacting on the United States was the Puerto Rican Horizontal Property Regime Act of 1958.

Since that time, all of the states have enacted legislation permitting the condominium form of ownership. Such statutes are necessary to allow or provide for:

1. *Individual and joint ownership of distinct areas*—with respect to a single real property the state statues recognize the distinction between individual ownership and common elements and allow for the transferability of interest.
2. *Contractual relationships among parties*—the state statutes universally require a "declaration of condominium" which is a binding contract among all unit owners.
3. *Common areas and usage*—enabling statutes recognize common areas and further provide that "tenants in common" should not be allowed to partition an undivided common interest.
4. *Equitable levying of property taxes*—state laws recognize that property taxes may be levied against a condominium and its undivided interest in common areas and require that units be assessed separately and fairly for purposes of such taxes.
5. *Financing*—condominium statutes facilitate lending on condominium units by allowing for such necessities as the recognition of three-dimensional legal descriptions and not merely the traditional flat plane–type of description.

Although the legalities of a condominium are complex and the potential investor would be well advised to approach them with the aid of legal counsel, only three primary documents relate to the rights of the condominium owner. These documents, which are designed to protect both the individual unit owner and the unit owners as a group, are: the declaration, the bylaws, and the management agreement.

The Declaration. The declaration of the condominium sets out the rules and regulations which apply to the project. As a written statement of policy and procedures, the declaration specifies the rights and obligations of the unit owners, individually and collectively. It recites the master covenants for the development. It is, in fact, the instrument which technically creates the condominium by converting a given parcel of land into a condominium subdivision. It is the birth certificate of the condominium. The declaration of a condominium may be 20 to 40 pages long. It sets forth rules and obligations and sometimes complex provisions in needed detail. Generally, the declaration will make provision for the following matters with respect to the condomimium:

1.	Legal description of land.	8.	Sharing in common expenses.
2.	Transmission statement.	9.	Association formation and
3.	Project name.		membership.
4.	Definitions and terminology.	10.	Bylaws.
5.	Definition of condominium	11.	Reciprocal easements.
	unit.	12.	Management agreement.
6.	Description of common elements.	13.	Collection of common funds.
		14.	Tax apportionment.
7.	Survey, plan, and map.	15.	Assessment collections.

16. Liens and enforcement.	22. Maintenance and repairs.
17. Occupancy and use restrictions.	23. Remedies for violation.
	24. Provisions against animals.
18. Provisions for insurance.	25. Rights of mortgagees.
19. Restrictions and partitioning.	26. Provisions for declaration amendment.
20. Transfers.	
21. Subleasing.	27. Termination.

In some instances, numerous other items will be mentioned in the declaration. It should be borne in mind that such provisions are designed to protect the unit owner individually and all unit owners collectively. Accordingly, since the declaration is the master covenant of the condominium project, it is recorded and placed on the public record like a master deed. Prior to investing in a condominium, it is therefore incumbent upon the wise investor to carefully study the condominium declaration.

The Bylaws. The bylaws of a condominium set forth the rules and procedures of the condominium association and its governing body or council. The owners' association created by the bylaws is usually set up as a nonprofit association to serve as the legal framework through which the unit owners can govern themselves. Though not always recorded with the master deed, the bylaws of the association are binding on the members/unit owners. Thus, the bylaws may extend, clarify, or add to certain restrictions or covenants made in the declaration. At a minimum, the bylaws will address the following elements of the condominium or condominium association:

1. The identification and structure of the association.
2. The membership and meetings.
3. The authority of the association.
4. The voting rights of unit owners.
5. The responsibilities of the board of directors.
6. The election of officers.
7. The levying and collection of assessments.
8. The general fiscal management.
9. The relationship of the condominium association to the management firm.
10. The amendment of bylaws.

The developer or sponsor of the condominium project is initially responsible for drafting the bylaws of the association. He names the association's first board of directors and specifies their term of office. Generally, this term is specified to end when the sponsor has sold out all of the units in the condominium project or at some specified future date, whichever comes first. At such time, new officers of the association are elected by the unit owners as members of the association. When the new board is elected, it is simultaneously given all the powers and responsibilities associated with the board, including the power to levy assessments for maintenance, repair, and other expenses. Since the board members do not usually desire to become directly involved in the day-to-day management of the project, the operating functions of the association are delegated to a professional property manager under the terms of some management agreement.

The Management Agreement. One of the major motivations for purchasing a condominium is the desire for minimum maintenance and maximum management-free use. In order to experience increased freedom from the responsibilities of management, the condominium association must maintain a relationship with some management entity.

Usually, the management of a condominium project is two-tiered as to time. In the development phase, the sponsor or the real estate developer usually functions as the management of the project and maintains a management contract with the condominium association. During the absorption period for the sellout of the project, the burden of management problems—general maintenance, landscape care, repair work, and the handling of complaints—generally falls on the developer's shoulders. However, when the condominium project has been sold out (either completely or to a specified degree), the developer frequently relinquishes control over management and the condominium association then contracts directly with a management firm. In a small condominium project, the association may merely elect to employ one of its own members or individual subcontractors to take care of its general maintenance and record-keeping needs. In a larger development, a professional property management firm will usually be retained. For a fee, such a firm will supply an on-site resident manager and off-site services such as record keeping and payroll handling. In addition, the management firm contracts for landscape maintenance, trash removal, necessary janitorial services associated with the common areas, and general repairs, billing for such services being on a monthly basis.

An important element in the success and desirability of a condominium project is the quality of the management. It is therefore important for the potential investor in a condominium project to ascertain the quality of the existing management and to develop some feel as to its likely future quality.

Condominium Financing

Financing the condominium unit is similar to financing the traditional residential or commercial property. Generally, the down payment or loan-to-value requirements, the interest rates, and the loan terms are comparable. In addition, at least for the residential condominium, both conventional and FHA-backed financing are available.

There are two major steps in condominium financing.The first involves the developer's (or the sponsor's) initial financing of the project. The developer generally arranges for a construction loan to provide the bulk of the funds he needs to bring the condominium project to reality, with a takeout commitment for permanent financing to the potential unit purchasers. The usual procedure is for the developer to contract with a lender who will both advance his needed construction money and offer financing to the individual unit purchasers at the time of sale. Ideally, this arrangement should be set up so as to minimize closing costs to both the developer and unit purchasers and to tie down interest rates on permanent loans at the time of the initial construction loan. Having such a loan commitment available to potential purchasers is a helpful selling tool, even though some purchasers may want to pay cash for a unit or arrange their own financing.

Individual financing of the individual units is the second step in condominium financing. Generally the type of mortgage involved is the constant-pay amortized mortgage whereby the mortgagor (the unit owner) makes a constant monthly payment which both provides for his interest obligation and "kills off" the principal on the loan over its term. In the individual financing of condominium units, flexibility is the keynote. On the residential condominium, the financing may be conventional or FHA. Loan-to-value ratios may be as high as 95 percent or as low as 65 percent, or even lower if so desired. The term of the mortgage on the condominium will usually range from 20 to 35 years, with 29- and 30-year terms now being the most popular nationally. The financing of commercial or industrial condominiums is comparable to the traditional financing of commercial and industrial properties, with a 75 percent loan-to-value ratio, a 25-year term, and conventional financing being the customary package.

The Horizontal Property Regime Act of 1958 (the Puerto Rican statute which first created the condominium in the United States and its territories) led in short to the enactment of Section 234 of the National Housing Act of 1961. Section 234 makes the major contribution of extending FHA mortgage insurance to condominium units, permitting FHA mortgage insurance for condominium units in states that allow an individual to take title to a single unit in a project. Under Section 234, a lender designated by the FHA as an "approved mortgagee" is eligible to submit condominium mortgage loans for approval. Certain additional requirements must be met, including the following: (1) the mortgagor must be the fee owner of the unit located in the project or must hold the unit under a renewable 99-year lease; (2) the unit for which financing is sought must be located in a condominium project covered by FHA-insured project financing; and (3) the mortgagor must not own more than four of the units in the project and must be the actual or proposed occupant of one of those units. FHA financing is not applicable to condominiums without some strings attached. However, when it is applicable, the implications in terms of the down payment requirements are significant to the investor in a condominium unit.

As shown in Exhibit 4, from the borrower's standpoint, the down payment requirements of FHA-insured loans are very competitive with that of conventional financing even by way of a 95 percent loan. Prior to 1977 revisions in the FHA down payment requirements, this was not always the case. Today, however, FHA-insured loans do offer an advantage to the investor who is seeking a low down payment unless the unit that he is purchasing is in the luxury class.

Simply because an investor desires a low down payment does not mean that the condominium that he is interested in acquiring will qualify for an FHA-insured loan. Frequently, developers shy away from in-

EXHIBIT 4
Down Payment Requirements on Residential Condos: Conventional versus FHA*

	Conventional			
	80 Per-cent	90 Percent†	95 Percent‡	FHA§
$45,000 unit	$ 9,000	$4,500	$2,250	$ 1,750
$60,000 unit	$12,000	$6,000	$3,000	$ 2,500
$80,000 unit	$16,000	$8,000	n.a.‖	$20,000#

* Exclusive of closing costs, points, and miscellaneous financing costs.
† FHLBB maximum loan of $75,000 assumed.
‡ FHLBB maximum loan of $60,000 assumed.
§ FHA down payment of 3 percent of first $25,000 of loan; 5 percent of rest; maximum loan of $60,000.
‖ Maximum 95 percent loan of $60,000 would require that mortgagor obtain only 90 percent financing.
Reflects $60,000 maximum FHA-insured loan.

volvement with the FHA because of the red tape involved in obtaining approval. In addition, sellers and lenders may lose interest in FHA-insured loans because of the points necessitated by the interest rate spread between FHA-insured and conventional loans.

Whether an insured finances conventionally or through an FHA-insured loan, an installment purchase, or a purchase-money mortgage, most of the additional financing considerations in the purchase of a condominium are similar to those in the purchase of a conventional property. The borrower must still show that he is creditworthy and that his income qualifies him for the loan desired.

Potential Consumer Problems

It is an undeniable fact of condominium life that the investor in a unit does not always find ownership to be carefree. Numerous problems can develop. Frequently, such problems take the form of complaints and claims directed at developers or sponsors of condominium projects—the "suppliers" of the condominium. At other times, grievances are directed at the board of directors of the condominium association or the management entity—the overseers of the common good of the unit owners. There are also potential problems which have no specific focal point. Exhibit 5 briefly identifies some of the problems that may arise. These problems may be associated with the developers of the condominium project, with the board of directors of the condominium association, or with the management entity or the resident manager of the project, or they may simply be general problems that are associated with condominium ownership. Each of these types of problems deserves some elaboration.

Problems Associated with the Developer. Developer-associated problems are often the most critical to the consumer of a condominium unit. Often, such problems arise even prior to actual occupancy.

EXHIBIT 5
Potential Consumer Problems
in Condominium Ownership

Developer associated

   1. Initial delivery date.
   2. Maintenance fee overruns.
   3. Recreational leases.
   4. Continuing control.
   5. Warranty shortcomings.

Board of director associated

   1. Governing practices.
   2. Budget estimates.
   3. Managing financial costs.
   4. Covenant enforcement.

Management entity associated

   1. Spending controls.
   2. Inadequate management.

General

   1. Failure to understand ownership risks.
      (a). Renting.
      (b). Resale.
   2. Risk management and insurance.
   3. Regulation.

Unrealistic Delivery Dates.   One of the most frequent complaints made by unit purchasers against developers is that the developers promise occupancy dates that they fail to meet. Such promises facilitate the initial sale of units, but they result in disgruntled purchasers. Associated with this problem is the use of "down payment money" by a few as they see fit instead of putting it into an escrow account for disbursement at the time of close. Such developers sometimes use down payment funds to provide working capital for the construction of a project which they fail to complete because of a general shortage of funds.

Maintenance Fee Overruns.   One of the most common abuses associated with developer involvements in condominiums is that of maintenance fee overruns. The share of condominium unit owners in the maintenance fee of the project is generally based on the relative size of their unit to the total of all units. However, the developer or the sponsor may quote unrealistically low maintenance fees in order to sell the units. In some cases, maintenance fees as low as $20 per month are quoted, when monthly fees of $100 or more would be more realistic. This problem is compounded by often unintentional failures of the estimators of maintenance fees to consider replacement reserves or future repairs in estimating the fee levels.

Recreational Leases. Perhaps the most publicized problem associated with the developers of condominium projects relates to leases on recreational facilities. Condominium unit owners often complain of the exorbitant fees charged for the use of recreational facilities. Though the availability of recreational facilities—swimming pools, tennis courts, handball courts, and so on—may be prime marketing factors for a condominium project, the fees for the use of such facilities are frequently felt to be too high. Furthermore, the inclusion of escalation clauses in the lease agreements on recreational facilities (based on the cost-of-living index or some other standard) leads to additional polarization between developer and unit owners.

Recreation leases have been a major problem only in the State of Florida. There, developers, as early as the late 1960s, seized on the 99-year recreational lease as a means of charging lower initial prices for their units, while loading the profit center of the project in the rec lease. It was not claimed that the rec lease rent was related to the value of the underlying fee. The developer saw this vehicle as a profit deferring, financing device with the advantage to him of an inflation hedge when tied in to a cost-of-living escalation provision.

Statutes, common law decisions, and market reaction have greatly limited the use of recreational leases in regard to condominium developments which have taken place since 1975. It is doubtful that the rec lease will be considered a major problem in the condominium marketplace beyond a few more years.

Continuing Control. Continuing management control of the condominium project after the completion and full occupancy of the units can also cause a problem from the unit owner's viewpoint. The problem revolves around a management agreement under which an agent selected by the developer continues to exert influence on the project after the developer has supposedly departed. This problem can be quite serious if the builder/developer has actually formed a subsidiary to function as the management company. In such cases, the management company may be suspected of being self-serving and of charging inflated fees. Since this situation does sometimes exist, the investor in the condominium unit should look into the management agreement, the managing agent, and any relationship that may exist between the management company and the builder/developer.

Warranties and Guarantees. One final area in which developer-associated problems may arise concerns the guarantees and warranties that are associated with the project or with individual units. In the solicitation phase of the sale process, room sizes, quality standards, and energy-saving features are sometimes grossly overstated. What the consumer actually receives may be substantially less desirable than what he has been promised. If an investor purchases a unit on the basis of "seller's puffs," only to experience a low-grade completed product, he will be understandably disappointed. A problem here is that the sale agreement and the condominium papers will generally prevail over any oral statements to the contrary. The condominium unit purchaser should thus be aware of the limitations on warranties and should in fact demand certain written understandings. Otherwise, the warranties and guarantees on condominium units are generally limited to one year (on items ranging from the building roof to appliances), with this period sometimes running from the date that the certificate of occupancy is issued rather than from the date that title to the condominium unit actually passes to the purchaser.

Problems Associated with the Board of Directors. The developer is not the only party against whom criticisms may be lodged by condominium unit owners. Occasionally, complaints arise against the cotenants who are serving as the board of directors of the condominium unit owner's association.

Governing Practices. The board often makes rules covering such items as procedures for the approval of new tenants, the number of guests at the pool, expenditures on upkeep and garbage removal. Too frequently, participants on the board are inexperienced managers who make naive and dangerous business decisions. Complaints against condominium boards often relate to such things as their failure to ascertain the existence of a quorum at meetings, their gross manipulations of proxies, their domination of nominating procedures, and their use of petitions in lieu of secret ballots.

Budgeting. The condominium board of directors may also be criticized for inaccurate budget estimates. Unit owners sometimes claim that board budget estimates are not meaningful and that condominium officers fail to consult with either their own board or with the membership on large expenditures. Another criticism is that condominium boards fail to ensure proper internal controls over the assets of condominium unit owner's associations.

An investor in a condominium unit should be satisfied that, at the least, the board will prepare an annual operating budget which is reviewed by the directors, with the assistance of a knowledgeable adviser if necessary. Expenses over a certain minimum level should require approval by the entire board. In addition, at least two officers should be required to sign all checks, and all cash and check receipts should be controlled by immediate remittance acknowledgments or restricting endorsements.

Covenant Enforcement. A final problem that arises with regard to condominium boards is the loose enforcement of covenants. It is sometimes charged that the officers of condominium associations fail to enforce association rules because of their desire to maintain popularity and circumvent dissension. Since the covenants were developed for the protection of all unit owners, it is important that they be properly enforced.

Problems Associated with the Management Entity. Although the board of directors is the ultimate overseer of the common good of the condominium association, the day-to-day operations of a condominium project are generally addressed by the project resident manager and by the property management firm employed by the condominium association. The problems associated with those day-to-day operations can be significant.

Spending Controls.   The property management firm will devote some portion of the overall maintenance fees to see that such services as lawn and landscape maintenance, cleanup, and general repairs are provided. In order to establish what appears to be a good track record of low-cost management, a management firm may pay daily bills with dollars that should be allocated to refurbishing, replacement, and repairs. Unfortunately, a day of reckoning eventually comes, and when the deferred maintenance is finally attended to, massive jumps in condominium assessments may be necessary. Thus, the unit owner can be faced with a large increase in his contribution to maintenance fees which he did not anticipate when he purchased his unit.

Inadequate Management.   Most of the problems associated with condominium management arise from the use of an inadequately trained resident manager. The resident manager is the person with the greatest potential for managing the "people problems" of the condominium project. In the small project, there may not be a resident manager. In the larger project, however, he is a critical element in the creation of overall project harmony. He should be able to enforce the house rules, and he must understand the rights and obligations of the unit owners as expressed in the declaration and bylaws. Since resident managers are often underpaid, condominium projects often fail to obtain the professionally trained managers they need. Moreover, given the increasing number of condominium projects, there will also be an increasing shortage of qualified resident managers.

General Problems.   There are some general problems associated with the ownership of condominium units for which no specific blame can be assigned. These may be the most serious problems of certain unit owners.

The Failure to Understand Ownership Risk.   Investors do lose money in condominium ventures. This is true for both developer-investors and for purchasers of individual units. Although some condominium projects—perhaps most—provide all of the psychic and economic returns that were anticipated by the investor, not all condominium projects are successful. One of the major problems of condominiums is that unit buyers do not fully understand the risks associated with ownership. The risks that relate to problems associated with the developer, the board of directors, and the management entity have been discussed above. However, of even more direct concern to a unit owner are the risks connected with the renting of a unit that he has acquired for investment/ income purposes and the risks connected with the resale of a unit.

The rental problem is most clearly associated with the vacation condominium. As many investors in resort or vacation condominiums have discovered, management can become a second career. The investor may spend many more hours managing and attempting to rent his unit than he ever expected to spend when he bought it. It is true that a management company will handle these tasks for a percentage of the rents, but that percentage is often high.

Absentee ownership can give rise to significant problems. Rental agents may pocket the proceeds, with the owner not realizing that his unit has been rented. Unless there is a rental pool, there is always uncertainty as to how hard the rental agent is working to rent a particular unit. In addition, tenant selection poses difficulties—vandalism and theft by tenants can be serious problems in rental condominiums.

When an individual invests in a condominium unit, he is often given a projection of the expected return on investment, given the probable rental that he will receive and the probable selling price at some hypothetical future sale date. Although such projections occasionally prove to be correct, they are usually overoptimistic. Condominium overbuilding, particularly in resort regions, may make it difficult to rent or sell one's unit. If the unit owner decides to leave his unit uninhabited while it is up for sale, this can create severe security problems. Perhaps the worst possibility is buying a unit in a project on which the lender forecloses or in a project which is in a "workout" situation with a lender. In such cases, the investor could experience a severe loss in the value of his condominium unit and could even find that his equity has been impaired significantly.

Risk Management and Insurance. Unique problems in risk management are associated with the ownership of a condominium unit. The distinction between individually owned airspace (and its contents) and jointly owned common elements creates two distinct property and liability insurance needs. These are: (1) the need to cover the property in which the unit owner has an *individual* interest and (2) the need to cover the common areas in which the unit owners have an undivided, *collective* interest. Segregating condominium properties into categories of insurance needs is sometimes difficult. The basic problem is distinguishing sole interest properties from undivided common interest properties. Each of these categories can include real property (land and the structures permanently attached thereto) and personal property (contents, some fixtures, and chattels) in numerous combinations, depending on the characteristics of the particular condominium project.

An accident or loss to property on the premises of a condominium project may fall either on the association or on the individual unit owner. Since there can be a gap in insurance protection or overlapping insurance protection between the policies of the association and policies of the unit owners, it is important to have the insurance needs of each clearly delineated.

There are several risks or exposures to loss which the condominium association faces and which it may want to insure. The two major exposures (or potential sources of loss) are the property exposure and the liability exposure. The property exposure reflects the association's statutory duty to repair or build common elements that have been damaged or destroyed by fire or other perils. The liability exposure exists because of the potential legal liability that arises out of injury to persons or damage to the property of others. A condominium association may protect itself by carrying a business package policy that would provide it with sufficient funds, either directly or through an insurance trustee, to meet its statutory duty to repair any property damage and to satisfy any legal liability claims. Such insurance coverages are usually written on the condominium property in the name of the project manager or the board of directors, with the premiums normally being treated as a common expense.

The association would carry a tailored form of the Special Multi-Peril (SMP) Policy. This policy would cover the unit owners collectively and would name an insurance trustee as specified in the condominium agreement. The basic coverages provided by the policy would include: (1) *Property coverage relating to all buildings* (except those in which individual unit owners have a sole interest). That coverage would include fixtures, equipment, and other items in which the owners collectively have an undivided interest, regardless of who paid for them (e.g., the swimming pool or the tennis courts), and personal property belonging to the condominium association (e.g., lawn chairs, recreation equipment, and pool tables). (2) *Liability coverage arising out of the condominium properties.* That coverage applies to the association and its members collectively and also to the unit owners individually as regards their liability in connection with the common elements. If the condominium association does not have proper and adequate insurance coverage, the individual unit owners and investors may become residually liable.

The existence of a business package policy in the name of the association does not in any way negate the need of each individual unit owner to insure his own unit. The individual unit owner will need insurance to cover his sole properties and any additional assessments that may result from the loss of common property elements whose costs each unit owner must share. The condominium unit owner will want to insure his personal property and his personal liability. He may also want to insure carpeting, paneling, light fixtures, cabinets, sinks, bathtubs, and similar personal property, if such items are considered to be his individual property or if the declaration or the bylaws make him responsible for insuring them.

The condominium unit owner may obtain property and liability insurance protection by purchasing a condominium unit owner's policy. Until recently, the unit owner would have had to purchase a homeowner's policy to meet his needs, with alterations in coverage being necessary in order to adapt this policy to the condominium. However, special policy forms are now available which meet the unique needs of the condominium form of ownership. It is extremely important that the condominium investor realize the need for such coverage and that he obtain it prior to acquiring title to his unit.

Regulation. As has been stated, the states began to enact condominium legislation in the 1960s. Today, all of the states have some form of condominium enabling legislation. However, much of this legislation is very general, lacks enforcement provisions, and has become outdated. There is, however, a trend toward improved state regulation of condominiums. Florida provides a good example.

Effective in October 1973, Florida enacted a Deceptive and Unfair Trade Practices Act which gave all consumers, including condominium unit purchasers, new rights in the marketplace. The declared purpose of the act is: "To protect consumers from suppliers who commit deceptive and unfair trade practices." The rules concerning condominiums focus primarily on the problems of disclosure and the transfer of control. For example, the developer must disclose, in writing, to his prospective unit purchasers the schedule and the formula for transferring the control of the association from the developer to the unit owners. The rules also requires full disclosure of the unit purchaser's right to cancel the contract under certain conditions. Failure to make these disclosures subjects the developer to a variety of legal sanctions. Similar sanctions are imposed if any of the developer's sales or promotion materials are deceptive or misleading.

The rules also establish guidelines for transferring the control of the condominium association from the developer to the unit owners. When sales on 90 percent of the units have been closed, the unit owners are entitled to elect at least the majority of the board of directors. Within a reasonable time after the unit owners elect this majority, the developer must relinquish control and deliver to the association all condominium property that he still holds or controls.

A series of amendments were appended to Florida's act in 1974. These amendments have been popularly referred to as the "Condominium Unit Owners' Bill of Rights." The impact of the amendments has been substantial. The so-called bill of rights: (1) redefines certain terms and provides definitions not previously included in Florida's condominium legislation; (2) revises the minimum-content requirements of the declaration for the condominium ownership contract; (3) provides for new processes, such as those allowed for the amendment of the declaration; (4) stipulates minimum-content requirements for condominium bylaws and explicitly provides for certain mandatory inclusions; (5) details the treatment of unit sale proceeds prior to closing; (6) mandates that all implied warranties of fitness and merchantability be attached to condominium unit purchase agreements; and (7) provides for effective methods of full disclosure prior to sale.

In some states that have failed to keep their condominium legislation current, local governments have filled this need. More and more municipalities and counties have been adopting condominium ordinances. The major emphasis of such local regulations has been to promote a better balance in terms of bargaining power between the unit purchaser and the project developer and to promote the full disclosure of all information that might be pertinent to purchases of condominium units. Another area that has frequently been addressed by legislation at the local level is that of continuing management over the condominium by the developer. Some localities now require that control of the condominium pass from the developer to the owners' association upon the closing of a particular percentage of all units. It remains to be seen just how far state and local regulations will go with respect to condominiums.

All of the problems of condominium ownership that have been described above are *potential* problems only. They need not exist, and in most condominium developments they do not exist. They are presented only as a warning that certain items should be considered prior to the purchase of a condominium unit. Most condominium developers and sponsors are of high capability and integrity. Most condominium unit owners end up being very pleased with their investments. Those who do not, however, are usually persons who did not attempt to foresee what problems might arise.

Summary

The condominium is a unique form of real property ownership. It offers the investor significant potential in terms of equity buildup through principal amortization, value appreciation, tax shelter, flexible financing, and desirable amenities. Whether the purchase is for owner occupancy or for investment purposes, the legalities are largely the same. Though there is much more legal paperwork (the declaration, the bylaws, the management agreement, the house rules) associated with the creation of a condominium than with the purchase of a single-family residence or an individual commercial industrial property, that paperwork is necessary to protect the condominium unit owner. Overall, if the potential purchaser of a condominium unit is aware of the problems that may arise in connection with that purchase, condominium ownership can prove to be a very enjoyable and rewarding experience.

Chapter

58

SMALL APARTMENT BUILDINGS

Frank J. Muriello

*F*RANK J. MURIELLO, MAI, SRPA, Muriello/Meyer & Associates, *Real Estate Appraisers and Consultants, Elk Grove Village, Illinois.*

General partner, Muriello/Meyer & Associates. Thesis reviewer, Institute of Financial Education. Secretary-treasurer, Village of Oak Park Housing Authority. Recipient of professional Recognition Award, American Institute of Real Estate Appraisers. Formerly Appraisal Division chairman, Chicago Real Estate Board; member, Multiple Family and Non-Residential Property Examining committees, American Institute of Real Estate Appraisers, and instructor in real estate appraisal, American Savings and Loan Institute.

With the exception of public housing, the building of 4–12 flats is virtually the entire new construction market for rental housing in most parts of the United States. The lack of new starts of large apartment complexes since 1974 has resulted in shortages of rental units in numerous areas and appears to be the basis for a throwback to the days when the investor in a small apartment building was so important to the rental market. In some instances, the owner-investor lives in the small apartment building. A growing number, however, have no intention of occupying one of the units. They buy on the assumption that the rental market will remain strong, due to a shortage of new rental housing. Real estate analysts classify such properties as owner-amenity income properties.

The Owner-Amenity Income Property

An owner-amenity income property can be described as falling into the 4–12-unit category. The equity requirements range from $20,000 to $60,000. To make the property work, the owner must have the time, talent, and energy to be his own property manager, janitor, and maintenance staff. This, of course, is in sharp contrast to the classic investment property, whose cash flow is sufficient to support management and maintenance expenses over the long pull. The key to the success of the owner-amenity investment property is the person with a more than modest accumulation of money who prefers to be an active investor (as opposed to a passive investor) but cannot afford to invest in a large property.

Bases for Purchase. Our staff recently made a survey of owner-amenity properties which has been purchased through our office. Buyers, brokers, and lenders were interviewed. Over 100 sales in Chicago and its suburbs were reviewed. First of all, we asked the buyers why they bought. Here are some of their answers:

1. I prefer to put my money in brick and mortar because bricks will cost more next year and the dollar will go down.
2. People always need two things—shelter and food.
3. Income is taxable at ordinary rates. Some of it must now be sheltered.
4. I know how to take care of a house. A six-flat is merely six houses stacked up. I know what I am doing in small housing.
5. Inflation is increasing about 10% per year, which is more than I can make on a CD.
6. If I work hard, I can live rent-free, and perhaps increase my family estate.
7. If the location is good, value will increase as costs and rents go up. $30,000 is not all of my savings (I keep some for emergencies), but a small apartment building is what I can afford. What's more, it's what I understand. I don't understand small industrial buildings or commercial. I do what I know best.

Next, we asked the buyers about their type of employment, their age, and their income range. We found that nearly all of the buyers were in business, trade, municipal, educational, and professional employment. They fell largely into the age range from 35 to 55, and their incomes ranged from $20,000 to $75,000, those at the top end being professionals. More than 60 percent of the buyers were going to live in the building, and 40 percent either lived close by or had some other method of caring for it. In any event, the vast majority seemed to realize that, in order to make the property pay, the management functions and janitorial maintenance services would have to be virtually free of charge to the owner.

The value analysis of small multifamily apartment buildings differs little from that of single-family homes. The basic research into physical considerations, neighborhood economic level, and property facilities is the same. The principal difference in the approach to the final determination of value arises from the reasons for the purchase of semi-income properties. In addition to believing that small multifamily apartment houses are investment properties, purchasers have the following reasons for buying them:

1. The use of an apartment or apartments by members of the family or close relatives.
2. Feeling of security that is derived from receiving rent.

3. The possibility of doing spare-time maintenance work and thus receiving indirect income.
4. The use of rental income for interest and mortgage payments.
5. The superior yields of real estate investment as compared to investment in savings, bonds, and so on.
6. The belief that the owner can live in his complex rent-free.
7. The belief that a six-flat requires only slightly more managerial effort than a home.
8. The possibility of future refinancing in order to buy additional apartment houses.
9. The tax advantages of depreciation, tax deferral of profits, and so on.

Analysis of Investment Potential. The market is a phenomenon that exists in the minds and the acts of real estate purchasers. However, it is necessary to assess the soundness of the assumptions and beliefs of the persons who buy small apartment buildings. The analyst's problem is to determine the fair cash market value of these properties by applying valid appraisal methods.

Most purchasers of small multifamily apartment buildings believe that such properties possess investment value because the rental from the apartments other than the one which they intend to occupy produces a net return and thus assists them to carry the burden of their investment. This belief becomes a matter for appraisal analysis. The analysis should ascertain whether the purchase prices found in the market are justified and when the market price and the market value are in balance.

Experience has taught the real estate analyst that the prices of small multi-unit apartments fluctuate more widely than do the prices of single-family dwellings. Moreover, when the real estate market is depressed, recovery of the market for small multifamily apartments is slower than that of the market for single-family dwellings.

A small multi-unit apartment property is an amenity income property with investment potential. Analysis reveals that if the owner calculates the expense and depreciation charges properly, the returns are not commensurate with the investment. The typical owner of a small multi-unit apartment building performs many maintenance duties which, in other investment properties, are performed by skilled workers. The self-employment of the owner creates a pseudoprofit. Owners of small apartment units appear not to be disturbed by the small return on their investment. The amenity returns are sufficient to satisfy them, just as homeowners are satisfied with the pure amenity returns that they receive from single-family home ownership and occupancy. Thus, a small multi-unit apartment property is a hybrid form of investment, and the appraisal process must be adjusted to take this into account.

A phenomenon of the market for small multi-unit apartment properties is that it lags the market for single-family properties. When single-family houses require high equities and demand high prices, people turn to multi-unit apartment building for assistance in meeting the costs of home ownership. At such times the equity required to purchase a single-family home is nearly as great as, and often greater than, the equity required to purchase a two-flat.

The life stage of the property should be an important consideration for the purchaser of a small multi-unit building. The need to accumulate a fund for replacement is often not apparent to the purchasers of new properties. However, purchasers of older properties have to contend with the costs of replacement and repair items from the day of purchase. The purchaser will suffer if he fails to consider this very important fact before making his purchase.

Purchasing a new apartment building rather than an older building seems to create a temporary advantage. The cost of repairs, maintenance, replacements, and short-life items of depreciation are not apparent during the early life of the property. The net rents, are therefore greater, and more money may be applied to interest and to debt amortization. In older properties, however, replacements and repairs are immediate items of expense.

A Case Example.   A new project located in a southwest suburb of Chicago appeared to typify the findings of our interviews. The project consisted of 16 six-flats and 2 twelve-flats situated on a nine-acre site (see Figures 1 and 2). On one side of the project was a golf course and

FIGURE 1

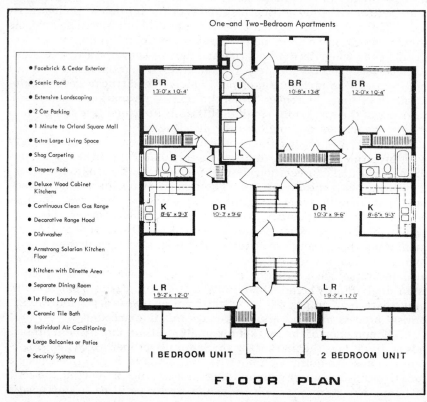

One-and Two-Bedroom Apartments

- Facebrick & Cedar Exterior
- Scenic Pond
- Extensive Landscaping
- 2 Car Parking
- 1 Minute to Orland Square Mall
- Extra Large Living Space
- Shag Carpeting
- Drapery Rods
- Deluxe Wood Cabinet Kitchens
- Continuous Clean Gas Range
- Decorative Range Hood
- Dishwasher
- Armstrong Solarian Kitchen Floor
- Kitchen with Dinette Area
- Separate Dining Room
- 1st Floor Laundry Room
- Ceramic Tile Bath
- Individual Air Conditioning
- Large Balconies or Patios
- Security Systems

B R 13'-0" x 10'-4'   U   B R 10'-8" x 13'-8'   B R 12'-0" x 10'-4'

B   L   B

K 8'-6" x 9'-3'   D R 10'-3" x 9'-6'   D R 10'-3" x 9'-6'   K 8'-6" x 9'-3'

L R 19'-2" x 12'-0'   L R 19'-2" x 12'-0'

I BEDROOM UNIT   2 BEDROOM UNIT

FLOOR   PLAN

FIGURE 2

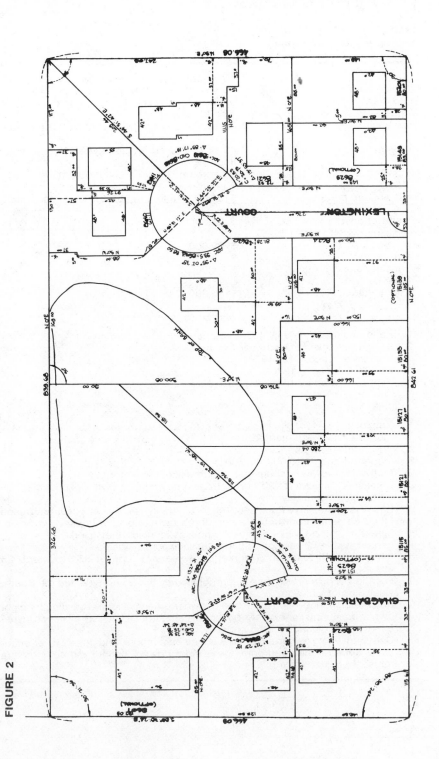

TABLE 1
Shagbark Hills Apartments

Location ....+.........	151st and Orland Brook Drive, Orland Park
Development	16 six-flat sites; 2 twelve-flat sites
Land area	9.1 acres, including 1.2-acre pond
Density	13.18 D.U. per acre
Typical site	80 sq ft × 200 sq ft—16,000 sq ft, irregular shape
Building size	48 sq ft × 42 sq ft plus bays—2,095 sq ft per floor
Unit size....................	2 bedroom, 1 bath × 5—915 sq ft
	1 bedroom, 1 bath × 1—745 sq ft
Base six unit price	$156,000—add $10,000 for full basement
Price allocation	
Land at cost	$ 23,700
Building 6,284 sq ft	
at $15.75 sq ft	$ 99,000
Landscaping	$ 4,800
Financing, closing, etc.	$ 4,000
O&P	$ 24,500
Total	$156,000

Marketing story

1. Land acquisition in July 1974—29 percent down, terms on takeout basis.
2. Began advertising December 24, 1875.
3. First sale January 13, 1976.
4. Sold out April 15, 1976.
5. First six-flat under roof April 15, 1976.

Buyer profile

1. Employment—four businesspersons, four skilled workers, four professionals, four municipal—all married.
2. Age range—35–55.
3. Income range—$20,000–$75,000.
4. Motivation—owner-occupants, 9; nonresident investors, 7.
5. Equities—7 investors: 20 percent down payment; 9 owner-occupants: 25–35 percent down payment.
6. Equity source—investors used cash on hand; six owner-occupants used funds obtained from house sales; three owner-occupants used funds obtained from the sale of apartment houses in which they lived.
7. Lender type—12 savings and loan associations; 4 banks.
8. Financing—15 loans at 9 percent, 25 years; 1 loan at 8.75 percent, 25 years.
9. Location of buyer residences—predominantly the South Side and the Southwest Side of Chicago.
10. Buyer experience—first purchase of owner-amenity income building for eight owner-occupants; one owner-occupant came from a two-flat; all seven investors already owned income property.
11. Comment—two owner-occupants added basements, and three owner-occupants added a third bedroom; these strictly owner options did not increase rents.

an active, new single-family subdivision in the $55,000–$69,000 price range.

The marketing story summarized in Table 1 is noteworthy. The sellout period was unusually brief. Similar buildings may take longer to sell. But, on balance, properly located buildings that require a low degree of maintenance should enjoy excellent sales. Owner-amenity properties appear to be selling with ease. This is borne out by the fact that numerous developers are resubdividing apartment land into owner-amenity properties.

The buyer profile shown in Table 1 is typical of our overall survey sample. It is noteworthy that all of the investors put the minimum amount down, preferring to link high-leverage financial incentives with certain depreciation incentives. The financing was favorable, indicating the general acceptance of owner-amenity property by lenders. This is particularly true when the owner intends to live in the building. Lenders did, however, indicate some reluctance where a nonoccupant investor was invovled.

The nonresident investors were the hardest to sell because their basic interests lay in tax shelter, whereas the owner-occupants were the easiest to sell, as their basic motivation was some cash flow and a free apartment. (The free apartment goal is one which most owners eventually find unattainable.) You will note from the site plan that eight of the buildings were partially joined in sets of two. The market reaction to this was poor, and the freestanding six-flats sold first. The site plan was therefore revised so that only one set of two buildings are joined. These were the last buildings to sell. It seems logical to conclude from this experience that a prudent site plan may have certain common areas, but that buildings should be freestanding if at all possible.

The developer presented each prospective purchaser with a typical first-year operating statement (see Table 2). Primary to the developer's operating statement was a guarantee to fill the building with acceptable tenants at the prescribed rents and to maintain the building during the first full year. On this basis, the annual cash flow of $3,266 was attainable. As an additional sales tool, the developer presented a rather simple tax savings pro forma for the first year (see Table 3). Although this impressed most owner-occupants, it was more interesting to investors. The rental income projections in this instance were most certainly above those currently being charged for apartments of comparable size. However, the inactivity in apartment construction had caused occupancy ratios to increase, thus creating shortages in certain areas, which inured to the benefit of the few projects being built. At any rate, it is not unusual for the rentals of small owner-amenity buildings to be $5–$10 per month higher than the rentals of larger investment-type properties, as tenants feel that on premise management by the owner is worth the difference.

The projected expenses proved to be reasonable. An interesting aspect of real estate taxes, at least in Cook County, is that the assessed value is 16 percent of the market price for buildings with six or fewer flats. For larger buildings, the assessed value increases to 33 percent of the market price.

TABLE 2
Financing the Property

Sale price		$156,000
Income		
Five 2 bedroom apartments at $295	$1,475	
One 1 bedroom apartment at $260	260	
Laundry commission	35	
Monthly total	$1,770	
Gross Annual Income		$ 21,240
Operating expenses		
Real estate taxes	$3,600	
Insurance	430	
Heat and cooking gas	648	
Water and sewer	300	
Electric	120	
Scavenger	96	
Miscellaneous expenses	200	
Annual expenses		5,394
Net annual income		$ 15,846

Mortgage of $124,800, 9 percent, 25 years, 1½ percent service charge.*

Monthly principal and interest, $1,048.32	$	12,580
Annual cash flow	$	3,266 (10.46%)
First-year mortgage principal reduction	$	1,412
Tax savings (see Table 3)	$	887
Anticipated property value appreciation	$	7,800 (5%)
Total annual return for a $31,200 investment	$	13,365 (42.83%)

* The mortgage terms are based on the most recent quotations by lending savings and loan associations. The amount of the loan service charge is basically offset by a credit for security deposits at the time of closing.

TABLE 3
Tax Savings

Annual income	$21,240
Less annual operating expense	5,394
Gross annual income	$15,846
Less first year's interest (will	
decrease each year)	11,168
Adjusted gross income	$ 4,678
Less depreciation based on double	
declining balance on building	
cost of $126,000 over 33	
years, at 6.06 percent per year	7,635
Net operating loss	($ 2,957)

Net tax savings based on 30 percent tax bracket = $887.

You will note from the site plan in Figure 2 that two 12-flats were planned. The asking price of a 12-flat was less than that of two 6-flats, due to certain savings in construction costs. Whereas the price per 6-flat unit was $26,000 for land and building, the price per 12-flat unit was $24,000, or a total of $288,000 for the 12 flats. The cost savings of $24,000 was more than offset by higher taxes per unit and slightly lower rentals. These factors were coupled with a much higher down payment, in this case $72,000—because the lender lowered his loan-to-value ratio to 75 percent. Even a 20 percent down payment requirement greatly reduces the supply of buyers, as the typically available equity is about $35,000–$40,000. Equally important, the typical buyer may be unable to manage and maintain the increased number of units.

The Role of the Appraiser.   Although the owner-amenity property is a hybrid investment, real estate analysis must deal with it in light of all market factors. The real estate appraiser's classic income approach to value is not applicable. Rather, the appraiser should prepare an operating statement which estimates with some accuracy what the building will probably produce over the long pull, after the developer has left the owner on his own (see Table 4). Such an analysis enables the lender to apply proper underwriting procedures, mindful that this is a combination credit and real estate loan, wherein the owner personally endorses the note. Debt service for large investment properties is usually based entirely on the income stream that such properties generate. The operating statement of the owner-amenity income property indicates a

TABLE 4
Reconstructed Operating Statement (over the long pull)

Gross income potential		$21,240
Vacancy factor 5 percent over the long pull		1,062
Effective gross income		$20,178
Less expenses		
Real estate taxes	$3,600	
Insurance	430	
Gas	648	
Water and sewage	300	
Scavenger	96	
Public electric	120	
Miscellaneous	200	
Advertising, legal, and audit*	325	
Mechanical repairs*	250	
Snow removal and lawn maintenance*	300	
Replacements*	300	
Decorating materials*	175	6,744
Net income before debt service		$13,434
Less debt service		12,580
Cash flow		$ 854

Equity dividend: $854 ÷ $31,200 = 2.75 percent.

* Denotes items beyond the first year.

monthly rental for each apartment, including the owner's. Therefore, the lender will evaluate the soundness of his loan based upon the cash flow and upon the present employment and the managerial ability of the buyer. An analysis of the long pull is also a basic aid to the appraiser in rating and comparing market data, since for owner-amenity income properties the most germane approach to value is clearly the market comparison approach (see Chapter 14).

It should be obvious from the long-pull statement that the free apartment is unattainable in most cases. In the early years of a newer building, the owner is not faced with replacement expense or with any noteworthy maintenance expense. In those years, therefore, his cash flow may be higher than the amount indicated on the long-pull statement. An occupancy ratio higher than 95 percent would also help. Depending upon locational factors, investors and lenders feel that a property will appreciate in value, particularly if it is a building of good construction and design. The investor in a small apartment building cannot expect a cash flow of any consequence. Still, even with the owner performing janitorial and management services, his equity dividend is only 2.75 percent. The question is, Why sacrifice the safety and liquidity of a high-yield certificate of deposit for a mere 2.75 percent?

Notwithstanding the minimal cash flow, most owners and nonresident investors believe that depreciation and the inflation hedge provided by real estate are the key elements contributing to the overall return from small apartment buildings. The aforementioned buyer motivations help explain this market phenomenon. Most buyers do not have a wide choice of active real estate investments, principally because the high equity requirements are beyond their reach.

Management Operational Controls

An apartment building is in full use 24 hours a day, 365 days a year. Whether the owner lives in one of the dwelling units or prefers to manage from a nearby location, an apartment building must have full-time attention and regular care. Tenants' demand for services and the competition from similar buildings will ultimately dictate the overall quality of life of the apartment house. It is axiomatic that the owner of a small apartment building must provide general management and many maintenance functions in order to produce a minimal cash flow. The owner-manager has to do more than collect rents and pay bills if he wishes to keep operating costs to a minimum while providing a high level of care and maintenance.

The selection of competitive rent levels must be done in light of the existing market conditions. Apartment buildings located in the same neighborhood generally tend to arrive at similar monthly rent levels, principally because they possess the same community and neighborhood amenities. Within the same neighborhood, however, higher rentals will occur where, for example, dwelling units have exposures that afford more natural light and ventilation.

Competition from apartment houses in other neighborhoods must be considered, as those apartment houses are a part of the broad market. The overall rent schedule must be weighed and tested in relation to building location, transportation factors, the availability of parking, consumer demand, and neighborhood amenities. For example, a dwelling unit situated within walking distance of varying work locations should perhaps command a higher rental in direct relation to the transportation savings.

In order to minimize costly tenant turnover, the manager should always consider providing a level of care that is somewhat above the norm. Although a certain uniformity in types of tenants is desirable in any apartment building, large or small, it is especially important to have a compatible mix of tenant types, if not a single tenant type, in the small apartment house. It is not unusual for tenants to be on a first-name basis in small complexes. Obviously a swinging single may cause disharmony in a four-flat, whose other tenants are senior citizens. A well-maintained building may suffer undue vacancy losses if the tenants are incompatible. The small apartment house has a natural rental advantage over the large complex by virtue of the fact that its tenants generally feel a kinship with the owner-manager and can more easily communicate with him. The ease with which the tenant of a small apartment house can seek out a responsive owner is a significant amenity that is not ordinarily available in a large complex.

It is prudent ownership and management to have a well-prepared and easily understood lease agreement which spells out the rights and responsibilities of the owner and the tenant. A security deposit in excess of one month's rent is highly desirable. This enables the owner to levy damage assessments on tenants who "live out" their last month's rent. However, the owner must be sure to require the same deposit from all tenants.

Management must constantly make studies regarding the highest rent attainable at a given time. When upward adjustments in rent levels are warranted, these adjustments must be accomplished on an individual basis, and not suddenly. The property manager may decide to raise the rent of a highly desirable, longtime tenant only minimally, because such tenants reduce vacancy and collection losses as well as the expense that accompanies tenant turnover. The best time to raise rentals to the maximum possible is when a vacancy occurs and the apartment is spruced up. However, although tenants are naturally reluctant to accept rent raises, they have come to expect annual upward adjustments that are at least equivalent to nationally publicized inflation percentages.

Owners of older apartment houses have the opportunity to upgrade and modernize kitchens and baths. A plan of work attach is necessary to prevent dwelling units that are being modernized from being vacant for too long a time. It is vital to make a careful study of the costs and time that are required in order to modernize and of the rent level that is attainable after modernization. An expenditure of $2,500 to gain a rental increase of $35 to $40 per month is obviously justified.

The Maintenance Program

Maintenance is usually classified as preventive and corrective. Preventive maintenance is intended to preclude the necessity of making major future repairs. Corrective maintenance runs parallel with the replacement of certain short-lived items, parts which are likely to wear out before the bone structure. Preventive or regular maintenance items should be categorized into schedules of varying intervals (daily, weekly, monthly, etc.) and will include hallway cleaning, the painting of the exterior trim, tuckpointing, and inspections and repair of heating and other mechanical equipment. Obviously, regular care goes hand in hand with obtaining quality tenants and higher rentals. Corrective maintenance comprises items which are normally budgeted and reserved on an annual basis, but are taken care of when a building component reaches the end of its physical life. Physical life estimates will vary, depending upon climatic conditions and the quality of construction. Roofs are generally replaced in 15 to 20 years, water heaters in 8 to 10 years, air conditioning compressors in 6 to 8 years, and hallway carpeting in 4 to 6 years. Carpeting in dwelling units usually lasts seven to ten years, assuming good material and a quality tenant. The owner-manager should annually prepare a budget and a maintenance schedule based upon his experience and that of other knowledgeable people, and should carefully project an income and expense statement. This will enhance the owner's ability to control his costs.

Regular expenditures for real estate taxes, insurance, and utilities are sometimes erroneously regarded as uncontrollable expense items. It is only prudent for management to constantly monitor tax assessment levels in the neighborhood to ensure equitable treatment. If an inequity is apparent, a complaint should be made to the supervisor of tax assessments (see Chapter 23). Although an owner cannot shop for taxes, he can shop for insurance. Modern package insurance should be examined for savings, and more than one insurance agent should be interviewed. Insurance should be seasonally adjusted to allow for general construction cost increases.

Because of sharply rising utility costs, new apartment developments tend to use individual electric heating systems, which are metered to the tenant. However, it is usually economically unfeasible to switch existing facilities from central heat. Instead, the installation of utility-saving devices has become commonplace. These include insulation, storm windows and doors, and dialing down at night. The efficiency of the heating system should be intensively evaluated. Plumbing leaks should be repaired immediately, especially since the tendency has been to raise water rates as consumption increases, whereas the opposite was once true. Many local water companies will assist owners in locating leaks.

The importance of a preventive and corrective maintenance program cannot be overemphasized. Apartment houses which fail to show a pride of ownership are drags on their neighborhood and eventually decline in market value.

LARGE-SCALE RENTAL HOUSING

John C. Hart

*J*OHN C. HART, Indianapolis, Indiana.

Developer of land, residential, commercial, and industrial sites. Member, Metropolitan Indianapolis Board of Realtors®; Great Lakes Planning Commission; and Federal National Mortgage Association Advisory Board (chairman in 1979). Director, Hoosier Motor Club and Fidelity Bank of Indiana. Economic adviser to Governor Otis R. Bowen of Indiana and Mayor William Hudnut of Indianapolis. Chairman, Indiana State Housing Finance Board. Lecturer on housing, economics, and finance at Butler University, Ball State University, Indiana University, Purdue University, and IUPUI. Faculty member, Graduate Real Estate Institute, Indiana University. Past president, National Association of Home Builders, Indiana Home Builders, Builders Association of Greater Indianapolis, and Marion County Planning Commission. Formerly Indiana state representative; chairman, Ways and Means Committee; and chairman, Governor's State Budget Committee. Formerly member, Advisory Committee, Federal Home Loan Bank Board.

The American dream is obviously to own one's personal residence—preferably a detached single-family dwelling. This life-style, however, is beyond the means of many Americans.

The Need for Rental Housing

Many people still require a rental apartment during some period of their lives. The developer of multifamily rental apartments must study the needs, the desires, and the movements of such people in order to determine:

1. The best possible locations.
2. The optimum square footage of the living area.
3. The desired amenities.
4. The cost of the necessary land and improvements.
5. The availability of short-term and long-term funds.
6. The equity requirement.
7. The achievable rental rates.

The potential market for apartments comprises a wide variety of groups: for example, young and old singles; young couples with preschool children; older couples whose children have left home; transferees to new jobs; and widows, widowers, and divorced persons. Apartment dwellers may be high school dropouts or college graduates, wealthy or poor, conservative or radical, working or retired, members of any race, religion, or nationality.

The average rental occupancy period of apartment dwellers is two years. Given the diversity of a relatively transient clientele, it is obvious that complex management problems must be solved if large-scale rental housing is to be successful.

Cycles in U.S. Apartment Construction

The first major apartment boom occurred in the late 20s. This boom was stimulated by a combination of population growth, new family formations, economic expansion, and an increase in credit for apartment financing. New-home financing was nearly unattainable, with a 50 percent loan-to-value ratio over a five-year term. Apartments were feasible because cash flows could repay the stiff credit terms—9 percent rates, maturities of 10 to 15 years. Moreover, property taxes were practically nonexistent in this period.

The crash of the 30s caused a moratorium on new apartment construction and financing. The Roosevelt Administration created the Federal Housing Administration and the nation's thrift industry during the 30s. However, apartment construction first began to revive during World War II. After World War II, the FHA reawakened the dormant apartment market with the Section 608 program. The Section 608 program helped developers to meet demand, but scandals led to its failure. Initially, the Section 608 program achieved its purpose of providing housing for newly formed families at reasonable rents.

In the 40s the federal government guaranteed the cost of constructing public housing units which were financed by the tax-exempt bonds of newly created local housing authorities. Although these units provided shelter for the very poor, their value is still being debated. In the 40s and 50s the combination of newly created savings and loan associations with FHA-insured loans that permitted longer terms and reduced down payments really began to make home buying feasible for the masses. The result was a considerable rise in the proportion of home-owning households.

By the early 60s major insurance companies had become large lenders in multifamily projects. For several years 100 percent (or even 110 percent) financing was available to developers. Large-scale rental apartment projects began to be built. Their amenities—clubhouses, tennis courts, golf courses, pools, saunas, and the like—permitted a life-style that prior generations had been unable to achieve without considerable sacrifice.

During the 60s the percentage of multifamily housing starts increased dramatically in most large cities. In the early 70s, nearly 50 percent of U.S. housing starts were multifamily rental units, and in some major urban centers the level was 70 percent.

In the early 60s it seemed impossible to make a mistake building apartments. The post–World War II babies had hit the marketplace, and the demand for such housing was at an all-time peak. By the late 60s and early 70s, however, inexperienced developers had come into the apartment market and for the first time a number of major apartment projects were foreclosed. These projects were unfeasible from the beginning, but it was a swinging market with plenty of money and great demand. The foreclosures were an outcome of the developers' inexperience and the unfeasibility of their projects.

The feasible, soundly planned projects continued to thrive, and lenders began to put their major trust in experienced developers. During the late 60s, the postwar baby boom, which created major apartment demand, also placed tremendous pressures on public facilities. Property taxes in every major city or county became a very costly burden on real estate, particularly apartment houses. The amount that had to be allocated to property taxes varied from a low of 12 percent to a high of 35 percent of the gross rental income. Naturally, the higher property taxes rose, the less feasible it became to build apartments. The cost of new schools and the cost of providing expanded public services to meet the needs of new single-family and multifamily communities were the main reasons for the escalation of property taxes. In addition, the surge in the production of housing created shortages of usable land, building materials, labor, and financing, thus triggering serious inflationary trends in housing costs.

Prior to this first major inflationary period an apartment developer could fairly well predict his equity requirements, and with fixed costs and fixed interest rates, apartment projects came out as targeted. As inflation accelerated, however, many major apartment projects were faced with the need for "gap" financing because of cost overruns or because of construction delays that resulted from shortages.

During the early period of the apartment boom, many builders retained ownership of projects whose equity needs they met with their own capital. However, inflation forced many builders to seek additional capital or secondary financing. At the same time, the long-term and construction lenders began to take more precautions and to demand sufficient equity or collateral before they approved new projects. This first occurred in the early 70s. The larger, more experienced developers found fresh sources of equity capital by preselling projects to limited partners who would benefit from the built-in tax shelters which were available. Some apartment developers used this method to presyndicate their projects in a nationwide investment market.

By 1973 and 1974, when the prime rate on interest reached a high of 12 percent, some major apartment developers were paying 17 percent for construction and development loans. During the same period there were critical materials shortages and a 15 to 20 percent inflation in building costs. Syndicators who had presold projects on the basis of what proved to be erroneous judgments of equity capital needs, came out short, and many of the country's largest apartment producers were forced into bankruptcy.

Contributing to the difficulties of the time were the new sources of funds for apartment building that were made available by newly formed real Estate investment trusts. These inexperienced investors came to the real estate marketplace loaded with cash but with a glaring lack of knowledge of the real estate financial markets. They contributed to the instability of a real estate marketplace that was already in serious jeopardy because of inflation, shortages, and the high cost of money.

By 1975, the apartment market was a shambles. Thousands of units were strung out in unfinished projects, and many completed and occupied projects were unable to meet their financial commitments. The result was a wringing out of the market. For about 24 months, through 1976, new apartment projects were unfeasible.

On the other hand, the single-family housing market seemed to thrive on the same inflationary conditions that caused the apartment market to flounder. Why the difference?

Regardless of inflation, single-family housing costs can always be adjusted upon completion of the product. Since all new housing built during the same period of time goes to the marketplace with the same inflationary costs, these costs are recoverable in the marketplace. Moreover, during the highly inflationary periods people who profited from the sale of their older homes were willing to pay inflated prices for their new homes because they expected to be able to resell them at a profit. In the apartment market, however, every newly built apartment had to compete against thousands of existing units, and the free marketplace in rentals just did not allow the rents necessary to cover the inflationary costs of the new units.

As the new apartment construction stopped, the high vacancy ratios which had been caused by the overbuilding of 1973 and 1974 began to disappear. Landlords whose projects were not yielding a fair return began to increase their rents, except in certain large urban areas where well-organized tenants successfully lobbied for rent control. In those areas rents moved upward much more slowly and new projects remained unfeasible.

In 1976 the federal government made two major infusions into the apartment market that spurred some major activity in apartment construction. It provided loans at below-market interest rates through the Brooke-Cranston funds which were specifically set aside for FHA multifamily projects. The 7½ percent interest rate provided by these funds plus presyndicating tax-sheltered apartment projects to limited partners made some new projects feasible. In addition, Section 8 of the Federal Housing Act, a new rental subsidy program, was enacted in 1976. The use of Section 8 subsidy funds along with Brooke-Cranston funds and the presyndication of projects also made some new apartment projects feasible.

Factors Affecting the Feasibility of a New Large-Scale Housing Project

Remembering that the apartment business is risky and not for amateurs, let us now see how the feasibility of a new multifamily apartment project is determined.

Location. By far the most important way to ensure the feasibility of a new apartment project is to secure the best possible location. Even in a successful project, 100 percent turnover in tenants occurs over a two–three-year period. It is therefore essential that a large-scale apartment project be accessible, visible, and easily identifiable, so that it can be marketed day in and day out, year in and year out.

The most successful large-scale apartment developments have been situated near large modern retail shopping centers. Proximity to interstate highways and expressways is highly desirable, though the projects should be far enough away from such developments to avoid pollution. The high land costs of a prime location will be recovered many times over in lower advertising costs.

The Cost of Land per Unit. The land costs for apartment projects generally range from a minimum of $500 per unit to a maximum of $1,500 per unit. A bargain in raw land costs may be more than offset by the difficulty of developing a site.

The Density of the Site. Town houses or one-story freestanding units can usually be built at a density of from six to eight units per acre. If two-story walk-ups are built in combination with town houses, a density of from 8 to 14 units per acre is possible. Two-story garden apartments can be built with a density of 15 to 20 units per acre. To build more than 20 units per acre, 2½-story garden apartments or elevator-type buildings would be needed. Most large-scale apartment projects combine ranch, town house, and garden units according to a formula devised to meet the demands of the given marketplace.

Market. Once a potential location has been discovered, a thorough market study of the existing competition should be prepared. The impact of competitive housing on the proposed project would depend on the distance of that housing from the location under consideration.

The market study should include data on the available types of units, the rentable square footage of units, the number of bedrooms and baths of units, the rental charges per square foot, and landlord and tenant responsibilities. The study should also contain information on the date the units were constructed, the history of the project, its present occupancy level, and the type of financing that it is using. A checklist should be made in order to itemize the amenities and the faults of each competing project.

The market study will show that the new project will be competing against existing apartments that were built at lower costs and are financed at lower interest rates. New apartment units can be competitive only at rental levels 10 to 15 percent higher than those of the older units. (In most cases the landlords of the older units will adjust their rents upward to a level slightly below that of the new schedule. Consequently, unless there has been little activity in new-apartment construction and occupancy rates are very high (96 percent or higher), the new units must possess better amenities than those of the existing units.

Financing.   Most conventional lenders require 75 to 100 more basis points for multifamily mortgages than for single-family mortgages. The Federal National Mortgage Association auction rate on single-family mortgages is a fairly good gauge of current market rates. If the FNMA auction rate is 9 percent, the rates for multifamily commitments will probably be 9¾ percent to 10 percent. The normal length of amortization on multifamily mortgage commitments is from 25 to 30 years.

Before leaving office as secretary of housing and urban development, Carla Hills split the FHA rate for the first time in its history, allowing a rate differential between single-family and multifamily commitments. Future FHA multifamily rates are expected to be from 50 to 100 basis points higher than the current market rates on single-family FHA mortgages. There is little if any activity today in conventionally financed multifamily projects because the currently quoted rates in excess of 11 percent are not feasible. The only major present activity in multifamily building is in FHA-insured loans where the builder or sponsor has secured Brooke-Cranston funds which reduce the FHA market rate to a subsidized rate of 7½ percent. Most of the FHA-insured projects have used either Brooke-Cranston funding or special tax-exempt bonds issued by local or state housing authorities. These bonds are also being used on projects at rates considerably below the current market level. In order for conventional mortgages to become feasible without special interest subsidies, the rates would have to drop to below 9 percent. At that point there would begin some activity in conventionally financed apartments, because of less red tape and lower costs.

Subsidies.   The 1976 Housing Act provided for the use of a new Section 8 rental subsidy program. The Section 8 subsidies are available for both new and existing apartment projects. The FHA determines the fair market rent of a rental unit which has been designated for Section 8 assistance and then pays the rental cost in excess of 25 percent of the tenant's adjusted income. Projects that use the subsidy of Brooke-Cranston interest rates (7½ percent) and/or housing authority bonds plus Section 8 allocations are the major current multifamily activity in the United States.

Presyndication

The nearly 50 percent equity that is required on a conventionally financed market rate project today is totally unattainable. Today the major apartment developers presyndicate their projects and use FHA-insured programs. FHA projects are structured to give the builder an allowance for overhead and a 90 percent to value loan. The builder's profit is his contribution to such projects.

No one can stay in the apartment construction business without making a profit and turning over cash. It is therefore necessary for large-scale developers to obtain outside equity capital which allows them to take their profit on each project. This is called preselling or presyndicating a project. In the current marketplace the typical FHA project using Brooke-Cranston funds and having Section 8 supplemental support could be sold for about 25 percent above the FHA mortgage commitment.

Some developers do their own syndicating; others sell their projects through third-party syndicators. The developer who uses a third-party syndicator usually nets from 17 to 18 points as the entrepreneur, developer, builder, and general partner. The builder is required to put up completion bonds and letters of credit for certain cash requirements. Unless a builder can recover the dollars allocated for the letters of credit during the rent-up period and prior to the final endorsement, he is forced to use some of his syndication funds to meet the shortages.

In order to enable equity capital investors to get the fair return that is obtainable from a combination of cash flow and legal tax shelter, the payments of syndicate funds to the builder are sometimes structured over a four- or five-year period. Most of the current syndicatable projects allow an investor to recapture each dollar of investment capital in the tax year in which it is invested if his tax bracket is 50 percent or higher. Congress has been pecking away at the advantages of this type of tax-sheltered real estate deal with minimum taxes and recapture provisions, so that syndication will become more difficult as time goes by. However, it is obvious that without presyndication, without Section 8, and without interest subsidies of some kind, there would be little or no current activity in rental apartment construction.

Assessing the Feasibility of a Large-Scale Housing Project

To assess the feasibility of an apartment project, it is necessary to prepare a pro forma statement that follows this format:

Gross rental income		100%
Vacancy		5
Net effective income ...		95%
Operating expenses	35%	
Debt service	45%	
		80%
Net cash flow		15%

The Gross Rental Income. After you have made your market analysis, take the rental square footage of a projected apartment and multiply that square footage by a per month rent per square foot. This will give you the monthly rental of the apartment. Multiply that amount by the number of apartments to obtain the maximum possible rental income.

Since the construction of a large project takes from 12 to 24 months, the projected rents on the pro forma statement should take into consideration the rents that can be obtained at that time. The amount of money that you can borrow is directly related to the achievable gross rents.

The Vacancy Factor. The vacancy rate of popular, well-designed, attractive projects in strong market areas can run as low as 3 percent. However, most lenders, including the FHA, require that a minimum 5 percent vacancy rate be shown. Some lenders require a 7 percent vacancy factor.

The Operating Expenditures. The operating costs of the apartment project include advertising, insurance, real and personal property taxes, maintenance and repair costs, management fees, utilities, legal and accounting costs, supply costs, and miscellaneous expenses. (Lenders today require tenant responsibility for heating and cooling expenses.) There must also be an adequate replacement reserve for items that depreciate in less than ten years, such as appliances and carpeting. The operating expenses on apartment projects vary from a low of 32 percent to a high of 45 percent. Any project with operating expenses in excess of 40 percent could be heading for trouble. Although most lenders use a formula of effective gross, less operating to net the cash available to determine the capitalization rate and thus the mortgage amount, the debt service will usually vary from 45 to 55 percent of the gross projected rents. When the product design has been determined and the rent schedules has been projected, it is important to make some basic judgments on the current costs of land, development costs, and building costs. These costs should then be compared with the mortgage financing that would be available. The mortgage interest rate and term develop a constant annual percentage of repayment. This constant annual percentage should be multiplied by the mortgage amount to obtain the annual debt service. You will then know your gap, or need for equity capital.

The Net Cash Flow. The net cash flow of 15 percent shown in the pro forma statement is overly optimistic in today's market. Most major current apartment projects are declared feasible and are being built with zero cash flow because the developer expect fixed debt service combined with future rent increases to generate future positive cash flows. Most syndicators do not expect positive cash flow in FHA-insured projects during the first three to five years. However, they anticipate a minimum 6 percent cash flow on the invested equity after three to five years. Syndicators require developers to make up negative cash flows in projects during the four- or five-year period in which the investors are paying in their equity capital.

Every potential project should be analyzed so that the bottom line net cash flow can be pinpointed and the risk of the developer minimized. This requires site and market selection that will ensure future cash flows and a mortgage commitment that is sufficient to hold the equity requirements at their lowest possible level.

The equity investor is looking for tax shelter, minimal cash flow, and possible capital gain advantages in the future resale of the property. The developer is hoping to retain as much of the syndication fee as possible, realizing that he must make up for any shortages, letters of credit, or negative cash flow for a contracted period of time (three to five years). A major benefit of apartment developers is to continue as the managing general partner of the projects they develop. Most syndicators look for strong, competent managers with proven apartment development background.

In an FHA project you are required to fill out forms which will allow the HUD processing office to determine the maximum mortgage commitment that will be available for the project. It is suggested that once this figure is available to the developer that he must commit himself to draw final plans to the point of getting firm bids from suppliers and subcontractors.

It is at this point where many projects are proven to be not feasible. There must be enough dollars allocated in the mortgage commitment to meet construction costs, land acquisition, and financing of the project. If there are projected overruns at this point, go back to the drawing board.

The Size of the Project

This chapter is oriented toward large-scale multifamily projects. A large-scale apartment project may be defined as any project with more than 100 units. Most major large-scale apartment projects have 200 to 750 units. The ideal number seems to be about 250 to 350 units. Large-scale apartment projects must offer various types of units in order to keep high occupancy levels. They should have a mixture of efficiency units and one-, two-, and three-bedroom units. Certain areas should be set aside for adults only, and if the market is strong enough, it is recommended that pets not be allowed.

Many major apartment developers try to stay away from large family units. Too many children in an apartment tend to increase management and maintenance problems. There is always a demand for one-bedroom units, and these stay well occupied, though sometimes it is just not feasible to build them. The two-bedroom apartment has a much lower proportional cost in square footage and brings in a much greater return per square foot in rent. It also permits two single adults to split the cost of a unit.

If various types of units are separated within a project, two sets of recreational facilities may be required. The developer should avoid overbuilding clubhouses and other common area facilities which might pose an unnecessary financial burden on the project.

Selecting the Proper Products

It is extremely important that suitable materials and products be used in large-scale rental housing. The high turnover necessitates constant repairs and maintenance on the entry ways within each apartment. Public hallways are expensive to maintain, and they provide no income. The products selected should have long life and be able to stand excess wear and tear. Exterior finish materials should be as maintenance free as possible.

The most successful large-scale apartment builders in the United States have usually found a plan that is to their liking and have then used this plan time and time again, making only minor modifications to either floor plans or exteriors. Being able to make use of their past experience enables them to avoid cost overruns and omissions in their new projects. It also enables them to avoid costly architectural fees.

Popular and noncontroversial colors and decor should be used, and the unit exteriors should blend in with the surrounding environment. Investment dollars should be set aside for a perimeter fence that will give the project a prestigious appearance and will make the tenants feel more secure.

The Future of Large-Scale Multifamily Housing

The specific characteristics of large-scale multifamily housing make it attractive to certain people. The principal asset of apartment projects is probably the maintenance-free, flexible life-style that they make possible.

The federal and state tax systems which grant the deductibility of real property taxes and interest on mortgages make it advantageous to own property instead of renting it. A highly inflationary period benefits owners over renters. Moreover, public sentiment can be expected to force Congress to take away the so-called tax shelters of multifamily rental projects. These factors endanger the future of rental apartments.

In moderate and luxury apartments, condominiums will probably replace rental units. These units will give their owners the benefits of tax deductions and the profits of inflation. The developer may retain a few units in a project for rental to temporary residents of a community or may enter into sale and buy-back arrangements with such residents with a buyer.

Rental units for low-income families will probably have to be built under special federally insured programs. The unavailability of tax shelters will destroy the ability to raise equity capital. The new programs would require the FHA to insure 100 percent of project costs, along with the allowance for the builder's overhead and profit. Such programs would incorporate many of the characteristics of the old Section 608 program. Congress may be hard pressed not to retain certain tax shelters for some low-income rental projects in order to preserve some sources of equity capital. Congress cannot abolish the present so-called tax shelters for multifamily rental units until it provides an alternative program.

Many large rental projects are sold after having been in existence for ten years or longer. At this time a project begins to show profits in excess of the net cash flow. Owners then have two major alternatives: to sell the project or to refinance it. A great fear regarding possible congressional action on tax shelters concerns the effect that this would have on second-, third-, and fourth-time buyers of rental apartment projects. Then the only escape for project owners would be to refinance them or to convert the rental apartments to condominiums.

With 65 percent of U.S. families owning their own homes, it seems unlikely that Congress will withdraw any of the federal income tax advantages of home ownership. At some point, therefore, multifamily rental apartments will probably take on the characteristics of ownership so that their occupants can also receive favorable tax treatment.

The rebuilding of the urban cores of our nation will require the use of new or rehabilitated multifamily structures. However, until Congress makes a definitive determination of its tax policy on multifamily housing, urban redevelopment will be stalled or delayed. If inflation cannot be restrained, rental housing will be greatly reduced.

Conclusion

Multifamily housing is a venturesome business. It requires foresight, knowledge, experience, and strong organizational support. The building of a large-scale apartment project is costly and time consuming. The potential profits and losses are very high. The future of multifamily rental apartments is very questionable because of the effect of inflation on interest rates, housing costs, and the renter and because of the constant shifts in federal tax policy toward single-family and multifamily housing.

INVESTMENT IN RETAIL SPACE

Marion Blackwell, Jr.

*M*ARION BLACKWELL, Jr., CCIM, President, Sharp-Boylston Co.,
Atlanta, Georgia.
   President, Atlanta Real Estate Associates, Inc. Past president,
Atlanta Board of Realtors®, Association of Georgia Real Estate
Exchangers, and Georgia CCIM chapter. Author of articles in
Real Estate Today, Real Estate Atlanta, Sales Talk, *and* Atlanta
Real Estate Journal.

The investments discussed in this chapter are defined as buildings
containing one or more retail businesses. Examples of such investments
are found in any city. They may vary from a freestanding building housing a McDonald's restaurant or a branch bank to a small group of stores
containing such businesses as barbershops, restaurants, dress shops,
hardware stores, or an occasional service operation such as an insurance
office or a real estate office.

Types of Retail Investment Properties

The three most common types of retail investments are properties
with long-term leases to national chain stores, buildings with short-term
leases, and small strip shopping centers.

Properties with long-term leases to national chain stores are in considerable demand because of the security of the investment and the freedom
from management. Pension funds, trust funds, and large investment
organizations invest in such properties. Since national chain stores usually have considerable financial strength, ordinarily the investor does
not have to worry about the tenant's ability to pay the rent and can be
sure that his capital will be well protected.

The use of a net lease frees the investor from any of the responsibilities of looking after the property or paying its expenses. In net leases

all expenses are paid by the tenant. The investor's only responsibility is to deposit the rent check each month. The tenant pays property taxes, insurance, maintenance, and all other costs relating to the real estate. These net leases are very popular with investors because they ensure the stability of the landlord's income.

Long term leases are also much preferred, again because of their security and lack of management problems. A long term lease is generally considered to be a lease of 15 years or more. Such a lease would relieve the investor of any worries about potential vacancies, problems of renegotiating leases with the tenant, or the task of locating a new tenant.

Freestanding buildings with short-term leases confront the owner of a property with the frequent need to renegotiate the lease or find a new tenant. Some investors deliberately arrange short-term leases and welcome the opportunity to renegotiate them. This gives them an opportunity to increase the rent if the neighborhood improves or if inflation continues to push rents upward. A short-term lease can be an advantage or a disadvantage, depending on the quality of a property. A low-grade building in a poor neighborhood could stand vacant for many months before an interested tenant comes along.

Owners of freestanding buildings with short-term leases should always keep in mind the advantages of diversification. If the investor's capital position permits it, properties of this type should be acquired in a variety of locations. Lease expiration dates should be staggered so that all of the investor's buildings will not be vacant at the same time. A single freestanding building can be a very dangerous investment for an investor, particularly if it is heavily financed. Mortgage payments have to be made even though no rent may be coming in. The investor could lose his real estate through default. However, if the investor owns several freestanding buildings with staggered leases, it is unlikely that all of them would become vacant at the same time.

Small strip shopping centers provide in one location the advantage of staggered lease diversification recommended above but not geographic diversification. Such shopping centers usually contain from three to five tenants (larger shopping centers are covered in Chapter 61. Managing a five-unit strip shopping center is much simpler than managing five freestanding buildings scattered over various parts of the city.

Assessing Rent Potentials

Before an investment is made in an income-producing property, its income stream should be carefully analyzed. An income stream is characterized by quantity, quality, and durability. These characteristics affect the value of the property under consideration.

Quantity has to do with how much revenue is produced. *Quality* has to do with the security of that revenue. Properties whose revenue is very secure, such as those leased to General Motors, would be worth more than properties whose revenue depends on something as uncertain as an individuals health. *Durability* involves the period of time over which a property will produce revenue. New, well-constructed buildings will produce revenue for a longer period of time than old, obsolete buildings; properties with longer leases will produce revenue for a longer time than will properties with shorter leases (see Chapters 12 and 13).

The three characteristics of the income stream are interrelated. For example, take two restaurants, one leased to McDonald's, another leased to "Bill and Joe." McDonald's may be paying $1,000 per month, and Bill and Joe may be paying $1,200 per month. Although the *quantity* of the income received from Bill and Joe is greater, the *quality* of the income from McDonald's is higher, so that the property leased to McDonald's could be worth more than the property leased to Bill and Joe.

A close look at the tenant's credit standing is essential in evaluating an investment. A certain amount of risk must be taken in any investment, but this risk can be properly evaluated if the investor carefully investigates the tenant's ability to pay the rent.

The tenant should always be requested to furnish a financial statement, preferably an audited statement. When leasing vacant space to a tenant, references should be requested. However, if an investor is considering buying a building which already has a tenant in place, information on the tenant's reputation and business ability may be obtained by asking the opinion of nearby business operators and his suppliers.

The general business experience of the tenant should also be determined. The chance that a business will fail is much greater in its earlier years. A building with a new tenant who has very little experience, and little financial backing, would be a very high risk investment unless there is a strong demand for the space by substitute tenants. In the case of very small businesses, it is always preferable for the owner of the business to personally endorse the lease.

Percentage leases are fairly common in retail properties. Many landlords have negotiated leases of five or ten years at a fixed rent only to find that their true income from the investment decreases each year for many reasons. Expense items paid by the landlord usually increase gradually through the years, and inflation also erodes the buying power of the diminishing net income. If the location of a property improves, fixed rentals prevent the owner from enjoying the benefits of the improvement. To make this situation more equitable, many landlords negotiate percentage leases which will protect them against the diminishing returns caused by a fixed rent.

In a percentage lease, the tenant usually pays a fixed guaranteed rent and in addition pays the landlord a certain percentage of his gross sales volume over a base level. For example, a sporting goods store might pay $1,000 per month rent plus 6 percent of its annual sales in excess of $200,000. If the volume of the store's business increases to $250,000, then the tenant would pay the landlord 6 percent of $50,000, providing the landlord with an additional $3,000 in rental income. The percentages paid by tenants vary greatly, depending on the type and the size of the business.

In buying a particular retail investment, an investor should carefully evaluate the tenant's ability to continue paying the present rent. If the present rent is too high, the tenant would demand a reduction at the expiration of the lease and the return from the investment would be reduced. If the present rent is too low, the landlord could renegotiate the lease at a higher rate with this tenant or another tenant. For example, assume that the investor is considering the purchase of a freestanding 6,000-square-foot hardware store that is leased for $2 per square foot per year, or $12,000 annually. If the annual sales volume is $360,000, and the potential landlord feels that a fair rent would be 4 percent of gross sales, or $14,400 per year, this would indicate that if the lease were renegotiated in the near future, the investor could increase his revenue by $2,400 annually.

Statistical information on average percentage rates for various businesses, average business volume per square foot, and average rent per square foot is available in publications put out by numerous real estate–related organizations, such as the Urban Land Institute and the Realtors' National Marketing Institute.

Locational Factors

In real estate the importance of location can never be overemphasized. Unlike other investments, such as cash, securities, or art, a real estate property is *immobile.* Once an investor puts his hard-earned cash into a particular spot, it is there until the market conditions allow him to take it out. He cannot move his property to another location in which conditions may be more favorable. For this reason, the location of a particular property needs to be carefully evaluated before the purchase decision is made. There are a number of factors which must be considered in evaluating a particular location.

Growth Trends. These can usually be ascertained by observing the frequency of new building construction and by analyzing statistics obtained from chambers of commerce. Most prudent investors like to acquire properties "in the path of progress." People create value, and properties acquired in areas whose population is growing will usually increase in value. This principle is more applicable to retail space than to many other forms of investment. The retail tenant's ability to pay rent depends upon the ability of his customers to buy goods. The more customers a retail tenant has, and the more money the customers have to spend, the more business the retail tenant will do, and the more rent he will be able to pay the investor. Contrarily, in an area of declining population or of declining purchasing power, retail businesses fail, the rents received for retail space decreases, and retail properties decline in value.

Most areas tend to go through cycles of productivity. They begin as sparsely populated neighborhoods. Then as people and new businesses move in, a neighborhood improves up to a certain point. At that point, the aging of buildings and a change in population makeup initiate a decline. After many years of decline, the neighborhood gets so bad that investors acquire properties for their land value alone. As some older buildings are demolished and others are refurbished, and as new buildings are built, the neighborhood will begin to revive and the cycle will be repeated. An investor considering a retail investment in a given neighborhood should try to determine the neighborhood's position in this cycle.

Neighborhood Features. Certain neighborhood features may have a significant favorable or unfavorable impact upon freestanding retail space. Among the features which the investor must look at carefully are the following.

Shopping Centers. In most cases a nearby shopping center will help generate traffic and will benefit smaller retail establishments. Smaller properties can "feed" off the customers who are pulled into the shopping center by the promotional activities of merchants.

Highways. The thoroughfare on which the retail building is located can be too busy or not busy enough. If traffic is too fast and too heavy, customers may be afraid to slow down and make a turn into the property. They may also pass the property without seeing it. If they do frequent the business, their difficulty in getting back out into extremely heavy traffic may discourage them from doing so again. Corner locations are usually much preferred over inside locations, since they provide alternative means of ingress and egress. Traffic lights and stop signs can help improve a retail location, but they will hurt it if they cause traffic to back up in front of the property and block the driveways. The ideal retail location is on the right side of the street for "going home" traffic and on the far side of an intersection from a traffic light or a stop sign. This allows traffic to clear the intersection at a moderate rate of speed and then to turn into the driveway without fear of a rear end collision. It also allows customers to leave the parking lot while oncoming traffic is stopped at the intersection. A median strip down the center of a highway can greatly improve traffic flow, but it can also prevent traffic on the far side of the thoroughfare from turning into a property. The width of the median, the height of the barrier, and the location of drive-throughs must be considered.

Market Area. Any retail location will have a definable market area or trade area, that is, a territory from which it draws its customers. This area must be defined as accurately as possible, and the investor should try to determine whether it contains enough potential customers to support his merchant tenants. If the business in the investor's retail space caters to a particular income group, the investor needs to determine whether there are enough available people within that income group to continue to support the business.

The boundaries of market areas can usually be distinguished by scrutinizing maps and aerial photographs. These boundaries are usually formed by such things as railroads, rivers, mountain ranges, large lakes, parks, major highways, expressways, airports, or anything that might discourage people from freely moving into an area.

Airports. Major commercial airports generate a lot of traffic and can have a very favorable influence on retail locations. Such businesses as restaurants, motels and automobile-leasing facilities usually flourish on the main thoroughfare leading to an airport.

Airports affect a very few properties unfavorably. Sites which are located close to the end of an airport runway have the disadvantage of being in a danger zone and a nuisance area. Zoning restrictions and avigation easements will sometimes prohibit the erection of the large signs that certain merchants may need.

Industrial Districts. A peculiar characteristic of large industrial districts is that they are usually heavily populated during the week, and almost empty on weekends. Businesses which serve their industries must operate on a five-day-a-week basis.

Low-Income Residential Areas. The very high incidence of crime and vandalism in retail districts which are near low-income residential areas has caused many merchants to refuse to do business in such areas. This creates a much higher than normal vacancy rate in retail buildings in low income neighborhoods. In projecting the net income from an investment in such an area, the investor should take this abnormally high vacancy rate into consideration and should also consider the higher operating costs that result from theft, vandalism, and so on.

Expense Control

Maintaining careful control over what goes out is just as important as carefully evaluating what is going to come in.

Property taxes usually constitute the single largest expense item in income-producing properties. Percentage leases, discussed above, are one method of protecting the investor against increasing taxes.

Another frequently used method is to require that the tenant pay all of the taxes on the property or any increase in the taxes. This is done through a lease provision which states what part of the taxes are to be paid by the landlord and what part are to be paid by the tenant. A common arrangement is to have the landlord pay the taxes for the first full tax year of the lease and the tenant pay any increases in the taxes after that first year. Each year, upon receiving the tax bill, the landlord sends a statement to the tenant showing him the amount of the increase and billing the tenant for his proportionate share.

Some landlords try to save money by deferring the maintenance of certain items. This is a very shortsighted approach to real estate investing. Items whose maintenance has been deferred become more expensive to repair as time goes on. Moreover, tenants may move out if the property is not kept in good condition.

In considering a potential investment, the buyer needs to look for evidence of deferred maintenance—that is, for evidence that repairs which should have been made were not made. The cost of deferred maintenance items should be estimated as accurately as possible and deducted from the normal market value of the property.

Vacancies occur sooner or later in all income properties. Even if a property is highly desirable, there may be a short interval between tenants. If an investor is considering acquiring a particular retail property, he should determine the exact cause and duration of any vacancies. A tenant may have moved out simply because he outgrew the space, but he may also have moved out because there is something basically wrong with the property which the investor needs to discover. If a space has been vacant for a long time, this may indicate that a new owner will require an even longer period of time to fill it.

Some landlords create an abnormal vacancy problem by trying to get too much rent for a property. Other landlords feel that they are better off by renting at a lower rate and keeping vacancies down to a minimum. There are arguments in favor of both policies.

Future vacancies should be allowed for by estimating a vacancy rate. The vacancy rate is lost income expressed as a percentage of gross potential income. This rate can be estimated in two ways. The first, and sometimes the most accurate, method is to look at the operating history of a property. If there have been no significant changes in the property, and if no changes are contemplated, then there is every reason to believe that the property's future productivity will duplicate its previous productivity and that past vacancy rates will be repeated in the future.

In the absence of accurate statistics on a property's operating history, an investor can project vacancy rates by using the following system. Let us say that there are five tenants in a particular building. The investor determines the number of *tenant months* by multiplying the number of tenants—five—by the number of months in a year. Then the investor uses his best judgment to estimate how many tenants will move out each year and how long it will take to find new tenants for the vacant spaces. The investor may decide that two tenants will move out each year and that in each case the vacant units will be unproductive for three months. *Two* vacant spaces at *three* months each means that a total number of six tenant months would be lost. That is, out of a potential of 60 tenant months, the property would be vacant for a total of 6 tenant months. Since 6 is 10 percent of 60, a reasonable projected vacancy estimate would be 10 percent.

Property Management

Some real estate investments require a wide variety of decisions, and in some instances these decisions have to be made on an almost daily basis. If an investor feels that he is unable or unwilling to make these decisions himself, he will want to consider retaining professional property management.

Property managers will take over any or all of the management responsibility. Their fees will depend on the extent of their responsibility and on the time that is needed to manage the property. In most cases, these fees will range from 3 percent to 10 percent of the gross income.

Rates of Return

Investors and real estate agents use a wide variety of formulas to measure and compare income-producing properties. Some of the more common rates used are the *capitalization rate,* the *cash flow rate,* the *equity rate,* and the *internal rate of return.* The same property will produce different rates, depending on which of these four systems is applied.

In purchasing retail properties, the investor needs to determine which method of calculating the rate of return will fit his personal situation best, and then be sure that the sellers and real estate agents with whom he communicates are quoting the same rate of return.

For example, an investor may determine that he needs a 10 percent rate of return. A particular investment could have an 8 percent capitalization rate, a 9 percent cash flow rate, a 10 percent equity rate, and an 11 percent internal rate of return. Anytime that two individuals discuss the rate of return, they need to be sure they are talking about the same rate (see Chapters 12 and 13).

The Capitalization Rate. The most widely used capitalization rate is sometimes called the overall rate. It does not take financing into consideration, and it assumes that the property is free and clear. The capitalization rate (overall rate) is calculated by dividing the net operating income by the price (or value) of the property.

For example, if an investor has an opportunity to purchase a retail building for $100,000, and the figures show that the building will produce a net operating income of $12,000, the capitalization rate can be calculated by dividing the $100,000 into the $12,000, producing an answer of 0.12. This 0.12 is then stated as being a 12 percent capitalization rate, or "cap rate" as it is often called.

The Cash Flow Rate. This rate ignores the total price of the property and considers only the cash flow as a percentage of the cash down payment (cash flow is net operating income minus all debt service).

For example, assume that the same property used in the example above, which had a net operating income of $12,000, also has an $80,000 mortgage on it. This $80,000 mortgage requires annual debt service—payments of principal and interest—totaling $9,000. After the $9,000 debt service has been subtracted from the $12,000 net operating income, the property produces an annual cash flow of $3,000.

With an $80,000 mortgage on a property priced at $100,000, the investor will have to invest $20,000 in cash to acquire the property. Thus he will be receiving a return of $3,000 in cash on his $20,000 cash investment. The cash flow rate is then calculated by dividing the $3,000 annual cash flow by the $20,000 equity, producing a figure of 0.15, which is a 15 percent cash flow rate.

The Equity Rate. This will usually be one of the highest rates of return that a property will produce, since any increase in the equity is added to the cash flow to calculate the rate. The above $9,000 debt service consists of principal and interest. When an investor makes principal payments, he is increasing his equity in his property and his personal net worth. The equity rate takes this into consideration as a part of the return on the investment.

For example, if the $9,000 mortgage payment consists of $7,000 in interest and $2,000 in principal, this means that the investor's equity in the property will increase by $2,000 in the first year. This increase in equity is added to the $3,000 cash flow, producing a total benefit to the owner of $5,000. This benefit was produced with a cash investment of $20,000. Dividing the $5,000 total benefit by the $20,000 investment produces an equity rate of 25 percent.

The Internal Rate of Return. This is the most accurate way to measure the productivity of income-producing properties.

The internal rate of return is a "summary" rate. It takes into consideration various advantages and disadvantages of owning a property, including the net operating income, equity buildup, and the tax shelter from depreciation and interest, and it assumes a hypothetical sale of the property at some point in the future. Ordinary income taxes on the taxable income which the property produces during the holding period and the capital gains taxes on the hypothetical sale are also taken into consideration. The resulting cash from the hypothetical sale is discounted back to today's value, and the annual cash flows from operating the property are also discounted on a compound basis back to today's value.

Financing

Good institutional financing is frequently very difficult to obtain on the types of properties that this chapter discusses, that is, moderately priced commercial income-producing properties. The large institutional lenders, such as insurance companies, are primarily interested in making loans of at least $500,000 to $1,000,000. Some retail properties, particularly freestanding buildings leased to major tenants, fall into this category and can easily be financed. However, the strip center containing four or five smaller tenants is usually priced far below the minimum requirements of the institutional lenders.

Savings and loan associations will sometimes step in to fill this gap. However, savings and loan associations are allowed to lend only a small percentage of their assets on commercial properties. They are sometimes a good source of financing on retail buildings.

The sellers themselves are an excellent source of financing for small- and moderate-sized commercial properties. However, unless a seller has experience in financing his own property, he will usually object to the idea of anything other than a straight cash sale. A real estate agent or investor who is familiar with all of the many varieties of purchase-money loans can frequently show a seller why it is to his advantage to finance the sale himself.

Conclusion

Retail income-producing properties are one of the most popular forms of investment. Retail buildings will usually provide many of the advantages of investments in apartment buildings, industrial properties, large shopping centers, and land. Retail buildings require much less personal contact with the tenants than do apartment buildings, because there are usually fewer tenants involved and because commercial tenants are usually more sophisticated than the typical apartment tenant. The steady income stream of retail buildings is usually much preferred over the one lump-sum profit that a land investment would produce. Depending on location and market conditions, retail space will usually stand vacant for a much shorter period of time than highly specialized industrial buildings or warehouses. When wisely purchased, retail buildings can form a most important part of the investor's portfolio.

SHOPPING CENTER INVESTMENT

Homer Hoyt

*H*OMER HOYT, JD, PhD, MAI, President, Homer Hoyt Associates, *Washington, D.C.*
Market analysis and appraisal of 500 shopping centers in the United States, Canada, and Puerto Rico, 1948–79. Award, American Institute of Real Estate Appraisers, 1964. Citation for Distinguished Service, University of Kansas, 1976. Member, Bar, Supreme Court of the United States, Phi Beta Kappa, Lambda Alpha, Rho Epsilon, Delta Sigma Rho. Chairman of the board, Homer Hoyt Institute. Author, "Appraisal of Shopping Centers," in Encyclopedia of Real Estate Appraising *(Englewood Cliffs, N.J.: Prentice-Hall, 1959, 1968, 1978);* One Hundred Years of Land Values in Chicago*(1933); and* Structure and Growth of Residential Neighborhoods in American Cities *(Federal Housing Administration, 1939). Coauthor,* Real Estate *(1st ed., 1939), 7th ed. (Santa Barbara, Calif.: Wiley/Hamilton, 1978).*

This chapter is devoted to the evaluation of shopping centers. These centers, usually in suburban locations, consist of a group of stores with adjacent automobile parking.

Investors evaluate these centers in their entirety, though the sales and rents of individual stores are considered in arriving at the valuation of an entire center. The different stores are not valued separately, because a single person, a group of persons, or a corporation owns and develops the entire center. The center is subject to a single mortgage, except in the case of department stores in regional centers, and the rents of the stores are based on their sales volume and on their effectiveness in attracting customers to the center.

The evaluation of the planned shopping center is based chiefly on net income. The cost basis can be used to determine whether a new shopping center will yield sufficient rent to cover the cost of construction. A new shopping center built without tenants may not be worth the cost required to build it. The market comparison method can seldom be used, because no two shopping centers have the same construction costs, interest and amortization rates on mortgages, types of stores, and leasing rates.

An appraiser may be asked to make a valuation of an existing shopping center or to make an estimate of the value that would be derived by developing a new shopping center on a vacant site. The investor should understand how that value is based upon income production and income production potentials.

Types of Shopping Centers

There are a number of different types of shopping centers. These include the regional or superregional, community, neighborhood, and discount centers.

Leading Regional or Superregional Shopping Centers. The regional shopping center contains at least one large department store, together with a group of fashion goods stores, women's and men's clothing stores, shoe stores, jewelry stores, restaurants, and numerous other stores which seek to offer the variety found in a central retail district. Such centers at first consisted of a group of stores built around an open mall surrounded by a belt of parking. These regional centers usually had a department store at each end, and some later added one or two department stores in the middle. The newest regional centers have enclosed malls, and many of the early centers have enclosed their malls. The regional centers with three or four department stores are now called superregional centers.

The regional center with 700,000 to 1,000,000 square feet of store area and 2,100,000 to 3,000,000 square feet of surface parking requires a ground area of 2,800,000 to 4,000,000 square feet, or 65 to 100 acres. To support sales of $75 million to $150 million in a large regional center requires a trade area with families having a total personal income of $600 million to $1,200 million. If the families in the trade area had average family incomes of $15,000, this would require a total of 50,000 to 100,000 families, or 150,000 to 300,000 population.

Table 1 presents a tabulation of the types of stores, typical square foot area, sales per square foot, total sales, and rents of a superregional center with four department stores. There are no typical centers, for there are hardly any two alike.

In a regional shopping center the department stores are the magnets that attract the smaller stores or mall stores. It is an almost universal practice to sell or lease the land and parking area required to the department store on a break-even basis. Sometimes such department stores as Sears and J. C. Penney own the entire shopping center site and lease to the mall tenants and other department stores. The valuation of a regional center is based almost entirely on the net income derived from the mall stores.

TABLE 1
A Superregional Shopping Center: Square Foot Area, Sales, and Rentals

No.	Type of Store	Total Square Feet of Gross Leasable Area	Sales per Square Foot	Total Sales	Rents Percent of Sales	Rents Total Charged per Square Foot	Total Rents Percent of Sales	Total Rents Per Square Foot
4	Department stores	600,000	$140	$ 84,000,000	2.5	$ 4.00	$2,100,000	$2,400,000
16	Women's ready-to-wear	100,000	150	15,000,000	6	11.00	900,000	1,100,000
10	Menswear	40,000	150	6,000,000	6	10.00	360,000	400,000
3	Family wear	20,000	100	2,000,000	5	10.00	100,000	200,000
1	Children's wear	2,000	100	200,000	6	10.00	12,000	20,000
6	Women's shoes	20,000	150	3,000,000	6	10.00	180,000	200,000
3	Men's and boys' shoes	10,000	150	1,500,000	6	10.00	60,000	100,000
2	Children's shoes	2,000	100	200,000	6	10.00	12,000	20,000
3	Family shoes	10,000	150	1,500,000	6	10.00	60,000	100,000
1	Barbershop	1,000	150	150,000	8	15.00	12,000	15,000
1	Hosiery	1,000	150	150,000	8	15.00	12,000	15,000
1	Beauty shop	2,000	150	300,000	8	15.00	24,000	30,000
1	Millinery	1,000	100	100,000	10	15.00	10,000	15,000
1	Records and tapes	2,000	250	500,000	6	20.00	30,000	40,000

1	Drugstore	15,000	200	3,000,000	3.6	12.00	90,000	180,000
1	Cleaner	2,000	70	140,000	8	8.00	11,200	16,000
7	Restaurants and cafeterias	45,000	150	6,750,000	6	15.00	405,000	675,000
1	Fast food	6,000	300	1,800,000	7	30.00	128,000	180,000
1	Candy and nuts	1,000	300	300,000	10	30.00	30,000	30,000
1	Books and stationery	5,000	150	750,000	6	10.00	45,000	50,000
2	Jewelry	5,000	300	1,500,000	5	20.00	75,000	100,000
1	Cards and gifts	2,000	150	300,000	7	20.00	21,000	40,000
1	Camera and photographer	1,000	300	300,000	5	20.00	15,000	20,000
1	Toys	3,000	200	600,000	5	10.00	30,000	30,000
1	Key shop	150	400	60,000	12.5	100.00	7,500	15,000
2	Sporting goods	10,000	200	2,000,000	5	10.00	100,000	100,000
2	Musical instruments	5,000	200	1,000,000	6	15.00	60,000	75,000
1	Post office	2,000	—	—	—	10.00	—	20,000
1	Bank	10,000	—	—	—	10.00	—	100,000
1	Savings and loan	2,000	—	—	—	10.00	—	20,000
1	Offices	54,850	—	—	—	10.00	—	548,500
1	Cinema	20,000	—	—	—	10.00	—	200,000
	Total	1,000,000		$132,210,000				$7,044,500
	Total except department stores	400,000		$48,100,000		$ 11.61		$4,644,500

In the United States and Canada there are now approximately 1,200 regional centers.

The Community Shopping Center. The community shopping center consists of a cluster of stores with a small department store 40,000–50,000 square feet in area, a few fashion stores, and neighborhood-type stores or supermarkets, drugstores, cleaners, and prestige shops.

Community centers are losing their attractiveness because they cannot compete effectively for fashion goods with the larger regional centers and for convenience goods with the neighborhood centers. However, there are community centers which are potential investments. These usually have the advantage of being constructed at lower costs, and hence they can be rented for less than stores in regional centers with air-conditioned malls. Their supermarkets, drugstores, and cleaners should be as attractive as those in neighborhood centers.

The Neighborhood Shopping Center. Neighborhood shopping centers specializing in convenience goods and services—supermarkets, drugstores, restaurants, cleaners, and branch banks—often contain 100,000 square feet of store area in 10 to 12 acres.

The Discount Shopping Center. Discount shopping centers featuring self-service general merchandise stores, such as K mart, have grown rapidly in the last few decades. These centers frequently have an adjoining supermarket. They occupy about ten acres.

The Specialty Shopping Center. Specialty shopping centers, such as Trolley Square in Salt Lake City and Ghirardelli Center in San Francisco, feature boutiques, restaurants, and other tourist attractions.

Evaluating an Existing Shopping Center

If the owner of an existing shopping center offers it for sale, or if a prospective purchaser is interested in buying a center, the owner should furnish the potential investor with the following information:

1. The terms of all leases, the percentage of sales, and the minimum guarantees actually paid over a series of years.
2. The expiration dates of the leases and the prospects for renewing or the expected rentals after the expirations.
3. The record of each store's sales over a period of years.
4. The terms of the mortgages on the property, the interest rates, and the expiration dates.
5. The annual record of expenses over a period of years, including real estate taxes and utility costs.
6. The condition of the buildings as disclosed by an examination to see whether repairs are needed.
7. Income tax statements.

After securing all of this information, the investor should estimate the current cash flow, allowances for depreciation, and the capitalized value based on income. He should assess the prospects for increased rental income when the present leases expire.

After analyzing the sales records, the investor should make a survey of new shopping centers that have been built or proposed to evaluate their actual or potential effects on the sales of the subject center. The new centers analyzed should be of the same type as the subject center.

Finally, the potential investor should assess the prospects for the growth of the population and income of the trade area, allowing for inflation.

Evaluating a Proposed Shopping Center

The investor may ask the developer to make an estimate of the sales and net income of a new shopping center that is to be built on a vacant site. These questions should be answered:

1. What type of center will be built—regional, community, discount, or neighborhood?
2. Does the developer own or control sufficient land for the proposed center—60–100 acres for the regional center, 30–40 acres for the community center, and 10–15 acres for the neighborhood or discount center?
3. Has the necessary commercial zoning been obtained?
4. Has a key tenant—such as a department store for a regional center or a supermarket for a neighborhood center—indicated an interest in the proposed center?

If the responses to these questions are favorable the population and income of the trade area should be determined and a market analysis should be made.

Market Analysis.   A market analysis is necessary in evaluating a proposed shopping center. It consists of the following steps:

1. Define the trade area of the proposed shopping center.
2. Determine the population, the number of families, and the income of the families in the trade area by means of tracts from the latest decennial census or later local censuses. To bring these figures up to date, use the information on added dwelling units contained in the U.S. housing census.
3. From the U.S. retail census, calculate the percentage of family income that is spent in department stores, women's clothing stores, supermarkets, shoe stores, and so on.
4. Estimate the total expenditures of families in each type of store in each census tract of the trade area.
5. Estimate what percentage of these total expenditures will be made in each store of the proposed center.
6. Estimate the total sales of each store in the proposed center during the center's first year of full operation.
7. From the sales of each store, calculate what its area should be.
8. Obtain an architect's drawings of the stores.

Cost Analysis.   Even if the sales estimate for the stores are favorable, a cost analysis is required to see whether it will pay to develop the proposed shopping center. The following must be done:

1. Determine the land value of the proposed shopping center site. What price will it bring from some other developer for some other use than the proposed use?
2. From the architect's drawings, obtain an estimate of how much it will cost to build the stores.
3. Determine what rents on minimum guarantees and percentage leases can be obtained from the proposed tenants, and estimate the total rental return.
4. Estimate the real estate taxes, building maintenance costs, insurance costs, and utility costs that will be incurred.
5. Determine what the interest rate and the amortization rate on the mortgages that will finance the building.
6. Estimate the net return on the land by deducting vacancy allowances, operating costs, and interest and amortization on the mortgages from the estimated rents.
7. Capitalize the expected net return, if any, to determine the land value of the developed shopping center. The project should be undertaken if this capitalized net return is greater than the land value that could be realized without developing.

This initial appraisal would be based on the rentals usually paid at similar shopping centers and on the mortgage interest rates for similar centers. The final appraisal cannot be made until all of the leases have been negotiated and the mortgage has been secured.

For existing centers, the investor should conduct a similar analysis in order to determine whether the price to be paid (rather than the cost to build) is worthwhile.

Postwar Trends in Shopping Centers

The movement to build planned shopping centers, which started slowly after World War II, accelerated until July 1977.

There are 19,000 shopping centers in the United States, of which approximately 1,200 are regional. The sales of department stores and fashion goods stores in nearly all central business districts have declined. The growth of the suburbs, free automobile parking, and the attractions of the air-conditioned mall and of centers with several department stores within easy under-roof walking distance have drawn shoppers from the central business districts to the new regional shopping centers. K mart has built 1,200 discount centers at which buyers can shop for medium-priced clothing, refrigerators, and hard goods.

However, the golden era of shopping center expansion may be over. Most large metropolitan areas now appear to have enough of them and the costs of building new shopping centers have skyrocketed. Land for the centers, which formerly sold for $200–$2,000 an acre, or at the most $10,000 an acre, has shot up to $150,000–$200,000 an acre. Interest rates on mortgages, which were once 5–6 percent, are now 9–10 percent. Construction costs, which were once $7–$15 a square foot, are now $20–$40 a square foot. A small store in a regional center that once rented for $2 a square foot annually now rents for $10 a square foot.

Although the market for shopping centers in big metropolitan areas may be saturated, there may be opportunities for expansion in the smaller cities. There is now a movement toward building minimalls in small cities that are some distance away from large metropolitan centers. These minimalls have three or four department stores, each of which is 50,000 square feet in size rather than 150,000–200,000 square feet in size. These stores are designed to provide most of the fashion goods that the local communities need, thus obviating the need for trips to a large metropolitan area.

There is now a great demand for shopping centers already built as a hedge against inflation because almost all stores have a percentage lease clause, in which rents based on sales rise with prices. Hence, there is a great investment opportunity in the 19,000 shopping centers that are already in existence.

Typical Rents and Sales in Shopping Centers

Data on typical rents and sales in three types of shopping centers— the superregional with four department stores, the community center, and the neighborhood center—will be presented below. The sales and rents given are based on the Urban Land Institute's *Dollars and Cents of Shopping Centers, 1975,* but the figures used are the author's approximations and do not correspond exactly to the data contained in *Dollars and Cents of Shopping Centers.*

The Regional or Superregional Shopping Center. The principal components of the hypothetical superregional shopping center of Table 1 reveals are four department stores with a total floor area of 600,000 square feet. If these stores have three levels, they will occupy a ground area of 200,000 square feet. They will require three square feet of parking area on the ground for each square foot of building area—1,800,000 square feet of parking area in addition to the 200,000 square feet of building area, or a total of 46 acres.

Although these department stores are the indispensable magnets of a regional center and occupy 60 percent of its aggregate area, they usually enter only incidentally into the calculation of the value of a regional shopping center. The ground they use is generally sold or leased to them. The value of the regional shopping center is based on the net return derived from the rents on the smaller stores or the mall stores that are attracted to the regional center by the presence of the department stores. In our hypothetical example, the gross leasable area of these stores, which may number 100 or more, is 400,000 square feet. The stores usually occupy ground area only (except in the case of two-level malls) and would require 1,200,000 square feet of parking, usually on the ground. Thus the total area required for these stores would be 1,600,000 square feet, or 37 acres.

Thus, the total area required for the superregional center would be 83 acres, unless part of its parking needs were met by multilevel parking garages.

Second to the department stores as an attraction of the regional center are the women's apparel stores, the men's apparel stores, and the shoe stores. These usually have a high volume of sales and pay a rent that is second only to that of the department stores. In Table 1, they are shown to occupy 204,000 square feet of space, or slightly more than half of all the space occupied by the mall stores. There are 46 of these apparel shops in our hypothetical center, and their size ranges from 1,000 square feet to 15,000 square feet.

A fashion center in an enclosed mall is an attractive place for restaurants, cafeterias, and fast-food shops, of which there are seven in the hypothetical center, ranging in size from 7,000 to 15,000 square feet.

Jewelry stores are also important in a fashion center.

A large regional shopping center usually requires some local convenience stores, such as a drugstore, a beauty shop, a barbershop, cleaners, and a key shop. However, supermarkets are seldom located in such centers.

A large regional shopping center is also an excellent location for the types of small shops that are found in central business districts, such as bookstores, camera stores, musical instrument stores, candy stores, toy stores, and sporting goods stores. Motion-picture theaters also thrive in some regional shopping centers.

Regional shopping centers are favored locations for banks, savings and loan associations, medical and dental offices, and real estate and insurance offices, all of which are also found in central business districts.

A branch post office adds to the attraction of the regional center.

The Evaluation of a Superregional Shopping Center. All of the elements in the appraisal of a superregional shopping center can vary greatly—the sales, rentals, and building costs fluctuate over a wide range.

The sales figures in Table 1 have been realized in many actual cases, but those figures are not the averages or the high and low sales figures which are shown in detail in *Dollars and Cents of Shopping Centers.* The rents percentage are paid commonly, and the total charges per square foot are within the ranges now being paid.

The developers of our hypothetical superregional shopping center have the problem of acquiring 83 acres of land, of which they lease 46 acres to the four department stores, and of securing sufficient rents to build 400,000 square feet of mall stores. As Table 1 shows, the assumed rent for the 400,000 square feet of mall stores is $4,644,500. Is this sufficient to build the mall stores at today's costs?

In the superregional shopping center it is a common practice to lease the ground to the department stores. The value of the shopping center is based entirely on the rents and costs of the mall stores. The high rents from the other stores are based on the drawing power of the department stores.

The highest rents are paid by some small-area stores, such as jewelry, key, and camera stores, but stores of this type occupy only small prime areas and do not yield a large aggregate rent.

According to *Dollars and Cents of Shopping Centers,* the median land cost of regional shopping centers in 1974 was $2.50 a square foot, and the land cost per square foot ranged from $1.10 to $22.59 a square foot. The median land cost of shell and mall buildings was $24.93 a square

TABLE 2
Rents and Operating Expenses of the Mall Stores in a Superregional Shopping Center

	Low	Median	High
Potential rents	$ 4,644,500	$ 4,644,500	$ 4,644,500
Five percent vacancy allowance	232,225	232,225	232,225
Rents collected	$ 4,412,275	$ 4,412,275	$ 4,412,275
Operating costs for 400,000 square feet .	$ 232,000 ($0.58/sq ft)	$ 457,000 ($1.13/sq ft)	$ 1,132,000 ($2.83/sq ft)
Balance available for debt service	4,180,275	3,955,275	3,280,275
Debt service cost	11,344,000 ($28.36/sq ft)	17,148,000 ($42.87/sq ft)	28,346,000 ($70.87/sq ft)
Interest and amortization	1,349,260	2,057,760	3,401,520
Annual net income	$ 2,831,015	$ 1,897,515	$ 121,245

TABLE 3
The Community Shopping Center: Store Types, Store Areas, Sales, and Rents

Type of Store		Gross Building Area (sq ft)	Sales per Square Foot	Rent as Percent of Sales	Total Rent per Square Foot
Junior department store	(141)	40,000	$ 50–$120	2–4	$2.50–$ 6.00
Variety store	(103)	20,000	33– 100	2½–5	1.60– 3.00
Women's ready-to-wear	(212)	4,000	60– 160	4–6	4.00– 10.00
Menswear	(138)	3,000	65– 130	4–6	4.00– 10.00
Women's specialty	(102)	3,000	62– 160	4–6	4.00– 10.00
Supermarket	(170)	20,000	135– 260	1–1½	2.00– 4.00
Restaurants	(88– 70)	4,000	64– 200	4–7	4.00– 11.00
Fast food	(60)	1,750	80– 200	4–8	6.00– 12.00
Family shoe store	(154)	3,200	50– 133	4–6	3.00– 9.50
Yard goods	(113)	4,000	44– 90	3–5	3.00– 6.00
Furniture	(46)	13,000	43– 100	4–6	2.40– 14.00
Hardware	(43)	6,000	40– 78	3–5	2.00– 6.00
Automotive TBEA	(54)	7,500	50– 70	3–5	2.00– 7.00
Records and tapes	(41)	2,000	60– 125	4–6	4.20– 21.00

Musical instruments (45)	1,500	68– 210	2–6	3.50– 8.00
Pet shops (37)	1,200	50– 124	4½–6	4.00– 6.00
Books and stationery (63)	2,000	58– 149	4–6	4.00– 10.00
Drugstore (131)	10,000	50– 200	2–4	2.50– 5.00
Jewelry (106)	1,800	77– 200	4–6	5.00– 20.00
Sporting goods (41)	2,000	62– 150	5	4.00– 8.00
Cards and gifts (118)	2,500	36– 115	6–8	4.00– 12.00
Liquors and wine (57)	2,500	62– 400	2–5	4.00– 11.00
Banks (96)	3,000			3.50– 12.00
Savings and loan associations (52)	2,000			4.00– 20.00
Beauty shops (157)	1,200	50– 111	5–10	4.00– 8.00
Barbershops (124)	600	35– 112	8–10	4.00– 8.00
Cleaners (99)	2,000	30– 60	5–10	3.00– 6.00
Medical and dental (159)	800			5.00– 7.50
Real estate (65)	800			4.00– 6.50
Total	161,150 square feet			

161,150 square feet
 of store area
483,450 square feet of parking
644,600 square feet, or 14.8 acres

The total number in the sample of a total of 253 types of stores is listed in the Urban Land Institute classification of community shopping centers.

foot in 1974, and the land cost of such buildings ranged from $18.43 to $35.88 a square foot.[1]

The total cost of land and buildings for regional centers that opened in 1974 ranged from $28.36 a square foot to $70.87 a square foot, with a median cost of $42.87 a square foot.[2]

The $4,644,500 rent for the mall-type stores of our hypothetical super-regional center—$11.61 per square foot of gross leasable area—is sufficient to yield a net return on low or medium operating and capital costs but not on high operating or capital costs. (Table 2).

The Community Shopping Center. The distinguishing feature of a community center is the junior department store with 40,000 square feet of selling area. Such a store is too small to offer the variety of a superregional center with three or four department stores, each of which has 150,000–6,200,000 square feet of selling area. The community center has all the stores of the neighborhood center—supermarkets, drugstores, beauty shops, barbershops, cleaners, banks, restaurants—and in addition it has a few more women's ready-to-wear stores, banks, and other stores (see Table 3). The community center also has a few ladies' specialty stores and shoe stores.

Fewer community centers have been built in recent years because of the current high construction costs and interest rates. Some community centers in smaller towns have been converted to mini–regional centers. If a large regional center is built near a community center, the junior department store of the community center may be converted to another use, such as a furniture store.

In analyzing community centers, the appraiser must take into consideration the lower cost of construction, the lower land values, and the lower interest rates that prevailed when most of those centers were built.

In community shopping centers the median rental cost per square foot is $1.93. The cost per square foot of the bottom decile is $1.07; that of the top decile is $3.37.[3]

The capital cost of community centers that opened in 1974 ranged from $18.69 a square foot for the bottom decile to $48.55 for the top decile, with a median cost of $28.20.

However, it is possible to calculate the total rent that a community center would have to receive to earn an economic return if it were built today.[4]

	Low	Median	High
Operating expenses	$1.07	$1.93	$3.37
Annual capital expenses—			
12 percent of cost....	2.24 ($18.69)	3.38 ($28.20)	5.84 ($48.55)
Total	$3.31	$5.31	$9.20

---

[1] *Dollars and Cents of Shopping Centers, 1975* (Washington, D.C.: Urban Land Institute, 1975), table 8–2, p. 282.

[2] Ibid.

[3] Ibid., table 5–18, p. 119.

[4] Ibid., table 8–3, p. 283.

TABLE 4
The Rents, Operating Expenses, and Capital Costs of a Community Shopping Center

	Low	Median	High
Potential rents	$ 626,200	$ 626,200	$ 626,200
Five percent vacancy allowance	31,310	31,310	31,310
Rents collected	594,890	594,890	594,890
Operating costs for 140,000 square feet	159,600 ($1.14/sq ft)	250,600 ($1.79/sq ft)	379,400 ($2.71/sq ft)
Balance available for debt service	435,290	344,290	215,490
Cost of construction	2,616,600 ($18.69/sq ft)	3,948,000 ($28.20/sq ft)	6,797,000 ($48.55/sq ft)
Twelve percent	313,920	473,760	815,640
Profit (loss)	$ 121,370	($ 129,470)	($ 600,150)

As Table 4 shows, a community shopping center will not yield a profit unless it is built at a low cost and has low operating expenses. However, many of the community shopping centers now in existence were built at a time when construction costs, land values, and interest rates on mortgages were lower than they are now, and such shopping centers may be able to yield a net return even if their junior department store and fashion goods stores are converted to uses that yield lower rents.

The Neighborhood Shopping Center. The neighborhood shopping center caters to persons living in the immediate vicinity who make frequent visits to buy food, drugstore items, greeting cards, and the services of barbershops, beauty parlors and cleaners. Such shopping centers often have a bank or a savings and loan association and medical and dental offices. These are the typical ingredients of a neighborhood shopping center. The other types of establishments in neighborhood shopping centers vary greatly. The hypothetical neighborhood shopping center of Table 5 includes a small women's ready-to-wear store, a jewelry store, a hardware store, and a small variety store. The total store area of that hypothetical shopping center is 80,000 square feet, and the parking required by the shopping center is 240,000 square feet, or a total of 7.35 acres. Neighborhood shopping centers vary in size from five to ten acres.

Neighborhood shopping centers cost far less to build than regional shopping centers because they have no covered malls and because their stores command a much lower rent. The rents in our hypothetical neighborhood shopping center total $367,200, or $4.60 a square foot.

The neighborhood shopping centers are by far the most numerous type of planned shopping centers. They are also the type for which the future demand will probably be greatest, since any substantial growth of new suburban residential areas will create a demand for neighborhood stores. Since families spend more for food in supermarkets than for clothing in regional centers (15 percent of income compared to 6 percent), and since they patronize food stores and cleaners weekly, the neighborhood shopping centers can be supported by the families in the immediate vicinity.

The indispensable basis for a neighborhood shopping center is the 20,000–30,000-square-foot supermarket, the center's largest store. Accompanying it in nearly every neighborhood center are the drugstore, the cleaners, the beauty shop, the barbershop, and the medical and dental offices. Among the types of establishments that may be found in many neighborhood centers are restaurants, banks, savings and loan associations, women's ready-to-wear stores, a card and gift shops, liquor and wine stores, family shoe stores, coin laundries, jewelry stores, menswear stores, and flower shops.

The number of neighborhood shopping centers reporting the presence of such stores is listed in Table 5. In addition to the 26 types of stores listed in Table 5, 69 other types of stores that are found in some neighborhood shopping centers are listed in *Dollars and Cents of Shopping Centers, 1975.*[5] The composition of neighborhood shopping centers varies

---

[5] Ibid., pp. 178–205.

TABLE 5
The Neighborhood Shopping Center Types of Stores, Store Areas, Sales, and Rents

Type of Store		Gross Building Area (sq ft)	Sales per Square Foot	Rent as Percent of Sales	Total Rent per per Square Foot
Supermarkets	(137)	20,000	$130–$300	1–1½	$2.00–$ 4.00
Drugstores	(114)	12,000	64– 168	2–4	2.50– 4.50
Beauty shops	(144)	1,200	45– 120	5–8	4.00– 11.00
Barbershops	(100)	600	40– 80	5–10	3.80– 7.00
Cleaners and dyers	(165)	1,600	30– 80	8	3.50– 6.50
Variety store	(41)	7,500	35– 145	4	2.00– 3.00
Restaurants	(92)	3,000	60– 100	5	5.00– 6.00
Women's ready-to-wear ..	(59)	2,000	46– 200	5	3.50– 10.00
Cards and gifts	(45)	1,800	37– 95	5–10	4.00– 9.00
Banks	(41)	2,400			5.00– 6.00
Savings and loan asso-ciations	(26)	1,500			4.50– 10.00
Hardware	(37)	5,400	28– 80	3–5	2.50– 5.00
Radio–TV–hi-fi	(34)	2,200	50– 88	2.50–6	3.30– 5.00
Yard goods	(36)	3,000	35– 85	5	3.00– 5.70
Family shoe store	(32)	3,000	35– 150	4–6	3.00– 8.50
Fast food	(33)	1,600	45– 190	5	4.00– 10.00
Women's specialty	(38)	1,600	50– 135	6	4.00– 7.80
Medical and dental	(115)	850			5.10– 7.50
Other offices	(51)	1,000			3.50– 6.90
Coin laundries	(43)	1,500	15– 70	7–10	3.00– 5.00
Service stations	(33)	1,700			6.00– 15.00
Real estate	(34)	950			4.50– 6.00
Liquors and wine	(42)	2,500	80– 300	1.50–5	4.00– 14.00
Flowers	(28)	1,000	50– 100	6–8	3.50– 16.00
Jewelry	(28)	1,100	80– 200	3–6	4.00– 12.00
Menswear	(33)	2,000	65– 173	4–6	4.50– 15.00
Total		83,000	square feet, or 7.6 acres		

The total number in the sample of a total of 253 types of stores is listed in the Urban Land Institute classification of neighborhood shopping centers.

greatly from city to city, and the types of stores represented besides the supermarket, the drugstore, the beauty shop, the barbershop, the cleaners, and medical and dental offices will depend on the kinds of other stores that are situated in the vicinity of the center, the distance of the center from a regional shopping center, and other factors.

The Evaluation of a Neighborhood Shopping Center. As Table 5 indicates, the sales of the stores in a neighborhood shopping center vary greatly. The rent as a percentage of sales varies from the low 1–1½ percent on sales paid by supermarkets to a high of 8 percent on beauty shops, cleaners, card and gift shops, and flowershops. The actual rent received per square foot generally depends on whether the type of store has a relatively low or high volume of sales per square foot. However, supermarkets, which have a high volume of sales, pay only $2–$4 a square foot in rent. Since their cost of construction per square foot is lower than that of the smaller stores, and since they are the indispensable magnet for attracting other stores to the neighborhood center, their rent per square foot is the lowest.

The value of an existing shopping center depends on the rents on minimum guarantees and percentages of all existing leases, the dates when the leases terminate, the present value of the rents that are expected to be received when the present leases expire, the interest and amortization rates on existing mortgages and the expected future interest rates when the present mortgages terminate, and the expected future real estate taxes and other operating expenses. The final evaluation is the capitalization of the expected future net income.

The capital costs of neighborhood centers which opened in 1974 varied from $16.59 a square foot in the bottom decile to $35.95 a square foot in the top decile, with a median cost of $28.20 a square foot.[6] The operating expenses of 130 shopping centers in the sample varied from 0.97 cents per square foot in the bottom decile to $3.59 a square foot in the top decile, with a median of $1.88 a square foot.[7] It can be calculated from these figures how much rent must be received from a neighborhood shopping center in order to cover the operating expenses and the interest and amortization on the capital cost.

	Low	Median	High
Operating expenses	$0.97	$1.88	$3.59
Annual capital expenses— 12 percent of cost....	1.87 ($16.59)	3.38 ($28.20)	4.31 ($35.95)
Total............	$2.84	$5.26	$7.90

Since the median cost per square foot of a neighborhood shopping center is $5.26, it is obvious that unless the costs are lower than the median, the stores shown in Table 5 would need to have a high volume of sales per square foot and to pay the higher rent indicated in the table in order to yield a net return on the investment.

However, neighborhood centers built in the 1950s were constructed at a much lower level of costs than the costs of the neighborhood centers that are being built at present, and they were financed at much lower interest rates than the present rates. The potential investor should examine the sales record of every store in a neighborhood center, the rents paid, the construction costs as indicated by the mortgage, and the rate of interest in order to estimate the cash flow and the net return. It is important to determine when the present leases will terminate and at what rental rate they will be renewed, and to determine when the present mortgages will terminate. Neighborhood shopping centers have different mixes of stores, different sales and rentals, different mortgage expira-

---

[6] Ibid., table 8–4, p. 283.
[7] Ibid., table 6–18, p. 173.

tion dates, different competitors, and each neighborhood shopping center can be properly appraised only after all of the pertinent facts are known.

The Effects of New Planned Shopping Centers on Retail Stores in Central Cities

The new planned shopping centers that have been built since 1948 have had a drastic effect on the retail stores of the central cities. In nearly every city the growth of the downtown department and apparel stores have lagged far behind that of the department stores in the regional and superregional centers. Small shopping strips in inner-city neighborhoods have frequently suffered declines as their inhabitants have moved into areas that have planned neighborhood shopping centers with parking facilities. For example, 63d Street and Halsted Street, once the leading shopping center in Chicago outside the Loop, now has a vacant lot where the Sears store once stood, and the former Wieboldt department store is now boarded up. To counter the drive to the suburban stores, department stores in the downtown areas have joined forces to copy the malls of the planned regional centers.

Although there have been some exceptions—for example, fast-food and furniture stores—to the general decline in the retail stores that existed without parking prior to World War II, an investment in the old-style retail store must be examined with great care. The small food store, if it is not a 7–11, has been superseded by the large 30,000-square-foot supermarket. W. T. Grant, the five-cent to one-dollar store, went into bankruptcy; Kresge, the five-and-ten store, expanded into the 100,000-square-foot K mart in suburban locations; and Woolworth, another five-and-ten, expanded into the Woolco of planned shopping centers.

SELECTED REFERENCES

Dollars and Cents of Shopping Centers (Washington, D.C.: Urban Land Institute).

Encyclopedia of Real Estate Appraising (Englewood Cliffs, N.J.: Prentice-Hall, 1978).

New Real Estate Investment Strategies.

OFFICE BUILDING INVESTMENTS

David M. Kaufman

*D*AVID M. KAUFMAN, CCIM, President, David M. Kaufman Associates, Inc., Realtors® and Auctioneers, Chicago, Illinois.
President, City Investor's Group, Ltd. (condominium conversion firm). Chairman, Commercial Investment Trader's Pit, Real Estate Board. Instructor, Real Estate Institute, YMCA Community College. Member, Chicago Real Estate Board, Junior Real Estate Board, South West Real Estate Board, National Association of Realtors®, and Realtors® National Marketing Institute. Formerly senior vice president, Sheldon F. Good & Co.; and member, Mayor Daley's Advisory Committee on Building Code Amendments. Author of articles in such publications as Guarantor, Real Estate Today, Mortgage and Real Estate Executives Report, Chicago Sun-Times, and Washington Post.

Psychologists tell us that ignorance breeds fear and that knowledge will dispel it. Investors or speculators in real estate will most often direct their attention to the areas of real estate which are most readily understood—apartment buildings, shopping centers, and industrial properties. However, with a bit more research, astute investors can profitably enter the office building investment market. This market offers a wide variety of opportunities for investment and speculation. The market includes both the 80,000-square-foot freestanding headquarters of a Fortune 500 company and the 7,500-square-foot neighborhood property. How is a "price tag" to be placed on such very different properties? This chapter is meant to help persons who are interested in office building investments. The prime concern is the value of the office building determined by analyzing the income that the building produces.

The Determinants of Office Rentals

For existing office properties, rentals are normally based on empirical observations of the market place. Rentals will vary to the extent that the location or the condition of the subject property differs from that of comparable properties. However, for new office properties, the rentals are heavily influenced by land and construction costs. In either case, the rent generated by the property should support the price paid for it.

Among the items that must be taken into account when an investment in a new office building is under consideration are the costs of site preparation, the costs of demolishing existing structures (less their salvage value), and the costs of the holding period, which are normally represented by interest charges and attendant expenses. The investors in a new office building will also have to decide whether or not to own the land on which the building will stand. Inasmuch as land is not a depreciable asset, it might make good sense to have a long-term lease on the land, so that the rent payments on the ground lease can be deducted in addition to the depreciation on the improvements. (More will be said below about this method of investment.) Interim alternative uses which can help pay the interest costs of an office building while it is under construction include the use of the unoccupied space and the uncompleted structure for parking, storage, and seasonal retail sales endeavors.

Figures on the construction costs of a particular building are readily obtainable from contractors or architects. The costs per square foot will vary widely, depending on the quality of the building to be constructed. If a group of investors is constructing a property for a particular tenant with whom a lease has already been signed, then the tenant will provide the investors with his plans for the property, and the construction costs can be readily determined from these plans.

In setting up the pro forma for the development, particular attention should be paid to the "soft costs," including the legal, accounting, and financing charges; the points; the appraisal fees; the interim interest charges; permanent loan costs; the leasing commissions; and the outlays for advertising and promotion.

To the hard costs and the soft costs should be added the operating expenses which will have to be met until the property comes "on line" and the tenants begin paying rent. This gives the total cost of the finished product. Once that is known, it is possible to calculate the net operating income (the income remaining after operating expenses are subtracted from the gross income) that will be required to make the office building under consideration an economically feasible project.

The last item of cost that should be calculated is the interim interest expense. Until all of the costs are known, it will be impossible to structure the total capitalization of the venture, particularly the equity investment versus the financed portion.

Projections for determining the necessary rentals should be done on the total costs. For example, let us assume that the costs are as follows:

Land	$ 200,000
Building	700,000
Soft Costs (including interest)	100,000
Interim operating Expenses	50,000
Total cost of development	$1,050,000

If an investor were satisfied with a 7 percent return, the net operating income to justify this investment would be $73,500. (0.07 × $1,050,000). In order to arrive at the gross annual income which this property would have to generate, it is merely necessary to add to the $73,500 net operating income an amount equal to the "on line" annual operating expenses which are projected for the property.

Projecting Operating Expenses

One of the most difficult aspects of any branch of real estate investment is the projection of operating expenses. Once an investor has been in office buildings for a while, he will develop a feeling for what the operating expenses of any particular office structure should be. But what should he do when he first invests in office properties? All too often, good projects fail because the projections of their operating expenses were based on rules of thumb. Office building expenses generally run from 35 percent to 50 percent of the gross annual income. However in order to be competitive, the investor must be able to project expenses more closely than that.

One good method for projecting the operating expenses of an office building is to review information provided by brokers on available office properties or to obtain actual operating costs from real estate management firms. A good source of information on the operating expenses of office building is the Institute of Real Estate Management, a division of the National Association of Realtors®.

One of the best methods of determining what the real estate taxes will be on a given office building is to consult either with the appraiser who is doing the appraisal for the intended lender or with an attorney who specializes in efforts to reduce real estate taxes. Such consultations have resulted in tremendous real estate tax savings through the use of little-known portions of the assessor's formula. One builder, for example, brought down the tax bill of a building by putting a metal roof on it. Doing this qualified the structure as a brick-and-frame building rather than a brick building, and it was therefore taxed at a lower rate.

However, it should be borne in mind that not only are real estate taxes an operating expense, but so are the costs of keeping real estate taxes low. If a given property is reassessed every four years, as is true for most properties, one might regard the cost of keeping down the taxes on that property as being amortized over a four-year period.

The cost of utilities can be determined most accurately by utility companies. Upon request, such companies will normally provide the assistance of their experts without charge. These experts arrive at their projections by analyzing an existing building or a projected development from the standpoint of total cubic footage, type of insulation, the projected number of occupants, and so on. Upon request, the experts of the utilities companies will also provide sound ideas for reducing the costs of electricity, fuel, and other utilities through the latest energy-saving materials.

We all know that there are lawyers and that there are real estate lawyers, and a similar distinction may be made among insurance brokers. An insurance broker who specializes in underwriting real estate losses will be able to provide invaluable assistance in projecting what the premium of a given office building will be and in recommending the proper amounts of coverage as well.

The maintenance, repair, and decorating costs of office buildings vary widely among different owners, so that it is difficult to make generalizations as to what those costs should be. The janitorial payroll can be determined quickly from the local union, if there is one, or from building maintenance engineers in other buildings.

A reserve for replacement is one of the more difficult items to provide for. The best method is to set up a ten-year table of cash requirements for the replacement of various items as they are projected to require replacement. Once this table has been established, it is possible to determine what monthly deposit should be made into a sinking fund that will grow into the amount necessary to meet the projected replacement costs. Admittedly, it is difficult to project when a roof will go out and how much it will cost to replace that roof when it does go out. However, in setting up reserves for replacement, one error seems to cancel out another, and maintaining a reserve fund of some kind is far better than having to reach into one's pocket for the cost of replacing major items or, worse yet, having to go back to investors for the necessary funds.

Leasing the Property

A very important aspect of managing office building investments is the quarterly review of income and operating expenses. The purpose of that review is not only to maintain the desired net operating income, but also to make sure that the net operating income continually increases to keep pace with the appreciation of the value of the property. Whether the investor is developing an office property or purchasing a vacated or partially vacated property, his most important effort will be leasing the vacant portions of the property. No matter how attractive an office building is and no matter how desirable its location is, unless the available space is marketed by a true professional who knows how to enhance its appeal, maximize its exposure, and handle the lease negotiations properly, the building can fail to bring in adequate returns. When all is said and done, the value of a developed or an existing building depends, not simply on its costs, but, as we will be shown below, on the quality and mortgagability of the lease documents and the quality of the rentals derived therefrom.

If the investor does not possess leasing expertise and the time that is needed to apply such expertise properly, then he should engage a Realtor® with established expertise in the leasing of office buildings as his exclusive leasing agent. This Realtor® will be responsible for promoting and leasing the space in the investor's building. In addition to overseeing a thorough marketing program for the space to be leased, he will enlist the cooperation of other Realtors®. Although brokerage commissions will probably be paid on most of the leases signed, what the investor gains from the active assistance that the Realtors® give him will more than compensate for the commission that he pays his agent.

The commissions of Realtors® are negotiable, and the amount of a reasonable commission the investor can usually determine by asking two or three Realtors® what their rates would be for handling the leasing of a particular office building. In order to create the right motivations for the broker, the broker and the owner should agree upon a commission rate per square foot of space leased, regardless of the length of the lease term. The commission can be the greater of a stated number of cents per square foot leased or of a stated percentage of the rents required under the lease. It makes sense to pick an overall dollar amount of commission that the broker would earn if he leased all of the available space and then to divide that amount by the entire square footage of the available space in order to arrive at the commission that the broker would earn per square foot leased.

There is less negotiation in leasing than in the sale and purchase of real estate, and therefore the offering rentals on office space should be kept as close to the market rentals as possible. One should always keep in mind that two important reasons why available office space is not leased are that the agent is neglecting to merchandise it or that the rental being asked is too high. If the agent is exhibiting good merchandising activity and leases are still not being entered into, an adjustment of the rental structure may prove appropriate.

The advertising program for office space should include both classified advertising and display advertising in the financial sections of appropriate media. Large but tasteful well-placed signs are essential. As tenants sign leases, additional signs can say that the community "welcomes XYZ Company," or that "XYZ Company moves in July 1." Such signs advertise the desirability of the property and develop a fear of failing to obtain space in it among prospective tenants. Brochures are highly important in an active advertising campaign for office space. These should avoid wordiness. "Billboard effect" brochures—with backup data sheets that go into the real detail of the property—are strongly recommended. Logical mailing lists for brochures can be obtained from many mailing companies at a reasonable cost. Radio advertisements can be a very important part of a leasing program and are less expensive than one might think.

In addition to advertising, the agent who is conducting a leasing program should develop a public relations effort on the space that is being leased. A good press release picked up in the right media has been known to lease out an entire property. The object is to create news by giving a nonnews item the proper slant. A good public relations program, marketed to the right media, can, almost without cost, create exposure worth thousands of dollars.

At the base of the leasing program should be a "shoe leather" campaign for distributing the brochure to users of office space in the area of the office building that is being leased or in areas from which it is hoped that tenants will be drawn. Space in buildings that are located in busy business districts has been leased successfully by standing in front of the buildings and handing out brochures to passersby. In addition, the brochure should be presented personally to the decision makers of the surrounding office buildings. In the process of doing this, agents often come in contact with salespeople who are promoting copy machines, business equipment, and other business services, and through a referral arrangement with such people, the Realtors® are able to multiply their efforts to lease office space.

Leasing Conventions

Leases of office space must not only stipulate rentals that make sound economic sense to both the lessor and the lessee but must also state exactly what the tenant gets in return for the rent he pays. Does the tenant pay for the thickness of the exterior walls or of a portion of the interior walls? Or does he pay for the space up to four feet outside the window on the exterior of the building? Does he pay for the rooms in which the telephone or mechanical equipment is kept, for common washrooms, for hallway space, for closets, and so on, and so on? There are many different conventions for leasing office space, and many confusing terms. An understanding of what the investor is trying to accomplish should really take the place of all those terms, and in the final analysis an investor should try to create renting arrangements that will best fit the needs of his particular property.

In a multitenant office building, there are only so many things that have to be defined and negotiated. The total space of the building to the very exterior portions (sometimes one half the depth) of all walls, could be called the gross rentable space of the building. This would include all areas within the outermost walls. Given the gross rentable space, one might measure the so-called usable amount of space within any demised premise and determine its relationship to the gross rentable space, so that when prospective tenants pick out usable square footages within the building, the rental for that square footage can be readily determined.

For example, if a building contained a gross rentable area of 100,000 square feet and all of the common areas added up to 11,000 square feet, then the usable area of the building would total 89,000 square feet, or 89 percent of the gross rentable square footage. Therefore, if a prospective tenant wanted 8,900 square feet of usable space in the building, the average rental for that space would be determined by dividing 8,900 square feet by the decimal equivalent of the percentage of the gross rentable square footage of the entire building that this usable space represents, in this case 0.89. The quotient is 10,000 square feet. Therefore, if the rental rate is $9 per square foot per year, the annual rental would be equal to $90,000, and the monthly rental would be one twelfth of that.

One office building promoter may include the exterior wall dimensions in calculating the usable square footage; another may include half of the exterior walls and half of the interior perimeter walls. The General Services Administration of the federal government measures only the space up to the walls, regardless of whether those walls are interior or exterior walls, and then deducts 10 percent to allow for posts and unusable space within the demised premises. Certainly, the lessors who deal with the GSA should remain flexible enough to meet its requirements, provided that the GSA is willing to pay the proper rental rate to make up for the differences in measuring techniques.

Meeting the Needs of Prospective Tenants

The demand of a particular business for office space is sometimes based on the old question of "Should I buy or should I rent"? In order to understand a prospective tenant, it is necessary to determine whether he needs capital to further his business, which is a reason not to tie up capital in the costly acquisition of real estate, or whether he has accumulated cash that could be put into the purchase of the building that he occupies. A prospective tenant of the latter type will not be able to obtain from smaller facilities the amenities and other benefits which a larger office property offers today. In designing modern office space, it is important not to overlook the employee amenities that prospective tenants now expect. The amenities considered should be reviewed from a standpoint of their economic value and their extent of use. The possible amenities can include common lunchroom facilities with vending machines for the employees of all tenants, on-premise copy and quick printing services, on-premise phone answering and secretarial services, minor repair and moving services, an on-premise health racquetball club, an on-premise luncheon club, a small auditorium or a conference meeting room for the tenants, and so forth. A proper package of amenities may make a tenant out of a would be owner-occupant.

Location. In meeting tenants' needs and desires, one item which should never be ignored is, of course, location. If one begins an office building development with a certain amount of space preleased, then this can be traded off for the competitive advantage of a specific location. Needless to say, a completely filled office building investment can be a good investment even if the location is not ideal.

Although certain generalizations can be made about locations, a good feasibility study should always be conducted before an office property is developed or purchased. In general, however, good locations for office properties include the central business district, the county seat, the vicinity of airports, shopping centers and across from shopping centers, the cloverleafs of major expressways, and finally the neighborhood of special use centers such as hospitals where office buildings for doctors, etc. would make sense.

Physical Characteristics of the Property. The physical arrangement of the property will certainly affect the demand for office space. Normally setbacks with good landscaping and artwork in the form of modern sculptures or fountains are preferred, and plazas are great enhancements. Among the most important requirements of tenants are privacy and professional appearance, and therefore, buildings that are designed to enhance these features should prosper.

Single-Tenant Use versus Multitenant Use. Whether an investor purchases a single-tenant facility and turns it into a multitenant facility,
or develops a single-tenant facility, or has a specific user for space but
decides to build a property which offers more space than that user needs,
the investor should consider the various aspects of single-tenant space
versus multitenant space. For example, from the standpoint of both merchandising and acquisition it is important to recognize that a tenant
with a strong need for corporate identity would normally prefer a single-
user building. Such a building will tend to be more expensive for the
investor, but it frees the investor from having to worry about common
areas and therefore permits usable square footage to become gross rentable square footage.

Single-tenant facilities and multitenant facilities also differ greatly
in their allocation of the responsibility for various expenses. A property
which is rented to a single tenant can be rented to that tenant on a
net basis. This means that the tenant pays all of the building expenses,
including the real estate taxes and the insurance expense. The only
cost to the landlord will be his mortgage payment, if he has one. The
big objection of tenants to this arrangement is that it puts them in the
real estate business. For example, they must maintain the building,
which can be especially costly in older buildings. Some multitenanted
buildings have provisions for escalation clauses in its lease so the rents
will rise to offset increased expenses.

Market Considerations. A major consideration in developing office
projects or investing or speculating in such projects is the cyclic nature
of the market demand for office space. Even an investor who commissions the most sophisticated feasibility studies is unable to know what
other feasibility studies are being conducted at the same time as his.
Quite often, certain localities wind up with a proliferation of office building developments that not only affect one another but also affect existing
office properties. At this writing, about ten major office buildings are
beginning construction in the downtown Chicago area. It is not too difficult to predict that within two or so the downtown office space market
will become very soft, and that the downtown tenant will be at a premium.

What does one do in a market where there is an oversupply of office
space? To begin with, one does not launch a new development unless
he thinks that it will be on line when the market is hardening. But
more important, one looks into the possibility of getting some really
good buys in existing office buildings with vacancy problems. As with
the stock market, in real estate when things are bad, the average investor
thinks that they are never going to get better, and when things are great,
he thinks that they can never become bad. Of course, the opposite is
normally true.

Rental Concessions. Now whether the investor has purchased a
building with vacancies at an excellent price or owns a building with
vacancies going into a soft market, what can he do?

One of his most obvious options is to offer prospective tenants rental
concessions and to get them into the properties on as short a lease as
they will accept, hoping that when the lease is up he will be able to

increase their rent. The prospective tenants are normally aware of what is going on. However they need space anyway, and although they are going to be paying the market rentals ultimately, they figure that they may as well take advantage of the reduced rental rate for as long as they can.

In a soft market the need for an intensified marketing program is, of course, stronger than ever, and such a program might be funded a little bit more heavily than it would be in a good market. It might also make sense to allow the Realtor® who is handling the project to offer full commissions to cooperating brokers. In order to permit this, the building owners would have to pay a commission and a half, with half a commission going to the Realtor® who is the exclusive agent and a full commission going to the cooperating broker who brings in the prospective tenant. In addition, the lease requirements might be softened as regards personal liabilities, subletting rights, and various other matters in order to make the subject space more favorable than its competition.

Financial Safeguards for the Investor

Certain safeguards may be added into the ability to carry the investment during a period of oversupply of office space in the market. The financial position of the investor should dictate the size of his office building investment. All too often, purchasers overleverage themselves, so that they lack the backup to see an investment through a difficult period. The old saying "You'll be worth tomorrow what you owe today" should have this corollary tacked onto it: "If you can, make the payments while you owe it." Sometimes the difference between purchasing a $500,000 property with $100,000 down rather than a $750,000 property with $100,000 down will make all the difference in the world to the investor because he will be able to carry the lesser leveraged property through difficult times whereas he would have a forced sale with the highly leveraged properties. In addition, with less leveraging he will be able to strike better terms on the balance owed and therefore would probably have a longer amortization schedule and a lower interest rate. This would result in a lower loan constant on an overall smaller balance, substantially reducing the monthly principal and interest.

During a period of soft rentals the building reserve account could provide the cushion necessary to see an investment through. Although it is preferable to leave this cushion untouched, tapping it is better than losing the property and the reserve account can be refunded when better times roll around. If a property is owned through a syndication, the syndicator, or general partner, would be wise to have the partnership agreements allow him to call upon limited partners for additional capitalization of a fractional amount of their initial investment. However, it is important for investors in any branch of real estate to build up good credit lines with banks so that they will be able to borrow on an interim basis in order to help carry an investment property through a difficult period.

The Value of Office Buildings

As was written earlier, the value of an office building investment is a direct function of the quality and quantity of its income stream. The qualitative analysis of the income stream includes a review of the various aspects of the income flow to determine what capitalization rate can be applied to the income stream in determining value. A close look should be taken at the rental rate. If the triple-A tenant who nows occupies the property were to leave in two years, could he be replaced by a tenant of similar quality at a similar rent? This might not be possible if the rent now being paid has been forced to match the value of the real estate desired by the present owner, as is the case for many sale-leaseback situations?

What is the length of the lease? For a poorly maintained building in a poorer part of town, it doesn't help much if a Fortune 500 company has a lease on it if the lease has only two years left to go. If there is a long lease—for 20 or 25 years—is the lease net, or are there expense stops with the tenant paying the overages, or does the lease provide that the rent will increase in the same proportion as the local consumer price index?

The degree of vacancy and low rents have a very direct bearing on the qualitative analysis of the office building income stream, and it is very difficult to judge how they should affect the capitalization rate. It must certainly be borne in mind that a vacant building should not necessarily be faulted by giving it a high capitalization rate. Buildings that have no tenants at all, that are built purely on speculation, may be financed by sophisticated lending institutions. If the major tenant of a well-located building, or even a building in a mediocre location, decides to move out, the same rent or even a higher rent may be achieved from just as good a company under certain circumstances.

Of course, vacancy cannot be ignored. Therefore, when looking at an office building as a possible investment, one should determine whether it is a "downside investment" or an "upside investment." A property which is fairly well filled, which commands a high price and gives a safe but low return, but without much chance of great appreciation, is a downside investment. A property which is underrented or vacant but has a good potential for being leased at higher rentals presents possibilities for rapid appreciation and is therefore an upside investment.

The Capitalization Rate and the Loan Constant

In the current marketplace, the influence of foreign investors on American real estate, coupled with rising energy prices and an inflationary spiral of operating expenses, has tended to decrease the returns on all types of real estate investments. Inflation has kept causing the value of properties to go up. However, operating net incomes have not been increasing commensurately. Therefore, the capitalization rates upon which investment properties are purchased have been decreasing.

The loan constant for a given loan is determined by the annual principal and interest payments on the loan by the original balance of the loan. For example, if $100,000 were borrowed at 8 percent interest on a 20-year amortization schedule, the total annual principal and interest payments would be about $10,040. Therefore, the loan constant for 8 percent interest on a 20-year amortization schedule is 10.04 percent.

Working backward, if an investor knew that he had $10,040 available from a property to service debt, and if he knew that he could borrow money at 8 percent to be amortized over a 20-year schedule, then he would know that he could service a debt in the amount of $100,000, as $10,040 divided by 0.1004 equals $100,000.

The term *leverage* is used quite often in real estate investment situations, and it figures greatly in office building investments. Most people feel that leverage means controlling a property with a low down payment, so that when that property appreciates, the investor is making money not only on the equity portion of the property but on the financed portion as well. An equally important aspect of leverage in office building investment also involves making money on borrowed money. If the income generated from an office property is greater than the financing cost, then there will be a cash flow from the financed portion of the investment. More technically stated, if the capitalization rate is greater than the loan constant, then positive leverage will exist and money will be made on the financed portion of the investment.

For example, consider a $1,000,000 dollar office building that is purchased with a $200,000 down payment. Assuming that the capitalization rate on the property is 12 percent (the net operating income would then be $120,000) and that the loan constant on the $800,000 financed portion of the investment is 10 percent, then the difference between the loan constant and the capitalization rate would be 2 percent. The cash flow would then be equal to 0.12 × $200,000 (the capitalization rate times the equity) plus 0.02 × $800,000 (the positive leverage percentage times the financed portion of the investment), which totals $40,000.

In the same manner that the difference between the capitalization rate and the loan constant cited in this example produced a positive 2 percent cash flow on the financed portion of the investment, which when added to the 12 percent return on the equity portion boosted the entire cash flow percentage to 20 percent, that difference could work exactly in reverse to produce negative leverage. Therefore, the investor should try to arrange financing so that the loan constant on a property does not exceed the capitalization rate. If it does, the investor will have to get his benefits from tax shelter or appreciation.

The Cash on Cash Method

As a quick tool of analysis, the cash on cash method is a good one. All that is involved is to deduct the amount of the operating expenses from the gross annual income, and then to subtract from that difference the principal and interest required for debt service. The resulting balance will be the cash flow. When divided by the down payment or equity (and multiplied by 100 to get the decimal in the right place), this will give the cash on cash percentage.

This method is also useful for "backing into" real estate values. Consider a property with a gross annual income of $200,000 and operating expenses (not including depreciation or interest) of $84,000. This leaves a net operating income of $116,000. The cash on cash method of determining the value of the property is based on the simple premise of paying the return on the investment to the investor before paying for the mortgage. In our example, if the purchaser makes a down payment of $250,000 upon which he wishes to receive an 8 percent cash on cash return, or $20,000, then the $20,000 is immediately subtracted from the $116,000 net operating income, leaving $96,000 available to service the debt of the investment. If the investor has determined that the owner in this particular situation will carry back owner financing at 8 percent for 20 years, then we know from loan constant tables that the loan constant for this percentage rate and amortization schedule is 10.04 percent. Now if the amount available for debt service, namely $96,000, is divided by the loan constant, namely 0.1004, the quotient will be the amount of debt that can be serviced by this payment of principal and interest, namely $956,175.30. Therefore, in this example the real estate is worth the total of the down payment of $250,000 plus the serviceable debt of $956,175.30, for a total value of $1,206,175.30.

The major drawback of the cash on cash method of computing the return on investment is that it ignores the effect of time on value. Is the cash flow which the investor receives in the fifth year as valuable to him as the cash flow which he receives in the first year? A brief examination of time and money tables will demonstrate that the answer to that question is no. In addition, what about other benefits of real estate ownership, such as appreciation, amortization of the loan balance, and tax benefits? The average pro forma offered by a seller tries to deal with these benefits by showing them as returns in the current year of analysis, which is erroneous, because for benefits other than tax benefits, the appreciation and amortization of the loan balance are not actually received by the investor until he sells the investment.

Once the office building investor has determined the cash return, he should consider the effect of income taxes on his cash flow. As with any other real estate investment, taxable income on an office building is calculated by subtracting from the net operating income the total of the interest plus the depreciation. Once a taxable income is known, then it can be multiplied by the investor's tax bracket (for a rule-of-thumb approach) or actually worked into his entire income situation for a more analytic view.

Depreciation

The amount of interest that is to be deducted from income is fairly easy to calculate, but let us spend a moment on depreciation. The depreciation which can be taken for an office building investment will be a function of two items, namely the useful life of the asset and the method of depreciation. (Of course, the portion of value attributable to land cannot be depreciated.)

The useful life of a new office building is normally between 33 and 40 years. The useful life of an existing office building can be based upon the amortization schedule which a lender is willing to lend money on or upon a bonafide appraisal of the property that specifically sets forth its remaining useful life.

The method of depreciation that can be used has recently been limited by revision in the federal income tax code. For new office buildings, the maximum allowable method is the 150 percent declining balance method. For existing office buildings, the maximum allowable method is the straight-line method. If architectural studies can substantiate the values claimed for the component parts of an office building, then a component form of depreciation can be used. This would probably result in a larger amount of depreciation in the early years.

At the time of the initial purchase, some transactions can be structured so as to convert part of the down payment from a capitalized amount to ordinary expense by considering that part to be payment to the seller for certain rights, such as noncompetition; the payment of expenses that would normally be the seller's, such as prepayment penalties on mortgages being paid off; commission; and so on. Unfortunately, one of the greatest boons in this area, prepaid interest, is no longer available to the investor under the current IRS regulations.

One pitfall to avoid is structuring a purchase so that the amortization period of the loan is too short. Because of the taxable nature of amortized principal, this could result in taxes which are in excess of the cash flow from the property. In addition, the lender must be extremely careful in situations where the depreciation method combined with the amortization schedule of the loan will place the adjusted cost basis of the investment below the mortgage balance. If a property loan is foreclosed and the investor loses his equity in the property when the foreclosure becomes final, or if the lender accepts a deed in lieu of foreclosure, the owner will wind up with a capital gain equal to the difference between the smaller adjusted cost basis and the larger mortgage balance. As in any other investment or business situation, competent accounting and legal counsel should be sought.

The Internal Rate of Return Method

One of the better methods of quantitatively analyzing the income stream is to use the discounted cash flow analysis to obtain the internal rate of return that an investment will yield. This method of analysis not only considers the four benefits of real estate ownership, but *when* those benefits are received. If one could project for a period of, say, seven years, the cash flows of a property after taxes, and if the property were sold at the end of the seventh year so that one could add to the cash flow for year 7 the projected net sale proceeds after all sale expenses, including the long-term capital gains tax, one could then search for a discount rate which would discount all of those future benefits to their present values. If those total present values equaled the initial down payment, then the discount percentage would equal the yield, or the so-called internal rate of return. Perhaps the example shown in Table 1 can make this method of analysis a little clearer.

The discounted cash flow analysis can also handle negative cash flows after taxes during the initial years of an investment, or even during its later years, by discounting those negative cash flows back to the present values at a safe rate (the passbook rate) and adding them to the

TABLE 1
Internal Rate of Return

Year	Cash Flow after Taxes	Down Payment on Office Building = $608,290.38 Present Values Discounted at 12 Percent
1	$26,000	$ 23,124.29
2	52,000	41,454.09
3	73,000	51,959.96
4	70,000	44,486.27
5	78,000	44,259.29
6	81,000	41,037.12
7	80,000 + 720,000* = 800,000	361,870.37
Total of present values discounted at 12 percent		608,290.38

* Net sale proceeds after long-term capital gains tax.
Initial investment = $608,290.38 (after prorations). The initial investment equals the total of present values when discounted at 12 percent. Therefore, the yield (internal rate of return) equals 12 percent, after taxes.

initial investment. The factors that should be used to obtain the present value amounts can be found in tables of financial constants or by means of some of the more sophisticated financial calculators that are now available. One must test several different discount rates until they zero in on the initial investment.

Like any analytic method, the internal rate of return method has its drawbacks. First, it could be argued that projecting out seven years is becoming a guessing game or that the farther out into the future one guesses, the less accurate one will be. Second, this method ignores possible tax law changes that can have a profound affect on future returns.

In any event, the method is a fairly sophisticated approach to quantitative analysis of income streams on office building properties. However, it is time consuming, in that it requires the analyst to test many discount rates on the actual cash flow after taxes, plus reversion amounts, in order to approximate the discount rate which will actually set all the present values equal to the initial investment amount.

An interesting application of this method is its use to work backward from it to arrive at the price to be paid for the investment. In other words, if in the previous example the investor desired a 12 percent yield and therefore discounted all the future benefits by 12 percent and wound up with $608,290.38, he would then know that this would have to be his initial investment (after prorations) for the investment to give him a 12 percent yield. Once he has discovered this, all he need do is add to the $608,290.38, the amount of money being borrowed under the mortgage or mortgages to arrive at the total value of the real estate. This is certainly an interesting appraisal technique.

Financing Strategies

Many get-rich-quick books are promoted as having the secrets of how to own properties through the use of OPM (other people's money), and 100 percent financing, and so on. This is possible, but it normally takes a good personal financial statement, a good name, and a track record. However, it is correct to say that the investor who knows his way around lenders and investors and how to deal with them will be way ahead of the game.

Let us review, then, financing strategies to maximize office building investment. As we will see later, there are many good tax and economic reasons why an owner should carry back the financing for the purchaser. Therefore when buying an office building, it would be wise to attempt to have the owner carry back all of the financing, inasmuch as he can charge as little as 6 percent interest (if he attempted to charge less than 6 percent interest, the government would impute 6 percent interest for tax purposes, etc.). This method of financing, as we saw when we examined the cash on cash approach to value, can have a big impact on making or breaking an office building purchase. Aside from its attractive interest rates and longer amortization schedules, this method also eliminates the payment of closing points on the loan, which could add up to a considerable expense.

If owner financing is unavailable, then a conventional source will have to be sought, and normally a mortgage banker or a mortgage broker will be as valuable to the purchaser as any other professional whom he engages in this transaction. A mortgage banker or a mortgage broker will be able to package all of the details on the property and the borrower and to present those details to various lenders in such a manner as to optimize the amount, the interest rate, the amortization schedule, and various other mortgage terms.

Many investors in office buildings attempt to obtain a "free" option on an office property by negotiating a contract to purchase which contains unreasonable terms upon which a mortgage cannot be gotten. In this way, the investor can at his discretion accept the terms of the mortgage which he is able to get, renegotiate the price to come into line with the appraisal done by the lender, or cancel the agreement, receive the return of his earnest money, and look for another deal. The investor who does this should make sure that contracts to purchase do not have passive clauses requiring him to give the owner notice that he has not received or is not able to fulfill the mortgage contingency. If they do, in the absence of such notice the owner could insist that the investor close the transaction for cash. Here again competent counsel is recommended.

Although many savings and loan associations make mortgages on office buildings, insurance companies and pension funds are the usual sources for financing.

When the investor is purchasing an office building for speculation or renovation improvement, it sometimes makes sense to buy the property for cash (or to borrow the entire amount of the sale price from his bank on a one-year loan), complete the leasing of the project or the increasing of the rentals after renovation, and then go to a savings and loan association or an insurance company for a permanent loan. This will not only enable him to pay back his bank, but will also give him cash beyond his costs (which in most situations is nontaxable).

During his ownership of office property, the investor's equity should increase due to amortization of the loan balance and appreciation in the value of the property. The investor may therefore decide to refinance the existing first mortgage for an amount in excess of that mortgage, especially if he is in a good mortgage market with low interest rates and high lender confidence. This allows the investor to take his equity out of the property without paying a long-term capital gains tax. The adjusted cost basis will almost certainly be below the mortgage balance once the property is refinanced.

Another popular method of getting additional financing on an office building is to sell the land under the property to a third party and then to lease it back for a long term. Such leases often give the owner of the improvements the right to reacquire title to the land at some future date at the greater of the original sale price of the land plus a certain appreciation rate or the then-appraised value of the land determined by two or three appraisers. This method has the advantage of removing the owner's capital from the nondepreciable portion of the investment, namely the land. In addition, it enables the investor to write off lease payments made on the land. (Land rental is normally set by having it independently appraised and establishing the rental as a percentage of value.)

It might be noted that purchasing land in this manner is a good investment for certain types of taxpayers that are either in a low-income tax bracket or in a no-income tax bracket, such as pension funds or retired persons. Since all of the land rental is unsheltered ordinary income, an investment of this kind is well suited to the needs of such investors. It must be remembered that the interests of the land purchaser will usually have to be subordinated to those of the first-mortgage holder.

Tax Strategies

All other things equal, the strategy in office building investment should be to avoid taxes whenever possible. The simplest procedure of selling one investment property and buying another is often the costliest. Unless an existing office building becomes a management headache, it will often make a lot of sense to refinance that building and use the proceeds of the refinancing to purchase additional office buildings. One benefit of such refinancing is the setting up of a new, higher balance upon which interest will be paid. This will give additional interest write-offs to offset additional income. Some of the proceeds of refinancing should be spent on maintaining the building and curing its obsolescence. The new capital improvements will give the investor a new, higher base for depreciation.

If a property is a management problem, then the investor might consider trading his equity under an Internal Revenue Code Section 1031, that is, a tax-deferred exchange for a larger property. The benefit here is that the equity taken from the smaller property is transferred into the larger property without paying taxes at the time. In doing the investment analysis on the larger property, it must be remembered that the new basis in the larger property will be influenced by the basis in the previously owned property, and competent counsel should be sought in setting up the depreciation schedule even for the purpose of initial analysis.

Another method of heightening the tax ramifications of an office building investment is to split the fee simple title interest, thereby taking title to the land in one entity and title to the improvements in another. This has become a bit more difficult since the passage of the Pension Reform Act of 1969, but it can still be accomplished. Basically, it involves having the investor's pension and profit-sharing trust take title to the land and then lease it to the investor, while the investor leases the office building to his tenants or perhaps even his own company. The ground lease is ordinary income to the nontaxable pension and profit-sharing trust, and the depreciation in the building is taken by the investor. Another way of taking advantage of this situation would be to set up two limited partnerships, one to own strictly the land under improvements and the other to own strictly improvements. Needless to say, the landowning partnerships should be in the lower tax brackets and the improvement-owning partnership should be in the higher tax brackets.

If an investor has been successful in refinancing and exchanging his way to larger and larger office properties, and he has accumulated a rather large portfolio, then the sale of the entire portfolio slowly and in different years should be considered. One of the biggest advantages of real estate can now be used if the investor sells his properties and portfolio on an installment method of reporting capital gains.

Taxes may be paid on capital gains as they are received by the seller, provided that the down payments and the principal paid in the year of the sale—plus certain other pro rata items which are picked up by the buyer and any net loan relief which the seller receives through the buyer's assumption of any of the seller's indebtedness—do not exceed 30 percent of the sale price and that the sale proceeds are spread over several years. In this manner, the initial down payment and funds received by the seller are considered to be a pro rata return of his undepreciated adjusted cost basis, and the long-term capital gains are reported when received. A big advantage of this method is that it gives the seller control of the interest rate and the amortization schedule, so that by varying these factors he can vary the value of the office property that he is selling.

The best way to sell an office property by the installment method would be to charge no interest and to add the amount that would have been paid in interest to the sale price, so that as the seller receives the payments of principal only, he pays lower taxes on them than he would if part of those payments were interest, which would be treated as ordinary income to the seller. The only problem with this is that the government is aware of this possibility and imputes the minimum of 6 percent interest on the unpaid balance to the seller. However, a sale at 6 percent interest at a 25-year amortization schedule will carry a loan constant which when put through the cash on cash approach to value will still enable the seller to receive a much higher price for the office property than he would receive if the purchaser were to go to a conventional source and borrow money at 9¾ percent amortized over 20 years.

In addition, effecting the installment sale enables the investor to even out his estate by converting a cumbersome real estate investment into a purchase-money mortgage or an articles of agreement contract which is more similar to a bond than it is to the ownership of real estate. This solves the problem of having an office building given away if the investor dies and his heirs do not know what to do with the real estate. Should the investor live for a long time after he has sold his portfolio on an installment basis, he has established an annuity for himself which will provide for him in retirement. Interest rates normally received by the seller on articles of agreement or purchase-money mortgage sales are normally in the range of 7–9 percent, and are payable monthly. It is hard to find an investment vehicle which provides the safety and high return of these instruments when the seller has sold his properties for cash. Unless the seller has some overriding need for the cash, it almost always makes sense for the seller to try to effect an installment-type sale. In a pinch, the seller can always make a loan on the paper carried as collateral.

Many investors mistakenly believe that in order to have an installment sale, the deed cannot pass. This is not true inasmuch as the unpaid balance can be secured by a wraparound trust deed or a part purchase-money mortgage and still qualify, provided that the purchaser does not fully assume any underlying financing which the seller has on the property.

The Investment Decision

What type of office property should an investor purchase? In order to answer that question intelligently, the investor has to analyze his needs and set his goals. The following example should give the prospective investor an idea of how to go about doing this.

An investor wants to retire in 26 years with an income of $60,000 per year.

$60,000 ÷ 0.07 (return on sale paper held) = $857,142.86

Therefore, the estate required in 26 years is $857,142.86, which will produce the desired $60,000 annual income.

Cash currently available for investment: $45,000	26 years	Estate required in 26 years: $958,142.86

By using the table of financial constants or one of the more sophisticated hand calculators, it can easily be calculated that in order to turn a $45,000 initial investment into $857,142.86 in 26 years, an aftertax yield of 12 percent must be maintained on the investment.

This gives the investor a yardstick by which to measure investments to see whether they match his goal-setting requirements. If an office building is analyzed by the discounted cash flow analysis method mentioned above and it is found to yield 12 percent or more through conservative projections, then it makes sense to acquire that building. If it does not yield 12 percent based on the owner's offering price, then it makes sense for the investor to offer the owners an amount at which it will yield 12 percent or more. If that offer is not accepted, the investor can look into other properties.

Office buildings offer a wonderful vehicle for investment in estate building. The tenants in office buildings are usually business people, and as such they are a bit easier to deal with than the tenants of apartment properties. Lenders are very familiar with office buildings as investments and are quite anxious to make loans on them. Although investments in office buildings are not management free, the management of office properties is a good deal easier than the management of apartment properties or shopping centers. The ratio of expenses to gross income is low enough to permit professional management fees, which should always be added in as an operating expense, whether or not professional management is used. If the investor is spending his time managing his investment himself, he should recognize that time is money and he should compensate himself for the time he is investing in this way.

INDUSTRIAL PROPERTY

Donald J. Hartman

*D*ONALD J. HARTMAN, MAI, SIR, ASA, Executive Vice President, Carl Rosman & Co., Southfield, Michigan.

Chairman, National Research Committee, Society of Industrial Realtors® and former president of Michigan chapter. Member, National Awards Committee, American Institute of Real Estate Appraisers, and former president of Michigan chapter. Twice recipient of Professional Recognition Award, American Institute of Real Estate Appraisers. Senior member, American Society of Appraisers. Instructor, Society of Industrial Realtors® courses in industrial real estate. Adjunct lecturer, Real Estate Program, University of Michigan Extension Service. Member, Community Advisory Council, Real Estate Program, Eastern Michigan University. Author of Appraisal Journal *articles on appraisal of industrial real estate.*

Real estate investors tend to invest in the types of property which they understand and with which they are most familiar. Although such developments as apartment buildings, shopping centers, and multiple-occupancy office buildings are nearly always structured around investment criteria, industrial plants are frequently developed, occupied, and owned by industrial firms. Only in recent years has investment in industrial real estate begun to approach the popularity of other types of real estate investment.

Investment in industrial real estate offers financial advantages at least equal to those offered by other real estate investments. And like investments in other types of property, it also has pitfalls that it is important for the investor to understand.

The purpose of this chapter is to explain the elements of an industrial real estate investment so that investors will become better equipped to evaluate investment opportunities in industrial real estate and so that persons in the real estate business who may be called upon to deal in such properties will be able to do so with greater competence.

This is not to imply that investment in industrial real estate is so special and so peculiar that it requires strange new formulas and investment criteria. Such is not the case with any type of real estate investment. Certain basic practices, customs, and criteria tend to apply, no matter what type of real estate is involved. For example, the basic objective in any investment can be said to be: "Buy low, sell high." The objectives in most real estate investments include maximizing income, protecting the equity, and obtaining tax benefits. The same objectives apply to investment in industrial real estate. However, the vehicle is different, and in order to maximize one's results it is important to understand what is involved.

Industrial Real Estate Defined

What constitutes industrial real estate? Industrial real estate has been defined to include all land and buildings that are either utilized or suited for industrial activities. Industry is said to include all activities involved in the production, storage, and distribution of tangible economic goods, rather than intangible services.[1] It can be seen that this very broad definition includes virtually every type of commercial activity other than retail sales and intangible services. In some cases, retail sales will be conducted as part of an industrial operation.

The precise classification of every aspect of an operation is more the problem of the broker and the zoning authorities than of the investor. What the investor should understand is that the locational criteria for industrial real estate are very different from those for commercial and residential investments. Those criteria involve the specific needs aspects of the industrial firm. However, the investor is primarily concerned with the investment benefits that he will derive from future rent payments, and he will be concerned with location only to the extent that it affects those benefits.

Types of Owners

Many industrial firms build or buy and occupy their own real estate. Substantial amounts of industrial real estate are owned by private individuals or groups of individuals who lease the property to industrial firms that they own or control. Much industrial real estate is owned by pure investors who lease the property to companies with which they enter into a landlord-tenant relationship. Much industrial real estate is leased to industrial firms by institutions seeking returns on their invested capital, such as life insurance companies. Some still undeveloped industrial real estate is owned by land speculators or developers who are hoping for an opportunity to sell at a profit or to create an income producing investment at some future date.

The ownership of industrial real estate seems to shift from one group

---

[1] William N. Kinnard, Jr., and Stephen D. Messner, *Industrial Real Estate,* 2d ed. (Washington, D.C.: Society of Industrial Realtors®, 1971), p. 4.

to another. In recent years, for example, certain life insurance companies have been making heavy purchases of income-producing industrial real estate, thus creating a shortage of sound industrial investments which can be purchased by noninstitutional investors. The life insurance companies purchased much of this property from developers who had built and leased the improvements. In addition, as sites in industrial parks have been absorbed by recent heavy demand, some developers of those parks have stopped selling land, planning instead to construct buildings for lease and retain the equities. Another recent development is the proliferation of syndicates, groups of investors who combine their resources to enable them to invest in properties that require more capital than they are willing or able to invest individually. The ownership vehicle is usually a form of limited partnership.

Investor Objectives

Like investors in other types of real estate, investors in industrial real estate are primarily interested in safe investments that will provide protection against inflation and an adequate return on the invested dollars. Thus, such investors look closely at the credit of tenants, at the likelihood that the value of a property will appreciate, and at the level of income that will remain after all expenses have been paid. Also important to these investors is the use of financing to leverage and diversify the investment portfolio. These factors will be discussed below.

Types of Industrial Investment Properties

Owner-Occupied Properties. People who own or control industrial firms have excellent opportunities to create industrial real estate investments for themselves by using their companies as tenants. This frequently comes about when an industrial firm is seeking to buy a plant. When the time comes to execute the purchase contract, the chief executive must decide what entity will become the owner. If he buys the property personally, with a group of relatives or friends or with any separate entity, his company can then lease the property on a basis that will give the investors an adequate return. The owner of such a firm will generally consider his company to be an adequately secure tenant financially, and the tenant will have the advantage of deducting the rent as a business expense. Whatever tax shelter is available can be enjoyed by the owning entity. An additional advantage of this arrangement is that the operating company conserves its working capital by not investing it in real estate. On the other hand, the money necessary to buy the real estate must be available to the purchasing entity.

Single-Tenant Properties. Another type of investment in industrial real estate is a single-tenant building that is owned by a person or an entity unrelated to the tenant. This type of investment is usually created by a lease. Since the investor must rely upon the financial strength of a single tenant for the return on his investment, the financial strength of that tenant is of critical importance to the investor. If the tenant experiences financial reverses or bankruptcy, the investor's rental income may decline sharply or disappear, and he will still have to cover the fixed expenses connected with the ownership of the real estate. Of course, given an active market, he may find a new tenant, but he may have to spend money on alterations that will make the building suitable for the tenant.

From this it can be seen that careful evaluation of the tenant is essential in the single-tenant industrial investment. The credit of the tenant is an important factor in all real estate investments, but it is particularly important in this situation because there is only one tenant to secure the investment. On the other hand, property management is greatly simplified if there is only one tenant to deal with.

Multiple-Tenant Properties. Many industrial real estate investments consist of buildings that are divided into rental units occupied by several tenants. Some of these investments have been created by constructing buildings for lease in small units, and some have been created by dividing large existing buildings into smaller rental units when single tenants cannot be found for the entire building. Multitenant industrial buildings are frequently called "incubator buildings" because they attract small companies that hope to become larger.

Although the credit of the tenants is important, the failure of one or two tenants is not likely to bring financial disaster to a multiple-tenant property. On the other hand, it is much more difficult to manage a multiple-tenant property than a single-tenant property. The owners of multiple-tenant buildings must concern themselves with such things as the prorating of taxes, common area maintenance, and security services, whereas in single-tenant buildings these matters can generally be left to the tenant.

Incidentally, some profitable incubator building investments have been created by owners of industrial firms who have bought for their own operations buildings much larger than they need, with the intent of occupying part and leasing out the remainder.

Sale-Leasebacks

Sale-leasebacks abound in industrial real estate investment, and many investors and even industrial firms seek such transactions without fully understanding what they are. Simply stated, the sale-leaseback is a transaction in which a company operating a business at premises which it owns sells those premises to an investor at an agreed price and simultaneously leases them back from the investor at an agreed rental for an agreed period of time. The investor then becomes the owner of the premises, and the former owner becomes a tenant.

A sale-leaseback is primarily a financing transaction that is designed to provide 100 percent financing to the seller as if he were mortgaging 100 percent of the value of a property. Instead of mortgage principal and interest payments, he makes rental payments. The difference is that at the end of the lease term he will not own the property, as he would if he paid off a mortgage. It is possible to write an option to repurchase into the sale-leaseback. However, doing this may have tax ramifications.

The industrial concern seeking a sale-leaseback is usually hoping to turn a fixed asset, the real estate, into working capital of which it can make better use elsewhere. However, the sale-leaseback may not always be a bonanza, as may be seen by considering two extreme types of sale-leasebacks.

One type is created by a substantial company which has a large amount of cash and wishes to build a new plant. The company can build this plant for cash, thus saving money that is normally expended for construction financing. Since this is a strong company with good credit, it can offer the completed package for sale to several institutions or investors on a leaseback basis, thus obtaining the maximum financing for the property and the lease rate which requires the lowest rate of return to the investor.

At the other extreme a sale-leaseback transaction may be offered by a company of marginal financial strength that is seeking an excessive price for its real estate. Typically, the real estate will be offered for sale at a price that may be as high as double its actual value in the market. The industrial firm will express its willingness to lease the property back at a correspondingly high rent, but under the circumstances there is reason to question whether the firm can afford to pay the rent throughout the life of the lease. If the tenant's business fails during the term of the lease, the purchaser-lessor will have vacant property on his hands which has cost him more than its value on the market, and he will find that the rent obtainable in the market is substantially less than the amount that he was receiving from the seller-tenant.

Between two extremes, sale-leasebacks with various levels of safety and return can be found. When offered a sale-leaseback, the potential investor should determine what the market value of the real estate would be *if it were* vacant and should investigate the financial strength of the tenant.

Industrial Land Development

In recent years, fortunes have been made and lost in the development of industrial land. Land development consists of buying raw land in large parcels; installing roads, utility lines, and other necessary improvements; and then selling individual lots to builders or users. In effect, the developer buys at wholesale and sells at retail.

The field of industrial land development is no place for the unsophisticated. The cost of providing improvements has risen sharply in recent years, and the time needed to get through the myriad of regulations and permits has lengthened. As a result, more construction money has to be borrowed and higher interest costs have to be paid.

Obtaining an acceptable absorption rate is the key to making money in industrial land development. That is, the developer sells the finished lots quickly enough to recover his costs before the carrying charges consume all of the profits. At present, many institutions that make construction loans for the development of industrial parks require that they be out of the development within three years. As a result, many current land development projects are staged for small amounts of acreage at a time, say, under 40 acres. Previously, industrial park projects were as large as 1,000 acres or more.

Some developers of industrial parks build industrial buildings on speculation without having tenants at hand. They find that this helps develop sales activity and that they can create investments for themselves by leasing the buildings.

When it is available, the build-to-suit project, sometimes called a "package deal," is a preferred approach for investors. This approach can be used when an investor finds a company which wishes to occupy a building on a site that he owns. It can also be used if the investor purchases a site that a company has selected. If the company has good enough credit and is willing to sign a proper lease, the investor will construct a building on his land to the company's specifications, thus creating an investment in industrial real estate for himself. This type of transaction is greatly preferred by developers because it enables them to eliminate the need to find a tenant for a building that has already been constructed.

Industrial Land Speculation

It is possible to buy industrial acreage, hold it for a period of time, and resell it at a profit without going through the expense and trouble of development. Certainly, many investors have profited from such transactions in the past. This type of speculation, however, is extremely risky, as it seems that when industrial land is not selling, virtually nothing can be done to make it move.

A rough rule of thumb that investors in vacant land frequently use should be kept in mind. It is generally considered that if vacant land—land that is not producing income—does not approximately double in value every five years, then the investor is losing money.

Types of Buildings

Since most industrial real estate investments involve buildings, an investor should understand what types of buildings may be involved and the significance of building design. An industrial building has been described as nothing more than a "shell" or "container" constructed around industrial equipment to provide shelter for it. For this reason, it is often true that when industrial equipment no longer has utility, the building that houses it is also obsolete. Industrial buildings are generally divided into three categories: general purpose, special purpose, and single purpose.

General-Purpose Buildings. General-purpose industrial buildings are suitable for a variety of industrial uses without substantial conversion.

Examples include warehouse buildings, office-warehouse buildings, and manufacturing buildings that do not require substantial amounts of customized construction.

A general-purpose building is characterized by flexibility of design. Ideally, a general-purpose building will have wide-open shop space without dividing walls, ceiling clearances that permit most industrial operations, and the capability for drive-in doors and truck-high loading facilities. In addition, it will be on a site that has adequate parking space and its zoning will permit some flexibility of occupancy. It may also have railroad siding or other specialized features.

This is not to say that a general-purpose building cannot have dividing walls, limited ceiling heights, and so on. But the features mentioned above are among those which create maximum flexibility of use, and the potential uses of a building will be determined by such features.

Special-Purpose Buildings. The special-purpose industrial building is designed for a specific use. It can be converted to alternative uses only at some expense or at some sacrifice in the efficient use of its space. For example removing the partition walls and the refrigeration equipment of a small milk-processing plant can adapt it for use as a warehouse or a light manufacturing facility. Similarly, a high-ceiling crane-bay building can be adapted to operations not requiring cranes. However, if this were done, the height advantage of the building might be lost, and in that case the cost of heating and maintaining the unneeded height would become a penalty to the new user.

Single-Purpose Buildings. Single-purpose buildings are designed for a single use and cannot be economically converted to an alternative use. The word *economically* is the key here, as a single-purpose building can, of course, be demolished and another building constructed in its place. However, it may not be feasible for an investor to undertake that type of project.

If single-purpose buildings are put to alternative uses, the sacrifice in utility is usually so great as to eliminate any advantages to an investor. In other words, the rental income that the investor would receive from a secondary use of a single-purpose building is likely to be too low to justify the original investment. Examples of single-purpose properties include electric generating plants, petroleum processing plants, and some metal refinishing plants.

In some cases, ingenuity can go a long way. For example, in a market of small buildings a building that is apparently single purpose due to its extremely large size can be converted to a general-purpose building by offering it for lease in smaller units. The cost of doing this is usually manageable, but the potential advantages of the changeover should be carefully explored before it is undertaken.

From the point of view of the industrial real estate investor, the more general in purpose a building is, the greater is the flexibility of occupancy and the greater is the likelihood that the investor will not have to suffer long periods of vacancy. Experts sometimes disagree as to whether a property should be labeled general purpose or special purpose, but what is important for the investor is the ability of a building to economically satisfy the demand for space in the market in which it is situated.

The Evaluation of Industrial Investments

Thus far, we have described industrial real estate investment and its relationship to other types of real estate investment. We have also described the various types of industrial real estate investments. Our next step is into the heart of the matter—dealing with the numbers.

Some investors tend to examine proposed investments from the purview of their personal dollar goals without considering the total picture. Some investors base their investment decisions solely upon the answer to the question "What is my first year cash on cash?" However, more sophisticated investors will examine the total investment package and every facet of the investment.

When an investor buys industrial real estate, he is acquiring two things: an income stream and the right to the reversion. Very simply, the income stream is the net proceeds from rent which he is able to keep each year, and the reversion is the remaining value of the real estate after the lease expires.

The Income Stream. As used here, the term *income stream* means net operating income (NOI) before income taxes. Each investor has his own income tax computations and obligations, and thus must compare investment opportunities on the basis of his own aftertax considerations. For simplicity, however, this discussion is based upon before-tax considerations, leaving the investor to take it from there.

Net operating income is the amount which remains after all operating expenses (fixed and variable) have been deducted from the rent required by the lease. It is calculated before any deduction is made for financing expenses. Fixed expenses usually include such things as real estate taxes and casualty insurance. Operating expenses usually include a charge for management and an allowance for maintenance and may include some common area expenses and some allowance for the amortization of improvements made specifically for the tenant. Depending upon the length of the lease, prudent investors will also deduct some vacancy factor from the rent. As will be seen later, under the terms of some leases some or all of these expenses can be the tenant's direct obligation.

Depending on the terms of the lease, net operating income can be fixed, or it can fluctuate from year to year based upon variations in expenses. Variable net operating income that the investor represents by a number that will be the same each year is called "stabilized income."

> *Example A:* A new industrial building is leased to a national concern for 15 years at a gross rental of $5,500 per month, with the tenant responsible for all real estate taxes and insurance costs in excess of those for the year of inception of the lease. The landlord's maintenance obligations are limited to the roof and outer walls.

Gross annual income $5,500 × 12		$66,000
Less vacancy 1%		660
Effective gross income		$65,340
Landlord expenses		
Base real estate taxes	$10,000	
Base insurance premiums	1,500	
Maintenance allowance	1,000	
Management*	0	
Total		$12,500
Net operating income (NOI)		$52,840

* Most investors will not inject a management charge for the single-tenant long-term lease invest-ment. In fact they may also omit a vacancy allowance, but the latter has been used here as an illustration.

Reversion. As defined above, the reversion is the value of the real estate when the lease expires or when all of the rights of occupancy of the real estate revert to the owner. If the investor owns the real estate when the lease expires he will have to dispose of it or rerent it. Conse-quently, the investor will be vitally concerned with the value of the property at that time. His purchase decision may be based upon whether he thinks the value of the property will appreciate or decline over his term of ownership. The value of the reversion can have a dramatic impact upon the actual return on his investment. The prudent investor should bear in mind that the future value of investment industrial real estate influences its present value. This influence is estimated in dis-counted cash flow studies.

Investment Considerations. Several factors that potential investors in industrial real estate should consider have already been mentioned in this chapter. One is the marketability of the industrial real estate if it becomes vacant. This has been shown to be influenced by the extent to which the property can be classified as general purpose. It is also a function of location (where the action is), the existence of competing projects, the investor's view of future economic conditions, and so on.

Another factor that has been mentioned is the potential for apprecia-tion of the real estate. Some investors will not consider purchasing prop-erty in a declining area. Others thrive on such investments. This question may also be related to the size of the income stream and the rate of return offered.

Return on investment is another important factor that is considered by investors in industrial real estate. Industrial real estate must compete for dollars with other potential investments, and the available rates of return are scaled accordingly. The rate of return on a free-and-clear basis, sometimes called the "overall rate," is calculated by dividing the net operating income by the purchase price (or value) of the property.

Example B: If an investor purchases the real estate from Example A for $540,000 cash, his rate of return on investment on a free and clear basis, or the overall rate, is:

$$\$52,840 \div \$540,000 = 9.79\%$$

If the property is encumbered by a mortgage, then the rate of return, usually called the "cash flow rate" or the "cash on cash rate," is calculated by subtracting the annual debt service (ADS) from the net operating income and dividing that result, called the "cash flow before taxes" (CFBT), by the amount of the equity investment.

> *Example C:* If the investor from Example B obtains a first mortgage in the amount of $405,000 requiring monthly payments of $3,538, including interest at 9½ percent per year, and amortizing in 25 years, his cash flow rate is:
>
> | | |
> |---|---:|
> | Net operating income .... | $52,840 |
> | Annual debt service $3,538 × 12 .... | 42,456 |
> | Cash flow before taxes .... | $10,384 |
>
> Equity: $540,000 − $405,000 = $135,000
> Cash flow rate: $10,384 ÷ $135,000 = 7.69%

These rate of return calculations provide the industrial real estate investor with a basis for comparing his investment, or his potential investment, with other investment opportunities that are available to him. From his standpoint, industrial real estate is no different from other types of real estate investments.

Another important factor that the investor in industrial real estate must consider is the credit of the tenant. The lease is the tenant's contract to pay rent, and the lease may be meaningless if the tenant does not have the financial capability to pay the rent. Therefore, an investor in industrial real estate should explore the credit of his tenant or tenants and take his findings into consideration when making his investment decision. Naturally, the weaker the tenant, the riskier the investment, and greater risk can be compensated for only by a greater rate of return or by the promise of substantial appreciation in value.

Leases and Leasing

This chapter has made several references to the existence of leases in industrial real estate investment. Although land leases are common in industrial real estate, we will concern ourselves here primarily with the lease of an industrial building. If an investor can effectively analyze an industrial real estate lease and investment involving a building, he should have no difficulty in doing the same for an investment in land only.

A lease is a contract between two parties by which one (the lessee, or tenant) is granted the right by the other (the lessor, or landlord) to occupy and use a specific parcel of real estate under a set of specific terms and conditions. Lease documents vary from simple one-page agreements to quagmires of documentation. This discussion will be limited to the basic economic terms and other covenants that are most frequently encountered in leases of industrial real estate. Needless to say, an investor considering purchase of leased property should read the lease. If necessary, he should obtain legal counsel to interpret it for him.

Leases can be categorized in a number of different ways. In industrial real estate, it is customary to classify them as either gross leases or net leases.

The Gross Lease. In the gross lease, the tenant pays a gross rental amount, and it is the landlord's obligation to pay the real estate taxes; fire, extended coverage, and vandalism insurance on the real estate; and for a certain amount of maintenance (this is frequently limited to the maintenance of the roof and the outer walls). The tenant is responsible for his own utilities. There is usually an escalator clause that limits the landlord's obligation for real estate taxes and provides that the tenant will pay any increase in real estate taxes over and above a stated amount. Such a clause is sometimes called a "tax stop." An "insurance stop" operates in the same way in relation to the fire, extended coverage, and vandalism insurance premiums.

The Net Lease. A net lease is one in which the tenant pays the landlord a net rental and also pays the real estate taxes; fire, extended coverage, and vandalism insurance; and for all maintenance on the building. This is sometimes called an "absolute net lease."

A lease can be constructed under which the tenant pays some of the lease expenses described above and the landlord pays others. This changes the degree of netness and accounts for the fact that leases are sometimes called net leases, net-net leases, net-net-net leases, and so on. Difficulties arise because those terms mean different things to different people. Therefore, if a lease is represented as a net lease, it is still important for the investor to verify the respective obligations of the landlord and the tenant.

Lease Terms and Options. Probably the most important financial term of the lease is the specified monthly rental. Leases vary in the way the rental amounts are expressed, so this portion of the lease should be read carefully to determine whether the dollar amount expressed is payable monthly or annually. Some leases even specify the total dollar rental for the entire term of the lease.

The duration of the lease in months or years is another important financial consideration, since it determines how long the given tenant will pay rent, and this can have an important influence upon the finance-ability of the property. In connection with the duration of the lease, the lease should be carefully scrutinized for options. It is not uncommon for tenants in industrial buildings to be granted options to renew their leases or options to purchase the leased property. If there are options to renew, the investor should examine the rent called for on those options and the length of extension permitted. From this he can evaluate the protection against inflation, or the absence of such protection, that is built into the lease. An option to purchase obviously places an upper limit of value upon the real estate, and it should be carefully examined for price and terms.

In the present inflationary times, investors negotiating leases are reluctant to grant options, since they believe that properties can be remarketed for sale or lease at much higher prices later on. The options that are negotiated usually contain provisions for substantial escalations in rental for the renewal periods. Since such options are a "one-way street," binding the landlord and not the tenant, tenants are usually willing to accept provisions for escalations in exchange for them. Many rental escalators are based upon government cost-of-living indices.

The Security Deposit.   Another financial consideration in the lease is the provision for a security deposit. This is money deposited by the tenant with the landlord, usually to ensure that the tenant will pay his rent and fulfill his other obligations under the terms of the lease, specifically the obligation to return the property to the landlord in sound condition.

This type of provision should be carefully studied to determine what obligations, if any, the landlord has as a result of obtaining the security deposit. Furthermore, if an investor is buying property subject to an existing lease containing a security provision, the seller should turn over the security deposit to the investor at closing, because eventually the new owner will be required to account for the deposit to the tenant.

The Maintenance Clauses.   The maintenance clauses should be studied to determine the respective maintenance obligations of the landlord and the tenant. Along the same line, the lease should state who is obligated to rebuild the property in the event of partial or total destruction by fire.

The Right to Assign or Sublet.   An important covenant in most leases is the right to assign or sublet. For the protection of the landlord, the tenant is frequently prohibited from subletting or assigning his lease without the landlord's permission. It is customary for the original tenant of an assigned or sublet property to remain responsible for the complete performance of all the covenants and terms of the lease.

The Eminent Domain Clause.   The eminent domain clause specifies the distribution of condemnation awards and the terms for the continuance of the lease in the event that the appropriate authorities exercise the power of eminent domain. Sometimes a net lease will require that the tenant purchase the real estate from the landlord in the event of a partial take by condemnation or of a partial loss by fire or other casualty. A lease containing this requirement is called a bond-type lease.

The Use of the Property.   Most leases contain language describing the use to which the property may be put by the tenant. This provision can be important to both parties, but the investor will be particularly concerned with wear and tear on the building that can result from its permitted uses.

Many other covenants may be included in leases, depending upon state laws and local custom. There is no such thing as a standard lease form. In most cases, industrial leases are tailored to suit the particular transaction. The investor should realize that the important thing is to have the lease represent the agreement of the parties and provide both parties with the protections necessary. To the investor, however, the lease is the document which identifies the rental income that will be translated into the net operating income upon which he bases his investment decision.

The Financing of Industrial Real Estate

Industrial real estate can be financed by utilizing virtually all of the methods applicable to other types of investment real estate. In addition, a few other vehicles are available for the creative investor.

Cash. Any discussion of the financing of real estate investments should begin with the simplest method of all—cash. There are people who do not believe in using borrowed funds for anything, and if they invest in industrial real estate they will wish to pay cash. However, many industrial real estate investments bring high prices, so that in many cases the investor is unable to come up with all of the cash for the purchase.

The Mortgage. The most common financing tool for investment in industrial real estate is the mortgage. The mortgage is actually a pledge of the real estate as security against the note upon which the loan is made. There can be several mortgages on a single property, and these are typically numbered in the order of their recording against the property. Thus, the first loan is the first mortgage; a loan on the remaining equity is the second mortgage; if a loan can be made on additional equity, it will be called the third mortgage; and so on.

Equity. The word *equity* has been used frequently in this chapter. Equity is the difference between the value of the real estate and the total of the loans outstanding against it. At the time of purchase, assuming that the purchaser buys at market value, his equity is the amount of his cash investment over and above any mortgages that he gives on the property. As time goes on, the equity will fluctuate as the mortgage balance is reduced through amortization and as the actual market value of the property increases or decreases.

> *Example D:* The investor from Examples B and C invested $135,000 over the first mortgage of $405,000, so that his original equity was $135,000 at the time of purchase. Assuming that the property value does not change, the investor's equity at the end of the fifth year of his ownership will be:
>
> | | |
> |---|---|
> | Property value .... | $540,000 |
> | Mortgage balance at end of fifth year .... | 379,647 |
> | Equity .... | $160,353 |
>
> If during the five years the property appreciates in value by 10 percent,* the investor's equity will be:
>
> | | |
> |---|---|
> | Property value .... | $594,000 |
> | Mortgage balance .... | 379,647 |
> | Equity .... | $214,353 |
>
> If during that period the property instead depreciates in value by 10 percent,* the equity will be:
>
> | | |
> |---|---|
> | Property value .... | $486,000 |
> | Mortgage balance .... | 379,647 |
> | Equity .... | $106,353 |
>
> * At the end of the fifth year, there will still be ten years remaining on the lease, and it is likely that the investment market will determine the property value. Therefore, a 10 percent change in value may be a remote possibility. That number is used here for illustrative purposes, but there are factors that can affect market value in these examples, assuming that the rent remains fixed. Those factors include a substantial reduction in real estate taxes and a substantial change in the overall rates or the cash flow rates in the investment market.

Mortgage Classifications. Mortgages on industrial real estate can be classified as "credit oriented" or "real estate oriented." In a credit-oriented loan, the lender looks primarily to the credit of the tenant for the security. The lender is more interested in the credit of the tenant than in the value of the real estate. In such cases, it is customary for the rent to be assigned to the lender in the event of default in the mortgage.

In the credit-oriented mortgage, the lender will establish his loan amount based upon a percentage of the net operating income (NOI) that he will accept to cover the mortgage payments (usually called the "annual debt service"). This percentage is called the "debt coverage ratio." The stronger the credit of the tenant, the greater the percentage of the NOI that the lender will apply to the annual debt service (ADS). Given a particular interest rate and amortization period allowed by the lender, the greater the ADS, the greater the loan can be.

Although mortgages are frequently based upon the lease or upon the real estate, the credit of the borrower is always a consideration. It is not unusual for the lender, especially in development loans, to request a personal guarantee of the entire loan or some portion of the loan from the borrower. The inherent risks of such a guarantee for the borrower are obvious, and most borrowers try very hard to avoid giving a personal guarantee, even at the expense of a higher interest rate or some other concession in mortgage terms.

In a real estate–oriented loan, the lender looks primarily to the real estate for his security. In such cases, the lender will usually limit the amount of loan to a percentage of the value of the property. This is called the "loan-to-value ratio."

Amortization. An important element in mortgages is the amortization period, that is, the period of time upon which the debt service (principal and interest payments) is computed. The amortization period is frequently longer than the term of the loan, in which case the balance of the loan is due in a lump sum at the end of the term. This lump sum is called a "balloon" or a "balloon payment." When borrowing with amortization that will create a balloon, such as a 20-year loan with a 25-year amortization, the investor must plan either on paying the balloon at the end of the 20 years or on obtaining a new mortgage (refinancing) at that time.

> *Example E:* In the previous examples, a loan of $405,000 was projected for a $540,000 property, and annual debt service of $42,456 was applied against net operating income of $52,840.
>
> The loan-to-value ratio is $405,000 ÷ $540,000 = 75 percent.
> The debt coverage ratio is $52,840 ÷ $42,456 = 1.24.
>
> The amortization period of the loan is 25 years. If the loan is due at the end of the lease (15 years), the balloon will be $273,644. If, instead, the loan is due at the end of 20 years, the balloon will be $168,819.
>
> If the lease is originally negotiated for a term of 25 years with the same NOI* and the strength of the tenant's credit is such that the lender will accept a debt coverage ratio of 1.10 instead of 1.24, then the investment will show:

```
Net operating income  . . . .   $52,840
Debt coverage ratio . . . . . .     1.10   (÷)
Annual debt service . . . . . .   $48,036
```

With the same 9½ percent annual interest and 25-year amortization, this ADS will pay a loan of $458,168 instead of $405,000.

The equity then is $540,000 − $458,168 = $81,832.

The cash flow before taxes is $52,840 − $48,036 = $4,804.

The cash flow rate is $4,804 ÷ $81,832 = 5.87%.

However, since the mortgage amount is based upon the NOI and not upon the property value (cost), the investor might decide:

The CFBT is $4,804.

The required return on invested cash, which is available in the market from competing investments, is 9.7%.

```
Value of equity ($4,804 ÷ 9.7%)   $ 49,526
Mortgage available . . . . . . . . . . . .    458,168
Property value . . . . . . . . . . . . . . .   $507,694
```

This investment is worth $507,700 to this investor

* Long-term leases are now usually structured with periodic rental escalations built in, possibly every five years and possibly tied to the consumer price index.

Mortgage Lenders. Virtually anybody can make a loan on investment real estate. Most industrial real estate investments are financed through mortgages from insurance companies. Loans on smaller transactions are available from banks and savings and loan associations. Some loans have been made by real estate investment trusts (REITs), and mortgage loans can also be made by syndicates, pension trusts, and private investors.

The Purchase-Money Mortgage. The purchase-money mortgage is a loan made by the seller of a property to cover the portion of the purchase price which the buyer is unable to provide in cash or through other loans. A purchase-money mortgage can be a first mortgage or a mortgage of any other number. The key ingredient is that it is a mortgage given to the seller of the property. The terms of purchase-money mortgages are not limited by banking or insurance requirements, and these terms may be negotiated on any basis that is agreeable to the parties as long as they stay within the usury limits.

Contract for Deed. Industrial real estate can be purchased on an installment basis, provided that this is permitted by local law. This is another method by which the seller helps finances the purchase. In some states this type of transaction is referred to as a "land contract" or contract for deed. In such a transaction, title typically does not pass until the final installment has been paid. The terms can be negotiated between the parties on any mutually agreeable basis, and the terms of installment sales are frequently similar in magnitude and structure to the terms of mortgages. The installment sale is frequently used where mortgages are unavailable or where the mortgage terms are unsatisfactory to the purchaser. (See Chapters 5 and 9.)

The Sale-Leaseback. The sale-leaseback has been discussed above as a type of industrial real estate investment. As such, it is actually a means of financing industrial real estate. A sale-leaseback can be further financed by the purchaser through a mortgage loan.

Syndication. Investments in industrial real estate can be financed by syndication. Groups of individuals can be assembled into limited partnerships or other types of entities in order to provide funds for financing investments such as industrial real estate development. Such syndicates can actually assume ownership or can act as mortgage lenders.

Revenue Bonds. Recent federal legislation makes revenue bond financing available for industrial real estate at rates lower than the usual mortgage rates. Not all communities have established the procedures necessary to utilize this tool, and the investor will have to make inquiries in his community to determine whether bond financing is available for his particular project.

Leverage. Perhaps the simplest way to define leverage is to say that it is the use of borrowed funds. In particular, leverage is considered here as the use of borrowed funds in the purchase of investment real estate. Positive leverage will increase the rate of return on equity, and negative leverage will decrease that rate of return.

Some of the advantages of leverage are obvious. For one, if an investor has a limited amount of cash to invest, using borrowed funds enables him to invest in more projects, thus diversifying his portfolio. In addition, it enables him to pay the loan back with cheaper money as inflation continues. Furthermore, the investor reduces his exposure to loss by having less of an investment in a particular project. For example, an investor with $200,000 in cash to invest may be able to buy four properties costing $250,000 each by investing $50,000 in each of them and borrowing the balance, instead of simply buying one property costing $200,000. By the use of leverage, he increases his investment assets from $200,000 to $1,000,000.

However, the use of mortgages means that the investor must make payments regularly, even if the tenant stops paying rent for some reason. The investor who uses leverage must be careful not to spread himself too thin and thus limit his staying power in case trouble develops in one or more of his investments, especially if he has given personal guarantees.

Conclusion

The various elements of investment in industrial real estate have been discussed here. It is not possible to structure rules to fit each element so that an investor need only apply a formula and gain a fortune. The investor must apply judgment when he compares investment opportunities.

One principle seems to be of general benefit, however. It is important to understand the market forces that apply to each part of the investment—the lease, the mortgage, the value of the property as if it were vacant, the credit of the tenant, and so on—and if any of the parts do not fit the market in which that part competes, caution is indicated and further investigation is warranted. For example, an offering price that appears to be "below the market" or a lease rental rate that seems to be "above the market" should be checked out to determine whether the investment contains unexpected pitfalls.

FARMS AND ACREAGE

Dwight W. Jundt

*D*WIGHT W. JUNDT, AFLM, ARA, President, Jundt Associates, Inc., Fort Lauderdale, Florida.
   Certified general contractor, State of Florida, and registered real estate broker in eight states. Director, Builders Association of South Florida. Past president, Farm and Land Institute. Past member, Executive Committee, National Association of Realtors®. A Lecturer at over 200 national, state, and regional real estate seminars and institutes. Author of numerous articles.

THIS LAND OF OURS

The United States is a land of city dwellers. Yet many of us are more at home in the country than in the city. Our relationship with trees and mountains and meadows becomes personal. The character and challenge and wonders of the outdoors weave an attachment to our inner longings which concrete and tall buildings can never replace.

But there's more to the land than idyllic escapism. Land is a factory—it produces our food and fiber. It is also a trade commodity, an investment, a future homesite, or a park. This chapter is devoted to a discussion of land as farms and acreage, or more exactly, as real estate and how it relates to its present and future owners.

There are nearly 2.3 billion acres of land in our 50 states. Of this, Alaska comprises over 365 million acres, Hawaii slightly over 4 million acres. There are over 1 billion acres of land in farms in the United States. In early 1979, the average price of farmland, according to the U.S. Department of Agriculture, exceeded $560 per acre. This translates to an asset in excess of $560 billion.

When the forefathers of our country came to this land, it was to find a place of freedom for a new life. None of them could have dared hope to find the rich resources which have fostered the strongest nation on earth. The underlying strength of our nation has always been and continues to be that land which has provided such a bountiful source of food, clothing, and housing. The strength of the United States is founded in large part upon the endowment of natural resources with which we have been blessed.

Although less than 5 percent of our people now reside on land to which they look for their economic livelihood, the importance of farms to the strength of the nation and the dynamics of the real estate industry is far more significant.

Production Regions and Types of Farming

The major types of farming found in particular parts of the United States can be classified into broad production regions (see Figure 1). One should realize that such classifications are oversimplified and represent partial images of complex farming situations. Wide variations in the types of farming are found within each region. Although the U.S. Department of Agriculture employs slightly different classifications, for the purposes of our discussion the regions and farming types have been classified as follows:

Production Region	*Predominant Type of Farming*
Northeast, Lake States	Dairy
Corn Belt, Northern Plains	Corn, wheat, general farming
Appalachian	General farming and tobacco
Delta States, Southeast	Cotton, soybeans, citrus fruits
Southern Plains	Cotton, soybeans, livestock
Mountain	Livestock, wheat
Pacific	Dairy, specialty crops

The Northeast and the Lake States. Dairying is the main farm enterprise in this region. The region has rougher, less productive soils than does the Corn Belt, but the cool climate is well adapted to the production of pasture and forage. The proximity of the area to centers of population makes it particularly well adapted to dairy operations. Milk is expensive to ship long distances, and it is generally produced within 200 miles of where it is consumed.

The operation of dairy farms has become highly specialized. Gone are the days when nearly every farmer kept cows and chickens for his own use and for the sale of cream and eggs to supplement his income. Now, nearly every farmer buys his dairy and poultry products in the same manner as any urban consumer.

Most of the commercial dairy farms are family operated, utilizing some outside labor. Milk production is a labor-intensive enterprise, requiring early and long hours every day of the week. A high degree of management is required for an efficient dairy, and a dairy can seldom be a successful operation with the use of hired labor only. Consequently, dairies seldom make satisfactory investment properties.

Many major farming types other than dairy farms can be found in this region. The southern portions of Minnesota, Michigan, and Wiscon-

FIGURE 1
Farm Production Regions

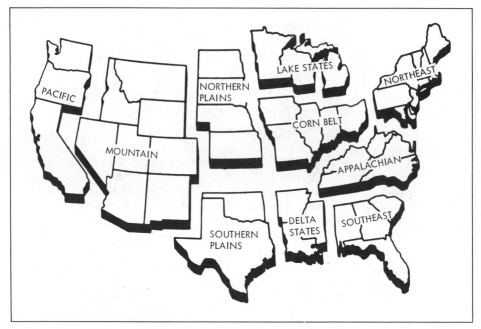

Source: Economic Research Service, U.S. Department of Agriculture.

sin contain many large row-crop farms which resemble those of the Corn Belt. The production of poultry, fruit, potatoes, and truck crops is extremely important in many areas of this region.

Almost half of the land in this region is wooded. Some of it has been used for farming in the past and could be farmed again.

The region is so far north as to have a short growing season. Although oats, barley, and wheat can be grown in most of the region, many of the fields are small and quite stony because of the rough terrain. Modern, large-scale machinery is difficult to use in these areas.

In addition, much of the land in this region has been diverted from farming to urban or estate-type use, thus reducing the amount of farmland that is available for production. The high concentration of population in these states ensures a constant demand for land of all types.

The Corn Belt and the Northern Plains. The Corn Belt contains the most uniform type of agricultural production in the United States. Within the limits of the Corn Belt and the Northern Plains is found the most productive land of any area of equal size in the world. Thus, this is a favorite area of domestic and foreign investors alike.

Land found in the Corn Belt is normally level or gently rolling. The soils are deep, rich, and fertile and are well adapted to the production of corn, soybeans, and other row crops. The climate is favorable, with good rainfall in most years, and the growing season is adequate for the production of most feed grain crops. Over 50 percent of the world's output of corn is grown in the Corn Belt and the Northern Plains.

Because of the abundance of feed crops, the production of cattle, hogs, and poultry is also very important in this region. The unique features of the Corn Belt have contributed to a greater use of modern technology. The fields are well adapted to the use of large machinery, insecticides and herbicides, and other modern technology. As a consequence, the farms have become larger and fewer each year. Since good land attracts good operators, a high level of management and technology is found in this region.

Although the southeastern portion of the Northern Plains is identified with the Corn Belt, the soils of much of the Northern Plains area are less productive than those found in the Corn Belt and the annual precipitation of the Northern Plains is considerably less than that of the Corn Belt. Much winter wheat is grown in the Corn Belt and the Northern Plains. The advent of sprinkler irrigation has become a very important factor in portions of Nebraska and Kansas.

Both cow-calf production and cattle feedlot operations are important to agricultural production in Nebraska and Kansas. The ideal location of these states between the feeder calf-producing regions of the West and the feed grain production regions of the Corn Belt has made the Northern Plains a leader in the production of fat cattle.

The Appalachian Region.   Although much of this region is mountainous and wooded, it is still an important segment of agriculture. The wide range of soils, topography, and climate makes it almost impossible to generalize about this area. Tobacco of all types is one of the most important crops. Lumber and other forest products are major commodities. Corn, small grains, and hay are grown as feed for hogs, sheep, and cattle. Cotton and soybeans are also important crops of this area. Since the climate and the rainfall are conducive to a long growing season, this is one of the best pasture regions in the United States. However, the farms and fields are often small, so that the returns are low as compared with those of farms in many other areas.

The Delta States and the Southeast.   The Delta States and the northern states of the Southeast region have long been known as the Cotton Belt. Cotton requires a long growing season and rather high temperatures. Mechanization and other technological changes have vastly increased the yields and changed the economics of cotton production.

Important as cotton is to these regions, many changes have occurred in the last decade. The timber was removed from hundreds of thousands of acres of delta land during the mid-1960s, and most of that land was converted to the production of soybeans and wheat. The importance of soybeans in the world market has reduced the reliance of the Delta States and the Southeast upon cotton as the primary cash crop.

Timber remains an important cash crop in many of the Southeastern states, and it supplies the large demands for construction in the South. In addition, the Sun Belt, as this area is often called, has boomed with industrial uses and population expansion. This has changed the nature of the area's agriculture.

Because of the high land prices in the Corn Belt, many farmers accustomed to a higher input of technology moved to the Delta States and the Southeast. As a consequence, general farming is being taken much more seriously.

Florida is probably the most distinctive state of the Southeastern region although it is thought of as a resort state, agriculture is a very important segment of its economy. The production of timber, cattle, citrus, and vegetable crops is extremely important to the economy of the state. Since it is possible to acquire large tracts of land in north and central Florida, outside investments are prevalent.

The Southern Plains. This region, comprising of Texas and Arkansas, includes highly specialized cotton farms; soybean, rice, and timber production; and the traditional cattle country. The production of calves from cow herds and of feeder cattle from hundreds of feedlots contributes substantially to the agricultural economy. In addition, southern Texas is important in the production of citrus and vegetable crops.

Arkansas has two distinct regions. The Mississippi delta region of the east is highly productive for cotton, rice, and soybeans. The heavily timbered western region is used for resort purposes as well as timber production. Most of the crop production in western Arkansas is restricted to the Red River Valley.

Texas contains nearly every type of agricultural enterprise that can be found in the country as a whole. Huge cattle operations are centered in much of its southwest region, where the rainfall is scanty, the productivity of the land is low, and the grazing is sparse. Drought and a shortage of range feed are frequent hazards of the rancher.

The Mountain Region. The Mountain Region is made up primarily of grazing land. The lower country includes a complex of desert and semidesert grasses and shrubs, which are used mainly for winter grazing or for spring and fall grazing. The higher elevations slope primarily into oak brush and timber types. Some of the rangeland can be used only seasonally. Livestock must be moved long distances at different times of the year. Much of the rangeland in this area is owned by the federal government.

As with other regions, it is difficult to generalize about the Mountain Region, because its southern portions are important in the production of citrus and vegetable crops where irrigation can be utilized. Its northwestern portion is important for the production of many grain crops, potatoes, and sugar beets, particularly where irrigation can be utilized.

The Pacific Region. The most important crops of this region are the fruits, nuts, and vegetables that are raised in California. Washington and Oregon contain the chief wheat-growing region of the West. Timber production is a major crop as well, and general farming can be found in much of the Pacific Region.

Summary of U.S. Production Regions and Farming Types. The predominant crops of each region have been mentioned, but it must also be noted that each region contains many overlapping types of production. For example, each region has pockets of specialty production. California produces some of the finest cotton in the country. Michigan produces some of the finest potatoes in the country. Colorado sugar beet production has a substantial impact on the region. The production of alfalfa for dehydration is important to the economy of Nebraska. Such pockets illustrate the great diversification in farm production that the country has available to it.

U.S. Land Value Trends

From 1935 to 1977, average land values in the United States increased consistently. Probably the sharpest increase was recorded during the year ending February 1, 1977, when land values increased an average of 17 percent. This raised the average value of U.S. land from $390 per acre to $456 per acre (see Tables 1 and 2). Land values in the Corn Belt and the Lake States increased as much as 36 percent during that year. Farmland values increased 14% from February 1978 to February 1979.

Land prices more than doubled in the nation from 1972 to 1979 (see Figure 2). Annual increases of over 35 percent were recorded for individual states during this period. Figure 3 indicates the average value per acre as measured on March 1 during the years 1940–79.

Averages only indicate trends, however. The prime land in the Corn Belt in a few cases was selling at more than $4,000 per acre and in many cases at more than $3,000 per acre. These prices were obviously averaged out with many sales of farmland at considerably lower prices. Large, minimally productive acreages of ranches, cutover timberlands, and pastureland selling at under $200 per acre brought the average land price in the country to the $560 per acre average estimated on February 1, 1979.

Several events combined to create the rapid increase in land prices during the 1970s. The strong influence of inflation encouraged farmers and nonfarmers alike to invest in land as a hedge against inflation. Other factors included the depletion of crop surpluses and the increase in demand for U.S. farm products throughout the world. These factors caused farm owners to buy more and bigger machinery, and this magnified their long-standing demand for farm enlargement. Since land prices had continued to go up, farmers had accumulated more equity in land that they already owned, and this gave them more borrowing power and a strong incentive to bid up available land.

There is good reason to doubt that land values will continue to show the rapid upward spiral that occurred during the 1970s. Indeed, adjustments took place in 1977 that saw the best land in the Corn Belt declining from more than $4,000 per acre to as much as 20 percent lower. Later increases have created new highs.

Factors Affecting Land Values. Land values are always affected by two critical forces:

1. *The first and most important force is what the land will return.* Although this force has seemingly been ignored during periods of steady appreciation in land values, it must be remembered that the returns on land are not always directly related to the individual prices of farm

TABLE 1

Farm Real Estate: Indices of Average Value per Acre, by State, Grouped by Farm Production Region, March 1, 1972, and March 1, 1974, to February 1, 1979 (March 1, 1967, equals 100)*

State	1972 March	1974 March	1975 March	1976 February	1977 February	1978 February	1979 February
Northeast							
New England†	174	231	257	278	301	332	365
New York	155	233	275	296	313	318	347
New Jersey	180	278	340	377	377	387	418
Pennsylvania	167	262	315	350	422	471	539
Delaware	134	199	242	288	334	374	430
Maryland	162	227	248	299	316	368	420
Lake States							
Michigan	127	174	184	201	256	287	319
Wisconsin	148	214	240	271	322	381	446
Minnesota	127	186	242	294	369	413	483
Corn Belt							
Ohio	127	184	208	252	331	373	448
Indiana	113	161	200	244	321	361	415
Illinois	116	173	209	260	353	390	441
Iowa	122	189	234	294	397	413	475
Missouri	143	207	214	241	284	325	364
Northern Plains							
North Dakota	127	193	265	310	349	369	413
South Dakota	118	172	214	241	287	336	380
Nebraska	127	183	215	271	307	295	360
Kansas	118	178	211	235	267	270	310
Appalachian							
Virginia	149	223	250	278	302	327	386
West Virginia	177	275	317	398	417	426	498
North Carolina	138	200	216	232	246	253	299
Kentucky	137	182	203	239	281	317	374
Tennessee	142	206	236	251	275	307	338
Southeast							
South Carolina	162	238	273	284	311	319	373
Georgia	175	264	298	299	322	357	386
Florida‡	136	200	224	237	253	273	303
Alabama	146	211	233	258	275	288	328
Delta							
Mississippi	129	182	204	205	217	249	279
Arkansas	143	186	191	213	238	261	316
Louisiana	139	174	191	201	218	251	286
Southern Plains							
Oklahoma	131	183	212	234	258	284	312
Texas	138	191	193	213	228	252	282
Mountain							
Montana	142	203	237	278	321	355	394
Idaho	141	203	243	264	296	320	349
Wyoming	134	191	218	254	273	285	322
Colorado	128	194	209	244	285	305	369
New Mexico	136	186	197	206	227	236	253
Arizona	159	208	211	217	227	237	254
Utah	173	216	232	261	289	305	326
Nevada	213	299	299	307	307	341	365
Pacific							
Washington	130	160	178	213	249	268	297
Oregon	170	213	228	242	254	277	302
California§	112	122	133	136	137	155	191
48 states§	132	187	213	242	283	308	351

* Includes improvements.
† Includes Maine, New Hampshire, Vermont, Massachusetts, Rhode Island, and Connecticut.
‡ Index based on percentage change in Georgia and Alabama.
§ Revised.

TABLE 2
Farm Real Estate Values: Average Value per Acre, March 1, 1971–1975, February 1, 1976–1979

State	March 1971	March 1972	March 1973	March 1974	March 1975	Feb. 1976	Feb. 1977	Feb. 1978	Feb. 1979
Northeast									
Maine*	$ 187	$ 218	$ 255	$ 306	$ 345	$ 373	$ 400	$ 441	$ 485
New Hampshire*	286	341	407	498	570	617	661	729	802
Vermont*	256	295	341	402	452	489	541	597	657
Massachusetts*	623	693	775	886	976	1,054	1,126	1,242	1,365
Rhode Island*	854	997	1,166	1,392	1,578	1,707	1,758	1,939	2,133
Connecticut*	1,034	1,171	1,332	1,549	1,725	1,866	1,779	1,962	2,158
New York	288	325	359	452	520	560	580	589	642
New Jersey	1,135	1,232	1,352	1,611	1,850	2,051	2,004	2,057	2,222
Pennsylvania	393	422	497	631	747	830	978	1,092	1,245
Delaware	553	564	640	800	956	1,138	1,340	1,500	1,723
Maryland	688	736	851	994	1,078	1,300	1,355	1,578	1,799
Lake States									
Michigan	333	373	450	530	563	615	767	860	955
Wisconsin	255	275	331	394	441	498	583	690	807
Minnesota	231	241	270	341	436	530	652	730	854
Corn Belt									
Ohio	416	439	506	630	711	861	1,121	1,263	1,516
Indiana	423	436	496	596	726	886	1,159	1,303	1,498
Illinois	494	523	570	728	857	1,066	1,431	1,581	1,786
Iowa	392	414	467	600	725	911	1,219	1,268	1,458
Missouri	236	261	294	385	399	449	526	602	674
Northern Plains									
North Dakota	95	99	110	146	196	229	258	273	306
South Dakota	85	87	94	120	146	164	194	227	257
Nebraska	157	170	194	244	285	359	401	385	470
Kansas	162	174	200	256	301	335	376	380	437
Appalachian									
Virginia	309	345	392	502	560	623	676	732	864
West Virginia	151	174	206	266	305	383	394	403	472
North Carolina	372	398	466	560	603	648	675	694	819
Kentucky	268	297	330	391	435	512	595	671	792
Tennessee	277	303	349	421	477	507	545	608	669
Southeast									
South Carolina	277	316	340	425	475	494	529	543	635
Georgia	256	292	333	432	486	488	509	564	609
Florida†	378	404	466	613	692	732	777	838	930
Alabama	227	238	270	337	370	410	432	452	515
Delta									
Mississippi	238	242	271	344	386	388	404	464	520
Arkansas	255	297	339	409	421	470	521	571	691
Louisiana	350	382	406	474	518	545	581	669	763
Southern Plains									
Oklahoma	183	195	221	267	307	339	365	402	442
Texas	156	174	199	248	252	278	286	316	354
Mountain									
Montana	63	68	76	97	114	134	152	168	186
Idaho	188	206	230	289	343	373	412	445	485
Wyoming	42	48	56	72	84	98	101	105	119
Colorado	103	116	139	179	193	225	256	274	332
New Mexico	46	51	59	77	82	86	89	93	100
Arizona	77	89	96	119	120	123	120	125	134
Utah	111	132	146	179	197	222	235	248	265
Nevada	60	69	79	92	92	94	87	97	104
Pacific									
Washington	224	239	276	313	358	428	491	528	586
Oregon	168	189	209	240	258	274	278	303	330
California	471	495	511	581	669	684	673	761	936
48 states	202	218	245	303	343	390	450	490	560

* The average rate of change for the six New England states was used to project dollar values for each of these six states.

† Values are based upon the average percentage change in the Georgia and Alabama index.

FIGURE 2

Percent Change in Average Value of Farm Real Estate Per Acre, March 1972–February 1979

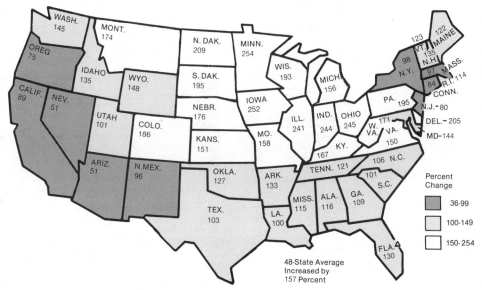

Note: Index numbers of average value per acre are based on estimates provided by USDA crop reporters through the Statistical Reporting Service.
* Average increase for Maine, New Hampshire, Vermont, Massachusetts, Rhode Island, and Connecticut.
△ Average of the percentage change in Georgia and Alabama index values.
Source: U.S. Department of Agriculture.

products. Because farmers increased their efficiency through the use of larger machinery and other technology, they were able to increase their overall returns even though the prices of farm products were not keeping pace with land costs. However, there is a point at which the returns become so marginal that they will not support additional land price increases. Lenders then become concerned about the impact that higher land prices and heavy debt have on a farmer's cash flow. Over any projectable period of time, the ability to of land to generate returns is a major determinant of land values.

2. *The second force is the attitude of the people who buy land.* As long as the farmer wants to expand his operations he will take a bullish approach when land comes up for sale. As long as people believe that inflation will continue they will look to land as a hedge. The investor who looks to land as a secure place for his money, both for returns and for appreciation, will continue to have a strong effect on land that comes up for sale.

The productivity of the U.S. farm operator is strongly recognized by both the Democratic party and the Republican party as a major source of U.S. strength in the world balance of power. The federal government

FIGURE 3
Farm Real Estate Values: Average Value Per Acre, 1940–1979

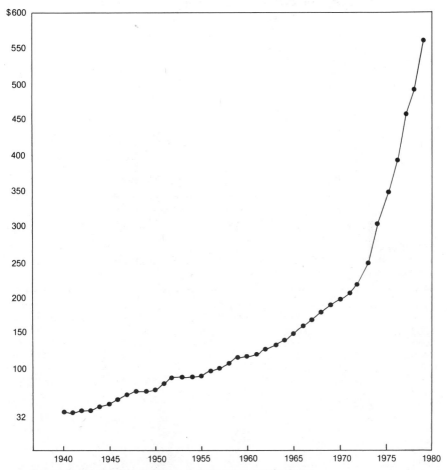

Source: Economic Research Service, U.S. Department of Agriculture.

is strongly committed to maintaining the prices of farm products in order to encourage ample food and fiber supplies. The importance of food in the export market is increasing annually.

The U.S. consumer spends a lower proportion of his money for food than does the consumer in the rest of the world (see Table 3). Higher prices for farm products, which are capitalized into higher land prices, are inevitable and acceptable.

Farmland versus Other Investments. If land proves to be a more reliable and rewarding investment than the traditional common stock market, other capital sources will attempt to find a medium through which to participate in the ownership of farmland (see Table 4).

TABLE 3
Expenditures for Food as a Proportion of
Private Consumer Expenditures

Country	Percent
United States	16.1
United Kingdom	19.3
Denmark	19.6
Australia	20.0
Sweden	22.5
France	25.8
Venezuela	26.0
Germany	27.2
Japan	34.4
Poland	46.7
USSR	52.5
Ghana	62.0

Source: U.S. Department of Agriculture, April 1974.

TABLE 4
Index of Farmland Values versus the Values of Common Stocks (January 1, 1963 = 100)

Year	Farmland Index	Common Stock Index
1963	100	100
1964	106	119
1965	112	134
1966	121	147
1967	130	127
1968	139	153
1969	147	165
1970	152	146
1971	158	146
1972	171	162
1973	195	187
1974	243	155
1975	277	109
1976	314	143
1977	368	170

Source: U.S. Department of Agriculture; and Standard & Poor's listing of 500 common stocks.

The Number, Size, and Ownership of U.S. Farms

The operation and ownership of farms in the United States are widely diversified. Because of this broad spectrum of control, no mass selling or buying of farms occurs in any one year and there are no sudden fluctuations in the market for farmland. The manipulation of the market by individuals or groups is not possible.

Since most farms are owner operated and since farmers tend to increase the size of their operations for greater efficiency of scale, the demand for farmland is constantly increasing, whereas the available supply of farmland is decreasing slightly. Thus, in 1940, excluding Hawaii and Alaska, there were 6,096,000 U.S. farms, containing 1,061 million acres, or an average of 174 acres per farm. By 1970, there were 2,726,000 farms containing about 1,060 million acres, or an average of 389 acres per farm. And in 1974 there were 2,450,000 farms, containing about 1,000 million acres, or an average of 408 acres per farm.

Looking further at the 1974 figures, we see that if small farms (under $2,500 annual gross sales) are excluded, there were only 1,680,689 farms. Their operators were classified as follows:

Full owner-operators	900,729
Own part–rent part	558,170
All tenant	221,790
Total	1,680,689

The ownership of farmland is centered in individuals, most of whom are owner-operators (see Tables 5 and 6).

Traditionally, there has been little interchange among the U.S. regions with regard to land prices. No central "exchange" monitors comparative land prices versus land values across the country. It is possible,

TABLE 5
Ownership of Farms (over $2,500 in annual sales)

Type of Owner	Number of Farms
Individuals or families	1,506,966
Partnerships	141,811
Corporate (including family)	28,090
Other	3,822
Total	1,680,069

Source: 1974 U.S. Census of Agriculture.

TABLE 6
Types of Farm Buyers for the Year Ended March 1976

Type	Percent
Individuals	86
Partnerships	8
Private closely held corporations	4
Public corporations	1
Other	1
	100

however, to chart land values accurately on a relative scale, and thus to gauge where land is relatively underpriced and to predict where land prices will increase most rapidly. Value judgments can be made based on the relative productive capacities and opportunities of various areas.

Finally, based on comparative productive capacity agricultural land prices in the United States are low as compared to land prices in other parts of the world. Moreover, improvements continue to be made in U.S. agricultural production technology, and these improvements are, in turn, capitalized into higher land values.

GUIDES TO THE SELECTION OF A FARM FOR BUSINESS AND PLEASURE

Understanding Land Descriptions

To properly locate and identify a farm, you must be able to understand the legal description. Such a description is based on a survey of the land. Different types of land surveys are used in various parts of the country.

The 13 original colonies followed the "metes and bounds" method. The surveyor began at some point in the boundary of the tract to be described and then listed distances and directions from point to point around the boundary. Disputes were not uncommon, because the monuments may have been stumps, rocks, or other items that disappeared over the years. This system is still used to describe irregularly shaped parcels, but recent surveys use concrete markers, steel pipes, or other types of more permanent monuments.

An example of an old metes and bounds description might be:

> the point of beginning is a large oak stump situated in the west sideline of John Appleseed's land and on the south side of the Julesberg Road; from the point of beginning running thence north, five degrees east, nineteen chains and thirty-two links to a large triangular-shaped rock; thence running east two degrees, three minutes south a distance of fifty chains and twelve links to a hickory stump . . .

and so on, until you are returned to the point of beginning.

The obvious weaknesses of this system led the federal government to adopt the "rectangular survey" system in 1785. This system applies uniformly to 30 states, but only partially in some of the states other than the 13 colonies. The merit of this system is that it is simple and accurate and that it permits land to be described in concise symbols and words, resulting in a kind of land description shorthand.

Under this system a north-south line, called a meridian, and a baseline running east and west were established through the area to be surveyed. Further subdivision of these areas resulted in squares, called townships, which are six miles on each side. Each township is divided into 36 squares. Each of these squares, termed a section, is a mile on each side and contains 640 acres more or less. The sections are further divided into quarters, each being 160 acres in size, and these quarters are further quartered until the description of a particular piece of ground can be reduced to its exact size and location. (Figure 4 shows a township plat and a map of the areas and distances of a section of land.)

A typical description using this system might be: "the Northeast Quarter NE 1/4) of the Northeast Quarter (NE 1/4) of Section Nine (9), Township 12 North, Range 5 West, of the fifth Principal Meridian in Blank County, containing 40 acres, more or less."

Finding What is Available

Assuming that the prospective land buyer has determined the general area in which he wishes to locate, he can find properties for sale in many ways, but there are shortcuts that he can take. Certainly the fastest way to get started is to go to a real estate broker who specializes in farms and acreage.

FIGURE 4

Land Description and Survey (map of a section of land showing area and distances; a section of land contains 1 square mile or 640 acres)

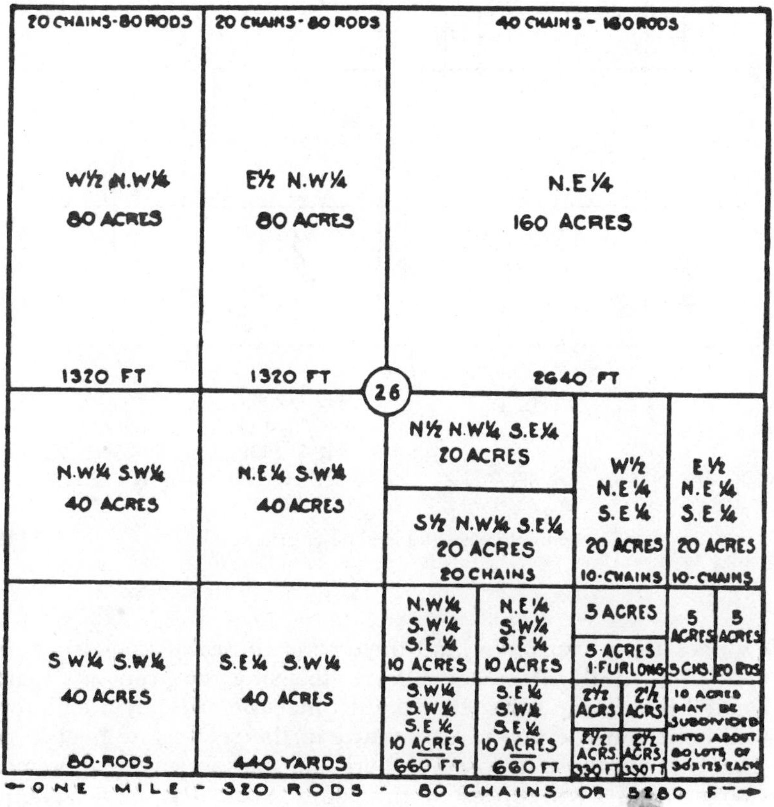

FIGURE 4 *(continued)*

N. W. 1/4 SEC. 18
100 ACRES

N. 1/2 SEC. 15
220 ACRES

6	5	4	3	2	1
7	8	9	10	11	12
18	17	16	15	14	13
19	20	21	22	23	24
30	29	28	27	26	25
31	32	33	34	35	36

W. 1/2 OF S. E. 1/4 SEC. 19
40 ACRES

N.E. 1/4 OF S.W. 1/4 SEC. 21
40 ACRES

N. 1/2 SEC. 23
S.W. 1/4 SEC. 23
N. 1/2 OF N.W. 1/4 SEC. 26
S.E. 1/4 OF N.W. 1/4 SEC. 26
600 ACRES

Township plat showing lead descriptions.

How does the prospective land buyer find the most knowledgeable broker? Although all of the states have licensing requirements which real estate brokers and salespersons must meet before they are allowed to act in behalf of the public, the nature of the real estate business is such that some of these licensed brokers and salespersons will be more knowledgeable and will represent him better. Normally, the most active brokers in an area are members of the National Association of Realtors®

and of their state and local boards of Realtors®. Within these organizations, the brokers who specialize in land are frequently members of the Farm and Land Institute, a branch of the National Association of Realtors®. If these brokers have undergone extensive study and testing, they may hold the designation of Accredited Farm and Land Member (AFLM). If a person is not satisfied with the service he obtains from one broker, there is nothing to prevent him from going to other brokers. However, a buyer is usually better off if he is represented by a single qualified broker that he has confidence in, and a broker should also feel that he has the loyalty of his client. A qualified broker should be able to tell his client which properties are available and to provide the client with complete and reliable information on each property. Much of the background information that the buyer needs concerning the crops, yields, and operating techniques of an area should be available through the broker.

Many state chapters of the Farm and Land Institute publish lists of land properties that are available across the state. Many brokers and owners advertise properties in newspapers. A buyer who is making a serious search for a property will check such advertisements regularly. Bankers and other prominent persons in a rural community will frequently be aware of properties for sale.

Tools to Help the Land Buyer

Soil Maps. The Soil Conservation Service (SCS) of the U.S. Department of Agriculture maintains offices in many U.S. counties, usually at the county seat. The technicians at such an office have frequently mapped much or all of the soil in the given county by type and capabilities. Frequently, a publication is available which includes a map of all the soils in the county. A wealth of other information is normally included, such as information on appropriate uses and production data. The SCS office may also prepare an individual land-capability map for a farmer who asks it for help. The map is superimposed on an aerial photograph. The soil types, slope, extent of erosion, and other land characteristics are identified. The SCS will prepare a conservation and production plan that considers alternative uses and treatments of land. It will make recommendations to the landowner, and financial assistance may be available for cost-sharing under conservation programs.

Aerial Photographs. Aerial photographs have been made of nearly every property in the United States. Copies of such photographs may be viewed at the county offices of the Agricultural Stabilization and Conservation Service (ASCS), which, like the SCS, is a part of the U.S. Department of Agriculture. The ASCS office may be located near that of the Soil Conservation Service. The office has forms for ordering enlarged individual copies of aerial photographs from the federal government, and photographs on a smaller scale are usually available at the office. The ASCS office is also able to furnish information on such matters as the crop allotments and the number of cultivated acres of each property.

For certain portions of the country, especially urban areas, private sources of aerial photographs are also available.

Topographic Maps.   The U.S. Geological Survey has prepared topographical maps of every part of the country. These maps describe properties by section, township, and range and also include descriptions of many physical features, such as wells, streams, schools, lakes, and roads. Elevations are shown by contour line, which illustrate the relative slope of the property.

The Federal Extension Service.   In cooperation with the state governments, this agency of the U.S. Department of Agriculture has established educational programs in most counties. These programs are centered in a local Agricultural Extension Service. The programs are organized and operated by the land-grant colleges in cooperation with the local county government and the Federal Extension Service. The county agricultural agent is the local representative of the Federal Extension Service. His office, usually at the county seat, is a source of information on many types of land and production problems.

County Highway Maps.   Highway and transportation maps are available either through the county courthouse or the state highway department. Such maps identify the sections, townships, and ranges or survey numbers of all property in a county. In addition, the maps include demographic information and information on streams, rivers, school sites, and towns. The maps are extremely helpful for locating properties and for charting comparable data on recently sold properties.

Other Maps and Plat Books.   Several other sources will assist the buyer in locating individual properties and in identifying the ownership of certain properties. County assessors may maintain individual plats of every parcel of land, identified by the owner and his address. Private mapping companies frequently prepare county plat Books that identify the owner and the size of individual farms and acreages.

Other Tools and Checklists.   An experienced land buyer will use checklists to make certain that he does not overlook key information when he is inspecting a property. In inspecting acreages, the following checklist might be used:

Size	Zoning	Topography	Price
Location	Sewer	Cover	Terms
County	Water	Taxes	Mortgage
City	Access	Status	Other

In inspecting farms or ranches, additional data are needed:

Tillable acres (by class)	Mineral rights
Irrigation acres	Merchantable timber
Pasture acres	Crop allotments
Wooded acres	Drainage
Carrying capacity (ranch)	Soil types
Buildings	Possession date
Other improvements	Crop leases
Fences	Wells

Analyzing a Specific Property

The gathering of information is probably the most important aspect of this analytic process.

The prospective buyer or his broker should make an exhaustive personal inspection of the property in company with the owner or his agent. He should ask every question having any bearing on the property, and make notes of the data he obtains.

He must obtain information on the availability of water, road access, mineral rights, crop yields, taxes, easements, improvements, and any other matters that affect the value of the property. He should take pictures of the improvements and other features of the property. He should inspect the buildings inside and out and make notations as to their size, condition, and uses. His inspection should be made with the use of an aerial photograph or at least a boundary map of the property, so that he can note important features. (Aerial photographs frequently spot erosion problems, and a trained eye can tell almost as much about a property from an aerial photograph as from a walk over the property.)

Once the collection of information is complete, the analytic process begins. The property should be dissected. The total acreage should be allocated into uses. These uses may include the best tillable land, the marginal tillable land, the pastureland, the wasteland, and the land occupied by improvements and roads. This allocation of assets will permit of comparison with like properties that have been sold. Unless the prospective buyer knows precisely what he is considering and how it compares with similar properties which have sold, no conclusion of value is possible for him.

Information that falls within the realm of government regulations should be analyzed independently from other sources. Information on the zoning of a property or its land use classification should be obtained from county or city offices. Information on the availability of water or sewerage, and its distance from the property must be verified. Information on taxes and special assessments can be confirmed at the assessor's office.

By the time this detailed collection of information and analysis is complete, the prospective buyer should have a good working knowledge of the property under consideration and of its value.

Financing the Purchase

As with other types of real estate, successful financing is frequently the most important factor in the purchase of farms and acreage. Over 80 percent of all farms sold are sold to people who have to borrow money in order to buy them.

Even if borrowing were not necessary, as long as farm values are appreciating at a rate greater than the net cost of interest to the borrower, the sensible approach for the buyer is to use as much leverage as is prudently possible. For example, for a buyer who is in the 50 percent tax bracket and can borrow 80 percent of the purchase price at 8 percent interest, the net aftertax cost of interest would be 4 percent. In that case, the required appreciated rate is substantially less than 8 percent.

The financing for a land purchase would normally be sought from one of the following sources:

1. Sellers.
2. The Federal Land Bank.
3. Insurance companies.
4. The Farmers Home Administration.
5. The Small Business Administration.
6. Commercial banks.

For the years 1970–76 the percentage of credit volume extended by type of lender was:

Sellers	48%
Federal Land Bank	25
Insurance companies	8
Commercial banks	10
Others	9
Total	100%

Sellers. By far the largest single segment of financing for land is the seller. Seller financing of land is popular among sellers for several reasons:

1. Frequently the seller of a property is a farm operator who is nearing retirement. The chances are that he has owned the land for some years. Consequently, the sale price is much higher than the price he paid for it. If he does not require the full proceeds of the sale immediately and is able to sell the land on an installment basis, the capital gains tax should be much lower over the payment period because his annual income in retirement will frequently be low. For a sale to qualify as an installment sale, the seller must receive not more than 30 percent of the purchase price in the year of sale. The less the seller takes in the first year, the better his tax position will be. The longer the period in which he receives the balance of the purchase price, the more dollars he will net after taxes.

2. The seller may be willing to accept a reasonably low down payment because, having operated the land for a number of years, he has high confidence in the land as security for the note. He may also have limited alternative possibilities for earning money on the full proceeds. If he is thinking of investing the proceeds in nothing more sophisticated than his local sávings and loan association, then the interest rate that he will receive from the purchaser will no doubt be higher.

3. Doing his own financing may give the seller more flexibility in negotiating a sale. In this way, he may be able to obtain a higher price for the property by attracting more people who are able to purchase it.

The disadvantages of seller financing to the seller include the following:

1. Since the purchaser is investing less equity, if land prices fall, the buyer may forfeit the land and the seller will have it back when it is worth

less. At the same time, the interest and principal payments which he may have been depending upon for his retirement income would also cease.

2. If the seller should need emergency funds, he may find it difficult to sell his interest in the installment contract or mortgage.

The advantages of seller financing to the buyer are as follows:

1. If the seller is willing to accept 30 percent or less as a down payment, this will give the buyer a greater loan than he would be able to get from any other source.
2. The seller may be willing to accept a lower interest rate and easier payment terms than would other financing sources.
3. The buyer may be able to effect tax savings through the trade-off between interest and principal payments. Since the buyer and the seller may be in substantially different income brackets, a deal that is favorable to both can frequently be worked out.

The buyer who is utilizing seller financing should be aware that in many states, the typical financing instrument for land is not a note and mortgage. Certain states utilize a deed of trust. However, the majority of agricultural states use an instrument called a "contract for deed" (also known as a "land contract").

The installment land contract is basically a conditional sale of real property in which the buyer makes principal and interest payments to the seller over an extended period of time, but the seller retains title to the property until all of the specified payments have been made. Moreover, even though the buyer takes possession and becomes the "beneficial owner," he is charged with exacting requirements as to interest and principal payments, tax payments, and other matters specified by the contract.

Should the buyer fail to substantially comply with the terms of the contract, he will be in default. When the buyer is in default, the forfeiture provision of the contract will allow the seller to declare the contract null and void, thus extinguishing the buyer's interest in the property. This is referred to as a nonjudicial foreclosure. It allows the seller to keep all of the payments he has received and to repossess the property, including any permanent improvements that have been made by the buyer.

The Federal Land Bank. The Federal Land Bank is part of the Cooperative Farm Credit System. Although it is not a government organization, it is supervised by the Farm Credit Administration, an independent federal agency. A borrower must make his initial contact with the Federal Land Bank through the local Federal Land Bank Association serving the given area. One office may serve several rural counties.

The maximum Federal Land Bank loan is 85 percent of the appraised value of the security. However, Federal Land Bank appraisals tend to be conservative as compared to the sale price. Loans for up to 40 years are available, and farmers or farm-related entities are favored applicants.

Insurance Companies. Insurance companies were formerly a major force in the farm-lending field, providing about 25 percent of the money loaned to buy farms. This proportion has been reduced by about one half. During the tight money periods of the 1960s and 1970s, many insurance companies stopped lending on farms. Those that are still active have full-time salaried staff representatives who can make decisions quickly. Insurance companies prefer low-risk, high-quality farmland areas, so that these companies may be willing to make loans in some areas but not in others.

The Farmers Home Administration. The Farmers Home Administration is a government lending agency whose funds are supplied by private sources. The agency has great flexibility in the amount and terms of its farm loans, but it limits these loans to persons who will own, manage, and operate the land they buy. FmHA also provides rural housing loans.

The Small Business Administration. The SBA is a minor force in farm lending, but it should be considered by borrowers who cannot get commercial credit.

Users of farm financing must compete with nonfarm borrowers for SBA funds. Inquiries regarding a SBA loan should be directed to the SBA office nearest to the property in question.

Commercial Banks. Commercial banks prefer to make farm loans to customers with whom they are familiar. Since serving client needs is a major consideration, banks normally tailor their loans to individual situations. Their loans to persons other than close customers are normally short term and at a low percentage of value.

EXPECTED RETURNS FROM LAND INVESTMENT

From Increase in Value

Average farm real estate values in 48 states increased 85 percent in the five years from March 1974 to February 1979, or 17 percent per year (see Figure 2). Although this rate is not expected to continue, it is reasonable to expect an average annual increase of 8 percent per year over a long period of time.

The ideal land investor does not depend on income from his land for his livelihood and can subsidize the amortization of debt with income from other sources. For such an investor, appreciation is more important than his annual return, because the rates at which his annual returns are taxed are higher than the capital gains rates he will pay on his equity buildup from appreciation when he sells. However, not everyone is as fortunate as such an investor. The person who needs the income from his farm property needs to analyze his cash flow position very carefully, particularly if he is financing 50 percent or more of the land. He cannot use appreciation in value to make his principal and interest payments.

Projecting Income and Expenses

Historically, the operating profit on land has been fairly low, averaging 4 or 5 percent when all costs are figured in. But each parcel of land is different from all other parcels, and levels of management, weather, yields, and prices are all so variable that it is not possible to use averages or even past experience with a specific farm to accurately project any one year's annual income. It is possible, however, to project a range of possible incomes.

Although cash rents normally provide a lower return, they provide a more certain return, since they are not subject to the vagaries of prices and yields. The ratios of cash rent to value in the primary crop-producing states ranged from 5.1 percent to 7.7 percent in the years 1973–76. Crop-share lease arrangements should yield returns that are 1–2 percent higher than those of cash rents (see Table 7).

Table 8 projects the returns from a hypothetical 200-acre parcel under a 50–50 crop-share lease. Assume that 160 acres of the parcel are tillable and that the remaining 40 acres of pastureland and buildings can be rented for cash.

If the hypothetical property is priced at $1,500 per acre, or $300,000, the net return is 4.84 percent of the purchase price. More important is the cash flow. Assume that the farm can be bought with seller financing for a down payment of 25 percent, or $75,000, with interest due annually on the balance at the rate of 6 percent. Assume further that the principal is payable at $10,000 per year for ten years, with a balloon payment due for the balance in the 11th year. The annual interest on $225,000 at 6 percent is $13,500. This cost essentially absorbs the net income, leaving an out-of-pocket cost of $10,000 per year for the principal. Since the interest cost and the depreciation on the buildings will offset all income, there are minimal tax consequences.

Projecting Net Returns

If the property appreciates in value for ten years at the same average rate as from 1974–1979, or 17% per year, the investment will look like this:

Value in ten years		$810,000
Debt at end of ten years		
Initial	$225,000	
Less payments	100,000	
Equity		125,000
		$685,000

Obviously, if there is less appreciation, there will be less improvement in the capital position.

OPERATING A FARM OR ACREAGE INVESTMENT

Some people own land for speculation; other landowners are serious farm or ranch operators intent on making a profit; still others are waiting until development comes closer; and some people own land purely for the sake of ownership. Depending on the goals of the owner, a basic

TABLE 7
Cropland Rented for Cash: Gross Cash Rent per Acre and Rent-to-Value Ratio, Selected States, March 1, 1973–1976*

State	Rent per Acre (dollars)				Rent-to-Value Ratio (percent)			
	1973	1974	1975	1976	1973	1974	1975	1976
Northeast								
Pennsylvania	17.50	19.20	21.80	23.50	3.3	2.9	2.6	2.7
Maryland†	17.60	20.00	21.90	23.90	2.1	2.2	2.3	2.1
Lake States								
Michigan	22.10	24.10	25.50	28.80	5.4	5.3	4.9	5.0
Wisconsin	24.10	28.10	32.50	37.10	7.1	7.0	7.3	7.0
Minnesota	22.30	30.20	38.30	45.20	7.2	7.3	7.4	7.0
Corn Belt								
Ohio	29.20	33.90	40.40	47.80	5.7	5.2	5.5	5.1
Indiana	37.80	47.90	63.00	71.70	6.9	7.1	7.6	6.7
Illinois	41.60	52.60	63.00	75.20	6.4	6.0	6.1	5.7
Iowa	43.70	57.00	69.50	77.70	7.6	7.4	7.4	6.3
Missouri	27.10	33.80	35.40	38.20	7.4	7.5	7.1	6.7
Northern Plains								
North Dakota	11.50	17.40	20.30	25.00	8.6	8.9	8.1	7.7
South Dakota	12.00	15.00	17.50	20.00	8.2	7.9	7.6	7.1
Nebraska (nonirrigated)	21.60	25.70	28.00	33.70	7.7	7.3	7.0	6.5
Kansas	16.70	21.60	25.10	26.80‡	7.2	7.0	6.6	6.6

Appalachian								
Virginia	20.20	23.20	26.20	31.20	4.8	4.1	4.1	4.1
North Carolina	23.40	26.00	26.40	26.80	4.8	4.8	4.2	3.9
Kentucky§	29.40	34.80	37.50	40.00	7.4	7.8	7.2	6.7
Tennessee	26.70	33.40	35.30	37.10	6.6	7.0	6.7	6.4
Southeast								
South Carolina	15.40	16.20	17.40	19.50	4.9	4.3	3.8	3.8
Georgia	20.90	23.30	26.50	27.20	5.2	4.8	4.9	4.7
Alabama	18.80	20.40	21.60	23.30	6.3	5.7	5.9	5.6
Delta								
Mississippi	24.40	27.10	28.80	30.40	7.4	6.9	6.8	6.8
Arkansas	24.60	28.20	30.10	32.30	6.9	6.6	6.7	6.6
Southern Plains								
Oklahoma	15.10	18.80	20.60	22.50	5.1	5.0	4.9	4.8

* Based on data obtained from crop reporters, Statistical Reporting Service, U.S. Department of Agriculture. The selection of states is based upon the adequacy of the data.
† The figures omit Crop District No. 1.
‡ The weighted average of irrigated land and dry cropland rents.
§ The figures omit Crop District No. 4.

TABLE 8

Income						
Crop	Acres	Yield	Total Bushels	Price	Total Value	Owner's Share
Corn	80	120	9,600	$2.50	$24,000	$12,000
Soybeans	80	40	3,200	5.00	16,000	8,000
Annual cash rent on pastureland and buildings						2,000
Owner's total income						$22,000
Less owner's share of expenses						
Taxes			$2,000			
Insurance			250			
Building maintenance			800			
Other maintenance			200			
Seed			640			
Chemicals			640			
Fertilizer			1,200			
Harvesting			400			
Drying			250			
Management			1,100			
Owner's total expense						7,480
Owner's net income						$14,520

land management plan must be established. Within the limitations imposed by the owner, the appropriate objective may be to maximize profit or to deduct losses against current income so as to achieve greater values later.

Typical Operating Methods

A number of options are available to the landowner. Which option he chooses will frequently be based upon his capability and upon how active he intends to be. The most common operating methods are described here.

The Cash Rent Basis. This is the most management-free arrangement, but it often returns the lowest net income. Since the tenant has to pay a stipulated amount of cash, regardless of how much the property produces, he will be conservative in the amount of expense incurred as rent.

Under a cash rent agreement, the landlord rents land and improvements to a tenant for a specified annual rental. The tenant assumes all the expenses of operation except taxes. Frequently he is responsible for the maintenance of fences and other improvements. The owner may wish to impose limitations on the use of the property in order to conserve its value. For example, he may limit the number of livestock or the kinds of crops that are planted.

The Crop-Share Lease. Under this arrangement the landlord receives an agreed share of the crops as his rental. The landlord shares in the cost of such crop expenses as seed, fertilizer, chemical treatments, and harvesting. In prime land areas, the owner may receive as much as half of the crop income and will typically pay half of the production expenses and all of the taxes. In less desirable areas, the landlord may receive one third or two fifths of the crop income. Where buildings or pastureland are on the property, the tenant may pay a cash rent for the use of these facilities or other arrangements may be made. Under the crop-share lease, relatively little management is required of the owner, and the income he receives from his portion of the crops would normally be higher than the income he would receive on a cash rent basis. Obviously, the qualifications of the tenant play a major part in the returns to the owner.

The Livestock-Share Lease. This variation of the crop-share lease is used where livestock is important in the farm operation. Under the terms of this lease the tenant normally furnishes labor, machinery, and a share of the feed and livestock expense. The landlord furnishes the land, buildings, and his share of the feed and livestock expense. Typical Midwestern livestock-share leases are 50–50 arrangements. There is a greater risk to the landlord under this operation than with a crop-share lease, but the returns are normally higher.

Direct Operation. Here the owner assumes total management responsibility. In addition, he provides the land, machinery, seed, fertilizer, livestock, feed, and operating capital. Labor is hired on a monthly or annual basis, and it does not normally share in the returns from the operation. Because skilled management and labor are often difficult to find, only unusual operations, generally large crop farms, lend themselves to direct operation. Large corporations have attempted to utilize this method with extremely varied results.

Custom Farming. This is a derivative of direct operation. It differs from direct operation in that an independent contractor who furnishes his own machinery is hired to handle all of the farming operations. The contractor is paid, normally on a per acre basis, for plowing, planting, harvesting, and so on.

The landlord assumes all of the risk and receives the entire crop. The risk is high, but often the reward is a higher return than where the income and expenses are shared. Owner-employed management is required, and this lease method is normally used only in cases where the property is 100 percent tillable.

Pitfalls to Avoid

If the landowner is going to provide relatively limited management input and is not very knowledgeable about farm operations, he should select and operate property in such a manner as to ensure the lowest risk possible. This means that he should probably purchase land that is capable of being operated under the traditional cash rent or crop-share basis, thus eliminating the need to purchase machinery and equipment or to hire expensive labor which he could not properly supervise.

He should avoid labor-intensive and speciality operations, such as vegetable farms, livestock breeding, dairy farms, and feedlots. The risk and management requirements of such operations are beyond the capability of most nonresident owners.

Obtaining Professional Farm Management

If the owner lacks the ability or the time to manage a farm property, he should consider employing a professional farm management firm. In almost all parts of the country, numerous private companies are available for full or partial management. Such dramatic advances have been made in farm technology and farming methods, that persons who have been trained specifically for the farm management function are often required. Prominent professional farm managers will usually be members of the American Society of Farm Managers and Rural Appraisers. This is an association whose members specialize in farm management and rural appraising. It offers courses and an accreditation program. It will provide owners with a list of farm managers who are available for service in different parts of the country. Its address is 470 South Colorado Boulevard, Suite 8, Denver, Colorado 80222.

A professional farm manager will supervise all of the details of a farm operation, including the following:

1. Preparing immediate and long-range operating plans to develop an economical farming operation on a property, in light of the property's resources, improvements, and crop and livestock potentials and in light of the owner's objectives and capital.   .
2. Leasing farms—selecting tenants and working out leasing arrangements.
3. Supervising the farm operation by consulting with the tenant or the resident manager at frequent intervals.
4. Selling livestock and crops at the most advantageous times.
5. Keeping clients informed about activities at their farms through formal quarterly reports, monthly financial statements, correspondence, and personal visits.
6. Participating in government farm programs when this is practical and economical.

LAND INVESTMENT

Alan J. Inbinder

Roy D. Gottlieb

A*LAN J. INBINDER, AFLM, Partner, Kenroy Associates, Skokie, Illinois.*

Land developer and broker responsible for acquisition, development, and sale of vacant land for residential uses. Past president, State of Illinois chapter 11, Farm and Land Institute. Past president, Chicago Real Estate Board Salesmen Club. Recipient, Chicago Real Estate Board Salesman of the Year Award.

ROY D. GOTTLIEB, Chairman, President, and Chief Operating Officer, Kenroy Inc., Skokie, Illinois.

Realtor®, developer, and real estate consultant specializing in land development, office buildings and subsidized housing. Lecturer on land development and land economics.

This chapter will not give you any pat answers as to how to go about buying, selling, or developing land. Instead, it will indicate what questions you must pose to yourself or your consultants before you invest in or sell land. The underlying theme of the chapter is that a profit is made on land investment when you purchase the property, not when you sell it. You only realize the profit when you sell it.

The chapter will also demonstrate that land investment is a complex and risky procedure in which both professionals and neophytes can make or lose large amounts of money, and that leveraging makes the risks even greater. The chapter will try to convince you that you must employ the best available talent or develop your own expertise through education or partnership association before you make a decision about investment in land. You must be aware of the risk/reward ratios, or you must find some company in which you have full faith and invest with it. In order to gain that faith, however, you should investigate the company's performance and its ability to correctly analyze and apply changing circumstances to property values.

Professional Input Necessary for Prudent Land Investment

Appraisals are not confined to real estate—they enter into all kinds of human activities. Whenever you buy something you make a value judgment—an appraisal—that takes into consideration your needs, your desires, your ability to pay, and your alternative uses for the funds. Appraisals also enter into your social relations—how and with whom you will spend your time are governed by value judgments. Throughout your life, consciously or unconsciously, you have been appraising alternative uses for your time, alternative interests, alternative short-term and long-range goals.

Appraisals of real estate do not require mysterious capacities but skills very similar to those you have employed in making your own appraisals. It takes a lot of time to properly put together the necessary data, and it takes logical thinking to come to a rational conclusion. It is only natural that those people whose business is real estate appraising and who spend most of their time in this endeavor should do it better than the average person. As a prospective purchaser or seller of real property, you should be able to set realistic guidelines for analyzing a prospective investment or for directing a professional appraiser or real estate consultant to evaluate your alternatives.

You should expect the appraiser to give you sufficient data to enable you, as a logical, thinking person, to follow the analysis of the appraiser and to review his procedures so as to come to the same conclusion that he did. You should insist that the appraiser, either orally or in writing, provide data on properties which have a reasonable degree of comparability with the subject property and not merely numbers from sales that are inserted without confirmation in order to support his predetermined conclusion. The appraiser should state in what respects the properties from which a conclusion is reached are comparable to the subject property and in what respects they are not comparable. He should briefly explain how he derived the indicated value of the subject property from the values of the comparable properties. The appraisal data should include a location map relating the comparable properties to the subject property and a brief description of each comparable property, together with its date of sale, its price, its zoning and utility characteristics, and if possible, the length of time that the property was on the market and the difference between the asking price and the selling price.

The appraiser must make one evaluation based on the zoning which now exists and other evaluations based on the zoning alternatives that might be accomplished. Within each zoning category other than the single-family category (and to a certain extent even within the single-family category), there are several uses to which property can be put. The as-zoned value is generally the least that you can expect for the property (except, as well be discussed below, if there is a change in administration or in the availability of utilities). The alternative use values must consider the length of time it will take to accomplish the zoning, the cost of the zoning (and of possible litigation proceedings), and the timing and the terms of sale if the zoning is accomplished.

The real estate market moves in a wavelike ebb and flow, with troughs and crests, swings from high demand to oversupply to reduced demand to scarcity to high demand. In 1974–75 buying land for speculation was perhaps the worst real estate investment you could make in the Chicago metropolitan area—unless, of course, you had the foresight and the holding power to predict and wait out the boom conditions that prevailed from 1976 through 1978. In that case, land was perhaps the best investment you could have made in real estate in 1974–75, but only if you had picked the properties which were later in demand, such as land zoned and with utilities for single-family detached housing, for three-story walk-up apartments in six-unit buildings, or for commercial property in prime locations. Suburban land for condominium high rises was a slow market commodity in 1974–75 and remained a slow market commodity through 1978, as did large tracts of industrial land for speculation.

It is difficult to predict how long high demand will continue for any one potential use of vacant land. The trend we have seen over the past 20 years, however, indicates that except during war or a deep recession, the demand starts with land for single-family houses and continues until such houses are priced at a level that is no longer affordable for the mass market. The exact price level will vary in different regions of the country and in different areas within a region, and it will certainly vary with inflation and with the average level of family income in each community. Rather than try to predict a price, you can follow the trend of house sales. In the Chicago area, for example, Bell Savings lists the number of new building permits issued for each community. Statistics can be obtained on the number of lines of house advertising.

If the seasonal sales level in a strong market is dropping for single-family houses, and that seems to be the trend, you can anticipate that the next phase of the housing market will swing more actively into attached housing, which can take the form of town houses, duplexes, and low-rise condos. These types of units reflect an attempt by the buying public to seek alternatives to a single-family home on its own individual lot because they can afford these alternatives and they cannot afford the freestanding single-family home. If the shift in demand from single-family homes to units in multifamily buildings drives the prices of the latter up, the demand for rental housing as an alternative to ownership will increase. If the land in certain suburban areas is too scarce to meet the demand for single-family housing, the demand for elevator, fire-resistant (and therefore higher priced) condominium and apartment housing will increase in those areas and demand will also leap to suburban areas that are farther out, because some people will be willing to trade off the additional driving time for the saving in money. This is not a long-lived phase in a housing cycle except in the areas of a community which are in greatest demand (these are generally areas with semi luxury-level and luxury-level housing).

The selection of land for commercial use requires analysis of the demography of an area, including its rate of population growth. Generally convenience centers of up to 80,000–100,000 square feet are built in response to a demonstrated need in the community, and which location is chosen usually depends on which developer can recognize the need first and convince the anchor tenant, generally a food/drug chain, to rent in his center. As shopping centers get larger, the preplanning period gets longer and greater dependence in placed on ease of access and prominence of location for present and anticipated future needs. Land for a major shopping center should not be acquired unless the investors have a clear working arrangement with the major anchor tenants that they will need to ensure their ability to get financing and the other tenants they will need in order to make the center a success. The acquisition of land for shopping centers should be an outgrowth of a business in commercial real estate development, not a speculation in land.

Speculative office buildings in the suburban areas move with the population trends as demonstrated by housing demand, the development of shopping centers, and ease of access on major highways. The same can be said to a certain extent of the demand for industrial land. Obviously, the development of both types of property is also conditioned by supply and demand. A major determinant of office and industrial relocation is generally the ease of reaching the new location from the homes of the key executives of the company that will be occupying the space. It is generally best to begin with expertise in developing commercial and industrial properties and then to acquire land that suits the conditions of a particular program rather than to begin by acquiring land and then trying to find a commercial or industrial use for it.

In order to properly plan land investment, you must anticipate end use. It is often said that if a certain property were worth buying, somebody would have bought it already. But you might see something in the property or in the area that the people who came before you did not see, or you may just happen to come along as someone else is getting ready to sell. Keep in mind that nobody sells property for less than he thinks it is worth. If you maintain a property in its present use you are rarely going to buy a bargain. What is going to make the difference between profit and loss is your ability to correctly assess what change might be made in the use of that property, and whether that change can, in fact, be effected, and how soon this can be done.

You must be aware that in most markets you are competing with people who spend most of their business time seeking out exactly the same thing you are looking for, namely a sound land investment that will make a lot of money in a short time with little risk. There are not very many such investments, however, and so it is nearly always a question of who will compromise what in order to make a purchase. When you are seeking property of a particular kind you should review all of the property within the market area of your property, not only to determine whether the price and terms you have been offered are reasonable (because the asking prices of every property in an area could be uneconomical), but also to determine the potential competition for as yet undeveloped sites.

It is obvious that anyone acquiring land must look both at the property itself and at what surrounds it (and at what in turn surrounds that). The influence of the surroundings are directly related to their nearness to your subject site. You should observe and anticipate what existing and potential developments on nearby property will have on the development of alternative uses for your property.

You must know values and make specific analyses of a property in order to determine its potential uses. Surveying and engineering are necessary to determine the size, topography, and soil-bearing capacity of a property as well as the availability and the likelihood of the continuing availability of all the necessary utilities. Planning consideration helps you determine what you physically can put on the property irrespective of zoning. Zoning may set limit to what you can do, but the physical constraints of a property generally limit its usability further. Community services are generally available to help you decide what to do with a property, but such services are more readily understandable to professional engineers and planners than they will be to you. Moreover, engineers and planners typically have closer rapport with community officials than do land investors, and will usually be able to get more detailed information than might be made accessible to you and to get that information with less difficulty than you might experience.

The real estate tax impact on various land is becoming a more prominent issue each year. Investment in land requires carrying costs. In addition to paying interest on borrowed capital, you have the indefinite costs of widely varying tax assessments. In the Chicago metropolitan area it is not uncommon to experience increases of 400–500 percent in a tax bill on a property that is unbuildable because it lacks utilities or zoning. Generally, only limited success can be achieved in reducing these taxes.

Unless you are ready to build on vacant land at the time you acquire it, there will undoubtedly be a change in community administration or state or county jurisdiction levels between the time that you acquire the land and the time that you can market or develop it. The likelihood is that from your point of view the attitude of the governing authorities toward land development, will change for the worse. In smaller communities, for example, many homeowners want to place more restrictions on future builders than were placed on the builders of their homes. It is therefore necessary for the prospective land investor to become strongly aware of the needs and demands of village or city officials, school boards, park districts, library districts, fire protection districts, forest preserve districts, or any other potential condemning authorities. Because many community officials are influenced by petitions and potential threats to their incumbency, you must analyze the attitude of homeowner groups toward your development plan in order to determine how easily and how soon you will be able to put the vacant land you contemplate purchasing into a marketable position for development or resale. Since it is not always possible to assess the attitudes of municipalities or homeowners before property is acquired, you should try to acquire land on a contingent basis which will enable you to work out zoning and utility problems and to determine the community's attitude to your development. If your investment and development goals are sound, you may have to "fight city hall." Your risk of loss can be minimized if you purchase property which can be resold for its minimum uses at a price close to your acquisition price.

It is obvious that you need a lawyer for legal matters. It may be less obvious that you need a lawyer who specializes in real estate. Before you buy any property, or certainly as a precondition to the purchase of a property, a thorough investigation must be made of the various ordinances and codes that determine whether you can proceed as you would like to or, for that matter, in any economically viable manner. If the four corners of an intersection are in four different municipal jurisdictions, one corner could be ten times as valuable as another corner. One property might be unbuildable because of a lack of utilities, another because of a lack of zoning, and a third because the topographic or soil conditions are unsuitable for development without extreme cost, whereas the zoning, the utilities, and a positive community attitude might make the fourth property eminently suitable for building. Your lawyer can advise you as to the restrictions of the applicable municipal building, zoning, and other codes. He can also give you guidelines for satisfying Environmental Protection Agency requirements and utility standards and for making zoning and annexation applications to park, library, forest preserve, school, and municipal districts.

You should learn about the nature of the hearings that take place in the different communities. What is essential in one community may be superfluous in others. Some jurisdictions view school board recommendations as just another consideration. Other jurisdictions require a written agreement between the investor and the school board before they will even consider a development plan. When you go into contract for land investment, whether you build yourself or sell to a developer, your ability to pay and your holding time will be directly affected by how long it takes you to arrive at solutions for the zoning, utilities, and other problems that must be resolved before it is possible to build upon your property. As the buyer of the property, you must anticipate the problems that will arise in converting land to ultimate use. Otherwise you are a gambler, not an investor.

Coordinating Professional Skills for Land Investment

Whether you invest in land on your own or you bring other people in to invest with you, you must be able to finance the land you buy for as long as you will need to carry it. You must negotiate the acquisition, the zoning, and if necessary, the development, and you must be able to coordinate the efforts of the professionals whose skills will be necessary to you. Generally you will need to put together an investment package. This will enable you to present to potential partners the information that impelled you to acquire the property.

However, you may have decided by now that all you want to do is put up your money, make profits, and have someone else mail checks to you. If so, you can buy stock in real estate companies. A few have done well in that way, but many have lost money. Investing in the stocks of real estate companies is no different from investing in the stocks of any other public company. However, since real estate development is an entrepreneurial business that is performed most successfully by individuals with high motivation and a high degree of professionalism, the basic incentive to the entrepreneur may considerably diluted once he has made his company public since he will probably have sold a large portion of it. His interest will be diluted much further after he has had to deal with stock analysts and regulatory agencies. Consequently, the authors do not recommend the purchase of real estate stocks as a means of getting into land investment unless you happen to know the individuals who run the company and you have confidence in them.

Public limited partnerships which are frequently marketed by stock and investment houses generally serve a specific purpose—some are cash flow ventures and some are tax shelter ventures. To an investor whose goals correspond to the objective of such a limited partnership, this may be a worthwhile investment vehicle, but it still requires a great deal of faith in the ability of the company to perform.

That faith is no less necessary in a private limited partnership. However there are generally fewer investors in such a limited partnership, and these investors are more likely to have a closer relationship with the general partner. The entrepreneurial benefits to the general partner are still there—he takes the risk and a large share of the profits. Our view—perhaps because of our past experience—is that investing in a private limited partnership with people in whom you have confidence is likely to be better than investing in a public limited partnership. Although the general partner in the private placement generally takes a larger share of the profits than does the general partner in a public placement, he also generally takes a much larger risk and smaller fees, so that he has a greater need for success.

The Rewards and Risks of Land Investment

Great fortunes have been made from real estate investments, including investments in vacant land. People have undoubtedly bought land whose value increased rapidly because of changing circumstances. However, very few people, regardless of their experience, have been able to do this often or even to make a profit on everything they bought.

Our approach has always been to project total costs versus anticipated selling prices for various alternative uses against a time line. Based on what we think are realistic factors in all categories, we project an investor return of at least 20 percent per year (not compounded) in addition to any profit we may be seeking for ourselves. With proper leveraging, good timing, and successful zonings, some of our investments have brought returns of 100 percent per year. In other cases—where interest rates rose to over 12 percent, taxes increased by 300–400 percent, farm rentals increased only slightly, and we had to carry the property for years longer than we anticipated—we have barely salvaged a break-even.

During the period of ownership, there are income tax deductions for interest and taxes which may be of benefit to you. Land is also an inflationary hedge, in that the price of properly located land which has zoning for realistic use or which can be rezoned for a variety of uses to meet changing market conditions will generally rise at least as much as the prices of other goods and services. Up until the last few years the price of land had been appreciating much faster than that. Now we find that in the Chicago area the appreciation depends on the use to which the land can be put.

Owning property and holding it for a long enough time for development to take place all around you or selling some of it to recoup your original investment and retaining a portion can put you in the enviable position of being able to participate in the development of buildings. In a joint venture of this kind you put in your land at a price equal to the market value, which is generally much higher than your cost, and with proper legal and accounting guidance you will be able to avoid paying an immediate tax on the increased value, thus increasing your participation in the venture. Contributing land to a venture will enable you to develop a cash flow through your participation in the ownership of buildings and to build up equity as the mortgages on the buildings are paid off.

Buying land requires money or credit, or both. Keeping land through good and bad times requires more money or credit, or both. The inability to carry the land until it can be properly zoned or until market conditions will allow you to sell it at a profit can make the difference between an excellent profit and total disaster. In our opinion, "staying power" may be even more important than location in the acquisition of land, although a prime location for anticipated use is generally regarded as the principal criterion of any land investment.

Another risk in land acquisition is buying too soon or too late. Buying too soon can be corrected by adequate staying power and the will to wait. Many people who buy land years in advance of the proper market conditions will tire of holding the property and sell it at the first opportunity to make a small profit. Buying after the market has been substantially saturated will generally be done at too high a price, so that there will be too little increase in value relative to the amount of investment that you must put at risk.

It is obvious that land is an illiquid asset. You only learn how illiquid it is when you need funds for other investments and you decide to sell a piece of land. Illiquidity is not a drawback of landownership, however, if the land owned is so-called ready-to-go land which is already developed for uses that have an immediate market. Such land can be highly liquid (a 30–90-day selling period).

Changing demand in the marketplace is another large risk of landownership. This may occur for several reasons. (1) The end use for the zoning you have may lose its demand by the time your property is ready to be developed. (2) As a result of changes in the attitude of a community, you may find it difficult to obtain approval for development, even when you propose developing your property for the uses for which it is already zoned (which brings you into costly litigation), or you may be denied zoning changes. (3) Changes in the regulations and the methods of enforcing regulations of the EPA and other agencies may restrict the development of your property.

Anyone who acquires land runs the risk of condemnation, the eminent domain right of a public body to acquire property for its anticipated needs. Normally you can expect to get the purchase price you paid or more. The rules of evidence in condemnation cases are so restrictive, however, that under certain circumstances you may not even get an amount equal to the price you paid even though the condemning authorities are required to pay fair market value. However, fair market value is a matter of interpretation, and the per acre price you get, may or may not adequately reflect the damages to the remainder of your property after the condemnation and the development of the improvements contemplated by the condemnation.

On the other hand, the condemning authorities may take your least valuable property for park or flood control or may skirt your property with roads or other developments that enhance the value of the remainder, a possibility that few property owners will admit during the course of a condemnation case. With expert legal counsel and properly prepared cases, some property owners have received far more from condemnations than they could have received had their property remained subject to the whims of the marketplace.

But condemnation in any form that takes less than all of your property will change your plans for the remainder and may complicate your development program. It is wise to investigate the potential of condemnation for any property you buy, either by inquiring or by having your attorney inquire (generally discreetly) as to the intended goals of highway departments, school districts, park districts, forest preserve districts, and other agencies that are likely to need property in your area.

Selecting Land to Meet the Future Demands of the Marketplace

You now know a number of the pitfalls of land investment, and you have guidelines for the factors which must be considered in acquiring land of any kind. The criteria of land acquisition will be discussed next. It is rarely necessary to explore all of these criteria fully, but depending upon the complexity and the amount of your investment, you will have to decide how extensive your investigation and analysis should be.

In seeking land, you start either with an anticipated use or with a site that has been offered to you. If you start with an anticipated use you will generally restrict yourself to a location that is easily accessible to you unless you are seeking a series of locations for a chain of similar uses. If the latter is the case, your criteria will have already been established by the end user. Assuming, therefore, that you have a specific use in mind, you will determine what standards must be met to have a successful use of the type you propose. You will then seek sites which fit those standards or which fit most of those standards. The people whom you will approach to find such sites for you will include real estate brokers, attorneys, and accountants whose clients may have properties of the kind you are seeking. In some areas the Farm Bureau can be helpful. Builders or maintenance suppliers relating to the industry which services your end use can also be a source of information. Home builders and organizations of real estate brokers can often refer you to people who are in the business of locating the type of site you are seeking.

If, on the other hand, a site is presented to you, and you have no end use in mind, you must go through the analysis of alternative uses that was described in previous sections and then make a financial analysis of the economic viability of the proposed investment.

Once you have determined that you wish to acquire a property, then unless you can make an immediate cash purchase, you will have to develop a financing program. The best program is to get an option or a conditional purchase agreement from the seller that gives you as much time as possible—for as many reasons as you can think of—to delay the payment of money. This chapter has spelled out many reasons why you should not put too much money at risk until you have learned a lot about the property and the market. Many of these are reasons that will not warm the heart of the seller or encourage him to give you lots of time. The most legitimate (and the most convenient) reasons relate to:

1. Soil conditions. These are normally determined in 30–60 days.
2. Engineering feasibility. Depending upon the available sources of utilities, you could ask for between 60 days and one year, but typically 60 to 120 days are requested.
3. Bank financing. This is generally not too popular with sellers, since they like to feel that you have the money to proceed, but the seller may give you from 90 to 180 days for this purpose, depending upon how anxious he is to sell.
4. Zoning, subdivision, and annexation. The time that you will be allowed for this purpose will vary widely, depending upon the state of the property when you approach the seller and upon the seller's knowledgeability concerning community attitudes. Typically zoning clauses permit six months to one year unless litigation is contemplated, in which case the time may be extended to three years and if the seller does not have a good real estate attorney, some contracts may run until all litigation opportunities are exhausted.

Some lending institutions make land loans. The criteria will vary with the institution and with your credit standing. Individuals frequently bring in partners who have limited funds and a desire to be involved in a land investment that is larger than any one of them can afford. We have had groups as large as 25 in private placement funding. You can bring in a lending institution as a cogeneral partner. Generally, you will need an excellent record of performance in order to be considered for the type of joint venture in which the lending institution puts up most of the money.

Any investors worth having will expect a financial analysis setting forth the cost of the land, the cost and timing of anticipated improvements, and a schedule of sales and anticipated selling prices together with related marketing expenses. These investors will want to know what is expected of them, what your contribution and your risk position will be, and how well you can back up the risk you are taking if the venture fails.

Don't fool yourself when you prepare your analysis. If anything, be more conservative than you think necessary. Our experience has been that we can generally predict values for various uses two or three years ahead and be fairly certain that if any of the uses we project are approved, our numbers on sales prices and selling expenses will be reasonably accurate. We have found, however, that changes in community attitudes and market conditions make it extremely hard to predict how long it will take to sell a property and what zoning we will achieve. We therefore provide investors with alternative projections on various time schedules.

Marketing Land Investments

Now that you have the land, what are you going to do with it? We assume that before you bought it you developed a program which outlined the steps needed to convert the raw property into a marketable commodity. Some of the things you need to do may take you out of the category of investor, which would most likely give you capital gains income tax treatment, and into the category of developer, which would most likely give you ordinary income if you were fortunate enough to make a profit. You should get competent legal and tax guidance on what your tax position permits you to do.

Even if you don't intend to do anything more than acquire land and resell it "as is," you should make an initial analysis of the property, and you should periodically reanalyze it—alone or in consultation with others—as if you were buying it all over again. Each time the reanalysis is done (this should be at least annually), you will arrive at a value for the property. When you arrive at a value at which you would not even consider purchasing the property, then you should attempt to sell it at close to that price. There is always an area of value at which you might not buy the property but you do not wish to sell it. At this point you should either consider selling the property or you should attempt to change the zoning of the property or to convert the property from raw land to improved land. Generally, when you reach this plateau level, unless a change in use potential is likely, the increase in value thereafter will not give you an adequate additional return on the market value of the property at that time.

You should also undertake a reanalysis of your property when there is a significant change in circumstances. The acquisition or development of nearby property for major uses is one such change. Others are impending or actual changes of administrations, changes in the rules or enforcement procedures of regulatory agencies, or condemnation proceedings affecting your property.

The highest resale value will always be attributed to property which is zoned, improved, and ready to be built upon, and the lowest resale value will generally be attributed to as-is unimproved land, (though such land may have a "romance" value, depending upon how good a salesperson you are and upon how well you can convince a prospective purchaser of its future potential).

To bring property to a fully improved ready-to-be-built-upon state takes a lot of time and a lot of money. It also takes a willingness to limit the number of possible end uses, since a fixed development program will generally restrict the number of uses to which a property can be put.

We have found that for most people who are not in need of cash but who wish to maximize the return on their investment, the sale of their land to a competent builder or developer on a "subject to zoning" basis will generally bring the greatest return with the least effort. However, you should have confidence in the ability and good judgment of your buyer because a buyer's efforts may not only fail but may also give rise to a hostile attitude toward your property. Moreover, selling in this way ties up your property for an extensive period of time and prohibits its sale to others.

You must also consider a term sale versus a cash sale. Most people will pay much more than just the interest difference to gain time. The risk of a term sale is one of default. Personal liability or an earnest money buffer will reduce that risk.

What you paid originally may determine whether or not you make a profit, but it does not determine the value of your property, except perhaps for purposes of condemnation. Never sell your property for too little or too much because of what you paid. The selling price of your property should relate to its value as a part of its end use, allowing for some land profit to your purchaser.

If your landholding is substantial, then it may be prudent to make several sales in acreage parcels to several builders or developers or to sell the land by zoning designations. You may also want to consider the partial improvement of the land by your ownership group. That is, you may extend the major utilities to the site and obtain an overall bulk plan approval for zoning categories, and in this way confirm the existence and the availability of the required utility services and provide the groundwork for builder efforts to obtain approval for site plans.

Another method of sale is not a sale at all. As was stated previously, you can participate with a builder or a financial institution in the development of your land, so that your profit will be based not only on the appreciation of the land but on the profits that may be reaped from the sale of the end product being developed or from the ownership of income-producing property. You can also give a builder or a developer very lenient terms, provided that he intends to proceed with end uses immediately, and you can have him pay you a bonus for having arranged matters so that he will not have to seek substantial financing for your land. That bonus can be made payable only as he sells the end product.

Conclusions

The land business brings you into contact with farmers and financiers, with promoters who have ideas and nothing more and with highly liquid investors and investment houses. In land investment, you must deal in politics, whether you want to or not, and you must acquire a rudimentary knowledge of engineering, planning, law, and accounting in order to succeed. Unless you are extremely wealthy, your timing needs to work out well, and although luck has not been stressed here, it certainly helps. Fortunes have been made and lost in the land business. Regardless of what you hear about how the "other fellow" is doing and about how fast he is doing it, in the land business, as in any other business, a conservative approach to investment, a well-planned development program, a conscientious periodic review of all the factors that relate to the value and the marketability of your property, and thorough follow-through are the best road to continued profitability.

Land Investment Checklist

Owner's status

1. Date of original contract.
2. Common name.
3. Location and municipality.
4. Original total acreage.
5. Beneficiaries of trust agreement.
6. Remaining acreage.
7. Zoning breakdown of remaining acreage.
8. Estimated value of remaining acreage.

Municipal considerations

1. Present zoning.
2. Summary of conditions of annexation agreement, if applicable.
3. Conditions relating to zoning or PUD.
4. Contribution requirements—land and dollars.
5. Zonings pending or contemplated.
6. Subdivisions pending or contemplated.
7. Litigations, including present or threatened condemnations.
8. If zoning or subdivisions are pending, schedule of dates for hearings and approvals.

General utility considerations

1. Public or private—if private, list company and representative; if public, list director or village engineer.
2. Location of sanitary sewer, water, and other utilities relative to subject property.
3. Tap-on costs, if any.

Land Investment Checklist *(continued)*

---

4. Potential topographical or soil problems.
5. Flooding considerations.
6. Access problems, including required easements, road widening, and traffic lights.

Mortgage summary

1. Dates of payment.
2. Interest.
3. Nonmonetary requirements.

Partnership agreement summary

1. Requirements of limited partners for funding or refunding.
2. Requirements of general partners.
3. Nonmonetary obligations of general partners.
4. Obligations for repayment of limited partners.

Pending contracts

1. Sales summary by specific dates, including principal and interest.
2. A reduced copy of land release planned.
3. Seller's monetary requirements.
4. Seller's nonmonetary requirements.
5. Schedule of completion for seller's nonmonetary requirements, including critical path breakdown to accomplish requirements.
6. Commission obligations and schedule of payments due and to whom.
7. Buyer's requirements.

Sources of funds to satisfy ownership requirements and contract contingencies

1. Anticipated sources of funds with which buyer will make payment on contract.

Consultants involved in owning, developing, and selling

1. Zoning attorney.
2. Contract attorney.
3. Special counsel, if any.
4. Tax consultant.
5. Engineer.
6. Surveyor.
7. Architect.
8. Planner.
9. Appraiser.
10. Traffic engineer/consultant.
11. Other.

Development

1. Staging and breakdown.
2. Contractors and subcontractors.
3. Name of coordinator.

Land Investment Checklist *(concluded)*

4. Obligations of the various parties.
5. Source of funds to pay obligations of land developer—if in mortgage, get mortgage terms
6. Critical path breakdown on development stages and anticipated completion dates.

Negotiations pending

1. Potential buyers.
2. Proposed price and terms.

SYNDICATES AND JOINT VENTURES

William L. Ramseyer

*W*ILLIAM L. RAMSEYER, *Executive Vice President, Questor Associates, San Francisco, California.*

Senior management responsibility for creating research, control, and management systems for company's legal, economics, real estate consultation, public sector advisory, financial feasibility, and transaction implementation services. Guest lecturer, Stanford Graduate School of Business and University of California Graduate School of Business. Member, Real Estate Advisory Committee, Golden Gate University MBA Program. Graduate, Advanced Management Program, Harvard Business School. Formerly publisher/editor, Real Estate Syndication Digest; *director of research, Association of Metropolitan San Jose; and legislative assistant to Senator Henry M. Jackson.*

Definitions and Dimensions

Syndicates and joint ventures are not an investment invention of our generation. As far back as the mid-19th century, Boston financial people were legally pooling assets for investment in real property. Since that time, although syndicates and joint ventures have often been in the forefront of investment activity, especially throughout the 1950s and into the early 1970s, they have received little or no mention in standard real estate texts. They are rarely mentioned even in general dictionaries or glossaries of real estate terms.

Unlike their counterparts of the 19th century, the current syndicates and joint ventures are complex and multidisciplinary. To be successful, even modest programs require considerable resources and sophistication. Organizing a program, choosing a sound economic strategy, locating and acquiring a property, finding investors, meeting regulatory requirements, providing competent project management, and being able to sense the optimal economic climate for achieving one's goals require untold hours and extensive research as well as expertise in law, economics, finance, psychology, and real estate itself.

Syndicates and joint ventures involve the issuing of shares of one kind or another. Relative to the market for corporate securities, the market for syndicate shares is inefficient—some would even say nonexistent. Nevertheless, millions of dollars are frequently involved in single offerings.

Over the last decade, a time of dramatic expansion for syndicates in the form of limited partnerships, the performance of many of these ventures has been anything but encouraging and the expectations of all too many investors have been unfulfilled. The resultant surge of regulation has perhaps inhibited syndicate activity as much as or more than it has provided investors with the protection intended.

For all of the obvious deterrents and the seeming failures, investment in real property through syndicates and joint ventures has been attracting the increased interest it deserves from both major institutional and private investors. Admittedly, part of that interest has been generated by the disappointing performance of the stock market; and in part stems from legal developments, such as the requirements for greater diversity in portfolios that are specified in the Employee Retirement Income Security Act of 1974 (ERISA). But the greatest part, perhaps, has arisen from the developing awareness that properly structured real estate securities programs represent a desirable alternative to more traditional forms of investment.

This opinion is confirmed by Stephen E. Roulac and Donald A. King, Jr., in an article that appeared in the summer 1977 issue of the *Journal of Portfolio Management.*

> But today there are several significant facts to suggest that real estate will assume an increasingly important role in institutional portfolios. Perhaps most significant, investment grade income-producing real estate enjoys risk and return characteristics that compare most favorably with common stocks and bonds, the traditional institutional investment assets. In any case, the discouraging stock market performance since the late 1960's and major changes in the structure of the securities markets generally have prompted asset managers to reexamine the ingrained prejudice favoring equity and fixed income securities to the virtual exclusion of other investment forms.

As applied to real estate, people use the terms *syndicate* and *joint venture* somewhat interchangeably. However, the former term generally refers to an investment activity that is subject to rules and regulations; the latter term more nearly describes an ownership relationship. In either case, we are talking about a group of two or more persons or companies organized by mutual agreement to invest in one or more properties. In the past, such agreements were often informal. Increasingly, however, they have assumed the form of a legal document—a must if the opportunity for investment is offered to individual investors.

Variations

Syndicates and joint ventures are as varied as the individuals or the entities that form them. Perhaps a developer conceives of a sizable project, such as a shopping center or a multiple-unit warehousing arrangement, but finds that his resources are insufficient to provide the capital he needs during the planning stages. Accordingly, he may enter into a joint venture partnership through a large investing organization, such as a brokerage house or a bank. This was the sponsor's rationale in the Public Storage, Inc., syndication offerings in 1976–77.

A number of offerings are in the form of "blind pools." Funds are raised either publicly or privately with no specific property in mind— yet with the promise that they will be used to acquire and operate income properties. The various Robert A. McNeil Funds that Pacific Investments has sponsored since 1965 represent this concept of syndication.

Or a sponsor may be in a position to apply the considerable expertise that is needed to plan a project and then to acquire and manage a property—yet lack the capital for such an undertaking. Organizing a syndicate and offering shares to individuals with funds to invest but little or no desire to be actively involved can enable the sponsor to achieve these goals. An example of this kind of arrangement is the Walnut Properties, a 1976 limited partnership whose shares were privately placed in the San Francisco Bay Area. The return to investors depends on how well the property is chosen and managed and on what appreciation in value, if any, takes place by the time of sale.

Still another arrangement is a syndicate that is formed to further public housing policy. In order to sell the shares of such an offering, the sponsor frequently utilizes the services of an underwriter, with the shares sold much as corporate securities are sold. The National Housing Partnership offerings that financed several Section 236 projects represent this kind of joint venture. Because the cash distributions of such syndicates are limited in amount, investors are generally attracted to them by the benefits they offer in the form of tax deductions which create sufficient tax savings to provide a satisfactory overall investment return.

Whatever the circumstances, the coming together into a joint venture relationship (frequently in some form of syndication) takes place for the most part because alone an individual or a company finds the real estate holdings of interest to be too costly, the risk involved to be too great, or the acquisition and management of the investment to be too complex.

Indicative of the volume of syndication during the 1970s are the figures in Table 1. These figures represent only offerings registered with the National Association of Securities Dealers, Inc. (NASD); they exclude public programs that are sold by companies and persons not affiliated with the NASD.

Comparable figures for private offerings are more difficult to quantify due to the lack of centralized reporting. However, the NASD has indicated on a preliminary basis that its members participated in $539,-

TABLE 1
Volume of Real Estate Syndication Offerings

Year	Volume ($000)	Number of Programs
1970	$ 256,000	54
1971	524,000	139
1972	1,911,000	207
1973	849,000	172
1974	521,458	94
1975	341,425	76
1976	272,705	44
1977	292,973	47
1978	782,672	70
1979*	399,685	31

Source: National Association of Securities Dealers, Inc.
* Period ending July 31.

928,000 of privately offered real estate investment situations between December 1, 1976, and November 30, 1977. Considering that this figure is only preliminary and that many other real estate private placements are offered by non-NASD members, the ratio of nonpublic real estate offerings to fully registered (SEC) programs may well be ten to one.

The decline in the popularity of real estate syndications, as measured by the figures in Table 1, has not arisen from any inherent weaknesses in this form of investment or any lack of faith in its potential. Marginal investment performance caused by ill-defined strategies, inadequate understanding of economic realities, inefficient management, adverse publicity, and stringent regulation has taken its toll. Yet with certain modifications, based on changes in tax laws and in the general investment climate, real estate securities continue to grow in number and to offer distinct advantages in the field of capital investment.

Economic Advantages

In addition to deriving psychological satisfaction from a sense of ownership, especially from a piece of land or a building, or even the smallest portion thereof, sellers and buyers alike feel that investment in syndicates has certain underlying economic advantages over investment in other kinds of securities. That feeling has not been eroded even by the recognition of previous syndicate failures or by the regulatory response to those failures. The following economic advantages of syndicates still exert a major influence.

Syndicates in Noncorporate Form Are a Single Tax Entity. Federal and some state authorities do not tax syndicates organized as partnerships—that is, the profits of such syndicates are taxable only against the interests of their members and not against the syndicate itself. Historically, syndicated investments in the form of limited partnerships were arranged so as to include extraordinary income tax protection. The gains (or losses) realized could be applied to the total income picture of the partners. This "shelter," however, has been considerably eroded, beginning with the Tax Reform Act of 1969, which substantially reduced the available tax deductions.

Professional Skill and Judgment Are Available to Syndicates. Few investors, even those who control tremendous sums and are relatively skilled in financial matters, are qualified to make decisions regarding the feasibility of real estate investment ventures. Purchasing securities in a syndicated program immediately makes investors partners with real estate professionals and provides access to the backup services that these professionals provide.

Although misrepresentation of ability unfortunately does occur, investors who carefully select the syndicates in which they invest enjoy all the benefits of association with the considerable resources and experience of major institutions and successful entrepreneurs. Most investors seem to be more capable of choosing a managing partner wisely than of attempting the almost impossible task of assessing a real estate program in all its complexities.

Syndicates Offer Economies of Scale. Because syndicates involve the pooling of funds, they make possible investment in large properties—projects that would normally be beyond the means of all but the wealthiest individuals. Large properties offer a chance for considerable efficiency over small properties, both at the time of acquisition and during their operation. The time and money needed to evaluate a geographic area, acquire permits, arrange financing, wait for approvals, negotiate terms, and handle the details of planning are not proportionate to the size of a property. Similar things have to be done whether a property is small or large.

The larger property is also able to realize competitive advantages because its operating expenses are proportionately lower than those of a smaller property. It can provide attractive extra features, such as recreational facilities, landscaping, and parking, at a lower per unit cost, and its on-site and off-site property management is more efficient and therefore less costly than that of a smaller property because it is spread over a larger number of units.

Syndicates Offer Opportunity for Diversification. Because of its greater opportunity to raise substantial amounts of capital, a syndicate can invest not only in larger projects but in multiple properties. Individual purchasers are traditionally threatened by the risks associated with having all one's eggs in one basket. Diversification means that an investment is not dependent on a single property or tied to a particular location. Should there be a loss in one unit, that loss can be spread over the entire investment.

Similarly the reserves or the additional funds that are needed to overcome temporary cash flow difficulties with a particular portion of an investment will be proportionately less for a number of diverse properties than for only one or two properties. However, it must be remembered that diversification can also have disadvantages. While it lowers the downside risk, it also dilutes the returns from an outstanding property.

The Elements of Syndication

Every real estate investment program—whether it is in corporate, trust, partnership, or some other form; whether its offering is public or private; and whether it involves a single property or multiple properties—passes through the three phases of origination, operation, and completion. These phases are known as the real estate investment life cycle. These phases are all equally vital to the success of the total program.

The Origination Phase. This earliest phase of every real estate investment program involves planning and marketing as well as the acquisition of whatever property is chosen. The planning phase, during which the program is defined, includes such policy considerations as risk-return objectives, portfolio diversification, and the anticipated holding period. Once a program has been defined, in order to ascertain its feasibility attention must be given to decisions concerning investor expectations, registration tactics, the preparation of offering documents, and marketing strategies. Each of these decisions necessarily entails its own research and analysis.

More or less concurrently, the sponsor will be seeking to locate a suitable property by conducting field research and analyzing all of the possible choices from the standpoint of income and expense, seller information and personal records, title and zoning, competition, and price. Once a choice has been made, the sponsor has to conduct a thorough financial analysis, negotiate terms and conditions, and go over the applicable plans, specifications, tax bills, leases, and permits. A formal appraisal and an audit of the property also have to be made, and escrow and purchase-and-sale agreements have to be prepared.

The Operations Phase. As the initial phase nears completion, the many components of both entity management and property management must be attended to. (See Table 2.) These matters commonly fall under the heading "operations."

The Completion Phase. The completion phase is just what its name suggests—that time in the investment program when the property is sold and distribution or reinvestment is consummated. During this phase, the value of the property has to be ascertained and an asking price determined. Marketing information regarding the sale of the property is prepared, and financial figures are made available. The property is shown to prospective buyers, and once a buyer has been found, documentation is provided and negotiations are entered into.

Upon the sale of the property, all of the necessary papers must be filed, all of the necessary reports must be prepared, and a complete accounting must be made to the partners, along with the distribution of the proceeds and the final payment of bills. A sale may be executed in such a way that the proceeds are reinvested and the process of origination, operation, and completion is repeated. More commonly, a joint ven-

TABLE 2
Components of Real Estate Syndicate Operations Phase

Property Management

Revenue gathering.
  Lease negotiation.
  Rent collection and provision for delinquent payments.
Expense control.
  Hiring and supervision of personnel.
  Purchase of supplies and services.
  Disbursement of funds.
Record keeping.
Maintenance and safety.
  Insurance coverage.
  Repair scheduling.
  Inspection.
Tenant relationships.
Property taxes.
Community and local government contacts.

Entity Management

Maintain investor relationships.
Provide on-site management and legal and accounting services.
Supervise on-site manager and major activities.
Establish accounting controls.
Prepare tax returns.
Provide and review reports.
Process transfer of interests.
Monitor overall status of the investment.
Monitor money markets and political and economic climate to determine
  investment strategies.
Negotiate new loans and contracts.

ture, however extensive in its scope or its participation, dissolves as
soon as its original objective has been fulfilled.

Structuring a Syndicate Offering

The specifics of structuring a real estate investment program are too
numerous and complex to be covered in a single chapter. It is scarcely
possible to treat the subject without knowing the parameters of the given
program. As an example, is the organization a corporation, a partnership, or a trust? Is this a blind pool, or is the property known? How
many classes of shares are there? Is this an open-end or a closed-end
offering? Will the offering be public or private? Is the property undeveloped, under construction, or fully developed? Is the property new or

old? How large is the property, and how much will it cost? Are the investors fully subject to income tax, or are they tax-exempt entities?

Until such questions are answered, it is virtually impossible to discuss structuring with any specificity. In addition, there is no one generally preferred method of structuring. Only regulations and the imagination of the originator limit how a program will be put together. There are, however, certain broad considerations and procedures that in some way apply to all real estate investment programs.

Whatever form of organization is chosen, the relationships among investors, sponsors, managers, and tenants must be clearly defined and their goals made as congruent as possible. The responsibilities, rights, and obligations of all participants need to be specified. Policy regarding compensation and investment return deserves special consideration. Although specific amounts cannot be determined, percentages and the timing of financial flows can and should be.

There must be a complete legal description of any property, together with a description of the improvements contemplated and an agreement as to what changes may be made under what circumstances. If construction is involved, there should be a statement specifying the completion dates and the penalties that are to be assessed in the event of delays. At the same time, the question of performance bonding should be resolved. A written agreement should specify the obligations of the buyers and sellers in detail, especially with regard to insurance and inspection.

According to many acquisition specialists, financing is the key to feasibility and sound structuring. Financing can take many forms. Whatever form is chosen, it should allow for sound accounting practice and it should be analyzed from the perspectives of the investors and the sponsors and with special regard to the holding period. Some of the major financial decisions will be in the areas of debt/equity ratio (leverage policy), regulatory approvals, depreciation schedules, and tax elections.

The structuring of a real estate investment program should concern itself with the management of the property and should include a management contract. The responsible parties must be clearly determined, and such matters as which party pays obligations during the initial operating stage (including debt service and taxes as well as the costs of operation) must be accounted for. Such details can often influence cash flow during a most critical period of the program, and it can greatly affect the viability of the responsible party.

Critical Issues

Fiduciary Obligation. In some business matters a fiduciary relationship exists whenever one person looks to another person to act on his behalf—not as agent, as in the case of a broker, but as principal. It is commonly accepted that all persons and organizations with ongoing management and administrative responsibility, such as general partners in an investment program, have fiduciary responsibilities. They are expected to act with due diligence. That is, as far as investment matters are concerned, they are expected to make "reasonable" efforts to investigate the economic viability of an offering and to fully disclose this information in the offering document. "Reasonable" has been interpreted to mean that which a prudent person would do in the management of his own property.

The concept is not a new one. Under 17th-century common law a fiduciary was required to "observe how men of prudence, discretion and intelligence manage their own affairs, not in regard to speculation, but in regard to the permanent disposition of their funds, considering the probable income as well as the probable safety of the capital invested." Time has brought no change in that interpretation.

In the past, many sponsors in the investment business did not accept the full intent of this definition of fiduciary responsibility. Some were totally unaware of what their role was expected to be. Present-day regulations, however, pay increasing attention to the requirements of the fiduciary role and impose ever higher standards of disclosure and accountability upon the general partner/sponsor. These regulations make clear that the fiduciary obligation applies in all aspects of the origination, operation, and completion phases of a real estate investment program.

So pervasive has the notion of fiduciary responsibility become that regulatory agencies apply it to persons associated with the planning of a real estate investment program—those experts who act as advisers in investment transactions, such as attorneys and accountants. It is often advice of such experts that determines whether or not an investment is made, and their accountability is therefore held to be similar to that of the general partner/sponsor.

Sponsor Compensation.   Any successful real estate investment program requires a suitable economic climate. Even given such a climate, entrepreneurial sophistication of the highest order is needed. For a favorable outcome, sponsors are needed who are able to plan, acquire, operate, and bring to completion a program involving, in part, economics, marketing, finance, law, construction management, and even behavioral psychology in dealing with the many people of contrary interests. In addition to specific knowledge and skill, the sponsors of successful programs must possess unusual energy, resourcefulness, and integrity. No one disputes that such talent deserves to be compensated. The problem lies in deciding how much, when, and in what form.

Every fee paid and every return granted to one element of a partnership inevitably dilutes the returns of the other elements. Thus, the more the sponsor receives, the less the other partners receive. The resolution of this problem is particularly difficult, since the sponsor is a fiduciary whose first duty is to protect the best interests of those who trust his expertise.

The issue concerns not only regulators who seek to do away with abuses, but members of the industry as well. The latter attempt to resolve the problem in a way that will permit beneficial decisions regarding the structuring of programs. They wish to preserve as much flexibility of behavior as possible in order to make programs economically worthwhile despite the increasing demands of regulators.

For the most part, the compensation of sponsors is based on their structuring strategies, managerial talent, and marketing skill. That compensation is most likely to take the form of specific fees, a percentage of revenues, and/or a participation interest. Increasingly, compensation arrangements have provided for some type of incentive payment for achieving performance levels higher than those of specified minimums. Traditionally, sponsors have received either fixed fees or stipulated percentages of gross amounts for acquisition, financing, management, leasing, and disposition.

The participation interest is a legal claim on some portion of the assets of a partnership, including net income or future cash distributions. It can be calculated by either a "net" or a "gross" revenue method. That is, the base used can be either the balance remaining after the limited partners have received their preferential return or the total return before any payment has been made to the limited partners. Occasionally, the partnership interest is paid in lieu of front-end compensation. In such instances, the timing of the dilution of return to the investors changes, but the dilution itself still occurs.

Certain arrangements with regard to sponsor compensation are more likely to achieve favorable tax results than are other arrangements. That is, the investor's tax position is enhanced when payments to sponsors generate tax deductions, though it is important to ensure that such payments are in fact made for services with real value.

As will be seen from the discussion that follows, regulation has effected significant changes in the sources and forms of sponsor compensation. The resolution of the problem of sponsor compensation, however, is unlikely to take place until the goals of the sponsor and the investor are somehow made more congruent.

The Regulation of Syndication.   Real estate syndication investments are highly regulated. In fact, such regulation and its administration are among the most dynamic areas of modern law. The guidelines covering what sponsors can and cannot do, when they can or must do something, and how they must do it are in a constant state of change. The growing sophistication of the persons who are involved in real estate syndication activity combined with a trend toward financial consumerism among syndicate investors has given use to requirements for more thorough documentation disclosure of syndicate transactions.

The regulation of real estate syndication involves a dual federal and state system. At the federal level, the Securities and Exchange Commission has jurisdiction over all private-sector investment activity. At the state level, the agency responsible for regulating securities of all types usually has jurisdiction over real estate syndication, and often the state real estate department is involved as well. In addition, the National Association of Securities Dealers, a quasi-governmental agency that operates under the general supervision of the Securities and Exchange Commission, has responsibility for regulating the distribution of syndicate securities by its members. These include securities dealers ranging in size from small insurance and mutual fund sales organizations to the largest member firms of the New York Stock Exchange.

The regulation of real estate investment in the form of securities is extraordinarily complex, and considerable expertise and experience are needed to deal with it. Because of this, the major participants in a syndicated real estate investment need the assistance of knowledgeable legal counsel both to plan the investment offering and to ensure compliance with regulatory standards. Six issues related to the issuance of securities must be addressed: the status of the securities, the registration requirements, the disclosure standards, the distribution procedures, the reporting requirements, and enforcement activity.

Although the term *security* encompasses many concepts, the one that is most germane to real estate syndication is the theory of the investment contract. According to this theory, the crucial characteristic of a security is not the nature of the underlying asset, but rather the manner in which the asset is marketed and managed. Where an investment is sold on the basis that there will be continuing management by either the sponsor or a third party, and where investors buy for the purpose of achieving a return on their investment, the essential attributes of an investment contract are present.

Unless a specific exemption from registration is available, one should expect to register the offering with the appropriate securities regulator. Some types of securities are exempt and certain types of offerings are exempt. Available exemptions include the Section 3(a)(11) interstate exemption, which exempts from registration offerings where the sponsor, investors, all offerees, and the business of the offering are all generally confined to the boundaries of one state. SEC Rule 147 provides a more explicit statement as to these requirements.

Another available exemption is the SEC Section 4(2) private placement exemption, which is available for transactions not involving a "public offering." While the definition of what is "not a public offering" is both vague and elusive, certain factors are significant, including the number of offerings and their relationships, the relationship of the sponsor to the offerings, the investor sophistication, how the offering is sold, the quality of disclosure and the accessibility to all the information, the size of the investment units and the size of the total offering, and the nature and character of the investment being offered. Recently, the SEC provided more clarification to their expectations by Rule 146. It should be emphasized, however, that the private placement requires a standard of disclosure at least equal to that which would be provided a public offering.

Other exemptions are also available for offerings involving contribution capital of less than $500,000, and SEC Rule 240 permits a specialized registration for very small issues. On the state level, all offerings must be registered unless they qualify as private placements.

To meet the federal registration requirements, the sponsor of a securities offering is required to make full and fair disclosure of all the material facts that would influence an investment decision. This emphasis on disclosure is somewhat misleading, since in the past the federal regulatory authorities have displayed a strong bias against providing information having to do with future investment prospects. More recently, there have been increasing indications that these authorities will not only accept but encourage forecast information. In contrast with the federal full disclosure emphasis, many states apply a merit standard which requires that an offering be "fair, just, and equitable" to the prospective purchaser. This standard has been very controversial, since it is difficult to define "fair, just, and equitable" in a satisfactory way.

The distribution of securities is also regulated. This is primarily the responsibility of the NASD, although the SEC is also involved. Persons who sponsor securities offerings on a recurring basis and persons who sell such offerings must be registered and licensed for this activity.

Just as corporations are required to make regular reports to their shareholders, so too are sponsors of real estate securities programs required to make regular reports to their investors. Since there has been a characteristic of near silence on the part of some program sponsors, the regulatory authorities have become increasingly adamant in insisting on a high standard of communication of information to investors in real estate syndications.

When an investor believes that he has been defrauded in connection with a real estate syndication, the persons who are charged with the responsibility for enforcing federal and state securities regulations will investigate the degree to which the offering has complied with those regulations. If a violation has occurred, an enforcement action will be taken. This may require the sponsor to offer to refund the investor's money plus interest thereon or to agree not to violate the securities laws in the future. This sponsor may also be banned from participation in real estate syndication for a designated period of time, or he may be subjected to criminal sanctions.

Choosing a Syndicate

An investor seeking to fulfill certain financial goals through the purchase of real estate securities must evaluate many factors—some obviously more important than others. In choosing a syndicate, the critical factors are the financial information, the sponsor's qualifications, and the partnership agreement.

The Financial Information.   Except in the case of a blind pool, a reasonable basis for the investor's choice of a syndicate would be its financial information. The investor should pay special attention to any projections made by the sponsor and should check the figures provided against the market and against those for similar properties. The relationships of gross revenues, price, estimated operating expenses, and the anticipated vacancy rate can all be compared to the usual standards.

The offering document will enable the prospective investor to ascertain what fees the sponsor expects and what distributions of cash flow will be made. Recasting a pro forma statement into seemingly more logical form may help the investor to determine what assumptions in the pro forma statement are or are not reasonable. For example, the investor may conclude from information contained in the offering document that the promised rate of return is unlikely to be realized. A careful reading and analysis of all the financial information provided by a syndicate can materially assist a prospective investor in arriving at a decision.

The Sponsor's Qualifications. Not every would-be investor has the time or the knowledge that are needed to choose a real estate investment program wisely. The would-be investor may feel far more qualified to select a sponsor, even though this too involves getting information. In such instances, he would do well to seek answers to questions such as the following:

1. Does the sponsor (individual or firm) have proven experience and knowledge in real estate investment (equity financing), or are the sponsor's experience and knowledge confined to mortgage placement (debt financing) or brokerage only?
2. Is the sponsor oriented to professional real property asset management? In other words, is the sponsor's primary concern simply to make a sale and collect commissions and fees, or will the sponsor's compensation be based on performance on the net invested capital under the sponsor's management? Is the sponsor concerned with the goals of the investors and prepared and qualified to fulfill the fiduciary role? Are there likely to be unresolvable conflicts of interest between the investor and the sponsor?
3. Does the sponsor have staying power—that is, does the sponsor have sufficient resources to adequately manage the contemplated investment throughout the full life cycle? Does the sponsor have a high credit rating?
4. When acquiring property, what emphasis will the sponsor place on field research and financial analysis? What professional advisers is the sponsor relying on for assistance in the planning and operational phases of the real estate investment program?
5. What kinds of reports will the sponsor make to investors, and how often?
6. Is the overall quality of the sponsor's organization and staff consistent with the highest professional standards?

The Partnership Agreement. The investor's satisfaction with his investment will depend in part on the terms of the legal agreement that is made among the participants and on how those terms are implemented. In whatever form a real estate venture is organized, the contracts drawn must serve to further the objectives that originally brought the participants together.

If the venture is in the form of a limited partnership, for example, the investor's concern will be with tax benefits and limitation of liability as well as a good return on his money. The partnership agreement should reflect that concern. Even if the limited partners have no voice in management, some provision should be made for keeping them informed. The rights of the limited partners to approve major changes in financing, to have a voice in sale arrangements and timing, to replace the general partner for failure to perform as promised, and even to dissolve a calamitous venture should be stipulated in precise terms. And every partnership agreement should include specific information as to how assessments (if any) are to be handled.

The partnership agreement should also address the sponsor's concerns. The sponsor's fees should be stated. If a participation interest is to be part of the sponsor's compensation, its terms should be clearly specified. The partnership agreement should also specify what costs will be paid by the partnership and what costs will be paid by the sponsor. The allocation and distribution of profits (or losses) must be provided for in precise language so as to avoid any misunderstandings as to their timing, proportion, priority, and conditions.

Such concepts as income, revenue, return, asset, and profit must be defined in the partnership agreement. No one interpretation is better than another so long as there is mutual understanding and accord.

Conclusion

Syndication and joint venture relationships are based on combining active management and passive capital to pursue a common investment objective. Fundamental to the success of syndicates and joint ventures are common goals, compatible business relationships, careful planning, effective implementation, and disciplined control. When properly executed, syndicates make possible the leveraging of expertise and capital resources.

Because of the comprehensive tasks that syndication involves and the complex overlay of regulations by which syndications are governed, syndication can be considered the ultimate challenge for the real estate professional. As such, it demands the highest levels of knowledge, experience, and responsibility. When a syndication is properly executed, its rewards can be above the norm for all involved.

SELECTING REAL ESTATE INVESTMENT OPPORTUNITIES*

Maury Seldin

Arthur M. Weimer

*M*AURY SELDIN, DBA, Professor of Finance and Real Estate, School of Business Administration, The American University, Washington, D.C.

Editor in Chief, The Real Estate Handbook (Dow Jones-Irwin). President, Metro Metrics, Inc., Washington-based real estate research and counseling firm. President, Homer Hoyt Institute. Past president, American Real Estate and Urban Land Economics Association; George Washington chapter of Lambda Alpha. Research fellow, Urban Land Institute. Author, Land Investment (Homewood, Ill.: Dow Jones-Irwin, 1975); and Real Estate Investment for Profit through Appreciation (Reston, Va: Reston Publishing Co, in press). Coauthor, Housing Markets (Homewood, Ill.: Dow Jones-Irwin, 1977); and Real Estate Investment Strategy, 2d ed. (New York: John Wiley, 1979).

ARTHUR M. WEIMER, PhD, LLD, MAI, CRE, Economic Consultant, United States League of Savings Associations, Washington, D.C.

Advisory Board member, The Real Estate Handbook (Dow Jones-Irwin). President, Weimer Business Advisory Service, Inc. Formerly savings association professor of real estate and land economics, special assistant to the president, and dean, Graduate School of Business, Indiana University, Bloomington. Member, Board of Directors, Chamber of Commerce of the United

---

* Portions of this chapter were adapted from Maury Seldin, *How to Look for Real Estate Opportunities* (Bloomington, Ind.: Weimer Business Advisory Service, 1978).

States; Midwest Research Institute; Railroadmen's Federal Savings and Loan Association, Indianapolis, Indiana; Unifirst Federal Savings and Loan Association, Jackson, Mississippi; and Ball Corporation, Muncie, Indiana. Coauthor, Real Estate 7th ed. (Santa Barbara, Calif.: Wiley/Hamilton, 1978); and Introduction to Business, 5th ed. (Homewood, Ill.: Richard D. Irwin.)

Most investors consider each real estate opportunity on its own merits, whenever and however they find it. They evaluate each opportunity as it comes along. This is called an opportunistic strategy.

Such an approach requires looking over and evaluating a lot of properties. It can be very time consuming and expensive. Nevertheless, many investors opt for this approach because it seems easiest.

In order to reduce the time and expense that are required to review properties, investors may develop a set of investment policies. For example, they may decide on one or more preferred localities. They may narrow down the range of offerings to those meeting specified criteria related to price, down payment, leverage, diversification, cash flow, tax shelter, type of property, and so on.

Investors often set up the price range of the properties that they would like to consider. For those who wish to set a price policy, there are a few techniques which are quite useful. The first deals with the down payment.

A decision is needed on the amount of leverage to use. (Leverage refers to the amount of borrowed money in relation to the amount of the investor's money. The higher the percentage of borrowed money, the greater the leverage.) A high-leverage purchaser will put 10 percent of the purchase price down, or perhaps as little as 5 percent or as much as 15 percent. A typical investor who does not use high leverage will put 20–30 percent down and use only a first-mortgage.

The amount of money available for a down payment multiplied by the reciprocal of the down payment ratio gives the price range desired. If the investor has $20,000 for a down payment and wants to buy with 10 percent down, he or she can buy a $200,000 property. If the investor pays 20 percent down, a $100,000 property can be bought (0.20 = 1/5; reverse the 1/5 to give the multiplier of 5).

If the investor wishes to diversify, then the money available is split into down payments for a number of investments. A very high leveraged, nondiversified investor should keep substantial cash reserves. The amount of those reserves affects the amount available for a down payment.

Highly leveraged properties may produce no cash flow. If the cash flow is negative, there is a continuous requirement of providing additional funds. Unimproved land is the classic case of such an investment.

Investments with negative cash flow require reserves. Sometimes those reserves are set aside by using previously accumulated funds.

Some investors use future income as the basis for potential reserves.

That is, they get more income than they spend, so the excess is available for investment. They may then program some of that excess to be used as reserves and thus to meet negative cash flow requirements.

If the investor's strategy is based upon using future personal income to meet the cash requirements, then the amount of future money may limit the size of purchase. For example, an investor with $20,000 cash may be looking for land to buy at 10 percent down. Although he or she could manage a down payment on $200,000 worth of land, the mortgage-carrying cost might be $1,800 per month. If the investor can only afford a monthly investment of half that, or $900, then the amount of the debt that could be serviced might be, say, $90,000 instead of $180,000. The property to look for would be priced at $100,000, not $200,000.

A variety of locations should be analyzed to determine which is of major interest. Investors often emphasize income-producing potential in selecting locations.

Properties go through life cycles. These life cycles are related to the physical age of structures, their maintenance and, to a great degree, their location. Investors who want the least risk select the properties that are newest but have established tenancies. Investors who want the greatest returns and are prepared to take higher risks select older properties with buildings that may not be occupied for very long before they are torn down to make way for new uses of the land. If a building is likely to be abandoned, however, and the land not reused, it should be avoided.

Brokers

Real estate brokers are an obvious route to finding property. The foregoing policies provide the basis for telling them what the investor prefers. The opportunistic investor will chase down many ads and brokers. The systematic investor tries to identify brokers who will serve his or her interests best. The investor should qualify the agent and the property and consider those properties which seem to be reasonable candidates for acquisition.

Sometimes, the properties on the market are not attractive to the investor. Many investors with good properties find them difficult to replace. They sell only under special circumstances. Thus, much of what is on the market at a given time may be the result of an adverse selection process. This means that the properties available for purchase are generally not as good as the average investment property.

Properties may be overpriced because there are sellers who will sell, but only at very high prices. The owners of investment properties producing a good cash flow may demand outlandish prices. They can afford to wait a long time. In fact, they can make money while waiting. By way of contrast, in sales of owner-occupied houses a genuine desire to sell at acceptable prices may exist for a number of reasons, such as a transfer to another city or a change in household size and composition due to death or divorce.

Despite the problems, reading the newspaper ads, finding a responsive broker, and working with the broker is the way in which many investors proceed. Reading the newspaper ads and finding the seller is another way to proceed.

Investors typically talk to lots of people—accountants, attorneys, bankers, insurance agents, and others who have constant contact with property owners. Such people often know of property which is for sale or, better yet, property which will be on the market soon.

Property that is identified before it comes on the market is often the best kind to buy. The owner may be anxious to sell and may accept a reasonable price. A good property is frequently bought before it reaches the open market. Such property is often found through people who know of the motivations of the prospective sellers. These may be professional and business people who have the prospective sellers as clients. They may also be astute real estate brokers who knows what is happening and will match up a buyer and a property even before the seller has fully decided to sell.

The opportunistic strategy is based upon responding to what is offered and picking the best property available.

Systematic Search Strategies

A systematic strategy is based upon deciding what to buy and then going out to find it. Such a strategy is not widely used because it seems more difficult than the opportunistic approach. But it is likely to be more profitable.

The first step in a systematic strategy is to set objectives. This means specifying what types of property will be considered, the price range, the financing, the location, and other characteristics.

These objectives are based upon an analysis of the risks that the investor is prepared to bear and on the type of rewards desired.

For example, one investor might specify that he or she is looking for rental houses priced in the low 40s which would rent for $300 to $325 per month in a particular section that is expected to get a new freeway. The investor would look for a seller who has an assumable loan and would carry back secondary financing.

A second investor might be looking for a 12-unit apartment building with one- and two-bedroom units with rents in the $200 to $300 range. She might be looking for something priced at about $250,000, with $50,000 down, and located in a suburban community now being engulfed by metropolitan expansion.

A third investor might be looking for a 40,000-square-foot office building priced at about $1 million in a close-in community which is now a part of a metropolitan area. He may be looking for an older building which could be upgraded after a new mall is built nearby.

A fourth investor may be looking for a freestanding store that is leased to a national chain organization with a high credit standing. She may be looking for something which requires about $60,000 cash, but the amount of cash can vary substantially. The preferred location is along one of several major suburban arteries or bypasses.

In each of these instances, the investor's selection will be based on policies that the investor has established. Those policies help to define some set of properties which will qualify for the investor's purposes.

A Workable Program. If the specifications are too stringent, there will not be enough properties to choose from. If the specifications are too broad, there will be too many properties to choose from. What is necessary is to define a workable program.

The multiple listing system is an easy way to identify properties which come on the market. A real estate broker who is a member of the multiple listing service can check weekly for new listings. This is likely to be most helpful in the case of single-family houses and doubles.

For small apartment buildings the easiest technique may be to find the real estate office that does the most volume in the particular type of property that the investor is interested in.

In some cases the only way to get suitable properties is to build them. There are two basic ways to start. One is to find the right land and then build for a tenant, or in some cases to build speculatively and to look for tenants while building. The other way is to find locations that will suit a prospective tenant under an arrangement in which the investor will build and lease. This alternative means finding the tenant first and then meeting his or her needs. This is frequently done with chain and franchise operations.

The search process for land is somewhat different in that the analysis required is heavily oriented to developability, which is related to zoning and to the timing and possible location of public improvements. But a systematic approach can be used to identify what types of land may be increasing in demand, where such land is located, and who owns it.

The investor's program may utilize many sources and extend over a long period of time. Some investors advertise, which is often a good approach. It is often necessary to scout the potential locations for properties and to check the public records for ownership or to have them checked. Some investors pay brokers a fee or commission to identify desirable properties.

The acquisition process requires compromises. Thus, when a candidate property is selected, a program for acquisition is set up which includes the terms and conditions under which the investor will buy. Some of those terms and conditions will be negotiable, others not.

The Use of Financing

Leverage. Investors who want high cash flow may use leverage to increase that cash flow relative to the cash invested by borrowing at low annual constants.

The annual constant is the ratio of the annual mortgage payment (which includes principal and interest) to the original amount of the mortgage. For example, $7.50 per month per $1,000 adds up to $90 per year, including principal and interest. The interest rate might be 8 percent, with the balance devoted to the payment of principal. The annual constant, then, is 9 percent ($90 divided by $1,000).

If the annual constant is lower than the ratio of the net operating income to the purchase price, then the leverage will increase the cash flow. For example, if the property sells for $100,000 and produces a net operating income of $10,000 (that is, rents less expenses, *excluding* mortgage payments), the ratio of the operating income to the purchase price is 10 percent ($10,000 divided by $100,000). Borrowing at a 9 percent annual constant will increase the cash flow relative to the cash investment as follows:

1. With no mortgage:

   Net operating income $10,000
   Less mortgage payment   0
   Cash flow $10,000

   $$\frac{\text{Cash flow}}{\text{Amount invested}} = \frac{\$10,000}{\$100,000} = 10\%$$

2. With a 50 percent mortgage.

   Net operating income 10,000
   Less mortgage payment
   ($50,000 × 0.09)   4,500
   Cash flow .... $ 5,500

   $$\frac{\text{Cash flow}}{\text{Amount invested}} = \frac{\$5,500}{\$50,000} = 11\%$$

3. With a 70 percent mortgage.

   Net operating income $10,000
   Less mortgage payment
   ($70,000 × 0.09)   6,300
   Cash flow .... $ 3,700

   $$\frac{\text{Cash flow}}{\text{Amount invested}} = \frac{\$3,700}{\$30,000} = 12.3\%$$

4. With a 90 percent mortgage.

   Net operating income $10,000
   Less mortgage payment
   ($90,000 × 0.09)   8,000
   Cash flow .... $ 1,900

   $$\frac{\text{Cash flow}}{\text{Amount invested}} = \frac{\$1,900}{\$10,000} = 19\%$$

The cash flow relative to the down payment on money invested is thus increased as the amount borrowed is increased, provided that the ratio of the net operating income to the purchase price is higher than the annual constant. The more that ratio exceeds the annual constant, the more the amount of money borrowed will increase the cash flow relative to the down payment.

With interest rates high and with real estate prices high, about the only way to get a low annual constant is to borrow on a low loan-to-value ratio. Even then, it may be difficult if the price of the property is high relative to its income.

An alternative is seller financing. Many sellers who have big taxable gains will want to report their gains on an installment basis. In order to do so, they need to get less than 30 percent of the purchase price in the year of sale. That 30 percent includes both the down payment and the principal payments (amortization) in the year of sale.

When a property is offered for sale at 29 percent down, this indicates that the seller may provide the financing. Many sellers will trade off lower interest rates for higher prices. If the price is not too high, there may be good cash flows with 20–29 percent down payments.

Tax Shelter.   Investors who want high tax shelter may use leverage to advantage.

Depreciable property, such as a building, will on a straight-line basis provide a fixed amount of depreciation each year, regardless of the type of financing. For example, a $100,000 property with $80,000 of the value in the building and $20,000 in the land has a depreciable base of $80,000. With a remaining economic life of 25 years, the depreciation is 4 percent of the $80,000, or $3,200, each year. The investor can write off that $3,200 each year, regardless of whether he or she pays all cash or borrows part of the purchase price.

If the investor pays all cash—$100,000—and the net operating income is $10,000, he or she will get $3,200 of the $10,000 in tax-sheltered income. Tax will be paid on income of $6,800, and this reduces the basis for tax purposes by $3,200 each year. Taxable income of $6,800 represents 68 percent of a $10,000 cash flow.

If the investor uses a $50,000 mortgage at 8 percent interest with a 9 percent constant, the mortgage payment will be $4,500 and the interest for the first year will be a little less than $4,000. (The interest is on the unpaid balance so that each month the amount of interest is less than the previous month. Thus, the annual interest will be a little less than 8 percent of $50,000.) The amortization will be a little over $500.

With the $50,000 mortgage the cash flow will be the $10,000 less the mortgage payment of $4,500, leaving $5,500. The taxable income, however, will be this $5,500 plus $500 amortization less the $3,200 depreciation, or $2,800. In other words, for the $50,000 down payment the investor gets $5,500 cash flow, of which the $2,800 taxable income represents about 51 percent.

The numbers will change slightly as the loan is reduced and the amount going to interest declines. But it is clear that the proportion of the cash flow which is sheltered may increase as the amount borrowed increases. For a 70 percent loan, the figures are as follows:

Net operating income		$10,000
Mortgage payment		
Interest (0.08 × $70,000)	$5,600	
Principal, first year (approximate) . . .	700	
		6,300
Cash flow		$ 3,700
Plus amortization (approximate)		700
		$ 4,400
Less depreciation		3,200
Taxable income		$ 1,200

Thus with the cash flow of $3,700 there is a taxable income of only $1,200. This $1,200 represents only 32 percent of the cash flow.

If 90 percent financing were available on similar terms (it is not likely to be), all of the cash flow would be sheltered and there would be a tax loss to write off against ordinary income. For example:

Net operating income	$10,000
Less mortgage payment	
($90,000 × 0.09 constant) . .	8,100
Cash flow	$ 1,900

On the $90,000 loan the interest at 8 percent is $7,200 for the year (or a little less with monthly payments). The amortization for the first year is $900.

Cash flow	$1,900
Plus amortization	900
	$2,800
Less depreciation	3,200
Tax loss	$ (400)

Thus, the entire cash flow of $1,900 is sheltered and there is a $400 tax loss which may be applied against ordinary income.

Accelerated depreciation would make these illustrations better in the earlier years of an investment but worse in the later years.

Many investors use lots of leverage in order to get tax shelter. Using more leverage, however, tends to push up the *rate* of interest. Lenders usually get higher interest rates for loans which are 80 percent of value than they do for loans which are 70 percent of value. For some types of property, the lowest rate may be at loan-to-value ratios as low as 60 percent.

Investors in income property generally obtain high leverage by using more than one mortgage. For example, an institutional lender may provide 70 percent of value, the seller may carry back 15 percent, and the purchaser thus puts up 15 percent. That would be $15,000 down with a $70,000 first mortgage and a $15,000 second mortgage.

Favorable terms may push up the price. In the above example, the sale price might really be $105,000, with $15,000 down and a $70,000 first mortgage. The seller would then have a $20,000 second mortgage, which in the open market might sell for only $15,000.

Some investors will gladly pay extra for favorable financing. They purchase a property expecting it to rise in value quickly. Thus, if the investor thinks that he can net $130,000 on a sale without waiting too long, he would rather capture the $30,000 increase in value with a down payment of $15,000 as compared to a down payment of $30,000.

With $30,000 down, he would get the whole $30,000 increase in value, which is doubling his initial investment. With $15,000 down, he could get only $25,000 of the $30,000 increase. But getting a $25,000 gain on a $15,000 investment is more profitable than getting a $30,000 gain on a $30,000 investment.

Such benefits are obviously influenced by a number of factors, including the interest costs and the tax consequences. In addition, the use of the added leverage is risky.

The point is, however, that many investors want to use leverage to capture the increase in value and look to types of investments that can be highly leveraged.

The availability of financing is influenced by the type of property, the willingness and ability of the seller to cooperate, the existing financing, the financial strength of the borrower, and the borrower's willingness to assume liability.

Location

It is hard to find good real estate investment opportunities where the local economy is on the decline. An area which is suffering from a persistent unemployment problem and is experiencing an exodus of population is usually not the most desirable place to look for profitable real estate investment opportunities. For example, many investors avoid one-industry towns if there is a danger that the industry will move elsewhere.

Growing communities, on the other hand, may provide some real opportunities. Sometimes it is difficult to pick a poor property in a rapidly growing area.

The future is not necessarily a projection of the past. But there is relative safety in investing in an area with a good solid growth rate. Even if the future growth rate is a little worse than the past growth rate has been, the area would still be a good one to invest in. It is the marginal areas that investors may find dangerous.

Within any local economy there develops a pattern of land use. Clusters of land use make up subareas of a metropolitan area. Different subareas have different growth potentials. These potentials differ because not all localities in a metropolitan area are equally desirable.

How any particular area performs relative to other areas depends on its competitive ability. If an area is in a high-income sector, then a growth of employment among high-income professionals will help it.

If a community consists mostly of blue-collar workers, then a growth of factory employment will increase real estate demand there. Look for those communities which are likely to get the lion's share of the local economic growth.

The investments which turn out best are usually those which are at locations that will benefit from increasing demand.

Zoning regulations and the potential for changes in those regulations are often critical factors. Limitations on land use through deed restrictions are another important factor.

The quality of a location changes over time. Thus, some locations get better and some worse. Some superb locations with older houses are currently the subject of renewed interest, for example. Many investors try to find the locations that are likely to improve in the future.

Monitoring Investments. Few real estate investments can be made and forgotten. Even getting into an investment often requires careful personal attention and some delicate timing.

The markets for most properties tend to be cyclical. The demand for real estate is volatile because expectations change and the cost and availability of mortgage money change. Thus, at one time there may be a great many buyers and at another time there may be very few.

The physical supply of real estate changes much more slowly than the demand for it. Building takes time. Furthermore, the stock added by building is a small percentage of the total stock. Typically, the demand intensifies before there is a change in the rate at which new properties are developed. Then the supply often overshoots the real needs and the market is overbuilt.

Careful investors try to buy in the early stages of a boom to and avoid buying too late.

If the political leadership of an area favors slow growth or managed growth, some investments will be hurt. Land, for example, may not be developed for a long time. Slow-growth policies tend to protect present investors by slowing down competition from new developments.

Avoiding Personal Liability. Investors may consider a variety of alternatives in order to avoid personal liability on loans. They can ask to have the property as the sole security for a loan. This is sometimes arranged through what is termed an "exculpatory clause." If an existing loan is taken over, the investor may be able to take title subject to the existing loan rather than assuming and agreeing to pay the existing loan. Even if there is personal liability on the first mortgage, an investor may be able to avoid it on the second, especially if the second mortgage is provided by the seller.

Protections. There are lots of other arrangements that can be made, especially in purchases of land. But if there are too many contingencies, the seller will not accept the deal. Decide what you think you are buying, and then make sure that the contract provides for it and that the necessary contingencies are covered. Thus you will only buy if your financing is right, if the title is good, if you get the right kind of deed, and if the property is in the condition that you believe it to be.

At times the contract overlooks something or circumstances may change after the initial contract has been signed but before the closing of escrow or settlement. The buyer may be protected from losing more than the deposit if it is agreed that forfeiture of the deposit will be the sole remedy in the event of default. Otherwise the buyer is potentially liable for damages on specific performance. Unlike labor contracts, real estate contracts can be enforced exactly. This is called "specific performance."

The size of the deposit is of some importance. Bigger deposits are more impressive when negotiating. The deposit can be put in an interest-bearing savings account so that the cost of tying up the money is reduced.

In addition to looking for suitable properties, the buyer should also look for agreeable sellers. Dealing with such sellers can make the contracting and the negotiating easier.

Negotiating Strategies

There are numerous negotiating strategies. Some strategies take much greater risks of losing a purchase than do others. And after you have worked hard to find a suitable investment you don't want to lose it. But you don't want to be taken advantage of either.

The Offer. The negotiating process starts with an offer to purchase. You set forth the terms and conditions on which you are prepared to buy. You spell them out, sign them, and give them to the seller as an offer together with a deposit.

Your offer should fall within an acceptable range. Wild offers can kill a deal. And sometimes an offer not meant to be accepted but rather to elicit a counteroffer is actually accepted. The first offer should be a serious one.

Legal Matters. The time to get your legal counsel is before you sign, not after. Your counsel can check the contract to see that it provides what you think it provides and that the legal aspects will not cause problems.

Some attorneys get involved in the business decision, and some are even good at it. You should decide whether you want business advice from your attorney or only legal advice.

Sometimes attorneys are so protective of their clients that they protect them out of deals. It is far better to decide what you want done and then to have your attorney make sure that the contract does it. Be sure you know how to do what you want to do, and find out *before* you sign the first piece of paper.

Most of the legal considerations will be noncontroversial. You don't want the settlement date to be postponed forever. You want clear title, and if you can't get it you want out. You want a warranty deed or its equivalent. Some of the more controversial issues have more business aspects than legal aspects. You want possession at settlement and proration of taxes, insurance, rents, and so on.

Basic Provisions. There may be some controversial contract items, such as finance terms, contingencies, forfeiture provisions, and time to settlement.

For strategic purposes, however, you should decide what provisions are most important to you and then be sure that they are in the contract. You may also propose some other provisions, so that in the negotiations you have something to give away if you are pressing for something extra or if the seller is pressing not to give you a key provision.

It is easiest to start with a "standard" form. The statement "It's OK, it's a standard form" falls into the same class as the statement "The check is in the mail."

Realtor® groups and others have forms which are pretty good as starters and may need no adjustment. But read them carefully, remembering that "the big print giveth and the small print taketh away." If you don't find a form you like, have a contract typed up, preferably by your attorney's office.

As has been noted earlier, the contract may have negative points. For example, you may pay a little higher price or make a little larger down payment than you had hoped to pay. You may agree to pay the second mortgage off in seven years, not ten, or even eight. You may agree to settle in 60 days, not 120.

You may not be willing to buy unless you get the desired new first mortgage. And you will want to limit your personal liability in certain ways as well as approve the existing leases.

Some of these things can be taken care of during the negotiation process without being part of the contract. You could be provided copies of the lease, and you could conduct your physical inspection of the property. The contract could then be silent on these matters.

The Seller's Response. The seller may respond to your offer by stating the written terms that are acceptable to him or her. You can hold firm on the important items and give in on the unimportant.

It helps to have an astute broker. You may want to be represented by an attorney who negotiates for you. Third-party negotiators make things easier because they can better see what the seller considers to be most important and work out mutually advantageous trade-offs.

Acceptance. When you finally get something acceptable, you are usually better off to take it than to push things to the hilt. A lot of work goes into finding suitable investments. You should not jeopardize a good deal in order to make it just a little better. Minor differences are just that, minor differences.

Crossing the threshold of a commitment to buy is difficult for many people. The decisions are not easy, but even making no decision is a decision. The best way to handle the situation may be to build a set of policies which guide you in your decision. In this way you will get great comfort from knowing that what you are doing conforms to your general plan. Then when you must take your first step, it will not seem so big.

Plan your steps in looking for real estate opportunities. Monitor your program. If the program is not working, replan it. But take your steps one at a time, and with enough steps you'll get where you want to go.

Have a safe and successful journey.

APPENDIX

Professional Designations:
A Compilation of
Requirements and
Organizations*

Lynn N. Woodward

*L*YNN N. WOODWARD, *Assistant Professor of Administration, Professorship of Real Estate and Land Use Economics, Wichita State University, Wichita, Kansas.*

Teaches real estate feasibility analysis, appraisal, finance, development, and equity investment. Has completed research projects on zoning, residential brokerage and commissions, computer applications in real estate, advanced appraisal and counseling techniques, and retail site location. President, American Real Estate Analysts, Inc.; serves on the board of directors of a mortgage banker; and is active in real estate development. Author of monthly column in Wichita Journal *and* The Wichitan *and of articles in* Appraisal Journal, Real Estate Review, Real Estate Today, *and other publications.*

The number of designations granted in real estate professional specialities has been increasing rapidly in recent years. This appendix summarizes the requirements of 41 real estate designations in the United States and Canada. The professional areas in real estate covered by designations include real estate residential marketing, industrial and commercial-investment brokerage and development, property management, appraisal, assessment, counseling, corporate finance, and related fields, and the university designations.

Professional designations, noted by initials following a name, are generally recognized as an indication of competence and special achieve-

* Mr. Woodward appreciates and wishes to acknowledge the help of Marcella Roberts, a graduate student in urban affairs and real estate at Wichita State University.

ment in a field. Academic degrees, such as MD, MBA, DBA, PhD, and LLD, are universally recognized. A number of organizations in the real estate field offer designations that indicate professional competence in particular real estate specialties. Each of these organizations seeks to professionalize its discipline by providing education and contact with other persons working in the field, and, above all, to bring such professionalism to the attention of the public being served.

Universally recognized designations in fields other than real estate include the CPA, or certified public accountant, designation, which recognizes competence in accounting and auditing and is administered by state boards of accountancy. The Institute of Chartered Analysts offers a certifed financial analyst designation which has educational, experience, and course requirements similar to those of the CPA. The initials *AIA* are associated in the public mind with architectural competence, but are not a professional designation based on particular requirements of the American Institute of Architects, other than licensing or certification by the state in which the architect practices. The experience requirements for such licensing keep AIA standards consistent, but the initials *AIA* after an architect's name merely recognize membership in the American Institute of Architects.

Twenty-four real estate organizations offering designations are discussed in this appendix. Seven of them are concerned with the appraisal of real property, including residential, income, industrial, farm and rural, and right-of-way property. The remaining 17 organizations concentrate in the areas of industrial development and sales, counseling services, various management specialties, marketing, corporate administration, and mortgage banking.

Seven of the 24 organizations offering real estate designations are affiliated with the National Association of Realtors®. They are: the American Institute of Real Estate Appraisers; the American Society of Real Estate Counselors; the Farm and Land Institute; the Institute of Real Estate Management; the Real Estate Securities and Syndication Institute; the Realtors® National Marketing Institute; and the Society of Industrial Realtors®. In addition, the Graduate Realtors® Institute programs of the NAR attempt to professionalize and advance the expertise of sales practitioners. The GRI is administered through state Realtor® associations that determine the specific requirements for the GRI designation.

Eight of the 24 organizations operate specifically in the appraisal field. These are: the American Association of Certified Appraisers, Inc.; the American Institute of Real Estate Appraisers; the Appraisal Institute, Canada; the National Association of Review Appraisers; the Society of Real Estate Appraisers; the American Society of Farm Managers and Rural Appraisers, Inc.; the American Society of Appraisers; and the International Association of Assessing Officers. The Society of Industrial Realtors® also requires appraisal experience.

Attempts to improve the quality of real estate counseling service and to bring together the top practitioners in the field of real estate counseling are made by the American Society of Real Estate Counselors and

TABLE 1
Summary Chart

Designation	Number Holding Designation	Has Stated Purpose	Has Age Requirement	Has Experience Requirement	Has Educational Level Requirement	Offers Own Courses	Exams (comprehensive)	Written	Oral	Accepts Course Equivalents	Requires Demonstration Reports	Interview/Recommendation	Contribution	Requires Memberships	Requires Other Designations	Initiation/Application Fee	Membership Dues	Time Limit on Candidacy	Other Requirements	Offering Organization
Real estate sales																				
CRB		X	X	X		X	X				X	X		X		X	X	X		Realtors® National Marketing Institute
CRS		X	X	X		X					X		X	X		X	X	X		Realtors® National Marketing Institute
GRI		X			X	X								X						Graduate, Realtors® Institute
MIRM		X	X	X	X	X					X	X		X		X	X	X		Institute of Residential Marketing
Industrial, commercial investment																				
CCIM	341	X	X	X		X	X	X				X		X		X	X	X		Realtors® National Marketing Institute
CID		X	X	X		X	X	X		X	X	X	X			X	X	X		American Industrial Development Council
CRSS		X	X	X	X	X	X	X	X	X	X	X		X	X	X	X	X		Real Estate Securities and Syndication Institute
SIR	1275	X		X		X	X	X	X	X	X	X		X	X	X	X	X	X	Society of Industrial Realtors®
Management																				
CPM		X	X	X	X	X	X	X		X	X	X		X		X	X	X	X	Institute of Real Estate Management
AMO		X	X	X		X		X				X		X	X	X	X	X	X	Institute of Real Estate Management
ARM		X	X	X		X		X			X	X				X	X	X		Institute of Real Estate Management
RAM	400	X	X	X	X	X	X	X			X			X		X	X	X	X	National Association of Home Builders
AFM		X	X	X	X	X	X	X	X	X	X	X		X		X	X	X	X	American Society of Farm Managers and Rural Appraisers
AFLM													X				X			Farm & Land Institute
CSM	461	X	X	X	X	X	X	X	X	X		X		X		X	X	X	X	International Council of Shopping Centers
ASPD	269	X		X	X	X	X	X	X	X		X			X	X	X	X	X	International Council of Shopping Centers

Appraisal

Designation	No.	Organization
SRA	3900	Society of Real Estate Appraisers
SRPA	2100	Society of Real Estate Appraisers
SREA	450	Society of Real Estate Appraisers
RM		American Institute of Real Estate Appraisers
MAI		American Institute of Real Estate Appraisers
SR/WA		American Right of Way Association
ARA		American Society of Farm Managers and Rural Appraisers
CRA	7000	Appraisal Institute, Canada
AACI		Appraisal Institute, Canada
CRA	5123	National Association of Review Appraisers
RRA (Canada)		National Association of Review Appraisers
RPA	350	Building Owners and Managers Institute International
CA-R	2300	American Association of Certified Appraisers
CA-S		American Association of Certified Appraisers
CA-C		American Association of Certified Appraisers
ASA		American Society of Appraisers

Assessment

Designation	No.	Organization
CAE		International Association of Assessing Officers
AAE		International Association of Assessing Officers
CPE		International Association of Assessing Officers
RES		International Association of Assessing Officers

Counseling

Designation	No.	Organization
CRE	467	American Society of Real Estate Counselors
SEC	45	Society of Exchange Counselors

Financial

Designation	No.	Organization
CMB	116	Mortgage Bankers Association

Corporate

Designation	No.	Organization
CREA		National Association of Corporate Real Estate Executives
CRES		National Association of Corporate Real Estate Executives
DCI		National Association of Corporate Real Estate Executives

Other fields

Designation	No.	Organization
AIA		American Institute of Architects
CPA		Certified Public Accountant
CFA		Institute of Chartered Financial Analysts

Universities

Designation	No.	Organization
PhD/DBA		7 universities
MBA/MS		37 universities

the Society of Exchange Counselors. Both of these organizations are highly selective in their membership requirements, and each of their members is entitled to use the organizational designation as an indication of his or her competence.

The professionalization of apartment building managers has been undertaken by the National Association of Home Builders through its Registered Apartment Manager (RAM) program. Other property management designations include those offered by the Institute of Real Estate Management, the International Council of Shopping Centers, and the Society of Real Property Administrators, a recently organized arm of the Building Owners and Managers Institute International.

Farm and rural areas receive attention through the American Society of Farm Managers and Rural Appraisers, Inc., and through NAR's Farm and Land Institute. The management and appraisal designations of the Farm Managers and Rural Appraisers society require appraisal experience and a college degree; the Farm and Land Institute designation requires a high school diploma and experience in farm, ranch, recreation, urban, or suburban real estate.

Marketing is stressed by the Realtors® National Marketing Institute and the Institute of Residential Marketing as well as the organizations mentioned above. Real estate syndications and other forms of real estate securities, including certain types of condominiums, real estate investment trusts, and mortgage securities, are emphasized by the Real Estate Securities and Syndication Institute of NAR. The National Association of Corporate Real Estate Executives (NACORE) is developing three designations for real estate specialists within major corporations. Financial expertise is the focus of the Mortgage Bankers Association of America.

Similarities and differences among the various organizations and designations are summarized in Table 1. When an organization has a particular requirement for one of its designations, the fact that the requirement exists is indicated by an *X* in the column. The particulars of the requirement are stated in summary fashion in the space devoted to each organization. These particulars may not be completely accurate. Requests for information were sent to every known real estate organization, but not all responded or responded with all of the information needed. Nevertheless, the information contained in this appendix should help real estate organizations to update their designation requirements and should help present and potential real estate practitioners in their career planning.

	Certified Real Estate Brokerage Manager (CRB)	Certified Residential Salesman (CRS)	Certified Commercial-Investment Member (CCIM)
Designation			
Offered by	Realtors® National Marketing Institute 430 North Michigan Avenue Chicago, Illinois 60611 (312) 440-8593	(312) 440-8592	(312) 440-8532
Number holding designation in 1978			
Purpose	Seeks to promote professional standing of Realtors® by providing practical education and helping establish sound and ethical practices		
Age requirement	21		
Experience	Candidate: Two years full time as licensed broker or salesperson. Currently in real estate brokerage Designation: Five consecutive years as active principal and hold current broker's license	Three years in residential sales. Prequalification: Five years of residential sales experience and 100 closed residential transactions (listings or sales)	One year as real estate broker or salesperson in commercial-investment real estate
Educational level	High school or equivalent		
Courses	MM101: How to Manage a Real Estate Office Successfully For designation: MM101, 102, 103, 104, 105 + 30 elective points	All required courses or equivalents	Introduction to Commercial/Investment Real Estate or CI101: Fundamentals of Real Estate Investment Taxation Designation: CI101, 102, 103, 104, 105 + 45 points
Examinations and examination dates	Comprehensive exam		Comprehensive exam
Course equivalents			
Demonstration reports	One demonstration report of effective management concepts	Document activity and experience in residential sales; document completion of four areas of related experience	Resume of completed commercial-investment transactions; three demos from six categories of sales to investors or to users, exchange, land sale lease, syndication

Interview	Field interviews at discretion of Admissions Committee; after exam		After exam
Contribution		Be actively selling; personally execute 150 closed transactions	
Memberships required	GRI, local board of NAR, RNMI (in own name)	GRI, NAR, RNMI	National Association of Realtors®, RNMI
Designations required	Realtor®	Realtor®	Realtor®
Initiation/application fee	Annual candidate's service fee of $25 + exam grading fee (if taken outside regular course)	Prequalification: $100 application service fee	Application service fee $25 + annual candidate's dues
Membership dues	RNMI $35; annual designated dues, local board of Realtors®		
Time limit on candidacy	Minimum one year, maximum five years + 2 1-year extensions	Five years	Minimum one year, maximum five years + 2 1-year extensions
Other requirements			

Designation	Graduate, Realtors® Institute (GRI)
Offered by	State associations of the National Association of Realtors®; state associations manage and maintain their own GRI programs, with review by the National Association of the course outline
Number holding designation in 1978	
Purpose	To educate and train persons to function effectively in the residential real estate brokerage business
Age requirement	
Experience	
Educational level	

Courses	Ninety hours of instruction, usually divided into three 30-hour courses organized in sequence in order to establish performance capabilities
Examinations and examination dates	
Course equivalents	
Demonstration reports	
Interview	
Contribution	
Memberships required	Realtor® or Realtor®-Associate
Designations required	
Initiation/application fee	
Membership dues	
Time limit on candidacy	
Other requirements	

Member of the Institute of Residential Marketing (MIRM)

Designation	
Offered by	NAHB Sales and Marketing Council Institute of Residential Marketing 15th and M Streets, N.W. Washington, D.C. 20005 (Obtain forms from Admissions Committee at above address)
Number holding designation in 1978	
Purpose	Increase professional competence of sales and marketing people in the industry and educate new people for the industry

	Candidate: 18
	Designation: 21
Age requirement	
Experience	Three years full time in housing industry
Educational level	High school or equivalent
Courses	Pilot program started in 1975 at California State University; gradually being added to curricula of colleges and universities around country, including Auburn University, Montgomery, Alabama; UCLA, Westwood, California; California State University, Fullerton; New York University, New York, New York; Rockhurst College, Kansas City, Missouri; Roosevelt University, Chicago; and Tulane University, New Orleans
Examinations and examination dates	IRM Courses I, II, III, and IV; 80 required credits + 25 elective credits
Course equivalents	
Demonstration reports	Article or case study (subject matter to be approved by Education Committee) for publication
Interview	
Contribution	
Memberships required	Member or employed by member of National Association of Home Builders; member of National Sales and Marketing Council.
Designations required	
Initiation/application fee	$50 with application for candidacy
Membership dues	$50 annually
Time limit on candidacy	Six years; grandfather clause for two years
Other requirements	Designation awarded where experience and knowledge exceed Institute requirements

Designation	*Certified Industrial Developer (CID)*
Offered by	American Industrial Development Council 1207 Grand Avenue, Suite 845 Kansas City, Missouri 64106 (Address inquiries to: Secretary, AIDC Certification Board)
Number holding designation in 1978	341 active (420 certified since program began)
Purpose	Identify knowledgeable professionals having the varied skills necessary to provide services for facility planners in industrial development field
Age requirement	None specified
Experience	Eight years
Educational level	
Courses	Must attend seminars, conferences, and meetings of recognized development organizations, such as AIDC, Urban Land Institute, National Association of Industrial and Office Parks, National Association of State Development Agencies, and Society of Industrial Realtors®
Examinations and examination dates	Written examinations at annual conferences of AIDC, at Industrial Development Institute at University of Oklahoma, and at regional ID meetings in United States and Canada; exam has 50 true-false, completion, and multiple-choice questions, as well as a case study problem and an oral portion; exam is open to all AIDC members or nonmembers who qualify
Course equivalents	
Demonstration reports	
Interview	
Contribution	Annual recertification to confirm that certified member is continuing with his or her ID education

Memberships required	
Designations required	
Initiation/application fee	Examination fee $10 for AIDC members, $25 for non-members
Membership dues	
Time limit on candidacy	
Other requirements	

Certified Real Estate Securities Sponsor
(CRSS)

Designation	
Offered by	Real Estate Securities and Syndication Institute (RESSI) 430 North Michigan Avenue Chicago, Illinois 60611 (312) 440-8183
Number holding designation in 1978	
Purpose	To establish standards of practice and to offer educational courses and professional designation
Age requirement	21
Experience	One year as licensed real estate or securities broker sponsoring, issuing, marketing, or managing an interest in real estate defined as a security (LPs, REITs, condo securities) *Candidate:* One year of experience *Before designation:* Two years of experience
Educational level	High school or equivalent
Courses	RESSI I and II plus CI's 101 and 103 or FLI's Agricultural and Urban Land Brokerage and Land Return Analysis

Examinations and examination dates	Exams for above courses
Course equivalents	125 points required, 75 of which are electives from experience, required courses, college education, demo reports, other designations, other courses
Demonstration reports	One demonstration report + résumé of consummated real estate securities transactions
Interview	Recommendation of state chapter
Contribution	
Memberships required	RESSI (in own name); local board of Realtors® (Realtor®, Realtor®-Associate, or affiliate)
Designations required	
Initiation/application fee	Candidate service fee, annual candidate dues, grading fee
Membership dues	Annual dues in RESSI and state chapter
Time limit on candidacy	Five years
Other requirements	

		SIR		
	Active	Salesman Affiliate	Associate	International Associate
Designation	SIR			
Offered by	Society of Industrial Realtors® of the National Association of Realtors® 925 15th Street, N.W. Washington, D.C. 20005 (202) 637-6880			
Number holding designation in 1978	1,275 members and associates in United States, Canada, England, and France			
Purpose	Unite Realtors® buying, selling, or leasing land and buildings to industry; foster knowledge, education, integrity, and quality workmanship in industrial real estate; exchange information and listings; cooperation; certification			

Age requirement	28 years	25 years (or demonstrate special ability)	None	None
Experience	Be active industrial real estate broker; have creditable record in industrial real estate for at least eight years (three yrs. may be educational, engineering, or appraisal)	Creditable record in selling and leasing real estate for five years (two years may be educational, engineering, or appraisal); with active member two years	Open to public utilities, established industrial real estate development companies, insurance companies, with major industrial portfolios, Canadian chartered banks, and major investment funds	Foreign brokers must conduct a substantial amount of industrial real estate business; open to qualified real estate brokers, corporate real estate executives, and established industrial real estate development companies in foreign countries (Canada same as United States)
Educational level	None specified, but may substitute for experience (three years) MA, MS, or PhD; law or real estate–related degree; CPA;	None specified, but may substitute for experience (two years) SIR I and II; or AIREA VII and SIR II		
Courses	SIR Course I, SIR Course II	SIR Course I, SIR Course II		
Examinations and examination dates	Exam given by Admissions Committee at national meeting or complete SIR Courses I and II or AIREA VII and SIR II			
Course equivalents	AIREA Course VII (Industrial Properties) for SIR Course I			
Demonstration reports				
Interview	By member of a chapter committee and a district vice president			
Contribution				
Memberships required	National Association of Realtors®; licensed broker	Realtor® or Realtor®-Associate	SIR chapter in territory of principal office	
Designations required	MAI, CPM, CCIM, CRB, or FRI may substitute for one year of experience			
Initiation/application fee	$250	$150	None	None

Membership dues	$325	$225	$250 ($125 for additional designee)	$250 ($125 for additional designee)
Time limit on candidacy			
Other requirements	Reputation for sincerity, integrity, and ability		

	Certified Property Manager (CPM)	Accredited Management Organization (AMO)	Accredited Resident Manager (ARM)
Designation			
Offered by	Institute of Real Estate Management (IREM) 430 North Michigan Avenue Chicago, Illinois 60611 (312) 440-8600		
Number holding designation in 1978			
Purpose	Serve professional needs of resident, supervisory, and executive property managers; gather and disseminate property management information and certify managers and firms		
Age requirement	Legal	Designation is for firms	None specified
Experience	*For candidate:* One year of property management *For designation:* College degree + 5 years of experience; be actively employed in property management when applying	Three years in property management; employ at least one CPM who directs and supervises	Additional standards of experience and professional qualification
Educational level	*For candidate:* High school or equivalent		
Courses	60 points: 300 series (basic theories and techniques of managing investment real estate); 401 (Managing Real Estate as an Investment); 500 series (Management Plan)	CPM must take Course 701 (Managing the Management Office) before accreditation	REM 101 (Successful On-Site Management) or REM 102 (Successful Management of Public Housing)

Examinations and examination dates	Three exams; may challenge; $150, series 300 and 400; $200, series 500		
Course equivalents	30 points of electives: IREM and NAR courses leading to MAI, CCIM, CRE, or SIR		
Demonstration reports	500 series (Management Plan)		
Interview	Yes	IREM chapter must endorse organization	Yes
Contribution			
Memberships required	*Candidate:* Real estate license *Designation:* NAR	CPM must head management department of firm	
Designations required		Independent credit check; meet IREM financial criteria	
Initiation/application fee	$75 + $100 annual service fee	$150	$30
Membership dues	$150	$150 accrediting fee	$40
Time limit on candidacy	One year minimum, five years maximum	Reaccredit every three years	
Other requirements		Insurance	

Designation	*Registered Apartment Manager (RAM)*
Offered by	National Association of Home Builders 15th and M Streets, N.W. Washington, D.C. 20005
Number holding designation in 1978	
Purpose	Signify completion of professional educational programs and fulfillment of rigid standards for apartment and property managers
Age requirement	
Experience	First three years of full-time apartment management
Educational level	High school graduate

Courses	National Registered Apartment Manager exam (given locally or by NAHB), 80 points required for designation; required credits include NAHB RAM school, 48 hours of instruction; discretionary points for additional experience, degree, broker's or salesperson's license, other approved NAHB seminars, and articles submitted to and published by NAHB
Examinations and examination dates	National Registered Apartment Manager exam (given locally or by NAHB)
Course equivalents	
Demonstration reports	Apartment management case study or article, subject to be approved by Education Committee; minimum 2,000 words
Interview	Must be approved by area home builders association and RAM Board of Governors
Contribution	
Memberships required	NAHB (or employed by member of NAHB)
Designations required	
Initiation/application fee	$100 ($50 application fee + first year's dues of $50)
Membership dues	$50 per year (for both candidates and RAMs)
Time limit on candidacy	Three years; may apply for extension
Other requirements	Agree to abide by RAM's Code of Ethics; earn a minimum of two CEUs per year for maintaining certification
Designation	*Accredited Farm Manager (AFM)* *Accredited Rural Appraiser (ARA)*
Offered by	American Society of Farm Managers and Rural Appraisers, Inc. P.O. Box 6857 360 South Monroe, # 460 Denver, Colorado 80206 (303) 388-4858

Number holding designation in 1978	Approximately 400	
Purpose	To develop and promote the professions of farm management and rural appraisal	
Age requirement	None specified	None specified
Experience	Five years (contact secretary for management report criteria)	Five years; 75 appraisals on approximately 200-acre units
Educational level	College degree	College degree
Courses	Society's management course	After 1981, society's basic and appraisal course or approved equivalent, plus a principles course
Examinations and examination dates	Comprehensive written and oral exam; offered twice a year (August and/or September)	Comprehensive written and oral exam; offered twice a year (August and/or September)
Course equivalents		
Demonstration reports	Two management reports giving complete farm management operating plans	Three reports showing ability in rural appraisals (at least two narrative reports)
Interview		
Contribution		
Memberships required	One year of society membership as a non-accredited professional	One year of society membership as a non-accredited professional
Designations required		
Initiation/application fee	$150 + $75 if applicant passes	$150 + $75 if applicant passes

Membership dues	$25 annually for title + $100 for professional members or $30 for academic or associate members or candidate members
Time limit on candidacy	
Other requirements	

Designation	*Accredited Farm and Land Member (AFLM)*
	(Accredited Farm and Land Broker (AFLB) was changed to AFLM in 1975; members who hold AFLB may continue to use it at their option)
Offered by	Farm and Land Institute
	National Association of Realtors®
	430 North Michigan Avenue
	Chicago, Illinois 60611
	(313) 440-8040
Number holding designation in 1978	
Purpose	To establish professional standards, to provide education for members, and to influence formulation of public policies affecting farm and land
Age requirement	25
Experience	Five years in farm, ranch, recreational, urban, or suburban real estate
	For candidacy: Hold license as real estate broker or salesperson and have at least two years of full-time experience immediately preceding application
Educational level	High school or equivalent
Courses	FLI Introduction to Agricultural and Urban Land Brokerage, FLI Federal Taxes and Real Estate, FLI Land Return Analysis, + one required elective + one or two additional electives (may be courses offered by other approved associations)

Examinations and examination dates	Written comprehensive examination
Course equivalents	Approved courses offered by AIREA, ASREC, IREM, RESSI, RNMI, and SIR may be substituted for "required elective" point credit
Demonstration reports	
Interview	Recommendation of chapter
Contribution	One or more years on FLI Board of Governors or national commitee; attendance at two national meetings and candidate orientation sessions
Memberships required	Minimum two years in FLI, Realtor®
Designations required	
Initiation/application fee	$100 with application for candidacy
Membership dues	Annual dues for candidates and accredited members are the same and are established by Board of Governors
Time limit on candidacy	Five years
Other requirements	

	Certified Shopping Center Manager (CSM)	*Accredited Shopping Center Promotion Director (ASPD)*
Designation		
Offered by	International Council of Shopping Centers 665 Fifth Avenue New York, New York 10022 (212) 421-8181	
Number holding designation in 1978	461	269
Purpose	Establish high professional standards in shopping center management and promotion; recognize those persons who meet high standards; and establish educational standards

Age requirement	21	
Experience	Be or have been a shopping center manager; four years in shopping center management, including maintenance, leasing, promotion, and shopping center income and expense accounting (may substitute for one year of experience ICSC courses Management I and II or equivalent college-level courses)	Three years of full-time experience in shopping center promotion; may also count up to two years of full-time activity in advertising, newspaper, radio, TV, public relations, or shopping center management
Educational level	None specified	None specified (may count completion of two college-level courses in advertising, journalism, marketing, or public relations toward general educational requirements)
Courses	During written and oral examinations, demonstrate professional knowledge and abilities in maintenance and construction, leasing, promotion, center accounting, mortgage and finance, center retailing and merchandising, insurance, legal, and community relations	During written and oral examinations, demonstrate professional knowledge and abilities in retailing, marketing, tenant relations, merchants associations, advertising, public relations, communications, insurance, legal, budget planning and record keeping, and promotion
Examinations and examination dates	Written and oral exam offered once each year	Written and oral exam offered once each year
Course equivalents		ICSC Marketing or Promotion Institute
Demonstration reports		
Interview	Field screening process; final review before exam	Field screening process; final review before exam
Contribution	Share expertise, participate in meetings, and help develop new ideas and concepts	
Memberships required		
Designations required		
Initiation/application fee	Examination fee with application: ICSC members, $100; nonmembers, $200.	
Membership dues		
Time limit on candidacy	Apply in January for May exam	Apply in May for September exam
Other requirements		

	Senior Residential Appraiser (SRA)	Senior Real Property Appraiser (SRPA)	Senior Real Estate Analyst (SREA)
Designation			
Offered by	Society of Real Estate Appraisers 7 South Dearborn Street Chicago, Illinois 60603 (312) 346-7422		
Number holding designation in 1978	3,900	2,100	450
Purpose	To promote professional and educational interests of real estate appraisers and analysts, to define and elevate standards, to promulgate a code of ethical practice, and to provide technical training courses		
Age requirement	21 (waived for college students)	21 (waived for college students)	
Experience	Experience evaluated on basis of point system for calendar time and "frequency of exposure to practical appraisal problems"		Eight to 12 years in income-property appraising
Educational level	If born after Dec. 31, 1979, have college degree or pass an academic substitute acceptable to Society		
Courses	Course 101: An Introduction to Appraising Real Property; a Study Guide to review for Exam R-2 to test ability to apply knowledge from experience and courses	Course 101, Exam R-2, Course 201: Principles of Income Property Appraising	Course 101, Exam R-2, Course 201, + Course 301: Special Application of Appraisal Analysis
Examinations and examination dates	Six-hour exam for 101, six-hour exam for R-2	Course 101, R-2, eight-hour exam for 201	Oral exams by admissions committee; recertify every five years
Course equivalents	AIREA Course 1-A for 101	AIREA Courses 1-A and 1-B for 101 and 201	AIREA Courses 1-A and 1-B for 101 and 201
Demonstration reports	One demonstration report on a residential property	One demonstration report on an income property	
Interview			

	Residential Member (RM)	Member, Appraisal Institute (MAI)	
Designation	Residential Member (RM)	Member, Appraisal Institute (MAI)	
Offered by	American Institute of Real Estate Appraisers 430 North Michigan Avenue Chicago, Illinois 60611 (312) 664-9700		
Number holding designation in 1978			
Purpose	To create a qualified corps of competent appraisers through education and testing		
Age requirement	None specified	None specified	
Experience	Three years of real estate, including two years of residential field (appraisal) experience	Five years of "creditable appraisal experience," with three years of "field variety experience"	
Contribution			Advance appraisal profession through participation in organization work, teaching, or developing courses, writing, or research
Memberships required			
Designations required			SRPA
Initiation/application fee	$25	$25	
Membership dues	$60 + chapter dues	$90 + chapter dues	$120 + chapter dues
Time limit on candidacy	Ten years	Ten years	
Other requirements			

Educational level	High school or equivalent	College degree or equivalent of a four-year college education
Courses	#1-A: Basic Appraisal Principles, Methods, and Techniques; #1-B; #8: Single-Family Residential Appraisal	#1-A; #1-B: Capitalization Theory and Techniques; #2: Urban Properties; one elective exam; and one comprehensive exam
Examinations and examination dates	#1-A and #8; taken at end of course or in May and September of each year	#1-A, #1-B, and #2; one elective exam; and comprehensive exam
Course equivalents	SREA 101 for #1-A + $150 for transfer of credit; SREA #R-2 for #8 (may be included in above fee)	SREA 101 and 201 for #1-A and #1-B, + $150 each for transfer of credit
Demonstration reports	Three single-family residential demo reports (one short narrative + two form reports); or two single-family residential reports (one narrative meeting standards for MAI demo and 1 form report)	Two demo appraisal reports, at least one of which is on income-producing property
Interview	Local chapter recommendation on "good moral character, integrity, sincerity of purpose, and general fitness"	
Contribution		
Memberships required		
Designations required	National Association of Realtors®	

Initiation/application fee	$50	$50
Membership dues		
Time limit on candidacy	Ten years	Ten years
Other requirements		

Designation	*Senior Member (SR/WA)*
Offered by	American Right of Way Association International Headquarters 3727 West Sixth Street—Suite 504 Los Angeles, California 90020 (213) 383-2117
Number holding designation in 1978	More than 11,000 members in Canada, Puerto Rico, and United States; those with designations: 2,550
Purpose	To better the conditions of the individual member, promote high standards and cooperative spirit among members, and engender attributes which elevate the profession
Age requirement	21
Experience	*For candidacy:* Prejourneyman three years (can substitute one year + four-year college degree or two years + two-year college degree) *For senior application:* Five additional years of journeyman experience; minimum of 600 experience credits required (10 credits per month of "journeyman" experience)
Educational level	Minimum of one college-level course in each of four fields of engineering, appraisal, law, and negotiation; since 1/1/78, college degree required before filing senior application; may be fulfilled by: (1) bachelor's degree, or (2) earning 480 additional education credits, or (3) CLEP score of 400 or above

Courses	1,200 credits earned by combination of experience, examination, and education (400 total minimum education credits: education credits from SR/WA exams, 155; education credits by course attendance, 245); complete AR/WA Courses 101, 201, 202 (Principles of ROW Acquisition, Communications in Real Estate Acquisition, and Interpersonal Relations of Real Estate Acquisition)
Examinations and examination dates	Four comprehensive exams in right-of-way engineering, appraisal, law, and negotiation (155 education credits)
Course equivalents	Approved courses include those from AIREA, IREM, SREA, American Society of Farm Managers and Rural Appraisers, and college and university courses
Demonstration reports	
Interview	For senior applications: two AR/WA references and chapter interview of candidate
Contribution	
Memberships required	American Right of Way Association (by vote of chapter executive board)
Designations required	
Initiation/application fee	$10 candidacy application fee, $5 annual renewal fee; $10 with exam request form; $20 senior application fee, $10 annual renewal fee; $10 fee to challenge exam
Membership dues	
Time limit on candidacy	Indefinite; exam reports valid for seven years
Other requirements	

	Canadian Residential Appraiser (CRA)	Accredited Appraiser Canadian Institute (AACI)
Designation		
Offered by	Appraisal Institute of Canada Suite 309—93 Avenue Lombard Winnipeg, Manitoba R3B 3B1 (204) 942-0751	
Number holding designation in 1978	Membership of approximately 7,000	
Purpose	Dedicated to high and uniform standards for members of the appraisal profession (is the national professional institute of real estate appraisers)	
Age requirement	None specified	None specified
Experience	Three years; CRA is an intermediate designation and may be used by holder only in connection with appraisal and valuation of individual undeveloped residential dwelling sites and dwellings containing not more than three self-contained family housing units	Five years; AACI designates fully accredited membership in the institute and may be used by the holder in connection with the appraisal of all types of property within limits prescribed in the Code of Ethics and Standards of Professional Conduct
Educational level	Exemptions are available for all or partial credits from the institute's program of education to members and/or graduates of complete programs of other organizations or educational institutions; must have approval of National Governing Council	

Courses	Available on correspondence and lecture basis; Course 100, Introduction to Real Estate Appraising; Economics I; Building Construction and Cost Estimating; Law	Same + Appraisal II and III, Economics II, and Communication Concepts and Strategies
Examinations and examination dates	National exams in appraisal in January, April, and September, ber, exams in other subjects in April and September	
Course equivalents	National Admissions Committee may approve educational programs from time to time; activities allied to the real estate or construction industry and related to the appraisal process may also be recognized for credit	
Demonstration reports	One single-family appraisal report	Three (?) demo reports
Interview	Chapter committee	Chapter committee
Contribution	Continuing professional development of members by presentation of local, regional, and national seminars and conferences	
Memberships required	Registration restricted to candidates for Appraisal II and III	
Designations required		
Initiation/application fee	By correspondence: contact National Executive office; by lecture program: contact local chapter	
Membership dues		
Time limit on candidacy		
Other requirements		

Certified Review Appraiser (CRA)

or

Registered Review Appraiser (RRA) (Canada)

Designation	
Offered by	National Association of Review Appraisers (NARA) Suite 410, Midwest Federal Building St. Paul, Minnesota 55101 (612) 227-6696
Number holding designation in 1978	5,123
Purpose	Maintenance of professional standards in the field of review appraising; goals include education, ethics, and the enhancement of the review appraiser
Age requirement	Be of legal age
Experience	Have five full years of appraisal review experience or its equivalent; be engaged in real estate review appraisal profession (investigation, analysis, estimation of cost, forecast of earning power, and determination of value of properties of every description and review analysis thereof)
Educational level	None specified
Courses	Sponsors professional development seminars for review appraisers each spring: Practical Procedures for Review Appraisers
Examinations and examination dates	Nationally administered certifying/testing examination
Course equivalents	
Demonstration reports	
Interview	
Contribution	
Memberships required	
Designations required	

Initiation/application fee	One-time processing fee of $10 plus an examination fee of $25
Membership dues	$85
Time limit on candidacy	
Other requirements	

Designation	*Real Property Administrator (RPA)*
	Certificate of Achievement after completion of three of seven parts: #1, #2, + any other part; RPA designation and diploma on completion of remaining four parts
Offered by	Building Owners and Managers Institute International 1221 Massachusetts Avenue, N.W. Washington, D.C. 20005 (202) 638-2929
Number holding designation in 1978	350
Purpose	To increase the level of proficiency of those who are managing commercial office property
Age requirement	21
Experience	No requirement
Educational level	High school graduate or equivalent
Courses	Seven courses and exams (may be taken in any order; offered through lecture, group study, or self-study): Engineering and Building Structures; Real Property Maintenance; Accounting and Financial Concepts; Risk Management and Insurance; The Judicial System and Legal Concepts; Real Estate Finance and Economics; and Management Concepts

	Affiliate (not certified)	Residential First Level R-1 (not certified)	Certified Appraiser— Residential (CA-R)	Certified Appraiser— Senior (CA-S)	Certified Appraiser— Consultant (CA-C)
Examinations and examination dates	January and May of each year; preregistration required by November 1 and April 1; review classes (ten hours) available before exams				
Course equivalents					
Demonstration reports					
Interview					
Contribution					
Memberships required					
Designations required					
Initiation/application fee	$100 enrollment fee; exam fee included in order for learning materials: $150 each for Parts 1–3 and $110 each for Parts 4–7				
Membership dues					
Time limit on candidacy					
Other requirements					
Designation	Affiliate (not certified)	Residential First Level R-1 (not certified)	Certified Appraiser— Residential (CA-R)	Certified Appraiser— Senior (CA-S)	Certified Appraiser— Consultant (CA-C)
Offered by	American Association of Certified Appraisers, Inc. (AACA) 7 Eswin Drive Greenhills Shopping Plaza Cincinnati, Ohio 45218 (513) 825-1603				
Number holding designation in 1978	2300				
Purpose	To advance the standards of professionalism and ethical appraisal procedures, and provide services to qualified appraisers				

Age requirement	None	None	None	None
Experience	Interest in furthering professionalism of appraisal profession	Three years of experience in appraising residential property and "show acceptable residential appraising expertise"	Five years of experience in appraising residential and commercial property and "show acceptable residential and commercial appraising expertise"	CA–S designation for two years and/or meet requirements of Educational Committee
Educational level				
Courses/examinations	After Charter designation period, demonstration appraisal reports and formal examinations may be required for accreditation	After Charter designation period, demonstration appraisal reports and formal examinations may be required for accreditation	After Charter designation period, demonstration appraisal reports and formal examinations may be required for accreditation; advancement to higher tier (in five-tier designation structure) is attained through notifying national office of change in experience and qualifications since initial application and providing evidence of acceptable appraisal expertise in a higher tier	
Examination dates				
Course equivalents				
Demonstration reports				
Interview				
Contribution				
Memberships required	None			
Designations required	None			
Initiation/application fee	$15	$15	$15	$15
Membership dues	$45	$45	$45	$45
Time limit on candidacy	None			
Other requirements	Certified Appraisers—those satisfying present designation criteria; Charter Designates—for a limited period, those approved shall be Charter Designates			

	Senior Member (ASA)
Designation	
Offered by	American Society of Appraisers (ASA)
	Dulles International Airport
	P.O. Box 17266
	Washington, D.C. 20041
Number holding desig-	
nation in 1978	
Purpose	
Age requirement	30
Experience	Six years
Educational level	
Courses	
Examinations and ex-	Written and oral examination
amination dates	
Course equivalents	
Demonstration reports	Two representative appraisal reports in particular field
Interview	Yes
Contribution	
Memberships required	
Designations required	
Initiation/application	
fee	
Membership dues	
Time limit on candidacy	
Other requirements	By invitation only

	Certified Assessment Evaluator (CAE)	Accredited Assessment Evaluator (AAE)	Certified Personalty Evaluator (CPE)	Residential Evaluation Specialist (RES)
Designation				
Offered by	International Association of Assessing Officers 1313 East 60th Street Chicago, Illinois 60637 (312) 947-2041			
Number holding designation in 1978				
Purpose	Improve standards of assessment practice and convey to the taxpaying public the true nature and importance of the work performed by assessing officers			
Age requirement	None specified	None specified	None specified	None specified
Experience	*For application:* Two years of appraisal experience or one year + approved appraisal course; one year in assessing field (may be concurrent) *By certification:* Five years or four years + approved appraisal courses; two years in assessing field	Same Same Assessing experience may be in public or private sector	Same Same as CAE Same	Three years of appraisal experience + one year in assessing (may run concurrently with appraisal experience requirement)
Educational level	None specified	None specified	None specified	Within preceding ten years must have passed IAAO exam for Courses 1 and 2 or have passed exams on comparable courses

Courses	Course 1: Fundamentals of Real Property Appraisal; Course 2: Appraisal of Income-Producing Property; plus one other course (Course 3: Development and Analysis of Narrative Appraisal Reports or comparable approved courses)	Course 2 or Course 5: Personal Property Valuation	Same	Same as AAE
		Same		
Examinations and examination dates	Written exam at conclusion of each course. May include oral exam.	Written exam at conclusion of each course. May include oral exam.	Same	Written exam. May include oral portion.
Course equivalents				
Demonstration reports	Two narrative appraisals—one single-family and one income-producing improved real estate (if hold MAI, demo report waived)	Same or (1) personal property (retail business); (2) personal property (service or manufacturing)	Same as AAE	If hold RM or SRA or CRA (Canada), demo report requirement waived; one complete narrative appraisal of a property acceptable to Admissions Committee
Interview	At discretion of Professional Admissions Committee			
Contribution				
Memberships required	Regular member IAAO	Subscribing member IAAO or associate	Regular member IAAO	Regular member IAAO
Designations required				
Initiation/application fee	$45	$45	$45	$45
Membership dues	$45 regular + $35 designation dues (annual)	$90 subscribing, $35 associate	$45 regular	$45 regular + $35 designation dues

	Counselor of Real Estate (CRE)
Time limit on candidacy	Three years
Other requirements	Affidavit on employment
Designation	Counselor of Real Estate (CRE) (Membership by invitation after person has been found to be qualified; designation awarded to all members)
Offered by	American Society of Real Estate Counselors 430 North Michigan Avenue Chicago, Illinois 60611 (312) 440-8091
Number holding designation in 1978	467
Purpose	Promote the growth and improve the quality of counseling service
Age requirement	
Experience	Three years in real estate counseling on fee, retainer, or per diem basis; ten years of real estate experience (postgraduate academic and degree activity may be substituted)
Educational level	
Courses	
Examinations and examination dates	
Course equivalents	
Demonstration reports	
Interview	
Contribution	
Memberships required	National Association of Realtors®

Three years   Three years   Three years

Designations required	Be sole proprietor, principal, or principal officer in firm, partnership, or corporation providing real estate services, or have major decision-making role
Initiation/application fee	$500
Membership dues	$375
Time limit on candidacy	
Other requirements	

Designation	SEC (full counselor member of the Society of Exchange Counselors)
Offered by	Society of Exchange Counselors 956 Willow Street Reno, Nevada 89502 (702) 786-1616
Number holding designation in 1978	45 (all members of society hold designation; membership by invitation only)
Purpose	To disseminate information; to more highly professionalize counseling, exchanging, and exchange counseling; and to provide technical assistance to members and to the business
Age requirement	None specified
Experience	In real estate counseling and exchanging; emphasis on candidate's success, knowledge, and integrity, and on what he has to offer the society in opportunities to do business
Educational level	No requirement
Courses	Regular SEC meetings are held quarterly, on third week of month; invitations extended only to guest being considered for candidacy; invitational meetings provide opportunities for SEC members to participate in a marketing meeting of a select group of production-oriented brokers

Examinations and examination dates	
Course equivalents	
Demonstration reports	
Interview	Accepted candidates must be accompanied by sponsor or approved sponsor substitute to three national meetings during candidacy year
Contribution	
Memberships required	National Association of Realtors®
Designations required	Realtor®
Initiation/application fee	Application sent by Regional Director to potential candidate; completed application to include financial statement, résumé, letters from sponsor
Membership dues	
Time limit on candidacy	One year for candidate applicant

Designation	Certified Mortgage Banker (CMB)
Offered by	Mortgage Bankers Association of America 1125 15th Street, N.W. Washington, D.C. 20005 (Attention: Cecil Sears, CMB Coordinator)
Number holding designation in 1978	116
Purpose	Establish high professional stature in real estate finance
Age requirement	
Experience	Two years in activities related to real estate finance (additional experience may count toward evaluation points)

Educational level	
Courses	150 or more evaluation points (may be earned through years of experience; possession of other real estate–related designations; attendance at MBA educational seminars; MBA correspondence courses; serving as chairman of an MBA committee, member of MBA Board of Governors, or MBA faculty member; submission of acceptable original paper; or unusual contributions to mortgage banking industry)
Examinations and examination dates	One-day written examination + individual oral examination by CMB Board of Review
Course equivalents	See list given above
Demonstration reports	Acceptable original paper may count toward evaluation points
Interview	Oral examination by CMB Board of Review
Contribution	Unusual contributions to mortgage banking industry may count toward evaluation points
Memberships required	Be employee of firm that has been member of Mortgage Bankers Association for at least one year
Designations required	Other real estate–related designations may count toward evaluation points
Initiation/application fee	$250 (nonrefundable) designation fee; $250 (nonrefundable) with application for candidacy
Membership dues	
Time limit on candidacy	Five years
Other requirements	Recommendation by senior officer of member firm + two personal references

	Certified Corporate Real Estate Analyst (CREA)	Certified Corporate Development Analyst (CRES)	Dean of the Corporate Institute (DCI)
Designation			
Offered by	National Association of Corporate Real Estate Executives 7799 Southwest 62d Avenue South Miami, Florida 33143 (305) 661-1585		
Number holding designation in 1978	Designations now being developed; first course offered in December 1978; 1,100 corporate members and 225 associates in NACORE		
Purpose			
Age Requirements			
Experience			Some years of experience will be required
Educational level			
Courses	NACORE 101: Corporate Real Estate Negotiations; other courses being developed in retail site location, basics of appraising, property management, property disposal, office and retail leasing, industrial facility planning, and corporate communication	Deal with in-depth valuation and operations of development; will have courses in development and management of office buildings, apartments, shopping centers, industrial properties, advanced property management, land development, construction and housing, basic construction engineering and architecture, marketing, development law, and advanced appraising	Advanced courses in finance, accounting, and law; preparation of in-depth projections for senior management relating projects to balance sheet, P&L statements, cash flow, and earnings; also advanced courses in management training
Examinations	Student exercises monitored & critiqued by experienced corporate professionals.		

Course equivalents

Demonstration reports

Interview

Contribution

Memberships required

Designations required

Initiation/application fee

Membership dues

Time limit on candidacy

Other requirements

Designation — AIA (member of American Institute of Architects)

Offered by — American Institute of Architects
1735 New York Avenue, N.W.
Washington, D.C. 20006

Number holding designation in 1978

Purpose — To serve and promote the public interest in improving the human environment

Age requirement — None specified

Experience — To be AIA member, must have sufficient experience to be licensed as architect by state; to be associate member, must be employed by a licensed architect

Educational level — Architectural training and practice sufficient for licensing by state

Courses

Examinations and examination dates	
Course equivalents	
Demonstration reports	
Interview	
Contribution	
Memberships required	Architectural license or registration by any state, District of Columbia, or territory of United States
Designations required	
Initiation/application fee	$50 for first year's dues plus $10 fee
Membership dues	National AIA dues, $100 per year, plus state dues
Time limit on candidacy	
Other requirements	

Certified Public Accountant (CPA)

Designation	Certified Public Accountant (CPA)
Offered by	State boards of accountancy
Number holding designation in 1978	
Purpose	To certify competence in accounting and auditing fields
Age requirement	21
Experience	Two years of practical public accounting experience
Educational level	Baccalaureate, master's, or higher academic degree from college or university recognized by the board of accountancy, with a concentration in accounting; or baccalaureate, master's, or higher academic degree from recognized college or university, without regard to course of study completed, plus two years of practical accounting experience

Courses

Examinations and examination dates
Written exam in accounting and auditing and in such other related subjects as the board may determine to be appropriate; exam offered at least once each year; may be retaken as many times as necessary

Demonstration reports

Interview

Contribution

Memberships required

Designations required

Initiation/application fee
Fee not to exceed $75

Membership dues
Annual fee for permit to practice as certified public accountant

Time limit on candidacy
No limit

Other requirements

Designation
Certified Financial Analyst (CFA)

Offered by
Institute of Chartered Financial Analysts

Number holding designation in 1978

Age requirement

Experience
Must be currently and primarily engaged in financial analysis related to securities investment one year before CFA Exam I, three years before Exam II, and five years before Exam III

Educational level
Bachelor's degree or other educational training or work experience

Preexamination requirements	Accounting: two years of academic exposure to accounting principles; economics: basic principles of macroeconomics and monetary systems; financial analysis: equivalent of two years of academic exposure to business administration, including corporate finance and corporate financial policies
Courses/examinations	Five basic subject matter areas: accounting, economics, financial analysis, portfolio management, and ethical standards
Examination dates	
Course equivalents	
Demonstration reports	
Contribution	
Memberships required	Financial Analysts Federation membership required before Exams II and III are taken
Designations required	
Initiation/application fee	
Membership dues	
Time limit on candidacy	
Other requirements	Professional conduct must conform to institute's Code of Ethics and Standards of Professional Conduct

Designation	*Doctor of Philosophy (PhD) in Real Estate*	*Master of Business Administration (MBA)* *Master of Science in Business (MS) in Real Estate*
Offered by	Seven universities	37 universities
Number holding designation in 1978		

Age requirements	None	None
Experience	Some schools require five years of experience	Business core courses only
Educational level	Master's degree with GMAT test and/or high grades	Bachelor's degree with GMAT test and/or high grades
Courses	Two to three years in residence at university	30 to 36 credits above core courses
Examinations	One to three comprehensive exams	Comprehensive exam in some cases
Examination dates		
Course equivalents		
Demonstration reports	Dissertation, major research paper	Thesis required in some cases
Interview	Defense	Defense required in some cases
Contribution	Research, teaching, service	
Memberships required		
Designations required		
Initiation/application fee		
Membership dues		
Time limit on candidacy		
Other requirements		

INDEX